Goldmine
Country Western

RECORD & CD PRICE GUIDE

Fred Heggeness

Published by

 **krause publications**

700 E. State Street • Iola, WI 54990-0001
Telephone: 715/445-2214

Please call or write for our free catalog. Our toll-free number to
place an order or obtain a free catalog is 800-258-0929 or please use our regular business telephone
715-445-2214 for editorial comment and further information.

Library of Congress Catalog Number: 96-76683
ISBN: 0-87341-470-5
Printed in the United States of America

Back cover photo courtesy of Ted Fiskevold

GOLDMINE COUNTRY WESTERN RECORD AND CD PRICE GUIDE

CONTENTS

Foreword

In Search of Those Rare Country Records

It is 1:00 p.m. on a quiet Sunday afternoon in mid-March as we pull a U-Haul moving van onto the main drag of Anaconda, Montana. There is no snow on the ground in the city, but big, quiet flakes fall from bulging clouds that hang in the nearby mountains. Nobody is on the streets, and there are few cars around.

"Either they're all still in church, or they're having Sunday dinners somewhere," I say to my partner.

He nods and wheels the big van up to a huge second-hand store, parking at the curb of the one-way street. "I stopped in here several years ago looking for furs and antlers. This dude had a bunch, but he was sky-high on all of it. I'm sure this is the place, and if I recall, a whole back room was full of records."

We were on our way from Minnesota to Seattle, moving a load of furniture for my partner's friend. I was tagging along to keep him company and help with loading and unloading, but with the understanding that I would be able to browse some second-hand, antique, and used record shops for rare records.

I've been collecting records for years. Originally, most were country music LPs. Then in 1983 I went to the Jimmie Rodgers Fifty-Year Memorial in Meridian, Mississippi. I decided I had to have some Jimmie Rodgers 78s, and started browsing through piles of those old platters. (There aren't a whole lot of Jimmie Rodgers 78s out there, but I started picking up a few country 78s and 10-inch LPs … if I'd only known, but I'm getting ahead.) My work had me living and traveling in a lot of states between 1983 and 1987 and I looked through a lot of records.

I lived in St. Paul, Minnesota, from 1987 to 1992, and shortly after I moved back to Minnesota, I started picking up 45s with the idea of buying a jukebox. In 1989, I bought a '76 Seeburg jukebox and my search for 45s intensified. I also started picking up more 78s, figuring someday I'd get a jukebox that played them.

We lock up the cab of the truck and walk inside. ("It's the same dude who ran the place four years ago," Patrick whispers to me.) There's a big old wood-burning barrel stove by the checkout counter to keep the chill off, and the dude and his woman friend are sitting awfully close to it. The place looks like an old warehouse, with assorted items piled everywhere. The smell of wood smoke prevails, but there is also a prominent underlying odor of mildew, musk, and old things.

We casually browse for ten minutes or so. "Nah, just passing through and looking around," I answer when the dude asks if he can help us. Then I slowly make my way to the back of the building. And there they are! Racks of LPs! Stacks of 78s and 45s! A roomful of records!

Before diving gleefully into those stacks of wax, I ask the dude, "How much do you want for these old records, anyway?"

"Oh, I guess I need a buck for the 45s and a buck-an'-a-half for the 78s," he says, eyeing me up. He's wearing a black leather biker-style jacket now. The heat from the wood stove has not made it back to the record room, and a cloud of dust rises about a foot above my cowboy boots every time I take a step.

"Really! You get that much for those old things. They look pretty beat up … and dirty. How come you want more for those old 78s? Most record players can't even play 'em."

"Well, they're older and more collectible, I guess…."

This tells me something right away: This "dealer" doesn't have any idea what his records are worth. In fact, the last time he probably touched any of them was when he dumped a box that he bought at an auction or a yard sale. Truth be told, most of his 45s will be worth more than the 78s. The dust on the records tells me something else right away: It's been a long time since anyone took as many of these records off his hands as I probably will, and I'm gonna get the ones I want for less than what he says. He thinks we're lookers, not buyers.

Here's the bottom line on searching for country and western 78 rpms. You have to dig through a lot of Bing Crosby on Decca to find one Ernest Tubb. And you'll find a lot of Ernest Tubb on Decca before you ever find one on Bluebird. You'll hear the slap and shuffle of a whole bunch of Joni James MGM 78s long before you bump into a Hank Williams 78 on MGM, and you will have left behind a lot of scratched, cracked, chipped, or broken Hank Williams MGM 78s long before you find a Luke the Drifter MGM 78 promo. That is, unless you are real lucky, or you want to pay big bucks for your country and western 78s.

For rare 45s and EPs, it's the same thing: You have to pick through a lot of rocks before you find those jewels!

Before you start searching for rare country and western records, it's good also to know what's rare in pop, R & B, rock, and jazz, and to have a decent grip on Top 40 music over the past fifty years or so, so you don't miss rare records in those genres. (If for nothing else, they're great for selling or trading.)

So I knew how to handle a roomful of records. Patrick, however, had no idea what he was getting into.

Two hours later, my hands are black and numb. My back aches. My nose and throat are dusty, dry, and scratchy. My jeans have dirty, greasy stains. By now, Patrick knows every fur, horn, bone, and lunch pail in the place, and I have a stack of about one hundred 45s, maybe a dozen 78s, two LPs, and two pieces of sheet music—"This Ole House" and "You Are My Sunshine" with photographs of Stuart Hamblen and Jimmy Davis, respectively, on the covers. (In well-tended antique stores, these would have been in plastic covers, but I found them in with a box of moldy magazines and other publications.) Patrick and I haul it all up to the checkout counter and dump it. The dude and his woman friend are huddled over by the wood stove. He ambles over to the counter.

"How many you got?"

"Well, I'm gonna take a hundred of these 45s off your hands if they're fifty cents a piece, and I got a dozen 78s and two sheet musics. What ya askin' for the sheet music?"

He's got me pegged by now. "Sheet music's $5 each," he says, fondling them as if he were holding the napkin on which Jimmie Davis might have scrawled the lyrics to "You Are My Sunshine." "These are great. I should have a dollar each on those 45s, but I might go eighty-five cents."

"If you want eighty-five cents, I'm gonna cut the stack in half...."

"Cut the stack in half and I'll charge you a buck," he says with a smirk.

"Hmmm, it's beginning to look like we're not going to be able to deal. It's a quiet Sunday afternoon and there hasn't been a soul in this store except me and Patrick for two hours. And most of these records are scratched up and probably won't even play through. Oh well, if nothin' else, I've dusted off your record stacks for you...."

"You ready to go?" Patrick says impatiently. "We still want to get over Lookout Pass and on into Wallace, Idaho, tonight, you know."

"Yeah, let's roll," I answer.

There are four inches of feathery snow on the ground when we leave. The wipers are busy as Patrick stores his jacket under the seat and fastens his seat belt. I'm on the passenger side, burrowing deep into Fred Heggeness's 1991 price guide *Rarest of the Rare, COUNTRY MUSIC*.

"Damn it, Patrick," I say. "There's records sitting on that counter that I've never seen before and probably won't see again. Some of them are in worse than fair condition, most are fair to good, and a few are excellent. But I'm probably never again gonna see a 45 rpm Lefty Frizzell singing "Brakeman's Blues" (which Fred listed at $15 in 1991) or Ernest Tubb singin' "Waiting for a Train" (which Fred doesn't even list because he probably didn't know it existed—the Decca number is lower than one he lists at $45). And I picked out a pile of about twenty Johnny Cash Sun 45s."

"Well," Patrick muses. "Let's let him stew for five minutes and then go back in...."

"Yeah. He's thinkin' the same way I am, that he should've dealt."

I ended up giving the dude seventy cents each for the 45s and he threw in the 78s and the sheet music for nothing. We were both happy.

As we drive out of Anaconda heading for Missoula, I check all of the records against Fred's book, highlighting the ones I have found and taking some notes. Finally I say, "Patrick, assuming these records were in very good to excellent shape, which they are not, and assuming that the value of these records has not gone up since 1991, I just picked up $555 worth of country records for $70. Now, this Fred guy only lists records in this book that are $10 or more. I've got his 1991 Rock Price Guide too, and I think these Fats Domino and Bobby Darin EPs and some of this Platters stuff might list in it. Then of course, all the rest of these are probably worth more than seventy cents each.

"This Fred fellow lives right in Detroit Lakes. People have been telling me for the last four years that I should meet Fred. You know, people who come over to listen to the jukebox or jam—folks who know I collect records. There was an article in the paper about Fred—had a photo with him and all his Beatles records and Beatles memorabilia—man, he's got a bunch of it. Seems to me there was a jukebox in the photo, too. I found these two price guides for fifty cents each at a used book store in Detroit Lakes, so I bought 'em. The cover price was $15.95 each. I started marking off the records I have, and based on these 1991 prices, my records are worth thousands of dollars to the right buyers. 'Course, I got no intentions of sellin' 'em, but it's interesting.

"Anyway, I called this Fred up about a month ago or so and left a message on his answering machine to 'come on over sometime and check out the museum.' He called me back. Said he'd love to come by and visit and see my stuff. I told him a little about all of my old and new country photographs, my autographed guitars, etc. He said he'd call me in a couple of weeks, but he hasn't yet. When we get back home I'm gonna call him again...."

As we pull into Missoula, it's getting dark and I can smell anti-freeze. We end up spending the night in a motel there and we have four hours down time the next day while we wait to have a new water pump put into the U-Haul moving van. I call up a woman I know in town who is a state legislator, and she takes us to pawn shops and second-hand shops on the north side of town. I pick up another bunch of records: some dandy LPs like a Marvin Rainwater and some Loretta Lynn Deccas for a couple bucks each, a few 78s for a buck or two, and a bunch of 45s including some Merle Haggards. Most are good to excellent, and twenty-five cents each.

By the time Patrick drops me off at home ten days later, in the trunk of our rental car sits a huge box of records that had come from shops, friends, and family in Montana, Washington, Oregon, and Idaho. I had spent about $200 on the whole bunch.

One of the other things we found was a very rare recording done by "Weyland Jennings" on the obscure Golden State label out of San Francisco. On this 45, #656, Waylon sings "Nashville Bum" and "Gulf Coast Belle" and I had to play it on a phonograph at the shop to be sure this "Weyland" was indeed our

Waylon. It's marked "PROMOTIONAL COPY/NOT FOR SALE." Fred and I suspect this might be a bootleg. Does anyone know anything about this record?

Also, Patrick and I, to battle driving fatigue and kill some time on the road, sketched out the beginnings of a composition that may some day be entitled "An Ode to Country Record Collectors," which goes like this:

I found a rare ol' seventy-eight, (twang-twang)

It was Lefty Frizzell's "Always Late." (twang-twang)

Somebody was gonna use it for home plate, (twang-twang)

Or for target practice, hang it on a gate. (twang-twang-twang)

I cleaned it up, it sounded great. (twang-twang)

I'm gonna look for more in another state. (twang-twang, another dang twang)

A couple of days after I got home, I called Fred Heggeness again and he visited. We are both avid record collectors and appreciators of music, and we also both collect autographs, photographs, and other memorabilia. Fred's whole house is similar to my basement. We both have very impressive "museums."

As fate would have it, at the time Fred and I finally met, Fred was putting the finishing touches on this book. And sure enough, I have country, western, and cowboy records that Fred had either never seen before or didn't know existed. Thus came about this foreword to Fred's latest book on rare country records. (By the way, I am a writer/photographer/journalist/p.r. man by trade.)

I am doing this with pleasure. I hope this book will help educate country record collectors, dealers, buyers, and sellers.

Of course, from my standpoint, there is an up side and a down side to this "education." Some "educated" dealers may start asking $25 for scratched-up Johnny Cash Sun records that they paid three cents for and may be lucky to get seventy cents for, making it difficult for collectors like myself to continue to collect. On the other hand, if price guides like Fred's become widely circulated (and used), it will drive record prices up. The Red River Dave 10-inch LP that I paid a buck for might net me $300 if I decide to sell some or all of my record collection twelve or thirteen years from now to put my kids through college!

Fred and I took our first (and likely not our last) record-collecting road trip recently. We went to two radio stations in Bemidji, Minnesota, stopping at a half dozen antique and second-hand shops as well. We found some jewels, and I found someone who understands that you have to go through every record to find them. (My wife, Marysia, and friends like Patrick are patient, but only to a point.)

Not long ago, I called Fred and told him I had purchased a $50 ticket to see Loretta Lynn's one night/one performance show at the Shooting Star Casino in Mahnomen, Minnesota, on the White Earth Indian Reservation, thirty-five miles north of Detroit Lakes. "I plan to get Loretta's autograph on the Epiphone and a couple of album jackets signed," I said. "Maybe you've got something you want me to bring along for her to sign."

"That'd be nice," Fred answered. "I'll tell you what I'll do. I'll give you four sleeves from the 'Coal Miner's Daughter' 45, and four sleeves from the 'We've Come a Long Way Baby' 45 and you can have half of them."

"That'll work," I said.

When I arrived at the casino, I was told by Loretta's manager and members of her band that she was not very likely to come out after the show to sign any autographs. Loretta's husband, Mooney, whom she refers to as "Do-Little" or "Do," has been very ill lately, her concert schedule has been light, and she hasn't been up to meeting with crowds after shows. Her manager did agree to take my guitar and other items to her dressing room to see if she'd sign the stuff before the show.

Loretta and her entourage gave us more than $50 worth of entertainment, performing for over two hours. She was in great form and voice. When the show ended, about 460 of the 500 people who had attended left, leaving about 40 fans and autograph seekers who'd crowded down into the corner closest to where Loretta's dressing room was located. Security informed everyone that she wasn't coming out, but true country fans are devoted and hopeful. Soon, Lane, her manager, came out on the stage shoulder and beckoned to me. I walked over and he leaned over and said, "Loretta really likes your stuff. In fact, she doesn't own a copy of the sleeve to the 'Coal Miner's Daughter' 45, and she wants to know if she can have one."

"Well, I think that's possible, but we better go back into the dressing room and talk this over," I said.

Loretta, a member of the Country Music Hall of Fame since 1988, was dressed in an all-white gown covered with sparkling silver sequins, and she looked like a queen right out of a fairy tale, standing beside a small table that was covered with my stuff. "You better hang on to those Decca albums, young man," she drawled as I walked in. "Those are worth a lot of money already." (I was born in 1953, so being addressed as "young man" really tickled me.)

I glanced down at the table and noticed she'd already signed the whole lot. "They're going to mean a lot more to me now that they're autographed by you," I answered.

She gave me a big hug. "I don't even have a copy of the 'Coal Miner's Daughter' sleeve, and I'd sure like to have one," she said, smiling that beautiful apple-cheeked smile of hers that makes her look like everybody's favorite aunt. "Do you think I could have one?"

"I'd be proud to give you one," I said, and she offered me one of those big, rosy cheeks that I happily kissed. "I'll tell you what, Loretta," I said reaching down and picking up two each of the 45 sleeves. Do you think you could sign a couple of these 'To Fred' and 'To Ted F'?"

"Sure," she drawled. "Who's Ted 'F'?" And smiling she added, "And what's that 'F' stand for?" I laughed and told her what my last name was. "Well Ted, efff," she said, "I've added my autograph to your guitar, along the signatures of a lot of friends of mine. You'd better think of me every time you play that thing."

To Loretta I say thank you, and I most certainly will.

Fred, incidentally, has the Gold Record awarded to Willie Nelson for the LP "Somewhere Over the Rainbow" hanging on his wall. He says he'd be willing to give it back to Willie in trade for maybe an autographed guitar or if Willie'd stop by and sign a few items the next time he comes to the Detroit Lakes area to perform at the We Fest Country Music Festival or the Shooting Star Casino. And I reckon that deal will eventually be cut.

I've gained a lot of insight into record collecting by getting to know Fred, his well-researched record price guides, and his knowledge, expertise, and historical perspective of the recording industry. I'm sure you will too. Enjoy this book, and learn from it. Happy hunting, happy dealing, and happy record trails!

Ted Fiskevold

Introduction

FORMAT OF LISTINGS

The **ARTIST** is listed in bold print alphabetically by last name or name of the act. Soundtracks and various artists material are listed by the title of the album. Following the artist identification is the **MUSIC FORMAT**.

Example:

HANK WILLIAMS (CW)

MUSIC FORMAT ABBREVIATIONS used in this book:

(CW)   Country Western
(C)   Country
(G)   Gospel
(I)   Instrumental
(R & B)   Rhythm and Blues
(RB)   Rockabilly

Following the artist identification is sometimes information about the artist, followed by "blanket" values of items generally worth less than $10. To list all releases of major country artists would take a book ten times the size of this book.

Example:

HANK WILLIAMS (CW)
Also recorded as Luke the Drifter
Audrey was his first wife and mother of Hank Jr.
MGM Golden Circle 45s with black bar on label $5-10 each
MGM Golden Circle 45s $3-5 each
MGM Band of Gold 45s $2-3 each
Other MGM 45s $2-3 each

The listings of individual titles begin after this general information. The **TITLE** line begins with the record format.

RECORD FORMAT ABBREVIATIONS used in this book:

45, 78, 33   Record speed (rpm)
2LP   Two-record set
3LP   Three-record set
10"   10-inch single
12"   12-inch single
CD   Compact disc
Cass   Cassette
EP   Extended play 45rpm

LP   Album
PS   Picture sleeve
(JB)   Jukebox release
(P)   Promo version
(RS)   Radio show
(S)   Stereo

The **TITLE** is after the record format. On a single, the song title of the "A" side is listed; on an extended play or LP, the title of the album is listed. The number that follows is the year representing either the year of release or the year of peak sales or chart.

The record label and number follow. The label represents the record company. The next column lists the price (or price range) for that item.

Example:

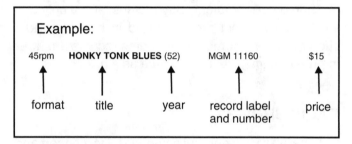

| 45rpm | **HONKY TONK BLUES** (52) | | MGM 11160 | $15 |
| format | title | year | record label and number | price |

The records listed are separated into groups of singles (45rpm, 78rpm), EPs (including jukebox releases), LPs (albums), and radio shows. For radio shows the name of the syndication company (Westwood One, NBC, DIR, etc.) is listed rather than the name of a record company. This is because radio shows are not for release or use by the public; therefore, they are not released by record companies.

STEREO VS MONO

Some stereo albums are rechanneled (remixed to create stereo effect) and are not "true stereo." Most of these LPs sound bad and are not as collectible, and their prices reflect that. True stereo albums will usually price higher than mono. In the late '60s some albums that are mono (especially RCA Victor) are priced very high because monaural recordings were being phased out and are rare.

In this book, stereo/mono values that are $5 or more in difference are listed. In many cases the stereo and mono versions have less than a $5 difference and are not listed separately or identified as either. You may assume both have the same value.

STOCK COPY VS PROMO

A stock copy is the version of a record/CD that is manufactured for sale to the public. A promo record is pressed for promotional use and is identified on the label as such. Most promo records are for radio/TV use and in some cases for jukebox use. The record label is responsible for royalty payments for stock copies sold for profit. The label does not pay royalties on promo records and that is why they are identified on the label as promo. Again, both stock copy and promo versions of a record are listed and priced if the difference is $5 or more. In many cases the stock and promo versions are worth about the same and are not listed separately. In some cases the promo may be a different version of a song; in all cases the promo has a different label.

Some collectors only buy promos, some only buy stock copies. Most are interested in both. All radio shows are considered promo. Some records are rarer in promo, some are more scarce as stock copies.

RADIO SHOWS

There are two general categories, live concert and music/interview. Live concerts are for the most part designed for one-time broadcast and are not available to the public in any other form. These live shows are very collectible and are good investments. Music/interview shows feature the artist (as a DJ) talking about and introducing his/her/their music, which is probably off a record that is available to the public. These shows are less desirable because the only attractive feature of the recording is the interview segment(s). Radio shows are generally priced in a range: $40-75, for example.

PRICING AND CONDITION

Very important when using this book. Read carefully: Prices listed are for **mint condition records!** That means new, unplayed, not off-center, no writing on labels, near-perfect to perfect condition. A record can be played and still be mint (call it near-mint). When you see a Hank Snow album for sale for $40 (as listed in this book) that means it is **new!** Don't pay $40 if it isn't! If it's in nice condition but shows wear from playing (still plays clean) it's in very good condition, which is 35-50% of the mint value. If there are some marks on the vinyl or markings on the cover, its value drops to about 25% of the mint price. If the record is beat (noisy when playing) and/or the cover is damaged, it's only worth 5-10% of the mint price! Read this paragraph every day and learn that **condition is everything** when determining the value. Don't pay too much for junk. But don't feel guilty if you have just paid too much for a mint condition classic!

PRICING IS GEOGRAPHICAL

Another very important factor. Hank Snow albums may sell for $40 in Canada, New York, Japan, or Dallas. But in Minneapolis a dealer at a show may be lucky to get $5 for a mint release. There is a big difference in prices in various parts of the country. Keep that in mind when digesting the prices in this book.

WHAT IS COUNTRY?

That was the tough part: deciding who is country enough to be in the book. Maybe I went too far in including Creedence Clearwater Revival, Ricky Nelson, or maybe Gene Vincent and Eddie Cochran. Or, should I have included the Byrds ("Sweethearts of the Rodeo")? Their music is today's country. But under that theory there should be many others: Billy Joe Royal, Joe Dowell. But there is not room in this edition.

What is country you ask? Well ... it's country, western, cowboy, string band, bluegrass, gospel, western swing, swing, southern, hard country, country rock, Southern rock, old-time, polka, fiddle, downhome, rockabilly, hillbilly, Tex-Mex, Nashville, bayou, boogie-woogie, West Coast, honky tonk, folk, chic, hot country, jive, drinkin', bar, countrypolitan, waltz, Southern roots, inspiration, steel guitar, sacred, trail, gunfighter (thanks, Marty), buckskin, guitar, skootin' farm, sod bustin' classic, gold, and oldie music!

Where is country now? I believe it is a combination of late '50s-early '60s ballad rock and '70s soft pop music. It is not the same as hillbilly/rockabilly jive '50s music or the honky tonk '60s/'70s Kitty Wells/George Jones/Waylon Jennings music. Where are Willie and Waylon? The honky tonk '60s/'70s country music and artists are not charting now, or being played as oldies on country stations. The recent Billboard chart of the 100 all-time country singles from '50s/'90s does not include any honky tonk records of the '60s/'70s era. I would go as far as to say that today's country music is not country (generally speaking). Agree? But then what is country?

HELP!

This is a first edition and I have overpriced, underpriced, left out, and misrepresented many records. There are plenty of errors. Maybe even a record is listed that doesn't exist. And there are many records that should be in this book. (I didn't purposely make these errors.) The coverage of 78s is weak. (Are they really that collectible among the general population of music fans? Do *you* have a 78 player?)

So, please send your additions, corrections, comments to *Goldmine* or me for inclusion in the next edition. I have a mail bag full of letters from the *Promo Record/CD Price Guide* (November 1995) and they all are welcome and full of information that I did not know about! I am just one person compiling this first edition book.

My address is:
Fred Heggeness
313 West Front Street
Detroit Lakes, Minnesota 56501

And *thank you* in advance!

OTHER BOOKS

There are many on the market, many available from Krause Publications. Look for books (price guides) on rock 45s, albums, jazz, doo-wop, novelty, personality, soundtracks, and others by fine authors like Les Docks, Neal Umphred, Jerry Osborne, Perry Cox, Joe Lindsay, Joel Whitburn, and many others.

Since Osborne's first book in the early '70s, I have been a guide collector and love them all! Many of these price guides are updated often. Some of the titles in this book have been taken from these other price guides, but the prices may be different.

IN CONCLUSION

Why are there so many Hank Williams MGM records? The god of country music was overpressed on MGM. There are so many reissues. So many releases. Sure, he had classics. But there were a lot of releases that never got played. The key to collecting Hank Williams, *find one in mint!*

On the other hand, the father of country music, Jimmie Rodgers, is very hard to find on any label. His original records (1929-1933) are 78s. RCA Victor has not re-released a lot of his material.

A friend of mine asked me what artist I would delete from this book if I went over my allotted pages. I said CCR or Ricky Nelson (borderline country?) and he said, "Leave them in and take out Slim Whitman!" For those of you that don't dig Slim, listen to his RCA material! It's great; he sounds like an early Hank Snow.

Top 25 Most Collectible Country Western Records

The list below considers only records that are country western; not those that might be crossover rock or rockabilly. Therefore, Elvis, Roy Orbison, the Johnny Burnette Trio, and so on are not on the list. If crossover records were part of the list, Presley would rank twenty titles worth $2,000-$4,000 each; Roy Orbison and the Teen Kings would rank $6,000 and $2,000; Paul McCartney $3,000; and Carl Mann, Ray Smith, and Bill Haley $2,000 each. The "Jamboree" LP is valued at $5,000 and the Billy Barrix rockabilly Chess 45 at $7,500! Also not included in the list below are the Fendermen, Charlie Feathers, Lou Giordano, and Buddy Holly.

So, here we go, strictly country western acts only:

$1,500 JIM REEVES SINGS (Mono only) — Abbott 5001

Very rare and very much in demand. Most of the tracks were released as singles, but the album is impossible to find at any price!

$1,500 HERE'S TO VETERANS (Merle Haggard) — Radio Show 1477

So what's the big difference between this $1,500 disc and show 1454, which is the same show but a different record? Glad you asked! Show 1477 features the Beatles on the other side. Enough said!

$1,200 GRAND OLE OPRY'S NEW STAR (George Jones) — Starday 101

George's first album, also his rarest. Some of these tracks were released as singles.

$1,000 BLUE YODEL No. 12 (Jimmie Rodgers) — Victor 6000

Released as a picture disc in 1935, this gem is very collectible among fans of all music formats. This title was also released as a (non-picture disc) regular 78rpm, Victor 24458, worth at least $100. Look for all Jimmie Rodgers records to rise fast in value, as he is the "Father of Country Music!"

$800 ROCK'N ROLL'N ROBBINS (Marty Robbins) — Columbia 2601

Marty's first album is his only solo 10-inch LP. Features many of his collectible rockabilly tracks. Valued here at $800, you'll probably have to pay more if you are buying!

$800 JERRY LEE LEWIS' GREATEST (White promo label version) — Sun 1265

His second Sun LP was released as a promo, unlike the first (Sun 1230). Very rare. The stock copy of Sun 1265 is worth $250!

$750 CALLING YOU (Hank Williams) — Sterling 201

Available as an original 78rpm record in 1947. This is Hank's first recording.

$500 WEALTH WON'T SAVE YOUR SOUL (Hank Williams) — Sterling 204

Hank's second 78rpm. Two versions, both worth $500 each. One version reads on the flip side, "When God Comes and Gathers His Jewels." The other version reads on the flip, "When God Comes and Fathers His Jewels." I challenge you to find them both!

$500 I DON'T CARE IF TOMORROW NEVER COMES (Hank Williams) — Sterling 208

Still 1947, Hank's third release, also only on 78rpm.

$500   MOON OVER MULLICAN (Moon Mullican)   Coral 57235
Price is for the stock copy, rarer than the promo. Great music too!

$500   WAYLON JENNINGS AT JDs   Bat 1001
His first LP is very rare. Reissued first on Sounds 1001, worth $200 and later on Vocalion in 1969, still collectible at $30-40.

$500   ROCKIN' WITH WANDA (Wanda Jackson)   Capitol promo 1384
This price is for the yellow promo label version. Classic album! Stock copy is listed later. Its reissue as a Starline label version is still collectible at $50.

$500   HANK SNOW   RCA Victor
Thesaurus Series

Promo collection of ten albums from RCA Victor Music Service to radio stations. You'd be lucky to find one, let alone all ten! When word gets around about this set, its value will skyrocket!

$500   SONS OF THE PIONEERS   RCA Victor
Thesaurus Series

Promo collection of eleven albums from RCA Victor Music Service to radio stations. Again, you'll be lucky to see just one disc of the set!

$500   THE SUN KEEPS SHINING (Everly Brothers) (45 rpm)   Columbia 21496
Yes, the Everly Brothers are rock crossover. But this is a country record! It's also their first release and only on Columbia. Very rare on the red label. The white promo label version is much easier to find, but still worth $250.

$400   HONKY TONKIN' (Hank Williams)   Sterling 210
This is the final Sterling 78rpm release and the easiest to find. The Sterling 78s are a great investment if you should get the opportunity!

$400   ROCKIN' WITH WANDA (Wanda Jackson)   Capitol 1384
The stock copy. Promo version is listed above.

$400   MOON OVER MULLICAN (Moon Mullican)   Coral 57235
Price is for the blue promo label version, more common than the stock copy, which is ranked above.

$400   ARKANSAS TWIST (Bobby Lee Trammell)   Atlantic 1503
Again, is this country or rockabilly? You buy it for $400 and listen to it, then let me know. Still, it's a great album!

$400   BBC TRANSCRIPTION DISC (Johnny Cash) (Radio show)
Not just a radio show, it's a country artist live in a rock concert format, it's a British release of an American artist for the American radio market, and it's the rarest and most collectible of all radio series. Also, it's very rare within the series. And there may be fewer than ten copies of this LP left. Yes, $400 is a very conservative price!

$400   **OLD TIME FAVORITES** (Bob Wills)   Antone's 6000

Were you a member of the Bob Wills Fan Club in the early '50s? This 10-inch LP was sent to you as a gift.

$400   **OLD TIME FAVORITES** (Bob Wills)   Antone's 6010

A second gift from the club. Bob Wills died in 1996, which may give these 10-inch LPs a boost in value.

$400   **LONELY WEEKENDS** (Charlie Rich)   Philips 1970

This LP was country/rock crossover like most of the Sun label artists and releases. Philips Records was owned by Sam Philips, who also owned Sun. Charlie Rich can be considered a genuine country artist.

$300   **AMERICAN EAGLE** Features Marty Robbins (Radio show)

Three-LP set features live music from Marty Robbins and other country artists, recorded in the early '80s. Live radio shows featuring top country artists will always be a good investment!

$300   **HANK WILLIAMS SINGS**   MGM 107

From 1952, this is Hank's first LP and is a 10-inch version.

$300   **MOANIN' THE BLUES** (Hank Williams)   MGM 168

This 10-inch LP was also released in 12-inch format with both a 1956 yellow label version and a 1960 black label version. The 12-inchers are worth $150 and $25.

$300   **THE HANK WILLIAMS MEMORIAL ALBUM**   MGM 202

Another 10-inch LP re-released as a 12-incher worth $150 (yellow label) and $25 (black label).

$300   **HANK WILLIAMS AS LUKE THE DRIFTER**   MGM 203

Released in 1953 as a 10-inch LP. Again, later versions are 12-inchers worth $150 (yellow label) and $25 (black).

$300   **HONKY TONKIN'** (Hank Williams)   MGM 242

Hank coined the phase "Honky Tonkin'" and this is the first record released with that title. It's another 10-inch LP with 12-inch re-releases.

$300   **I SAW THE LIGHT** (Hank Williams)   MGM 243

Only one version of this 10-inch LP was pressed. Later versions are 12-inchers. One has a green cover and yellow label and is worth $200; another version has a church on the cover and a yellow label, worth $150. The black label version goes for $25.

$300   **RAMBLIN' MAN** (Hank Williams)   MGM 291

The last of the 10-inch LPs. Later 12-inch versions worth $150 and $25.

$300   **IT'S ONLY MAKE BELIEVE** (Conway Twitty)   MGM EP 1623

The first MGM EP for Conway Twitty, yellow label 1958 release. Later EPs on the MGM label are worth up to $250 each.

$300   AMERICA'S FAVORITE FOLK ARTIST (Slim Whitman)   Imperial 3004

This 10-inch LP was released in 1954 and is very hard to find. Love him or hate him, this is a classic LP. Another 10-inch LP on RCA Victor (3217) was released in 1954 and is worth $200.

$300   JOLE BLON (Waylon Jennings)   Brunswick 55130

Waylon's first record, recording during his association and membership with Buddy Holly & the Crickets. Holly plays guitar on this release. The $300 price tag is for the maroon-colored label stock copy. The promo version lists at $250!

Charlie Feathers is considered rockabilly but I think many will agree that he belongs on the list above. "Tongue Tied Jill," a maroon-colored label 45 rpm on Meteor (5032) is worth over $1,000! Other versions on Meteor range in value from $300-$750, including 78s. Sun label 78s and 45s by Feathers range from $400-750 each. The Flip label, pressed by Sun, ranges from $500-$750 for "I've Been Deceived" (Flip 503).

You'll discover that the twenty-nine-plus highest priced records in this book are either rockabilly or rock crossover country songs (like Elvis). The country western-only artists don't rank until Jim Reeves's Ab-bott LP is listed at $1,500. Rockabilly and rock cross-over records represented the bridge of country western music changing to rock and roll. Most rockabilly records were released in 1958, give or take a year.

Also listed at $1,500 is the Merle Haggard radio show. The reason for that high price tag is the Beatles show on the flip side.

Hopefully this book will help to open the country music market with more respect and value for genuine country/country western artists like Jimmie Rodgers, Hank Williams, Hank Snow, Kitty Wells, Roy Acuff, and so on.

A

ABBOTT SINGERS (CW)
Jim Edward Brown, Maxine Brown, and Bonnie with Dido Rowley and Lafawn Paul
See the Browns

ACORN SISTERS (RB)

-singles-

45rpm	**COME DANCE WITH ME** (58)	Acorn 593	$15

-EPs-

EP	**ACORN SISTERS** (58)	Starday 119	$15
EP	**ACORN SISTERS** (59)	Acorn 160	$18

ROY ACUFF (CW)
Conqueror 78s worth $15-25 each
Perfect, Melotone, Oriole, Banner, Romeo 78s $15-20 each
Other Vocalion and Okeh 78s $10-20 each
Other Columbia 78s $10 each
Other Columbia 45s $8 each
Other Capitol 45s $6 each
Other Decca 45s $6-8 each
United Artists 45s $6 each
    (With the Nitty Gritty Dirt Band)
Other Hickory 45s $5 each
Capitol Starline 45s $2 each
MCA 45s $2
    (Some duets with Bill Anderson)
Columbia HOF 45s $2 each
Other Columbia LPs $6 each
Other Hickory/MGM LPs $8 each
Elektra 45s $2 each
Hal Kat color vinyl 45s $5 each
    (With Charlie Louvin)
Elektra LPs $8 each
Elektra 2LP sets $12 each
Pickwick (Hilltop) LPs $5 each
Golden Country LPs $8 each

-singles-

78rpm	**GREAT SPECKLED BIRD** (38)	Vocalion 4252	$50
78rpm	**WABASH CANNONBALL** (38)	Vocalion 4466	$40
78rpm	**THE PRODIGAL SON** (44)	Okeh 6716	$25
78rpm	**I'LL FORGIVE YOU, BUT I CAN'T FORGET** (44)	Okeh 6723	$25
78rpm	**JOLE BLON** (47)	Columbia 37287	$18
45rpm	**TENNESSEE WALTZ** (52)	Columbia 20551	$30
45rpm	**A PLASTIC HEART** (53)	Columbia 20792	$25
45rpm	**DOUG MACARTHUR** (54)	Columbia 20828	$25
45rpm	**ADVICE TO JOE** (54)	Columbia 20858	$20
45rpm	**JUST A FRIEND** (54)	Columbia 20877	$15
45rpm	**CHEATING** (54)	Columbia 20951	$15
45rpm	**SHE ISN'T GUARANTEED** (55)	Columbia 21018	$15
45rpm	**WHAT WILL I DO** (52)	Capitol 2385	$15
45rpm	**IS IT LOVE OR IS IT LIES** (52)	Capitol 2460	$10
45rpm	**16 CHICKENS** (53)	Capitol 2548	$10
45rpm	**SWAMP LILY** (53)	Capitol 2642	$10
45rpm	**WHOA MULE** (54)	Capitol 2738	$10
45rpm	**SUNSHINE SPECIAL** (54)	Capitol 2820	$12
45rpm	**THAT'S WHAT MAKES THE JUKEBOX PLAY** (55)	Capitol 3115	$12
45rpm	**CRAZY WORRIED MIND** (57)	Decca 29748	$10
45rpm	**MOTHER HOLD ME TIGHT** (58)	Decca 29935	$12
	(Duet with Kitty Wells)		
45rpm	**ONCE MORE** (58)	Hickory 1073	$12
45(P)	**ONCE MORE** (58)	Hickory 1073	$18
	(White promo label)		
45rpm	**THEY'LL NEVER TAKE HER LOVE FROM ME** (59)	Hickory 1090	$15
45rpm	**MY LOVE CAME BACK TO ME** (59)	Hickory 1097	$15
45rpm	**DON'T KNOW WHY** (59)	Hickory 1113	$12
45rpm	**MOUNTAIN GUITAR** (60)	Hickory 1134	$10
45rpm	**LOST JOHN, HE'S GONE** (61)	Hickory 1149	$12
33rpm	**WABASH CANNONBALL** Hall of Fame 33rpm single	Columbia 3-33024	$20
	(Black label with small center hole)		

-EPs-

EP	**REVIVAL TIME** (51)	Columbia 1514	$35
EP	**SONGS OF THE SMOKY MOUNTAINS** (55)	Capitol 1-617	$25
	(Various spellings on Smoky/Smokey)		
EP	**SONGS OF THE SMOKY MOUNTAINS** (55)	Capitol 2-617	$25
EP	**SONGS OF THE SMOKY MOUNTAINS** (55)	Capitol 3-617	$25

EP	**ROY ACUFF & THE SMOKY MOUNTAIN BOYS** (57)	Columbia 2803	$25
EP	**ROY ACUFF & THE SMOKY MOUNTAIN BOYS** (57)	Columbia 2825	$25
EP(P)	**KING OF COUNTRY MUSIC** (61) Promo-only EP for radio	Hickory H LPM 109	$50
	(Price includes paper sleeve, six songs on EP)		
EP(P)	**1976 FIFTH INTERNATIONAL FAN FAIR** (76)	CMA Nashville UR699	$20
	(16 PSA spots, one by Acuff)		

–albums–

10"LP	**SONGS OF THE SMOKEY MOUNTAINS** (49)	Columbia 9004	$200
	(Various spellings on Smoky/Smokey)		
10"LP	**OLD TIME BARN DANCE** (49)	Columbia 9010	$150
10"LP	**SONGS OF THE SADDLE** (50)	Columbia 9013	$125
LP	**SONGS OF THE SMOKY MOUNTAINS** (55)	Capitol 617	$60
	(Various spellings on Smoky/Smokey)		
LP	**FAVORITE HYMNS** (58)	MGM 3707	$40
LP(P)	**FAVORITE HYMNS** (58) White promo label	MGM 3707	$50
LP	**GREAT SPECKLED BIRD** (58)	Harmony 7082	$25
	(Reissue in 1968 is number 12289, worth $5)		
LP(P)	**GREAT SPECKLED BIRD** (58)	Harmony 7082	$35
	(White promo label)		
LP	**THAT GLORY BOUND TRAIN** (61)	Harmony 7294	$20
LP(P)	**THAT GLORY BOUND TRAIN** (61)	Harmony 7294	$30
	(White promo label)		
LP	**HYMN TIME** (62)	MGM 4044	$18
LP(P)	**HYMN TIME** (62)	MGM 4044	$25
	(White promo label)		
LP	**SONGS OF THE SMOKY MOUNTAINS** (63)	Capitol 1870	$25
LP(P)	**SONGS OF THE SMOKY MOUNTAINS** (63) Yellow promo label	Capitol 1870	$35
LP	**ONCE MORE** (61)	Hickory 101	$30
	(The first LP released by Hickory)		
LP	**ALL TIME GREATEST HITS** (62)	Hickory 109	$25
LP	**STAR OF THE GRAND OL' OPRY** (63)	Hickory 113	$25
LP	**THE WORLD IS HIS STAGE** (63)	Hickory 114	$25
LP	**ROY ACUFF SINGS AMERICAN FOLK SONGS** (63)	Hickory 115	$25
LP	**HAND-CLAPPING SONGS** (63)	Hickory 117	$25
	(With the Jordanaires)		
LP	**COUNTRY MUSIC'S HALL OF FAME** (63)	Capitol 1870	$25
	(Reissue in 1979 has SM prefix, worth $5)		
LP(P)	**COUNTRY MUSIC'S HALL OF FAME** (63)	Capitol 1870	$35
	(Blue promo label)		
LP	**THE GREAT ROY ACUFF** (64)	Capitol 2103	$25
LP(P)	**THE GREAT ROY ACUFF** (64)	Capitol 2103	$30
	(Blue promo label)		
LP	**COUNTRY MUSIC HALL OF FAME** (64)	Hickory 119	$20
LP	**GREAT TRAIN SONGS** (65)	Hickory 125	$18
LP	**THE GREAT ROY ACUFF** (65)	Harmony 7342	$12
LP(P)	**THE GREAT ROY ACUFF** (65)	Harmony 7342	$18
	(White promo label)		
LP	**ROY ACUFF** (65)	Metro (MGM) 508	$18
	(Sacred songs)		
LP(P)	**ROY ACUFF** (65)	Metro 508	$25
	(Yellow promo label)		
LP	**THE VOICE OF COUNTRY MUSIC** (65)	Capitol 2276	$25
LP(P)	**THE VOICE OF COUNTRY MUSIC** (65)	Capitol 2276	$35
	(Blue promo label)		
LP	**ROY ACUFF SINGS HANK WILLIAMS** (66)	Hickory 134	$40
LP	**WAITING FOR MY CALL TO GLORY** (66)	Harmony 7376	$18
	(Reissue in 1969 is number 11334, worth $6)		
LP(P)	**WAITING FOR MY CALL TO GLORY** (66)	Harmony 7376	$25
	(White promo label)		
LP(P)	**IN THE COUNTRY WESTERN MANNER** (70s)	U. S. Dept Health	$30
	(Twenty-one PSA spots, Roy does one 60-second spot)		
LP	**FAMOUS OPRY FAVORITES** (67)	Hickory 139	$18
LP	**LIVING LEGEND** (68)	Hickory 145	$18
LP	**TREASURY OF COUNTRY HITS** (69)	Hickory 147	$15
LP	**ROY ACUFF TIME** (70)	Hickory 156	$15
LP	**I SAW THE LIGHT** (70)	Hickory 158	$15
LP	**ROY ACUFF'S GREATEST HITS**	Columbia 1034	$12
LP	**NIGHT TRAIN TO MEMPHIS** (70)	Harmony 11403	$10
LP(P)	**NIGHT TRAIN TO MEMPHIS** (70)	Harmony 11403	$15
	(White promo label)		
2LP	**WHY IS ROY ACUFF** (73)	Hickory 162	$18
LP	**BACK IN THE COUNTRY** (74)	Hickory (MGM) 4507	$12
3LP	**COUNTRY & WESTERN CLASSICS** (75)	Time Life 09	$12
3LP	**HANK WILLIAMS AND ROY ACUFF** (70s)	Lamb & Lion (MGM) 706	$20
	(One disc is Acuff, two discs are Williams)		
LP(P)	**INTERVIEW WITH ROY ACUFF** (78) By Joe Smith	Elektra 78	$25
	(White promo label, promo-only release)		

	-radio shows-		
16"(RS)	**LEATHERNECK JAMBOREE** Public service radio show	Leatherneck Show 21	$100-150
	(Radio show from the 50s)		
LP(RS)	**GRAND OL' OPRY** (60s)	WSM show 13	$40-50
	(With guests Loretta Lynn and the Wilburn Brothers)		
LP(RS)	**GRAND OL' OPRY** (60s)	WSM show 19	$40-50
	(Guests include Wilburn Brothers)		
LP(RS)	**GRAND OL' OPRY** (60s)	WSM show 68	$40-50
	(Guests include Wilburn Brothers and Wilma Lee/Stoney Cooper)		
LP(RS)	**GRAND OL' OPRY** (60s)	WSM show 80	$40-50
	(Guests include the Carter Family and Don Gibson)		
LP(RS)	**GRAND OL' OPRY** (60s)	WSM show 85	$40-50
	(Guests include Wilburn Brothers and Loretta Lynn)		
LP(RS)	**GRAND OL' OPRY** (60s)	WSM show 93	$40-50
	(With guests)		
LP(RS)	**GRAND OL' OPRY** (60s)	WSM show 113	$40-50
	(Guests include June Carter and the Wilburn Brothers)		

ROY ACUFF JR. (CW)
Hickory 45s $3 each

-albums-

LP	**ROY ACUFF JR.** (70)	Hickory 150	$15

ART ADAMS (RB)

-singles-

45rpm	**ROCK CRAZY BABY** (57)	Cherry 1005	$100
45rpm	**DANCIN' DOLL** (58)	Cherry 1019	$75

BILLY ADAMS (RB)

-singles-

45rpm	**YOU GOTTA HAVE A DUCKTAIL** (58)	Nav Voo 802	$60
45rpm	**THE RETURN OF THE ALL AMERICAN BOY** (58)	Nav Voo 805	$50
45rpm	**BABY, I'M BUGGED** (58)	Decca 30724	$18
45(P)	**BABY, I'M BUGGED** (58)	Decca 30724	$15
	(Pink promo label)		
45rpm	**CAN'T GET ENOUGH** (59)	Capitol 4373	$18
45(P)	**CAN'T GET ENOUGH** (59)	Capitol 4373	$12
	(Red promo label)		

CHARLIE ADAMS (RB)

-singles-

45rpm	**CATTIN' AROUND** (57)	Columbia 21355	$20
45(P)	**CATTIN' AROUND** (57)	Columbia 21355	$15
	(White promo label)		
45rpm	**PISTOL PACKIN' MAMA HAS LAID HER PISTOL DOWN** (57)	Columbia 21443	$15
45(P)	**PISTOL PACKIN' MAMA HAS LAID HER PISTOL DOWN** (57)	Columbia 21443	$10
	(White promo label)		

KAY ADAMS (CW)
Tower 45s $3 each

-albums-

LP	**WHEELS & TEARS** (66)	Tower 5033	$15
LP	**MAKE MINE COUNTRY** (67)	Tower 5069	$12
LP	**ALCOHOL & TEARS** (68)	Tower 5087	$10
	(Same value promo or stock on all three)		

GEN ADKINS (Polka)
Singer with the Tune Toppers

-singles-

45rpm	**MOON KISSES** (55)	SRC 12	$15
	(With the Tune Toppers)		

HAZEL ADKINS (RB)

-singles-

45rpm	**SHE'S MINE** (58)	Air 5045	$50
45rpm	**SHE'S MINE** (58)	Jody 1000	$40

JACK ADKINS (CW)
Starday 45s $2 each

-albums-

LP	**JACK ADKINS** (62)	Starday 168	$18

ADMIRAL TONES (RB)

-singles-

45rpm	**HEY HEY PRETTY BABY** (57)	Future 1006	$50
45rpm	**HEY HEY PRETTY BABY** (58)	Felsted 8563	$40

LARRY AGAN (RB)

-singles-

45rpm	**FRANKIE'S NEW LOVER** (58)	Squire 103	$40

VARIOUS ARTISTS

-radio shows-

LP(P)	**AIR FORCE COUNTRY** (74-76) Air Force PSA ads	U.S. Air Force	each $25
	(Includes ten to sixteen spots by top artists and each is issued with a special hard cover)		

AL & JIM (RB)

-singles-

45rpm	**ROCK-A-BILLY MUSIC** (58)	Logan 3117	$30

ALABAMA (C)

RCA Victor 45s $2 each
Other RCA Victor promo 45s $3 each
RCA Victor LPs $4 each

-singles-

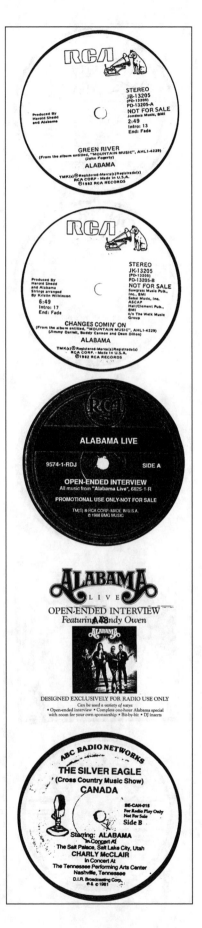

45rpm	**I WANNA COME OVER** (79)	MDJ 7906	$10
	(Multicolored label)		
45(P)	**I WANNA COME OVER** (79)	MDJ 7906	$18
	(Colored vinyl promo)		
45(P)	**MOUNTAIN MUSIC** (81)	RCA Victor 13019	$18
	(Green vinyl promo, gold label)		
45(P)	**I WANNA BE WITH YOU TONIGHT** (82)	Sun 1173	$25
	(Yellow vinyl promo-only release)		
45(P)	**FIRE IN THE NIGHT** (84)	RCA Victor 13926	$12
	(Blue vinyl promo, silver label)		
45(P)	**TOUCH ME WHEN WE'RE DANCING** (86)	RCA Victor 5003	$10
	(Gold promo label, black vinyl, includes insert)		
PS(P)	**TAR TOP** (88) Promo-only picture sleeve	RCA Victor 5222	$10
	(Record is black vinyl, red promo label)		
45(P)	**PASS IT ON** (90) Includes twelve-second PSA	RCA Victor 2519	$10
	(Picture sleeve includes PSA script and "Not for Sale")		

-12-inch singles-

12"(P)	**GREEN RIVER** (82) Green vinyl, yellow label	RCA Victor 13205	$18
	(Twelve-inch single issued in printed clear plastic cover)		

-albums-

LP	**WILD COUNTRY** (81) Recalled	Plantation 44	$60
	(Group did not want this LP released)		
LP(P)	**WILD COUNTRY** (81) White promo label	Plantation 44	$40
	(Also recalled)		
LP	**STARS** (82) Release unknown	Sun 148	Unknown
	(Same material as Plantation 44)		
LP(P)	**STARS** (82) Release unknown	Sun 148	Unknown
	(White promo label, if it exists)		
LP(P)	**OPEN-ENDED INTERVIEW WITH ALABAMA** (88)	RCA Victor	$30
	(Promo-only release, music and interviews)		

-radio shows-

LP(RS)	**COUNTRY NEWS** (Aug 81) Randy Cook		$10-15
	(Six of the fourteen five-minute shows about Alabama)		
3LP(RS)	**THE SILVER EAGLE** (81) Charlie McClain	DIR	$40-75
	(Live concert, label error reads "Charlie McClair")		
3LP(RS)	**THE SILVER EAGLE** (81) With Razzy Bailey	DIR	$40-80
	(Live concert)		
3LP(RS)	**THE SILVER EAGLE** (Apr 82)	DIR	$50-100
	(Live concert)		
3LP(RS)	**THE ALABAMA STORY** (Jun 83) Box set	United Stations	$20-40
	(Music and interviews)		
3LP(RS)	**TRIPLE** (Jun 83) Janie Fricke and Ricky Skaggs	Mutual Radio	$20-30
	(Music and interviews, box set)		
LP(RS)	**LIVE AT GILLEY'S** (Sep 83)	Westwood One	$25-40
	(Live concert)		
LP(RS)	**LIVE AT GILLEY'S** (Apr 85)	Westwood One	$25-40
	(Live concert different from above)		
LP(RS)	**LIVE AT GILLEY'S** (May 88) With Loretta Lynn	Westwood One	$25-40
	(Live concert)		
2LP(RS)	**A LOOK AT ALABAMA** (80s) "A Look at the Future"		$20-30
	(Music and interviews)		
3LP(RS)	**GOLDEN DECADE** (Jan 88) Box set		$25-50
	(Music and interviews)		
LP(RS)	**AUSTIN ENCORE** (88) With Johnny Rodriguez	Mainstreet Broadcasting	$20-30
	(Live concert)		
3CD(RS)	**WESTWOOD ONE SPECIAL** (Nov 94)	Westwood One	$20-40
	(Music and interviews from "Once Upon a Lifetime")		

MAX ALEXANDER (RB)
-singles-

45rpm	**LITTLE ROME** (58)	Caprock 116	$90

ALL AMERICAN RAMBLES (CW)
-albums-

LP	**DESTINATION DIXIE** (58)	Gone 5006	$40

VARIOUS ARTISTS (CW)
-singles-

2LP	**ALL-STAR COUNTRY & WESTERN JAMBOREE**	Starday 7001	$25
	(Features most past and present Starday artists, packaged for RCA Record Club members)		

VARIOUS ARTISTS (R)
-albums-

LP	**ALL STAR ROCK 'N' ROLL REVUE** (59)	King 513	$40

CHUCK ALAIMO (RB)
The Chuck Alaimo Quartet
Other MGM 45s $10 each
-singles-

45rpm	**HOP IN MY JALOP** (58) Stock or promo copy	MGM 12636	$18
45(P)	**HOP IN MY JALOP** (58)	MGM 12636	$15
	(Yellow promo label)		

UREL ALBERT (C)
World's greatest country imitator
Other 45s $2-5 each
-singles-

45rpm	**I'M AN IMITATOR** (69)	Spar 30023	$12
45(P)	**I'M AN IMITATOR** (69)	Spar 30023	$15
	(White promo label)		
45rpm	**COUNTRY AND POP MUSIC** (73)	Toast 311	$15
45rpm	**BREAK ONE NINE** (76)	Column One 198	$10

BILL ALLEN (RB)
-singles-

45rpm	**OO-WE-BABY** (57)	Eldorado 505	$10
45rpm	**PLEASE GIVE ME SOMETHING** (58)	Imperial 5500	$50

CLAY ALLEN (C)
Longhorn label 45s have Clay's photo and signature on the label, worth $3-5 each

DEBORAH ALLEN (C)
Other RCA, Capitol, and MCA 45s $2 each
RCA, Capitol, and MCA LPs $3 each
-singles-

45(P)	**HEARTACHE AND A HALF** (84)	RCA Victor 13921	$10
	(Red label, yellow vinyl, price includes picture sleeve)		

-radio shows-

LP(RS)	**COUNTRY MUSIC TIME** (80s)	U.S. Air Force	$10-15
	(Music and interviews)		

HAROLD ALLEN (RB)
-singles-

45rpm	**HONKY TONKIN' WOMEN** (57)	Mar-vel 1200	$30
45rpm	**I NEED SOME LOVIN'** (57)	Mar-vel 1201	$25

JERRY ALLEN (C)
Cardinal label 45s are mostly instrumentals, worth $3-5 each

KIRBY ALLEN (RB)
-singles-

45rpm	**MOTHER DON'T 'LLOW ROCK 'N' ROLL** (58)	Maze 140	$50

LONNIE ALLEN (RB)
-singles-

45rpm	**YOU'LL NEVER CHANGE ME** (58)	Val-Hill 1005	$30

MILTON ALLEN (RB)
-singles-

45rpm	**DON'T BUG ME BABY** (60)	RCA Victor 7116	$40

REX ALLEN (CW)

Decca 78s $8 each
Other Decca 45s $3-6 each
Mercury 45s $5 each
Hilltop 45s $3 each
MCA 45s $2 each
JMI and Collector Classics LPs $4 each
MCA LPs $3 each

-singles-

45rpm	**AS LONG AS THE RIVER FLOWS ON** (52)	Decca 27952	$12
	(With the Anita Kerr Singers)		
45rpm	**TILL THE WELL GOES DRY** (52)	Decca 28146	$12
45rpm	**JAMBALAYA** (52)	Decca 28341	$12
	(With the Nashville Dixielanders)		
45rpm	**CRYING IN THE CHAPEL** (53)	Decca 28758	$10
	(His biggest country hit)		
45rpm	**WHY, DADDY?** (54)	Decca 28933	$10
	(With Janice Klein)		
45rpm	**HE PLAYED A STEEL GUITAR** (55)	Decca 28998	$10
45rpm	**YOU TOOK MY NAME** (55)	Decca 29297	$10
	(With Eva Summers)		
45rpm	**L-O-N-E-S-O-M-E LETTER BLUES** (55)	Decca 29397	$10
45rpm	**THAT'S WHAT MAKES THE JUKEBOX PLAY** (56)	Decca 29586	$10
45rpm	**DADDY, YOU KNOW WHAT** (56) With son Curtis Allen	Decca 29610	$10
	(Both of the above are for stock copies)		
45rpm	**THE LAST ROUNDUP** (58)	Decca 29729	$10
	(With Victor Young)		
45rpm	**THE LAST FRONTIER** (58)	Decca 29871	$10
	(With Victor Young)		
45rpm	**TRAIL OF THE LONESOME PINE** (58)	Decca 30066	$12
	(With Victor Young)		
45rpm	**KNOCK KNOCK RATTLE** (58) Stock copy	Decca 30651	$18
45(P)	**KNOCK KNOCK RATTLE** (58) Pink promo label	Decca 30651	$15
45rpm	**BAREFOOT COUNTRY BOY** (58) With son Curtis Allen	Vista 355	$18
45rpm	**RIDERS IN THE SKY** (76) Grady Martin	Monument 202	$10
	(Narration by Rex Allen)		

-EPs-

EP	**REX ALLEN SINGS** (55)	Mercury 3111	$25
EP	**REX ALLEN SINGS** (55)	Mercury 3113	$25
EP	**PATTI PAGE & REX ALLEN SING** (55)	Mercury 3114	$25
	(With Patti Page)		
EP	**SONG TALES** (56)	Mercury 3193	$25
EP	**WESTERN STYLE** (56)	Mercury 3198	$25
EP	**REX ALLEN SINGS** (56)	Mercury 3209	$25
EP	**WESTWOOD HO THE WAGONS** (57)	Decca 2448	$30
EP	**REX ALLEN SINGS** (59) Includes "Bronco Boogie"	Vista 3302	$40
	(Stock or promo copy)		

-albums-

LP	**UNDER WESTERN SKIES** (56)	Decca 8402	$50
LP(P)	**UNDER WESTERN SKIES** (56)	Decca 8402	$40
	(Pink promo label)		
LP	**MISTER COWBOY** (59)	Decca 8776	$40
LP(P)	**MISTER COWBOY** (59)	Decca 8776	$35
	(Pink promo label)		
LP	**REX ALLEN SINGS** (60)	Hacienda 101	$175
	(Very hard to find)		
LP	**REX ALLEN SINGS** (61)	Buena Vista 3307	$50
LP(P)	**REX ALLEN SINGS** (61)	Buena Vista 3307	$40
	(White promo label)		
LP	**FAITH OF A MAN** (62)	Mercury 20719	$25
LP(P)	**FAITH OF A MAN** (62)	Mercury 20719	$30
	(White promo label)		
LP	**MELODIES OF THE PLAINS** (62)	Design 612	$10
LP	**REX ALLEN SINGS AND TELLS TALES** (62)	Mercury 20752	$25
LP(P)	**REX ALLEN SINGS AND TELLS TALES** (62)	Mercury 20752	$30
	(White promo label)		
LP	**REX ALLEN SINGS AND TELLS TALES** (66)	Wing 16324	$15
LP(P)	**REX ALLEN SINGS AND TELLS TALES** (66)	Wing 16324	$18
	(White promo label)		
LP	**REX ALLEN** (62)	Wing 16268	$15
LP(P)	**REX ALLEN** (62)	Wing 16268	$18
	(White promo label)		
LP	**WESTERN BALLADS** (65)	Hilltop (Pickwick) 6009	$10
LP	**SMOOTH COUNTRY SOUND** (68)	Decca 5011	$15
LP(P)	**SMOOTH COUNTRY SOUND** (68)	Decca 5011	$12
	(White promo label)		
LP	**THE TOUCH OF GOD'S HAND** (70)	Decca 5205	$18

LP(P)	**THE TOUCH OF GOD'S HAND** (70)	Decca 5205	$15
	(White promo label)		
LP	**FAVORITE SONGS** (70)	Disneyland 1337	$12
LP	**SONGS OF THE GOLDEN WEST** (70)	Vocalion 3885	$15
	(Reissued Decca material)		
LP	**LOVE GONE COLD** (72)	Longhorn 1234	$10

REX ALLEN, JR. (C)
Son of Rex Allen
Other Warner 45s $2 each
Warner LPs $3 each

-singles-

45(P)	**COUNTRY COMFORT** (74)	SSS 837	$12
	(Elton John song, blue vinyl)		
45(P)	**LAST OF THE SILVER SCREEN COWBOYS** (82) w/Rex Allen	Warner 50035	$10
	(Price includes classic picture sleeve, the record is a see-through black vinyl)		

-radio shows-

LP(RS)	**LIVE AT GILLEY'S** (85)	Westwood One	$10-15
	(Live concert)		

RONNIE ALLEN (RB)

-singles-

45rpm	**JUVENILE DELINQUENT** (58)	San 208	$40
45rpm	**HIGH SCHOOL LOVE** (58)	San 209	$40

ROSALIE ALLEN (CW)
Bluebird 78s $15 each
   (With the Black River Riders)
Other RCA Victor 45s and 78s $5-8 each

-singles-

45rpm	**SHOOT HIM HIGH PAW** (51)	RCA Victor 4425	$18
45rpm	**THE WALLFLOWER WALTZ** (52)	RCA Victor 4752	$12
	(With Elton Britt)		
45rpm	**BRING YOUR SWEET SELF BACK TO ME** (53)	RCA Victor 5308	$10
45rpm	**ON AND ON WITH YOU** (53)	RCA Victor 5322	$12
	(With Elton Britt)		
45rpm	**CASTAWAY** (53)	RCA Victor 5379	$10

-EPs-

EP	**HE TAUGHT ME HOW TO YODEL** (55)	RCA Victor 592	$40
	(With Patsy Montana)		

-albums-

10"LP	**ROSALIE ALLEN SINGS COUNTRY & WESTERN** (54)	Waldorf 150	$75
	(Budget label)		
LP	**SONGS OF THE GOLDEN WEST** (57)	Grand Award 330	$40
	(Budget label)		
LP	**RODEO** (59)	Grand Award 350	$20
	(With Tex Fletcher)		
LP	**ROSALIE ALLEN** (61)	RCA Victor 2313	$20
2LP	**ROSALIE ALLEN** (75)	Camden	$18
	(Reissue of RCA Victor material)		

TONY ALLEN (RB)

-singles-

45rpm	**CALL MY NAME** (57)	Imperial 5523	$15
45(P)	**CALL MY NAME** (57)	Imperial 5523	$12
	(Promo label)		
45rpm	**ROCKIN' SHOES** (58)	Imperial 5547	$20
45(P)	**ROCKIN' SHOES** (58)	Imperial 5547	$15
	(Promo label)		

ALLEN BROTHERS (CW)
Bluebird 78s $12 each
Columbia 78s $25 each
Other Victor 78s $40 each
Vocalion 78s $20 each

-singles-

78rpm	**WINDOW SHADE BLUES**	Victor 23692	$100
78rpm	**GLORIOUS NIGHT BLUES**	Victor 23707	$75
	The Allen Brothers recorded several albums in the '80s including Red Allen. See (Red Allen and the) Osborne Brothers for listings of collectible MGM albums from 1959		

JIM ALLEY (RB)

-singles-

45rpm	**DIG THAT ROCK & ROLL** (58)	Pearl 4468	$65

GLORIA ALLEYNE (R)

-singles-

45rpm	**WHEN I SAY MY PRAYERS** (58)	Josie 767	$40

ALLMAN BROTHERS BAND (R)
Other Hour Glass 45s on Liberty $8 each
Other label 45s $2-4 each
LPs $4-8 each

-singles-

45(P)	**POWER OF LOVE** (67) Hour Glass	Liberty 56029	$15
45(P)	**MORNING DEW** (72) (Red vinyl)	Bold Records	$50

-EPs-

EP(JB)	**BEGINNINGS** (73) Jukebox LLP (Issued with a hard cover)	Atlantic 805	$18
EP(JB)	**BROTHERS AND SISTERS** (73) Jukebox LLP (Issued with a paper cover)	Capricorn 229	$20
EP(JB)	**LAID BACK** (73) Jukebox LLP (Issued with a paper cover)	Capricorn 0116	$20

-albums-

LP(P)	**DUANE ALLMAN DIALOGS** (72) (Promo-only release)	Capricorn PRO 545	$100
CD(P)	**ACOUSTIC EVENING** (93) Eight tracks by the Allmans (Also eight tracks by the Indigo Girls)	Epic CD	$75

-radio shows-

2LP(RS)	**TOYOTA PRESENTS** (70s) (Gregg Allman)	Toyota Presents	$25-50
LP(RS)	**ROCK AROUND THE WORLD** (June 77) (Music and interviews)	ABC Radio	$75-125
3LP(RS)	**SUPERGROUPS** (82) Allman Brothers (Live concert)	DIR	$75-125
LP(RS)	**INNERVIEW** (70s) Allman Brothers (Music and interviews)	Inner View	$10-20
3LP(RS)	**SOURCE SPECIAL** (Nov 81) Allman Brothers (Music and interviews)	NBC Source	$25-50
3LP(RS)	**A NIGHT ON THE ROAD** (82) (Box set with scripts and time clock)	ABC Radio	$75-125
2LP(RS)	**KING BISCUIT FLOWER HOUR** (81) Allman Brothers (Live concert)	DIR/ABC	$25-50
CD(RS)	**KING BISCUIT FLOWER HOUR** (87) Allman Brothers (Live concert)	DIR	$29-30
CD(RS)	**KING BISCUIT FLOWER HOUR** (Nov 87) w/CSN & Y (Live concert)	DIR	$20-30
CD(RS)	**KING BISCUIT FLOWER HOUR** (Dec 87) Gregg Allman (Live concert)	DIR	$20-30
2CD(RS)	**KING BISCUIT FLOWER HOUR** (July 89) (Two shows, live concert)	DIR	$40-60
CD(RS)	**KING BISCUIT FLOWER HOUR** (Dec 90) Allman Brothers (Live concert)	DIR	$20-30
CD(RS)	**KING BISCUIT FLOWER HOUR** (Mar 92) Gregg Allman (Live concert)	DIR	$20-30
CD(RS)	**KING BISCUIT FLOWER HOUR** (Nov 94) Gregg Allman (Live concert)	DIR	$20-30
2LP(RS)	**IN CONCERT** (88) Allman Brothers (Live concert)	Westwood One	$20-40
2LP(RS)	**IN CONCERT** (Oct 90) Allman Brothers (Live concert)	Westwood One	$20-35
CD(RS)	**IN CONCERT** (Oct 94) New Allman Band (Live concert)	Westwood One	$25-40
2LP(RS)	**OFF THE RECORD** (89) Allman Brothers (Music and interviews)	Westwood One	$15-25
CD(RS)	**OFF THE RECORD** (91) Allman Brothers (Music and interviews)	Westwood One	$15-25
2LP(RS)	**WORLD OF ROCK** (Aug 89) Gregg Allman (Allman is cohost, music and interviews)	DIR	$15-25
2CD(RS)	**ROCK STARS** (July 89) Allman Brothers (Music and interviews)	Radio Today	$20-40
3CD(RS)	**ROCK AT THE CORE** (89) Various artists (Music and interviews, includes Allman Brothers)	Rock Core	$25-50
2CD(RS)	**UP CLOSE** (88) Gregg Allman (Music and interviews)	Media America	$25-40
4CD(RS)	**UP CLOSE** (89) Allman Brothers (Music and interviews)	Media America	$25-50
CD(RS)	**IN THE STUDIO** (90s) Profile of an album (Music and interviews)	Album Network	$10-15
3LP(RS)	**SUPERSTAR CONCERT** (90) Allman Brothers (Box set, live concert)	Westwood One	$20-40

2CD(RS)	**SUPERSTAR CONCERT** (90) Allman Brothers	Westwood One	$20-40
	(Live concert)		
3CD(RS)	**GLOBAL SATELLITE SPECIAL** (92) Allman Brothers	Global Satellite	$20-40
	(Music and interviews)		
2CD(RS)	**CRY OF LOVE IN CONCERT** (Jan 94)	Westwood One	$20-35
	(Music and interviews)		
2CD(RS)	**ALBUM NETWORK SPECIAL** (Aug 94) Allman Brothers	Album Network	$20-40
	(Music and interviews)		

TOMMY ALLSUP (R)
Of the Crickets
Reprise 45s $5 each

-albums-

LP	**TOMMY ALLSUP** (65)	Reprise 6182	$50
LP(P)	**TOMMY ALLSUP** (65)	Reprise 6182	$60
	(White promo label)		

LUCKY JOE ALMOND (RB)

-singles-

45rpm	**OO OO ANYTHING GOES** (58)	Globe 240	$30
45rpm	**ROCK ME** (58)	Trumpet 199	$12
45rpm	**GONNA ROCK & ROLL** (59)	Trumpet 221	$15

JOHNNY AMELIO (RB)

-singles-

45rpm	**JUGUE** (57)	Blue Moon 405	$125
45rpm	**JO-ANN JO-ANN** (59)	Blue Moon 408	$75

VARIOUS ARTISTS (C)
Weekly versions of American Country Countdown are worth less than $10 per set

-radio shows-

8LP(RS)	**AMERICAN COUNTRY COUNTDOWN** (80s)	Westwood One	$25-50
	Year-end countdown of one hundred country songs		
	(Two weekly 3LP, 4LP sets)		

DOUG AMERSON (RB)

-singles-

45rpm	**BOP MAN TOP** (57)	G & G 105	$60
45rpm	**BOP MAN TOP** (58)	Intrastate 25	$50

BETTY AMOS (CW)

-singles-

45rpm	**I WILL FOR YOU** (55)	Mercury 70456	$10

ANDY ANDERSON (RB)

-singles-

45rpm	**I-I-I LOVE YOU** (58)	Felsted 8508	$20
45rpm	**YOU SHAKE ME UP** (58)	Apollo 535	$40
45rpm	**GIMMIE A LOCK O' YOUR HAIR** (58)	Century Ltd.	$40

BILL ANDERSON (C)
Other Decca 45s $2-4 each
MCA 45s including duets $2 each
Other Decca LPs $4-6 each
Vocalion LPs $6 each
MCA LPs $3 each

-singles-

45rpm	**CITY LIGHTS** (58)	TNT 9015	$75
	(Rockabilly, written by Anderson)		
45(P)	**CITY LIGHTS** (58)	TNT 9015	$85
	(White promo label)		
45rpm	**NINETY-NINE** (59)	Decca 30914	$10
45rpm	**DEAD OR ALIVE** (60)	Decca 30993	$10
45rpm	**8 X 10** (63)	Decca 31521	$10
	(Price includes picture sleeve)		

-EPs-

EP	**PO' FOLKS** (63)	Decca 2740	$18
EP	**STILL** (64)	Decca 2761	$18
EP	**FIVE LITTLE FINGERS** (65)	Decca 2776	$18
EP	**ME** (65)	Decca 2790	$18
EP	**CERTAIN** (65)	Decca 2798	$18
33(P)	**1965 MARCH OF DIMES** (65) Sings "Still"	March of Dimes 5501	$25
	(Two spots, 4:24 and :30)		
33(P)	**1976 FIFTH INTERNATIONAL FAN FAIR** (76) Radio spots	CMA UR699	$25
	(Sixteen spots, Anderson does one)		

-albums-

LP(P)	**COUNTRY & WESTERN DRUMMERS** (60) Production aids	Seasac 159	$50
	(With Roy Drusky and Darrell McCall)		
LP	**BILL ANDERSON SINGS COUNTRY SONGS** (62)	Decca 4192	$20
LP(P)	**BILL ANDERSON SINGS COUNTRY SONGS** (62)	Decca 4192	$25
	(White promo label)		
LP	**STILL** (63)	Decca 4427	$18
LP(P)	**STILL** (63)	Decca 4427	$20
	(White promo label)		
LP	**BILL ANDERSON SINGS** (64)	Decca 4499	$15
LP(P)	**BILL ANDERSON SINGS** (64)	Decca 4499	$18
	(White promo label)		
LP	**BILL ANDERSON SHOWCASE** (64)	Decca 4600	$15
LP(P)	**BILL ANDERSON SHOWCASE** (64)	Decca 4600	$18
	(White promo label)		
LP	**FROM THIS PEN** (65) With the Jordanaires	Decca 4646	$15
LP(P)	**FROM THIS PEN** (65)	Decca 74646	$18
	(White promo label)		
LP	**BRIGHT LIGHTS AND COUNTRY MUSIC** (65)	Decca 4686	$15
LP(P)	**BRIGHT LIGHTS AND COUNTRY MUSIC** (65)	Decca 4686	$18
	(White promo label)		
LP	**I LOVE YOU DROPS** (66)	Decca 4771	$12
LP(P)	**I LOVE YOU DROPS** (66)	Decca 4771	$15
	(White promo label)		
LP	**GET WHILE THE GETTIN'S GOOD** (67) With Jordanaires	Decca 4855	$12
LP(P)	**GET WHILE THE GETTIN'S GOOD** (67)	Decca 4855	$15
	(White promo label)		
LP	**BILL ANDERSON'S GREATEST HITS** (67)	Decca 4859	$12
LP(P)	**BILL ANDERSON'S GREATEST HITS** (67)	Decca 4859	$15
	(White promo label)		
LP	**I CAN DO NOTHING ALONE** (67)	Decca 4886	$10
LP(P)	**I CAN DO NOTHING ALONE** (67)	Decca 4886	$12
	(White promo label)		
LP	**FOR LOVING YOU** (67) With Jan Howard	Decca 4959	$10
LP(P)	**FOR LOVING YOU** (67)	Decca 4959	$12
	(White promo label)		
LP	**WILD WEEKEND** (68)	Decca 4998	$10
LP(P)	**WILD WEEKEND** (68)	Decca 4998	$12
	(White promo label)		
LP	**HAPPY STATE OF MIND** (68)	Decca 5056	$10
LP(P)	**HAPPY STATE OF MIND** (68)	Decca 5056	$12
	(White promo label)		
2LP	**THE BILL ANDERSON STORY** (69)	Decca 7198	$25
	(Repackaged version has label number 7213)		
2LP(P)	**THE BILL ANDERSON STORY** (69)	Decca 7198	$30
	(White promo label)		

-radio shows-

LP(RS)	**GRAND OL' OPRY** (60s) Radio show	WSM show 72	$25-40
	(Guests include the Browns and Connie Smith)		
LP(RS)	**HOOTENAVY** Radio show with Connie Smith	U.S. Navy 40H	$25-40
	(One fifteen-minute show on each side)		
LP(RS)	**CHRISTMAS WITH ...** (70s) Radio show	Diamond P 515	$25-40
	(Music and interviews)		
2LP(RS)	**COUNTRY COOKIN'** (Mar 77) Fifteen-minute shows	U.S. Air Force	$10-15
	(Music and interviews)		
LP(RS)	**COUNTRY MUSIC TIME** (78)	U.S. Air Force	$10-12
	(Music and interviews)		
LP(RS)	**COUNTRY CROSSROADS** (80s)	Southern Baptists	$10-12
	(Music and interviews)		

JOHN ANDERSON (C)
Warner 45s $2 each
Other MCA promo colored vinyl 45s $8 each
MCA 45s $1 each
Warner and MCA LPs $3 each

-singles-

45(P)	**WHEN YOUR YELLOW BRICK ROAD TURNS BLUE** (87)	MCA 53155	$10
	(Red vinyl, white promo label)		

-radio shows-

LP(RS)	**COUNTRY MUSIC TIME** (80s)	U.S. Air Force	$10-12
	(Music and interviews)		
3LP(RS)	**AMERICAN EAGLE** (July 86)	DIR	$15-25
	(Live concert)		
LP(RS)	**LIVE FROM GILLEY'S** (Dec 86)	Westwood One	$15-25
	(Live concert)		
CD(RS)	**SUMMER CONCERT SERIES** (July 94) With Boy Howdy	Westwood One	$25-50
	(Live concert)		

LIZ ANDERSON (C)
Mother of Lynn Anderson
RCA Victor 45s $2 each
RCA Victor and Camden LPs $3-5 each

LONNIE ANDERSON (RB)

-singles-

45rpm	**TEENAGE BABY** (58)	Lads 700	$125

LYNN ANDERSON (C)
Other Chart 45s $3 each
Other Columbia 45s $2 each
MCA 45s $1 each
Permain 45s $1 each
Album Globe LPs $6 each
Columbia LPs $3-5 each
Harmony LPs $4 each
MCA LPs $3 each

-singles-

33(P)	**FRANK JONES INTERVIEW** (70)	Columbia AS7 1024	$10
	(Price includes black/white picture sleeve)		
45(P)	**LISTEN TO A COUNTRY SONG** (70)	Columbia AE7 1052	$10
	(Promo-only medley of songs from the LP)		
45(P)	**DING-A-LING THE CHRISTMAS BELL** (70)	Columbia 45251	$10
	(Promo record and picture sleeve)		

-EPs-

EP	**THE BEST OF LYNN ANDERSON** (69) Jukebox LLP	Chart 009	$15
	(Issued with a hard cover)		
EP	**ROSE GARDEN** (70) Jukebox LLP	Columbia 30411	$12
	(Red label, hard cover)		
EP	**LYNN ANDERSON** (71) Jukebox LLP	Chart 1028	$12
	(Issued with a hard cover)		

-albums-

LP	**RIDE, RIDE, RIDE (67)**	Chart 1001	$18
	(Red label, later orange label worth $8-10)		
LP	**BIG GIRLS DON'T CRY** (69)	Chart 1008	$12
	(Orange label)		
LP	**THE BEST OF LYNN ANDERSON** (69)	Chart 1009	$12
	(Orange label)		
LP	**WITH LOVE FROM LYNN** (69)	Chart 1013	$12
LP	**AT HOME WITH LYNN** (69)	Chart 1017	$12
LP	**SONGS THAT MADE COUNTRY GIRLS FAMOUS** (69)	Chart 1022	$10
LP	**UPTOWN COUNTRY GIRL** (70)	Chart 1028	$10
LP	**SONGS MY MOTHER WROTE** (70)	Chart 1032	$10
	(Lynn's mother is Liz Anderson)		
LP	**I'M ALRIGHT** (70)	Chart 1037	$10
	(Light blue label)		
LP	**LYNN ANDERSON'S GREATEST HITS** (70)	Chart 1040	$10
LP	**LYNN ANDERSON WITH STRINGS** (71)	Chart 1043	$10
2LP	**LYNN ANDERSON** (72)	Chart 1050	$12

MARIAN ANDERSON (P)
A black singer of mostly gospel music, she recorded some country songs in a RCA Victor EP-313 box set
of three 45s, all on red vinyl, worth $8 each disc

SLIM ANDERSON (Polka)
Arcola 45s $4-8 each

PATTY ANDREWS (R,P)

-singles-

45rpm	**TOO OLD TO ROCK 'N' ROLL** (56)	Capitol 3295	$10

NICK ANTHONY (RB)

-singles-

45rpm	**YOU'RE REAL KEEN, JELLY BEAN** (57)	ABC Paramount 9919	$18
45(P)	**YOU'RE REAL KEEN, JELLY BEAN** (57)	ABC Paramount 9919	$15
	(White promo label)		

PAUL ANTHONY (RB)

-singles-

45rpm	**BOP! BOP! BOP!** (58)	Roulette 4099	$10

TONY ARATA (C)
MCA color vinyl 45s $5 each

THE ARKANSAS BLUEGRASS BOYS (BG)
-albums-

LP	**BLUEGRASS SPECIAL** (62)	Smigar 6275	$30

VARIOUS ARTISTS
-albums-

LP(P)	**ARMY RESERVE PRESENTS SPOTS** (74-76) PSA radio ads	Army Reserve	each $25

(Each disc represents three months, includes twenty-eight spots
by top current rock and country artists, issued with a special
hard cover)

EDDY ARNOLD (CW)
If you don't include Elvis, Eddy Arnold has sold more country records than anyone in history!
Other Victor 78s $5-8 each
RCA Victor 78s $5-8 each
RCA Victor promo 78s $8 each
Other RCA Victor green vinyl 45s (before 1950) $35 each
Other RCA Victor colored vinyl 45s (after 1970) $8 each
MGM 45s $2 each
Other RCA Victor picture sleeves (45s) $2-8 each
Other RCA Victor jukebox LLPs $6-8 each
Other RCA Victor LPs $1-3 each
Other Camden LPs $2-5 each
MGM LPs $2-4 each

-singles-

78rpm	**MOMMIE PLEASE STAY HOME WITH ME** (44)	Bluebird 0520	$75
	(First record by Eddy Arnold)		
	Later released on RCA Victor		
78rpm	**CATTLE CALL** (45)	Bluebird 0527	$45
	(First charted record)		
	Later released on RCA Victor		
78rpm	**DID YOU SEE MY DADDY** (45)	Bluebird 0535	$35
78rpm	**YOU MUST WALK THE LINE** (46)	Bluebird 0540	$25
78rpm	**I TALK TO MYSELF ABOUT YOU** (46)	RCA Victor 1801	$25
78rpm	**CAN'T WIN, CAN'T PLACE, CAN'T SHOW** (46)	RCA Victor 1855	$20
78rpm	**MOMMY PLEASE STAY HOME WITH ME** (46)	RCA Victor 1871	$20
78rpm	**THAT'S HOW MUCH I LOVE YOU** (47)	RCA Victor 1948	$18
78rpm	**WHAT IS LIFE WITHOUT LOVE** (47)	RCA Victor 2058	$10
	(First number one charted record)		
78rpm	**IT'S A SIN** (47)	RCA Victor 2241	$10
78rpm	**I'LL HOLD YOU IN MY HEART** (47)	RCA Victor 2332	$10
	(Mega hit)		

-box sets-

78s/45s	**ALL TIME HITS** (53)	RCA Victor 195	$50
	(Three record set, 45s are green vinyl)		
78s/45s	**TO MOTHER** (53)	RCA Victor 239	$30
	(Three record box set, black vinyl)		
78s/45s	**EDDY ARNOLD SINGS** (54)	RCA Victor 260	$50
	(Three record set, 45s are green vinyl)		

-45s-

45rpm	**THEN I TURNED AND WALKED SLOWLY AWAY** (49)	RCA Victor 0025	$25
	(Aqua label)		
45rpm	**MY DADDY IS ONLY A PICTURE** (49)	RCA Victor 0026	$20
	(Aqua label, black vinyl)		
45rpm	**MY DADDY IS ONLY A PICTURE** (49)	RCA Victor 0026	$40
	(Aqua label, green vinyl)		
45rpm	**DON'T BOTHER TO CRY** (49)	RCA Victor 0030	$20
	(Aqua label)		
45rpm	**DON'T ROB ANOTHER MAN'S CASTLE** (49)	RCA Victor 0042	$10
	(Aqua label)		
45rpm	**ONE KISS TOO MANY** (49)	RCA Victor 0051	$10
	(Aqua label)		
45rpm	**I'M THROWING RICE** (49)	RCA Victor 0080	$20
	(Aqua label)		
45rpm	**THE ECHO OF YOUR FOOTSTEPS** (49)	RCA Victor 0083	$10
	(Aqua label)		
45rpm	**C-H-R-I-S-T-M-A-S** (50)	RCA Victor 0127	$18
	(Aqua label)		
45rpm	**C-H-R-I-S-T-M-A-S** (50)	RCA Victor 0127	$10
	(Black label)		
45rpm	**THERE'S NO WINGS ON MY ANGEL** (50)	RCA Victor 0137	$10
	(Aqua label)		
45rpm	**TAKE ME IN YOUR ARMS AND HOLD ME** (50)	RCA Victor 0150	$10
	(Aqua label)		
45rpm	**EVIL TEMPT ME NOT** (50)	RCA Victor 0165	$40
	(Aqua label, green vinyl)		

45rpm	**BEAUTIFUL ISLE OF SOMEWHERE** (50)	RCA Victor 0166	$40
	(Aqua label, green vinyl)		
45rpm	**HILLS OF TOMORROW** (50)	RCA Victor 0167	$40
	(Green vinyl, box set of all three worth $125)		
45rpm	**LITTLE ANGEL WITH THE DIRTY FACE** (50)	RCA Victor 0300	$40
	(Aqua label, green vinyl)		
45rpm	**LITTLE ANGEL WITH THE DIRTY FACE** (50)	RCA Victor 0300	$10
	(Aqua label)		
45rpm	**CUDDLE BUGGIN' BABY** (50)	RCA Victor 0342	$10
	(Aqua label)		
45rpm	**A PRISON WITHOUT WALLS** (50)	RCA Victor 0382	$18
	(Aqua label)		
45rpm	**A PRISON WITHOUT WALLS** (50)	RCA Victor 0382	$10
	(Black label)		
45rpm	**WHITE CHRISTMAS** (51)	RCA Victor 0390	$40
	(Aqua label, green vinyl)		
45rpm	**THERE'S BEEN A CHANGE IN ME** (51)	RCA Victor 0412	$15
	(Aqua label)		
45rpm	**MAY THE GOOD LORD BLESS AND KEEP YOU** (51)	RCA Victor 0425	$15
	(Aqua label)		
45rpm	**KENTUCKY WALTZ** (51)	RCA Victor 0444	$15
	(Aqua label)		
45rpm	**I WANNA PLAY HOUSE WITH YOU** (52)	RCA Victor 0476	$25
	(Aqua label)		
45rpm	**I WANNA PLAY HOUSE WITH YOU** (52)	RCA Victor 0476	$15
	(Black label)		
45rpm	**CALL HER YOUR SWEETHEART** (52)	RCA Victor 4413	$15
	(Aqua label)		
45rpm	**ANYTHING THAT'S PART OF YOU** (52)	RCA Victor 4569	$12
	(Aqua label)		
45rpm	**A FULL TIME JOB** (52)	RCA Victor 4787	$10
	(Black label)		
45rpm	**OLDER AND BOLDER** (53)	RCA Victor 4954	$10
	(Black label)		
45rpm	**I WANT TO THANK YOU LORD** (53)	RCA Victor 5020	$15
	(Black label)		
45rpm	**CONDEMNED WITHOUT TRIAL** (53)	RCA Victor 5108	$12
	(Black label)		
45rpm	**MOONLIGHT AND ROSES** (53)	RCA Victor 5192	$12
	(Black label)		
45rpm	**YOU ALWAYS HURT THE ONE YOU LOVE** (53)	RCA Victor 5193	$12
	(Black label)		
45rpm	**HOW'S THE WORLD TREATING YOU** (54)	RCA Victor 5305	$12
	(Black label)		
45rpm	**MAMA, COME GET YOUR BABY BOY** (54)	RCA Victor 5415	$10
	(Black label)		
45rpm	**I REALLY DON'T WANT TO KNOW** (54)	RCA Victor 5525	$12
	(Black label)		
45rpm	**MY EVERYTHING** (54)	RCA Victor 5634	$10
	(Black label)		
45rpm	**HEP CAT BABY** (54)	RCA Victor 5805	$12
	(Black label)		
45(P)	**HEP CAT BABY** (54)	RCA Victor 5805	$10
	(White promo label)		
45rpm	**ROCKIN' MOCKIN' BIRD** (55)	RCA Victor 6502	$10
	(Dog on top label)		
45(P)	**THE FABULOUS 45** (56) Eleven cuts, one by Arnold	RCA Victor SPD-21	$40
	(Promotion by RCA to demonstrate 45rpm format)		
45(P)	**NEW YEAR'S GREETINGS/CHRISTMAS GREETINGS** (56)	RCA Victor SP-45-128	$40
	(Twelve cuts each side, one each by Arnold)		
45(P)	**I'LL HOLD YOU IN MY HEART** From "Music in the Air"	U. S. A. F. 42	$15
	(Public service programming includes full song)		
45rpm	**LITTLE MISS SUNBEAM** (58)	RCA Victor 7040	$12
	(Record and picture sleeve)		
45(P)	**NEW WORLD IN THE MORNING** (60)	RCA Victor SPS-45-227	$10
	(White label promo-only release)		
45rpm	**SITTIN' BY SITTIN' BULL** (61)	RCA Victor 7619	$15
	(Stereo single)		
33rpm	**JUST CALL ME LONESOME** (62)	RCA Victor 7861	$15
	(Compact-33 single)		
33rpm	**WRECK OF THE OLD '97** (62)	RCA Victor 2668	$12
	(Jukebox stereo single)		
45(P)	**MARY CARTER PAINTS** (68)	Mary Carter Paints 1421	$30
	(One-sided single, yellow label)		
45(P)	**DON'T GIVE UP ON ME** (82)	RCA Victor 13094	$10
	(Blue vinyl, blue promo label)		

-EPs-

2EP	**COUNTRY CLASSICS** (52)	RCA Victor 3027	$75
	(Very hard to find with both records intact)		
2EP	**ALL TIME HITS FROM THE HILLS** (54)	RCA Victor 3031	$50
	(Hard to find with both records)		
2EP	**AN AMERICAN INSTITUTION** (54)	RCA Victor 3230	$50
	(Hard to find with both records)		
EP	**TO MOTHER** (54)	RCA Victor 239	$40
EP	**EDDY ARNOLD SINGS** (54)	RCA Victor 260	$35
EP	**EDDY ARNOLD'S FAVORITE SACRED SONGS** (54)	RCA Victor 261	$30
	(Previously a three-record 45rpm color vinyl box set)		
EP	**ALL TIME HITS FROM THE HILLS** (54)	RCA Victor 328	$25
EP	**CATTLE CALL** (55)	RCA Victor 712	$25
EP	**THE OLD RUGGED CROSS** (55)	RCA Victor 427	$30
EP	**ALL TIME FAVORITES** (55)	RCA Victor 428	$25
EP	**ALL TIME FAVORITES** (55)	RCA Victor 429	$25
EP	**CHRISTMAS GREETINGS** (55)	RCA Victor 473	$30
EP	**OPEN THY MERCIFUL ARMS** (55)	RCA Victor 500	$25
EP	**SONGS OF HOPE AND INSPIRATION** (55)	RCA Victor 544	$20
EP	**I REALLY DON'T WANT TO KNOW** (55)	RCA Victor 573	$25
EP	**TOP HITS ROUNDUP** (55)	RCA Victor 624	$25
2EP	**WANDERIN' WITH EDDY ARNOLD** (55)	RCA Victor 1111	$40
2EP	**ALL TIME FAVORITES** (55)	RCA Victor 1223	$40
EP	**ALL TIME FAVORITES** (55)	RCA Victor 786	$18
2EP	**ANYTIME** (55)	RCA Victor 787	$18
2EP	**ANYTIME** (55)	RCA Victor 1224	$25
2EP	**CHAPEL ON THE HILL** (55)	RCA Victor 1225	$25
EP	**THE MOST HAPPY FELLA** (56)	RCA Victor 900	$18
	(With Chet Atkins)		
EP	**TENNESSEE WALTZ** (56)	RCA Victor 913	$18
EP	**TENNESSEE WALTZ** (56)	RCA Victor 914	$18
EP	**A LITTLE ON THE LONELY SIDE** (56)	RCA Victor 972	$15
EP	**THE VERY THOUGHT OF YOU** (56)	RCA Victor 973	$15
EP	**SEPTEMBER SONG** (56)	RCA Victor 974	$15
EP	**WHEN THEY WERE YOUNG** (57)	RCA Victor 1484	$15
3EP	**MY DARLING, MY DARLING** (57)	RCA Victor 1575	$15 each
	(Vol. 1, 2, 3 $45 for all three)		
EP	**EDDY ARNOLD TIME** (57)	RCA Victor 4109	$15
EP	**SPECIALLY FOR LITTLE ONES** (57)	RCA Victor 4220	$15
3EP(P)	**POP SAMPLER** (57)	RCA Victor SP-7-13	$25
	(One song by Eddy Arnold, "Wanderin'")		
EP	**EDDY ARNOLD** (58)	RCA Victor 5019	$12
EP	**BOUQUET OF ROSES** (58)	RCA Victor 5055	$12
EP(P)	**THE BALLAD OF WES TANCRED** (58)	RCA Victor DJ-14	$20
	(White promo label, four-song EP, flip is Vaughn Monroe)		
EP(P)	**DO YOU LOVE ME** (59) With Jaye P. Morgan	RCA Victor DJ-88	$18
	(White promo label, four-song EP, flip is Eddie Fisher)		
EP	**KENTUCKY WALTZ** (59)	RCA Victor 5087	$12
EP	**TENNESSEE'S EDDY ARNOLD** (59)	RCA Victor 5126	$12
EP	**TAKE ME IN YOUR ARMS** (59)	RCA Victor 5150	$12
EP	**EDDY ARNOLD SINGS THEM AGAIN** (61)	RCA Victor 115	$18
	(Compact-33 double)		
EP(JB)	**SOMETIMES I'M HAPPY** (67) Jukebox LLP	RCA Victor 2909	$12
	(Issued with a hard cover, blank on back)		
EP(JB)	**MY WORLD** (67) Jukebox LLP	RCA Victor 3466	$10
	(Issued with a hard cover, blank on back)		
EP(JB)	**THE LAST WORD IN LONESOME** (68) Jukebox LLP	RCA Victor 3622	$10
	(Issued with a hard cover, blank on back)		
EP(JB)	**THE BEST OF EDDY ARNOLD** (72) Jukebox LLP	RCA 4320 (LLP #141)	$10
	(Issued with a paper sleeve)		
33(P)	**HIGH BLOOD PRESSURE** (82) PSA radio ads	NR 14128	$18
	(Fourteen cuts, Arnold does two)		
33(P)	**HIGH BLOOD PRESSURE** (83) PSA radio ads	NR 14344	$18
	(Ten cuts, Arnold does two)		
33(P)	**ARE YOU BEHAVIN'?** (83)	NR 14951	$15
	(Radio spots)		

-albums-

10"LP	**ANYTIME** (Country Classics) (52)	RCA Victor 3027	$125
	(First album, first pressing is ten-inch)		
LP	**ANYTIME** (Country Classics) (55)	RCA Victor 1224	$50
	(Second pressing is twelve-inch)		
10"LP	**ALL TIME HITS FROM THE HILLS** (52)	RCA Victor 3031	$100
	(This pressing is ten-inch)		
10"LP	**ALL TIME FAVORITES** (53)	RCA Victor 3117	$80
	(First pressing is ten-inch)		
LP	**ALL TIME FAVORITES** (55)	RCA Victor 1223	$50
	(Second pressing is twelve-inch)		

10"LP	**CHAPEL ON THE HILL** (54)	RCA Victor 3219	$85
	(First pressing is ten-inch)		
LP	**CHAPEL ON THE HILL** (55)	RCA Victor 1225	$50
	(Second pressing is twelve-inch)		
10"LP	**AN AMERICAN INSTITUTION** Fold-out cover	RCA Victor 3230	$125
	(First pressing is ten-inch, with booklet)		
	The booklet is about $25 of the value		
LP	**WANDERIN' WITH EDDY ARNOLD** (55)	RCA Victor 1111	$60
	(The first twelve-inch-only LP)		
LP	**A DOZEN HITS** (56)	RCA Victor 1293	$45
	(All the following LP listings are twelve-inch)		
LP	**A LITTLE ON THE LONELY SIDE** (56)	RCA Victor 1377	$40
LP	**WHEN THEY WERE YOUNG** (57)	RCA Victor 1484	$35
LP	**MY DARLING, MY DARLING** (57)	RCA Victor 1575	$35
LP	**PRAISE HIM, PRAISE HIM** (58)	RCA Victor 1733	$30
LP	**HAVE GUITAR, WILL TRAVEL** (59) Mono	RCA Victor 1928	$25
	(Mono versions of this LP are hard to find)		
LP	**HAVE GUITAR, WILL TRAVEL** (59) Stereo	RCA Victor 1928	$30
	(Stereo, more common)		
LP	**THEREBY HANGS A TALE** (59) Mono	RCA Victor 2036	$20
LP	**THEREBY HANGS A TALE** (59) Stereo	RCA Victor 2036	$25
LP	**EDDY ARNOLD** (59) Mono	Camden 471	$18
	(Stereo version, released in 1966, worth $8)		
LP	**EDDY ARNOLD SINGS AGAIN** (60) Mono	RCA Victor 2185	$20
LP	**MORE EDDY ARNOLD** (60) Mono	Camden 563	$15
	(Stereo version, released in 1966, worth $8)		
LP	**EDDY ARNOLD SINGS AGAIN** (60) Stereo	RCA Victor 2185	$25
LP	**YOU GOTTA HAVE LOVE** (60) Stereo	RCA Victor 2268	$20
	(From this point on, LPs are mono or stereo)		
LP	**LET'S MAKE MEMORIES TONIGHT** (61) Stereo	RCA Victor 2337	$20
LP	**ONE MORE TIME** (61)	RCA Victor 2471	$20
LP	**CHRISTMAS WITH EDDY ARNOLD** (61) Mono	RCA Victor 2554	$20
LP(P)	**CHRISTMAS WITH EDDY ARNOLD** (61)	RCA Victor PRS 346	$50
	(White label promo-only version for radio)		
LP	**CATTLE CALL** (63)	RCA Victor 2578	$18
LP	**OUR MAN DOWN SOUTH** (62)	RCA Victor 2596	$18
LP	**FAITHFULLY YOURS** (63)	RCA Victor 2629	$20
LP	**FOLK SONG BOOK** (64)	RCA Victor 2811	$15
LP	**EDDY'S SONGS** (64)	Camden 798	$10
	(Camden was RCA's budget label)		
LP	**SOMETIMES I'M HAPPY, SOMETIMES I'M BLUE** (64)	RCA Victor 2909	$12
LP	**POP HITS FROM THE COUNTRY SIDE** (64)	RCA Victor 2951	$12
LP	**THE EASY WAY** (65)	RCA Victor 3361	$12
LP	**I'M THROWING RICE** (65)	Camden 897	$10
LP	**MY WORLD** (65)	RCA Victor 3466	$10
	(These LPs in the mid-60s were all big sellers)		
LP	**I WANT TO GO WITH YOU** (66)	RCA Victor 3507	$10
LP	**THE BEST OF EDDY ARNOLD** (66)	RCA Victor 3565	$10
LP	**THE LAST WORD IN LONESOME** (66)	RCA Victor 3622	$10
LP	**SOMEBODY LIKE ME** (66)	RCA Victor 3715	$10
LP	**LONELY AGAIN** (67)	RCA Victor 3753	$10
LP	**TURN THE WORLD AROUND** (67)	RCA Victor 3869	$10
LP	**THE EVERLOVIN' WORLD OF EDDY ARNOLD** (68) Mono	RCA Victor 3931	$40
	(Very rare in mono, the last mono LP)		
LP	**THE EVERLOVIN' WORLD OF EDDY ARNOLD** (68) Stereo	RCA Victor 3931	$10
LP	**THE ROMANTIC WORLD OF EDDY ARNOLD** (68)	RCA Victor 4009	$10
2LP	**CHAINED TO A MEMORY** (72)	Camden 9007	$10
LP(P)	**SO MANY WAYS** (73)	MGM 4878	$12
	(Yellow promo label)		
LP(P)	**SHE'S GOT EVERYTHING I NEED** (74)	MGM 4912	$10
	(Yellow promo label)		
LP	**LIVING LEGEND** (74)	K-Tel 307	$10
	(RCA material, price includes 8x10 photo)		
	-radio shows-		
16"(RS)	**NAVY HOEDOWN** (50s) Shows other than listed below	U.S. Navy	$15-30
	(Music and interviews)		
16"(RS)	**NAVY HOEDOWN** (55) Show on other side is Patsy Cline	U.S. Navy	$50-100
	(Music and interviews)		
16"(RS)	**MARCH OF DIMES** (54)	MOD show 5436	$40-60
	(Full show plus spots for the March of Dimes)		
16"(RS)	**COUNTRY MUSIC TIME** (55) Public service	CM show 70	$25-40
	(Music and interviews)		
16"(RS)	**COUNTRY MUSIC TIME** (56) Public service	CM show 92	$25-40
	(Music and interviews)		
LP(RS)	**EDDY ARNOLD TIME** Six five-minute PSA shows	U.S. Dept Health	$20-30 each
	(This is a series with over forty records in the series)		
LP(RS)	**CHRISTMAS WITH ...** Radio show	Diamond P 502	$25-40
	(For radio, green label)		

JERRY ARNOLD (RB)

-singles-

45rpm	**RACE FOR TIME** (58)	Security 106	$75
45rpm	**HIGH CLASSED BABY** (58)	Security 107	$60
45rpm	**RACE FOR TIME** (58)	Cameo 120	$40

LLOYD ARNOLD (RB)

-singles-

45rpm	**RED COAT, GREEN PANTS & RED SUEDE SHOES** (58)	Myers 113	$60

ASHER & LITTLE JIMMY (CW)

-albums-

LP	**MOUNTAIN BALLADS AND OLD HYMNS** (66)	Decca 4785	$50
LP(P)	**MOUNTAIN BALLADS AND OLD HYMNS** (66)	Decca 4785	$40
	(Pink promo label)		

JOHN ASHLEY (RB)
Other Dot 45s $10-15 each

-singles-

45rpm	**LITTLE LOU** (57)	Capehart 5006	$30
45(P)	**LITTLE LOU** (57)	Capehart 5006	$25
	(White promo label)		
45rpm	**BORN TO ROCK** (58)	Dot 15775	$25
45rpm	**LET THE GOOD TIMES ROLL** (58)	Dot 15878	$10

LEON ASHLEY (CW)
RCA Victor 45s $3 each
Ashley 45s $2-3 each

-singles-

45rpm	**IT'S ALRIGHT BABY** (58)	Imperial 5795	$18
45(P)	**IT'S ALRIGHT BABY** (58)	Imperial 5795	$15
	(Promo label)		

-albums-

LP	**LAURA** (67)	RCA Victor 3900	$15
LP	**A NEW BRAND OF COUNTRY** (69)	Ashley 3695	$12
	(With Margie Singleton)		
LP	**MENTAL JOURNEY** (69)	Ashley 3700	$12
LP	**BEST OF LEON ASHLEY** (70)	Ashley 54001	$12

ROBERT ASHLEY (RB)

-singles-

45rpm	**COMIC STRIP ROCK 'N' ROLL** (59)	Mercury 71365	$25
45(P)	**COMIC STRIP ROCK 'N' ROLL** (59)	Mercury 71365	$20
	(White promo label)		

ERNEST ASHWORTH (CW)
Hickory 45s $2 each
Starday 45s $2 each
Other LPs $5-8 each

-albums-

LP	**HITS OF TODAY & TOMORROW** (67)	Hickory 118	$18
LP	**BEST OF ERNEST ASHWORTH** (68)	Hickory 146	$12
LP	**GREATEST HITS** (76)	Starday 964	$10

ASLEEP AT THE WHEEL (C)
Featuring Ray Benson
Other Capitol 45s $2-3 each
United Artists, Epic, and MCA 45s $2-4 each
Capitol, UA, Epic, and MCA LPs 3-8 each

-singles-

45(P)	**LOUISIANA** (78) Promo-only single	Capitol PRO-8868	$12
	(Price includes attractive promo-only picture sleeve)		

-albums-

LP	**COMIN' RIGHT AT YA** (73)	United Artists 038	$12
	(Group's first LP)		
2LP	**FATHERS & SONS** (75)	Epic 33782	$20
	(First pressing, label number must include "BG" and the other LP in the set is by Bob Wills)		

-radio shows-

LP(RS)	**LIVE AT GILLEY'S** (Dec 85)	Westwood One	$25-50
	(Live concert)		
LP(RS)	**LIVE AT GILLEY'S** (May 86)	Westwood One	$20-40
	(Live concert)		
LP(RS)	**LIVE AT GILLEY'S** (Dec 88)	Westwood One	$25-40
	(Live concert)		
Cass(RS)	**AUSTIN ENCORE** (90s)	Mainstreet Entertainment	$25-50
	(Live concert on cassette)		

BOB ATCHER (CW)
Capitol 45s $5 each
Columbia 45s $2 each

-albums-

10"LP	**BOB ATCHER'S EARLY AMERICAN FOLK SONGS** (53)	Columbia 9006	$75
	(First pressing is ten-inch)		
LP	**BOB ATCHER'S EARLY AMERICAN FOLK SONGS** (55)	Columbia 7313	$30
	(Second pressing is twelve-inch)		
10"LP	**SONGS OF THE SADDLE** (54)	Columbia 9013	$60
LP	**THE DEAN OF COWBOY SINGERS** (64)	Columbia 2232	$20
LP(P)	**THE DEAN OF COWBOY SINGERS** (64)	Columbia 2232	$25
	(White promo label)		

CHET ATKINS (CW)
RCA Victor dog on top 45s $3-6 each
RCA Victor dog on side 45s $2 each
Other RCA Victor jukebox LLPs $8 each
Columbia duet 45s $3 each
Other RCA Victor LPs $3-8 each
Other Camden LPs $3-8 each
Time-Life series LPs $5 each
Pickwick LPs $4 each
Columbia LPs $4 each
  (Chet Atkins C.G.P.)
Columbia duet LPs $6 each

-singles-

45rpm	**GOOD-BYE BLUES** (52) Green label	RCA Victor 4491	$15
	(With the Beasley Singers)		
45rpm	**RUSTIC DANCE** (54)	RCA Victor 5010	$10
	(Black label)		
45rpm	**COUNTRY GENTLEMAN** (54)	RCA Victor 5300	$10
	(The original version, black label)		
45rpm	**BARBER SHOP RAG** (55)	RCA Victor 5565	$10
	(Black label)		
45rpm	**THE SLOP** (61) Record and picture sleeve	RCA Victor 7847	$10
	(Most of the value is for the scarce sleeve)		
45rpm	**CHET'S TUNE** (67) Twenty years at RCA for Chet	RCA Victor 9229	$10
	(Various artists, price includes picture sleeve)		

-EPs-

2EP	**CHET ATKINS' GALLOPIN' GUITAR** (53)	RCA Victor 3079	$50
2EP	**STRINGIN' ALONG WITH CHET ATKINS** (53)	RCA Victor 3163	$40
2EP	**STRINGIN' ALONG WITH CHET ATKINS** (55)	RCA Victor 1236	$30
EP	**STRINGIN' ALONG WITH CHET ATKINS** (56)	RCA Victor 796	$20
EP	**CHET ATKINS & HIS GUITAR** (54)	RCA Victor 588	$25
EP	**PICKIN' THE HITS** (54)	RCA Victor 594	$25
2EP	**SESSION WITH CHET ATKINS** (54)	RCA Victor 1090	$25
2EP	**CHET ATKINS IN THREE DIMENSIONS** (55)	RCA Victor 1197	$50
	(This EP set is also available as RCA 685, 686, and 687)		
2EP	**FINGER STYLE GUITAR** (56)	RCA Victor 1383	$25
	(EPs separate are worth $12-15 each)		
2EP	**HI-FI IN FOCUS** (56)	RCA Victor 1577	$25
	(EPs separate are worth $12-15 each)		
EP	**CHET ATKINS AT HOME** (58)	RCA Victor 4194	$12
EP	**HUM AND STRUM** (59)	RCA Victor 4343	$12
	(Includes booklet)		
EP	**ONE MINUTE JULIP** (59)	RCA Victor 4356	$10
EP	**POOR PEOPLE OF PARIS** (59)	RCA Victor 5052	$10
EP	**CHET ATKINS GUITAR** (59)	RCA Victor 5125	$10
EP	**CHET ATKINS FAVORITES** (59)	RCA Victor 5154	$10
EP(P)	**MR. ATKINS, IF YOU PLEASE** (59) Promo-only EP	Sesac 13	$40
	(With the Anita Kerr Singers)		
EP(P)	**NO GREATER LOVE** (59) Promo-only EP	Sesac 48	$25
	(With Faron Young, each artist has two cuts)		
EP	**PLAYS GREAT MOVIE THEMES** (61)	RCA Victor 124	$18
	(Compact-33 double)		
EP(JB)	**BEST OF CHET ATKINS** (66) Jukebox LLP	RCA Victor 3558	$15
	(Issued with a hard cover, back is blank)		

-albums-

10"LP	**GALLOPIN' GUITAR** (53)	RCA Victor 3079	$75
	(First album)		
10"LP	**STRINGIN' ALONG WITH** (53)	RCA Victor 3163	$60
	(First pressing, ten-inch LP)		
LP	**STRINGIN' ALONG WITH** (55)	RCA Victor 1236	$40
	(Second pressing, twelve-inch)		
LP	**A SESSION WITH CHET ATKINS** (54)	RCA Victor 1090	$30
LP	**CHET ATKINS IN THREE DIMENSIONS** (55)	RCA Victor 1197	$25
LP	**CHET ATKINS FINGER STYLE GUITAR** (56)	RCA Victor 1383	$25

LP	**HI-FI IN FOCUS** (57)	RCA Victor 1577	$25
LP	**CHET ATKINS IN HOLLYWOOD** (59)	RCA Victor 1993	$25
LP	**HUM AND STRUM ALONG WITH CHET** (59) Mono	RCA Victor 2025	$25
	(Price includes music booklet)		
LP	**HUM AND STRUM ALONG WITH CHET** (59) Stereo	RCA Victor 2025	$30
	(Price includes music booklet)		
LP	**MISTER GUITAR** (59) Mono	RCA Victor 2103	$25
LP	**MISTER GUITAR** (59) Stereo	RCA Victor 2103	$30
LP	**CHET ATKINS TEENSVILLE** (60) Mono	RCA Victor 2161	$25
LP	**CHET ATKINS TEENSVILLE** (60) Stereo	RCA Victor 2161	$35
LP	**THE OTHER CHET ATKINS** (60)	RCA Victor 2175	$20
LP	**THE MOST POPULAR GUITAR** (61)	RCA Victor 2346	$20
LP	**CHRISTMAS WITH CHET ATKINS** (61)	RCA Victor 2423	$20
LP	**CHET ATKINS & HIS GUITAR** (61) Mono	Camden 659	$12
LP	**CARIBBEAN GUITAR** (62)	RCA Victor 2549	$12
LP	**GUITAR GENIUS** (63)	Camden 753	$10
LP	**THE POPS GO COUNTRY** (66) With Boston Pops	RCA Victor 2870	$18
	(RCA Victor Red Seal classical series)		
LP	**THE BEST OF CHET ATKINS** (64)	RCA Victor 2887	$12
LP	**REMINISCING** (64)	RCA Victor 2952	$20
	(Hank Snow and Chet Atkins)		
LP	**MUSIC FROM NASHVILLE** (66)	Camden 981	$10
LP	**PLAY GUITAR WITH CHET ATKINS** (67)	Dolton 17506	$25
	(Includes booklet)		
LP	**CHET** (67)	Camden 2182	$12
LP	**CHET PICKS ON THE POPS** (69) With Boston Pops	RCA Victor 3104	$18
	(RCA Victor Red Seal classical series)		
LP	**BY SPECIAL REQUEST** (70) C. B. Atkins and C. E. Snow	RCA Victor 4254	$25
	(Hank Snow and Chet Atkins)		
2LP	**COUNTRY PICKIN'** (71)	Camden 9006	$10

-radio shows-

16"(RS)	**LEATHERNECK JAMBOREE** (55) Public service radio	Leatherneck Show 19	$40-75
	(Music and interviews)		
16"(RS)	**NAVY HOEDOWN** (50s)	U.S. Navy	$15-25
	(Music and interviews)		
LP(RS)	**CHRISTMAS WITH ...** Radio show (70s)	Diamond P 514	$25-50
	(Music and interviews)		

JIM ATKINS (CW)

-singles-

45rpm	**I'M A DING DONG DADDY** (53)	Coral 64147	$25
	(Flip side, Juke Joint Johnny)		

ATLANTA (C)
MDJ Color vinyl 45s $5 each with picture sleeve
MDJ LPs $3 each

-radio shows-

LP(RS)	**LIVE AT GILLEY'S** (Jan 85)	Westwood One	$15-25
	(Live concert)		

BOBBY AUSTIN (CW)
Capitol 45s $2 each

-albums-

LP	**APARTMENT NO. 9** (67)	Capitol 2773	$15
LP	**OLD LOVE NEVER DIES** (68)	Capitol 2915	$10

GENE AUSTIN (CW)
Fraternity 45s $5 each

-radio shows-

16"(RS)	**TREASURY DEPARTMENT** (50s)	Treasury Department	$10-20
	(Music and interviews)		

SIL AUSTIN (I/CW)

-EPs-

EP(P)	**SLOW WALK ROCK** (57) Green promo-only label	Mercury 19A	$15
	(Excerpts from Slow Walk LP)		

GENE AUTRY (CW)

-singles-

Other early 78s on Champion, Gennett, Q. R. S., Superior, Supertone, Perfect, and Victor are worth
   $40-50 and up, all released before 1944
Other Conqueror 78s, except two below, are worth $20-$35 each
Other Perfect 78s $20-$40 each
Vocalion 78s $10-$20 each
Other Columbia 78s $3 each
Okeh 78s $6 each

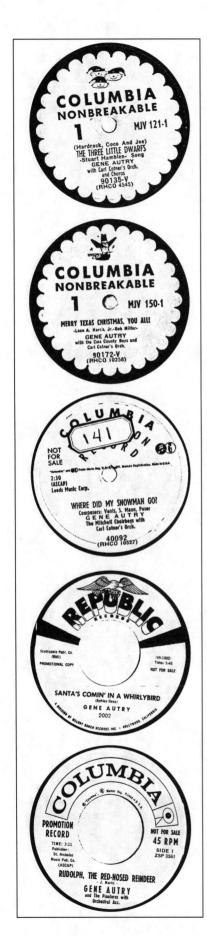

Columbia and Okeh promo 78s $6-8 each
Other Columbia 45s before 1965 $4-8 each
Other Columbia 45s after 1965 $2-5 each
Birchmount LPs $8 each
Hurrah LPs $6 each
Other Columbia LPs $5-8 each
Other Republic LPs $4-8 each

-singles-

78rpm	**DAD IN THE HILLS**	Conqueror 7702	$75
78rpm	**A GANGSTER'S WARNING**	Conqueror 7704	$75
78rpm	**BACK TO OLD SMOKY MOUNTAIN**	Conqueror 7999	$60
78rpm	**TUMBLING TUMBLEWEEDS**	Conqueror 8465	$50
	(By the Gene Autry Trio)		
78rpm	**RHYTHM OF THE HOOF BEATS**	Conqueror 9450	$50
78rpm	**THEY CUT DOWN THE OLD PINE TREE**	Supertone 9704	$50
78rpm	**DAD IN THE HILLS**	Champion 16372	$75
78rpm	**THAT'S HOW I GOT MY START**	Champion 16485	$75
78rpm	**COWBOY YODEL**	Gennett 7243	$100
78rpm	**HOBO BILL'S LAST RIDE**	Gennett 7290	$100
78rpm	**TRAIN WHISTLE BLUES**	Gennett 7310	$100
78rpm	**LIVING IN THE MOUNTAINS**	Q. R. S. 1044	$125
78rpm	**THE GIRL I LEFT BEHIND**	Superior 2561	$150
78rpm	**DAD IN THE HILLS**	Superior 2596	$75
78rpm	**PISTOL PACKIN' PAPA**	Superior 2637	$60
78rpm	**MEAN MAMA BLUES**	Superior 2660	$50
78rpm	**THAT'S HOW I GOT MY START**	Superior 2681	$50
78rpm	**HOBO BILL'S LAST RIDE**	Superior 2769	$50
78rpm	**BEAR CAT PAPA**	Victor 23530	$100
78rpm	**DO RIGHT DADDY**	Victor 23548	$85
78rpm	**THERE'S A GOOD GAL IN THE MOUNTAINS**	Victor 23561	$80
78rpm	**HIGH STEPPIN' MAMA**	Victor 23589	$75
78rpm	**SHE'S A LOW DOWN MAMA**	Victor 23617	$75
78rpm	**RHEUMATISM BLUES**	Victor 23630	$75
78rpm	**WILD CAT MAMA**	Victor 23642	$85
78rpm	**I'M ALWAYS DREAMING OF YOU**	Victor 23673	$50
78rpm	**BLACK BOTTOM BLUES**	Victor 23707	$75
78rpm	**KENTUCKY LULLABY**	Victor 23720	$60
78rpm	**THE GANGSTER'S WARNING**	Victor 23725	$100
78rpm	**BACK TO OLD SMOKY MOUNTAIN**	Victor 23726	$100
78rpm	**COWBOY'S HEAVEN**	Victor 23783	$80
78rpm	**LOUISIANA MOON**	Victor 23792	$75
78rpm	**YOUR VOICE IS CALLING**	Victor 23810	$75
78rpm	**MY ALABAMA HOME**	Victor 40200	$75
45rpm	**LET ME CRY ON YOUR SHOULDER** (49)	Columbia 9-901	$25
	(One of the first Columbia 45rpm releases)		
45rpm	**RED RIVER VALLEY** (52)	Columbia 20085	$30
45rpm	**THE LAST ROUNDUP** (53)	Columbia 20541	$25
45rpm	**THERE'S A GOLDMINE IN THE SKY** (53)	Columbia 20542	$25
45rpm	**WHEN IT'S ROUNDUP TIME IN HEAVEN** (53)	Columbia 20543	$25
45rpm	**COWBOY'S HEAVEN** (53)	Columbia 20544	$20
	(The four above 45s part of a $100 box set)		
45rpm	**AT MAIL CALL TODAY** (53)	Columbia 20814	$15
	(Issued earlier on Okeh 78rpm)		
45rpm	**A VOICE IN THE CHOIR** (53)	Columbia 21229	$12
45rpm	**THE FUNNY LITTLE BUNNY** (53)	Columbia 68	$20
	(Yellow label children's series, with picture cover)		
78rpm	**THE THREE LITTLE DWARFS** (53)	Columbia 121	$25
	(Price includes picture sleeve)		
45rpm	**THE THREE LITTLE DWARFS** (53)	Columbia 121	$18
	(Price includes picture sleeve)		
2/45s	**THE STORY OF LITTLE CHAMP** (53)	Columbia 104	$18
	(Yellow label children's series, with cover)		
78rpm	**MERRY TEXAS CHRISTMAS, YOU ALL!** (53)	Columbia 150	$25
	(Price includes picture sleeve)		
45rpm	**MERRY TEXAS CHRISTMAS, YOU ALL!** (53)	Columbia 150	$20
	(Children's series, with open-label picture sleeve)		
45rpm	**RUDOLPH, THE RED-NOSED REINDEER** Hall of Fame series	Columbia 33165	$18
	("Not for Sale" on label, scarce picture sleeve)		
45rpm	**SANTA, SANTA, SANTA** (53)	Columbia 39464	$15
45rpm	**WHERE DID MY SNOWMAN GO?** (53)	Columbia 40092	
45rpm	**ROUND, ROUND THE CHRISTMAS TREE** (56)	Columbia 40589	$12
45rpm	**EVERYONE IS A CHILD AT CHRISTMAS** (56)	Columbia 40790	$15
45rpm	**JOHNNY REB & BILLY YANK** (57)	Columbia 40931	$12
45rpm	**HALF YOUR HEART** (57)	Columbia 40960	$10
45rpm	**NINE LITTLE REINDEER** (58)	Republic 2001	$12
45rpm	**SANTA'S COMIN' IN A WHIRLYBIRD** (59)	Republic 2002	$10

45(P)	**RUDOLPH, THE RED-NOSED REINDEER** (60)	Columbia ZSP 3581	$25
	(Promo-only single, two versions)		
45rpm	**RUDOLPH, THE RED-NOSED REINDEER** (67)	Mistletoe 801	$10
	(Record and picture sleeve)		

-EPs-

EP	**GENE AUTRY AT THE RODEO** (51)	Columbia 1528	$60
EP	**STORY OF THE LITTLE CHAMP** (51)	Columbia 1605	$50
EP	**GENE AUTRY** (52)	Columbia 1663	$50
EP	**GENE AUTRY** (53)	Columbia 1721	$50
EP	**SINGING TIME WITH GENE AUTRY** (53)	Columbia 1776	$40
EP	**CHRISTMAS FUN** (53)	Columbia 1782	$40
EP	**WESTERN CLASSICS** (54)	Columbia H 4-1	$40
	(Singles set)		
EP	**WESTERN CLASSICS VOL. 2** (54)	Columbia H 4-7	$40
	(Singles set)		
EP	**STAMPEDE** (54)	Columbia 1791	$35
EP	**EASTER FUN** (54)	Columbia 1844	$30
EP	**MERRY CHRISTMAS** (55)	Columbia 270	$35
	(Columbia Christmas series)		
EP	**CHILDREN'S CHRISTMAS** (56)	Columbia 2612	$25
	(With the Cass County Boys)		
EP(P)	**SANTA'S HIT PARADE** (56) Columbia Record Club EP	Columbia D-17	$40
	(Issued with a paper cover, with Rosemary Clooney)		

-albums-

10"LP	**STORY OF THE NATIVITY** (55)	Columbia 82	$100
	(Special Columbia children's series)		
10"LP	**LITTLE JOHNNY PILGRIM AND GUFFY** (55)	Columbia 83	$100
	(Special Columbia children's series)		
10"LP	**RUSTY THE ROCKING HORSE**	Columbia 94	$100
	(Special Columbia children's series)		
10"LP	**MERRY CHRISTMAS WITH GENE AUTRY** (55)	Columbia 2547	$125
	(Available only as a ten-inch album)		
10"LP	**GENE AUTRY SINGS PETER COTTONTAIL** (55)	Columbia 2568	$125
	(Available only as a ten-inch album)		
10"LP	**STAMPEDE** (55)	Columbia 8009	$150
	(Includes Jackie Robinson and Pee Wee Reese)		
10"LP	**WESTERN CLASSICS** (55)	Columbia 6020	$75
10"LP	**WESTERN CLASSICS** (56)	Columbia 9001	$75
10"LP	**WESTERN CLASSICS VOL. 2** (56)	Columbia 9002	$75
LP	**GENE AUTRY AND CHAMPION WESTERN ADVENTURES** (55)	Columbia 677	$125
	(The first twelve-inch album by Autry)		
LP	**GENE AUTRY AND CHAMPION WESTERN ADVENTURES** (59)	Harmony 9505	$30
LP	**GENE AUTRY AT THE RODEO** (58)	Columbia 8001	$100
	(Very hard to find)		
4LP	**MELODY RANCH RADIO SHOW** (65)	Murray Hill 897296	$75
	(Commercial version of old radio shows)		
LP	**CHRISTMAS WITH GENE AUTRY** (58)	Challenge 600	$50
	(Later released on Republic)		
LP	**CHRISTMAS WITH GENE AUTRY** (76)	Republic 600	$12
LP	**GENE AUTRY'S GREATEST HITS** (61) Red label	Columbia 1575	$25
	(Red label stock copy)		
LP(P)	**GENE AUTRY'S GREATEST HITS** (61)	Columbia 1575	$40
	(White promo label)		
LP	**GENE AUTRY'S GOLDEN HITS** (62)	RCA Victor 2623	$40
LP	**CHRISTMAS FAVORITES** (64)	Harmony 9550	$25
	(With Rosemary Clooney and Art Carney)		
LP(P)	**CHRISTMAS FAVORITES** (64)	Harmony 9550	$30
	(White promo label)		
LP	**GENE AUTRY'S GREAT WESTERN HITS** (65)	Harmony 7332	$30
LP	**GENE AUTRY'S GREAT WESTERN HITS** (65)	Harmony 7332	$35
	(White promo label)		
LP	**MELODY RANCH** (65)	Melody Ranch 101	$40
	(Includes Johnny Bond)		
LP	**BACK IN THE SADDLE AGAIN** (66)	Harmony 7376	$18
LP(P)	**BACK IN THE SADDLE AGAIN** (66)	Harmony 7376	$20
	(White promo label)		
LP	**GENE AUTRY SINGS** (66)	Harmony 7399	$12
LP(P)	**GENE AUTRY SINGS** (66)	Harmony 7399	$15
	(White promo label)		
LP	**GENE AUTRY SINGS** (67)	Hallmark 582	$10
LP	**RUDOLPH THE RED-NOSED REINDEER** (68)	Grand Prix 11	$12
	(Budget label)		
LP	**RUDOLPH THE RED-NOSED REINDEER** (68)	Design 5	$12
	(Budget label)		
2LP	**LIVE FROM MADISON SQUARE GARDEN** (68)	Republic 1968	$15
LP	**LIVE FROM MADISON SQUARE GARDEN** (76)	Republic 6014	$10

LP	**COUNTRY MUSIC HALL OF FAME ALBUM** (70)	Columbia 1035	$12
LP	**MELODY RANCH—A RADIO ADVENTURE** (75)	Radiola 1048	$12
	(Commercial versions of old radio shows)		
2LP	**ALL AMERICAN COWBOY** (76)	Republic 1970	$15
2LP	**ALL AMERICAN COWBOY** (76)	Republic 6011	$10
2LP	**22 ALL TIME FAVORITES** (77)	GRT 2103-720	$12
2LP	**50TH ANNIVERSARY** (78)	Republic 6022	$12
LP	**CHRISTMAS CLASSICS** (78)	Starday 1038	$12
LP	**GENE AUTRY BACK IN THE SADDLE AGAIN** (80)	Encore 14380	$10
	(Budget label)		
LP	**GENE AUTRY CHRISTMAS FAVORITES** (81)	Columbia 15766	$12
	(Columbia Special Products)		
LP	**EVERYONE'S A CHILD AT CHRISTMAS** (81)	Columbia 15767	$10
	(Columbia Special Products)		

-radio shows-

LP(RS)	**COUNTRY CROSSROADS** (Dec 81) Special Christmas	Southern Baptist	$25-40
	(Music and interviews)		
LP(RS)	**COUNTRY CROSSROADS** (80s)	Southern Baptist	$15-25
	(Music and interviews)		

HOYT AXTON (C)
Horizon and Vee Jay 45s $5-8 each
  (Folk and folk-rock music)
A&M 45s $2 each
Other 45s $1 each
Other Vee Jay and Horizon LPs $5-8 each
Other LPs $2-5 each

-albums-

LP	**THUNDER'N LIGHTNING** (63)	Horizon 1613	$25
LP	**SATURDAY'S CHILD** (63)	Horizon 1621	$25
LP	**HOYT AXTON EXPLODES** (64)	Vee Jay 1098	$20
LP	**BEST OF HOYT AXTON** (64)	Vee Jay 1118	$18
LP	**GREENBACK DOLLAR** (65)	Vee Jay 1126	$15
LP	**SATURDAY'S CHILD** (65)	Vee Jay 1127	$12
	(Reissue of Horizon album)		
LP	**THUNDER'N LIGHTNING** (65)	Vee Jay 1128	$10
	(Reissue of Horizon album)		
LP	**MY GRIFFIN IS GONE** (69)	Columbia 9766	$10
LP(P)	**MY GRIFFIN IS GONE** (69)	Columbia 9766	$12
	(White promo label)		

-radio shows-

2LP(RS)	**COUNTRY COOKIN'** (75) Four fifteen-minute radio shows	Army Reserve	$25-40
	(Music and interviews)		
LP(RS)	**LIVE AT GILLEY'S** (July 84)	Westwood One	$20-30
	(Live concert)		

EARL AYCOCK (CW)

-albums-

LP	**EARL AYCOCK** (58)	Mercury 20282	$20
LP(P)	**EARL AYCOCK** (58)	Mercury 20282	$15
	(White promo label)		

B

THE BACHELORS (CW)
Wolf, Andre, and Haskell

-singles-

78rpm	**TE-E-E-E-EX-AS** (54)	Excel 106	$15

DEFORD BAILEY (CW)
78s on Bluebird and Brunswick worth $30-$50 each

RAZZY BAILEY (C)
MGM 45s $3 each
RCA 45s or picture sleeves $1 each
Other RCA color vinyl 45s $8 each
SOA color vinyl 45s $3 each
MCA 45s $1 each

-singles-

45rpm	**I HATE HATE** (74)	Aquarian 601	$10
	(Razzy and the Neighborhood Kids)		

45(P)	**I KEEP COMING BACK** (80)	RCA Victor 12120	$12
	(Yellow label, green vinyl)		
45(P)	**MIDNIGHT HAULER** (81)	RCA Victor 12268	$12
	(Brown label, blue vinyl)		
45(P)	**EVERYTIME YOU CROSS MY MIND** (82)	RCA Victor 13084	$10
	(Orange label, red vinyl)		
45(P)	**PEACE ON EARTH** (82)	RCA Victor 13359	$12
	(Red label, green vinyl)		
45(P)	**POOR BOY** (82)	RCA Victor 13383	$10
	(Blue label, blue vinyl)		
45(P)	**AFTER THE GREAT DEPRESSION** (83)	RCA Victor 13512	$10
	(Red label, red vinyl)		

-radio shows-

LP(RS)	**COUNTRY SESSIONS** (80s)	NBC Radio	$10-15
	(Live concert)		
3LP(RS)	**THE SILVER EAGLE** (81) With Ronnie Milsap	DIR 012	$25-40
	(Live concert)		
3LP(RS)	**THE SILVER EAGLE** (Apr 82)	DIR	$10-12
	(Live concert)		
3LP(RS)	**THE SILVER EAGLE** (Apr 83) With John Conley	DIR	$10-20
	(Live concert)		
3LP(RS)	**THE SILVER EAGLE** (Aug 85) With Gus Hardin	Westwood One	$10-15
	(Live concert)		
3LP(RS)	**AMERCIAN EAGLE** (Jan 87) With Joe Stampley	Westwood One	$10-15
	(Live concert)		

ABE BAKER (RB)

-singles-

45rpm	**MOCCASIN ROCK** (58)	Laurel 1010	$60

BUTCH BAKER (CW)

-radio shows-

LP(RS)	**COUNTRY MUSIC TIME** (70s)	U.S. Air Force	$10-15
	(Music and interviews)		

FRED BAKER (CW)
Other Capitol 45s $5-8 each

-singles-

45rpm	**I GOTTA DO WHAT I GOTTA DO** (53)	Capitol 3091	$12
45(P)	**I GOTTA DO WHAT I GOTTA DO** (53)	Capitol 3091	$10
	(White promo label)		

JOHNNY BALMER (Polka)
And the Grand Canyon Boys
Old Timer 45s $5-10 each

THE BAND (R)
Featuring Robbie Robertson
Capitol 45s $3-5 each

-albums-

LP(P)	**THE LAST WALTZ** (78)	Warner 737	$15
	(Promo-only release, edited version of stock copy)		

-radio shows-

CD(RS)	**KING BISCUIT FLOWER HOUR** (Mar 88)	DIR	$30-50
	(Live concert)		
CD(RS)	**KING BISCUIT FLOWER HOUR** (Apr 91)	DIR	$30-50
	(With Blues Traveler)		
CD(RS)	**IN THE STUDIO** (Sep 88)	Album Network	$15-25
	(Music and interviews)		
2CD(RS)	**UP CLOSE** (94) Profile of the group	Media America	$25-50
	(Music and interviews)		

MOE BANDY (C)
GRC 45s $2 each
MCA, Columbia 45s $1 each

-albums-

LP	**I JUST STARTED HATIN' CHEATIN' SONGS TODAY** (74)	GRC 10005	$18
LP	**IT WAS ALWAYS SO EASY** (75)	GRC 10007	$15
LP	**BANDY, THE RODEO CLOWN** (75)	GRC 10016	$15

-radio shows-

3LP(RS)	**THE SILVER EAGLE** (81) With Joe Stampley	DIR 003	$25-40
	(Live concert)		
3LP(RS)	**THE SILVER EAGLE** (Jan 82)	DIR	$10-15
	(Live concert)		
LP(RS)	**COUNTRY SESSIONS** (80s)	NBC Radio	$10-12
	(Live concert)		

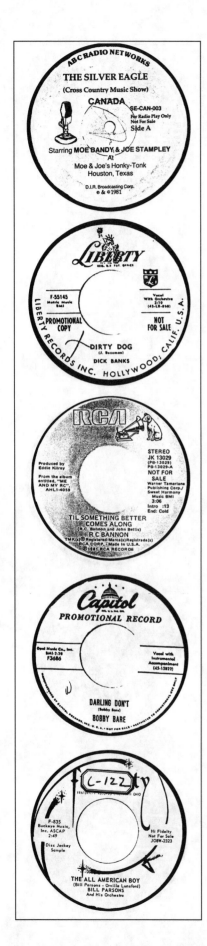

LP(RS)	**LIVE AT GILLEY'S** (Oct 86)	Westwood One	$10-15
	(Live concert)		
3LP(RS)	**AMERICAN EAGLE** (Jan 87) With Joe Stampley	Westwood One	$10-15
	(Live concert)		

DICK BANKS (RB)

-singles-

45rpm	**DIRTY DOG** (58)	Liberty 55145	$15
45(P)	**DIRTY DOG** (58)	Liberty 55145	$10
	(White promo label)		

R. C. BANNON (C)

RCA Victor color vinyl 45s $6 each
Other RCA Victor 45s $1 each

GLENN BARBER (CW)

Hickory 45s $2 each

-albums-

LP	**NEW STAR** (70)	Hickory 152	$12
LP	**BEST OF GLENN BARBER** (72)	Hickory 167	$10

PHIL BARCLAY (RB)

-singles-

45rpm	**YOUNG LONG JOHN** (58)	Doke 101	$60
45rpm	**I LOVE 'EM ALL** (58)	Doke 102	$40

BOBBY BARE (C)

The names of Bobby Bare and Bill Parsons were mixed up at Fraternity Records in 1958 and Bobby
   did not get credit for his greatest selling rock single! The label used the same name for the follow-up
   single, "Educated Rock and Roll."
RCA Victor 45s $3-5 each
RCA Victor picture sleeves $8 each
Mercury 45s $2-4 each
Columbia 45s $2 each
Collectibles 45s (reissues) $1 each
Other RCA Victor and Mercury LPs $5-10 each
Other Pickwick LPs $3-5 each
Other United Artists LPs $3-5 each

-singles-

45rpm	**ANOTHER LOVE HAS ENDED** (57)	Capitol 3557	$18
45(P)	**ANOTHER LOVE HAS ENDED** (57)	Capitol 3557	$15
	(White promo label)		
45rpm	**DARLING DON'T** (57)	Capitol 3686	$18
45(P)	**DARLING DON'T** (57)	Capitol 3686	$15
	(White promo label)		
45rpm	**THE LIVIN' END** (57)	Capitol 3771	$15
45(P)	**THE LIVIN' END** (57)	Capitol 3771	$10
	(White promo label)		
45rpm	**THE ALL-AMERICAN BOY** (58) Bill Parsons	Fraternity 835	$12
	(Dark blue label)		
45(P)	**THE ALL-AMERICAN BOY** (58) Bill Parsons	Fraternity 835	$20
	(White promo label)		
45rpm	**EDUCATED ROCK AND ROLL** (59) Bill Parsons	Fraternity 838	$15
	(Dark blue label)		
45(P)	**EDUCATED ROCK AND ROLL** (59) Bill Parsons	Fraternity 838	$18
	(White promo label)		
45rpm	**I'M HANGIN' UP MY RIFLE** (59)	Fraternity 861	$10
45(P)	**I'M HANGIN' UP MY RIFLE** (59)	Fraternity 861	$12
	(White promo label)		
45rpm	**SWEET SINGIN' SAM** (59)	Fraternity 867	$10
45(P)	**SWEET SINGIN' SAM** (59)	Fraternity 867	$15
	(White promo label)		
45rpm	**BROOKLYN BRIDGE** (59)	Fraternity 890	$12
45(P)	**BROOKLYN BRIDGE** (59)	Fraternity 890	$15
	(White promo label)		
45(P)	**WHAT'S IT ALL ABOUT** (Feb 79)	Southern Baptist MA1575	$10
	(Flip side features Gino Vanelli)		

-EPs-

EP(P)	**BOBBY BARE PROMO EP** (72)	Mercury MELP-16	$12
	(Promo-only release)		

-albums-

LP	**DETROIT CITY** (63)	RCA Victor 2776	$25
LP	**500 MILES AWAY FROM HOME** (63)	RCA Victor 2835	$25
LP	**THE TRAVELIN' BARE** (64)	RCA Victor 2955	$25
LP	**SPECIAL DELIVERY** (64)	Camden 820	$25
	(With Roy Orbison and Joey Powers)		

LP	TUNES FOR TWO (65)	RCA Victor 3336	$18
	(Duets with Skeeter Davis)		
LP	CONSTANT SORROW (65)	RCA Victor 3395	$20
LP	TENDER YEARS (65)	Hilltop 6026	$12
	(Budget label)		
LP	THE BEST OF BOBBY BARE (66)	RCA Victor 3479	$20
LP	TALK ME SOME SENSE (66)	RCA Victor 3515	$20
LP	THE STREETS OF BALTIMORE (66)	RCA Victor 3618	$20
LP	THIS I BELIEVE (67)	RCA Victor 3688	$20
LP	THE GAME OF TRIANGLES (67)	RCA Victor 3764	$18
	(With Liz Anderson and Norma Jean)		
LP	A BIRD NAMED YESTERDAY (67)	RCA Victor 3831	$18
LP	ENGLISH COUNTRYSIDE (67)	RCA Victor 3896	$20
	(Flip side is "The Hillsiders" from the UK)		
LP	FOLSOM PRISON BLUES (68)	Camden 2290	$15
LP	BEST OF BOBBY BARE VOL. 2 (68)	RCA Victor 3994	$18
LP	LINCOLN PARK INN (69)	RCA Victor 4177	$15
LP	YOUR HUSBAND, MY WIFE (70)	RCA Victor 4335	$12
	(Duets with Skeeter Davis)		
LP	THIS IS BARE COUNTRY (70)	Mercury 61290	$15
LP(P)	THIS IS BARE COUNTRY (70)	Mercury 61290	$18
	(White promo label)		
LP	WHERE HAVE ALL THE SEASONS GONE (71)	Mercury 61316	$12
LP(P)	WHERE HAVE ALL THE SEASONS GONE (71)	Mercury 61316	$15
	(White promo label)		
LP	I NEED SOME GOOD NEWS BAD (71)	Mercury 61342	$10
LP(P)	I NEED SOME GOOD NEWS BAD (71)	Mercury 61342	$12
	(White promo label)		
LP	WHAT AM I GONNA DO (72)	Mercury 61363	$12
LP(P)	WHAT AM I GONNA DO (72)	Mercury 61363	$15
	(White promo label)		
LP	I'M A LONG WAY FROM HOME (71)	Camden 2465	$12
LP	BOBBY BARE (73)	RCA Victor 0290	$15
LP	MEMPHIS, TENNESSEE (73)	Camden 0150	$10
2LP	THIS IS BARE COUNTRY (73)	RCA Victor 6090	$15
LP	BOBBY BARE'S GREATEST HITS (74)	Sun 136	$30
	(Stock copies are rare)		
LP(P)	SINGIN' IN THE KITCHEN (74)	RCA Victor DJL1-0079	$25
	(Promo only)		
LP	THE VERY BEST OF BOBBY BARE (75)	United Artists 427	$10
LP	THIS IS BARE COUNTRY (76)	United Artists 621	$12
LP(P)	THE BOBBY BARE RADIO SHOW (80)	Columbia AS-747	$25
	(Promo-only LP released by the record label)		
LP(P)	COUNTRY & WESTERN PSA radio spots for Marines	U.S. Marines	$25
	(Twenty artists including one spot by Bobby Bare)		

-radio shows-

LP(RS)	COUNTRY MUSIC TIME (70s)	U.S. Air Force	$10-12
	(Music and interviews)		
2LP(RS)	COUNTRY COOKIN' (Sept 85) Various artists	U.S. Navy	$10-15
	(Music and interviews)		
3LP(RS)	THE SILVER EAGLE (81) Live concert	DIR 005	$20-25
	(Bobby Bare and Lacy J. Dalton)		
3LP(RS)	THE SILVER EAGLE (Jan 82)	DIR	$10-15
	(Live concert)		
LP(RS)	LIVE AT GILLEY'S (Apr 83)	Westwood One	$10-15
	(Live concert)		

WILEY BARKDULL (CW)

-singles-

45rpm	HEY, HONEY (57)	Hickory 1074	$25
45(P)	HEY, HONEY (57)	Hickory 1074	$20
	(White promo label)		

DELBERT BARKER (RB)

-singles-

| 45rpm | BIMBO (55) | Top Tunes 1058 | $20 |
| 45rpm | NO GOOD ROBIN HOOD (56) | King 4951 | $40 |

GLENN BARKER (RB)

-singles-

| 45rpm | SHADOW MY BABY (58) | Starday 249 | $60 |

THE BARKER BROTHERS (RB)

-singles-

| 45rpm | HEY LITTLE MAMA (58) | Kent 302 | $40 |
| 45rpm | WELL ALL RIGHT ... FRIDAY NIGHT (59) | Decca 30753 | $15 |

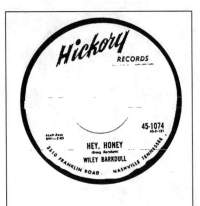

45(P)	**WELL ALL RIGHT … FRIDAY NIGHT** (59)	Decca 30753	$12
	(Pink promo label)		
45rpm	**LOVIN' HONEY** (59)	Decca 30811	$25
45(P)	**LOVIN' HONEY** (59)	Decca 30811	$20
	(Green promo label)		

JACK BARLOW (CW)
Dot 45s $2 each

-albums-

LP	**BABY, THAT AIN'T LOVE** (69)	Dot 25923	$12
LP	**CATCH THE WIND** (70)	Dot 25995	$10

BENNY BARNES (CW)

-singles-

45rpm	**POOR MAN'S RICHES** (57)	Starday 262	$10
45rpm	**YOU GOTTA PAY**	Starday 401	$10
45rpm	**POOR MAN'S RICHES** (57)	Mercury 71048	$12
45(P)	**POOR MAN'S RICHES** (57)	Mercury 71048	$10
	(White promo label)		
45rpm	**NICKEL'S WORTH OF DREAMS** (57)	Mercury 71119	$12
45(P)	**NICKEL'S WORTH OF DREAMS** (57)	Mercury 71119	$10
	(White promo label)		
45rpm	**GOLD RECORDS IN THE SNOW** (59)	D 1052	$30
	(Tribute to Buddy Holly, Big Bopper, and Richie Valens)		

BILLY BARNETT (RB)

-singles-

45rpm	**ROMP AND STOMP** (58)	Double B 1113	$60

BOBBY BARNETT (C)
Other Sims 45s $5-8 each

-singles-

45rpm	**MOANIN' THE BLUES** (63)	Sims 198	$18
	(Price includes picture sleeve)		
45(P)	**MOANIN' THE BLUES** (63)	Sims 198	$10
	(White promo label)		

-albums-

LP	**BOBBY BARNETT AT THE WORLD FAMOUS CRYSTAL PALACE** (64)	Sims 118	$30
LP	**LYIN' LOVIN' & LEAVIN'** (68)	Columbia 9790	$10
LP(P)	**LYIN' LOVIN' & LEAVIN'** (68)	Columbia 9790	$12
	(White promo label)		

MAC BARNS (RB)

-singles-

45rpm	**BE BOPPIN' DADDY** (58)	Fame 580	$60

ROB BARRAN (RB)

-singles-

45rpm	**TOM TOM ROCK** (58)	Silver Streak 311	$100

BARRIER BROTHERS (BG)

-albums-

LP	**GOLDEN BLUEGRASS HITS** (62)	Philips 60003	$25
LP(P)	**GOLDEN BLUEGRASS HITS** (62)	Philips 60003	$30
	(White promo label)		
LP	**MORE GOLDEN BLUEGRASS HITS** (62)	Philips 60049	$25
LP(P)	**MORE GOLDEN BLUEGRASS HITS** (62)	Philips 60049	$30
	(White promo label)		
LP	**GOSPEL SONGS, BLUEGRASS STYLE** (63)	Philips 60083	$25
LP(P)	**GOSPEL SONGS, BLUEGRASS STYLE** (63)	Philips 60083	$30
	(White promo label)		
LP	**GOSPEL SONGS, BLUEGRASS STYLE** (65)	Cumberland 69522	$30

BILLY BARRIX (RB)

-singles-

45rpm	**COOL OFF BABY** (58)	Chess 1662	$7,500

TEDDY BART (RB)

-singles-

45rpm	**HEADIN' FOR A WEDDIN'** (58)	Felsted 8514	$18

BART BARTON (RB)

-singles-

45rpm	**AIN'T I'M A MESS** (58)	EEM 1651	$50
	(Price includes rare picture sleeve)		

LOUIE BASHELL (Polka)
With His Silk Umbrella Orchestra
RCA Victor 45s $5-10 each

KENNY BASS (Polka)
Coral 45s $4-8 each
Decca 45s $3-6 each

LEON BASS (RB)
-singles-

45rpm	**COUNTRY HIX'S** (58)	Whirl-A-Way 1058	$40

SHIRLEY BATES (CW)
-singles-

45rpm	**CARLOS YBARRA** (54)	Fabor 106	$12

PHIL BAUGH (C)
Guitar player
Other Longhorn 45s $5-8 each
-singles-

45rpm	**COUNTRY GUITAR** (65) Picture on label	Longhorn 559	$10
	(Vocal by Vern Stovall)		

-albums-

LP	**COUNTRY GUITAR** (65)	Longhorn 002	$35
LP	**CALIFORNIA GUITAR** (69)	Era 801	$18
LP(P)	**CALIFORNIA GUITAR** (69)	Era 801	$25
	(White promo label)		

ALAN BAUM (RB)
-singles-

45rpm	**MY KIND OF WOMAN** (58)	Red Robin 124	$40

BILL BEACH (RB)
-singles-

45rpm	**PEG PANTS** (58)	King 4940	$60

TOMMY JIM BEAM (RB)
-singles-

45rpm	**MY LITTLE JEWEL** (58)	100 Proff 101	$125

DEAN BEARD (RB)
-singles-

45rpm	**RAKIN' & SCRAPIN'** (58)	Edmoral 1011	$60
45rpm	**SING SING SING** (59)	Fox 408	$60
45rpm	**PARTY PARTY** (59)	Sangelo 55	$50

BEAVER VALLEY SWEETHEARTS (CW)
-singles-

45rpm	**I CARE NO MORE** (52)	RCA Victor 4955	$10
	See Elton Britt		

FRITZ BECHTEL (Polka)
Decca 45s $4-8 each

MOLLY BEE (CW)
Capitol 45s $5-10 each
MGM 45s $3-6 each
-EPs-

EP	**YOUNG ROMANCE** (58)	Capitol 1097	$18

-albums-

LP	**YOUNG ROMANCE** (58)	Capitol 1097	$25
LP(P)	**YOUNG ROMANCE** (58)	Capitol 1097	$20
	(Promo label)		
LP	**IT'S GREAT, IT'S MOLLY BEE** (65)	MGM 4303	$15
LP(P)	**IT'S GREAT, IT'S MOLLY BEE** (65)	MGM 4303	$18
	(Yellow promo label)		
LP	**SWINGING COUNTRY** (67)	MGM 4423	$12
LP(P)	**SWINGING COUNTRY** (67)	MGM 4423	$15
	(Yellow promo label)		

CARL BELEW (CW)
Decca 45s $4-8 each
RCA Victor 45s $3-5 each
-EPs-

EP	**CARL BELEW** (60)	Decca 2687	$15

	-albums-		
LP	**CARL BELEW** (60)	Decca 4074	$18
LP(P)	**CARL BELEW** (60)	Decca 4074	$15
LP	**CARL BELEW** (62)	Wrangler 1007	$15
LP	**HELLO OUT THERE** (64)	RCA Victor 2848	$15
LP	**AM I THAT EASY TO FORGET** (65)	RCA Victor 3381	$15
LP	**COUNTRY SONGS** (66)	Vocalion 3774	$12
LP	**LONELY STREET** (67)	Vocalion 3791	$12
LP	**TWELVE SHADES OF BELEW** (68)	RCA Victor 3919	$12
LP	**WHEN MY BABY SINGS HIS SONG** (72)	Decca 5337	$10
	(Duets with Betty Jean Robinson)		

BILL BELL (RB)

	-singles-		
45rpm	**LITTLE BITTY GIRL** (58)	Mida 112	$40

DWAIN BELL (RB)

	-singles-		
45rpm	**ROCK & ROLL ON A SATURDAY NIGHT** (57)	Summit 110	$150

EDDIE BELL (RB)

	-singles-		
45rpm	**JOHNNY B. GOODE IS IN HOLLYWOOD** (58)	Lucky Four 1005	$60
45rpm	**THE MASKED MAN** (59)	Mercury 71677	$15
45(P)	**THE MASKED MAN** (59)	Mercury 71677	$10
	(White promo label)		

FREDDIE BELL & THE BELLBOYS (R)
Mercury 45s $5-8 each

	-albums-		
LP	**ROCK & ROLL** (59)	Mercury 20289	$40
LP(P)	**ROCK & ROLL** (59)	Mercury 20289	$50
	(White promo label)		

JOHNNY BELL (R)

	-singles-		
45rpm	**THE THIRD DEGREES** (59)	Brunswick 55142	$50
45(P)	**THE THIRD DEGREES** (59)	Brunswick 55142	$40
	(Yellow promo label)		

TOMMY BELL (R)

	-singles-		
45rpm	**SWAMP GAL** (58)	ZII 9001	$60

BELLAMY BROTHERS (C)
Elektra 45s $2 each
Warner 45s $2-3 each
MCA 45s $1-2 each
Other MCA color vinyl 45s $8 each
Warner LPs $5-8 each

	-singles-		
45(P)	**FEELIN' THE FEELIN'** (85) Yellow vinyl	MCA 52747	$10
	(White promo label)		
45(P)	**COUNTRY RAP** (86) Yellow vinyl	MCA 52834	$12
	(White promo label)		
45(P)	**TOO MUCH IS NOT ENOUGH** (86) Red vinyl	MCA 52917	$10
	(White promo label)		
	-EPs-		
EP(P)	**AN OPEN END INTERVIEW** (85)	Warner 002	$20
	(Promo-only release)		
	-radio shows-		
LP(RS)	**COUNTRY MUSIC TIME** (80s)	U.S. Air Force	$10-12
	(Music and interviews)		
3LP(RS)	**THE SILVER EAGLE** (Apr 83)	DIR	$10-20
	(Live concert)		
3LP(RS)	**AMERICAN EAGLE** (Jan 87)	Westwood One	$10-20
	(Live concert)		
LP(RS)	**WESTWOOD ONE PRESENTS** (Feb 87)	Westwood One	$10-15
	(Live concert)		
LP(RS)	**LIVE AT GILLEY'S** (Aug 88)	Westwood One	$10-15
	(Live concert)		

ERNIE BENEDICT (CW)
And the Range Riders
RCA Victor 78s $10-15 each

-singles-

45rpm	**WHEN I COMB MY HANDS THROUGH THE SANDS OF TEXAS** (49) RCA Victor 0106		$15
	(Green vinyl)		

BOYD BENNETT (RB)
And His Rockets

-singles-

78rpm	**SEVENTEEN** (55) Blue label	King 1470	$10
78(P)	**SEVENTEEN** (55)	King 1470	$15
	(White promo label)		
78(P)	**SEVENTEEN** (55)	King 1470	$18
	(White promo label with profile)		
45rpm	**SEVENTEEN** (55) Blue label	King 1470	$15
45(P)	**SEVENTEEN** (55)	King 1470	$18
	(White promo label)		
45(P)	**SEVENTEEN** (55)	King 1470	$15
	(White promo label with profile)		
78rpm	**MY BOY FLAT TOP** (55) Blue label	King 1494	$10
78(P)	**MY BOY FLAT TOP** (55)	King 1494	$18
	(White promo label)		
45rpm	**MY BOY FLAT TOP** (55) Blue label	King 1494	$15
45(P)	**MY BOY FLAT TOP** (55)	King 1494	$18
	(White promo label)		
78rpm	**THE MOST** (55)	King 4853	$15
78(P)	**THE MOST** (55)	King 4853	$10
	(White promo label)		
45rpm	**THE MOST** (55)	King 4853	$15
45(P)	**THE MOST** (55)	King 4853	$10
	(White promo label)		
78rpm	**RIGHT AROUND THE CORNER** (55)	King 4874	$15
78(P)	**RIGHT AROUND THE CORNER** (55)	King 4874	$10
	(White promo label)		
45rpm	**RIGHT AROUND THE CORNER** (55)	King 4874	$15
45(P)	**RIGHT AROUND THE CORNER** (55)	King 4874	$18
	(White promo label)		
78rpm	**BLUE SUEDE SHOES** (56)	King 4903	$10
78(P)	**BLUE SUEDE SHOES** (56)	King 4903	$18
	(White promo label)		
45rpm	**BLUE SUEDE SHOES** (56)	King 4903	$15
45(P)	**BLUE SUEDE SHOES** (56)	King 4903	$18
	(White promo label)		
45rpm	**BOOGIE BEAR** (59) Black label	Mercury 71479	$12
45(P)	**BOOGIE BEAR** (59)	Mercury 71479	$15
	(White promo label)		
45rpm	**NAUGHTY ROCK & ROLL** (59)	Mercury 71537	$20
45(P)	**NAUGHTY ROCK & ROLL** (59)	Mercury 71537	$15
	(White promo label)		

-EPs-

EP	**ROCK AND ROLL** (57)	King 377	$80
EP	**ROCK AND ROLL** (57)	King 383	$75

-albums-

LP	**BOYD BENNETT** (57)	King 532	$100
LP	**BOYD BENNETT** (57)	King 594	$75

CLIFF BENNETT (RB)

-singles-

45rpm	**I'M IN LOVE WITH YOU** (61)	Capitol 4621	$30
45(P)	**I'M IN LOVE WITH YOU** (61)	Capitol 4621	$25
	(Capitol promo label)		

JOE BENNETT (RB)
And the Sparkletones

-singles-

78rpm	**BLACK SLACKS** (57)	ABC Paramount 9837	$12
45rpm	**BLACK SLACKS** (57)	ABC Paramount 9837	$10
45(P)	**BLACK SLACKS** (57)	ABC Paramount 9837	$15
	(White promo label)		
78rpm	**PENNY LOAFERS AND BOBBY SOCKS** (57)	ABC Paramount 9867	$15
45rpm	**PENNY LOAFERS AND BOBBY SOCKS** (57)	ABC Paramount 9867	$10
45(P)	**PENNY LOAFERS AND BOBBY SOCKS** (57)	ABC Paramount 9867	$15
	(White promo label)		
45rpm	**I DIG YOU, BABY** (57)	ABC Paramount 9885	$10
45(P)	**I DIG YOU, BABY** (57)	ABC Paramount 9885	$15
	(White promo label)		

45rpm	**LITTLE TURTLE** (58)	ABC Paramount 9929	$10
45(P)	**LITTLE TURTLE** (58)	ABC Paramount 9929	$15
	(White promo label)		
45rpm	**DO THE STOP** (58)	ABC Paramount 9959	$10
45(P)	**DO THE STOP** (58)	ABC Paramount 9959	$15
	(White promo label)		
45rpm	**BAYOU ROCK** (59)	Paris 530	$10
45(P)	**BAYOU ROCK** (59)	Paris 530	$15
	(White promo label)		
45rpm	**ARE YOU FROM DIXIE** (60)	Paris 542	$10
45(P)	**ARE YOU FROM DIXIE** (60)	Paris 542	$15
	(White promo label)		

WALT BENTON (RB)

-singles-

45rpm	**STUCK UP** (58)	20th Fox 143	$40
45(P)	**STUCK UP** (58)	20th Fox 143	$50
	(White promo label)		

MIKE BERRY (RB)

-singles-

45rpm	**TRIBUTE TO BUDDY HOLLY** (62)	Coral 62341	$25
	(Major hit in the UK, home of Mike Berry & the Outlaws)		
45(P)	**TRIBUTE TO BUDDY HOLLY** (62)	Coral 62341	$20
	(Yellow promo label)		

BEVERLY HILLBILLIES (CW)
Elton Britt and Zeke Manners

-albums-

LP	**THOSE FABULOUS BEVERLY HILLBILLIES**	Rar-Arts 1000	$75
	(Gold vinyl)		
	See Elton Britt		
	See Zeke Manners		

BIG BOB (R)

-singles-

45rpm	**YOUR LINE WAS BUSY** (58)	Jaro 77003	$50

BIG BOPPER (R)
J. P. Richardson

-singles-

45rpm	**CHANTILLY LACE** (57) The Big Bopper	D 1008	$350
45rpm	**BEGGAR TO A KING** (57) Jape Richardson	Mercury 71219	$50
45(P)	**BEGGAR TO A KING** (57) Jape Richardson	Mercury 71219	$40
	(White promo label)		
45rpm	**TEENAGE MOON** (58) Jape Richardson	Mercury 71312	$50
45(P)	**TEENAGE MOON** (58) Jape Richardson	Mercury 71312	$40
	(White promo label)		
45rpm	**CHANTILLY LACE** (58) The Big Bopper	Mercury 71343	$25
45(P)	**CHANTILLY LACE** (58) The Big Bopper	Mercury 71343	$35
	(White promo label)		
45rpm	**CHANTILLY LACE** (58) The Big Bopper	Mercury 30072	$15
	(Celebrity Series)		
45(P)	**CHANTILLY LACE** (58) The Big Bopper	Mercury 30072	$25
	(Rare white promo label)		
45rpm	**BIG BOPPER'S WEDDING** (58) The Big Bopper	Mercury 71375	$20
45(P)	**BIG BOPPER'S WEDDING** (58) The Big Bopper	Mercury 71375	$25
	(White promo label)		
45rpm	**WALKING THROUGH MY DREAMS** (59) The Big Bopper	Mercury 71416	$20
45(P)	**WALKING THROUGH MY DREAMS** (59) The Big Bopper	Mercury 71416	$25
	(White promo label)		
45rpm	**IT'S THE TRUTH, RUTH** (59) The Big Bopper	Mercury 71451	$25
45(P)	**IT'S THE TRUTH, RUTH** (59) The Big Bopper	Mercury 71451	$30
	(White promo label)		
45rpm	**PINK PETTICOATS** (59) The Big Bopper	Mercury 71482	$20
45(P)	**PINK PETTICOATS** (59) The Big Bopper	Mercury 71482	$25
	(White promo label)		

-albums-

LP	**CHANTILLY LACE** (57)	Mercury 20402	$75
LP(P)	**CHANTILLY LACE** (57)	Mercury 20402	$80
	(White promo label)		

BIG ROCKER (RB)

-singles-

45rpm	**ROCK 'N' ROLL ROMANCE** (58)	Lucky Four 1009	$40

BILLBOARD (Various Artists)

-radio shows-

5LP(RS)	**SOUND OF '77** (Dec 77) Country version	Billboard Magazine	$125
	(Includes an Elvis Presley tribute)		

THE BILL-WILL BAND (Polka)

-singles-

45rpm	**JOEY'S POLKA** (59)	Double Eagle 45-1A	$15
	(Green vinyl)		

CLINT BLACK (C)
RCA Victor 45s $2 each
RCA Victor LPs $4 each

JEANNE BLACK (CW)
Jeanne and Janie
Capitol 45s $4-8 each

-albums-

LP	**A LITTLE BIT LONELY** (60)	Capitol 1513	$20
LP(P)	**A LITTLE BIT LONELY** (60)	Capitol 1513	$25
	(Capitol promo label)		

SONNY BLAIR (RB)

-singles-

45rpm	**PLEASE SEND MY BABY BACK** (52)	Meteor 5006	$125

TOMMY BLAKE (RB)

-singles-

45rpm	**FLAT FOOT** (58)	Sun 278	$25
45rpm	**I DIG YOU BABY** (59)	Sun 300	$100

CLIFF BLAKELY (RB)

-singles-

45rpm	**WANT TO BE WITH YOU** (59)	Starday 352	$30
45rpm	**GET OFF MY TOE** (59)	Starday 365	$35

JIMMY BLAKELY (CW)
And His Western Swing Band

-singles-

45rpm	**THE PLACE IS NOT THE SAME** (66)	United Artists 412	$10

BLANCHARD & MORGAN (N)
Jack Blanchard and Misty Morgan
Wayside 45s $3 each
Mega 45s $2 each
Mega LPs $8 each

-albums-

LP	**BIRDS OF A FEATHER** (70)	Wayside 001	$15

GLENN BLAND (R)

-singles-

45rpm	**MEAN GENE** (58)	Sarg 159	$45
45rpm	**WHEN MY BABY PASSES BY** (58)	Sarg 164	$40

BLANKENSHIP BROTHERS (RB)

-singles-

45rpm	**THAT'S WHY I'M BLUE** (58)	Skyline 106	$60

JULES BLATTNER (RB)

-singles-

45rpm	**ROCK AND ROLL BLUES** (58)	Bobbin 105	$60

BLUE BOYS (CW)
Backing group for Jim Reeves
RCA Victor 45s $2 each

-albums-

LP	**WE REMEMBER JIM** (65)	RCA Victor 3331	$30
	(Reissue LP is "Memories of Jim Reeves")		
LP	**SOUNDS OF JIM REEVES** (66)	RCA Victor 3529	$25
LP	**THE BLUE BOYS IN PERSON** (67)	RCA Victor 3696	$25
LP	**HIT AFTER HIT** (67)	RCA Victor 3794	$25

BLUE RIDGE MOUNTAIN BOYS (CW)
Time 45s $3 each

-albums-

LP	HOOTENANNY & BLUEGRASS (63)	Time 2083	$15
LP	BLUEGRASS DOWN HOME (63)	Time 2103	$12

BLUE SKY BOYS (CW)
Bluebird label 78s are worth $18-$25 each
Other RCA Victor 78s $10 each
Other RCA VIctor 45s $15 each

-singles-

45rpm	DUST ON THE BIBLE (49) Green vinyl	RCA Victor 0036	$50
45rpm	LITTLE MOTHER OF THE HILLS (49) Green vinyl	RCA Victor 0111	$40
78(P)	WHEN HEAVEN COMES DOWN (49) White promo label	RCA Victor DJ-58	$50
	(Special release promo-only version)		
45rpm	WHEN HEAVEN COMES DOWN (49) Green vinyl	RCA Victor 0163	$20

-albums-

LP	THE BLUE SKY BOYS (62)	Starday 205	$25
LP	TOGETHER AGAIN (63)	Starday 257	$20
LP	THE BLUE SKY BOYS (63)	Starday 269	$30
LP	THE BLUE SKY BOYS (63)	Camden 797	$15
LP	THE BLUE SKY BOYS (66)	Capitol 2483	$20
LP	THE BLUE SKY BOYS (66)	Capitol 2483	$15
	(Capitol promo label)		
2LP	BLUEGRASS MOUNTAIN MUSIC (74)	Camden 0726	$25
2LP	THE BLUE SKY BOYS (76)	Bluebird 5525	$15

THE BLUEGRASS GENTLEMEN (CW)
-albums-

LP	THE BLUEGRASS GENTLEMEN (62)	Liberty 3214	$15
LP(P)	THE BLUEGRASS GENTLEMEN (62)	Liberty 3214	$20
	(White promo label)		

THE BLUEGRASS HOPPERS (CW)
-albums-

LP	THE COUNTRY'S COME TO TOWN (68)	Cuca 1160	$25

STERLING BLYTHE (C)
-albums-

LP	A NIGHT AT THE SHOWBOAT (60) Red vinyl	Sage & Sand 14	$40
	(Lettering on the label is red and black)		
LP	A NIGHT AT THE SHOWBOAT (68) Red vinyl	Sage & Sand 14	$25
	(Label lettering is in several colors)		
LP	STERLING BLYTHE SINGS (62)	Crown 5179	$12
	(Budget label)		

TOOTER BOATMAN (RB)
-singles-

45rpm	POOR GAL (58)	Rebel 108	$125
45rpm	THUNDER AND LIGHTNING (58)	Twinkle 501	$125

BOB & LUCILLE (R & B)
-singles-

45rpm	EENIE MEENIE MINEY MO (58)	Ditto 121	$55

BOBBY & HIS ORBITS (RB)
-singles-

45rpm	FELICIA (57)	Seeco 6005	$12
45(P)	FELICIA (57)	Seeco 6005	$15
	(White promo label)		

BOBBY BOBO (CW)
-singles-

45rpm	AUCTIONEER (63)	Boone 1020	$12

NOEL BOGGS (CW)
-albums-

LP	MAGIC STEEL GUITAR (60)	Shasta 503	$18
LP	HOLLYWOOD & VINE (62)	Shasta 530	$15
LP	NOEL BOGGS WITH FRIENDS (63)	Shasta 531	$12

CALVIN BOLES (RB)
-singles-

45rpm	STOMPIN' ON A HARDWOOD FLOOR (58)	Yucca 161	$60

BOBBY BOND (CW)

-albums-

LP	**BOBBY BOND** (64)	Time 2122	$10

EDDIE BOND (RB)

-singles-

45rpm	**TALKIN' OFF THE WALL** (57)	Ekko 1015	$100
45rpm	**MONKEY AND THE BABOON** (57)	Diplomat 8566	$55
45rpm	**ROCKIN' DADDY** (58)	Mercury 70826	$40
45(P)	**ROCKIN' DADDY** (58)	Mercury 70826	$25
	(White promo label)		
45rpm	**SLIP SLIP SLIPIN' IN** (58)	Mercury 70882	$40
45(P)	**SLIP SLIP SLIPIN' IN** (58)	Mercury 70882	$25
	(White promo label)		
45rpm	**BOPPIN' BONNIE** (58)	Mercury 70941	$40
45(P)	**BOPPIN' BONNIE** (58)	Mercury 70941	$25
	(White promo label)		
45rpm	**YOU'RE PART OF ME** (58)	Mercury 71067	$15
45(P)	**YOU'RE PART OF ME** (58)	Mercury 71067	$10
	(White promo label)		
45rpm	**LOVE, LOVE, LOVE** (58)	Mercury 71237	$15
45(P)	**LOVE, LOVE, LOVE** (58)	Mercury 71237	$10
	(White promo label)		

-albums-

LP	**EDDIE BOND SINGS THE GREATEST COUNTRY GOSPEL** (61)	Philips 1980	$35

JOHNNY BOND (CW)

Columbia 78s in the 20700 series are worth $8-15 each
Other Columbia 45s $5-8 each
Starday 45s $3-6 each
Gusto 45s $2-3 each

-singles-

45rpm	**STAR SPANGLED WALTZ** (51)	Columbia 20726	$10
45rpm	**BARREL HOUSE BESSIE** (51)	Columbia 20734	$15
45rpm	**STEPPIN' OUT** (52)	Columbia 20738	$10
45rpm	**JINGLE BELLS BOOGIE** (52)	Columbia 20756	$15
45rpm	**GLAD RAGS** (51)	Columbia 20787	$15
	(Released again in 1955)		
45rpm	**ALABAMA BOOGIE BOY** (52)	Columbia 20909	$15
45rpm	**LOUISIANA LUCY** (52)	Columbia 20948	$12
45rpm	**I WENT TO YOUR WEDDING** (53)	Columbia 21007	$10
	(Johnny Bond with Helen Carter)		
45rpm	**ANYBODY'S BABY** (53)	Columbia 21082	$10
45rpm	**WILD CAT BOOGIE** (54)	Columbia 21160	$20
45(P)	**WILD CAT BOOGIE** (54)	Columbia 21160	$18
	(White promo label)		
78rpm	**TEN LITTLE BOTTLES** (54)	Columbia 21222	$20
	(Original version, later a hit on Starday)		
78(P)	**TEN LITTLE BOTTLES** (54)	Columbia 21222	$25
	(White promo label)		
45rpm	**TEN LITTLE BOTTLES** (54)	Columbia 21222	$18
45(P)	**TEN LITTLE BOTTLES** (54)	Columbia 21222	$20
	(White promo label)		
45rpm	**STEALIN'** (54)	Columbia 21294	$10
45(P)	**STEALIN'** (54)	Columbia 21294	$12
	(White promo label)		
45rpm	**GLAD RAGS** (55) Red label	Columbia 21369	$18
	(Bond wrote this song which was a hit for Tennessee Ernie Ford)		
45(P)	**GLAD RAGS** (55)	Columbia 21369	$15
	(White promo label)		
45rpm	**LOUISIANA SWING** (55)	Columbia 21383	$12
45(P)	**LOUISIANA SWING** (55) With photo on label	Columbia 21383	$18
	(White promo label)		
45rpm	**LIVIN' IT UP** (56)	Columbia 21448	$12
45(P)	**LIVIN' IT UP** (56)	Columbia 21448	$10
	(White promo label)		
45rpm	**LOADED FOR BEAR** (56)	Columbia 21494	$10
45(P)	**LOADED FOR BEAR** (56)	Columbia 21494	$12
	(White promo label)		
45rpm	**THE LITTLE ROCK AND ROLL** (57)	Columbia 21521	$25
45(P)	**THE LITTLE ROCK AND ROLL** (57)	Columbia 21521	$18
45rpm	**LONESOME TRAIN** (57)	Columbia 21565	$12
45(P)	**LONESOME TRAIN** (57)	Columbia 21565	$10
	(White promo label)		

45rpm	**HONKY TONK FEVER** (58)		Columbia 40842	$12
45(P)	**HONKY TONK FEVER** (58)		Columbia 40842	$10
	(White promo label)			
45rpm	**BROKEN DOLL** (58)		Columbia 41034	$12
45(P)	**BROKEN DOLL** (58)		Columbia 41034	$10
	(White promo label)			
45rpm	**HOT ROD LINCOLN** (59) Blue label		Republic 2005	$10
	(Written and also recorded by Charlie Ryan)			
45(P)	**HOT ROD LINCOLN** (59)		Republic 2005	$15
	(White promo label)			
45rpm	**X-15** (60)		Republic 2008	$10
45(P)	**X-15** (60)		Republic 2008	$12
	(White promo label)			
45rpm	**SIDE CAR CYCLE** (60)		Republic 2010	$10
45(P)	**SIDE CAR CYCLE** (60)		Republic 2010	$12
	(White promo label)			

-EPs-

EP	**JOHNNY BOND & HIS RED RIVER BOYS** (58)		Columbia 2820	$50
EP	**HOT ROD LINCOLN** (60)		Republic 100	$40
	(The first EP for Gene Autry's label)			
EP(JB)	**TEN LITTLE BOTTLES** (65) Jukebox LLP		Starday 333	$15
	(Price includes cover and title strips)			

-albums-

LP	**THAT WILD, WICKED, BUT WONDERFUL WEST** (61)		Starday 147	$40
LP	**LIVE IT UP, LAUGH IT UP** (62)		Starday 187	$25
	(Includes Cowboy Copas, Justin Tubb and others)			
LP	**SONGS THAT MADE HIM FAMOUS** (63)		Starday 227	$25
LP	**JOHNNY BOND RIDES AGAIN** (63)		Shasta 516	$15
LP	**HOT ROD LINCOLN** (64)		Starday 298	$30
LP	**JOHNNY BOND'S BEST** (64) Brown label		Harmony 7308	$25
LP(P)	**JOHNNY BOND'S BEST** (64) White promo label		Harmony 7308	$35
LP	**TEN LITTLE BOTTLES** (65)		Starday 333	$25
LP	**FAMOUS HOT RODDERS I HAVE KNOWN** (65)		Starday 354	$40
LP	**THE MAN WHO COMES AROUND** (66)		Starday 368	$18
LP	**BOTTLES UP** (66)		Starday 378	$20
LP	**BRANDED STOCK OF JOHNNY BOND** (66)		Starday 388	$18
LP	**TEN NIGHTS IN A BARROOM** (67)		Starday 402	$15
LP	**DRINK UP AND GO HOME** (68)		Starday 416	$15
LP	**THE BEST OF JOHNNY BOND** (69)		Starday 444	$15
LP	**HERE COME THE ELEPHANTS** (71)		Starday 472	$12
LP(P)	**BOTTLED IN BOND** (65) White promo label		Harmony 7353	$25

-radio shows-

LP(RS)	**HOOTENAVY** (60s) Fifteen-minute radio show		U.S. Navy 19/20	$25-40
	(Music and interviews)			

JIMMY BONE (RB)

-singles-

45rpm	**LITTLE MAMA** (58)		Grace 510	$40

BONNIE LOU (CW)

-singles-

45rpm	**SEVEN LONELY DAYS** (52)		King 1192	$10
45rpm	**TENNESSEE WIG WALK** (53)		King 1237	$12
45rpm	**BARNYARD HOP** (55)		King 1506	$10
45rpm	**BO WEEVIL** (56)		King 4900	$10
45(P)	**BO WEEVIL** (56)		King 4900	$12
	(White promo label)			

-EPs-

EP	**BONNIE LOU SINGS** (58)		King 335	$25
EP	**DADDY-O** (58)		King 389	$25

-albums-

LP	**BONNIE LOU SINGS** (58)		King 595	$25

LARRY BOONE (CW)

-radio shows-

LP(RS)	**LIVE AT GILLEY'S** (Sept 88)		Westwood One	$10-15
	(Live concert)			

RICK BOUNTY (RB)

-singles-

45rpm	**IT'LL BE ME** (58)		Bow 6144	$50

BILL BOWEN (RB)

-singles-

45rpm	**HAVE MYSELF A BALL** (58)		Meteor 5033	$125

JIMMY BOWEN (R)
Other Roulette 45s $10 each

-singles-

45rpm	I'M STICKIN' WITH YOU (57)	Blue Moon 402	$100
45rpm	I'M STICKIN' WITH YOU (57)	Triple D 797	$75
78rpm	I'M STICKIN' WITH YOU (58)	Roulette 4001	$40
	(The first Roulette release)		
45rpm	I'M STICKIN' WITH YOU (58)	Roulette 4001	$40
	(Orange "Roulette" label)		
45rpm	I'M STICKIN' WITH YOU (59)	Roulette 4001	$15
	(Red label)		

-albums-

LP	JIMMY BOWEN (57) First pressing	Roulette 25004	$75

MARGIE BOWES (CW)
Decca 45s $2-5 each

-albums-

LP	MARGIE BOWES SINGS (67)	Decca 4816	$15
LP(P)	MARGIE BOWES SINGS (67)	Decca 4816	$18
	(White promo label)		
LP	TODAY'S COUNTRY SOUND (69)	Decca 5023	$10
LP(P)	TODAY'S COUNTRY SOUND (69)	Decca 5023	$12
	(White promo label)		

DON BOWMAN (N)
RCA Victor 45s $3-6 each
Other RCA Victor LPs $5-8 each
Mega LPs $3-5 each

-albums-

LP	OUR MAN IN TROUBLE (64)	RCA Victor 2831	$15
LP	FRESH FROM THE FUNNY FARM (65)	RCA Victor 3345	$15
LP	FUNNY FOLK FLOPS (68)	RCA Victor 3920	$12
	(Duets with Skeeter Davis)		
LP	STILL FIGHTING MENTAL HEALTH (69)	Lone Star 4605	$12

DONNIE BOWSER (RB)

-singles-

45rpm	TALK TO ME BABY (57)	Bamboo 508	$10
45rpm	I LOVE YOU BABY (58)	Sage 265	$12
45rpm	GOT THE BEST OF ME (58)	Sage 276	$10
45rpm	I LOVE YOU BABY (58)	Fraternity 801	$10
45(P)	I LOVE YOU BABY (59)	Fraternity 801	$12
	(White promo label)		

DONNIE BOWSHIRE (RB)

-singles-

45rpm	ROCK AND ROLL JOYS (58)	Dess 7002	$150
45rpm	I LOVE YOU BABY (58)	Robbins 1009	$75

BOXCAR WILLIE (C)
Marty Martin
Column One 45s $4-8 each
Other Main Street 45s $3-5 each
Column One LPs $5-8 each
Main Street LPs $3-5 each

-singles-

45rpm	BOXCAR WILLIE (76) Marty Martin & the Rangers	Roto 7493	$25
	(First record, the song title became his recording name)		
45rpm	TRIBUTE TO JIMMIE RODGERS (83)	Main Street	$12
	(Price includes picture sleeve)		

-albums-

LP	MARTY MARTIN SINGS COUNTRY MUSIC (76) Marty Martin	AHMC AA118	$50
	(First LP)		

-radio shows-

3LP(RS)	INTERNATIONAL FESTIVAL (Oct 82) Various artists	Mutual Broadcasting	$30-50
	(Live concert includes Boxcar Willie)		
LP(RS)	COUNTRY CROSSROADS (May 86)	Southern Baptist	$10-15
	(Music and interviews)		

BILL BOYD (CW)
Other RCA Victor green vinyl 45s $25 each
Other RCA Victor 45s $5-10 each

-singles-

45rpm	JINGLE BELLS (48)	RCA Victor 0129	$20
	(Green vinyl)		

EDDIE BOYD (RB)

-singles-

45rpm	SAVE HER DOCTOR (51)	JOB	$50
45rpm	I'M PLEADING (52)	JOB 1005	$50
45rpm	BLUE COAT MAN (52) Red vinyl	JOB 1007	$85
45rpm	I'M GOING DOWNTOWN (53)	Herald 406	$85
45rpm	IT'S MISERABLE TO BE ALONE (53)	JOB 1009	$50
45rpm	I LOVE YOU (54)	JOB 1114	$50
45rpm	COOL KIND TREATMENT (54)	Chess 1523	$40

JIMMY BOYD (RB)

Other MGM 45s $5-8 each

-singles-

45rpm	CREAM PUFF (58)	MGM 12788	$40

SLIM BOYD (CW)

Premier, Coronet and Spin-O-Rama LPs $10 each
  (All are budget labels)

HAROLD BRADLEY (CW)

Columbia 45s $3 each

-albums-

LP	BOSSA NOVA GUITAR GOES TO NASHVILLE (63)	Columbia 8814	$18
LP(P)	BOSSA NOVA GUITAR GOES TO NASHVILLE (63)	Columbia 8814	$15
LP	MISTY GUITAR (63)	Columbia 8873	$15
LP(P)	MISTY GUITAR (63)	Columbia 8873	$12

OWEN BRADLEY (CW)

Other Coral 45s $5-8 each
Other Decca LPs $5-8 each

-singles-

78rpm	BLUES STAY AWAY FROM ME (49)	Coral 60107	$12
45rpm	I WILL STILL LOVE YOU (53)	Coral 60892	$10
45rpm	GRANADA (55)	Decca 28732	$10

-EPs-

EP	DANCE TIME (55)	Coral 81014	$25
EP	CHRISTMAS TIME (55)	Coral 82015	$25
EP	CHERISHED HYMNS (55)	Coral 82016	$30
EP	BANDSTAND HOP (58)	Decca 2593	$30

-albums-

LP	CHRISTMAS TIME (55)	Coral 56012	$25
LP	STRAUSS WALTZES (55)	Coral 56022	$20
LP	LAZY RIVER (56)	Coral 56035	$20
LP	SINGIN' IN THE RAIN (56)	Coral 56047	$20
LP	CHERISHED HYMNS (56)	Coral 56065	$25
LP	BANDSTAND HOP (58)	Decca 8724	$25
LP(P)	BANDSTAND HOP (58)	Decca 8724	$30
	(Pink promo label)		
LP	BIG GUITAR (59) Mono	Decca 8868	$25
LP	BIG GUITAR (59) Stereo	Decca 8868	$35
LP(P)	BIG GUITAR (59)	Decca 8868	$30
	(Pink promo label)		
LP	PARADISE ISLAND (60)	Decca 4078	$18
LP(P)	PARADISE ISLAND (60)	Decca 4078	$15
	(White promo label)		

CAROLYN BRADSHAW (CW)

-singles-

45rpm	MARRIAGE OF MEXICAN JOE (53)	Abbott 141	$15
	(Answer song to Jim Reeves's "Mexican Joe")		

JACK BRADSHAW (RB)

-singles-

45rpm	JO-JO (57)	Mar-Vel 753	$50

DOUG BRAGG (RB)

-singles-

45rpm	DAYDREAMING AGAIN (58)	D 1018	$60

JOHNNY BRANDON (RB)

-singles-

45rpm	HEY PRETTY BABY (57)	London 1744	$12
45(P)	HEY PRETTY BABY (57)	London 1744	$15
	(White promo label)		

BOBBY BRANT (RB)
-singles-

45rpm	PIANO NELLIE (58)	White Rock 1114	$65
45rpm	PIANO NELLIE (58)	East West 124	$40

WALTER BRENNAN (CW)
Other label 45s $3-5 each
Other Dot and Liberty LPs $6-8 each

-singles-

45rpm	DUTCHMAN'S GOLD (60)	Dot 16066	$25
	(Price includes picture sleeve)		

-albums-

LP	DUTCHMAN'S GOLD (60)	Dot 3309	$25
LP(P)	MAMA SANG A SONG (62)	Liberty 3266	$25
	(White promo label)		

JAY BRINKLEY (R)
-singles-

45rpm	GUITAR SMOKE (58)	Kliff 101	$40

ELTON BRITT (CW)
Other label 78s $5-10 each
Other RCA Victor 45s $5-8 each

-singles-

78rpm	NEW LONDON TEXAS SCHOOL TRAGEDY	Conqueror 8809	$40
78rpm	THERE'S A STAR-SPANGLED BANNER WAVING SOMEWHERE (42)	Bluebird 9000	$15
78rpm	WAVE TO ME, MY LADY (46)	Victor 1789	$12
45rpm	CHIME BELLS (49) Green aqua label	RCA Victor 0143	$18
	(With the Skytoppers)		
45rpm	CHIME BELLS (53) Black label	RCA Victor 0143	$10
45rpm	LOST AND FOUND BLUES (49) Green vinyl	RCA Victor 0408	$15
78rpm	ROTATION BLUES (49)	RCA Victor 0494	$20
45rpm	ROTATION BLUES (49)	RCA Victor 0494	$25
45rpm	THE TALE A SAILOR TOLD (49)	RCA Victor 4324	$18
	(With the Beaver Valley Sweethearts and the Skytoppers)		
45rpm	GOD'S LITTLE CANDLES (52)	RCA Victor 4786	$12
	(With the Jordanaires)		
45rpm	CANNONBALL YODEL (53)	RCA Victor 5251	$15
45(P)	CANNONBALL YODEL (53)	RCA Victor 5251	$10
	(White promo label)		
45rpm	JUST FOR YOU (53)	RCA Victor 5322	$12
	(With the Beaver Valley Sweethearts)		
45(P)	JUST FOR YOU (53)	RCA Victor 5322	$10
	(White promo label)		
45rpm	I FEEL THE BLUES COMIN' ON (54)	RCA Victor 5402	$12
45(P)	I FEEL THE BLUES COMIN' ON (54)	RCA Victor 5402	$10
	(White promo label)		
45rpm	THAT'S HOW THE YODEL WAS BORN (54)	RCA Victor 5509	$12
45(P)	THAT'S HOW THE YODEL WAS BORN (54)	RCA Victor 5509	$10
	(White promo label)		
45rpm	ONE WAY TICKET (54)	RCA Victor 5795	$12
45(P)	ONE WAY TICKET (54)	RCA Victor 5795	$10
	(White promo label)		
45rpm	THE SINGING HILLS (55)	RCA Victor 5868	$12
45(P)	THE SINGING HILLS (55)	RCA Victor 5868	$10
	(White promo label)		

-EPs-

EP	GREAT COUNTRY SONGS (55)	RCA Victor 425	$20
EP	DUETS (55)	RCA Victor 505	$20
	(With Rosalie Allen)		
EP	ELTON BRITT YODEL SONGS (55)	RCA Victor 817	$15
2EP	ELTON BRITT YODEL SONGS (55)	RCA Victor 1288	$25

-albums-

10"LP	ELTON BRITT YODEL SONGS (54)	RCA Victor 3222	$75
LP	ELTON BRITT YODEL SONGS (56)	RCA Victor 1288	$50
LP	ROSALIE ALLEN & ELTON BRITT (57)	Waldorf 1206	$40
	(With Rosalie Allen)		
LP	THE WANDERING COWBOY (59) Mono	ABC Paramount 293	$25
LP	THE WANDERING COWBOY (59) Stereo	ABC Paramount 293	$40
LP(P)	THE WANDERING COWBOY (59)	ABC Paramount 293	$30
	(White promo label)		
LP	BEYOND THE SUNSET (60) Mono	ABC Paramount 322	$25
LP	BEYOND THE SUNSET (60) Stereo	ABC Paramount 322	$30
LP(P)	BEYOND THE SUNSET (60)	ABC Paramount 322	$30
	(White promo label)		
LP	I HEARD A FOREST PRAYING (60) Mono	ABC Paramount 331	$25

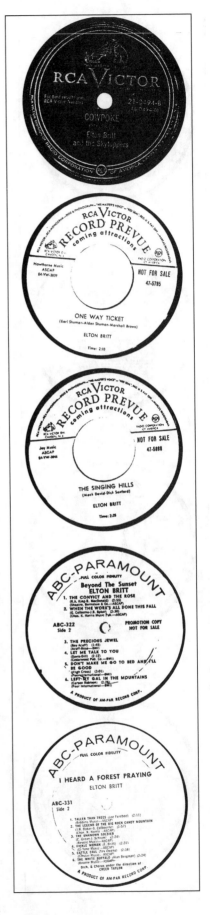

LP	**I HEARD A FOREST PRAYING** (60) Stereo	ABC Paramount 331	$30
LP(P)	**I HEARD A FOREST PRAYING** (60)	ABC Paramount 331	$30
	(White promo label)		
LP	**THOSE FABULOUS BEVERLY HILLBILLIES** (61) Gold vinyl	Rar-Arts 1000	$50
	(Features Britt and Zeke Manners)		
LP	**THE BEST OF ELTON BRITT** (63)	RCA Victor 2669	$25
LP	**THE SINGING HILLS** (65)	ABC Paramount 521	$15
LP(P)	**THE SINGING HILLS** (65)	ABC Paramount 521	$25
	(White promo label)		
LP	**SOMETHIN' FOR EVERYONE** (66)	ABC Paramount 566	$15
LP(P)	**SOMETHIN' FOR EVERYONE** (66)	ABC Paramount 566	$25
	(White promo label)		
LP	**STARRING ELTON BRITT & ROSALIE ALLEN** (66)	Grand Award 262	$20
	(Budget label, with Rosalie Allen)		
LP	**WHEN EVENING SHADOWS FALL** (68)	RCA Victor 4073	$18
LP	**ELTON BRITT SINGS** (69)	Spin-O-Rama 169	$15
	(Budget label, with Bill Emerson)		
LP	**THE JIMMIE RODGERS BLUES** (69)	Camden 2295	$15
LP	**16 GREAT COUNTRY PERFORMANCES** (71)	ABC 744	$12
LP(P)	**16 GREAT COUNTRY PERFORMANCES** (71)	ABC 744	$15
	(White promo label)		

GARTH BROOKS (C)
Capitol 45s $2-5 each
Liberty 45s $2-4 each

-singles-

45(P)	**IF TOMORROW NEVER COMES** (89)	Capitol 44430	$10
	(White promo label)		
45(P)	**LEARNING TO LIVE AGAIN** (92) Red vinyl	Liberty 56973	$10
	(For Jukeboxes only)		
45(P)	**CALLING BATON ROUGE** (94) Colored vinyl	Liberty	$10
	(For jukeboxes only)		

-albums-

CD(P)	**GOTTA DRIVE** (93) With Steve Wariner	Arista 2638	$20
	(Garth and Steve discuss Steve's new LP)		
CD(P)	**INTERVIEW FOR IN PIECES ALBUM** (93)	Liberty DPRO-79004	$25
	(Promo-only thirty-minute interview for album)		

-radio shows-

CD(RS)	**ENTERTAINER OF THE YEAR** (May 92)	Unistar	$25-40
	(Music and interview profile)		

BROTHER PHELPS (C)

-radio shows-

CD(RS)	**COUNTRY CUTTING EDGE** (Nov 93)	Westwood One	$15-20
	(Music and interviews)		

COUSIN CECIL BROWER (CW)

-albums-

LP	**AMERICA'S FAVORITE SQUARE DANCES** (62)	Smash 67014	$18
	(With calls)		
LP	**AMERICA'S FAVORITE SQUARE DANCES** (62)	Smash 67015	$18
	(Without calls)		

BOBBY BROWN (RB)

-singles-

45rpm	**DOWN AT MARY'S HOUSE** (58)	Vaden 100	$75
45rpm	**PLEASE PLEASE BABY** (58)	Vaden 109	$60

CHARLIE BROWN (RB)

-singles-

45rpm	**MEAN MEAN MAMA** (58)	Rose 101	$40
45rpm	**HAVE YOU HEARD THE GOSSIP** (58)	Rose 102	$40

HYLO BROWN (CW)
Other Capitol 45s $5-10 each

-singles-

45rpm	**LOST TO A STRANGER** (55)	Capitol 3124	$10
45rpm	**THE PRISONER'S SONG** (57)	Capitol 3554	$10

-albums-

LP	**HYLO BROWN** (59)	Capitol 1168	$75
LP(P)	**HYLO BROWN** (59)	Capitol 1168	$85
	(Capitol promo label)		
LP	**BLUEGRASS BALLADEER** (62)	Starday 185	$25
LP	**BLUEGRASS GOES TO COLLEGE** (62)	Starday 204	$25
LP	**HYLO BROWN MEETS THE LONESOME PINE FIDDLERS** (63)	Starday 220	$30
	(With the Lonesome Pine Fiddlers)		

LP	**HYLO BROWN WITH THE LONESOME PINE FIDDLERS** (63)	Starday 222	$30
	(With the Lonesome Pine Fiddlers)		
LP	**SING ME A BLUEGRASS SONG** (63)	Starday 249	$18
LP	**BLUEGRASS GOES TO COLLEGE** (65)	Nashville 2025	$18
	(Budget label)		
LP	**HYLO BROWN SINGS BLUEGRASS** (66)	Diplomat 2604	$12
	(Budget label)		

JAMES BROWN (CW)
And the Trail Winers
Star of TV's *Rin Tin Tin* show

-singles-

78rpm	**THE BALLAD OF DAVY CROCKETT** (55)	MGM 11941	$40
78(P)	**THE BALLAD OF DAVY CROCKETT** (55)	MGM 11941	$30
	(Yellow promo label)		
45rpm	**THE BALLAD OF DAVY CROCKETT** (55)	MGM 11941	$30
45(P)	**THE BALLAD OF DAVY CROCKETT** (55)	MGM 11941	$25
	(Yellow promo label)		
45rpm	**THE WHITE BUFFALO** (55)	MGM 12080	$15
	(From the TV show *Rin Tin Tin*)		
45(P)	**THE WHITE BUFFALO** (55)	MGM 12080	$20
	(Yellow promo label)		

MILTON BROWN (CW)
Decca 45s $5-8 each

-EPs-

EP	**DANCE-O-RAMA** (55)	Decca 2221	$15
EP	**DANCE-O-RAMA** (55)	Decca 2222	$10

-albums-

10"LP	**DANCE-O-RAMA** (55)	Decca 1001	$30
LP	**DANCE-O-RAMA** (55) Black label	Decca 5561	$25
LP(P)	**DANCE-O-RAMA** (55) Pink promo label	Decca 5561	$20

T. GRAHAM BROWN (C)
Capitol 45s $1 each

-radio shows-

3LP(RS)	**AMERICAN EAGLE** (Aug 86)	Westwood One	$40-60
	(Rare live concert)		
LP(RS)	**LIVE AT GILLEY'S** (Aug 88)	Westwood One	$10-15
	(Live concert)		
LP(RS)	**LIVE AT GILLEY'S** (90)	Westwood One	$10-12
	(Live concert)		
LP(RS)	**BEST OF WESTWOOD ONE** (90) With Desert Rose Band and	Westwood One	$40-75
	the Judds		
	(Live concert)		
3LP(RS)	**THE SILVER EAGLE** (June 90)	Westwood One	$10-15
	(Live concert)		
LP(RS)	**WESTWOOD ONE PRESENTS** (93)	Westwood One	$25-40
	(Rare live concert)		

WALTER BROWN (RB)

-singles-

45rpm	**ALLEY CAT** (58)	Zip 4686	$45

JACKSON BROWNE (R)
Asylum 45s $3 each
Asylum twelve-inch singles $8-12 each
Other Asylum LPs $4-8 each
Other Asylum promo LPs $12 each

-singles-

12"(P)	**STAY/THE LOAD-OUT/STAY** (77) White promo label 45rpm	Asylum 11389	$15
	(Classic 8:51 version)		
12"(P)	**BEFORE THE DELUGE** (79) 33rpm	Asylum 11442	$300
	(Must be the 33rpm version)		
12"(P)	**BEFORE THE DELUGE** (79) 45rpm	Asylum 11442	$75
	(Must be the 45rpm version)		

-albums-

LP	**FOR EVERYMAN** (73)	Asylum 5067	$15
LP(P)	**FOR EVERYMAN** (73)	Asylum 5067	$25
	(White promo label)		
2CD(P)	**RETROSPECTIVE** (93)		$75
	(Promo-only greatest hits CD)		

-radio shows-

3LP(RS)	**SUPERSTAR CONCERT** (Oct 86) Box set	Westwood One	$30-50
	(Live concert)		
3LP(RS)	**SUPERSTAR CONCERT** (Sept 90) Box set	Westwood One	$30-40
	(Live concert with Eddie Money)		

NOTES

2LP(RS)	**POP CONCERT** (Apr 87)	Westwood One	$100-200
	(Rare live concert)		
2LP(RS)	**OFF THE RECORD** (Oct 89)	Westwood One	$15-20
	(Music and interviews)		

BILL BROWNING (RB)

-singles-

45rpm	**DON'T PUSH, DON'T SHOVE**	Starday 432	$50
45rpm	**BORNED WITH THE BLUES**	Island 7	$60
45rpm	**SINFUL WOMAN**	Island 11	$60

THE BROWNS (C)

Recorded as the Abbott Singers
Includes listings of Jim Brown and Maxine Brown
RCA Victor 45s before 7555 $5-8 each
RCA Victor 45s after 7555 $2-5 each
RCA Victor 45s by Jim Edward Brown $2-3 each
Chart 45s by Maxine Brown $5 each
Other RCA Victor LPs by the Browns $4-8 each
Other RCA Victor LPs by Jim Edward Brown $4-8 each
RCA Victor LPs by Jim Edward Brown and Helen Cornelius $3-6 each

-singles-

45rpm	**LOOKING BACK TO SEE** (54)	Fabor 107	$20
	(Jim Edward Brown and Maxine Brown)		
45(P)	**LOOKING BACK TO SEE** (54)	Fabor 107	$25
	(Black promo label)		
45rpm	**DRAGGIN' MAIN STREET** (54)	Fabor 118	$30
	(Jim Edward and Maxine Brown)		
45(P)	**DRAGGIN' MAIN STREET** (54)	Fabor 118	$40
	(Black promo label)		
45rpm	**HERE TODAY AND GONE TOMORROW** (55)	Fabor 126	$18
	(Jim Edward, Maxine, and Bonnie)		
45(P)	**HERE TODAY AND GONE TOMORROW** (55)	Fabor 126	$20
	(Black promo label)		
45rpm	**THE GRASS IS GREENER** (55)	Fabor 129	$18
	(The Abbott Singers)		
45(P)	**THE GRASS IS GREENER** (55) Abbott Singers	Fabor 129	$25
	(Black promo label)		
45rpm	**THE THREE BELLS** (59)	RCA Victor 7555	$10
45(S)	**SCARLET RIBBONS** (59) Stereo single	RCA Victor 7614	$18
45rpm	**THE OLD LAMPLIGHTER** (60)	RCA Victor 7700	$15
	(Price includes picture sleeve)		
45rpm	**MARGO** (60)	RCA Victor 7755	$15
	(Price includes picture sleeve)		

-EPs-

EP	**JIM EDWARD, MAXINE & BONNIE BROWN** (57)	RCA Victor 1438	$30
EP	**THE BROWNS SING THE 3 BELLS** (59)	RCA Victor 4347	$40
EP	**SCARLET RIBBONS** (59)	RCA Victor 4352	$25
EP	**THE OLD LAMPLIGHTER** (60)	RCA Victor 4364	$25
EP	**THE BROWNS** (68)	RCA Victor 5089	$30
	(Gold standard series, mostly Fabor material)		

-albums-

LP	**JIM EDWARD, MAXINE & BONNIE BROWN** (57)	RCA Victor 1438	$50
LP	**SWEET SOUNDS BY THE BROWNS** (59) Stereo	RCA Victor 2144	$25
LP	**TOWN & COUNTRY** (60) Stereo	RCA Victor 2174	$25
LP	**THE BROWNS SING THEIR HITS** (60) Stereo	RCA Victor 2260	$25
LP	**OUR FAVORITE FOLK SONGS** (61)	RCA Victor 2333	$25
LP	**SONGS FROM THE LITTLE BROWN CHURCH HYMNAL** (61)	RCA Victor 2345	$18
LP	**GRAND OL' OPRY FAVORITES** (64)	RCA Victor 2784	$18
LP	**THIS YOUNG LAND** (64)	RCA Victor 2860	$18
LP	**THREE SHADES OF BROWN** (65)	RCA Victor 2987	$18
LP	**WHEN LOVE IS GONE** (65)	RCA Victor 3423	$18
LP	**I HEARD THE BLUEBIRDS SING** (65)	Camden 885	$15
LP(P)	**COUNTRY & WESTERN** PSA radio ads for Marines	U.S. Marines	$25
	(Twenty artists including one spot featuring Jim Edward Brown)		
LP	**BEST OF THE BROWNS** (66)	RCA Victor 3561	$15
LP	**ALONE WITH YOU** (66) Jim Edward Brown	RCA Victor 3569	$12
	(First solo album)		
LP	**OUR KIND OF COUNTRY** (66)	RCA Victor 3668	$15
LP	**THE OLD COUNTRY CHURCH** (67)	RCA Victor 3798	$15
LP	**BROWNS SING THE BIG ONES FROM THE COUNTRY** (67)	RCA Victor 2142	$15
LP	**A HARVEST OF COUNTRY SONGS** (68)	Camden 2262	$15
LP	**SUGAR CANE COUNTY** (69) Maxine Brown	Chart 1012	$12

BROWN'S FERRY FOUR (CW)
Grandpa Jones, Delmore Brothers, Merle Travis

-EPs-

EP	SACRED SONGS (57) Vol 1	King 237	$45
EP	SCARED SONGS (57) Vol 2	King 238	$40
EP	SACRED SONGS (57) Vol 3	King 239	$35

-albums-

LP	SACRED SONGS (57)	King 551	$35
LP	SACRED SONGS (58)	King 590	$30
LP	WONDERFUL SACRED SONGS (64)	King 943	$25
LP	16 GREATEST HITS (68)	Starday 3017	$12
	See Delmore Brothers		
	See Grandpa Jones		
	See Merle Travis		

EDWIN BRUCE (RB)
RCA Victor, Monument 45s $4 each
United Artists 45s $2 each
Epic 45s $2 each
MCA 45s $1 each
Epic and United Artists LPs $5 each
MCA LPs $4 each

-singles-

45rpm	ROCK BOPPIN' BABY (58)	Sun 276	$12
45rpm	SWEET WOMAN (58)	Sun 292	$10

-albums-

LP	IF I COULD JUST GO HOME (68)	RCA Victor 3948	$25
LP	SHADES OF ED BRUCE (69)	Monument 18118	$20

-radio shows-

LP(P)	COUNTRY MUSIC TIME (80s)	U.S. Air Force	$10-12
	(Music and interviews)		
3LP(RS)	THE SILVER EAGLE (Mar 84)	DIR	$15-25
	(Live concert)		

VIN BRUCE (CW)

-singles-

45rpm	MY MAMA SAID (53)	Columbia 21120	$10

AL BRUMLEY (C)

-albums-

LP(P)	THE AL BRUMLEY SHOWCASE (60)	Sesac 1701/1702	$25
	(Promo-only release)		
LP	AL BRUMLEY SINGS AL BRUMLEY (65)	American Artists 1020	$10

WES BRYAN (R)

-singles-

45rpm	TINY SPACEMAN (58)	United Artists 102	$50
	(Price includes picture sleeve)		
45(P)	TINY SPACEMAN (58)	United Artists 102	$20
	(White promo label)		
45rpm	WAIT FOR ME BABY (58)	United Artists 122	$15
45(P)	WAIT FOR ME BABY (58)	United Artists 122	$12
	(White promo label)		

FELICE & BOUDLEAUX BRYANT
Writers

-singles-

45rpm	WAKE UP LITTLE SUSIE (66)	Monument 857	$10
45(P)	WAKE UP LITTLE SUSIE (66)	Monument 857	$12
	(Promo label with a star)		

-albums-

LP	BOUDLEAUX BRYANT'S BEST SELLERS (63)	Monument 18007	$20
LP(P)	COUNTRY STANDARDS FROM HOUSE OF BRYANT Vol 1	Bryant 1001	$35
	(Yellow cover, original songs written by Felice and Boudleaux Bryant)		
LP(P)	COUNTRY STANDARDS FROM HOUSE OF BRYANT Vol 2	Bryant 1002	$35
	(Blue cover, both LPs for radio airplay only)		
LP(P)	A TOUCH OF BRYANT (80) Promo only	CMH 6243	$25
	(Nashville session artist versions of songs written by Felice and Boudleaux)		

JIMMY BRYANT (CW)
Other Capitol 45s $5-8 each

-singles-

45rpm	STRATOSPHERE BOOGIE (54) With Speedy West	Capitol 2964	$18
45(P)	STRATOSPHERE BOOGIE (54) With Speedy West	Capitol 2964	$12
	(White promo label)		

45rpm	**CAFFEINE PATROL** (56) With Speedy West	Capitol 3208	$15
45(P)	**CAFFEINE PATROL** (56) With Speedy West	Capitol 3208	$10
	(White promo label)		

-EPs-

EP	**TWO GUITARS COUNTRY STYLE** (54)	Capitol 1-520	$20
EP	**TWO GUITARS COUNTRY STYLE** (54)	Capitol 2-520	$15
EP	**COUNTRY CABINJAZZ** (60)	Capitol 1314	$20

-albums-

10"LP	**TWO GUITARS COUNTRY STYLE** (54)	Capitol 520	$65
LP	**TWO GUITARS COUNTRY STYLE** (54)	Capitol 520	$55
	(Jimmy Bryant and Speedy West)		
LP	**COUNTRY CABIN JAZZ** (60) Mono	Capitol 1314	$25
LP	**COUNTRY CABIN JAZZ** (60) Stereo	Capitol 1314	$35
LP(P)	**COUNTRY CABIN JAZZ** (60)	Capitol 1314	$30
	(Capitol promo label)		
LP	**BRYANT'S BACK IN TOWN** (66)	Imperial 12310	$10
LP(P)	**BRYANT'S BACK IN TOWN** (66)	Imperial 12310	$12
	(White promo label)		
LP	**LAUGHING GUITAR, CRYING GUITAR** (66)	Imperial 12315	$18
LP(P)	**LAUGHING GUITAR, CRYING GUITAR** (66)	Imperial 12315	$20
	(White promo label)		
LP	**WE ARE YOUNG** (66)	Imperial 12338	$18
LP	**WE ARE YOUNG** (66)	Imperial 12338	$20
	(White promo label)		
LP	**PLAY COUNTRY GUITAR** (67)	Dolton 17505	$30
	(Price includes booklet)		
LP	**THE FASTEST GUITAR IN THE COUNTRY** (67)	Imperial 12360	$18
LP(P)	**THE FASTEST GUITAR IN THE COUNTRY** (67)	Imperial 12360	$20

BUCCANEERS (RB)

-singles-

45rpm	**BYE BYE BABY** (58)	Cupid 5006	$60

CORINNE BUCEY (CW)
Decca 45s $2 each

-albums-

LP	**NEW VOICE IN TOWN** (64)	Decca 4550	$15
LP(P)	**NEW VOICE IN TOWN** (64)	Decca 4550	$12
	(Decca promo label)		

WES BUCHANAN (R)

-singles-

45rpm	**GIVE SOME LOVE MY WAY** (58)	Prep 114	$50
45(P)	**GIVE SOME LOVE MY WAY** (58)	Prep 114	$40
	(Yellow promo label)		

GARY BUCK (CW)
Tower 45s $2 each

-albums-

LP	**GARY BUCK'S COUNTRY SCENE** (67)	Tower 5054	$10

RAY BUDZILEK (Polka)
And the Boys in the Band
Capitol 45s $5 each

JIMMY BUFFET (R)
ABC 45s $2 each
MCA colored vinyl 45s $6 each
MCA 45s $2 each

-radio shows-

LP(RS)	**ROBERT W. MORGAN** (78)	Watermark	$30-50
	(Music and interviews)		
2LP(RS)	**STARFLEET** (July 80)		$200-300
	(Rare live concert)		
2LP(RS)	**IN CONCERT** (July 81)	Westwood One	$100-200
	(Live concert)		
2LP(RS)	**POP CONCERT** (Nov 86)	Westwood One	$175-250
	(Live concert)		

NORMAN BULLOCK (RB)

-singles-

45rpm	**LIES LIES LIES** (58)	M & J 2	$25

RAY BURDEN (R)

-singles-

45rpm	**THAT KIND OF CARRYING ON** (58)	Cullman 6403	$55

SONNY BURGESS (RB)

-singles-

45rpm	MARY LOU (57)	Razorback 120	$12
45rpm	SADIE'S BACK IN TOWN (58)	Philips 3551	$15
45(P)	SADIE'S BACK IN TOWN (58)	Philips 3551	$18
	(Philips promo label)		
45rpm	RED HEADED WOMAN (58)	Sun 247	$25
45rpm	AIN'T GOT A THING (58)	Sun 263	$10
45rpm	MY BUCKET'S GOT A HOLE IN IT (58)	Sun 285	$10

WILMA BURGESS (CW)

Decca 45s $2-4 each
Coral 45s $2 each

-albums-

LP	DON'T TOUCH ME (66)	Decca 4788	$12
LP(P)	DON'T TOUCH ME (66)	Decca 4788	$10
	(White promo label)		
LP	WILMA BURGESS SINGS MISTY BLUE (67)	Decca 4852	$12
LP(P)	WILMA BURGESS SINGS MISTY BLUE (67)	Decca 4852	$10
	(White promo label)		
LP	TEAR TIME (67)	Decca 4935	$12
LP(P)	TEAR TIME (67)	Decca 4935	$10
	(White promo label)		
LP	THE TENDER LOVIN' COUNTRY SOUND (68)	Decca 5024	$12
LP(P)	THE TENDER LOVIN' COUNTRY SOUND (68)	Decca 5024	$10
	(White promo label)		
LP	PARTING IS SUCH SWEET SORROW (69)	Decca 5090	$12
LP(P)	PARTING IS SUCH SWEET SORROW (69)	Decca 5090	$10
	(White promo label)		

JIM BURGETT (RB)

-singles-

45rpm	PICK-UP-A-COUPLA RECORDS (58)	Go 6565	$40

BUDDY BURKE (RB)

-singles-

45rpm	THAT BIG OLD MOON (58)	Bullseye 1002	$40

FRENCHIE BURKE (CW)

-albums-

LP	FIDDLIN' FRENCHIE BURKE (75)	20th Century Fox	$15

BUZZ BURNAM (RB)

-singles-

45rpm	MAMA LOU (57)	Viv 498	$60
45rpm	MAMA LOU (58)	Viv 4000	$60

DORSEY BURNETTE (RB)

Of the Johnny Burnette Trio

-singles-

45rpm	LET'S FALL IN LOVE (57)	Abbott 188	$20
45rpm	BERTHA LOU (58)	Cee-Jam 16	$15
45rpm	GREAT SHAKIN' FEVER (59)	Era 3045	$10
45(P)	GREAT SHAKIN' FEVER (59)	Era 3045	$12
	(White promo label)		
45rpm	WAY IN THE MIDDLE OF THE NIGHT (58)	Imperial 5668	$18
45(P)	WAY IN THE MIDDLE OF THE NIGHT (58)	Imperial 5668	$15
	(White promo label)		
45rpm	CIRCLE ROCK (60)	Imperial 5987	$18
45(P)	CIRCLE ROCK (60)	Imperial 5987	$15
	(White promo label)		
45(P)	BE A NAVY MAN (60s) Song to promote the U.S. Navy	Navy Recruiting	$75
	(Promo includes picture sleeve)		

-albums-

LP	DORSEY BURNETTE SINGS (63)	Dot 25456	$25
LP	TALL OAK TREE (60)	Era 102	$40
LP	DORSEY BURNETTE'S GREATEST HITS (69)	Era 800	$50
LP(P)	DORSEY BURNETTE'S GREATEST HITS (69)	Era 800	$60
	(Era promo label)		

-radio shows-

LP(RS)	HERE'S TO VETERANS (70s) Fifteen-minute PSA show	Veterans Administration	$100-200
	(Music and interviews)		
	See Johnny Burnette		
	See the Burnette Brothers		

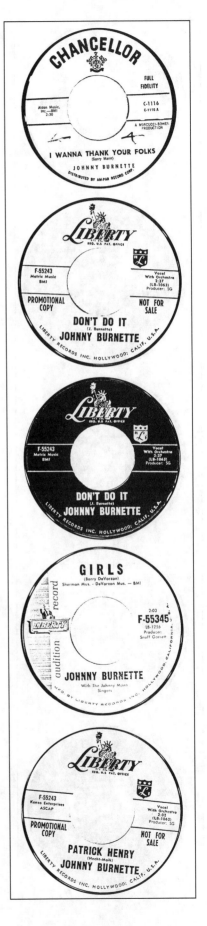

JOHNNY BURNETTE (RB)

Of the Johnny Burnette Trio
Other Liberty 45s $4-8 each
Other Liberty promo 45s $20 each
Chancellor 45s $6-8 each
Chancellor promo 45s $18 each

-singles-

45rpm	**YOU'RE UNDECIDED**		Von 1006	$150
	("Go Mule Go" on the flip)			
45rpm	**KISS ME** (57) Blue label		Freedom 44001	$15
45(P)	**KISS ME** (57)		Freedom 44001	$12
	(White promo label)			
45rpm	**GUMBO** (58) Blue label		Freedom 44011	$12
45(P)	**GUMBO** (58)		Freedom 44011	$10
	(White promo label)			
45rpm	**SWEET BABY DOLL** (58) Blue label		Freedom 44017	$45
45rpm	**SWEET BABY DOLL** (58)		Freedom 44017	$40
	(White promo label)			
45rpm	**BIGGER MAN** (64)		Magic Lamp 515	$100
	(Price includes picture sleeve)			
45rpm	**YOU'RE SIXTEEN** (60)		Liberty 55285	$40
	(Price includes picture sleeve)			
45(P)	**YOU'RE SIXTEEN** (69)		Liberty 55285	$25
	(White promo label)			

-EPs-

EP	**JOHNNY BURNETTE'S HITS** (61)		Liberty 1011	$50

-albums-

LP	**DREAMIN'** (60) Mono		Liberty 3179	$30
LP	**DREAMIN'** (60) Stereo		Liberty 7179	$40
LP(P)	**DREAMIN'** (60)		Liberty 3179	$75
	(White promo label)			
LP	**JOHNNY BURNETTE** (61) Mono		Liberty 3183	$25
LP	**JOHNNY BURNETTE** (61) Stereo		Liberty 7183	$35
LP(P)	**JOHNNY BURNETTE** (61)		Liberty 3183	$60
	(White promo label)			
LP	**JOHNNY BURNETTE SINGS** (61) Mono		Liberty 3190	$25
LP	**JOHNNY BURNETTE SINGS** (61) Stereo		Liberty 7190	$35
LP(P)	**JOHNNY BURNETTE SINGS** (61)		Liberty 3190	$60
	(White promo label)			
LP	**HITS AND OTHER FAVORITES** (62) Mono		Liberty 3206	$25
LP	**HITS AND OTHER FAVORITES** (62) Stereo		Liberty 7206	$35
LP(P)	**HITS AND OTHER FAVORITES** (62)		Liberty 3206	$60
	(White promo label)			
LP	**ROSES ARE RED** (63) Stereo		Liberty 7255	$30
LP(P)	**ROSES ARE RED** (63)		Liberty 7255	$40
	(White promo label)			
LP	**THE JOHNNY BURNETTE STORY** (64) Stereo		Liberty 7389	$30
LP(P)	**THE JOHNNY BURNETTE STORY** (64)		Liberty 7389	$40
	(White promo label)			

LINDA BURNETTE (RB)

-singles-

45rpm	**RATTLE BONES ROCK** (58)		Perry 5	$60

SMILEY BURNETTE (N)

Other Capitol 45s $4-8 each

-singles-

45rpm	**BLUE BOTTLE FLY** (50)		Capitol 30129	$25
	(Price includes picture sleeve)			

-albums-

LP	**OLE FROG** (62)		Starday 191	$20

-radio shows-

16"(RS)	**RADIOZARK** (50s)		Radiozark	$25-50
	(Music and interviews)			

BURNETTE BROTHERS (RB)

Johnny and Dorsey Burnette

-singles-

45rpm	**MY HONEY** (58)		Imperial 5509	$60
45(P)	**MY HONEY** (58)		Imperial 5509	$50
	(Cream-colored promo label)			
45rpm	**GREEN GRASS OF TEXAS**		Infinity 001	$12
	(By The Texans)			
45rpm	**GREEN GRASS OF TEXAS**		Starcrest 6004	$10
	(By The Jim Dandees)			

45rpm	**BLUES STAY AWAY FROM ME**	Coral 62190	$25
45(P)	**BLUES STAY AWAY FROM ME**	Coral 62190	$20
	(Blue promo label)		
	See Dorsey Burnette		
	See Johnny Burnette		

JOHNNY BURNETTE TRIO (RB)
Johnny and Dorsey Burnette with Paul Burlison

-singles-

45rpm	**TEAR IT UP** (57)	Coral 61651	$250
45(P)	**TEAR IT UP** (57)	Coral 61651	$150
	(Blue promo label)		
45rpm	**MIDNIGHT TRAIN** (57)	Coral 61675	$250
45(P)	**MIDNIGHT TRAIN** (57)	Coral 61675	$150
	(Blue promo label)		
45rpm	**HONEY HUSH** (57)	Coral 61719	$250
45(P)	**HONEY HUSH** (57)	Coral 61719	$150
	(Blue promo label)		
45rpm	**LONESOME TRAIN** (57)	Coral 61758	$250
45(P)	**LONESOME TRAIN** (57)	Coral 61758	$150
	(Blue promo label)		
45rpm	**EAGER BEAVER BABY** (57)	Coral-61829	$250
45(P)	**EAGER BEAVER BABY** (57)	Coral 61829	$150
	(Blue promo label)		
45rpm	**DRINKING WINE SPO-DEE-O-DEE** (57)	Coral 61869	$250
45(P)	**DRINKING WINE SPO-DEE-O-DEE** (57)	Coral 61869	$150
	(Blue promo label)		
45rpm	**ROCKBILLY BOOGIE** (57)	Coral 61918	$250
45(P)	**ROCKBILLY BOOGIE** (57)	Coral 61918	$150
	(Blue promo label)		

-albums-

LP	**JOHNNY BURNETTE & THE ROCK 'N' ROLL TRIO** (57)	Coral 57080	$2,000
	(Unknown as promo)		

SONNY BURNS (RB)

-singles-

45rpm	**TOO HOT TO HANDLE** (53)	Starday 118	$30
45rpm	**WRONG ABOUT YOU** (53) with George Jones	Starday 146	$20
45rpm	**ANOTHER WOMAN LOOKING FOR A MAN** (54)	Starday 152	$10
45rpm	**TELL HER** (55)	Starday 165	$15
	(Flip side, "Heartbroken Me," features George Jones)		
45rpm	**A REAL COOL CAT**	Starday 209	$40

HAROLD BURRAGE (RB)

-singles-

45rpm	**MESSED UP** (56)	Cobra 5012	$18
45rpm	**SHE KNOCKS ME OUT** (56)	Cobra 5022	$15
45rpm	**BETTY JEAN** (57)	Cobra 5026	$12

NEAL BURRIS (CW)

-singles-

45rpm	**I BET MY HEART** (53)	Columbia 21081	$10

THE (FLYING) BURRITO BROTHERS (C)
Includes Gram Parsons, Chris Hillman, Rick Roberts, Bernie Leadon, and Chris Ethridge
Members went on to be in pop groups McQuinn and Clark, Firefall, The Eagles
A&M 45s $5 each
Curb 45s $2 each

-albums-

2LP	**CLOSE UP THE HONKY TONKS** (80)	A&M 6510	$12
2LP(P)	**CLOSE UP THE HONKY TONKS** (80)	A&M 6510	$15
	(White promo label)		

-radio shows-

LP(RS)	**WESTWOOD ONE PRESENTS** (Jan 83)	Westwood One	$100-175
	(Rare live concert)		
2CD(LP)	**UP CLOSE** (94) Profile of the group	Media America	$25-40
	(Music and interviews)		

BOB BURTON (RB)

-singles-

45rpm	**BOOGIE WOOGIE BABY OF MINE** (58)	Mar-Vel 951	$15
45rpm	**TIRED OF ROCKING** (58)	Mar-Vel 953	$50

GARY BURTON (CW)

-albums-

LP	**TENNESSEE FIREBIRD** (66)	RCA Victor 3719	$15

JAMES BURTON (R)

-albums-

LP	**CORN PICKIN' & SLICK SLIDIN'** (68)	Capitol 2822	$75
LP(P)	**CORN PICKIN' & SLICK SLIDIN'** (68) Yellow promo	Capitol 2822	$100
LP	**JAMES BURTON** (71)	A&M 4293	$50
LP(P)	**JAMES BURTON** (71) White promo label	A&M 4293	$40

(Best known as guitarist for Elvis Presley, Ricky Nelson, Waylon Jennings, and others)

WAYNE BUSBY (RB)

-singles-

45rpm	**GOIN' BACK TO DIXIE** (57)	Ott 201	$50
45rpm	**GOIN' BACK TO DIXIE** (58)	Empire 506	$50

DICK BUSH (RB)

-singles-

45rpm	**HOLLYWOOD PARTY** (58)	Era 1067	$45
45(P)	**HOLLYWOOD PARTY** (58)	Era 1067	$35

(White promo label)

JOHNNY BUSH (CW)

Stop and Million 45s $3 each
Starday and RCA Victor 45s $2 each

-albums-

LP	**THE SOUND OF A HEARTACHE** (68)	Stop 10002	$25
LP	**UNDO THE RIGHT** (68)	Stop 10005	$20
LP	**YOU GAVE ME A MOUNTAIN** (69)	Stop 10008	$20
LP	**JOHNNY BUSH** (70)	Stop 10014	$20
LP	**THE BEST OF JOHNNY BUSH** (72)	Million 1001	$25
LP	**BUSH COUNTRY** (72)	Stop 1028	$15
LP	**HERE'S JOHNNY BUSH** (72)	Starday 475	$15
LP	**WHISKEY RIVER** (73)	RCA Victor 4817	$15
LP	**HERE COMES THE WORLD AGAIN** (73)	RCA Victor 0216	$12
LP	**TEXAS DANCE HALL GIRL** (73)	RCA Victor 0369	$12

BOB BUSSO (RB)

-singles-

45rpm	**BOO HOO** (58)	Vargo 1000	$25

DWIGHT BUTCHER (C)

-singles-

45rpm	**JIMMIE RODGERS IN RETROSPECT** (60)	Certified 531	$15

SAM BUTERA (RB)

-singles-

45rpm	**BIM BAM** (58) Blue label	Capitol 4014	$25
45(P)	**BIM BAM** (58) Yellow promo label	Capitol 4014	$20
45rpm	**CHANTILLY LACE** (60) Capitol promo label	Capitol 4683	$10
45rpm	**TEN LITTLE WOMEN** (60) Yellow label	Prep 105	$12
45(P)	**TEN LITTLE WOMEN** (60) White promo label	Prep 105	$15
45rpm	**DON'T KNOCK IT** (61)	Dot 16012	$10

CARL BUTLER & PEARL (CW)

Columbia 45s $3-6 each
CMH LPs $5 each

-albums-

LP	**DON'T LET ME CROSS OVER** (63) Carl Butler	Columbia 8802	$20
LP(P)	**DON'T LET ME CROSS OVER** (63)	Columbia 8802	$25
	(White promo label)		
LP	**LOVIN' ARMS** (64) Carl Butler & Pearl	Columbia 8925	$20
LP(P)	**LOVIN' ARMS** (64)	Columbia 8925	$25
	(White promo label)		
LP	**THE OLD AND THE NEW** (65) Carl Butler & Pearl	Columbia 9108	$15
LP(P)	**THE OLD AND THE NEW** (65)	Columbia 9108	$18
	(White promo label)		
LP	**THE GREAT CARL BUTLER SINGS** (66)	Harmony 11185	$12
LP(P)	**THE GREAT CARL BUTLER SINGS** (66)	Harmony 11185	$15
	(White promo label)		
LP	**AVENUE OF PRAYER** (67) Carl Butler & Pearl	Columbia 9440	$15
LP(P)	**AVENUE OF PRAYER** (67)	Columbia 9440	$18
	(White promo label)		
LP	**OUR COUNTRY WORLD** (68) Carl Butler & Pearl	Columbia 9651	$15
LP(P)	**OUR COUNTRY WORLD** (68)	Columbia 9651	$18
	(White promo label)		
LP	**HONKY TONKIN'** (69) Carl Butler & Pearl	Columbia 9769	$15
LP	**HONKY TONKIN'** (69)	Columbia 9769	$12
	(White promo label)		

LP	**CARL & PEARL BUTLER'S GREATEST HITS** (70)	Columbia 1039	$10
LP	**CARL & PEARL BUTLER'S GREATEST HITS** (70)	Columbia 1039	$12
	(White promo label)		
LP	**FOR THE FIRST TIME** (71) Carl Butler	Harmony 30674	$12
LP(P)	**FOR THE FIRST TIME** (71)	Harmony 30674	$15
	(White promo label)		
LP	**WATCH & PLAY** (72) Carl Butler & Pearl	Harmony 31182	$10
LP(P)	**WATCH & PLAY** (72)	Harmony 31182	$12
	(White promo label)		
LP	**TEMPTATION KEEPS TWISTIN' HER ARM** (72)	Chart 1051	$15

LARRY BUTLER (CW)
Imperial 45s $2 each

-albums-

LP	**TWELVE TOP COUNTRY HITS OF THE YEAR** (67)	Imperial 12365	$10

JERRY BYRD (I,R)
Mercury 45s $2-5 each
Decca 45s $2-4 each
Monument 45s $1 each
Other Mercury LPs $6-10 each
Other Monument LPs $5-8 each

-EPs-

EP	**NANI HAWAII** (54)	Mercury 3024	$12
EP	**JERRY BYRD'S BEST** (55)	Mercury 3279	$12
EP	**HI-FI GUITAR** (58)	Decca 2558	$12

-albums-

LP	**NANI HAWAII** (53)	Mercury 25077	$25
LP	**GUITAR MAGIC** (54)	Mercury 25134	$25
LP(P)	**GUITAR MAGIC** (54)	Mercury 25134	$20
	(White promo label)		
LP	**BYRD'S EXHIBITION** (54)	Mercury 25169	$25
LP(P)	**BYRD'S EXHIBITION** (54)	Mercury 25169	$20
	(White promo label)		
LP	**HI-FI GUITAR** (58)	Decca 8643	$25
LP(P)	**HI-FI GUITAR** (58)	Decca 8643	$30
	(Pink promo label)		
LP	**ON THE SHORES OF WAIKIKI** (60)	Wing 16183	$12
LP	**BYRD OF PARADISE** (61)	Monument 18009	$18
LP	**MEMORIES OF MARIA** (62)	Monument 14008	$15
LP	**BLUE HAWAIIAN STEEL GUITAR** (63)	Mercury 60856	$18
LP(P)	**BLUE HAWAIIAN STEEL GUITAR** (63)	Mercury 60856	$15
	(White promo label)		
LP	**MAN OF STEEL** (64)	Mercury 60932	$12
LP(P)	**MAN OF STEEL** (64)	Mercury 60932	$10
	(White promo label)		
LP	**COUNTRY STEEL GUITAR GREATS** (66)	Wing 16315	$12

C

C. COMPANY (C)
Featuring Terry Nelson
Other Plantation 45s $4 each

-singles-

45(P)	**BATTLE HYMN OF LT. CALLEY** (71)	Plantation 73	$15
	(Green vinyl promo only)		

-albums-

LP	**WAKE UP AMERICA** (71)	Plantation 15	$10
LP(P)	**WAKE UP AMERICA** (71)	Plantation 15	$15
	(White promo label)		

JOHNNY CABBOT (R)

-singles-

33rpm	**NIGHT & DAY** (62)	Columbia 42283	$40
	(Compact single)		

FREDDIE CADDELL (RB)

-singles-

45rpm	**AT THE ROCKHOUSE** (58)	Ardent 12	$100

AUBREY CAGLE (RB)

-singles-

45rpm	**REAL COOL** (57)	House Sounds 504	$125
45rpm	**BE-BOP BLUES** (58)	Glee 1000	$60
45rpm	**COME ALONG LITTLE GIRL** (58)Glee 1001		$60

BUDDY CAGLE (CW)

Imperial 45s $2-3 each

-albums-

LP	**THE WAY YOU LIKE IT** (66)	Imperial 12318	$12
LP	**MI CASA, TU CASA** (67)	Imperial 12348	$10
LP	**LONGTIME TRAVELING** (67)	Imperial 12361	$10
LP	**THROUGH A CRACK IN A BOXCAR DOOR** (67)	Imperial 12374	$10

AL CAIOLA (R)

-albums-

LP	**HIGH STRUNG** (59)	RCA Victor 2031	$25

CAJUN PETE (CW)

-albums-

LP	**TALES OF THE BAYOU** (61) Stereo	Mercury 60633	$25
LP	**TALES OF THE BAYOU** (61) Mono	Mercury 20633	$18
LP(P)	**TALES OF THE BAYOU** (61)	Mercury 20633	$30
	(White promo label)		

CHARLIE CALHOUN (RB)

-singles-

45rpm	**WHY THE CAR WON'T GO** (55)	MGM 11989	$18
45(P)	**WHY THE CAR WON'T GO** (55)	MGM 11989	$15
	(Yellow promo label)		

DUDLY CALLICUTT (RB)

-singles-

45rpm	**GET READY BABY** (58)	DC 0412	$40

MIKE CALLAHAN (RB)

-singles-

45/PS	**I CAN'T HELP IT** (58)	Protone 204	$40
	(Price includes picture sleeve)		

BOB CALLOWAY (RB)

-singles-

45rpm	**WAKE UP, LITTLE BOY BLUE** (58)	UBC 1013	$100

ALEX CAMPBELL (CW)

-albums-

LP	**SIXTEEN RADIO FAVORITES** (63)	Starday 214	$18
LP	**TRAVEL ON** (66)	Starday 342	$15

ARCHIE CAMPBELL (CW)

Other RCA Victor 45s $4-8 each
Nashville and Elektra LPs $4-6 each

-singles-

45rpm	**CHRISTMAS EVE IN HEAVEN** (66)	RCA Victor 9028	$10

-albums-

LP	**MAKE FRIENDS WITH ARCHIE CAMPBELL** (62)	Starday 162	$25
LP	**BEDTIME STORIES FOR ADULTS** (62)	Starday 167	$25
LP	**THE JOKER IS WILD** (63)	Starday 223	$18
LP	**THE GRAND OL' OPRY'S GOOD HUMOR MAN** (66)	Starday 377	$15
LP	**HAVE A LAUGH ON ME** (66)	RCA Victor 3504	$18
LP	**COCKFIGHT** (66)	RCA Victor 3699	$15
LP	**KIDS, I LOVE 'EM** (67)	RCA Victor 3780	$15
LP	**THE GOLDEN YEARS** (67)	RCA Victor 3892	$15
LP	**BULL SESSION AT BULL'S GAP** (68)	Chart 1007	$15
	(With Junior Samples)		
LP	**ARCHIE & LORENE TELL IT LIKE IT IS** (68)	RCA Victor 4068	$10
	(With Lorene Mann)		
LP	**THE BEST OF ARCHIE CAMPBELL** (69)	RCA Victor 4280	$12
LP	**DIDN'T HE SHINE** (70)	RCA Victor 4582	$10

CECIL CAMPBELL (CW)

-singles-

45rpm	**DIXIELAND ROCK** (57)	MGM 12245	$12
45rpm	**ROCK AND ROLL FEVER** (58)	MGM 12482	$25

-albums-

LP	**STEEL GUITAR JAMBOREE** (63)	Starday 254	$25

DICK CAMPBELL (RB)

-singles-

45rpm	**SHE'S MY GIRL** (58)	Great 4703	$18

GLEN CAMPBELL (CW)
Starday 45s $6-8 each
Other Capitol 45s $2-5 each
Warner, MCA and Atlantic America 45s $1-2 each
Other Capitol LPs $3-8 each
Surrey LPs $5 each
Buckboard LPs $1-2 each
Pickwick LPs $2-3 each
Atlantic America LPs $2 each

-singles-

45rpm	**TURN AROUND, LOOK AT ME** (61)	Crest 1087	$15
45rpm	**TURN AROUND, LOOK AT ME** (61)	Crest 1087	$12
	(White promo label)		
45rpm	**THE MIRACLE OF LOVE** (61)	Crest 1096	$18
45(P)	**THE MIRACLE OF LOVE** (61)	Crest 1096	$15
	(White promo label)		
45rpm	**DEATH VALLEY** (61)	Capehart 5008	$25
45(P)	**DEATH VALLEY** (61)	Capehart 5008	$18
	(White promo label)		
45rpm	**DREAMS FOR SALE** (61)	Ceneco 1324	$25
45rpm	**I WONDER** (61)	Ceneco 1356	$20
45rpm	**DELIGHT, ARKANSAS** (61)	Everest 2500	$10
45(P)	**DELIGHT, ARKANSAS** (61)	Everest 2500	$12
	(White promo label)		
45rpm	**LONG BLACK LIMOUSINE** (62)	Capitol 4856	$25
	(Price includes picture sleeve)		
45rpm	**DARK AS A DUNGEON** (62)	Capitol 4990	$15
	(Green River Boys featuring Glen Campbell)		
45rpm	**SUMMER, WINTER, SPRING AND FALL** (64)	Capitol 5279	$18
	(Price includes picture sleeve)		
45rpm	**GUESS I'M DUMB** (64)	Capitol 5441	$75
	(Written by Brian Wilson, vocals by the Honeys)		
45rpm	**UNIVERSAL SOLDIER** (65)	Capitol 5504	$10
	(Written by Buffy St. Marie)		
45rpm	**HEY LITTLE ONE** (68)	Capitol 2076	$12
	(Price includes picture sleeve)		
45(P)	**WHAT'S IT ALL ABOUT** (Feb 79) PSA five-minute program	Southern Baptist MA1622	$10
	(Flip side features the Pointer Sisters)		

-EPs-

EP(JB)	**WICHITA LINEMAN** (68) Jukebox LLP	Capitol 103	$12
	(Issued with a paper cover)		
EP(JB)	**GALVESTON** (69) Jukebox LLP	Capitol 210	$10
	(Issued with a paper cover)		
EP(P)	**GLEN CAMPBELL GOOD TIME HOUR** (69)	Capitol SP 55	$30
	(Promo only from Chevrolet)		
EP(JB)	**GREATEST HITS** (70) Jukebox LLP	Capitol 752 (LLP 156)	$10
	(Issued with a paper cover)		

-albums-

LP	**BIG BLUEGRASS SPECIAL** (62)	Capitol 1810	$100
	(Green River Boys featuring Glen Campbell)		
LP	**TOO LATE TO WORRY, TOO BLUE TO CRY** (63)	Capitol ST-1881	$25
LP	**ASTOUNDING 12-STRING GUITAR OF GLEN CAMPBELL** (64)	Capitol ST-2023	$25
	(Must have the ST-prefix)		
LP	**BIG BAD ROCK GUITAR OF GLEN CAMPBELL** (65) Stereo	Capitol ST-2392	$35
LP	**BIG BAD ROCK GUITAR OF GLEN CAMPBELL** (65) Mono	Capitol T-2392	$25
LP(P)	**SILVER PLATTER SERVICE** (65) Various artists	Capitol PRO 3171	$25
	(With Jack Wagner, includes Campbell interview)		
LP	**BURNING BRIDGES** (67)	Capitol 2679	$15
LP	**BY THE TIME I GET TO PHOENIX** (67)	Capitol 2851	$15
LP	**GENTLE ON MY MIND** (67)	Capitol 2809	$12
LP	**CHRISTMAS WITH GLEN CAMPBELL** (69)	Capitol 6699	$15
	("CP" Creative Products release)		
LP	**COUNTRY SOUL** (69)	Starday 414	$15
LP	**GALVESTON** (69)	Capitol 210	$12
LP	**TRUE GRIT** (69)	Capitol 263	$30
2LP	**GLEN CAMPBELL LIVE** (69)	Capitol 268	$10
LP	**COUNTRY MUSIC STAR NO. 1** (69)	Starday 437	$25
LP	**NORWOOD** (70)	Capitol 475	$12
2LP	**COUNTY FAIR** (70)	Capitol 562	$12

2LP	**ARTISTRY OF GLEN CAMPBELL** (72)	Capitol 94469	$18
	(Capitol Record Club release)		

-radio shows-

2LP(RS)	**COUNTRY COOKIN'** (June 76) Various artists	U.S. Army Reserve	$10-15
	(One show is Campbell, music and interviews)		
LP(RS)	**RALPH EMERY SHOW** (70s)		$10-15
	(Campbell is guest, music and interviews)		
2LP(RS)	**GLEN CAMPBELL SPECIAL** (May 82)	NBC Source	$20-30
	(Some live material)		
3LP(RS)	**ON A COUNTRY ROAD** (Jun 83) Box set	U.S. Army	$10-15
	(Live segment features Glen Campbell)		
Cass(RS)	**AUSTIN CITY LIMITS** (94) With Eddy Raven	Mainstreet	$20-40
	(Live concert on cassette)		

RAY CAMPI (RB)

-singles-

45rpm	**IT AIN'T ME** (57)	Dot 15617	$40
45rpm	**PLAY IT COOL** (57)	TNT 145	$40
45rpm	**MY SCREAMIN' MIMI** (57)	Domino 700	$12
45rpm	**THE BALLAD OF DONNA AND PEGGY SUE** (58)	D 1047	$12
45rpm	**BILLIE JEAN** (58)	Winsor 001	$10

CANADIAN SWEETHEARTS (RB)
Featuring Lucille Starr and Bob Regan
A&M 45s $5-8 each
Epic 45s $3-5 each
Epic 45s by Lucille Starr $2 each
A&M LPs $6-8 each
Epic LPs $5-8 each

-singles-

45rpm	**NO HELP WANTED** (58)	Soma 1156	$35

-albums-

LP	**INTRODUCING THE CANADIAN SWEETHEARTS** (64)	A&M 106	$50
LP(P)	**INTRODUCING THE CANADIAN SWEETHEARTS** (64)	A&M 106	$40
	(White promo label)		
LP	**SIDE BY SIDE** (67)	Epic 26243	$12
LP(P)	**SIDE BY SIDE** (67)	Epic 26243	$15
	(White promo label)		

JACKIE CANNON (RB)

-singles-

45rpm	**PROOF OF YOUR LOVE** (58)	Chan 103	$25

JUDY CANOVA (CW)
TV personality

-singles-

45rpm	**GO TO SLEEP LITTLE BABY** (54)	Royale 54	$25
45rpm	**I AIN'T GOT NOBODY** (55)	Varsity 45243	$18

JUDY CAPPS (R)

-singles-

45rpm	**YOU CAN HAVE MY LOVE** (58)	Cherry 1009	$50
45rpm	**THERE'S A MOON OUT TONIGHT** (60)	Planet 1010	$50

BOB CARAWAY (RB)

-singles-

45rpm	**BALLIN' KEEN** (58)	Crest 1065	$50
45(P)	**BALLIN' KEEN** (58)	Crest 1065	$45
	(White promo label)		

JACK CARD (CW)

-singles-

78rpm	**WILL ROGERS** (44)	Montgomery Ward 4941	$50
	(Flip side "The Last Flight of Wiley Post")		

JACK CARDWELL (CW)
Other King and Decca 78s and 45s $4-8 each

-singles-

45rpm	**YOU HID YOUR CHEATING HEART** (53)	King 1163	$12
78rpm	**THE DEATH OF HANK WILLIAMS** (53)	King 1172	$25
78(P)	**THE DEATH OF HANK WILLIAMS** (53)	King 1172	$30
	(White promo "Bio" label)		
45rpm	**THE DEATH OF HANK WILLIAMS** (53)	King 1172	$25
45rpm	**YOU'RE LOOKING FOR SOMETHING** (54)	King 1269	$10

HENSON CARGILL (CW)
Monument 45s $2-4 each
Other Monument LPs $4-6 each

-albums-

LP	**SKIP A ROPE** (68)	Monument 18094	$10

STEVE CARL (RB)

-singles-

45rpm	**CURFEW** (58)	Meteor 5046	$75

THOMAS CARLISLE (CW)
"Thumbs" Carlisle

-albums-

LP	**ROGER MILLER PRESENTS THUMBS CARLISLE** (65)	Smash 67074	$15
LP(P)	**ROGER MILLER PRESENTS THUMBS CARLISLE** (65)	Smash 67074	$20
	(White promo label)		
LP	**ALL THUMBS** (66)	Smash 67085	$15
LP(P)	**ALL THUMBS** (66)	Smash 67085	$18
	(White promo label)		

CARLISLES (CW)
Featuring Bill and Clifford Carlisle
78s by Cliff Carlisle on Bluebird worth $8-$15 each, on
   Champion $18 each, Decca $15 each as just Cliff Carlisle
Hickory 45s $5-8 each
Vanguard 45s $3 each
Other RCA Victor 45s $3-5 each

-singles-

78rpm	**RATTLIN' DADDY** (46)	Bluebird 6478	$18
78rpm	**RAINBOW AT MIDNIGHT** (46)	King 535	$10
78rpm	**TOO OLD TO CUT THE MUSTARD** (53)	Mercury 6348	$10
45rpm	**TOO OLD TO CUT THE MUSTARD** (53)	Mercury 6348	$12
78rpm	**NO HELP WANTED** (54)	Mercury 70028	$10
45rpm	**NO HELP WANTED** (54)	Mercury 70028	$15
45(P)	**NO HELP WANTED** (54)	Mercury 70028	$10
	(White promo label)		
78rpm	**KNOTHOLE** (54)	Mercury 70109	$10
45rpm	**KNOTHOLE** (54)	Mercury 70109	$15
45(P)	**KNOTHOLE** (54)	Mercury 70109	$12
	(White promo label)		
78rpm	**IS ZAT YOU, MYRTLE** (53)	Mercury 70174	$10
45rpm	**IS ZAT YOU, MYRTLE** (53)	Mercury 70174	$18
	(Red label)		
45rpm	**IS ZAT YOU, MYRTLE** (53)	Mercury 70174	$15
	(Black label)		
45(P)	**IS ZAT YOU, MYRTLE** (53)	Mercury 70174	$12
	(White promo label)		
78rpm	**TAIN'T NICE** (53)	Mercury 70232	$10
45rpm	**TAIN'T NICE** (53)	Mercury 70232	$15
	(Black label)		
45(P)	**TAIN'T NICE** (53)	Mercury 70232	$12
	(White promo label)		
78rpm	**SHAKE A LEG** (54)	Mercury 70351	$10
45rpm	**SHAKE A LEG** (54)	Mercury 70351	$12
45(P)	**SHAKE A LEG** (54)	Mercury 70351	$10
	(White promo label)		
78rpm	**MOODY'S GOOSE** (54)	Mercury 70405	$15
45rpm	**MOODY'S GOOSE** (54)	Mercury 70405	$15
45(P)	**MOODY'S GOOSE** (54)	Mercury 70405	$12
	(White promo label)		
78rpm	**HONEY LOVE** (54)	Mercury 70434	$15
45rpm	**HONEY LOVE** (54)	Mercury 70434	$15
45(P)	**HONEY LOVE** (54)	Mercury 70434	$10
	(White promo label)		
78rpm	**BUSY BODY BOOGIE** (54)	Mercury 70484	$15
45rpm	**BUSY BODY BOOGIE** (54)	Mercury 70484	$20
	(Green label)		
45rpm	**BUSY BODY BOOGIE** (54)	Mercury 70484	$15
	(Black label)		
45(P)	**BUSY BODY BOOGIE** (54)	Mercury 70484	$12
	(White promo label)		
78rpm	**IT'S BEDTIME BILL/RUSTY OLD HALO** (54)	Mercury 70544	$15
45rpm	**IT'S BEDTIME BILL/RUSTY OLD HALO** (54)	Mercury 70544	$18
	(Green label)		
45rpm	**IT'S BEDTIME BILL/RUSTY OLD HALO** (54)	Mercury 70544	$15
	(Black label)		
45(P)	**IT'S BEDTIME BILL/RUSTY OLD HALO** (54)	Mercury 70544	$12
	(White promo label)		

78rpm	**BARGAIN DAY, HALF OFF** (55)	Mercury 70604	$15
45rpm	**BARGAIN DAY, HALF OFF** (55)	Mercury 70604	$12
	(Green label)		
45rpm	**BARGAIN DAY, HALF OFF** (55)	Mercury 70604	$12
	(Black label)		
45(P)	**BARGAIN DAY, HALF OFF** (55)	Mercury 70604	$10
	(White promo label)		
45rpm	**ON MY WAY TO THE SHOW** (56)	Mercury 70712	$12
45rpm	**ON MY WAY TO THE SHOW** (56)	Mercury 70712	$10
	(White promo label)		
45rpm	**RUN, BOY** (56)	Mercury 70754	$12
45(P)	**RUN, BOY** (56)	Mercury 70754	$10
	(White promo label)		
45rpm	**PICKIN' PEAS** (56)	Mercury 70828	$12
45(P)	**PICKIN' PEAS** (56)	Mercury 70828	$10
	(White promo label)		
45rpm	**MIDDLE AGE SPREAD** (57)	Mercury 70887	$12
45(P)	**MIDDLE AGE SPREAD** (57)	Mercury 70887	$10
	(White promo label)		
45rpm	**I'M ROUGH STUFF** (57)	Mercury 71035	$12
45(P)	**I'M ROUGH STUFF** (57)	Mercury 71035	$10
	(White promo label)		
45rpm	**LADDER OF LOVE** (57)	Mercury 71110	$15
45(P)	**LADDER OF LOVE** (57)	Mercury 71110	$12
	(White promo label)		
45rpm	**DOWN BOY** (58)	Mercury 71490	$12
45(P)	**DOWN BOY** (58)	Mercury 71490	$10
	(White promo label)		
45rpm	**TINY SPACEMAN** (58) Bill Carlisle	RCA Victor 7132	$12
45(P)	**TINY SPACEMAN** (58)	RCA Victor 7132	$10
	(White promo label)		

-EPs-

EP	**CUTTING CAPERS WITH THE CARLISLES** (56)	Mercury 3118	$50
EP	**BOUNDING BILLY & THE LITTLE CARLISLES** (56)	Mercury 3280	$40

-albums-

LP	**ON STAGE WITH THE CARLISLES** (58)	Mercury 20359	$40
LP(P)	**ON STAGE WITH THE CARLISLES** (58)	Mercury 20359	$50
	(White promo label)		
LP	**FRESH FROM THE COUNTRY** (59)	King 643	$25
LP	**THE BEST OF BILL CARLISLE** (66)	Hickory 129	$15
LP(P)	**THE BEST OF BILL CARLISLE** (66)	Hickory 129	$25
	(Stock copy worth $15, as by Bill Carlisle)		
LP	**SONGS & HYMNS** Clifford Carlisle	Rem 1002	$25
LP	**CARLISLES** (68)	Guest Star 1446	$15

-radio shows-

16"(RS)	**US ARMY BAND** (50s)	U.S. Army	$20-40
	(Guest stars are the Carlisles)		
16"(RS)	**US ARMY BAND** (50s)	U.S. Army	$30-60
	(The Carlisles with guest Hank Snow)		
16"(RS)	**COUNTRY MUSIC TIME** (50s)	Country Music Show 82	$15-25
	(Music and interviews)		

PAULETTE CARLSON (C)
Original member of Skunk Hollow
Lead singer of Highway 101
Other RCA Victor color vinyl 45s $8 each
RCA Victor 45s $2 each
Warner 45s by Highway 101 $1 each
Warner picture sleeves $2 each

-singles-

45rpm	**SWEETIE** (78) Paulette Carlson	Skunk Hollow 0014	$18
	(First record)		
45rpm	**MERRILL ISN'T MAGIC ANYMORE** (78)	Skunk Hollow 0012	$12
	(Featuring Merrill Piepkorn and Paulette Carlson)		
45rpm	**SIX DAYS ON THE ROAD** (78) Skunk Hollow	Skunk Hollow 0013	$12
	(Featuring Merrill Piepkorn and Paulette Carlson)		
45rpm	**YOU GOTTA GET TO MY HEART** (83) Paulette Carlson	RCA Victor 13546	$10
	(Tan label, red vinyl)		
45(P)	**I'D SAY YES** (83) Paulette Carlson	RCA Victor 13599	$10
	(Yellow vinyl promo)		
45(P)	**CAN YOU FOOL** (84) Paulette Carlson	RCA Victor 13745	$10
	(Yellow vinyl promo)		
	See Highway 101		

TEX CARMAN (CW)
Jenks Carman

	-singles-		
45rpm	HILLBILLY HULA (53)	Decca 28771	$15
45rpm	I'M A POOR LONESOME FELLOW (53)	Capitol 2345	$12
45rpm	DIXIE CANNON BALL (54)	Capitol 2886	$10
	-albums-		
LP	COUNTRY CARAVAN (59)	Modern 7037	$60
LP	JENKS TEX CARMAN (60)	Sage 9	$50
LP	THE OLE INDIAN (62)	Sage 26	$75
	(Red vinyl)		
LP	JENKS TEX CARMAN PLAYS AND SINGS (63)	Sage 40	$50

HOAGY CARMICHAEL (CW)
The great songwriter

-singles-

45rpm	IDA RED (54) With the Cass County Boys	Decca 28951	$18

(Of the hundreds of records recorded by Carmichael, this one is country)

PAUL CARNES (RB)
-singles-

45rpm	I'M A MEAN MEAN DADDY (58)	Pro 101	$40

EVERETT CARPENTER (RB)
-singles-

45rpm	LET YOUR HAIR DOWN BABY (58)	Square Deal 501	$70

FREDDIE CARPENTER (RB)
-singles-

45rpm	MONEY MONEY MONEY (57)	East West 112	$25
45(P)	MONEY MONEY MONEY (57)	East West 112	$20
	(White promo label)		

MARY-CHAPIN CARPENTER (C)
Columbia 45s $2 each

STEVE CARPENTER (RB)
-singles-

45rpm	YOU'RE PUTTING ME ON (60)	Brunswick 55322	$40
45(P)	YOU'RE PUTTING ME ON (60)	Brunswick 55322	$35
	(Yellow promo label)		

THELMA CARPENTER (R,CW)
-singles-

45rpm	YES, I'M LONESOME TONIGHT (59)	Coral 62241	$15

(Answer song to Elvis's "Are You Lonesome Tonight")

45(P)	YES, I'M LONESOME TONIGHT (59)	Coral 62241	$12
	(Blue promo label)		

BILL CARROLL (RB)
-singles-

45rpm	I FEEL GOOD (58)	Dixie 2010	$45

JOHNNY CARROLL (RB)
-singles-

45rpm	I THINK OF YOU (57)	Sarg 144	$25
45rpm	THAT'S THE WAY I LOVE (57)	Philips 3520	$20
45(P)	THAT'S THE WAY I LOVE (57)	Philips 3520	$25
	(White promo label)		
45rpm	ROCK 'N' ROLL RUBY (58)	Decca 29940	$50
45(P)	ROCK 'N' ROLL RUBY (58)	Decca 29940	$40
	(Pink promo label)		
45rpm	WILD WILD WOMEN (58)	Decca 29941	$45
45(P)	WILD WILD WOMEN (58)	Decca 29941	$35
	(Pink promo label)		
45rpm	HOT ROCK (59)	Decca 30013	$45
45(P)	HOT ROCK (59)	Decca 30013	$35
	(Pink promo label)		
45rpm	BANDSTAND DOLL (59)	Warner 5042	$12
45(P)	BANDSTAND DOLL (59)	Warner 5042	$10
	(White promo label)		
45rpm	SUGAR (59)	Warner 5080	$12
45(P)	SUGAR (59)	Warner 5080	$10
	(White promo label)		

CARROLL BROTHERS (RB)
-singles-

45rpm	**RED HOT** (58)	Cameo 140	$40

CHUCK CARSON (RB)
Circle Dot 45s $10 each
-singles-

45rpm	**THE LITTLE STINKER** (57) With the Melody Ramblers	Soma 1061	$12
45rpm	**THE NAVAJO TRAIL** (58) With the Arbach Three	Soma 1085	$12
45rpm	**MOONLIGHT ROCK** (58)	Hep 2142	$75

JOE CARSON (CW)
Liberty 45s $4-8 each
-albums-

LP	**IN MEMORIAM** (64)	Liberty 7360	$15
LP(P)	**IN MEMORIAM** (64) (White promo label)	Liberty 7360	$18

JOHN CARSON (CW)
78s on Bluebird are worth $25 each

MARTHA CARSON (CW)
Martha Lou Carson
Other RCA Victor 45s $5-8 each
Starday and Sims 45s $3-5 each
-singles-

45rpm	**ALL THESE THINGS** (56)	RCA Victor 6603	$10
45rpm	**NOW STOP** (57)	RCA Victor 6948	$15

-EPs-

2EP	**JOURNEY TO THE SKY** (55)	RCA Victor 1145	$25
EP	**JOURNEY TO THE SKY** (55)	RCA Victor 1145	$15

-albums-

LP	**JOURNEY TO THE SKY** (55)	RCA Victor 1145	$25
LP	**ROCK-A MY SOUL** (57)	RCA Victor 1490	$40
LP	**SATISFIED** (60)	Capitol 1507	$25
LP(P)	**SATISFIED** (60) (Capitol promo label)	Capitol 1507	$30
LP	**A TALK WITH THE LORD** (62)	Capitol 1607	$30
LP(P)	**A TALK WITH THE LORD** (62) (Capitol promo label)	Capitol 1607	$25
LP	**MARTHA CARSON** (63) Stereo	Sims 100	$25

-radio shows-

16"(RS)	**US ARMY BAND** (50s) (Martha Carson with guest Ray Price)	U.S. Army	$15-25

MINDY CARSON (CW)
-radio shows-

16"(RS)	**NATIONAL GUARD** (50s) (Different show on each side, music and interviews)	National Guard	$10-15

FRED CARTER (R)
-singles-

45rpm	**FREELOADERS** (58)	Lode 2001	$40

HARRY CARTER (RB)
-singles-

45rpm	**JUMP BABY JUMP** (59)	Mar-Vel 1300	$50
45rpm	**I DON'T WANT YOU** (59)	Mar-Vel 1301	$50

WILF CARTER See Montana Slim

CARTER FAMILY (CW)
Includes Helen Carter, June Carter, Anita Carter, and Carlene Carter
78s on Bluebird worth $20 each, Decca $15-$18 each
Other label 78s $5-10 each
Other Columbia promo 78s $4-8 each
Other Columbia 45s $4-8 each
Other label 45s $3-6 each
-singles-

78rpm	**BURY ME UNDER THE WEEPING WILLOW** (28)	Victor 21074	$20
78rpm	**WILDWOOD FLOWER** (28)	Victor 40000	$15
78rpm	**KEEP ON THE SUNNY SIDE** (28)	Victor 21434	$12
78rpm	**LITTLE DARLIN' OF MINE** (29)	Victor 21638	$12
78rpm	**I'M THINKING TONIGHT OF MY BLUE EYES** (29)	Victor 40089	$10
78rpm	**WORRIED MAN BLUES** (30)	Victor 40319	$10
78rpm	**LONESOME VALLEY** (31)	Victor 23541	$12

78rpm	**CAN THE CIRCLE BE UNBROKEN** (35)	Banner 33465	$15
45rpm	**BABY IT'S COLD OUTSIDE** (49) June Carter	RCA Victor 0075	$18
	(With Homer & Jethro)		
45rpm	**BLUEBIRD ISLAND** (51) Anita Carter	RCA Victor 0441	$12
45rpm	**YOU FLOPPED WHEN YOU GOT ME ALONE** (53) June Carter	Columbia 21128	$10
78rpm	**WELL I GUESS I TOLD YOU OFF** (53) With Mother Maybelle	Columbia 21262	$15
	(White promo label)		
45rpm	**SET THE WEDDING** (56) Helen Carter	Hickory 1076	$18
45(P)	**SET THE WEDDING** (56) Helen Carter	Hickory 1076	$15
45rpm	**THAT'S WHAT MAKES THE JUKEBOX PLAY** (56) Anita Carter	RCA Victor 6129	$12
45(P)	**THAT'S WHAT MAKES THE JUKEBOX PLAY** (56) Anita Carter	RCA Victor 6129	$10
45rpm	**THE MASK ON YOUR HEAD** (56) Anita Carter	RCA Victor 6228	$10
45rpm	**I WORE DARK GLASSES** (56) Anita Carter	RCA Victor 6364	$10
45rpm	**BLUE DOLL** (58) Anita Carter	Cadence 1333	$10
45(P)	**BLUE DOLL** (58)	Cadence 1333	$12
	(White promo label)		
45rpm	**MAMA DON'T CRY AT MY WEDDING** (59) Anita Carter	Jamie 1154	$12
45(P)	**MAMA DON'T CRY AT MY WEDDING** (59)	Jamie 1154	$10
	(White/brown promo label)		

-EPs-

45(P)	**IF I HAD A NEEDLE & THREAD** (58)	RCA Victor DJ-34	$15
	(Promo-only EP, two songs on each side, flip side by the Country Partners)		
45(P)	**HE'S A REAL GONE GUY** (58) Anita Carter	RCA Victor DJ-60	$15
	(Promo-only EP, two songs on each side, flip side by Porter Wagoner)		
45rpm	**SET THE WEDDING** (58) Helen Carter	Hickory 1076	$12
45(P)	**SET THE WEDDING** (58) Helen Carter	Hickory 1076	$10
	(White promo label)		

-EPs-

EP(P)	**HE'S A REAL GONE GUY** (59)	RCA Victor 6805 DJ-60	$10
	(Flip side is two songs by Porter Wagoner)		
EP	**THE CARTER FAMILY** (65)	Decca 2788	$40
EP	**THE CARTER FAMILY EXTENDED PLAY ALBUM**	Acme 101	$50
EP	**THE CARTER FAMILY EXTENDED PLAY ALBUM**	Acme 102	$50
EP	**THE CARTER FAMILY EXTENDED PLAY ALBUM**	Acme 103	$50

-albums-

LP	**ALL TIME FAVORITES** (60)	Acme LP-1	$150
LP	**IN MEMORY OF A. P. CARTER** (60)	Acme LP-2	$150
LP	**MOTHER MAYBELLE CARTER**	Ambassador 98069	$125
LP	**TOGETHER AGAIN** (62)	RCA Victor 2580	$30
	(Hank Snow and Anita Carter)		
LP	**ANITA CARTER SINGS FOLK SONGS OLD & NEW** (63)	Mercury 20770	$30
LP(P)	**ANITA CARTER SINGS FOLK SONGS OLD & NEW** (63)	Mercury 20770	$25
	(White promo label)		
LP	**THE CARTER FAMILY** (63) Original title	Decca 4404	$50
LP(P)	**THE CARTER FAMILY** (63)	Decca 4404	$60
	(Pink promo label)		
LP	**A COLLECTION OF FAVORITES** (63) Retitled	Decca 4404	$40
LP(P)	**A COLLECTION OF FAVORITES** (63)	Decca 4404	$50
	(Pink promo label)		
LP	**MORE FAVORITES BY THE CARTER FAMILY** (65)	Decca 4557	$40
LP(P)	**MORE FAVORITES BY THE CARTER FAMILY** (65)	Decca 4557	$50
	(Pink promo label)		

-radio shows-

16"(RS)	**COUNTRY STYLE USA** (50s) The Carter Family	Country Style 113	$40-75
	(Music and interviews)		
16"(RS)	**COUNTRY STYLE USA** (50s) June Carter	Country Style 211	$30-60
	(Music and interviews)		
CD(RS)	**COUNTRY CUTTING EDGE** (Nov 93) Carlene Carter	Westwood One	$25-50
	(Live concert)		
CD(RS)	**LIVE FROM THE CRAZY HORSE** (94) Carlene Carter	Westwood One	$25-50
	(Live concert)		
	See Johnny Cash		

RIC CARTEY (RB)

-singles-

45rpm	**OOOH-EEE** (57)	Stars 539	$50
45rpm	**YOUNG LOVE** (57)	RCA Victor 6751	$15

JOHNNY CARVER (CW)

Imperial 45s $3-5 each
Other Imperial LPs $5-8 each
United Artists, ABC, and Harmony LPs $3-6 each

-albums-

LP	**REALLY COUNTRY** (68)	Imperial 12347	$10

EDDIE CASH (RB)

-singles-

45rpm	**DOING ALL RIGHT** (58)	Peak 1001	$100

JOHNNY CASH (CW)

Other Columbia 45s $3-8 each
Other Columbia picture sleeves $5 each
Other Sun 45s 1100 series $2 each
Other Sun 45s #2, #7 $2-3 each
Scotti Brothers 45s $3 each
Mercury 45s $2 each
Other Columbia LPs $2-8 each
Other Columbia promo label LPs $5-8 each
Priority LPs $2-5 each
Other Pickwick/Hilltop LPs $2-5 each
Other Harmony LPs $3-6 each
Other Harmony promo label LPs $6-8 each
Share, Power Pak, Out of Town, Allegiance, Nashville, Accord, Album Globe, Everest LPs $2-4 each
Mercury LPs $4 each
Sun LPs duet with Jerry Lee Lewis $6-8 each
Columbia duet LP with Tammy Wynette $8 each

-singles-

78rpm	**HEY PORTER** (55)	Sun 221	$30
	(First Sun single, other side, "Cry Cry Cry," was first hit)		
45rpm	**HEY PORTER** (55)	Sun 221	$25
78rpm	**FOLSOM PRISON BLUES** (56)	Sun 232	$25
45rpm	**FOLSOM PRISON BLUES** (56)	Sun 232	$20
78rpm	**I WALK THE LINE** (56)	Sun 241	$25
45rpm	**I WALK THE LINE** (56)	Sun 241	$18
78rpm	**THERE YOU GO** (56)	Sun 258	$25
45rpm	**THERE YOU GO** (56)	Sun 258	$18
78rpm	**NEXT IN LINE** (57)	Sun 266	$25
45rpm	**NEXT IN LINE** (57)	Sun 266	$15
78rpm	**GIVE MY LOVE TO ROSE** (57)	Sun 279	$20
45rpm	**GIVE MY LOVE TO ROSE** (57)	Sun 279	$15
78rpm	**BALLAD OF A TEENAGE QUEEN** (57)	Sun 283	$20
45rpm	**BALLAD OF A TEENAGE QUEEN** (57)	Sun 283	$15
78rpm	**GUESS THINGS HAPPEN THAT WAY** (58)	Sun 295	$20
45rpm	**GUESS THINGS HAPPEN THAT WAY** (58)	Sun 295	$15
45rpm	**GUESS THINGS HAPPEN THAT WAY** (58)	Sun 295	$50
	(Price includes picture sleeve)		
78rpm	**THE WAYS OF A WOMAN IN LOVE** (58)	Sun 302	$20
45rpm	**THE WAYS OF A WOMAN IN LOVE** (58)	Sun 302	$15
78rpm	**IT'S JUST ABOUT TIME** (59)	Sun 309	$25
45rpm	**IT'S JUST ABOUT TIME** (59)	Sun 309	$15
78rpm	**LUTHER PLAYED THE BOOGIE** (58)	Sun 316	$40
45rpm	**LUTHER PLAYED THE BOOGIE** (58)	Sun 316	$12
45rpm	**I FORGOT TO REMEMBER** (59)	Sun 321	$12
45rpm	**GOODBY LITTLE DARLIN'** (59)	Sun 331	$10
45rpm	**I LOVE YOU BECAUSE** (59)	Sun 334	$10
45rpm	**THE STORY OF A BROKEN HEART** (59)	Sun 343	$12
45rpm	**MEAN EYED CAT** (59)	Sun 347	$10
45rpm	**OH LONESOME ME** (59)	Sun 355	$10
45rpm	**SUGARTIME** (60)	Sun 363	$10
45rpm	**BLUE TRAIN** (60)	Sun 376	$10
45rpm	**WIDE OPEN ROAD** (60)	Sun 392	$10
45(P)	**WIDE OPEN ROAD** (60)	Sun 392	$12
	(White promo label)		
45rpm	**WHAT DO I CARE** (60)	Columbia 41251	$12
45(P)	**WHAT DO I CARE** (60)	Columbia 41251	$10
	(White promo label)		
45rpm	**DON'T TAKE YOUR GUNS TO TOWN** (60)	Columbia 41313	$10
45rpm	**DON'T TAKE YOUR GUNS TO TOWN** (60)	Columbia 41313	$35
	(Price includes picture sleeve)		
45(P)	**DON'T TAKE YOUR GUNS TO TOWN** (60)	Columbia 41313	$15
	(White promo label)		
45rpm	**LITTLE DRUMMER BOY** (60)	Columbia 41481	$15
45rpm	**LITTLE DRUMMER BOY** (60)	Columbia 41481	$50
	(Price includes picture sleeve)		
5-45s	**RIDE THIS TRAIN** (60) Set of five stereo singles	Columbia JS7-JS12	$12 each
	(Jukebox singles, $75 for the set with paper insert)		
45(P)	**LITTLE DRUMMER BOY** (60)	Columbia 41481	$18
45rpm	**TENNESSEE FLAT-TOP BOX** (61)	Columbia 42147	$20
	(Price includes picture sleeve)		
33rpm	**TENNESSEE FLAT-TOP BOX** (61) 33rpm single	Columbia 42147	$25
	(Stereo single)		
45rpm	**THE BIG BATTLE** (62)	Columbia 42301	$20
	(Price includes picture sleeve)		

33rpm	**THE BIG BATTLE** (62) 33rpm single	Columbia 42301	$25
	(Stereo single)		
45rpm	**IN THE JAILHOUSE NOW** (62)	Columbia 42425	$18
	(Price includes picture sleeve that has the same photo as "Tennessee Flat-Top Box")		
33rpm	**IN THE JAILHOUSE NOW** (62) 33rpm single	Columbia 42425	$25
	(Stereo single)		
45/PS	**BONANZA!** (63)	Columbia 42425	$18
	(Price includes picture sleeve)		
33rpm	**BONANZA!** (63) 33rpm single	Columbia 42425	$25
	(Stereo single)		
45rpm	**BUSTED** (63)	Columbia 42665	$18
	(Price includes picture sleeve with the same photo as "Bonanza!)		
33rpm	**BUSTED** (63) 33rpm single	Columbia 42665	$25
	(Stereo single)		
45rpm	**RING OF FIRE** (64)	Columbia 42788	$25
	(Price includes picture sleeve)		
5-45s	**RING OF FIRE** (64) Set of five stereo singles	Columbia 8853	$10 each
	(Jukebox singles, set of five $50)		
45rpm	**ROLL CALL** (67)	Columbia 44373	$18
	(Price includes picture sleeve)		
45rpm	**FOLSOM PRISON BLUES** (68)	Columbia 44513	$15
	(Price includes picture sleeve)		
45(P)	**GET RHYTHM** (69)	Sun 1103	$12
	(White label, blue vinyl)		
45(P)	**BIG RIVER** (70)	Sun 1121	$12
	(White label, yellow vinyl)		
45rpm	**WINGS IN THE MORNING** (80)	Cachet 4506	$10
	(Price includes picture sleeve)		

-EPs-

EP(P)	**THE JOHNNY CASH SHOW** Demo for radio series, seven-inch	U.S. Dept Health	$20
	(Johnny's photo is on the label)		
EP	**JOHNNY CASH SINGS HANK WILLIAMS** (58)	Sun 111	$100
EP	**JOHNNY CASH** (58)	Sun 112	$75
EP	**JOHNNY CASH** (58)	Sun 113	$75
EP	**JOHNNY CASH WITH THE TENNESSEE TWO** (58)	Sun 114	$75
EP	**JOHNNY CASH** (58)	Sun 116	$75
EP	**JOHNNY CASH** (58)	Sun 117	$75
EP	**THE FABULOUS JOHNNY CASH** (58) Vol. 1	Columbia 12531	$25
EP	**THE FABULOUS JOHNNY CASH** (58) Vol. 2	Columbia 12532	$25
EP	**THE FABULOUS JOHNNY CASH** (58) Vol. 3	Columbia 12533	$25
	(All issued with hard covers)		
EP	**HYMNS BY JOHNNY CASH** (59) Vol. 1	Columbia 12841	$25
EP	**HYMNS BY JOHNNY CASH** (59) Vol. 2	Columbia 12841	$25
EP	**HYMNS BY JOHNNY CASH** (59) Vol. 3	Columbia 12841	$25
	(All issued with hard covers)		
EP	**SONGS OF OUR SOIL** (59) Vol. 1	Columbia 13392	$25
EP	**SONGS OF OUR SOIL** (59) Vol. 2	Columbia 13392	$25
EP	**SONGS OF OUR SOIL** (59) Vol. 3	Columbia 13392	$25
	(All issued with hard covers)		
EP	**JOHNNY CASH SINGS THE REBEL** (59)	Columbia 2155	$25
	(From the television series)		
EP	**NOW THERE WAS A SONG** (60)	Columbia 14631	$20
EP	**NOW THERE WAS A SONG** (60)	Columbia 14631	$20
EP	**NOW THERE WAS A SONG** (60)	Columbia 14631	$20
	(All issued with a hard cover)		
EP(JB)	**JOHNNY CASH-THE LEGEND** (66) Jukebox LLP	Sun 2-118	$30
	(Price includes paper cover and title strips)		
EP(JB)	**I WALK THE LINE** (66) Jukebox LLP	Columbia 8990	$20
	(Issued with a paper cover)		
EP(JB)	**HAPPINESS IS YOU** (66) Jukebox LLP	Columbia 9337	$20
	(Issued with a paper cover)		
EP(JB)	**JOHNNY CASH'S GREATEST HITS VOL 1** (67) Jukebox LLP	Columbia 9478	$20
	(Issued with a paper cover)		
EP(JB)	**JOHNNY CASH AT FOLSOM PRISON** (68) Jukebox LLP	Columbia 9639	$20
	(Issued with a hard cover)		
EP(JB)	**HELLO, I'M JOHNNY CASH** (70) Jukebox LLP	Columbia 9943	$25
	(Issued with a hard cover)		
EP(P)	**THE SURVIVORS** (82) w/Carl Perkins and Jerry Lee Lewis	Columbia AE7 1505	$25
	(Price includes promo picture sleeve)		

-albums-

LP	**JOHNNY CASH WITH HIS HOT AND BLUE GUITAR** (56)	Sun 1220	$50
	(First album, released before signing with Columbia)		
LP	**JOHNNY CASH SINGS THE SONGS THAT MADE HIM FAMOUS** (58)	Sun 1235	$40
	(Original Sun label)		
LP	**THE FABULOUS JOHNNY CASH** (58) Mono	Columbia 1253	$25
LP	**THE FABULOUS JOHNNY CASH** (58) Stereo	Columbia 8122	$30

LP	**GREATEST! JOHNNY CASH** (59)	Sun 1240	$40
	(Original Sun label)		
LP	**SONGS OF OUR SOIL** (59) Mono	Columbia 1339	$25
LP	**SONGS OF OUR SOIL** (59) Stereo	Columbia 8148	$30
LP	**HYMNS BY JOHNNY CASH** (59) Mono	Columbia 1722	$25
LP	**HYMNS BY JOHNNY CASH** (59) Stereo	Columbia 8125	$30
LP	**NOW, THERE WAS A SONG** (60) Mono	Columbia 1463	$25
LP	**NOW, THERE WAS A SONG** (60) Stereo	Columbia 8254	$30
LP	**RIDE THIS TRAIN** (60) Mono	Columbia 1464	$20
LP	**RIDE THIS TRAIN** (60) Stereo	Columbia 8255	$25
LP	**JOHNNY CASH SINGS HANK WILLIAMS** (60)	Sun 1245	$35
	(Original Sun label)		
LP	**NOW HERE'S JOHNNY CASH** (61)	Sun 1255	$30
	(Original Sun label)		
LP	**THE LURE OF THE GRAND CANYON** (61) Mono	Columbia 1622	$30
	(With Andre Kostelanetz)		
LP	**THE LURE OF THE GRAND CANYON** (61) Stereo	Columbia 8422	$40
	(Johnny Cash does narration)		
LP(P)	**THE LURE OF THE GRAND CANYON** (61) Red label promo	Columbia 1622	$50
	(Stock red label with "Not for Sale" in white letters)		
LP	**HYMNS FROM THE HEART** (62)	Columbia 8522	$18
LP	**THE SOUND OF JOHNNY CASH** (62)	Columbia 8602	$18
LP	**ALL ABOARD THE BLUE TRAIN** (63)	Sun 1270	$30
	(Original Sun label)		
LP	**BLOOD, SWEAT & TEARS** (63)	Columbia 8730	$20
LP	**RING OF FIRE** (63)	Columbia 8853	$12
LP	**CHRISTMAS SPIRIT** (63)	Columbia 8917	$20
LP	**I WALK THE LINE** (64)	Columbia 8990	$18
	(Not the same as the 1970 soundtrack version)		
LP	**THE ORIGINAL SUN SOUND OF JOHNNY CASH** (64)	Sun 1275	$30
	(Original Sun label)		
LP	**BITTER TEARS** (64)	Columbia 9048	$20
LP	**ORANGE BLOSSOM SPECIAL** (64)	Columbia 9109	$12
2LP	**JOHNNY CASH SINGS BALLADS OF THE TRUE WEST** (65)	Columbia 838	$25
LP	**JOHNNY CASH'S COUNTRY ROUNDUP** (65)	Hilltop 6010	$15
	(With the Wilburn Brothers and Billy Grammer)		
LP	**MEAN AS HELL** (65)	Columbia 9246	$15
LP(P)	**MEAN AS HELL** (65)	Columbia 2446	$25
	(White promo label)		
LP	**EVERYBODY LOVES A NUT** (66)	Columbia 9292	$15
LP(P)	**EVERYBODY LOVES A NUT** (66)	Columbia 9292	$18
	(White promo label)		
LP	**HAPPINESS IS YOU** (66)	Columbia 9337	$12
LP(P)	**HAPPINESS IS YOU** (66)	Columbia 9337	$18
	(White promo label)		
LP	**FROM SEA TO SHINING SEA** (67)	Columbia 9447	$12
LP(P)	**FROM SEA TO SHINING SEA** (67)	Columbia 9447	$18
	(White promo label)		
LP	**CARRYIN' ON** (67) With June Carter	Columbia 9528	$10
LP(P)	**CARRYIN' ON** (67)	Columbia 9528	$12
	(White promo label)		
LP	**GOLDEN SOUNDS OF COUNTRY MUSIC** (68)	Harmony 11249	$10
LP(P)	**GOLDEN SOUNDS OF COUNTRY MUSIC** (68)	Harmony 11249	$12
	(White promo label)		
LP	**THIS IS JOHNNY CASH** (69)	Harmony 11342	$10
LP(P)	**THIS IS JOHNNY CASH** (69)	Harmony 11342	$12
	(White promo label)		
LP	**LEGENDS & LOVE SONGS** (68)	Columbia 363	$15
	(Columbia Record Club release)		
LP	**GRAND CANYON SUITE** (69) With Andre Kostelanetz	Columbia 7425	$30
	(Gray Masterworks label, promo has timing strip on cover)		
LP	**THE HOLY LAND** (69)	Columbia 9726	$25
	(With a 3-D cover)		
LP	**THE HOLY LAND** (69)	Columbia 9726	$10
	(Without the 3-D cover)		
LP	**LITTLE FAUSS & BIG HALSY** (70) With Carl Perkins	Columbia 30385	$25
	(Soundtrack album)		
LP	**I WALK THE LINE** (70)	Columbia 30397	$20
	(Soundtrack version)		
2LP	**JOHNNY CASH-THE LEGEND** (70)	Sun 118	$25
	(Price includes booklet, later Sun label)		
2LP(P)	**JOHNNY CASH-THE LEGEND** (70)	Sun 118	$25
	(White promo labels, later Sun labels)		
2LP	**JOHNNY CASH: THE MAN, THE WORLD, HIS MUSIC** (71)	Sun 126	$25
LP(P)	**JOHNNY CASH: THE MAN, THE WORLD, HIS MUSIC** (71)	Sun 126	$25
	(White promo labels)		
LP(P)	**THE DORAL ALBUM** (72)	Doral CSP (CBS)	$40
	(Mail order from Doral)		

LP	**GIVE MY LOVE TO ROSE** (72) With June Carter	Harmony 31256	$10
2LP	**THE GOSPEL ROAD** (73)	Columbia 32253	$25
2LP	**A BELIEVER SINGS THE TRUTH** (79)	Cachet 9001	$12
LP(P)	**CLASSIC CHRISTMAS** (80)	Columbia 36866	$25
	(White promo label)		

-ads-

LP(P)	**1970 PEPSI-COLA RADIO** (70) Various artists	Pepsi-Cola 1706	$100
	(Radio ads)		
LP(P)	**1970 PEPSI-COLA RADIO** (70) INTERIM version	Pepsi-Cola 1718	$100
	(Cash does two cuts on each of the above two discs)		
LP(P)	**1971 PEPSI-COLA RADIO** (71) Various artists	Pepsi-Cola 1722	$100
	(Radio ads)		
LP(P)	**1971 PEPSI-COLA RADIO** (71) other versions	Pepsi-Cola 1723	$100
	(Cash does two cuts on each of the above two discs)		
LP(P)	**GOOD EARTH** (73) Radio spots and songs	Farm Sales Team	$80
	(Blue label, normal LP format with hard cover and includes TV ads)		
LP(P)	**SOMEBODY CARES ABOUT YOU** (70s) Radio PSA spots	U.S. Dept Labor	$25
	(Twenty cuts including one by Johnny Cash)		

-radio shows-

16"(RS)	**TREASURY DEPARTMENT** (59)	U.S. Treasury	$30-60
	(Cash is host, music and interviews)		
LP(RS)	**THE JOHNNY CASH SHOW** (60s) Public service series	U.S. Dept Health	$25-40 each
	(There are several shows in the series, which had a folk/ country-western flavor)		
LP(RS)	**JOHNNY CASH-THE WORLD OF FOLK MUSIC** (67) Series	Social Security	$25-50 each
	(Several shows in the series)		
LS(RS)	**JOHNNY CASH-THE WORLD OF FOLK MUSIC** (68) w/Bob Dylan	Social Security	$50-100
	(From the above series, with Bob Dylan the guest)		
2LP(RS)	**COUNTRY COOKIN'** (Feb 77)	U.S. Army Reserve	$25
	(Music and interviews)		
LP(P)	**AIR FORCE COUNTRY** (70s) PSA spots	U.S. Air Force	$25
	(Fourteen cuts, two by Cash, issued with hard cover)		
LP(RS)	**CHRISTMAS WITH ...** Radio show	Diamond P	$25
	(Music and interviews)		
LP(RS)	**BBC TRANSCRIPTION DISC** (78)	BBC Transcription	$300-400
	(Very rare live Christmas concert)		
Cass(RS)	**AUSTIN CITY LIMITS** (93)	Mainstreet	$40-75
	(Live concert issued on cassette to radio stations)		
	See the Carter Family		
	See Roseanne Carter		

ROSEANNE CASH (C)
Daughter of Johnny Cash and June Carter

-radio shows-

3LP(RS)	**THE SILVER EAGLE** (81) Live concert	DIR	$30-50
	(Roseanne Cash and Rodney Crowell, also Don Williams)		
LP(RS)	**WESTWOOD ONE PRESENTS** (Sept 89)	Westwood One	$50-100
	(Live concert)		
	See Johnny Cash		

TOMMY CASH (CW)
The brother of Johnny Cash
Epic 45s $3-6 each
Epic Memory Lane promo 45s $5 each
Epic LPs $5-8 each
Monument LPs $2-5 each

-albums-

LP	**HERE COMES TOMMY CASH** (68)	United Artists 6628	$12
LP(P)	**HERE COMES TOMMY CASH** (68)	United Artists 6628	$15
	(White promo label)		

BOB CASS (RB)

-singles-

45rpm	**CORVETTE BABY** (58)	RBC 100	$60

TOMMY CASSEL (R)

-singles-

45rpm	**GO AHEAD ON** (58)	Cassel 58X1	$60
45rpm	**ROCKIN' ROCK AND ROLLIN' STONE** (58)	Cassel 58X3	$60

PETE CASSELL (CW)
The Blind Minstrel

-singles-

45rpm	**THE LETTER EDGED IN BLACK** (55)	Varsity 45219	$20

-albums-

LP	**THE LEGEND OF PETE CASSELL** (65)	Hilltop 6023	$30

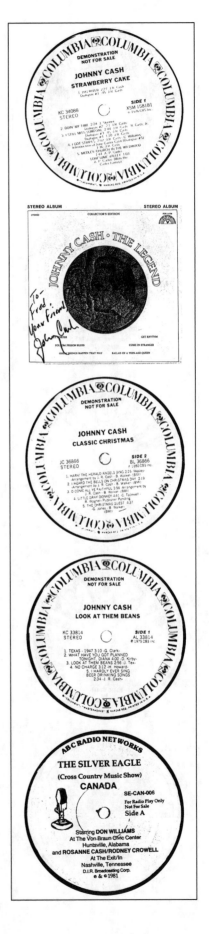

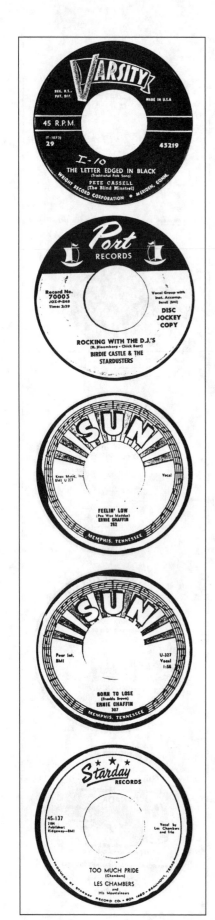

BIRDIE CASTLE & THE STARDUSTERS (RB)
-singles-

45rpm	ROCKING WITH THE DJS' (57)		Port 70005	$15
45(P)	ROCKING WITH THE DJS' (57)		Port 70005	$18
	(Port promo label)			

JOEY CASTLE (RB)
-singles-

45rpm	ROCK AND ROLL DADDY (59)		Headline 1008	$40

FRANK CATHEY (RB)
-singles-

45rpm	MY ROCK 'N' ROLL DADDY (57)		Cathey 201	$60

JIMMY CAVELLO (RB)
-singles-

45rpm	ROCK THE JOINT (58)		BSD 1005	$50

JOHN WESLEY CAVES (RB)
-singles-

45rpm	ROCKET TO THE MOON (58)		Memory Lane 102	$40

PHIL CAY (RB)
-singles-

45rpm	MEET ME IN THE BARNYARD (58)		Hart 1001	$65

ERNIE CHAFFIN (RB)
-singles-

45rpm	STOP LOOK & LISTEN (57)		Fine 1010	$15
45rpm	FEELIN' LOW (57)		Sun 262	$12
45rpm	BORN TO LOSE (58)		Sun 307	$10

CURLY CHALKER (CW)
Columbia 45s $3 each
Crescendo LPs $5-8 each
-albums-

LP	BIG HITS ON BIG STEEL (67)		Columbia 9396	$18
LP(P)	BIG HITS ON BIG STEEL (67)		Columbia 9396	$15
	(White promo label)			

LES CHAMBERS (CW)
-singles-

45rpm	TOO MUCH PRIDE (55)		Starday 137	$12
45rpm	KISS LIKE THAT (56)		Starday 158	$10
45rpm	WILL IT ALWAYS BE (57) With Country Johnny Mathis		Starday 181	$10

RAY CHAMPA (Polka)
With His Polka Champs
-singles-

45rpm	CASTLE ROCK POLKA (58)		Piknik 1010	$10

THE CHAMPS (R,I)
Including listings of Chuck Rio and Dave Burgess
Members of the group included Glen Campbell, Jim Seals, and Dash Crofts
Tops EPs with Dave Burgess $8 each
Other 45s by members of the Champs $3-6 each
-singles-

78rpm	TEQUILA (58)		Challenge 1016	$25
45rpm	TEQUILA (58)		Challenge 1016	$10
	(Original first pressing shows Tequila as Side 2)			
45(P)	TEQUILA (58)		Challenge 1016	$12
	(White promo label)			
45(P)	MAYBELLE (58) Dave Burgess with the Champs		Challenge 1018	$10
78rpm	EL RANCHO ROCK (58)		Challenge 59007	$35
45rpm	LOVEY DOVEY BABY (59) Dave Burgess		Challenge 59007	$15
45(P)	LOVEY DOVEY BABY (59)		Challenge 59032	$18
	(White promo label)			
45rpm	LULU (59) Dave Burgess		Challenge 59032	$12
45(P)	LULU (59)		Challenge 59037	$15
	(White promo label)			
45rpm	EVERLOVIN' (59) Dave Burgess		Challenge 59045	$12
45(P)	EVERLOVIN' (59)		Challenge 59045	$15
	(White promo label)			
45rpm	AKIKO (60) Chuck Rio		Challenge 59073	$12
45(P)	AKIKO (60)		Challenge 59073	$15
	(White promo label)			

-EPs-

EP	**4-HITS** (57) Three of the four cuts are by Dave Burgess	Tops 303	$18
EP	**THE CHAMPS** (58)	Challenge 101	$25

-albums-

LP	**GO CHAMPS GO** (58) Limited blue vinyl	Challenge 601	$300
LP	**GO CHAMPS GO** (58) Black vinyl	Challenge 601	$60
LP	**EVERYBODY'S ROCKIN' WITH THE CHAMPS** (59) Mono	Challenge 605	$50
LP	**EVERYBODY'S ROCKIN' WITH THE CHAMPS** (59) Stereo	Challenge 605	$80
LP	**GREAT DANCE HITS** (62) Mono	Challenge 613	$40
LP	**GREAT DANCE HITS** (62) Stereo	Challenge 613	$50
LP	**ALL AMERICAN MUSIC FROM THE CHAMPS** (62) Mono	Challenge 614	$40
LP	**ALL AMERICAN MUSIC FROM THE CHAMPS** (62) Stereo	Challenge 614	$50
	See Glen Campbell		

HOWARD CHANDLER (RB)

-singles-

45rpm	**WAMPUS CAT** (58)	Wampus 100	$65

CHAPARRAL BROTHERS (CW)

Capitol 45s $2-4 each
Other Capitol LPs $6 each

-albums-

LP	**INTRODUCING THE CHAPARRAL BROTHERS** (68)	Capitol 2922	$10

RAY CHARLES (CW)

Recorded four "Country-Western" LPs on ABC Paramount in the '60s, and with Willie Nelson and as
a solo act on Columbia in the '80s

-singles-

5-33(S)	**MODERN SOUNDS IN COUNTRY & WESTERN** (62) Jukebox set	ABC Paramount 410	$40
	(Five 7" stereo singles with small center holes)	1 thru 5	
	(Price is for all five singles, or $8 each)		

-albums-

LP	**MODERN SOUNDS IN COUNTRY & WESTERN MUSIC** (62)	ABC Paramount 410	$12
LP(P)	**MODERN SOUNDS IN COUNTRY & WESTERN MUSIC** (62)	ABC Paramount 410	$25
	(White promo label)		
LP	**MODERN SOUNDS IN COUNTRY & WESTERN MUSIC VOL. 2** (62)	ABC Paramount 435	$12
LP(P)	**MODERN SOUNDS IN COUNTRY & WESTERN MUSIC VOL. 2** (62)	ABC Paramount 435	$25
	(White promo label)		

-radio shows-

Cass(RS)	**AUSTIN ENCORE** (94)	Mainstreet Broadcasting	$20-40
	(Live concert with Lee Greenwood issued on cassette)		

TOMMY CHARLES (CW)

-singles-

45rpm	**HEY THERE BABY** (57)	Willett 1010	$30
45rpm	**AFTER SCHOOL** (58)	Decca 29946	$12
45(P)	**AFTER SCHOOL** (58)	Decca 29946	$10
	(Pink promo label)		

CHARLES RIVER BOYS (C)

Prestige LPs $5-10 each

-albums-

LP	**BEATLE COUNTRY** (66)	Elektra 4006	$15
LP(P)	**BEATLE COUNTRY** (66)	Elektra 4006	$18
	(White promo label)		

JODY CHASTIN (RB)

-singles-

45rpm	**MY MY** (58)	Kay 1002	$65

CARL CHERRY (RB)

-singles-

45rpm	**THE ITCH** (58)	Tene 1023	$60

DON CHERRY (C)

Monument 45s $2 each

LEW CHILDRE (CW)

-albums-

LP	**OLD TIME GET TOGETHER** (61)	Starday 153	$15
	(With Cowboy Copas)		
	See Cowboy Copas		

HARRY CHOATES (CW)

-singles-

78rpm	**JOLE BLON** (47) (The original version, written by Choates)	Modern Mountain 511	$18
45rpm	**JOLE BLON** (55) (The flip side is sung in French)	Starday 187	$25

-albums-

LP	**JOLE BLON** (60s) (Original title)	D 7000	$40
LP	**ORIGINAL CAJUN FIDDLE** (60s) (Retitled version)	D 7000	$15

CHARLES CHRISTY (RB)

-singles-

45rpm	**COME ON BABY** (58)	Mammal	$40

VARIOUS ARTISTS

-singles-

33(P)	**CHRONOLOGY OF AMERICAN MUSIC** 33rpm demo disc (One side of this demo disc features about one-second each clips from each record to reach #1 on Billboard Hot 100 from 1955-1972, a classic and rare seven-inch collectible.)	$40

-albums-

LP(RS)	**CHRONOLOGY OF AMERICAN MUSIC** The complete show (Features the #1 Billboard Hot 100 records from 1955-1972) Many country artists are featured in the production.	$100

CHUCK & BILL (RB)

-singles-

45rpm	**WAY OUT THERE** (57)	Brunswick 55011	$15
45(P)	**WAY OUT THERE** (57) (Yellow promo label)	Brunswick 55011	$12
45rpm	**I WANNA MOVE A LITTLE CLOSER** (58)	Brunswick 55034	$15
45(P)	**I WANNA MOVE A LITTLE CLOSER** (58) (Yellow promo label)	Brunswick 55034	$12

CHUCK WAGON GANG (G)

Columbia 45s $3-8 each

CHUCKY FROM KENTUCKY (N)

-singles-

78rpm	**WHAT IT WAS, WAS FOOTBALL** (51) Part 1, Part 2 (Could this be the original version?)	Republic 500/501	$75
45rpm	**WHAT IT WAS, WAS FOOTBALL** (51) Part 1, Part 2 (Later versions by The Duke of Paducah and Andy Griffth)	Republic 500/501	$50

VARIOUS ARTISTS (CW)

-albums-

LP	**CHURCH IN THE WILDWOOD** (59) (Includes classic original gospel songs by Louvin Brothers, Chester Smith, Tex Ritter, Martha Carson, Tommy Collins and others)	Capitol 1113	$25
LP(P)	**CHURCH IN THE WILDWOOD** (59) (Black promo label)	Capitol 1113	$30

PETE CIOLINO (RB)

-singles-

45rpm	**DADDY JOE** (58)	Recorte 40	$65

GUY CLARK (C)

RCA Victor color vinyl promo 45s $6-8 each

KEN CLARK (CW)

-albums-

LP	**FIDDIN' COUNTRY STYLE** (59) (With Don Anthony)	Starday 114	$25

ROY CLARK (C)

Dot 45s $2-5 each
Dot/ABC 45s $2 each
Other Capitol LPs $5 each
Dot, Hilltop, MCA LPs $2-5 each

-singles-

45(P)	**WHAT'S IT ALL ABOUT** (Nov 78) Public service show (Flip side features Roberta Flack)	W. I. A. A. 342	$12

33(P)	**AIR FORCE PUBLIC SERVICE SPOTS** (79) PSA ads	Air Force 79-19R	$15
	(Twelve cuts, Clark does two, issued with hard cover)		
45(P)	**WHAT'S IT ALL ABOUT** (Nov 82) PSA five-minute show	Southern Baptist MA 3054	$10
	(Includes interview, flip side is Waylon Jennings)		
33(P)	**ELECTRONIC INDUSTRIES** (84) PSA ads	EIA 79791	$15
	(Nine cuts all with Clark, issued with soft cover)		
33(P)	**NEW MINIMUM WAGE PSAS** (86)	U.S. Dept Labor 77281	$15
	(Public service ads)		

-albums-

LP	**THE LIGHTNING FINGERS OF ROY CLARK** (62)	Capitol 1780	$15
LP	**ROY CLARK SINGS THE TIP OF MY FINGERS** (63)	Capitol 1972	$12
LP	**ROY CLARK GUITAR SPECTACULAR** (65)	Capitol 2425	$12
LP	**ROY CLARK SINGS LONESOME LOVE BALLADS** (66)	Capitol 2452	$10
2LP	**ROY CLARK** (74)	Dot 1040	$10

SANFORD CLARK (RB)
Dot blue promo label 45s $15 each
Jamie and Trey 45s $8 each

-singles-

45rpm	**THE FOOL** (55)	MCI 1003	$40
45rpm	**USTA BE MY BABY** (56)	Dot 15516	$10
45rpm	**OOO BABY** (56)	Dot 15534	$18
45rpm	**THE GLORY OF LOVE** (57)	Dot 15556	$10
45rpm	**LOU BE DOO** (58)	Dot 15585	$10
45rpm	**SWANEE RIVER ROCK** (58)	Dot 15646	$15
45rpm	**MODERN ROMANCE** (58)	Dot 15738	$40
45rpm	**THE FOOL** (66) Produced by Waylon Jennings	Ramco 1972	$10

YODELING SLIM CLARK (CW)
Paris, Plymouth, and Palace LPs $5-10 each

-EPs-

EP	**FAMOUS COWBOY SONGS**	Remington 32	$40

-albums-

10"LP	**WESTERN SONGS & DANCES** (54)	Playhouse 2017	$40
LP	**COWBOY AND YODEL SONGS** (62)	Continental 1505	$30
LP	**COWBOY SONGS** (63)	Masterseal 57	$25
	(Budget label)		
LP	**COWBOY SONGS VOL. 2** (64)	Masterseal 135	$25
	(Budget label)		
LP	**YODELING SLIM CLARK SINGS JIMMY ROGERS** (66)	Palomino 300	$75
LP	**YODELING SLIM CLARK SINGS & YODELS FAVORITE MONTANA SLIM SONGS OF THE MOUNTAINS & PLAINS VOL. 1** (66)	Palomino 301	$60
LP	**YODELING SLIM CLARK SINGS & YODELS FAVORITE MONTANA SLIM SONGS OF THE MOUNTAINS & PLAINS VOL. 2** (66)	Palomino 303	$50
LP	**I FEEL A TRIP COMING ON** (66)	Palomino 306	$30
LP	**OLD CHESTNUTS** (67)	Palomino 307	$40
LP	**YODELING SLIM CLARK'S 50TH ANNIVERSARY ALBUM** (68)	Palomino 314	$50
	(Limited gold vinyl version)		

JOE CLAY (RB)

-singles-

45rpm	**DUCK TAIL** (58)	Vik (RCA) 0211	$30
45(P)	**DUCK TAIL** (58)	Vik 0211	$25
	(White promo label)		
45rpm	**GET ON THE RIGHT TRACK** (58)	Vik 0218	$25
45(P)	**GET ON THE RIGHT TRACK** (58)	Vik 0218	$20
	(White promo label)		

PAUL CLAYTON (CW)
Folk artist
Also recorded for Elektra, Riverside, and Stinson

-albums-

These are the only LPs considered country

10"LP	**FOLK SONGS & BALLADS OF VIRGINIA** (56)	Folkways 47	$40
10"LP	**CUMBERLAND MOUNTAIN FOLK SONGS** (57)	Folkways 2007	$25

TOMMY CLAYTON (CW)

-singles-

45rpm	**ONE HAS MY NAME** (55)	Royale 45203	$10

DON CLEARY (CW)

-albums-

LP	**DON CLEARY SONGS TRADITIONAL COWBOY SONGS** (66)	Palomino 302	$50
	(Don Cleary owned the label)		

EDDIE CLEARY (RB)

-singles-

45rpm	**THINK IT OVER BABY** (58)	Kawana 102	$65

BILL TAYLOR & THE CLEFS (R)

-singles-

45rpm	**LITTLE JEWEL** (58)	Fame 502	$50

VASSAR CLEMENTS (CW)
One of the most recorded country studio musicians
Recorded solo with several modern labels

-albums-

LP	**VASSAR CLEMENTS** (75)	Mercury 1022	$10
LP	**SUPERBOW** (76)	Mercury 1058	$10

ZEKE CLEMENTS (CW)

-albums-

LP	**THE MAN FROM MUSIC MOUNTAIN** (70)	Guest Star 1443	$15
	(Budget label)		

EDDIE CLETRO (RB)

-singles-

45rpm	**FLYIN' SAUCER BOOGIE** (58)	Lariat 101	$75

BENNY CLIFF (RB)

-singles-

45rpm	**SHAKE UM UP ROCK** (58)	Drift 1441	$150

BILL CLIFTON (CW)
With the Dixie Mountain Boys
Mercury 45s $5-8 each

-albums-

LP	**MOUNTAIN FOLK SONGS** (59)	Starday 111	$30
LP	**THE CARTER FAMILY MEMORIAL ALBUM** (61)	Starday 146	$25
LP	**THE BLUEGRASS SOUND OF BILL CLIFTON** (61)	Starday 159	$20
LP	**SOLDIER, SING ME A SONG** (63)	Starday 213	$18
LP	**CODE OF THE MOUNTAINS** (64)	Starday 271	$18
LP	**MOUNTAIN BLUEGRASS SONGS** (66)	Nashville 2004	$15
LP	**BLUEGRASS IN THE AMERICAN TRADITION** (67)	Nashville 2018	$15

PATSY CLINE (CW)
Decca 78s including and after 30221 are worth $10 each
4-Star 45s $4-6 each
Decca 45s in the 25000 series $4-8 each
RCA Victor duet 45s $3 each
MCA 45s $2 each
Longines Symphonette LPs $10-12 each
Accord LPs $4 each
51 West LPs $3 each
Country Fidelity $4 each
Album Globe, HSRD and Allegiance LPs $3 each
Other MCA LPs $2-5 each

-singles-

45rpm	**HUNGRY FOR LOVE** (56)	Everest 2011	$15
45(P)	**HUNGRY FOR LOVE** (56)	Everest 2011	$10
	(White promo label)		
45rpm	**LOVE ME LOVE ME HONEY DO** (57)	Everest 2052	$15
45(P)	**LOVE ME LOVE ME HONEY DO** (57)	Everest 2052	$10
	(White promo label)		
45rpm	**THERE HE GOES** (57)	Everest 2060	$15
45(P)	**THERE HE GOES** (57)	Everest 2060	$10
	(White promo label)		
78rpm	**WALKING AFTER MIDNIGHT** (57)	Decca 30221	$20
78(P)	**WALKING AFTER MIDNIGHT** (57)	Decca 30221	$25
	(Pink promo label)		
45rpm	**WALKING AFTER MIDNIGHT** (57)	Decca 30221	$12
45rpm	**WALKING AFTER MIDNIGHT** (57)	Decca 30221	$30
	(Price includes picture sleeve)		
45(P)	**WALKING AFTER MIDNIGHT** (57)	Decca 30221	$12
	(Pink promo label)		
45rpm	**TODAY, TOMORROW AND FOREVER** (58)	Decca 30339	$15
45(P)	**TODAY, TOMORROW AND FOREVER** (58)	Decca 30339	$12
	(Pink promo label)		
45rpm	**I DON'T WANTA** (58) Blue label	Everest 20005	$15
45(P)	**I DON'T WANTA** (58)	Everest 20005	$18
	(White promo label)		
45rpm	**I DON'T WANTA** (59) Black label	Decca 30504	$25
45(P)	**I DON'T WANTA** (59)	Decca 30504	$20
	(Green promo label)		

45rpm	**JUST OUT OF REACH** (60)	Decca 30746	$15
45(P)	**JUST OUT OF REACH** (60)	Decca 30746	$12
	(Pink promo label)		
45rpm	**DEAR GOD** (60)	Decca 30794	$15
45(P)	**DEAR GOD** (60)	Decca 30794	$12
	(Pink promo label)		
45rpm	**CRY NOT FOR ME** (60)	Decca 30846	$15
45(P)	**CRY NOT FOR ME** (60)	Decca 30846	$12
	(Pink promo label)		
45rpm	**GOTTA LOTTA RHYTHM** (60)	Decca 30929	$18
45(P)	**GOTTA LOTTA RHYTHM** (60)	Decca 30929	$15
	(Pink promo label)		
45rpm	**LOVESICK BLUES** (60)	Decca 31061	$15
45(P)	**LOVESICK BLUES** (60)	Decca 31061	$12
	(Pink promo label)		
45rpm	**I FALL TO PIECES** (61)	Decca 31205	$12
45(P)	**I FALL TO PIECES** (61)	Decca 31205	$15
	(Pink promo label)		
45rpm	**CRAZY** (61)	Decca 31317	$10
45(P)	**CRAZY** (61)	Decca 31317	$12
	(Pink promo label)		
45rpm	**SHE'S GOT YOU** (61)	Decca 31354	$12
45(P)	**SHE'S GOT YOU** (61)	Decca 31354	$10
	(Pink promo label)		
45rpm	**WHEN I GET THROUGH WITH YOU** (62)	Decca 31377	$12
45rpm	**WHEN I GET THROUGH WITH YOU** (62)	Decca 31377	$25
	(Price includes picture sleeve)		
45(P)	**WHEN I GET THROUGH WITH YOU** (62)	Decca 31377	$10
	(Pink promo label)		
45rpm	**HEARTACHES** (62)	Decca 31429	$12
45(P)	**HEARTACHES** (62)	Decca 31429	$10
	(Pink promo label)		
45rpm	**TRA LE LA LE LA TRIANGLE** (63)	Decca 31455	$12
45(P)	**TRA LE LA LE LA TRIANGLE** (63)	Decca 31455	$10
	(Pink promo label)		
45rpm	**BACK IN BABY'S ARMS** (63)	Decca 31483	$12
45(P)	**BACK IN BABY'S ARMS** (63)	Decca 31483	$10
	(Pink promo label)		
45rpm	**FADED LOVE** (63)	Decca 31522	$12
45(P)	**FADED LOVE** (63)	Decca 31522	$10
	(Pink promo label)		
45rpm	**HE CALLED ME BABY** (63)	Decca 31671	$12
45(P)	**HE CALLED ME BABY** (63)	Decca 31671	$10
	(Pink promo label)		
45rpm	**I CAN'T HELP IT** (64)	Decca 31754	$10
45(P)	**I CAN'T HELP IT** (64)	Decca 31754	$12
	(Pink promo label)		

-EPs-

EP(P)	**I DON'T WANTA** (56) Plus three other songs	Patsy Cline (4-Star) 25	$40
	(Promo only, no cardboard sleeve)		
EP(P)	**PATSY CLINE** (57)	Patsy Cline (4-Star)	$40
	(Promo only, no cardboard sleeve)		
EP	**SONGS BY PATSY CLINE** (58)	Coral 81159	$50
	(Sacred songs)		
EP	**PATSY CLINE** (58)	Decca 2542	$40
EP	**PATSY CLINE** (61)	Decca 2703	$25
	(Featuring "I Fall To Pieces")		
EP	**PATSY CLINE** (61)	Decca 2707	$25
	(Featuring "Crazy")		
EP	**PATSY CLINE** (62)	Decca 2719	$25
	(Featuring "She's Got You")		
EP	**PATSY CLINE** (62)	Decca 2729	$25
	(Featuring "So Wrong")		
EP	**PATSY CLINE** (63)	Decca 2757	$25
	(Featuring "Leavin' On Your Mind")		
EP	**DEAR GOD** (63)	Decca 2759	$25
EP	**PATSY CLINE** (64)	Decca 2768	$25
	(Featuring "I'm Blue Again")		
EP	**SOMEDAY YOU'LL WANT ME TO WANT YOU** (64)	Decca 2770	$25
EP	**PORTRAIT OF PATSY CLINE** (65)	Decca 2794	$25
EP	**LOVE LETTERS IN THE SAND** (65)	Decca 2802	$25
EP(P)	**PATSY CLINE** (63) Jukebox LLP	Decca 34130	$25
	(Issued with a hard cover)		
EP(P)	**PATSY CLINE** (64) Jukebox LLP	Decca 34131	$25
	(Issued with a hard cover)		
EP(P)	**PATSY CLINE** (64) Jukebox LLP	Decca 34132	$25
	(Issued with a hard cover)		

EP(P)	**PATSY CLINE** (64) Jukebox LLP		Decca 34133	$25
	(Issued with a hard cover)			
		-albums-		
LP	**PATSY CLINE** (57)		Decca 8611	$40
LP(P)	**PATSY CLINE** (57)		Decca 8611	$50
	(Pink promo label)			
LP	**PATSY CLINE SHOWCASE** (61) With the Jordanaires		Decca 4202	$25
LP(P)	**PATSY CLINE SHOWCASE** (61)		Decca 4202	$35
	(Pink promo label)			
LP	**SENTIMENTALLY YOURS** (62)		Decca 4282	$25
LP(P)	**SENTIMENTALLY YOURS** (62)		Decca 4282	$35
	(Pink promo label)			
LP	**PATSY CLINE'S GOLDEN HITS** (62)		Everest 1200	$25
LP(P)	**PATSY CLINE'S GOLDEN HITS** (62)		Everest 1200	$40
	(White promo label)			
2LP	**THE PATSY CLINE STORY** (63)		Decca 176	$30
2LP(P)	**THE PATSY CLINE STORY** (63) Pink promo labels		Decca 176	$40
	(Price on Decca 176 includes booklet)			
LP	**ENCORES** (63)		Everest 1204	$25
LP	**IN MEMORIAM** (63)		Everest 1217	$20
LP	**A LEGEND** (63)		Everest 1223	$20
LP	**REFLECTIONS** (64)		Everest 1229	$20
LP	**A PORTRAIT OF PATSY CLINE** (64)		Decca 4508	$25
LP(P)	**A PORTRAIT OF PATSY CLINE** (64)		Decca 4508	$30
	(Decca promo label)			
LP	**THAT'S HOW A HEARTACHE BEGINS** (64)		Decca 4586	$25
LP(P)	**THAT'S HOW A HEARTACHE BEGINS** (64)		Decca 4586	$30
	(Decca promo label)			
LP	**TODAY, TOMORROW, FOREVER** (64)		Hilltop 6001	$20
LP	**GONE BUT NOT FORGOTTEN** (65)		Starday 346	$35
	(Patsy Cline, Cowboy Copas and Hawkshaw Hawkins)			
LP	**HERE'S PATSY CLINE** (65)		Vocalion 3753	$25
LP(P)	**HERE'S PATSY CLINE** (65)		Vocalion 3753	$35
	(White promo label)			
LP	**GOTTA LOT OF RHYTHM IN MY SOUL** (65)		Metro 540	$20
LP(P)	**GOTTA LOT OF RHYTHM IN MY SOUL** (65)		Metro 540	$25
	(Yellow promo label)			
LP	**I CAN'T FORGET YOU** (65)		Hilltop 6016	$18
LP	**STOP THE WORLD & LET ME GET OFF** (66)		Hilltop 6039	$15
LP	**PATSY CLINE'S GREATEST HITS** (67)		Decca 4854	$15
LP(P)	**PATSY CLINE'S GREATEST HITS** (67)		Decca 4854	$18
	(White promo label)			
LP	**MISS COUNTRY MUSIC** (67)		Hilltop 6054	$18
LP	**IN CARE OF THE BLUES** (68)		Hilltop 6072	$15
LP	**PATSY CLINE IN CARE OF THE BLUES** (68)		Sears 127	$20
2LP	**A PORTRAIT OF PATSY** (69)		Columbia 5280	$25
	(Columbia Record Club release)			
LP	**COUNTRY GREAT** (69)		Vocalion 3872	$18
LP(P)	**COUNTRY GREAT** (69)		Vocalion 3872	$25
	(White promo label)			
2LP	**THE PATSY CLINE STORY** (80)		MCA 4038	$12
	(Reissue of Decca 176)			
		-radio shows-		
16"(RS)	**NAVY HOEDOWN** (50s)		U.S. Navy	$30-60
	(Music and interviews, Patsy Cline is guest)			
LP(RS)	**COUNTRY MUSIC TIME** (60s) Show 227		U.S. Air Force	$175-225
	(Flip side features Benny Martin)			
LP(RS)	**COUNTRY MUSIC TIME** (70s) Show 258		U.S. Air Force	$30-50
	(Flip side features the Jordanaires)			

LOY CLINGMAN (RB)

-singles-

45rpm	**IT'S NOTHING TO ME** (57) w/Al Casey on guitar	Liberty Bell 106	$20
45rpm	**IT'S NOTHING TO ME** (57)	Dot 15567	$15

JESSIE COATES (RB)

-singles-

45rpm	**NOBODY CAN TAKE MY BABY** (58)	Headline 101	$50

EDDIE COCHRAN/COCHRAN BROTHERS (RB)

Includes listings by Jewel and Eddie, The Kelly Four

-singles-

45rpm	**WALKIN' STICK BOOGIE** (56)	Cash 1021	$100
45rpm	**TIRED AND SLEEPY** (56)	Ekko 3001	$125
45rpm	**TWO BLUE SINGING STARS** (56)	Ekko 1003	$85
45rpm	**GUILTY CONSCIENCE** (56)	Ekko 1005	$85
	(Above singles by the Cochran Brothers)		

45rpm	**SKINNY JIM** (56)	Crest 1026	$125
45(P)	**SKINNY JIM** (56)	Crest 1026	$150
	(White promo label)		
45rpm	**STROLLIN' GUITAR** (57) By The Kelly Four	Silver 1001	$15
	(Eddie Cochran and Jerry Capehart)		
45(P)	**STROLLIN' GUITAR** (57) White promo label	Silver 1001	$30
	(White promo label)		
45rpm	**STROLLIN' GUITAR** (57) By Jewel and Eddie	Silver 1004	$15
	(Eddie Cochran and Jewel Atkins)		
45(P)	**STROLLIN' GUITAR** (57)	Silver 1004	$30
	(White promo label)		
45rpm	**OPPORTUNITY** (57) By Jewel and Eddie	Silver 1004	$15
	(Eddie Cochran and Jewel Atkins)		
45(P)	**OPPORTUNITY** (57) White promo label	Silver 1004	$30
	("Opportunity" and "Strollin' Guitar" have the same label number)		
45rpm	**ANNIE HAD A PARTY** (57) By The Kelly Four	Silver 1006	$15
45(P)	**ANNIE HAD A PARTY** (57)	Silver 1006	$25
	(White promo label)		
45rpm	**ROUGH STUFF** (57)	Capehart 5003	$20
45rpm	**ROUGH STUFF** (57)	Capehart 5003	$175
	(Price includes picture sleeve)		
45(P)	**ROUGH STUFF** (57)	Capehart 5003	$35
	(White promo label)		
78rpm	**SITTIN' IN THE BALCONY** (57)	Liberty 55056	$100
45rpm	**SITTIN' IN THE BALCONY** (57)	Liberty 55056	$15
45(P)	**SITTIN' IN THE BALCONY** (57)	Liberty 55056	$100
	(White promo label)		
78rpm	**MEAN WHEN I'M MAD** (57)	Liberty 55070	$85
45rpm	**MEAN WHEN I'M MAD** (57)	Liberty 55070	$25
45rpm	**MEAN WHEN I'M MAD** (57)	Liberty 55070	$400
	(Price includes picture sleeve)		
45(P)	**MEAN WHEN I'M MAD** (57)	Liberty 55070	$75
	(White promo label)		
78rpm	**DRIVE IN SHOW** (57)	Liberty 55087	$150
45rpm	**DRIVE IN SHOW** (57)	Liberty 55087	$20
45(P)	**DRIVE IN SHOW** (57)	Liberty 55087	$75
	(White promo label)		
78rpm	**TWENTY FLIGHT ROCK** (58)	Liberty 55112	$125
45rpm	**TWENTY FLIGHT ROCK** (58)	Liberty 55112	$25
45(P)	**TWENTY FLIGHT ROCK** (58)	Liberty 55112	$75
	(White promo label)		
78rpm	**JEANNIE JEANNIE JEANNIE** (58)	Liberty 55123	$125
45rpm	**JEANNIE JEANNIE JEANNIE** (58)	Liberty 55123	$20
45(P)	**JEANNIE JEANNIE JEANNIE** (58)	Liberty 55123	$25
	(White promo label)		
78rpm	**PRETTY GIRL** (58)	Liberty 55138	$150
45rpm	**PRETTY GIRL** (58)	Liberty 55138	$20
45(P)	**PRETTY GIRL** (58)	Liberty 55138	$75
	(White promo label)		
78rpm	**SUMMERTIME BLUES** (58)	Liberty 55144	$400
	(One of the rarest rock 78s)		
45rpm	**SUMMERTIME BLUES** (58)	Liberty 55144	$20
45(P)	**SUMMERTIME BLUES** (58)	Liberty 55144	$75
	(White promo label)		
45rpm	**TEENAGE HEAVEN** (58)	Liberty 55177	$20
45(P)	**TEENAGE HEAVEN** (58)	Liberty 55177	$40
	(White promo label)		
45rpm	**SOMETHING ELSE** (59)	Liberty 55203	$20
45(P)	**SOMETHING ELSE** (59)	Liberty 55203	$40
	(White promo labels)		
45rpm	**LITTLE ANGEL** (59)	Liberty 55217	$20
45(P)	**LITTLE ANGEL** (59)	Liberty 55217	$40
	(White promo labels)		
45rpm	**CUT ACROSS SHORTY** (59)	Liberty 55242	$20
45(P)	**CUT ACROSS SHORTY** (59)	Liberty 55242	$40
	(White promo label)		
45rpm	**SWEETIE PIE** (59)	Liberty 55278	$20
45(P)	**SWEETIE PIE** (59)	Liberty 55278	$30
	(White promo label)		
45rpm	**WEEKEND** (60)	Liberty 55389	$18
45(P)	**WEEKEND** (60)	Liberty 55389	$30
	(White promo label)		

-EPs-

EP	**SINGIN' TO MY BABY** (58)	Liberty 3061-1	$100
EP	**SINGIN' TO MY BABY** (58)	Liberty 3061-2	$100
EP	**SINGIN' TO MY BABY** (58)	Liberty 3061-3	$100

NOTES

-albums-

LP	**SINGIN' TO MY BABY** (58)	Liberty 3061	$150
LP(P)	**SINGIN' TO MY BABY** (58)	Liberty 3061	$300
	(White promo label)		
LP	**EDDIE COCHRAN MEMORIAL ALBUM** (60)	Liberty 3172	$75
LP(P)	**EDDIE COCHRAN MEMORIAL ALBUM** (60)	Liberty 3172	$150
	(White promo label)		
LP	**NEVER TO BE FORGOTTEN** (62)	Liberty 3220	$75
LP(P)	**NEVER TO BE FORGOTTEN** (62)	Liberty 3220	$125
	(White promo label)		
	See Hank Cochran		

HANK COCHRAN (C)
Recorded with, but not related to, Eddie Cochran
RCA Victor 45s $2-4 each
Capitol 45s $1-2 each
Capitol LPs $5-10 each
Elektra LPs $3 each

-albums-

LP	**HITS FROM THE HEART** (63)	RCA Victor 3303	$20
LP	**GOING IN TRAINING** (65)	RCA Victor 3431	$18
LP	**THE HEART OF HANK COCHRAN** (68)	Monument 18089	$15
	See Eddie Cochran		

-radio shows-

LP(RS)	**COUNTRY MUSIC TIME** (60s)	U.S. Air Force	$10-20
	(Music and interview)		

JACKIE LEE COCHRAN (RB)

-singles-

45rpm	**ENDLESS LOVE** (57)	Spry 120	$150
45rpm	**I WANNA SEE YOU** (57)	Jaguar 3031	$50
45rpm	**BUY A CAR** (58)	Viv 102	$100
45rpm	**BUY A CAR** (58)	Viv 988	$100
45(P)	**BUY A CAR** (58)	ABC Paramount 9930	$75
	(White promo label)		
45rpm	**HIP SHAKIN' MAMA** (58)	Sims 107	$100
45(P)	**HIP SHAKIN' MAMA** (58)	Sims 107	$100
	(White promo label)		
45rpm	**MAMA, DON'T YOU THINK I KNOW** (59)	Decca 30206	$75
45rpm	**MAMA, DON'T YOU THINK I KNOW** (59)	Decca 30206	$75
	(Decca promo label)		

DAVID ALLAN COE (CW)
Columbia 45s $2-5 each
Columbia LPs $3-6 each

-albums-

LP	**PENITENTIARY BLUES** (77)	SSS International 9	$75
	(Withdrawn early, rare)		
LP(P)	**THE UNDERGROUND ALBUM** (78)	DAC Records	$60
	(Black and white cover, "X" material)		

-radio shows-

LP(RS)	**COUNTRY MUSIC TIME** (80s)	U.S. Air Force	$40-60
	(Live concert)		

COKE (COCA-COLA) JINGLES (ADS)

-singles-

45(P)	**COCA-COLA JINGLE A GO-GO** (62) Seven-inch	Coca-Cola Vol 1	$75
	(With small center hole)		
45(P)	**COCA-COLA JINGLE A GO-GO** (62) Seven-inch	Coca-Cola Vol 2	$200
	(With small center hole, artists are Ray Charles and Everly Brothers)		
45(P)	**COCA-COLA JINGLE A GO-GO** (63) Seven-inch	Coca-Cola Vol 1	$200
	(With small center hole)		
45(P)	**COCA-COLA JINGLE A-GO-GO** (63) Seven-inch	Coca-Cola Vol 2	$50
	(Small center hole)		
33(P)	**BUBBLE-UP** (Coca-Cola) (65) With Stan Freberg	Coca-Cola 2227	$75
	(Issued with a cover, pressed by Capitol)		

-EPs-

EP(P)	**SWING THE JINGLE** Price includes picture sleeve	Coca-Cola	$100
	(This 45rpm includes the Drifters, Lou Bravos, Lesley Gore and Roy Orbison)		
EP(P)	**THINGS GO BETTER WITH COKE** Mail-in offer	Coke GMBH 105 112	$100
	(Artists; Supremes, Ray Charles, Petula Clark and Dave Dee, Becky, Mick & Tich)		
	(German press, available in USA, flip side is "I'll Lose You")		

There are many other Coke records with 30 and 60-second
radio ads featuring top artists on both seven and twelve-inch
discs. Starting in 1970 Coke issued spots for various music
formats. Johnny Cash was one country artist to sing for Coke.

-albums-

LP(P)	**SWING THE JINGLE** (60s) The Four Seasons	Coca-Cola	$400
	(Six tracks, price includes special cover)		

COKER FAMILY (CW)
Al Coker, Alvadean Coker, Sandy Coker

-singles-

45rpm	**SUGAR DOLL** (54) Alvadean Coker	Abbott 163	$15
45rpm	**MEADOWLARK MELODY** (54) Sandy Coker and His Coker Band	Abbott 171	$10
45rpm	**WE'RE GONNA BOP** (54) Alvadean Coker	Abbott 176	$35
45rpm	**ARE YOU THE ONE** (55) Jim Reeves and Alvadean Coker	Abbott 184	$18
45rpm	**ROCK ISLAND RIDE** (56) Sandy Coker	Decca 30051	$15
45(P)	**ROCK ISLAND LINE** (56)	Decca 30051	$10
	(Green promo label)		
45rpm	**THERE'S A TEAR IN THE EYE OF THE MAN IN THE MOON** (56)	Decca 30052	$15
	(Alvadean Coker)		
45(P)	**THERE'S A TEAR IN THE EYE OF THE MAN IN THE MOON** (56)	Decca 30052	$10
	(Green promo label)		
45rpm	**DON'T GO BABY** (57) Al Coker	Decca 30053	$30
45(P)	**DON'T GO BABY** (57)	Decca 30053	$20
	(Green promo label)		
45rpm	**ONE MORE CHANCE** (58) Al Coker	Decca 30490	$18
45(P)	**ONE MORE CHANCE** (58)	Decca 30490	$15
	(Green promo label)		

BEN COLDER See Sheb Wooley

CURLEY COLDIRON (CW)
And the Circle C Boys
Other Sullivan 45s $4-8 each

-singles-

45(P)	**CHEROKEE BABY** (58)	Sullivan 520	$10

-EPs-

EP(P)	**CURLEY COLDIRON & THE CIRCLE C BOYS** (58)	Sullivan 1000	$10

DON COLE (RB)

-singles-

45rpm	**SWEET LOVIN' HONEY** (58)	Kent 305	$25
45rpm	**SNAKE EYED MAMA** (58)	RPM 502	$30

LEE COLE (RB)

-singles-

45rpm	**COOL BABY** (58)	Mist 1010	$40

LES COLE (RB)

-singles-

45rpm	**BEE BOPPIN' DADDY** (58)	D 1010	$100

SONNY COLE (RB)

-singles-

45rpm	**I DREAMED I WAS ELVIS** (57)	Excel 123	$50

RAY COLEMAN (R & B)

-singles-

45rpm	**JUKEBOX ROCK & ROLL** (58)	Arcade 147	$60

MARGIE COLLIE (CW)
Other Decca 45s $4-8 each

-singles-

45rpm	**HIS NEW WAR BRIDE** (54)	Decca 28701	$12

EDDIE COLLINS (RB)

-singles-

45rpm	**PATIENCE BABY** (58)	Fernwood 104	$40

ROBERT COLLINS (Polka)
MGM 45s $5-8 each

TOMMY COLLINS (CW)
Other Columbia 45s $4-8 each

-singles-

78rpm	**YOU GOTTA HAVE A LICENSE** (53)	Capitol 2584	$20
78(P)	**YOU GOTTA HAVE A LICENSE** (53)	Capitol 2584	$18
	(White promo label)		
45rpm	**YOU GOTTA HAVE A LICENSE** (53)	Capitol 2584	$18

45(P)	**YOU GOTTA HAVE A LICENSE** (53)	Capitol 2584	$15
	(White promo label)		
78rpm	**YOU BETTER NOT DO THAT** (54)	Capitol 2701	$18
78(P)	**YOU BETTER NOT DO THAT** (54)	Capitol 2701	$15
	(White promo label)		
45rpm	**YOU BETTER NOT DO THAT** (54)	Capitol 2701	$18
45(P)	**YOU BETTER NOT DO THAT** (54)	Capitol 2701	$15
	(White promo label)		
78rpm	**I ALWAYS GET A SOUVENIR** (54)	Capitol 2806	$15
78(P)	**I ALWAYS GET A SOUVENIR** (54)	Capitol 2806	$12
	(White promo label)		
45rpm	**I ALWAYS GET A SOUVENIR** (54)	Capitol 2806	$15
45(P)	**I ALWAYS GET A SOUVENIR** (54)	Capitol 2806	$10
	(White promo label)		
78rpm	**WHATCHA GONNA DO NOW** (54)	Capitol 2891	$18
78(P)	**WHATCHA GONNA DO NOW** (54)	Capitol 2891	$15
	(White promo label)		
45rpm	**WHATCHA GONNA DO NOW** (54)	Capitol 2891	$18
45(P)	**WHATCHA GONNA DO NOW** (54)	Capitol 2891	$15
	(White promo label)		
78rpm	**UNTIED/BOOB-I-LAK** (55)	Capitol 3017	$15
78(P)	**UNTIED/BOOB-I-LAK** (55)	Capitol 3017	$12
	(White promo label)		
45rpm	**UNTIED/BOOB-I-LAK** (55)	Capitol 3017	$15
45(P)	**UNTIED/BOOB-I-LAK** (55)	Capitol 3017	$12
	(White promo label)		
78rpm	**UNTIED/EVER SINCE YOU WENT AWAY** (55)	Capitol 3065	$15
78(P)	**UNTIED/EVER SINCE YOU WENT AWAY** (55)	Capitol 3065	$12
	(White promo label)		
45rpm	**UNTIED/EVER SINCE YOU WENT AWAY** (55)	Capitol 3065	$15
45(P)	**UNTIED/EVER SINCE YOU WENT AWAY** (55)	Capitol 3065	$12
	(White promo label)		
78rpm	**IT TICKLES** (55)	Capitol 3082	$15
78(P)	**IT TICKLES** (55)	Capitol 3082	$12
	(White promo label)		
45rpm	**IT TICKLES** (55)	Capitol 3082	$15
45(P)	**IT TICKLES** (55)	Capitol 3082	$12
	(White promo label)		
78rpm	**I'LL BE GONE** (55)	Capitol 3289	$12
78(P)	**I'LL BE GONE** (55)	Capitol 3289	$10
	(White promo label)		
45rpm	**I'LL BE GONE** (55)	Capitol 3289	$12
45(P)	**I'LL BE GONE** (55)	Capitol 3289	$10
	(White promo label)		
78rpm	**WHAT KIND OF SWEETHEART ARE YOU** (55)	Capitol 3370	$12
78(P)	**WHAT KIND OF SWEETHEART ARE YOU** (55)	Capitol 3370	$10
	(White promo label)		
45rpm	**WHAT KIND OF SWEETHEART ARE YOU** (55)	Capitol 3370	$12
45(P)	**WHAT KIND OF SWEETHEART ARE YOU** (55)	Capitol 3370	$10
	(White promo label)		
78rpm	**NO LOVE HAVE I** (56)	Capitol 3466	$12
78(P)	**NO LOVE HAVE I** (56)	Capitol 3466	$10
	(White promo label)		
45rpm	**NO LOVE HAVE I** (56)	Capitol 3466	$12
45(P)	**NO LOVE HAVE I** (56)	Capitol 3466	$10
	(White promo label)		
78rpm	**I WISH I HAD DIED IN MY CRADLE** (56)	Capitol 3591	$10
45rpm	**I WISH I HAD DIED IN MY CRADLE** (56)	Capitol 3591	$10
78rpm	**ALL OF THE MONKEES AIN'T IN THE ZOO** (57)	Capitol 3665	$12
45rpm	**ALL OF THE MONKEES AIN'T IN THE ZOO** (57)	Capitol 3665	$12
45rpm	**A LOVE IS BORN** (58)	Capitol 3789	$12
45rpm	**A HUNDRED YEARS FROM NOW** (58)	Capitol 4263	$12
45rpm	**THE WRECK OF THE OLD 97** (58)	Capitol 4327	$15
45(P)	**THE WRECK OF THE OLD 97** (58)	Capitol 4327	$10
	(Red promo label)		
45rpm	**SUMMER'S ALMOST GONE** (58)	Capitol 4421	$12
45(P)	**SUMMER'S ALMOST GONE** (58)	Capitol 4421	$10
	(Red promo label)		
45rpm	**BLACK CAT** (58)	Capitol 4495	$25
45(P)	**BLACK CAT** (58)	Capitol 4495	$20
	(Red promo label)		
45rpm	**IF I COULD JUST GO BACK** (62)	Capitol 5117	$12
45rpm	**ALL OF THE MONKEES AIN'T IN THE ZOO** (64)	Capitol 5345	$12
45rpm	**TAKE ME BACK TO THE GOOD OLD DAYS** (66)	Tower 213	$10
45(P)	**TAKE ME BACK TO THE GOOD OLD DAYS** (66)	Tower 213	$12
	(White promo label)		

45rpm	**ERNEST TUBB 78'S** (80)	Music America 106	$10
	The song "Leonard," recorded by Merle Haggard (MCA 51048)		
	in 1980 is about Tommy Collins		

-EPs-

EP	**TOMMY COLLINS** (55)	Capitol 607	$25
EP	**WORDS AND MUSIC COUNTRY STYLE** (57) Vol 1	Capitol 1-776	$30
EP	**WORDS AND MUSIC COUNTRY STYLE** (57) Vol 2	Capitol 2-776	$30
EP	**WORDS AND MUSIC COUNTRY STYLE** (57) Vol 3	Capitol 3-776	$30
EP	**LIGHT OF THE LORD** (59) Vol 1	Capitol 1-1125	$25
	(Gospel album)		
EP	**LIGHT OF THE LORD** (59) Vol 2	Capitol 2-1125	$25
EP	**LIGHT OF THE LORD** (59) Vol 3	Capitol 3-1125	$25
EP	**THIS IS TOMMY COLLINS** (59) Vol 1	Capitol 1-1196	$20
EP	**THIS IS TOMMY COLLINS** (59) Vol 2	Capitol 2-1196	$20
EP	**THIS IS TOMMY COLLINS** (59) Vol 3	Capitol 3-1196	$20

-albums-

LP	**WORDS AND MUSIC COUNTRY STYLE** (57)	Capitol 776	$100
LP(P)	**WORDS AND MUSIC COUNTRY STYLE** (57)	Capitol 776	$125
	(Capitol promo label)		
LP	**LIGHT OF THE LORD** (59)	Capitol 1125	$40
LP(P)	**LIGHT OF THE LORD** (59)	Capitol 1125	$50
	(Capitol promo label)		
LP	**THIS IS TOMMY COLLINS** (59)	Capitol 1196	$50
LP(P)	**THIS IS TOMMY COLLINS** (59)	Capitol 1196	$60
	(Capitol promo label)		
LP	**SONGS I LOVE TO SING** (61)	Capitol 1436	$40
LP(P)	**SONGS I LOVE TO SING** (61)	Capitol 1436	$45
	(Capitol promo label)		
LP	**THE DYNAMIC TOMMY COLLINS** (66)	Columbia 9310	$25
LP(P)	**THE DYNAMIC TOMMY COLLINS** (66)	Columbia 9310	$30
	(Capitol promo label)		
LP	**LET'S LIVE A LITTLE** (66)	Tower 5021	$25
LP(P)	**LET'S LIVE A LITTLE** (66)	Tower 5021	$30
	(White promo label)		
LP	**TOMMY COLLINS ON TOUR** (68)	Columbia 9578	$25
LP(P)	**TOMMY COLLINS ON TOUR** (68)	Columbia 9578	$30
	(White promo label)		
LP	**SHINDIG** (68)	Tower 5107	$25
LP(P)	**SHINDIG** (68)	Tower 5107	$30
	(White promo label)		
LP	**TOMMY COLLINS CALLIN'** (72)	Starday 474	$15

COLLINS KIDS (RB)

-singles-

45rpm	**BEETLE BUG BOP/HUSH MONEY** (55)	Columbia 21470	$25
45(P)	**BEETLE BUG BOP/HUSH MONEY** (55)	Columbia 21470	$20
	(White promo label)		
45rpm	**ROCKAWAY ROCK** (56)	Columbia 21514	$25
45(P)	**ROCKAWAY ROCK** (56)	Columbia 21514	$20
	(White promo label)		
45rpm	**I'M IN MY TEENS** (56)	Columbia 21543	$20
45(P)	**I'M IN MY TEENS** (56)	Columbia 21543	$18
	(White promo label)		
45rpm	**ROCK AND ROLL POLKA** (56)	Columbia 21560	$20
45(P)	**ROCK AND ROLL POLKA** (56)	Columbia 21560	$18
	(White promo label)		
45rpm	**YOU ARE MY SUNSHINE** (57)	Columbia 40760	$12
	(With Carl Smith, Rosemary Clooney, Gene Autry, and		
	Don Cherry)		
45(P)	**YOU ARE MY SUNSHINE** (57)	Columbia 40760	$10
	(White promo label)		
45rpm	**MOVE A LITTLE CLOSER** (57)	Columbia 40824	$18
45(P)	**MOVE A LITTLE CLOSER** (57)	Columbia 40824	$15
	(White promo label)		
45rpm	**HOP, SKIP AND JUMP** (57)	Columbia 40921	$18
45(P)	**HOP, SKIP AND JUMP** (57)	Columbia 40921	$15
	(White promo label)		
45rpm	**PARTY** (57)	Columbia 41012	$30
45(P)	**PARTY** (57)	Columbia 41012	$25
	(White promo label)		
45rpm	**HOY HOY** (57)	Columbia 41087	$25
45(P)	**HOY HOY** (57)	Columbia 41087	$20
	(White promo label)		
45rpm	**MERCY** (58) Lorrie and Larry Collins	Columbia 41149	$25
45(P)	**MERCY** (58)	Columbia 41149	$20
	(White promo label)		
45rpm	**ROCK BOPPIN' BABY/WHISTLE STOP** (58)	Columbia 41225	$30

45(P)	**ROCK BOPPIN' BABY/WHISTLE STOP** (58)	Columbia 41225	$25
	(White promo label)		
45rpm	**SUGAR PLUM** (61)	Columbia 41329	$12
45(P)	**SUGAR PLUM** (61)	Columbia 41329	$10
	(White promo label)		
45rpm	**THE LONESOME ROAD** (61) Lorrie and Larry Collins	Columbia 41541	$12
45(P)	**THE LONESOME ROAD** (61)	Columbia 41541	$10
	(White promo label)		
45rpm	**THAT'S YOUR AFFAIR** (62) Lorrie Collins	Columbia 41673	$12
45(P)	**THAT'S YOUR AFFAIR** (62)	Columbia 41673	$10
	(White promo label)		
45rpm	**GET ALONG HOME CINDY** (62) Larry Collins	Columbia 41953	$12
45(P)	**GET ALONG HOME CINDY** (62)	Columbia 41953	$10
	(White promo label)		
45rpm	**HEY MAMA BOOM-A-LACKA** (62) Larry Collins	Columbia 42534	$12
45(P)	**HEY MAMA BOOM-A-LACKA** (62)	Columbia 42534	$10
	(White promo label)		

-albums-

LP	**INTRODUCING LARRY & LORRIE** (83)	Columbia 38457	$12

JESSI COLTER (CW)
Capitol 45s $2-3 each
RCA Victor LPs $10 each
Capitol LPs $3-6 each

-singles-

45rpm	**YOUNG & INNOCENT** (59) Miriam Johnson	Jamie 1181	$25
	(Miriam Johnson is her real name and this first record is written and produced by Duane Eddy. She later married Eddy and more recently married Waylon Jennings.)		

COMMANDER CODY (C)
Paramount 45s $5 each
Arista, MCA, and Warner 45s $2-4 each
Arista, MCA LPs $5-10 each
Other Warner LPs $10-12 each

-albums-

LP	**LOST IN THE OZONE** (71)	Paramount 6017	$18
LP	**LIVE FROM DEEP IN THE HEARTS OF TEXAS** (74)	Paramount 1017	$15
2LP	**WE'VE GOT A LIVE ONE HERE** (76)	Warner 2939	$10

COMPTON BROTHERS (CW)
Other Dot 45s $2 each
Other Dot LPs $8-10 each

-singles-

45rpm	**PINE GROVE** (71)	Dot 17378	$10
	(Price includes picture sleeve)		

-albums-

LP	**ON TOP OF THE COMPTON BROTHERS** (68)	Dot 25867	$12

LEW CONETTA (RB)

-singles-

45rpm	**YOU GOT ME CRAZY** (57)	Decca 30365	$15
45(P)	**YOU GOT ME CRAZY** (57)	Decca 30365	$10
	(Pink promo label)		
45rpm	**HOLLER LOVE** (59)	Decca 30601	$15
45(P)	**HOLLER LOVE** (59)	Decca 30601	$10
	(Decca promo label)		

JOHN CONLEE (C)
ABC 45s $2-3 each
MCA 45s $1-2 each
Curb 45s $1 each
Columbia 45s $1 each

-radio shows-

LP(RS)	**COUNTRY MUSIC TIME** (80s)	U.S. Air Force	$10-15
	(Music and interviews)		
3LP(RS)	**ON A COUNTRY ROAD** (Mar 83) Box set	Mutual Broadcasting	$10-20
	(Live concert segment features John Conlee)		

EARL THOMAS CONLEY (C)
Sunbird 45s $2-5 each

-singles-

45(P)	**SMOKEY MOUNTAIN MEMORIES** (82)	RCA Victor 13053	$12
	(Yellow label, red vinyl)		
45(P)	**SOMEWHERE BETWEEN RIGHT AND WRONG** (82)	RCA Victor 13320	$10
	(White label, blue vinyl)		

45(P)	**YOUR LOVE'S ON THE LINE** (83)	RCA Victor 13525	$12
	(Gold label, gold vinyl)		
45(P)	**ANGEL IN DISGUISE** (84)	RCA Victor 13758	$10
	(Yellow label, red vinyl)		
45(P)	**HONOR BOUND** (84)	RCA Victor 13960	$10
	(Blue label, blue vinyl)		

-radio shows-

LP(RS)	**COUNTRY MUSIC TIME** (80s)	U.S. Air Force	$10-15
	(Music and interviews)		
3LP(RS)	**SILVER EAGLE** (Jan 83)	Westwood One	$10-20
	(Live concert)		
3LP(RS)	**SILVER EAGLE** (Oct 84) With the Judds	Westwood One	$50-100
	(Live concert)		
3LP(RS)	**SILVER EAGLE** (May 85) With John Anderson	Westwood One	$10-20
	(Live concert)		
3LP(RS)	**AMERICAN EAGLE** (Dec 86) With Nicolette Larson	Westwood One	$15-30
	(Live concert)		
LP(RS)	**LIVE AT GILLEY'S** (Jan 88)	Westwood One	$10-20
	(Live concert)		

TONY CONN (RB)

-singles-

45rpm	**LIKE WOW** (57)	Decca 30813	$45
45(P)	**LIKE WOW** (57)	Decca 30813	$40
	(Pink promo label)		
45rpm	**YOU PRETTY THING** (58)	Decca 30865	$45
45(P)	**YOU PRETTY THING** (58)	Decca 30865	$40
	(Pink promo label)		

RAY CONNIFF (RB,AC)
Best known for adult instrumental music; recorded rockabilly as Jimmy Richards
Columbia color vinyl 45s $3 each
Columbia Stereo EPs (Jukebox use) $3 each

-singles-

45rpm	**PIGGY BANK BOOGIE** (54)	Brunswick 80244	$25
45(P)	**PIGGY BANK BOOGIE** (54)	Brunswick 8024	$18
	(White promo label)		
45rpm	**STROLLIN' AND BOPPIN'** (59) Jimmy Richards	Columbia 41083	$15
45(P)	**STROLLIN' AND BOPPIN'** (59)	Columbia 41083	$12
	(White promo label)		
45(P)	**HOLIDAY GREETINGS VOICE TRACKS** (60s) Green vinyl	Columbia 111922	$15
	(Thirteen cuts, ten seconds each, four by Conniff)		

-albums-

LP	**DANCE THE BOP** (57)	Columbia 1004	$25
	(Includes "The Drop," version of "Singing the Blues")		
LP(P)	**DANCE THE BOP** (57)	Columbia 1004	$20
	(White promo label)		

Ray did orchestra and backing voices on many '50s hits on Columbia and Epic, like Guy Mitchell, Marty Robbins and Roy Hamilton, among others

GEORGE COOK (Polka)
Decca 45s $3-6 each

SPADE COOLEY (CW)

-singles-

78rpm	**SHAME ON YOU** (45)	Okeh 6731	$10
78rpm	**DETOUR** (46)	Columbia 36935	$10
45rpm	**SPANISH FANDANGO** (50)	RCA Victor 0027	$18
	(Green vinyl)		
45rpm	**FOOLISH TEARS** (50)	RCA Victor 0157	$18
	(Green vinyl)		

-EPs-

2EP	**ROY ROGERS SOUVENIR ALBUM** (52)	RCA Victor 3041	$30
EP	**DANCE-O-RAMA** (55)	Decca 2225	$18
EP	**DANCE-O-RAMA** (55)	Decca 2226	$15

-albums-

10"LP	**SAGEBRUSH SWING** (52)	Columbia 9007	$40
10"LP	**ROY ROGERS SOUVENIR ALBUM** (52)	RCA Victor 3041	$50
10"LP	**DANCE-O-RAMA** (55)	Decca 5563	$40
LP	**FIDOODLIN'** (59) Mono	Raynote 5007	$25
LP	**FIDOODLIN'** (59) Stereo	Raynote 5007	$35
LP	**FIDOODLIN'** (61) Mono	Roulette 25145	$25
LP	**FIDOODLIN'** (61) Stereo	Roulette 25145	$30

DOLLY COOPER (RB)

-singles-

45rpm	**BIG ROCK INN** (56) Maroon label	Dot 15495	$15
45rpm	**BIG ROCK INN** (56) Black label	Dot 15495	$10

WILMA LEE & STONEY COOPER See Wilma Lee

COWBOY COPAS (CW)

Other King 45s after 5000 $2-5 each
Other Starday 45s $4-6 each

-singles-

78rpm	**FILIPINO BABY** (46)	King 505	$25
78rpm	**BREEZE** (48)	King 618	$18
78rpm	**SIGNED SEALED AND DELIVERED** (48)	King 658	$20
78rpm	**TENNESSEE WALTZ** (48)	King 696	$20
78rpm	**TENNESSEE MOON** (48)	King 714	$18
78rpm	**I'M WALTZING WITH TEARS IN MY EYES** (49)	King 775	$15
78rpm	**CANDY KISSES** (49)	King 777	$12
78rpm	**HANGMAN'S BOOGIE** (49)	King 811	$12
78rpm	**THE STRANGE LITTLE GIRL** (51)	King 951	$10
45rpm	**I CAN'T REMEMBER TO FORGET** (52)	King 1080	$15
45rpm	**IT'S NO SIN TO LOVE YOU** (53)	King 1136	$10
45rpm	**DOLL OF CLAY** (53)	King 1166	$12
45rpm	**PLEDGING MY LOVE** (55)	King 1456	$12
45rpm	**THE PARTY'S OVER** (55)	King 1464	$10
45rpm	**YOU WALKED RIGHT OUT OF MY DREAMS** (58)	King 5479	$12
45(P)	**YOU WALKED RIGHT OUT OF MY DREAMS** (58) (White promo label)	King 5479	$10
45rpm	**ALABAM** (60)	Starday 501	$10

-EPs-

EP	**COWBOY COPAS SINGS HIS FAVORITE SONGS VOL. 1** (57)	King 319-1	$40
EP	**COWBOY COPAS SINGS HIS FAVORITE SONGS VOL. 2** (57)	King 319-2	$40
EP	**COWBOY COPAS** (60)	Starday 145	$20
EP	**COWBOY COPAS** (60)	Starday 146	$20

-albums-

LP	**COWBOY COPAS SINGS HIS ALL-TIME HITS** (57)	King 553	$50
LP	**FAVORITE SACRED SONGS** (57)	King 556	$45
LP	**SACRED SONGS BY COWBOY COPAS** (59)	King 619	$45
LP	**TRAGIC TALES OF LOVE & LIFE** (60)	King 714	$40
LP	**BROKEN HEARTED MELODIES** (60)	King 720	$35
LP	**ALL TIME COUNTRY MUSIC GREAT** (60)	Starday 118	$25
LP	**INSPIRATIONAL SONGS BY COWBOY COPAS** (61)	Starday 133	$25
LP	**COWBOY COPAS** (61)	Starday 144	$25
LP	**MISTER COUNTRY MUSIC** (62)	Starday 175	$30
LP	**SONGS THAT MADE HIM FAMOUS** (62)	Starday 184	$25
LP	**COWBOY COPAS COUNTRY MUSIC ENTERTAINER NO. 1** (63)	Starday 208	$30
LP	**AS YOU REMEMBER COWBOY COPAS** (63)	King 824	$30
LP	**IN MEMORY-COWBOY COPAS & HAWKSHAW HAWKINS** (63) (With Hawkshaw Hawkins)	King 835	$25
LP	**LEGEND OF COWBOY COPAS & HAWKSHAW HAWKINS** (64) (With Hawkshaw Hawkins)	King 850	$25
LP	**BEYOND THE SUNSET** (63)	Starday 212	$30
LP	**THE UNFORGETTABLE COWBOY COPAS** (63)	Starday 234	$30
LP	**COWBOY COPAS—STAR OF THE GRAND OL' OPRY** (63)	Starday 247	$25
LP	**COWBOY COPAS HYMNS** (64)	King 894	$45
LP	**COWBOY COPAS & HIS FRIENDS** (64)	Starday 268	$25
LP	**GONE BUT NOT FORGOTTEN** (65) (Patsy Cline, Cowboy Copas and Hawkshaw Hawkins)	Starday 346	$25
2LP	**THE COWBOY COPAS STORY** (65)	Starday 347	$25
LP	**24 GREAT HITS** (66) (Cowboy Copas and Hawkshaw Hawkins)	King 984	$20
LP	**A SATISFIED MIND** (66)	Hilltop 6032	$12
LP	**THE LATE AND GREAT COWBOY COPAS** (66)	Nashville 2013	$18
LP	**ALABAM** (68)	Nashville 2036	$15
LP	**SIGNED, SEALED & DELIVERED** (69)	Nashville 2050	$15
LP	**FILIPINO BABY** (69)	Nashville 2077	$15
LP	**STAR OF THE OPRY** (70) (Budget label)	Guest Star 1460	$10

-radio shows-

16"(RS)	**U.S. ARMY BAND** (50s) (Music and interviews)	U.S. Army	$20-40
16"(RS)	**U.S. ARMY BAND** (50s) With Ernest Tubb (Music and interviews)	U.S. Army	$25-50
16"(RS)	**U.S. ARMY BAND** (50s) With George Morgan (Music and interviews)	U.S. Army	$25-50
16"(RS)	**U.S. ARMY BAND** (50s) With Jimmy Newman (Music and interviews)	U.S. Army	$20-40

16"(RS)	**COUNTRY STYLE USA** (50s)	Country Style USA 167	$20-40
	(Music and interviews)		
LP(RS)	**COUNTRY MUSIC TIME** (70s)	U.S. Air Force	$10-20
	(Music and interviews)		

LLOYD COPAS (RB)

-singles-

45rpm	**CIRCLE ROCK** (58)	Dot 15686	$50

JOHNNY COPELAND (RB)

-singles-

45rpm	**ROCK AND ROLL LILY** (58)	Mercury 71280	$15
45(P)	**ROCK AND ROLL LILY** (58)	Mercury 71280	$10
	(White promo label)		

KEN COPELAND (RB)

-singles-

45rpm	**FANNY BROWN** (57)	Lin 5017	$18
45rpm	**WHERE THE RIO DE ROSA FLOWS** (57)	Dot 15686	$10

HENRY CORDING (RB)
From France

-singles-

45rpm	**ROCK AND ROLL MOPS/HICCOUGH ROCK** (58)	Columbia 40762	$18
45(P)	**ROCK AND ROLL MOPS/HICCOUGH ROCK** (58)	Columbia 40762	$15
	(White promo label)		

RANDY CORNER (C)
Dot 45s $2 each

-albums-

LP	**MY FIRST ALBUM** (76)	Dot 2048	$12

ORVILLE COUCH (CW)
VJ 45s $3-6 each
Monument 45s $2-4 each

-albums-

LP	**HELLO TROUBLE** (64)	Vee Jay 1087	$20

VARIOUS ARTISTS (CW)

-EPs-

EP(P)	**(1964) COUNTRY AND WESTERN AWARD WINNERS** (64)	Decca 34325	$15
	(Jukebox LLP, price includes hard cover and title strips)		

COUNTRY COUSINS (CW)

-radio shows-

16"(RS)	**U.S. ARMY BAND** (50s) With Wilburn Brothers	U.S. Army	$15-25
	(Music and interviews)		

COUNTRY CUT-UPS (CW)

-albums-

LP	**COUNTRY CUT-UPS GO TO COLLEGE**	Town House 1000	$75

COUNTRY GENTLEMEN (CW)
Gusto LPs $5-8 each
Vanguard and Folkways LPs $6-8 each
Design LPs $5 each

-EPs-

EP	**DIXIE, LOOK AWAY** (59)	Starday 408	$18
EP	**ORANGE BLOSSOM SPECIAL** (61)	Starday 440	$15

-albums-

LP	**TRAVELING DOBRO BLUES** (59)	Starday 109	$45
LP	**SONGS OF THE PIONEERS** (62)	Cimarron 2001	$40
LP	**SONGS OF THE PIONEERS** (62)	Starday 311	$20

COUNTRY GOSPELAIRES (CW)
Starday 45s $3-5 each

-albums-

LP	**THE CHURCH BACK HOME** (59)	Starday 105	$18

THE COUNTRY GUITARS (CW)

-albums-

LP	**WELCOME TO GUITAR COUNTRY** (68)	Mercury 16373	$10

NOTES

COUNTRY HAMS (R)
Paul and Linda McCartney

-singles-

45rpm	**WALKING IN THE PARK WITH ELOISE** (74)	EMI 3977	$30
45rpm	**WALKING IN THE PARK WITH ELOISE** (74)	EMI 3977	$75
	(Price includes picture sleeve)		
45(P)	**WALKING IN THE PARK WITH ELOISE** (74)	EMI 3977	$40
	(Brown promo label)		
	See Chet Atkins		
	See Paul McCartney		

VARIOUS ARTISTS (CW)

-albums-

LP	**COUNTRY JUBILEE** (62)	Decca 38237	$25
	(Top Decca artists with some of their better tracks)		
LP(P)	**COUNTRY JUBILEE** (62)	Decca 38237	$30
	(Pink promo label)		

COUNTRY LADS (CW)
Other Columbia 45s $4-8 each

-singles-

45rpm	**I WON'T BEG YOUR PARDON** (58)	Columbia 41062	$10

VARIOUS ARTISTS (CW)

-albums-

2LP	**THE COUNTRY MUSIC HALL OF FAME** (62)	Starday 164	$25
	(Includes the best tracks from most Starday artists to 1962)		

COUNTRY PARDNERS (CW)
Other RCA Victor 45s $4-8 each

-singles-

45rpm	**PLEASURE KISSES** (58)	RCA Victor 6665	$10
	(Vocal by Bill Price)		

VARIOUS ARTISTS (C)

-radio shows-

LP(RS)	**COUNTRY SESSIONS** (81) CMA awards show	Country Sessions	$15-30
LP(RS)	**COUNTRY SESSIONS** (82) CMA awards show	NBC Radio	$15-30
	(Other Country Sessions CMA shows are worth $10 each)		
3LP(RS)	**CMA AWARDS SHOW** (80s)	Westwood One	$20-40
	(Price is for each show of any year)		

VARIOUS ARTISTS (CW)

-albums-

LP(P)	**COUNTRY STANDARDS FROM HOUSE OF BRYANT** Vol. 1	Bryant 1001	$35
	(For airplay only, includes original versions written by Boudleaux and Felice Bryant, yellow cover)		
LP(P)	**COUNTRY STANDARDS FROM HOUSE OF BRYANT** Vol. 2	Bryant 1002	$35
	(Blue cover, both LPs have great tracks!)		

VARIOUS ARTISTS (CW,R)

-albums-

LP	**COUNTRY WESTERN HITS** Vol. 1 (68)	Bud-Jet 301	$25
	(Minnesota-area artists including Dave Dudley, Texas Bill Strength, and the Muleskinners)		
LP	**COUNTRY WESTERN HITS** Vol. 2 (68)	Bud-Jet 302	$25
	(Mostly same artists, different songs)		
LP	**COUNTRY WESTERN HITS** Vol. 3 (68)	Bud-Jet 303	$25
	(These three LPs are a mix of CW with Minnesota garage-rock of the '60s; this series is the country version of the Big Hits of Mid-America rock set)		

COUSIN FUZZY (Polka)
And His Cousins
Other Polkaland 45s and 78s $5-10 each

-singles-

45rpm	**TRUST ME DARLING** (55)	Polkaland 189	$15
45rpm	**WHY DO YOU GALS WEAR BRITCHES?** (56)	Polkaland 210	$18
	(Red label)		
45rpm	**GUITAR POLKA** (56)	Polkaland 511	$15
45rpm	**LAUGHING POLKA** (57) With Bob Conley	Polkaland 532	$25
45rpm	**SQUEEZE BOX POLKA** (58)	Polkaland 541	$12
45rpm	**ROCK AND ROLL POLKA** (59)	Polkaland 580	$20

COUSIN LEROY (R)
-singles-

45rpm	**WILL A MATCHBOX HOLD MY CLOTHES** (57)	Ember 1016	$50
45(P)	**WILL A MATCHBOX HOLD MY CLOTHES** (57)	Ember 1016	$40
	(White promo label)		
45rpm	**I'M LONESOME** (58)	Ember 1023	$50
45(P)	**I'M LONESOME** (58)	Ember 1023	$40
	(White promo label)		

COUSIN WILBUR (CW)
-albums-

LP	**THE COUSIN WILBUR SHOW**	C. W. 100	$50

BUDDY COVELLE (RB)
-albums-

45rpm	**BILLY BOY** (59)	Brunswick 55151	$40
45(P)	**BILLY BOY** (59)	Brunswick 55151	$30
	(Yellow promo label)		
45rpm	**LORRAINE** (59)	Coral 62181	$150
45(P)	**LORRAINE** (59)	Coral 62181	$125
	(Blue promo label)		

RICKY COYNE (RB)
-singles-

45rpm	**ROLLIN' PIN MIM** (58)	Ferwick 1011	$50

BILLY CRADDOCK (RB)
Billy "Crash" Craddock
Cartwheel 45s $4-8 each
Capitol 45s $3-5 each
ABC 45s $2-5 each
ABC LPs $6-12 each
Capitol LPs $3-5 each
Starday LPs $6 each
MCA LPs $2-4 each

-singles-

45rpm	**I WANT THAT** (57)	Cornet	$18
45rpm	**BETTY BETTY** (58)	King 5912	$15
45(P)	**BETTY BETTY** (58)	King 5912	$12
	(White promo label)		
45rpm	**BOOM BOOM BABY** (59)	Columbia 41470	$12
45rpm	**BOOM BOOM BABY** (59)	Columbia 41470	$30
	(Price includes picture sleeve)		
45(P)	**BOOM BOOM BABY** (59)	Columbia 41470	$10
	(White promo label)		

-EPs-

33(JB)	**RUB IT IN** (74) Jukebox LLP	ABC 817 (LLP #265)	$12
	(Issued with a paper sleeve)		

-albums-

LP	**I'M TORE UP** (64)	King 912	$75
LP	**KNOCK THREE TIMES** (71)	Cartwheel 193	$20
LP	**YOU BETTER MOVE ON** (72)	Cartwheel 05001	$15
LP	**BILLY CRASH CRADDOCK** (73)	Harmony 32186	$18
	(Columbia singles included)		
LP(P)	**BILLY CRASH CRADDOCK** (73)	Harmony 32186	$20
	(White promo label)		
LP	**BEST OF BILLY CRASH CRADDOCK** (73)	Chart 1053	$12

FLOYD CRAMER (C)
Other MGM 45s $4-6 each
RCA Victor 45s $2-5 each
Other RCA Victor picture sleeves $2-5 each
RCA Victor jukebox LLPs $5-8 each
Other MGM LPs $5-8 each
Other RCA Victor LPs $3-8 each

-singles-

78rpm	**JOLLY CHOLLY** (55)	Abbott 159	$12
45rpm	**JOLLY CHOLLY** (55)	Abbott 159	$10
78rpm	**RAG-A-TAG** (56)	Abbott 181	$12
45rpm	**RAG-A-TAG** (56)	Abbott 181	$10
45rpm	**JEALOUS, COLD, CHEATING HEART** (55)	MGM 12059	$10
	(Medley of Hank Williams songs)		
33rpm	**ON THE REBOUND** (61)	RCA Victor 7840	$15
	(Compact-33 single, price includes picture sleeve)		
33rpm	**YOUR LAST GOODBYE** (61)	RCA Victor 7907	$10
	(Compact-33 single)		

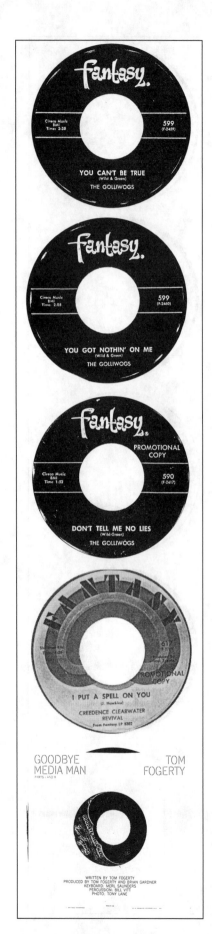

-EPs-

EP	**THAT HONKY-TONK PIANO** (57)	MGM 1379	$15
EP	**THAT HONKY-TONK PIANO** (57)	MGM 1380	$15
EP	**THAT HONKY-TONK PIANO** (57)	MGM 1381	$15
EP	**ON THE REBOUND** (61)	RCA Victor 134	$15
	(Compact-33 Double)		
EP	**I REMEMBER HANK WILLIAMS** (62)	RCA Victor 4373	$12
EP	**LAST DATE** (62)	RCA Victor 4377	$15
EP(P)	**THE YOUNG AND THE RESTLESS** (74)	RCA Victor 0272	$10
	(Promo-only EP with promo-only picture sleeve)		

-albums-

LP	**THAT HONKY-TONK PIANO** (57)	MGM 3502	$25
LP(P)	**THAT HONKY-TONK PIANO** (57)	MGM 3502	$30
	(Yellow promo label)		
LP	**FLOYD CRAMER GOES HONKY-TONKIN'** (64)	MGM 4223	$10
	(Reissue of MGM 3502)		
LP(P)	**FLOYD CRAMER GOES HONKY-TONKIN'** (64)	MGM 4223	$12
	(White promo label)		
LP	**HELLO BLUES** (60)	RCA Victor 2151	$18
LP	**LAST DATE** (61)	RCA Victor 2350	$15
LP	**I REMEMBER HANK WILLIAMS** (62)	RCA Victor 2544	$12

-radio shows-

3LP(RS)	**AMERICAN EAGLE** (80s) With Marty Robbins	Westwood One	$150-300
	(Very rare live concert)		

BLACKIE CRAWFORD (CW)

-singles-

45rpm	**BABY BUGGY BLUES** (54)	Coral 64118	$15

JACKIE CRAY (RB)

-singles-

45rpm	**MAYBELLE** (58)	Limelight 3001	$40

CREEDENCE CLEARWATER REVIVAL (R)

CCR
Includes listings by the Golliwogs, John Fogerty, Tom Fogerty, and the Blue Ridge Rangers
Other Fantasy 45s $5-8 each
RCA Test Pressing 45s $25 each
   (Yellow label)
Fantasy promo label 45s after 617 $10-15 each
Fantasy red/green label 45s of Blue Ridge Rangers $10 each
Fantasy brown label promo 45s of Blue Ridge Rangers $8 each
Asylum promo 45s by John Fogerty $5 each
Elektra promo 45s by John Fogerty $4 each
Warner promo 45s by John Fogerty $4 each
Warner promo 12-inch John Fogerty singles $12 each
Fantasy brown promo label 45s by Tom Fogerty after 715 $4 each
Fantasy lightning label promo 45s by Tom Fogerty $3 each
Fantasy LPs $3-8 each
Fantasy promo LPs by Blue Ridge Rangers $20 each

-singles-

45rpm	**LITTLE GIRL** (65) Golliwogs	Fantasy 590	$50
45(P)	**LITTLE GIRL** (65)	Fantasy 590	$75
	(Red promo label)		
45rpm	**YOU CAME WALKING** (65) Golliwogs	Fantasy 597	$50
45(P)	**YOU CAME WALKING** (65)	Fantasy 597	$75
	(Red promo label)		
45rpm	**YOU CAN'T BE TRUE** (65) Golliwogs	Fantasy 599	$50
45(P)	**YOU CAN'T BE TRUE** (65)	Fantasy 599	$75
	(Red promo label)		
45rpm	**BROWN EYED GIRL** (65) Golliwogs	Scorpio 404	$50
45(P)	**BROWN EYED GIRL** (65)	Scorpio 404	$75
	(Scorpio promo label)		
45rpm	**FIGHT FIRE** (66) Golliwogs	Scorpio 405	$50
45(P)	**FIGHT FIRE** (66)	Scorpio 405	$75
	(Scorpio promo label)		
45rpm	**WALKING ON THE WATER** (66) Golliwogs	Scorpio 408	$50
45(P)	**WALKING ON THE WATER** (66)	Scorpio 408	$75
	(Scorpio promo label)		
45(P)	**PORTERVILLE** (67) Golliwogs	Scorpio 412	$100
	(Promo only as listed by Golliwogs)		
45rpm	**PORTERVILLE** (67) Creedence Clearwater Revival	Scorpio 412	$75
45(P)	**PORTERVILLE** (67) Creedence Clearwater Revival	Scorpio 412	$75
	(Scorpio promo label)		
45rpm	**SUSIE Q** (68) Creedence Clearwater Revival	Fantasy 616	$12
45(P)	**SUSIE Q** (68)	Fantasy 616	$25
	(Red/green promo label)		

45rpm	**I PUT A SPELL ON YOU** (68)	Fantasy 617	$12
45(P)	**I PUT A SPELL ON YOU** (68)	Fantasy 617	$25
	(Red/green promo label)		
45(P)	**BAD MOON RISING** (69)	Fantasy 622	$18
	(Red/green promo label)		
45(P)	**GREEN RIVER** (69)	Fantasy 625	$18
	(Red/green promo label)		
45rpm	**DOWN ON THE CORNER** (69)	Fantasy 634	$15
	(Price includes picture sleeve)		
45(P)	**45 REVOLUTIONS PER MINUTE** (69)	Fantasy 2838	$50
	(Promo only, price includes picture sleeve, which was also a promo-only release)		
45rpm	**TRAVELIN' BAND** (70)	Fantasy 637	$15
	(Price includes picture sleeve)		
45(P)	**TRAVELIN' BAND** (70)	Fantasy 637	$18
	(Red/green promo label)		
45rpm	**UP AROUND THE BEND** (70)	Fantasy 641	$15
	(Price includes picture sleeve)		
45rpm	**LOOKIN' OUT MY BACK DOOR** (70)	Fantasy 645	$15
	(Price includes picture sleeve)		
45(P)	**LOOKIN' OUT MY BACK DOOR** (70)	Fantasy 645	$18
	(Red/green promo label)		
45(P)	**HAVE YOU EVER SEEN THE RAIN** (70)	Fantasy 655	$18
	(Red/green promo label)		
45rpm	**GOODBYE MEDIA MAN** (71) Tom Fogerty	Fantasy 661	$30
	(Price includes picture sleeve)		
45(P)	**GOODBYE MEDIA MAN** (71) Tom Fogerty	Fantasy 661	$15
	(Brown promo label)		
45rpm	**SWEET HITCH-HIKER** (71)	Fantasy 665	$15
	(Price includes picture sleeve)		
45(P)	**SOMEDAY NEVER COMES** (72)	Fantasy 676	$10
	(Brown promo label)		
45rpm	**LADY OF FATIMA** (72) Tom Fogerty	Fantasy 680	$10
45rpm	**LADY OF FATIMA** (72)	Fantasy 680	$15
	(Brown promo label)		
45(P)	**JAMBALAYA** (72) Blue Ridge Rangers	Fantasy 689	$12
	(Red/green promo label)		
45rpm	**FACES, PLACES, PEOPLE** (72) Tom Fogerty	Fantasy 691	$10
45(P)	**FACES, PLACES, PEOPLE** (72)	Fantasy 691	$12
	(Brown promo label)		
45(P)	**HEARTS OF STONE** (72) Blue Ridge Rangers	Fantasy 700	$12
	(Brown promo label)		
45(P)	**JOYFUL RESURRECTION** (73) Tom Fogerty	Fantasy 702	$10
	(Brown promo label)		
45(P)	**YOU DON'T OWE ME** (73) Blue Ridge Rangers	Fantasy 710	$12
	(Brown promo label)		
45(P)	**REGGIE** (73) Tom Fogerty	Fantasy 715	$10
	(Brown promo label)		
45rpm	**COMIN' DOWN THE ROAD** (73) John Fogerty	Fantasy 717	$10
45(P)	**COMIN' DOWN THE ROAD** (73)	Fantasy 717	$15
	(Brown promo label)		
45rpm	**SWEET THINGS TO COME** (75) Tom Fogerty	Fantasy 737	$10
	(Brown promo label)		
45rpm	**I HEARD IT THROUGH THE GRAPEVINE** (76)	Fantasy 759	$10
	(Price includes picture sleeve)		
12"(P)	**I HEARD IT THROUGH THE GRAPEVINE** (76)	Fantasy 759 DJ	$20
	(Promo-only twelve-inch single)		
45(P)	**COMMOTION** (81)	Fantasy 908	$10
	(Brown promo label)		
45(P)	**MEDLEY U. S. A.** (81) Seven-song medley of hits	Fantasy 917	$10
	(Promo lightning label)		
45(P)	**CHAMPAGNE LOVE** (81) Tom Fogerty	Fantasy 923	$10
	(Lightning promo label)		
45(P)	**COTTONFIELDS** (81)	Fantasy 920	$10
	(Blue promo label)		
45(P)	**MEDLEY** (85) Two four-song medleys	Fantasy 957	$10
	(Blue promo label)		
12"(P)	**MEDLEY** (85) eight-song medley (7:08)	Fantasy 238	$15
	(Blue promo label)		
45(P)	**VANZ KANT DANZ** (85) John Fogerty	Warner PRO 2363	$18
	(Promo only, 4:04 version)		
12"(P)	**VANZ KANT DANZ** (85) John Fogerty	Warner PRO 2362	$25
	(Promo-only twelve-inch single, 5:30 and 4:04 versions)		

-albums-

LP	**CREEDENCE CLEARWATER REVIVAL** (68) Blue label	Fantasy 8382	$18
LP	**BAYOU COUNTRY** (69) Blue label	Fantasy 8387	$15
LP	**GREEN RIVER** (69) Blue label	Fantasy 8393	$15

LP	**WILLY AND THE POOR BOYS** (69) Blue label	Fantasy 8397	$15
LP	**COSMO'S FACTORY** (70) Blue label	Fantasy 8402	$15
LP	**PENDULUM** (70) Blue label	Fantasy 8410	$15
LP	**PENDULUM** (70) Black label	Liberty	$75
	(Pressed in USA for foreign distribution)		
LP(P)	**PENDULUM** (70)	Fantasy 8410	$75
	(White promo label)		
LP	**MARDI GRAS** (72) Blue label	Fantasy 9404	$12
LP(P)	**MARDI GRAS** (72)	Fantasy 9404	$40
	(Brown promo label)		

-radio shows-

2LP(RS)	**OFF THE RECORD** (May 85) John Fogerty	Westwood One	$20-40
	(Music and interview)		
LP(RS)	**BBC TRANSCRIPTION DISC** (86)	BBC Transcription	$300-450
	(Very rare live concert)		
2LP(RS)	**KING BISCUIT FLOWER HOUR** (Feb 86)	DIR	$50-100
	(Live concert, with the Divinyls)		
2LP(RS)	**KING BISCUIT FLOWER HOUR** (July 87)	DIR	$40-75
	(Live concert)		
CD(RS)	**OFF THE RECORD** (Mar 93) CCR	Westwood One	$20-40
	(Music and interview)		
CD(RS)	**OFF THE RECORD** (Aug 94) CCR	Westwood One	$25-40
	(Music and interview)		
4LP(RS)	**ROCK ROLL & REMEMBER** (80s) Various artists	United Stations	$10-20
	(With Dick Clark and members of CCR)		
2LP(RS)	**LEGENDS OF ROCK** (Apr 88) CCR	NBC Radio	$20-40
	(Music and interview)		
LP(RS)	**BIRTHDAY TRIBUTE** (Nov 90) Tom Fogerty	Unistar	$10-15
	(Part of the 5LP "Solid Gold Scrapbook")		
2CD(RS)	**THE STORY OF CREEDENCE CLEARWATER REVIVAL** (Aug 92)	Unistar	$20-40
	(Music and interview)		
3CD(RS)	**CREEDENCE CLEARWATER REVIVAL SPECIAL** (0ct 92)	Unistar	$25-50
	(Music and interview)		
2CD(RS)	**WESTWOOD ONE SPECIAL** (Sept 93)	Westwood One	$75-125
	(Live concert)		
CD(RS)	**IN CONCERT-NU ROCK** (Nov 94)	Westwood One	$50-100
	(Live concert)		

CRICKETS (RB)

-singles-

45rpm	**MORE THAN I CAN SAY** (60) Crickets	Coral 62198	$25
45(P)	**MORE THAN I CAN SAY** (60)	Coral 62198	$50
	(Blue promo label)		
45rpm	**PEGGY SUE GOT MARRIED** (60) Crickets	Coral 62238	$25
45(P)	**PEGGY SUE GOT MARRIED** (60)	Coral 62238	$50
	(Blue promo label)		

-albums-

LP	**IN STYLE WITH THE CRICKETS** (60)	Coral 57320	$50
LP(P)	**IN STYLE WITH THE CRICKETS** (60) Blue promo label	Coral 57320	$75
	(Above LP does not feature Buddy Holly)		

VARIOUS ARTISTS/SOUNDTRACK
DAVY CROCKETT
Collectible records from Walt Disney's *Davy Crockett*
The Kentucky Headhunters on Mercury $2 each

-singles-

78rpm	**DAVID CROCKETT** (49) The Happy Students	Records of Knowledge 1002	$25
	(Two-record set with picture cover, not the same song as		
	"The Ballad of Davy Crockett")		
78rpm	**THE BALLAD OF DAVY CROCKETT** (54) Children's series	Columbia J-242	$10
	(Original soundtrack version by Fess Parker		
78(PS)	**THE BALLAD OF DAVY CROCKETT** (54) Picture sleeve	Columbia J-242	$35
	(Same prices for the 45rpm version of J-252)		
78rpm	**THE BALLAD OF DAVY CROCKETT** (54)	Columbia 40449	$20
78(P)	**THE BALLAD OF DAVY CROCKETT** (54)	Columbia 40449	$25
	(White promo label)		
45rpm	**THE BALLAD OF DAVY CROCKETT** (54)	Columbia 40449	$15
45(P)	**THE BALLAD OF DAVY CROCKETT** (54)	Columbia 40449	$20
	(White promo label)		
	Columbia 40449 is the first single in a series from the TV show,		
	the Columbia singles include Buddy Ebson, who later was Jed		
	on *The Beverly Hillbillies.*		
78rpm	**THE BALLAD OF DAVY CROCKETT** (54) Tennessee Ernie Ford	Capitol 3058	$40
78(P)	**THE BALLAD OF DAVY CROCKETT** (54)	Capitol 3058	$25
	(White promo label)		
45rpm	**THE BALLAD OF DAVY CROCKETT** (54)	Capitol 3058	$25

45(P)	**THE BALLAD OF DAVY CROCKETT** (54)	Capitol 3058	$20
	(White promo label)		
45(P)	**THE BALLAD OF DAVY CROCKETT** (55) Fess Parker & Frontiersmen	Wonderland Music 252	$25
	(Promo only, Capitol Custom label)		
45rpm	**THE BALLAD OF DAVY CROCKETT** (55) Sandpipers	Golden D197	$15
45rpm	**THE BALLAD OF DAVY CROCKETT** (55) Children's record	Golden D197	$25
	(The Sandpipers with Mitchell Miller and Orchestra, price includes picture sleeve and six-inch record yellow vinyl)		
78rpm	**BALLAD OF DAVY CROCKETT** (55) James Brown & Trailwinders	MGM 11941	$40
78(P)	**BALLAD OF DAVY CROCKETT** (55)	MGM 11941	$30
	(Yellow promo label)		
45rpm	**BALLAD OF DAVY CROCKETT** (55) James Brown & Trailwinders	MGM 11941	$30
	(James Brown was a star on TV's *Rin Tin Tin*)		
45(P)	**BALLAD OF DAVY CROCKETT** (55)	MGM 11941	$25
	(Yellow promo label)		
78rpm	**THE BALLAD OF DAVY CROCKETT** (55) Mac Wiseman	Dot 1240	$25
45rpm	**THE BALLAD OF DAVY CROCKETT** (55)	Dot 1240	$20
78rpm	**THE BALLAD OF DAVY CROCKETT** (55) Rusty Draper	Mercury 70555	$20
78(P)	**THE BALLAD OF DAVY CROCKETT** (55)	Mercury 70555	$25
	(White promo label)		
45rpm	**THE BALLAD OF DAVY CROCKETT** (55) Rusty Draper	Mercury 70555	$25
45(P)	**THE BALLAD OF DAVY CROCKETT** (55)	Mercury 70555	$20
	(White promo label)		
78rpm	**THE BALLAD OF DAVY CROCKETT** (55) Bill Hayes	Cadence 1256	$25
78(P)	**THE BALLAD OF DAVY CROCKETT** (55)	Cadence 1256	$20
	(White promo label)		
45rpm	**THE BALLAD OF DAVY CROCKETT** (55) Bill Hayes	Cadence 1256	$20
45(P)	**THE BALLAD OF DAVY CROCKETT** (55)	Cadence 1256	$30
	(White promo label)		
78rpm	**THE BALLAD OF DAVY CREW-CUT** (55) Homer & Jethro	RCA Victor 6178	$25
78(P)	**THE BALLAD OF DAVY CREW-CUT** (55)	RCA Victor 6178	$20
	(White promo label)		
45rpm	**THE BALLAD OF DAVY CREW-CUT** (55) Homer & Jethro	RCA Victor 6178	$12
45(P)	**THE BALLAD OF DAVY CREW-CUT** (55)	RCA Victor 6178	$10
	(White promo label)		
45rpm	**PANCHO LOPEZ** (57) Lalo Guerrero	Real 1301	$18
	(Latin version)		
45rpm	**THE BALLAD OF DAVY CROCKETT** (58) Bill Hayes	Cadence 1601	$18
	(Gold record series) This is the same Bill Hayes that played Doug Williams on TV's "Days of our Lives"		
78rpm	**THE BALLAD OF DAVY CROCKETT** (58) Steve Allen	Coral 61368	$50
78(P)	**THE BALLAD OF DAVY CROCKETT** (58)	Coral 61368	$40
	(Blue promo label)		
45rpm	**THE BALLAD OF DAVY CROCKETT** (55) Steve Allen	Coral 61368	$30
45(P)	**THE BALLAD OF DAVY CROCKETT** (55)	Coral 61368	$25
	(Blue promo label)		
78rpm	**THE BALLAD OF DAVY CROCKETT** (55) Burl Ives	Decca 29423	$30
78(P)	**THE BALLAD OF DAVY CROCKETT** (55)	Decca 29423	$40
	(Pink promo label)		
45rpm	**THE BALLAD OF DAVY CROCKETT** (55) Burl Ives	Decca 29423	$25
45(P)	**THE BALLAD OF DAVY CROCKETT** (55)	Decca 29423	$18
	(Pink promo label)		
45rpm	**THE BALLAD OF DAVY CROCKETT** (55) The Wellingtons	Disneyland 557	$40
45(P)	**THE BALLAD OF DAVY CROCKETT** (55)	Disneyland 557	$50
	(White promo label)		
45rpm	**THE BALLAD OF DAVY CROCKETT** (55) Louis Armstrong	Vista 471	$25
45(P)	**THE BALLAD OF DAVY CROCKETT** (55)	Vista 471	$18
	(Pink promo label)		
45rpm	**THE BALLAD OF DAVY CROCKETT** (55) The Forty-Niners	Columbia 752	$25
	(Children's series)		
45rpm	**THE BALLAD OF DAVY CROCKETT** (55) Sons of the Pioneers	RCA WBY 25	$25
	(Children's series)		
45rpm	**THE BALLAD OF OLE SVENSON** (55) Yogi Yorgesson	Capitol 3089	$15
45(P)	**THE BALLAD OF OLE SVENSON** (55)	Capitol 3089	$12
	(White promo label)		
45rpm	**DUVID CROCKETT** (55) Mickey Katz	Capitol 3144	$18
45(P)	**DUVID CROCKETT** (55) Mickey Katz	Capitol 3144	$15
	(White promo label)		
45rpm	**THE BALLAD OF DAVY CROCKETT** (55) Voices of Walter Schumann	RCA 6041	$15
45(P)	**THE BALLAD OF DAVY CROCKETT** (55)	RCA Victor 6041	$12
	(White promo label)		
45rpm	**THE BALLAD OF DAVY CROCKETT** (64) Fess Parker	RCA Victor 8429	$15
45(P)	**THE BALLAD OF DAVY CROCKETT** (64)	RCA Victor 8429	$12
	(White promo label)		
45rpm	**DAVY CROCKETT** (70) Fess Parker	Gusto 900	$15
45(P)	**DAVY CROCKETT** (70) Fess Parker	Gusto 900	$12
	(White promo label)		

-other related singles-

45rpm	**FAREWELL** (55) Fess Parker		Columbia 40450	$25
45(P)	**FAREWELL** (55)		Columbia 40450	$20
	(White promo label)			
45rpm	**OLD BETSY** (55) Fess Parker and Buddy Ebsen		Columbia 40510	$25
45(P)	**OLD BETSY** (55)		Columbia 40510	$20
	(White promo label)			
45rpm	**KING OF THE RIVER** (55) Fess Parker as Davy Crockett		Columbia 40568	$25
45(P)	**KING OF THE RIVER** (55)		Columbia 40568	$20
	(White promo label)			
45rpm	**KING OF THE RIVER** (55) Lou Monte		RCA Victor 6246	$20
45(P)	**KING OF THE RIVER** (55)		RCA Victor 6246	$18
	(White promo label)			

-EPs-

EP	**THE BALLAD OF DAVY CROCKETT** (55) The Rhythmaires		Tops 254	$30
	(Four-song EP, other three by Sherri Lynn)			
EP	**TALES OF DAVY CROCKETT** (56) Tennessee Ernie Ford		Capitol 3235	$20
	(Includes "The Ballad of Davy Crockett")			
EP(P)	**TALES OF DAVY CROCKETT** (56)		Capitol 3235	$30
	(White promo label)			
EP	**THE ORIGINAL DAVY CROCKETT** (56) Fess Parker		Columbia 2031	$40
	("At the Alamo")			
EP	**THE ORIGINAL DAVY CROCKETT** (56) Fess Parker		Columbia 2032	$40
	("Goes to Congress")			
EP	**THE ORIGINAL DAVY CROCKETT** (56) Fess Parker		Columbia 2033	$40
	("Indian Fighter")			

-albums-

LP	**TALES OF DAVY CROCKETT** (55) Tennessee Ernie Ford		Capitol 3235	$100
	(Stories and songs)			
LP(P)	**TALES OF DAVY CROCKETT** (55)		Capitol 3235	$75
	(Capitol promo label)			
LP	**THREE ADVENTURES OF DAVY CROCKETT** (58)		Disneyland 1315	$75
	(Yellow label, yellow border on cover-original version)			
LP	**THREE ADVENTURES OF DAVY CROCKETT** (62)		Disneyland 1926	$50
	(Blue label, white border on cover-later pressings)			

G. L. CROCKETT (RB)

-singles-

45rpm	**LOOK OUT MABEL** (58)		Chief 7010	$65

HOWARD CROCKETT (RB)

-singles-

45rpm	**IF YOU'LL LET ME** (57)		Dot 15593	$25

GEORGE CROMWELL (RB)

-singles-

45rpm	**WASHED UP** (57)		Brunswick 55131	$18
45(P)	**WASHED UP** (57)		Brunswick 55131	$15
	(Yellow promo label)			

CROOM BROTHERS (R)

-singles-

45rpm	**ROCK AND ROLL BOOGIE** (58)		Vee Jay 283	$40

RODNEY CROWELL (C)
Married to Roseanne Cash, best known as a writer
Warner 45s $1 each
Columbia 45s $1 each

-albums-

LP(P)	**INTERCHORDS** (86)		Columbia	$15
	(Promo-only LP with music and interviews)			

-radio shows-

3LP(RS)	**THE SILVER EAGLE** (81) Live concert		DIR 006	$20-40
	(Roseanne Cash and Crowell, Don Williams)			
LP(RS)	**WESTWOOD ONE PRESENTS** (Dec 89)		Westwood One	$20-40
	(Live concert)			
Cass(RS)	**AUSTIN ENCORE** (94)		Mainstreet Broadcasting	$40-75
	(Live concert with Emmylou Harris, issued only on cassette)			

J. C. CROWLEY (C)
RCA Victor 45s $2 each

BOBBY CROWN (RB)

-singles-

45rpm	**ONE WAY TICKET** (58)		Felco 102	$150

VARIOUS ARTISTS
-albums-

13LP	**CRUISIN'** (70 and 73) Complete set of thirteen LPs	Increase LPs	$150
	(Each LP highlights a year from 1955-1967, price is for first pressing, which must feature a DJ and include a copyright date of 1970 or 1973, early dates were pressed in 1970, later years in 1973)		
LP(P)	**CRUISIN** (73) Promo-only sampler	Increase DJ	$50
	(This rare LP was sent to radio stations with no cover issued, has six cuts)		

SIMON CRUM See Ferlin Huskey

RICK CUNHA (C)
GRC 45s $2 each

-albums-

LP	**CUNHA SONGS** (74)	GRC 5004	$20
	(Recording features Waylon Jennings)		

DICK CURLESS (CW)
Other Tower 45s $3-6 each
Capitol 45s $2 each
Other Capitol LPs $5-8 each
Hilltop LPs $8 each
Interstate LPs $6 each

-singles-

45(P)	**A TOMBSTONE EVERY MILE** (65)	Tower 124	$10
	(White promo label)		

-albums-

LP	**DICK CURLESS SINGS SONGS OF THE OPEN COUNTRY** (58)	Tiffany 1016	$75
LP	**SINGING JUST FOR FUN** (59)	Tiffany 1028	$50
LP	**I LOVE TO TELL A STORY** (60)	Tiffany 1033	$40
LP	**A TOMBSTONE EVERY MILE** (65)	Tower 5005	$30
LP	**HYMNS** (65)	Tower 5012	$30
LP	**THE SOUL OF DICK CURLESS** (66)	Tower 5013	$25
LP	**TRAVELIN' MAN** (66)	Tower 5015	$20
LP	**AT HOME WITH DICK CURLESS** (66)	Tower 5016	$30
LP	**A DEVIL LIKE ME NEEDS AN ANGEL LIKE YOU** (66)	Tower 5025	$25
	(With Kay Adams)		
LP	**ALL OF ME BELONGS TO YOU** (67)	Tower 5066	$25
LP	**RAMBLIN' COUNTRY** (67)	Tower 5089	$15
LP	**THE LONG LONESOME ROAD** (68)	Tower 5108	$15
LP	**THE WILD SIDE OF TOWN** (68)	Tower 5137	$12
LP	**THE LAST BLUES SONG** (73)	Capitol 11211	$25
	(First cover shows Curless with eye patch)		
LP	**THE LAST BLUES SONG** (73)	Capitol 11211	$15
	(No eye patch)		

JIM CURLY (RB)
-singles-

45rpm	**ROCK AND ROLL ITCH** (57)	Metro 100	$125
45rpm	**ROCK AND ROLL ITCH** (58)	Mida 100	$60
45rpm	**SLOPPY, SLOPPY SUZIE** (58)	Mida 108	$50

DON CURTIS (RB)
-singles-

45rpm	**ROUGH TOUGH MAN** (58)	Kliff 104	$50

EDDIE CURTIS (RB)
-singles-

45rpm	**YOU'RE MUCH TOO PRETTY FOR ME** (56)	Dot 15505	$15
45rpm	**SHAKE, PRETTY BABY, SHAKE** (58)	Gee 9	$125

MAC CURTIS (RB)
GRT 45s $3-5 each

-singles-

45rpm	**IF I HAD ME A WOMAN** (57)	King 4927	$75
45rpm	**GRANDADDY'S ROCKIN'** (57)	King 4949	$75
45rpm	**YOU AIN'T TREATIN' ME RIGHT** (57)	King 4965	$60
45rpm	**THAT AIN'T NOTHIN' BUT RIGHT** (58)	King 4995	$50
45rpm	**YOU'RE THE ONE** (62)	Dot 16315	$10
45rpm	**HONEY, DON'T** (70)	Epic 10574	$12
45(P)	**HONEY, DON'T** (70)	Epic 10574	$10
	(White promo label)		

-albums-

LP	**SUNSHINE MAN** (68)	Epic 26419	$15

LP(P)	**SUNSHINE MAN** (68)	Epic 26419	$20
	(White promo label)		
LP	**EARLY IN THE MORNING** (71)	GRT 20002	$15
LP(P)	**EARLY IN THE MORNING** (71)	GRT 20002	$18
	(White promo label)		

SONNY CURTIS (RB)

Of the Crickets
Capitol 45s $3-5 each
Elektra 45s 2-5 each
Elektra LPs $5-8 each
Steem 45s $3 each
Steem picture sleeve $5 each

-singles-

45rpm	**WRONG AGAIN** (58)	Dot 15754	$40
45rpm	**WILLA MAE JONES** (58)	Dot 15799	$35
45rpm	**RED HEADED STRANGER** (59)	Coral 62207	$30
45(P)	**RED HEADED STRANGER** (59)	Coral 62207	$40
	(Blue promo label)		
45rpm	**LAST SONG I'M EVER GOING TO SING**	Dimension 1017	$10
45(P)	**LAST SONG I'M EVER GOING TO SING**	Dimension 1017	$12
	(Black promo label)		
45rpm	**I WANNA GO BUMMIN' AROUND** (68)	Viva 617	$12
45(P)	**I WANNA GO BUMMIN' AROUND** (68)	Viva 617	$15
45rpm	**DAY DRINKER** (69)	Viva 626	$10
45rpm	**THE STRAIGHT LIFE** (69)	Viva 630	$10
45(P)	**CHRISTMAS COUNTRY MESSAGES** (81) Various artists	Elektra 47254	$10
	(Promo only for radio stations, includes Sonny Curtis)		

-albums-

LP	**BEATLE HITS** (64)	Imperial 12276	$25
LP(P)	**BEATLE HITS** (64)	Imperial 12276	$40
	(White promo label)		
LP	**THE FIRST OF SONNY CURTIS** (68)	Viva 36012	$30
LP	**THE SONNY CURTIS STYLE** (69)	Viva 36021	$25
	See Crickets		
	See Sonny West		

D

D. J. AND THE CATS (RB)

-singles-

45rpm	**SITTING IN SCHOOL** (58)	Hep 2100	$45

TED DAFFAN (CW)

And His Texans

-singles-

78rpm	**NO LETTER TODAY/BORN TO LOSE** (43)	Okeh 6706	$10

DICK D'AGOSTIN (RB)

-singles-

45rpm	**I'M YOUR DADDY-O** (57)	Accent 1046	$15
45rpm	**NANCY LYNNE** (58)	Dot 15773	$25
45rpm	**IT'S YOU** (59)	Liberty 55218	$15
45(P)	**IT'S YOU** (59)	Liberty 55218	$10
	(White promo label)		

TED DAIGLE (CW)

And His Westerners

-albums-

LP	**WESTERN SONGS** (68)	Altone 221	$15

DAKOTA ROUNDUP (CW)

Jimmy Wells

-singles-

45rpm	**CURLEY'S TOM-CAT BOOGIE** (55)	North Star 2040	$18
45rpm	**SELLING CHANCES** (56) With Ardis Wells	North Star 2041	$15

JIMMY DALEY and the Ding-A-Lings (RB)

-singles-

45rpm	**ROCK, PRETTY BABY** (57)	Decca 30163	$15
45(P)	**ROCK, PRETTY BABY** (57)	Decca 30163	$12
	(Pink promo label)		

45rpm	**RED LIPS AND GREEN EYES** (58)	Decca 30358	$15
45(P)	**RED LIPS AND GREEN EYES** (58)	Decca 30358	$12
	(Pink promo label)		
45rpm	**HOLE IN THE WALL** (58)	Decca 30532	$15
45(P)	**HOLE IN THE WALL** (58)	Decca 30532	$12
	(Pink promo label)		

-EPs-

EP	**ROCK, PRETTY BABY** (57) Vol 1	Decca 2482	$40
EP	**ROCK, PRETTY BABY** (57) Vol 2	Decca 2483	$40
EP	**ROCK, PRETTY BABY** (57) Vol 3	Decca 2484	$40

-albums-

LP	**ROCK, PRETTY BABY** (57) Soundtrack LP	Decca 8429	$35
LP(P)	**ROCK, PRETTY BABY** (57)	Decca 8429	$40
	(Pink promo label)		

VERN DALHART (CW)
Other label 78s $5-10 each

-singles-

78rpm	**WRECK OF THE NO. 9** (25)	Lincoln 2712	$25
78rpm	**THE PRISONER'S SONG** (25)	Victor 19427	$15
	(Country music's first major hit)		

DUSTY DALTON (RB)

-singles-

45rpm	**SHOTGUN** (58)	Unique 100	$15
45(P)	**SHOTGUN** (58)	Unique 100	$12
	(White promo label)		

LACY J. DALTON (C)
Jill Croston
Columbia 45s $1 each

-albums-

LP	**JILL CROSTON** (78)	Harbor 001	$25

-radio shows-

3LP(RS)	**THE SILVER EAGLE** (81)	DIR 005	$15-25
	(Live concert)		
3LP(RS)	**AMERICAN EAGLE** (81) With T. Graham Brown	Westwood One	$20-40
	(Live concert)		
LP(RS)	**LIVE AT GILLEY'S** (June 88)	Westwood One	$10-15
	(Live concert)		

TERRY DALY (RB)

-singles-

45rpm	**YOU DON'T BUG ME** (58)	Mark 122	$100

CHARLIE DANIELS BAND (C)
Other Kama Sutra 45s $3-6 each
Epic 45s $2-5 each
Epic picture sleeves $2-4 each
Epic promo picture sleeves $3-5 each
Capitol LP $8
Epic LPs $2-5 each

-singles-

45rpm	**THE MIDDLE OF A HEARTACHE** (72)	Paula 418	$20
45(P)	**THE MIDDLE OF A HEARTACHE** (72)	Paula 418	$15
	(White promo label)		
45(P)	**UNEASY RIDER** (73) Long (5:19) and short (3:53)	Kama Sutra 576	$10
	(Stock copy is 5:19)		
45(P)	**WHAT'S IT ALL ABOUT** (Feb 77) Public service show	W. I. A. A. 1058	$25
	(Flip side features Boston)		
45(P)	**WHAT'S IT ALL ABOUT** (Sep 80) Public service show	W. I. A. A. 1803	$18
	(Flip side features Willie Nelson)		

-EPs-

(See "Fire on the Mountain" LPs)

-albums-

LP	**THE JOHN, GREASE & WOLFMAN** (72)	Kama Sutra 2060	$12
LP	**HONEY IN THE ROCK** (73)	Kama Sutra 2071	$10
LP	**WHISKEY** (73)	Kama Sutra 2076	$10
LP	**FIRE ON THE MOUNTAIN** (74)	Kama Sutra 2603	$10
	(Includes EP and EP cover Volunteer Jam)		
LP(P)	**FIRE ON THE MOUNTAIN** (74)	Kama Sutra 2603	$15
	(Promo label, includes promo version of the EP and stock EP picture sleeve)		
LP	**NIGHT RIDER** (74)	Kama Sutra 2607	$10
2LP	**THE ESSENTIAL CHARLIE DANIELS** (76)	Kama Sutra 2612	$15

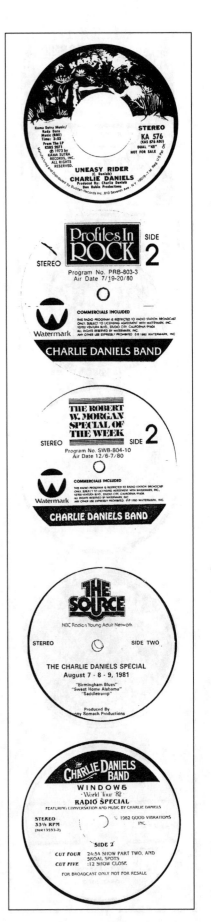

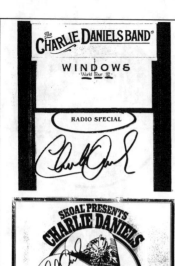

2LP(P)	**THE ESSENTIAL CHARLIE DANIELS** (76)	Kama Sutra 2612	$18
	(Blue promo label)		

-radio shows-

LP(RS)	**INNERVIEW** (70s)	Inner View	$10-15
	(Profile of "Uneasy Rider")		
LP(RS)	**PROFILES IN ROCK** (July 80)	Watermark	$10-15
	(Music and interview)		
LP(RS)	**ROBERT W. MORGAN** (Dec 80)	Watermark	$10-15
	(Music and interviews)		
2LP(RS)	**THE CHARLIE DANIELS SPECIAL** (Aug 81)	NBC Source	$40-75
	(Live concert)		
3LP(RS)	**SPRITE PRESENTS** (Oct 81)	DIR	$20-40
	(Rare live concert)		
LP(RS)	**WINDOWS** (82) Issued with hard cover	Good Vibrations	$15-25
	(Music and interviews)		
3LP(RS)	**SILVER EAGLE** (80s)	Westwood One	$20-30
	(Live concert from Volunteer Jam X)		
3LP(RS)	**SKOAL PRESENTS, THANKSGIVING 1982** (Nov 82) Box set	United Stations	$20-30
	(Music and interviews)		
LP(RS)	**LIVE AT GILLEY'S** (Nov 84)	Westwood One	$25-40
	(Live concert)		
LP(RS)	**LIVE AT GILLEY'S** (Feb 87)	Westwood One	$20-40
	(Live concert)		
2LP(RS)	**PIONEERS IN MUSIC** (Jun 86) Southern Rockers	DIR Show 46	$20-30
	(With Lynyrd Skynyrd, Molly Hatchet, and .38 Special)		
3LP(RS)	**TRIPLE** (83) Box set featuring three artists	Mutual Radio	$20-30
	(With Larry Gatlin and Barbara Mandrell)		
LP(RS)	**THE CHARLIE DANIELS STORY- RADIO SPECIAL** (Jan 90)	Epic 1780	$10-15
	(Album format blue promo label, music and interviews)		
CD(RS)	**CHARLIE DANIELS HOLIDAY RADIO SPECIAL** (Dec 90)	Epic 2204	$10-15
	(From Cabin Fever Productions)		
Cass(RS)	**AUSTIN ENCORE** (94)	Mainstreet Broadcasting	$20-30
	(Live concert available on cassette)		

JEFF DANIELS (RB)

-singles-

45rpm	**DADDY-O-ROCK** (58)	Meladee 117	$65
45rpm	**FOXY DAN** (59)	Astro 108	$50
45rpm	**SWITCH BLADE SAM** (59)	Big Howdy 777	$50

TOMMY DANTON (RB)

-singles-

45rpm	**OH YEAH** (57)	Par 235	$40
45rpm	**OH YEAH** (57)	Dot 15650	$25

DENVER DARLING (C)

-albums-

LP	**SONGS OF THE TRAIL** (58)	Audio Lab 1507	$20

JOHNNY DARRELL (C)

United Artists 45s $2 each
United Artists picture sleeves $3-6 each
United Artists LPs $5-8 each
Sunset LPs $5 each
  (Budget label)
Capricorn LPs $4 each
Gusto LPs $3 each

CHUCK DARTY (RB)

-singles-

45rpm	**MY STEADY GIRL** (57)	Chart 649	$10

FRANKIE DASH (RB)

-singles-

45rpm	**ROCK TO THE MOON**	Cool 106	$50

DAVE & SUGAR (C)

Dave Rowland
Other RCA Victor 45s $2 each
Other RCA Victor LPs $2-5 each
Elektra LPs $4 each

-albums-

LP	**DAVE & SUGAR** (76)	RCA Victor 1818	$10
	(Price includes poster)		

-radio shows-

LP(RS)	**LIVE AT GILLEY'S** (Mar 87)	Westwood One	$10-15
	(Live concert)		

GAIL DAVIES (C)
Warner 45s $1 each
Warner LPs $2-5 each

-albums-

LP	**GAIL DAVIES** (78)	Lifesong 35504	$12

-radio shows-

3LP(RS)	**THE SILVER EAGLE** (81)	DIR 018	$20-30
	(Live concert with Mel Tillis)		

BO DAVIS (RB)

-singles-

45rpm	**LET'S COAST AWHILE** (56)	Crest 1027	$60
45(P)	**LET'S COAST AWHILE** (56)	Crest 1027	$50
	(White promo label)		

CLIFF DAVIS (RB)

-singles-

45rpm	**HARD HEARTED GIRL** (58)	Banana 501	$75

DALE DAVIS (RB)

-singles-

45rpm	**GOTTA ROCK** (58)	Stardale 100	$65

GAIL DAVIS (RB)

-singles-

45rpm	**ROCK TO THE MOON** (58)	Holiday 102	$50

HANK DAVIS (RB)

-singles-

45rpm	**GET LOST BABY** (58)	Dauphin 105	$100

JIMMIE DAVIS (CW)
78s on Bluebird worth $15 each, Decca before 5435 $10 each
Decca 45s $2-6 each
Other Decca LPs $4-10 each
Coral, MCA, Plantation, Caanan LPs $2-5 each
Vocalion and Paula LPs $3-6 each

-singles-

45rpm	**SUPPERTIME** (59)	Decca 28799	$10

-EPs-

EP	**NEAR THE CROSS** (55)	Decca 732	$18
EP	**HYMN TIME** (57)	Decca 2536	$15
EP	**HYMN TIME** (57)	Decca 2560	$15
EP	**THE DOOR IS ALWAYS OPEN** (58)	Decca 2582	$15
EP	**MANSION OVER THE HILLTOP** (59)	Decca 2625	$15
EP	**HAIL HIM WITH A SONG** (59)	Decca 2642	$12
EP	**YOU ARE MY SUNSHINE** (59) Mono	Decca 2654	$12
EP	**YOU ARE MY SUNSHINE** (59) Stereo	Decca 2654	$18
	(All other Jimmie Davis EPs are mono only)		
EP	**SOMEONE TO CARE** (59)	Decca 2690	$12
EP	**JIMMIE DAVIS** (62)	Decca 2711	$10
EP	**TIME CHANGES EVERYTHING** (62)	Decca 2733	$10
EP	**DO LORD** (63)	Decca 2755	$10
EP	**HIGHWAY TO HEAVEN** (65)	Decca 2795	$10

-albums-

LP	**NEAR THE CROSS** (55)	Decca 8174	$20
LP	**HYMN TIME** (57)	Decca 8572	$20
	(With the Anita Kerr Singers)		
LP(P)	**HYMN TIME** (57)	Decca 8572	$25
	(Pink promo label)		
LP	**THE DOOR IS ALWAYS OPEN** (58)	Decca 8729	$18
LP(P)	**THE DOOR IS ALWAYS OPEN** (58)	Decca 8729	$20
	(Pink promo label)		
LP	**HAIL HIM WITH A SONG** (58)	Decca 8786	$18
LP(P)	**HAIL HIM WITH A SONG** (58)	Decca 8786	$20
	(Pink promo label)		
LP	**YOU ARE MY SUNSHINE** (59)	Decca 8896	$12
LP(P)	**YOU ARE MY SUNSHINE** (59)	Decca 8896	$15
	(Pink promo label)		
LP	**SUPPERTIME** (60)	Decca 8953	$20
LP(P)	**SUPPERTIME** (60)	Decca 8953	$25
	(Pink promo label)		

LARRY DAVIS (RB)

-singles-

45rpm	**GONNA LIVE IT UP** (58)	Kangaroo 13	$45

LINK DAVIS (RB)

-singles-

45rpm	**SIXTEEN CHICKS** (58)	Starday 235	$40

-albums-

LP	**CAJUN COWBOY** (69)	Mercury 61243	$15
LP(P)	**CAJUN COWBOY** (69)	Mercury 61243	$20
	(White promo label)		

MAC DAVIS (C)

Capitol 45s $4-6 each
Columbia and Casablanca 45s $1-2 each
MCA color vinyl 45s $5 each
Columbia and Casablanca LPs $2-5 each
Columbia quad LPs $10

-singles-

45(P)	**WHAT'S IT ALL ABOUT** (Jan 75) Public service show	W. I. A. A. 253	$10
	(Flip side features Roberta Flack)		

ROCKY DAVIS (RB)

-singles-

45rpm	**HOT ROAD BABY** (58)	Blue Sky 102	$125

SKEETER DAVIS (CW)

The Davis Sisters
   (With Betty Davis)
Other RCA Victor 78s by the Davis Sisters $5-10 each
Other RCA Victor 45s by the Davis Sisters $6-10 each
RCA Victor 45s by Skeeter Davis $3-6 each
RCA Victor picture sleeves by Skeeter Davis $4-8 each
Other RCA Victor LPs $5-10 each
Other Camden LPs $4-8 each

-singles-

78rpm	**I FORGOT MORE THAN YOU'LL EVER KNOW** (53)	RCA Victor 5345	$15
	(The Davis Sisters)		
78(P)	**I FORGOT MORE THAN YOU'LL EVER KNOW** (53)	RCA Victor 5345	$10
	(White promo label)		
45rpm	**I FORGOT MORE THAN YOU'LL EVER KNOW** (53)	RCA Victor 5345	$12
45(P)	**I FORGOT MORE THAN YOU'LL EVER KNOW** (53)	RCA Victor 5345	$10
	(White promo label)		
45rpm	**SORROW AND PAIN** (53) The Davis Sisters	RCA Victor 5460	$12
45(P)	**SORROW AND PAIN** (53)	RCA Victor 5460	$10
	(White promo label)		
45rpm	**GOTTA GIT A-GOIN'** (54) The Davis Sisters	RCA Victor 5607	$12
45(P)	**GOTTA GIT A-GOIN'** (54)	RCA Victor 5607	$10
	(White promo label)		
45rpm	**JUST LIKE ME** (55) The Davis Sisters	RCA Victor 5843	$12
45(P)	**JUST LIKE ME** (55)	RCA Victor 5843	$10
	(White promo label)		

-EPs-

EP	**I'M SAVING MY LOVE** (63)	RCA Victor 4374	$18

-albums-

LP	**I'LL SING YOU A SONG & HARMONIZE TOO** (60)	RCA Victor 2197	$18
LP	**HERE'S THE ANSWER** (61)	RCA Victor 2327	$18
LP	**THE END OF THE WORLD** (62)	RCA Victor 2699	$20
	(Reissued on Camden in 1973, worth $8)		
LP	**CLOUDY WITH OCCASIONAL TEARS** (63)	RCA Victor 2736	$18
LP	**THE BEST OF SKEETER DAVIS** (65)	RCA Victor 3374	$12
LP	**SKEETER DAVIS SINGS BUDDY HOLLY** (67)	RCA Victor 3790	$40
	(With Waylon Jennings on guitar)		

RONNIE DAWSON (RB)

-singles-

45rpm	**ROCKIN' BONES** (58)	Rockin' 1	$60

CURLEY DAY (CW)

-singles-

45rpm	**SORROW CITY 1963** (63)	Day 2001	$15

JIMMY DAY (CW)

-albums-

LP	**GOLDEN STEEL GUITAR STRINGS** (62)	Philips 600016	$20

LP(P)	**GOLDEN STEEL GUITAR STRINGS** (62)	Philips 600016	$18
	(White promo label)		
LP	**STEEL & STRINGS** (63)	Philips 600075	$18
LP(P)	**STEEL & STRINGS** (63)	Philips 600075	$15
	(White promo label)		

CHARLES DEAN (RB)

-singles-

45rpm	**ITCHY** (58)	Benton 103	$125

DIZZY DEAN (CW)
Hall of Fame baseball pitcher

-singles-

45rpm	**WABASH CANNON BALL** (55)	Colonial No. 4	$35
	(Rare 45rpm pressed by Capitol)		

EDDIE DEAN (CW)
Other Conqueror 78s $10 each
Capitol 78s $10 each
Other label 78s $5-10 each
Other Capitol 45s $5-8 each
Shasta LPs $5-8 each

-singles-

78rpm	**THE OREGON TRAIL** (43) With Jimmie Dean	Conqueror 8596	$25
45rpm	**TEARS ON MY GUITAR** (51)	Capitol 1915	$15
78rpm	**I DREAMED OF A HILL-BILLY HEAVEN** (55)	Sage & Sand 180	$25
45rpm	**I DREAMED OF A HILL-BILLY HEAVEN** (55)	Sage & Sand 180	$20
	(The original version cowritten with Hal Southern)		
45rpm	**OPEN UP YOUR DOOR, BABY** (56)	Sage & Sand 207	$10
	(Eddie Dean and Joanie Hall)		
45rpm	**SOMEBODY GREAT** (57)	Sage & Sand 208	$10
45rpm	**ROCK AND ROLL COWBOY** (58)	Sage & Sand 226	$20

-albums-

LP	**GREATER WESTERNS** (56)	Sage 1	$45
LP	**HI-COUNTRY** (57)	Sage 5	$40
LP	**GREATEST WESTERNS** (57)	Sound 603	$40
LP	**FAVORITES OF EDDIE DEAN** (61)	King 686	$30
LP	**HILLBILLY HEAVEN** (61)	Sage 16	$30
LP	**THE GOLDEN COWBOY** (67)	Crown 320	$12
	(Budget label)		
LP	**LITTLE GREEN APPLES** (68)	Crown 578	$10
	(Budget label)		
LP	**RELEASE ME** (68)	Crown 581	$12
	(Budget label)		
LP	**EDDIE DEAN SINGS COUNTRY & WESTERN** (68)	Crown 583	$12
	(Budget label)		
LP	**HILLBILLY HEAVEN** (68)	Crown 5258	$15
	(Budget label)		
LP	**I DREAMED OF A HILLBILLY HEAVEN** (68)	Sutton 333	$12
	(Budget label)		
LP	**EDDIE DEAN SINGS** (70)	Crown 5434	$12
	(Budget label)		
LP	**EDDIE DEAN SINGS A TRIBUTE TO HANK WILLIAMS** (70)	Design 1026 (DLP 89)	$10
	(Budget label and very common)		

JIMMY DEAN (C)
Any 78s $5-10 each
Other Columbia 45s $2-8 each
Other Columbia 33rpm singles $8 each
Other Columbia picture sleeves $8 each
Hilltop 45s $5 each
Casino 45s $2 each
Churchill 45s $1 each
Other Columbia LPs $4-8 each
Other RCA Victor LPs $4-8 each
Other Harmony LPs $5-10 each
Accord, Hilltop, GRT, and Casino LPs $2-5 each
Spin-O-Rama LP duet $6
Wyncote LP duet $4

-singles-

45rpm	**BUMMING AROUND** (53)	Four Star 1613	$12
45(P)	**BUMMING AROUND** (53)	Four Star 1613	$10
	(White promo label)		
45rpm	**QUEEN OF HEARTS** (54)	Four Star 1640	$12
45(P)	**QUEEN OF HEARTS** (54)	Four Star 1640	$10
	(White promo label)		
45rpm	**BIG BLUE DIAMONDS** (56)	Mercury 70691	$12

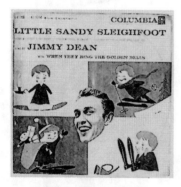

45(P)	**BIG BLUE DIAMONDS** (56)	Mercury 70691	$10
	(White promo label)		
45rpm	**FIND 'EM, FOOL 'EM, AND LEAVE 'EM ALONE** (56)	Mercury 70745	$10
45(P)	**FIND 'EM, FOOL 'EM, AND LEAVE 'EM ALONE** (56)	Mercury 70745	$12
	(White promo label)		
45rpm	**FREIGHT TRAIN BLUES** (57)	Mercury 70786	$12
45(P)	**FREIGHT TRAIN BLUES** (57)	Mercury 70786	$10
	(White promo label)		
45rpm	**LITTLE SANDY SLEIGHFOOT** (57)	Columbia 41025	$25
	(Price includes picture sleeve)		
45rpm	**BIG JOHN** (61) Original version	Columbia 42175	$18
	(Lyric includes "One Hell of a Man")		
45rpm	**BIG BAD JOHN** (61) Common version	Columbia 42175	$18
	(Price includes picture sleeve)		
45rpm	**BIG BAD JOHN** (61) Common version	Columbia 42175	$10
	(Lyric was rewritten)		
33rpm	**BIG BAD JOHN** (61)	Columbia 42175	$15
	(33rpm single)		
45rpm	**DEAR IVAN** (62)	Columbia 42259	$15
	(Price includes picture sleeve)		
45rpm	**TO A SLEEPING BEAUTY** (62)	Columbia 42282	$15
	(Price includes picture sleeve)		
45rpm	**P. T. 109** (62)	Columbia 42338	$15
	(Price includes picture sleeve)		
5-33s	**PORTRAIT OF JIMMY DEAN** (62) Five stereo singles	Columbia JS7-63	$6 each
	(For jukeboxes, with paper cover, $30 for set)		
45rpm	**STEEL MEN** (63)	Columbia 42483	$15
	(Price includes picture sleeve)		
45rpm	**PLEASE PASS THE BISCUITS** (63)	Columbia 42529	$12
	(Price includes picture sleeve)		
45(P)	**BLUE CHRISTMAS** (67)	Columbia 111915	$10
	(Promo-only white label, green vinyl)		

-EPs-

EP	**JIMMY DEAN'S HOUR OF PRAYER** (57)	Columbia 10251	$12
EP	**JIMMY DEAN'S HOUR OF PRAYER** (57)	Columbia 10252	$12
EP	**JIMMY DEAN'S HOUR OF PRAYER** (57)	Columbia 10253	$12
EP(JB)	**PORTRAIT OF JIMMY DEAN** (62) Jukebox LLP	Columbia 1894	$18
	(Issued with a hard cover)		

-albums-

LP	**JIMMY DEAN SINGS HIS TELEVISION FAVORITES** (57)	Mercury 20319	$25
LP(P)	**JIMMY DEAN SINGS HIS TELEVISION FAVORITES** (57)	Mercury 20319	$30
	(White promo label)		
LP	**JIMMY DEAN SINGS HIS TELEVISION FAVORITES** (64)	Wing 12292	$15
LP	**JIMMY DEAN'S HOUR OF PRAYER** (57)	Columbia 1025	$20
LP(P)	**JIMMY DEAN'S HOUR OF PRAYER** (57)	Columbia 1025	$25
	(White promo label)		
LP	**HYMNS BY JIMMY DEAN** (60)	Harmony 11042	$12
LP(P)	**HYMNS BY JIMMY DEAN** (60)	Harmony 11042	$15
	(White promo label)		
LP	**BIG BAD JOHN** (61)	Columbia 8535	$12
LP(P)	**BIG BAD JOHN** (61)	Columbia 8535	$15
	(White promo label)		
LP	**FAVORITES OF JIMMY DEAN** (61)	King 686	$18
LP	**PORTRAIT OF JIMMY DEAN** (62)	Columbia 8694	$10
LP(P)	**PORTRAIT OF JIMMY DEAN** (62)	Columbia 8694	$12
	(White promo label)		
LP	**BUMMIN' AROUND** (65)	Starday 325	$30
	(With Johnny Horton)		
LP	**MOST RICHLY BLESSED** (68)	RCA Victor 3824	$10
LP	**A THING CALLED LOVE** (68)	RCA Victor 3999	$10

-radio shows-

16"(RS)	**NAVY HOEDOWN** (50s)	U.S. Navy	$15-25
	(Music and interview, with Chet Atkins)		

JUNIOR DEAN (RB)

-singles-

45rpm	**CHICK CHICK** (58)	Mike 7328	$100

FRANK DEATON (R)

-singles-

45rpm	**MY LOVE FOR YOU** (57)	Bally 1042	$40

BUD DECKELMAN (R)

-singles-

45rpm	**DAYDREAMING** (58)	Meteor 5014	$65
	(Red vinyl)		

BILLY DEE (CW)

-singles-

45rpm	**DRINKING TEQUILA** (54)	Fabor 104	$15

JIMMY DEE (RB)

-singles-

45rpm	**RICK TICK TOCK** (58)	TNT 161	$60
45rpm	**YOU'RE LATE MISS KATE** (58)	TNT 152	$40
45rpm	**HENRIETTA** (57)	Dot 15644	$15
45rpm	**YOU'RE LATE MISS KATE** (58)	Dot 15721	$25
45rpm	**GUITAR PICKIN' MAN** (59)	Inner-Glo 105	$60

JOHNNY DEE See John D. Loudermilk

TOMMY DEE (R)
Starday 45s $5 each

-singles-

45rpm	**THREE STARS** (59) With Carol Kay	Crest 1057	$20
	(Tribute to Buddy Holly, Big Bopper, and Richie Valens)		
45(P)	**THREE STARS** (59)	Crest 1057	$30
	(White promo label)		
45/PS	**THREE STARS** Later pressing (80s) with Carol Kay	Crest 1057	$10
	(Longer reissue version includes radio broadcasts and		
	Waylon Jennings interview, price includes title sleeve,		
	which was not issued with the original)		
45rpm	**THERE'S A STAR SPANGLED BANNER WAVING**	Challenge 59083	$10
	SOMEWHERE		
	(Price is for stock or promo copy)		

DELMORE BROTHERS (CW)
Featuring Alton Delmore
Any 78rpm on Bluebird is worth $10-$15, Decca 78s are worth just under $10 each
Other King 45s $5-10 each
Country (label) LPs $5 each

-singles-

78rpm	**GOT THE KANSAS CITY BLUES**	Columbia 15724	$75
78rpm	**FREIGHT TRAIN BOOGIE** (46)	King 570	$12
45rpm	**FREIGHT TRAIN BOOGIE** (50)	King 570	$25
78rpm	**BLUES STAY AWAY FROM ME** (49)	King 803	$10
78rpm	**PAN AMERICAN BOOGIE** (50)	King 826	$12
45rpm	**PAN AMERICAN BOOGIE** (50)	King 826	$35
45rpm	**I'LL LET THE FREIGHT TRAIN CARRY ME ON** (52)	King 927	$25
45rpm	**TENNESSEE CHOO CHOO** (53)	King 966	$25
45rpm	**GOT NO WAY OF KNOWING** (54)	King 1084	$18
45rpm	**GOOD TIMES IN MEMPHIS** (58) Alton Delmore	Linco 1315	$30

-EPs-

EP	**SACRED SONGS VOL. 1** (57) Brown's Ferry Four	King 237	$15
EP	**SACRED SONGS VOL. 2** (57) Brown's Ferry Four	King 238	$15
EP	**SACRED SONGS VOL. 3** (57) Brown's Ferry Four	King 320	$15
	(Brown's Ferry Four is Grandpa Jones, Merle Travis, and		
	the Delmore Brothers)		
EP	**TRADITIONAL SACRED SONGS** (59)	King 313	$15
EP	**TRADITIONAL SACRED SONGS** (59)	King 322	$15

-albums-

LP	**SACRED SONGS** (57) Brown's Ferry Four	King 551	$40
LP	**SONGS BY THE DELMORE BROTHERS** (58)	King 589	$30
LP	**SACRED SONGS VOL. 2** (58) Brown's Ferry Four	King 590	$25
LP	**THE DELMORE BROTHERS 30TH ANNIVERSARY ALBUM** (62)	King 785	$20
LP	**IN MEMORY** (64)	King 910	$20
LP	**IN MEMORY VOL 2** (64)	King 920	$20
LP	**WONDERFUL SACRED SONGS** (65) Brown's Ferry Four	King 943	$25
LP	**24 GREAT COUNTRY SONGS** (66)	King 983	$15
LP	**BEST OF THE DELMORE BROTHERS** (69)	Starday 962	$15
LP	**BEST OF THE DELMORE BROTHERS** (70)	King 1090	$15

JERRY DEMAR (RB)

-singles-

45rpm	**CROSS-EYED ALLEY CAT** (58)	Ford 501	$65

LITTLE JIMMY DEMPSEY (RB)
Starday and ABC 45s $2 each
Starday LPs $6 each

-singles-

45rpm	**BOP HOP** (58)	Fox 5	$75

-albums-

LP	**GUITAR COUNTRY OF LITTLE JIMMY DEMPSEY** (67)	ABC 619	$10
LP	**STRINGS OF MY GUITAR** (69)	ABC 670	$10

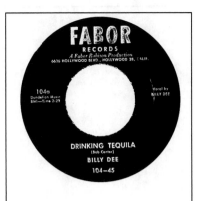

NOTES

LEE DENSON (RB)

-singles-

45rpm	**HIGH SCHOOL HOP** (57)	Kent 306	$25
45rpm	**HEART OF A FOOL** (58)	Vik (RCA) 0251	$18
45(P)	**HEART OF A FOOL** (58)	Vik 0251	$15
	(White promo label)		
45rpm	**NEW SHOES** (59)	Vik 0281	$18
45(P)	**NEW SHOES** (59)	Vik 0281	$12
	(White promo label)		

JOHN DENVER (R)

Other RCA Victor 45s $1-3 each
RCA Victor jukebox LLPs $5 each
RCA Victor LPs $2-4 each

-singles-

45(P)	**A BABY JUST LIKE YOU** (79)	RCA Victor 11767	$10
	(Green promo label, red vinyl)		

-albums-

LP(P)	**HOLIDAY RADIO SPECIAL** (85) John Denver	RCA Victor 5398	$10
	(Promo-only concert from RCA Victor)		

-radio shows-

3LP(RS)	**TRIPLE** (83) Box set	Mutual Radio	$15-25
	(Music and interviews, with Emmylou Harris and Lee Greenwood)		
LP(RS)	**SALUTE TO AMERICA** (July 90) John Denver/George Bush	Department Interior	$10-20
	(Unusual live concert)		

DEPUTIES (C)

Backing group for Faron Young

-albums-

LP	**SOUNDS OF THE DEPUTIES** (65)	Faron Young Record Co. 002	$30
	(Solo LP)		

LARRY DERIEUX (RB)

-singles-

45rpm	**CHICKEN SESSION** (58)	Arco 102	$50

THE DESERT ROSE BAND (C)

Includes Chris Hillman, former member of the Byrds
Other MCA 45s $1 each
Other MCA color vinyl 45s $8 each
MCA LPs $3 each

-singles-

45(P)	**ASHES OF LOVE** (87)	MCA 53048	$10
	(Blue vinyl)		

-radio shows-

LP(RS)	**WESTWOOD ONE PRESENTS** (Oct 89) Live concert	Westwood One	$40-75
	(With T. Graham Brown and The Judds)		
LP(RS)	**WESTWOOD ONE PRESENTS** (Feb 90)	Westwood One	$50-100
	(Rare live concert)		

AL DEXTER (CW)

-singles-

78rpm	**NEW JELLYROLL BLUES**	Vocalion 03435	$10
78rpm	**PISTOL PACKIN' MAMA/ROSALITA** (44)	Okeh 6708	$12
78rpm	**SO LONG, PAL/TOO LATE TO WORRY, TO BLUE TO CRY** (44)	Okeh 6718	$12
	(Both sides of the two above singles were hits)		
78rpm	**I'M LOSING MY MIND OVER YOU** (45)	Okeh 6727	$10
78rpm	**GUITAR POLKA** (46)	Columbia 36898	$10
45rpm	**PISTOL PACKIN' MAMA** (57)	Ekko 1020	$20
	(Rockabilly version)		

-albums-

10"LP	**SONGS OF THE SOUTHWEST** (54)	Columbia 9005	$50
LP	**PISTOL PACKIN' MAMA** (61)	Harmony 7293	$12
LP(P)	**PISTOL PACKIN' MAMA** (61)	Harmony 7293	$15
	(White promo label)		
LP	**AL DEXTER SINGS & PLAYS HIS GREATEST HITS** (62)	Capitol 1701	$30
LP	**THE ORIGINAL PISTOL PACKIN' MAMA** (68)	Hilltop 6070	$12

DIAMONDS (R)

Listed here are the only records considered to be country by this pop doo-wop group
Other Diamonds records are very collectible also

-EPs-

EP(P)	**CHOICE SELECTIONS FROM** (59) White promo EP w/cover	Mercury MEP 72	$20
	(Includes one song from Out West, San Antonio Rose)		

	-albums-		
LP	**THE DIAMONDS OUT WEST** (59)	Mercury 18940	$50
	(Only Diamonds LP considered country)		
LP(P)	**THE DIAMONDS OUT WEST** (59)	Mercury 18940	$75
	(White promo label)		

VARIOUS ARTISTS

-EPs-

EP(P)	**DIAMONDS BY THE DOZEN** (63) Jukebox LLP	RCA Victor 2668	$18
	(Price includes hard cover and title strips)		

DENNY DIANTE (R)

-singles-

45rpm	**LITTLE LOVER** (58)	Holiday 1210	$55

(Little) JIMMY DICKENS (CW)

Other Columbia 78s $6-10 each
Other Columbia 45s $5-10 each

-singles-

78rpm	**PENNIES FOR PAPA** (50)	Columbia 20548	$12
78(P)	**PENNIES FOR PAPA** (50)	Columbia 20548	$15
	(Columbia promo label)		
45rpm	**PENNIES FOR PAPA** (50)	Columbia 20548	$25
45(P)	**PENNIES FOR PAPA** (50)	Columbia 20548	$20
	(White promo label)		
78rpm	**COUNTRY BOY** (50)	Columbia 20585	$10
78(P)	**COUNTRY BOY** (50)	Columbia 20585	$15
	(Columbia promo label)		
45rpm	**COUNTRY BOY** (50)	Columbia 20585	$15
45(P)	**COUNTRY BOY** (50)	Columbia 20585	$10
	(White promo label)		
78rpm	**SLEEPIN' AT THE FOOT OF THE BED** (50)	Columbia 20644	$10
78(P)	**SLEEPIN' AT THE FOOT OF THE BED** (50)	Columbia 20644	$12
	(Columbia promo label)		
45rpm	**SLEEPIN' AT THE FOOT OF THE BED** (50)	Columbia 20644	$12
45(P)	**SLEEPIN' AT THE FOOT OF THE BED** (50)	Columbia 20644	$10
	(White promo label)		
78rpm	**HILLBILLY FEVER** (50)	Columbia 20677	$10
45rpm	**HILLBILLY FEVER** (50)	Columbia 20677	$10
78rpm	**WALK CHICKEN WALK** (51)	Columbia 20722	$10
45rpm	**WALK CHICKEN WALK** (51)	Columbia 20722	$10
78rpm	**OUT OF BUSINESS** (51)	Columbia 20744	$10
45rpm	**OUT OF BUSINESS** (51)	Columbia 20744	$10
78rpm	**I'M LITTLE BUT I'M LOUD** (51)	Columbia 20769	$10
78(P)	**I'M LITTLE BUT I'M LOUD** (51)	Columbia 20769	$12
	(Tan promo label)		
45rpm	**I'M LITTLE BUT I'M LOUD** (51)	Columbia 20769	$12
45(P)	**I'M LITTLE BUT I'M LOUD** (51)	Columbia 20769	$10
	(White promo label)		
78rpm	**COLD FEET** (51)	Columbia 20786	$10
45rpm	**COLD FEET** (51)	Columbia 20786	$10
78rpm	**SIGN ON THE HIGHWAY** (52)	Columbia 20835	$10
45rpm	**SIGN ON THE HIGHWAY** (52)	Columbia 20835	$10
78rpm	**THEY LOCKED GOD OUTSIDE** (52)	Columbia 20925	$10
45rpm	**THEY LOCKED GOD OUTSIDE** (52)	Columbia 20925	$10
78rpm	**HOT DIGGITY DOG** (52)	Columbia 20943	$10
78(P)	**HOT DIGGITY DOG** (52)	Columbia 20943	$12
	(Tan promo label)		
45rpm	**HOT DIGGITY DOG** (52)	Columbia 20943	$12
45(P)	**HOT DIGGITY DOG** (52)	Columbia 20943	$10
	(White promo label)		
78rpm	**WAITRESS WAITRESS** (52)	Columbia 20976	$10
45rpm	**WAITRESS WAITRESS** (52)	Columbia 20976	$10
78rpm	**TEARDROPS** (52)	Columbia 21093	$10
45rpm	**TEARDROPS** (52)	Columbia 21093	$10
78rpm	**BAREFOOTED LITTLE COWBOY** (54)	Columbia 21167	$12
78(P)	**BAREFOOTED LITTLE COWBOY** (54)	Columbia 21167	$15
	(Tan promo label)		
45rpm	**BAREFOOTED LITTLE COWBOY** (54)	Columbia 21167	$15
45(P)	**BAREFOOTED LITTLE COWBOY** (54)	Columbia 21167	$12
	(White promo label)		
78rpm	**THAT LITTLE COUNTRY CHURCH** (54)	Columbia 21203	$10
45rpm	**THAT LITTLE COUNTRY CHURCH** (54)	Columbia 21203	$10
78rpm	**ROCK ME** (54)	Columbia 21206	$20
78(P)	**ROCK ME** (54)	Columbia 21206	$25
	(Tan promo label)		

45rpm	ROCK ME (54)	Columbia 21206	$20
45(P)	ROCK ME (54)	Columbia 21206	$18
	(White promo label)		
78rpm	YOU BETTER NOT DO THAT (54)	Columbia 21216	$15
78(P)	YOU BETTER NOT DO THAT (54)	Columbia 21216	$18
	(Tan promo label)		
45rpm	YOU BETTER NOT DO THAT (54)	Columbia 21216	$12
45(P)	YOU BETTER NOT DO THAT (54)	Columbia 21216	$10
	(White promo label)		
78rpm	OUT BEHIND THE BARN (54)	Columbia 21247	$12
78(P)	OUT BEHIND THE BARN (54)	Columbia 21247	$15
	(Tan promo label)		
45rpm	OUT BEHIND THE BARN (54)	Columbia 21247	$12
45(P)	OUT BEHIND THE BARN (54)	Columbia 21247	$10
	(White promo label)		
78rpm	TAKE ME AS I AM (55)	Columbia 21296	$10
45rpm	TAKE ME AS I AM (55)	Columbia 21296	$10
78rpm	STINKY PASS THE HAT AROUND (55)	Columbia 21341	$10
45rpm	STINKY PASS THE HAT AROUND (55)	Columbia 21341	$10
78rpm	SALTY BOOGIE (55)	Columbia 21384	$15
78(P)	SALTY BOOGIE (55)	Columbia 21384	$18
	(Tan promo label)		
45rpm	SALTY BOOGIE (55)	Columbia 21384	$15
45(P)	SALTY BOOGIE (55)	Columbia 21384	$12
	(White promo label)		
78rpm	WHEN THEY GET TOO ROUGH (55)	Columbia 21434	$10
45rpm	WHEN THEY GET TOO ROUGH (55)	Columbia 21434	$10
78rpm	HEY WORM! (55)	Columbia 21491	$10
45rpm	HEY WORM! (55)	Columbia 21491	$10
45rpm	BIG SANDY (55)	Columbia 21515	$10
78rpm	I NEVER THOUGHT IT WOULD HAPPEN TO ME (56)	Columbia 21555	$10
45rpm	I NEVER THOUGHT IT WOULD HAPPEN TO ME (56)	Columbia 21555	$10
78rpm	I NEVER HAD THE BLUES (56)	Columbia 40890	$15
45rpm	I NEVER HAD THE BLUES (56)	Columbia 40890	$10
78rpm	MAKING THE ROUNDS (57)	Columbia 40961	$15
45rpm	MAKING THE ROUNDS (57)	Columbia 40961	$10
45rpm	FAMILY REUNION (57)	Columbia 41079	$10
45rpm	I GOT A HOLE IN MY POCKET (57)	Columbia 41173	$30
45(P)	I GOT A HOLE IN MY POCKET (57)	Columbia 41173	$25
	(White promo label)		

-EPs-

EP	LITTLE JIMMY DICKENS (52)	Columbia 1664	$25
EP	RAISIN' THE DICKENS (57)	Columbia 10471	$20
EP	LITTLE JIMMY DICKENS (57)	Columbia 2807	$18
EP	LITTLE JIMMY DICKENS (57)	Columbia 2813	$18
EP	LITTLE JIMMY DICKENS (57)	Columbia 2824	$15

-albums-

10"LP	OLD COUNTRY CHURCH (54)	Columbia 9053	$75
LP	RAISIN' THE DICKENS	Columbia 1047	$75
LP	BIG SONGS BY LITTLE JIMMY DICKENS (60)	Columbia 8345	$25
LP(P)	BIG SONGS BY LITTLE JIMMY DICKENS (60) Promo copy (Red promo label with "Demonstration Not for Sale" in white letters)	Columbia 8345	$35
LP	LITTLE JIMMY DICKENS SINGS OUT BEHIND THE BARN (62) (Includes original "Violet & the Rose")	Columbia 8687	$25
LP(P)	LITTLE JIMMY DICKENS SINGS OUT BEHIND THE BARN (62) (Red promo label with "Demonstration Not for Sale" in white letters)	Columbia 8687	$35
LP	LITTLE JIMMY DICKENS' BEST (64) (Includes rockabilly songs)	Harmony 7311	$25
LP(P)	LITTLE JIMMY DICKENS' BEST (64) (White promo label)	Harmony 7311	$35
LP	ALONE WITH GOD (65)	Harmony 7326	$15
LP(P)	ALONE WITH GOD (65) (White promo label)	Harmony 7326	$18
LP	HANDLE WITH CARE (65)	Columbia 9088	$18
LP(P)	HANDLE WITH CARE (65) (White promo label)	Columbia 9088	$20
LP	MAY THE BIRD OF PARADISE FLY UP YOUR NOSE (65)	Columbia 9242	$18
LP(P)	MAY THE BIRD OF PARADISE FLY UP YOUR NOSE (65) (White promo label)	Columbia 9242	$20
LP	LITTLE JIMMY DICKENS GREATEST HITS (66) (Reissued in 1967)	Columbia 9351	$18
LP(P)	LITTLE JIMMY DICKENS GREATEST HITS (66) (White promo label)	Columbia 9351	$20
LP	AIN'T IT FUN (67)	Harmony 11220	$12
LP(P)	AIN'T IT FUN (67) (White promo label)	Harmony 11220	$15

LP	**BIG MAN IN COUNTRY MUSIC** (68)	Columbia 9648	$15
	(Reissued in 1973)		
LP	**JIMMY DICKENS SINGS** (68)	Decca 4967	$15
LP(P)	**JIMMY DICKENS SINGS** (68)	Decca 4967	$10
	(White promo label)		
LP	**JIMMY DICKENS COMES CALLIN'** (69)	Decca 5091	$15
LP(P)	**JIMMY DICKENS COMES CALLIN'** (69)	Decca 5091	$18
	(White promo label)		
LP	**JIMMY DICKENS GREATEST HITS** (69)	Decca 5133	$15
LP(P)	**JIMMY DICKENS GREATEST HITS** (69)	Decca 5133	$18
	(White promo label)		

-radio shows-

3LP(RS)	**THE SILVER EAGLE** (80s) With George Jones	DIR	$75-150
	(Live concert)		

DUB DICKERSON (CW)

-singles-

45rpm	**THE BELLS OF MONTEREY** (54)	Capitol 2504	$12
45rpm	**MY GAL GERTIE** (56)	Capitol 2947	$12
45(P)	**MY GAL GERTIE** (56)	Capitol 2947	$10
	(White promo label)		
45rpm	**UNDER THE HEADING OF MY BUSINESS** (57)	Capitol 3099	$12
45(P)	**UNDER THE HEADING OF MY BUSINESS** (57)	Capitol 3099	$10
	(White promo label)		
45rpm	**SHOTGUN WEDDING** (58)	Sims 106	$25
45(P)	**SHOTGUN WEDDING** (58)	Sims 106	$30
	(White promo label)		
45rpm	**NAME YOUR PRICE** (59)	Sims 127	$10

-albums-

LP	**SAD AND LONELY** (62)	Sims 102	$25

ELROY DIETZEL (RB)

-singles-

45rpm	**TEENAGE BALL** (58)	Bo-Kay 101	$60
45rpm	**ROCK-N-BONES** (58)	Bo-Kay 102	$60

DANNY DILL (RB)
Liberty and MGM 45s $2-5 each

-singles-

45rpm	**HUNGRY FOR YOUR LOVIN'** (57)	ABC Paramount 9734	$15
45(P)	**HUNGRY FOR YOUR LOVIN'** (57)	ABC Paramount 9734	$12
	(White promo label)		

-albums-

LP	**FOLK SONGS FROM THE WILD WEST** (60)	MGM 3819	$15
LP(P)	**FOLK SONGS FROM THE WILD WEST** (60)	MGM 3819	$18
	(Yellow promo label)		
LP	**FOLK SONGS FROM THE COUNTRY** (63)	Liberty 7301	$15
LP(P)	**FOLK SONGS FROM THE COUNTRY** (63)	Liberty 7301	$18
	(White promo label)		

DILLARD & CLARK (R)
Doug Dillard and Gene Clark
Clark was a member of the Byrds
A&M 45s by Dillard & Clark $5 each
Capitol 45s by McGuinn, Clark & Hillman $5 each

-albums-

LP	**THE BANJO ALBUM** (62) Doug Dillard	Together 1003	$80
	(Early Byrds material on this label)		
LP	**FANTASTIC EXPEDITION OF DILLARD & CLARK** (68)	A&M 4158	$15
LP(P)	**FANTASTIC EXPEDITION OF DILLARD & CLARK** (68)	A&M 4158	$18
	(White promo label)		
LP	**THROUGH THE MORNING, THROUGH THE NIGHT** (69)	A&M 4203	$12
LP(P)	**THROUGH THE MORNING, THROUGH THE NIGHT** (69)	A&M 4203	$15
	(White promo label)		
	See the Dillards		

THE DILLARDS (BG)
Featuring Doug and Rodney Dillard
Any 45s $2-5 each
Anthem and Poppy LPs $5-10 each
Flying Fish LPs $5 each

-albums-

LP	**THE BANJO ALBUM** (62) Doug Dillard	Together 1003	$80
	(Label for early Byrds material)		
LP	**BACK PORCH BLUEGRASS** (63) Stereo	Elektra 232	$40
	(First pressing)		

LP	**BACK PORCH BLUEGRASS** (67)	Elektra 7232	$15
LP	**BACK PORCH BLUEGRASS** (67)	Elektra 7232	$18
	(White promo label)		
LP	**THE DILLARDS LIVE! ALMOST!** (64) Stereo	Elektra 265	$25
	(First pressing)		
LP	**THE DILLARDS LIVE! ALMOST!** (67)	Elektra 7265	$12
LP	**PICKIN' & FIDDLIN' WITH BYRON BERLINE** (65) Stereo	Elektra 285	$25
	(First pressings)		
LP	**PICKIN' & FIDDLIN' WITH BYRON BERLINE** (65)	Elektra 7285	$12
LP	**THE DILLARDS-COPPERFIELDS** (69)	Elektra 74054	$10
LP	**DUELIN' BANJO** (73)	20th Century Fox	$12

DEAN DILLON (C)
RCA Victor 45s $1 each
RCA Victor color vinyl 45s $5 each
RCA Victor duet color vinyl 45s $8-10 each

DIXIE GENTLEMEN (BG)
United Artists 45s $2 each

-albums-

LP	**COUNTRY STYLE OF THE DIXIE GENTLEMEN** (63)	United Artists 6296	$18

CARL DOBKINS JR. (R)
Other Decca 45s $5-10 each
Chalet 45s $2-3 each

-singles-

45rpm	**TAKE HOLD OF MY HAND** (58)	Fraternity 794	$20
45(P)	**TAKE HOLD OF MY HAND** (58)	Fraternity 794	$25
	(White promo label)		
45rpm	**MY HEART IS AN OPEN BOOK** (59)	Decca 30803	$18
45(P)	**MY HEART IS AN OPEN BOOK** (59)	Decca 30803	$15
	(Pink promo label)		
45rpm	**IF YOU DON'T WANT MY LOVIN'** (59)	Decca 30856	$15
45(P)	**IF YOU DON'T WANT MY LOVIN'** (59)	Decca 30856	$12
	(Pink promo label)		
45rpm	**LUCKY DEVIL** (59)	Decca 31020	$15
45rpm	**LUCKY DEVIL** (59)	Decca 31020	$30
	(Price includes picture sleeve)		
45rpm	**EXCLUSIVELY YOURS** (60)	Decca 31088	$15
45(P)	**EXCLUSIVELY YOURS** (60)	Decca 31088	$12
	(Pink promo label)		

-albums-

LP	**CARL DOBKINS JR.** (59)	Decca 8938	$40
LP(P)	**CARL DOBKINS JR.** (59)	Decca 8938	$45
	(Pink promo label)		

CHUCK DOCKERY (RB)

-singles-

45rpm	**BABY LET'S DANCE** (58)	New Song 123	$50

DODGER & JOHNNY ANGEL (RB)
-singles-

45rpm	**BOOGIE MAN** (58)	Skyway 117	$90

RAY DOGGETT (RB)
-singles-

45rpm	**NO DOUBT ABOUT IT** (58)	Pearl 716	$100
45rpm	**GO GO HEART** (58)	Spade 1928	$50

RAMBLIN' JIMMIE DOLAN (CW)
Other Capitol 78s and 45s $5-8 each

-singles-

78rpm	**HOT ROD RACE** (51)	Capitol 1322	$15
45rpm	**HOT ROD RACE** (51)	Capitol 1322	$20
	("Hot Rod Lincoln" was the answer song)		
78rpm	**RACK UP THE BALLS BOYS** (52)	Capitol 2118	$12
45rpm	**RACK UP THE BALLS BOYS** (52)	Capitol 2118	$15
78rpm	**HOT ROD MAMA** (53)	Capitol 2244	$15
78(P)	**HOT ROD MAMA** (53)	Capitol 2244	$12
	(Capitol promo label)		
45rpm	**HOT ROD MAMA** (53)	Capitol 2244	$20
78rpm	**TOOL PUSHER ON A ROTARY RIG** (54)	Capitol 2713	$15
45rpm	**TOOL PUSHER ON A ROTARY RIG** (54)	Capitol 2713	$10
78rpm	**LOOK-A HERE, BABY** (55)	Capitol 2830	$15
45rpm	**LOOK-A HERE, BABY** (55)	Capitol 2830	$15
78rpm	**A SAILOR'S LETTER** (56)	Capitol 2977	$15
45rpm	**A SAILOR'S LETTER** (56)	Capitol 2977	$12

JOHNNY DOLLAR (C)
Date and Charts 45s $2 each

-albums-

LP	**JOHNNY DOLLAR** (67)	Date 4009	$15
LP(P)	**JOHNNY DOLLAR** (67)	Date 4009	$18
	(White promo label)		
LP	**BIG RIG ROLLIN' MAN** (69)	Chart 1023	$12
LP	**COUNTRY HIT PARADE** (69)	Chart 3000	$10

NORM DOMBROWSKI (Polka)
With the Happy Notes

-singles-

45rpm	**I LOVE YOU WALTZ** (62)	Gold Records 107	$12
45rpm	**ASTRONAUT POLKA** (63)	Gold Records 109	$15
45rpm	**ENJOY YOURSELF POLKA** (64)	Gold Records 112	$18

DON AND DEWEY (R)

-singles-

45rpm	**MISS YOU** (58)	Shade 1000	$40

DON (GUESS) & HIS ROSES (RB)

-singles-

45rpm	**RIGHT NOW** (58)	Dot 15755	$40
45rpm	**LEAVE THOSE CATS ALONE** (58)	Dot 15784	$100

JIMMY DONLEY (RB)

-singles-

45rpm	**KICKIN' MY HOUND AROUND** (57)	Decca 30308	$15
45(P)	**KICKIN' MY HOUND AROUND** (57)	Decca 30308	$12
	(Decca promo label)		

RAL DONNER (R)
Rising Sons 45s $5-10 each
MJ, Sunlight, Starfire, Chicago Fire, and Mid-Eagle 45s $3-6 each
Starfire green vinyl 45s $6 each
Starfire picture sleeves $5 each

-singles-

45rpm	**TELL ME WHY** (59)	Scottie 1310	$50
45rpm	**GIRL OF MY BEST FRIEND** (61)	Gone 5102	$35
	(Black label)		
45rpm	**GIRL OF MY BEST FRIEND** (61)	Gone 5102	$20
	(Multicolored label)		
45rpm	**TO LOVE** (61)	Gone 5108	$30
	(Different tracks, same record number)		
45rpm	**YOU DON'T KNOW WHAT YOU'VE GOT** (61)	Gone 5108	$20
45rpm	**PLEASE DON'T GO** (61)	Gone 5114	$20
45rpm	**SCHOOL OF HEARTBREAKERS** (61)	Gone 5119	$20
45rpm	**SHE'S EVERYTHING** (62)	Gone 5121	$20
	(Flip side, "Will You Love Me in Heaven")		
45rpm	**SHE'S EVERYTHING** (62)	Gone 5121	$30
	(Flip side, "Because We're Young")		
45rpm	**TO LOVE SOMEONE** (62)	Gone 5125	$20
45rpm	**LOVELESS LIFE** (62)	Gone 5129	$20
45rpm	**TO LOVE** (62)	Gone 5133	$20
45rpm	**YOU DON'T KNOW WHAT YOU'VE GOT** (63)	End 19	$25
45rpm	**LONELINESS OF A STAR** (63)	Tau 105	$30
45rpm	**CHRISTMAS DAY** (63)	Reprise 20,135	$25
45(P)	**CHRISTMAS DAY** (63)	Reprise 20,135	$30
	(White promo label)		
45rpm	**I GOT BURNED** (63)	Reprise 20,141	$25
45rpm	**I GOT BURNED** (63)	Reprise 20,141	$200
	(Price includes picture sleeve)		
45(P)	**I GOT BURNED** (63)	Reprise 20,141	$30
	(White promo label)		
45rpm	**I WISH THIS NIGHT WOULD NEVER END** (63)	Reprise 20,176	$25
45(P)	**I WISH THIS NIGHT WOULD NEVER END** (63)	Reprise 20,176	$30
	(White promo label)		
45rpm	**RUN, LITTLE LINDA** (63)	Reprise 20,192	$30
45(P)	**RUN, LITTLE LINDA** (63)	Reprise 20,192	$35
	(White promo label)		
45rpm	**POISON IVY LEAGUE** (64)	Fontana 1502	$20
	(Flip, "Finally Said Something Good")		
45rpm	**POISON IVY LEAGUE** (64)	Fontana 1502	$18
	(Flip, "Tear in My Eye")		
45(P)	**POISON IVY LEAGUE** (64)	Fontana 1502	$25
	(White promo label, either version)		

45rpm	**GOOD LOVIN'** (64)		Fontana 1515	$20
45(P)	**GOOD LOVIN'** (64)		Smash 34774	$40
	(White promo label)			
45rpm	**LOVE ISN'T LIKE THAT** (66)		Red Bird 057	$75
45(P)	**LOVE ISN'T LIKE THAT** (66)		Red Bird 057	$50
	(Red Bird promo label)			
45rpm	**THE DAY THE BEAT STOPPED** (78)		Thunder 7801	$15
	(Small center hole, clear vinyl)			

-albums-

LP	**TAKIN' CARE OF BUSINESS** (61)		Gone 5012	$250

DONNY AND THE DUKE (RB)

-singles-

45rpm	**ROCK BABY** (58)		MGM 12641	$15
45(P)	**ROCK BABY** (58)		MGM 12641	$10
	(Yellow promo label)			

JERRY DOSTAL (Polka)
Other Soma 78s $15 each
Coral 45s $5-10 each
Little Crow 45s $2-4 each

-singles-

78rpm	**LAKE SIDE WALTZ** (53)		Soma 1001	$30
	(The first Soma record)			
45rpm	**LAKE SIDE WALTZ** (53)		Soma 1001	$25
45rpm	**BLUE SKIRT WALTZ** (54)		Soma 1002	$18
	(Yellow label)			
45rpm	**BLUE SKIRT WALTZ** (60)		Soma 1002	$10
	(Black label)			
45rpm	**ROSALINDA WALTZ** (55)		Soma 1026	$12
45rpm	**YOU PROMISED ME** (56)		Soma 1033	$10

GLENN DOUGLAS (RB)
Nephew of Ernest Tubb
Decca 45s $8 each

-albums-

LP	**HEARTBREAK ALLEY** (58)		Decca 8748	$50
LP(P)	**HEARTBREAK ALLEY** (58)		Decca 8748	$40
	(Pink promo label)			

MEL DOUGLAS (RB)

-singles-

45rpm	**CADILLAC BOOGIE** (58)		San 1506	$50

TONY DOUGLAS (C)
Any 45s $1 each

-albums-

LP	**HIS & HERS** (64)		Sims 121	$18
LP(P)	**HIS & HERS** (64)		Sims 121	$20
	(White promo label)			
LP	**MR. NICE GUY** (66)		Sims 131	$15
LP(P)	**MR. NICE GUY** (66)		Sims 131	$18
	(White promo label)			
LP	**HEART** (67)		Paula 2198	$12
LP	**THE VERSATILE TONY DOUGLAS** (69)		Paula 2206	$12
LP	**THANK YOU FOR TOUCHING MY LIFE** (70)		Dot 26009	$10
LP(P)	**THANK YOU FOR TOUCHING MY LIFE** (70)		Dot 26009	$12
	(White promo label)			

JERRY DOVE (RB)

-singles-

45rpm	**PINK BOW TIE** (58)		TNT 141	$60

LARRY DOWD (RB)

-singles-

45rpm	**BLUE SWINGIN' MAMA** (59)		Spinning 6009	$50

JOE DOWELL (R)
Other Smash 45s $5-8 each
Journey 45s and picture sleeves $1 each
Other Smash LPs $15 each

-singles-

45rpm	**WOODEN HEART** (61)		Smash 1708	$25
	(Price includes picture sleeve)			
45(P)	**WOODEN HEART** (61)		Smash 1708	$10
	(White promo label)			

45rpm	**THE BRIDGE OF LOVE** (62)	Smash 1717	$15
	(Price includes picture sleeve)		
45rpm	**LITTLE RED RENTED ROWBOAT** (63)	Smash 1759	$18
	(Price includes picture sleeve)		
45rpm	**NGA-BRANGA-BROUGHT** (64)	Smash 1799	$12
	(Price includes picture sleeve)		

-albums-

LP	**WOODEN HEART** (61) Stereo	Smash 67000	$25
LP	**WOODEN HEART** (61) Mono	Smash 27000	$18
LP(P)	**WOODEN HEART** (61)	Smash 27000	$30
	(White promo label)		

(BIG) AL DOWNING (RB)

-singles-

45rpm	**DOWN ON THE FARM** (58)	White Rock 1111	$50
45rpm	**DOWN ON THE FARM** (58)	Challenge 59006	$40
45(P)	**DOWN ON THE FARM** (58)	Challenge 59006	$25
	(White promo label)		
45rpm	**MISS LUCY** (58)	White Rock 1113	$50
45rpm	**MISS LUCY** (58)	Carlton 489	$30
45(P)	**MISS LUCY** (58)	Carlton 489	$20
	(Green promo label)		
45rpm	**WHEN MY BLUE MOON TURNS TO GOLD AGAIN** (59)	Carlton 507	$20
45(P)	**WHEN MY BLUE MOON TURNS TO GOLD AGAIN** (59)	Carlton 507	$18
	(Green promo label)		

RUDY DOZIER (RB)

-singles-

45rpm	**WICKED** (58)	Teen Time 108	$40

GUY DRAKE (N)

-albums-

LP	**WELFARE CADILLAC** (70)	Royal American 1001	$25

JIMMY DRAKE See Nervous Norvus

PETE DRAKE (C)
Smash 45s $2 each
Hilltop LPs $8 each
Mountain Dew LPs $6 each

-albums-

LP	**THE FABULOUS STEEL GUITAR SOUND OF PETE DRAKE** (62)	Starday 180	$20
LP	**COUNTRY STEEL GUITAR** (63)	Cumberland 69503	$15
LP	**FOREVER** (64)	Smash 67053	$18
LP(P)	**FOREVER** (64)	Smash 67053	$20
	(White promo label)		
LP	**TALKING STEEL GUITAR** (64)	Smash 67060	$15
LP(P)	**TALKING STEEL GUITAR** (64)	Smash 67060	$18
	(White promo label)		
LP	**TALKING STEEL & SINGING STRINGS** (65)	Smash 67064	$15
LP(P)	**TALKING STEEL & SINGING STRINGS** (65)	Smash 67064	$18
	(White promo label)		
LP	**THE AMAZING INCREDIBLE PETE DRAKE** (65)	Starday 319	$30
LP	**STEEL AWAY** (68)	Canaan 9640	$10
LP	**THE PETE DRAKE SHOW** (70)	Stop 10011	$12

RUSTY DRAPER (CW)
Other Mercury 78s and 45s $5-8 each

-singles-

78rpm	**THE BALLAD OF DAVY CROCKETT** (55)	Mercury 70555	$20
78(P)	**THE BALLAD OF DAVY CROCKETT** (55)	Mercury 70555	$25
	(White promo label)		
45rpm	**THE BALLAD OF DAVY CROCKETT** (55)	Mercury 70555	$25
45(P)	**THE BALLAD OF DAVY CROCKETT** (55)	Mercury 70555	$20
	(White promo label)		
78rpm	**THE SHIFTING, WHISPERING SANDS** (56)	Mercury 70696	$18
78(P)	**THE SHIFTING, WHISPERING SANDS** (56)	Mercury 70696	$20
	(White promo label)		
45rpm	**THE SHIFTING, WHISPERING SANDS** (56)	Mercury 70696	$12
45(P)	**THE SHIFTING, WHISPERING SANDS** (56)	Mercury 70696	$10
	(White promo label)		
45rpm	**PINK CADILLAC** (56) Maroon label	Mercury 70921	$12
45rpm	**PINK CADILLAC** (56) Black label	Mercury 70921	$10
45(P)	**PINK CADILLAC** (56) White promo label	Mercury 70921	$12

JIMMY DRIFTWOOD (CW)
Other RCA Victor 45s $3-6 each
Monument 45s $2-3 each
Other Monument LPs $4-8 each
Rimrock and Rackensack LPs $2-4 each

-singles-

45rpm	**THE BATTLE OF NEW ORLEANS** (59)	RCA Victor 7534	$12
	(Original version of the Johnny Horton hit)		
45(P)	**THE BATTLE OF NEW ORLEANS** (59)	RCA Victor 7534	$10
	(White promo label)		
45(P)	**THE MARSHALL OF SILVER CITY** (59)	RCA Victor SP-92	$12
	(Promo only, black label)		
45(P)	**JOHN PAUL JONES** (60)	RCA Victor 7603	$12
	(White promo label)		
45(S)	**JOHN PAUL JONES** (60)	RCA Victor 7603	$10
	(Stereo single used in jukeboxes)		

-EPs-

EP	**SOLDIER'S JOY** (59)	RCA Victor 4345	$12

-albums-

LP	**NEWLY DISCOVERED EARLY AMERICAN FOLK SONGS** (58)	RCA Victor 1635	$40
LP	**WILDERNESS ROAD & JIMMIE DRIFTWOOD** (59) Stereo	RCA Victor 1994	$25
	(Mono version worth $20)		
LP	**THE WESTWOOD MOVEMENT** (60)	RCA Victor 2171	$25
LP	**TALL TALES IN SONG** (60)	RCA Victor 2228	$25
LP	**SONGS OF BILLY YANK & JOHNNY REB** (61)	RCA Victor 2316	$25
LP	**DRIFTWOOD AT SEA** (62)	RCA Victor 2443	$25
LP	**VOICE OF THE PEOPLE** (63)	Monument 18006	$15

ROY DRUSKY (CW)
Decca 45s $4-8 each
Mercury 45s $2-4 each
Other Mercury LPs $4-8 each
   (Including Priscilla Mitchell duets)
Vocalion LPs $5-10 each
Wings and Capitol LPs $4-6 each
Plantation LPs $4 each
Scorpion and Hilltop LPs $3 each

-albums-

LP(P)	**PAIR OF ACES** (50s) Drusky and McCall	Sesac	$40
	(Promo-only duet album)		
LP	**ANYMORE WITH ROY DRUSKY** (61)	Decca 4160	$18
LP(P)	**ANYMORE WITH ROY DRUSKY** (61)	Decca 4160	$20
	(Pink promo label)		
LP	**IT'S MY WAY** (62)	Decca 4340	$15
LP(P)	**IT'S MY WAY** (62)	Decca 4340	$18
	(Pink promo label)		
LP	**SONGS OF THE CITIES** (64)	Mercury 60883	$10
LP	**YESTERDAY'S GONE** (64)	Mercury 60919	$10

-radio shows-

16"(RS)	**U.S. ARMY BAND** (50s) With Hank Snow	U.S. Army	$20-40
	(Music and interviews)		
LP(RS)	**GRAND OL' OPRY** (62)	WSM Radio 63	$25-40
	(Music and interviews)		
LP(RS)	**GRAND OL' OPRY** (63)	WSM Radio 75	$25-40
	(Music and interviews)		
LP(RS)	**GRAND OL' OPRY** (64)	WSM Radio 112	$25-40
	(Music and interviews)		
LP(RS)	**HOOTENAVY** (60s) Fifteen-minute show	U.S. Navy 29/30	$25-40
	(Two shows, one on each side)		
LP(RS)	**HOOTENAVY** (60s)	U.S. Navy 39/40	$25-40
	(Music and interviews)		

JIMMY DRY (CW)

-singles-

45rpm	**NEVER TOO LATE** (64)	D 1266	$10

LAWRENCE DUCHOW (Polka)
And His Red Ravens
RCA Victor 78s $2-4 each
Other RCA Victor 45s $4-8 each

-singles-

45rpm	**WHEN WE PARTED** (52) Aqua label	RCA Victor 4462	$18
45rpm	**HA, HA-HO, HO** (52) Aqua label	RCA Victor 4573	$15
45rpm	**DUTCH GARDEN** (53)	RCA Victor 4825	$15
45rpm	**I WANT A GIRL** (53)	RCA Victor 5165	$15
45rpm	**MAMBO POLKA** (53) With Frenchy Boutan	RCA Victor 5282	$12

45rpm	**POLISH PIANO POLKA** (54)	RCA Victor 5464	$12
45rpm	**BARBARA POLKA** (54) With Dick Metro and Gene Tebo	RCA Victor 5394	$15
45rpm	**SHOEMAKER POLKA** (56)	Potter 1003	$12
45rpm	**SAXOPHONE WALTZ** (57)	Potter 1004	$10
45rpm	**WHEN MY BLUE MOON TURNS TO GOLD AGAIN** (58)	Potter 2002	$12

DAVE DUDLEY (CW)

Mercury 45s $2-4 each
United Artists 45s $2-4 each
Rice 45s $2 each
Sun black vinyl 45s $3 each
Sun colored vinyl 45s $6 each
Other jukebox LLPs $10 each
Other Mercury LPs $5-8 each
United Artists LPs $8-10 each
Sun and Plantation LPs $5 each
Sun and Coronet duet LPs $3 each
Rice LPs $4 each
Mountain Dew and Guest Star LPs $3 each
Nashville LPs $2-3 each

-singles-

45rpm	**MAYBE I DO** (57)	Vee 7003	$40
	(Record company from Moorhead, Minnesota)		
45rpm	**ROCK AND ROLL NURSERY RHYME** (58)	King 4933	$18
45(P)	**ROCK AND ROLL NURSERY RHYME** (58)	King 4933	$15
	(White promo label)		
45rpm	**SIX DAYS ON THE ROAD** (59)	Golden Wing 3020	$10
45(P)	**SIX DAYS ON THE ROAD** (59)	Golden Wing 3020	$15
	(White promo label)		
45rpm	**COWBOY BOOTS** (59)	Golden Ring 3030	$12
	(Golden Ring printed on label in a ring)		
45rpm	**COWBOY BOOTS** (59)	Golden Ring 3030	$15
	(No ring on the label, block letters)		
45(P)	**COWBOY BOOTS** (59)	Golden Ring 3030	$18
	(White promo label)		

-EPs-

EP(P)	**DAVE DUDLEY COUNTRY** (67) Jukebox LLP	Mercury 669	$15
	(Price includes title strips and hard cover)		
EP(P)	**ORIGINAL TRAVELING MAN** (72) White promo-only EP	Mercury MEPL-17	$15
	(Released to radio stations only, in paper sleeve)		

-albums-

LP	**SIX DAYS ON THE ROAD** (63)	Golden Ring 110	$50
LP	**SONGS ABOUT THE WORKING MAN** (64)	Mercury 60899	$15
LP(P)	**SONGS ABOUT THE WORKING MAN** (64)	Mercury 60899	$18
	(White promo label)		
LP	**TRAVELING WITH DAVE DUDLEY** (64)	Mercury 60927	$12
LP(P)	**TRAVELING WITH DAVE DUDLEY** (64)	Mercury 60927	$15
	(White promo label)		
LP	**TALK OF THE TOWN** (64)	Mercury 60970	$12
LP(P)	**TALK OF THE TOWN** (64)	Mercury 60970	$15
	(White promo label)		
LP	**TRUCK DRIVIN' SON-OF-A-GUN** (65)	Mercury 61028	$10
LP(P)	**TRUCK DRIVIN' SON-OF-A-GUN** (65)	Mercury 61028	$12
	(White promo label)		

-radio shows-

LP(RS)	**COUNTRY MUSIC TIME** (70s)	U.S. Army	$10-15

ARLIE DUFF (CW)

-singles-

45rpm	**YOU ALL COME** (54)	Starday 104	$15
45rpm	**STUCK-IN-A-MUD HOLE** (54)	Starday 106	$12
45rpm	**LET ME BE YOUR SALTY DOG** (55)	Starday 132	$12
45rpm	**I DREAMED OF A HILL-BILLY HEAVEN** (55)	Decca 29428	$15
45(P)	**I DREAMED OF A HILL-BILLY HEAVEN** (55)	Decca 29428	$12
	(Pink promo label)		
45rpm	**ALLIGATOR COME ACROSS** (57)	Decca 29987	$18
45(P)	**ALLIGATOR COME ACROSS** (57)	Decca 29987	$15
	(Pink promo label)		
45rpm	**SEND ME AN ANGEL**	Smartt 1001	$15
	(Red vinyl special release)		

JOHN DUFFY (BG)

-albums-

LP	**BLUEGRASS HOOTENANNY** (60s)	International Award 227	$35

EDDIE DUGOSH (RB)

-singles-

45rpm	ONE MILE (59)	Award 116	$15
45rpm	STRANGE KINDA FEELING (59)	Sarg 135	$25

ROY DUKE (RB)

-singles-

45rpm	BEHAVE, BE QUIET OR BE GONE (57)	Reject 1002	$12
45rpm	BEHAVE, BE QUIET OR BE GONE (57)	Decca 29962	$18
45(P)	BEHAVE, BE QUIET OR BE GONE (57)	Decca 29962	$15
	(Pink promo label)		
45rpm	HONKY TONK QUEEN (58)	Decca 30095	$15
45(P)	HONKY TONK QUEEN (58)	Decca 30095	$12
	(Pink promo label)		
45rpm	HARD HEARTED MAMA (58)	Decca 30235	$15
45(P)	HARD HEARTED MAMA (58)	Decca 30235	$12
	(Pink promo label)		

DUKE OF PADUCAH (N)
Benjamin "Whitey" Ford

-singles-

78rpm	WHAT IT WAS (54) Part 1, Part 2	Mercury 70290	$30
	(Earlier version of the Andy Griffith classic)		
45rpm	WHAT IT WAS (54) Part 1, Part 2	Mercury 70290	$25

-albums-

LP	BUTTON SHOES, BELLY LAUGHS & MONKEY BUSINESS (61)	Starday 148	$25

DON DUNCAN (RB)

-singles-

45rpm	SOMETHING SPECIAL (58)	Venture 111	$50

HERBIE DUNCAN (RB)

-singles-

45rpm	HOT LIPS BABY (58)	Glenn 1400	$60
45rpm	THAT'S ALL (58)	Glenn 1402	$40

JOHNNY DUNCAN (C)
Columbia 45s $1 each
Columbia LPs $3-5 each
  (Including Janie Fricke and June Stearns duets)
Harmony LPs $2-5 each

TOMMY DUNCAN (RB)

-singles-

45rpm	DADDY LOVES MOMMY (58)	Fire 101	$25

TOMMY DURDEN (CW)

-singles-

45rpm	DEEP IN THE HEART OF A FOOL (60)	D 1076	$15

HUELYN DUVALL (RB)

-singles-

45rpm	IT'S NO WONDER (57)	Starfire 600	$40
45rpm	COMIN' OR GOIN' (58)	Challenge 1012	$50
45(P)	COMIN' OR GOIN' (58)	Challenge 1012	$30
	(White promo label)		
45rpm	YOU KNOCK ME OUT (58)	Challenge 59002	$15
45(P)	YOU KNOCK ME OUT (58)	Challenge 59002	$10
	(White promo label)		
45rpm	THREE MINUTES TO KILL (59)	Challenge 59014	$15
45(P)	THREE MINUTES TO KILL (59)	Challenge 59014	$10
	(White promo label)		
45rpm	JULIET (59)	Challenge 59025	$12
45(P)	JULIET (59)	Challenge 59025	$10
	(White promo label)		
45rpm	PUCKER PAINT (59)	Challenge 59069	$18
45(P)	PUCKER PAINT (59)	Challenge 59069	$12
	(White promo label)		

E

EAGLES (R)
Including Don Henley, Glenn Frey, and Don Felder
Asylum promo 45s $3-6 each
Asylum 45s $2-4 each
Geffen 45s by Don Henley $2-3 each
MCA 45s by Glenn Frey $2-3 each
Any 45s by Don Felder $1-2 each

-singles-

45(P)	**WHAT'S IT ALL ABOUT** (Mar 75) Public service show	W. I. A. A. 256	$25
	(Label misprint reads "Rick Frey" and Don Henley)		
45(P)	**WHAT'S IT ALL ABOUT** (Mar 77) Public service show	W. I. A. A. 362	$25
	(Flip side features Kris Kristofferson)		
45(P)	**HEARTACHE TONIGHT** (79)	Asylum 12394	$15
	(Price is for the version with a small center hole)		

-EPs-

12"(P)	**PLEASE COME HOME FOR CHRISTMAS** (78)	Asylum 11402	$20
	(Also "Funky New Year")		

-albums-

CD(P)	**TOUR COLLECTION** (94) Ten tracks	PRCD 8983	$30
	(Promo-only release)		

-radio shows-

LP(RS)	**INNERVIEW** (70s) Don Felder	Inner View	$10-15
	(Music and interviews)		
2LP(RS)	**THE EAGLES SPOTLIGHT SPECIAL** (80) Box set	ABC Radio	$50-100
	(Profile of the group)		
5LP(RS)	**KING BISCUIT FLOWER HOUR** A conversation with …	DIR	$125-200
	(Rare profile of the group)		
3LP(RS)	**SUPERSTAR CONCERT** (80s)	Westwood One	$40-75
	(Live concert)		
LP(RS)	**BBC ROCK HOUR** (Nov 83) Don Felder	London Wavelength	$30-50
	(Thanksgiving show)		
3CD(RS)	**ON THE BORDER** (90)		$75-100
	(Music and interviews)		
2LP(RS)	**OFF THE RECORD** (90s) Glenn Frey	Westwood One	$10-20
	(Music and interviews)		
2LP(RS)	**OFF THE RECORD** (90s) Don Henley	Westwood One	$15-25
	(Music and interviews)		
2CD(RS)	**OFF THE RECORD** (Aug 94)	Westwood One	$25-50
	(Music and interviews of reunion)		
CD(RS)	**OFF THE RECORD** (Aug 94)	Westwood One	$15-30
	(Music and interviews of reunion)		
CD(RS)	**OFF THE RECORD** (Dec 94)	Westwood One	$20-30
	(Music and interviews)		
3CD(RS)	**PINK CHAMPAGNE ON ICE** (Nov 90)		$75-100
	(Music and interviews)		
CD(RS)	**IN THE STUDIO** (Oct 92)	Media America	$15-25
	(Profile of an album, music and interviews)		
3CD(RS)	**COMMON THREAD SPECIAL** (Oct 93) Various artists		$40-60
	(Tribute LP and radio show of Eagles songs)		

JIM EANES (CW)
And the Shenandoah Valley Boys
Other Decca 78s and 45s $5-8 each
Starday 45s $4-6 each
Rural Rhythm LPs $5-10 each
County LPs $3-6 each

-singles-

78rpm	**THEY LOCKED GOD OUTSIDE THE IRON CURTAIN** (53)	Decca 46403	$15
45rpm	**THEY LOCKED GOD OUTSIDE THE IRON CURTAIN** (53)	Decca 46403	$25
78rpm	**A PRISONER OF WAR** (53)	Decca 28387	$12
45rpm	**A PRISONER OF WAR** (53)	Decca 28387	$20
78rpm	**WHEN THE ONE THAT YOU LOVE IS IN LOVE WITH YOU** (54)	Decca 28609	$10
45rpm	**WHEN THE ONE THAT YOU LOVE IS IN LOVE WITH YOU** (54)	Decca 28609	$10
78rpm	**DON'T GO LOOKIN' FOR TROUBLE** (57)	Decca 29841	$15
78(P)	**DON'T GO LOOKIN' FOR TROUBLE** (57)	Decca 29841	$12
	(Decca promo label)		
45rpm	**DON'T GO LOOKIN' FOR TROUBLE** (57)	Decca 29841	$12
45(P)	**DON'T GO LOOKIN' FOR TROUBLE** (57)	Decca 29841	$10
	(Pink promo label)		

-EPs-

EP	**JIM EANES** (59)	Starday 108	$20

	-albums-		
LP	**STATESMAN OF BLUEGRASS MUSIC** (70s)	Jessup 152	$18

JOHNNY EARL (RB)

-singles-

45rpm	**PULL IT MAN** (58)	Gyro 102	$40

STEVE EARLE (C)
And the Dukes
Other Epic 45s $2-5 each
Uni 45s $3 each
Other MCA black vinyl 45s $2-4 each
Other MCA color vinyl 45s $8 each

-singles-

45(P)	**A LITTLE BIT IN LOVE** (85)	Epic 04784	$10
	(Price includes promo-only picture sleeve)		
45(P)	**HILLBILLY HIGHWAY** (86)	MCA 52785	$10
	(White promo label, green vinyl)		
45(P)	**SOMEDAY** (86)	MCA 52920	$10
	(White promo label, red vinyl)		
12"(P)	**SOMEDAY** (86) Three-song twelve-inch single	MCA L33-17129	$10
	(White promo label, special hard cover)		
45(P)	**NOWHERE ROAD** (87)	MCA 53103	$10
	(White promo label, blue vinyl)		

-radio shows-

3LP(RS)	**AMERICAN EAGLE** (July 86) With Forester Sisters	Westwood One	$20-30
	(Live concert)		
3LP(RS)	**AMERICAN EAGLE** (Jan 87) With T. Graham Brown	Westwood One	$30-50
	(Live concert)		

JACK EARLS (RB)

-singles-

45rpm	**SLOW DOWN** (58)	Sun 240	$25

BERNIE EARLY (RB)

-singles-

45rpm	**ROCK DOLL** (58)	MGM 12640	$12
45(P)	**ROCK DOLL** (58)	MGM 12640	$10
	(Yellow promo label)		

CLINT EASTWOOD (C)

-albums-

LP	**COWBOY FAVORITES** (60s)	Cameo 1056	$40

CONNIE EATON (C)
ABC and Chart 45s $2 each
ABC and Chart duet LPs $5 each

LEE EBERT (RB)

-singles-

45rpm	**LET'S JIVE IT** (58)	Rocket 801	$125

ECHOMORES (RB)

-singles-

45rpm	**LITTLE CHICK** (58)	Rocket 1042	$60

ECO-NASHVILLE (PSA/Ads)
Earth Communications Office

-albums-

CD(P)	**WE ONLY HAVE 10 YEARS TO SAVE OUR PLANET** (90-91)	ECO Nashville 4043	$25
	(Public service radio ads, sixty-three cuts, ten to sixty seconds each with top country artists including Emmylou Harris, Randy Travis, Roseanne Cash, Alabama, Bellamy Brothers, Lionel Cartwright, Dan Seals, and others)		

EDDIE EDDINGS (CW)

-singles-

45rpm	**SMOOCHIN'** (53)	Starday 163	$10

DUANE EDDY (R)
Includes Jimmy (Delbridge) & Duane and Miriam Johnson (Jessi Colter)
Gregmark, Colpix, Reprise, Congress 45s $5-8 each
    (Not including promos)
Other Jamie yellow promo label 45s $15 each
Gregmark promo 45s $12 each
Reprise white promo label 45s $10 each

Colpix white promo label 45s $10 each
Congress white promo label 45s $8 each
Elektra 45s $2-3 each
Capitol 45s $3-5 each
Capitol picture sleeves $3 each
Stacy white promo label 45s by Al Casey $10 each
   (Most records include Duane Eddy)
RCA Victor LPs $10 each
Capitol LPs $3 each

-singles-

45rpm	**SODA FOUNTAIN GIRL**	Eb. X. Preston 212	$125
	(By Jimmy & Duane)		
45rpm	**RAMROD** (57)	Ford 500	$1,000
	(Very rare on Ford)		
78rpm	**MOVIN' N' GROOVIN'** (58)	Jamie 1101	$25
45rpm	**MOVIN' N' GROOVIN'** (58)	Jamie 1101	$15
45rpm	**MOVIN' N' GROOVIN'** (58)	Jamie 1101	$50
	(Pink promo label)		
78rpm	**REBEL ROUSER** (58)	Jamie 1104	$20
45rpm	**REBEL ROUSER** (58)	Jamie 1104	$15
45rpm	**RAMROD** (58)	Jamie 1109	$20
45rpm	**CANNONBALL** (59)	Jamie 1111	$20
45rpm	**THE LONELY ONE** (59)	Jamie 1117	$15
45(P)	**THE LONELY ONE** (59)	Jamie DE-8	$40
	(Rare yellow promo label)		
45(S)	**THE LONELY ONE** (59)	Jamie 1117	$20
	(Yellow label, stereo single)		
45rpm	**YEP!** (59)	Jamie 1122	$12
45rpm	**YEP!** (59)	Jamie 1122	$40
	(Price includes picture sleeve)		
45(S)	**YEP!** (59)	Jamie 1122	$25
	(Stereo single)		
45rpm	**FORTY MILES OF BAD ROAD** (59)	Jamie 1126	$30
	(Price includes picture sleeve)		
45rpm	**FORTY MILES OF BAD ROAD** (59)	Jamie 1126	$25
	(Stereo single)		
45rpm	**SOME KIND OF EARTHQUAKE** (59)	Jamie 1130	$30
	(Price includes picture sleeve)		
45rpm	**SOME KIND OF EARTHQUAKE** (59)	Jamie 1130	$25
	(Stereo single)		
45rpm	**BONNIE COME BACK** (59)	Jamie 1144	$25
	(Price includes picture sleeve)		
45rpm	**SHAZAM!** (60)	Jamie 1151	$25
	(Price includes picture sleeve)		
45rpm	**BECAUSE THEY'RE YOUNG** (60)	Jamie 1156	$25
	(Price includes picture sleeve)		
5-45s	**(JUKEBOX STEREO SINGLES SET)** Five 45s	Jamie JLP 71-75	$25 each
	(Stereo singles, $125 for the set)		
45rpm	**KOMOTION** (60)	Jamie 1163	$25
	(Price includes picture sleeve)		
45rpm	**PETER GUNN** (60)	Jamie 1168	$25
	(Price includes picture sleeve)		
45rpm	**PEPE** (61) Red picture sleeve	Jamie 1175	$30
	(Price includes picture sleeve)		
45rpm	**PEPE** (61) Yellow picture sleeve	Jamie 1175	$25
	(Price includes picture sleeve)		
45rpm	**YOUNG AND INNOCENT** (60) Miriam Johnson	Jamie 1181	$18
	(Miriam Johnson married Duane Eddy after this record, then after a divorce, married Waylon Jennings and recorded as Jessi Colter)		
45rpm	**THEME FROM DIXIE** (61)	Jamie 1183	$20
	(Price includes picture sleeve)		
45rpm	**RING OF FIRE** (61)	Jamie 1187	$20
	(Price includes picture sleeve)		
45rpm	**DRIVIN' HOME** (61)	Jamie 1195	$20
	(Price includes picture sleeve)		
45rpm	**MY BLUE HEAVEN** (61)	Jamie 1200	$18
	(Price includes picture sleeve)		
45rpm	**DEEP IN THE HEART OF TEXAS** (62)	RCA Victor 7999	$18
	(Price includes picture sleeve)		
45rpm	**DANCE WITH THE GUITAR MAN** (62)	RCA Victor 8047	$20
	(Price includes picture sleeve)		
45rpm	**GUITAR MAN** (62)	RCA Victor 8087	$18
	(Price includes picture sleeve)		
45rpm	**BOSS GUITAR** (63)	RCA Victor 8183	$18
	(Price includes picture sleeve)		
45rpm	**LONELY BOY, LONELY GUITAR** (63)	RCA Victor 8180	$18
	(Price includes picture sleeve)		

45rpm	**YOUR BABY'S GONE SURFIN'** (63)		RCA Victor 8214	$20
	(Price includes picture sleeve)			
45rpm	**THE SON OF REBEL ROUSER** (64)		RCA Victor 8276	$15
	(Price includes picture sleeve)			
45rpm	**GUITAR CHILD** (63)		RCA Victor 8335	$15
	(Price includes picture sleeve)			
45rpm	**THEME FROM A SUMMER PLACE** (64)		RCA Victor 8376	$15
	(Price includes picture sleeve)			
45rpm	**GUITAR STAR** (64)		RCA Victor 8442	$15
	(Price includes picture sleeve)			
45rpm	**MOONSHOT** (65)		RCA Victor 8507	$15
	(Price includes picture sleeve)			

-EPs-

EP	**DUANE EDDY** (59)		Jamie 101	$75
EP	**SHAZAM** (60)		Jamie 301	$75
EP	**YEP!** (60)		Jamie 302	$75
EP	**BECAUSE THEY'RE YOUNG** (60)		Jamie 304	$75
EP(JB)	**DUANE EDDY** (62) Jukebox LLP from Wurlitzer		RCA Wurlitzer 100	$50
	(Issued with a hard cover)			
EP	**DUANE EDDY** (63)		RCA Victor 8200	$50
EP(JB)	**GUITAR MAN** (68)		RCA Victor 1100	$30
	(Issued with a cover and title strips)			
EP(JB)	**TWANGIN' THE GOLDEN HITS** (68)		RCA Victor 2993	$30
	(Issued with a cover and title strips)			

-albums-

LP	**HAVE TWANGY GUITAR WILL TRAVEL** (58) Mono		Jamie 3000	$75
	(First pressing has a white cover)			
LP	**HAVE TWANGY GUITAR WILL TRAVEL** (58) Stereo		Jamie 3000	$250
	(Yellow label)			
LP	**HAVE TWANGY GUITAR WILL TRAVEL** (58) Mono		Jamie 3000	$40
	(Gold and white label)			
LP	**HAVE TWANGY GUITAR WILL TRAVEL** (58) Stereo		Jamie 3000	$75
	(Gold and white label)			
LP	**ESPECIALLY FOR YOU** (59)		Jamie 3006	$40
LP	**THE TWANGS THE THANG** (59)		Jamie 3009	$40
LP	**SONGS FROM OUR HERITAGE** (59)		Jamie 3011	$50
	(Gatefold cover)			
LP	**SONGS FROM OUR HERITAGE** (59) Red vinyl		Jamie 3011	$250
LP	**SONGS FROM OUR HERITAGE** (59) Blue vinyl		Jamie 3011	$250
	(These versions have a gatefold cover)			
LP	**SONGS FROM OUR HERITAGE** (59)		Jamie 3011	$25
	(Common single cover)			
LP	**$1,000,000 WORTH OF TWANG** (60)		Jamie 3014	$25
LP	**GIRLS! GIRLS! GIRLS!** (61)		Jamie 3019	$25
LP	**$1,000,000 WORTH OF TWANG VOL. 2** (62)		Jamie 3022	$25
LP	**DUANE A-GO-GO** (65)		Colpix 490	$30
LP(P)	**DUANE A-GO-GO** (65)		Colpix 490	$50
	(White promo label)			
LP	**DUANE EDDY DOES BOB DYLAN** (65)		Colpix 494	$40
LP(P)	**DUANE EDDY DOES BOB DYLAN** (65)		Colpix 494	$75
	(White promo label)			
LP	**THE BIGGEST TWANG OF THEM ALL** (66)		Reprise 6218	$18
LP(P)	**THE BIGGEST TWANG OF THEM ALL** (66)		Reprise 6218	$25
	(White promo label)			
LP	**THE ROARING TWANGIES** (67)		Reprise 6240	$18
LP(P)	**THE ROARING TWANGIES** (67)		Reprise 6240	$25
	(White promo label)			
2LP(P)	**VINTAGE YEARS** (75)		Sire 3707	$20
	(White promo labels)			

JIM EDDY (CW)
Mercury 45s $8-10 each

-singles-

45rpm	**LIVIN' DOLL** (58)		Soma 1091	$18

PEARL EDDY (CW)

-singles-

45rpm	**THAT'S WHAT A HEART IS FOR** (53)		Vik (RCA) 0043	$10

JIMMY EDWARDS (RB)

-singles-

45rpm	**LOVE BUG CRAWL** (57)		Mercury 71209	$12
45(P)	**LOVE BUG CRAWL** (57)		Mercury 71209	$10
	(White promo label)			
45rpm	**MY HONEY** (58)		Mercury 71272	$12

45(P)	**MY HONEY** (58) (White promo label)	Mercury 71272	$10

-EPs-

EP(P)	**DISC JOCKEY SIXTY SECOND SPECIAL** (57) (Includes sixty-second version of "Love Bug Crawl")	Mercury MEP-33	$15

JOHNNY EDWARDS (RB)
-singles-

45rpm	**ROCK & ROLL SADDLES** (58)	Northland 7002	$75

JONATHAN EDWARDS (C)
Capricorn 45s $3 each
MCA 45s $2 each

STONEY EDWARDS (C)
Capitol 45s $2 each
Capitol LPs $5-10 each
Music America LPs $4 each

TIBBY EDWARDS (CW)
-singles-

45rpm	**ONE MORE NIGHT** (57)	D 1081	$10

VERN EDWARDS (RB)
-singles-

45rpm	**COOL, BABY COOL** (58)	Probe 100	$75

BILLY ELDRIDGE (RB)
-singles-

45rpm	**LET'S GO BABY** (58)	Vulco 1501	$85
45rpm	**LET'S GO BABY** (58)	Unart 2011	$50
45(P)	**LET'S GO BABY** (58) (White promo label)	Unart 2011	$35

RAMBLIN' JACK ELLIOT (F)
Folksinger
Only his country LPs are listed
-albums-

LP	**RAMBLIN' COWBOY** (62)	Monitor 379	$25
LP	**RAMBLIN' JACK ELLIOT SINGS JIMMIE RODGERS** (62) (Also Woody Guthrie songs)	Monitor 380	$25
LP	**JACK ELLIOT COUNTRY STYLE** (62)	Prestige 13045	$20
LP	**COUNTRY STYLE** (64)	Prestige 14029	$18
LP	**COUNTRY STYLE** (70)	Prestige 7804	$10

DOLAN ELLIS (C)
Member of the New Christy Minstrels
Only his country EP is listed
-EPs-

EP(P)	**DOLAN ELLIS SINGS FOR WESTERN SAVINGS** (This LLP has a paper picture cover and was recorded in Phoenix)	Audio Recorders	$10

JIMMY ELLIS See Orion

RED ELLIS (BG)
Starday 45s $2 each
-albums-

LP	**HOLY CRY FROM THE CROSS** (62)	Starday 168	$15
LP	**THE SACRED SOUND OF BLUEGRASS MUSIC** (62)	Starday 203	$12
LP	**OLD TIME RELIGION BLUEGRASS STYLE** (63)	Starday 273	$10

REX ELLIS (RB)
-singles-

45rpm	**BOP HOP JAMBOREE** (58)	Rivermont 1160	$150

ELMO & PATSY (N)
Epic 45s $3 each
Epic picture sleeves $3 each
Oink LPs $5-8 each

TED EMBRY (RB)
-singles-

45rpm	**NEW SHOES** (57)	Ac'cent 1057	$25

BILL EMERSON (BG)
And His Virginia Mountaineers
Coronet and Design LPs $5 each

BILLY EMERSON (RB)

-singles-

45rpm	**NO TEASIN' AROUND** (54)	Sun 195	$150
45rpm	**THE WOODCHUCK** (54)	Sun 203	$125
45rpm	**MOVE BABY MOVE** (54)	Sun 214	$50
45rpm	**RED HOT** (55)	Sun 219	$50

-radio shows-

LP(RS)	**WE PICK THE NAVY** (60s) U.S. Navy Band (Featuring Bill Emerson)	U.S. Navy	$40

RAPLH EMERY (CW)
Host of the Grand Ol' Opry

-singles-

45rpm	**HELLO FOOL** (61) (Answer song to "Hello Walls")	Liberty 55352	$10
45rpm	**LEGEND OF SLEEPY HOLLOW** (62)	Liberty 55383	$15
45(P)	**LEGEND OF SLEEPY HOLLOW** (62) (White promo label)	Liberty 55383	$12

MELVIN ENDSLEY (CW)
Other RCA Victor 45s $6-8 each
Hickory 45s $5 each

-singles-

45rpm	**KEEP A-LOVIN' ME, BABY** (58)	RCA Victor 6968	$12
45rpm	**HUNGRY EYES** (58)	RCA Victor 7062	$12
45rpm	**I GOT A FEELIN'** (58)	RCA Victor 7147	$12
45rpm	**LET'S FALL OUT OF LOVE** (59)	RCA Victor 7216	$10

-EPs-

EP(P)	**I AIN'T GETTIN' ANYWHERE WITH YOU** (57) (Two songs on each side, Doree Post on flip side)	RCA Victor DJ-58	$15

BOB ENSIGN (BG)
And the Stump Jumpers
Other Rural Rhythm LPs $5-8 each

-singles-

LP	**BOB ENSIGN & THE STUMP JUMPERS** (71) (With Dallas Turner)	Rural Rhythm 177	$15
LP	**OLD TIME FAVORITES** (73) (Cover lists Nevada Slim as artist)	Rural Rhythm 186	$50
LP	**OLD TIME FAVORITES** (73) (Cover lists Bob Ensign as artist)	Rural Rhythm 186	$15

ESQUERITA (R)

-EPs-

EP	**ESQUERITA** (59)	Capitol 1186	$55

-albums-

LP	**ESQUERITA** (59)	Capitol 1186	$125
LP(P)	**ESQUERITA** (59) (Capitol promo label)	Capitol 1186	$100

BOB EUBANKS (R)

-singles-

45rpm	**HEAVEN OF THE STARS** (59)	Tracy 6101	$10

JIMMY EVANS (RB)

-singles-

45rpm	**THE JOINT'S REALLY JUMPIN'** (58)	Caveman 502	$100
45rpm	**THE JOINT'S REALLY JUMPIN'** (58)	Clearmont 502	$75

LEON EVERETT (C)
Other RCA Victor 45s $2-3 each
RCA Victor LPs $4-6 each

-singles-

45rpm	**GOODBYE KING OF ROCK 'N' ROLL** (77) (Tribute to Presley)	True 107	$12
45(P)	**GOODBYE KING OF ROCK 'N' ROLL** (77) (Red/white promo label)	True 107	$10
45(P)	**SOUL SEARCHIN'** (82) (Yellow promo label, red vinyl)	RCA Victor 13282	$10
45(P)	**SHADOWS OF MY MIND** (82) (Cream-colored promo label, blue vinyl)	RCA Victor 13391	$10

45(P)	**MY LADY LOVES ME** (83)	RCA Victor 13466	$10
	(Yellow promo label, yellow vinyl)		
45(P)	**THE LADY, SHE'S RIGHT** (83)	RCA Victor 13584	$10
	(Blue promo label, blue vinyl)		
45(P)	**I COULD'A HAD YOU** (84)	RCA Victor 13717	$10
	(Orange label, green vinyl)		

-albums-

LP	**GOODBYE KING OF ROCK & ROLL** (77)	True 1002	$15
	(Tribute to Presley, includes poster)		

-radio shows-

3LP(RS)	**SILVER EAGLE** (82) With Jerry Reed	Westwood One	$20-40
	(Live concert)		
3LP(RS)	**SILVER EAGLE** (83) With McGuffy Lane	Westwood One	$20-40
	(Live concert)		
3LP(RS)	**SILVER EAGLE** (May 85) With Gus Hardin	Westwood One	$20-40
	(Live concert)		
LP(RS)	**LIVE AT GILLEY'S** (Jan 86)	Westwood One	$10-15
	(Live concert)		

VINCE EVERETT (RB)

-singles-

45rpm	**SUCH A NIGHT** (62)	ABC Paramount 10313	$25
45(P)	**SUCH A NIGHT** (62)	ABC Paramount 10313	$20
	(White promo label)		
45rpm	**I AIN'T GONNA BE YOUR LOW DOWN DOG ANYMORE** (62)	ABC Paramount 10360	$25
45(P)	**I AIN'T GONNA BE YOUR LOW DOWN DOG ANYMORE** (62)	ABC Paramount 10360	$20
	(White promo label)		
45rpm	**BABY LET'S PLAY HOUSE** (63)	ABC Paramount 10472	$30
45(P)	**BABY LET'S PLAY HOUSE** (63)	ABC Paramount 10472	$20
	(White promo label)		
45rpm	**TO HAVE, TO HOLD AND LET GO** (65)	ABC Paramount 10624	$18
45(P)	**TO HAVE, TO HOLD AND LET GO** (65)	ABC Paramount 10624	$15
	(White promo label)		
45rpm	**BUTTERCUP**	Town 1964	$10

EVERLY BROTHERS (R)
Don and Phil Everly
Other Warner 45s $5-10 each
Other Warner promo 45s $10-12 each
RCA Victor 45s $5-8 each
Other RCA Victor promo 45s $8-10 each
Mercury 45s $2-5 each
Mercury picture sleeves $3 each
Ode, ABC, and Polydor 45s by Don Everly $3-5 each
Pye 45s by Phil Everly $6 each
Elektra, Curb, and Capitol 45s by Phil Everly $2-4 each
Capitol 45s by Everly Brothers and Beach Boys $6 each
Other Warner LPs $8 each
Other Warner promo LPs $12 each
Harmony LPs $8-12 each
RCA Victor LPs $8-12 each
Ode and Hickory LPs by Don Everly $8-10 each
RCA Victor and Pye LPs by Phil Everly $8-10 each

-singles-

45rpm	**THE SUN KEEPS SHINING** (56) Red label	Columbia 21496	$500
45(P)	**THE SUN KEEPS SHINING** (56)	Columbia 21496	$250
	(White promo label)		
78rpm	**BYE BYE LOVE** (57)	Cadence 1315	$40
45rpm	**BYE BYE LOVE** (57)	Cadence 1315	$15
78rpm	**WAKE UP LITTLE SUSIE** (57)	Cadence 1337	$40
45rpm	**WAKE UP LITTLE SUSIE** (57)	Cadence 1337	$15
45rpm	**WAKE UP LITTLE SUSIE** (57)	Cadence 1337	$175
	(Price includes picture sleeve)		
78rpm	**THIS LITTLE GIRL OF MINE** (57)	Cadence 1342	$40
45rpm	**THIS LITTLE GIRL OF MINE** (57)	Cadence 1342	$15
78rpm	**ALL I HAVE TO DO IS DREAM** (58)	Cadence 1348	$40
45rpm	**ALL I HAVE TO DO IS DREAM** (58)	Cadence 1348	$15
78rpm	**BIRD DOG** (58)	Cadence 1350	$50
45rpm	**BIRD DOG** (58)	Cadence 1350	$15
78rpm	**PROBLEMS** (58)	Cadence 1355	$75
45rpm	**PROBLEMS** (58)	Cadence 1355	$15
PS	**PROBLEMS** (58)	Cadence 1355	$45
	(Price includes picture sleeve)		
45rpm	**TAKE A MESSAGE TO MARY** (59)	Cadence 1364	$15
45(P)	**TAKE A MESSAGE TO MARY** (59)	Cadence 1364	$25
	(White promo label)		

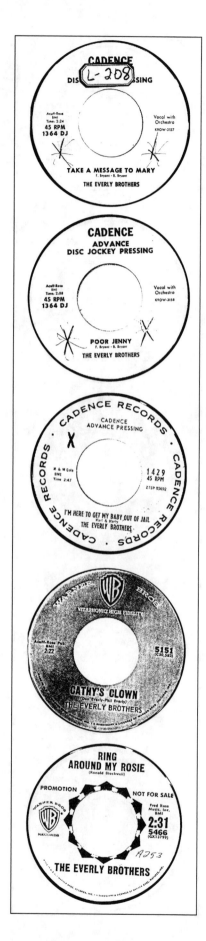

45rpm	TILL I KISSED YOU (59)	Cadence 1369	$15
45rpm	TILL I KISSED YOU (59)	Cadence 1369	$40
	(Price includes picture sleeve)		
45(P)	TILL I KISSED YOU (59)	Cadence 1369	$18
	(White promo label)		
45rpm	LET IT BE ME (60)	Cadence 1376	$12
45rpm	LET IT BE ME (60)	Cadence 1376	$35
	(Price includes picture sleeve)		
45(P)	LET IT BE ME (60)	Cadence 1376	$15
	(White promo label)		
45rpm	WHEN WILL I BE LOVED (60)	Cadence 1380	$12
45(P)	WHEN WILL I BE LOVED (60)	Cadence 1380	$15
	(White promo label)		
45rpm	LIKE STRANGERS (60)	Cadence 1388	$10
45(P)	LIKE STRANGERS (60)	Cadence 1388	$15
	(White promo label)		
45rpm	I'M HERE TO GET MY BABY OUT OF JAIL (62)	Cadence 1429	$10
45rpm	I'M HERE TO GET MY BABY OUT OF JAIL (62)	Cadence 1429	$25
	(Price includes picture sleeve)		
45(P)	I'M HERE TO GET MY BABY OUT OF JAIL (62)	Cadence 1429	$12
	(White promo label)		
45rpm	CATHY'S CLOWN (60)	Warner 5151	$15
45rpm	CATHY'S CLOWN (60)	Warner 5151	$40
	(Price includes picture sleeve)		
45rpm	CATHY'S CLOWN (60)	Warner 5151	$50
	(Stereo single)		
45(P)	CATHY'S CLOWN (60)	Warner 5151	$20
	(White promo label)		
45(P)	CATHY'S CLOWN (60)	Warner 5151	$100
	(Gold promo label, gold vinyl)		
45rpm	SO SAD (60)	Warner 5163	$10
45rpm	SO SAD (60)	Warner 5163	$30
	(Price includes picture sleeve)		
45(P)	SO SAD (60)	Warner 5163	$18
	(White promo label)		
45(P)	SO SAD (60)	Warner 5163	$75
	(Gold promo label, gold vinyl)		
45rpm	EBONY EYES (61)	Warner 5199	$10
45rpm	EBONY EYES (61)	Warner 5199	$20
	(Price includes picture sleeve)		
45(P)	EBONY EYES (61)	Warner 5199	$15
	(White promo label)		
45(P)	EBONY EYES (61)	Warner 5199	$75
	(Gold promo label, gold vinyl)		
45rpm	TEMPTATION (61)	Warner 5220	$20
	(Price includes picture sleeve)		
45(P)	TEMPTATION (61)	Warner 5220	$12
	(White promo label)		
45rpm	CRYING IN THE RAIN (61)	Warner 5250	$20
	(Price includes picture sleeve)		
45(P)	CRYING IN THE RAIN (61)	Warner 5250	$12
	(White promo label)		
45rpm	MUSKRAT +3 (62) Four-song EP-single	Warner 5501	$10
	(Two of the four tracks are edited)		
45rpm	MUSKRAT +3 (62)	Warner 5501	$20
	(Price includes picture sleeve)		
45(P)	MUSKRAT +3 (62)	Warner 5501	$20
	(White promo label)		
45rpm	THAT'S OLD FASHIONED (62)	Warner 5273	$20
	(Price includes picture sleeve)		
45(P)	THAT'S OLD FASHIONED (62)	Warner 5273	$12
	(White promo label)		
45rpm	DON'T ASK ME TO BE FRIENDS (62)	Warner 5297	$20
	(Price includes picture sleeve)		
45(P)	DON'T ASK ME TO BE FRIENDS (62)	Warner 5297	$10
	(White promo label)		
45rpm	LOVE IS STRANGE (65)	Warner 5649	$20
	(Price includes picture sleeve)		
45(P)	BOWLING GREEN (66)	Warner Bros 7020	$12
	(White promo label)		
45(P)	LOVE OF THE COMMON PEOPLE (67)	Warner Bros 7088	$12
	(White promo label)		
45(P)	RIDIN' HIGH (71)	RCA Victor SP-45-326	$30
	(Yellow promo label, promo-only release)		

-EPs-

EP	THE EVERLY BROTHERS (57)	Cadence 104	$100
EP	THE EVERLY BROTHERS (57)	Cadence 105	$100
EP	THE EVERLY BROTHERS (58)	Cadence 107	$100

Type	Title	Label	Price
EP	SONGS OUR DADDY TAUGHT US (58) Vol 1	Cadence 108	$75
EP	SONGS OUR DADDY TAUGHT US (58) Vol 2	Cadence 109	$75
EP	SONGS OUR DADDY TAUGHT US (58) Vol 3	Cadence 110	$75
EP(P)	SONGS OUR DADDY TAUGHT US (58) (White promo label with typewritten titles)	Cadence 3016	$60
EP	THE EVERLY BROTHERS (59)	Cadence 111	$75
EP	THE EVERLY BROTHERS (59)	Cadence 118	$75
EP	THE VERY BEST OF THE EVERLY BROTHERS (60)	Cadence 121	$50
EP	FOREVERLY YOURS (60)	Warner Bros 1381	$40
EP	FOREVERLY YOURS VOL 2 (60)	Warner Bros 1381	$40
EP(P)	FOREVERLY YOURS (60) (Gold vinyl special release)	Warner Bros 1381	$150
EP(P)	COCA-COLA JINGLE A GO-GO Vol 1 (With another track by Ray Charles)	Coca-Cola	$200
EP(P)	EVERLY FAMILY SHOW (61) (Special promo release)	Warner 306	$50
EP(P)	ROCKIN' WITH THE EVERLY BROTHERS (61) (Special promo release)	Warner 333	$50
EP(JB)	ROCKIN' WITH THE EVERLY BROTHERS (68) Jukebox LLP (Issued with a hard cover)	Cadence LLP-3	$75
EP(JB)	DREAM WITH THE EVERLY BROTHERS (68) Jukebox LLP (Issued with a hard cover)	Cadence LLP-4	$75
EP(JB)	EVERLY BROTHERS GOLDEN HITS (68) Jukebox LLP (Issued with a cover)	Warner 1471	$40
EP(JB)	THE VERY BEST OF THE EVERLY BROTHERS (68) Jukebox LLP (Issued with a cover)	Warner 1554	$40
EP(JB)	EVERLY BROTHERS SHOW (68) Jukebox LLP (Price includes title strips and paper sleeve)	Warner 1858	$40

-albums-

Type	Title	Label	Price
LP	THE EVERLY BROTHERS (58)	Cadence 3003	$125
LP	SONGS OUR DADDY TAUGHT US (59)	Cadence 3016	$100
LP	THE EVERLY BROTHERS BEST (59) Blue cover	Cadence 3025	$75
LP	THE FABULOUS STYLE OF THE EVERLY BROTHERS (60) Mono	Cadence 3040	$50
LP	THE FABULOUS STYLE OF THE EVERLY BROTHERS (60) Stereo	Cadence 25040	$75
LP	FOLK SONGS OF THE EVERLY BROTHERS (62) Mono	Cadence 3059	$50
LP	FOLK SONGS OF THE EVERLY BROTHERS (62) Stereo	Cadence 25059	$25
LP	15 EVERLY HITS (63) Mono	Cadence 3062	$40
LP	15 EVERLY HITS (63) Stereo	Cadence 25062	$25
10"(P)	SOUVENIR SAMPLER - 10 SONGS (61) (White label promo with special cover)	Warner Bros 135	$750
LP	IT'S EVERLY TIME (60)	Warner 1381	$25
LP(P)	IT'S EVERLY TIME (60) (White promo label)	Warner 1381	$100
LP	A DATE WITH THE EVERLY BROTHERS (60) (Includes fold-open cover and photos)	Warner 1395	$25
LP(P)	A DATE WITH THE EVERLY BROTHERS (60) (White promo label)	Warner 1395	$50
LP	BOTH SIDES OF AN EVENING (61)	Warner 1418	$20
LP(P)	BOTH SIDES OF AN EVENING (61) (White promo label)	Warner 1418	$40
LP	INSTANT PARTY (62)	Warner 1430	$20
LP(P)	INSTANT PARTY (62) (White promo label)	Warner 1430	$40
LP	GOLDEN HITS (62)	Warner 1471	$15
LP(P)	GOLDEN HITS (62) (White promo label)	Warner 1471	$40
LP	CHRISTMAS WITH THE EVERLY BROTHERS (62)	Warner 1483	$20
LP(P)	CHRISTMAS WITH THE EVERLY BROTHERS (62) (White promo label)	Warner 1483	$40
LP	GREAT COUNTRY HITS (63)	Warner 1513	$12
LP(P)	GREAT COUNTRY HITS (63) (White promo label)	Warner 1513	$40
LP	VERY BEST OF THE EVERLY BROTHERS (64)	Warner 1554	$10
LP(P)	VERY BEST OF THE EVERLY BROTHERS (64) (White promo label)	Warner 1554	$25
LP	ROCK 'N' SOUL (65)	Warner 1578	$10
LP(P)	ROCK 'N' SOUL (65) (White promo label)	Warner 1578	$20
LP	GONE, GONE, GONE (65)	Warner 1585	$10
LP(P)	GONE, GONE, GONE (65) (White promo label)	Warner 1585	$20
LP	BEAT 'N' SOUL (65)	Warner 1605	$10
LP(P)	BEAT 'N' SOUL (65) (White promo label)	Warner 1605	$20
LP	IN OUR IMAGE (66)	Warner 1620	$10

LP(P)	**IN OUR IMAGE** (66)	Warner 1620	$20
	(White promo label)		
LP	**TWO YANKS IN ENGLAND** (66) Mono	Warner 1646	$15
	(The Hollies are featured on this LP)		
LP	**TWO YANKS IN ENGLAND** (66) Stereo	Warner 1646	$30
LP(P)	**TWO YANKS IN ENGLAND** (66)	Warner 1646	$30
	(White promo label)		
LP	**THE HIT SOUND OF THE EVERLY BROTHERS** (67) Mono	Warner 1676	$20
LP	**THE HIT SOUND OF THE EVERLY BROTHERS** (67) Stereo	Warner 1676	$30
LP(P)	**THE HIT SOUND OF THE EVERLY BROTHERS** (67)	Warner 1676	$30
	(White promo label)		
LP	**THE EVERLY BROTHERS SING** (67) Mono	Warner 1708	$25
LP	**THE EVERLY BROTHERS SING** (67) Stereo	Warner 1708	$30
LP(P)	**THE EVERLY BROTHERS SING** (67)	Warner 1708	$30
	(White promo label)		
LP	**ROOTS** (68)	Warner 1752	$20
LP(P)	**ROOTS** (68)	Warner 1752	$25
	(White promo label)		
LP(P)	**EVERLY BROTHERS REUNION CONCERT** (Oct 83)	Passport 4006DJ	$75
	(Recorded live at Albert Hall in September 1983, promo-only release with special cover)		

-radio shows-

2LP(RS)	**ROYALTY OF ROCK** (83)	RKO Radio	$30-50
	(Music and interviews, also features Buddy Holly)		

EXILE (C)
Warner and Epic 45s $1 each
Warner and Epic LPs $2 each

-radio shows-

LP(RS)	**LIVE FROM DISNEY WORLD** (July 86) With the Judds	NBC Radio	$40-75
	(Live concert)		
LP(RS)	**LIVE FROM GILLEY'S** (Dec 87)	Westwood One	$10-15
	(Live concert)		
LP(RS)	**WESTWOOD ONE PRESENTS** (May 90)	Westwood One	$15-25
	(Live concert)		

F

TOMMY FACENDA (R)

-singles-

45rpm	**HIGH SCHOOL U. S. A. VIRGINIA** (57)	Legrand 1001	$25
	(Original version, recorded in Norfolk for Virginia area high schools)		
45rpm	**HIGH SCHOOL U. S. A.** (57) 28 Versions	Atlantic (28 versions)	$25 each
	(Some versions have sold in local areas for $50-$75 each)		

TOMMY FAILE (C)
Choice 45s $5 each

JIM FAIR (CW)

-singles-

45rpm	**YOU ALL COME** (53)	Top Tunes 1060	$10

WERLY FAIRBURN (CW)
Capitol 78s $10 each

-singles-

45rpm	**GOOD DEAL LUCILLE** (53)	Capitol 2770	$15
45(P)	**GOOD DEAL LUCILLE** (53)	Capitol 2770	$12
	(White promo label)		
45rpm	**LOVE SPELLED BACKWARDS IS EVOL** (54)	Capitol 2844	$12
45(P)	**LOVE SPELLED BACKWARDS IS EVOL** (54)	Capitol 2844	$10
	(White promo label)		
45rpm	**PRISON CELL OF LOVE** (54)	Capitol 2963	$12
45(P)	**PRISON CELL OF LOVE** (54)	Capitol 2963	$10
	(White promo label)		
45rpm	**IT'S A COLD WEARY WORLD** (55)	Capitol 3101	$12
45(P)	**IT'S A COLD WEARY WORLD** (55)	Capitol 3101	$10
	(White promo label)		
45rpm	**I GUESS I'M CRAZY** (54)	Columbia 21432	$12
45(P)	**I GUESS I'M CRAZY** (54)	Columbia 21432	$10
	(White promo label)		
45rpm	**EVERYBODY'S ROCKIN'** (57)	Columbia 21528	$30

45(P)	EVERYBODY'S ROCKIN' (57)	Columbia 21528	$25
	(White promo label)		
45rpm	CAMPING WITH MARIE	Trumpet 195	$12
45rpm	YOU ARE MY SUNSHINE	Milestone 2013	$10
45rpm	I'M A FOOL ABOUT YOUR LOVE	Savoy 1503	$15
45(P)	I'M A FOOL ABOUT YOUR LOVE	Savoy 1503	$12
	(White promo label)		
45rpm	SPEAK TO ME BABY	Savoy 1509	$12
45(P)	SPEAK TO ME BABY	Savoy 1509	$10
	(White promo label)		
45rpm	TELEPHONE BABY	Savoy 1521	$15
45(P)	TELEPHONE BABY	Savoy 1521	$12
	(White promo label)		

BARBARA FAIRCHILD (C)
Norman 45s $8 each
Kapp 45s $3-5 each
Columbia 45s $1 each
Paid, Autiograph, and Capitol 45s $1 each
All LPs $2 each

JOHNNY FAIRE (RB)

-singles-

45rpm	BERTHA LOU (58)	Surf 5019	$25

JOHN FALLIN (RB)

-singles-

45rpm	PARTY KISS (59)	Capitol 4216	$15
45(P)	PARTY KISS (59)	Capitol 4216	$12
	(Yellow promo label)		
45rpm	WILD STREAK (60)	Capitol 4283	$15
45(P)	WILD STREAK (60)	Capitol 4283	$12
	(Red promo label)		

FAMILY BROWN (C)
Featuring Tracy and Barry Brown
RCA Victor color vinyl 45s $5 each
Other RCA Victor 45s $1 each
RCA Victor LPs $4 each

VARIOUS ARTISTS

-EPs-

33(P)	FAN FAIR PROMO SPOTS (80s) Public service ads	CMA Nashville	$18 each
	(Top country artists promote Nashville Fan Fair in June)		

DONNA FARGO (C)
Dot and Warner 45s $2-3 each
Dot picture sleeves $3 each
RCA Victor color vinyl 45s $6 each
RCA Victor and MCA 45s $1 each
Dot and Warner LPs $5-8 each
RCA Victor and MCA LPs $2-3 each

FARMER BOYS (CW)
Capitol 78s $10 each

-singles-

45rpm	YOU'RE A HUMDINGER (55)	Capitol 3077	$20
45(P)	YOU'RE A HUMDINGER (55)	Capitol 3077	$15
	(White promo label)		
45rpm	LEND A HELPING HAND (55)	Capitol 3162	$15
45(P)	LEND A HELPING HAND (55)	Capitol 3162	$12
	(White promo label)		
45rpm	YOU LIED (56)	Capitol 3246	$12
45(P)	YOU LIED (56)	Capitol 3246	$10
	(White promo label)		
45rpm	FLIP FLOP (56)	Capitol 3322	$15
45(P)	FLIP FLOP (56)	Capitol 3322	$12
	(White promo label)		
45rpm	COOL DOWN MAME (57)	Capitol 3569	$12
45(P)	COOL DOWN MAME (57)	Capitol 3569	$10
	(White promo label)		
45rpm	NO ONE (58)	Capitol 3827	$12
45(P)	NO ONE (58)	Capitol 3827	$10
	(White promo label)		

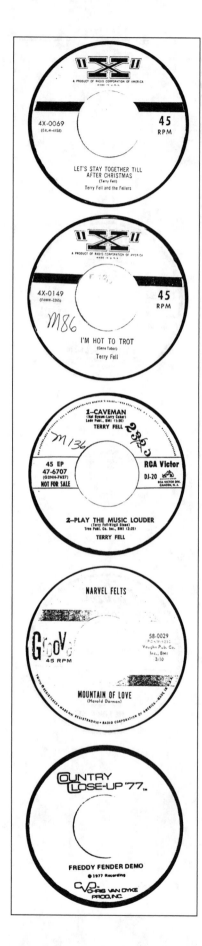

CHARLIE FEATHERS (RB)

-singles-

78rpm	I'VE BEEN DECEIVED (55)		Flip 503	$750
45rpm	I'VE BEEN DECEIVED (55)		Flip 503	$500
78rpm	I'VE BEEN DECEIVED (55)		Sun 503	$500
45rpm	I'VE BEEN DECEIVED (55)		Sun 503	$400
78rpm	DEFROST YOUR HEART (56)		Sun 231	$750
45rpm	DEFROST YOUR HEART (56)		Sun 231	$600
78rpm	ALL MESSED UP (56)		Meteor 5025	$750
45rpm	ALL MESSED UP (56)		Meteor 5025	$600
78rpm	TONGUE TIED JILL (56)		Meteor 5032	$750
45rpm	TONGUE TIED JILL (56) Maroon label		Meteor 5032	$1,000
45rpm	TONGUE TIED JILL (56) Black label		Meteor 5032	$300
45rpm	EVERYBODY'S LOVIN' MY BABY (57)		King 4971	$300
45(P)	EVERYBODY'S LOVIN' MT BABY (57)		King 4971	$250
	(White promo label)			
45rpm	BOTTLE TO THE BABY (57)		King 4997	$250
45(P)	BOTTLE TO THE BABY (57)		King 4997	$200
	(White promo label)			
45rpm	NOBODY'S WOMAN (57)		King 5022	$150
45(P)	NOBODY'S WOMAN (57)		King 5022	$125
	(White promo label)			
45rpm	TOO MUCH ALIKE (57)		King 5043	$150
45(P)	TOO MUCH ALIKE (57)		King 5043	$125
	(White promo label)			
45rpm	JUNGLE FEVER (58)		Kay 1001	$200
45rpm	DINKY JOHN (60)		Wall-May 101	$200
45rpm	WILD WILD PARTY (62)		Memphis 103	$100
45rpm	DEEP ELM BLUES (63)		Holiday Inn 144	$150

TERRY FELL (CW)
Other "X" 78s $12 each

-singles-

45rpm	DON'T DROP IT (54)		"X" (RCA) 0010	$12
45(P)	DON'T DROP IT (54)		"X" 0010	$15
	(White promo label)			
45rpm	LET'S STAY TOGETHER TILL AFTER CHRISTMAS (54)		"X" 0069	$20
45(P)	LET'S STAY TOGETHER TILL AFTER CHRISTMAS (54)		"X" 0069	$15
	(White promo label)			
45rpm	GET ABOARD MY WAGON (55)		"X" 0078	$12
45(P)	GET ABOARD MY WAGON (55)		"X" 0078	$10
	(White promo label)			
45rpm	MISSISSIPPI RIVER SHUFFLE (55)		"X" 0114	$12
45(P)	MISSISSIPPI RIVER SHUFFLE (55)		"X" 0114	$10
	(White promo label)			
78rpm	I'M HOT TO TROT (55)		"X" 0149	$15
78(p)	I'M HOT TO TROT (55)		"X" 0149	$18
	(White promo label)			
45rpm	I'M HOT TO TROT (55)		"X" 0149	$12
45(P)	I'M HOT TO TROT (55)		"X" 0149	$15
	(White promo label)			
45rpm	OVER AND OVER (56)		RCA Victor 6444	$10
45rpm	I CAN HEAR YOU CLUCKIN' (57)		RCA Victor 6621	$12
45rpm	CAVEMAN (57)		RCA Victor 6707	$10

-EPs-

EP(P)	CAVEMAN/PLAY THE MUSIC LOUDER (57) Promo-only EP		RCA Victor 6707 DJ-20	$15
	(Two songs on each side, flip side is by Homer & Jethro)			

DICK FELLER (C)
United Artists and Asylum 45s $2-5 each
Asylum LPs $4-6 each

-albums-

LP	DICK FELLER WROTE (73)		United Artists 094	$10

DARRELL FELTS (RB)

-singles-

45rpm	PLAYMATES (58)		Dixie 2008	$75

NARVEL FELTS (C)
Cinnamon 45s $4 each
Dot and MCA 45s $1-2 each
Hi LPs $8 each
ABC/Dot and MCA LPs $5-8 each
Power Pac and Gusto LPs $3 each

-singles-

45rpm	CUTIE BABY (57)		Pink 701	$18
45rpm	HONEY LOVE (57)		Pink 702	$18

45rpm	**DARLING SUE** (57)	Pink 706	$18
45rpm	**MOUNTAIN OF LOVE** (57)	Groove 0029	$15
45(P)	**MOUNTAIN OF LOVE** (57)	Groove 0029	$12
	(White promo label)		
45rpm	**KISS-A-ME BABY** (57)	Mercury 71140	$15
45(P)	**KISS-A-ME BABY** (57)	Mercury 71140	$12
	(White promo label)		
45rpm	**CRY, CRY, CRY** (57)	Mercury 71190	$12
45(P)	**CRY, CRY, CRY** (57)	Mercury 71190	$10
	(White promo label)		
45rpm	**ROCKET RIDE** (58)	Mercury 71249	$12
45(P)	**ROCKET RIDE** (58)	Mercury 71249	$10
	(White promo label)		

-albums-

LP	**DRIFT AWAY** (73)	Cinnamon 5000	$18

-radio shows-

LP(RS)	**COUNTRY MUSIC TIME** (80s)	U.S. Air Force	$10-15
	(Music and interviews)		
LP(RS)	**LIVE FROM THE LONE STAR** (Mar 80)		$15-25
	(Live concert)		
LP(RS)	**LIVE FROM GILLEY'S** (Apr 87)	Westwood One	$15-25
	(Live concert)		

FREDDIE FENDER (C)
Other Norco 45s $5-8 each
Other Imperial 45s $8 each
ABC/Dot 45s $2-3 each
MCA and GRC 45s $1 each
GRT LPs $8 each
ABC/Dot LPs $4-6 each
Starflite, MCA, and Accord LPs $3 each
Hilltop duet LPs $4 each

-singles-

45rpm	**GOING OUT WITH THE TIDE**	Norco 103	$10
45rpm	**BONY MORONIE**	Norco 107	$15
45rpm	**MEAN WOMAN** (57)	Duncan 1000	$30
45rpm	**WASTED DAYS & WASTED NIGHTS** (58) Original version	Duncan 1001	$20
45rpm	**WILD SIDE OF LIFE** (58)	Duncan 1002	$12
45rpm	**MEAN WOMAN** (57)	Imperial 5659	$15
45(P)	**MEAN WOMAN** (57)	Imperial 5659	$12
	(Cream-colored promo label)		
45rpm	**WASTED DAYS & WASTED NIGHTS** (58)	Imperial 5670	$15
45(P)	**WASTED DAYS & WASTED NIGHTS** (58)	Imperial 5670	$12
	(Cream-colored promo label)		
45rpm	**A MAN CAN CRY** (59)	Argo 5375	$15
45(P)	**A MAN CAN CRY** (59)	Argo 5375	$12
	(White promo label)		
45rpm	**LITTLE MAMA** (59)	Duncan 1004	$15
45(P)	**COUNTRY CLOSEUP '77** (77)	Chris Van Dyke	$10
	(Demo disc for radio show)		

THE FENDERMEN (R)

-singles-

45rpm	**MULE SKINNER BLUES** (59)	Cuca 1003	$150
	(Original version, different from Soma version)		
45rpm	**MULE SKINNER BLUES** (60)	Soma 1137	$20
	(Idea for this song came from the Joe D. Gibson version on the Tetra label)		
45rpm	**DON'T YOU JUST KNOW IT** (60)	Soma 1142	$20
45rpm	**HEARTBREAKIN' SPECIAL** (61) Black label	Soma 1155	$20
45(P)	**HEARTBREAKIN' SPECIAL** (61) White label promo	Soma 1155	$40

-albums-

LP	**MULE SKINNER BLUES** (60)	Soma 1240	$4,000
	(Blue vinyl, very rare)		
LP	**MULE SKINNER BLUES** (60)	Soma 1240	$1,000
	(Black vinyl)		

AL FERRIER (RB)

-singles-

45rpm	**I'M THE MAN** (57)	Excello 2105	$40
45rpm	**NO NO BABY** (58)	Goldband 1031	$15
45rpm	**MY BABY DONE GONE AWAY** (58)	Goldband 1035	$12
45rpm	**LET'S GO BOPPING TONIGHT** (58)	Goldband 1072	$15
45rpm	**HONEY BABY** (59)	Goldband 1212	$10

SONNY FISHER (RB)

-singles-

45rpm	**ROCKIN' DADDY** (58)	Starday 179	$50
45rpm	**SNEAKY PETE** (58)	Starday 190	$50
45rpm	**ROCKIN' AND A ROLLIN'** (59)	Starday 207	$50
45rpm	**PINK AND BLACK** (59)	Starday 244	$50

DICK FLANNIGAN (RB)

-singles-

45rpm	**ROUGH AND TOUGH** (58)	Alpine	$60

FLATT & SCRUGGS (CW)

Lester Flatt and Earl Scruggs
Other Columbia 78s $10 each
Other Columbia 45s $3-8 each
RCA Victor 45s by Lester Flatt $2-4 each
Nugget 45s by Lester Flatt $3 each
CMA, Canaan, and Columbia 45s by Lester Flatt $1-2 each
Columbia 45s by Earl Scruggs or the Earl Scruggs Revue $2-3 each
RCA Victor and Columbia LPs by Lester Flatt $5-10 each
CMH and Canaan LPs by Lester Flatt $4-6 each
Flying Fish and Power Pac LPs by Lester Flatt $3 each
RCA Victor LPs by Lester Flatt and Bill Monroe $8 each
Other Columbia LPs by Flatt & Scruggs $5-10 each
Other Harmony LPs by Flatt & Scruggs $5-8 each
Power Pac, Nashville, County, 51 West, Rounder, Everest, and Hilltop LPs by Flatt & Scruggs $3-5 each
Rounder LPs by Flatt & Scruggs and Bill Monroe $5 each

-singles-

78rpm	**I'M GONNA MAKE HEAVEN MY HOME** (50)	Mercury 6161	$20
45rpm	**I'M GONNA MAKE HEAVEN MY HOME** (50)	Mercury 6161	$25
78rpm	**WE'LL MEET AGAIN SWEETHEART** (50)	Mercury 6181	$20
45rpm	**WE'LL MEET AGAIN SWEETHEART** (50)	Mercury 6181	$25
78rpm	**CORA IS GONE** (51)	Mercury 6181	$18
45rpm	**CORA IS GONE** (51)	Mercury 6302	$20
78rpm	**I'LL JUST PRETEND** (51)	Mercury 6372	$15
45rpm	**I'LL JUST PRETEND** (51)	Mercury 6372	$18
78rpm	**OLD COUNTRY DOG BLUES** (51)	Mercury 6396	$15
45rpm	**OLD COUNTRY DOG BLUES** (51)	Mercury 6396	$18
78rpm	**WILL ROSES BLOOM** (52)	Mercury 70016	$12
45rpm	**WILL ROSES BLOOM** (52)	Mercury 70016	$10
78rpm	**BACK TO THE CROSS** (52)	Mercury 70064	$12
45rpm	**BACK TO THE CROSS** (52)	Mercury 70064	$10
78rpm	**'TIS SWEET TO BE REMEMBERED** (52)	Columbia 20886	$18
78(P)	**'TIS SWEET TO BE REMEMBERED** (52)	Columbia 20886	$25
	(White promo label)		
45rpm	**'TIS SWEET TO BE REMEMBERED** (52)	Columbia 20886	$15
45(P)	**'TIS SWEET TO BE REMEMBERED** (52)	Columbia 20886	$12
	(White promo label)		
78rpm	**FOGGY MOUNTAIN SPECIAL** (54)	Columbia 21295	$15
78(P)	**FOGGY MOUNTAIN SPECIAL** (54)	Columbia 21295	$12
	(White promo label)		
45rpm	**FOGGY MOUNTAIN SPECIAL** (54)	Columbia 21295	$15
45(P)	**FOGGY MOUNTAIN SPECIAL** (54)	Columbia 21295	$10
	(White promo label)		
45rpm	**RANDY LYNN RAG** (56)	Columbia 21501	$15
45(P)	**RANDY LYNN RAG** (56)	Columbia 21501	$12
	(White promo label)		
45rpm	**GIVE MOTHER MY CROWN** (56)	Columbia 21536	$12
45(P)	**GIVE MOTHER MY CROWN** (56)	Columbia 21536	$10
	(White promo label)		
45rpm	**DIM LIGHTS, THICK SMOKE** (56) Hall of Fame series	Columbia 52009	$12
45(P)	**DIM LIGHTS, THICK SMOKE** (56)	Columbia 52009	$15
	(White promo label)		
45rpm	**EARL'S BREAKDOWN** (56) Hall of Fame series	Columbia 52010	$10
45(P)	**EARL'S BREAKDOWN** (56)	Columbia 52010	$12
	(White promo label)		
45rpm	**SIX WHITE HORSES** (56)	Columbia 40853	$10
45rpm	**DON'T LET YOUR DEAL GO DOWN** (58)	Columbia 40990	$10
45rpm	**MAMA'S AND DADDY'S LITTLE GIRL** (58)	Columbia 41244	$10
45rpm	**THE BALLAD OF JED CLAMPETT** (63)	Columbia 42606	$15
45(P)	**THE BALLAD OF JED CLAMPETT** (63)	Columbia 42606	$18
	(White promo label)		
33rpm	**THE BALLAD OF JED CLAMPETT** (63)	Columbia 42606	$25
	(33rpm single)		
45rpm	**PEARL PEARL PEARL** (63)	Columbia 42755	$25
	(From *Beverly Hillbillies*, price includes picture sleeve)		
45(P)	**PEARL PEARL PEARL** (63)	Columbia 42755	$12
	(White promo label)		

33rpm	**PEARL PEARL PEARL** (63)	Columbia 42755	$12
	(33rpm single)		
45rpm	**FOGGY MOUNTAIN BREAKDOWN** (65)	Columbia 43412	$12
	(Theme song for movie *Bonnie and Clyde*)		
45(P)	**FOGGY MOUNTAIN BREAKDOWN** (65)	Columbia 43412	$10
	(White promo label)		
45rpm	**CALIFORNIA UP TIGHT BAND** (67)	Columbia 44194	$10
	(Price includes picture sleeve)		
45(P)	**WHAT'S IT ALL ABOUT** (May 76) Public service show	W. I. A. A. 318	$10
	(Interviews with Earl Scruggs, flip side features Elvin Bishop)		

-EPs-

EP	**FOGGY MOUNTAIN JAMBOREE** (57)	Columbia 10191	$30
EP	**LESTER FLATT & EARL SCRUGGS** (57)	Columbia 2811	$30
EP	**LESTER FLATT & EARL SCRUGGS** (57)	Columbia 2823	$30
EP	**SONGS OF GLORY** (60) Vol 1	Columbia 14241	$25
EP	**SONGS OF GLORY** (60) Vol 2	Columbia 14242	$25
EP	**SONGS OF GLORY** (60) Vol 3	Columbia 14243	$25
EP(P)	**FLATT & SCRUGGS** (65) Jukebox LLP	Columbia 8751	$20
	(Issued with a hard cover)		

-albums-

LP	**FOGGY MOUNTAIN JAMBOREE** (57)	Columbia 1019	$50
LP	**COUNTRY MUSIC** (58) Stereo	Mercury 20358	$40
LP	**COUNTRY MUSIC** (58) Mono	Mercury 20358	$30
LP(P)	**COUNTRY MUSIC** (58)	Mercury 20358	$50
	(White promo label)		
LP	**LESTER FLATT & EARL SCRUGGS** (59) Stereo	Mercury 20542	$40
LP	**LESTER FLATT & EARL SCRUGGS** (59) Mono	Mercury 20542	$30
LP(P)	**LESTER FLATT & EARL SCRUGGS** (59)	Mercury 20542	$50
	(White promo label)		
LP	**SONGS OF GLORY** (60) Stereo	Columbia 8221	$25
LP	**SONGS OF GLORY** (60) Mono	Columbia 8221	$20
LP(P)	**SONGS OF GLORY** (60) White promo label	Columbia 8221	$30
	(Mono version worth around $20)		
LP	**FLATT & SCRUGGS & THE FOGGY MOUNTAIN BOYS** (60)	Harmony 7250	$18
LP(P)	**FLATT & SCRUGGS & THE FOGGY MOUNTAIN BOYS** (60)	Harmony 7250	$25
	(White promo label)		
LP	**FOGGY MOUNTAIN BANJO** (61) Stereo	Columbia 8364	$25
LP	**FOGGY MOUNTAIN BANJO** (61) Mono	Columbia 1564	$20
LP(P)	**FOGGY MOUNTAIN BANJO** (61)	Columbia 1564	$30
	(Red promo label "Demonstration Not for Sale" in white letters)		
LP	**SONGS OF THE FAMOUS CARTER FAMILY** (61) Stereo	Columbia 8464	$25
	(With Mother Maybelle Carter)		
LP	**SONGS OF THE FAMOUS CARTER FAMILY** (61) Mono	Columbia 1664	$20
LP(P)	**SONGS OF THE FAMOUS CARTER FAMILY** (61) Promo copy	Columbia 1664	$30
	(Red promo label with promo identification in white)		
LP	**FOLK SONGS OF OUR LAND** (62) Stereo	Columbia 8630	$18
LP(P)	**FOLK SONGS OF OUR LAND** (62) Promo copy	Columbia 1830	$25
	(Red promo label with promo letters in white)		
LP	**THE ORIGINAL SOUND OF FLATT & SCRUGGS** (63) Stereo	Mercury 60773	$25
LP	**THE ORIGINAL SOUND OF FLATT & SCRUGGS** (63) Mono	Mercury 20773	$20
LP(P)	**THE ORIGINAL SOUND OF FLATT & SCRUGGS** (63) Promo	Mercury 20773	$30
	(White promo label)		
LP	**THE BALLAD OF JED CLAMPETT** (63)	Columbia 8751	$18
LP(P)	**THE BALLAD OF JED CLAMPETT** (63)	Columbia 1951	$25
	(White promo label)		
LP	**FLATT & SCRUGGS AT CARNEGIE HALL** (63)	Columbia 8845	$18
LP(P)	**FLATT & SCRUGGS AT CARNEGIE HALL** (63)	Columbia 2045	$25
	(White promo label)		
LP	**RECORDED LIVE AT VANDERBILT UNIVERSITY** (64)	Columbia 8934	$18
LP(P)	**RECORDED LIVE AT VANDERBILT UNIVERSITY** (64)	Columbia 2134	$25
	(White promo label)		
LP	**THE FABULOUS SOUND OF FLATT & SCRUGGS** (64)	Columbia 9055	$20
LP(P)	**THE FABULOUS SOUND OF FLATT & SCRUGGS** (64)	Columbia 2255	$25
	(White promo label)		
LP	**THE VERSATILE FLATT & SCRUGGS** (65)	Columbia 9154	$18
LP(P)	**THE VERSATILE FLATT & SCRUGGS** (65)	Columbia 2354	$25
	(White promo label)		
LP	**GREAT ORIGINAL RECORDINGS** (65)	Harmony 7340	$15
LP(P)	**GREAT ORIGINAL RECORDINGS** (65)	Harmony 7340	$20
	(White promo label)		
LP	**STARS OF THE GRAND OL' OPRY** (66)	Starday 365	$25
	(With Jim & Jesse)		
LP	**TOWN & COUNTRY** (66)	Columbia 9243	$15
LP	**WHEN THE SAINTS GO MARCHING IN** (66)	Columbia 9313	$12
LP	**FLATT & SCRUGGS GREATEST HITS** (66)	Columbia 9370	$12

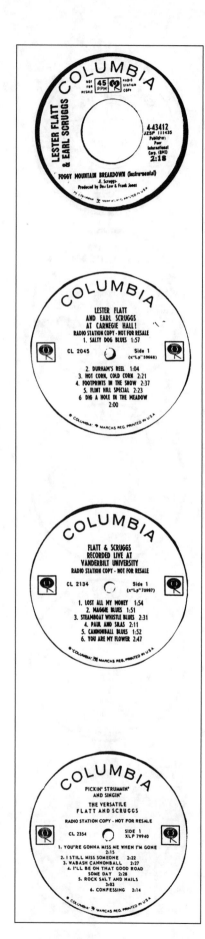

LP	**STRICTLY INSTRUMENTAL** (67)		Columbia 9443	$15
	(With Doc Watson)			
LP	**HEAR THE WHISTLE BLOW** (67)		Columbia 9486	$10
LP	**SACRED SONGS** (67)		Harmony 11202	$10
LP(P)	**SACRED SONGS** (67)		Harmony 11202	$12
	(White promo label)			
LP	**CHANGING TIMES** (68)		Columbia 9596	$10
LP	**THE STORY OF BONNIE & CLYDE** (68)		Columbia 9649	$10
LP	**NASHVILLE AIRPLANE** (68)		Columbia 9741	$10
LP	**ORIGINAL THEME FROM BONNIE & CLYDE** (68)		Mercury 61162	$15
LP(P)	**ORIGINAL THEME FROM BONNIE & CLYDE** (68)		Mercury 61162	$18
	(White promo label)			
LP	**THE ORIGINAL FOGGY MOUNTAIN BREAKDOWN** (68)		Mercury Wing 16376	$15
LP(P)	**THE ORIGINAL FOGGY MOUNTAIN BREAKDOWN** (68)		Mercury Wing 16376	$18
	(White promo label)			
LP	**THE ONE AND ONLY** (68) Lester Flatt		Nugget 104	$25
LP	**SONGS TO CHERISH** (68)		Harmony 11265	$10
LP	**DETROIT CITY** (69)		Columbia 493	$10
	(Columbia Musical Treasures)			
LP	**FINAL FLING** (70)		Columbia 9945	$10
2LP	**FLATT & SCRUGGS** (70)		Columbia 30	$12
LP	**BREAKING OUT** (70)		Columbia 30347	$10
2LP	**WORLD OF FLATT & SCRUGGS** (73)		Columbia 31964	$15
LP	**A BOY NAMED SUE** (73)		Columbia 32244	$10
3LP	**COUNTRY & WESTERN CLASSICS** (82)		Time-Life 04	$25
	(Box set issued with a booklet)			

-radio shows-

16"(RS)	**LEATHERNECK JAMBOREE** (50s)		Leatherneck Show 24	$50-75
	(Music and interviews)			
LP(RS)	**GRAND OL' OPRY** (62)		WSM Radio 88	$25-40
	(Music and interviews)			
LP(RS)	**GRAND OL' OPRY** (63)		WSM Radio 95	$25-40
	(Music and interviews)			

GEORGE FLEMING (RB)

-singles-

45rpm	**THE SHAKE** (58)		Fleming 501	$65

PHIL FLOWERS (RB)

-singles-

45rpm	**NO KISSIN' AT THE HOP** (58)		Wing 2100	$25
45rpm	**NO KISSIN' AT THE HOP** (58)		Dot	$15

FRANK FLOYD (RB)

-singles-

45rpm	**ROCK A LITTLE BABY** (57)		F & L 100	$100

RED FOLEY (CW)

Other Conqueror 78s $10 each
Other Decca 78s $5-10 each
Other Decca 45s $3-8 each
Other Vocalion LPs $5-8 each
Hilltop LPs $5 each
MCA LPs $4 each

-singles-

78rpm	**THE 1936 FLOODS** (44)		Conqueror 8676	$25
78rpm	**SMOKE ON THE WATER** (44)		Decca 6102	$12
78rpm	**HANG YOUR HEAD IN SHAME** (44)		Decca 6108	$10
78rpm	**AT MAIL CALL TODAY** (46)		Decca 18698	$12
	(With Lawrence Welk)			
78rpm	**NEW JOLE BLONDE** (47)		Decca 46034	$10
78rpm	**FREIGHT TRAIN BOOGIE** (47)		Decca 46035	$10
78rpm	**OLD SHEP** (47)		Decca 46052	$12
45rpm	**OLD SHEP** (47) First pressing		Decca 46052	$25
	(Black label, rays on sides of Decca)			
45rpm	**OLD SHEP** (47) Second pressing		Decca 46052	$10
	(Black label, star under Decca)			
78rpm	**TENNESSEE SATURDAY NIGHT** (48)		Decca 46136	$10
45rpm	**TENNESSEE SATURDAY NIGHT** (48)		Decca 46136	$15
45rpm	**TENNESSEE POLKA** (49)		Decca 46170	$10
45rpm	**SUNDAY DOWN IN TENNESSEE** (49)		Decca 46197	$10
45rpm	**TENNESSEE BORDER NO. 2** (49)		Decca 46200	$10
	(With Ernest Tubb)			
45rpm	**CHATTANOOGIE SHOE SHINE BOY** (50)		Decca 46205	$15
45rpm	**STEAL AWAY** (50) Purple label		Decca 14505	$15
45rpm	**STEAL AWAY** (58) Black label		Decca 30470	$12

45(P)	STEAL AWAY (58) Pink promo label	Decca 30470	$10
45rpm	BIRMINGHAM BOUNCE (50)	Decca 46234	$12
45rpm	HILLBILLY FEVER NO. 2 (50)	Decca 46255	$10
45rpm	CINCINNATI DANCING PIG (50)	Decca 46261	$15
45rpm	HOT ROD RACE (51)	Decca 46286	$15
45rpm	IT IS NO SECRET (51)	Decca 14566	$10
45rpm	HOBO BOOGIE (51)	Decca 46304	$15
45rpm	PEACE IN THE VALLEY (51)	Decca 46319	$10
	(Re-released several times)		
45rpm	TOO OLD TO CUT THE MUSTARD (52)	Decca 46387	$10
	(Red Foley and Ernest Tubb)		
45rpm	ALABAMA JUBILEE (52)	Decca 27810	$10
45rpm	MILK BUCKET BOOGIE (52)	Decca 27981	$15
45rpm	I'M BOUND FOR THE KINGDOM (52)	Decca 28147	$10
45rpm	MIDNIGHT (52)	Decca 28420	$10
45rpm	DON'T LET THE STARS GET IN YOUR EYES (53)	Decca 28460	$10
45rpm	HOT TODDY (53)	Decca 28587	$12
45rpm	NO HELP WANTED (53)	Decca 28634	$10
	(Red Foley and Ernest Tubb)		
45rpm	MANSION OVER THE HILLTOP/I BELIEVE (54)	Decca 28694	$12
45rpm	GOODBYE, BOBBY BOY (53)	Decca 28944	$10
45rpm	TENNESSEE WHISTLING MAN (54)	Decca 29000	$10
45rpm	ONE BY ONE (54)	Decca 29065	$10
	(Red Foley with Kitty Wells)		
45rpm	PINBALL BOOGIE (54)	Decca 29100	$15
45(P)	PINBALL BOOGIE (54)	Decca 29100	$12
	(Pink promo label)		
45rpm	MY FRIEND (54)	Decca 29159	$10
45rpm	SKINNIE MINNIE (54)	Decca 29228	$10
45rpm	WHEN YOU COME TO THE END OF THE DAY (55)	Decca 29667	$10
45rpm	I WANT TO BE WITH YOU (55)	Columbia 20799	$10
45rpm	THE HOOT OWL BOOGIE (56)	Decca 29894	$12
45(P)	THE HOOT OWL BOOGIE (56)	Decca 29894	$10
	(Pink promo label)		
45rpm	ROCK 'N REELIN' (57)	Decca 30067	$20
45(P)	ROCK 'N REELIN' (57)	Decca 30067	$15
	(Pink promo label)		
45rpm	STRIKE WHILE THE IRON IS HOT (58)	Decca 30452	$15
45(P)	STRIKE WHILE THE IRON IS HOT (58)	Decca 30452	$12
	(Green promo label)		
45rpm	STROLLING THE BLUES (58)	Decca 30639	$10
45rpm	CRAZY LITTLE GUITAR MAN (58)	Decca 30674	$20
45(P)	CRAZY LITTLE GUITAR MAN (58)	Decca 30674	$15
	(Pink promo label)		
45(P)	IF I CAN HELP SOMEBODY (58)	Decca 38057	$20
	(White promo-only label, release of the "Official Christmas Seal song" of 1958)		
45rpm	IF I CAN HELP SOMEBODY (58) Black label	Decca 30710	$12
	(Version released to the public)		
45(P)	IF I CAN HELP SOMEBODY (58)	Decca 30710	$10
	(Pink promo label)		

-EPs-

EP	ERNEST TUBB & RED FOLEY (52)	Decca 2024	$15
	(With Ernest Tubb)		
EP	RED FOLEY SINGS (53)	Decca 2025	$15
EP	A TRIBUTE TO JIMMIE RODGERS (53)	Decca 2059	$25
	(With Ernest Tubb)		
EP	SING A SONG OF CHRISTMAS (53)	Decca 2090	$15
EP	SOUVENIR ALBUM PART 1 (55)	Decca 2145	$25
	(Includes "Old Shep")		
EP	SOUVENIR ALBUM PART 2 (55)	Decca 2146	$20
EP	SOUVENIR ALBUM PART 3 (56)	Decca 2363	$20
EP	LIFT UP YOUR VOICE (55) Vol 1	Decca 2184	$15
EP	LIFT UP YOUR VOICE (55) Vol 2	Decca 2185	$15
EP	BEYOND THE SUNSET (55)	Decca 2207	$18
EP	RED & ERNIE VOL 1 (56)	Decca 2367	$15
	(Red Foley and Ernest Tubb)		
EP	RED & ERNIE VOL 2 (56)	Decca 2368	$15
	(Red Foley and Ernest Tubb)		
EP(P)	RED FOLEY'S GOLDEN FAVORITES (61) Jukebox LLP	Decca 34295	$30
	(Includes six of his best early "boogie" songs, issued with hard cover)		
EP(P)	THE RED FOLEY SHOW (63) Jukebox LLP	Decca 34112	$30
	(Songs with Patsy Cline, Ernest Tubb, Kitty Wells and the Wilburn Brothers)		

-albums-

10"LP	RED FOLEY SOUVENIR ALBUM (51)	Decca 5303	$50

10"LP	**LIFT UP YOUR VOICE** (54)		Decca 5338	$35
LP	**RED & ERNIE** (56)		Decca 8298	$30
	(Red Foley and Ernest Tubb)			
LP(P)	**RED & ERNIE** (56)		Decca 8298	$40
	(Pink promo label)			
LP(P)	**RED FOLEY DICKIES SOUVENIR ALBUM** (58)		Decca LP	$75
	(Promo-only release)			
LP	**SOUVENIR ALBUM** (58)		Decca 8294	$40
LP(P)	**SOUVENIR ALBUM** (58)		Decca 8294	$45
	(Pink promo label)			
LP	**BEYOND THE SUNSET** (58)		Decca 8296	$25
LP(P)	**BEYOND THE SUNSET** (58)		Decca 8296	$30
	(Pink promo label)			
LP	**HE WALKS WITH THEE** (58)		Decca 8767	$25
LP(P)	**HE WALKS WITH THEE** (58)		Decca 8767	$30
	(Pink promo label)			
LP	**MY KEEPSAKE ALBUM** (58)		Decca 8806	$40
LP(P)	**MY KEEPSAKE ALBUM** (58)		Decca 8806	$50
	(Pink promo label)			
LP	**LET'S ALL SING WITH RED FOLEY** (59)		Decca 8847	$18
LP(P)	**LET'S ALL SING WITH RED FOLEY** (59)		Decca 8847	$20
	(Pink promo label)			
LP	**LET'S ALL SING TO HIM** (59)		Decca 8903	$15
LP(P)	**LET'S ALL SING TO HIM** (59)		Decca 8903	$18
	(Pink promo label)			
LP	**RED FOLEY'S GOLDEN FAVORITES** (61)		Decca 4107	$15
LP(P)	**RED FOLEY'S GOLDEN FAVORITES** (61)		Decca 4107	$18
	(Pink promo label)			
LP	**COMPANY'S COMIN'** (61)		Decca 4140	$30
LP(P)	**COMPANY'S COMIN'** (61)		Decca 4140	$40
	(Pink promo label)			
LP	**SONGS OF DEVOTION** (61)		Decca 4198	$15
	(With the Jordanaires)			
LP(P)	**SONGS OF DEVOTION** (61)		Decca 4198	$20
	(Pink promo label)			
LP	**DEAR HEARTS AND GENTLE PEOPLE** (62)		Decca 4290	$15
LP(P)	**DEAR HEARTS AND GENTLE PEOPLE** (62)		Decca 4290	$18
	(Pink promo label)			
LP	**THE RED FOLEY SHOW** (63)		Decca 4341	$25
	(With Patsy Cline, Ernest Tubb, Kitty Wells, Wilburn Brothers, and others)			
LP(P)	**THE RED FOLEY SHOW** (63)		Decca 4341	$35
	(Pink promo label)			
2LP	**THE RED FOLEY STORY** (64)		Decca 177	$25
2LP(P)	**THE RED FOLEY STORY** (64)		Decca 177	$35
	(White promo labels)			
LP	**SONGS EVERYBODY KNOWS** (65)		Decca 4603	$10
LP(P)	**SONGS EVERYBODY KNOWS** (65)		Decca 4603	$12
	(White promo labels)			
LP	**I'M BOUND FOR THE KINGDOM** (65)		Vocalion 3745	$10
LP(P)	**I'M BOUND FOR THE KINGDOM** (65)		Vocalion 3745	$12
	(White promo label)			
LP	**RED FOLEY** (66)		Vocalion 3751	$10
LP(P)	**RED FOLEY** (66)		Vocalion 3751	$12
	(White promo label)			
LP	**SONGS FOR THE SOUL** (67)		Decca 4849	$10
LP(P)	**SONGS FOR THE SOUL** (67)		Decca 4849	$12
	(White promo label)			

-radio shows-

16"(RS)	**RADIOZARK** (50s) Public service radio		Radiozark Show 87	$25-40
	(Music and interviews)			

WEBB FOLEY (C)
M (label) 45s $4 each

BILLY FOLGER (CW)
Other North Star 45s $15 each

-singles-

45rpm	**WEEP NO MORE** (55)		North Star 2047	$40

EDDIE FONTAINE (RB)

-singles-

45rpm	**WHERE IS DE WOMAN** (57)		Jalo 102	$25
45rpm	**NOTHIN' SHAKIN'** (57)		Argo 5309	$12
45rpm	**HEY MARIE, ROCK WITH ME** (58)		Decca 30338	$15
45(P)	**HEY MARIE, ROCK WITH ME** (58)		Decca 30338	$12
	(Pink promo label)			

FRANK FONTAINE (RB)

-singles-

45rpm	**EVERYBODY ROCKS** (55)	MGM 12129	$25
45(P)	**EVERYBODY ROCKS** (55)	MGM 12129	$20
	(Yellow promo label)		

HENRY FORD (RB)

-singles-

45rpm	**IS THERE PEACE IN KOREA** (58)	Delta 417	$25

JIMMY FORD (RB)

-singles-

45rpm	**DON'T HANG AROUND ME** (57)	Stylo 2102	$25

TENNESSEE ERNIE FORD (CW)

Other Capitol 78s $5-10 each
Other Capitol 45s $2-8 each
Other Capitol EPs $4-8 each
Other Capitol LPs $3-8 each
Capitol duet LPs $5-8 each

-singles-

78rpm	**TENNESSEE BORDER** (49)	Capitol 15400	$15
78rpm	**SMOKEY MOUNTAIN BOOGIE** (49)	Capitol 40212	$15
45rpm	**SMOKEY MOUNTAIN BOOGIE** (49)	Capitol 40212	$20
45rpm	**MULE TRAIN** (49)	Capitol 40258	$15
45rpm	**THE CRY OF THE WILD GOOSE** (50)	Capitol 40280	$15
78rpm	**THE SHOTGUN BOOGIE** (51)	Capitol 1295	$15
45rpm	**THE SHOTGUN BOOGIE** (51)	Capitol 1295	$20
45rpm	**THE STRANGE LITTLE GIRL** (51)	Capitol 1470	$10
78rpm	**SHOTGUN BOOGIE** (52)	Capitol 1626	$12
45rpm	**SHOTGUN BOOGIE** (52)	Capitol 1626	$15
78rpm	**KISSING BUG BOOGIE** (52)	Capitol 1775	$12
45rpm	**KISSING BUG BOOGIE** (52)	Capitol 1775	$15
78rpm	**ROCK CITY BOOGIE** (52)	Capitol 1911	$12
45rpm	**ROCK CITY BOOGIE** (52)	Capitol 1911	$15
78rpm	**BLACKBERRY BOOGIE** (52)	Capitol 2170	$12
45rpm	**BLACKBERRY BOOGIE** (52)	Capitol 2170	$18
78rpm	**CATFISH BOOGIE** (53)	Capitol 2602	$12
45rpm	**CATFISH BOOGIE** (53)	Capitol 2602	$15
45(P)	**CATFISH BOOGIE** (53)	Capitol 2602	$12
	(White promo label)		
45rpm	**RIVER OF NO RETURN** (54)	Capitol 2810	$10
78rpm	**BALLAD OF DAVY CROCKETT** (54)	Capitol 3058	$40
78(P)	**BALLAD OF DAVY CROCKETT** (54)	Capitol 3058	$25
	(Capitol promo label)		
45rpm	**BALLAD OF DAVY CROCKETT** (54)	Capitol 3058	$25
45(P)	**BALLAD OF DAVY CROCKETT** (54)	Capitol 3058	$20
	(White promo label)		
78rpm	**SIXTEEN TONS** (55)	Capitol 3262	$10
78(P)	**SIXTEEN TONS** (55)	Capitol 3262	$15
	(Capitol promo label)		
45rpm	**SIXTEEN TONS** (55)	Capitol 3262	$10
45(P)	**SIXTEEN TONS** (55)	Capitol 3262	$12
	(White promo label)		
78rpm	**ROCK, ROLL, BOOGIE** (56)	Capitol 3474	$20
78(P)	**ROCK, ROLL, BOOGIE** (56)	Capitol 3474	$18
	(Yellow promo label)		
45rpm	**ROCK, ROLL, BOOGIE** (56)	Capitol 3474	$12
45(P)	**ROCK, ROLL, BOOGIE** (56)	Capitol 3474	$10
	(Yellow promo label)		
45(P)	**FIRST BORN** (57)	Capitol 3553	$12
	(Yellow promo label, Ford's photo on the label)		
45rpm	**GLAD RAGS** (58)	Capitol 4107	$15
45(P)	**GLAD RAGS** (58)	Capitol 4107	$12
	(White promo label)		
45rpm	**LITTLE RED ROCKIN' HOOD** (60)	Capitol 4577	$12
45(P)	**LITTLE RED ROCKIN' HOOD** (60)	Capitol 4577	$10
	(Red promo label)		

-EPs-

EP	**BACKWOODS BOOGIE & BLUES** (53)	Capitol 413	$40
EP	**TENNESSEE ERNIE FORD & KAY STARR** (55)	Capitol 621	$15
	(With Kay Starr)		
EP	**TENNESSEE ERNIE FORD** (56)	Capitol 639	$20
EP	**SIXTEEN TONS** (56)	Capitol 693	$25
EP	**OL' ROCKIN' ERN'** (56) Vol 1	Capitol 1-888	$30
EP	**OL' ROCKIN' ERN'** (56) Vol 2	Capitol 2-888	$30

EP	OL' ROCKIN' ERN' (56) Vol 3	Capitol 3-888	$30
EP	TALES OF DAVY CROCKETT (56)	Capitol 3235	$20
EP(P)	TALES OF DAVY CROCKETT (56)	Capitol 3235	$30
	(White promo label)		
EP	TENNESSEE ERNIE FORD (61)	Capitol 1380	$15
	(Compact-33 EP)		
EP(P)	WHEN PEA PICKERS GET TOGETHER (63) Mail order item	Green Giant 2566	$12
	(From Jolly Green Giant, Le Sueur, Minnesota, issued with cover)		
33(P)	NATIONAL WILDLIFE FEDERATION (64) Radio ads	NWF 1964	$12
	(Ads by Ford, Andy Griffith, and Lorne Greene, issued with a cover)		

-albums-

LP	THIS LUSTY LAND (56)	Capitol 700	$15
LP(P)	THIS LUSTY LAND (56)	Capitol 700	$12
	(Capitol promo label)		
LP	HYMNS-TENNESSEE ERNIE (56)	Capitol 756	$15
LP(P)	HYMNS-TENNESSEE ERNIE (56)	Capitol 756	$12
	(Capitol promo label)		
LP	TENNESSEE ERNIE FORD FAVORITES (57)	Capitol 841	$15
LP(P)	TENNESSEE ERNIE FORD FAVORITES (57)	Capitol 841	$12
	(Capitol promo label)		
LP	OL' ROCKIN' ERN' (57)	Capitol 888	$50
LP(P)	OL' ROCKIN' ERN' (57)	Capitol 888	$40
	(Yellow promo label)		
LP	GATHER 'ROUND (59)	Capitol 1227	$12
LP(P)	GATHER 'ROUND (59)	Capitol 1227	$10
	(Yellow promo label)		
LP	WHAT A FRIEND WE HAVE (60)	Capitol 1272	$12
	(With the Jordanaires)		
LP(P)	WHAT A FRIEND WE HAVE (60)	Capitol 1272	$10
	(Yellow promo label)		
LP	SIXTEEN TONS (60)	Capitol 1380	$18
LP(P)	SIXTEEN TONS (60)	Capitol 1380	$15
	(Yellow promo label)		
LP	COME TO THE FAIR (60)	Capitol 1473	$12
LP	COME TO THE FAIR (60)	Capitol 1473	$10
	(Yellow promo label)		
LP	SINGS CIVIL WAR SONGS OF THE NORTH (61)	Capitol 1539	$12
LP	SINGS CIVIL WAR SONGS OF THE SOUTH (61)	Capitol 1539	$12
3LP	TENNESSEE ERNIE FORD DELUXE SET (68)	Capitol 2942	$12

FORESTER SISTERS (C)
Warner 45s $2 each
Warner LPs $4 each

-radio shows-

LP(RS)	LIVE AT GILLEY'S (May 86)	Westwood One	$10-15
	(Live concert)		
3LP(RS)	AMERICAN EAGLE (July 86) With Steve Earle	Westwood One	$15-25
	(Live concert)		
3LP(RS)	AMERICAN EAGLE (July 86) With Bellamy Brothers	Westwood One	$15-20
	(Live concert)		
3LP(RS)	AMERICAN EAGLE (Nov 86)	Westwood One	$10-20
	(Live concert)		
LP(RS)	WESTWOOD ONE PRESENTS (June 90)	Westwood One	$10-15
	(Live concert)		

BEANON FORSE (RB)
-singles-

45rpm	YOU BETTER GO NOW (58)	Rodney 514	$25

FOSTER & LLOYD (C)
RCA Victor LPs $3 each

-radio shows-

LP(RS)	WESTWOOD ONE PRESENTS (Nov 89)	Westwood One	$15-20
	(Live concert)		

THE FOUR CHORDS QUARTET (CW)
-singles-

45rpm	MAY THE GOOD LORD BLESS AND KEEP YOU (53)	Royale 157	$10
	(Red vinyl)		

FOUR TUNES (R & B)
One of the most collectible R & B groups recorded one single that might be considered country
-singles-

78rpm	COOL WATER (50)	RCA Victor 3967	$25
45rpm	COOL WATER (50)	RCA Victor 3967	$40

WALLY FOWLER (G)
Decca 45s $3-6 each
King 45s $3-6 each
Starday 45s $2-5 each
Vocalion LPs $5-8 each
Hilltop, Nashwood, and Pickwick LPs $2 each

-EPs-

EP	**CALL OF THE CROSS** (60)	Decca 2602	$10

-albums-

LP	**CALL OF THE CROSS** (60)	Decca 8560	$15
	(With the Anita Kerr Singers)		
LP(P)	**CALL OF THE CROSS** (60)	Decca 8560	$12
	(Pink promo label)		
LP	**GOSPEL SONG FESTIVAL** (60)	King 702	$30
	(With the Oak Ridge Quartet)		
LP	**WALLY FOWLER'S ALL NIGHT SINGING GOSPEL CONCERT** (60)	Starday 112	$25
	(Also with the Oak Ridge Quartet)		
LP	**WALLY FOWLER'S ALL NIGHT SINGING CONCERT** (64)	Starday 301	$15
LP	**WALLY FOWLER SINGS A TRIBUTE TO ELVIS** (77)	Dove 1000	$15
	(Recorded with several artists)		

CURLEY FOX (C)

-albums-

LP	**CURLEY FOX & TEXAS RUBY** (62)	Starday 235	$18
	(With Texas Ruby)		
LP	**TRAVELING BLUES** (63)	Harmony 7302	$15
LP(P)	**TRAVELING BLUES** (63)	Harmony 7302	$18
	(White promo label)		

ORVILLE FOX (RB)

-singles-

45rpm	**HONEY YOU TALK TO MUCH** (58)	Ellis 101	$90

CONNIE FRANCIS (R)
This pop singer did release some country LPs on MGM, which were also released as jukebox LLPs. The LPs on MGM that are country are worth around $10 each and the LLPs $10-15 each.

TILLMAN FRANKS (RB)

-singles-

45rpm	**HI-TONE PAPA** (58)	Gotham 7412	$35

FRANTICS FOUR (RB)

-singles-

45rpm	**TV MAMA** (58)	Gulfstream 1000	$40

DALLAS FRAZIER (C)
Capitol and RCA Victor 45s $2-3 each
Other Capitol and RCA Victor LPs $5-8 each

-albums-

LP	**ELVIRA** (66)	Capitol 2552	$15

VARIOUS ARTISTS

-albums-

LP(P)	**FREEDOMLAND U. S. A.** (61) Red promo label	Columbia 1484	$25
	(Includes Johnny Horton and Charlie Weaver)		

HUGH FRIAR (RB)

-singles-

45rpm	**I CAN'T STAY MAD AT YOU** (58)	Clix 805	$50

JANIE FRICKE (C)
Columbia 45s $1 each

-radio shows-

3LP(RS)	**TRIPLE** (May 83) Box set	Mutual Broadcasting	$20-30
	(With Alabama and Ricky Skaggs)		
3LP(RS)	**SILVER EAGLE** (Nov 83) With Bellamy Brothers	Westwood One	$10-15
	(Live Concert)		

FEZZ FRITSCHE (Polka)
FM 78s $10 each
MGM 78s $6 each
Soma 78s $5 each
Black Soma label 45s $5 each

-singles-

45rpm	**INNOCENCE WALTZ** (52)	FM 10,003	$25
	(And His Goosetown Band)		

NOTES

45rpm	BLUE EYES WALTZ (53)	Soma 1004	$20
45rpm	WALTZ QUADRILLE (53)	Soma 1005	$20
45rpm	BEAUTIFUL YOUTH (53)	MGM 11341	$25
	(With His Goosetown Band)		
45rpm	FISHERMAID POLKA (54)	MGM 11986	$12
	(With His Goosetown Band)		
45(P)	FISHERMAID POLKA (54)	MGM 11986	$15
	(Yellow promo label)		
45rpm	NEW ULM FAVORITE (55)	Soma 1038	$10
45rpm	PARADE POLKA (56)	Soma 1058	$10
	(With His Goosetown Band)		
45rpm	PEPPER POT POLKA (56)	Soma 1059	$10

DAVID FRIZZELL (C)
Warner and Viva 45s $1-2 each
Warner and Viva LPs $2-4 each
(Including duet LPs with Shelly West)

-radio shows-

3LP(RS)	SILVER EAGLE (May 84)	Westwood One	$10-15
	(Live concert)		
3LP(RS)	SILVER EAGLE (Aug 84) With Shelly West	Westwood One	$10-20
	(Live concert)		
LP(RS)	COUNTRY MUSIC TIME (80s)	U.S. Air Force	$10-15
	(Music and interviews)		

LEFTY FRIZZELL (CW)
Other Columbia 78s $5-8 each
Other Columbia 45s $3-8 each
Other Columbia LPs $4-8 each
Other Harmony LPs $4-8 each
ABC LPs $4-8 each
MCA and Rounder LPs $2-3 each

-singles-

78rpm	IF YOU'VE GOT THE MONEY I'VE GOT THE TIME (50)	Columbia 20739	$10
45rpm	IF YOU'VE GOT THE MONEY I'VE GOT THE TIME (57)	Columbia 52019	$10
	(Columbia Hall of Fame series)		
45(P)	IF YOU'VE GOT THE MONEY I'VE GOT THE TIME (57)	Columbia 52019	$12
	(Columbia Hall of Fame series, white promo label)		
45(P)	IF YOU'VE GOT THE MONEY I'VE GOT THE TIME Promo	Columbia 33040	$10
	(Red promo label Columbia Hall of Fame series)		
78rpm	LOOK WHAT THOUGHTS WILL DO (51)	Columbia 20772	$10
45rpm	LOOK WHAT THOUGHTS WILL DO (51)	Columbia 20772	$15
45rpm	I WANT TO BE WITH YOU ALWAYS (51)	Columbia 20799	$12
45rpm	I WANT TO BE WITH YOU ALWAYS (57)	Columbia 52020	$10
45(P)	I WANT TO BE WITH YOU ALWAYS (57)	Columbia 52020	$15
	(White promo label)		
78rpm	ALWAYS LATE (51)	Columbia 20837	$10
45rpm	ALWAYS LATE (51)	Columbia 20837	$12
78rpm	BRAKEMAN'S BLUES (51)	Columbia 20837	$12
45rpm	BRAKEMAN'S BLUES (51)	Columbia 20841	$15
78rpm	BLUE YODEL NO. 6 (51)	Columbia 20842	$12
45rpm	BLUE YODEL NO. 6 (51)	Columbia 20842	$15
78rpm	LULLABY YODEL (51)	Columbia 20843	$12
45rpm	LULLABY YODEL (51)	Columbia 20843	$15
45box	LEFTY FRIZZELL (51) 45rpm Box set	Columbia 4-15-4	$50
	(Price is for all three singles and box)		
45box	LISTEN TO LEFTY (52) 45rpm Box set	Columbia 4-17-4	$50
	(Price is for all three singles and box)		
45rpm	HOW LONG WILL IT TAKE (52)	Columbia 20885	$12
45rpm	DON'T STAY AWAY (52)	Columbia 20911	$12
45rpm	IF YOU CAN SPARE THE TIME (52)	Columbia 20950	$12
45rpm	FOREVER (52)	Columbia 20997	$12
45rpm	I'M AN OLD, OLD MAN (53)	Columbia 21034	$12
78rpm	BRING YOUR SWEET SELF BACK TO ME (53)	Columbia 21084	$10
45rpm	BRING YOUR SWEET SELF BACK TO ME (53)	Columbia 21084	$12
78rpm	BEFORE YOU GO, MAKE SURE YOU KNOW (53)	Columbia 21142	$10
45rpm	BEFORE YOU GO, MAKE SURE YOU KNOW (53)	Columbia 21142	$12
78rpm	HOPELESS LOVE (54)	Columbia 21169	$10
45rpm	HOPELESS LOVE (54)	Columbia 21169	$12
78rpm	RUN 'EM OFF (54)	Columbia 21194	$12
45rpm	RUN 'EM OFF (54)	Columbia 21194	$15
78rpm	TWO HEARTS BROKEN NOW (54)	Columbia 21284	$10
45rpm	TWO HEARTS BROKEN NOW (54)	Columbia 21284	$12
45(P)	TWO HEARTS BROKEN NOW (54)	Columbia 21284	$15
	(White promo label)		
78rpm	I LOVE YOU MOSTLY (54)	Columbia 21328	$10
45rpm	I LOVE YOU MOSTLY (54)	Columbia 21328	$12
45(P)	I LOVE YOU MOSTLY (54)	Columbia 21328	$15
	(White promo label)		

78rpm	MAKING BELIEVE (55)	Columbia 21366	$10
45rpm	MAKING BELIEVE (55)	Columbia 21366	$12
78rpm	YOUR TOMORROWS WILL NEVER COME (55)	Columbia 21458	$10
45rpm	YOUR TOMORROWS WILL NEVER COME (55)	Columbia 21458	$12
78rpm	FIRST TO HAVE A SECOND CHANCE (56)	Columbia 21488	$10
45rpm	FIRST TO HAVE A SECOND CHANCE (56)	Columbia 21488	$12
78rpm	YOU CAN'T LIVE THAT FAST (57)	Columbia 21530	$15
45rpm	YOU CAN'T LIVE THAT FAST (57)	Columbia 21530	$15
45(P)	YOU CAN'T LIVE THAT FAST (57)	Columbia 21530	$12
	(White promo label)		
45rpm	YOU'RE HUMBUGGIN' ME (58)	Columbia 41268	$20
45(P)	YOU'RE HUMBUGGIN' ME (58)	Columbia 41268	$15
	(White promo label)		
45(P)	SAGINAW, MICHIGAN (64)	Columbia 42924	$20
	(White promo label, blue vinyl)		

-EPs-

EP	JIMMIE RODGERS MEMORIAL (51)	Columbia 1667	$40
EP	LEFTY FRIZZELL (52)	Columbia 2061	$25
EP	THE SONGS OF JIMMIE RODGERS (53)	Columbia 2087	$25
EP	LEFTY FRIZZELL (57)	Columbia 2802	$20
EP	LEFTY FRIZZELL (58)	Columbia 2822	$20
EP	THE ONE & ONLY LEFTY FRIZZELL (59) Vol 1	Columbia 13421	$15
EP	THE ONE & ONLY LEFTY FRIZZELL (59) Vol 2	Columbia 13422	$15
EP	THE ONE & ONLY LEFTY FRIZZELL (59) Vol 3	Columbia 13423	$15

-albums-

10"LP	SONGS OF JIMMIE RODGERS (51)	Columbia 9019	$100
10"LP	LISTEN TO LEFTY (52)	Columbia 9021	$75
10"LP	CARL, LEFTY & MARTY (56)	Columbia 2544	$250
	(Carl Smith, Lefty Frizzell, and Marty Robbins)		
LP	ONE ONE & ONLY LEFTY FRIZZELL (59)	Columbia 1342	$35
LP	LEFTY FRIZZELL SINGS THE SONGS OF JIMMIE RODGERS (60)	Harmony 7241	$30
LP(P)	LEFTY FRIZZELL SINGS THE SONGS OF JIMMIE RODGERS (68)	Harmony 7241	$40
	(White promo label)		
LP	SAGINAW, MICHIGAN (64) Stereo	Columbia 8969	$25
LP	SAGINAW, MICHIGAN (64) Mono	Columbia	$20
LP(P)	SAGINAW, MICHIGAN (64)	Columbia	$25
	(White promo label)		
LP	THE SAD SIDE OF LOVE (65)	Columbia 9186	$12
LP(P)	THE SAD SIDE OF LOVE (65)	Columbia 9186	$15
	(White promo label)		
LP	LEFTY FRIZZEL'S COUNTRY FAVORITES (66)	Harmony 11186	$10
LP(P)	LEFTY FRIZZEL'S COUNTRY FAVORITES (66)	Harmony 11186	$15
	(White promo label)		
LP	LEFTY FRIZZEL'S GREATEST HITS (66)	Columbia CS-9288	$12
	(First pressings must have the CS-prefix)		
LP(P)	LEFTY FRIZZEL'S GREATEST HITS (66)	Columbia	$15
	(White promo label)		
LP	MOM & DAD'S WALTZ (67)	Harmony 11219	$12
LP(P)	MOM & DAD'S WALTZ (67)	Harmony 11219	$15
	(White promo label)		
LP	LEFTY FRIZZELL PUTTIN' ON (67)	Columbia 9572	$15
LP(P)	LEFTY FRIZZELL PUTTIN' ON (67)	Columbia	$18
	(White promo label)		

FRANK FROST (R)

-albums-

LP	HEY BOSS MAN (61)	Philips International 1975	$50

BOBBY FULLER (R)

Bobby Fuller Four
Eric 45s $3 each
Capitol 45s $5-8 each

-singles-

45rpm	YOU'RE IN LOVE (62)	Yucca 140	$15
45rpm	MY HEART JUMPED (62)	Yucca 144	$12
45rpm	I FOUGHT THE LAW (64)	Exeter 124	$40
45rpm	I FOUGHT THE LAW (65)	Mustang 3014	$10
45rpm	LOVE'S MADE A FOOL OF YOU (66)	Mustang 3016	$10
45rpm	THE MAGIC TOUCH (66)	Mustang 3018	$10

-albums-

LP	KRLA-KING OF THE WHEELS (66) Mono	Mustang 900	$40
LP	KRLA-KING OF THE WHEELS (66) Stereo	Mustang 900	$50
LP	I FOUGHT THE LAW (66) Mono	Mustang 901	$25
LP	I FOUGHT THE LAW (66) Stereo	Mustang 901	$40

JERRY FULLER (C)
Other Challenge 45s $5-10 each
MCA LPs $2-4 each

-singles-

45rpm	I'VE FOUND A NEW LOVE (57)	Lin 5011	$10
45rpm	MOTHER GOOSE AT THE BANDSTAND (58)	Lin 5019	$20
45rpm	ANNA FROM LOUISIANA (58)	Challenge 59085	$10
45(P)	ANNA FROM LOUISIANA (58)	Challenge 5908	$12
	(White promo label)		

-albums-

LP	TEENAGE LOVE (60)	Lin 100	$75

JOHNNY FULLER (R)

-singles-

45rpm	COMIN' ROUND THE CORNER (53)	Hollywood 1063	$40
45rpm	BUDDY (53)	Flair 1054	$40

ANNETTE FUNICELLO (C)
Annette
Only her country material is listed here; she recorded much pop material

-albums-

LP	ANNETTE FUNICELLO COUNTRY ALBUM (84)	Starview 4001	$10
	(Includes many Nashville studio artists)		

G

GABBART & HOLT (RB)

-singles-

45rpm	HEY BABY (58)	Sage 287	$50

EDDIE GAINES (RB)

-singles-

45rpm	BE-BOP BATTLING BALL (58)	Summit 101	$150

JAMES GALLAGHER (RB)

-singles-

45rpm	CRAZY CHICKEN (57)	Decca 29984	$25
45(P)	CRAZY CHICKEN (57)	Decca 29984	$18
	(Pink promo label)		

BOB GALLION (RB)

-singles-

45rpm	MY SQUARE DANCIN' MAMA (58)	MGM 12195	$60
45(P)	MY SQUARE DANCIN' MAMA (58)	MGM 12195	$50
	(Yellow promo label)		

AUGIE GARCIA (Quintet) (RB)

-singles-

45rpm	DRINKING WINE (58)	North Star 2023	$50
45rpm	HI YO SILVER (58)	North Star 2025	$45
45rpm	RING-A-LING (59)	North Star 2065	$40

DAVE GARDNER (RB)

-singles-

45rpm	HOP ALONG ROCK (58)	Decca 30548	$15
45(P)	HOP ALONG ROCK (58)	Decca 30548	$10
	(Pink promo label)		
45rpm	WILD STREAK (58)	Decca 30627	$15
45(P)	WILD STREAK (58)	Decca 30627	$10
	(Pink promo label)		

JOHNNY GARNER (RB)

-singles-

45rpm	KISS ME SWEET (58)	Imperial 5536	$15
45(P)	KISS ME SWEET (58)	Imperial 5536	$12
	(Imperial promo label)		
45rpm	DIDI DIDI (58)	Imperial 5548	$25
45(P)	DIDI DIDI (58)	Imperial 5548	$20
	(Imperial promo label)		

GLEN GARRISON (C)
Imperial 45s $1-2 each

-albums-

LP	**COUNTRY! COUNTRY!** (67)	Imperial 12346	$15
LP(P)	**COUNTRY! COUNTRY!** (67)	Imperial 12346	$18
	(White promo label)		
LP	**THE COUNTRY SOUL OF GLEN GARRISON** (68)	Imperial 12378	$10

GLENN GARRISON (RB)

-singles-

45rpm	**LOVIN' LORENE** (58)	Crest 1047	$25
45(P)	**LOVIN' LORENE** (58)	Crest 1047	$20
	(White promo label)		
45rpm	**PONYTAIL GIRL** (58)	Lode 106	$30

DAVID GATES (R)
Lead singer of Bread

-singles-

45rpm	**SWINGIN' BABY DOLL** (59)	East West 123	$75
45(P)	**SWINGIN' BABY DOLL** (59)	East West 123	$60
	(White promo label)		
45rpm	**LOVIN' AT NIGHT** (61) With the Accents	Robbins 1008	$50

THE GATLINS (C)
The Gatlin Brothers
Larry Gatlin
Monument 45s $2 each
Columbia 45s $1 each
Columbia one-sided singles $5 each
Monument LPs $5 each
Columbia LPs $3-4 each

-radio shows-

LP(RS)	**COUNTRY MUSIC TIME** (70s-80s)	U.S. Air Force	$10-12
	(Music and interviews)		
3LP(RS)	**THE SILVER EAGLE** (Apr 82)	DIR	$10-15
	(Live concert)		
3LP(RS)	**ON A COUNTRY ROAD** (Jan 83) Box set	Mutual Radio	$10-15
	(Includes live segment by Gatlins)		
3LP(RS)	**AMERICAN EAGLE** (Jul 86)	DIR	$10-15
	(Live concert)		
LP(RS)	**WESTWOOD ONE PRESENTS** (Sept 89)	Westwood One	$10-15
	(Live concert)		
Cass(RS)	**AUSTIN ENCORE** (94)	Mainstreet Broadcasting	$20-30
	(Live concert on cassette only)		

CRYSTAL GAYLE (C)
Younger sister of Loretta Lynn
United Artists 45s $1-3 each
Columbia, Elektra, and Liberty 45s $1 each
Other United Artists LPs $5 each
Columbia, Elektra, and Liberty LPs $2-4 each

-albums-

LP(P)	**CRYSTAL GAYLE SAMPLER** (77)	United Artists 163	$25
	(Promo-only release)		

-radio shows-

3LP(RS)	**THE SILVER EAGLE** (Feb 81)	DIR	$15-25
	(Live concert)		
3LP(RS)	**TRIPLE** (Jun 82) With Anne Murray and Ronnie Milsap	Mutual Broadcasting	$15-25
	(Music and interviews)		
LP(RS)	**ROBERT W. MORGAN** (Jul 83)	Watermark	$15-25
	(Music and interviews)		

GEEZINSLAW BROTHERS (N)
Sam Allred and Dewayne Smith
    (Not brothers or father and son)
Capitol 45s $3-5 each
Step One 45s $2 each
Lone Star LPs $5 each

-albums-

LP	**THE KOOKY WORLD OF THE GEEZINSLAW BROTHERS** (63)	Columbia 8900	$25
LP(P)	**THE KOOKY WORLD OF THE GEEZINSLAW BROTHERS** (63)	Columbia 8900	$30
	(White promo label)		
LP	**CAN YOU BELIEVE** (66)	Capitol 2570	$25
LP	**MY DIRTY, LOWDOWN, ROTTEN, COTTON-PICKIN' LITTLE DARLIN'** (67)	Capitol 2771	$20
LP	**CHUBBY** (68)	Capitol 2885	$20
LP	**THE GEEZINSLAWS ARE ALIVE** (69)	Capitol 130	$15

BOBBIE GENTRY (C)
Capitol 45s $2-5 each
Capitol LPs $5-10 each
Capitol 2LPs $8-12 each

-albums-

LP(P)	**ODE TO BILLY JOE** (76)	Warner LP	$20
	(Special radio salute, promo only)		

GEORGE & EARL (RB)

-singles-

45rpm	**DONE GONE** (56)	Mercury 70852	$40

GEORGIA SATELLITES (R)

-radio shows-

2LP(RS)	**KING BISCUIT FLOWER HOUR** (Apr 87)	DIR	$15-30
	(Live concert)		

SOUNDTRACK

-albums-

LP	**GIANT** (57)	Capitol 773	$40
	(With James Dean, Rock Hudson, and Liz Taylor)		

ETHAN GIANT (RB)

-singles-

45rpm	**WHERE'S MY BABY** (58)	Mark 141	$65

TERRI GIBBS (C)
MCA 45s $1-2 each
MCA LPs $2-4 each

-radio shows-

3LP(RS)	**THE SILVER EAGLE** (Feb 82) With Lee Greenwood	DIR	$10-20
	(Live concert)		
3LP(RS)	**THE SILVER EAGLE** (Sept 84) With Razzy Bailey	DIR	$10-15
	(Live concert)		

DON GIBSON (CW)
Other RCA Victor 45s $3-6 each
Hickory 45s $2-3 each
Other RCA Victor LPs $5-10 each
RCA Victor duet LPs $6-8 each
Other Camden LPs $4-8 each
Hickory LPs, solo and duet, $3-6 each
ABC LPs $3-5 each

-singles-

78rpm	**NO SHOULDER TO CRY ON** (52)	Columbia 20999	$25
45rpm	**NO SHOULDER TO CRY ON** (52)	Columbia 20999	$20
78rpm	**WALKIN' IN THE MOONLIGHT** (53)	Columbia 21109	$20
45rpm	**WALKIN' IN THE MOONLIGHT** (53)	Columbia 21109	$18
78rpm	**RUN BOY** (56)	MGM 12109	$40
78(P)	**RUN BOY** (56)	MGM 12109	$30
	(Yellow promo label)		
45rpm	**RUN BOY** (56)	MGM 12109	$25
45(P)	**RUN BOY** (56)	MGM 12109	$18
	(Yellow promo label)		
78rpm	**SWEET DREAMS** (56)	MGM 12194	$30
78(P)	**SWEET DREAMS** (56)	MGM 12194	$25
	(Yellow promo label)		
45rpm	**SWEET DREAMS** (56)	MGM 12194	$15
45(P)	**SWEET DREAMS** (56)	MGM 12194	$12
	(Yellow promo label)		
45rpm	**I AIN'T GONNA WASTE MY TIME** (57)	MGM 12290	$18
45(P)	**I AIN'T GONNA WASTE MY TIME** (57)	MGM 12290	$15
	(Yellow promo label)		
45rpm	**I AIN'T A-STUDYING YOU, BABY** (58)	MGM 12494	$25
45(P)	**I AIN'T A-STUDYING YOU, BABY** (58)	MGM 12494	$20
	(Yellow promo label)		
33rpm	**WHAT ABOUT ME** (61)	RCA Victor 7841	$10
	(33rpm compact single)		
45rpm	**HEAD OVER HEELS IN LOVE WITH YOU** (62)	RCA Victor 8144	$10
	(Price includes picture sleeve)		

-EPs-

EP	**DON GIBSON** (56)	Columbia 2146	$20
EP	**BLUE BLUE DAY** (58)	RCA Victor 4323	$15
EP	**THAT LONESOME VALLEY** (59)	RCA Victor 4335	$15
EP	**BLUE & LONESOME** (59) Blue label	RCA Victor 5114	$15

EP	**BLUE & LONESOME** (59) Maroon label	RCA Victor 5114	$20
EP(P)	**I CAN'T LEAVE/I LOVE YOU STILL** (59) Promo only	RCA Victor 6860 DJ-94	$18
	(Two songs on each side, Benny Martin is on the flip)		

-albums-

LP	**OH LONESOME ME** (58)	RCA Victor 1743	$50
LP	**SONGS BY DON GIBSON** (58)	Lion 70069	$25
	(Budget label)		
LP(P)	**SONGS BY DON GIBSON** (58)	Lion 70069	$35
	(White promo label)		
LP	**NO ONE STANDS ALONE** (59) Mono	RCA Victor 1918	$25
LP	**NO ONE STANDS ALONE** (59) Stereo	RCA Victor 1918	$30
LP	**THAT GIBSON BOY** (59) Mono	RCA Victor 2038	$18
LP	**THAT GIBSON BOY** (59) Stereo	RCA Victor 2038	$25
LP	**LOOK WHO'S BLUE** (60) Mono	RCA Victor 2184	$18
LP	**LOOK WHO'S BLUE** (60) Stereo	RCA Victor 2184	$25
LP	**SWEET DREAMS** (60) Mono	RCA Victor 2269	$18
LP	**SWEET DREAMS** (60) Stereo	RCA Victor 2269	$25
LP	**GIRLS, GUITARS & GIBSON** (61)	RCA Victor 2361	$20
LP	**SOME FAVORITES OF MINE** (62)	RCA Victor 2448	$20
LP	**I WROTE A SONG** (63)	RCA Victor 2702	$20
LP	**GOD WALKS THESE HILLS** (64)	RCA Victor 2878	$20
LP	**THE BEST OF DON GIBSON** (65)	RCA Victor 3376	$18
LP	**TOO MUCH HURT** (65)	RCA Victor 3470	$18
LP	**A BLUE MILLION TEARS** (65)	Camden 852	$18
LP	**DON GIBSON** (65)	Metro 529	$15
	(Early MGM tracks)		
LP(P)	**DON GIBSON** (65)	Metro 529	$20
	(Yellow promo label)		
LP	**THE FABULOUS DON GIBSON** (65)	Harmony 7358	$15
LP(P)	**THE FABULOUS DON GIBSON** (65)	Harmony 7358	$18
	(White promo label)		
LP	**DON GIBSON WITH SPANISH GUITARS** (66)	RCA Victor 3594	$18
	(With the Jordanaires)		
LP	**GREAT COUNTRY SONGS** (66)	RCA Victor 3680	$18
	(With the Jordanaires)		
LP	**HURTIN' INSIDE** (66)	Camden 2101	$15
LP	**MORE COUNTRY SOUL** (68)	RCA Victor 4053	$15
LP(P)	**CAROLINA BREAKDOWN**	RCA Victor 0424	$25
	(Special release green vinyl)		

-radio shows-

16"(RS)	**COUNTRY STYLE USA** (56)	Country Style USA 177	$25-40
	(Music and interviews)		
16"(RS)	**COUNTRY STYLE USA** (56)	Country Style USA 188	$25-40
	(Music and interviews)		
16"(RS)	**U.S. ARMY BAND** (60s)	U.S. Army	$20-30
	(Music and interviews)		
16"(RS)	**GRAND OL' OPRY** (61) Fifteen-minute show	WSM Radio 16	$20-35
	(Music and interviews)		
16"(RS)	**GRAND OL' OPRY** (63)	WSM Radio 71	$20-35
	(Music and interviews)		

RONNIE GILL (R)

-singles-

45rpm	**STANDING ON THE MOUNTAIN** (58)	Rip 129	$40

VINCE GILL (C)

Pure Prairie League
Casablanca 45s by Pure Prairie League $4 each
RCA Victor 45s by Pure Prairie League $2 each
(Not featuring Vince Gill)
RCA Victor 45s $2-5 each
Other RCA Victor color vinyl 45s $10 each
MCA 45s $2 each
Casablanca LPs by Pure Prairie League $3-5 each
RCA Victor LPs by Pure Prairie League $2-3 each
(Not featuring Vince Gill)
RCA Victor and MCA LPs $3 each

-singles-

45(P)	**OH CAROLINA** (84)	RCA Victor 13809	$15
	(Yellow label, yellow vinyl)		

MICKEY GILLEY (RB)

Other Paula 45s $5-8 each
Playboy 45s $4 each
Playboy picture sleeves $4 each
Fox Family 45s $5 each
Other Epic 45s $1 each
Airbourne 45s $3 each
Epic LPs $2-4 each
Columbia LPs $8 each
Other Playboy LPs $6-8 each
Plantation, Hilltop, and 51 West LPs $3-5 each

-singles-

45rpm	OOH WEE BABY		Minor 106	$175
45rpm	DOWN THE LINE		Astro 102	$20
45rpm	SUSIE Q		Astro 104	$18
45rpm	IS IT WRONG		Astro	$20
45rpm	IS IT WRONG		Potomac 901	$10
45rpm	DRIVE IN MOVIE (58)		Khourys 712	$40
45rpm	DRIVE IN MOVIE (58)		Princess 4004	$20
45rpm	CAUGHT IN THE MIDDLE (58)		Princess 4006	$12
45rpm	I'LL KEEP ON DREAMING (58)		Princess 4011	$10
45rpm	I STILL CARE (58)		Princess 4015	$10
45rpm	VALLEY OF TEARS		Sabra 518	$12
45rpm	CALL ME SHORTY (58)		Dot 15706	$60
45rpm	I AIN'T BO DIDDLEY (59)		San 1513	$15
45rpm	YOUR SELFISH PRIDE (59)		Lynn 503	$15
45rpm	MY BABY'S BEEN CHEATING AGAIN (60)		Lynn 508	$12
45rpm	SLIPPIN' AND SLIDIN' (60)		Lynn 512	$15
45rpm	MY BABY (60)		Lynn 515	$15
45rpm	GRAPEVINE		Rex 1007	$10
45rpm	WHAT HAVE I DONE		Daryl 101	$10
45rpm	WHOLE LOT OF TWISTIN' GOIN' ON (62)		Eric 7021	$10
45rpm	NOW THAT I HAVE YOU		Supreme 101	$10
45(P)	LOVE IN THE WANT ADS (67)		Paula 269	$10
	(White promo label)			
45(P)	AIR FORCE SPOTS (81) Public service ads		Air Force GS 81-4	$15
	(Gilley does one thirty-second spot, record with small center hole, issued with paper cover)			
45(P)	MICKEY GILLEY CHRISTMAS MEDLEY (81)		Epic AE7 1356	$10
	(Special live version for radio only)			

-EPs-

33(P)	USO ADS (82) Public service ads		USO	$10
	(Thirty-two PSA spots, one by Gilley)			

-albums-

LP	LONELY WINE (64)		Astro 101	$100
LP	DOWN THE LINE (67) Red label		Paula 2195	$25
LP(P)	DOWN THE LINE (67) White promo label		Paula 2195	$30
LP	ROOM FULL OF ROSES (74)		Playboy 128	$18
LP	CITY LIGHTS (74)		Playboy 403	$18
LP	MICKEY GILLEY AT HIS BEST (74)		Paula 2224	$18
LP	MICKEY GILLEY (78)		Paula 2234	$15
	(Reissue of earlier material)			

-radio shows-

LP(RS)	COUNTRY MUSIC TIME (78)		U.S. Air Force	$10-15
	(Music and interviews)			
LP(RS)	LIVE AT GILLEY'S (Jan 85)		Westwood One	$20-40
	(Live concert)			
LP(RS)	WESTWOOD ONE PRESENTS (Nov 89)		Westwood One	$15-25
	(Live concert)			
Cass(RS)	AUSTIN ENCORE (94)		Mainstreet Broadcasting	$20-40
	(Live concert on cassette only)			

DEL GILLMAN (CW)
And His Bar-X Boys
Tops 78s and 45s $5 each

JIMMY GILMORE (R)

-singles-

LP	BUDDY'S BUDDY (64)		Dot 25577	$75

LOU GIORDANO (R & B)

-singles-

45rpm	STAY CLOSE TO ME (59) Maroon label		Brunswick 55115	$225
	(Buddy Holly on guitar)			
45(P)	STAY CLOSE TO ME (59)		Brunswick 55115	$200
	(Yellow promo label)			

THE GIRLS NEXT DOOR (C)

-radio shows-

3LP(RS)	**AMERICAN EAGLE** (Feb 87) With Marty Haagard	DIR	$10-20
	(Live concert)		

LOUIS GITTINS (RB)

-singles-

45rpm	**MY HOT MAMA** (57)	Kat 100	$50

WILL GLAHE (Polka)
London 45s $4-10 each

JIM GLASER (C)
Of Tompall & the Glaser Brothers

-albums-

LP	**JUST LOOKING FOR A HOME** (61)	Starday 158	$40

-radio shows-

LP(RS)	**LIVE AT GILLEY'S** (Feb 86)	Westwood One	$10-20
	(Live concert)		

TOMPALL GLASER (CW)
And the Glaser Brothers
 (Jim and Charles)
Decca 45s $3-5 each
MGM 45s $2 each
United Artists 45s $2 each
ABC 45s $2 each
Elektra 45s $1 each
Other MGM LPs $5-8 each
ABC LPs $3-5 each
Elektra LPs $3 each

-albums-

LP	**THIS LAND FOLK SONGS** (60) Mono	Decca 4041	$30
LP	**THIS LAND FOLK SONGS** (60) Stereo	Decca 4041	$40
LP	**THIS LAND FOLK SONGS** (60)	Decca 4041	$35
	(Pink promo label)		
LP	**JUST LOOKING FOR A HOME** (61) Jim Glaser	Starday 158	$40
LP	**TOMPALL SINGS THE BALLAD OF NAMI THE KILLER WHALE**	United Artists 6540	$30
	& OTHER BALLADS OF ADVENTURE (66)		
LP(P)	**TOMPALL SINGS THE BALLAD OF NAMI THE KILLER WHALE**	United Artists 6540	$25
	& OTHER BALLADS OF ADVENTURE (66)		
	(White promo label)		
LP	**COUNTRY FOLKS** (67)	Vocalion 3807	$15
LP	**COUNTRY FOLKS** (67)	Vocalion 3807	$18
	(White promo label)		
LP	**TOMPALL & THE GLASER BROTHERS** (67)	MGM 4465	$15
LP(P)	**TOMPALL & THE GLASER BROTHERS** (67)	MGM 4465	$18
	(Yellow promo label)		
LP	**TICK TICK TICK** (77)	MGM 4667	$12
	(Soundtrack with Mike Curb)		
LP(P)	**TICK TICK TICK** (77)	MGM 4667	$15
	(White promo label)		

-radio shows-

LP(RS)	**LIVE AT GILLEY'S** (Feb 86) Jim Glaser	Westwood One	$10-20
	(Live concert)		

CLIFF GLEAVES (RB)

-singles-

45rpm	**LOVE IS MY BUSINESS** (58)	Summer 501	$12
45rpm	**LONG BLACK HEARSE** (58)	Liberty 55263	$15
45(P)	**LONG BLACK HEARSE** (58)	Liberty 55263	$10
	(White promo label)		

DARRELL GLENN (CW)
NRC 45s $4-8 each

-albums-

LP	**CRYING IN THE CHAPEL** (59)	NRC 5	$30

GLEN GLENN (RB)

-singles-

45rpm	**EVERYBODY'S MOVIN'** (58)	Era 1061	$40
45(P)	**EVERYBODY'S MOVIN'** (58)	Era 1061	$30
	(White promo label)		
45rpm	**ONE CUP OF COFFEE** (59)	Era 1070	$18
45(P)	**ONE CUP OF COFFEE** (59)	Era 1070	$12
	(White promo label)		

SOUNDTRACK

LP	**GO JOHNNY GO** (58)	(No label name)	$125

TOMMY GODDARD (C)
Sage 45s $5-10 each

RAY GODFREY (C)
Other Sims 45s $6-8 each
Other Columbia 45s $2-4 each

-singles-

45rpm	**BETTER TIMES A COMIN'** (65)	Sims 130	$10
45rpm	**KEEP YOUR CHIN UP SOLDIER** (68)	Columbia 43618	$10
	(Price includes picture sleeve)		

CAL GOLDEN (SD)
And His Arkansas Mountain Boys

-singles-

45rpm	**IF YOU'VE GOT THE MONEY** (50)	Old Timer 8052	$12
	(Yellow label, with Harry Raby)		

RONNIE GOODE (R)

-singles-

45rpm	**ROCKIN' BUG** (58)	Demon 1510	$10

ANITA GORDON (CW)

-singles-

45rpm	**SCARE-DY CAT** (63)	RCA Victor 8274	$10

CURTIS GORDON (RB)

-singles-

45rpm	**SITTIN' ON TOP OF THE WORLD** (58)	Mercury 71097	$20
45(P)	**SITTIN' ON TOP OF THE WORLD** (58)	Mercury 71097	$18
	(White promo label)		
45rpm	**CRY CRY** (59)	Mercury 71121	$15
45(P)	**CRY CRY** (59)	Mercury 71121	$10
	(White promo label)		

ROSCOE GORDON (RB)

-singles-

78rpm	**ROSCO BOOGIE** (50)	RPM 322	$18
45rpm	**ROSCO BOOGIE** (50)	RPM 322	$45
78rpm	**SADDLE THE COW** (50)	RPM 324	$20
45rpm	**SADDLE THE COW** (50)	RPM 324	$60
78rpm	**DIME A DOZEN** (58)	RPM 336	$20
45rpm	**DIME A DOZEN** (50)	RPM 336	$40
45rpm	**BOOTED** (51)	RPM 344	$40
45rpm	**BOOTED** (51)	Chess 1487	$60
45rpm	**NO MORE DOGGIN'** (51)	RPM 350	$40
78rpm	**TELL DADDY** (53)	Duke 101	$20
45rpm	**TELL DADDY** (53)	Duke 101	$30
78rpm	**T-MODEL BOOGIE** (53)	Duke 106	$20
45rpm	**T-MODEL BOOGIE** (53)	Duke 106	$40
78rpm	**TOO MANY WOMEN** (53)	Duke 109	$20
45rpm	**TOO MANY WOMEN** (53)	Duke 109	$40
45rpm	**WEEPING BLUES** (55)	Flip 227	$200
45rpm	**WEEPING BLUES** (55)	Sun 227	$375
45rpm	**THE CHICKEN** (56)	Flip 237	$25
45rpm	**THE CHICKEN** (56)	Sun 237	$125
45rpm	**SHOOBIE OOBIE** (57)	Sun 257	$12

PAPA JOHN GORDY (CW)

-albums-

LP	**FATHER OF HONKY TONK** (65)	Camden 862	$15

CHARLIE GORE (C)

-albums-

LP	**THE COUNTRY GENTLEMAN** (60)	Audio Lab 1526	$40

VERN GOSDIN (C)
Of the Gosdin Brothers
Elektra 45s $1 each
Elektra, Ovation, and Complete LPs $2-4 each

-albums-

LP	**SOUNDS OF GOODBYE** (68) The Gosdin Brothers	Capitol 2852	$15

-radio shows-

3LP(RS)	**THE SILVER EAGLE** (Apr 85) With the Judds	DIR	$40-75
	(Live concert)		
Cass(RS)	**AUSTIN ENCORE** (94)	Mainstreet Broadcasting	$20-25
	(Live concert on cassette only)		

JACKIE GOTROE (RB)

-singles-

45rpm	**LOBO JONES** (57)	Vortex 102	$125
45rpm	**RAISED ON ROCK AND ROLL** (58)	Rhythm 111	$60

SONNY GOWANS (RB)

-singles-

45rpm	**ROCKIN' BY MYSELF** (58)	United Artists 114	$40

CHARLIE GRACIE (RB)

Cameo 45s $10-15 each
Coral 45s $10 each
Roulette, Felsted 45s $8 each
Other 45s $2-3 each

-singles-

45rpm	**BOOGIE WOOGIE BLUES** (58)	Cadillac 141	$60
45rpm	**ROCKIN' AND ROLLIN'** (58)	Cadillac 144	$60

LOU GRAHAM (RB)

-singles-

45rpm	**WEE WILLIE BROWN** (58)	Clymax 318	$40

SONNY GRAHAM (CW)

RCA Victor 45s $5 each

BILLY GRAMMER (CW)

Monument 45s $5-8 each
Decca 45s $2-5 each
Epic 45s $2 each

-EPs-

EP	**BILLY GRAMMER** (64)	Decca 2767	$15

-albums-

LP	**TRAVELIN' ON** (61) Mono	Monument 4000	$50
LP	**TRAVELIN' ON** (61) Stereo	Monument 14000	$40
LP	**GOSPEL GUITAR** (62)	Decca 4212	$15
LP(P)	**GOSPEL GUITAR** (62)	Decca 4212	$12
	(Pink promo label)		
LP	**GOLDEN GOSPEL FAVORITES** (64)	Decca 4460	$15
LP(P)	**GOLDEN GOSPEL FAVORITES** (64)	Decca 4460	$12
	(Pink promo label)		
LP	**GOTTA TRAVEL ON** (64)	Decca 4542	$15
LP(P)	**GOTTA TRAVEL ON** (64)	Decca 4542	$12
	(Pink promo label)		
LP	**COUNTRY GUITAR** (65)	Decca 4642	$15
LP(P)	**COUNTRY GUITAR** (65)	Decca 4642	$12
	(Pink promo label)		
LP	**SUNDAY GUITAR** (67)	Epic 26233	$12
LP(P)	**SUNDAY GUITAR** (67)	Epic 26233	$15
	(White promo label)		
LP	**COUNTRY FAVORITES** (68)	Vocalion 3826	$15
LP(P)	**COUNTRY FAVORITES** (68)	Vocalion 3826	$10
	(White promo label)		

-radio shows-

LP(RS)	**GRAND OL' OPRY** (61) Fifteen-minute show	WSM Radio 14	$20-40
	(Music and interviews)		

GRANDPA JONES (CW)

Louis Jones
Other RCA Victor 45s and 78s $5-10 each
Decca 45s $4-8 each
Other King 45s $4-8 each
Monument 400 series 45s $4-8 each
Monument 800 series 45s $3-6 each
Monument (CBS) 8500 series 45s $2-4 each
Warner 45s $5 each
Other Monument LPs $3-5 each
CMH 2LPs $5-8 each
Nashville LPs $6 each
Coral and Starday LPs $5 each

-singles-

78rpm	**T. V. BLUES** (51)	RCA Victor 4660	$18

45rpm	**T. V. BLUES** (51)	RCA Victor 4660	$25
45(P)	**T. V. BLUES** (51)	RCA Victor 4660	$30
	(White promo label)		
78rpm	**BREAD AND GRAVY** (54)	RCA Victor 5234	$15
45rpm	**BREAD AND GRAVY** (54)	RCA Victor 5234	$20
45(P)	**BREAD AND GRAVY** (54)	RCA Victor 5234	$25
	(White promo label)		
45rpm	**DOWN IN DIXIE** (54)	King 1061	$15
45rpm	**FIX ME A PALLET** (55)	King 1069	$12
45rpm	**PAPA LOVES MAMBO** (55)	RCA Victor 5891	$12
45rpm	**MATRIMONY RIDGE** (56)	RCA Victor 6088	$15
	(With Minnie Pearl)		

-EPs-

EP	**GRANDPA JONES** (56)	King 223	$18
EP	**GRANDPA JONES** (59)	Decca 2648	$15
EP(P)	**GRANDPA JONES MAKES THE RAFTERS RING** (62)	Monument 013	$15
	(Jukebox LLP)		

-albums-

LP	**GRANDPA JONES SINGS HIS GREATEST HITS** (58)	King 554	$40
LP	**STRICTLY COUNTRY TUNES** (59)	King 625	$30
LP	**ROLLIN' ALONG WITH GRANDPA JONES** (63)	King 809	$25
LP	**16 SACRED GOSPEL SONGS** (63)	King 822	$25
	(With Brown's Ferry Four)		
LP	**DO YOU REMEMBER** (62)	King 845	$25
LP	**GRANDPA JONES MAKES THE RAFTERS RING** (62)	Monument 4006	$20
LP	**GRANDPA JONES YODELING HITS** (63)	Monument 8001	$18
LP	**THE OTHER SIDE OF GRANDPA JONES** (64)	King 888	$18
LP	**AN EVENING WITH GRANDPA JONES** (63)	Decca 4364	$25
LP(P)	**AN EVENING WITH GRANDPA JONES** (63)	Decca 4364	$30
	(Pink promo label)		
LP	**GRANDPA JONES SINGS REAL FOLK SONGS** (64)	Monument 18021	$18
LP	**GRANDPA JONES** (66)	Monument 18041	$40
	(Songs from the Brown's Ferry Four days)		
LP	**EVERYBODY'S GRANDPA** (68)	Monument 18083	$15
LP	**GRANDPA JONES** (69)	King 1042	$12
LP	**GRANDPA JONES SINGS HITS FROM HEE HAW** (69)	Monument 18131	$15
LP	**PICKIN' TIME** (70)	Vocalion 3900	$12
LP(P)	**PICKIN' TIME** (70)	Vocalion 3900	$15
	(White promo label)		
LP	**GRANDPA JONES LIVE** (70)	Monument 18138	$15
LP	**GRANDPA JONES LIVE** (72)	Harmony 31396	$12
LP(P)	**GRANDPA JONES LIVE** (72)	Harmony 31396	$15
	(Pink promo label)		
	See Brown's Ferry Four		

BILLY GRAY (CW)
The Western Oakies
Other Decca 45s $5-8 each

-singles-

45rpm	**YOU'D BE THE FIRST TO KNOW** (55) With Wanda Jackson	Decca 29267	$25
45(P)	**YOU'D BE THE FIRST TO KNOW** (55)	Decca 29267	$18
	(Pink promo label)		

-EPs-

EP	**DANCE-O-RAMA** (56)	Decca 2233	$12
EP	**DANCE-O-RAMA** (56)	Decca 2234	$12

-albums-

10"LP	**DANCE-O-RAMA** (56)	Decca 5567	$40

CLAUDE GRAY (CW)
And the Graymen
Decca and Mercury 45s $2-4 each
Million 45s $3 each

-albums-

LP	**SONGS OF BROKEN LOVE AFFAIRS** (62)	Mercury 60658	$20
LP(P)	**SONGS OF BROKEN LOVE AFFAIRS** (62)	Mercury 60658	$18
	(White promo label)		
LP	**COUNTRY GOES TO TOWN** (62)	Mercury 60718	$18
LP(P)	**COUNTRY GOES TO TOWN** (62)	Mercury 60718	$15
	(White promo label)		
LP	**CLAUDE GRAY SINGS** (67)	Decca 4882	$15
LP(P)	**CLAUDE GRAY SINGS** (67)	Decca 4882	$12
	(Pink promo label)		
LP	**TREASURE OF LOVE** (67)	Hilltop 6051	$10
LP	**THE EASY WAY OF CLAUDE GRAY** (68)	Decca 4963	$15
LP(P)	**THE EASY WAY OF CLAUDE GRAY** (68)	Decca 4963	$12
	(Pink promo label)		

LP	**PRESENTING CLAUDE GRAY** (72)	Million 1002	$12

RUDY GRAYZELL (RB)
Rudy Gray

-singles-

45rpm	**LOOKING AT THE MOON AND WISHING ON A STAR** (53)	Abbott 145	$12
45rpm	**BONITA CHIQUITA** (53)	Abbott 147	$12
45rpm	**THERE'S GONNA BE A BALL** (54) Rudy Gray	Capitol 2946	$15
45(P)	**THERE'S GONNA BE A BALL** (54)	Capitol 2946	$10
	(White promo label)		
45rpm	**YOU BETTER BELIEVE IT** (54) Rudy Gray	Capitol 3044	$12
45(P)	**YOU BETTER BELIEVE IT** (54)	Capitol 3044	$10
	(White promo label)		
45rpm	**PLEASE BIG MAMA** (55) Rudy Gray	Capitol 3149	$15
45(P)	**PLEASE BIG MAMA** (55)	Capitol 3149	$10
	(White promo label)		
45rpm	**THE MOON IS UP** (57)	Starday 229	$35
45rpm	**DUCK TAIL** (57)	Starday 241	$30
45rpm	**JIG-GA-LEE-GA** (57)	Starday 270	$30
45rpm	**LET'S GET WILD** (58)	Starday 321	$30
45rpm	**LET'S GET WILD** (58)	Mercury 71138	$25
45(P)	**LET'S GET WILD** (58)	Mercury 71138	$20
	(White promo label)		
45rpm	**JUDY** (58)	Sun 290	$10

JOE GRCEVICH (Polka)
With Joe Kuchinick

-singles-

45rpm	**PALME** (52)	Stanchel 1025	$25

BOBBY GREEN (RB)

-singles-

45rpm	**LITTLE HEART ATTACKS** (58)	Dak 4429	$50

LLOYD GREEN (C)
Chart, Monument, MGM, and Little Darlin' LPs $4-6 each

-albums-

LP	**BIG STEEL GUITAR** (64)	Time 2152	$15

GREENBRIAR BOYS (BG)

-albums-

LP	**THE GREENBRIAR BOYS** (62)	Vanguard 9104	$20
LP(P)	**THE GREENBRIAR BOYS** (62)	Vanguard 9104	$25
	(White promo label)		
LP	**RAGGED BUT RIGHT!** (64)	Vanguard 9159	$20
LP(P)	**RAGGED BUT RIGHT!** (64)	Vanguard 9159	$25
	(White promo label)		
LP	**DIAN & THE GREENBRIAR BOYS** (64)	Elektra 233	$25
LP	**BETTER LATE THAN NEVER** (66)	Vanguard 9233	$18
LP(P)	**BETTER LATE THAN NEVER** (66)	Vanguard 9233	$25
	(White promo label)		

JACK GREENE (CW)
Decca 45s $2-3 each
Decca LPs $5-10 each
Decca LPs by Jack Greene and Jeannie Sealy $6-8 each
MCA LPs by Jack Greene and Jeannie Sealy $2-4 each

LORNE GREENE (P)
Bonanza TV star
Other RCA Victor 45s $4-8 each
Artists of America 45s $3 each
Artists of America picture sleeves $3 each
Other RCA Victor LPs $5-10 each

-singles-

45rpm	**I'M THE SAME OLE ME** (63)	RCA Victor 8229	$10
	(RCA dog-on-top label)		
45rpm	**RINGO** (64)	RCA Victor 8444	$10
45(P)	**RINGO** (64)	RCA Victor 8444	$15
	(White promo label)		

-EPs-

33(P)	**NATURAL WILDLIFE FEDERATION** (64) Radio ads	NWF 1964	$12
	(Spots featuring Greene, Andy Griffith, and Ernie Ford)		
EP(P)	**WELCOME TO THE PONDEROSA** (64) Jukebox LLP	RCA Victor 2843	$40
	(Price includes title strips and hard cover)		

NOTES

-albums-

LP	**WELCOME TO THE PONDEROSA** (64)	RCA Victor 2843	$20

LEE GREENWOOD (C)
Other Dot 45s $5 each
Other MCA color vinyl 45s $8 each
Other MCA 45s $2 each
MCA LPs $2-4 each

-singles-

45(P)	**MARIA** (70) Lee Greenwood Affair (White promo label)	Dot 17312	$10
45(P)	**CHRISTMAS TO CHRISTMAS** (85) (Green promo label, red vinyl)	MCA 52733	$12
45(P)	**HEARTS ARE NOT MADE TO BREAK** (86) (White promo label, red vinyl)	MCA 52807	$10
45(P)	**MORNIN' RIDE** (86) (White promo label, yellow vinyl)	MCA 52984	$10
45(P)	**SOMEONE** (87) (White promo label, yellow vinyl)	MCA 53096	$10
45(P)	**IF THERE'S ANY JUSTICE** (87) Long/short versions (White promo label, red vinyl)	MCA 53156	$10

-EPs-

33(P)	**AIR FORCE PUBLIC SERVICE** (82) (Issued with a cover)	Air Force	$18
33(P)	**AIR FORCE PUBLIC SERVICE** (86) (Lee does two spots using "God Bless the USA" as a theme, price includes the paper picture sleeve)	Air Force	$15
33(P)	**SELECTIVE SERVICE MONSTER HITS** (88) PSAs (Four public service cuts, Greenwood does one, issued with paper cover)	Selective Service 16989	$10

-radio shows-

3LP(RS)	**THE SILVER EAGLE** (Feb 82) With Terri Gibbs (Live concert)	Westwood One	$10-20
3LP(RS)	**TRIPLE** (May 84) Box set (Music and interviews, includes Emmylou Harris and John Denver)	Mutual Radio	$20-30
LP(RS)	**LIVE AT GILLEY'S** (Nov 86) (Live concert)	Westwood One	$15-25
LP(RS)	**WESTWOOD ONE PRESENTS** (Nov 86) (Live concert)	Westwood One	$15-25

BOBBY GREGORY (C)
-EPs-

EP	**VALLEY OF THE BLUES** (60) (Plus three other songs, standard paper sleeve)	Gregorian 110	$15
EP	**I'M A WORKER FOR THE LORD** (60) (Plus three other songs, all gospel, paper sleeve)	Gregorian 111	$12
EP	**TRAIN LOAD OF BLUES** (60) (Plus three other songs, some gospel, paper sleeve)	Gregorian 112	$15

IVAN GREGORY (RB)
-singles-

45rpm	**ELVIS PRESLEY BLUES** (58)	G & G 110	$60

CHUCK GRAY (RB)
-singles-

45rpm	**PUSH THE PANIC BUTTON** (58)	Fable 616	$60

RAY GRIFF (C)
Boot, ABC, Capitol, and Dot 45s $1 each
Royal American 45s $2 each
Other Dot LPs $5 each
Boot, ABC, Capitol, Royal American LPs $3-6 each
-albums-

LP	**A RAY OF SUNSHINE** (68)	Dot 24868	$12

ALLENDER GRIFFIN (C)
Roadster 45s $3-5 each
Roadster picture sleeves $3 each

BUCK GRIFFIN (RB)
-singles-

45rpm	**PRETTY LOU** (57)	Holiday Inn 109	$12
45rpm	**MEADOWLARK BOOGIE** (57)	Lin 1005	$25
45rpm	**BALLIN' AND SQUALLIN'** (57)	Lin 1015	$60
45rpm	**GO-STOP-O** (57)	Lin 1016	$15
45rpm	**FIRST MAN ON THE MOON** (58)	Lin 5030	$12

45rpm	STUTTERIN' PAPA (57)	MGM 12284	$60
45(P)	STUTTERIN' PAPA (57)	MGM 12284	$50
	(Yellow promo label)		
45rpm	BOW MY BACK (58)	MGM 12439	$50
45(P)	BOW MY BACK (58)	MGM 12439	$40
	(Yellow promo label)		
45rpm	JESSIE LEE (58)	MGM 12597	$50
45(P)	JESSIE LEE (58)	MGM 12597	$40
	(Yellow promo label)		
45rpm	THE PARTY (58)	Metro 20007	$15
45(P)	THE PARTY (58)	Metro 20007	$18
	(Blue promo label)		

CURLEY GRIFFIN (RB)
-singles-

| 45rpm | GOT ROCKIN' ON MY MIND (58) | Atomic 305 | $50 |

ANDY GRIFFITH (N)
From the *Andy Griffith Show*
Other Capitol 45s $5-10 each
Columbia 45s $3 each
Other Capitol LPs $4-6 each
Columbia LPs $3-5 each

-singles-

78rpm	WHAT IT WAS, WAS FOOTBALL (54)	Capitol 2693	$30
45rpm	WHAT IT WAS, WAS FOOTBALL (54)	Capitol 2693	$25
45(P)	WHAT IT WAS, WAS FOOTBALL (54)	Capitol 2693	$20
	(White promo label)		
78rpm	SWAN LAKE (55)	Capitol 2855	$12
45rpm	SWAN LAKE (55)	Capitol 2855	$15
45rpm	SWAN LAKE (55)	Capitol 2855	$12
	(White promo label)		
45rpm	CARMEN (57)	Capitol 3402	$10
45rpm	NO TIME FOR SERGEANTS (57)	Capitol 3498	$10
45rpm	HAMLET (58)	Capitol 4157	$10
45rpm	ROMEO & JULIET (63)	Capitol 2571	$18
	(Price includes picture sleeve)		
45(P)	ROMEO & JULIET (63)	Capitol 2571	$12
	(Record only, red/orange promo)		

-EPs-

EP	WHAT IT WAS, WAS FOOTBALL (54)	Capitol 498	$18
	(One of the all-time biggest selling EPs)		
33(P)	NATIONAL WILDLIFE FEDERATION (64) Radio ads	NWF 1964	$12
	(Featuring Griffith, Lorne Greene, and Ernie Ford)		

-albums-

LP	JUST FOR LAUGHS (58)	Capitol 962	$25
LP(P)	JUST FOR LAUGHS (58)	Capitol 962	$30
	(Yellow promo label)		
LP	SHOUTS THE BLUES AND OLD TIMEY SONGS (59)	Capitol 1105	$30
LP(P)	SHOUTS THE BLUES AND OLD TIMEY SONGS (59)	Capitol 1105	$40
	(Yellow promo label)		
LP(P)	SILVER PLATTER SERVICE (May 67)	Capitol PRO 3245	$25
	(Includes interview and "Andy and Cleopatra")		

GAYLE GRIFFITH (RB)
-singles-

| 45rpm | ROCKIN' AND KNOCKIN' (58) | Emerald 2003 | $50 |

JOE GRIFFITH (R)
-singles-

| 45rpm | CRAZY SACK (57) | Reelfoot 1250 | $20 |

NANCY GRIFFITH (C)
-radio shows-

| Cass(RS) | AUSTIN ENCORE (94) | Mainstreet Broadcasting | $25-40 |
| | (Live concert on cassette only) | | |

CARL GROVES (RB)
-singles-

| 45rpm | CANTEEN BABY (58) | Musicale 116 | $40 |

BILLY GUITAR (R)
-singles-

45rpm	HERE COMES THE NIGHT (58)	Decca 30634	$40
45(P)	HERE COMES THE NIGHT (58)	Decca 30634	$30
	(Pink promo label)		

BONNIE GUITAR (CW)
Dot 45s $5-10 each
Other Dot LPs $5-10 each
Paramount, Hamilton, Pickwick, and Camden LPs $3-5 each

-albums-

LP	**MOONLIGHT & SHADOWS** (57) Mono	Dot 3069	$20
LP	**MOONLIGHT & SHADOWS** (59) Stereo	Dot 3069	$25
LP	**WHISPERING HOPE** (59)	Dot 25151	$15
LP	**DARK MOON** (62)	Dot 3335	$25

JEFF GUITAR (RB)
-singles-

45rpm	**JUMP AND SHOUT** (57)	Rocket 502	$60
45rpm	**WAIT A MINUTE BABY** (58)	Creole 1762	$50

GUITAR JR. (CW)
-albums-

LP	**PICK ME UP ON YOUR WAY DOWN** (60)	Goldband 1085	$25

HARDROCK GUNTER (RB)
-singles-

78rpm	**GONNA DANCE ALL NIGHT** (54)	Sun 201	$75
45rpm	**GONNA DANCE ALL NIGHT** (54)	Sun 201	$175
45rpm	**WHOO! I MEAN WHEE!** (55)	Emperor 57	$75
45rpm	**WHOO! I MEAN WHEE!** (55)	Emperor 112	$50

JACK GUTHRIE (CW)
Capitol 45s $2 each

-singles-

78rpm	**OKLAHOMA HILLS** (45)	Capitol 201	$12
78rpm	**OAKIE BOOGIE** (47)	Capitol 341	$10

-albums-

LP	**JACK GUTHRIE'S GREATEST SONGS** (66)	Capitol 2456	$25
	(Folk singer Woody Guthrie was Jack's cousin)		

CHARLES GUY (C)
Capitol 45s $2 each

-albums-

LP	**PRISONER'S DREAM** (63)	Capitol 1920	$20

H

MARTY HAAGARD (C)
-radio shows-

3LP(RS)	**AMERICAN EAGLE** (Feb 87) With Girls Next Door	DIR	$10-20
	(Live concert)		
LP(RS)	**LIVE AT GILLEY'S** (May 87)	Westwood One	$10-15
	(Live concert)		

EDDIE HABAT (Polka)
Decca 45s $4-8 each

VALINE HACKERT (RB)
-singles-

45rpm	**BILLY BOY** (57)	Brunswick 55151	$60
45(P)	**BILLY BOY** (57)	Brunswick 55151	$50
	(Yellow promo label)		

RED HADLEY (RB)
-singles-

45rpm	**BROTHER THAT'S ALL** (57)	Meteor 5017	$125
	(Red vinyl)		
45rpm	**BROTHER THAT'S ALL** (57)	Meteor 5017	$75
	(Black vinyl)		

ERNIE HAGAR (CW)
-albums-

LP	**SWINGIN' STEEL GUITAR** (65)	Sage & Sand 42	$18

DON HAGER (RB)

-singles-

45rpm	**BEBOP BOOGIE** (57)	Oak 0357	$55
45rpm	**LITTLE LIZA JANE BOP** (57)	Oak 0358	$55

THE HAGERS (C)

Twins Jim and John
From *Hee Haw*
Capitol 45s $3 each
Capitol LPs $5-10 each
Barnaby and Elektra LPs $3-6 each

MERLE HAGGARD (C)

Other Capitol 45s $3-6 each
Capitol picture sleeves $4-8 each
Elektra 45s $2 each
Elektra picture sleeves $2 each
MCA 45s $1 each
Epic 45s $1 each
Epic one-sided small center hole 45s $3 each
Mercury 45s $2 each
Curb 45s $1 each
Other Capitol Jukebox LLPs $6-10 each
Other Capitol LPs $3-8 each
Elektra LPs $3 each
MCA and Epic LPs $2-4 each
Mercury and Curb LPs $2 each

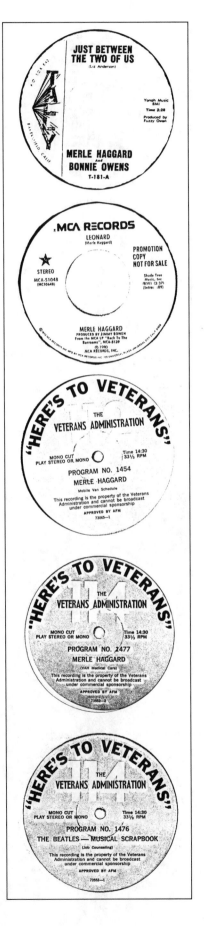

-singles-

45rpm	**SING A SAD SONG** (64)	Tally 155	$10
45rpm	**SAM HILL** (64)	Tally 178	$10
45rpm	**STRANGERS** (65)	Tally 179	$10
45rpm	**JUST BETWEEN THE TWO OF US** (65)	Tally 181	$12
	(Merle Haggard and Bonnie Owens)		
45(P)	**OKIE FROM MUSKOGEE** (69)	Capitol PRO-4829	$15
	(Special promo release)		
45(P)	**JESUS, TAKE A HOLD** (70)	Capitol PRO-5042	$15
	(Red/orange promo-only label)		
45(P)	**I CAN'T BE MYSELF** (70)	Capitol PRO-6003	$12
	(Red/orange promo only)		
45(P)	**LEONARD** (80) White promo label	MCA 51048	$10
	(Price includes paper insert that explains why the song was written about Tommy Collins)		

-EPs-

EP(JB)	**OKIE FROM MUSKOGEE** (70) Jukebox LLP	Capitol 384	$10
	(Issued with a paper cover)		

-albums-

LP	**STRANGERS** (65)	Capitol 2373	$30
LP	**JUST BETWEEN THE TWO OF US** (66)	Capitol 2453	$20
	(Duet album with Bonnie Owens)		
LP	**SWINGING DOORS** (66)	Capitol 2585	$25
LP	**I'M A LONESOME FUGITIVE** (67)	Capitol 2702	$25
LP	**I THREW AWAY THE ROSE** (67)	Capitol 2789	$25
LP	**KILLERS THREE** (68)	Tower 5141	$15
	(With Dick Curless, Bonnie Owens, and Kay Adams)		
LP	**THE LEGEND OF BONNIE & CLYDE** (68)	Capitol 2912	$18
LP	**MAMA TRIED** (68)	Capitol 2972	$18
2LP	**SAME TRAIN, A DIFFERENT TIME** (69)	Capitol 223	$25
	(A Tribute to Jimmie Rodgers)		
LP	**CLOSE UP** (69)	Capitol 259	$18
LP	**TRIBUTE TO THE BEST DAMN FIDDLE PLAYER IN THE WORLD**	Capitol 638	$18
	(Tribute to Bob Wills)		
2LP	**HIGH ON A HILLTOP** (71)	Capitol 707	$12
LP	**HAGGARD'S STRANGERS & FRIENDS HONKY TONKIN'** (71)	Capitol 796	$40
2LP	**LAND OF MANY CHURCHES** (71)	Capitol 803	$75
	(With Bonnie Owens and the Carter Family)		
LP	**TRULY THE BEST OF MERLE HAGGARD** (71)	Capitol 823	$40

-radio shows-

LP(RS)	**COUNTRY MUSIC TIME** (60s)	U.S. Navy	$25-50
	(Flip side features Merle Travis)		
LP(RS)	**HERE'S TO VETERANS** (60s) Fifteen-minute PSA show	Vets Administration	$25-40
	(Program 1454, flip side is Margie Evans)		
LP(RS)	**HERE'S TO VETERANS** (60s)	Vets Administration	$750-1,500
	(Program 1477, high value is because the flip side features the Beatles!)		
LP(RS)	**LIVE FROM THE LONE STAR** (Jun 80)		$20-40
	(Live concert)		
3LP(RS)	**THE SILVER EAGLE** (Feb 85) With George Strait	DIR	$40-75
	(Live concert)		

3LP(RS)	**THE SILVER EAGLE** (Jan 81)	DIR 002	$30-60
	(Live concert)		
2LP(RS)	**SILVER EAGLE II** (81) Live concert	TBS Synd (DIR)	$30-60
	(Pressed in USA for use in Canada)		
3LP(RS)	**WILLIE & MERLE** (Jun 82) Box set	Mutual Broadcasting	$25-40
	(Willie Nelson and Merle Haggard)		
3LP(RS)	**ON A COUNTRY ROAD** (Jan 83) Box set	Mutual Broadcasting	$15-25
	(Live concert segment by Haggard)		
3LP(RS)	**THE MERLE HAGGARD STORY** (Oct 84) Box set		$30-40
	(Music and interviews)		
Cass(RS)	**AUSTIN ENCORE** (94)	Mainstreet Broadcasting	$30-50
	(Live concert on cassette only)		

JIMMY HAGGETT (RB)

-singles-

45rpm	**THEY CALL OUR LOVE A SIN** (58)	Sun 236	$600
45rpm	**GONNA SHUT YOU OFF BABY** (58)	Meteor 5043	$500

RONNIE HAIG (RB)

-singles-

45rpm	**DON'T YOU HEAR ME CALLING, BABY?** (58)	Note 10010	$50
45rpm	**ROCKING WITH RHYTHM AND BLUES** (58)	Note 11014	$75
45rpm	**DON'T YOU HEAR ME CALLING, BABY?** (58)	ABC Paramount 9912	$35
45(P)	**DON'T YOU HEAR ME CALLING, BABY?** (58)	ABC Paramount 9912	$25
	(White promo label)		
45rpm	**DON'T YOU HEAR ME CALLING, BABY?** (61)	ABC Paramount 10209	$25
45(P)	**DON'T YOU HEAR ME CALLING, BABY?** (61)	ABC Paramount 10209	$15
	(White promo label)		

REX HALE (RB)

-singles-

45rpm	**DOWN AT BIG MAMA'S HOUSE** (58)	Rhythm 303	$125

BILL HALEY & HIS COMETS (RB)

Johnny Clifton
   (And His String Band)
The Saddlemen
Other Decca 45s $4-8 each
Logo, New Town, United Artists 45s $4-8 each
Janis, MCA, Odean and Rag 45s $2-4 each
Other Decca LPs $10-15 each
Other Warner LPs $10-15 each
Guest Star, Kama Sutra, Janis, Ambassador, Valiant, Crescendo, and Sun LPs $5-10 each

-singles-

78rpm	**STAND UP AND BE COUNTED** (48) Johnny Clifton	Center 102	$1,000
	(First record)		
78rpm	**VOGUE PICTURE DISC** (49) Saddlemen	Vogue Records	$200
	(This is the only rockabilly record in the Vogue picture disc series)		
78rpm	**DEAL ME A HAND** (50)	Keystone 5101	$250
78rpm	**I'M GONNA DRY EV'RY TEAR WITH A KISS** (50)	Atlantic 727	$200
78rpm	**ROCKET 88** (51) With the Saddlemen	Holiday 105	$125
78rpm	**GREEN TREE BOOGIE** (51) With the Saddlemen	Holiday 108	$125
78rpm	**PRETTY BABY** (51) With the Saddlemen	Holiday 110	$100
78rpm	**A YEAR AGO THIS CHRISTMAS** (52) With the Saddlemen	Holiday 111	$100
78rpm	**JUKEBOX CANNONBALL** (52) With the Saddlemen	Holiday 113	$100
78rpm	**ROCK THE JOINT** (52) With the Saddlemen	Essex 303	$75
45rpm	**ROCK THE JOINT** (52)	Essex 303	$80
	(Black label)		
45rpm	**ROCK THE JOINT** (52)	Essex 303	$40
	(Script label)		
45rpm	**ROCK THE JOINT** (52)	Essex 303	$2,000
	(Very rare red vinyl)		
78rpm	**ROCKING CHAIR ON THE MOON** (52) With the Saddlemen	Essex 305	$75
45rpm	**ROCKING CHAIR ON THE MOON** (52)	Essex 305	$60
78rpm	**REAL ROCK DRIVE** (52)	Essex 310	$75
45rpm	**REAL ROCK DRIVE** (52)	Essex 310	$125
	(Blue label)		
45rpm	**REAL ROCK DRIVE** (52)	Essex 310	$60
	(Orange label)		
78rpm	**CRAZY MAN CRAZY** (53)	Essex 321	$75
45rpm	**CRAZY MAN CRAZY** (53)	Essex 321	$35
78rpm	**FRACTURED** (53)	Essex 327	$75
45rpm	**FRACTURED** (53)	Essex 327	$40
78rpm	**LIVE IT UP** (53)	Essex 332	$75
45rpm	**LIVE IT UP** (53)	Essex 332	$40
78rpm	**STRAIGHT JACKET** (53)	Essex 340	$75
45rpm	**STRAIGHT JACKET** (53)	Essex 340	$40

78rpm	**JUKEBOX CANNONBALL** (53)	Essex 374	$100
45rpm	**JUKEBOX CANNONBALL** (53)	Essex 374	$60
78rpm	**ROCKET 88** (54)	Essex 381	$100
45rpm	**ROCKET 88** (54)	Essex 381	$125
78rpm	**ROCKET 88** (54)	Transworld 381	$75
45rpm	**ROCKET 88** (54)	Transworld 381	$50
78rpm	**ROCK THE JOINT** (54)	Essex 399	$100
45rpm	**ROCK THE JOINT** (54)	Essex 399	$75
78rpm	**REAL ROCK DRIVE** (54)	Transworld 718	$150
45rpm	**REAL ROCK DRIVE** (54)	Transworld 718	$200
78rpm	**ROCK AROUND THE CLOCK** (54)	Essex 102	$100
45rpm	**ROCK AROUND THE CLOCK** (54)	Essex 102	$50
	(Blue vinyl version is a bootleg)		
78rpm	**ROCK AROUND THE CLOCK** (54) Gold print on black	Decca 29124	$40
78rpm	**ROCK AROUND THE CLOCK** (54) Silver print on black	Decca 29124	$25
78(P)	**ROCK AROUND THE CLOCK** (54)	Decca 29124	$75
	(Pink promo label)		
45rpm	**ROCK AROUND THE CLOCK** (54) First pressing	Decca 29124	$18
	(All Decca first pressings thru 29970 have rays on the sides		
	of "Decca" on the label)		
45rpm	**ROCK AROUND THE CLOCK** (55) Second pressing	Decca 29124	$15
	(All Decca second pressings thru 29970 have rays under		
	"Decca" on the label)		
45(P)	**ROCK AROUND THE CLOCK** (55)	Decca 29124	$40
	(Pink promo label)		
78rpm	**SHAKE, RATTLE AND ROLL** (55) Gold on black	Decca 29204	$30
78rpm	**SHAKE, RATTLE AND ROLL** (55) Silver on black	Decca 29204	$25
78(P)	**SHAKE, RATTLE AND ROLL** (55)	Decca 29204	$40
	(Pink promo label)		
45rpm	**SHAKE, RATTLE AND ROLL** (55) First pressing	Decca 29204	$50
45rpm	**SHAKE, RATTLE AND ROLL** (55) Second pressing	Decca 29204	$15
45(P)	**SHAKE, RATTLE AND ROLL** (55)	Decca 29204	$40
	(Pink promo label)		
78rpm	**DIM, DIM THE LIGHTS** (55) Gold on black	Decca 29317	$30
78rpm	**DIM, DIM THE LIGHTS** (55) Silver on black	Decca 29317	$25
78(P)	**DIM, DIM THE LIGHTS** (55)	Decca 29317	$40
	(Pink promo label)		
45rpm	**DIM, DIM THE LIGHTS** (55) First pressing	Decca 29317	$18
45rpm	**DIM, DIM THE LIGHTS** (55) Second pressing	Decca 29317	$12
45(P)	**DIM, DIM THE LIGHTS** (55)	Decca 29317	$15
	(Pink promo label)		
78rpm	**BIRTH OF THE BOOGIE** (55)	Decca 29418	$30
78(P)	**BIRTH OF THE BOOGIE** (55)	Decca 29418	$25
	(Pink promo label)		
45rpm	**BIRTH OF THE BOOGIE** (55) First pressing	Decca 29418	$18
45rpm	**BIRTH OF THE BOOGIE** (55) Second pressing	Decca 29418	$12
45(P)	**BIRTH OF THE BOOGIE** (55)	Decca 29418	$15
	(Pink promo label)		
78rpm	**TWO HOUND DOGS** (55)	Decca 29552	$30
78(P)	**TWO HOUND DOGS** (55)	Decca 29552	$25
	(Pink promo label)		
45rpm	**TWO HOUND DOGS** (55) First pressing	Decca 29552	$18
45rpm	**TWO HOUND DOGS** (55) Second pressing	Decca 29552	$12
45(P)	**TWO HOUND DOGS** (55)	Decca 29552	$15
	(Pink promo label)		
78rpm	**ROCK-A-BEATIN' BOOGIE** (55)	Decca 29713	$30
78(P)	**ROCK-A-BEATIN' BOOGIE** (55)	Decca 29713	$25
	(Pink promo label)		
45rpm	**ROCK-A-BEATIN' BOOGIE** (55) First pressing	Decca 29713	$18
45rpm	**ROCK-A-BEATIN' BOOGIE** (55) Second pressing	Decca 29713	$12
45(P)	**ROCK-A-BEATIN' BOOGIE** (55)	Decca 29713	$15
	(Pink promo label)		
78rpm	**SEE YOU LATER, ALLIGATOR** (56)	Decca 29791	$30
78(P)	**SEE YOU LATER, ALLIGATOR** (56)	Decca 29791	$25
	(Pink promo label)		
45rpm	**SEE YOU LATER, ALLIGATOR** (56) First pressing	Decca 29791	$18
45rpm	**SEE YOU LATER, ALLIGATOR** (56) Second pressing	Decca 29791	$12
45(P)	**SEE YOU LATER, ALLIGATOR** (56)	Decca 29791	$15
	(Pink promo label)		
78rpm	**R-O-C-K** (56)	Decca 29870	$50
78(P)	**R-O-C-K** (56)	Decca 29870	$40
	(Pink promo label)		
45rpm	**R-O-C-K** (56) First pressing	Decca 29870	$18
45rpm	**R-O-C-K** (56) Second pressing	Decca 29870	$12
45(P)	**R-O-C-K** (56)	Decca 29870	$15
	(Pink promo label)		
78rpm	**ROCKIN' THROUGH THE RYE** (56)	Decca 29948	$50

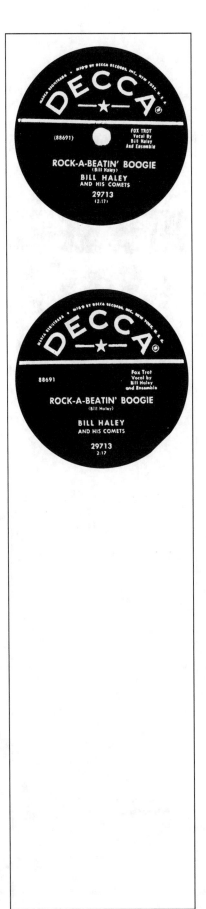

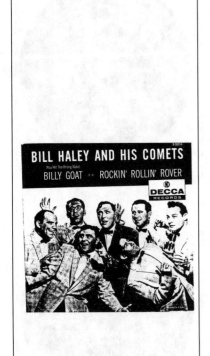

78(P)	**ROCKIN' THROUGH THE RYE** (56)	Decca 29948	$40
	(Pink promo label)		
45rpm	**ROCKIN' THROUGH THE RYE** (56) First pressing	Decca 29948	$18
45rpm	**ROCKIN' THROUGH THE RYE** (56) Second pressing	Decca 29948	$12
45(P)	**ROCKIN' THROUGH THE RYE** (56)	Decca 29948	$15
	(Pink promo label)		
45rpm	**RIP IT UP** (57) First pressing	Decca 30028	$15
45rpm	**RIP IT UP** (57) Second pressing	Decca 30028	$12
45(P)	**RIP IT UP** (57)	Decca 30028	$12
	(Pink promo label)		
45rpm	**RUDY'S ROCK** (56) First pressing	Decca 30058	$15
45rpm	**RUDY'S ROCK** (56) Second pressing	Decca 30058	$12
45(P)	**RUDY'S ROCK** (56)	Decca 30058	$12
	(Pink promo label)		
45rpm	**DON'T KNOCK THE ROCK** (56) First pressing	Decca 30148	$15
45rpm	**DON'T KNOCK THE ROCK** (56) Second pressing	Decca 30148	$12
45(P)	**DON'T KNOCK THE ROCK** (56)	Decca 30148	$12
	(Pink promo label)		
45rpm	**FORTY CUPS OF COFFEE** (56) First pressing	Decca 30214	$15
45rpm	**FORTY CUPS OF COFFEE** (56) Second pressing	Decca 30214	$12
45(P)	**FORTY CUPS OF COFFEE** (56)	Decca 30214	$12
	(Pink promo label)		
45rpm	**BILLY GOAT** (57) First pressing	Decca 30314	$100
	(Price includes picture sleeve)		
45rpm	**BILLY GOAT** (57) First pressing	Decca 30314	$15
45rpm	**BILLY GOAT** (57) Second pressing	Decca 30314	$12
45(P)	**BILLY GOAT** (57)	Decca 30314	$12
	(Pink promo label)		
45rpm	**THE DIPSY DOODLE** (57) First pressing	Decca 30394	$15
45rpm	**THE DIPSY DOODLE** (57) Second pressing	Decca 30394	$12
45(P)	**THE DIPSY DOODLE** (57)	Decca 30394	$12
	(Pink promo label)		
45rpm	**ROCK THE JOINT** (58) First pressing	Decca 30461	$15
45rpm	**ROCK THE JOINT** (58) Second pressing	Decca 30461	$12
45(P)	**ROCK THE JOINT** (58)	Decca 30461	$12
	(Pink promo label)		
45rpm	**MARY, MARY LOU** (58) First pressing	Decca 30530	$60
	(Price includes picture sleeve)		
45rpm	**MARY, MARY LOU** (58) First pressing	Decca 30530	$15
45rpm	**MARY, MARY LOU** (58) Second pressing	Decca 30530	$12
45(P)	**MARY, MARY LOU** (58)	Decca 30530	$12
	(Pink promo label)		
45rpm	**SKINNY MINNIE** (58) First pressing	Decca 30592	$15
45rpm	**SKINNY MINNIE** (58) Second pressing	Decca 30592	$12
45(P)	**SKINNY MINNIE** (58)	Decca 30592	$12
	(Pink promo label)		
45rpm	**LEAN JEAN** (58) First pressing	Decca 30681	$15
45rpm	**LEAN JEAN** (58) Second pressing	Decca 30681	$12
45(P)	**LEAN JEAN** (58)	Decca 30681	$12
	(Pink promo label)		
45rpm	**WHOA, MABEL** (58) First pressing	Decca 30741	$15
45rpm	**WHOA, MABEL** (58) Second pressing	Decca 30741	$12
45(P)	**WHOA, MABEL** (58)	Decca 30741	$12
	(Pink promo label)		
45rpm	**CORRINE, CORRINA** (58)	Decca 30781	$15
45(P)	**CORRINE, CORRINA** (58)	Decca 30781	$12
	(Pink promo label)		
45rpm	**I GOT A WOMAN** (58)	Decca 30844	$15
45(P)	**I GOT A WOMAN** (58)	Decca 30844	$12
	(Pink promo label)		
45rpm	**A FOOL SUCH AS I** (59)	Decca 30873	$15
45(P)	**A FOOL SUCH AS I** (59)	Decca 30873	$12
	(Pink promo label)		
45rpm	**CALDONIA** (59)	Decca 30926	$15
45(P)	**CALDONIA** (59)	Decca 30926	$12
	(Pink promo label)		
45rpm	**JOEY'S SONG** (59)	Decca 30956	$15
45(P)	**JOEY'S SONG** (59)	Decca 30956	$12
	(Decca promo label)		
45rpm	**SKOKIAAN** (59)	Decca 31030	$15
45(P)	**SKOKIAAN** (59)	Decca 31030	$12
	(Decca promo label)		
45rpm	**MUSIC, MUSIC, MUSIC** (60)	Decca 31080	$15
45(P)	**MUSIC, MUSIC, MUSIC** (60)	Decca 31080	$12
	(Decca promo label)		
45rpm	**CANDY KISSES** (60)	Warner 5145	$12
45(P)	**CANDY KISSES** (60)	Warner 5145	$50
	(Yellow vinyl, promo label)		

45(P)	**CANDY KISSES** (60)	Warner 5145	$15
	(White promo label)		
45rpm	**HAWK** (60)	Warner 5154	$12
45(P)	**HAWK** (60)	Warner 5154	$15
	(White promo label)		
45rpm	**SO RIGHT TONIGHT** (60)	Warner 5171	$12
45(P)	**SO RIGHT TONIGHT** (60)	Warner 5171	$10
	(White promo label)		
45rpm	**FLIP, FLOP & FLY** (61)	Warner 5228	$12
45(P)	**FLIP, FLOP & FLY** (61)	Warner 5228	$10
	(White promo label)		
45rpm	**THE SPANISH TWIST** (61)	Gone 5111	$12
45rpm	**RIVIERA** (61)	Gone 5116	$10
45rpm	**THE GREEN DOOR** (64)	Decca 31650	$10
45(P)	**THE GREEN DOOR** (64)	Decca 31650	$15
	(Yellow promo label)		
45rpm	**BURN THAT CANDLE** (65)	Apt 25081	$10
45rpm	**HALEY A-GO-GO** (65)	Apt 25087	$10
45rpm	**ROCK AROUND THE CLOCK** (70)	Kama Sutra 508	$15
45(P)	**ROCK AROUND THE CLOCK** (70)	Kama Sutra 508	$12
	(Yellow promo label)		
45rpm	**ROCK AROUND THE CLOCK** (70)	Buddah 169	$10
45(P)	**ROCK AROUND THE CLOCK** (70)	Buddah 169	$12
	(Yellow promo label)		
45rpm	**ROCK AROUND THE CLOCK** (71)	Warner 7124	$10
45(P)	**ROCK AROUND THE CLOCK** (71)	Warner 7124	$12
	(White promo label)		
45rpm	**ROCK AROUND THE CLOCK** (75)	Kasey 7006	$10
	(Price includes picture sleeve)		
45rpm	**YODEL YOUR BLUES AWAY** (78)	Arvee 4677	$12

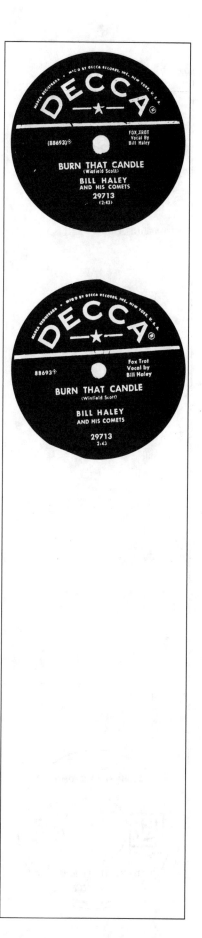

-EPs-

EP	**FOR YOUR DANCE PARTY** (54)	Essex 102	$250
EP	**BILL HALEY'S DANCE PARTY** (54)	Essex 102	$200
EP	**ROCK WITH BILL HALEY AND HIS COMETS** (54)	Essex 117	$200
EP	**ROCK WITH BILL HALEY AND HIS COMETS VOL 2** (54)	Essex 118	$200
EP	**ROCK WITH BILL HALEY AND HIS COMETS VOL 3** (54)	Essex 119	$200
	(Two different pre-label number prefixes for each of the Essex EPs)		
EP	**ROCK WITH BILL HALEY AND HIS COMETS** (55)	Transworld 117	$200
EP	**ROCK WITH BILL HALEY AND HIS COMETS VOL. 2** (55)	Transworld 118	$200
EP	**ROCK WITH BILL HALEY AND HIS COMETS VOL. 3** (55)	Transworld 119	$200
	(Transworld EPs are reissues of the Essex EPs)		
EP	**SHAKE, RATTLE AND ROLL** (55)	Decca 2168	$150
EP	**DIM, DIM THE LIGHTS** (55)	Decca 2209	$125
EP	**ROCK AND ROLL DANCE PARTY** (56)	Decca 2322	$100
EP	**HE DIGS ROCK AND ROLL** (56)	Decca 2398	$100
EP	**HE DIGS ROCK AND ROLL** (56)	Decca 2399	$100
EP	**HE DIGS ROCK AND ROLL** (56)	Decca 2400	$100
EP	**ROCK AND ROLL STAGE SHOW** (56)	Decca 2416	$75
EP	**ROCK AND ROLL STAGE SHOW** (56)	Decca 2417	$75
EP	**ROCK AND ROLL STAGE SHOW** (56)	Decca 2418	$75
EP	**ROCKIN' THE OLDIES** (57)	Decca 2532	$75
EP	**ROCK AND ROLL PARTY** (57)	Decca 2533	$75
EP	**ROCKIN' AND ROLLIN'** (57)	Decca 2534	$75
EP	**ROCKIN' AROUND THE WORLD** (57)	Decca 2564	$75
EP	**ROCKIN' AROUND EUROPE** (57)	Decca 2576	$75
EP	**ROCKIN' AROUND THE AMERICAS** (57)	Decca 2577	$75
EP	**ROCKIN' THE JOINT** (58)	Decca 2615	$75
EP	**ROCKIN' THE JOINT** (58)	Decca 2616	$75
EP	**BILL HALEY'S CHICKS** (58) First pressing	Decca 2638	$75
EP	**BILL HALEY'S CHICKS** (58) Second pressing	Decca 2638	$40
EP	**BILL HALEY AND HIS COMETS** (58) Mono first pressing	Decca 2670	$75
EP	**BILL HALEY AND HIS COMETS** (58) Mono second pressing	Decca 2670	$40
EP	**BILL HALEY AND HIS COMETS** (58) Stereo	Decca 72670	$100
EP	**TOP TEEN HITS** (59) Mono first pressing	Decca 2671	$75
EP	**TOP TEEN HITS** (59) Mono second pressing	Decca 2671	$40
EP	**TOP TEEN HITS** (59) Stereo	Decca 72671	$100
EP(P)	**DEMONSTRATION RECORD** (59)	Decca 38088	$25
	(One Haley song, "Eloise")		
EP	**ROCK AROUND THE CLOCK** (79)	Claire 4779	$20

-albums-

LP	**ROCK WITH BILL HALEY AND HIS COMETS**	Essex 202	$250
10"LP	**SHAKE, RATTLE AND ROLL** (54)	Decca 5560	$500
LP	**ROCK AROUND THE CLOCK** (55) First pressing	Decca 8225	$125
	(Black label)		
LP	**ROCK AROUND THE CLOCK** (55) Second pressing	Decca 8225	$30
	(Rainbow label)		

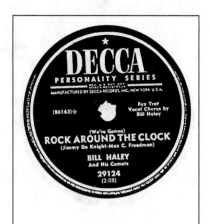

LP	**ROCK AROUND THE CLOCK** (55) Stereo		Decca 78225	$40
	(Rainbow label)			
LP(P)	**ROCK AROUND THE CLOCK** (55)		Decca 8225	$250
	(Pink promo label)			
LP	**HE DIGS ROCK AND ROLL** (55)		Decca 8315	$125
LP(P)	**HE DIGS ROCK AND ROLL** (55)		Decca 8315	$100
	(Pink promo label)			
LP	**ROCK AND ROLL STAGE SHOW** (55)		Decca 8345	$125
LP(P)	**ROCK AND ROLL STAGE SHOW** (55)		Decca 8345	$200
	(Pink promo label)			
LP	**ROCK WITH BILL HALEY AND HIS COMETS** (56)		Transworld 202	$275
	(Reissue of the Essex album)			
LP	**ROCK WITH BILL HALEY AND HIS COMETS** (57)		Somerset 4600	$125
	(Reissue of the Essex/Transworld LP)			
LP	**ROCKIN' THE OLDIES** (57)		Decca 8569	$125
LP(P)	**ROCKIN' THE OLDIES** (57)		Decca 8569	$150
	(Pink promo label)			
LP	**ROCKIN' AROUND THE WORLD** (57)		Decca 8692	$125
LP(P)	**ROCKIN' AROUND THE WORLD** (57)		Decca 8692	$125
	(Pink promo label)			
LP	**ROCKIN' THE JOINT** (58)		Decca 8775	$100
LP(P)	**ROCKIN' THE JOINT** (58)		Decca 8775	$100
	(Pink promo label)			
LP	**BILL HALEY'S CHICKS** (59) Mono		Decca 8821	$100
LP	**BILL HALEY'S CHICKS** (59) Stereo		Decca 8821	$150
LP(P)	**BILL HALEY'S CHICKS** (59)		Decca 8821	$125
	(Pink promo label)			
LP	**STRICTLY INSTRUMENTAL** (59) Mono		Decca 8964	$100
LP	**STRICTLY INSTRUMENTAL** (59) Stereo		Decca 8964	$150
LP(P)	**STRICTLY INSTRUMENTAL** (59)		Decca 8964	$100
	(Pink promo label)			
LP	**BILL HALEY AND HIS COMETS** (60)		Warner 1378	$40
LP(P)	**BILL HALEY AND HIS COMETS** (60)		Warner 1378	$65
	(White promo label)			
LP	**BILL HALEY'S JUKEBOX** (60)		Warner 1391	$40
LP(P)	**BILL HALEY'S JUKEBOX** (60)		Warner 1391	$50
	(White promo label)			
LP	**BILL HALEY AND THE COMETS** (63)		Vocalion 3696	$25
LP	**TWISTIN' KNIGHTS AT THE ROUND TABLE** (62) Stereo		Roulette 25174	$25
LP	**ROCK 'N' ROLL** (73)		Crescendo 2077	$15
LP(P)	**ROCK 'N' ROLL** (73)		Crescendo 2077	$20
	(White promo label)			

BILLY HALL (RB)

-singles-

45rpm	**MOVE OVER ROVER** (58)		Mar-Vel 1002	$50

CONNIE HALL (C)
Decca 45s $3 each

-albums-

LP	**CONNIE HALL** (62)		Decca 4217	$18
LP(P)	**CONNIE HALL** (62)		Decca 4217	$15
	(Pink promo label)			
LP	**COUNTRY SONGS** (65)		Vocalion 3752	$15
LP	**COUNTRY STYLE** (65)		Vocalion 3801	$15

DICKSON HALL (CW)
Kapp EPs $8 each

-EPs-

EP	**OUTLAWS OF THE OLD WEST** (54)		MGM 329	$20

-albums-

10"LP	**OUTLAWS OF THE OLD WEST** (54)		MGM 329	$50
LP	**OUTLAWS OF THE OLD WEST** (56)		MGM 3263	$25
LP(P)	**OUTLAWS OF THE OLD WEST** (56)		MGM 3263	$30
	(Yellow promo label)			
LP	**FABULOUS COUNTRY HITS** (57)		Kapp 1067	$25
LP	**24 FABULOUS COUNTRY HITS** (66)		Kapp 3464	$15
LP(P)	**24 FABULOUS COUNTRY HITS** (66)		Kapp 3464	$18
	(White promo label)			
LP	**25 ALL-TIME COUNTRY & WESTERN HITS** (58)		Epic 3427	$25
LP	**COUNTRY & WESTERN MILLION SELLERS** (60)		Perfect 14016	$20

JOANIE HALL (CW)
And the Frontiersmen
Recorded with Eddie Dean

-singles-

45rpm	**OPEN UP YOUR DOOR, BABY** (62)	Sage & Sound 207	$15
	(Joanie Hall with Eddie Dean)		

-albums-

LP	**WESTERN MEETS COUNTRY** (62)	Sage & Sound 34	$20

ROY HALL (RB)

-singles-

45rpm	**ONE MONKEY DON'T STOP THE SHOW** (57)	Pierce 1918	$60
45rpm	**THREE ALLEY CATS** (57)	Hi-Q 5045	$40
45rpm	**ALL BY MYSELF** (57)	Decca 29697	$30
45(P)	**ALL BY MYSELF** (57)	Decca 29697	$25
	(Pink promo label)		
45rpm	**SEE YOU LATER ALLIGATOR** (58)	Decca 29786	$35
45(P)	**SEE YOU LATER ALLIGATOR** (58)	Decca 29786	$30
	(Pink promo label)		
45rpm	**BLUE SUEDE SHOES** (58)	Decca 29880	$30
45(P)	**BLUE SUEDE SHOES** (58)	Decca 29880	$25
	(Pink promo label)		
45rpm	**DIGGIN' THE BOOGIE** (58)	Decca 30060	$40
45rpm	**DIGGIN' THE BOOGIE** (58)	Decca 30060	$30
	(Pink promo label)		

SONNY HALL (RB)

-singles-

45rpm	**MY BIG FAT BABY** (57)	D 1009	$60

TOM T. HALL (C)
Mercury 45s $3-6 each
RCA Victor 45s $2-4 each
Columbia duet 45s $2 each
Mercury LPs $5-8 each
RCA Victor LPs $4-6 each

-EPs-

EP(P)	**60-SECOND RADIO PROGRAM FILLERS** (71)	Smash DJ-136	$10
	(Eight sixty-second cuts including one by Hall, issued with a paper cover)		
EP(P)	**TOM T. HALL'S GREATEST HITS** (71)	Mercury MEPL-23	$12
	(Four songs by Hall from LP)		
EP(P)	**TOM T. HALL ... THE STORY TELLER** (72)	Mercury MEPL-24	$12
	(Four songs by Hall from LP)		
33(P)	**1976 FIFTH INTERNATIONAL FAN FAIR** (76)	CMA Nashville UR699	$20
	(16 spots, Hall does one)		
33(P)	**EMPLOYER SUPPORT OF THE GUARD & RESERVE** (82)	EGR 1282	$10
	(Public service spots for radio, same ad on each side)		

-radio shows-

LP(RS)	**COUNTRY MUSIC TIME** (80s)	U.S. Air Force	$10-15
	(Music and interviews)		
LP(RS)	**COUNTRY SESSIONS** (80s)	NBC Radio	$10-15
	(Music and interviews)		
LP(RS)	**COUNTRY CROSSROADS** (80s)	Southern Baptists	$10-15
	(Music and interviews)		
LP(RS)	**LIVE AT GILLEY'S** (Mar 83)	Westwood One	$10-15
	(Live concert)		

STUART HAMBLEN (G)
Other Columbia 45s $5-8 each
Other RCA Victor 45s $4-8 each
Voss 45s $6 each
Word, Lamb & Lion, and Sacred (label) LPs $2-4 each

-singles-

45rpm	**BUT I'LL GO CHASIN' WOMEN** (50)	Columbia 20625	$10
45rpm	**I'M THE ONE WHO LOVES YOU** (50)	Columbia 20714	$10
45rpm	**THIS OLE HOUSE** (54)	RCA Victor 5739	$10

-EPs-

2EP	**IT IS NO SECRET** (54)	RCA Victor 3265	$18
2EP	**IT IS NO SECRET** (56)	RCA Victor 1253	$15
EP	**IT IS NO SECRET** (56)	RCA Victor 804	$10
EP	**GRAND OLD HYMNS** (57)	RCA Victor 1-1436	$10
EP	**GRAND OLD HYMNS** (57)	RCA Victor 2-1436	$10
EP	**STUART HAMBLEN** (58)	Columbia 2827	$10
EP	**THIS OLE HOUSE** (59)	RCA Victor 5115	$10

-albums-

10"LP	**IT IS NO SECRET** (54)		RCA Victor 3265	$40
LP	**IT IS NO SECRET** (56)		RCA Victor 1253	$25
LP	**GRAND OLD HYMNS** (57)		RCA Victor 1436	$20
LP	**HYMNS** (57)		Harmony 7009	$25
LP	**BEYOND THE SUN** (59)		Camden 537	$15
LP	**REMEMBER ME** (60)		Coral 57254	$18
LP(P)	**REMEMBER ME** (60)		Coral 57254	$15
	(Blue promo label)			
LP	**THE SPELL OF THE YUKON** (61)		Columbia 8388	$15
LP	**OF GOD I SING** (62)		Columbia 8569	$15
LP	**IN THE GARDEN** (66)		Camden 973	$12
LP	**THIS OLD HOUSE HAS GOT TO GO** (66)		Kapp 3469	$12
LP	**I BELIEVE** (67)		Harmony 11203	$12
LP(P)	**I BELIEVE** (67)		Harmony 11203	$15
	(White promo label)			

GEORGE HAMILTON IV (CW)

RCA Victor 45s $3-6 each
Uni 45s $5 each
Other Colonial 45s, 1000 series, $2 each
Other RCA Victor LPs $5-10 each
Other Camden LPs $4-8 each
Lamb & Lion LPs $4 each
Hilltop, ABC, and Harmony LPs $3-4 each
Grand Award LPs $3 each
Camden and RCA Victor duet LPs $8 each

-singles-

45rpm	**IF YOU DON'T KNOW** (56)		Colonial 420	$75
45(P)	**IF YOU DON'T KNOW** (56)		Colonial 420	$50
	(White promo label)			
45rpm	**I'VE GOT A SECRET** (57)		Colonial 451	$60
45(P)	**I'VE GOT A SECRET** (57)		Colonial 451	$40
	(White promo label)			
78rpm	**A ROSE AND A BABY RUTH** (57)		ABC Paramount 9765	$15
45rpm	**A ROSE AND A BABY RUTH** (57)		ABC Paramount 9765	$15
45(P)	**A ROSE AND A BABY RUTH** (57)		ABC Paramount 9765	$15
	(White promo label)			
45rpm	**ONLY ONE LOVE** (57)		ABC Paramount 9782	$15
45(P)	**ONLY ONE LOVE** (57)		ABC Paramount 9782	$18
	(White promo label)			
78rpm	**EVERYBODY'S BODY** (58)		ABC Paramount 9838	$25
45rpm	**EVERYBODY'S BODY** (58)		ABC Paramount 9838	$20
45(P)	**EVERYBODY'S BODY** (58)		ABC Paramount 9838	$18
	(White promo label)			
45rpm	**WHY DON'T THEY UNDERSTAND** (58)		ABC Paramount 9862	$15
45(P)	**WHY DON'T THEY UNDERSTAND** (58)		ABC Paramount 9862	$18
	(White promo label)			
45rpm	**NOW AND FOR ALWAYS** (58)		ABC Paramount 9898	$12
45(P)	**NOW AND FOR ALWAYS** (58)		ABC Paramount 9898	$15
	(White promo label)			
45rpm	**I KNOW WHERE I'M GOING** (58)		ABC Paramount 9924	$12
45(P)	**I KNOW WHERE I'M GOING** (58)		ABC Paramount 9924	$15
	(White promo label)			
45rpm	**YOUR CHEATIN' HEART** (59)		ABC Paramount 9946	$10
45(P)	**YOUR CHEATIN' HEART** (59)		ABC Paramount 9946	$15
	(White promo label)			
45rpm	**LUCY, LUCY** (59)		ABC Paramount 9966	$15
45(P)	**LUCY, LUCY** (59)		ABC Paramount 9966	$18
	(White promo label)			
45rpm	**THE TEEN COMMANDMENTS** (59)		ABC Paramount 9974	$20
45(P)	**THE TEEN COMMANDMENTS** (59)		ABC Paramount 9974	$25
	(George Hamilton with Paul Anka and Johnny Nash)			
45rpm	**LITTLE TOM** (59)		ABC Paramount 10059	$10
45rpm	**WHY I'M WALKIN'** (60)		ABC Paramount 10090	$10
45rpm	**BEFORE THIS DAY ENDS** (60)		ABC Paramount 10125	$10

-EPs-

EP(P)	**GEORGE HAMILTON IV-ON CAMPUS** (58)		ABC Paramount A-220	$40
	(White label EP for radio only, issued without sleeve)			

-albums-

LP	**GEORGE HAMILTON IV-ON CAMPUS** (58) Mono		ABC Paramount 220	$30
LP	**GEORGE HAMILTON IV-ON CAMPUS** (58) Stereo		ABC Paramount 220	$40
LP(P)	**GEORGE HAMILTON IV-ON CAMPUS** (58)		ABC Paramount 220	$40
	(White promo label)			
LP	**SING ME A SAD SONG** (58) Mono		ABC Paramount 251	$30
	(Album is a tribute to Hank Williams)			

LP	SING ME A SAD SONG (58) Stereo	ABC Paramount 251	$40
LP(P)	SING ME A SAD SONG (58)	ABC Paramount 251	$40
	(White promo label)		
LP	TO YOU & YOURS (61)	RCA Victor 2373	$20
LP	GEORGE HAMILTON IV-BIG 15 (63) Mono	ABC Paramount 461	$25
LP	GEORGE HAMILTON IV-BIG 15 (63) Stereo	ABC Paramount 461	$30
LP(P)	GEORGE HAMILTON IV-BIG 15 (63)	ABC Paramount 461	$30
LP	ABILENE (63)	RCA Victor 2778	$20
LP	FORT WORTH, DALLAS OR HOUSTON (64)	RCA Victor 2972	$15
LP	MISTER SINCERITY (65)	RCA Victor 3371	$15
LP	STEEL RAIL BLUES (66)	RCA Victor 3601	$15
LP	BY GEORGE (66)	ABC Paramount 535	$25
LP(P)	BY GEORGE (66)	ABC Paramount 535	$35
	(White promo label)		

-radio shows-

16"(RS)	NAVY HOEDOWN (60s) With Faron Young	U.S. Navy	$20-35
	(Music and interviews)		

JOHN HAMPTON (RB)

-singles-

45rpm	HONEY HUSH (57)	United 210	$75
45(P)	HONEY HUSH (57)	United 210	$50
	(White promo label)		

PAUL HAMPTON (RB)

-singles-

45rpm	ROCKIN' DOLL (58)	Columbia 41089	$18
45(P)	ROCKIN' DOLL (58)	Columbia 41089	$15
	(White promo label)		
45rpm	SLAM BAM THANK YA MA'AM (58)	Columbia 41145	$18
45(P)	SLAM BAM THANK YA MA'AM (58)	Columbia 41145	$15
	(White promo label)		

JIM HARDIMAN (CW)

-singles-

45rpm	A COWBOY'S DREAM OF LOVE (59)	RCM 7551	$15
	(Flip side is "Abilene")		

GUS HARDIN (C)
RCA Victor color vinyl 45s $6 each
RCA Victor 45s $2 each

RICK HARDIN (C)

-albums-

LP	A TASTE OF COUNTRY & WESTERN (63)	Time 2126	$20

WES HARDIN (RB)

-singles-

45rpm	ANYWAY (58)	AFS 302	$100

HARDIN TRIO (C)
Arlene, Bobby, and Robbie Hardin
Columbia 45s $2-5 each
Columbia LPs $5-10 each
Columbia LPs by Arlene Hardin $4-8 each
Capitol LPs by Arlene Hardin $5 each

-singles-

45rpm	CRYING (68) Arlene Hardin	Columbia 45203	$12
	(Price includes picture sleeve)		

-albums-

LP	TIPPY TOEING (66) Hardin Trio	Columbia 9306	$20
LP(P)	TIPPY TOEING (66)	Columbia 9306	$25
	(White promo label)		
LP	SING ME BACK HOME (68) Hardin Trio	Columbia 9633	$15
LP(P)	SING ME BACK HOME (68)	Columbia 9633	$18
	(White promo label)		
LP	NASHVILLE SENSATION (69) Bobby Hardin	Starday 443	$15
LP	GREAT COUNTRY HITS (70) Hardin Trio	Harmony 11396	$10
LP(P)	GREAT COUNTRY HITS (70)	Harmony 11396	$12
	(White promo label)		

JOHNNY HARGETT (RB)

-singles-

45rpm	ROCK THE TOWN TONIGHT (58)	Cherry 1016	$40

Emmylou Harris
Light of the Stable

RON HARGRAVE (RB)

-singles-

45rpm	LATCH ON (57)	MGM 12412	$18
45(P)	LATCH ON (57)	MGM 12412	$15
	(White promo label)		

LINDA HARGROVE (C)

Capitol and Elektra LPs $5-8 each

BILLY HARLAND (RB)

-singles-

45rpm	SCHOOL HOUSE ROCK (58)	Brunswick 55066	$100
45(P)	SCHOOL HOUSE ROCK (58)	Brunswick 55066	$75
	(Yellow promo label)		

JANICE HARPER (R)

Prep 45s $4-8 each

REDD HARPER (G)

Velvet 78s $10 each

-albums-

LP	I WALK THE GLORY ROAD (58)	Christian Faith 1253	$25
	(LP recorded for a Christian format)		

EMMYLOU HARRIS (C)

Other Reprise 45s $2-4 each
Warner 45s $2 each
Other Reprise LPs $6-8 each
Warner LPs $3-6 each

-singles-

45rpm	I'LL BE YOUR BABY TONIGHT (69)	Jubilee 5679	$20
45(P)	I'LL BE YOUR BABY TONIGHT (69)	Jubilee 5679	$15
	(White promo label)		
45rpm	LIGHT OF THE STABLE (75)	Reprise 1341	$15
	(Price includes picture sleeve, with Dolly Parton, Linda Ronstadt, and Neil Young)		
45(P)	LIGHT OF THE STABLE (75)	Reprise 1341	$10
	(Brown promo label)		
45(P)	LIGHT OF THE STABLE (87)	Warner 2872	$10
	(Promo-only release)		

-albums-

LP	GLIDING BIRD (69)	Jubilee 8031	$75
LP	GLIDING BIRD (69)	Emus 12052	$25
LP	PIECES OF THE SKY (75)	Reprise 2213	$15
LP(P)	PIECES OF THE SKY (75)	Reprise 2213	$18
	(White promo label)		
LP	ELITE MOTEL (75)	Reprise 2236	$15
LP(P)	ELITE MOTEL (75)	Reprise 2236	$18
	(White promo label)		

-radio shows-

LP(RS)	LIVE AT GILLEY'S (Apr 83)	Westwood One	$50-100
	(Rare live concert)		
3LP(RS)	TRIPLE (May 84) Box set	Mutual Radio	$20-30
	(Music and interviews, with John Denver and Lee Greenwood)		
3LP(RS)	THE SILVER EAGLE (May 85)	DIR	$75-125
	(Live concert)		
3LP(RS)	AMERICAN EAGLE (Jan 87) With Don Williams	DIR	$50-100
	(Live concert)		

RAY HARRIS (RB)

-singles-

45rpm	COME ON LITTLE MAMA (58)	Sun 254	$25
45rpm	GREENBACK DOLLAR, WATCH & CHAIN (58)	Sun 272	$18

DANNY HARRISON (RB)

-singles-

45rpm	ROCK-A-BILLY BOOGIE (58)	Event 4273	$40

WILBERT HARRISON (R)

-singles-

78rpm	KANSAS CITY (58)	Fury 1023	$60
45rpm	THIS WOMAN OF MINE (52)	Rockin' 526	$50

FREDDIE HART (CW)
Other Capitol and Columbia 78s $8-10 each
Other Columbia 45s $3-6 each
Capitol 45s $2-4 each
Sunbird 45s $3 each
Kapp 45s $2 each
Kapp picture sleeves $4 each
MCA 45s $1-2 each
Capitol jukebox LLPs $5-8 each
Other Columbia LPs $5-8 each
Harmony LPs $5 each
Other Kapp LPs $4-6 each
Capitol LPs $4-8 each
Hilltop, Vocalion, and Coral LPs $3-5 each

-singles-

45rpm	**IT JUST DON'T SEEM LIKE HOME** (54)	Capitol 2873	$10
45rpm	**I'M GOING OUT ON THE FRONT PORCH AND CRY** (55)	Capitol 2991	$10
78rpm	**DIG BOY DIG** (56)	Columbia 21512	$18
45rpm	**DIG BOY DIG** (56)	Columbia 21512	$25
45(P)	**DIG BOY DIG** (56)	Columbia 21512	$20
	(White promo label)		
45rpm	**SNATCH IT AND GRAB IT** (56)	Columbia 21550	$12
45(P)	**SNATCH IT AND GRAB IT** (56)	Columbia 21550	$10
	(White promo label)		
45rpm	**DRINK UP AND GO HOME** (56)	Columbia 21558	$12
45(P)	**DRINK UP AND GO HOME** (56)	Columbia 21558	$10
	(White promo label)		
45rpm	**FRAULEIN** (57)	Columbia 40896	$12
45(P)	**FRAULEIN** (57)	Columbia 40896	$10
	(White promo label)		
45rpm	**CANADA TO TENNESSEE** (57)	Capitol 3203	$10

-albums-

LP	**THE SPIRITED FREDDIE HART** (62)	Columbia 1792	$40
LP	**STRAIGHT FROM THE HEART** (66)	Kapp 3492	$20

LARRY HART (RB)

-singles-

45rpm	**A LOOKA-A LOOKA** (57)	Okeh 7077	$12
45(P)	**A LOOKA-A LOOKA** (57)	Okeh 7077	$10
	(White promo label)		

ROD HART (C)
Novelty
45s $3-5 each

JOHN HARTFORD (BG)
Also known as a folk singer
RCA Victor 45s $3-5 each
MCA color vinyl 45s $6 each
MCA 45s $2 each
Flying Fish and Warner 45s $2-4 each
Ampex 45s $4 each
Other RCA Victor LPs $10 each
Flying Fish LPs $4-8 each

-albums-

LP	**JOHN HARTFORD LOOKS AT LIFE** (67)	RCA Victor 3687	$20

-radio shows-

LP(RS)	**COUNTRY MUSIC TIME** (80s)	U.S. Air Force	$10-20
	(Music and interviews)		

DALE HAWKINS (R)
Other Checker 45s $10-12 each

-singles-

45rpm	**BE-BOP-A-JEAN** (57)	Cha Cha 701	$75
45(P)	**BE-BOP-A-JEAN** (57)	Cha Cha 701	$50
	(White promo label)		
45rpm	**SEE YOU SOON BABOON** (58)	Checker 843	$18
45(P)	**SEE YOU SOON BABOON** (58)	Checker 843	$15
	(White promo label)		
45rpm	**BABY BABY** (58)	Checker 876	$18
45(P)	**BABY BABY** (58)	Checker 876	$15
	(White promo label)		

-albums-

LP	**OH! SUZY-Q** (60)	Checker 1429	$1,000
	(Black label and yellow cover)		
LP	**LET'S ALL TWIST** (62) Mono	Roulette 25175	$125
LP	**LET'S ALL TWIST** (62) Stereo	Roulette 25175	$200

LP	**DALE HAWKINS** (76)	Chess 703	$10
LP(P)	**DALE HAWKINS** (76)	Chess 703	$15
	(White promo label)		

HAWKSHAW HAWKINS (CW)

Died with Patsy Cline and Cowboy Copas in a 1963 plane crash; at that time he was married
  to Jean Shepard
Other King and RCA Victor 78s $5-10 each
Other King red label 45s $8-10 each
King blue label 45s $5 each
Other RCA Victor 45s $5-10 each
Columbia 45s $3-6 each
Starday LPs $8-10 each

-singles-

78rpm	**PAN AMERICAN** (48)	King 689	$12
78rpm	**DOG HOUSE BOOGIE** (48)	King 720	$12
45rpm	**I WASTED A NICKEL** (51)	King 821	$20
78rpm	**RATTLESNAKIN' DADDY** (52)	King 944	$12
45rpm	**RATTLESNAKIN' DADDY** (52)	King 944	$20
78rpm	**SLOW POKE** (52)	King 998	$12
45rpm	**SLOW POKE** (52)	King 998	$18
45rpm	**I LOVE THE WAY YOU SAY GOODNIGHT** (52)	King 1081	$18
45rpm	**I HOPE YOU'RE CRYING TOO** (53)	King 1134	$15
45rpm	**TANGLED HEART** (53)	King 1154	$15
45rpm	**IF I EVER GET RICH MOM** (53)	King 1175	$15
45rpm	**I'LL TRADE YOURS FOR MINE** (53)	RCA Victor 5333	$15
45rpm	**A HEAP OF LIVIN'** (54)	RCA Victor 5444	$15
45rpm	**REBOUND** (54)	RCA Victor 5702	$15
45rpm	**HOW COULD ANYTHING SO PRETTY BE SO MEAN** (55)	RCA Victor 6103	$10
45rpm	**SUNNY SIDE OF THE MOUNTAIN** (57)	RCA Victor 6509	$10
45(P)	**LONESOME 7-7203** (63) Promo-only gold label	King LP-808	$25
	(Special promo single released right after his death with flip side "Love Died Tonight" not scheduled to be released as single)		
45(P)	**LONESOME 7-7203** (63) Promo-only gold label	King 5712	$25
	(Billboard Spotlight and Cash Box Pick special release, with "Seagrams" by the Viceroys [Bethlehem 3045] on the flip side)		

-EPs-

EP	**THE HAWK OF THE WEST VIRGINIA HILLS** (62)	King 231	$18
EP(P)	**THE ALL NEW HAWKSHAW HAWKINS** (63) Jukebox LLP	King 808	$25
	(Price includes hard cover and title strips)		

-albums-

LP	**COUNTRY WESTERN CAVALCADE WITH HAWKSHAW HAWKINS**	Gladwynne 2006	$100
LP	**HAWKSHAW HAWKINS**	La Brea 8020	$80
LP	**HAWKSHAW HAWKINS VOL. 1** (58)	King 587	$40
LP	**SINGS GRAND OL' OPRY FAVORITES VOL 2** (58)	King 592	$40
LP	**HAWKSHAW HAWKINS** (59)	King 599	$40
LP	**THE ALL NEW HAWKSHAW HAWKINS** (63)	King 808	$40
LP	**TAKEN FROM OUR VAULTS VOL 1** (63)	King 858	$30
LP	**TAKEN FROM OUR VAULTS VOL 2** (63)	King 870	$30
LP	**THE GREAT HAWKSHAW HAWKINS** (63)	Harmony 11044	$20
LP(P)	**THE GREAT HAWKSHAW HAWKINS** (63)	Harmony 11044	$25
	(White promo label)		
LP	**TAKEN FROM OUR VAULTS VOL 3** (64)	King 873	$25
LP	**HAWKSHAW HAWKINS SINGS** (64)	Camden 808	$20
LP	**GONE, BUT NOT FORGOTTEN** (65)	Starday 346	$25
	(Hawkshaw Hawkins, Patsy Cline, and Cowboy Copas)		
LP	**THE COUNTRY GENTLEMEN** (66)	Camden 931	$20
LP	**HAWKSHAW HAWKINS** (69)	Nashville 2070	$15
LP	**LONESOME 7-7203** (69)	King 1043	$15

-radio shows-

16"(RS)	**LEATHERNECK JAMBOREE** Fifteen-minute show	Leatherneck Jamboree 25	$20-40
	(Music and interviews)		
16"(RS)	**U.S. ARMY BAND** (60s) With George Morgan	U.S. Army	$20-30
	(Music and interviews)		
16"(RS)	**U.S. ARMY BAND** (60s) With Jean Shepard	U.S. Army	$20-30
	(Music and interviews)		
16"(RS)	**U.S. ARMY BAND** (60s) With Carl Smith	U.S. Army	$20-30
	(Music and interviews)		

RONNIE HAWKINS (R)

Other Roulette 45s $10 each
Monument 45s $2-3 each
Monument LPs $3-6 each

-singles-

45rpm	**KANSAS CITY** (57) Rockin' Ronald	End 1043	$40
	(With the Rebels)		

45rpm	**FORTY DAYS** (58)	Roulette 4154	$15
45(P)	**FORTY DAYS** (58)	Roulette 4154	$20
	(Colored promo label)		
45rpm	**MARY LOU** (58) And the Hawks	Roulette 4177	$15
45(P)	**MARY LOU** (58)	Roulette 4177	$18
	(Colored promo label)		
45rpm	**LONELY HOURS** (59) And the Hawks	Roulette 4228	$12
45(P)	**LONELY HOURS** (59)	Roulette 4228	$15
	(Colored promo label)		

-albums-

LP	**RONNIE HAWKINS** (59) Mono	Roulette 25078	$100
LP	**RONNIE HAWKINS** (59) Stereo	Roulette 25078	$150
LP	**RONNIE HAWKINS** (59)	Roulette 25078	$500
	(Very rare red vinyl)		
LP	**MR. DYNAMO** (60) Mono	Roulette 25102	$100
LP	**MR. DYNAMO** (60) Stereo	Roulette 25102	$150
LP	**MR. DYNAMO** (60)	Roulette 25102	$400
	(Very rare red vinyl)		
LP	**THE FOLK BALLADS OF RONNIE HAWKINS** (60) Mono	Roulette 25120	$50
LP	**THE FOLK BALLADS OF RONNIE HAWKINS** (60) Stereo	Roulette 25120	$75
LP	**THE SONGS OF HANK WILLIAMS** (61) Mono	Roulette 25137	$75
LP	**THE SONGS OF HANK WILLIAMS** (61) Stereo	Roulette 25137	$100

MICKEY HAWKS (RB)

-singles-

45rpm	**BIP BOP BOOM**	Profile 4002	$30
	(Mickey Hawks with Moon Mullins, who is Moon Mullican)		
45rpm	**HIDI HIDI HIDI**	Profile 4007	$40
45rpm	**SCREAMIN' MIMI JEANIE**	Profile 4010	$50

RON HAYDOCK (RB)

-singles-

45rpm	**BOP HOP**	Cha Cha 1002	$50
45rpm	**BE-BOP-A-JEAN** (59)	Cha Cha 701	$75
	(White label first pressing)		
	See Dale Hawkins		

BILL HAYES (R)
Doug Williams on *Days of Our Lives*
MGM 45s and 78s $2 each

-singles-

78rpm	**THE BALLAD OF DAVY CROCKETT** (55)	Cadence 1256	$25
78(P)	**THE BALLAD OF DAVY CROCKETT** (55)	Cadence 1256	$20
	(White promo label)		
45rpm	**THE BALLAD OF DAVY CROCKETT** (55)	Cadence 1256	$20
45(P)	**THE BALLAD OF DAVY CROCKETT** (55)	Cadence 1256	$30
	(White promo label)		
45rpm	**THE BALLAD OF DAVY CROCKETT** (58)	Cadence 1601	$18
	(Gold record series)		
45rpm	**RAMSHAKLE DADDY** (57)	ABC Paramount 9809	$12
45(P)	**RAMSHAKLE DADDY** (57)	ABC Paramount 9809	$10
	(White promo label)		
45rpm	**BOP BOY** (58)	ABC Paramount 9895	$50
45(P)	**BOP BOY** (58)	ABC Paramount 9895	$40
	(White promo label)		

RED HAYS (CW)

-singles-

45rpm	**DOGGONE WOMAN** (53)	Starday 164	$12

DON HEAD (RB)

-singles-

45rpm	**GOIN' STRONG** (58)	Dub 2840	$25

ROY HEAD (R)
Other Back Beat 45s $5-10 each
Mercury 45s $4 each
TMI 45s $2 each
TMI LPs $5-10 each
ABC (Dot) LPs $4-8 each
Elektra LPs $3-6 each

-singles-

45rpm	**ONE MORE TIME** (65)	TNT 194	$15
45rpm	**TREAT HER RIGHT** (65)	Backbeat 546	$10
45(P)	**TREAT HER RIGHT** (65)	Backbeat 546	$15
	(Colored promo label)		

-albums-

LP	ROY HEAD & THE TRAITS (65)	TNT 101	$100
LP	TREAT ME RIGHT (65) Mono	Scepter 532	$25
LP	TREAT ME RIGHT (65) Stereo	Scepter 532	$40
LP(P)	TREAT ME RIGHT (65)	Scepter 532	$40
	(White promo label)		
LP	SOME PEOPLE (70)	Dunhill 50080	$12
LP(P)	SOME PEOPLE (70)	Dunhill 50080	$15
	(White promo label)		

JIMMY HEAP (RB)

-singles-

45rpm	LITTLE JEWEL (58)	Fame 502	$125

JIMMY HEAP (CW)
With Perk Williams
Other Capitol 78s and 45s $4-8 each

-singles-

45rpm	LIFETIME OF SHAME (50) With Perk Williams	Capitol 1958	$10
45rpm	RELEASE ME (52) With Perk Williams	Capitol 2518	$10
45rpm	CRY, CRY DARLING (54) With Perk Williams	Capitol 2767	$10
45rpm	ETHEL IN MY GAS TANK (55) With Perk Williams	Capitol 2866	$10
45rpm	I TOLD YOU SO (56) With Perk Williams	Capitol 2990	$10

VARIOUS ARTISTS

-singles-

45(P)	DICK HEARD ARTIST MANAGEMENT, HOLIDAY ANNOUNCEMENTS	Bandbox 373	$15
	(Three sixty-second PSA spots, one each from Van Trevor, Penny Starr, and Johnny $ Dollar, flip side is "Christmas in the Country" by Trevor)		

JIMMY HEATH (RB)

-singles-

45rpm	LITTLE DARLIN' (58)	Mega 2261	$60

BOBBY HELMS (CW)
Other Decca 78s $8-10 each
Other Decca 45s $4-8 each
Kapp 45s $4 each
Little Darlin' 45s $3 each
Certron 45s $2 each
Certron picture sleeves $3 each
MCA, Certron, Mistletoe, and Power Pak LPs $3-5 each
Little Darlin' LPs $5 each

-singles-

78rpm	TENNESSEE ROCK & ROLL (56)	Decca 29947	$12
45rpm	TENNESSEE ROCK & ROLL (56)	Decca 29947	$15
45(P)	TENNESSEE ROCK & ROLL (56)	Decca 29947	$12
	(Pink promo label)		
45rpm	FRAULEIN (57)	Decca 30194	$12
45(P)	FRAULEIN (57)	Decca 30194	$10
	(Pink promo label)		
45rpm	MY SPECIAL ANGEL (57)	Decca 30423	$12
45(P)	MY SPECIAL ANGEL (57)	Decca 30423	$10
	(Pink promo label)		
45rpm	JINGLE BELL ROCK (58)	Decca 30513	$15
45(P)	JINGLE BELL ROCK (58)	Decca 30513	$12
	(Green promo label)		
45rpm	SCHOOLBOY CRUSH (58)	Decca 30682	$12
45(P)	SCHOOLBOY CRUSH (58)	Decca 30682	$10
	(Pink promo label)		

-EPs-

EP	BOBBY HELMS SINGS TO MY SPECIAL ANGEL (57)	Decca 2555	$30
EP	TONIGHT'S THE NIGHT (58)	Decca 2586	$30
EP	BOBBY HELMS (59)	Decca 2629	$25

-albums-

LP	BOBBY HELMS SINGS TO MY SPECIAL ANGEL (57)	Decca 8638	$40
LP(P)	BOBBY HELMS SINGS TO MY SPECIAL ANGEL (57)	Decca 8638	$50
	(Pink promo label)		
LP	THE BEST OF BOBBY HELMS (63)	Columbia 8860	$20
LP	BOBBY HELMS (65)	Vocalion 3743	$15
LP(P)	BOBBY HELMS (65)	Vocalion 3743	$20
	(White promo label)		
LP	I'M THE MAN (66)	Kapp 3463	$10
LP	SORRY MY NAME ISN'T FRED (66)	Kapp 3505	$10

LP	**BOBBY HELMS SINGS FRAULEIN** (67)	Harmony 11209	$15
LP(P)	**BOBBY HELMS SINGS FRAULEIN** (67)	Harmony 11209	$18
	(White promo label)		
LP	**MY SPECIAL ANGEL** (69)	Vocalion 3874	$15
LP(P)	**MY SPECIAL ANGEL** (69)	Vocalion 3874	$18
	(White promo label)		

DON HELMS (CW)
One of the original Drifting Cowboys

-albums-

LP	**STEEL GUITAR SOUNDS OF HANK WILLIAMS** (62)	Smash 67001	$20
LP(P)	**STEEL GUITAR SOUNDS OF HANK WILLIAMS** (62)	Smash 67001	$25
	(White promo label)		
LP	**DON HELMS' STEEL GUITAR** (62)	Smash 67019	$18
LP(P)	**DON HELMS' STEEL GUITAR** (62)	Smash 67019	$25
	(White promo label)		

JIMMIE HELMS (RB)

-singles-

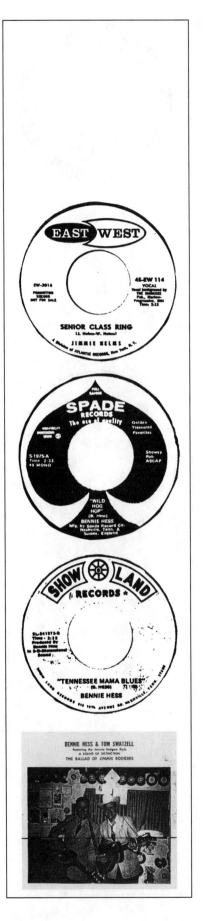

45rpm	**SENIOR CLASS RING** (57)	East West 114	$25
45(P)	**SENIOR CLASS RING** (57)	East West 114	$20
	(White promo label)		

CHUCK HENDERSON (RB)

-singles-

45rpm	**ROCK AND ROLL BABY** (58)	Ozark 959	$100

AL HENDRIX (RB)

-singles-

45rpm	**RHONDA LEE** (57)	Tally 119	$18
45rpm	**RHONDA LEE** (57)	ABC Paramount 9901	$12
45(P)	**RHONDA LEE** (57)	ABC Paramount 9901	$10
	(White promo label)		
45rpm	**YOUNG AND WILD** (57)	LaGree 701	$25

EARL HENRY (RB)

-singles-

45rpm	**WHATCHA GONNA DO?** (58)	Dot 15756	$25

WALTER HENSLEY (CW)

-albums-

LP	**THE FIVE-STRING BANJO TODAY** (64)	Capitol 2149	$20
	(With the Jordanaires and Boots Randolph)		

HERB AND KAY (G)
Other King 45s $5-10 each

-singles-

45rpm	**THIS OLE HOUSE** (55)	King 1376	$20

DENNIS HERROLD (RB)

-singles-

45rpm	**HIP HIP BABY** (58)	Imperial 5482	$50
45(P)	**HIP HIP BABY** (58)	Imperial 5482	$40
	(Cream-colored promo label)		

BENNIE HESS (RB)

-singles-

45rpm	**WILD HOG HOP** (57)	Major 1001	$75
45(P)	**WILD HOG HOP** (57)	Major 1001	$150
	(Very rare promo, only a few copies exist)		
45rpm	**TRUCKERS BLUES** (58)	Musicode 5691	$15
45rpm	**WILD HOG HOP** (59)	Musicode 5693	$35
45rpm	**WALKING THAT LAST MILE** (59)	Major 1006	$75
45(P)	**WALKING THAT LAST MILE** (59)	Major 1006	$75
	(Promo label)		
45rpm	**WILD HOG HOP** (59)	Spade 1975	$40
45rpm	**COUNTRY STYLE BOOGIE** (60)	Jet 1926	$25
45rpm	**ELVIS PRESLEY BOOGIE** (60)	Spade 2202	$45
45rpm	**TENNESSEE MAMA BLUES** (60)	Tap 1016	$40
45rpm	**THE LIFE OF JIMMIE RODGERS** (61) With Tom Swatzell	Showland 241973	$75
	(Price includes picture sleeve)		

CHUCK HESS (CW)

-albums-

LP	**COUNTRY & WESTERN FAVORITES** (60)	Strand 1084	$20

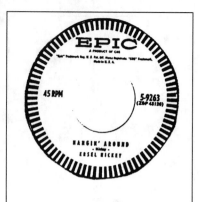

ERSEL HICKEY (RB)

-singles-

45rpm	**UPSIDE DOWN LOVE** (57)		Apollo 761	$10
45rpm	**HANGIN' AROUND** (57)		Epic 9263	$15
45(P)	**HANGIN' AROUND** (57)		Epic 9263	$10
	(White promo label)			
45rpm	**GOIN' DOWN THAT ROAD** (58)		Epic 9278	$15
45(P)	**GOIN' DOWN THAT ROAD** (58)		Epic 9278	$10
	(White promo label)			
45rpm	**YOU NEVER CAN TELL** (58)		Epic 9298	$15
45(P)	**YOU NEVER CAN TELL** (58)		Epic 9298	$10
	(White promo label)			
45rpm	**YOU THREW A DART** (58)		Epic 9309	$15
45(P)	**YOU THREW A DART** (58)		Epic 9309	$10
	(White promo label)			

JOHNNY HICKS (RB)

-singles-

45rpm	**PICK UP BLUES** (55)		Columbia 21064	$45

ROBERT HICKS (RB)

-singles-

45rpm	**ROCK BABY ROCK** (58)		Mirasonic 1001	$50

DEAN HIGHTOWER (CW)
ABC Paramount 45s $3 each

-albums-

LP	**TWANGY GUITAR WITH A BEAT** (59)		ABC Paramount 312	$25
LP(P)	**TWANGY GUITAR WITH A BEAT** (59)		ABC Paramount 312	$30
	(White promo label)			

HIGHWAY 101 (C)
Featuring Paulette Carlson
  (Only Paulette Carlson, from Skunk Hollow, recorded with Highway 101)
Warner 45s $1 each
Warner picture sleeves $2 each
Other RCA Victor 45s by Paulette Carlson $2 each

-singles-

45rpm	**TUMBLEWEED RAG** (78) Skunk Hollow		Skunk Hollow 0012	$15
	(Featuring Merrill Piepkorn and Paulette Carlson)			
45rpm	**SIX DAYS ON THE ROAD** (76) Skunk Hollow		Skunk Hollow 0013	$15
	(Featuring Merrill Piepkorn and Paulette Carlson)			
45rpm	**SWEETIE** (76) Paulette Carlson		Skunk Hollow 0014	$20
	(Paulette Carlson's first solo record)			
45(P)	**YOU GOTTA GET TO MY HEART** (83) Paulette Carlson		RCA Victor 13546	$10
	(Tan label, red vinyl)			
45(P)	**I'D SAY YES** (83) Paulette Carlson		RCA Victor 13599	$10
	(Colored vinyl)			
45(P)	**CAN YOU FOOL** (84) Paulette Carlson		RCA Victor 13745	$10
	(Colored vinyl)			
45(P)	**IT CAME UPON A MIDNIGHT CLEAR** (87) Highway 101		Warner 2872	$10
	(Promo-only single)			

-radio shows-

LP(RS)	**COUNTRY MUSIC TIME** (80s) Highway 101		U.S. Air Force	$10-20
	(Music and interviews)			
LP(RS)	**LIVE AT GILLEY'S** (80s) Highway 101		Westwood One	$20-40
	(Live concert)			
LP(RS)	**WESTWOOD ONE PRESENTS** (80s) Highway 101		Westwood One	$20-40
	(Live concert)			

THE EDDIE HILL TRIO (CW)
Other Columbia 45s $5-10 each

-singles-

45rpm	**UNREDEEMED DIAMONDS** (54)		Columbia 21556	$10

GOLDIE HILL (CW)
Goldie Hill Smith
The Golden Hillbilly
Married to Carl Smith
Decca 78s $4-8 each
Decca 45s $5-8 each
Vocalion LPs $5-10 each
Epic LPs $3-6 each

-singles-

5-45s	**GOLDIE HILL** (60) Five jukebox singles		Decca 38190	$5 each
	(For the set of five singles $25)			

		-EPs-		
EP	**GOLDIE HILL SINGS** (55)		Decca 2162	$20
EP	**GOLDIE HILL** (60)		Decca 2679	$15
EP	**GOLDIE HILL** (61)		Decca 2688	$12
		-albums-		
LP	**GOLDIE HILL** (60)		Decca 4034	$25
LP(P)	**GOLDIE HILL** (60)		Decca 4034	$30
	(Pink promo label)			
LP	**LONELY HEARTACHES** (61)		Decca 4148	$18
LP(P)	**LONELY HEARTACHES** (61)		Decca 4148	$25
	(Pink promo label)			
LP	**ACCORDING TO MY HEART** (62)		Decca 4219	$18
LP(P)	**ACCORDING TO MY HEART** (62)		Decca 4219	$25
	(Pink promo label)			
LP	**COUNTRY HIT PARADE** (64)		Decca 4492	$15
LP(P)	**COUNTRY HIT PARADE** (64)		Decca 4492	$18
	(Pink promo label)			

JAYCEE HILL (RB)

		-singles-		
45rpm	**ROMP STOMPIN' BOOGIE** (55)		Epic 9185	$40
45(P)	**ROMP STOMPIN' BOOGIE** (55)		Epic 9185	$30
	(White promo label)			

JOEL HILL (RB)

		-singles-		
45rpm	**LITTLE LOVER** (58)		Trans American 519	$20

TINY HILL (CW)
Mercury 78s $2-4 each
Other Mercury 45s $3-6 each
Other Mercury LPs $3-5 each

		-singles-		
45rpm	**BATTLE WITH THE BOTTLE** (53)		Mercury 5726	$15
45rpm	**IT'S ENOUGH TO MAKE A PREACHER CUSS** (54)		Mercury 70005	$12
45rpm	**DEW-DEW-DEWY DAY** (55)		Mercury 70079	$10
		-EPs-		
EP(P)	**DANCIN' AND SINGIN' WITH TINY HILL** (55)		Mercury MEP-76	$15
	(Promo-only release)			
		-albums-		
LP	**DANCIN' AND SINGIN' WITH TINY HILL** (55)		Mercury 20630	$10

TOMMY HILL (CW)
One of country's great songwriters
Decca 78s $4-8 each
Other Decca 45s $5-10 each

		-singles-		
45rpm	**I AIN'T SITTIN' WHERE I WAS** (53)		Decca 28474	$10

VARIOUS ARTISTS (CW)

		-albums-		
LP	**HILLBILLY JAMBOREE** (57)		Starday 101	$40

CLAYTON HILLIS (RB)

		-singles-		
45rpm	**DON'T YOU KNOW I LOVE YOU** (58)		Linco 1319	$40

HILLMEN (R)
Featuring Chris Hillman

		-albums-		
LP	**THE HILLMEN** (70)		Together 1012	$75
	(With Chris Hillman and Vern Gosdin)			
LP	**SLIPPIN' AWAY** (76) Chris Hillman		Asylum 1062	$12
LP(P)	**SLIPPIN' AWAY** (76)		Asylum 1062	$15
	(White promo label)			
LP	**CLEAR SAILIN'** (77) Chris Hillman		Asylum 1104	$12
LP(P)	**CLEAR SAILIN'** (77)		Asylum 1104	$15
	(White promo label)			
LP	**THE HILLMEN** (81)		Sugar Hill 3719	$18
	(Reissue of the Together LP)			
LP	**DESERT ROSE** (84) Chris Hillman		Sugar Hill 3743	$15
	(With James Burton)			

VARIOUS ARTISTS (CW)

-radio shows-

52LP(RS)	**HISTORY OF COUNTRY MUSIC** (Jun 82)		Drake Chenault	$150-250
	(Fifty-two-hour documentary with scripts, quite scarce)			

STAN HITCHCOCK (C)
GRT, Epic, and Cinnamon 45s $2 each
GRT, Epic LPs $4-8 each
Cinnamon LPs $3-6 each

HI-TOMBS (RB)

-singles-

45rpm	**SWEET ROCKIN' MAMA** (58)		Cannon 832	$75

BUD HOBBS (CW)

-singles-

45rpm	**GOOSE ROCK** (53)		MGM 11579	$75
	(Features that man around town, Buck Owens)			
45(P)	**GOOSE ROCK** (53)		MGM 11579	$50
	(Yellow promo label)			

RANDY HOBBS (RB)

-singles-

45rpm	**YOU BETTER RUN** (58)		Gator 1000	$50

BOBBY HODGE (RB)

-singles-

45rpm	**SITTING ON TOP OF THE WORLD** (58)		Cuca 1066	$45

RALPH HODGES (R)

-singles-

45rpm	**MONEY TALK** (58)		Whispering Pine	$40

SONNY HODGES (RB)

-singles-

45rpm	**SHAKE A LEG** (58)		Larry 802	$60

ADOLPH HOFNER (Polka)
And His San Antonians
Columbia 45s $5 each

BILLY HOGAN (RB)

-singles-

45rpm	**SHAKE IT OVER SPUTNIK** (58)		Vena 101	$30

EDDIE HOLBROOK (RB)

-singles-

45rpm	**WORRY MY MIND** (58)		Ace 1001	$65

BUDDY HOLLY & THE CRICKETS (RB)
Includes listings of the Crickets, Camps, Ivan
Includes Niki Sullivan, Sonny Curtis, Jerry Allison, and Jerry Naylor
Other MCA 45s $5 each
Any promo 45s by Tommy Allsup $3 each
Metromedia or Reprise promo LPs by Tommy Allsup $5-10 each
Capitol promo 45s by Sonny Curtis $4 each
Other Elektra promo 45s by Sonny Curtis $3 each
Elektra promo LPs $10 each

-singles-

Coral and Brunswick promo 78s were probably never pressed

The Crickets (With Buddy Holly)

78rpm	**THAT'LL BE THE DAY** (57) The Crickets		Brunswick 55009	$400
45rpm	**THAT'LL BE THE DAY** (57) Maroon label		Brunswick 55009	$40
	(First pressing)			
45rpm	**THAT'LL BE THE DAY** (57) Orange label		Brunswick 55009	$20
	(Second pressing)			
45rpm	**THAT'LL BE THE DAY** (57) Black label		Brunswick 55009	$10
	(Third pressing)			
45(P)	**THAT'LL BE THE DAY** (57) Yellow promo label		Brunswick 55009	$150
78rpm	**OH BOY** (57) The Crickets		Brunswick 55035	$350
45rpm	**OH BOY** (57) Maroon label		Brunswick 55035	$40
45rpm	**OH BOY** (57) Orange label		Brunswick 55035	$20
45rpm	**OH BOY** (57) Black label		Brunswick 55035	$10
45(P)	**OH BOY** (57) Yellow promo label		Brunswick 55035	$150
78rpm	**MAYBE BABY** (57) The Crickets		Brunswick 55053	$350
45rpm	**MAYBE BABY** (57) Maroon label		Brunswick 55053	$40

45rpm	**MAYBE BABY** (57) Orange label	Brunswick 55053	$20
	MAYBE BABY (57) Black label	Brunswick 55053	$10
45(P)	**MAYBE BABY** (57) Yellow promo label	Brunswick 55053	$150
78rpm	**THINK IT OVER** (58) The Crickets	Brunswick 55072	$300
45rpm	**THINK IT OVER** (58) Maroon label	Brunswick 55072	$40
45rpm	**THINK IT OVER** (58) Orange label	Brunswick 55072	$20
45rpm	**THINK IT OVER** (58) Black label	Brunswick 55072	$10
45(P)	**THINK IT OVER** (58) Yellow promo label	Brunswick 55072	$150
78rpm	**IT'S SO EASY** (58) The Crickets	Brunswick 55094	$300
45rpm	**IT'S SO EASY** (58) Maroon label	Brunswick 55094	$40
45rpm	**IT'S SO EASY** (58) Orange label	Brunswick 55094	$20
45rpm	**IT'S SO EASY** (58) Black label	Brunswick 55094	$10
45(P)	**IT'S SO EASY** (58) Yellow promo label	Brunswick 55094	$150
45rpm	**LOVE'S MADE A FOOL OF YOU** (59) Maroon label	Brunswick 55124	$30
45rpm	**LOVE'S MADE A FOOL OF YOU** (59) Orange label	Brunswick 55124	$18
45rpm	**LOVE'S MADE A FOOL OF YOU** (59) Black label	Brunswick 55124	$10
45(P)	**LOVE'S MADE A FOOL OF YOU** (59) Yellow promo label	Brunswick 55124	$150
45rpm	**WHEN YOU ASK ABOUT LOVE** (59) Maroon label	Brunswick 55153	$30
45rpm	**WHEN YOU ASK ABOUT LOVE** (59) Orange label	Brunswick 55153	$18
45rpm	**WHEN YOU ASK ABOUT LOVE** (59) Black label	Brunswick 55153	$10
45(P)	**WHEN YOU ASK ABOUT LOVE** (59) Yellow promo label	Brunswick 55153	$150

Buddy Holly, Buddy Holly and the Three Tunes (The Crickets)

78rpm	**BLUE DAYS-BLACK NIGHTS** (56)	Decca 29854	$400
45rpm	**BLUE DAYS-BLACK NIGHTS** (56) First pressing	Decca 29854	$500
	(First pressings have rays at sides of "Decca")		
45rpm	**BLUE DAYS-BLACK NIGHTS** (56) Second pressing	Decca 29854	$200
	(Second pressings have rays below "Decca")		
45(P)	**LOVE ME** (56) Blue promo label	Decca 29854	$300
78rpm	**MODERN DON JUAN** (56)	Decca 30166	$400
45rpm	**MODERN DON JUAN** (56) First pressing	Decca 30166	$400
45rpm	**MODERN DON JUAN** (56) Second pressing	Decca 30166	$200
45(P)	**MODERN DON JUAN** (56) Blue promo label	Decca 30166	$300
78rpm	**THAT'LL BE THE DAY** (57)	Decca 30434	$400
45rpm	**THAT'LL BE THE DAY** (57) First pressing	Decca 30434	$300
45rpm	**THAT'LL BE THE DAY** (57) Second pressing	Decca 30434	$200
45(P)	**THAT'LL BE THE DAY** (57) Blue promo label	Decca 30434	$200
78rpm	**WORDS OF LOVE** (57)	Coral 61852	$300
45rpm	**WORDS OF LOVE** (57) Orange label	Coral 61852	$400
45rpm	**WORDS OF LOVE** (62) Black label	Coral 61852	$25
45(P)	**WORDS OF LOVE** (57) Blue promo label	Coral 61852	$300
45(P)	**WORDS OF LOVE** (62) Yellow promo label	Coral 61852	$75
78rpm	**PEGGY SUE** (57)	Coral 61885	$300
45rpm	**PEGGY SUE** (57) Orange label	Coral 61885	$40
45rpm	**PEGGY SUE** (62) Black label	Coral 61885	$20
45(P)	**PEGGY SUE** (57) Blue promo label	Coral 61885	$200
45(P)	**PEGGY SUE** (62) Yellow promo label	Coral 61885	$75
78rpm	**LOVE ME** (58)	Decca 30543	$300
45rpm	**LOVE ME** (58) First pressing	Decca 30543	$300
45rpm	**LOVE ME** (58) Second pressing	Decca 30543	$100
45(P)	**LOVE ME** (58) Green promo label	Decca 30543	$300
45(P)	**LOVE ME** (58) Blue promo label	Decca 30543	$200
78rpm	**TING-A-LING** (58)	Decca 30650	$300
45rpm	**TING-A-LING** (58) First pressing	Decca 30650	$250
45rpm	**TING-A-LING** (58) Second pressing	Decca 30650	$100
45(P)	**TING-A-LING** (58) Blue promo label	Decca 30650	$200
78rpm	**LISTEN TO ME** (58)	Coral 61947	$300
45rpm	**LISTEN TO ME** (58) Orange label	Coral 61947	$40
45rpm	**LISTEN TO ME** (62) Black label	Coral 61947	$20
45(P)	**LISTEN TO ME** (58) Blue promo label	Coral 61947	$200
45(P)	**LISTEN TO ME** (62) Yellow promo label	Coral 61947	$75
78rpm	**RAVE ON** (58)	Coral 61985	$300
45rpm	**RAVE ON** (58) Orange label	Coral 61985	$40
45rpm	**RAVE ON** (62) Black label	Coral 61985	$20
45(P)	**RAVE ON** (58) Blue promo label	Coral 61985	$200
45(P)	**RAVE ON** (62) Yellow promo label	Coral 61985	$75
78rpm	**EARLY IN THE MORNING** (58)	Coral 62006	$300
45rpm	**EARLY IN THE MORNING** (58) Orange label	Coral 62006	$40
45rpm	**EARLY IN THE MORNING** (62) Black label	Coral 62006	$20
45(P)	**EARLY IN THE MORNING** (58) Blue promo label	Coral 62006	$200
45(P)	**EARLY IN THE MORNING** (62) Yellow promo label	Coral 62006	$75
78rpm	**HEARTBEAT** (58)	Coral 62051	$400
45rpm	**HEARTBEAT** (58) Orange label	Coral 62051	$40
45rpm	**HEARTBEAT** (58) Black label	Coral 62051	$20
45(P)	**HEARTBEAT** (58) Blue promo label	Coral 62051	$200
45(P)	**HEARTBEAT** (62) Yellow promo label	Coral 62051	$75
45rpm	**IT DOESN'T MATTER ANYMORE** (59) Orange label	Coral 62074	$40
45rpm	**IT DOESN'T MATTER ANYMORE** (62) Black label	Coral 62074	$20

45(P)	IT DOESN'T MATTER ANYMORE (59) Blue promo label	Coral 62074	$200
45(P)	IT DOESN'T MATTER ANYMORE (62) Yellow promo label	Coral 62074	$75
45rpm	PEGGY SUE GOT MARRIED (59) Orange label	Coral 62134	$75
45rpm	PEGGY SUE GOT MARRIED (62) Black label	Coral 62134	$20
45(P)	PEGGY SUE GOT MARRIED (59) Blue promo label	Coral 62134	$200
45(P)	PEGGY SUE GOT MARRIED (59) Yellow promo label	Coral 62134	$75
45rpm	MORE THAN I CAN SAY (59) Orange label	Coral 62198	$40
45rpm	MORE THAN I CAN SAY (62) Black label	Coral 62198	$20
45(P)	MORE THAN I CAN SAY (59) Blue promo label	Coral 62198	$200
45(P)	MORE THAN I CAN SAY (62) Yellow promo label	Coral 62198	$75
45rpm	TRUE LOVE WAYS (60) Orange label	Coral 62210	$40
45rpm	TRUE LOVE WAYS (62) Black label	Coral 62210	$20
45(P)	TRUE LOVE WAYS (60) Blue promo label	Coral 62210	$200
45(P)	TRUE LOVE WAYS (62) Yellow promo label	Coral 62210	$75
45rpm	YOU'RE SO SQUARE (61) Maroon label	Coral 62283	$150
	(Canadian pressing)		
45rpm	REMINISCING (62) Orange label	Coral 62329	$30
45rpm	REMINISCING (62) Black label	Coral 62329	$20
45(P)	REMINISCING (62) Yellow promo label	Coral 62329	$175
45rpm	TRUE LOVE WAYS (63) Orange label	Coral 62352	$40
45rpm	TRUE LOVE WAYS (63) Black label	Coral 62352	$30
45(P)	TRUE LOVE WAYS (63) Yellow promo label	Coral 62352	$150
45rpm	BROWN EYED HANDSOME MAN (63) Orange label	Coral 62369	$30
45rpm	BROWN EYED HANDSOME MAN (63) Black label	Coral 62369	$20
45(P)	BROWN EYED HANDSOME MAN (63) Yellow promo label	Coral 62369	$125
45rpm	ROCK AROUND WITH OLLIE VEE (64) Orange label	Coral 62390	$30
45rpm	ROCK AROUND WITH OLLIE VEE (64) Black label	Coral 62390	$20
45(P)	ROCK AROUND WITH OLLIE VEE (64) Yellow promo label	Coral 62390	$100
45rpm	NOT FADE AWAY (64) Black label	Coral 62407	$30
45(P)	NOT FADE AWAY (64) Yellow promo label	Coral 62407	$80
45rpm	SLIPPIN' AND SLIDIN' (65) Black label	Coral 62448	$75
45(P)	SLIPPIN' AND SLIDIN' (65) Yellow promo label	Coral 62448	$75
45rpm	RAVE ON (68) Black label	Coral 62554	$25
45(P)	RAVE ON (68) Yellow promo label	Coral 62554	$50
45rpm	LOVE IS STRANGE (69) Black label	Coral 62558	$20
45rpm	LOVE IS STRANGE (69)	Coral 62558	$50
	(Price includes picture sleeve)		
45(P)	LOVE IS STRANGE (69) Yellow promo label	Coral 62558	$75
45(P)	LOVE IS STRANGE (69) Yellow promo label and insert	Coral 62558	$100
45rpm	I'M LOOKIN' FOR SOMEONE TO LOVE (69)	Coral 65618	$15
45(P)	I'M LOOKIN' FOR SOMEONE TO LOVE (69)	Coral 65618	$50
	(Blue Silver Star Series promo label)		
45(P)	IT DOESN'T MATTER ANYMORE (78)	MCA 40905	$10
	(Price includes promo record and picture sleeve)		
45(P)	WHAT'S IT ALL ABOUT (Jul 81) Public service show	W. I. A. A. 585	$40
	(Music and interviews)		

The Crickets (Without Buddy Holly)

Liberty, Parkway, MGM, Barnaby, and Epic 45s don't fit a country format, only the Coral releases follow

45rpm	MORE THAN I CAN SAY (60) The Crickets	Coral 62198	$25
45(P)	MORE THAN I CAN SAY (60)	Coral 62198	$50
	(Blue promo label)		
45rpm	PEGGY SUE GOT MARRIED (60) The Crickets	Coral 62238	$25
45(P)	PEGGY SUE GOT MARRIED (60)	Coral 62238	$50
	(Blue promo label)		

Other Buddy Holly related 45s that fit a country format are listed below; Rick Turner & The Picks, The Bowman Brothers, and Norman Petty Trio can't be considered country and are not listed despite Holly involvement

45rpm	WHOLE LOTTA LOVIN' (58) Jim Robinson	Epic 9234	$75
	(Holly on guitar)		
45(P)	WHOLE LOTTA LOVIN' (58)	Epic 9234	$50
	(White promo label)		
45rpm	THREE STEPS TO HEAVEN (58) Niki Sullivan	Dot 15751	$40
45(P)	THREE STEPS TO HEAVEN (58)	Dot 15751	$100
	(Rare Dot blue promo label)		
45rpm	ONE FADED ROSE (58) Charlie Phillips	Coral 61908	$75
	(Holly on guitar)		
45(P)	ONE FADED ROSE (58)	Coral 61908	$50
	(Blue promo label)		
45rpm	REAL WILD CHILD (58) Ivan	Coral 62017	$200
	(Buddy Holly and Jerry Allison)		
45(P)	REAL WILD CHILD (58)	Coral 62017	$100
	(Blue promo label)		
45rpm	FRANKIE FRANKENSTEIN (59) Ivan	Coral 62081	$400
	(Buddy Holly and Jerry Allison)		
45(P)	FRANKIE FRANKENSTEIN (59)	Coral 62081	$200
	(Blue promo label)		
45rpm	RED HEADED STRANGER (59) Sonny Curtis	Coral 62207	$30

45(P)	**RED HEADED STRANGER** (59)	Coral 62207	$40
	(Blue promo label)		
45rpm	**STAY CLOSE TO ME** (59) Lou Giordano	Brunswick 55115	$1,000
	(Holly on guitar)		
45(P)	**STAY CLOSE TO ME** (59)	Brunswick 55115	$500
	(Yellow promo label)		
45rpm	**JOLE BLON** (59) Waylon Jennings	Brunswick 55130	$300
	(Holly on guitar)		
45(P)	**JOLE BLON** (59)	Brunswick 55130	$150
	(Yellow promo label)		
45rpm	**STARLIGHT** (59) Jack Huddle	Petsy 207	$500
	(Holly on guitar)		
45rpm	**STARLIGHT** (59)	Kapp 207	$200
45(P)	**STARLIGHT** (59)	Kapp 207	$200
	(White/red promo label)		
45rpm	**FRANKIE FRANKENSTEIN** (67) Ivan	Coral 65607	$40
45(P)	**FRANKIE FRANKENSTEIN** (67)	Coral 65607	$100
	(Yellow Silver Star Series promo label)		

-EPs-

EP	**THE CHIRPING CRICKETS** (57) Maroon label	Brunswick 71036	$1,000
	(With Buddy Holly)		
EP	**SOUND OF THE CRICKETS** (58) Maroon label	Brunswick 71038	$750
	(With Buddy Holly)		
EP	**THAT'LL BE THE DAY** (58) First pressing	Decca 2575	$1,200
	(With liner notes on the back cover)		
EP	**THAT'LL BE THE DAY** (58) Second pressing	Decca 2575	$1,000
	(With ads on the back cover)		
EP	**LISTEN TO ME** (58) Orange label	Coral 81169	$1,000
	(Buddy Holly & The Crickets)		
EP	**THE BUDDY HOLLY STORY** (59) Orange label	Coral 81182	$1,000
	(Buddy Holly & The Crickets)		
EP	**PEGGY SUE GOT MARRIED** (62) Orange label	Coral 81191	$1,000
	(Buddy Holly & The Crickets)		
EP	**THE CRICKETS** (63) Orange label	Coral 81192	$1,000
	(Buddy Holly & The Crickets)		
EP	**BROWN EYED HANDSOME MAN** (63) Orange label	Coral 81193	$1,000
	(Buddy Holly & The Crickets)		

-albums-

LP	**THE CHIRPING CRICKETS** (57) Maroon label	Brunswick 54038	$500
LP(P)	**THE CHIRPING CRICKETS** (57) Yellow promo label	Brunswick 54038	$1,000
LP	**THAT'LL BE THE DAY** (58) Black label	Decca 8707	$1,250
LP	**THAT'LL BE THE DAY** (58) Multicolored label	Decca 8707	$250
LP(P)	**THAT'LL BE THE DAY** (58) Pink promo label	Decca 8707	$1,250
LP	**BUDDY HOLLY** (58) Maroon label	Coral 57210	$250
LP	**BUDDY HOLLY** (58) Black label	Coral 57210	$75
LP(P)	**BUDDY HOLLY** (58) Blue promo label	Coral 57210	$750
LP	**BUDDY HOLLY STORY** (59) Maroon label	Coral 57279	$200
	(Red and black print on the back cover)		
LP	**BUDDY HOLLY STORY** (59) Maroon label	Coral 57279	$150
	(All black print on the back cover)		
LP	**BUDDY HOLLY STORY** (59) Maroon label	Coral 57279	$75
	(Pictures on the back cover)		
LP	**BUDDY HOLLY STORY** (59) Black label	Coral 57279	$75
	(Red and black print on the back cover)		
LP	**BUDDY HOLLY STORY** (59) Black label	Coral 57279	$50
	(All black print on the back cover)		
LP	**BUDDY HOLLY STORY** (59) Black label	Coral 57279	$40
	(Pictures on the back cover)		
LP	**BUDDY HOLLY STORY** (59) Stereo	Coral 757279	$125
LP(P)	**BUDDY HOLLY STORY** (59)	Coral 57279	$600
	(Blue promo label)		
LP	**IN STYLE WITH THE CRICKETS** (59) The Crickets	Coral 57320	$150
	(Buddy Holly not on this album)		
LP	**IN STYLE WITH THE CRICKETS** (59) Stereo	Coral 57320	$300
LP(P)	**IN STYLE WITH THE CRICKETS** (59)	Coral 57320	$200
	(Blue promo label)		
LP	**BUDDY HOLLY STORY VOL 2** (60) Maroon label	Coral 57326	$150
LP	**BUDDY HOLLY STORY VOL 2** (60) Black label	Coral 57326	$50
LP(P)	**BUDDY HOLLY STORY VOL 2** (60) Blue promo label	Coral 57326	$600
LP	**BUDDY HOLLY & THE CRICKETS** (62) Maroon label	Coral 57405	$150
LP	**BUDDY HOLLY & THE CRICKETS** (62) Black label	Coral 57405	$50
LP	**BUDDY HOLLY & THE CRICKETS** (62) Maroon stereo	Coral 757405	$125
LP	**BUDDY HOLLY & THE CRICKETS** (62) Black stereo	Coral 757405	$75
LP(P)	**BUDDY HOLLY & THE CRICKETS** (62) Blue promo label	Coral 57405	$600
LP	**REMINISCING** (63) Maroon label	Coral 57426	$200
	(White sticker on the cover)		

LP	**REMINISCING** (63) Maroon label		Coral 57426	$150
LP	**REMINISCING** (63) Black label		Coral 57426	$40
LP	**REMINISCING** (63) Maroon stereo		Coral 757426	$125
LP	**REMINISCING** (63) Black stereo		Coral 757426	$50
LP(P)	**REMINISCING** (63) Yellow promo label		Coral 57426	$400
LP	**SHOWCASE** (64)		Coral 57450	$100
LP	**SHOWCASE** (64) Stereo		Coral 757450	$50
LP(P)	**SHOWCASE** (64) Yellow promo label		Coral 57450	$300
LP	**HOLLY IN THE HILLS** (65)		Coral 57463	$125
LP	**HOLLY IN THE HILLS** (65) Stereo		Coral 757463	$75
LP(P)	**HOLLY IN THE HILLS** (65) Yellow promo label		Coral 57463	$300
LP	**THE BEST OF BUDDY HOLLY** (66)		Coral 8	$75
LP	**THE BEST OF BUDDY HOLLY** (66) Stereo		Coral 8	$50
LP	**BUDDY HOLLY'S GREATEST HITS** (67)		Coral 57492	$75
LP	**BUDDY HOLLY'S GREATEST HITS** (67) Stereo		Coral 757492	$40
LP(P)	**BUDDY HOLLY'S GREATEST HITS** (67) (Yellow promo label)		Coral 57492	$250
LP	**THE GREAT BUDDY HOLLY** (67) Mono (Rare in mono)		Vocalion 3811	$75
LP	**THE GREAT BUDDY HOLLY** (67) Reprocessed stereo		Vocalion 73811	$40
LP	**GIANT** (69) Stereo		Coral 757504	$40
LP(P)	**GIANT** (69) (Yellow promo label)		Coral 757504	$175
LP	**GOOD ROCKIN' BUDDY HOLLY** (71) (Reprocessed stereo only)		Vocalion 3923	$75
6LP	**THE COMPLETE BUDDY HOLLY** (81) Box set of 6 LPs		MCA 80000	$50

-radio shows-

LP(RS)	**EARTH NEWS** (Jan 78) (Entire week of daily features devoted to Buddy Holly)		Earth News	$20-40
4LP(RS)	**BUDDY HOLLY SPECIAL** With host Jim Pewter (Four hour radio show)		Creative Radio	$50-100
2LP(RS)	**A TRIBUTE TO BUDDY HOLLY** (85) With host Jerry Naylor (Edited version)		Creative Radio	$30-50
2LP(RS)	**BUDDY HOLLY** (87) (Edited version)		Creative Radio	$40-75
LP(RS)	**ROYALTY OF ROCK** (82) Profile of Buddy Holly (Music and interviews)		RKO	$30-50
3LP(RS)	**AMERICAN EAGLE** (87) Various artists (Jerry Lee Lewis, Carl Perkins, and Buddy Holly)		DIR	$75-150

TOMMY HOLMES (RB)

-singles-

45rpm	**WA-CHIC-KA-NAKA** (58)		Cherry 112	$125
45rpm	**WITCH DOCTOR'S WEDDING** (58)		Cherry 113	$100

DAN HOLT (R)

With Bob Eveslage

-singles-

45(P)	**YOU DON'T KNOW WHAT YOU'VE GOT** (88) (Red promo label, only six promo copies pressed)		Clowd 8804	$50

JIM HOLT (RB)

-singles-

45rpm	**PARALYZED** (58)		Gulfstream 1061	$60

HOMER & JETHRO (CW)

Homer Haynes and Jethro Burns
Other RCA Victor 78s $8-10 each
Other RCA Victor promo 78s $10 each
Other RCA Victor 45s $5-10 each
Nashville LPs $5 each
RCA Victor LPs by The Nashville String Band $5-8 each
 (Homer & Jethro with Chet Atkins)
Flying Fish LPs by Jethro Burns $5 each

-singles-

78rpm	**I FEEL THAT OLD AGE COMING ON** (49)		King 749	$15
45rpm	**I FEEL THAT OLD AGE COMING ON** (49)		King 749	$25
78rpm	**TENNESSEE BORDER NO. 2** (49)		King 0113	$10
45rpm	**TENNESSEE BORDER NO. 2** (49)		King 0113	$25
78rpm	**BABY, IT'S COLD OUTSIDE** (49) With June Carter		RCA Victor 0075	$15
45rpm	**BABY, IT'S COLD OUTSIDE** (49) (Green vinyl)		RCA Victor 0075	$30
45rpm	**BABY, IT'S COLD OUTSIDE** (53) (Black vinyl)		RCA Victor 0075	$20
78rpm	**THAT TEXAS LAND** (50)		RCA Victor 0468	$12
45rpm	**THAT TEXAS LAND** (50)		RCA Victor 0468	$18

78rpm	JAM-BOWL-LIAR (51)	RCA Victor 5043	$15
45rpm	JAM-BOWL-LIAR (51)	RCA Victor 5043	$20
45(P)	JAM-BOWL-LIAR (51)	RCA Victor 5043	$18
	(White promo label)		
78rpm	THAT HOUND DOG IN THE WINDOW (53)	RCA Victor 5280	$15
45rpm	THAT HOUND DOG IN THE WINDOW (53)	RCA Victor 5280	$20
45(P)	THAT HOUND DOG IN THE WINDOW (53)	RCA victor 5280	$18
	(White promo label)		
78rpm	MY UPPER PLATE (54)	RCA Victor 5456	$10
45rpm	MY UPPER PLATE (54)	RCA Victor 5456	$20
45(P)	MY UPPER PLATE (54)	RCA Victor 5456	$18
	(White promo label)		
78rpm	HAY SHMO! (54)	RCA Victor 5555	$10
45rpm	HAY SHMO! (54)	RCA Victor 5555	$18
45(P)	HAY SHMO! (54)	RCA Victor 5555	$15
	(White promo label)		
45rpm	HERNANDO'S HIDEAWAY (54)	RCA Victor 5788	$15
45(P)	HERNANDO'S HIDEAWAY (54)	RCA Victor 5788	$12
	(White promo label)		
45rpm	THE NIGHT AFTER CHRISTMAS (54)	RCA Victor 5903	$18
45(P)	THE NIGHT AFTER CHRISTMAS (54)	RCA Victor 5903	$15
	(White promo label)		
78rpm	THE NUTTY LADY OF SHADY LANE (54)	RCA Victor 6029	$12
45rpm	THE NUTTY LADY OF SHADY LANE (54)	RCA Victor 6029	$18
45(P)	THE NUTTY LADY OF SHADY LANE (54)	RCA Victor 6029	$15
	(White promo label)		
78rpm	LET ME GO, BLUBBER (54)	RCA Victor 6053	$10
45rpm	LET ME GO, BLUBBER (54)	RCA Victor 6053	$15
45(P)	LET ME GO, BLUBBER (54)	RCA Victor 6053	$12
	(White promo label)		
78rpm	THE BALLAD OF DAVY CREW-CUT (54)	RCA Victor 6178	$25
78(P)	THE BALLAD OF DAVY CREW-CUT (54)	RCA Victor 6178	$20
	(White promo label)		
45rpm	THE BALLAD OF DAVY CREW-CUT (54)	RCA Victor 6178	$12
45(P)	THE BALLAD OF DAVY CREW-CUT (54)	RCA Victor 6178	$10
	(White promo label)		
78rpm	YALLER ROSE OF TEXAS, YOU-ALL (55)	RCA Victor 6241	$10
45rpm	YALLER ROSE OF TEXAS, YOU-ALL (55)	RCA Victor 6241	$15
45(P)	YALLER ROSE OF TEXAS, YOU-ALL (55)	RCA Victor 6241	$12
	(White promo label)		
45rpm	NUTTIN' FOR CHRISTMAS (55)	RCA Victor 6322	$18
45(P)	NUTTIN' FOR CHRISTMAS (55)	RCA Victor 6322	$15
	(White promo label)		
45rpm	SIFTING, WHIMPERING SANDS (55)	RCA Victor 6342	$15
45(P)	SIFTING, WHIMPERING SANDS (55)	RCA Victor 6342	$12
	(White promo label)		
45rpm	THIS IS A WIFE? (56)	RCA Victor 6374	$12
45rpm	HART BRAKE MOTEL (56)	RCA Victor 6542	$12
45rpm	JUST BE THERE (56)	RCA Victor 6651	$10
45rpm	HOUN' DAWG (56)	RCA Victor 6706	$10
45rpm	RAMBLIN' ROSE (57)	RCA Victor 6954	$10
45rpm	AT THE FLOP (58)	RCA Victor 7162	$12
45rpm	I GUESS THINGS HAPPEN THAT WAY (58)	RCA Victor 7342	$10
45rpm	THE BATTLE OF KOOKAMONGA (59)	RCA Victor 7585	$10
45rpm	SINK THE BISMARCK (60)	RCA Victor 7744	$10
45(S)	SINK THE BISMARCK (60)	RCA Victor 7744	$18
	(Stereo single)		
45rpm	PLEASE HELP ME, I'M FALLING (60)	RCA Victor 7790	$10
45rpm	ARE YOU LONESOME TONIGHT (61)	RCA Victor 7852	$10
45rpm	I WANT TO HOLD YOUR HAND (64)	RCA Victor 8345	$15
45(P)	I WANT TO HOLD YOUR HAND (64)	RCA Victor 8345	$20
	(White promo label)		

-EPs-

2EP	HOMER & JETHRO FRACTURE FRANK LOESSER (53)	RCA Victor 3112	$40
EP	HOMER & JETHRO MURDER THE STANDARDS (54)	RCA Victor 226	$20
EP	HOMER & JETHRO ASSAULT TOP POPS (54)	RCA Victor 429	$20
EP	SEASONED GREETINGS (54)	RCA Victor 534	$20
EP	HERNANDO'S HIDEAWAY (55)	RCA Victor 580	$20
EP	LET ME GO, BLUBBER (55)	RCA Victor 595	$20
EP	THIS IS A WIFE? SIXTEEN TONS! (56)	RCA Victor 716	$18
EP	BAREFOOT BALLADS (57) (Vol. 1)	RCA Victor 1-1412	$18
EP	BAREFOOT BALLADS (57) (Vol. 2)	RCA Victor 2-1412	$18
EP	THE WORST OF HOMER & JETHRO (57)	RCA Victor 1560	$18
EP	HOMER & JETHRO ENCORE! (58)	King 317	$30
EP	HOMER & JETHRO (59)	Audio Lab 4	$25
EP(P)	HOUN' DAWG/SCREEN DOOR (58)	RCA Victor 6706 DJ-20	$20
	(Flip side has two songs by Terry Fell)		

EP(P)	MAMA FROM THE TRAIN/I'M MY OWN GRANDPA (58)	RCA Victor 6765 DJ-47	$100
	(Flip side has two songs by the Four Lovers, who, as you know, are the Four Seasons)		

-albums-

10"LP	HOMER & JETHRO FRACTURE FRANK LOESSER (53)	RCA Victor 3112	$75
	(Rare ten-inch album)		
LP	BAREFOOT BALLADS (57)	RCA Victor 1412	$50
LP	WORST OF HOMER & JETHRO (57)	RCA Victor 1560	$50
LP	MUSICAL MADNESS (58)	Audio Lab 1513	$40
LP	LIFE CAN BE MISERABLE (58) Mono	RCA Victor 1880	$30
LP	LIFE CAN BE MISERABLE (58) Stereo	RCA Victor 1880	$50
LP	HOMER & JETHRO (59)	King 639	$30
LP	HOMER & JETHRO AT THE COUNTRY CLUB (60) Mono	RCA Victor 2181	$20
LP	HOMER & JETHRO AT THE COUNTRY CLUB (60) Stereo	RCA Victor 2181	$25
LP	SONGS MY MOTHER NEVER SANG (61)	RCA Victor 2286	$25
LP	ZANY SONGS OF THE 30S (62)	RCA Victor 2455	$20
LP	PLAYING IT STRAIGHT (62)	RCA Victor 2459	$20
	(Not a novelty album)		
LP	HOMER & JETHRO AT THE CONVENTION (62)	RCA Victor 2492	$30
LP	HOMER & JETHRO STRIKE BACK (62) Mono	Camden 707	$18
LP	HOMER & JETHRO STRIKE BACK (67) Stereo	Camden 707	$18
LP	HUMOROUS SIDE OF COUNTRY MUSIC (63)	Camden 768	$15
LP	CORNIER THAN CORN (63)	King 848	$20
LP	HOMER & JETHRO GO WEST (63)	RCA Victor 2674	$18
LP	OOH, THAT'S CORNY (63)	RCA Victor 2743	$20
LP	CORNFUCIUS SAY (64)	RCA Victor 2928	$18
LP	FRACTURED FOLK SONGS (64)	RCA Victor 2954	$18
LP	HOMER & JETHRO SING TENDERLY (65)	RCA Victor 3357	$18
LP	THE OLD CRUSTY MINSTRELS (65)	RCA Victor 3462	$18
LP	SONGS TO TICKLE YOUR FUNNY BONE (66)	Camden 948	$15
LP	THE BEST OF HOMER & JETHRO (66)	RCA Victor 3474	$18
LP	ANY NEWS FROM NASHVILLE (66)	RCA Victor 3638	$18
LP	WANTED FOR MURDER (66)	RCA Victor 3673	$15
LP	SONGS FOR THE OUT CROWD (67)	Camden 2137	$15
LP	IT AIN'T NECESSARILY SQUARE (67)	RCA Victor 3701	$18
LP	24 GREAT SONGS IN THE HOMER & JETHRO STYLE (67)	King 1005	$18
LP	NASHVILLE CATS (67)	RCA Victor 3822	$18
LP	SOMETHING STUPID (68)	RCA Victor 3877	$15
LP	THE PLAYBOY SONG (68)	Camden 2315	$15
LP	THERE'S NOTHING LIKE AN OLD HIPPIE (68)	RCA Victor 3973	$15
LP	COOL COOL CHRISTMAS (68)	RCA Victor 4001	$18
LP	HOMER & JETHRO AT VANDERBILT U (68)	RCA Victor 4024	$18
LP	HOMER & JETHRO'S NEXT ALBUM (69)	RCA Victor 4148	$15
LP	HOMER & JETHRO (69)	Guest Star 1428	$15
	(Budget label)		
LP	HOMER & JETHRO (70)	Diplomat 68	$10
	(Reissue on another budget label)		
2LP	COUNTRY COMEDY (71)	Camden 9012	$18
LP	THE FAR OUT WORLD OF HOMER & JETHRO (72)	RCA Victor 4648	$15

GLEN HONEYCUTT (RB)
-singles-

45rpm	CAMPUS LOVE (58)	Ferwood 142	$75

JESSIE HOOPER (RB)
-singles-

45rpm	ALL MESSED UP (58)	Cherry 602	$100
45rpm	ALL MESSED UP (58)	Meteor 5025	$100

DAN HOPKINS (RB)
-singles-

45rpm	TIDDLEY DIDDLEY (58)	Dart 147	$50

BILLIE JEAN HORTON (CW)
Widow of Johnny Horton and Hank Williams
-singles-

45rpm	I'D RATHER YOU DIDN'T LOVE ME (63)	ABC Paramount 10332	$15
45(P)	I'D RATHER YOU DIDN'T LOVE ME (63)	ABC Paramount 10332	$10
	(White promo label)		
45rpm	JOHNNY COME LATELY (64)	Atlantic 2249	$15
45(P)	JOHNNY COME LATELY (64)	Atlantic 2249	$10
	(White promo label)		

JOHNNY HORTON (CW)
Other Columbia LPs $5-10 each
Custom duet LPs with Sonny James or Billy Barton $5 each

-singles-

78rpm	**PLAID AND CALICO** (51)	Cormac 1193	$50
45rpm	**PLAID AND CALICO** (51)	Cormac 1193	$75
78rpm	**COAL SMOKE, VALVE OIL AND STEAM** (51)	Cormac 1197	$50
45rpm	**COAL SMOKE, VALVE OIL AND STEAM** (51)	Cormac 1197	$75
78rpm	**CANDY JONES** (51)	Abbott 100	$40
45rpm	**CANDY JONES** (51)	Abbott 100	$50
78rpm	**HAPPY MILLIONAIRE** (51)	Abbott 101	$40
45rpm	**HAPPY MILLIONAIRE** (51)	Abbott 101	$50
78rpm	**PLAID AND CALICO** (51) (Reissue of Cormac 1193)	Abbott 102	$40
45rpm	**PLAID AND CALICO** (51)	Abbott 102	$50
78rpm	**COAL SMOKE, VALVE OIL AND STEAM** (51) (Reissue of Cormac 1197)	Abbott 103	$40
45rpm	**COAL SMOKE, VALVE OIL AND STEAM** (51)	Abbott 103	$50
78rpm	**GO AND WASH YOUR DIRTY FEET** (51)	Abbott 104	$40
45rpm	**GO AND WASH YOUR DIRTY FEET** (51)	Abbott 104	$50
78rpm	**SHADOWS ON THE OLD BAYOU** (51)	Abbott 105	$40
45rpm	**SHADOWS ON THE OLD BAYOU** (51)	Abbott 105	$50
78rpm	**WORDS** (51)	Abbott 106	$35
45rpm	**WORDS** (51)	Abbott 106	$40
78rpm	**ON THE BANKS OF THE BEAUTIFUL NILE** (52)	Abbott 107	$35
45rpm	**ON THE BANKS OF THE BEAUTIFUL NILE** (52)	Abbott 107	$40
78rpm	**SOMEBODY'S ROCKIN' MY BROKEN HEART** (52)	Abbott 108	$35
45rpm	**SOMEBODY'S ROCKIN' MY BROKEN HEART** (52)	Abbott 108	$40
78rpm	**RHYTHM IN MY BABY'S WALK** (52)	Abbott 109	$35
45rpm	**RHYTHM IN MY BABY'S WALK** (52)	Abbott 109	$40
78rpm	**THE DEVIL SENT ME YOU** (52)	Mercury 6412	$25
45rpm	**THE DEVIL SENT ME YOU** (52)	Mercury 6412	$30
78rpm	**THE REST OF YOUR LIFE** (52)	Mercury 6418	$25
45rpm	**THE REST OF YOUR LIFE** (52)	Mercury 6418	$30
78rpm	**THE CHILD'S SIDE OF LIFE** (53)	Mercury 70014	$20
78(P)	**THE CHILD'S SIDE OF LIFE** (53) (White promo label)	Mercury 70014	$25
45rpm	**THE CHILD'S SIDE OF LIFE** (53)	Mercury 70014	$30
78rpm	**TENNESSEE JIVE** (53)	Mercury 70100	$15
78(P)	**TENNESSEE JIVE** (53) (White promo label)	Mercury 70100	$20
45rpm	**TENNESSEE JIVE** (53)	Mercury 70100	$20
45(P)	**TENNESSEE JIVE** (53) (White promo label)	Mercury 70100	$25
78rpm	**S. S. LURELINE** (53)	Mercury 70156	$15
78(P)	**S. S. LURELINE** (53) (White promo label)	Mercury 70156	$18
45rpm	**S. S. LURELINE** (53)	Mercury 70156	$15
45(P0	**S. S. LURELINE** (53) (White promo label)	Mercury 70156	$18
78rpm	**YOU YOU YOU** (53)	Mercury 70198	$15
78(P)	**YOU YOU YOU** (53) (White promo label)	Mercury 70198	$18
45rpm	**YOU YOU YOU** (53)	Mercury 70198	$15
45(P)	**YOU YOU YOU** (53) (White promo label)	Mercury 70198	$18
78rpm	**PLAID AND CALICO** (53)	Abbott 135	$15
45rpm	**PLAID AND CALICO** (53)	Abbott 135	$20
78rpm	**THE LOVE OF A GIRL** (53)	Mercury 70227	$15
78(P)	**THE LOVE OF A GIRL** (53) (White promo label)	Mercury 70227	$18
45rpm	**ALL FOR THE LOVE OF A GIRL** (53)	Mercury 70227	$15
45(P)	**ALL FOR THE LOVE OF A GIRL** (53) (White promo label)	Mercury 70227	$18
78rpm	**THE TRAIN WITH THE RHUMBA BEAT** (54)	Mercury 70325	$15
78(P)	**THE TRAIN WITH THE RHUMBA BEAT** (54) (White promo label)	Mercury 70325	$18
45rpm	**THE TRAIN WITH THE RHUMBA BEAT** (54)	Mercury 70325	$15
45(P)	**THE TRAIN WITH THE RHUMBA BEAT** (54) (White promo label)	Mercury 70325	$18
78rpm	**THE DOOR OF YOUR MANSION** (54)	Mercury 70399	$15
78(P)	**THE DOOR OF YOUR MANSION** (54) (White promo label)	Mercury 70399	$18
45rpm	**THE DOOR OF YOUR MANSION** (54)	Mercury 70399	$15
45(P)	**THE DOOR OF YOUR MANSION** (54) (White promo label)	Mercury 70399	$18
78rpm	**THERE'LL NEVER BE ANOTHER MARY** (55)	Mercury 70462	$15

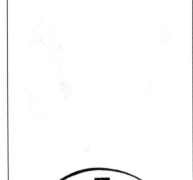

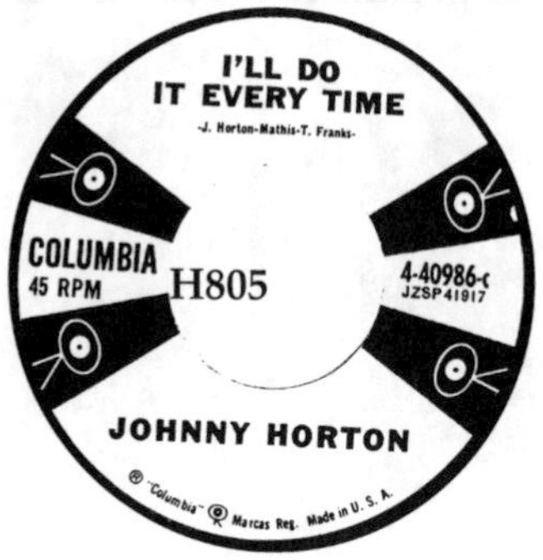

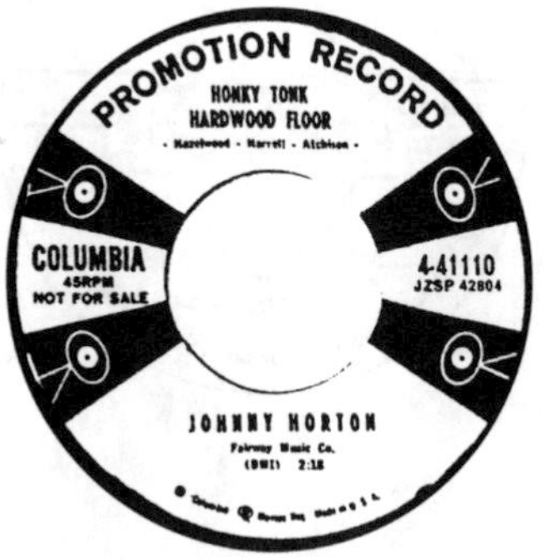

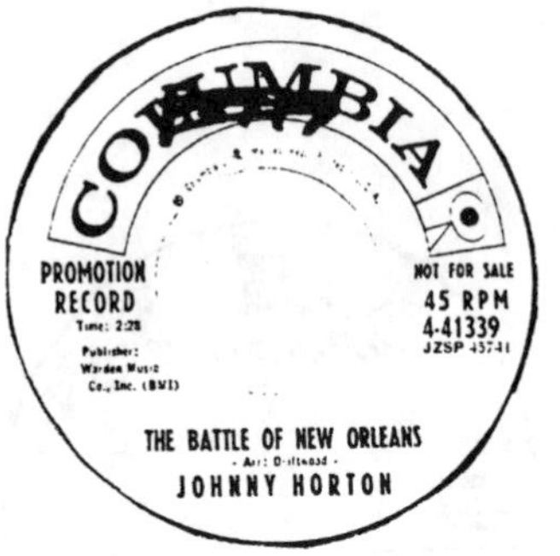

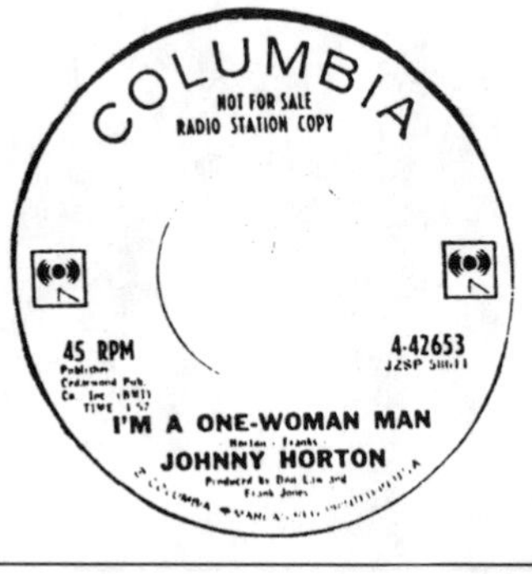

78(P)	**THERE'LL NEVER BE ANOTHER MARY** (55) (White promo label)	Mercury 70462	$18
45rpm	**THERE'LL NEVER BE ANOTHER MARY** (55) (Green label)	Mercury 70462	$15
45(P)	**THERE'LL NEVER BE ANOTHER MARY** (55) (White promo label)	Mercury 70462	$18
78rpm	**RIDIN' THE SUNSHINE SPECIAL** (55)	Mercury 70636	$15
78(P)	**RIDIN' THE SUNSHINE SPECIAL** (55) (White promo label)	Mercury 70636	$18
45rpm	**RIDIN' THE SUNSHINE SPECIAL** (55) (Green label)	Mercury 70636	$15
45(P)	**RIDIN' THE SUNSHINE SPECIAL** (55) (White promo label)	Mercury 70636	$18
78rpm	**BIG WHEELS ROLLIN'** (55)	Mercury 70707	$15
78(P)	**BIG WHEELS ROLLIN'** (55) (White promo label)	Mercury 70707	$18
45rpm	**BIG WHEELS ROLLIN'** (55) (Green label)	Mercury 70707	$15
45(P)	**BIG WHEELS ROLLIN'** (55) (White promo label)	Mercury 70707	$18
78rpm	**HONKY-TONK MAN** (56)	Columbia 21504	$20
78(P)	**HONKY-TONK MAN** (56) (White promo label)	Columbia 21504	$25
45rpm	**HONKY-TONK MAN** (56)	Columbia 21504	$20
45(P)	**HONKY-TONK MAN** (56) (White promo label)	Columbia 21504	$15
78rpm	**I'M A ONE-WOMAN MAN** (57)	Columbia 21538	$20
78(P)	**I'M A ONE-WOMAN MAN** (57) (White promo label)	Columbia 21538	$25
45rpm	**I'M A ONE-WOMAN MAN** (57)	Columbia 21538	$20
45(P)	**I'M A ONE-WOMAN MAN** (57) (White promo label)	Columbia 21538	$15
78rpm	**I'M COMING HOME** (58)	Columbia 40813	$18
78(P)	**I'M COMING HOME** (58) (White promo label)	Columbia 40813	$20
45rpm	**I'M COMING HOME** (58)	Columbia 40813	$20
45(P)	**I'M COMING HOME** (58) (White promo label)	Columbia 40813	$15
45rpm	**THE WOMAN I NEED** (58)	Columbia 40919	$15
45(P)	**THE WOMAN I NEED** (58) (White promo label)	Columbia 40919	$12
45rpm	**I'LL DO IT EVERY TIME** (58)	Columbia 40986	$15
45(P)	**I'LL DO IT EVERY TIME** (58) (White promo label)	Columbia 40986	$12
45rpm	**LOVER'S ROCK** (58)	Columbia 41043	$20
45(P)	**LOVER'S ROCK** (58) (White promo label)	Columbia 41043	$15
45rpm	**HONKY TONK HARDWOOD FLOOR** (59)	Columbia 41110	$40
45(P)	**HONKY TONK HARDWOOD FLOOR** (59) (White promo label)	Columbia 41110	$30
45rpm	**ALL GROWN UP** (58)	Columbia 41210	$15
45(P)	**ALL GROWN UP** (58) (White promo label)	Columbia 41210	$12
45rpm	**WHEN IT'S SPRINGTIME IN ALASKA** (58)	Columbia 41308	$10
45rpm	**THE BATTLE OF NEW ORLEANS** (59) (Record only)	Columbia 41339	$10
45rpm	**THE BATTLE OF NEW ORLEANS** (59) (Price includes picture sleeve)	Columbia 41339	$30
45(P)	**THE BATTLE OF NEW ORLEANS** (59) (White promo label)	Columbia 41339	$15
45rpm	**PLAID & CALICO** (59)	Dot 15966	$15
45rpm	**JOHNNY REB** (59)	Columbia 41437	$10
45rpm	**SINK THE BISMARCK** (60) (Record only)	Columbia 41568	$10
45rpm	**SINK THE BISMARCK** (60) (Price includes picture sleeve)	Columbia 41568	$25
45rpm	**NORTH TO ALASKA** (60) (Record only)	Columbia 41782	$10
45rpm	**NORTH TO ALASKA** (60) (Price includes picture sleeve)	Columbia 41782	$20
33rpm	**SLEEPY-EYED JOHN** (61) (33rpm single)	Columbia 41963	$15
45rpm	**SLEEPY-EYED JOHN** (61) (Price includes picture sleeve)	Columbia 41963	$18
33rpm	**HONKY-TONK MAN** (62) (33rpm single)	Columbia 42302	$15
45rpm	**HONKY-TONK MAN** (62) (Price includes picture sleeve)	Columbia 42302	$18

33rpm	**I'M A ONE-WOMAN MAN** (63)	Columbia 42653	$15
	(33rpm single)		
45rpm	**I'M A ONE-WOMAN MAN** (63)	Columbia 42653	$18
	(Price includes picture sleeve)		
33rpm	**WHEN IT'S SPRINGTIME IN ALASKA** (63)	Columbia 42774	$15
	(33rpm single)		
45rpm	**WHEN IT'S SPRINGTIME IN ALASKA** (63)	Columbia 42774	$18
	(Price includes picture sleeve)		

-EPs-

EP(P)	**FREE & EASY SONGS** (59) With the Four B's	Sesac AD-26	$75
	(Promo-only release to radio stations)		
EP	**REQUESTFULLY YOURS** (55)	Mercury 3091	$25
EP	**HONKY-TONK MAN** (57)	Columbia 2130	$20
EP	**THE SPECTACULAR JOHNNY HORTON** (60) Vol 1	Columbia 13621	$25
EP	**THE SPECTACULAR JOHNNY HORTON** (60) Vol 2	Columbia 13622	$25
EP	**THE SPECTACULAR JOHNNY HORTON** (60) Vol 3	Columbia 13623	$25
EP	**JOHNNY HORTON MAKES HISTORY** (60) Vol 1	Columbia 14781	$25
EP	**JOHNNY HORTON MAKES HISTORY** (60) Vol 2	Columbia 14782	$25
EP	**JOHNNY HORTON MAKES HISTORY** (60) Vol 3	Columbia 14783	$25

-albums-

LP	**HONKY TONK MAN** (57)	Columbia 1721	$50
LP	**DONE ROVIN'**	Briar International 104	$125
	(The material in this LP was originally to be released on Abbott)		
LP	**THE FANTASTIC JOHNNY HORTON** (59) Black label	Mercury 20478	$125
LP(P)	**THE FANTASTIC JOHNNY HORTON** (59)	Mercury 20478	$150
	(White promo label)		
LP(P)	**FREE & EASY SONGS** (59) With the Four B's	Sesac 1201,2	$175
	(Promo-only release to radio stations)		
LP	**THE SPECTACULAR JOHNNY HORTON** (60) Mono	Columbia 1362	$25
LP	**THE SPECTACULAR JOHNNY HORTON** (60) Stereo	Columbia 8167	$30
LP	**JOHNNY HORTON MAKES HISTORY** (60) Mono	Columbia 1478	$30
LP	**JOHNNY HORTON MAKES HISTORY** (60) Stereo	Columbia 8269	$35
LP	**JOHNNY HORTON'S GREATEST HITS** (61) Mono	Columbia 1596	$25
LP	**JOHNNY HORTON'S GREATEST HITS** (61) Stereo	Columbia 8396	$30
LP	**HONKY-TONK MAN** (62) Mono	Columbia 1721	$30
LP	**HONKY-TONK MAN** (63) Stereo	Columbia 8779	$25
LP	**JOHNNY HORTON COUNTRY STYLE** (63)	Crown 5290	$15
	(With Billy Barton and Don Hughes)		
LP	**JOHNNY HORTON** (62) Mono	Dot 3221	$30
LP	**JOHNNY HORTON** (65) Stereo	Dot 25221	$25
LP	**I CAN'T FORGET YOU** (65)	Columbia 9099	$18
LP(P)	**I CAN'T FORGET YOU** (65)	Columbia 9099	$25
	(White promo label)		
LP	**THE VOICE OF JOHNNY HORTON** (65)	Hilltop 6012	$15
	(Budget label)		
LP	**JOHNNY HORTON ON THE LOUISIANA HAYRIDE** (66)	Columbia 9366	$25
LP(P)	**JOHNNY HORTON ON THE LOUISIANA HAYRIDE** (66)	Columbia 9366	$30
	(White promo label)		
LP	**ALL FOR THE LOVE OF A GIRL** (68)	Hilltop 6060	$18
	(Mercury material)		
LP	**THE UNFORGETTABLE JOHNNY HORTON** (68)	Harmony 11291	$15
LP(P)	**THE UNFORGETTABLE JOHNNY HORTON** (68)	Harmony 11291	$18
	(White promo label)		
LP	**JOHNNY HORTON ON THE ROAD** (69)	Columbia 9940	$12
LP(P)	**JOHNNY HORTON ON THE ROAD** (69)	Columbia 9940	$15
	(White promo label)		
LP	**THE LEGEND OF JOHNNY HORTON** (70)	Sears 110	$15
	(Abbott material)		
LP	**THE LEGENDARY JOHNNY HORTON** (70)	Harmony 11384	$15
LP(P)	**THE LEGENDARY JOHNNY HORTON** (70)	Harmony 11384	$20
	(White promo label)		
LP	**THE BATTLE OF NEW ORLEANS** (71)	Harmony 30394	$15
LP(P)	**THE BATTLE OF NEW ORLEANS** (71)	Harmony 30394	$20
	(White promo label)		
2LP	**THE WORLD OF JOHNNY HORTON** (71)	Columbia KG 30884	$15
	(KG prefix on label number, first pressing)		

VAUGHN HORTON (Polka)
With the Pinetoppers
Decca 45s $2-4 each
Decca EPs $10 each
Decca LPs $10 each

DON HOSEA (RB)

-singles-

45rpm	**EVERLASTING LOVE** (58)	Crystal 501	$60

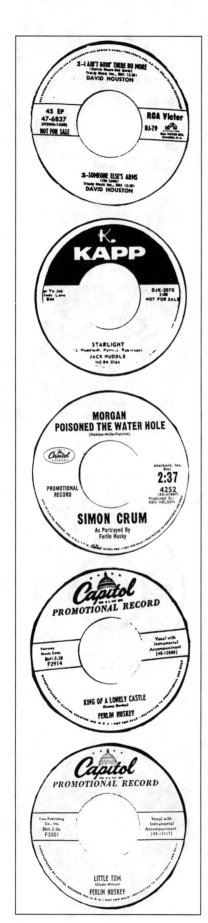

SOUNDTRACK

-EPs-

EP(P)	**HOT ROD GANG** (58) Promo label	Capitol PRO 985	$600
	(Promo-only release for radio stations)		

-albums-

LP	**HOT ROD GANG** (58)	Capitol 985	$100
	(Features the music of Gene Vincent & the Blue Caps)		
LP(P)	**HOT ROD GANG** (58) Promo label	Capitol 985	$500
	(Radio/TV use only on the label)		
	See Gene Vincent		

SOUNDTRACK

-albums-

LP	**HOT ROD RUMBLE** (57)	Liberty 3048	$75
LP(P)	**HOT ROD RUMBLE** (57)	Liberty 3048	$60
	(White promo label)		

DAVID HOUSTON (CW)
Other RCA Victor 45s $5-10 each
Epic 45s $2-4 each
Epic picture sleeves $2-4 each
Hilltop 45s $2 each
Epic jukebox LLPs $5-8 each
Other Epic LPs $2-8 each
Columbia LPs $5 each
Harmony and Camden LPs $5-10 each
Gusto, Exact, Delta, Excelsior, Derrick, and 51 West LPs $2 each

-singles-

45rpm	**SHERRY'S LIPS** (57)	Philips 3583	$18
45(P)	**SHERRY'S LIPS** (57)	Philips 3583	$25
	(Colored promo label)		
45rpm	**ALL I DO IS DREAM OF YOU** (57)	NRC 005	$12
45(P)	**ALL I DO IS DREAM OF YOU** (57)	NRC 005	$15
	(White promo label)		
45rpm	**SUGAR SWEET**	RCA Victor 6611	$18
45rpm	**TEENAGE FRANKIE & JOHNNY**	RCA Victor 7001	$10
45rpm	**SHERRY'S LIPS** (63)	Sun 403	$15
45(P)	**SHERRY'S LIPS** (63)	Sun 403	$20
	(White promo label)		

-EPs-

EP(P)	**BLUE PRELUDE** (57)	RCA Victor 6696 DJ-15	$15
	(Two songs on each side, flip is Porter Wagoner)		
EP(P)	**I AIN'T GOIN' THERE NO MORE** (57)	RCA Victor 6837 DJ-79	$12
	(Two songs on each side, flip is Bobby John)		

-albums-

LP	**DAVID HOUSTON** (64)	Epic 26112	$12
LP(P)	**DAVID HOUSTON** (64)	Epic 26112	$15
	(White promo label)		

JOE HOUSTON (R)

-albums-

LP	**WHERE'S JOE** (58)	Combo 100	$40
LP	**ROCKIN' AT THE DRIVE-IN** (58)	Combo 400	$40

CHUCK HOWARD (RB)

-singles-

45rpm	**GOSSIP** (58)	Flame 1020	$60
45rpm	**JOY GRAY** (58)	ESV 1017	$40

HARLAN HOWARD (C)
Married to Jan Howard
Monument, RCA Victor, and Capitol 45s $2-4 each
Nugget 45s $3-5 each

-albums-

LP	**HARLAN HOWARD SINGS HARLAN HOWARD** (61)	Capitol 1631	$30
LP	**TO THE SILENT MAJORITY**	Nugget 105	$30
LP	**ALL TIME FAVORITE COUNTRY SONGWRITER** (65)	Monument 18038	$25
LP	**MR. SONGWRITER** (67)	RCA Victor 3729	$25
LP	**DOWN TO EARTH** (68)	RCA Victor 3886	$25

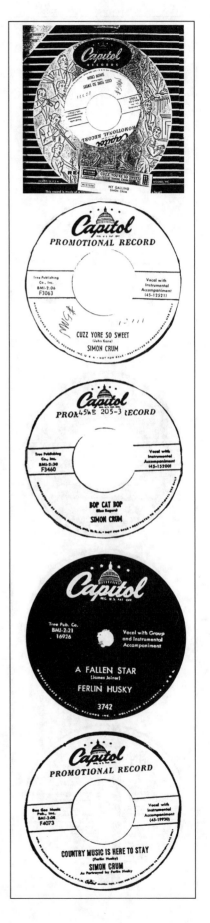

JAN HOWARD (CW)
Wife of Harlan Howard
Decca and Capitol 45s $2-4 each
Decca LPs $4-8 each

-albums-

LP	**JAN HOWARD** (62)	Wrangler 1005	$25
LP	**SWEET & SENTIMENTAL** (62) With the Jordanaires	Capitol 1779	$20
LP(P)	**SWEET & SENTIMENTAL** (62)	Capitol 1779	$25
	(Blue promo label)		

LEIGH HOWELL (RB)

-singles-

45rpm	**I SAW YOU STANDING** (58)	Mellotone 1001	$12

LOYD HOWELL (RB)

-singles-

45rpm	**LITTLE FROGGY WENT A COURTIN'** (59)	Nashville 5028	$100

ORANGIE HUBBARD (RB)

-singles-

45rpm	**LOOK WHAT I FOUND** (57)	Lucky 0007	$50

JACK HUDDLE (RB)

-singles-

45rpm	**STARLIGHT** (58)	Petsy 207	$125
	(Buddy Holly on guitar)		
45rpm	**STARLIGHT** (59)	Kapp 207	$100
45(P)	**STARLIGHT** (59)	Kapp 207	$75
	(White promo label)		

JOE HUDGINS (RB)

-singles-

45rpm	**WHERE'D YOU STAY LAST NIGHT** (59)	Robbins 1005	$45
45rpm	**WHERE'D YOU STAY LAST NIGHT** (59)	Decca 30854	$15
45(P)	**WHERE'D YOU STAY LAST NIGHT** (59)	Decca 30854	$12
	(Pink promo label)		

PAUL HUFFMAN (RB)

-singles-

45rpm	**SHE'S MINE** (58)	Winston 1015	$12

JOE HUGHES (RB)

-singles-

45rpm	**MAKE ME DANCE, LITTLE ANT** (60)	Kangaroo 105	$65

T. K. HULIN (RB)

-singles-

45rpm	**LITTLE BOY BLUE** (58)	L.K. 1001	$60

CON HUNLEY (C)
Warner 45s $1-2 each
Warner LPs $2-5 each

-radio shows-

3LP(RS)	**THE SILVER EAGLE** (Sept 82) With Loretta Lynn	DIR	$40-75
	(Live concert)		
LP(RS)	**LIVE AT GILLEY'S** (July 86)	Westwood One	$10-20
	(Live concert)		

HARVEY HURT (RB)

-singles-

45rpm	**BIG DOG LITTLE DOG** (58)	Master 1226	$60

FERLIN HUSKY (CW)
And His Hush Puppies
Ferlin Huskey (Sometimes spelled)
Also recorded as Terry Preston
Also recorded as Simon Crum
Other 78s $5-8 each
Other Capitol 45s $5-10 each
ABC 45s $2 each
Other Capitol 78s and 45s by Terry Preston $5-8 each
Other Capitol 45s by Simon Crum $5-8 each

-singles-

78rpm	**TIME** (50) Terry Preston	Capitol 1947	$15
45rpm	**TIME** (50)	Capitol 1947	$18
78rpm	**ROAD TO HEAVEN** (50) Terry Preston	4-Star 1516	$25

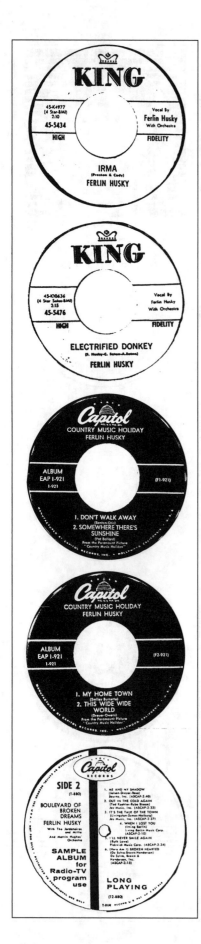

45rpm	ROAD TO HEAVEN (50)	4-Star 1516	$18
78rpm	MY FOOLISH HEART (51) Terry Preston	Capitol 2391	$15
45rpm	MY FOOLISH HEART (51)	Capitol 2391	$12
78rpm	HANK'S SONG (52)	Capitol 2391	$20
	(Hank Williams impersonation)		
45rpm	HANK'S SONG (52)	Capitol 2397	$25
	(Written by Tommy Collins)		
45rpm	I LOST MY HEART TODAY (53)	Capitol 2495	$10
45rpm	A DEAR JOHN LETTER (53)	Capitol 2502	$10
	(Jean Shepard and Ferlin Husky)		
45rpm	YOU'LL DIE A THOUSAND DREAMS (53)	Capitol 2558	$10
45rpm	I WOULDN'T TREAT A DOG LIKE YOU'RE TREATING ME (54)	Capitol 2627	$10
45rpm	THE DRUNKEN DRIVER (54)	Capitol 2835	$15
45(P)	THE DRUNKEN DRIVER (54)	Capitol 2835	$12
	(White promo label)		
45rpm	LAUGH, LAUGH, LAUGH (54) Cousin Herb Henson	Capitol 2824	$15
	(The trademark Husky laugh is theme)		
45(P)	LAUGH, LAUGH, LAUGH (54)	Capitol 2824	$12
	(White promo label)		
45rpm	KING OF A LONELY CASTLE (54)	Capitol 2914	$10
45rpm	LITTLE TOM (55)	Capitol 3001	$18
78rpm	CUZZ YORE SO SWEET (55) Simon Crum	Capitol 3063	$20
78(P)	CUZZ YORE SO SWEET (55)	Capitol 3063	$25
	(Yellow promo label)		
45rpm	CUZZ YORE SO SWEET (55) Simon Crum	Capitol 3063	$15
45(P)	CUZZ YORE SO SWEET (55)	Capitol 3063	$12
	(White promo label)		
45rpm	I'LL BABYSIT WITH YOU (55)	Capitol 3097	$10
45rpm	DEAR MISTER BROWN (55)	Capitol 3233	$10
45rpm	A HILLBILLY'S DECK OF CARDS (56) Simon Crum	Capitol 3270	$20
45(P)	A HILLBILLY'S DECK OF CARDS (56)	Capitol 3270	$15
	(White promo label)		
45rpm	SLOW DOWN BROTHER (56)	Capitol 3316	$10
45rpm	BOP CAT BOP (57) Simon Crum	Capitol 3460	$25
45(P)	BOP CAT BOP (57)	Capitol 3460	$18
	(White promo label)		
45rpm	GONE (57)	Capitol 3628	$10
45(P)	GONE (57) Smash Hit Record label	Capitol 3628	$15
	(Yellow promo label)		
45(P)	GONE (57)	Capitol 3628	$12.
	(White promo label)		
78rpm	A FALLEN STAR (58)	Capitol 3742	$18
45rpm	A FALLEN STAR (58)	Capitol 3742	$10
45rpm	WANG DANG DOO (58)	Capitol 3862	$15
45rpm	COUNTRY MUSIC IS HERE TO STAY (58) Simon Crum	Capitol 4073	$15
45(P)	COUNTRY MUSIC IS HERE TO STAY (58)	Capitol 4073	$12
	(White promo label)		
45rpm	BLACK SHEEP (59)	Capitol 4278	$10
45rpm	IRMA (59)	King 5434	$10
45rpm	ELECTRIFIED DONKEY (60)	King 5476	$10
45rpm	THE WALTZ YOU SAVED FOR ME (61)	Capitol 4650	$10
	(Price includes picture sleeve)		
45rpm	DON'T HURT ME ANYMORE (64)	Capitol 2048	$10
	(Price includes picture sleeve)		
45rpm	YOU SHOULD LIVE MY LIFE (65)	Capitol 2154	$10
	(Price includes picture sleeve)		

-EPs-

EP	FERLIN HUSKY (55)	Capitol 609	$15
EP	SONGS OF THE HOME & HEART (56) Vol 1	Capitol 1-718	$18
EP	SONGS OF THE HOME & HEART (56) Vol 2	Capitol 2-718	$18
EP	SONGS OF THE HOME & HEART (56) Vol 3	Capitol 3-718	$18
EP	BOULEVARD OF BROKEN DREAMS (57) Vol 1	Capitol 1-880	$15
EP	BOULEVARD OF BROKEN DREAMS (57) Vol 2	Capitol 2-880	$15
EP	BOULEVARD OF BROKEN DREAMS (57) Vol 3	Capitol 3-880	$15
EP	COUNTRY MUSIC HOLIDAY (58)	Capitol 921	$12
EP	FERLIN FAVORITES (60) Vol 1	Capitol 1280	$10
EP	FERLIN FAVORITES (60) Vol 2	Capitol 1280	$10
EP	FERLIN FAVORITES (60) Vol 3	Capitol 1280	$10
EP	WINGS OF A DOVE (61)	Capitol 1516	$12

-albums-

LP	FERLIN HUSKY & JEAN SHEPARD (55)	Capitol 609	$15
	(With Jean Shepard)		
LP(P)	FERLIN HUSKY & JEAN SHEPARD (55)	Capitol 609	$18
	(Yellow promo label)		
LP	FERLIN HUSKY'S SONGS OF THE HOME & HEART (56)	Capitol 718	$35
LP(P)	FERLIN HUSKY'S SONGS OF THE HOME & HEART (56)	Capitol 718	$40
	(Yellow promo label)		

LP	**BOULEVARD OF BROKEN DREAMS** (57)	Capitol 880	$30
LP(P)	**BOULEVARD OF BROKEN DREAMS** (57)	Capitol 880	$35
	(Yellow promo label)		
LP	**BORN TO LOSE** (59)	Capitol 1204	$25
LP(P)	**BORN TO LOSE** (59)	Capitol 1204	$30
	(Blue promo label)		
LP	**FERLIN HUSKY-COUNTRY TUNES SUNG FROM THE HEART** (59)	King 647	$50
LP	**SITTIN' ON A RAINBOW** (59)	Capitol 976	$25
LP(P)	**SITTIN' ON A RAINBOW** (59)	Capitol 976	$30
	(Blue promo label)		
LP	**EASY LIVIN'** (60)	King 728	$50
LP	**FERLIN'S FAVORITES** (60)	Capitol 1280	$20
LP(P)	**FERLIN'S FAVORITES** (60)	Capitol 1280	$25
	(Blue promo label)		
LP	**GONE** (63)	Capitol 1383	$25
LP(P)	**GONE** (63)	Capitol 1383	$30
	(Blue promo label)		
LP	**WALKIN' & HUMMIN'** (61)	Capitol 1546	$18
LP(P)	**WALKIN' & HUMMIN'** (61)	Capitol 1546	$25
	(Blue promo label)		
LP	**MEMORIES OF HOME** (63)	Capitol 1633	$18
LP(P)	**MEMORIES OF HOME** (63)	Capitol 1633	$25
	(Blue promo label)		
LP	**SOME OF MY FAVORITES** (63)	Capitol 1720	$18
LP(P)	**SOME OF MY FAVORITES** (63)	Capitol 1720	$25
	(Blue promo label)		
LP	**THE UNPREDICTABLE SIMON CRUM** (63) Simon Crum	Capitol 1880	$100
LP(P)	**THE UNPREDICTABLE SIMON CRUM** (63)	Capitol 1880	$125
	(Blue promo label)		
LP	**THE HEART & SOUL OF FERLIN HUSKY** (63)	Capitol 1885	$18
LP	**HITS OF FERLIN HUSKY** (63)	Capitol 1885	$15
LP	**BY REQUEST** (64)	Capitol 2101	$15
LP	**TRUE, TRUE LOVIN'** (65)	Capitol 2305	$12
LP	**SONGS OF MUSIC CITY, U. S. A.** (66)	Capitol 2439	$12
LP	**I COULD SING ALL NIGHT** (66)	Capitol 2548	$12
LP	**WHAT AM I GONNA DO NOW** (67)	Capitol 2705	$10
LP	**CHRISTMAS ALL YEAR LONG** (67)	Capitol 2793	$10
LP	**JUST FOR YOU** (68)	Capitol 2870	$10
LP	**WHERE NO ONE STANDS ALONE** (68)	Capitol 2913	$10
LP	**WHITE FENCES AND EVERGREEN TREES** (69)	Capitol 115	$10
LP	**THE BEST OF FERLIN HUSKY** (69)	Capitol 143	$10
LP	**THAT'S WHY I LOVE YOU SO MUCH** (69)	Capitol 239	$10

-radio shows-

16"(RS)	**COUNTRY STYLE USA** (56)	Country Style USA	$25-40
	(Music and interviews)		
16"(RS)	**COUNTRY STYLE USA** (56)	Country Style USA	$25-40
	(Music and interviews)		
16"(RS)	**COUNTRY MUSIC TIME** (57)	U.S. Army 72	$25-40
	(Music and interviews)		
16"(RS)	**COUNTRY MUSIC TIME** (57)	U.S. Army 101	$25-40
	(Music and interviews)		
16"(RS)	**COUNTRY MUSIC TIME** (58)	U.S. Army 108	$25-40
	(Music and interviews)		
16"(RS)	**COUNTRY MUSIC TIME** (58)	U.S. Army 118	$25-40
	(Music and interviews)		
16"(RS)	**NAVY HOEDOWN** (60s)	U.S. Navy	$25-35
	(Music and interviews)		
16"(RS)	**U.S. ARMY BAND** (60s) With Johnny & Jack	U.S. Army	$25-50
	(Music and interviews)		
16"(RS)	**U.S. ARMY BAND** (60s) With Ray Price	U.S. Army	$20-40
	(Music and interviews)		
16"(RS)	**U.S. ARMY BAND** (60s) With Jean Shepard	U.S. Army	$25-40
	(Music and interviews)		

I

VARIOUS ARTISTS

-albums-

10"(P)	**IMPERIAL SAMPLER** (55)	Imperial DJ LP-1	$40
	(Torok, Mark, Sanders and Henslee)		

BENNY INGRAM (RB)

-singles-

45rpm	JELLO SAL (58)		Bandera 1302	$50

AUTRY INMAN (CW)

Other Decca 45s $4-8 each
Other RCA Victor and Jubilee 45s $2-4 each
United Artists, Sims, and Epic 45s $2 each
Epic LPs $8 each
Guest Star and Alshire LPs $4-8 each

-singles-

45rpm	LET'S TAKE THE LONG WAY HOME (51)		Decca 46407	$12
45rpm	WHO DO YOU LOVE (52)		Decca 28290	$10
45rpm	I'LL MISS MY HEART (53)		Decca 28592	$10
45rpm	THAT'S ALL RIGHT (53)		Decca 28629	$20
45(P)	THAT'S ALL RIGHT (53)		Decca 28629	$15
	(Pink promo label)			
45rpm	PUCKER UP (54)		Decca 28778	$10
45rpm	A DEAR JOHN LETTER (54)		Decca 28798	$12
45(P)	A DEAR JOHN LETTER (54)		Decca 28798	$10
	(Pink promo label)			
45rpm	BE BOP BABY (55)		Decca 29936	$25
45(P)	BE BOP BABY (55)		Decca 29936	$20
	(Pink promo label)			
45rpm	NITECLUBBIN' (67)		Risque 103	$10

-albums-

LP	AUTRY INMAN (63)		Mountain Dew 7022	$25
LP	AUTRY INMAN AT THE FRONTIER CLUB (64)		Sims 107	$25
LP	RISCOTHEQUE SATURDAY NIGHT (64)		Jubilee 2055	$25
	(Adult comedy/party record)			
LP	RISCOTHEQUE ADULT COMEDY (64)		Jubilee 2056	$25
	(Another adult party record)			
LP	AUTRY INMAN (69)		Jubilee 8024	$18

JERRY IRBY (RB)

MGM 78s and 45s $5-10 each

-singles-

45rpm	TIME YOU STARTED LOOKING (57)		Daffan 106	$20
45rpm	CLICKETY CLACK (58)		Daffan 108	$40
45rpm	CHANTILLY LACE (59)		Jer-Ray 222	$20

SMITTY IRVIN (BG)

Monument 45s $3 each

ROBERT IRVINE (RB)

-singles-

45rpm	FASTEST HOT IN TOWN (58)		Presto 525	$40

BUD ISAACS (CW)

-EPs-

EP	CRYIN' STEEL GUITAR (55)		RCA Victor 590	$20

JIMMY ISLE (RB)

Everest 45s $10 each

-singles-

45rpm	GOIN' WILD (58) Stock or promo copy		Roulette 4065	$18
45(P)	GOIN' WILD (58)		Roulette 4065	$12
	(Colored promo label)			

IVAN (RB)

Jerry Ivan Allison
Original member of the Crickets

-singles-

45rpm	REAL WILD CHILD (59) Orange label		Coral 62017	$200
45(P)	REAL WILD CHILD (59) Blue promo label		Coral 62017	$100
45rpm	REAL WILD CHILD (61) Orange label		Coral 65607	$40
45(P)	REAL WILD CHILD (61) Blue promo label		Coral 65607	$100
45rpm	FRANKIE FRANKENSTEIN (59) Orange label		Coral 62081	$400
45(P)	FRANKIE FRANKENSTEIN (59) Blue promo label		Coral 62081	$200
	(Buddy Holly on guitar)			

SONNY JOE IVY (RB)

-singles-

45rpm	RUBY AND THE GAMBLER (58)		Jewel 738	$25

J

JACK & DANIEL (CW)
-singles-

45rpm	**DON'T MAKE LOVE IN A BUGGY** (53)	Decca 28467	$10
45rpm	**KNOTHOLE** (54)	Decca 28681	$15
45(P)	**KNOTHOLE** (54)	Decca 28681	$10
	(Pink promo label)		

JACK & JIM (RB)
-singles-

45rpm	**TARZAN & JANE** (59) Maroon label	Brunswick 55141	$50
45(P)	**TARZAN & JANE** (59)	Brunswick 55141	$40
	(Yellow promo label)		

CARL JACKSON (CW)
-radio shows-

LP(RS)	**COUNTRY MUSIC TIME** (70s)	U.S. Air Force	$10-15
	(Music and interviews)		

CORDELL JACKSON (RB)
-singles-

45rpm	**ROCK AND ROLL CHRISTMAS** (58)	Moon 80	$30

EDDIE JACKSON (RB)
-singles-

45rpm	**ROCK & ROLL BABY** (58)	Fortune 186	$10

HARRY JACKSON (F)
-albums-

2LP	**THE COWBOY, HIS SONGS, BALLADS & BRAG** (66)	Folkways 5723	$25

SHOT JACKSON (CW)
-albums-

LP	**SINGING STRINGS OF STEEL GUITAR** (62)	Starday 230	$20

STONEWALL JACKSON (CW)
Other Columbia 45s $4-8 each
Columbia jukebox LLPs $6-8 each
-singles-

45rpm	**WATERLOO** (59)	Columbia 41393	$20
	(Price includes picture sleeve)		
45(P)	**WATERLOO** (59)	Columbia 41393	$10
	(White promo label)		
45(P)	**B. J. THE D. J.** (62)	Columbia 42889	$15
	(White promo label, blue vinyl)		

-EPs-

EP	**THE DYNAMIC STONEWALL JACKSON** Vol 1 (59)	Columbia 13911	$15
EP	**THE DYNAMIC STONEWALL JACKSON** Vol 2 (59)	Columbia 13912	$15
EP	**THE DYNAMIC STONEWALL JACKSON** Vol 3 (59)	Columbia 13913	$15

-albums-

LP	**THE DYNAMIC STONEWALL JACKSON** (59) Mono	Columbia 1391	$20
LP	**THE DYNAMIC STONEWALL JACKSON** (59) Stereo	Columbia 8186	$25
LP	**SADNESS IN A SONG** (63)	Columbia 8570	$18
LP(P)	**SADNESS IN A SONG** (63)	Columbia 8570	$25
	(White promo label)		
LP	**I LOVE A SONG** (63)	Columbia 8859	$18
LP(P)	**I LOVE A SONG** (63)	Columbia 8859	$25
	(White promo label)		
LP	**TROUBLE & ME** (64)	Columbia 9078	$18
LP(P)	**TROUBLE & ME** (64)	Columbia 9078	$25
	(White promo label)		
LP	**STONEWALL JACKSON'S GREATEST HITS** (65)	Columbia 9177	$12
LP	**ALL'S FAIR IN LOVE 'N' WAR** (66)	Columbia 9309	$18
LP(P)	**ALL'S FAIR IN LOVE 'N' WAR** (66)	Columbia 9309	$25
	(White promo label)		

TOMMY JACKSON (CW)
Dot 45s $5-10 each
Decca 45s $4-8 each
Other Dot LPs $4-8 each
Hamilton LPs $6 each

-EPs-

EP	**SQUARE DANCE MUSIC** (57)	Dot 1030-1043	$12 each
	(A series of fourteen EPs, all with the same title and same value, all issued separately and at the same time)		

-albums-

LP	**POPULAR SQUARE DANCE MUSIC** (57)	Dot 3015	$30
	(Without calls)		
LP	**SQUARE DANCE TONIGHT** (58)	Dot 3085	$25
LP	**SQUARE DANCES WITHOUT CALLS** (59)	Decca 8950	$18
LP(P)	**SQUARE DANCES WITHOUT CALLS** (59)	Decca 8950	$25
	(Pink promo label)		
LP	**SQUARE DANCE FIDDLE HITS** (59)	Mercury 20346	$25
LP(P)	**SQUARE DANCE FIDDLE HITS** (59)	Mercury 20346	$30
	(White promo label)		
LP	**DO-SI-DO** (59)	Dot 3163	$15
LP	**SQUARE DANCE FESTIVAL** Vol 1 (60)	Dot 3330	$15
LP	**SQUARE DANCE FESTIVAL** Vol 2 (60)	Dot 3331	$15
LP	**SQUARE DANCE FESTIVAL** Vol 3 (60)	Dot 3532	$15
LP	**SWING YOUR PARTNER** (62)	Dot 25454	$20
LP	**GREATEST BLUEGRASS HITS** (62)	Dot 25471	$25
LP	**LET'S DANCE TO COUNTRY** (64)	Somerset 21800	$15
	(Budget label)		
LP	**GUITAR & FIDDLE COUNTRY STYLE** (65) With Lloyd Ellis	Mercury 12298	$18
LP(P)	**GUITAR & FIDDLE COUNTRY STYLE** (65)	Mercury 12298	$25
	(White promo label)		
LP	**TWIN FIDDLES** (65) With Pete Wade	Cumberland 69530	$18

-radio shows-

LP(RS)	**COUNTRY MUSIC TIME** (60s)	U.S. Air Force	$10-20
	(Flip side is the Jordanaires)		

WANDA JACKSON (CW)
And the Party Timers
Other Capitol 45s $3-8 each
Other Capitol LPs $8-15 each
Pickwick LPs $5 each
Myrrh LPs $4 each
Gusto and Word LPs $3 each

-singles-

45rpm	**YOU CAN'T HAVE MY LOVE** (54)	Decca 29140	$25
	(Wanda Jackson and Billy Gray)		
45(P)	**YOU CAN'T HAVE MY LOVE** (54)	Decca 29140	$18
	(Pink promo label)		
45rpm	**IF YOU KNEW WHAT I KNOW** (54)	Decca 29253	$25
45(P)	**IF YOU KNEW WHAT I KNOW** (54)	Decca 29253	$15
	(Pink promo label)		
45rpm	**IF YOU DON'T SOMEBODY ELSE WILL** (54)	Decca 29267	$20
45(P)	**IF YOU DON'T SOMEBODY ELSE WILL** (54)	Decca 29267	$12
	(Pink promo label)		
45rpm	**TEARS AT THE GRAND OLE OPRY** (55)	Decca 29514	$25
45(P)	**TEARS AT THE GRAND OLE OPRY** (55)	Decca 29514	$18
	(Pink promo label)		
45rpm	**IT'S THE SAME WORLD** (55)	Decca 29677	$20
45(P)	**IT'S THE SAME WORLD** (55)	Decca 29677	$15
	(Pink promo label)		
45rpm	**WASTED** (56)	Decca 29803	$15
45(P)	**WASTED** (56)	Decca 29803	$10
	(Pink promo label)		
45rpm	**I GOTTA KNOW** (56)	Capitol 3485	$50
45(P)	**I GOTTA KNOW** (56)	Capitol 3485	$40
	(White promo label)		
45rpm	**HOT DOG! THAT MADE HIM MAD** (57)	Capitol 3575	$50
45(P)	**HOT DOG! THAT MADE HIM MAD** (57)	Capitol 3575	$40
	(White promo label)		
45rpm	**BABY LOVES HIM** (57)	Capitol 3637	$60
45(P)	**BABY LOVES HIM** (57)	Capitol 3637	$50
	(White promo label)		
45rpm	**COOL LOVE** (57)	Capitol 3764	$40
45(P)	**COOL LOVE** (57)	Capitol 3764	$30
	(White promo label)		
45rpm	**FUJIYAMA MAMA** (58)	Capitol 3843	$40
45(P)	**FUJIYAMA MAMA** (58)	Capitol 3843	$35
	(White promo label)		

45rpm	**HONEY BOP** (58)	Capitol 3941	$40
45(P)	**HONEY BOP** (58)	Capitol 3941	$30
	(White promo label)		
45rpm	**MEAN MEAN MAN** (59)	Capitol 4026	$50
45(P)	**MEAN MEAN MAN** (59)	Capitol 4026	$40
	(White promo label)		
45rpm	**ROCK YOUR BABY** (59)	Capitol 4081	$25
45(P)	**ROCK YOUR BABY** (59)	Capitol 4081	$20
	(White promo label)		
45rpm	**SAVIN' MY LOVE** (59)	Capitol 4142	$12
45(P)	**SAVIN' MY LOVE** (59)	Capitol 4142	$10
	(Capitol promo label)		
45rpm	**LET'S HAVE A PARTY** (60)	Capitol 4397	$40
	(With Gene Vincent & the Blue Caps)		
45(P)	**LET'S HAVE A PARTY** (60)	Capitol 4397	$30
	(Red promo label)		
45rpm	**MEAN MEAN MAN** (60)	Capitol 4469	$15
45(P)	**MEAN MEAN MAN** (60)	Capitol 4469	$12
	(Red promo label)		
45rpm	**RIOT IN CELL BLOCK NUMBER NINE** (61)	Capitol 4520	$20
45(P)	**RIOT IN CELL BLOCK NUMBER NINE** (61)	Capitol 4520	$18
	(Red promo label)		
45rpm	**IF I CRIED EVERY TIME YOU HURT ME** (62)	Capitol 4723	$25
	(Price includes picture sleeve)		

-EPs-

EP	**WANDA JACKSON** (58)	Capitol 1041	$50
EP(P)	**WONDERFUL WANDA** (62) Jukebox LLP	Capitol 1776	$25
	(Price includes title strips and hard cover)		

-albums-

LP	**WANDA JACKSON** (58)	Capitol 1041	$200
LP(P)	**WANDA JACKSON** (58)	Capitol 1041	$250
	(Yellow promo label)		
LP	**ROCKIN' WITH WANDA** (60)	Capitol 1384	$400
LP	**ROCKIN' WITH WANDA** (62)	Capitol 1384	$200
	(Gold Starline label, reissue)		
LP	**ROCKIN' WITH WANDA** (63)	Capitol 1384	$50
	(Black Starline label, reissue)		
LP(P)	**ROCKIN' WITH WANDA** (60)	Capitol 1384	$500
	(Yellow promo label)		
LP	**THERE'S A PARTY GOIN' ON** (61) Mono	Capitol 1511	$150
LP	**THERE'S A PARTY GOIN' ON** (61) Stereo	Capitol 1511	$200
LP(P)	**THERE'S A PARTY GOIN' ON** (61)	Capitol 1511	$200
	(Yellow promo label)		
LP	**RIGHT OR WRONG** (61) Mono	Capitol 1596	$30
LP	**RIGHT OR WRONG** (61) Stereo	Capitol 1596	$40
LP(P)	**RIGHT OR WRONG** (61)	Capitol 1596	$50
	(Capitol promo label)		
LP	**WONDERFUL WANDA** (62)	Capitol 1776	$30
LP(P)	**WONDERFUL WANDA** (62)	Capitol 1776	$25
	(Capitol promo label)		
LP	**LOVIN' COUNTRY** (62)	Decca 4224	$60
	(With Billy Gray, older Decca material)		
LP(P)	**LOVIN' COUNTRY** (62)	Decca 4224	$50
	(Pink promo label)		
LP	**LOVE ME FOREVER** (63)	Capitol 1911	$20
LP	**TWO SIDES OF WANDA JACKSON** (64)	Capitol 2030	$50
LP	**BLUES IN MY HEART** (64)	Capitol 2306	$30
LP	**WANDA JACKSON SINGS COUNTRY SONGS** (66)	Capitol 2438	$25
LP	**WANDA JACKSON SALUTES THE COUNTRY MUSIC HALL OF FAME**	Capitol 2606	$25
LP	**RECKLESS LOVE AFFAIR** (67)	Capitol 2704	$25
LP	**YOU'LL ALWAYS HAVE MY LOVE** (67)	Capitol 2812	$20
LP	**THE BEST OF WANDA JACKSON** (67)	Capitol 2883	$20
LP	**CREAM OF THE CROP** (68)	Capitol 2976	$18
LP	**NOBODY'S DARLIN'** (69)	Vocalion 3861	$15
	(Repackage of Decca 4224)		
LP(P)	**NOBODY'S DARLIN'** (69)	Vocalion 3861	$20
	(White promo label)		
LP	**THE MANY MOODS OF WANDA JACKSON** (69)	Capitol 129	$18
LP	**THE HAPPY SIDE OF WANDA JACKSON** (69)	Capitol 238	$18
LP	**WANDA JACKSON IN PERSON** (69)	Capitol 345	$20

-radio shows-

2LP(RS)	**COUNTRY COOKIN'** (Sep 75) Four fifteen-minute shows	U.S. Army Reserve 227	$25-50
	(One of the four shows features Wanda Jackson)		

SOUNDTRACK

-45s and albums-

LP(P)	**JAMBOREE** (57)	Warner (No number)	$5,000
	(Various artists rock & roll soundtrack is promo only with no label number, neither this LP or the movie was released)		
	These 45s were released of songs from the *Jamboree* movie, not neccessary from the soundtrack		
45rpm	**UNCHAIN MY HEART** (55) Slim Whitman	Imperial 8312	$18
45rpm	**UNCHAIN MY HEART** (55)	Imperial 8312	$20
	(Cream-colored promo label)		
45rpm	**JAMBOREE** (57) Count Basie	Verve 89184	$18
78rpm	**HULA LOVE** (58) Buddy Knox	Roulette 4018	$40
	("From Jamboree" on label)		
45rpm	**HULA LOVE** (58)	Roulette 4018	$20

BOBBY JAMES (R)

45rpm	**I NEED YOU SO** (58)	Cub 51 104	$50

JESSE JAMES (RB)

45rpm	**RED HOT ROCKIN BLUES** (57)	Kent 314	$45
45(P)	**RED HOT ROCKIN BLUES** (57)	Kent 314	$50
	(White promo label)		

LEON JAMES (RB)

45rpm	**BABY, LET'S ROCK** (58)	Bumble Bee 501	$50

SONNY JAMES (CW)

Capitol 78s $5-8 each
Other Capitol 45s $3-8 each
Capitol picture sleeves $3-5 each
Dot 45s $6 each
Columbia 45s $1-2 each
Columbia picture sleeves $2 each
Columbia promo picture sleeves $3 each
Dimension 45s $1 each
Dimension picture sleeves $2 each
Other Capitol jukebox LLPs $8 each
Other Capitol LPs $4-8 each
Other Columbia LPs $2-4 each
Pickwick LPs $4 each
Crown, Monument, and TVP LPs $3-4 each
Dimension LPs $3 each

-singles-

45rpm	**THAT'S ME WITHOUT YOU** (53)	Capitol 2259	$10
45rpm	**I FORGOT MORE THAN YOU'LL EVER KNOW** (54)	Capitol 2508	$10
45rpm	**SHE DONE GIVE HER HEART TO ME** (54)	Capitol 2906	$10
45rpm	**YOUNG LOVE** (57)	Capitol 3602	$10
	(With the Jordanaires)		
45(P)	**YOUNG LOVE** (57)	Capitol 3602	$15
	(White promo label)		
45rpm	**YOUNG LOVE** (59)	Groove G4-1	$25
	(Different arrangement than the Capitol hit)		
45(P)	**DEAR LOVE** (57) Yellow promo label	Capitol 3734	$10
	(Promo version has James photo on the label)		
45rpm	**JENNY LOU** (60)	NRC 050	$10
45(P)	**JENNY LOU** (60)	NRC 050	$15
	(White promo label)		
45rpm	**BIMBO** (61)	NRC 061	$10
45(P)	**BIMBO** (61)	NRC 061	$15
	(White promo label)		
33s(JB)	**THE MINUTE YOU'RE GONE** (64) Set of five singles	Capitol 2017	$5 each
	(Compact-33 singles for jukebox use)		
45(P)	**SONNY JAMES** (66) Rowe AMI Promotion record	Play Me 1005A	$20
	(Red vinyl, thirty seconds long, for jukeboxes)		
45rpm	**BAREFOOT SANTA CLAUS** (66) With a bunch of kids	Capitol 5733	$12
	(Price includes picture sleeve)		

-EPs-

EP	**THE SOUTHERN GENTLEMAN** Vol 1 (57)	Capitol 1-779	$25
EP	**THE SOUTHERN GENTLEMAN** Vol 2 (57)	Capitol 2-779	$25
EP	**THE SOUTHERN GENTLEMAN** Vol 3 (57)	Capitol 3-779	$25
EP	**YOUNG LOVE** (57)	Capitol 827	$30
EP	**FIRST DATE, FIRST KISS, FIRST LOVE** (57)	Capitol 861	$25
EP	**SONNY** Vol 1 (57)	Capitol 1-867	$20
EP	**SONNY** Vol 2 (57)	Capitol 2-867	$20
EP	**SONNY** Vol 3 (57)	Capitol 3-867	$20
EP	**HONEY** Vol 1 (58)	Capitol 1-988	$18
EP	**HONEY** Vol 2 (58)	Capitol 2-988	$18

EP	HONEY Vol 3 (58)	Capitol 3-988	$18
EP(JB)	THE SENSATIONAL SONNY JAMES (71) Jukebox LLP	Capitol 806 (LLP 159)	$10
	(Issued with a paper cover)		

-albums-

LP	THE SOUTHERN GENTLEMAN (57)	Capitol 779	$30
LP(P)	THE SOUTHERN GENTLEMAN (57)	Capitol 779	$40
	(Yellow promo label)		
LP	SONNY (57)	Capitol 867	$30
LP(P)	SONNY (57)	Capitol 867	$40
	(Yellow promo label)		
LP	HONEY (58)	Capitol 988	$25
LP(P)	HONEY (58)	Capitol 988	$30
	(Yellow promo label)		
LP	THE SONNY SIDE (59)	Capitol 1178	$25
LP(P)	THE SONNY SIDE (59)	Capitol 1178	$30
	(Capitol promo label)		
LP(P)	NUMBER ONE HITS OF SONNY JAMES	Capitol SPRO-112	$50
	(Promo-only LP for radio stations)		
LP	YOUNG LOVE (62)	Dot 25462	$20
	("Young Love" is re-recorded for this Dot album)		
LP	THE MINUTE YOU'RE GONE (64)	Capitol 2017	$20
LP	YOU'RE THE ONLY WORLD I KNOW (65)	Capitol 2209	$18
LP	I'LL KEEP HOLDING ON (65)	Capitol 2317	$18
LP	BEHIND THE TEAR (65)	Capitol 2415	$18
LP	YOUNG LOVE (65)	Hamilton 12160	$15
	(Same material as Dot 25462)		
LP	TRUE LOVE'S A BLESSING (66)	Capitol 2500	$18
LP	TILL THE LAST LEAF SHALL FALL (66)	Capitol 2561	$18
LP	MY CHRISTMAS DREAM (66)	Capitol 2589	$20
LP	THE BEST OF SONNY JAMES (66)	Capitol 2615	$15
LP	THE SOUTHERN GENTLEMAN With Kathy Dee	Guest Star 1487	$15
	(Budget label)		
2LP	THAT SPECIAL COUNTRY FEELING	Capitol 31357	$18
	(Capitol Record Club release)		
LP	SONNY JAMES SINGS YOUNG LOVE (67)	Camden 2140	$15
	(RCA Victor material, "Young Love" is the version released as a single on Groove)		
LP	I'LL NEVER FIND ANOTHER YOU (67)	Capitol 2788	$15
2LP	I'LL NEVER FIND ANOTHER YOU (70)	Capitol 535	$15
2LP	WHEN THE SNOW IS ON THE ROSES (75)	Columbia 33627	$12
2LP	GREATEST HITS OF SONNY JAMES (75)	Brookville 6898	$12
	(Available only through the mail)		

-radio shows-

LP(RS)	GRAND OL' OPRY (62) Fifteen-minute show	WSM Radio 67	$25-40
	(Music and interviews)		

TOM JAMES (RB)

-singles-

45rpm	TRACK DOWN BABY (58)	Klix 001	$60

BILL JANES (RB)

-singles-

45rpm	SCHOOL'S OUT (58)	Muntab 104	$20

JOHNNY JANO (RB)

-singles-

45rpm	HAVING A WHOLE LOT OF FUN (58)	Excello 2099	$40

FELTON JARVIS (RB)

-singles-

45rpm	SWINGIN' CAT (58)	Thunder 1023	$40

J. D. JARVIS (G)
And the Rocky Mountain Boys
Jewel LPs $5-8 each

JOHNNY JAY (RB)

-singles-

45rpm	HAVIN' A WHOLE LOT OF FUN (57)	Excello 2099	$40
45(P)	HAVIN' A WHOLE LOT OF FUN (57)	Excello 2099	$30
	(White promo label)		
45rpm	SUGAR DOLL (58)	Mercury 71232	$15
45(P)	SUGAR DOLL (58)	Mercury 71232	$12
	(White promo label)		
45rpm	THAT'S WHAT I LIKE (59)	Play 1006	$15
45rpm	I'M GONNA KEEP IT (59)	Mercury 71267	$15

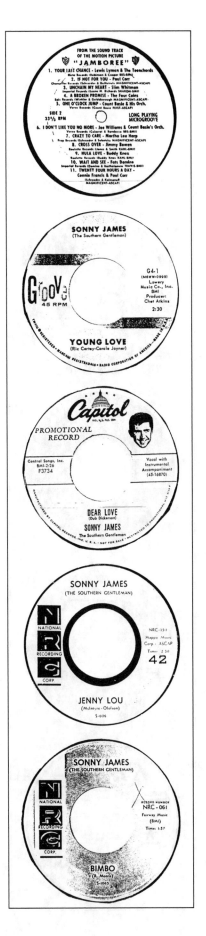

45(P)	**I'M GONNA KEEP IT** (59) (White promo label)	Mercury 71267	$12

P. JAY & THE HAYSTACKERS (RB)
-singles-

45rpm	**HIGH SCHOOL ROCK 'N' ROLL** (57)	Oak 1202	$40

JERRY JAYE (R)
Hi 45s $4-6 each
-albums-

LP	**MY GIRL JOSEPHINE** (67)	Hi 32038	$25
LP	**HONKY TONK MEN LOVE REDNECK MEN** (70)	Hi 32102	$15

JIMMY JEFFERS (RB)
-singles-

45rpm	**TEARDROPS FROM MY EYES** (58)	Fraternity 857	$12

WALLY JEFFERY (RB)
-singles-

45rpm	**OH YEAH** (57)	Do Ra Me 1402	$100

BOBO JENKINS (RB)
-singles-

45rpm	**NOTHING BUT LOVE** (58)	Boxer 202	$50

BILL JENNINGS (C)
-albums-

LP	**GUITAR VIBES** (60)	Audio Lab 1514	$20

BOB JENNINGS (C)
Jubilee and Challenge 45s $3 each

WAYLON JENNINGS (RB/CW)
Member of Buddy Holly's Crickets
RCA Victor black label, dog on side, 45s $4-8 each
RCA Victor white promo label 45s $5 each
Other RCA Victor 45s $2-4 each
RCA Victor "Waylon" printed white sleeves $2 each
Other MCA and RCA Victor color vinyl 45s $8 each
MCA 45s $1-2 each
Columbia duet 45s $3 each
Other RCA Victor LPs $4-8 each
Other United Artists LPs $4-8 each
   (Soundtracks)
Other Camden LPs $6-10 each
Time-Life LPs $5 each
Pickwick LPs $4 each
-singles-

45rpm	**JOLE BLON** (59) Maroon label	Brunswick 55130	$300
45(P)	**JOLE BLON** (59) Yellow promo label (Yellow promo label)	Brunswick 55130	$150
45rpm	**WHITE LIGHTNING** (64)	Bat 121636	$30
45rpm	**RAVE ON** (64)	A&M 722	$15
45(P)	**RAVE ON** (64) (White promo label)	A&M 722	$12
45rpm	**JUST TO SATISFY YOU** (64)	A&M 739	$15
45(P)	**JUST TO SATISFY YOU** (64) (White promo label)	A&M 739	$12
45rpm	**NEVER AGAIN** (64)	Trend 102	$25
45(P)	**NEVER AGAIN** (64) (Yellow and white promo label)	Trend 102	$30
45rpm	**THE STAGE** (64)	Trend 106	$100
45(P)	**THE STAGE** (64) (Yellow and white promo label)	Trend 106	$75
45rpm	**MY BABY WALKS ALL OVER ME** (66) Black label	Ramco 1989	$18
45(P)	**MY BABY WALKS ALL OVER ME** (66) (White/orange promo label)	Ramco 1989	$15
45rpm	**MY WORLD** (67) Black label	Ramco 1997	$15
45(P)	**MY WORLD** (67) (White/orange promo label)	Ramco 1997	$12
45(P)	**LUCKENBACH, TEXAS** (77) Waylon (Rare promo version, RCA in script, no "Victor")	RCA Victor 10924	$15
45(P)	**WHAT'S IT ALL ABOUT** (Oct 75) Public service show (Flip side features Dirt Band)	W. I. A. A. 288	$12
45(P)	**WHAT'S IT ALL ABOUT** (Nov 82) Public service show (Flip side features Roy Clark)	W. I. A. A. 3054	$12
45(P)	**AMANDA** (79) (Blue promo label, blue vinyl)	RCA Victor 11596	$15

45rpm	**THREE STARS** (80) Tommy Dee and Carol Kay	Crest 1057	$20
	(This is the reissue, NOT the original)		
	A Waylon Jennings interview from 1959 is dubbed into this		
	classic hit from 1959 and issued in very limited numbers with		
	a picture sleeve, the interview is not on the original version)		
45(P)	**I'LL BE ALRIGHT** (81)	RCA Victor 12245	$15
	(Orange promo label, yellow vinyl)		
45(P)	**JUST TO SATISFY YOU** (82) With Willie Nelson	RCA Victor 13073	$15
	(Silver promo label, blue vinyl)		
45(P)	**THE DOCK OF THE BAY** (82) With Willie Nelson	RCA Victor 13319	$15
	(Green promo label, red vinyl)		
45(P)	**BREAKIN' DOWN** (83)	RCA Victor 13543	$15
	(Red promo label, green vinyl)		
45(P)	**HOLD ON, I'M COMIN'** (83) With Jerry Reed	RCA Victor 13580	$12
	(Red promo label, red vinyl)		
45(P)	**AMERICA** (84)	RCA Victor 13908	$15
	(Silver label, blue vinyl, long 3:43 and short 3:25 versions)		
45(P)	**WALTZ ME TO HEAVEN** (84)	RCA Victor 13984	$12
	(Yellow promo label, yellow vinyl)		
33(P)	**SAVE THE CHILDREN** (87) PSA spots	DWP 126	$20
	(Twenty spots, Waylon does one thirty-second)		
45(P)	**WORKING WITHOUT A NET** (86)	MCA 52776	$10
	(White promo label, blue vinyl)		
45(P)	**WILL THE WOLF SURVIVE** (86)	MCA 52830	$10
	(White promo label, yellow vinyl)		
45(P)	**ROSE IN PARADISE** (87)	MCA 53009	$10
	(White promo label, red vinyl)		
45(P)	**FALLIN' OUT** (87)	MCA 53088	$10
	(White promo label, yellow vinyl)		

-albums-

LP	**WAYLON JENNINGS AT JDS** (64)	Bat 1001	$500
	(Reissued on Vocalion in 1969)		
LP	**WAYLON JENNINGS AT JDS** (64)	Sounds 1001	$200
	(Same material as Bat album)		
LP	**FOLK COUNTRY** (66) Mono	RCA Victor 3523	$25
LP	**FOLK COUNTRY** (66) Stereo	RCA Victor 3523	$40
LP	**LEAVIN' TOWN** (66) Mono	RCA Victor 3620	$25
LP	**LEAVIN' TOWN** (66) Stereo	RCA Victor 3620	$30
LP	**WAYLON SINGS OL' HARLAN** (67) Mono	RCA Victor 3660	$30
LP	**WAYLON SINGS OL' HARLAN** (67) Stereo	RCA Victor 3660	$40
LP	**NASHVILLE REBEL** (67) Mono	RCA Victor 3736	$30
	(Soundtrack recording)		
LP	**NASHVILLE REBEL** (67) Stereo	RCA Victor 3736	$40
LP	**LOVE OF THE COMMON PEOPLE** (67) Mono	RCA Victor 3825	$20
LP	**LOVE OF THE COMMON PEOPLE** (67) Stereo	RCA Victor 3825	$25
LP	**THE ONE & ONLY WAYLON JENNINGS** (67)	Camden 2183	$18
LP	**HANGIN' ON** (68) Mono	RCA Victor 3918	$100
	(Very limited press in mono)		
LP	**HANGIN' ON** (68) Stereo	RCA Victor 3918	$25
LP	**ONLY THE GREATEST** (68)	RCA Victor 4023	$20
LP	**JEWELS** (68)	RCA Victor 4085	$20
LP	**JUST TO SATISFY YOU** (69)	RCA Victor 4137	$20
	(Includes two tracks with Anita Carter)		
LP	**COUNTRY-FOLK** (69) With the Kimberleys	RCA Victor 4180	$20
LP	**DON'T THINK TWICE** (69)	RCA Victor 4238	$20
LP	**DON'T THINK TWICE** (69)	A&M 4238	$40
	(Produced by Herb Alpert)		
LP(P)	**DON'T THINK TWICE** (69)	A&M 4238	$50
	(White promo label)		
LP	**WAYLON JENNINGS** (69)	Vocalion 3873	$30
	(Material from the JDs' studio sessions)		
LP(P)	**WAYLON JENNINGS** (69)	Vocalion 3873	$40
	(White promo label)		
LP	**NED KELLY** (70)	United Artists 5213	$20
	(Soundtrack recording)		
LP(P)	**NED KELLY** (70)	United Artists 5213	$25
	(White promo label)		
LP(P)	**GET INTO WAYLON JENNINGS** (72)	RCA Victor SPS 570	$75
	(White promo-only sampler label)		
LP	**MACKINTOSH & T. J.** (76)	RCA Victor 1520	$12
	(Soundtrack recording)		
LP(P)	**WAYLON & WILLIE** (78) With Willie Nelson	RCA Victor 2686	$40
	(Gold vinyl)		
LP	**GREATEST HITS** (79)	RCA Victor 3406	$12
	(Picture disc)		

LP(RS)	**COUNTRY MUSIC TIME** (80s)	U.S. Air Force	$10-15
	(Music and interviews)		
3LP(RS)	**WAYLON & WILLIE** (Jan 82) Box set	Mutual Radio	$25-50
	(Music and interviews)		
3LP(RS)	**THE SILVER EAGLE** (Nov 83) With Jessi Colter	DIR	$25-50
	(Live concert)		
3LP(RS)	**THE SILVER EAGLE** (Aug 84)	DIR	$30-50
	(Live birthday tribute to Waylon)		
3LP(RS)	**THE SILVER EAGLE** (Oct 85) With Kris Kristofferson	DIR	$40-75
	(Live concert)		
3LP(RS)	**THE WAYLON JENNINGS STORY** (Nov 88) Box set		$20-40
	(Music and interviews)		
LP(RS)	**LIVE AT GILLEY'S** (Jan 89)	Westwood One	$25-40
	(Live concert)		
LP(RS)	**WESTWOOD ONE PRESENTS** (Jan 90)	Westwood One	$25-40
	(Live concert)		

JERRY JERICHO (CW)

-singles-

45rpm	**LETS CALL IT OFF** (53)	Starday 120	$10

RALPH JEROME (RB)

-singles-

45rpm	**ROCKHOUSE** (58)	KP 1007	$60

JEUJENE & THE JAYBOPS (R)

-singles-

45rpm	**THUNDERIN' GUITAR** (67)	Zero 3279	$75
	(Only one hundred copies pressed on red vinyl)		

JIM & JESSE (BG)

The McReynolds Brothers
Epic 45s $2-4 each
Capitol 45s $2 each
Other Epic LPs $5-10 each
Masterseal LPs $5
  (With the Sweet Mountain Boys)
Palace LPs $4 each
  (Masterseal and Palace are budget labels)
Other Capitol LPs $4-8 each
CMH LPs $3-6 each
CMH 2LPs $8 each
Other label LPs $3 each

-EPs-

EP(JB)	**JIM & JESSE** (70) Jukebox LLP	Epic 26031	$15
	(Issued with a cardboard cover)		

-albums-

LP	**BLUEGRASS SPECIAL** (63)	Epic 26031	$20
LP	**BLUEGRASS SPECIAL** (63)	Epic 26031	$25
	(White promo label)		
LP	**BLUEGRASS CLASSICS** (63)	Epic 26074	$15
LP	**BLUEGRASS CLASSICS** (63)	Epic 26074	$18
	(White promo label)		
LP	**THE OLD COUNTRY CHURCH** (64)	Epic 26107	$15
LP(P)	**THE OLD COUNTRY CHURCH** (64)	Epic 26107	$18
	(White promo label)		
LP	**Y'ALL COME** (64)	Epic 26144	$15
LP(P)	**Y'ALL COME** (64)	Epic 26144	$18
	(White promo label)		
LP	**SACRED SONGS OF VIRGINIA** (65)	Ultra Sonic 52	$18
LP	**BERRY PICKIN' THE COUNTRY** (65)	Epic 26176	$15
	(Chuck Berry songs)		
LP(P)	**BERRY PICKIN' THE COUNTRY** (65)	Epic 26176	$18
	(White promo label)		
LP	**DIESEL ON MY TAIL** (67)	Epic 26314	$12
LP(P)	**DIESEL ON MY TAIL** (67)	Epic 26314	$15
	(White promo label)		
LP	**ALL-TIME GREAT COUNTRY INSTRUMENTALS** (68)	Epic 26394	$12
LP(P)	**ALL-TIME GREAT COUNTRY INSTRUMENTALS** (68)	Epic 26394	$15
	(White promo label)		
LP	**SALUTING THE LOUVIN BROTHERS** (69)	Epic 26465	$15
LP(P)	**SALUTING THE LOUVIN BROTHERS** (69)	Epic 26465	$18
	(White promo label)		
2LP	**TWENTY GREAT SONGS** (69)	Capitol 264	$25
LP	**WILDWOOD FLOWER** (70)	Harmony 11399	$12

LP(P)	**WILDWOOD FLOWER** (70)	Harmony 11399	$15
	(White promo label)		
2LP	**WE LIKE TRAINS** (75)	Epic 33746	$12

JIM & JOE (CW)
Fabor 45s $4-8 each

JIM & ROD (RB)
-singles-

45rpm	**DIDN'T IT ROCK** (59)	Challenge 59034	$60
45(P)	**DIDN'T IT ROCK** (59)	Challenge 59034	$50
	(White promo label)		

JIMMY & JOHNNY (CW)
Jimmy Lee and Johnny Mathis
Other Decca 78s $4-8 each
Other Decca 45s $3-6 each
Little Darlin' 45s $3 each
-singles-

78rpm	**I'M BEGINNING TO REMEMBER** (55)	Chess 4859	$10
	(Jimmy Lee and Johnny Mathis)		
45rpm	**I'M BEGINNING TO REMEMBER** (55)	Chess 4859	$20
78rpm	**LOVE ME** (54)	Chess 4863	$50
	(Jimmy Lee and Johnny Mathis)		
45rpm	**LOVE ME** (54)	Chess 4863	$75
45rpm	**I CAN'T FIND THE DOOR KNOB** (55) Jimmy & Johnny	D 1004	$30
45rpm	**DON'T GIVE ME THAT LOOK** (56) Jimmy & Johnny	D 1018	$18
45rpm	**MY LITTLE BABY** (56) Jimmy & Johnny	D 1089	$15
45rpm	**DON'T CALL ME, I'LL CALL YOU** (56)	TNT 184	$20
	(Jimmy & Johnny)		
78rpm	**SWEET SINGING DADDY** (56) Jimmy & Johnny	Decca 29772	$15
78(P)	**SWEET SINGING DADDY** (56)	Decca 29772	$20
	(Pink promo label)		
45rpm	**SWEET SINGING DADDY** (56)	Decca 29772	$25
45(P)	**SWEET SINGING DADDY** (56)	Decca 29772	$20
	(Pink promo label)		
45rpm	**'TIL THE END OF THE WORLD** (56) Jimmy & Johnny	Decca 29954	$12
45(P)	**'TIL THE END OF THE WORLD** (56)	Decca 29954	$10
	(Pink promo label)		
78rpm	**SWEET LOVE ON MY MIND** (56) Jimmy & Johnny	Decca 30061	$30
78(P)	**SWEET LOVE ON MY MIND** (56)	Decca 30061	$40
	(Pink promo label)		
45rpm	**SWEET LOVE ON MY MIND** (56)	Decca 30061	$50
45(P)	**SWEET LOVE ON MY MIND** (56)	Decca 30061	$40
	(Pink promo label)		
45rpm	**WILL IT ALWAYS BE** (57)	Starday 181	$10
	(Les Chambers and Johnny Mathis)		
45rpm	**DON'T GIVE ME THAT LOOK** (57) Jimmy & Johnny	Decca 30278	$15
45(P)	**DON'T GIVE ME THAT LOOK** (57)	Decca 30278	$12
	(Pink promo label)		
45rpm	**WHAT CHA' DOIN' TO ME** (58) Jimmy & Johnny	Decca 30410	$15
45(P)	**WHAT CHA' DOIN' TO ME** (58)	Decca 30410	$12
	(Pink promo label)		

-albums-

LP	**COUNTRY JOHNNY MATHIS** (65) Country Johnny Mathis	Hilltop 7004	$25
LP	**HE KEEPS ME SINGIN'** (67) Country Johnny Mathis	Little Darlin' 8007	$20
LP	**COME HOME TO MY HEART** (70) Country Johnny Mathis	Little Darlin' 8016	$18
LP	**IN THE HOUSE OF THE LORD** (72) Johnny Mathis	Pickwick 7004	$10
	(Reissue of the Hilltop 7004)		

JIV-A-TONES (RB)
-singles-

45rpm	**FLIRTY GIRTY** (58)	Fox 1	$50
45rpm	**FLIRTY GIRTY** (58)	Felsted	$25

THE JODIMARS (RB)
Members of Bill Haley's Comets
-singles-

45rpm	**LET'S ALL ROCK TOGETHER** (56)	Capitol 3285	$25
45(P)	**LET'S ALL ROCK TOGETHER** (56)	Capitol 3285	$20
	(White promo label)		
45rpm	**DANCIN' THE BOP** (57)	Capitol 3360	$25
45(P)	**DANCIN' THE BOP** (57)	Capitol 3360	$20
	(White promo label)		
45rpm	**RATTLE MY BONES** (57)	Capitol 3436	$20
45(P)	**RATTLE MY BONES** (57)	Capitol 3436	$18
	(White promo label)		

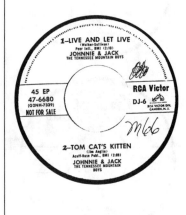

45rpm	**RATTLE SHAKIN' DADDY** (57)	Capitol 3512	$20
45(P)	**RATTLE SHAKIN' DADDY** (57)	Capitol 3512	$15
	(White promo label)		
45rpm	**MIDNIGHT** (57)	Capitol 3588	$20
45(P)	**MIDNIGHT** (57)	Capitol 3588	$15
	(White promo label)		
45rpm	**CLOUD 99** (58)	Capitol 3633	$20
45(P)	**CLOUD 99** (58)	Capitol 3633	$15
	(White promo label)		
45rpm	**ONE GRAIN OF SAND** (58) Marshall & Wes	Milestone 107	$25
	(With the Jodimars)		
45(P)	**ONE GRAIN OF SAND** (58)	Milestone 107	$20
	(Promo label)		
	See Bill Haley and The Comets		

GRADIE JOE (RB)

-singles-

45rpm	**ROCKABILLY MUSIC** (58)	Blue Moon 407	$100

JOHNNIE & JACK (CW)

Johnnie is John Wright (Johnny Wright)
Other RCA Victor 78s $5-10 each
Other RCA Victor 45s $5-10 each

-singles-

45rpm	**POISON LOVE** (51)	RCA Victor 0377	$12
45rpm	**CRYING HEART BLUES** (51)	RCA Victor 0478	$10
45rpm	**THREE WAYS OF KNOWING** (52)	RCA Victor 4555	$10
78(P)	**OH, BABY MINE** (54)	RCA Victor 4555	$15
	(White promo label)		
78rpm	**OH, BABY MINE** (54)	RCA Victor 4555	$15
78(P)	**OH, BABY MINE** (54)	RCA Victor 4555	$18
	(White promo label)		
45rpm	**YOU'RE MY DOWNFALL** (54)	RCA Victor 5483	$10
45rpm	**OH, BABY MINE** (54)	RCA Victor 5681	$25
	(A hit for the Four Knights)		
45(P)	**OH, BABY MINE** (54)	RCA Victor 5681	$18
	(White promo label)		
78rpm	**GOODNIGHT, SWEETHEART, GOODNIGHT** (54)	RCA Victor 5775	$12
78(P)	**GOODNIGHT, SWEETHEART, GOODNIGHT** (54)	RCA Victor 5775	$15
	(White promo label)		
45rpm	**GOODNIGHT, SWEETHEART, GOODNIGHT** (54)	RCA Victor 5775	$18
	(Another R & B hit)		
45(P)	**GOODNIGHT, SWEETHEART, GOODNIGHT** (54)	RCA Victor 5775	$15
	(White promo label)		
45rpm	**KISS CRAZY BABY** (55)	RCA Victor 5880	$12
45(P)	**KISS CRAZY BABY** (55)	RCA Victor 5880	$10
	(White promo label)		
45rpm	**BABY IT'S IN THE MAKING** (58) With Ruby Wells	RCA Victor 6508	$10

-EPs-

EP(P)	**LIVE AND LET LIVE** (56)	RCA Victor 6680 DJ-6	$18
	(Promo-only four-song EP, two Johnnie & Jack tracks)		
EP	**I HEARD MY SAVIOR CALL** (55)	RCA Victor 502	$18
EP	**THE TENNESSEE MOUNTAIN BOYS** (57)	RCA Victor 4053	$15
EP	**THE TENNESSEE MOUNTAIN BOYS** (57)	RCA Victor 1587	$15
EP	**SMILES AND TEARS** (62)	Decca 34115	$15

-albums-

LP	**THE TENNESSEE MOUNTAIN BOYS** (57)	RCA Victor 1587	$40
	(Also known as Johnnie & Jack)		
LP	**HITS BY JOHNNIE & JACK** (59)	RCA Victor 2017	$25
LP	**SMILES & TEARS** (62)	Decca 4308	$25
LP(P)	**SMILES & TEARS** (62)	Decca 4308	$30
	(Pink promo label)		
LP	**JOHNNIE & JACK SING POISON LOVE** (63)	Camden 747	$25
LP	**SINCERELY** (64)	Camden 822	$25
LP	**HERE'S JOHNNIE & JACK** (68)	Vocalion 3832	$12
	(Decca material)		
LP(P)	**HERE'S JOHNNIE & JACK** (68)	Vocalion 3832	$15
	(White promo label)		
2LP	**ALL THE BEST OF JOHNNIE & JACK** (70)	RCA Victor 6022	$25

-radio shows-

16"(RS)	**COUNTRY MUSIC TIME** (60s)	U.S. Army	$25-50
	(Music and interviews)		
LP(RS)	**COUNTRY MUSIC TIME** (60s)	U.S. Air Force	$15-25
	(Music and interviews)		

JOHN'S GOSPEL QUARTET (G)
The Stanley Brothers

-albums-

LP(P)	**JOHN'S GOSPEL QUARTET** (67)	Wango 103	$25
	(Promo-only release, no cardboard cover)		
LP(P)	**JOHN'S COUNTRY QUARTET** (67)	Wango 104	$25
	(Promo only, no cardboard cover)		
LP(P)	**JOHN'S GOSPEL QUARTET** Vol 2 (67)	Wango 105	$25
	(Promo only, no cardboard cover)		
LP(P)	**SONGS OF MOTHER & HOME** (67)	Wango 106	$25
	(Promo only, no cardboard cover)		
	See the Stanley Brothers		

BROWNIE JOHNSON (R)

-singles-

45rpm	**THE SUN WOULD NEVER SHINE** (58)	Lynn 101	$60

CLIFF JOHNSON (RB)

-singles-

45rpm	**GO 'WAY HOUND DOG** (58)	Columbia 40865	$50
45(P)	**GO 'WAY HOUND DOG** (58)	Columbia 40865	$40
	(White promo label)		

HOYT JOHNSON (RB)

-singles-

45rpm	**EENIE MEANY MINIE MOE** (58)	Erwin 555	$25

JIM JOHNSON (RB)

-singles-

45rpm	**MEAN WOMAN BLUES** (58)	Midwest 1002	$80

JOE JOHNSON (RB)

-singles-

45rpm	**RATTLESNAKE DADDY** (57)	Acme 47	$50
	(Silver label)		
45rpm	**RATTLESNAKE DADDY** (57)	Acme 47	$40
	(Orange label)		

RALPH JOHNSON (RB)

-singles-

45rpm	**HENPECKED DADDY** (58)	Ralph Johnson 639	$175

RAY JOHNSON (RB)

-singles-

45rpm	**GONNA ROLL LUCKY SEVEN TONIGHT** (58)	Blend 1002	$75
45rpm	**DIZZY, BABY, DIZZY** (58)	Liberty 55135	$18
45(P)	**DIZZY, BABY, DIZZY** (58)	Liberty 55135	$15
	(White promo label)		

THE JOHNSON FAMILY SINGERS (G)

-singles-

78rpm	**SHIFTING, WHISPERING SANDS** (55)	RCA Victor 6243	$15
78(P)	**SHIFTING, WHISPERING SANDS** (55)	RCA Victor 6243	$10
	(White promo label)		
45rpm	**SHIFTING, WHISPERING SANDS** (55)	RCA Victor 6243	$15
45(P)	**SHIFTING, WHISPERING SANDS** (55)	RCA Victor 6243	$12
	(White promo label)		

-albums-

LP	**OLD TIME RELIGION** (54)	RCA Victor 1128	$25

DON JOHNSTON (RB)

-singles-

45rpm	**BORN TO LOVE ONE WOMAN** (59)	Mercury 70991	$18
45(P)	**BORN TO LOVE ONE WOMAN** (59)	Mercury 70991	$15
	(White promo label)		

JOKERS (RB)

-singles-

45rpm	**LITTLE MAMA** (58)	Grace 510	$100

JOLLY LUMBERJACKS (Polka)
Other yellow label Soma 45s $6 each
Black label Soma 45s $5 each
Other label 45s $5-10 each

-singles-

45rpm	**BECAUSE YOU LOVE ME** (54)	Soma 1012	$15
45rpm	**TELL ME WALTZ** (55)	Soma 1015	$15
45rpm	**COTTAGE WALTZ** (55)	Soma 1016	$12
45rpm	**HI-LO WALTZ** (56)	Soma 1020	$12
45rpm	**GRANDMOTHER'S JOY WALTZ** (56)	Soma 1021	$12

ANN JONES (CW)
And Her American Sweethearts

-albums-

LP	**ANN JONES & HER AMERICAN SWEETHEARTS** (59)	Audio Lab 1521	$100
LP	**HIT & RUN** (60)	Audio Lab 1556	$100

ANTHONY ARMSTRONG JONES (C)
Chart 45s $3 each

-albums-

LP	**PROUD MARY** (69)	Chart 1019	$15
LP	**TAKE A LETTER MARIA** (70)	Chart 1027	$15
LP	**SUGAR IN THE FLOWERS** (70)	Chart 1036	$12
LP	**GREATEST HITS VOL 1** (71)	Chart 1047	$12

CHUCK JONES (RB)

-singles-

45rpm	**YOU'RE THE MOST** (58)	Belle Meade 1903	$15
45rpm	**BERTIE** (58)	Belle Meade 425	$10

CORKY JONES (RB)
Better known as Buck Owens

-singles-

45rpm	**HOT DOG** (56)	Prep 107	$100
	See Buck Owens		

DOTTIE JONES (CW)
Sarg 45s $6-10 each

GEORGE JONES (CW)
Thumper Jones
Hank Smith
Other Mercury 45s $4-8 each
Mercury Celebrity Series 45s $4 each
Mercury Celebrity Series promo 45s $5 each
United Artists 400-500 series 45s $6 each
Other United Artists 45s $3-6 each
Musicor 45s $3-5 each
Musicor 45s by George and Gene $4-6 each
  (With Gene Pitney)
Epic 45s $2-4 each
  (Including duets)
Epic picture sleeves $3 each
MCA duet 45s $2 each
Other duet 45s on other labels $2 each
Other Musicor (Musicor/RCA) LPs $4-8 each
  (Including duet LPs)
Unart LPs $10 each
Epic LPs from 70s $5-10 each
Epic promo LPs from 70s $6-12 each
Epic LPs from 80s $3-6 each
  (Including duets LPs)
RCA Victor LPs $4-8 each
Columbia LPs $4-8 each
  (Including duet LPs)
Liberty duet LPs $6 each
K-Tel, Hilltop, Buckboard, Time-Life, 51 West LPs, Allegiance, Ambassador, Rounder, Sunrise, Power Pak,
  Music Disc, Everest, Gusto, Album Globe, Trolly Car, Phoenix 10, Picadilly, Koala, Ruby, Trip,
  Accord, Grass Country, I & M, Design, International Award and TVP LPs $3 each
  (Mostly budget labels)
Other Mountain Dew and Nashville LPs $3 each

-singles-

78rpm	**NO MONEY IN THIS DEAL** (53)	Starday 130	$40
45rpm	**NO MONEY IN THIS DEAL** (53)	Starday 130	$50
78rpm	**PLAY IT COOL MAN- PLAY IT COOL** (53)	Starday 146	$30
45rpm	**PLAY IT COOL MAN- PLAY IT COOL** (53)		
	(Flip side is "Wrong About You" by George Jones and Sonny Burns)		
78rpm	**YOU ALL GOODNIGHT** (54)	Starday 162	$25
45rpm	**YOU ALL GOODNIGHT** (54)	Starday 162	$30
78rpm	**TELL HER** (54)	Starday 165	$25

45rpm	**TELL HER** (54) (Flip side is "Heartbroken Me" by George Jones and Sonny Burns)	Starday 165	$30
78rpm	**HOLD EVERYTHING** (55)	Starday 188	$20
45rpm	**HOLD EVERYTHING** (55)	Starday 188	$25
78rpm	**WHY, BABY, WHY** (55)	Starday 202	$30
45rpm	**WHY, BABY, WHY** (55)	Starday 202	$25
78rpm	**WHAT AM I WORTH** (56)	Starday 216	$20
45rpm	**WHAT AM I WORTH** (56)	Starday 216	$25
78rpm	**I'M RAGGED BUT I'M RIGHT** (56)	Starday 234	$20
45rpm	**I'M RAGGED BUT I'M RIGHT** (56)	Starday 234	$25
78rpm	**ROCK IT** (56) Thumper Jones	Starday 240	$125
45rpm	**ROCK IT** (56) (A rockabilly song)	Starday 240	$100
78rpm	**YOU GOTTA BE MY BABY** (56)	Starday 247	$20
45rpm	**YOU GOTTA BE MY BABY** (56)	Starday 247	$25
78rpm	**TAGGIN' ALONG** (56)	Starday 256	$20
45rpm	**TAGGIN' ALONG** (56)	Starday 256	$25
78rpm	**JUST ONCE MORE** (56)	Starday 264	$20
45rpm	**JUST ONCE MORE** (56)	Starday 264	$25
78rpm	**YEARNING** (56) With Jeanette Hicks	Starday 279	$20
45rpm	**YEARNING** (56) (Flip side is by Jeanette Hicks)	Starday 279	$25
78rpm	**DON'T STOP THE MUSIC** (57)	Mercury 71029	$25
78(P)	**DON'T STOP THE MUSIC** (57) (White promo label)	Mercury 71029	$35
45rpm	**DON'T STOP THE MUSIC** (57)	Mercury 71029	$12
45(P)	**DON'T STOP THE MUSIC** (57) (White promo label)	Mercury 71029	$15
45rpm	**TOO MUCH WATER** (57)	Mercury 71096	$10
45rpm	**FLAME IN MY HEART** (57) (Duet with Virginia Spurlock)	Mercury 71141	$18
45(P)	**FLAME IN MY HEART** (57) (White promo label)	Mercury 71141	$15
45rpm	**COLOR OF THE BLUES** (58)	Mercury 71257	$10
45rpm	**TREASURE OF LOVE** (58)	Mercury 71373	$10
45rpm	**NOTHING CAN STOP ME** (58) (Flip side is duet with Jeanette Hicks)	Mercury 71339	$12
45(P)	**NOTHING CAN STOP ME** (58) (White promo label)	Mercury 71339	$10
45rpm	**IT TAKES A LOTTA LIVIN'** (59)	Decca 30904	$18
45(P)	**IT TAKES A LOTTA LIVIN'** (59) (Pink promo label)	Decca 30904	$15
45rpm	**WHITE LIGHTNING** (59)	Mercury 71406	$15
45(P)	**WHITE LIGHTNING** (59) (White promo label)	Mercury 71406	$18
5-33s	**GEORGE JONES GREATEST HITS** (59-61) Set of five singles (Price is for the set, which includes envelope and color paper title sleeve)	Mercury 60621	$250
	GEORGE JONES GREATEST HITS (59-61) (Price is for just the color paper title sleeve) The individual records are listed below	Mercury 60621	$20
33(S)	**WHITE LIGHTNING** (59) 33rpm compact stereo single (For Jukeboxes, blue label and small center hole)	Mercury 7045	$50
33(S)	**WHY BABY WHY** (59) 33rpm compact stereo single (Blue label, small center hole)	Mercury 7046	$50
33(S)	**THE WINDOW UP ABOVE** (59) 33rpm compact stereo single (Blue label, small center hole)	Mercury 7047	$40
33(S)	**TALL TALL TREES** (59) 33rpm compact stereo single (Blue label, small center hole)	Mercury 7048	$40
33(S)	**WHO SHOT SAM** (59) 33rpm compact stereo single (Blue label, small center hole)	Mercury 7049	$50
45rpm	**WHO SHOT SAM** (59)	Mercury 71464	$12
45(P)	**WHO SHOT SAM** (59) (White promo label)	Mercury 71464	$10
45rpm	**SHE THINKS I STILL CARE** (62) (Price includes picture sleeve)	United Artists 424	$25
45rpm	**TARNISHED ANGEL** (64) (Price includes picture sleeve)	Mercury 72233	$25
45rpm	**THINGS HAVE GONE TO PIECES** (65) (Price includes picture sleeve)	Musicor 1067	$12
45rpm	**LOUISIANA MAN** (65) George Jones and Gene Pitney (Price includes picture sleeve)	Musicor 1097	$20
45rpm	**MAYBE NEXT CHRISTMAS** (65)	D 1226	$10

-EPs-

78EP	**HITS** (56) Hank Smith (With the Nashville Playboys)	Tops 280	$75

45EP	**HITS** (56) Various artists (Four songs, two by Hank Smith, "Blue Suede Shoes" and "Heartbreak Hotel")	Tops 280	$50
78EP	**CRAZY ARMS** (57) Hank Smith (Back side includes "I Take the Chance" with Betsy Green, all cuts feature the Nashville Playboys)	Tops 288	$75
45EP	**CRAZY ARMS** (57) Hank Smith (With the Nashville Playboys)	Tops 288	$50
78EP	**CONSCIENCE I'M GUILTY** (57) Hank Smith (With the Nashville Playboys)	Tops 291	$100
45EP	**CONSCIENCE I'M GUILTY** (57) Hank Smith (Also features Rusty Jones)	Tops 291	$75
78EP	**POOR MAN'S RICHES** (57) Hank Smith (With the Nashville Playboys)	Tops 3001	$125
45EP	**POOR MAN'S RICHES** (57) (Four songs, one by Hank Smith, Poor Man's Riches)	Tops 3001	$100
78EP	**THERE YOU GO/TRAIN OF LOVE** (57) Hank Thomas (With the Nashville Playboys)	Tops 3002	$100
45EP	**THERE YOU GO/TRAIN OF LOVE** (57) (Four songs, two by Hank Thomas & the Nashville Playboys)	Tops 3002	$75
78EP	**SAME TWO LIPS/AM I LOSING YOU** (57) Hank Smith (Other two songs feature the Nashville Playboys)	Tops 3003	$100
45EP	**SAME TWO LIPS/AM I LOSING YOU** (57) (Two songs by Hank Smith on four-song EP)	Tops 3003	$75
78EP	**HONKY TONK SONG** (57) Nashville Ramblers (Author unsure of George Jones/Hank Smith involvement)	Tops 3004	–
45EP	**HONKY TONK SONG** (57) (Three of four songs features Nashville Ramblers)	Tops 3004	–
EP	**EP** (58) Various artists (One George Jones song, "Why Baby Why," no cover)	Dixie 501	$200
EP	**THUMPER JONES** (58) (Songs by Thumper Jones, no cover)	Dixie 502	$175
EP	**EP** (58) Various artists (One George Jones song, "Heartbreak Hotel," no cover)	Dixie 505	$150
EP	**EP** (58) Various artists (One George Jones song, "Don't Do This to Me," no cover)	Dixie 525	$150
EP	**WHITE LIGHTNING** (59) Vol 1	Mercury 3399	$40
EP	**WHITE LIGHTNING** (59) Vol 2	Mercury 3400	$40
EP	**WHITE LIGHTNING** (59) Vol 3	Mercury 3401	$40
EP	**COUNTRY CHURCH TIME** (61) Vol 1	Mercury 4035	$25
EP	**COUNTRY CHURCH TIME** (61) Vol 2	Mercury 4036	$25
EP	**COUNTRY CHURCH TIME** (61) Vol 3	Mercury 4037	$25
EP	**GEORGE JONES GREATEST HITS** (61) Vol 1	Mercury 4048	$30
EP	**GEORGE JONES GREATEST HITS** (61) Vol 2	Mercury 4049	$30
EP	**GEORGE JONES GREATEST HITS** (61) Vol 3	Mercury 4050	$30
EP(P)	**GEORGE JONES** (65) Jukebox LLP (Issued with a hard cover)	Starday 335	$100
EP(P)	**FAN FAIR SPOTS** (76) Various artists (George does two thirty-second ads)	CMA Nashville 699	$20

-Starday albums-

LP	**GRAND OL' OPRY'S NEW STAR** (58) (First and rarest album)	Starday 101	$1,200
LP	**HILLBILLY HIT PARADE** (58) Various artists (Six tracks by George Jones)	Starday 102	$250
LP	**THE CROWN PRINCE OF COUNTRY MUSIC** (60)	Starday 125	$100
LP	**HIS GREATEST HITS** (62)	Starday 150	$40
LP	**THE FABULOUS COUNTRY MUSIC SOUND OF GEORGE JONES** (62)	Starday 151	$40
LP	**GEORGE JONES** (65)	Starday 335	$25
LP	**LONG LIVE KING GEORGE** (65)	Starday 344	$25
LP	**THE GEORGE JONES STORY** (66) (Add $15 for bonus photo)	Starday 366	$25
LP	**SONG BOOK & PICTURE ALBUM** (67) (Add $15 for book)	Starday 401	$25
LP	**GEORGE JONES & DOLLY PARTON** (68)	Starday 429	$25
LP	**THE GOLDEN COUNTRY HITS OF GEORGE JONES** (69)	Starday 440	$25

-Mercury albums-

LP	**SALUTES HANK WILLIAMS** (59) Mono	Mercury 20257	$40
LP	**SALUTES HANK WILLIAMS** (59) Stereo	Mercury 60257	$50
LP(P)	**SALUTES HANK WILLIAMS** (59) (White promo label)	Mercury 20257	$50
LP	**14 COUNTRY FAVORITES** (60) Mono	Mercury 20306	$75
LP	**14 COUNTRY FAVORITES** (60) Stereo	Mercury 60306	$80
LP(P)	**14 COUNTRY FAVORITES** (60) (White promo label)	Mercury 20306	$100
LP	**COUNTRY CHURCH TIME** (59) Mono	Mercury 20462	$100
LP	**COUNTRY CHURCH TIME** (59) Stereo	Mercury 60462	$125

LP(P)	**COUNTRY CHURCH TIME** (59)	Mercury 20462	$125
	(White promo label)		
LP	**WHITE LIGHTNING AND OTHER FAVORITES** (59) Mono	Mercury 20477	$100
LP	**WHITE LIGHTNING AND OTHER FAVORITES** (59) Stereo	Mercury 60477	$125
LP(P)	**WHITE LIGHTNING AND OTHER FAVORITES** (59)	Mercury 20477	$100
	(White promo label)		
LP	**SALUTES HANK WILLIAMS** (60) Mono	Mercury 20596	$40
LP	**SALUTES HANK WILLIAMS** (60) Stereo	Mercury 60596	$50
LP(P)	**SALUTES HANK WILLIAMS** (60)	Mercury 20596	$50
	(White promo label)		
LP	**GEORGE JONES GREATEST HITS** (61) Mono	Mercury 20621	$30
LP	**GEORGE JONES GREATEST HITS** (61) Stereo	Mercury 60621	$40
LP(P)	**GEORGE JONES GREATEST HITS** (61)	Mercury 20621	$40
	(White promo label)		
LP	**COUNTRY AND WESTERN HITS** (61) Mono	Mercury 20624	$30
LP	**COUNTRY AND WESTERN HITS** (61) Stereo	Mercury 60624	$40
LP(P)	**COUNTRY AND WESTERN HITS** (61)	Mercury 20624	$40
	(White promo label)		
LP	**FROM THE HEART** (62) Mono	Mercury 20694	$30
LP	**FROM THE HEART** (62) Stereo	Mercury 60694	$40
LP(P)	**FROM THE HEART** (62)	Mercury 20694	$40
	(White promo label)		
LP	**DUETS COUNTRY STYLE** (62) Mono	Mercury 20747	$30
	(With Margie Singleton)		
LP	**DUETS COUNTRY STYLE** (62) Stereo	Mercury 60747	$40
LP(P)	**DUETS COUNTRY STYLE** (62)	Mercury 20747	$40
	(White promo label)		
LP	**THE NOVELTY SIDE OF GEORGE JONES** (63) Mono	Mercury 20793	$40
LP	**THE NOVELTY SIDE OF GEORGE JONES** (63) Stereo	Mercury 60793	$50
LP(P)	**THE NOVELTY SIDE OF GEORGE JONES** (63)	Mercury 20793	$40
	(White promo label)		
LP	**THE BALLAD SIDE OF GEORGE JONES** (63) Mono	Mercury 20836	$30
LP	**THE BALLAD SIDE OF GEORGE JONES** (63) Stereo	Mercury 60836	$40
LP(P)	**THE BALLAD SIDE OF GEORGE JONES** (63)	Mercury 20836	$40
	(White promo label)		
LP	**BLUE AND LONESOME** (64)	Mercury 60906	$30
	(Stereo versions of many Mercury albums were released on Mercury/Wing)		
LP(P)	**BLUE AND LONESOME** (64)	Mercury 20906	$40
LP	**COUNTRY & WESTERN #1 MALE SINGER** (64)	Mercury 60937	$30
LP(P)	**COUNTRY & WESTERN #1 MALE SINGER** (64)	Mercury 20937	$40
	(White promo label)		
LP	**HEARTACHES AND TEARS** (65)	Mercury 60990	$30
LP(P)	**HEARTACHES AND TEARS** (65)	Mercury 20990	$40
	(White promo label)		
LP	**SINGING THE BLUES** (65)	Mercury 61029	$30
LP(P)	**SINGING THE BLUES** (65)	Mercury 21029	$40
	(White promo label)		
LP	**GEORGE JONES GREATEST HITS VOL 2** (65)	Mercury 61048	$25
LP(P)	**GEORGE JONES GREATEST HITS VOL 2** (65)	Mercury 21048	$35
	(White promo label)		
	-United Artists albums-		
LP	**THE NEW FAVORITES OF GEORGE JONES** (62)	United Artists 6193	$18
LP(P)	**THE NEW FAVORITES OF GEORGE JONES** (62)	United Artists 3193	$25
	(White promo label)		
LP	**SINGS THE HITS OF HIS COUNTRY COUSINS** (62)	United Artists 6218	$18
LP(P)	**SINGS THE HITS OF HIS COUNTRY COUSINS** (62)	United Artists 3218	$25
	(White promo label)		
LP	**HOMECOMING IN HEAVEN** (62)	United Artists 6219	$20
LP(P)	**HOMECOMING IN HEAVEN** (62)	United Artists 3219	$25
	(White promo label)		
LP	**MY FAVORITES OF HANK WILLIAMS** (62)	United Artists 6220	$25
LP(P)	**MY FAVORITES OF HANK WILLIAMS** (62)	United Artists 3220	$30
	(White promo label)		
LP	**GEORGE JONES SINGS BOB WILLS** (62)	United Artists 6221	$25
LP(P)	**GEORGE JONES SINGS BOB WILLS** (62)	United Artists 3221	$30
	(White promo label)		
LP	**I WISH TONIGHT WOULD NEVER END** (63)	United Artists 6270	$18
LP(P)	**I WISH TONIGHT WOULD NEVER END** (63)	United Artists 3270	$25
	(White promo label)		
LP	**THE BEST OF GEORGE JONES** (63)	United Artists 6291	$18
LP(P)	**THE BEST OF GEORGE JONES** (63)	United Artists 3291	$25
	(White promo label)		
LP	**WHAT'S IN OUR HEARTS** (63) With Melba Montgomery	United Artists 6301	$18
LP(P)	**WHAT'S IN OUR HEARTS** (63)	United Artists 3301	$25
	(White promo label)		
LP	**GEORGE JONES SINGS MORE NEW FAVORITES** (64)	United Artists 6338	$20

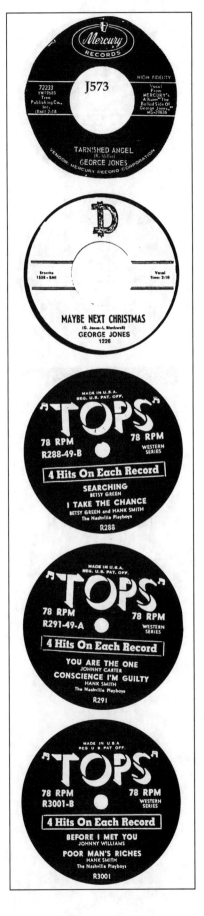

LP(P)	**GEORGE JONES SINGS MORE NEW FAVORITES** (64)	United Artists 3338	$30
	(White promo label)		
LP	**BLUEGRASS HOOTENANNY** (64) With Melba Montgomery	United Artists 6352	$20
LP(P)	**BLUEGRASS HOOTENANNY** (64)	United Artists 3352	$25
	(White promo label)		
LP	**GEORGE JONES SINGS LIKE THE DICKENS** (64)	United Artists 6364	$30
	(Songs of Jimmy Dickens)		
LP(P)	**GEORGE JONES SINGS LIKE THE DICKENS** (64)	United Artists 3364	$40
	(White promo label)		
LP	**A KING & TWO QUEENS** (64)	United Artists 6367	$20
	(With Melba Montgomery and Judy Lynn)		
LP(P)	**A KING & TWO QUEENS** (64)	United Artists 6367	$25
	(White promo label)		
LP	**I GET LONELY IN A HURRY** (64)	United Artists 6388	$18
LP(P)	**I GET LONELY IN A HURRY** (64)	United Artists 3388	$25
	(White promo label)		
LP	**TROUBLE IN MIND** (65)	United Artists 6408	$25
LP(P)	**TROUBLE IN MIND** (65)	United Artists 3408	$30
	(White promo label)		
LP	**THE RACE IS ON** (65)	United Artists 6422	$20
	(Red cover with photo of George)		
LP	**THE RACE IS ON** (65)	United Artists 6422	$18
	(Cartoon cover)		
LP(P)	**THE RACE IS ON** (65)	United Artists 3422	$25
	(White promo label)		
LP	**KING OF BROKEN HEARTS** (65)	United Artists 6442	$20
LP(P)	**KING OF BROKEN HEARTS** (65)	United Artists 3442	$25
	(White promo label)		
LP	**THE GREAT GEORGE JONES** (66)	United Artists 6457	$20
LP(P)	**THE GREAT GEORGE JONES** (66)	United Artists 3457	$25
	(White promo label)		
LP	**BLUE MOON OF KENTUCKY** (66) With Melba Mongomery	United Artists 6472	$15
LP(P)	**BLUE MOON OF KENTUCKY** (66)	United Artists 3472	$18
	(White promo label)		
LP	**GEORGE JONES GOLDEN HITS, VOL 1** (66)	United Artists 6532	$15
LP(P)	**GEORGE JONES GOLDEN HITS, VOL 1** (66)	United Artists 3532	$18
	(White promo label)		
LP	**THE YOUNG GEORGE JONES** (67)	United Artists 6558	$18
LP(P)	**THE YOUNG GEORGE JONES** (67)	United Artists 3558	$25
	(White promo label)		
LP	**GEORGE JONES GOLDEN HITS** (67)	United Artists 6566	$15
LP(P)	**GEORGE JONES GOLDEN HITS** (67)	United Artists 3566	$18
	(White promo label)		

-Musicor albums-

LP	**FOR THE FIRST TIME, TWO GREAT SINGERS** (65) Mono	Musicor 2044	$20
	(With Gene Pitney)		
LP	**FOR THE FIRST TIME, TWO GREAT SINGERS** (65) Stereo	Musicor 3046	$25
	(First pressing)		
LP	**RECORDED IN NASHVILLE** (65) Mono	Musicor 2044	$20
	(Same album as above, different title and cover)		
LP	**RECORDED IN NASHVILLE** (65) Stereo	Musicor 3044	$25
	(With Gene Pitney)		
LP	**MR. COUNTRY AND WESTERN** (65) With Melba Montgomery	Musicor 2046	$15
LP	**NEW COUNTRY HITS** (65)	Musicor 2060	$20
	(Mono numbers are listed, stereo numbers run in the 3000 series and have the same value)		
LP	**OLD BRUSH ARBORS** (66)	Musicor 2061	$20
LP	**IT'S COUNTRY TIME AGAIN** (66) With Gene Pitney	Musicor 2065	$20
	(The Jordanaires are on all Jones/Pitney albums)		
LP	**FAMOUS COUNTRY DUETS** (66) With Melba Montgomery	Musicor 2079	$18
	(Also features Gene Pitney)		
LP	**LOVE BUG** (66)	Musicor 2088	$20
LP	**COUNTRY HEART** (66)	Musicor 5094	$20
LP	**I'M A PEOPLE** (66)	Musicor 2099	$20
LP	**WE FOUND HEAVEN RIGHT HERE ON EARTH** (66)	Musicor 2106	$18
LP	**CLOSE TOGETHER AS YOU AND ME** (67)	Musicor 2109	$15
	(With Melba Montgomery)		
LP	**GEORGE JONES GREATEST HITS** (67)	Musicor 2116	$15
LP	**WALK THROUGH THIS WORLD WITH ME** (67)	Musicor 2119	$18
LP	**CUP OF LONELINESS** (67)	Musicor 2124	$18
LP	**LET'S GET TOGETHER** (67) With Melba Montgomery	Musicor 2127	$15
LP	**HITS BY GEORGE** (67)	Musicor 2128	$18
LP	**THE SONGS OF DALLAS FRAZIER** (68)	Musicor 3149	$15
	(All Musicor albums are now stereo only)		
LP	**IF MY HEART HAD WINDOWS** (68)	Musicor 3158	$15
2LP	**THE MUSICAL LOVES, LIFE AND SORROWS OF AMERICA'S GREAT COUNTRY STAR** (68)	Musicor 3159	$20
LP	**MY COUNTRY** (69)	Musicor 3169	$15

LP	I'LL SHARE MY WORLD WITH YOU (69)	Musicor 3177	$15
LP	WHERE GRASS WON'T GROW (69)	Musicor 3181	$15
LP	WILL YOU VISIT ME ON SUNDAY? (70)	Musicor 3188	$15
LP	THE BEST OF GEORGE JONES (70)	Musicor 3191	$12
LP	WITH LOVE (71)	Musicor 3194	$15
LP	THE BEST OF SACRED MUSIC (71)	Musicor 3203	$15
LP	THE GREAT SONGS OF LEON PAYNE (71)	Musicor 3204	$15

-other albums-

LP	GEORGE JONES & MELBA MONTGOMERY (68)	Guest Star 1465	$25
	(Budget label)		
LP	MAYBE LITTLE BABY (70s)	Sears 125	$15
LP	THE ONE & ONLY GEORGE JONES (70s)	White Lightning	$12
	(Budget label)		
LP	SEASONS OF MY HEART (70s)	Nashville 2076	$12
LP	THE RACE IS ON (70s)	Camden 0377	$10
LP	ROCK-IT (70s) Thumper Jones	Teenage Heaven 676	$18
LP	FLOWERS FOR MAMA (72)	Camden 2591	$15
2LP	WE GO TOGETHER (75) With Tammy Wynette	Epic 33752	$12
2LP(P)	WE GO TOGETHER (75)	Epic 33752	$15
	(White promo label)		

-radio shows-

2LP(RS)	RADIO INTERVIEW PROGRAM (73) With Tammy Wynette		$25-50
	(Music and interviews)		
16"(RS)	LEATHERNECK JAMBOREE (60s)	Leatherneck Jamboree 18	$125-150
	(Music and interviews)		
3LP(RS)	THE SILVER EAGLE (81) With Marshall Tucker Band	DIR 010	$75-125
	(Live concert)		
3LP(RS)	THE SILVER EAGLE (81) With Ronnie Milsap	DIR	$75-150
	(Live concert)		
3LP(RS)	THE SILVER EAGLE (May 84) With Little Jimmie Dickens	DIR	$75-150
	(Live concert)		
3LP(RS)	THE SILVER EAGLE (July 85) With Tammy Wynette	DIR	$50-100
	(Live concert)		
3LP(RS)	THE SILVER EAGLE (Dec 85)	DIR	$50-100
	(Live from the Austin Opera House)		
LP(RS)	COUNTRY SESSIONS (82)	NBC Radio	$40-75
	(Live concert)		
LP(RS)	LIVE FROM GILLEY'S (July 81)	Westwood One	$25-50
	(Live concert)		
LP(RS)	LIVE FROM GILLEY'S (Apr 82)	Westwood One	$25-50
	(Live concert)		
LP(RS)	LIVE FROM GILLEY'S (June 84)	Westwood One	$30-60
	(Live concert)		
LP(RS)	LIVE FROM GILLEY'S (Aug 85)	Westwood One	$40-75
	(Live concert)		
LP(RS)	LIVE FROM GILLEY'S (July 87)	Westwood One	$40-75
	(Live concert)		
LP(RS)	LIVE FROM GILLEY'S (Feb 88)	Westwood One	$40-75
	(Live concert)		
LP(RS)	LIVE FROM GILLEY'S (Oct 90)	Westwood One	$30-60
	(Live concert)		
3LP(RS)	THE AMERCIAN EAGLE (Jan 87) With Tammy Wynette	DIR	$75-100
	(Live concert)		
3LP(RS)	THE AMERICAN EAGLE (Apr 87) With Dwight Yoakam	DIR	$75-150
	(Live concert)		
LP(RS)	WESTWOOD ONE PRESENTS (June 87)	Westwood One	$40-75
	(Live concert)		
LP(RS)	WESTWOOD ONE PRESENTS (June 89)	Westwood One	$30-60
	(Live concert)		
LP(RS)	WESTWOOD ONE PRESENTS (Mar 90)	Westwood One	$30-60
	(Live concert)		

GRANDPA JONES Listed under Grandpa

LITTLE MONTE JONES (RB)

-singles-

45rpm	YOU'RE JUST THAT KIND (58)	Jean 100	$100

STAN JONES (CW)
Sons of the Pioneers

-albums-

LP	CREAKIN' LEATHER (60)	Buena Vista 3015	$25
	(Disneyland label)		
LP	CREAKIN' LEATHER (60)	Disneyland 3015	$15
LP	GHOST RIDERS IN THE SKY (61)	Buena Vista 3306	$20
	(Jones wrote this cowboy classic)		

THUMPER JONES Listed under George Jones

THE JORDANAIRES (All)

Gordon Stoker, Neal Matthews, Hoyt Hawkins, Hugh Jarrett, and Ray Walker
On more records than any individual or group in history!
    The Jordanaires have recorded on almost every major label and have backed many top singers in their forty-year history, including Elvis Presley, Roy Acuff, Patsy Cline, George Jones, Marty Robbins, Hank Snow, and hundreds of others!
-As the Jordanaires-
Capitol 78s $4-6 each
Other Capitol 45s $3-5 each

-singles-

45rpm	**PEACE IN THE VALLEY** (51) Purple label	Decca 14530	$15
	(Decca Faith Series)		
45rpm	**READ THAT BOOK** (51)	Capitol 1499	$15
45rpm	**BUGLE CALL FROM HEAVEN** (53)	Capitol 2815	$15
45(P)	**BUGLE CALL FROM HEAVEN** (53)	Capitol 2815	$10
	(White promo label)		
45rpm	**THIS OLD HOUSE** (54)	Capitol 2915	$12
45(P)	**THIS OLD HOUSE** (54)	Capitol 2915	$10
	(White promo label)		
45rpm	**ROCK 'N ROLL RELIGION** (56)	Capitol 3420	$12
45(P)	**ROCK 'N ROLL RELIGION** (56)	Capitol 3420	$10
	(White promo label)		
45rpm	**SUGAREE** (57)	Capitol 3610	$12
	(Written by Marty Robbins)		
45(P)	**SUGAREE** (57)	Capitol 3610	$10
	(White promo label)		
45(P)	**SUGAREE** (57)	Capitol 3610	$15
	(Photo of the group on yellow promo label)		
45rpm	**WELLA WELLA HONEY** (58)	Capitol 4025	$12
45(P)	**WELLA WELLA HONEY** (58)	Capitol 4025	$10
	(White promo label)		

-EPs-

2EP	**BEAUTIFUL CITY** (53)	RCA Victor 3081	$20
EP	**THE JORDANAIRES** (55)	Capitol 610	$18
EP	**HEAVENLY SPIRIT** (58)	Capitol 1-1011	$15
EP	**HEAVENLY SPIRIT** (58)	Capitol 2-1011	$15
EP	**HEAVENLY SPIRIT** (58)	Capitol 3-1011	$15
EP	**GLORYLAND** (59)	Capitol 1-1167	$12
EP	**GLORYLAND** (59)	Capitol 2-1167	$12
EP	**GLORYLAND** (59)	Capitol 3-1167	$12
EP	**LAND OF JORDAN** (60)	Capitol 1-1311	$10
EP	**LAND OF JORDAN** (60)	Capitol 2-1311	$10
EP	**LAND OF JORDAN** (60)	Capitol 3-1311	$10
EP(P)	**THE JORDANAIRES** (55)	Sesac AD-46	$25
	(Promo-only release)		

-albums-

10"LP	**BEAUTIFUL CITY** (53)	RCA Victor 3081	$50
LP(P)	**OF RIVERS AND PLAINS** (55)	Sesac 1401/1402	$40
	(Promo-only release)		
LP	**PEACE IN THE VALLEY** (57)	Decca 8681	$25
LP(P)	**PEACE IN THE VALLEY** (57)	Decca 8681	$30
	(Pink promo label)		
LP	**HEAVENLY SPIRIT** (58)	Capitol 1011	$25
LP(P)	**HEAVENLY SPIRIT** (58)	Capitol 1011	$30
	(Yellow promo label)		
LP	**GLORYLAND** (59)	Capitol 1167	$20
LP(P)	**GLORYLAND** (59)	Capitol 1167	$25
	(Yellow promo label)		
LP	**LAND OF JORDAN** (60)	Capitol 1311	$20
LP(P)	**LAND OF JORDAN** (60)	Capitol 1311	$25
	(Yellow promo label)		
LP	**TO GOD BE THE GLORY** (61) With Ray Walker	Capitol 1559	$20
LP(P)	**TO GOD BE THE GLORY** (61)	Capitol 1559	$25
	(Capitol promo label)		
LP	**SPOTLIGHT ON THE JORDANAIRES** (62)	Capitol 1742	$25
	(Hits they backed other artists on)		
LP(P)	**SPOTLIGHT ON THE JORDANAIRES** (62)	Capitol 1742	$30
	(Capitol promo label)		
LP	**THIS LAND** (64)	Columbia 9014	$20
LP(P)	**THIS LAND** (64)	Columbia 9014	$25
	(White promo label)		
LP	**THE BIG COUNTRY HITS** (66)	Columbia 2458	$20
LP(P)	**THE BIG COUNTRY HITS** (66)	Columbia 2458	$25
	(White promo label)		
LP	**CHRISTMAS TO ELVIS** (78)	Classic 1935	$15
	(With Scotty Moore and D. J. Fontana)		

-radio shows-

16"(RS)	**U.S. ARMY** (60s)	U.S. Army	$25-50
	(Music and interviews)		
16"(RS)	**COUNTRY STYLE USA** (60s)	Country Style 196	$25-40
	(Music and interviews)		
16"(RS)	**COUNTRY STYLE USA** (60s)	Country Style 210	$25-40
	(Music and interviews)		
16"(RS)	**COUNTRY STYLE USA** (60s)	Country Style 220	$25-40
	(Music and interviews)		
LP(RS)	**COUNTRY MUSIC TIME** (65)	U.S. Air Force 249	$25-50
	(Music and interviews, flip side is the Wilburn Brothers)		
LP(RS)	**COUNTRY MUSIC TIME** (60s)	U.S. Air Force	$10-20
	(Flip side features Tommy Jackson)		
LP(RS)	**COUNTRY MUSIC TIME** (60s)	U.S. Air Force	$15-30
	(Flip side features Ray Price)		
LP(RS)	**COUNTRY MUSIC TIME** (60s)	U.S. Air Force	$20-40
	(Flip side features Patsy Cline)		
LP(RS)	**COUNTRY MUSIC TIME** (60s)	U.S. Air Force	$10-20
	(Flip side features Jimmy Newman)		
LP(RS)	**COUNTRY MUSIC TIME** (66)	U.S. Air Force 309	$25-50
	(Music and interviews, flip side is Mac Wiseman)		
LP(RS)	**COUNTRY MUSIC TIME** (Feb 82)	U.S. Air Force	$10-15
	(Music and interviews, flip is Tom Grant)		
	The Jordanaires have backed almost every major artist in this book		

BENNIE JOY (RB)

-singles-

45rpm	**CRASH THE PARTY** (58)	Antler 41	$60
45rpm	**STEADY WITH BETTY** (58)	Dixie 2001	$65
45rpm	**ITTIE BITTIE EVERYTHING** (59)	Ram 1107	$45
45rpm	**SPIN THE BOTTLE** (59)	Tri Dec 8667	$55

CEE CEE JOY (CW)

-singles-

33rpm	**WHOLE LOTTA LOVIN'** (58) 33rpm compact single	Columbia 41815	$10
	(Yellow label, small center hole)		

THE JUDDS (C)
Wynonna and Naomi Judd
RCA Victor 45s $1 each
MCA 45s by Wynonna $1 each
RCA Victor LPs $2-4 each
MCA LPs by Wynonna $3 each

-singles-

45(P)	**HAD A DREAM** (83)	RCA Victor 13673	$10
	(Gold label, red vinyl)		

-albums-

LP(RS)	**COUNTRY MUSIC TIME** (80s)	U.S. Air Force	$10-20
	(Music and interviews)		
LP(RS)	**LIVE FROM GILLEY'S** (Dec 84)	Westwood One	$50-100
	(Rare live concert)		
3LP(RS)	**THE SILVER EAGLE** (Oct 84) With Earl Thomas Conley	DIR	$50-100
	(Live concert)		
3LP(RS)	**THE SILVER EAGLE** (Apr 85) With Vern Gosden	DIR	$40-75
	(Live concert)		
3LP(RS)	**THE SILVER EAGLE** (Sept 85) With Sawyer Brown	DIR	$50-100
	(Live concert)		
3LP(RS)	**THE SILVER EAGLE** (Nov 85)	DIR	$50-100
	(Live from Hampton, Virginia)		
LP(RS)	**LIVE FROM DISNEY WORLD** (July 86) With Exile	NBC Radio	$40-75
	(Live concert)		
3LP(RS)	**THE JUDDS CHRISTMAS PRESENT** (Dec 87)	Westwood One	$50-100
	(Mostly music and interviews, some rare unreleased tracks are included)		
3LP(RS)	**THE JUDDS STORY** (May 89)		$40-75
	(Music and interviews)		
LP(RS)	**BEST OF WESTWOOD ONE** (Oct 89) With T. Graham Brown	Westwood One	$40-75
	(Live concert, also Desert Rose Band)		
LP(RS)	**WESTWOOD ONE PRESENTS** (June 90)	Westwood One	$40-75
	(Live concert)		
3LP(RS)	**FAREWELL TO THE JUDDS** (Aug 91)		$40-75
	(Music and interviews)		

VARIOUS ARTISTS

-radio shows-

3LP(RS)	**JULY 4TH SILVER EAGLE SALUTE TO AMERICA** (Jun 85)	DIR	$40-75
	(Live concert)		

K

KALIN TWINS (R)

-singles-

45rpm	**WALKIN' TO SCHOOL** (58)	Decca 30552	$15
45(P)	**WALKIN' TO SCHOOL** (59)	Decca 30552	$10
	(Pink promo label)		
45rpm	**WHEN** (58)	Decca 30642	$15
45(P)	**WHEN** (58)	Decca 30642	$18
	(Pink promo label)		
45(P)	**WHEN** (58)	Decca 30642	$20
	(Green promo label)		

-EPs-

EP	**THE KALIN TWINS** (58)	Decca 2623	$18

-albums-

LP	**THE KALIN TWINS** (58)	Decca 8812	$100
LP(P)	**THE KALIN TWINS** (58)	Decca 8812	$75
	(Pink promo label)		

HILLARY KANTER (C)
RCA Victor promo yellow vinyl 45s $6 each
Other RCA Victor 45s $2 each

RAMSEY KEARNEY (RB)

-singles-

45rpm	**ROCK THE BOP** (58)	Jaxon 501	$50

MURRY KELLUM (C)

-singles-

45(P)	**MEMPHIS SUN** (78) Green vinyl	Sun 176	$10
	(Tribute song to Sun's artists in the '50s and '60s)		

JIMMY KELLY (RB)

-singles-

45rpm	**LITTLE CHICKIE** (57)	Cobra 5028	$12

PAT KELLY (RB)

-singles-

45rpm	**THE STRANGER DRESSED IN BLACK** (57)	Chic 1009	$12
45rpm	**HEY DOLL BABY** (58)	Jubilee 5315	$25
45(P)	**HEY DOLL BABY** (58)	Jubilee 5315	$20
	(White promo label)		

KENDALLS (C)
Royce and Jeannie Kendall
Stop 45s $3 each
Ovation 45s $1-2 each
Mercury 45s $1 each
Dot 45s $2 each
Ovation and Mercury LPs $2-4 each
Gusto and Power Pak LPs $2 each

-albums-

LP	**MEET THE KENDALLS** (70)	Stop 1020	$15
LP	**TWO DIVIDED BY LOVE** (72)	Dot 26001	$10

-radio shows-

LP(RS)	**LIVE FROM GILLEY'S** (Feb 87)	Westwood One	$10-20
	(Live concert)		

DAVE KENNEDY (CW)
The Dave Kennedy Group
With the Ambassadors
Other Cuca 45s $8 each

-singles-

45rpm	**JOANIE** (59) With Rose Marie	Cuca 1004	$15
45rpm	**WOODEN HEART** (60)	Cuca 1036	$25
	(Red label, "You Didn't Listen" on flip)		

45rpm	**YOU DON'T HAVE A WOODEN HEART** (61) Linda Hall	Cuca 1044	$20
	(Flip side is "Treat Me Nice")		
45rpm	**LITTLE RED RENTED ROWBOAT** (62)	Cuca 1093	$15

JERRY KENNEDY (C)
Played lead guitar on Elvis songs
Half of Tom & Jerry (On Mercury)
(Tom is Charlie Tomlinson)
One of the great producers of country music

-albums-

LP	**GUITAR'S GREATEST HITS** (61) Mono	Mercury 20626	$18
	(Tom & Jerry)		
LP	**GUITAR'S GREATEST HITS** (61) Stereo	Mercury 60626	$25
LP(P)	**GUITAR'S GREATEST HITS** (61)	Mercury 20626	$30
	(White promo label)		
LP	**GUITARS PLAY THE SOUND OF RAY CHARLES** (62) Mono	Mercury 20671	$18
	(Tom & Jerry)		
LP	**GUITARS PLAY THE SOUND OF RAY CHARLES** (62) Stereo	Mercury 60671	$25
LP(P)	**GUITARS PLAY THE SOUND OF RAY CHARLES** (62)	Mercury 20671	$25
	(White promo label)		
LP	**GUITAR'S GREATEST HITS VOL 2** (62) Mono	Mercury 20756	$18
	(Tom & Jerry)		
LP	**GUITAR'S GREATEST HITS VOL 2** (62) Stereo	Mercury 60756	$25
LP(P)	**GUITAR'S GREATEST HITS VOL 2** (62)	Mercury 20756	$25
	(White promo label)		
LP	**SURFIN' HOOTENANNY** (63) Mono	Mercury 20842	$25
	(Tom & Jerry)		
LP	**SURFIN' HOOTENANNY** (62) Stereo	Mercury 60842	$30
LP(P)	**SURFIN' HOOTENANNY** (62)	Mercury 20842	$35
	(White promo label)		
LP	**FROM NASHVILLE TO SOULVILLE** (65)	Smash 67006	$15
LP	**GUITARS & STRINGS PLAY THE GOLDEN STANDARDS** (63)	Smash 67024	$15
LP	**JERRY KENNEDY PLAYS** (71)	Mercury 61339	$12

KEN KENNINGTON (RB)
-singles-

45rpm	**IT GOES WITHOUT SAYING** (58)	Confederate 130	$20

KENNY & DOOLITTLE (RB)
-singles-

45rpm	**KITTY KAT** (57)	Sims 123	$65

KENTUCKY COLONELS (BG)
Sierra-Briar LPs $5-10 each
Liberty LPs $5 each
Rounder LPs $4 each

-albums-

LP	**APPALACHIAN SWING** (64)	World Pacific 1821	$50
LP	**LIVIN' IN THE PAST** (75)	Briar 7202	$30
LP	**THE NEW SOUNDS OF BLUEGRASS AMERICA** (76)	Briar 109	$40
LP	**KENTUCKY COLONELS** (78)	Shiloh 4048	$15

DOUG KERSHAW See Rusty & Doug

KID THOMAS (RB)
-singles-

45rpm	**ROCKIN' THIS JOINT TONIGHT** (58)	Transcontinental 1012	$50

KIDD ROCK (RB)
-singles-

45rpm	**LOOK WHAT YOU HAVE DONE** (58)	Arno 100	$50

KIDS FROM TEXAS (RB)
-singles-

45rpm	**LONG LEGGED LINDA** (58)	Hanover 4500	$25
45(P)	**LONG LEGGED LINDA** (58)	Hanover 4500	$18
	(White promo label)		

MERLE KILGORE (CW)
Starday 45s $4 each
Mercury 45s $5 each
Elektra 45s $2 each

-singles-

45rpm	**EVERYBODY NEEDS A LITTLE LOVIN'** (57)	Imperial 8300	$30
45(P)	**EVERYBODY NEEDS A LITTLE LOVIN'** (57)	Imperial 8300	$25
	(Imperial promo label)		

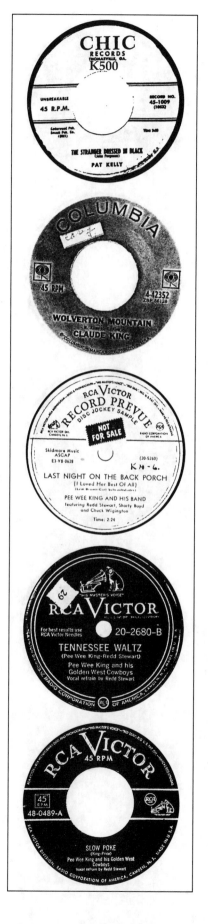

45rpm	**ERNIE** (57)		Imperial 5409	$30
45(P)	**ERNIE** (57)		Imperial 5409	$20
	(Cream-colored promo label)			
45rpm	**HANG DOLL** (58)		Imperial 5555	$15
45(P)	**HANG DOLL** (58)		Imperial 5555	$12
	(Cream-colored promo label)			

-albums-

LP	**THERE'S GOLD IN THEM THAR HILLS** (63)		Starday 251	$25
LP	**MERLE KILGORE, THE TALL TEXAN** (66)		Mercury/Wing 16316	$18
LP	**BIG MERLE KILGORE** (73)		Starday 479	$15

-radio shows-

LP(RS)	**COUNTRY MUSIC TIME** (70s)		U.S. Air Force	$10-15
	(Music and interviews)			

TED KILLEN (RB)

-singles-

45rpm	**HEY PRETTY WOMAN** (57)		Western Ranch 119	$50

BRADLEY KINCAID (CW)
The Kentucky Mountain Boy
Bluebonnet LPs $6-10 each
Round Robin, Old Homestad LPs $4-8 each

-EPs-

EP	**SINGS AMERICAN BALLADS & FOLK SONGS** (56)		Varsity 60	$18
EP	**SINGS AMERICAN BALLADS & FOLK SONGS** (56)		Varsity 61	$18

-albums-

10"LP	**AMERICAN BALLADS** (55)		Varsity 6988	$30
LP	**SINGS AMERICAN BALLADS & FOLK SONGS** (57)		Varsity 34	$20

CLAUDE KING (C)
Other Columbia 45s $3-6 each
Columbia picture sleeves $5 each
True 45s $1 each
Other Columbia LPs $5-10 each
Gusto and True LPs $4-8 each

-singles-

45rpm	**WOLVERTON MOUNTAIN** (62)		Columbia 42352	$10
	(Number one on country charts two months)			
45(P)	**WOLVERTON MOUNTAIN** (62)		Columbia 42352	$15
	(White promo label)			
45rpm	**THE BURNING OF ATLANTA** (63)		Columbia 42581	$10
	(Price includes picture sleeve)			

-albums-

LP	**MEET CLAUDE KING** (62)		Columbia 8610	$20
LP(P)	**MEET CLAUDE KING** (62)		Columbia 8610	$25
	(White promo label)			
LP	**TIGER WOMAN** (65)		Columbia 9215	$15
LP	**THE BEST OF CLAUDE KING** (68)		Harmony 11300	$15
LP(P)	**THE BEST OF CLAUDE KING** (68)		Harmony 11300	$18
	(White promo label)			

JESSE LEE KING (RB)

-singles-

45rpm	**ROCK AND ROLL ROVER** (57)		Pines 652	$100
45rpm	**ROCK AND ROLL ROVER** (58)		Pine 101	$100

PEE WEE KING (CW)
Featuring Redd Stewart
Other RCA Victor 78s $5-10 each
Other RCA Victor 45s $6-10 each
Top Rank 45s $6 each
Jaro 45s $5 each
Capitol 45s $4 each
Starday 45s $4 each
Landa 45s $3 each

-singles-

78rpm	**TENNESSEE WALTZ** (48)		RCA Victor 2680	$15
45rpm	**TENNESSEE WALTZ** (48) Aqua label		RCA Victor 2680	$18
78rpm	**TENNESSEE TEARS** (49)		RCA Victor 0037	$15
45rpm	**TENNESSEE TEARS** (49) Aqua label		RCA Victor 0037	$18
78rpm	**TENNESSEE POLKA** (49)		RCA Victor 0085	$15
45rpm	**TENNESSEE POLKA** (49) Aqua label		RCA Victor 0085	$18
45rpm	**BONAPARTE'S RETREAT** (50) Aqua label		RCA Victor 0114	$15
45rpm	**CINCINNATI DANCING PIG** (50) Aqua label		RCA Victor 0379	$25
	(Green vinyl)			
45rpm	**TENNESSEE WALTZ** (51) Aqua label		RCA Victor 0407	$15
	(Reissue charted Top Ten country)			

78rpm	**SLOW POKE** (51)	RCA Victor 0489	$12
	(Number one country record four months, also number one pop song)		
78(P)	**SLOW POKE** (51)	RCA Victor 0489	$18
	(White promo label)		
45rpm	**SLOW POKE** (51) Aqua label	RCA Victor 0489	$18
45rpm	**SILVER AND GOLD** (52) Aqua label	RCA Victor 4458	$20
45rpm	**BUSYBODY** (52)	RCA Victor 4655	$15
45rpm	**TWO-FACED CLOCK** (53)	RCA Victor 4883	$12
45rpm	**TENNESSEE TANGO** (53)	RCA Victor 5009	$12
45rpm	**SCREWBALL** (53)	RCA Victor 5260	$12
45rpm	**CHANGING PARTNERS/BIMBO** (54)	RCA Victor 5537	$15
	(Both sides were Top Ten country)		
45rpm	**HUGGIN' MY PILLOW** (54)	RCA Victor 5632	$12
45rpm	**BACKWARD, TURN BACKWARD** (54)	RCA Victor 5694	$12
45rpm	**TURN AROUND** (55)	RCA Victor 6270	$10
45rpm	**PEEK-A-BOO WALTZ** (56)	RCA Victor 6302	$12
45rpm	**BLUE SUEDE SHOES** (56)	RCA Victor 6450	$18
45rpm	**BALLROOM BABY** (57)	RCA Victor 6666	$15

-albums-

10"LP	**PEE WEE KING** (54)	RCA Victor 3028	$50
10"LP	**PEE WEE KING** (55)	RCA Victor 3071	$50
10"LP	**WALTZES** (55)	RCA Victor 3109	$50
10"LP	**SWING WEST** (55)	RCA Victor 3280	$50
LP	**SWING WEST** (56)	RCA Victor 1237	$40
	(Reissued in 1977)		
LP	**BACK AGAIN** (64)	Starday 965	$20
	(With the New Golden West Cowboys)		
LP	**COUNTRY BARN DANCE** (65)	Camden 876	$20
LP	**BIGGEST HITS** (66)	Capitol 2460	$20
LP	**THE LEGENDARY PEE WEE KING** (67)	Longhorn 1236	$25
LP	**TENNESSEE WALTZ & SLOWPOKE** (70s)	Nashville 2042	$12
	(Budget label)		
LP	**BEST OF PEE WEE KING AND REDD STEWART** (75)	Starday 965	$15
LP	**GOLDEN OLDE TYME DANCES** (75)	Briar 102	$75
	(Pee Wee King and His Lucky Seven)		

RAY KING (G)
With Jack Irwin
Alshire LPs $4-8 each

-albums-

LP	**PEACE IN THE VALLEY** (63)	Somerset 18500	$15

SID KING (RB)
And the Five Strings

-singles-

45rpm	**I LIKE IT** (55)	Columbia 21361	$20
45(P)	**I LIKE IT** (55)	Columbia 21361	$15
	(White promo label)		
45rpm	**DRINKIN' WINE SPO DEE-O-DEE** (56)	Columbia 21403	$25
45(P)	**DRINKIN' WINE SPO DEE-O-DEE** (56)	Columbia 21403	$18
	(White promo label)		
45rpm	**SAG DRAG AND FALL** (56)	Columbia 21449	$18
45(P)	**SAG DRAG AND FALL** (56)	Columbia 21449	$15
	(White promo label)		
45rpm	**MAMA I WANT YOU** (57)	Columbia 21489	$18
45(P)	**MAMA I WANT YOU** (57)	Columbia 21489	$15
	(White promo label)		
45rpm	**BLUE SUEDE SHOES** (57)	Columbia 21503	$25
45(P)	**BLUE SUEDE SHOES** (57)	Columbia 21503	$18
	(White promo label)		
45rpm	**GOOD ROCKIN' BABY** (57)	Columbia 21564	$18
45(P)	**GOOD ROCKIN' BABY** (57)	Columbia 21564	$15
	(White promo label)		
45rpm	**OOBIE DOOBIE** (57)	Columbia 40680	$25
45(P)	**OOBIE DOOBIE** (57)	Columbia 40680	$18
	(White promo label)		
45rpm	**IT'S TRUE, I'M BLUE** (58)	Columbia 40833	$18
45(P)	**IT'S TRUE, I'M BLUE** (58)	Columbia 40833	$15
	(White promo label)		
45rpm	**I'VE GOT THE BLUES** (58)	Columbia 41019	$15
45(P)	**I'VE GOT THE BLUES** (58)	Columbia 41019	$12
	(White promo label)		

PAUL KIRK (RB)

-singles-

45rpm	**READY LITTLE STEADY** (58)	Urania 5006	$50

JACK KITCHES (RB)

-singles-

45rpm	**RED HOT BOOGIE** (58)	(No Name) 12577	$75

SONNY KNIGHT (RB)
Other Dot 78s and 45s $5-10 each

-singles-

45rpm	**ONCE IN A WHILE** (56)	Starla 10	$10
45rpm	**CONFIDENTIAL** (56)	Vita 137	$15
78rpm	**CONFIDENTIAL** (56)	Dot 15507	$18
45rpm	**CONFIDENTIAL** (56) Maroon label	Dot 15507	$10

BUDDY KNOX (R)

-singles-

45rpm	**PARTY DOLL** (57)	Blue Moon 402	$175
	(Only a few hundred copies pressed)		
45rpm	**PARTY DOLL** (57)	Triple D 797	$75
45rpm	**PARTY DOLL** (57)	Roulette 4002	$25
	(Orange roulette label)		
45rpm	**PARTY DOLL** (57)	Roulette 4002	$15
	(Red label)		
45rpm	**ROCK YOUR LITTLE BABY TO SLEEP** (58)	Roulette 4009	$12
78rpm	**HULA LOVE** (58)	Roulette 4018	$40
	(Label mentions "Jamboree")		
45rpm	**HULA LOVE** (58)	Roulette 4018	$20
	(Label mentions "Jamboree")		
45rpm	**HULA LOVE** (58)	Roulette 4018	$15
45rpm	**SWINGIN' DADDY** (58)	Roulette 4042	$10
45rpm	**I THINK I'M GONNA KILL MYSELF** (58)	Roulette 4140	$10
45rpm	**LING-TING-TONG** (59)	Liberty 55305	$30
	(Price includes picture sleeve)		

-EPs-

EP	**BUDDY KNOX** (58)	Roulette 1-301	$500

-albums-

LP	**BUDDY KNOX** (58) Black label	Roulette 25003	$150
	(Price is for first pressing)		
LP	**BUDDY KNOX** (58)	Roulette 25003	$75
	(Multicolored label)		
LP	**BUDDY KNOX AND JIMMY BOWEN** (59)	Roulette 25048	$200
LP	**BUDDY KNOX'S GREATEST HITS** (62) Mono	Liberty 3251	$30
LP	**BUDDY KNOX'S GREATEST HITS** (62) Stereo	Liberty 7251	$40
LP(P)	**BUDDY KNOX'S GREATEST HITS** (62)	Liberty 3251	$50
	(White promo label)		
	See Jimmy Bowen		

FREDDY KOENIG (RB)

-singles-

45rpm	**HEY CLARICE** (58)	Lori 9548	$40

KRIS KRISTOFFERSON (C)
Monument 45s $2 each
Monument LPs $4-6 each

-singles-

45(P)	**WHAT'S IT ALL ABOUT** (70s) Public service show	W. I. A. A.	$12
	(Music and interviews)		

-radio shows-

LP(RS)	**ROBERT KLEIN** (Nov 79) With Janis Ian and Kenny Loggins	Watermark	$50-100
	(Music and interviews)		
3LP(RS)	**THE SILVER EAGLE** (Oct 85) With Waylon Jennings	DIR	$40-75
	(Live concert)		

L

SLEEPY LABEEF (RB)
Tommy LaBeef
Columbia 45s $5-10 each
Other Plantation 45s $3 each
Other Sun 45s $2 each

-singles-

45rpm	**TURN ME LOOSE** (57)	Cresent 102	$100

45rpm	I'M THROUGH (58)		Starday 292	$150
45rpm	I'M THROUGH (58)		Mercury 71112	$75
45(P)	I'M THROUGH (58)		Mercury 71112	$60
	(White promo label)			
45rpm	ALL THE TIME (59)		Mercury 71179	$75
45(P)	ALL THE TIME (59)		Mercury 71179	$60
	(White promo label)			
45rpm	RIDE ON, JOSEPHINE (59) Tommy LaBeef		Wayside 1651	$250
45rpm	WALKIN' SLOWLY (59) Tommy LaBeef		Wayside 1652	$250
45rpm	TORE UP (59) Tommy LaBeef		Wayside 1654	$250
45rpm	RIDE ON, JOSEPHINE (59) Tommy LaBeef		Picture 1937	$100
45(P)	ASPHALT COWBOY (71)		Plantation 66	$12
	(Green promo label, green vinyl)			
45(P)	GOOD ROCKIN' BOOGIE (78)		Sun 1137	$10
	(White promo label, yellow vinyl)			
45(P)	BOOGIE WOOGIE COUNTRY GIRL (79)		Sun 1145	$10
	(Yellow promo label, yellow vinyl)			

-EPs-

EP	BALLAD OF A TEENAGE QUEEN (56) Various Artists		Dixie 530	$100
	(One song by LaBeef, three other artists)			

-albums-

LP	THE BULLS NIGHT OUT (74)		Sun 130	$10
LP	WESTERN GOLD (76)		Sun 138	$12
LP	1977 ROCKABILLY (78)		Sun 1004	$18
	(Yellow vinyl)			
LP	DOWN HOME ROCKABILLY (79)		Sun 1014	$18
	(Yellow vinyl)			
LP	EARLY, RARE & ROCKIN' SIDES (79)		Baron 102	$18

LA COSTA (C)
La Costa Tucker
(Older sister of Tanya Tucker)
Capitol 45s $2-3 each
Capitol LPs $3-6 each

LENNY LACOUR (RB)

-singles-

45rpm	ROCKIN' ROSALIE (57)		Academy 3571	$50

PETER LAFARGE (F)
Folkways LPs $10 each

-albums-

LP	IRA HAYES & OTHER BALLADS (62)		Columbia 8595	$18
LP(P)	IRA HAYES & OTHER BALLADS (62)		Columbia 8595	$25
	(White promo label)			

LAFETS & KITTY (R)

-singles-

45rpm	CAN CAN ROCK AND ROLL (57)		Apollo 520	$60

FRANKIE LAINE (AC,CW)
Only his country records are listed
Mercury 78s $5 each
Columbia 78s $4-6 each
Other Mercury 45s $4-6 each
Other Columbia 45s $3-6 each
Other Columbia EPs $10-15 each
Mercury 10-inch LPs $25 each
Mercury LPs $5-10 each
Other Columbia LPs $4-10 each

-singles-

45rpm	THE CRY OF THE WILD GOOSE (51)		Mercury 5363	$12
45rpm	HIGH NOON (52)		Columbia 39770	$10
45rpm	THE KID'S LAST FIGHT (54)		Columbia 40170	$12
78rpm	MOONLIGHT GAMBLER (56)		Columbia 40780	$18
78(P)	MOONLIGHT GAMBLER (56)		Columbia 40780	$20
	(Columbia promo label)			
45rpm	MOONLIGHT GAMBLER (56)		Columbia 40780	$25
	(Price includes picture sleeve)			
45(P)	MOONLIGHT GAMBLER (56)		Columbia 40780	$10
	(White promo label)			
45rpm	GUNFIGHT AT O. K. CORRAL (57)		Columbia 40916	$12
45(P)	GUNFIGHT AT O. K. CORRAL (57)		Columbia 40916	$10
	(White promo label)			
45rpm	THE 3:10 TO YUMA (57)		Columbia 40962	$12
45(P)	THE 3:10 TO YUMA (57)		Columbia 40962	$10
	(White promo label)			

45rpm	RAWHIDE (58)	Columbia 41230	$12
45(P)	RAWHIDE (58)	Columbia 41230	$10
	(White promo label)		

-EPs-

EP	MOONLIGHT GAMBLER (57)	Columbia 2121	$25

-albums-

LP	ROCKIN' (57)	Columbia 975	$25
LP(P)	ROCKIN' (57)	Columbia 975	$30
	(White promo label)		
LP	HELL BENT FOR LEATHER! (61) Mono	Columbia 1615	$15
LP	HELL BENT FOR LEATHER! (61) Stereo	Columbia 1615	$25
LP	HELL BENT FOR LEATHER! (61)	Columbia 1615	$20
	(White promo label)		

TOMMY LAM (RB)

-singles-

45rpm	SPEED LIMIT (58)	Nabor 103	$60

GENE LA MARR (RB)

-singles-

45rpm	CRAZY LITTLE HOUSE ON THE HILL (58)	Spry 113	$50
45rpm	YOU CAN COUNT ON ME (58)	Spry 114	$50

TONY LAMBERT (RB)

-singles-

45rpm	HOT ROD SCOOTER (57)	Dawn 232	$18
45(P)	HOT ROD SCOOTER (57)	Dawn 232	$15
	(White promo label)		

JIMMY LAMBERTH (RB)

-singles-

45rpm	LATCH ON TO YOUR BABY (58)	Meteor 5044	$60

TONY & JACKIE LAMIE (R)

-singles-

45rpm	WORE TO A FRAZZELL (58)	Sunset 706	$60

DAVE LANDERS (CW)

-singles-

78rpm	I GOT A CINDER IN MY EYE (52)	MGM 11050	$10
45rpm	I GOT A CINDER IN MY EYE (52)	MGM 11050	$20
	(Imitations including Hank Williams)		

DIZZY LANDERS (RB)

-singles-

45rpm	UNCLE JOHN'S BONGOS (58)	Do Ra Me 1412	$35

BUDDY LANDON (RB)

-singles-

45rpm	RAUNCHY LITTLE BABY (57)	Jaguar 3026	$15
45rpm	OH YES (58)	Jaguar 3028	$12

NED LANDRY (SQD)
RCA Victor 45s $5-10 each

BOBBY LANE (RB)

-singles-

45rpm	YOU SHAKE ME (58)	Amco 002	$40

CRISTY LANE (C)
LS, Liberty, and United Artists 45s and LPs $1-2 each

KENNY LANE (RB)

-singles-

45rpm	FROGGY WENT A COURTIN' (58)	Strate-8 1504	$60

RALPH LANE (RB)

-singles-

45rpm	YOU GOTTA SHOW ME (58)	Cowtown	$50

LANE BROTHERS (RB)
RCA Victor 78s and 45s $10 each

-EPs-

EP	THE LANE BROTHERS (58)	RCA Victor 4175	$30

LANGNER SISTERS (C)

-albums-

LP	THE LANGNER SISTERS (66)	Studio City 9011	$30
LP	IT'S THE COUNTRY LIFE FOR ME (67)	Studio City 9012	$25

(A mix of almost-novel Minnesota garage-country-western old-time, and yes, they yodel!)

CURLEY LANGLEY (RB)

-singles-

45rpm	ROCKIN' AND ROLLIN' (58)	Arcadia 110	$75
45rpm	SHE WASN'T YOUR GIRL (58)	Arcadia 111	$75

BILLY LARGE (C)

Columbia 45s $2-3 each
Columbia picture sleeves $6 each

NICOLETTE LARSON (C)

Warner 45s $2-3 each
Other MCA 45s $2 each
MCA and Warner LPs $3 each

-singles-

45(P)	WHAT'S IT ALL ABOUT (May 79) Public service show	W. I. A. A. 474	$12
	(Flip side features Barbara Mandrell)		
45(P)	LET ME BE THE FIRST (86)	MCA 52797	$10
	(White promo label, blue vinyl)		
45(P)	THAT'S HOW YOU KNOW WHEN LOVE'S RIGHT (86)	MCA 52839	$10
	(White promo label, green vinyl)		
45(P)	THAT'S MORE ABOUT LOVE (86)	MCA 52937	$10
	(White promo label, blue vinyl)		

-EPs-

EP(P)	ONE BRIGHT STAR (85)	MCA 17046	$12
	(Promo-only EP also features John Schneider, Steve Wariner, and Jimmy Buffet, price includes picture sleeve)		

-radio shows-

3LP(RS)	THE AMERICAN EAGLE (July 86) With Mel Tillis	DIR	$50-100
	(Live concert)		
3LP(RS)	THE AMERICAN EAGLE (Dec 86)	DIR	$25-50
	(Live concert)		

ROC LA RUE (RB)

-singles-

45rpm	TEENAGE BLUES (58)	Rama 226	$60

LAUREL RIVER VALLEY BOYS (BG)

Judson LPs $8-10 each

-albums-

LP	DANCE ALL NIGHT WITH A BOTTLE IN YOUR HAND (64)	Riverside 7504	$18

ART LAW (RB)

-singles-

45rpm	KITTY KAT ROCK (58)	Gulfstream 1051	$100

BILL LAWRENCE (RB)

-singles-

45rpm	HEY BABY (58)	Freedom 44004	$40

BOBBY LAWSON (R)

-singles-

45rpm	BABY DON'T BE THAT WAY (58)	M.R.C. 600	$40

CURTIS LEACH (CW)

Longhorn 45s $3-5 each

-albums-

LP	INDESCRIBABLE (65)	Longhorn 003	$50

LED ZEPPELIN (R)

Only the group's country song is listed

-singles-

45rpm	HOT DOG (79) Stock copy only	Swan Song 71003	$3-5
	(Flip side of "Fool in the Rain," the promo version doesn't include "Hot Dog," because it is considered a "B" side, also the only item listed by title in this book worth under $10)		

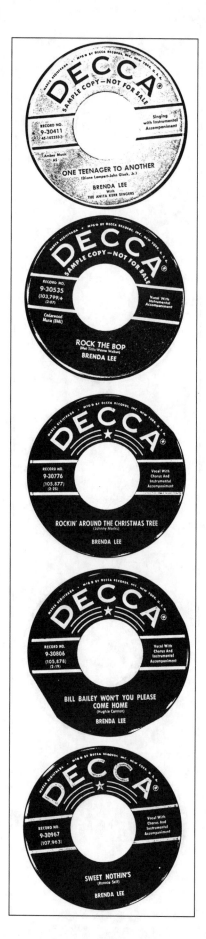

BRENDA LEE (RB)
Other Decca 45s $4-8 each
Other MCA color vinyl 45s $8 each
Other MCA 45s $2 each

-singles-

78rpm	**I AIN'T GONNA GIVE NOBODY NONE** (56)	Apollo 490	$30
78(P)	**I AIN'T GONNA GIVE NOBODY NONE** (56)	Apollo 490	$40
	(White promo label)		
45rpm	**I AIN'T GONNA GIVE NOBODY NONE** (56)	Apollo 490	$50
45(P)	**I AIN'T GONNA GIVE NOBODY NONE** (56)	Apollo 490	$40
	(White promo label)		
78rpm	**BIGELOW 6-200** (56)	Decca 30050	$18
78(P)	**BIGELOW 6-200** (56)	Decca 30050	$25
	(Pink promo label)		
45rpm	**BIGELOW 6-200** (56)	Decca 30050	$18
45(P)	**BIGELOW 6-200** (56)	Decca 30050	$15
	(Pink promo label)		
78rpm	**I'M GONNA LASSO SANTA CLAUS** (56)	Decca 88215	$40
	(Decca Children's Series)		
78rpm	**I'M GONNA LASSO SANTA CLAUS** (56)	Decca 88215	$60
	(Price includes picture sleeve)		
78rpm	**I'M GONNA LASSO SANTA CLAUS** (56)	Decca 30107	$40
78(P)	**I'M GONNA LASSO SANTA CLAUS** (56)	Decca 30107	$50
	(Pink promo label)		
45rpm	**I'M GONNA LASSO SANTA CLAUS** (56)	Decca 30107	$15
45rpm	**I'M GONNA LASSO SANTA CLAUS** (56)	Decca 30107	$40
	(Price includes picture sleeve)		
45(P)	**I'M GONNA LASSO SANTA CLAUS** (56)	Decca 30107	$12
	(Pink promo label)		
78rpm	**ONE STEP AT A TIME** (57)	Decca 30198	$15
78(P)	**ONE STEP AT A TIME** (57)	Decca 30198	$18
	(Pink promo label)		
45rpm	**ONE STEP AT A TIME** (57)	Decca 30198	$18
45(P)	**ONE STEP AT A TIME** (57)	Decca 30198	$15
	(Pink promo label)		
45rpm	**DYNAMITE** (57)	Decca 30333	$18
45(P)	**DYNAMITE** (57)	Decca 30333	$15
	(Pink promo label)		
45rpm	**ONE TEENAGER TO ANOTHER** (57)	Decca 30411	$18
45(P)	**ONE TEENAGER TO ANOTHER** (57)	Decca 30411	$15
	(Pink promo label)		
45rpm	**ROCK THE BOP** (58)	Decca 30535	$30
45(P)	**ROCK THE BOP** (58)	Decca 30535	$25
	(Green promo label)		
45rpm	**RING-A-MY PHONE** (59)	Decca 30673	$18
45(P)	**RING-A-MY PHONE** (59)	Decca 30673	$15
	(Green or pink promo label)		
45rpm	**ROCKIN' AROUND THE CHRISTMAS TREE** (58)	Decca 30776	$15
	(Black label with star under Decca)		
45rpm	**ROCKIN' AROUND THE CHRISTMAS TREE** (58)	Decca 30776	$25
	(Price includes picture sleeve)		
45(P)	**ROCKIN' AROUND THE CHRISTMAS TREE** (58)	Decca 30776	$12
	(Pink promo label)		
45rpm	**BILL BAILEY WON'T YOU PLEASE COME HOME** (59)	Decca 30806	$15
45(P)	**BILL BAILEY WON'T YOU PLEASE COME HOME** (59)	Decca 30806	$12
	(Pink promo label)		
45rpm	**LET'S JUMP THE BROOMSTICK** (59)	Decca 30885	$30
45(P)	**LET'S JUMP THE BROOMSTICK** (59)	Decca 30885	$25
	(Pink promo label)		
45rpm	**SWEET NOTHIN'S** (60)	Decca 30967	$15
45rpm	**SWEET NOTHIN'S** (60)	Decca 30967	$75
	(Price includes rare picture sleeve)		
45(P)	**SWEET NOTHIN'S** (60)	Decca 30967	$12
	(Pink promo label)		
45rpm	**I'M SORRY** (60)	Decca 31093	$12
45rpm	**I'M SORRY** (60)	Decca 31093	$25
	(Price includes picture sleeve)		
45(P)	**I'M SORRY** (60)	Decca 31093	$15
	(Pink promo label)		
45rpm	**I WANT TO BE WANTED** (60)	Decca 31149	$12
45rpm	**I WANT TO BE WANTED** (60)	Decca 31149	$25
	(Price includes picture sleeve)		
45(P)	**I WANT TO BE WANTED** (60)	Decca 31149	$12
	(Pink promo label)		
45rpm	**EMOTIONS** (61)	Decca 31195	$10
45rpm	**EMOTIONS** (61)	Decca 31195	$20
	(Price includes picture sleeve)		

45(P)	**EMOTIONS** (61)	Decca 31195	$12
	(Pink promo label)		
45rpm	**YOU CAN DEPEND ON ME** (61)	Decca 31231	$10
45rpm	**YOU CAN DEPEND ON ME** (61)	Decca 31231	$20
	(Price includes picture sleeve)		
45(P)	**YOU CAN DEPEND ON ME** (61)	Decca 31231	$12
	(Pink promo label)		
45rpm	**DUM DUM** (61)	Decca 31272	$10
45rpm	**DUM DUM** (61)	Decca 31272	$18
	(Price includes picture sleeve)		
45(P)	**DUM DUM** (61)	Decca 31272	$12
	(Pink promo label)		
45rpm	**FOOL #1** (61)	Decca 31272	$10
45rpm	**FOOL #1** (61)	Decca 31272	$18
	(Price includes picture sleeve)		
45(P)	**FOOL #1** (61)	Decca 31272	$10
	(Pink promo label)		
45rpm	**BREAK IT TO ME GENTLY** (62)	Decca 31348	$10
45rpm	**BREAK IT TO ME GENTLY** (62)	Decca 31348	$18
	(Price includes picture sleeve)		
45(P)	**BREAK IT TO ME GENTLY** (62)	Decca 31348	$10
	(Pink promo label)		
45rpm	**ALL ALONE AM I** (62)	Decca 31424	$10
45rpm	**ALL ALONE AM I** (62)	Decca 31424	$18
	(Price includes picture sleeve)		
45(P)	**ALL ALONE AM I** (62)	Decca 31424	$10
	(Pink promo label)		
45rpm	**YOUR USED TO BE** (63)	Decca 31454	$15
	(Price includes picture sleeve)		
45rpm	**LOSING YOU** (63)	Decca 31478	$15
	(Price includes picture sleeve)		
45rpm	**MY WHOLE WORLD IS FALLING DOWN** (63)	Decca 31510	$15
	(Price includes picture sleeve)		
45rpm	**THE GRASS IS GREENER** (63)	Decca 31539	$15
	(Price includes picture sleeve)		
45rpm	**THINK** (64)	Decca 31599	$15
	(Price includes picture sleeve)		
45rpm	**ALONE WITH YOU** (64)	Decca 31628	$12
	(Price includes picture sleeve)		
45rpm	**WHEN YOU LOVED ME** (64)	Decca 31654	$12
	(Price includes picture sleeve)		
45rpm	**JINGLE BELL ROCK** (64)	Decca 31687	$15
	(Price includes picture sleeve)		
45rpm	**CHRISTMAS WILL BE JUST ANOTHER LONELY DAY** (64)	Decca 31688	$15
	(Price includes picture sleeve)		
45rpm	**IS IT TRUE?** (64)	Decca 31690	$12
	(Price includes picture sleeve)		
45rpm	**TRULY, TRULY TRUE** (65)	Decca 31762	$12
	(Price includes picture sleeve)		
5-33s	**MERRY CHRISTMAS FROM BRENDA LEE** (65)	Decca 34265-34269	$12 each
	(Set of five jukebox stereo singles, $50 for the set with paper sleeve)		
5-33s	**SINCERELY** (67) Set of five jukebox stereo singles	Decca 38275-38279	$10 each
	($50 for the set with paper sleeve)		
5-33s	**EMOTIONS** (67) Set of five jukebox stereo singles	Decca 34060-34064	$10 each
	($50 for the set with paper sleeve)		
45rpm	**JOHNNY ONE TIME** (69)	Decca 32428	$15
	(Price includes picture sleeve)		
45(P)	**OPEN END INTERVIEW WITH BRENDA LEE** (72)	Decca 34370	$20
	(Promo-only release)		
45(P)	**GOOD LOVE DON'T COME THAT EASY** (81)	(MCA) 005	$10
	(Kentucky Fried Chicken songwriting contest winner, promo-only release)		
45(P)	**WHY HAVE YOU BEEN GONE SO LONG** (85)	MCA 52720	$10
	(White promo label, yellow vinyl)		
45(P)	**TWO HEARTS** (86)	MCA 52804	$10
	(White promo label, red vinyl)		

-EPs-

EP	**BRENDA LEE** (59)	Decca 2661	$50
EP	**SWEET NOTHIN'S** (60)	Decca 2678	$40
EP	**DECCA HITS** (60) Various artists	Decca 38167	$25
	(One Brenda Lee cut, "Sweet Nothin's")		
EP	**BRENDA LEE** (60)	Decca 2682	$30
	(Includes "Jambalaya")		
EP	**BRENDA LEE** (60)	Decca 2683	$30
	(Includes "I'm Sorry")		
EP	**BRENDA LEE** (60)	Decca 2695	$25
	(Includes "I Want to Be Wanted")		

EP	**BRENDA LEE** (61)	Decca 2702	$25
	(Includes "When I Fall in Love")		
EP	**LOVER COME BACK TO ME** (61)	Decca 2704	$25
EP	**BRENDA LEE** (61)	Decca 2712	$25
	(Includes "You Can Depend on Me")		
EP	**BRENDA LEE** (61)	Decca 2716	$25
	(Includes "Tragedy")		
EP	**EVERYBODY LOVES ME BUT YOU** (62)	Decca 2725	$25
EP	**BRENDA LEE** (62)	Decca 2730	$25
	(Includes "Heart in Hand")		
EP	**BRENDA LEE** (62)	Decca 2738	$25
	(Includes "All Alone Am I")		
EP	**FLY ME TO THE MOON** (62)	Decca 2745	$25
EP	**BRENDA LEE** (62)	Decca 2755	$25
EP	**BRENDA LEE** (63)	Decca 2764	$25
	(Includes "The Grass Is Greener")		
EP	**BRENDA LEE** (63)	Decca 2775	$18
	(Includes "As Usual")		
EP	**THANKS A LOT** (63)	Decca 2801	$18
EP(P)	**SINCERELY** (63) Jukebox LLP	Decca 34051	$15
	(Issued with a hard cover)		
EP(P)	**THAT'S ALL** (63) Jukebox LLP	Decca 34099	$15
	(Issued with a hard cover)		
EP(P)	**ALL ALONE AM I** (63) Jukebox LLP	Decca 34108	$15
	(Issued with a hard cover)		
EP(P)	**LET ME SING** (63) Jukebox LLP	Decca 34204	$15
	(Issued with a hard cover)		
EP(P)	**BY REQUEST ...** (64) Jukebox LLP	Decca 34242	$15
	(Issued with a hard cover)		
EP(P)	**BY REQUEST ...** (64) Jukebox LLP	Decca 34243	$15
	(Issued with a hard cover)		
EP(P)	**MERRY CHRISTMAS** (64) Jukebox LLP	Decca 34254	$18
	(Issued with a hard cover)		
EP(P)	**TOO MANY RIVERS** (65) Jukebox LLP	Decca 34341	$15
	(Issued with a hard cover)		
EP(P)	**FOR THE FIRST TIME** (68) Jukebox LLP	Decca 34528	$15
	(Brenda Lee with Pete Fountain)		

-albums-

LP	**GRANDMA, WHAT GREAT SONGS YOU SANG** (59) Mono	Decca 8873	$30
LP	**GRANDMA, WHAT GREAT SONGS YOU SANG** (59) Stereo	Decca 8873	$40
LP(P)	**GRANDMA, WHAT GREAT SONGS YOU SANG** (59)	Decca 8873	$50
	(Pink promo label)		
LP	**BRENDA LEE** (60) Mono	Decca 4039	$25
LP	**BRENDA LEE** (60) Stereo	Decca 4039	$30
LP(P)	**BRENDA LEE** (60)	Decca 4039	$35
	(Pink promo label)		
LP	**THIS IS BRENDA** (60) Mono	Decca 4082	$20
LP	**THIS IS BRENDA** (60) Stereo	Decca 4082	$25
LP(P)	**THIS IS BRENDA** (60)	Decca 4082	$30
	(Pink promo label)		
LP	**EMOTIONS** (61) Mono	Decca 4104	$20
LP	**EMOTIONS** (61) Stereo	Decca 4104	$25
LP(P)	**EMOTIONS** (61)	Decca 4104	$30
	(Pink promo label)		
LP	**ALL THE WAY** (61)	Decca 4176	$18
LP(P)	**ALL THE WAY** (61)	Decca 4176	$25
	(Pink promo label)		
LP	**SINCERELY** (62)	Decca 4216	$18
LP(P)	**SINCERELY** (62)	Decca 4216	$25
	(Pink promo label)		
LP	**THAT'S ALL** (62)	Decca 4326	$18
LP(P)	**THAT'S ALL** (62)	Decca 4326	$25
	(Pink promo label)		
LP	**ALL ALONE AM I** (63)	Decca 4370	$18
LP(P)	**ALL ALONE AM I** (63)	Decca 4370	$25
	(Pink promo label)		
LP	**SONGS EVERYBODY KNOWS** (64)	Decca 8873	$15
	(Repackage of Decca 8873)		
LP(P)	**SONGS EVERYBODY KNOWS** (64)	Decca 8873	$18
	(Pink promo label)		
LP	**LET ME SING** (64)	Decca 4439	$12
LP(P)	**LET ME SING** (64)	Decca 4439	$15
	(Pink promo label)		
LP	**BY REQUEST** (64)	Decca 4509	$12
LP(P)	**BY REQUEST** (64)	Decca 4509	$15
	(Pink promo label)		
LP	**MERRY CHRISTMAS FROM BRENDA LEE** (64)	Decca 4583	$18

LP(P)	**MERRY CHRISTMAS FROM BRENDA LEE** (64)	Decca 4583	$25
	(Pink promo label)		
LP	**TOP TEEN HITS** (65)	Decca 4626	$15
LP(P)	**TOP TEEN HITS** (65)	Decca 4626	$18
	(Decca promo label)		
LP	**THE VERSATILE BRENDA LEE** (65)	Decca 4661	$15
LP(P)	**THE VERSATILE BRENDA LEE** (65)	Decca 4661	$18
	(Decca promo label)		
LP	**TOO MANY RIVERS** (65)	Decca 4684	$10
LP(P)	**TOO MANY RIVERS** (65)	Decca 4684	$12
	(Decca promo label)		
LP	**BYE BYE BLUES** (65)	Decca 4755	$10
LP(P)	**BYE BYE BLUES** (65)	Decca 4755	$12
	(Decca promo label)		
LP	**10 GOLDEN YEARS** (66) First pressing	Decca 4757	$12
	(Album cover folds open)		
LP	**10 GOLDEN YEARS** (66) Normal cover	Decca 4757	$10
LP(P)	**10 GOLDEN YEARS** (66)	Decca 4757	$15
	(Decca promo label)		
LP	**COMING ON STRONG** (66)	Decca 4825	$10
LP(P)	**COMING ON STRONG** (66)	Decca 4825	$12
	(Decca promo label)		
LP	**HERE'S BRENDA LEE** (67)	Vocalion 3795	$10
LP(P)	**HERE'S BRENDA LEE** (67)	Vocalion 3795	$15
	(White promo label)		
LP	**REFLECTIONS IN BLUE** (67)	Decca 4941	$10
LP(P)	**REFLECTIONS IN BLUE** (67)	Decca 4941	$12
	(White promo label)		
LP(P)	**FOR CHRISTMAS SEALS** (68) Also Ernie Ford	Decca 9226	$75
	(Two public service shows, one by Brenda Lee, the other Tennessee Ernie Ford, promo only, issued with a hard cover)		
LP	**FOR THE FIRST TIME** (68) With Pete Fountain	Decca 4955	$10
LP(P)	**FOR THE FIRST TIME** (68)	Decca 4955	$12
	(Decca promo label)		
LP	**JOHNNY ONE TIME** (69)	Decca 5111	$10
LP(P)	**JOHNNY ONE TIME** (69)	Decca 5111	$12
	(White promo label)		
LP	**LET IT BE ME** (70)	Vocalion 3890	$10
LP(P)	**LET IT BE ME** (70)	Vocalion 3890	$12
	(White promo label)		
LP	**MEMPHIS PORTRAIT** (70)	Decca 5232	$10
LP(P)	**MEMPHIS PORTRAIT** (70)	Decca 5232	$12
	(White promo label)		

-radio shows-

16"(RS)	**COUNTRY STYLE U. S. A.** (60s)	Armed Forces	$50-100
	(Music and interviews)		

DICKEY LEE (R)
Other Smash 45s $4-8 each
Hallway 45s $ 5 each
TCF Hall 45s $4 each
Atco 45s $4 each
RCA Victor LPs $4-8 each
Mercury LPs $5 each

-singles-

45rpm	**STAY TRUE BABY** (58)	Tampa 10016	$30
45rpm	**GOOD LOVIN'** (58)	Sun 280	$30
45rpm	**FOOL, FOOL, FOOL** (58)	Sun 297	$75
45rpm	**WHY DON'T YOU WRITE ME** (60)	Dot 16087	$15
45rpm	**PATCHES** (62)	Smash 1758	$10
45(P)	**PATCHES** (62)	Smash 1758	$15
	(White promo label)		

-albums-

LP	**TALES OF PATCHES SUNG BY DICKEY LEE** (62) Mono	Smash 67020	$20
LP	**TALES OF PATCHES SUNG BY DICKEY LEE** (62) Stereo	Smash 67020	$35
LP(P)	**TALES OF PATCHES SUNG BY DICKEY LEE** (62)	Smash 27020	$30
	(White promo label)		
LP	**PEYTON PLACE** (65)	TCF Hall 8001	$20

ERNIE LEE (CW)
-singles-

45rpm	**MY HOME IS THE DUST OF THE ROAD** (49) Green vinyl	RCA Victor 0158	$15

FLOYD LEE (RB)
-singles-

45rpm	**GO BOY** (58)	Enterprise 1234	$60

HARRY LEE (RB)

-singles-

45rpm	ROCKIN' ON A REINDEER (58)	Igloo 101	$100

JACKIE LEE (CW)
Coral 45s and 78s $5-10 each

JIMMY LEE (RB)
Capitol 78s $4-8 each
Other Capitol 45s $5-10 each

-singles-

45rpm	LIPS THAT KISS SO SWEETLY (52)	Capitol 1924	$12
45rpm	HOW ABOUT A DATE (53)	Capitol 2491	$18
45(P)	HOW ABOUT A DATE (53)	Capitol 2491	$15
	(White promo label)		
45rpm	YOU AIN'T NO GOOD FOR ME	Fortune 191	$50
45rpm	SHE'S GONE	Clix 100	$15
45rpm	IT MUST BE LOVE	Apollo 525	$18
45(P)	IT MUST BE LOVE	Apollo 525	$25
	(White promo label)		
45rpm	LOVE ME (59) With Wayne Walker	Chess 4863	$100
45(P)	LOVE ME (59)	Chess 4863	$125
	(Rare white/blue promo label)		
45rpm	LOOK WHAT LOVE WILL DO	Vin 1010	$12

JOHNNY LEE (C)
Asylum and Full Moon 45s $2 each
Other label 45s $1 each
Asylum LPs $3 each
Other label LPs $2-3 each

-albums-

LP	FOR LOVERS ONLY (77)	JMS 1000	$15

-radio shows-

LP(RS)	LIVE FROM GILLEY'S (Apr 87)	Westwood One	$10-15
	(Live concert)		
LP(RS)	WESTWOOD ONE PRESENTS (Feb 90)	Westwood One	$10-15
	(Live concert)		

MYRON LEE (R)
And the Caddies

-singles-

45rpm	RONA BABY (59)	Hep 2076	$50
45rpm	LOVER'S HOLIDAY (59)	Hep 2102	$50
45rpm	HOMICIDE (60)	Hep 2146	$75
45rpm	RONA BABY (59)	Felsted 8570	$25
45rpm	COME BACK BABY (60)	Keen 2104	$18
	("Rona Baby" on the flip side)		
45rpm	PETER RABBITT (62)	M & L Label	$12
45rpm	BLUE LAWDY BLUE (62)	Nor-Va-Jak 1326	$10
45rpm	MARY'S SWINGIN' LAMB (62)	Soma 1114	$12
45rpm	FAT MAN (63)	Garrett 4009	$25
45rpm	TOWN GIRL (63)	Del-Fi 4180	$18
45(P)	TOWN GIRL (63)	Del-Fi 4180	$25
	(White promo label)		
45rpm	EVERYBODY'S GOING TO THE PARTY (65)	ABC Paramount 10610	$18
45(P)	EVERYBODY'S GOING TO THE PARTY (65)	ABC Paramount 10610	$25
	(White promo label)		

TERRY LEE (RB)
Bob Becker
And the Poor Boys
Poor Boys 45s by Bob Becker $5 each
MusicTown 45s by Bob Becker $4 each

-singles-

45rpm	MY LITTLE SUE (58) Not a promo, white label	Soma 1116	$300
	(The "other band" when Bobby Vee was discovered in Fargo as fill-in for Buddy Holly; in fact, Bob Becker/Terry Lee & The Poor Boys were the top draw teen band in the Fargo-Moorhead area at the time of the plane crash that killed Buddy Holly, The Big Bopper, and Richie Valens, and it was the Poor Boys that were first called to fill in that historic night in Moorhead)		

WILMA LEE & STONEY COOPER (CW)
Other Hickory 45s $6-10 each
Decca 45s by Stoney Cooper $3 each

-singles-

45rpm	THE TRAMP ON THE STREET (56)	Hickory 1058	$15

45rpm	THE TRAMP ON THE STREET (56)	Hickory 1058	$10
	(White promo label)		
45rpm	COME WALK WITH ME (59)	Hickory 1085	$15
45(P)	COME WALK WITH ME (59)	Hickory 1085	$10
	(White promo label)		
45rpm	BIG MIDNIGHT SPECIAL (59)	Hickory 1098	$15
45(P)	BIG MIDNIGHT SPECIAL (59)	Hickory 1098	$10
	(White promo label)		
45rpm	THERE'S A BIG WHEEL (59)	Hickory 1107	$12
45(P)	THERE'S A BIG WHEEL (59)	Hickory 1107	$10
	(White promo label)		
45rpm	JOHNNY, MY LOVE (60)	Hickory 1118	$12
45(P)	JOHNNY, MY LOVE (60)	Hickory 1118	$10
	(White promo label)		

-EPs-

EP	WILMA LEE & STONEY COOPER (53)	Columbia 2837	$15
EP(P)	FAMILY FAVORITES (62)	Hickory 106	$50
	(Promo-only release)		

-albums-

LP	THERE'S A BIG WHEEL (60)	Hickory 100	$50
	(Hickory's first LP release)		
LP(P)	THERE'S A BIG WHEEL (60)	Hickory 100	$60
	(White promo label)		
LP	SACRED SONGS (60)	Harmony 7233	$25
LP(P)	SACRED SONGS (60)	Harmony 7233	$30
	(White promo label)		
LP	FAMILY FAVORITES (62)	Hickory 106	$40
LP(P)	FAMILY FAVORITES (62)	Hickory 106	$50
	(White promo label)		
LP	SONGS OF INSPIRATION (62)	Hickory 112	$40
LP(P)	SONGS OF INSPIRATION (62)	Hickory 112	$50
	(White promo label)		
LP	SUNNY SIDE OF THE MOUNTAIN (66)	Harmony 11178	$25
LP(P)	SUNNY SIDE OF THE MOUNTAIN (66)	Harmony 11178	$30
	(White promo label)		
LP	WILMA LEE & STONEY COOPER SING (66)	Decca 4784	$20
LP(P)	WILMA LEE & STONEY COOPER SING (66)	Decca 4784	$25
	(Pink promo label)		
LP	A TRIBUTE TO ROY ACUFF (70)	Skylite 7301	$12

-radio shows-

16"(RS)	U.S. ARMY (60S)	U.S. Army	$25-50
	(Music and interviews)		
16"(RS)	COUNTRY MUSIC TIME	U.S. Army 98	$30-50
	(Music and interviews)		
16"(RS)	COUNTRY MUSIC TIME	U.S. Army 115	$30-50
	(Music and interviews)		
LP(RS)	GRAND OL' OPRY (61)	WSM Radio 52	$30-50
	(Music and interviews)		
LP(RS)	GRAND OL' OPRY (63)	WSM Radio 86	$25-50
	(Music and interviews)		

LEE BROTHERS (CW)
With Billy Don's Trail Riders of the Golden West

-singles-

45rpm	LOST ROMANCE (58)	North Star 2054	$25

LEGENDARY STARDUST COWBOY (R)
Other Mercury 45s $8 each

-singles-

45rpm	PARALYZED (68)	Psycho Suave 1033	$40
45(P)	PARALYZED (68)	Mercury 72862	$10
	(Play it before you buy it!)		
45(P)	PARALYZED (68)	Mercury 72862	$15
	(White promo label)		

LEON & CARLOS (RB)

-singles-

45rpm	ROCK EVERYBODY (58)	Liberty Tone 108	$150

BOBBY LEWIS (R)
Other Beltone 45s $6-10 each
United Artists 45s $3-6 each
Capricorn 45s $2 each
Other United Artists LPs $6-10 each
R. P. A. LPs $4-8 each
Ace of Hearts LPs $6 each
Album Globe LPs $3 each

-singles-

45rpm	MUMBLES BLUES (58)	Spot Records	$25
45rpm	YOU BETTER STOP (59)	Roulette 4182	$18
45(P)	YOU BETTER STOP (59)	Roulette 4182	$20
	(White/red promo label)		
45rpm	TOSSIN' AND TURNIN' (61)	Beltone 1002	$10
45rpm	ONE TRACK MIND (61)	Beltone 1012	$10

-albums-

LP	TOSSIN' AND TURNIN' (61)	Beltone 4000	$200
LP	THE BEST OF BOBBY LEWIS (70)	United Artists 6770	$20
LP(P)	THE BEST OF BOBBY LEWIS (70)	United Artists 6770	$25
	(White promo label)		

GENE LEWIS (RB)

-singles-

45rpm	CRAZY LEGS (57)	R-Dell 103	$25
45rpm	TOO YOUNG TO SETTLE DOWN (58)	Josie 819	$10

HUGH X. LEWIS (C)
Kapp 45s $2 each
Kapp LPs $5-10 each

JERRY LEE LEWIS (RB)
The Killer
Also recorded as the Hawk, George & Louis
Smash DJS series white promo label 45s $8 each
Other Smash 45s $4-8 each
Smash All Time Smash Hits 45s $3 each
Mercury DJ series white promo label 45s $6 each
Other Mercury 45s $2-4 each
Other Sun promo 45s (1100 series) $3 each
Other Sun singles (1100 series) $2 each
SCR 45s $3 each
Curb (MCA) duet 45s $3 each
Everest, Elektra, MCA LPs $4 each
Sears LPs $8 each
Trip, Polydor, Pickwick, Accord, Koala, Rhino, Power Pak, Buckboard, Aura, Design, and Sunnyvale
   LPs $3 each
Other Sun LPs (1000 series) $5 each
Pickwick 2LP sets $6 each

-singles-

78rpm	CRAZY ARMS (57)	Sun 259	$100
	(Jerry Lee Lewis)		
45rpm	CRAZY ARMS (57)	Sun 259	$100
	(Jerry Lee Lewis)		
45rpm	CRAZY ARMS (57)	Sun 259	$40
	(Jerry Lewis & His Pumping Piano)		
78rpm	WHOLE LOT OF SHAKIN' GOING ON (57)	Sun 267	$75
45rpm	WHOLE LOT OF SHAKIN' GOING ON (57)	Sun 267	$25
78rpm	GREAT BALLS OF FIRE (57)	Sun 281	$75
45rpm	GREAT BALLS OF FIRE (57)	Sun 281	$25
45rpm	GREAT BALLS OF FIRE (57)	Sun 281	$75
	(Price includes picture sleeve)		
78rpm	BREATHLESS (58)	Sun 288	$75
45rpm	BREATHLESS (58)	Sun 288	$25
78rpm	HIGH SCHOOL CONFIDENTIAL (58)	Sun 296	$75
45rpm	HIGH SCHOOL CONFIDENTIAL (58)	Sun 296	$25
45rpm	HIGH SCHOOL CONFIDENTIAL (58)	Sun 296	$75
	(Price includes picture sleeve)		
45rpm	RETURN OF JERRY LEE (58) George & Lewis	Sun 301	$30
	(Novelty cut-in record)		
45rpm	BREAK-UP (58)	Sun 303	$18
45rpm	I'LL SAIL MY SHIP ALONE (59)	Sun 312	$18
45rpm	LOVIN' UP A STORM (59)	Sun 317	$18
45rpm	IN THE MOOD (60) The Hawk	Philips 3559	$50
45(P)	IN THE MOOD (60)	Philips 3559	$75
	(Rare promo label)		
45rpm	LET'S TALK ABOUT US (60)	Sun 324	$18
45rpm	LITTLE QUEENIE (60)	Sun 330	$18
45rpm	BABY, BABY, BYE BYE (60)	Sun 337	$15
45rpm	HANG UP MY ROCK & ROLL SHOES (60)	Sun 344	$15
45rpm	WHEN I GET PAID (60)	Sun 352	$15
45rpm	WHAT'D I SAY (61)	Sun 356	$15
45rpm	IT WON'T HAPPEN WITH ME (61)	Sun 364	$15
45rpm	SAVE THE LAST DANCE FOR ME (61)	Sun 367	$15
45rpm	MONEY (61)	Sun 371	$12
45rpm	I'VE BEEN TWISTIN' (62)	Sun 374	$12

45rpm	**SWEET LITTLE SIXTEEN** (62)	Sun 379	$12
45rpm	**GOOD GOLLY MISS MOLLY** (62)	Sun 382	$12
45rpm	**TEENAGE LETTER** (63)	Sun 384	$12
45rpm	**CARRY ME BACK TO OLD VIRGINIA** (64)	Sun 396	$12
45(P)	**HIT THE ROAD, JACK** (64)	Smash 1857	$10
45rpm	**I'M ON FIRE** (64)	Smash 1886	$40
	(Rare record)		
45rpm	**I'M ON FIRE** (64)	Smash 1886	$25
	(White promo label)		
45rpm	**ROCKIN' PNEUMONIA** (65)	Smash 1992	$15
45(P)	**ROCKIN' PNEUMONIA** (65)	Smash 1992	$10
	(White promo label)		
45(P)	**I CAN'T SEEM TO SAY GOODBYE** (70)	Sun 1115	$12
	(White promo label, gold vinyl)		
45(P)	**WAITING FOR A TRAIN** (71)	Sun 1119	$10
	(Yellow promo label, yellow vinyl)		
45(P)	**YOUR LOVING WAYS** (71)	Sun 1128	$10
	(Yellow promo label, yellow vinyl)		
45(P)	**DRINKING WINE SPO-DEE O'DEE** (73)	Mercury 73374	$10
	(White promo label)		
45(P)	**SAVE THE LAST DANCE FOR ME** (78)	Sun 1139	$10
	(Yellow promo label, yellow vinyl)		
45(P)	**HELLO JOSEPHINE** (79)	Sun 1141	$10
	(Yellow promo label, yellow vinyl)		

-EPs-

EP	**THE GREAT BALL OF FIRE** (57)	Sun 107	$125
	(Issued with a paper sleeve)		
EP	**JERRY LEE LEWIS** (57)	Sun 108	$100
	(Issued with a hard cover)		
EP	**JERRY LEE LEWIS** (57)	Sun 109	$100
	(Issued with a hard cover)		
EP	**JERRY LEE LEWIS** (58)	Sun 110	$100
	(Issued with a hard cover)		
EP(JB)	**THE GOLDEN CREAM OF THE COUNTRY** (69) Jukebox LLP	Sun 108 #155	$30
	(Issued with a paper sleeve)		
EP(JB)	**JERRY LEE LEWIS** (69) Jukebox LLP	Smash 2	$30
	(Issued with a hard cover)		
EP(P)	**D. J. OPEN END INTERVIEW WITH JERRY LEE LEWIS** (70)	Smash DJS-28	$40
	(White promo label, for radio stations only)		
EP(JB)	**A TASTE OF COUNTRY** (70) Jukebox LLP	Sun 114	$25
	(Issued with paper cover)		
EP(P)	**SPECIAL RADIO CUTS FROM WOULD YOU TAKE ANOTHER CHANCE ON ME** (71)	Mercury 6	$25
	(White promo label for radio only)		
EP(P)	**SPECIAL RADIO CUTS FROM THE KILLER ROCKS ON** (72)	Mercury 14	$25
	(White promo label for radio only)		

-albums-

LP	**JERRY LEE LEWIS** (58)	Sun 1230	$200
LP	**JERRY LEE'S GREATEST** (62)	Sun 1265	$250
LP(P)	**JERRY LEE'S GREATEST** (62)	Sun 1265	$800
	(Very rare white promo label)		
LP	**ROCKIN' WITH JERRY LEE LEWIS** (63)	Design 165	$25
	(Budget label)		
LP	**THE GOLDEN HITS OF JERRY LEE LEWIS** (64) Mono	Smash 27040	$20
LP	**THE GOLDEN HITS OF JERRY LEE LEWIS** (64) Stereo	Smash 67040	$25
LP(P)	**THE GOLDEN HITS OF JERRY LEE LEWIS** (64)	Smash 27040	$30
	(White promo label)		
LP	**THE GREATEST LIVE SHOW ON EARTH** (64) Mono	Smash 27056	$75
LP	**THE GREATEST LIVE SHOW ON EARTH** (64) Stereo	Smash 67056	$100
LP(P)	**THE GREATEST LIVE SHOW ON EARTH** (64)	Smash 27056	$50
	(White promo label)		
LP	**THE RETURN OF ROCK** (65) Mono	Smash 27063	$25
LP	**THE RETURN OF ROCK** (65) Stereo	Smash 67063	$35
LP(P)	**THE RETURN OF ROCK** (65)	Smash 27063	$30
	(White promo label)		
LP	**COUNTRY SONGS FOR CITY FOLKS** (65) Mono	Smash 27071	$15
LP	**COUNTRY SONGS FOR CITY FOLKS** (65) Stereo	Smash 67071	$18
LP(P)	**COUNTRY SONGS FOR CITY FOLKS** (65)	Smash 27071	$20
	(White promo label)		
LP	**MEMPHIS BEAT** (66) Mono	Smash 27079	$15
LP	**MEMPHIS BEAT** (66) Stereo	Smash 67079	$18
LP(P)	**MEMPHIS BEAT** (66)	Smash 27079	$20
	(White promo label)		
LP	**BY REQUEST** (66) Mono	Smash 27086	$20
LP	**BY REQUEST** (66) Stereo	Smash 67086	$25
LP(P)	**BY REQUEST** (66)	Smash 27086	$30
	(White promo label)		

LP	**SOUL MY WAY** (67) Mono	Smash 27097	$20
LP	**SOUL MY WAY** (67) Stereo	Smash 67097	$25
LP(P)	**SOUL MY WAY** (67)	Smash 27097	$30
	(White promo label)		
LP	**THE RETURN OF ROCK** (67)	Wing 16340	$15
LP(P)	**THE RETURN OF ROCK** (67)	Wing 12340	$18
	(White promo label)		
LP	**IN DEMAND** (68)	Wing 16340	$15
	(Reissue of "The Return of Rock")		
LP	**ANOTHER PLACE, ANOTHER TIME** (68)	Smash 67104	$15
LP(P)	**ANOTHER PLACE, ANOTHER TIME** (68)	Smash 67104	$18
	(White promo label)		
LP	**GOLDEN ROCK HITS** (69)	Smash 67040	$15
	(Reissue of the original Smash 27040)		
LP(P)	**GOLDEN ROCK HITS** (69)	Smash 27040	$18
	(White promo label)		
LP	**ALL COUNTRY** (69)	Smash 67071	$15
	(Reissue of Smash 27071)		
LP(P)	**ALL COUNTRY** (69)	Smash 67071	$18
	(White promo label)		
LP	**SHE STILL COMES AROUND** (69)	Smash 67112	$12
LP	**SHE STILL COMES AROUND** (69)	Smash 27112	$15
	(White promo label)		
LP	**COUNTRY MUSIC HALL OF FAME HITS VOL 1** (69)	Smash 67117	$12
LP(P)	**COUNTRY MUSIC HALL OF FAME HITS VOL 1** (69)	Smash 27117	$15
	(White promo label)		
LP	**COUNTRY MUSIC HALL OF FAME HITS VOL 2** (69)	Smash 67118	$12
LP(P)	**COUNTRY MUSIC HALL OF FAME HITS VOL 2** (69)	Smash 27118	$15
	(White promo label)		
LP	**TOGETHER** (69) With Linda Gail Lewis	Smash 67126	$12
LP(P)	**TOGETHER** (69)	Smash 67126	$15
	(White promo label)		
2LP	**THE LEGEND OF JERRY LEE LEWIS** (69)	Wing 125	$18
2LP(P)	**THE LEGEND OF JERRY LEE LEWIS** (69)	Wing 125	$25
	(White promo labels)		
LP	**ORIGINAL GOLDEN HITS VOL 1** (69)	Sun 102	$12
LP(P)	**ORIGINAL GOLDEN HITS VOL 1** (69)	Sun 102	$15
	(White promo label)		
LP	**ORIGINAL GOLDEN HITS VOL 2** (69)	Sun 103	$12
LP(P)	**ORIGINAL GOLDEN HITS VOL 2** (69)	Sun 103	$15
	(White promo label)		
LP	**ROCKIN' RHYTHM & BLUES** (69)	Sun 107	$12
LP(P)	**ROCKIN' RHYTHM & BLUES** (69)	Sun 107	$15
	(White promo label)		
LP	**THE GOLDEN CREAM OF THE COUNTRY** (69)	Sun 108	$12
LP(P)	**THE GOLDEN CREAM OF THE COUNTRY** (69)	Sun 108	$15
	(White promo label)		
LP	**SHE EVEN WOKE ME UP TO SAY GOODBYE** (70)	Smash 67128	$12
LP(P)	**SHE EVEN WOKE ME UP TO SAY GOODBYE** (70)	Smash 27128	$15
	(White promo label)		
LP	**THE BEST OF JERRY LEE LEWIS** (70)	Smash 67131	$12
LP(P)	**THE BEST OF JERRY LEE LEWIS** (70)	Smash 27131	$15
	(White promo label)		
LP	**A TASTE OF COUNTRY** (70)	Sun 114	$12
LP(P)	**A TASTE OF COUNTRY** (70)	Sun 114	$15
	(White promo label)		
LP	**MONSTERS** (71)	Sun 124	$12
LP(P)	**MONSTERS** (71)	Sun 124	$15
	(White promo label)		
LP	**ORIGINAL GOLDEN HITS VOL 3** (71)	Sun 128	$10
LP(P)	**ORIGINAL GOLDEN HITS VOL 3** (71)	Sun 128	$15
	(White promo label)		
LP	**ROOTS** (71)	Sun 145	$10
LP(P)	**ROOTS** (71)	Sun 145	$15
	(White promo label)		
LP	**LIVE AT THE INTERNATIONAL** (71)	Mercury 61278	$12
LP(P)	**LIVE AT THE INTERNATIONAL** (71)	Mercury 61278	$15
	(White promo label)		
LP	**IN LOVING MEMORIES** (71)	Mercury 61318	$18
LP(P)	**IN LOVING MEMORIES** (71)	Mercury 61318	$25
	(White promo label)		
LP	**THERE MUST BE MORE TO LOVE THAN THIS** (71)	Mercury 61323	$15
LP(P)	**THERE MUST BE MORE TO LOVE THAN THIS** (71)	Mercury 61323	$18
	(White promo label)		
LP	**TOUCHING HOME** (71)	Mercury 61343	$25
	(Drawing on the cover)		
LP	**TOUCHING HOME** (71)	Mercury 61343	$15
	(Photo on the cover)		

LP(P)	**TOUCHING HOME** (71)	Mercury 61343	$18
	(White promo label)		
LP	**WOULD YOU TAKE ANOTHER CHANCE ON ME** (71)	Mercury 61346	$15
LP(P)	**WOULD YOU TAKE ANOTHER CHANCE ON ME** (71)	Mercury 61346	$18
	(White promo label)		
LP	**WHO'S GONNA PLAY THIS OLD PIANO** (72)	Mercury 61366	$15
LP(P)	**WHO'S GONNA PLAY THIS OLD PIANO** (72)	Mercury 61366	$18
	(White promo label)		
LP	**THE KILLER ROCKS ON** (72)	Mercury 637	$15
LP(P)	**THE KILLER ROCKS ON** (72)	Mercury 637	$18
	(White promo label)		
LP	**SOMETIMES A MEMORY AIN'T ENOUGH** (72)	Mercury 677	$12
LP(P)	**SOMETIMES A MEMORY AIN'T ENOUGH** (72)	Mercury 677	$15
	(White promo label)		
LP	**SOUTHERN ROOTS** (72)	Mercury 690	$12
LP(P)	**SOUTHERN ROOTS** (72)	Mercury 690	$15
	(White promo label)		
LP(P)	**SOUTHERN ROOTS A RADIO SPECIAL** (72)	Mercury MK-3 (690)	$75
	(White promo label)		
LP	**I-40 COUNTRY** (73)	Mercury 710	$20
LP(P)	**I-40 COUNTRY** (73)	Mercury 710	$25
	(White promo label)		
2LP	**THE SESSION** (73)	Mercury 803	$25
2LP(P)	**THE SESSION** (73)	Mercury 803	$30
	(White promo labels)		
LP	**BOOGIE WOOGIE COUNTRY MAN** (75)	Mercury 1030	$15
LP(P)	**BOOGIE WOOGIE COUNTRY MAN** (75)	Mercury 1030	$18
	(White promo label)		
LP	**ODD MAN IN** (75)	Mercury 1064	$15
LP(P)	**ODD MAN IN** (75)	Mercury 1064	$18
	(White promo label)		
LP	**COUNTRY CLASS** (76)	Mercury 1109	$15
LP(P)	**COUNTRY CLASS** (76)	Mercury 1109	$18
	(White promo label)		
LP	**COUNTRY MEMORIES** (77)	Mercury 5004	$12
LP(P)	**COUNTRY MEMORIES** (77)	Mercury 5004	$15
	(White promo label)		
LP	**BEST OF JERRY LEE LEWIS VOL 2** (78)	Mercury 5006	$12
LP(P)	**BEST OF JERRY LEE LEWIS VOL 2** (78)	Mercury 5006	$15
	(White promo label)		
LP	**JERRY LEE LEWIS KEEPS ROCKIN'** (78)	Mercury 5010	$12
LP(P)	**JERRY LEE LEWIS KEEPS ROCKIN'** (78)	Mercury 5010	$15
	(White promo label)		
LP	**TRIO** (78) With Jimmy Ellis and Carl Perkins	Sun 1018	$15
	(Gold vinyl)		

-radio shows-

LP(RS)	**COUNTRY SESSIONS** (81)	Country Sessions 107	$50-75
	(Live concert)		
3LP(RS)	**INTERNATIONAL FESTIVAL** (Oct 82)	Mutual Radio	$30-60
	(Live concert with other artists)		
LP(RS)	**COUNTRY SESSIONS** (Apr 83)	NBC Radio	$25-40
	(Live concert)		
3LP(RS)	**ON A COUNTRY ROAD** (May 83) Box set	Mutual Radio	$25-50
	(Live concert segment of Jerry Lee Lewis)		
LP(RS)	**LIVE AT GILLEY'S** (Jun 83)	Westwood One 83-24	$40-75
	(Live concert)		
3LP(RS)	**AMERICAN EAGLE** (87)	DIR	$100-200
	(Live show features Carl Perkins, Lewis, and the Crickets)		

LINDA GAIL LEWIS (C)
Married to Jerry Lee Lewis
Smash 45s $2 each

-albums-

LP	**TWO SIDES OF LINDA GAIL LEWIS** (69)	Mercury 67119	$15
LP(P)	**TWO SIDES OF LINDA GAIL LEWIS** (69)	Mercury 67119	$18
	(White promo label)		
LP	**TOGETHER** (69) With Jerry Lee Lewis	Mercury 67126	$15
LP(P)	**TOGETHER** (69)	Mercury 67126	$18
	(White promo label)		

SIDNEY LEWIS (RB)

-singles-

45rpm	**BOPPIN' TO GRANDFATHER'S CLOCK** (59)	Island 6	$75

NOTES

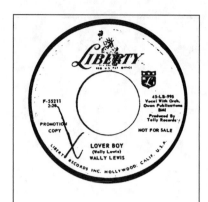

TEXAS JIM LEWIS (CW)
Coral 78s $6 each
Other Coral 45s $5-10 each

-singles-

45rpm	SWEET FACE BUT A COLD HEART (54)	Coral 60856	$15

-radio shows-

16"(RS)	THE STANDARD RADIO SHOW (50s)	Armed Forces	$10-20
	(Music and interviews)		

WALLY LEWIS (R)

-singles-

45rpm	KATHLEEN (57)	Tally 117	$12
45rpm	KATHLEEN (57)	Dot 15705	$10
45rpm	WHITE BOBBY SOCKS (58)	Dot 15763	$10
45rpm	SALLY GREEN (58)	Liberty 55196	$10
45rpm	LOVER BOY (58)	Liberty 55211	$10

LEWIS & CLARKE EXPEDITION (R,CW)
Michael Murphey and Boomer Castleman

-singles-

45rpm	I FEEL GOOD (67)	Colgems 1006	$18
	(Price includes picture sleeve)		

-albums-

LP	THE LEWIS & CLARKE EXPEDITION (67)	Colgems 105	$25
	See Michael Murphey		

THE LEWIS FAMILY (G)
Starday 45s $4-8 each
Other Starday LPs $5-8 each
Caanan LPs $5 each
Solid Rock LPs $4 each

-EPs-

EP	THE LEWIS FAMILY (58)	Starday 102	$18
EP	THE LEWIS FAMILY (59)	Starday 104	$18
EP	THE LEWIS FAMILY (59)	Starday 114	$15
EP	THE LEWIS FAMILY (60)	Starday 117	$15
EP	THE LEWIS FAMILY (62)	Starday 161	$12
EP	THE LEWIS FAMILY (64)	Starday 208	$12

-albums-

LP	SINGIN' TIME DOWN SOUTH (60)	Starday 121	$30
	(Reissued on Nashville label in 1969)		
LP	ANNIVERSARY CELEBRATION (62)	Starday 161	$25
LP	GOSPEL SPECIAL (62)	Starday 193	$25
LP	SING ME A GOSPEL SONG (62)	Starday 238	$20
LP	ALL NIGHT SINGING CONVENTION (63)	Starday 252	$20
LP	SINGING IN MY SOUL (64)	Starday 289	$20
LP	FIRST FAMILY OF GOSPEL MUSIC (65)	Starday 331	$20
LP	THE LEWIS FAMILY & CARL STORY (65)	Starday 364	$20
	(Featuring Carl Story)		
LP	THE LEWIS FAMILY ALBUM (65)	Starday 381	$18
LP	SHALL WE GATHER AT THE RIVER (66)	Starday 395	$18
LP	TIME IS MOVING ON (67)	Starday 408	$15
LP	ALL DAY SINGING & DINNER ON THE GROUND (68)	Starday 419	$15
LP	GOLDEN GOSPEL BANJO (68)	Starday 422	$15
LP	DID YOU EVER GO SAILING (69)	Starday 433	$15
LP	SINGIN' TIME DOWN SOUTH (69)	Nashville 2016	$12
	(Reissue of Starday 121)		
LP	GOLDEN GOSPEL OF THE LEWIS FAMILY (70)	Starday 450	$15
LP	GOSPEL SING OUT (70)	Nashville 2045	$12
	(Budget label)		
LP	BEST OF THE LEWIS FAMILY (70)	Starday 465	$15
LP	GOSPEL SINGING SENSATIONS FROM DIXIE (71)	Nashville 2062	$12
	(Budget label)		

LIGHT CRUST DOUGHBOYS (CW)
All-star swing band includes Leon McAulliff and Bob Wills
Texas Rose, Aolt, Doughboy, and Longhorn LPs $8-10 each

-albums-

LP	THE LIGHT CRUST DOUGHBOYS (59)	Audio Lab 1525	$50

LILLY BROTHERS (BG)

-albums-

LP	BLUEGRASS BREAKDOWN (63)	Folkways 14010	$20
LP	COUNTRY SONGS OF THE LILLY BROTHERS (64)	Folkways 14035	$18
LP	FOLK SONGS FROM THE SOUTHERN MOUNTAINS (66)	Folkways 2433	$15
	(With Don Stover)		

LIL' MISS WANDA (R)

-singles-

45rpm	**MY JOHNNY** (58)	Aires 1020	$100

LI'L WALLY (Polka)
Li'l Wally Jagiello
Jay Jay 78s $5 each
Other Jay Jay 45s $5-10 each
Jay Jay LPs $4 each

-singles-

45rpm	**LUCKY POLKA** (53)	Jay Jay 121	$25
45rpm	**WISH I WAS SINGLE AGAIN** (56)	Jay Jay 145	$10
45rpm	**WE LEFT OUR WIVES AT HOME** (56)	Jay Jay 148	$10
45rpm	**MEMORIES WALTZ** (56)	Jay Jay 152	$10
45rpm	**WHO DO YOU LIKE TO LOVE YOU** (57)	Jay Jay 154	$10
45rpm	**THE WEDDING WALTZ** (58)	Jay Jay 156	$10
45rpm	**ZIP ZIP POLKA** (58)	Jay Jay 157	$10
45rpm	**YOU WALTZ** (59)	Jay Jay 171	$30
	(Price includes very rare picture sleeve)		
45rpm	**KISSED AGAIN WALTZ** (60)	Jay Jay 172	$30
	(Price includes very rare picture sleeve)		
45rpm	**JULIDA** (60)	Jay Jay 173	$25
	(Price includes rare picture sleeve)		
45rpm	**LIVE IT UP** (61)	Jay Jay 177	$25
	(Price includes rare picture sleeve)		
45rpm	**YOU ARE MY SWEETHEART NOW POLKA** (63)	Jay Jay 211	$25
	(Price includes picture sleeve)		
45rpm	**CLAPPIN' POLKA** (63) Lee Morgan	Jay Jay 217	$25
	(Price includes picture sleeve)		
45rpm	**THANKS FOR A WONDERFUL EVENING POLKA** (64)	Jay Jay 218	$25
	(Price includes picture sleeve)		
45rpm	**KALINA W LESIE** (65)	Jay Jay 238	$25
	(Yellow label, green vinyl)		
45rpm	**CHURCH BELLS ARE BREAKING UP THAT OLD GANG OF MINE** (65)	Jay Jay 239	$25
	(Yellow label, green vinyl)		
45rpm	**CHURCH BELLS ARE BREAKING UP THAT OLD GANG OF MINE** (65)	Jay Jay 239	$12
	(Black vinyl)		
45rpm	**DUTCHMEN BOHEMIAN POLKA** (65) Michigan Dutchmen	Jay Jay 240	$25
	(Yellow label, green vinyl)		

LAWANDA LINDSEY (C)
Chart and Capitol 45s $2-3 each

-albums-

LP	**SWINGIN' AND SINGING MY SONG** (69)	Chart 1015	$15
LP	**PICKIN' WILD MOUNTAIN BERRIES** (70)	Chart 1030	$15
	(With Kenny Vernon)		
LP	**WE'LL SING IN THE SUNSHINE** (70)	Chart 1035	$12
LP	**LAWANDA LINDSEY'S GREATEST HITS** (71)	Chart 1048	$10
LP	**THIS IS LAWANDA LINDSEY** (74)	Capitol 11306	$10

SHERWIN LINTON (R)
Also recorded with the Cotton Kings and the Fenderbenders
Hickory 45s $4 each
Other Black Gold 45s $3-5 each
New World (Bell) 45s $3 each
ASI, Soundwaves, American Heritage, Little Richie, and Breaker 45s $2-3 each
Breaker picture sleeves $2 each
Circle 45s by Linda Lou $4 each

-singles-

45rpm	**MULESKINNER BLUES '65** (65) The Muleskinners	Twin Town 708	$15
45rpm	**HOUSE OF BLUE LIGHTS** (65)	Twin Town 716	$12
45(P)	**HOUSE OF BLUE LIGHTS** (65)	Twin Town 716	$18
	(White promo label)		
45rpm	**WHO BESIDES ME** (66)	Soma 1405	$10
	(Black Soma label)		
45rpm	**WOLFMAN** (66) The Muleskinners	Soma 1418	$10
45rpm	**TWIST A HOLE IN THE GROUND** (66) The Fenderbenders	RAKO 6201	$12
45rpm	**SADIE** (66) Bob Trebus with the Fenderbenders	Soma 1450	$15
	(Yellow Soma label)		
45rpm	**WHITE LIGHTNING** (66)	Agar 3577	$10
45rpm	**SIX DAYS ON THE ROAD** (66) The Fenderbenders	Agar 5407	$15
45rpm	**I'M NOT AMONG THE LOVING** (68)	Black Gold 6913	$18
	(Price includes picture sleeve)		

-albums-

LP	**SHERWIN LINTON AND THE COTTON KINGS** (68)	Re-Car 2018	$40
LP	**I'M NOT JOHNNY CASH** (72)	Black Gold 7116	$20

MAX LIPSCOMB (RB)

-singles-

45rpm	**BABY YOU'RE SO SQUARE** (58)	Squire 102	$60

LITTLE DENNY (RB)

-singles-

45rpm	**ROLL AND ROLL BLUES** (58)	Perry 1	$60

JAY B. LLOYD See Black's Combo

JIMMY LLOYD (RB)

-singles-

45rpm	**I GOT A ROCKET IN MY POCKET** (58)	Roulette 4062	$25
45(P)	**I GOT A ROCKET IN MY POCKET** (58)	Roulette 4062	$30
	(Roulette promo label)		
45rpm	**WHERE THE RIO DEL ROSA FLOWS** (58)	Roulette 7001	$25
45(P)	**WHERE THE RIO DEL ROSE FLOWS** (58)	Roulette 7001	$30
	(Roulette promo label)		

HANK LOCKLIN (CW)

Other 4-Star 78s $6-10 each
Decca 78s $4-6 each
RCA Victor 78s $3-5 each
Other RCA Victor 45s $3-5 each
Other RCA Victor LPs $4-8 each
RCA Victor duet LPs $6 each
Plantation LPs $4 each
International Award LPs $3 each

-singles-

78rpm	**THE SAME SWEET GIRL** (49)	4-Star 1313	$15
78rpm	**LET ME BE THE ONE** (53)	4-Star 1641	$12
	(Number one country song)		
45rpm	**LET ME BE THE ONE** (53)	4-Star 1641	$15
45rpm	**THE SAME SWEET GIRL** (54)	4-Star 1747	$10
45(P)	**THE SAME SWEET GIRL** (54)	4-Star 1747	$12
	(White promo label)		
45rpm	**I CAN'T RUN AWAY** (54)	Decca 28740	$10
45rpm	**LET ME CONFESS** (54)	Decca 29599	$10
45rpm	**YOUR HEART IS AN ISLAND** (56)	RCA Victor 6170	$10
45rpm	**WHO AM I TO CAST THE FIRST STONE** (56)	RCA Victor 6242	$10
45rpm	**WHY, BABY, WHY** (56)	RCA Victor 6247	$10
45rpm	**GEISHA GIRL** (57)	RCA Victor 6984	$10
33rpm	**HAPPY BIRTHDAY TO ME** (61)	RCA Victor 7921	$15
	(Compact-33 single)		

-EPs-

EP(P)	**FOURTEEN KARAT GOLD** (57) Four-song EP	RCA Victor 6778 DJ-53	$18
	(Two songs on the flip side by Dorothy Olsen)		
EP	**FOREIGN LOVE** (58)	RCA Victor 4221	$12
EP	**HANK LOCKLIN** (58)	RCA Victor 5096	$12
EP	**PLEASE HELP ME, I'M FALLING** (60)	RCA Victor 4366	$12
EP	**HANK LOCKLIN'S GREATEST HITS** (61)	RCA Victor LPC-116	$18
	(Compact-33)		

-albums-

LP	**FOREIGN LOVE** (58)	RCA Victor 1673	$40
LP	**PLEASE HELP ME, I'M FALLING**	RCA Victor 2291	$25
LP	**THE BEST OF HANK LOCKLIN** (61)	King 672	$25
LP	**HANK LOCKLIN ENCORES** (61)	King 738	$18
LP	**HANK LOCKLIN** (62)	Camden 705	$18
LP	**HANK LOCKLIN** (62)	Wrangler 1004	$25
LP	**TRIBUTE TO ROY ACUFF, THE KING OF COUNTRY MUSIC** (62)	RCA Victor 2597	$20
LP	**THIS SONG IS JUST FOR YOU** (63)	Camden 765	$18
LP	**HAPPY JOURNEY** (64)	RCA Victor 2464	$18
LP	**10 SONGS** (62)	Design 603	$18
	(Budget label)		
LP	**THE WAYS OF LIFE** (63)	RCA Victor 2680	$18
LP	**IRISH SONGS COUNTRY STYLE** (64)	RCA Victor 2801	$25
LP	**HANK LOCKLIN SINGS HANK WILLIAMS** (64)	RCA Victor 2997	$25
LP	**BORN TO RAMBLE** (65)	Hilltop 6003	$15
	(Budget label)		
LP	**DOWN TEXAS WAY** (65)	Metro 541	$18
LP(P)	**DOWN TEXAS WAY** (65)	Metro 541	$25
	(Yellow promo label)		
LP	**MY KIND OF COUNTRY MUSIC** (65)	Camden 912	$15
LP	**HANK LOCKLIN SINGS EDDY ARNOLD** (65)	RCA Victor 3391	$18

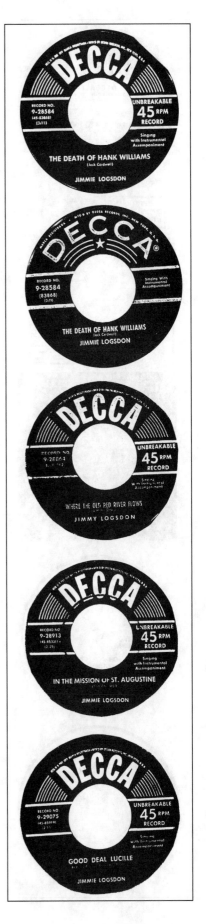

LP	ONCE OVER LIGHTLY (65)	RCA Victor 3465	$18
LP	THE BEST OF HANK LOCKLIN (66)	RCA Victor 3559	$18
LP	THE GIRLS GET PRETTIER (66)	RCA Victor 3588	$18
	(With the Jordanaires)		
LP	THE GLORYLAND WAY (66)	RCA Victor 3656	$18
LP	SEND ME THE PILLOW YOU DREAM ON (67)	RCA Victor 3770	$15
LP	NASHVILLE WOMEN (67)	RCA Victor 3841	$15
LP	BUMMIN' AROUND (67)	Camden 2121	$15
LP	QUEEN OF HEARTS (68)	Hilltop 6063	$12
LP	COUNTRY HALL OF FAME (68)	RCA Victor 3946	$15
LP	MY LOVE SONG FOR YOU (68)	RCA Victor 4030	$15
LP	SOFTLY (69)	RCA Victor 4113	$15
LP	THAT'S HOW MUCH I LOVE YOU (69)	Camden 2266	$15
LP	WABASH CANNONBALL (69)	Camden 2306	$12
LP	LOOKIN' BACK (69)	RCA Victor 4191	$15
LP	THE BEST OF TODAY'S COUNTRY HITS (69)	RCA Victor 6017	$15
LP	BLESS HER HEART, I LOVE HER (70)	RCA Victor 4392	$12
LP	CANDY KISSES (70)	Camden 2447	$12
LP	SEND ME THE PILLOW YOU DREAM ON (70)	Sears 104	$12
LP	THE FIRST FIFTEEN YEARS (71)	RCA Victor 4604	$12
LP	MAYOR OF MCLELLAN, TEXAS (71)	RCA Victor 4800	$12
LP	SEND ME THE PILLOW YOU DREAM ON (73)	Camden 2562	$12
LP	COUNTRY HALL OF FAME (74)	Camden 0427	$12

-radio shows-

LP(RS)	GRAND OL' OPRY (63)	WSM Radio 91	$25-50
	(Music and interviews)		
LP(RS)	HOOTENAVY (60s)	U.S. Navy 21/22	$25-50
	(Music and interviews, flip features Mel Tillis)		
LP(RS)	HOOTENAVY (60s)	U.S. Navy 51/52	$25-50
	(Music and interviews)		

BUD LOGAN (C)
Mercury 45s $2-3 each

TEX LOGAN (BG)
And the Charles River Valley Boys

-albums-

LP	BLUEGRASS GET TOGETHER (64)	Folkways 14024	$20

LOGAN VALLEY BOYS (RB)

-singles-

45rpm	ROCK AND ROLL COUNTRY STYLE (58)	Excellent 279	$50

JIMMIE LOGSDON (CW)
King 78s and 45s $4-6 each
Other Decca 78s $5 each
Other Decca 45s $4-6 each

-singles-

78rpm	THE DEATH OF HANK WILLIAMS (53)	Decca 28584	$25
78(P)	THE DEATH OF HANK WILLIAMS (53)	Decca 28584	$30
	(Pink promo label)		
45rpm	THE DEATH OF HANK WILLIAMS (53) First pressing	Decca 28584	$40
	(Flip side is "Hank Williams Sings the Blues No More," rays on side of Decca)		
45rpm	THE DEATH OF HANK WILLIAMS (53) Second pressing	Decca 28584	$25
	(Wide letters on Decca, star under Decca)		
45(P)	THE DEATH OF HANK WILLIAMS (53) Second pressing	Decca 28584	$18
	(Pink promo label)		
45rpm	WHERE THE OLD RED RIVER FLOWS (54)	Decca 28864	$15
45(P)	WHERE THE OLD RED RIVER FLOWS (54)	Decca 28864	$10
	(Pink promo label)		
45rpm	IN THE MISSION OF ST. AUGUSTINE (54)	Decca 28913	$18
45(P)	IN THE MISSION OF ST. AUGUSTINE (54)	Decca 28913	$12
	(Pink promo label)		
45rpm	GOOD DEAL LUCILLE (55)	Decca 29075	$15
45(P)	GOOD DEAL LUCILLE (55)	Decca 29075	$12
	(Pink promo label)		

-albums-

LP	HOWDY NEIGHBORS (63)	King 843	$30

BOBBY LOLLAR (RB)

-singles-

45rpm	BAD BAD BOY (58)	Benton 101	$125

THE LONE RANGER (CW)
Clayton Moore

-singles-

78rpm	**THE LONE RANGER** (51) Box set	Decca 864	$75
	(Three record 78-rpm box set)		
45rpm	**THE LONE RANGER** (51) Box set	Decca 864	$50
	(Three-record set)		
78rpm	**HE BECOMES THE LONE RANGER** (51)	Decca K-29	$30
	(Price includes picture sleeve)		
45rpm	**HE BECOMES THE LONE RANGER** (51)	Decca K-29	$25
	(Price includes picture sleeve)		
78rpm	**HE FINDS SILVER** (51)	Decca K-30	$30
	(Price includes picture sleeve)		
45rpm	**HE FINDS SILVER** (51)	Decca K-30	$25
	(Price includes picture sleeve)		
78rpm	**HE FINDS DAN REID** (51)	Decca K-31	$30
	(Price includes picture sleeve)		
45rpm	**HE FINDS DAN REID** (51)	Decca K-31	$25
	(Price includes picture sleeve)		
78rpm	**HE HELPS THE COLONEL'S SON** (51)	Decca K-32	$30
	(Price includes picture sleeve)		
45rpm	**HE HELPS THE COLONELS' SON** (51)	Decca K-32	$25
	(Price includes picture sleeve)		

THE LONE STAR RAMBLERS (CW)
-albums-

LP	**TEXAS SQUARE DANCING WITH RED AT THE 60 CLUB** (67)	Longhorn 600	$20

THE LONESOME PINE FIDDLERS (BG)
-albums-

LP	**14 MOUNTAIN SONGS** (61)	Starday 155	$25
LP	**BLUEGRASS** (62)	Starday 194	$25
LP	**MORE BLUEGRASS** (63)	Starday 222	$20
LP	**KENTUCKY BLUEGRASS** (70)	Nashville 2020	$15
	(Budget label)		

LONESOME RHODES (CW)
Sandy and Donna Rhodes

-albums-

LP	**LONESOME RHODES** (67)	RCA Victor 3759	$15

LONESOME RIVER BOYS (BG)
-albums-

LP	**RAISE A RUCKUS** (63)	Riverside 7535	$20
LP	**BLUEGRASS HOOTENANNY** (63)	Battle 96128	$18

CURTIS LONG (RB)
-singles-

45rpm	**HOOTCHY COOTCHY** (58)	Linco 1314	$60

HUEY LONG (RB)
-singles-

45rpm	**ELVIS STOLE MY GAL** (58)	Fidelity 4055	$50

JOHNNY LONG (CW)
-EPs-

EP(JB)	**GOLDEN HITS** (68) Jukebox LLP	Everest 1201	$20
	(Price includes hard cover and title strips)		

SHORTY LONG (CW)
-singles-

45rpm	**I-YI** (54)	X (RCA) 0039	$10

-albums-

LP	**COUNTRY JAMBOREE** (63)	Ford 712	$20

LONG HAIRS (RB)
-singles-

45rpm	**GO GO GO** (58)	Memphis 110	$40

CURTIS LONS (RB)
-singles-

45rpm	**HOOTCHY COOTCHY** (58)	Linco 1314	$18

LONZO & OSCAR (CW)
John and Rollin Sullivan
Decca 78s $3-4 each
Other Decca 45s $4-6 each
Starday 45s $4-6 each
GRC and Brylen LPs $4-6 each

-singles-

45rpm	KNOCK KNEED SUZY (53)	Decca 28510	$10
45rpm	BABY ME BABY (53)	Decca 28624	$10

-albums-

LP	AMERICA'S GREATEST COUNTRY COMEDIANS (60)	Starday 119	$40
LP	COUNTRY MUSIC TIME (63)	Starday 244	$40
LP	COUNTRY COMEDY TIME (63)	Decca 4363	$20
LP(P)	COUNTRY COMEDY TIME (63)	Decca 4363	$25
	(Pink promo label)		
LP	LONZO & OSCAR (65)	Hilltop 6021	$12
LP	MOUNTAIN DEW (68)	Columbia 9587	$15
LP(P)	MOUNTAIN DEW (68)	Columbia 9587	$18
	(White promo label)		
LP	HOLE IN THE BOTTOM OF THE SEA (69)	Nugget 001	$12

BOBBY LORD (CW)
Other Columbia 78s $5 each
Other Columbia 45s $3-6 each

-singles-

45rpm	NO MORE, NO MORE, NO MORE (55)	Columbia 21339	$25
45(P)	NO MORE, NO MORE, NO MORE (55)	Columbia 21339	$20
	(White promo label)		
45rpm	AIN'T CHA EVER GONNA? (55)	Columbia 21367	$12
45(P)	AIN'T CHA EVER GONNA? (55)	Columbia 21367	$10
	(White promo label)		
45rpm	SO DOGGONE LONESOME (56)	Columbia 21498	$15
45rpm	SO DOGGONE LONESOME (56)	Columbia 21498	$12
	(White promo label)		
78rpm	EVERYBODY'S ROCKIN' BUT ME (56)	Columbia 21539	$40
45rpm	EVERYBODY'S ROCKIN' BUT ME (56)	Columbia 21539	$30
45(P)	EVERYBODY'S ROCKIN' BUT ME (56)	Columbia 21539	$25
	(White promo label)		
45rpm	BEAUTIFUL BABY (57)	Columbia 40666	$15
45(P)	BEAUTIFUL BABY (57)	Columbia 40666	$12
	(White promo label)		
45rpm	HIGH VOLTAGE (57)	Columbia 40927	$15
45(P)	HIGH VOLTAGE (57)	Columbia 40927	$12
	(White promo label)		
45rpm	THE FIRE OF LOVE (58)	Columbia 41155	$10
45rpm	PARTY POOPER (58)	Columbia 41352	$10

-albums-

LP	BOBBY LORD'S BEST (64)	Harmony 7322	$25
LP(P)	BOBBY LORD'S BEST (64)	Harmony 7322	$30
	(White promo label)		
LP	THE BOBBY LORD SHOW (65)	Hickory 126	$18
LP(P)	THE BOBBY LORD SHOW (65)	Hickory 126	$25
	(White promo label)		
LP	BOBBY LORD (70)	Decca 5246	$12
LP(P)	BOBBY LORD (70)	Decca 5246	$15
	(White promo label)		

-radio shows-

LP(RS)	COUNTRY MUSIC TIME (60s)	U.S. Air Force	$10-20
	(Flip side features Cowboy Copas)		

JOHN D. LOUDERMILK (CW)
Also known as Johnny Dee and Ebe Sneezer
RCA Victor 45s $5 each
RCA Victor picture sleeves $5-10 each

-singles-

45rpm	SITTIN' IN THE BALCONY (57) Johnny Dee	Colonial 430	$30
	(Original version, later recorded by Eddie Cochran)		
45(P)	SITTIN' IN THE BALCONY (57)	Colonial 430	$40
	(White label promo)		
45rpm	IT'S GOTTA BE YOU/TEENAGE QUEEN (57) Johnny Dee	Colonial 433	$25
45(P)	IT'S GOTTA BE YOU/TEENAGE QUEEN (57)	Colonial 433	$30
	(White promo label)		
45rpm	1000 CONCRETE BLOCKS (58) Johnny Dee	Colonial 435	$25
45(P)	1000 CONCRETE BLOCKS (58)	Colonial 435	$30
	(White label promo)		
45rpm	ASIATIC FLU (58) Ebe Sneezer and the Epidemics	Colonial 436	$30

45(P)	ASIATIC FLU (58)	Colonial 436	$35
	(White promo label)		
45rpm	SOMEBODY SWEET (58)	Dot 15699	$25
45rpm	SUSIE'S HOUSE (58) John D. Loudermilk	Columbia 41165	$15
45rpm	SUSIE'S HOUSE (58)	Columbia 41165	$40
	(Price includes picture sleeve)		
45(P)	SUSIE'S HOUSE (58)	Columbia 41165	$12
	(White promo label)		
45rpm	TOBACCO ROAD (59) John D. Loudermilk	Columbia 41562	$15
	(Original version)		
45(P)	TOBACCO ROAD (59)	Columbia 41562	$12
	(White promo label)		

-albums-

LP	LANGUAGE OF LOVE (61)	RCA Victor 2434	$30
LP	TWELVE SIDES OF LOUDERMILK (62)	RCA Victor 2539	$25
LP	JOHN D. LOUDERMILK SINGS A BIZARRE COLLECTION OF THE MOST UNUSUAL SONGS (65)	RCA Victor 3497	$25
LP	SUBURBAN ATTITUDES IN COUNTRY VERSE (67)	RCA Victor 3807	$20
LP	COUNTRY LOVE SONGS (68)	RCA Victor 4040	$18
LP	THE OPEN MIND OF JOHN D. LOUDERMILK (68)	RCA Victor 4097	$15

LOUISIANA HONEYDRIPPERS (BG)
-albums-

LP	LOUISIANA BLUEGRASS (62)	Prestige 13035	$20

LOUVIN BROTHERS (CW)
Charlie and Ira
Capitol 78s $3-6 each
Other Capitol 45s $4-8 each
Capitol 45s by Charlie Louvin $2-4 each
Capitol 45s by Ira Louvin $4-5 each
Golden Eagle 45s by Charlie Louvin $2 each
Other Capitol LPs $5-10 each
Hilltop LPs $8-10 each
Other Capitol LPs by Charlie Louvin $8-10 each
Capitol LPs by Charlie and Melba $6 each
United Artists LPs by Charlie Louvin $8 each
Accord and Audiograph LPs by Charlie Louvin $4 each
-singles-

45rpm	IF WE FORGET GOD (54)	Capitol 2852	$10
45rpm	SATAN AND THE SAINT (55)	Capitol 2965	$10
45rpm	WHEN I STOP DREAMING (55)	Capitol 3177	$10
45rpm	I DON'T BELIEVE YOU'VE MET MY BABY (56)	Capitol 3300	$10
45rpm	CHILDISH LOVE (56)	Capitol 3413	$10
45rpm	YOU'RE RUNNING WILD (56)	Capitol 3523	$10

-EPs-

EP	THE LOUVIN BROTHERS (56)	Capitol 602	$25
EP	LOVE SONGS OF THE HILLS (56)	Capitol 744	$25
EP	TRAGIC SONGS OF LIFE (56) Vol 1	Capitol 1-769	$30
EP	TRAGIC SONGS OF LIFE (56) Vol 2	Capitol 2-769	$30
EP	TRAGIC SONGS OF LIFE (56) Vol 3	Capitol 3-769	$30
EP	NEARER MY GOD TO THEE (57) Vol 1	Capitol 1-825	$25
EP	NEARER MY GOD TO THEE (57) Vol 2	Capitol 2-825	$25
EP	NEARER MY GOD TO THEE (57) Vol 3	Capitol 3-825	$25
EP	THE LOUVIN BROTHERS (57) Vol 1	MGM 1324	$30
EP	THE LOUVIN BROTHERS (57) Vol 2	MGM 1325	$30
EP	THE LOUVIN BROTHERS (57) Vol 3	MGM 1326	$30
EP	IRA & CHARLIE (58) Vol 1	Capitol 1-910	$20
EP	IRA & CHARLIE (58) Vol 2	Capitol 2-910	$20
EP	IRA & CHARLIE (58) Vol 3	Capitol 3-910	$20
EP	THE FAMILY WHO PRAYS (58) Vol 1	Capitol 1-1061	$18
EP	THE FAMILY WHO PRAYS (58) Vol 2	Capitol 2-1061	$18
EP	THE FAMILY WHO PRAYS (58) Vol 3	Capitol 3-1061	$18
EP	COUNTRY LOVE BALLADS (59)	Capitol 1106	$15
EP	SATAN IS REAL (60) Vol 1	Capitol 1-1277	$18
EP	SATAN IS REAL (60) Vol 2	Capitol 2-1277	$18
EP	SATAN IS REAL (60) Vol 3	Capitol 3-1277	$18
EP(P)	LONESOME IS ME (66) Charlie Louvin	Capitol 2482	$15
	(Jukebox LLP with hard cover)		

-albums-

LP	TRAGIC SONGS OF LIFE (56)	Capitol 769	$100
LP(P)	TRAGIC SONGS OF LIFE (56)	Capitol 769	$80
	(Yellow promo label)		
LP	NEARER MY GOD TO THEE (57)	Capitol 825	$100
LP(P)	NEARER MY GOD TO THEE (57)	Capitol 825	$80
	(Yellow promo label)		

LP	THE LOUVIN BROTHERS (57)	MGM 3426	$200
LP(P)	THE LOUVIN BROTHERS (57)	MGM 3426	$175
	(Yellow promo label)		
LP	IRA & CHARLIE (58)	Capitol 910	$100
LP(P)	IRA & CHARLIE (58)	Capitol 910	$75
	(Yellow promo label)		
LP	THE FAMILY WHO PRAYS (58)	Capitol 1061	$75
LP(P)	THE FAMILY WHO PRAYS (58)	Capitol 1061	$60
	(Yellow promo label)		
LP	COUNTRY LOVE BALLADS (59)	Capitol 1106	$75
LP(P)	COUNTRY LOVE BALLADS (59)	Capitol 1106	$60
	(Yellow promo label)		
LP	SATAN IS REAL (60)	Capitol 1277	$75
LP(P)	SATAN IS REAL (60)	Capitol 1277	$60
	(Yellow promo label)		
LP	MY BABY'S GONE (60)	Capitol 1385	$75
LP(P)	MY BABY'S GONE (60)	Capitol 1385	$60
	(Capitol promo label)		
LP	A TRIBUTE TO THE DELMORE BROTHERS (60)	Capitol 1449	$80
LP(P)	A TRIBUTE TO THE DELMORE BROTHERS (60)	Capitol 1449	$75
	(Capitol promo label)		
LP	ENCORE (61)	Capitol 1547	$50
LP(P)	ENCORE (61)	Capitol 1547	$40
	(Capitol promo label)		
LP	COUNTRY CHRISTMAS (61) Mono	Capitol 1616	$50
LP	COUNTRY CHRISTMAS (61) Stereo	Capitol 1616	$75
LP(P)	COUNTRY CHRISTMAS (61)	Capitol 1616	$60
	(Capitol promo label)		
LP	WEAPON OF PRAYER (62)	Capitol 1721	$40
LP(P)	WEAPON OF PRAYER (62)	Capitol 1721	$30
	(Capitol promo label)		
LP	KEEP YOUR EYES ON JESUS (63)	Capitol 1834	$40
LP(P)	KEEP YOUR EYES ON JESUS (63)	Capitol 1834	$30
	(Capitol promo label)		
LP	SING & PLAY THEIR CURRENT HITS (64)	Capitol 2091	$25
LP(P)	SING & PLAY THEIR CURRENT HITS (64)	Capitol 2091	$20
	(Blue promo label)		
LP	LESS AND LESS (65) Charlie Louvin	Capitol 2208	$15
LP(P)	LESS AND LESS (65)	Capitol 2208	$18
	(Blue promo label)		
LP	THANK GOD FOR MY CHRISTIAN HOME (65)	Capitol 2331	$25
LP(P)	THANK GOD FOR MY CHRISTIAN HOME (65)	Capitol 2331	$20
	(Blue promo label)		
LP	THE UNFORGETTABLE IRA LOUVIN (65) Ira Louvin	Capitol 2413	$25
LP(P)	THE UNFORGETTABLE IRA LOUVIN (65)	Capitol 2413	$20
	(Blue promo label)		
LP	MANY MOODS OF CHARLIE LOUVIN (66) Charlie Louvin	Capitol 2437	$15
LP(P)	MANY MOODS OF CHARLIE LOUVIN (66)	Capitol 2437	$18
	(Blue promo label)		
LP	TWO DIFFERENT WORLDS (66)	Tower 5038	$20
LP(P)	TWO DIFFERENT WORLDS (66)	Tower 5038	$30
	(White promo label)		
LP	LONESOME IS ME (66) Charlie Louvin	Capitol 2482	$15
LP(P)	LONESOME IS ME (66)	Capitol 2482	$18
	(Blue promo label)		
LP	I'LL REMEMBER ALWAYS (67) Charlie Louvin	Capitol 2689	$12
LP	I FORGOT TO CRY (67) Charlie Louvin	Capitol 2787	$12
LP	THE LOUVIN BROTHERS (67)	Metro 598	$25
	(Reissue of the MGM album)		
LP(P)	THE LOUVIN BROTHERS (67)	Metro 598	$40
	(Yellow promo label)		
LP	THE GREAT ROY ACUFF SONGS (67)	Capitol 2827	$25
LP(P)	THE GREAT ROY ACUFF SONGS (67)	Capitol 2827	$20
	(Blue promo label)		
LP	WILL YOU VISIT ME ON SUNDAYS (68) Charlie Louvin	Capitol 2958	$12
LP	COUNTRY HEART & SOUL (68)	Tower 5122	$20
LP(P)	COUNTRY HEART & SOUL (68)	Tower 5122	$25
	(White promo label)		
LP	TWO DIFFERENT WORLDS (67)	Capitol 5038	$15
LP	COUNTRY HEART AND SOUL (68)	Capitol 5122	$15
LP	HEY DADDY (68) Charlie Louvin	Capitol 142	$15
LP	THE KIND OF MAN I AM (68) Charlie Louvin	Capitol 248	$15
LP	HERE'S A TOAST TO MAMA (69) Charlie Louvin	Capitol 416	$15
	-radio shows-		
LP(RS)	COUNTRY MUSIC TIME (60s)	U.S. Air Force	$50-100
	(Flip side features Ernest Tubb)		
LP(RS)	COUNTRY MUSIC TIME (60s)	U.S. Air Force 197	$40-75
	(Flip side features Hank Snow)		

LP(RS)	**COUNTRY MUSIC TIME** (60s)	U.S. Air Force 217	$20-40
	(Flip side features Hank Snow)		
LP(RS)	**LOUVIN BROTHERS AND ERNEST TUBB**	U.S. Air Force	$40-75
	(Public service radio show, USAF show #294)		

LOVE BROTHERS (RB)

-singles-

45rpm	**BABY, I'LL NEVER LET YOU GO** (58)	By-Love 843	$50

PATTY LOVELESS (C)
Other MCA 45s $2 each
MCA LPs $3 each

-singles-

45(P)	**LONELY DAYS, LONELY NIGHTS** (85)	MCA 52694	$12
	(White promo label, yellow vinyl, price includes picture sleeve)		
45(P)	**I DID** (86)	MCA 52787	$10
	(White promo label, blue vinyl)		
45(P)	**I DID** (87)	MCA 53040	$10
	(White promo label, blue vinyl)		
45(P)	**AFTER ALL** (87)	MCA 53097	$10
	(White promo label, yellow vinyl)		

-radio shows-

LP(RS)	**LIVE FROM GILLEY'S** (Sept 88)	Westwood One	$10-15
	(Live concert)		

LYLE LOVETT (C)
Other MCA 45s $2 each
MCA LPs $3 each

-singles-

45(P)	**COWBOY MAN** (86)	MCA 52951	$15
	(Black promo label, white print, clear vinyl, perhaps the most beautiful record in this book!)		
45(P)	**GOD WILL** (87)	MCA 53030	$10
	(White promo label, blue vinyl)		

-radio shows-

LP(RS)	**WESTWOOD ONE PRESENTS** (June 89)	Westwood One	$40-75
	(Rare live concert)		

JIM LOWE (R)
Other Dot 45s $5-10 each

-singles-

78rpm	**CLOSE THE DOOR** (55)	Dot 15381	$20
45rpm	**CLOSE THE DOOR** (55)	Dot 15381	$18
78rpm	**MAYBELLENE** (55)	Dot 15407	$20
45rpm	**MAYBELLENE** (55) Maroon label	Dot 15407	$18
78rpm	**BLUE SUEDE SHOES** (56)	Dot 15456	$25
45rpm	**BLUE SUEDE SHOES** (56) Maroon label	Dot 15456	$18
78rpm	**THE GREEN DOOR** (56) Maroon label	Dot 15486	$25
78rpm	**THE GREEN DOOR** (56) Black label	Dot 15486	$30
45rpm	**THE GREEN DOOR** (56) Maroon label	Dot 15486	$18
45rpm	**THE GREEN DOOR** (56) Black label	Dot 15486	$15
78rpm	**BY YOU, BY YOU, BY YOU** (56)	Dot 15525	$15
45rpm	**BY YOU, BY YOU, BY YOU** (56)	Dot 15525	$12
45rpm	**PRINCE OF PEACE** (56)	Mercury 71016	$12
45(P)	**PRINCE OF PEACE** (56)	Mercury 71016	$15
	(White promo label)		
45rpm	**FOUR WALLS** (57)	Dot 15569	$10
45rpm	**SLOW TRAIN** (57)	Dot 15611	$10
45rpm	**THE BRIGHT LIGHT** (57)	Dot 15665	$15
	(Flip side is "Rock-A-Chicka")		
45rpm	**THE LADY FROM JOHANNESBERG** (58)	Dot 15693	$12
45rpm	**CHAPEL BELLS ON CHAPEL HILL** (58)	Dot 15832	$18
45rpm	**PLAY NUMBER THEVEN** (58)	Dot 15869	$12
45rpm	**WITHOUT YOU** (59)	Dot 15954	$12
	(Written by David Seville)		

-EPs-

EP	**RAINBOW** (57)	Dot 1061	$25
	(Issued with a hard cover)		

-albums-

LP	**THE DOOR OF FAME** (57)	Mercury 20246	$100
LP(P)	**THE DOOR OF FAME** (57)	Mercury 20246	$125
	(White promo label)		
LP	**SONGS THEY SING BEHIND THE GREEN DOOR** (57) Mono	Dot 3051	$150
LP	**SONGS THEY SING BEHIND THE GREEN DOOR** (58) Stereo	Dot 25051	$125
LP	**WICKED WOMEN** (58)	Dot 3114	$100

BILL LOWERY (CW,G)
Other Capitol 45s $5 each

-singles-

45rpm	**I DREAMED OF A HILLBILLY HEAVEN** (57)	Capitol 3053	$15
45(P)	**I DREAMED OF A HILLBILLY HEAVEN** (57)	Capitol 3053	$12
	(White promo label)		

LS (C)
Elvis imitation

-singles-

45(P)	**SPELLING ON THE STONE** (88)	Curb 10522	$10
	(Mystery record, as were many Elvis-related post-1977 records)		

NICK LUCAS (CW)

-albums-

LP	**PAINTING THE CLOUDS WITH SUNSHINE** (57)	Decca 8653	$40
LP(P)	**PAINTING THE CLOUDS WITH SUNSHINE** (57)	Decca 8653	$25
	(Pink promo label)		

ROBIN LUKE (R)
Other Dot 45s $5-8 each

-singles-

45rpm	**SUSIE DARLIN'** (57)	International 206	$50
	(Original label)		
45rpm	**SUSIE DARLIN'** (57)	International 206	$150
	(Price includes picture sleeve)		
45rpm	**MY GIRL** (57)	International 208	$30
45rpm	**STROLLIN' BLUES** (58)	International 210	$30
45rpm	**FIVE MINUTES MORE** (58)	International 212	$30
45rpm	**SUSIE DARLIN'** (58)	Dot 15781	$15
45rpm	**CHICKA CHICKA HONEY** (58)	Dot 15879	$18
	(Flip side is "My Girl")		
45rpm	**YOU CAN'T STOP ME FROM DREAMING** (58)	Dot 15899	$15
	(Flip side is "Strollin' Blues")		
45rpm	**FIVE MINUTES MORE** (59)	Dot 15959	$15
45rpm	**MAKE ME A DREAMER** (59)	Dot 16001	$12
45rpm	**BAD BOY** (60)	Dot 16040	$10
45rpm	**EVERLOVIN'** (60)	Dot 16096	$50
	(Price includes picture sleeve)		

-EPs-

EP	**SUSIE DARLIN'** (58)	Dot 1092	$500
	(Issued with a hard cover)		

LULU BELLE & SCOTTY (CW)
Other Mercury 78s and 45s $5-10 each
Starday 45s $4 each
Old Homestead and Birch LPs $5-10 each

-singles-

78rpm	**SOME SUNDAY MORNING** (50) Vogue picture disc	Vogue 718	$50
78rpm	**I GET A KICK OUT OF CORN** (50) Vogue picture disc	Vogue 719	$40
78rpm	**TIME WILL TELL** (50) Vogue picture disc	Vogue 720	$40
78rpm	**THAT'S ONLY HALF OF IT** (53)	Mercury 70092	$10
78(P)	**THAT'S ONLY HALF OF IT** (53)	Mercury 70092	$15
	(White promo label)		
45rpm	**THAT'S ONLY HALF OF IT** (53)	Mercury 70092	$10

-albums-

LP	**LULU BELLE & SCOTTY** (63)	Super 6201	$50
LP	**THE SWEETHEARTS OF COUNTRY MUSIC** (63)	Starday 206	$30
LP	**DOWN MEMORY LANE** (64)	Starday 285	$30
LP	**LULU BELLE & SCOTTY** (65)	Starday 351	$30

BOB LUMAN (RB)
Other Warner 45s $5-8 each
Hickory 45s $3-5 each
Other Hickory LPs $5-10 each
Other Epic LPs $5-8 each
Other Harmony LPs $6 each
Polydor LPs $5 each

-singles-

45rpm	**RED CADILLAC & BLACK MUSTACHE** (58) Maroon label	Imperial 5705	$100
45rpm	**RED CADILLAC & BLACK MUSTACHE** (58) Black label	Imperial 5705	$50
45(P)	**RED CADILLAC & BLACK MUSTACHE** (58)	Imperial 5705	$75
	(Cream-colored promo label)		
45rpm	**RED CADILLAC & BLACK MUSTACHE** (58) Maroon label	Imperial 8311	$100
45rpm	**RED CADILLAC & BLACK MUSTACHE** (58) Black label	Imperial 8311	$50
45(P)	**RED CADILLAC & BLACK MUSTACHE** (58)	Imperial 8311	$75
	(Cream-colored promo label)		

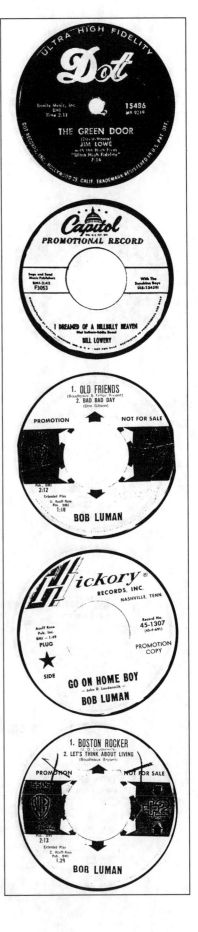

45rpm	**RED HOT** (58) Maroon label	Imperial 8313	$100
45rpm	**RED HOT** (58) Black label	Imperial 8313	$50
45(P)	**RED HOT** (58)	Imperial 8313	$75
	(Cream-colored promo label)		
45rpm	**MAKE UP YOUR MIND BABY** (56) Maroon label	Imperial 8315	$75
45rpm	**MAKE UP YOUR MIND BABY** (56) Black label	Imperial 8315	$40
45(P)	**MAKE UP YOUR MIND BABY** (56)	Imperial 8315	$50
	(Cream-colored promo label)		
45rpm	**TRY ME** (58)	Capitol 3972	$25
45(P)	**TRY ME** (58)	Capitol 3972	$30
	(Promotional debut record, yellow label)		
45(P)	**TRY ME** (58)	Capitol 3972	$20
	(White promo label)		
45rpm	**PRECIOUS** (58)	Capitol 4059	$18
45(P)	**PRECIOUS** (58)	Capitol 4059	$15
	(Capitol promo label)		
45rpm	**CLASS OF '59** (59)	Warner 5081	$18
45(P)	**CLASS OF '59** (59)	Warner 5081	$15
	(White promo label)		
45rpm	**DREAMY DOLL** (60)	Warner 5105	$18
45(P)	**DREAMY DOLL** (60)	Warner 5105	$15
	(White promo label)		
45rpm	**LET'S THINK ABOUT LIVING** (60)	Warner 5172	$18
45rpm	**LET'S THINK ABOUT LIVING** (60)	Warner 5172	$60
	(Price includes picture sleeve)		
45(P)	**LET'S THINK ABOUT LIVING** (60)	Warner 5172	$20
	(White promo label)		
45rpm	**OH LONESOME ME** (61)	Warner 5184	$50
	(Price includes picture sleeve)		
45(P)	**OH LONESOME ME** (61)	Warner 5184	$12
	(White promo label)		
45rpm	**THE GREAT SHOWMAN** (61)	Warner 5204	$40
	(Price includes picture sleeve)		
45(P)	**THE GREAT SHOWMAN** (61)	Warner 5204	$12
	(White promo label)		
45rpm	**YOU'VE TURNED DOWN THE LIGHT** (61)	Warner 5233	$40
	(Price includes picture sleeve)		
45(P)	**YOU'VE TURNED DOWN THE LIGHT** (61)	Warner 5233	$10
	(White promo label)		

-EPs-

EP	**LET'S THINK ABOUT LIVING** (60)	Warner Bros 1396	$300
	(Issued with a hard cover)		
EP	**BOSTON ROCKER/LET'S THINK ABOUT LIVING** (61)	Warner Bros 5506	$175
	(Four-song EP includes two oldies, red label)		
EP(P)	**BOSTON ROCKER/LET'S THINK ABOUT LIVING** (61)	Warner Bros 5506	$250
	(White and red promo label, issued without cover)		
EP(P)	**LIVIN,' LOVIN' SOUNDS** (65)	Hickory 124-006	$50
	(Promo six-pac, issued with paper picture sleeve)		

-albums-

LP	**LET'S THINK ABOUT LIVING** (60) Mono	Warner Bros 1396	$50
LP	**LET'S THINK ABOUT LIVING** (60) Stereo	Warner Bros 1396	$75
LP(P)	**LET'S THINK ABOUT LIVING** (60)	Warner Bros 1396	$100
	(White promo label)		
LP	**LIVIN' LOVIN' SOUNDS** (65)	Hickory 124	$18
LP(P)	**LIVIN' LOVIN' SOUNDS** (65)	Hickory 124	$25
	(White promo label)		
LP	**AIN'T GOT TIME TO BE UNHAPPY** (68)	Epic 26393	$10
LP(P)	**AIN'T GOT TIME TO BE UNHAPPY** (68)	Epic 26393	$12
	(White promo label)		
LP	**COME ON HOME AND SING THE BLUES TO DADDY** (69)	Epic 26463	$10
LP(P)	**COME ON HOME AND SING THE BLUES TO DADDY** (69)	Epic 26463	$12
	(White promo label)		
LP	**BOB LUMAN** (72)	Harmony 32006	$10
LP(P)	**BOB LUMAN** (72)	Harmony 32006	$12
	(White promo label)		

ROBERT LUNN (CW)
Starday 45s $2 each

-albums-

LP	**THE ORIGINAL TALKING BLUES MAN** (62)	Starday 228	$18

MICHAEL LUNSFORD (C)
-albums-

LP	**MIKE LUNSFORD** (75)	Starday 951	$12
LP	**MIKE LUNSFORD** (77)	Starday 969	$10

FRANK LUTHER See Carson Robison

GERRIE LYNN (C)
Columbia 45s $2 each

-albums-

LP	**PRESENTING GERRIE LYNN** (67)	Columbia 9385	$15
LP(P)	**PRESENTING GERRIE LYNN** (67)	Columbia 9385	$12
	(White promo label)		

JUDY LYNN (C)
United Artists 45s $2-3 each
United Artists picture sleeves $4 each
Musicor, Unart 45s $2-3 each
Columbia 45s $1-2 each
Musicor duet LPs $8 each
Amaret LPs $5 each

-albums-

LP	**JUDY LYNN SINGS AT THE GOLDEN NUGGET** (62)	United Artists 6226	$18
	(With the Sunshine Boys)		
LP(P)	**JUDY LYNN SINGS AT THE GOLDEN NUGGET** (62)	United Artists 6226	$25
	(White promo label)		
LP	**HERE IS OUR GAL JUDY LYNN** (63)	United Artists 6288	$15
LP(P)	**HERE IS OUR GAL JUDY LYNN** (63)	United Artists 6288	$18
	(White promo label)		
LP	**COUNTRY & WESTERN GIRL SINGER** (64)	United Artists 6342	$15
LP(P)	**COUNTRY & WESTERN GIRL SINGER** (64)	United Artists 6342	$18
	(White promo label)		
LP	**THE JUDY LYNN SHOW** (64)	United Artists 6390	$12
LP(P)	**THE JUDY LYNN SHOW** (64)	United Artists 6390	$15
	(White promo label)		
LP	**THE JUDY LYNN SHOW ACT 2** (65)	United Artists 6443	$12
LP(P)	**THE JUDY LYNN SHOW ACT 2** (65)	United Artists 6443	$15
	(White promo label)		
LP	**THE BEST OF JUDY LYNN** (66)	United Artists 6461	$10
LP	**THE JUDY LYNN SHOW PLAYS AGAIN** (66)	Musicor 3096	$15
LP	**HONEY STUFF** (66)	Musicor 3112	$15
	(With the Jordanaires)		
LP	**GOLDEN NUGGETS** (67)	Musicor 3126	$12
LP	**JUDY LYNN IN LAS VEGAS** (67)	Unart 21009	$10
LP	**JUDY LYNN SINGS AT CAESAR'S PALACE** (69)	Columbia 9879	$12
LP(P)	**JUDY LYNN SINGS AT CAESAR'S PALACE** (69)	Columbia 9879	$15
	(White promo label)		

-albums-

16"(RS)	**NAVY HOEDOWN** (60s) With Jean Shepard	U.S. Navy	$10-20
	(Music and interviews)		

LORETTA LYNN (CW)
Decca 45s $2-5 each
Other Decca picture sleeves $5 each
MCA LPs $3-6 each
Trolly Car LPs $8 each
Coral LPs $3 each

-singles-

45rpm	**HONKY TONK GIRL** (60)	Zero 107	$75
	(First pressing)		
45rpm	**HEARTACHES MEET MR. BLUES** (60)	Zero 110	$75
45rpm	**THE DARKEST DAY** (60)	Zero 112	$60
45rpm	**HONKY TONK GIRL** (60)	Zero 1011	$25
	(Second pressing, this version charted)		
45rpm	**COAL MINER'S DAUGHTER** (70)	Decca 32749	$10
	(Price includes picture sleeve)		
45(PD)	**SEASON'S GREETINGS** (72) Picture disc	(Decca) 7211281	$75
	(Conway Twitty and Loretta Lynn picture disc, small center hole, no label)		

-EPs-

EP(P)	**LORETTA LYNN SINGS** (63) Jukebox LLP	Decca 34226	$50
	(Issued with a hard cover and title strips)		
EP	**THE OTHER WOMAN** (64)	Decca 2762	$25
	(First stock copy EP, with hard cover)		
EP(P)	**SONGS FROM THE HEART** (64) Jukebox LLP	Decca 34318	$40
	(Issued with a hard cover and title strips)		
EP	**WINE, WOMEN & SONG** (65)	Decca 2784	$20
	(Issued with a hard cover)		
EP	**THE END OF THE WORLD** (65)	Decca 2793	$18
	(Issued with a hard cover)		
EP	**SONGS FROM THE HEART** (65)	Decca 2800	$15
	(Issued with a hard cover)		

EP(P)	**I LIKE 'EM COUNTRY** (66) Jukebox LLP	Decca 34374	$30
	(Hard cover and title strips included)		
EP(P)	**YOU AIN'T WOMAN ENOUGH** (66) Jukebox LLP	Decca 34418	$20
	(Hard cover and title strips included)		
EP(P)	**FIST CITY** (68) Jukebox LLP	Decca 34531	$25
	(Hard cover and title strips included)		
EP(P)	**ONE'S ON THE WAY** (72) Jukebox LLP	Decca 34877	$15
	(Paper sleeve and title strips included)		
PD(P)	**CHRISTMAS GREETINGS** (72) Seven-inch picture disc EP	Decca Records	$40
	(Promo-only picture disc with Conway Twitty)		

-albums-

LP	**LORETTA LYNN SINGS** (63) Mono	Decca 4457	$40
LP	**LORETTA LYNN SINGS** (63) Stereo	Decca 74457	$50
LP(P)	**LORETTA LYNN SINGS** (63)	Decca 4457	$50
	(Pink promo label)		
LP	**BEFORE I'M OVER YOU** (64) Mono	Decca 4541	$25
LP	**BEFORE I'M OVER YOU** (64) Stereo	Decca 4541	$30
LP(P)	**BEFORE I'M OVER YOU** (64)	Decca 4541	$30
	(Pink promo label)		
LP	**SONGS FROM MY HEART** (65) Mono	Decca 4620	$25
LP	**SONGS FROM MY HEART** (65) Stereo	Decca 4620	$30
LP(P)	**SONGS FROM MY HEART** (65)	Decca 4620	$30
	(Pink promo label)		
LP	**ERNEST TUBB & LORETTA LYNN** (65) Mono	Decca 4639	$25
LP	**ERNEST TUBB & LORETTA LYNN** (65) Stereo	Decca 4639	$30
LP(P)	**ERNEST TUBB & LORETTA LYNN** (65)	Decca 4639	$30
	(Pink promo label)		
LP	**BLUE KENTUCKY GIRL** (65) Mono	Decca 4665	$25
LP	**BLUE KENTUCKY GIRL** (65) Stereo	Decca 4665	$30
LP(P)	**BLUE KENTUCKY GIRL** (65)	Decca 4665	$30
	(Decca promo label)		
LP	**HYMNS** (65) Mono	Decca 4695	$25
LP	**HYMNS** (65) Stereo	Decca 4695	$30
LP(P)	**HYMNS** (65)	Decca 4695	$30
	(Decca promo label)		
LP	**I LIKE 'EM COUNTRY** (66) Mono	Decca 4744	$18
LP	**I LIKE 'EM COUNTRY** (66) Stereo	Decca 4744	$25
LP(P)	**I LIKE 'EM COUNTRY** (66)	Decca 4744	$30
	(Decca promo label)		
LP	**YOU AIN'T WOMAN ENOUGH** (66) Mono	Decca 4783	$18
LP	**YOU AIN'T WOMAN ENOUGH** (66) Stereo	Decca 4783	$25
LP(P)	**YOU AIN'T WOMAN ENOUGH** (66)	Decca 4783	$30
	(Decca promo label)		
LP	**A COUNTRY CHRISTMAS** (66) Mono	Decca 4817	$18
LP	**A COUNTRY CHRISTMAS** (66) Stereo	Decca 4817	$25
LP(P)	**A COUNTRY CHRISTMAS** (66)	Decca 4817	$30
	(Decca promo label)		
LP	**DON'T COME HOME A DRINKIN'** (67) Mono	Decca 4842	$18
LP	**DON'T COME HOME A DRINKIN'** (67) Stereo	Decca 4842	$25
LP(P)	**DON'T COME HOME A DRINKIN'** (67)	Decca 4842	$30
	(Decca promo label)		
LP	**ERNEST TUBB & LORETTA LYNN SINGIN' AGAIN** (67)	Decca 4872	$15
LP(P)	**ERNEST TUBB & LORETTA LYNN SINGIN' AGAIN** (67)	Decca 4872	$18
	(White promo label)		
LP	**WHO SAYS GOD IS DEAD!** (68)	Decca 4928	$15
LP(P)	**WHO SAYS GOD IS DEAD!** (68)	Decca 4928	$18
	(White promo label)		
LP	**SINGIN' WITH FEELIN'** (67)	Decca 4930	$15
LP(P)	**SINGIN' WITH FEELIN'** (67)	Decca 4930	$18
	(White promo label)		
LP	**FIST CITY** (68)	Decca 4997	$15
LP(P)	**FIST CITY** (68)	Decca 4997	$18
	(White promo label)		
LP	**HERE'S LORETTA LYNN** (68)	Vocalion 3853	$15
LP(P)	**HERE'S LORETTA LYNN** (68)	Vocalion 3853	$18
	(White promo label)		
LP	**LORETTA LYNN'S GREATEST HITS** (68)	Decca 75000	$12
LP	**YOUR SQUAW IS ON THE WARPATH** (69) With Barney	Decca 75084	$40
LP	**YOUR SQUAW IS ON THE WARPATH** (69) No Barney	Decca 75084	$15
LP(P)	**YOUR SQUAW IS ON THE WARPATH** (69) With Barney	Decca 75084	$50
	(White promo label)		
LP(P)	**YOUR SQUAW IS ON THE WARPATH** (69) No Barney	Decca 75084	$20
	(White promo label)		
LP	**A WOMAN OF THE WORLD** (69)	Decca 75113	$15
LP(P)	**A WOMAN OF THE WORLD** (69)	Decca 75113	$18
	(White promo label)		
LP	**IF WE PUT OUR HEADS TOGETHER** (69) With Ernest Tubb	Decca 75115	$15

LP(P)	**IF WE PUT OUR HEADS TOGETHER** (69)	Decca 75115	$18
	(White promo label)		
LP	**WINGS UPON YOUR HORNS** (70)	Decca 75163	$15
LP(P)	**WINGS UPON YOUR HORNS** (70)	Decca 75163	$18
	(White promo label)		
LP	**WRITES 'EM AND SINGS 'EM** (70)	Decca 75198	$15
LP(P)	**WRITES 'EM AND SINGS 'EM** (70)	Decca 75198	$18
	(White promo label)		
LP	**COAL MINER'S DAUGHTER** (71)	Decca 75253	$20
LP(P)	**COAL MINER'S DAUGHTER** (71)	Decca 75253	$25
	(White promo label)		
LP	**I WANNA BE FREE** (71)	Decca 75282	$12
LP(P)	**I WANNA BE FREE** (71)	Decca 75282	$15
	(White promo label)		
LP	**YOU'RE LOOKIN' AT COUNTRY** (71)	Decca 75310	$12
LP(P)	**YOU'RE LOOKIN' AT COUNTRY** (71)	Decca 75310	$10
	(White promo label)		
LP	**ONE'S ON THE WAY** (72)	Decca 75334	$12
LP(P)	**ONE'S ON THE WAY** (72)	Decca 75334	$10
	(White promo label)		
LP	**ALONE WITH YOU** (72)	Vocalion 3925	$12
LP(P)	**ALONE WITH YOU** (72)	Vocalion 3925	$15
	(White promo label)		
LP	**GOD BLESS AMERICA AGAIN** (72)	Decca 75351	$12
LP(P)	**GOD BLESS AMERICA AGAIN** (72)	Decca 75351	$10
	(White promo label)		
LP	**HERE I AM AGAIN** (72)	Decca 75381	$12
LP(P)	**HERE I AM AGAIN** (72)	Decca 75381	$10
	(White promo label)		
LP(P)	**LORETTA LYNN (GREATEST HITS)** (74)	MCA 1934	$50
	(Promo only with a white label)		
2LP	**THE BEST OF LORETTA LYNN** (76)	CM 1043	$20
	(Released through *Country Music Magazine*)		
2LP	**ON THE ROAD WITH LORETTA & THE COAL MINERS** (76)	Loretta Lynn 1001	$50
	(Double-LP sold at Lynn's concerts)		
LP(P)	**ALLIS-CHALMERS PRESENTS LORETTA LYNN** (78)	MCA 35013	$40
	(Promo-only release)		
2LP	**ALL MY BEST** (78)	Tee Vee 1024	$15
	(Mail-in offer from television)		
LP(P)	**CRISCO PRESENTS COUNTRY CLASSICS** (79)	MCA 35018	$40
	(Promo-only release)		

-radio shows-

3LP(RS)	**THE SILVER EAGLE** (Sept 82) With Con Hundley	DIR	$40-75
	(Live concert)		
3LP(RS)	**THE AMERICAN EAGLE** (Sept 86) With Dolly Parton	DIR	$50-100
	(Live concert)		
LP(RS)	**THE BEST OF GILLEY'S** (May 88) With Alabama	Westwood One	$25-40
	(Live concert)		
LP(RS)	**WESTWOOD ONE PRESENTS** (Apr 89)	Westwood One	$50-100
	(Rare live concert)		

M

LEON MACH (RB)

-singles-

45rpm	**YOU HURT ME SO** (58)	Lavender 1554	$50

BILL MACK (RB)

-singles-

45rpm	**KITTY KAT** (58)	Starday 231	$50
45rpm	**CAT JUST GOT IN TOWN** (58)	Starday 252	$40

WARNER MACK (CW)
Warner MacPherson
Other Decca 45s $3-6 each
Decca LPs $12 each

-singles-

45rpm	**BABY SQUEEZE ME** (57)	Decca 30301	$15
45(P)	**BABY SQUEEZE ME** (57)	Decca 30301	$12
	(Pink promo label)		
45rpm	**ROC-A-CHICKA** (58)	Decca 30471	$15

45(P)	**ROC-A-CHICKA** (58)		Decca 30471	$12
	(Pink promo label)			

-EPs-

EP	**SITTIN' IN A ALL NITE CAFE** (65)		Decca 2805	$12

-albums-

LP	**GOLDEN COUNTRY HITS** (61)		Kapp 3255	$15
LP	**GOLDEN COUNTRY HITS** Vol 2 (62)		Kapp 3279	$15

UNCLE DAVE MACON (CW, BG)

Bluebird 78s $25 each
Brunswick 78s $30-40 each
Champion 78s $25-$75 each
Decca and Ward 78s $10 each
Okeh 78s $50 each
Vocalion 78s $20-$35
Vetco, County, Rounder, Old Homestead, and Davis LPs $3-6 each
Folkways LPs $8 each

-albums-

LP	**UNCLE DAVE MACON** (66)		Decca 4760	$30
LP(P)	**UNCLE DAVE MACON** (66)		Decca 4760	$35
	(Pink promo label)			

MADDOX BROTHERS (CW)

With Rose Maddox
Decca 78s $5-10 each
Columbia 78s $5-10 each
Other Columbia 45s $8-10 each
Other Capitol 45s $5 each
Sears and Piccadilly LPs $8 each
Arhoolie LPs $6 each

-singles-

78rpm	**MIDNIGHT TRAIN** (50) Maddox Brothers and Rose		4-Star 1184	$12
78rpm	**MILK COW BLUES** (51) Maddox Brothers and Rose		4-Star 1185	$15
78rpm	**ROCK ALL OUR BABIES TO SLEEP** (52) Maddox Brothers		4-Star 3899	$12
45rpm	**WHY NOT CONFESS** (52) Maddox Brothers and Rose		Decca 28551	$18
45rpm	**THE HICCOUGH SONG** (53) Maddox Brothers and Rose		Columbia 21062	$15
45rpm	**NO HELP WANTED** (53) Maddox Brothers and Rose		Columbia 21065	$15
45rpm	**THE LIFE THAT YOU'VE LED** (54) Rose Maddox		Columbia 21297	$12
45(P)	**THE LIFE THAT YOU'VE LED** (54)		Columbia 21297	$10
	(White promo label)			
45rpm	**WILD WILD YOUNG MEN** (54) Maddox Brothers and Rose		Columbia 21394	$18
45(P)	**WILD WILD YOUNG MEN** (54)		Columbia 21394	$15
	(White promo label)			
45rpm	**NO MORE TIME** (55) Maddox Brothers and Rose		Columbia 21405	$10
45rpm	**THE DEATH OF ROCK AND ROLL** (55) Maddox Bros and Rose		Columbia 21559	$30
45(P)	**THE DEATH OF ROCK AND ROLL** (55)		Columbia 21559	$25
	(White promo label)			
45rpm	**LOOKY THERE OVER THERE** (55) Maddox Bros and Rose		Columbia 40814	$10
45rpm	**UGLY AND SLOUCHY** (56) Maddox Brothers and Rose		Columbia 40836	$15
45(P)	**UGLY AND SLOUCHY** (56)		Columbia 40836	$12
	(White promo label)			
45rpm	**TAKE A GAMBLE ON ME** (56) Rose Maddox		Columbia 40873	$10
45rpm	**LOVE IS STRANGE** (56) Maddox Brothers and Rose		Columbia 40895	$10
45rpm	**STOP WHISTLIN' WOLF** (57) Maddox Brothers and Rose		Columbia 41020	$15
45(P)	**STOP WHISTLIN' WOLF** (57)		Columbia 41020	$12
	(White promo label)			
45rpm	**MY LITTLE BABY** (59) Rose Maddox		Capitol 4241	$12
45(P)	**MY LITTLE BABY** (59) Rose Maddox		Capitol 4241	$10
	(Blue promo label)			

-EPs-

EP	**PRECIOUS MEMORIES** (58) Rose Maddox		Columbia 11591	$30
EP	**ONE ROSE** (60) Vol 1 Rose Maddox		Capitol 1-1312	$18
EP	**ONE ROSE** (60) Vol 2		Capitol 2-1312	$18
EP	**ONE ROSE** (60) Vol 3		Capitol 3-1312	$18

-albums-

LP	**PRECIOUS MEMORIES** (58) Rose Maddox		Columbia 1159	$35
LP	**A COLLECTION OF STANDARD SACRED SONGS** (59)		King 669	$50
	(Maddox Brothers and Rose)			
LP	**THE ONE ROSE** (60) Rose Maddox		Capitol 1312	$30
LP(P)	**THE ONE ROSE** (60)		Capitol 1312	$35
	(Capitol promo label)			
LP	**GLORYBOUND TRAIN** (60) Rose Maddox		Capitol 1437	$25
LP(P)	**GLORYBOUND TRAIN** (60)		Capitol 1437	$30
	(Capitol promo label)			
LP	**A BIG BOUQUET OF ROSES** (61) Rose Maddox		Capitol 1548	$25
LP(P)	**A BIG BOUQUET OF ROSES** (61)		Capitol 1548	$30
	(Capitol promo label)			

LP	THE MADDOX BROTHERS AND ROSE (61)	King 677	$25
LP	I'LL WRITE YOUR NAME IN THE SAND (61)	King 752	$25
	(Maddox Brothers and Rose)		
LP	THE MADDOX BROTHERS AND ROSE (62)	Wrangler 1003	$25
LP	THE MADDOX BROTHERS AND ROSE (62)	Forum 2503	$18
	(Reissue of above)		
LP	ROSE MADDOX SINGS BLUEGRASS (62)	Capitol 1799	$50
	(Rose Maddox with Bill Monroe)		
LP	ALONE WITH YOU (63) Rose Maddox	Capitol 1993	$25
LP	GO HONKY TONKIN' (65)	Hilltop 6007	$12
	(Later released on Sears)		

MADDY BROTHERS (RB)
-singles-

45rpm	ROCKIN' PARTY (58)	Celestial 109	$40

J. E. MAINER (CW)
And His Mountaineers
King 45s $4 each
Rural Rhythm LPs $8 each
Old Timey, Arhoolie, Blue Jay, and Old Homestead LPs $4 each
-albums-

LP	GOOD OLE MOUNTAIN MUSIC (60)	King 666	$25
LP	J. E. MAINER VARIETY ALBUM (61)	King 765	$20
LP	SOULFUL SACRED SONGS (62) Wade Mainer	King 769	$18

VINCE MALOY (RB)
-singles-

45rpm	I'VE BEEN AROUND YOUR DOOR BEFORE (58)	"1223" 0475	$50

GENE MALTAIS (RB)
-singles-

45rpm	THE RAGING SEA (58)	Lilac 3159	$150
45rpm	LOVEMAKIN' (58)	Regal 7502	$75
45rpm	CRAZY BABY (58)	Decca 30387	$75
45(P)	CRAZY BABY (58)	Decca 30387	$50
	(Pink promo label)		

TONY MANDARIN (C)
-singles-

45rpm	BRONCO ROCK White label, blue vinyl	Stofer 101	$40
	(Out of 10,000 copies pressed and sold, only 600 were blue vinyl)		
45rpm	BRONCO ROCK White label, orange vinyl	Stofer 101	$10

BARBARA MANDRELL (C)
Columbia 45s $3 each
ABC 45s $2 each
Other MCA 45s $1 each
MCA picture sleeves $3 each
Capitol 45s $1 each
ABC LPs $4-6 each
MCA LPs $3 each
Time-Life and Songbird LPs $6 each
Other Columbia LPs $4-6 each
-singles-

45(P)	WHAT'S IT ALL ABOUT (May 79) Public service show	W. I. A. A. 473	$12
	(Flip side features Nicolette Larson)		
45(P)	SANTA, BRING MY BABY BACK HOME (84)	MCA 1241	$10
	(Promo-only release, two songs on flip side)		
45(P)	FAST LANES AND COUNTRY ROADS (85)	MCA 52737	$10
	(White promo label, yellow vinyl)		
45(P)	WHEN YOU GET TO THE HEART (86)	MCA 52802	$10
	(White promo label, red vinyl)		

-albums-

LP	TREAT HIM RIGHT (71)	Columbia 30967	$12
LP(P)	TREAT HIM RIGHT (71)	Columbia 30967	$15
	(White promo label)		
LP	MIDNIGHT OIL (73)	Columbia 32743	$10
LP	THIS TIME I ALMOST MADE IT (74)	Columbia 32959	$10

-radio shows-

2LP(RS)	NAVY HOEDOWN (Jun 75) Four thirty-minute shows	U.S. Navy Series 16	$25-50
	(Music and interview)		
3LP(RS)	CHRISTMAS FROM THE HEART (Dec 90)	Westwood One	$20-30
	(Music and interviews)		

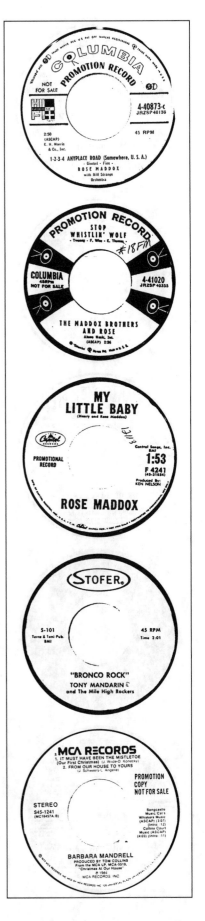

LOUISE MANDRELL (C)
Married to R. C. Bannon
RCA Victor 45s $1 each
RCA Victor picture sleeves $3 each
Epic LPs $8 each
RCA Victor LPs $5 each

-singles-

45(P)	**WHERE THERE'S SMOKE THERE'S FIRE** (81)	RCA Victor 12359	$12
	(With R. C. Bannon, silver label, red vinyl)		
45(P)	**AROUND MY HEART** (82)	RCA Victor 13039	$10
	(White promo label, green vinyl)		
45(P)	**ROMANCE** (82)	RCA Victor 13373	$10
	(Red promo label, green vinyl)		
45(P)	**SAVE ME** (83)	RCA Victor 13450	$10
	(Green promo label, yellow vinyl)		
45(P)	**TOO HOT TO SLEEP** (83)	RCA Victor 13567	$10
	(Yellow promo label, red vinyl)		

CARL MANN (R)

-singles-

45rpm	**GONNA ROCK & ROLL TONIGHT** (57)	Jaxon 502	$2,000
45rpm	**MONA LISA** (59)	Philips 3539	$15
45(P)	**MONA LISA** (59)	Philips 3539	$25
	(Promo label)		
45rpm	**ROCKIN' LOVE** (58)	Philips 3546	$15
45rpm	**SOME ENCHANTED EVENING** (60)	Philips 3550	$15
45rpm	**SOUTH OF THE BORDER** (60)	Philips 3555	$12
45rpm	**BORN TO BE BAD** (60)	Philips 3564	$12
45rpm	**I AIN'T GOT NO HOME** (60)	Philips 3569	$12
45rpm	**WHEN I GROW TOO OLD TO DREAM** (60)	Philips 3579	$12

-albums-

LP	**LIKE MANN** (60)	Philips 1960	$500

LORENE MANN (C)
RCA Victor 45s $2 each
Other RCA Victor LPs $8-10 each

-albums-

LP	**A MAN NAMED LORENE** (69)	RCA Victor 4243	$12

JOE MAPHIS (CW)
And Rose Lee Maphis
Other Republic and Columbia 45s $4-8 each
Starday 45s $3 each
CMH 2LP sets $8 each
CMH LPs $5 each
Sacred LPs $6 each

-singles-

45rpm	**YOU CAN'T TAKE THE HEART OUT OF ME** (52)	Lariat 45 1203	$20
	(Cousin Joe Maphis and Rose Lee with Billy Liebert)		
45rpm	**GREEN RIVER RAG** (Hoedown)	MacGregor 8505	$18
45rpm	**WATER BABY BOOGIE** (57)	Republic 2006	$15
45(P)	**WATER BABY BOOGIE** (57)	Republic 2006	$12
	(White promo label)		
45rpm	**GUITAR ROCK & ROLL** (57)	Columbia 21518	$25
45(P)	**GUITAR ROCK & ROLL** (57)	Columbia 21518	$20
	(White promo label)		
45rpm	**I GOTTA LOTTA LOVIN'** (59) Joe Maphis and Rose Lee	Columbia 41004	$12
45(P)	**I GOTTA LOTTA LOVIN'** (59)	Columbia 41004	$10
	(White promo label)		

-EPs-

EP	**KING OF THE STRINGS** (64)	Starday 235	$15

-albums-

LP	**FIRE ON THE STRINGS** (57)	Columbia 1005	$100
LP	**HI-FI HOLIDAY FOR BANJO** (59)	Harmony 11032	$25
LP(P)	**HI-FI HOLIDAY FOR BANJO** (59)	Harmony 11032	$30
	(White promo label)		
LP	**ROSE LEE MAPHIS** (61) Mono	Columbia 1598	$25
LP	**ROSE LEE MAPHIS** (61) Stereo	Columbia 8398	$30
LP(P)	**ROSE LEE MAPHIS** (61)	Columbia 1598	$40
	(White promo label)		
LP	**ROSE LEE & JOE MAPHIS** (62)	Capitol 1778	$30
	(With the Blue Ridge Mountain Boys)		
LP(P)	**ROSE LEE & JOE MAPHIS** (62)	Capitol 1778	$40
	(Yellow promo label)		
LP	**KING OF THE STRINGS** (62)	MacGregor 1205	$75
LP	**MERLE TRAVIS & JOE MAPHIS** (64)	Capitol T-2102	$40
	(First pressing)		

LP	MERLE TRAVIS & JOE MAPHIS (64)	Capitol SM-2101	$15
LP	MR. AND MRS. COUNTRY MUSIC (64)	Starday 286	$25
	(With Rose Lee Maphis)		
LP	HOOTENANNY STAR (64)	Kapp 3347	$20
LP	KING OF THE STRINGS (66)	Starday 316	$50
LP	GOLDEN GOSPEL (66)	Starday 322	$30
LP	COUNTRY GUITAR GOES TO THE JIMMY DEAN SHOW (66)	Starday 373	$40
	(Price includes thirty-four-page booklet)		
LP	NEW SOUND OF JOE MAPHIS (67)	Mosrite 400	$20
LP	GUITARATION GAP (71) Joe and Jody Maphis	Chart 1042	$12
LP	NASHVILLE GUITARS (73) With Jackie Phelps	Nashville 2091	$12

-radio shows-

| LP(RS) | COUNTRY MUSIC TIME (70s) | U.S. Air Force | $30-50 |
| | (Music and interviews) | | |

BOBBY MARCHAN (RB)

-singles-

| 45rpm | CHICKEN WAH-WAH (57) | Gale (RCA) 101 | $15 |

BENNY MARTIN (CW)
RCA Victor 45s $3-5 each
Starday and Mercury 45s $5-8 each
Other CMH LPs $5 each
Power Pak LPs $5 each
Flying Fish LPs $5 each

-EPs-

| EP(P) | THAT'S THE STORY OF MY LIFE (59) | RCA Victor DJ-94 | $25 |
| | (Two songs on each side, Don Gibson is on the flip side) | | |

-albums-

LP	COUNTRY MUSIC'S SENSATIONAL ENTERTAINER (61)	Starday 131	$50
LP	OLD TIME FIDDLIN' & SINGIN' (64)	Mercury Wing 16289	$15
LP(P)	OLD TIME FIDDLIN' & SINGIN' (64)	Mercury Wing 16289	$18
	(White promo label)		
LP	BENNY MARTIN WITH BOBBY SYKES (65)	Hilltop 6034	$12
	(With Bobby Sykes)		
2LP	THE FIDDLE COLLECTION (77)	CMH 9006	$18
2LP	BIG DADDY OF THE FIDDLE & BOW (79)	CMH 9019	$15

-radio shows-

| LP(RS) | COUNTRY MUSIC TIME (60s) | U.S. Air Force | $175-250 |
| | (Flip side features Patsy Cline) | | |

BOBBI MARTIN (C)
Coral 45s $5 each
United Artists 45s $4 each
Buddah 45s $3 each
United Artists LPs $8 each
Vocalion LPs $6 each
Sunset LPs $5 each

-EPs-

| EP | DON'T FORGET I STILL LOVE YOU (65) | Coral 81194 | $15 |

-albums-

| LP | DON'T FORGET I STILL LOVE YOU (65) | Coral 57472 | $15 |
| LP | I LOVE YOU SO (65) | Coral 57478 | $12 |

GRADY MARTIN (CW)
And His Slewfoot Five
Decca 45s $2 each
Monument 45s $1 each
Other Decca EPs $6-8 each
Other Decca LPs $4-8 each
Monument LPs $3 each

-EPs-

EP	DANCE-O-RAMA (55)	Decca 2231	$12
EP	DANCE-O-RAMA (55)	Decca 2232	$12
EP	POWERHOUSE DANCE PARTY VOL 1 (56)	Decca 2297	$10
EP	POWERHOUSE DANCE PARTY VOL 2 (56)	Decca 2298	$10
EP	POWERHOUSE DANCE PARTY VOL 3 (56)	Decca 2299	$10
EP	JUKE BOX JAMBOREE VOL 1 (56)	Decca 2358	$10
EP	JUKE BOX JAMBOREE VOL 2 (56)	Decca 2359	$10
EP	JUKE BOX JAMBOREE VOL 3 (56)	Decca 2360	$10

-albums-

10"LP	DANCE-O-RAMA (55)	Decca 5566	$25
LP	POWERHOUSE DANCE PARTY (56)	Decca 8181	$12
LP(P)	POWERHOUSE DANCE PARTY (56)	Decca 8181	$15
	(Pink promo label)		
LP	JUKE BOX JAMBOREE (56)	Decca 8292	$15

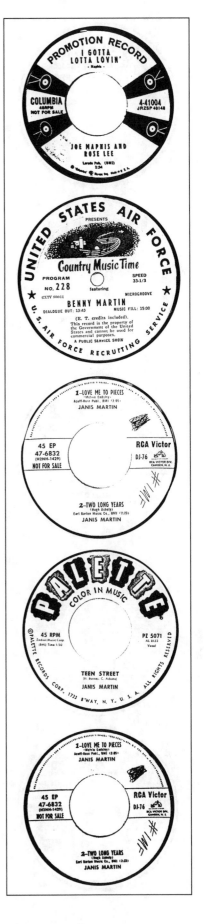

LP(P)	**JUKE BOX JAMBOREE** (56)	Decca 8292	$18
	(Pink promo label)		
LP	**THE ROARING TWENTIES** (57)	Decca 8648	$10
LP	**HOT TIME TONIGHT** (59)	Decca 8883	$10

JANIS MARTIN (RB)
She is the female Elvis

-singles-

45rpm	**DRUGSTORE ROCK & ROLL** (56)	RCA Victor 6491	$40
45rpm	**OOBY DOOBY** (56)	RCA Victor 6560	$50
45rpm	**MY BOY ELVIS** (56)	RCA Victor 6652	$50
45rpm	**BAREFOOT BABY** (57)	RCA Victor 6744	$30
45rpm	**LOVE ME TO PIECES** (57)	RCA Victor 6832	$30
45rpm	**LOVE AND KISSES** (57)	RCA Victor 6983	$30
45rpm	**ALL RIGHT BABY** (58)	RCA Victor 7104	$40
45rpm	**BANG BANG** (58)	RCA Victor 7318	$40
45rpm	**HARD TIMES AHEAD** (59)	Paulette 5058	$18
45rpm	**TEEN STREET** (59)	Paulette 5071	$18

-EPs-

EP	**JUST SQUEEZE ME** (56)	RCA Victor 4093	$400
EP(P)	**LOVE ME TO PIECES/TWO LONG YEARS** (57) Promo only	RCA Victor DJ-76	$75
	(Two songs on each side, Hank Snow is on the flip)		

JIMMY MARTIN (RB)

-singles-

45rpm	**ROCK THE BOP** (58)	Jaxon 501	$175

JIMMY MARTIN (CW)
And the Sunny Mountain Boys
Decca 45s $3-5 each
MCA 45s $1 each
Other Decca LPs $4-8 each
MCA LPs $3 each
Gusto LPs $3 each
Anthology of Country Music LPs $5 each

-EPs-

EP	**ROCK HEARTS** (59)	Decca 2649	$25
EP	**HI-DE DIDDLE** (64)	Decca 2752	$12
EP	**JIMMY MARTIN** (64)	Decca 2773	$10

-albums-

LP	**GOOD 'N COUNTRY** (60)	Decca 4016	$25
LP(P)	**GOOD 'N COUNTRY** (60)	Decca 4016	$30
	(Pink promo label)		
LP	**COUNTRY MUSIC TIME** (62)	Decca 4285	$20
LP(P)	**COUNTRY MUSIC TIME** (62)	Decca 4285	$25
	(Pink promo label)		
LP	**THIS WORLD IS NOT MY HOME** (63)	Decca 4360	$18
LP(P)	**THIS WORLD IS NOT MY HOME** (63)	Decca 4360	$20
	(White promo label)		
LP	**WIDOW MAKER** (64)	Decca 4536	$15
LP(P)	**WIDOW MAKER** (64)	Decca 4536	$18
	(White promo label)		
LP	**SUNNY SIDE OF THE MOUNTAIN** (65)	Decca 4643	$15
LP(P)	**SUNNY SIDE OF THE MOUNTAIN** (65)	Decca 4643	$18
	(White promo label)		

MAC MARTIN (CW)
With the Dixie Travelers
Rural Rhythm LPs $8-10 each

JAMES MASK (RB)

-singles-

45rpm	**SAVE YOU LOVE** (58)	Bandera 1306	$50

MASON DIXON (C)
Texas black vinyl 45s $4 each
Texas heavy cardboard picture sleeves $4 each
  (For any Texas single)
Premier green vinyl 45s $5 each
Premier 45s $2 each
NLT and Capitol 45s $2 each
Premier LPs $6 each
Capitol LPs $5 each

-singles-

45(P)	**HOUSTON HEARTACHE** (85)	Texas 5508	$10
	(Blue label, blue vinyl)		
45(P)	**ARMADILLO COUNTRY** (85)	Texas 5510	$18
	(Blue label, red marble vinyl, clear cover)		

45(P)	**ARMADILLO COUNTRY** (85)	Texas 5510	$10
	(Blue label, red vinyl)		
45(P)	**CIRCLE** (85)	Texas 5556	$10
	(Brown label, yellow vinyl)		
45(P)	**ONLY A DREAM AWAY** (85)	Texas 5558	$10
	(Blue label, blue vinyl)		

SALLY MASSEY & RHYTHM PALS (CW)
-singles-

45rpm	**WALKING AFTER MIDNIGHT** (54)	Vogue 8159	$12

SAMMY MASTERS (RB)
-singles-

45rpm	**PINK CADILLAC** (57)	Four Star 1695	$25
45rpm	**WHOP-T-BOP** (57)	Four Star 1697	$25

COUNTRY JOHNNY MATHIS (CW)
Jimmy Lee and Johnny Mathis
Jimmy & Johnny
Other Decca 78s $4-8 each
Other Decca 45s $3-6 each
Little Darlin' 45s $3 each
-singles-

78rpm	**I'M BEGINNING TO REMEMBER** (55)	Chess 4859	$10
	(Jimmy Lee and Johnny Mathis)		
45rpm	**I'M BEGINNING TO REMEMBER** (55)	Chess 4859	$20
78rpm	**LOVE ME** (56)	Chess 4863	$50
	(Jimmy Lee and Johnny Mathis)		
45rpm	**LOVE ME** (56)	Chess 4863	$75
45rpm	**I CAN'T FIND THE DOOR KNOB** (56) Jimmy & Johnny	D 1004	$30
45rpm	**DON'T GIVE ME THAT LOOK** (56) Jimmy & Johnny	D 1018	$18
45rpm	**MY LITTLE BABY** (56) Jimmy & Johnny	D 1089	$15
45rpm	**DON'T CALL ME, I'LL CALL YOU** (56) Jimmy & Johnny	TNT 184	$20
78rpm	**SWEET SINGING DADDY** (56) Jimmy & Johnny	Decca 29772	$15
78(P)	**SWEET SINGING DADDY** (56)	Decca 29772	$20
	(Pink promo label)		
45rpm	**SWEET SINGING DADDY** (56)	Decca 29772	$25
45(P)	**SWEET SINGING DADDY** (56)	Decca 29772	$20
	(Pink promo label)		
45rpm	**'TILL THE END OF THE WORLD** (56) Jimmy & Johnny	Decca 29954	$12
45(P)	**'TILL THE END OF THE WORLD** (56)	Decca 29954	$10
	(Pink promo label)		
78rpm	**SWEET LOVE ON MY MIND** (56) Jimmy & Johnny	Decca 30061	$30
78(P)	**SWEET LOVE ON MY MIND** (56)	Decca 30061	$40
	(Pink promo label)		
45rpm	**SWEET LOVE ON MY MIND** (56)	Decca 30061	$50
45(P)	**SWEET LOVE ON MY MIND** (56)	Decca 30061	$40
	(Pink promo label)		
45rpm	**HERE COMES MY BABY** (57) Jimmy & Johnny	Decca 30278	$15
45(P)	**HERE COMES MY BABY** (57)	Decca 30278	$12
	(Pink promo label)		
45rpm	**I'LL DO IT EVERYTIME** (57) Jimmy & Johnny	Decca 30410	$15
45(P)	**I'LL DO IT EVERYTIME** (57)	Decca 30410	$12
	(Pink promo label)		
45rpm	**WILL IT ALWAYS BE** (57)	Starday 181	$25
	(Les Chambers and Johnny Mathis)		

-albums-

LP	**HILLTOP GOSPEL** (65) Country Johnny Mathis	Hilltop 7004	$25
LP	**HE KEEPS ME SINGING** (67) Country Johnny Mathis	Little Darlin' 8007	$20
LP	**COME HOME TO MY HEART** (70) Country Johnny Mathis	Little Darlin' 8016	$18
LP	**IN THE HOUSE OF THE LORD** (72) Johnny Mathis	Pickwick 7004	$10
	(Reissue of Hilltop 7004)		

BILLY MATCH (RB)
-singles-

45rpm	**I WANT MY BABY** (57)	Starfire 664	$75

KATHY MATTEA (C)
Mercury 45s $1 each
Mercury LPs $3 each
-radio shows-

3LP(RS)	**SILVER EAGLE** (Nov 84) With Jim Glazer	DIR	$50-100
	(Live concert)		
LP(RS)	**WESTWOOD ONE PRESENTS** (Oct 89)	Westwood One	$50-100
	(Live concert)		
LP(RS)	**WESTWOOD ONE PRESENTS** (Jan 90)	Westwood One	$60-120
	(Live concert)		

LP(RS)	**LIVE AT GILLEY'S** (Jan 90)	Westwood One	$25-40
	(Live concert)		

RAMON MAUPIN (R)
-singles-

45rpm	**ROCKIN' RUFUS** (58)	Fernwood 105	$75

SMILEY MAXEDON (CW)
-singles-

45rpm	**GIVE ME A RED HOT MAMA AND AN ICE COLD BEER** (52)	Columbia 21188	$15
45rpm	**THAT'S ALL RIGHT** (53)	Columbia 21301	$12

HASKELL MAY (RB)
-singles-

45rpm	**PARTY LINE** (57)	Sundown 102	$60

LEON McAULIFF (CW)
Other Columbia 78s $4-8 each
Other Columbia 45s $4-8 each
Capitol 45s $6 each
Pine Mountain, Delta, and Stoneway LPs $4-8 each
-singles-

78rpm	**PANHANDLE WALTZ** (51)	Columbia 346	$15
45rpm	**PANHANDLE WALTZ** (51)	Columbia 346	$30
	(Small center hole, thick vinyl)		
78rpm	**STEEL GUITAR RAG** (54)	Columbia 20546	$10
45rpm	**STEEL GUITAR RAG** (54)	Columbia 20546	$18
45(P)	**STEEL GUITAR RAG** (54)	Columbia 20546	$12
	(White promo label)		
45rpm	**BLUE GUITAR STOMP** (54)	Columbia 20845	$12
45(P)	**BLUE GUITAR STOMP** (54)	Columbia 20845	$10
	(White promo label)		
45rpm	**EATING RIGHT OUT OF YOUR HAND** (54)	Columbia 21115	$12
45(P)	**EATING RIGHT OUT OF YOUR HAND** (54)	Columbia 21115	$10
	(White promo label)		
78rpm	**SH-BOOM** (55)	Columbia 21283	$12
45rpm	**SH-BOOM** (55)	Columbia 21283	$15
45(P)	**SH-BOOM** (55)	Columbia 21283	$10
	(White promo label)		
45rpm	**STEEL GUITAR RAG/PANHANDLE RAG** (59)	Cimarron 4039	$15
45(P)	**STEEL GUITAR RAG/PANHANDLE RAG** (59)	Cimarron 4039	$10
	(White promo label)		
45rpm	**CHOO CHOO CH'BOOGIE** (61)	Cimarron 4052	$12
45(P)	**CHOO CHOO CH'BOOGIE** (61)	Cimarron 4052	$10
	(White promo label)		
45rpm	**MY ACE IN THE HOLE** (61)	Cimarron 4054	$12
	(Flip side is Willie Nelson's "Night Life")		
45(P)	**MY ACE IN THE HOLE** (61)	Cimarron 4054	$10
	(White promo label)		
45rpm	**FADED LOVE** (62)	Cimarron 4057	$10
5-45s(S)	**COZY INN** (61) Jukebox set	ABC Paramount 394	$8 each
	(Yellow labels, five stereo singles and title strips)		

-EPs-

EP	**TAKE IT AWAY LEON** (58)	Dot 1063	$18
EP	**STEEL GUITAR RAG** (59)	Capitol 3001	$15

-albums-

LP(P)	**POINTS WEST** (57)	Sesac 1601	$75
	(Promo-only release)		
LP(P)	**JUST A MINUTE** (57)	Sesac	$75
	(Promo-only release)		
LP	**TAKE OFF** (58)	Dot 3139	$30
LP	**THE SWINGIN' WESTERN STRINGS OF LEON McAULIFF** (60)	Cimarron 2002	$40
LP	**COZY INN** (61)	ABC Paramount 394	$40
LP(P)	**COZY INN** (61)	ABC Paramount 394	$50
	(White promo label)		
LP	**MISTER WESTERN SWING** (62)	Starday 171	$50
LP	**THE SWINGIN' WEST WITH LEON McAULIFF** (64)	Starday 280	$25
LP	**THE SWINGIN' WESTERN STRINGS OF LEON McAULIFF** (64)	Starday 309	$30
LP	**THE DANCIN'EST BAND AROUND** (64)	Capitol 2016	$30
LP	**EVERYBODY DANCE! EVERYBODY SWING!** (64)	Capitol 2148	$30
LP	**GOLDEN COUNTRY HITS** (66)	Dot 3689	$18
LP	**AND HIS WESTERN SWING BAND** (84)	Columbia 38908	$12

JANET MCBRIDE (CW)
Longhorn 45s $3 each

-albums-

LP	**COUNTRY DOZEN** (67) With Vern Stovall	Longhorn 005	$20

C. W. MCCALL (C)
Bill Fries
MGM 45s $3 each
Polydor 45s $1 each
Other American Gramaphone 45s $2 each
Polydor LPs $3-5 each

-singles-

45rpm	**OLD HOME FILLER-UP AN' KEEP-ON-A-TRUCKIN' CAFE** (72) (Later released on MGM, this record was the result of a radio commercial for Old Home Bread)	American Gramaphone 351	$10

-EPs-

EP(P)	**SMOKEY THE COP** (78) C. W. McCall and others (Issued with hard cover, eight cuts, one by C. W.)	Ad Council 877	$15

-albums-

LP	**WOLF CREEK PASS** (75)	MGM 4989	$10
LP(P)	**WOLF CREEK PASS** (75) (White promo label)	MGM 4989	$12
LP	**BLACK BEAR ROAD** (75)	MGM 5008	$10
LP(P)	**BLACK BEAR ROAD** (75) (White promo label)	MGM 5008	$12

PAUL MCCARTNEY (R)
Of the Beatles
Country Hams
Thrillington
Listed is his material considered country

-singles-

45rpm	**COUNTRY DREAMER** (73) Paul McCartney and Wings ("A" side is Helen Wheels)	Apple 1869	$10
45(P)	**COUNTRY DREAMER** (73) (Same song on both sides)	Apple PRO-6787	$400
45rpm	**SALLY G** (74) Paul McCartney and Wings ("A" side is Junior's Farm)	Apple 1875	$10
45(P)	**SALLY G** (74) (Same song on both sides)	Apple P-1875	$75
45rpm	**WALKING IN THE PARK WITH ELOISE** (74) Country Hams	EMI 3977	$40
45rpm	**WALKING IN THE PARK WITH ELOISE** (74) Country Hams (Price includes picture sleeve)	EMI 3977	$75
45(P)	**WALKING IN THE PARK WITH ELOISE** (74)	EMI 3977	$40
45(P)	**WALKING IN THE PARK WITH ELOISE** (74) (Promo record and stock picture sleeve)	EMI 3977	$75
45(P)	**WHAT'S IT ALL ABOUT** (Aug 76) Public service show (Flip side features Johnny Ray)	W. I. A. A. 331	$60
45(P)	**WHAT'S IT ALL ABOUT** (Oct 77) Public service show (Flip side features Bobby Vinton)	W. I. A. A. 394	$60

-albums-

LP	**RAM** (71) Stereo (Includes "Heart of the Country")	Capitol 3375	$18
LP(P)	**RAM** (71) Mono (All mono copies of this LP were used as promos)	Capitol 3375	$3,000
LP(P)	**BRUNG TO EWE BY** (71) (Promo-only sampler from the LP "Ram," to radio stations only)	Apple 6210	$400
LP	**THRILLINGTON** (77) Percy Thrillington (Percy Thrillington is Paul McCartney, includes "Heart of the Country")	Capitol 11642	$150

CHARLY MCCLAIN (C)
Epic 45s $1-2 each
Kentucky Fried Chicken (RCA) 45s $3 each
Other Epic LPs $3-6 each

-albums-

LP	**HERE'S CHARLY** (77)	Epic 34447	$10
LP(P)	**LIVE AT THE LONE STAR** (80) (Promo-only release)	Epic PRO	$12

-radio shows-

3LP(RS)	**SILVER EAGLE** (Feb 84) With Johnny Rodriquez (Live concert)	DIR	$15-25
LP(RS)	**LIVE AT GILLEY'S** (Dec 86) (Live concert)	Westwood One	$10-15

DELBERT MCCLINTON (C)
Any label 45s $2 each
Capricorn LPs $6-10 each
Intermediate, MCA, Clean, and Accord LPs $3-6 each

-albums-

LP	**GENUINE COWHIDE** (76)	ABC 959	$10

O. B. MCCLINTON (C)
Enterprise 45s $2 each
Enterprise LPs $5-8 each

MEL MCCONNIGLE (RB)

-singles-

45rpm	**RATTLE SHAKIN' MAMA** (57)	Rocket 101	$100

MCCORMICK BROTHERS (CW)

-singles-

45rpm	**RED HEN BOOGIE** (54)	Hickory 1013	$25
45(P)	**RED HEN BOOGIE** (54)	Hickory 1013	$30
	(White promo label)		
45rpm	**BILLY GOAT BOOGIE** (55)	Hickory 1021	$25
45(P)	**BILLY GOAT BOOGIE** (55)	Hickory 1021	$30
	(White promo label)		
45rpm	**NO SUBSTITUTE WILL DO** (55)	Hickory 1067	$15
45(P)	**NO SUBSTITUTE WILL DO** (55)	Hickory 1067	$12
	(White promo label)		
45rpm	**BIG EYES** (56)	Hickory 1080	$20
45(P)	**BIG EYES** (56)	Hickory 1080	$15
	(White promo label)		
45rpm	**RUNNIN' ROUND ON ME** (57)	Hickory 1089	$12
45(P)	**RUNNIN' ROUND ON ME** (57)	Hickory 1089	$10
	(White promo label)		

-albums-

LP	**SONGS FOR HOME FOLKS** (61)	Hickory 102	$75
LP	**AUTHENTIC BLUEGRASS HITS** (62)	Hickory 108	$50
LP	**GRASS MEETS BRASS** (69)	Metromedia 1019	$18
LP(P)	**GRASS MEETS BRASS** (69)	Metromedia 1019	$25
	(White promo label)		

CHARLIE MCCOY (C)
Monument 45s $1 each
Monument jukebox LLPs $5 each
Other Monument LPs $3-6 each

-albums-

LP	**THE REAL MCCOY** (69)	Monument 18121	$12

-radio shows-

LP(RS)	**COUNTRY MUSIC TIME** (70s)	U.S. Air Force	$10-12
	(Music and interviews)		

RAY MCCOY (RB)

-singles-

45rpm	**ROCKIN' BABY** (57)	Fable 615	$50

JIM MCCRORY (RB)

-singles-

45rpm	**PARKING LOT** (57)	Key 5803	$50
45rpm	**ROCK YA BABY** (58)	Key 5805	$50

SUSAN MCCRORY (R)

-singles-

45rpm	**ROVIN' GAL** (57)	Arrow 1005	$35
	(Price includes picture sleeve)		

MEL MCDANIEL (C)
Capitol 45s $2 each
Capitol LPs $5 each

-radio shows-

LP(RS)	**LIVE AT GILLEY'S** (Mar 87)	Westwood One	$10-15
	(Live concert)		

JIM MCDONALD (R)

-singles-

45rpm	**LET'S HAVE A BALL** (58)	KCM 3700	$40

SKEETS MCDONALD (CW)
Other Capitol 78s $5 each
Other Capitol 45s $4-8 each
Columbia 45s $2-3 each

-singles-

78rpm	DON'T LET THE STARS GET IN YOUR EYES (51)	Capitol 2216	$10
45rpm	DON'T LET THE STARS GET IN YOUR EYES (51)	Capitol 2216	$20
45rpm	LET ME KNOW (52)	Capitol 2326	$10
45rpm	BABY, I'M COUNTIN' (53)	Capitol 2523	$12
45rpm	REMEMBER YOU'RE MINE (54)	Capitol 2774	$10
45rpm	YOUR LOVE IS LIKE A FAUCET (55)	Capitol 2885	$10
45rpm	SMOKE COMES OUT MY CHIMNEY JUST THE SAME (56)	Capitol 2976	$10
45rpm	NUMBER ONE IN YOUR HEART (56)	Capitol 3038	$10
45rpm	STROLLIN' (57)	Capitol 3215	$10
45rpm	YOU OUGHTA SEE GRANDMA ROCK (58)	Capitol 3461	$50
45(P)	YOU OUGHTA SEE GRANDMA ROCK (58)	Capitol 3461	$40
	(White promo label)		
45rpm	YOU BETTER NOT GO (58)	Capitol 3600	$15
45(P)	YOU BETTER NOT GO (58)	Capitol 3600	$10
	(White promo label)		
45rpm	FINGERTIPS (59)	Capitol 3778	$15
45(P)	FINGERTIPS (59)	Capitol 3778	$10
	(White promo label)		

-EPs-

EP	COUNTRY AND HILLBILLY SONGS BY SKEETS MCDONALD (54)	Capitol 451	$50
EP	GOIN' STEADY WITH THE BLUES (58)	Capitol 1040	$25

-albums-

LP	GOIN' STEADY WITH THE BLUES (58)	Capitol 1040	$50
LP(P)	GOIN' STEADY WITH THE BLUES (58)	Capitol 1040	$40
	(Yellow promo label)		
LP	THE COUNTRY'S BEST (59)	Capitol 1179	$40
LP(P)	THE COUNTRY'S BEST (59)	Capitol 1179	$30
	(Yellow promo label)		
LP	CALL ME SKEETS (64) Stereo	Columbia 8970	$25
LP(P)	CALL ME SKEETS (64)	Columbia 2170	$30
	(White promo label)		
LP	SKEETS (66)	Sears 116	$25

RONNIE MCDOWELL (C)
Scorpion 45s $5 each
Epic 45s $1 each
Other MCA colored vinyl 45s $8 each
Other MCA 45s $2 each
Other Scorpion LPs $5-8 each
Epic LPs $2-5 each
MCA LPs $2-4 each

-singles-

45(P)	LOVIN' THAT CRAZY FEELIN' (86)	MCA 52994	$10
	(White promo label, red vinyl)		

-albums-

LP	THE KING IS GONE (77)	Scorpion 8021	$10
LP	ELVIS (79)	Dick Clark TVLP 79	$15
	(Soundtrack album)		
LP	A TRIBUTE TO ELVIS (79)	Scorpion 0015	$12
	(With the Jordanaires)		

-radio shows-

LP(RS)	COUNTRY MUSIC TIME (70s)	U.S. Air Force	$10-15
	(Music and interviews)		
3LP(RS)	SILVER EAGLE (Sept 85) With Reba McEntire	DIR	$20-40
	(Live concert)		
LP(RS)	WESTWOOD ONE PRESENTS (May 81)	Westwood One	$40-75
	(Rare live concert)		

PAKE MCENTIRE (C)

-radio shows-

LP(RS)	LIVE AT GILLEY'S (Dec 86)	Westwood One	$10-15
	(Live concert)		

REBA MCENTIRE (C)
Mercury 45s 57000 series $4 each
Other Mercury 45s $2-4 each
Mercury picture sleeves $3 each
MCA 45s $2 each
Other Mercury LPs $5-10 each
MCA LPs $2-4 each

-singles-

45(P)	**WHAT AM I GONNA DO ABOUT YOU** (86)		MCA 52922	$12
	(White promo label, blue vinyl)			
45(P)	**THE CHRISTMAS SONG** (87)		MCA 17446	$10
	(Promo-only release)			
45(P)	**I'LL BE HOME FOR CHRISTMAS** (87)		MCA 17725	$10
	(Promo-only release)			
45(P)	**LET THE MUSIC LIFT YOU UP** (87)		MCA 52990	$12
	(White promo label, yellow vinyl)			
45(P)	**ONE PROMISE TOO LATE** (87)		MCA 53092	$12
	(White promo label, yellow vinyl)			

-albums-

LP	**REBA MCENTIRE** (77)	Mercury 1177	$75
LP	**REBA MCENTIRE** (79)	Mercury 5002	$25
LP	**OUT OF A DREAM** (79)	Mercury 5017	$40
LP	**FEEL THE FIRE** (80)	Mercury 5029	$30
LP	**UNLIMITED** (82)	Mercury 4049	$25
LP	**HEART TO HEART** (82)	Mercury 6003	$20
LP	**BEHIND THE SCENE** (83)	Mercury 812781	$18

-radio shows-

3LP(RS)	**SILVER EAGLE** (May 84) With Bill Anderson	DIR	$20-35
	(Live concert)		
3LP(RS)	**SILVER EAGLE** (Sept 85) With Roger McDowell	DIR	$20-40
	(Live concert)		
3LP(RS)	**SILVER EAGLE** (Dec 85) With Charlie Pride	DIR	$20-40
	(Live concert)		
LP(RS)	**LIVE AT GILLEY'S** (Apr 85) Patsy Cline Tribute	Westwood One	$25-50
	(Live concert)		
LP(RS)	**LIVE AT GILLEY'S** (Nov 85)	Westwood One	$20-40
	(Live concert)		
LP(RS)	**LIVE AT GILLEY'S** (Mar 89)	Westwood One	$20-35
	(Live concert)		
3LP(RS)	**MEMORIAL DAY SPECIAL** (May 87)		$40-75
	(Mostly music and interviews)		
2LP(RS)	**CHRISTMAS WITH REBA** (Dec 88) With Milsap and Parton	Westwood One	$25-40
	(Mostly music and interviews)		

SAM MCGEE (CW)
Sam and Kirk McGee
And the Crook Brothers
The Dixieliners
Starday 45s $5 each

-albums-

LP	**SAM & KIRK MCGEE & THE CROOK BROTHERS** (62)	Starday 182	$40

WAYNE MCGUINESS (RB)

-singles-

45rpm	**ROCK, ROLL & RHYTHM** (58)	Meteor 5035	$75

GENE MCKOWN (RB)

-singles-

45rpm	**ROCKABILLY RHYTHM** (58)	Aggie 1001	$50
45rpm	**LITTLE MARY** (58)	Aggie 1003	$60

BUTCH MCLAREY (RB)

-singles-

45rpm	**ROCKIN' HALL** (58)	Kliff 103	$60
45rpm	**MY SWEETHEART** (58)	Ballad 1013	$55

CURTIS MCPEAK (BG)
Power Pak LPs $4 each

-albums-

LP	**BLUEGRASS HILLBILLIES** (63)	ABC Paramount 446	$20
LP(P)	**BLUEGRASS HILLBILLIES** (63)	ABC Paramount 446	$18
	(White promo label)		

LEE (RED) MELSON (RB)

-EPs-

EP	**LEE (RED) MELSON** (58)	Ridgecrest 1007	$75

JAMES MELTON (Classical)
RCA Victor red vinyl 45s from WDM 1535 $5 each
   (Country western songs)

BUDDY MEREDITH (BG)

-albums-

LP	SING ME A HEART SONG (63)	Starday 225	$15

HELEN MERRILL (CW)

-albums-

LP	AMERICAN COUNTRY SONGS (59)	Atco 112	$25

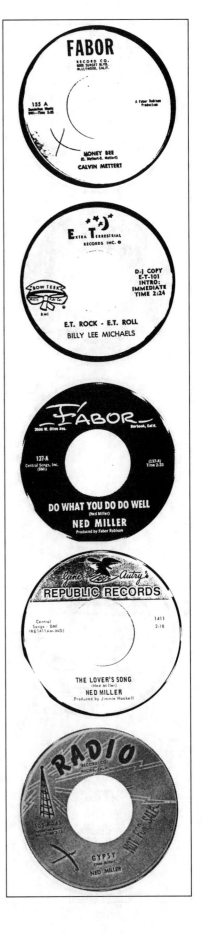

CALVIN METTERT (RB)

-singles-

45rpm	HONEY BEE (57)	Fabor 155	$12

JIMMY MEYERS (RB)

-singles-

45rpm	PRETTY BABY ROCK PRETTY BABY ROCK (57)	Fortune 211	$50

BILLY LEE MICHAELS (RB)

-singles-

45rpm	ROCK-A-BILLY BABY	Boptown 101	$20
	(Only 300 copies pressed)		
45rpm	DATE ON THE CORNER	Spinout 101	$10
	(Only 500 copies pressed)		
45(P)	E. T. ROCK-E. T. ROLL	Extra Terrestrial 101	$10
	(Only 500 copies pressed)		

ELMON MICKLE (RB)

-singles-

45rpm	FLAT FOOT SAM (58)	Elko 003	$40

ARLIE MILLER (RB)

-singles-

45rpm	LOU ANN (57)	Lucky 80	$150

CARL MILLER (RB)

-singles-

45rpm	RHYTHM GUITAR (57)	Lu 503	$50

CLINT MILLER (C)
Headline 45s $5 each

FRANKIE MILLER (CW)
Other Columbia 78s and 45s $5-10 each
Starday 45s $5-10 each

-singles-

45rpm	HEY! WHERE YA GOIN'? (54)	Columbia 21314	$20
45(P)	HEY! WHERE YA GOIN'? (54)	Columbia 21314	$15
	(White promo label)		

-EPs-

EP	FRANKIE MILLER (60)	Starday 122	$18

-albums-

LP	COUNTRY MUSIC'S NEW STAR (61)	Starday 134	$40
LP	TRUE COUNTRY STYLE OF FRANKIE MILLER (62)	Starday 199	$30
LP	FINE COUNTRY SINGING OF FRANKIE MILLER (63)	Audio Lab 1562	$25
LP	BLACKLAND FARMER (65)	Starday 338	$25

JODY MILLER (C)
Capitol 45s $3 each
Capitol picture sleeves $3 each
Epic 45s $1 each
Other Capitol LPs $5 each
Epic LPs $2 each
Pickwick LPs $6 each

-albums-

LP	WEDNESDAY'S CHILD IS FULL OF WOE (63)	Capitol 1913	$25
LP	QUEEN OF THE HOUSE (65)	Capitol 2349	$20
LP	HOME OF THE BRAVE (65)	Capitol 2412	$20

-radio shows-

LP(P)	SILVER PLATTER SERVICE (Nov 65) With Jack Wagner	Capitol 3176	$15
	(Label service, includes interview and music)		

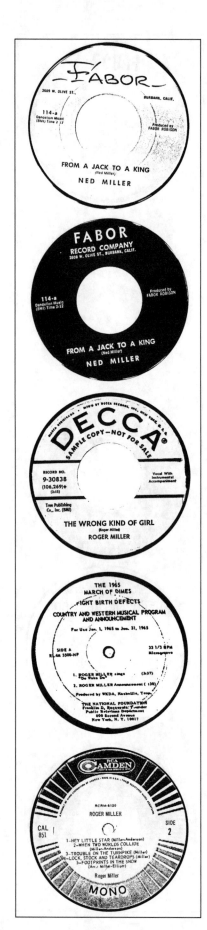

JOE MILLER (CW)

-albums-

LP	**COUNTRY MUSIC WITH JOE MILLER** (65)	Folkways 31093	$15

NED MILLER (CW)
Other Fabor 45s $4-6 each
Capitol 45s $3-4 each
Capitol Starline 45s $2 each
Republic 45s $4 each

-singles-

45rpm	**GYPSY** (57)	Radio 105	$20
45rpm	**FROM A JACK TO A KING** (57)	Dot 15601	$15
	(Pre-Fabor version)		
45rpm	**TURN BACK** (57)	Dot 15651	$10
45rpm	**FROM A JACK TO A KING** (62)	Fabor 114	$15
	(Yellow label)		
45rpm	**FROM A JACK TO A KING** (62)	Fabor 114	$10
	(Black label)		

-albums-

LP	**FROM A JACK TO A KING** (63)	Fabor 1001	$100
	(Special release multicolored vinyl)		
LP	**FROM A JACK TO A KING** (63) Black vinyl	Fabor 1001	$50
LP	**SINGS THE SONGS OF NED MILLER** (65)	Capitol 2330	$20
LP	**THE BEST OF NED MILLER** (66)	Capitol 2414	$18
LP	**TEARDROP LANE** (67)	Capitol 2586	$15
LP	**IN THE NAME OF LOVE** (68)	Capitol 2914	$15
LP	**NED MILLER'S BACK** (70)	Republic 1304	$12

ROGER MILLER (C)
Other RCA Victor 45s $8 each
Starday 45s $4 each
Other Smash 45s $3-6 each
Columbia 45s $2 each
Other Smash LPs $4-6 each
Other Mercury, Mercury Wing, 20th Century Fox LPs $4-6 each
Everest and Pickwick LPs $3 each
Columbia LPs $4 each

-singles-

45rpm	**MINE IS A LONELY LIFE** (58)	Decca 30792	$15
	(Justin Tubb with Roger Miller)		
45(P)	**MINE IS A LONELY LIFE** (58)	Decca 30792	$12
	(Pink promo label)		
45rpm	**THE WRONG KIND OF GIRL** (59)	Decca 30838	$15
45(P)	**THE WRONG KIND OF GIRL** (59)	Decca 30838	$12
	(Pink promo label)		
45rpm	**YOU DON'T WANT MY LOVE** (59)	RCA Victor 7776	$10
45rpm	**BURMA SHAVE** (60)	RCA Victor 7958	$15
45rpm	**DANG ME** (64)	Smash 1881	$15
	(Price includes picture sleeve)		
45rpm	**DO-WACKA-DO** (64)	Smash 1947	$12
	(Price includes picture sleeve)		
45rpm	**BALLAD OF WATERHOLE #3** (67)	Smash 2121	$10
	(Price includes picture sleeve)		
45rpm	**LITTLE GREEN APPLES** (68)	Smash 2148	$10
	(Price includes picture sleeve)		
45(P)	**THE TOM GREEN COUNTY FAIR** (70)	Smash DJS-43	$10
	(White promo label, promo-only version)		

-EPs-

EP(JB)	**ROGER AND OUT** (64) Jukebox LLP	Smash 702	$15
	(Issued with a hard cover)		
33(P)	**1965 MARCH OF DIMES** (65) One song and one PSA ad	March of Dimes 5500	$25
	(Sings Do-Waka-Do, 3:57 and does thirty-second spot)		
EP(JB)	**THE RETURN OF ROGER MILLER** (65) Jukebox LLP	Smash 705	$15
	(Issued with a hard cover)		
EP(JB)	**ROGER MILLER'S GOLDEN HITS** (65) Jukebox LLP	Smash 706	$15
	(Issued with a hard cover)		
EP(P)	**THE BEST OF ROGER MILLER** (72)	Smash MEPL-9	$12
	(Promo-only EP)		

-albums-

LP	**ROGER MILLER** (64)	Camden 851	$18
	(RCA Victor material)		
LP	**THE ONE & ONLY ROGER MILLER** (65)	Camden 903	$15
LP	**WILD CHILD** (65)	Starday 318	$25
LP	**THE COUNTRY SIDE OF ROGER MILLER** (65)	Starday 318	$20
	(Retitled)		
LP	**WATERHOLE #3** (67)	Smash 67096	$18
	(Soundtrack)		

LP(P)	**WATERHOLE #3** (67)	Smash 27096	$20
	(White promo label)		
LP	**DEAR FOLKS, SORRY I HAVEN'T WRITTEN LATELY** (73)	Columbia 32449	$10
	-radio shows-		
3LP(RS)	**AMERICAN EAGLE** (Oct 86) with Tom T. Hall	DIR	$50-100
	(Rare live concert)		

WALTER MILLER (RB)
-singles-

45rpm	**EVERYBODY'S GOT A BABY BUT ME** (59)	United Artists 104	$40

WARREN MILLER (RB)
-singles-

45rpm	**I WANNA ROCK AND ROLL** (57)	Goldband 1039	$25
45rpm	**EVERYBODY'S GOT A BABY BUT ME** (57)	United Artists 104	$30
45(P)	**EVERYBODY'S GOT A BABY BUT ME** (57)	United Artists 104	$25
	(White promo label)		

MILLER BROTHERS (CW)
Old Homestead LPs $5-10 each
-singles-

45rpm	**LOCO CHOO CHOO** (54)	King	$50
45rpm	**ROSE OF TIJUANA** (55)	4-Star 88	$10
45rpm	**BACK ROADS** (56)	4-Star 1730	$10

-EPs-

EP	**THE MILLER BROTHERS** (57)	4-Star 32	$20
	(Issued without a cover)		

MILLER SISTERS (R)
Some country ties on Sun and Flip
Other label 45s $10-20 each
-singles-

45rpm	**UNTIL YOU'RE MINE** (55)	Herald 455	$50
45(P)	**UNTIL YOU'RE MINE** (55)	Herald 455	$60
	(White promo label)		
45rpm	**I KNEW YOU WOULD** (55)	Sun 504	$150
45rpm	**I KNEW YOU WOULD** (55)	Flip 504	$200
45rpm	**THERE'S NO RIGHT WAY TO DO ME WRONG** (56)	Sun 230	$50
45rpm	**TEN CATS DOWN** (56)	Sun 255	$50
45rpm	**GUESS WHO** (56)	Ember 1004	$30
45(P)	**GUESS WHO** (56)	Ember 1004	$35
	(White promo label)		
45rpm	**DO YOU WANNA GO** (56)	Hull 718	$40
45rpm	**CRAZY BILLBOARD SONG** (57)	Acme 717	$40
45rpm	**THE FLIP SKIP** (57)	Acme 721	$40
45rpm	**MY OWN** (57)	Onyx 507	$30
45rpm	**UNTIL YOU'RE MINE** (58)	Herald 527	$25
	(Reissue of Herald 455)		
45(P)	**UNTIL YOU'RE MINE** (58)	Herald 527	$20
	(White promo label)		

CURLEY MILLIKEN (RB)
-singles-

45rpm	**ROCK 'N ROLL COUNTRY BOY** (58)	Talos 401	$75

HANK MILLS (RB)
-singles-

45rpm	**JUST A MEAN MEAN MAMA** (58)	Blaze 103	$15

RONNIE MILSAP (C)
Warner 45s $5-10 each
Other RCA Victor 45s $2-4 each
RCA Victor LPs $3-6 each
-singles-

45rpm	**YOUR TEARS LEAVE ME COLD** (77)	Festival 5002	$15
45(P)	**YOUR TEARS LEAVE ME COLD** (77)	Festival 5002	$18
	(White promo label)		
45(P)	**ONLY ONE LOVE IN MY LIFE** (78)	RCA Victor 11270	$15
	(Cream-colored promo label, white vinyl)		
45(P)	**LET'S TAKE THE LONG WAY AROUND THE WORLD** (78)	RCA Victor 11369	$15
	(Blue promo label, yellow vinyl)		
45(P)	**SANTA BARBARA** (78)	RCA Victor 11421	$15
	(White promo label, blue vinyl)		
45(P)	**WHAT'S IT ALL ABOUT** (Sep 79) Public service show	W. I. A. A. 1756	$12
	(Flip side features Styx)		
45(P)	**NOBODY LIKES SAD SONGS** (79)	RCA Victor 11553	$15
	(Cream-colored promo label, purple vinyl)		

45(P)	**NO GETTING OVER ME** (81)	RCA Victor 12264	$12
	(Cream-colored promo label, yellow vinyl)		
45(P)	**ANY DAY NOW** (82)	RCA Victor 13216	$15
	(Orange label, blue vinyl)		
45(P)	**STRANGER IN MY HOUSE** (83)	RCA Victor 13470	$15
	(Mustard promo label, green vinyl)		
45(P)	**DON'T YOU KNOW HOW MUCH I LOVE YOU** (83) New Mix	RCA Victor 13564	$12
	(Orange promo label, yellow vinyl)		
45(P)	**PRISONER OF THE HIGHWAY** (84)	RCA Victor 13876	$10
	(Green promo label, black vinyl)		
45(P)	**SHE KEEPS THE HOME FIRES BURNING** (85)	RCA Victor 14034	$12
	(Yellow label, green vinyl)		

-radio shows-

3LP(RS)	**THE SILVER EAGLE** (81) With Razzy Bailey	DIR 012	$25-40
	(Live concert)		
3LP(RS)	**TRIPLE** (Jun 82) Box set	Mutual Broadcasting	$20-30
	(With Anne Murray and Crystal Gayle)		
LP(RS)	**LIVE AT GILLEY'S** (May 88) With Mel Tillis	Westwood One	$20-40
	(Rare live concert)		
3LP(RS)	**CHRISTMAS WITH REBA** (Dec 88) With McEntire and Parton	Westwood One	$25-40
	(Mostly music and interviews)		

ROSS MINIMI (RB)

-singles-

45rpm	**OH! JANET** (58)	Gulfstream 7269	$60

MINNIE PEARL (CW)
Sarah Cannon
RCA Victor duet 78s and 45s $10 each

-albums-

LP	**HOWDEE** (63)	Starday 224	$40
LP	**AMERICA'S BELOVED MINNIE PEARL** (65)	Starday 380	$30
LP	**THE COUNTRY MUSIC STORY** (66)	Starday 397	$25
	(Minnie Pearl narrates over other artists hit songs)		
LP	**HOWDY** (67)	Sunset 5148	$15
LP	**LAUGH-A-LONG** (72)	Pickwick 6014	$15
LP	**LOOKIN' FOR A FELLER** (73)	Nashville 2043	$12

GUY MITCHELL (P)
Only the country listed
Other Columbia 78s and 45s $4-8 each

-singles-

45rpm	**NINETY NINE YEARS** (56)	Columbia 40631	$10
78rpm	**SINGING THE BLUES** (56)	Columbia 40769	$12
78(P)	**SINGING THE BLUES** (56)	Columbia 40769	$18
	(Columbia promo label)		
45rpm	**SINGING THE BLUES** (56)	Columbia 40769	$15
45rpm	**SINGING THE BLUES** (56)	Columbia 40769	$30
	(Price includes picture sleeve)		
45(P)	**SINGING THE BLUES** (56)	Columbia 40769	$18
	(White promo label)		
33(P)	**SINGING THE BLUES** (56)	Columbia 33005	$25
	(Hall of Fame series, flip side is "Heartaches By the Number")		
45rpm	**KNEE DEEP IN THE BLUES** (56)	Columbia 40820	$12
45(P)	**KNEE DEEP IN THE BLUES** (56)	Columbia 40820	$15
	(White promo label)		
45rpm	**ROCK-A-BILLY** (57)	Columbia 40877	$10
45rpm	**HEARTACHES BY THE NUMBER** (60)	Columbia 41476	$15
	(Price includes picture sleeve)		
33(P)	**HEARTACHES BY THE NUMBER** (60)	Columbia 30476	$15
	(Seven-inch jukebox stereo single)		
45rpm	**MY SHOES KEEP WALKING BACK TO YOU** (60)	Columbia 41725	$10

-albums-

10"LP	**SONGS OF THE OPEN SPACES** (53)	Columbia 6231	$50
	(First album)		
10"LP	**RED GARTERS** (54)	Columbia 6282	$100
	(Soundtrack)		
LP	**GUY MITCHELL'S GREATEST HITS** (59)	Columbia 1226	$25
LP	**SUNSHINE GUITAR** (60)	Columbia 1552	$25
LP(P)	**SUNSHINE GUITAR** (60)	Columbia 1552	$30
	(White promo label)		
LP	**TRAVELIN' SHOES** (68)	Starday 412	$12
LP	**SINGIN' UP A STORM** (69)	Starday 432	$12
LP	**HEARTACHES BY THE NUMBER** (70)	Nashville 2074	$10

LEE MITCHELL (RB)
-singles-

45rpm	**ROOTIE TOOTIE BABY** (59)	Sharp	$125

MARLON MITCHELL (RB)
-singles-

45rpm	**ICE COLD BABY** (58)	Vena 100	$50

TOMMY MITCHELL (RB)
-singles-

45rpm	**JUKE BOX, HELP ME FIND MY BABY** (58)	Mercury 70930	$18
45(P)	**JUKE BOX, HELP ME FIND MY BABY** (58)	Mercury 70930	$15
	(White promo label)		

BILLY MIZE (C)
Imperial and United Artists 45s $2-3 each
-albums-

LP	**THIS TIME AND PLACE** (69)	Imperial 12441	$15
LP	**YOU'RE ALRIGHT WITH ME** (70)	United Artists 6781	$12

HANK MIZELL (RB)
-singles-

45rpm	**JUNGLE ROCK** (58)	Eko 506	$100
45rpm	**JUNGLE ROCK** (59)	King 5236	$40
	(The same song on Amazon label, released around 1963, is worth $20)		

BOBBY MIZZELL (RB)
-singles-

45rpm	**KNOCKOUT** (58)	Kim 307	$75

RONNIE MOLLEEN (R)
-singles-

45rpm	**ROCKYN' UP** (58)	King 5365	$50

BILL MONROE (BG)
With his brothers James, Charlie, and Birch, became the Monroe Brothers
Bluebird 78s by the Monroe Brothers $15-20 each
Other Bluebird 78s $10 each
Other Decca 78s and 45s $4-8 each
MCA LPs $2-4 each
MCA LPs by The Monroe Brothers $5 each
MCA LPs by Bill and James Monroe $3-5 each
Atteiram LPs by Birch Monroe $5 each
Atteiram LPs by James Monroe $6 each
Rem LPs by Charlie Monroe $8-10 each
Old Homestead, Pine Mountain, Golden Country, County, and Pine Tree LPs by Charlie Monroe $4-6 each
-singles-

78rpm	**GREAT SPECKLED BIRD** (44) Charlie Monroe	Bluebird 7862	$12
78rpm	**MULE SKINNER BLUES** (45)	Bluebird 8568	$25
78rpm	**NO LETTER IN THE MAIL** (45)	Bluebird 8611	$20
78rpm	**DOG HOUSE BLUES** (46)	Bluebird 8692	$20
78rpm	**TENNESSEE BLUES** (46)	Bluebird 8813	$20
78rpm	**BLUE YODEL NO. 7** (47)	Bluebird 8861	$18
45rpm	**RAWHIDE** (52)	Decca 46392	$15
45rpm	**AN ANGEL IN DISGUISE** (52)	Decca 46406	$10
45rpm	**SAILOR'S PLEA** (52)	Decca 28183	$12
	(Both sides are Jimmie Rodgers songs)		
45rpm	**FIND 'EM, FOOL 'EM AND LEAVE THEM ALONE** (52)	Decca 28281	$10
	(Charlie Monroe)		
45rpm	**PIKE COUNTY BREAKDOWN** (52)	Decca 28356	$12
45rpm	**CABIN OF LOVE** (53)	Decca 28749	$10
45rpm	**I'M WORKING ON A BUILDING** (55)	Decca 29348	$10

-EPs-

EP	**BILL MONROE & HIS BLUEGRASS BOYS** (52)	Columbia 1709	$40
EP	**BILL MONROE & HIS BLUEGRASS BOYS** (57)	Columbia 2804	$30
EP	**BILL MONROE** (56)	Decca 2353	$20
EP	**BILL MONROE** (56)	Decca 2354	$20
EP	**KNEE DEEP IN BLUEGRASS** (58)	Decca 2585	$20
EP	**I SAW THE LIGHT** (58)	Decca 2610	$20
EP	**BILL MONROE & HIS BLUEGRASS BOYS** (62)	Decca 2713	$18
EP	**LITTLE JOE** (62)	Decca 2724	$20
EP	**BLUE RIDGE MOUNTAIN BLUES** (63)	Decca 2753	$18
EP	**DARK AS THE NIGHT** (64)	Decca 2764	$18
EP	**I'LL MEET YOU IN CHURCH SUNDAY MORNING** (65)	Decca 2792	$18

-albums-

LP	**KNEE DEEP IN BLUEGRASS**	Decca 8731	$40
LP(P)	**KNEE DEEP IN BLUEGRASS**	Decca 8731	$50
	(Pink promo label)		
LP	**MR. BLUEGRASS** (60)	Decca 4080	$25
LP(P)	**MR. BLUEGRASS** (60)	Decca 4080	$30
	(Pink promo label)		
LP	**GREAT BILL MONROE & THE BLUEGRASS BOYS** (61)	Harmony 7290	$25
LP(P)	**GREAT BILL MONROE & THE BLUEGRASS BOYS** (61)	Harmony 7290	$30
	(White promo label)		
LP	**BLUEGRASS RAMBLE** (62)	Decca 4266	$25
LP(P)	**BLUEGRASS RAMBLE** (62)	Decca 4266	$30
	(Pink promo label)		
LP	**BLUEGRASS SPECIAL** (62)	Decca 4382	$25
LP(P)	**BLUEGRASS SPECIAL** (62)	Decca 4382	$30
	(Pink promo label)		
LP	**MY ALL TIME COUNTRY FAVORITES** (62)	Decca 4527	$25
LP(P)	**MY ALL TIME COUNTRY FAVORITES** (62)	Decca 4527	$30
	(Pink promo label)		
LP	**FATHER OF BLUEGRASS MUSIC** (62)	Camden 719	$25
LP	**I'LL MEET YOU IN CHURCH SUNDAY MORNING** (64)	Decca 4537	$25
LP(P)	**I'LL MEET YOU IN CHURCH SUNDAY MORNING** (64)	Decca 4537	$30
	(Pink promo label)		
LP	**BILL MONROE SINGS COUNTRY SONGS** (64)	Vocalion 3702	$20
LP(P)	**BILL MONROE SINGS COUNTRY SONGS** (64)	Vocalion 3702	$25
	(White promo label)		
LP	**BILL MONROE'S BEST** (64)	Harmony 7315	$20
LP(P)	**BILL MONROE'S BEST** (64)	Harmony 7315	$25
	(White promo label)		
LP	**EARLY BLUEGRASS** (64)	Camden 774	$25
	(Bluebird material includes Charlie)		
LP	**ORIGINAL BLUEGRASS SOUND** (65)	Harmony 7338	$18
LP(P)	**ORIGINAL BLUEGRASS SOUND** (65)	Harmony 7338	$20
	(White promo label)		
LP	**BLUEGRASS INSTRUMENTALS** (65)	Decca 4601	$18
LP(P)	**BLUEGRASS INSTRUMENTALS** (65)	Decca 4601	$20
	(White promo label)		
LP	**HIGH LONESOME SOUND OF BILL MONROE** (66)	Decca 4780	$18
LP(P)	**HIGH LONESOME SOUND OF BILL MONROE** (66)	Decca 4780	$20
	(White promo label)		
LP	**LORD, BUILD ME A CABIN** (65) Charlie Monroe	Starday 361	$18
LP	**CHARLIE MONROE SINGS AGAIN** (66) Charlie Monroe	Starday 372	$18
LP	**BLUEGRASS TIME** (67)	Decca 4896	$18
LP(P)	**BLUEGRASS TIME** (67)	Decca 4896	$20
	(White promo label)		
LP	**BILL MONROE'S GREATEST HITS** (68)	Decca 5010	$15
LP(P)	**BILL MONROE'S GREATEST HITS** (68)	Decca 5010	$18
	(White promo label)		
LP	**THE MONROE BROTHERS, BILL & CHARLIE** (69)	Decca 5066	$15
LP(P)	**THE MONROE BROTHERS, BILL & CHARLIE** (69)	Decca 5066	$18
	(White promo label)		
LP	**I SAW THE LIGHT** (69)	Decca 8769	$15
LP(P)	**I SAW THE LIGHT** (69)	Decca 8769	$18
	(Decca promo label)		
LP	**WHO'S CALLING YOU SWEETHEART TONIGHT** (69)	Camden 2310	$15
	(Charlie Monroe)		
LP	**A VOICE FROM ON HIGH** (69)	Decca 5135	$15
LP(P)	**A VOICE FROM ON HIGH** (69)	Decca 5135	$18
	(White promo label)		
LP	**GREAT BILL MONROE & THE BLUEGRASS BOYS** (69)	Harmony 11335	$12
2LP	**BILL MONROE & HIS BLUEGRASS BOYS** (70)	Columbia 1065	$12
LP	**BLUEGRASS STYLE** (70)	Vocalion 3870	$12
LP(P)	**BLUEGRASS STYLE** (70)	Vocalion 3870	$15
	(White promo label)		
LP	**KENTUCKY BLUEGRASS** (70)	Decca 5213	$15
LP(P)	**KENTUCKY BLUEGRASS** (70)	Decca 5213	$18
	(White promo label)		
LP	**BILL MONROE'S COUNTRY HALL OF FAME** (71)	Decca 5281	$15
LP(P)	**BILL MONROE'S COUNTRY HALL OF FAME** (71)	Decca 5281	$18
	(White promo label)		
LP	**UNCLE PEN** (72)	Decca 5348	$15
LP(P)	**UNCLE PEN** (72)	Decca 5348	$18
	(White promo label)		
LP	**FEAST HERE TONIGHT** (75) Monroe Brothers	Bluebird 5510	$10

-radio shows-

LP(RS)	**GRAND OL' OPRY** (63) Fifteen-minute show	WSM Radio 61	$25-40
	(Music and interviews)		

LP(RS)	**COUNTRY MUSIC TIME** (70s)	U.S. Air Force	$10-20
	(Music and interviews)		
LP(RS)	**COUNTRY MUSIC TIME** (80s) With Nat Stuckey	U.S. Air Force	$10-20
	(Music and interviews)		
3LP(RS)	**SILVER EAGLE** (Mar 85) With Ricky Skaggs	DIR	$50-75
	(Rare live show)		

PATSY MONTANA (CW)
Ruby Blevins

-singles-

78rpm	**WHEN I GETS TO WHERE I'M GOING**	Vogue 721	$40
	(Vogue picture disc)		

-EPs-

EP	**HE TAUGHT ME HOW TO YODEL** (55)	RCA Victor 592	$20
	(Rosalie Allen and Patsy Montana)		

-albums-

LP	**NEW SOUND OF PATSY MONTANA** (64)	Sims 122	$50
LP(P)	**NEW SOUND OF PATSY MONTANA** (64)	Sims 122	$75
	(White promo label)		
LP	**EARLY COUNTRY FAVORITES** (83)	Old Homestead 307	$12
	(Featuring Waylon Jennings on guitar)		
LP	**PATSY MONTANA & THE PRAIRIE RAMBLERS** (84)	Columbia 38909	$15

MONTANA SLIM (CW)
Wilf Carter
And the Calgary Stampeders
Bluebird 78s are worth $12-$18 each
Other RCA Victor 78s and 45s $5-10 each
Other Decca 45s $4-8 each
Starday 45s $5 each

-singles-

45rpm	**BLUEBIRD ON YOUR WINDOWSILL** (49) Green vinyl	RCA Victor 0054	$40
45rpm	**MY OKLAHOMA ROSE** (52)	RCA Victor 4446	$25
78rpm	**THE NIGHT BEFORE CHRISTMAS** (54)	RCA Victor 5322	$15
	(Purple label)		
45rpm	**MY MOUNTAIN HIGH YODEL SONG** (55)	Decca 29384	$12
45(P)	**MY MOUNTAIN HIGH YODEL SONG** (55)	Decca 29384	$10
	(Pink promo label)		
45rpm	**THE SUNSHINE BIRD** (56)	Decca 29535	$12
45(P)	**THE SUNSHINE BIRD** (56)	Decca 29535	$10
	(Pink promo label)		
45rpm	**THERE'S A TREE ON EVERY ROAD** (57)	Decca 29671	$12
45(P)	**THERE'S A TREE ON EVERY ROAD** (57)	Decca 29671	$10
	(Pink promo label)		
45rpm	**I'M RAGGED BUT I'M RIGHT** (59)	Decca 29942	$12
45(P)	**I'M RAGGED BUT I'M RIGHT** (59)	Decca 29942	$10
	(Pink promo label)		

-EPs-

EP	**ALL TIME GREATS** (55)	Decca 2204	$40

-albums-

LP	**WILF CARTER-MONTANA SLIM** (58)	Camden 527	$40
LP	**I'M RAGGED BUT I'M RIGHT** (59)	Decca 8917	$75
LP(P)	**I'M RAGGED BUT I'M RIGHT** (59)	Decca 8917	$60
	(Pink promo label)		
LP	**THE DYNAMITE TRAIL** (60)	Decca 4092	$75
LP(P)	**THE DYNAMITE TRAIL** (60)	Decca 4092	$60
	(Pink promo label)		
LP	**REMINISCIN' WITH MONTANA SLIM** (62)	Camden 668	$25
LP	**WILF CARTER AS MONTANA SLIM** (64)	Starday 300	$25
LP	**32 WONDERFUL YEARS** (65)	Camden 846	$18
LP	**WILF CARTER** (66)	Starday 389	$25
LP	**NO LETTER TODAY** (67)	Camden 2171	$15
2LP	**MONTANA SLIM'S GREATEST HITS** (74)	Camden 0694	$15
LP	**HAVE A NICE DAY** (77)	RCA Victor 2313	$15

GARY MONTGOMERY (RB)

-singles-

45rpm	**RIGHT NOW** (58)	Beagle 101	$40

MELBA MONTGOMERY (C)
United Artists 45s $3 each
Musicor 45s $2 each
Musicor 45s with Gene Pitney $4-5 each
Capitol 45s $2 each
Buddah 45s $2 each
Elektra 45s $1 each

Capitol LPs $5-10 each
Buddah and Hilltop LPs $3-5 each

-albums-

LP	**AMERICA'S NUMBER ONE COUNTRY & WESTERN SINGER** (64)		United Artists 6341	$18
LP(P)	**AMERICA'S NUMBER ONE COUNTRY & WESTERN SINGER** (64) (White promo label)		United Artists 6341	$25
LP	**I CAN'T GET USED TO BEING LONELY** (64)		United Artists 6391	$18
LP(P)	**I CAN'T GET USED TO BEING LONELY** (64) (White promo label)		United Artists 6391	$25
LP	**DOWN HOME** (64)		United Artists 6399	$18
LP(P)	**DOWN HOME** (64) (White promo label)		United Artists 6399	$25
LP	**BEING TOGETHER** (64) (With Gene Pitney)		Musicor 3077	$18
LP(P)	**BEING TOGETHER** (64) (White promo label)		Musicor 3077	$25
LP	**COUNTRY GIRL** (66)		Musicor 3079	$15
LP(P)	**COUNTRY GIRL** (66) (White promo label)		Musicor 3079	$12
LP	**THE HALLELUJAH ROAD** (66)		Musicor 3097	$15
LP(P)	**THE HALLELUJAH ROAD** (66) (White promo label)		Musicor 3097	$12
LP	**MELBA TOAST** (66)		Musicor 3113	$12
LP(P)	**MELBA TOAST** (66) (White promo label)		Musicor 3113	$10
LP	**DON'T KEEP ME LONELY TOO LONG** (66) (With the Jordanaires)		Musicor 3114	$12
LP	**DON'T KEEP ME LONELY TOO LONG** (66) (White promo label)		Musicor 3114	$10
LP	**I'M JUST LIVING** (67)		Musicor 3129	$12
LP(P)	**I'M JUST LIVING** (67) (White promo label)		Musicor 3129	$10
LP	**THE MOOD I'M IN** (67)		Unart 21008	$15

CLYDE MOODY (CW)

Decca 45s $4-8 each
Starday 45s $3 each

-albums-

LP	**BEST OF CLYDE MOODY** (64)		King 891	$75
LP	**WE'VE PLAYED EVERY PLACE** (78) (With Tommy Scott)		Starday 999	$15

JOE MOON (RB)

-singles-

45rpm	**LIVE IT UP** (58)		Hill Crest 120	$60

BERNIE MOORE (RB)

-singles-

45rpm	**ROCK GUITAR ROCK** (58)		Planet X 9622	$60

BOB MOORE (C)

Monument 45s $2-4 each
Hickory 45s $2 each

-albums-

LP	**BOB MOORE AND HIS ORCHESTRA** (61)		Monument 18008	$18
LP	**MEXICO** (67) (Repackage reissue of first album)		Monument 18008	$12
LP	**VIVA BOB MOORE** (67)		Hickory 131	$15
LP(P)	**VIVA BOB MOORE** (67) (White promo label)		Hickory 131	$18

CHARLIE MOORE (CW)

With the Dixie Partners
King 45s $4 each
Starday 45s $3 each
Old Homestead LPs $4-8 each
Country Bluegrass, Leather, Wango LPs $3-6 each

-EPs-

EP	**CHARLIE MOORE** (59)		Starday 103	$25
EP	**CHARLIE MOORE** (60)		Starday 116	$20

-albums-

LP	**FOLK 'N' HILL** (63) (With Bill Napier)		King 828	$25
LP	**THE BEST OF CHARLIE MOORE & BILL NAPIER** (63)		King 880	$25
LP	**COUNTRY HYMNAL** (64) (With Bill Napier)		King 917	$18

LP	CITY FOLKS BACK ON THE FARM (65)	King 922	$18
	(With Bill Napier)		
LP	SONGS FOR LONESOME TRUCK DRIVERS (65)	King 936	$18
	(With Bill Napier)		
LP	COUNTRY MUSIC GOES TO VIET NAM (66)	King 982	$25
	(With Bill Napier)		
LP	SPECTACULAR INSTRUMENTALS (67)	King 1014	$18
	(With Bill Napier)		
LP	GOSPEL & SACRED SONGS SUNG BY MOORE & NAPIER (67)	King 1017	$18
LP	BRAND NEW COUNTRY & WESTERN SONGS (67)	King 1021	$20
LP	THE BEST OF CHARLIE MOORE & BILL NAPIER (75)	Starday 963	$12

LATTIE MOORE (CW)
-singles-

45rpm	JUKE JOINT JOHNNIE (52)	Speed 101	$25
45rpm	THEY'RE NOT WORTH THE PAPER THEY'RE PRINTED ON (55)	King 1327	$20
45rpm	LONESOME MAN BLUES (56)	King 4955	$20
45rpm	CAJUN DOLL (57)	King 5370	$18
45(P)	CAJUN DOLL (57)	King 5370	$12
	(White promo label)		
45rpm	JUKE JOINT JOHNNIE (57)	Arc 8005	$30

-albums-

LP	THE BEST OF LATTIE MOORE (60)	Audio Lab 1555	$30
LP	COUNTRY SIDE (62)	Audio Lab 1573	$25
LP	LATTIE MOORE (64)	Derbytown 102	$20

LUCKY MOORE (RB)
-singles-

45rpm	WALKING AND TALKING (58)	Wat-Vee 900	$60

MERRILL MOORE (CW)
Other Capitol 78s $8-$10 each

-singles-

45rpm	BIG BUG BOOGIE (51)	Capitol 2226	$20
45rpm	RED LIGHT (52)	Capitol 2386	$18
45(P)	RED LIGHT (52)	Capitol 2386	$15
	(White promo label)		
78rpm	HOUSE OF BLUE LIGHTS (53)	Capitol 2574	$12
45rpm	HOUSE OF BLUE LIGHTS (53)	Capitol 2574	$15
45(P)	HOUSE OF BLUE LIGHTS (53)	Capitol 2574	$12
	(White promo label)		
45rpm	SNATCHIN' AND GRABBIN' (54)	Capitol 2691	$15
45(P)	SNATCHIN' AND GRABBIN' (54)	Capitol 2691	$12
	(White promo label)		
45rpm	FLY RIGHT BOOGIE (55)	Capitol 2796	$15
45(P)	FLY RIGHT BOOGIE (55)	Capitol 2796	$12
	(White promo label)		
45rpm	DOGGIE HOUSE BOOGIE (55)	Capitol 2924	$15
45(P)	DOGGIE HOUSE BOOGIE (55)	Capitol 2924	$12
	(White promo label)		
45rpm	ROCK ROCKOLA (56)	Capitol 3034	$12
45(P)	ROCK ROCKOLA (56)	Capitol 3034	$10
	(White promo label)		
45rpm	HARD TOP RACE (56)	Capitol 3226	$12
45(P)	HARD TOP RACE (56)	Capitol 3226	$10
	(White promo label)		
45rpm	DOWN THE ROAD A PIECE (56)	Capitol 3311	$12
45(P)	DOWN THE ROAD A PIECE (56)	Capitol 3311	$10
	(White promo label)		
78rpm	BARREL HOUSE BESSIE (57)	Capitol 3721	$12
45rpm	BARREL HOUSE BESSIE (57)	Capitol 3721	$15
45(P)	BARREL HOUSE BESSIE (57)	Capitol 3721	$12
	(White promo label)		

RED MOORE (RB)
-singles-

45rpm	CRAWDAD SONG (58)	Red 840	$125

RONNIE MOORE (R)
-singles-

45rpm	YOU HAVE THIS AND MORE (58)	Stompertime 1157	$40

SCOTTY MOORE (R)
Backed Elvis Presley

-albums-

LP	THE GUITAR THAT CHANGED THE WORLD (64)	Epic 24103	$75

LP(P)	**THE GUITAR THAT CHANGED THE WORLD** (64) (White promo label)	Epic 24103	$75

SPARKLE MOORE (RB)
-singles-

45rpm	**ROCK-A-BOP** (57)	Fraternity 751	$30
45(P)	**ROCK-A-BOP** (57) (White promo label)	Fraternity 751	$25
45rpm	**KILLER** (58)	Fraternity 766	$12
45(P)	**KILLER** (58) (White promo label)	Fraternity 766	$10

TURNER MOORE (R)
-singles-

45rpm	**I'LL BE LEAVIN' YOU** (58)	Mel-O-Tone 1500	$50

TOMMY MORELAND (R)
-singles-

45rpm	**THE DRIFTER** (58)	Maid 1000	$100

AL MORGAN (CW)
-singles-

45rpm	**THAT SILVER-HAIRED DADDY OF MINE** (54)	"X" (RCA) 0015	$10

CHARLIE MORGAN (RB)
-singles-

45rpm	**DINKY JOHN** (58)	Walmay 100	$100

GEORGE MORGAN (CW)
Columbia 78s $5-8 each
Other Columbia 21000 series 45s $10 each
Columbia Hall of Fame 54000 series 45s $8 each
Columbia 40000 series 45s $4 each
Columbia yellow label 45s $5 each
Columbia orange label 45s $3 each
Starday 45s $3 each
Stop 45s $2 each
MCA 45s $1 each
MCA, Power Pak, and 4-Star LPs $3-5 each
Other Columbia and Harmony LPs $5-8 each

-singles-

45rpm	**CANDY KISSES** (49)	Columbia 20547	$25
45rpm	**RAINBOW IN MY HEART** (49)	Columbia 20563	$20
45rpm	**ROOM FULL OF ROSES** (49)	Columbia 20594	$18
45rpm	**CRY-BABY HEART** (49)	Columbia 20627	$18
45rpm	**ALMOST** (52)	Columbia 20944	$15
45rpm	**BE SURE YOU KNOW** (53)	Columbia 20945	$15
45rpm	**ONE WOMAN MAN** (53)	Columbia 21006	$18
45rpm	**A LOVER'S QUARREL** (53)	Columbia 21070	$15
45rpm	**WITHERED ROSES** (54)	Columbia 21071	$12
45rpm	**I PASSED BY YOUR WINDOW** (54)	Columbia 21108	$12
45rpm	**LOOK WHAT FOLLOWED ME HOME TONIGHT** (54)	Columbia 21178	$12
45rpm	**A CHEAP AFFAIR** (55)	Columbia 21344	$12

-EPs-

EP	**GEORGE MORGAN** (52)	Columbia 1708	$30
EP	**MORGAN, BY GEORGE** Vol 1 (57)	Columbia 10441	$18
EP	**MORGAN, BY GEORGE** Vol 2 (57)	Columbia 10442	$18
EP	**MORGAN, BY GEORGE** Vol 3 (57)	Columbia 10443	$18
EP	**TEARS BEHIND THE SMILE** (57)	Columbia 2136	$18
EP	**ALMOST** (58)	Columbia 2832	$18

-albums-

LP	**MORGAN, BY GEORGE** (57)	Columbia 1044	$50
LP	**GOLDEN MEMORIES** (61)	Columbia 8431	$25
LP(P)	**GOLDEN MEMORIES** (61) (White promo label)	Columbia 1831	$30
LP	**TENDER LOVIN' CARE** (64)	Columbia 8911	$20
LP(P)	**TENDER LOVIN' CARE** (64) (White promo label)	Columbia 2111	$25
LP	**SLIPPIN' AROUND** (64) (With Marion Worth)	Columbia 8997	$20
LP(P)	**SLIPPIN' AROUND** (64) (White promo label)	Columbia 2197	$25
LP	**RED ROSES FOR A BLUE LADY** (65)	Columbia 9133	$20
LP(P)	**RED ROSES FOR A BLUE LADY** (65) (White promo label)	Columbia 2333	$25
LP	**RED ROSES FOR A BLUE LADY** (67)	Harmony 11201	$15

LP(P)	**RED ROSES FOR A BLUE LADY** (67)	Harmony 11201	$18
	(White promo label)		
LP	**CANDY KISSES** (67)	Starday 400	$25
LP	**COUNTRY HITS BY CANDLELIGHT** (67)	Starday 410	$20
LP	**STEAL AWAY** (68)	Starday 413	$20
LP	**CANDY KISSES** (69)	Harmony 11331	$15
	(Columbia material)		
LP(P)	**CANDY KISSES** (69)	Harmony 11331	$18
	(White promo label)		
LP	**BARBARA** (69)	Starday 417	$25
LP	**SOUNDS OF GOODBYE** (69)	Starday 435	$18
LP	**GEORGE MORGAN SINGS LIKE A BIRD** (69)	Stop 10009	$15
	(Reissued on Power Pak)		
LP	**MISTY BLUE** (69)	Nashville 2061	$15
LP	**THE BEST OF GEORGE MORGAN** (70)	Starday 457	$12
LP	**THE BEST OF GEORGE MORGAN** (74)	Starday 957	$10
	(Reissue)		
LP	**REMEMBERING THE GREATEST HITS** (75)	Columbia 33894	$12
LP	**FROM THIS MOMENT ON** (75)	4-Star 002	$12

-radio shows-

16"(RS)	**COUNTRY STYLE USA** (60s)	Country Style USA 174	$20-35
	(Music and interviews)		
16"(RS)	**COUNTRY STYLE USA** (60s)	Country Style USA 200	$20-40
	(Music and interviews)		
16"(RS)	**COUNTRY MUSIC TIME** (60s)	U.S. Army 99	$20-40
	(Music and interviews)		
16"(RS)	**U.S. ARMY BAND** (60s)	U.S. Army	$25-40
	(Music and interviews)		
16"(RS)	**NAVY HOEDOWN** (60s)	U.S. Navy	$25-40
	(Music and interviews)		
LP(RS)	**GRAND OL' OPRY** (63)	WSM Radio 69	$20-40
	(Music and interviews)		

ROCKET MORGAN (RB)

-singles-

45rpm	**YOU'RE HUMBUGGIN' ME** (58)	Zynn 502	$12
45rpm	**TAG ALONG** (58)	Zynn 507	$18

JACKIE MORNINGSTAR (RB)

-singles-

45rpm	**ROCKIN' IN THE GRAVEYARD** (57)	Orange 1018	$100
45rpm	**ROCKIN' IN THE GRAVEYARD** (58)	Sandy 1018	$60

GARY MORRIS (C)
Warner 45s $2 each
Warner LPs $4 each

-radio shows-

3LP(RS)	**SILVER EAGLE** (81) with Con Hundley	DIR	$20-40
	(Live concert)		
LP(RS)	**LIVE FROM DISNEY WORLD** (Aug 86) With Saywer Brown		$50-100
	(Live concert)		
3LP(RS)	**AMERICAN EAGLE** (Dec 86)	DIR	$25-50
	(Live concert)		
LP(RS)	**WESTWOOD ONE PRESENTS** (88)	Westwood One	$10-20
	(Live concert)		
LP(RS)	**LIVE FROM GILLEY'S** (May 90)	Westwood One	$15-25
	(Live concert)		
LP(RS)	**WESTWOOD ONE PRESENTS** (90)	Westwood One	$15-30
	(Rare live concert)		

GENE MORRIS (RB)

-singles-

45rpm	**LOVIN' HONEY** (58)	Edmoral 1012	$60

GLEN MORRIS (RB)

-singles-

45rpm	**I GOT THE BLUES** (57)	Liberty Bell 9017	$12

MORRIS BROTHERS (RB)

-singles-

45rpm	**ROCKIN' COUNTRY FEVER** (58)	Morris 101	$50

HAROLD MORRISON (CW)

-albums-

LP	**HOSS, HE'S THE BOSS** (65)	Decca 4680	$18
LP(P)	**HOSS, HE'S THE BOSS** (65)	Decca 4680	$15
	(Pink promo label)		

NOTES

JIM MORRISON (RB)

-singles-

45rpm	READY TO ROCK (58)	Artic 2100	$100

JOHNNY & JONIE MOSBY (C)
Capitol and Columbia 45s $2-3 each
Other Capitol LPs $8 each

-albums-

LP	THE NEW SWEETHEARTS OF COUNTRY MUSIC (65)	Starday 328	$25
LP	MR. & MRS. COUNTRY MUSIC (65)	Columbia 9097	$12
LP(P)	MR. & MRS. COUNTRY MUSIC (65)	Columbia 9097	$15
	(White promo label)		
LP	MAKE A LEFT, THEN A RIGHT (68)	Capitol 2903	$15
LP	HOLD ME (69)	Capitol 286	$15
LP	I'LL NEVER BE FREE (69)	Capitol 414	$15
LP	MR. & MRS. COUNTRY MUSIC (70)	Harmony 11389	$10
LP(P)	MR. & MRS. COUNTRY MUSIC (70)	Harmony 11389	$15
	(White promo label)		

ROY MOSS (RB)

-singles-

45rpm	WIGGLE WALKIN' BABY	Fascination 1002	$125
45rpm	YOU'RE MY BIG BABY NOW (56)	Mercury 70770	$100
45(P)	YOU'RE MY BIG BABY NOW (56)	Mercury 70770	$75
	(White promo label)		
45rpm	CORRINNE, CORINNA (56)	Mercury 70858	$75 45
(P)	CORRINNE, CORINNA (56)	Mercury 70858	$60
	(White promo label)		

MOUNTAIN RAMBLERS (BG)

-albums-

LP	BLUE RIDGE MOUNTAIN MUSIC (62)	Atlantic 1347	$20

MOUNTAINEERS (BG)

-albums-

LP	BLUEGRASS BANJO PICKIN' (63)	Cumberland 69501	$15

MUDCRUTCH (R)
Features Tom Petty
Only country related listed

-singles-

45rpm	UP IN MISSISSIPPI (71)	Pepper 9449	$400
45rpm	DEPOT STREET (75)	Shelter 40357	$30
45(P)	DEPOT STREET (75)	Shelter 40357	$25
	(White promo label)		

MOON MULLICAN (RB)
Also recorded as Moon Mullins
Early 78s white promo label $20 each
Other King 78s $8-12 each
Other King 45s $8 each
Other Starday 45s $4-6 each
Musicor 45s $4 each
Western and Phonorama LPs $5-10 each

-singles-

78rpm	NEW PRETTY BLONDE (47)	King 578	$20
	(New version of Jole Blon)		
78rpm	JOLE BLON'S SISTER (47)	King 632	$15
78rpm	SWEETER THAN THE FLOWERS (48)	King 673	$15
78rpm	I'LL SAIL MY SHIP ALONE (50)	King 830	$15
45rpm	I'LL SAIL MY SHIP ALONE (50)	King 830	$40
78rpm	MONA LISA (50)	King 886	$15
45rpm	MONA LISA (50)	King 886	$30
78rpm	SHORT BUT SWEET (51)	King 931	$15
45rpm	SHORT BUT SWEET (51)	King 931	$25
78rpm	CHEROKEE BOOGIE (51)	King 965	$15
45rpm	CHEROKEE BOOGIE (51)	King 965	$18
78rpm	TRIFLIN' WOMAN BLUES (53)	King 1060	$15
45rpm	TRIFLIN' WOMAN BLUES (53)	King 1060	$18
78rpm	JAMBALAYA (54)	King 1106	$15
45rpm	JAMBALAYA (54)	King 1106	$18
78rpm	PIPELINER BLUES (54)	King 1137	$15
45rpm	PIPELINER BLUES (54)	King 1137	$18
45rpm	A CRUSHED RED ROSE (55)	King 1152	$18
78rpm	OOGLIE, OOGLIE, OOGIE (55)	King 1164	$15
45rpm	OOGLIE, OOGLIE, OOGIE (55)	King 1164	$18

78rpm	**ROCKET TO THE MOON** (56)	King 1198	$15
45rpm	**ROCKET TO THE MOON** (56)	King 1198	$18
45rpm	**GRANDPA STOLE MY BABY** (56)	King 1244	$18
45rpm	**GOOD DEAL LUCILLE** (57)	King 1337	$18
78(P)	**I'M HANGING UP ALL MY WORK CLOTHES** (57)	King 1366	$15
78rpm	**I'M HANGING UP ALL MY WORK CLOTHES** (57)	King 1366	$20
	(White promo label)		
45rpm	**I'M HANGING UP ALL MY WORK CLOTHES** (57)	King 1366	$12
45rpm	**SEVEN NIGHTS TO ROCK** (58)	King 4894	$20
	(Flip side is "Honolulu Rock-A Roll-A")		
45rpm	**ROCK AND ROLL MR. BULLFROG** (58)	King 4915	$20
45(P)	**ROCK AND ROLL MR. BULLFROG** (58)	King 4915	$18
	(White promo bio label)		
45rpm	**BIP BOP BOOM**	Mart 113	$125
	(Mickey Hawks with Moon Mullins)		
45rpm	**BIP BOP BOOM**	Profile 4002	$30
	(Mickey Hawks with Moon Mullins)		
45rpm	**HEY SHAH** (58)	King 4937	$20
45rpm	**SEVEN NIGHTS TO ROCK** (59)	King 5172	$20
	(Flip side is "I'll Sail My Ship Alone")		
45(P)	**SEVEN NIGHTS TO ROCK** (59)	King 5172	$18
	(White promo label)		
45rpm	**ROCKET TO THE MOON** (59)	King 5379	$18
45(P)	**ROCKET TO THE MOON** (59)	King 5379	$12
	(White promo label)		
45rpm	**THE WRITIN' ON THE WALL** (60)	Decca 30962	$18
45(P)	**THE WRITIN' ON THE WALL** (60)	Decca 30962	$15
	(Pink promo label)		
45rpm	**JENNY LEE** (60)	Coral 61994	$20
45(P)	**JENNY LEE** (60)	Coral 61994	$15
	(Blue promo label)		
45rpm	**MOON'S ROCK** (60)	Coral 62042	$20
45(P)	**MOON'S ROCK** (60)	Coral 62042	$15
	(Blue promo label)		
45rpm	**NEW JOLE BLON** (64)	Starday 527	$10

-EPs-

EP	**KING OF THE HILLBILLY PIANO PLAYERS** (55)	King 214	$50
EP	**PIANO SOLOS BY MOON MULLICAN** (56)	King 227	$30
EP	**MOON MULLICAN** (58)	King 314	$25
EP	**MOON MULLICAN** (60)	Starday 154	$25

-albums-

LP	**MOON OVER MULLICAN** (58)	Coral 57235	$500
LP(P)	**MOON OVER MULLICAN** (58)	Coral 57235	$400
	(Blue promo label)		
LP	**MOON MULLICAN PLAYS AND SINGS** (58)	Sterling 601	$150
LP	**MOON MULLICAN SINGS HIS ALL-TIME GREATEST HITS** (58)	King 555	$150
LP	**MOON MULLICAN PLAYS AND SINGS 16** (59)	King 628	$125
LP	**THE MANY MOODS OF MOON MULLICAN** (60)	King 681	$125
LP	**INSTRUMENTALS** (62)	Audio Lab 1568	$150
LP	**PLAYIN' AND SINGIN'** (63)	Starday 135	$100
LP	**MR. PIANO MAN** (64)	Starday 267	$50
LP	**MISTER HONKY TONK MAN** (65)	Spar 3005	$100
LP	**MOON MULLICAN SINGS 24 OF HIS FAVORITE TUNES** (65)	King 937	$40
LP	**GOOD TIMES GONNA ROLL** (66)	Hilltop 6033	$25
LP	**THE UNFORGETTABLE MOON MULLICAN** (67)	Starday 398	$40
LP	**SHOWCASE** (68)	Kapp 3600	$25
LP	**I'LL SAIL MY SHIP ALONE** (70)	Nashville 2080	$20

DEE MULLINS (C)
Other Plantation 45s $2-3 each

-singles-

45(P)	**REMEMBER BETHLEHEM** (68)	Plantation	$10
	(Yellow vinyl)		

-albums-

LP	**CONTINUING STORY OF HARPER VALLEY PTA** (69)	Plantation 4	$15

MICHAEL MURPHEY (C)
Michael Martin Murphey
Lewis & Clarke Expedition
The New Society
A&M 45s $5 each
A&M picture sleeves $4 each
Epic 45s $2-4 each
Epic picture sleeves $4 each
Liberty and EMI 45s $2 each
Liberty and EMI picture sleeves $2 each
Warner 45s $1 each

Chartmaker 45s by Lewis & Clarke $6 each
RCA Victor 45s by the New Society $6 each
Other A&M LPs $5-8 each
Epic LPs $4-8 each
Liberty and EMI LPs $3-5 each

-singles-

45rpm	**BLUE REVELATIONS** (67) Lewis & Clarke Expedition	Colgems 1006	$15
	(Price includes picture sleeve)		
45(P)	**BLUE REVELATIONS** (67)	Colgems 1006	$10
	(White promo label, no picture sleeve)		
45rpm	**DESTINATION UNKNOWN** (68) Lewis & Clarke Expedition	Colgems 1011	$15
	(Price includes picture sleeve)		
45(P)	**DESTINATION UNKNOWN** (68)	Colgems 1011	$10
	(White promo label, no picture sleeve)		
45(P)	**WHAT'S IT ALL ABOUT** (76) Public service show	W. I. A. A. 313	$15
	(Flip side features B. B. King)		

-EPs-

| EP(P) | **HEALING SPRINGS** (76) Michael Murphey | Playback 69 | $20 |
| | (With three other artists and songs) | | |

-albums-

LP	**LEWIS & CLARKE EXPEDITION** (67)	Colgems 105	$30
LP	**GERONIMO'S CADILLAC** (72)	A&M 4358	$15
	(Reissued in 1974 as A&M 3134)		
LP(P)	**GERONIMO'S CADILLAC** (72)	A&M 4358	$20
	(White promo label)		
LP	**COSMIC COWBOY** (73)	A&M 4388	$10
	(Reissued in 1974 as A&M 3317)		
LP(P)	**COSMIC COWBOY** (73)	A&M 4388	$15
	(White promo label)		

-radio shows-

LP(RS)	**COUNTRY SESSIONS** (83)	NBC Radio	$25-50
	(Rare live concert)		
3LP(RS)	**AMERICAN EAGLE** (Nov 86)	DIR	$10-20
	(Live concert)		
3LP(RS)	**AMERICAN EAGLE** (Mar 87)	DIR	$10-15
	(Live concert)		
LP(RS)	**LIVE AT GILLEY'S** (July 85)	Westwood One	$10-25
	(Live concert)		
LP(RS)	**LIVE AT GILLEY'S** (Sept 88)	Westwood One	$10-15
	(Live concert)		
LP(RS)	**WESTWOOD ONE PRESENTS** (Dec 89)	Westwood One	$10-20
	(Live concert)		
LP(RS)	**WESTWOOD ONE PRESENTS** (Apr 90)	Westwood One	$10-15
	(Live concert)		

CHUCK MURPHY (CW)

-singles-

45rpm	**WHO DRANK MY BEER WHILE I WAS IN THE REAR?** (53)	Coral 60800	$15
45rpm	**A 2-D GAL IN A 3-D TOWN** (54)	Coral 61014	$12
45rpm	**HARD HEADED** (54)	Columbia 21258	$15
45(P)	**HARD HEADED** (54)	Columbia 21258	$12
	(White promo label)		
45rpm	**RHYTHM HALL** (54)	Columbia 21305	$15
45(P)	**RHYTHM HALL** (54)	Columbia 21305	$12
	(White promo label)		

DON MURPHY (RB)

-singles-

| 45rpm | **MEAN MAMA BLUES** (57) | Cosmopolitan 2264 | $125 |

JIMMY MURPHY (RB)

-singles-

78rpm	**BIG MAMA BLUES** (50)	RCA Victor 0474	$15
78(P)	**BIG MAMA BLUES** (50)	RCA Victor 0474	$20
	(White promo label)		
45rpm	**HERE KITTY KITTY** (56)	Columbia 21486	$50
45(P)	**HERE KITTY KITTY** (56)	Columbia 21486	$40
	(White promo label)		
45rpm	**SIXTEEN TONS OF ROCK & ROLL** (56)	Columbia 21534	$75
45(P)	**SIXTEEN TONS OF ROCK & ROLL** (56)	Columbia 21534	$50
	(White promo label)		
45rpm	**BABOON BOOGIE** (56)	Columbia 21569	$40
45(P)	**BABOON BOOGIE** (56)	Columbia 21569	$30
	(White promo label)		
45rpm	**I'M GONE MAMA** (57)	Rev 3508	$15
45(P)	**I'M GONE MAMA** (57)	Rev 3508	$12
	(White promo label)		

45rpm	**I LOVE TO HEAR THE BLUES**	Ark 259	$10
45rpm	**HALF A LOAF OF BREAD**	Rem 340	$10

ANNE MURRAY (C)
Other Capitol 45s $1 each
Capitol picture sleeves $2 each
Other Capitol LPs $2-4 each
Pickwick LPs $8 each

-singles-

45(P)	**CHRISTMAS MEDLEY** (81)	Capitol SPRO-9723	$10
	(Promo-only release)		

-albums-

LP	**ANNE MURRAY** (71)	Capitol 667	$10
	(Her first album)		

-radio shows-

2LP(RS)	**ABC CHRISTMAS SPECIAL** (Dec 81)	ABC Radio	$15-25
	(Music and interviews)		
3LP(RS)	**TRIPLE** (Jun 82) Box set, with R. Milsap and C. Gayle	Mutual Broadcasting	$20-30
	(Music and interviews)		
2LP(RS)	**STARTRACK PROFILE** (July 84)	Westwood One	$15-25
	(Music and interviews)		
2LP(RS)	**STARTRACK PROFILE** (May 85)	Westwood One	$15-20
	(Music and interviews)		
3LP(RS)	**AMERICAN EAGLE** (Jan 87)	DIR	$75-125
	(Rare live concert)		
LP(RS)	**LIVE AT GILLEY'S** (Mar 90)	Westwood One	$25-40
	(Live concert)		
LP(RS)	**WESTWOOD ONE PRESENTS** (Apr 90)	Westwood One	$50-75
	(Rare live concert)		

VARIOUS ARTISTS

-albums-

LP(P)	**MUSIC CITY U. S. A.** (62)	Columbia 2590	$30
	(Live songs, CBS artists, Carl Smith host, white promo label, yellow vinyl)		

N

CLIFF NASH (RB)

-singles-

45rpm	**JENNIE LOU** (58)	Do Ra Me 5028	$60

NASHVILLE BRASS (C)
With Danny Davis
RCA Victor 45s $1 each
RCA Victor LPs $3 each

NASHVILLE STRING BAND (C)
Homer & Jethro and Chet Atkins
RCA Victor 45s $1 each
RCA Victor LPs $3-5 each

TEX NEIGHBORS (RB)

-singles-

45rpm	**ROCK AND ROLL DOT** (58)	Emerald 2109	$60

RICK NELSON (R)
Mainly a pop singer, he did country in the late '70s and early '80s; however, his pop music was very country as most of it featured the Jordanaires
Other Imperial 45s $8 each
Other Decca 45s $5-8 each
Decca pink promo 45s $9 each
Decca blue promo 45s $8 each
Decca yellow promo 45s $5 each
MCA 45s $3 each
MCA promo 45s $3-4 each
MCA picture sleeves $3 each
Capitol 45s $3 each
Capitol promo 45s $4 each
Epic 45s $3 each
Epic promo 45s $5 each
Other MCA LPs $8 each

NOTES

Capitol LPs $6 each
Other Epic LPs $6 each

-singles-

78rpm	**A TEENAGER'S ROMANCE** (56)	Verve 10047	$50
45rpm	**A TEENAGER'S ROMANCE** (56)	Verve 10047	$20
78rpm	**YOU'RE MY ONE AND ONLY LOVE** (57)	Verve 10070	$50
45rpm	**YOU'RE MY ONE AND ONLY LOVE** (57)	Verve 10070	$20
78rpm	**BE-BOP BABY** (57)	Imperial 5463	$40
45rpm	**BE-BOP BABY** (57) Maroon label	Imperial 5463	$25
45rpm	**BE-BOP BABY** (57)	Imperial 5463	$75
	(Price includes picture sleeve)		
45rpm	**BE-BOP BABY** (57) Black label	Imperial 5463	$18
45(P)	**BE-BOP BABY** (57)	Imperial 5463	$75
	(Cream-colored promo label)		
78rpm	**STOOD UP** (57)	Imperial 5483	$30
45rpm	**STOOD UP** (57)	Imperial 5483	$15
45rpm	**STOOD UP** (57)	Imperial 5483	$50
	(Price includes picture sleeve)		
45(P)	**STOOD UP** (57)	Imperial 5483	$60
	(Cream-colored promo label)		
78rpm	**BELIEVE WHAT YOU SAY** (57)	Imperial 5503	$30
45rpm	**BELIEVE WHAT YOU SAY** (57)	Imperial 5503	$15
45rpm	**BELIEVE WHAT YOU SAY** (57)	Imperial 5503	$50
	(Price includes picture sleeve)		
45(P)	**BELIEVE WHAT YOU SAY** (57)	Imperial 5503	$50
	(Cream-colored promo label)		
78rpm	**POOR LITTLE FOOL** (58)	Imperial 5528	$30
45rpm	**POOR LITTLE FOOL** (58)	Imperial 5528	$15
45(P)	**POOR LITTLE FOOL** (58)	Imperial 5528	$50
	(Cream-colored promo label)		
78rpm	**LONESOME TOWN** (58)	Imperial 5545	$30
45rpm	**LONESOME TOWN** (58)	Imperial 5545	$15
45rpm	**LONESOME TOWN** (58)	Imperial 5545	$50
	(Price includes picture sleeve)		
45(P)	**LONESOME TOWN** (58)	Imperial 5545	$50
	(Cream-colored promo label)		
78rpm	**IT'S LATE** (58)	Imperial 5565	$40
45rpm	**IT'S LATE** (58)	Imperial 5565	$15
45rpm	**IT'S LATE** (58)	Imperial 5565	$50
	(Price includes picture sleeve)		
45(P)	**IT'S LATE** (58)	Imperial 5565	$40
	(Cream-colored promo label)		
45rpm	**SWEETER THAN YOU** (59)	Imperial 5595	$15
45rpm	**SWEETER THAN YOU** (59)	Imperial 5595	$50
	(Price includes picture sleeve)		
45(P)	**SWEETER THAN YOU** (59)	Imperial 5595	$40
	(Cream-colored promo label)		
45rpm	**I WANNA BE LOVED** (59)	Imperial 5614	$15
45rpm	**I WANNA BE LOVED** (59)	Imperial 5614	$40
	(Price includes picture sleeve)		
45(P)	**I WANNA BE LOVED** (59)	Imperial 5614	$35
	(Cream-colored promo label)		
45rpm	**YOUNG EMOTIONS** (59)	Imperial 5663	$12
45rpm	**YOUNG EMOTIONS** (59)	Imperial 5663	$40
	(Price includes picture sleeve)		
45(P)	**YOUNG EMOTIONS** (59)	Imperial 5663	$30
	(Cream-colored promo label)		
45rpm	**I'M NOT AFRAID** (60)	Imperial 5685	$12
45rpm	**I'M NOT AFRAID** (60)	Imperial 5685	$40
	(Price includes picture sleeve)		
45(P)	**I'M NOT AFRAID** (60)	Imperial 5685	$25
	(Cream-colored promo label)		
45rpm	**YOU ARE THE ONLY ONE** (60)	Imperial 5707	$12
45rpm	**YOU ARE THE ONLY ONE** (60)	Imperial 5707	$40
	(Price includes picture sleeve)		
45(P)	**YOU ARE THE ONLY ONE** (60)	Imperial 5707	$25
	(White promo label)		
45rpm	**TRAVELIN' MAN** (61) Black vinyl	Imperial 5741	$12
45rpm	**TRAVELIN' MAN** (61)	Imperial 5741	$40
	(Price includes picture sleeve)		
45(P)	**TRAVELIN' MAN** (61) Red vinyl	Imperial 5741	$800
	(Very rare red vinyl)		
45rpm	**TRAVELIN' MAN** (61) Black vinyl	Imperial 5741	$25
45(P)	**TRAVELIN' MAN** (61) Red vinyl	Imperial 5741	$750
	(White promo label, red vinyl)		
45rpm	**A WONDER LIKE YOU** (61)	Imperial 5770	$12
45rpm	**A WONDER LIKE YOU** (61)	Imperial 5770	$35
	(Price includes picture sleeve)		

45(P)	**A WONDER LIKE YOU** (61) (White promo label)	Imperial 5770	$25
45rpm	**YOUNG WORLD** (62)	Imperial 5805	$12
45rpm	**YOUNG WORLD** (62) (Price includes picture sleeve)	Imperial 5805	$35
45(P)	**YOUNG WORLD** (62) (White promo label)	Imperial 5805	$20
45rpm	**TEEN AGE IDOL** (62)	Imperial 5864	$10
45rpm	**TEEN AGE IDOL** (62) (Price includes picture sleeve)	Imperial 5864	$35
45(P)	**TEEN AGE IDOL** (62) (White promo label)	Imperial 5864	$20
45rpm	**IT'S UP TO YOU** (62)	Imperial 5901	$10
45rpm	**IT'S UP TO YOU** (62) (Price includes picture sleeve)	Imperial 5901	$30
45(P)	**IT'S UP TO YOU** (62) (White promo label)	Imperial 5901	$15
45rpm	**THAT'S ALL** (63)	Imperial 5910	$10
45(P)	**THAT'S ALL** (63) (White promo label)	Imperial 5910	$15
45rpm	**OLD ENOUGH TO LOVE** (63) (Price includes picture sleeve)	Imperial 5935	$25
45(P)	**OLD ENOUGH TO LOVE** (63) (White promo label)	Imperial 5935	$15
45(P)	**A LONG VACATION** (63) (White promo label)	Imperial 5958	$15
45(P)	**TIME AFTER TIME** (63) (White promo label)	Imperial 5958	$15
33s(P)	**RICK NELSON** (63) Set of five jukebox singles ($250 for the set of five)	Decca 34194	$50 each
45rpm	**TODAY'S TEARDROPS** (64)	Imperial 66004	$25
45rpm	**TODAY'S TEARDROPS** (64) (Price includes picture sleeve)	Imperial 66004	$40
45(P)	**TODAY'S TEARDROPS** (64) (White promo label)	Imperial 66004	$20
45rpm	**CONGRATULATIONS** (64)	Imperial 66017	$25
45(P)	**CONGRATULATIONS** (64) (White promo label)	Imperial 66017	$20
45rpm	**LUCKY STAR** (64)	Imperial 66019	$25
45(P)	**LUCKY STAR** (64) (White promo label)	Imperial 66019	$20
45rpm	**I GOT A WOMAN** (63) (Price includes picture sleeve)	Decca 31475	$25
45rpm	**STRING ALONG** (63) (Price includes picture sleeve)	Decca 31495	$25
45rpm	**FOOLS RUSH IN** (63) (Price includes picture sleeve)	Decca 31533	$25
45rpm	**FOR YOU** (63) (Price includes picture sleeve)	Decca 31574	$25
45rpm	**THE VERY THOUGHT OF YOU** (64) (Price includes picture sleeve)	Decca 31612	$25
45rpm	**THERE'S NOTHING I CAN SAY** (64) (Price includes picture sleeve)	Decca 31656	$25
45rpm	**A HAPPY GUY** (64) (Price includes picture sleeve)	Decca 31703	$25
45rpm	**MEAN OLD WORLD** (65) (Price includes picture sleeve)	Decca 31756	$25
45rpm	**YESTERDAY'S LOVE** (65) (Price includes picture sleeve)	Decca 31800	$25
45rpm	**LOVE AND KISSES** (65) (Price includes picture sleeve)	Decca 31845	$25
45rpm	**LOUISIANA MAN** (65) (Price includes picture sleeve)	Decca 31900	$20
45rpm	**THINGS YOU GAVE ME** (66) (Price includes picture sleeve)	Decca 32026	$20
45rpm	**I'M CALLED LONELY** (67) (Price includes picture sleeve)	Decca 32120	$20
45rpm	**EASY TO BE FREE** (70) (Price includes picture sleeve)	Decca 32635	$20
45(P)	**DREAM LOVER** (86) Rick Nelson (Price includes promo picture sleeve)	Epic 06066	$10

-EPs-

EP	**RICKY** (57) (Three of the four songs are by Ricky Nelson)	Verve 5048	$300
EP	**RICKY** Vol 1 (57)	Imperial 153	$150
EP(P)	**RICKY** Vol 1 (57) (Cream-colored promo label)	Imperial 153	$250

NOTES

EP	**RICKY** Vol 2 (57)	Imperial 154	$150
EP(P)	**RICKY** Vol 2 (57)	Imperial 154	$250
	(Cream-colored promo label)		
EP	**RICKY** Vol 3 (57)	Imperial 155	$150
EP(P)	**RICKY** Vol 3 (57)	Imperial 155	$250
	(Cream-colored promo label)		
EP	**RICKY NELSON** Vol 1 (58)	Imperial 156	$150
EP(P)	**RICKY NELSON** Vol 1 (58)	Imperial 156	$200
	(Cream-colored promo label)		
EP	**RICKY NELSON** Vol 2 (58)	Imperial 157	$150
EP(P)	**RICKY NELSON** Vol 2 (58)	Imperial 157	$200
	(Cream-colored promo label)		
EP	**RICKY NELSON** Vol 3 (58)	Imperial 158	$150
EP(P)	**RICKY NELSON** Vol 3 (58)	Imperial 158	$200
	(Cream-colored promo label)		
EP	**RICKY SINGS AGAIN** Vol 1 (59)	Imperial 159	$150
EP(P)	**RICKY SINGS AGAIN** Vol 1 (59)	Imperial 159	$175
	(Cream-colored promo label)		
EP	**RICKY SINGS AGAIN** Vol 2 (59)	Imperial 160	$150
EP(P)	**RICKY SINGS AGAIN** Vol 2 (59)	Imperial 160	$175
	(Cream-colored promo label)		
EP	**RICKY SINGS AGAIN** Vol 3 (59)	Imperial 161	$150
EP(P)	**RICKY SINGS AGAIN** Vol 3 (59)	Imperial 161	$175
	(Cream-colored promo label)		
EP	**SONGS BY RICKY** Vol 1 (59)	Imperial 162	$125
EP(P)	**SONGS BY RICKY** Vol 1 (59)	Imperial 162	$150
	(Cream-colored promo label)		
EP	**SONGS BY RICKY** Vol 2 (59)	Imperial 163	$125
EP(P)	**SONGS BY RICKY** Vol 2 (59)	Imperial 163	$150
	(Cream-colored promo label)		
EP	**SONGS BY RICKY** Vol 3 (59)	Imperial 164	$125
EP(P)	**SONGS BY RICKY** Vol 3 (59)	Imperial 164	$150
	(Cream-colored promo label)		
EP	**RICKY SINGS SPIRITUALS** (60)	Imperial 165	$150
EP(P)	**RICKY SINGS SPIRITUALS** (60)	Imperial 165	$200
	(White promo label)		
EP(JB)	**ONE BOY TOO LATE** (65) Jukebox LLP	Decca 2760	$125
	(Issued with hard cover and title strips)		
EP(JB)	**FOR YOUR SWEET LOVE** (68) Jukebox LLP	Decca 4419	$75
	(Issued with hard cover and title strips)		
EP(JB)	**BEST ALWAYS** (68) Jukebox LLP	Decca 4660	$75
	(Issued with hard cover and title strips)		
	-albums-		
LP	**TEEN TIME** (57)	Verve 2083	$40
	(Various artists with three Ricky Nelson songs)		
LP	**RICKY** (57) Stars on the label	Imperial 9048	$100
LP	**RICKY** (66) Black green label	Imperial 9048	$20
LP(P)	**RICKY** (57)	Imperial 9048	$175
	(White promo label)		
LP	**RICKY NELSON** (58)	Imperial 9050	$100
LP(P)	**RICKY NELSON** (58)	Imperial 9050	$175
	(White promo label)		
LP	**RICKY SINGS AGAIN** (59)	Imperial 9061	$100
LP(P)	**RICKY SINGS AGAIN** (59)	Imperial 9061	$175
	(White promo label)		
LP	**SONGS BY RICKY** (60)	Imperial 9082	$75
LP(P)	**SONGS BY RICKY** (60)	Imperial 9082	$175
	(White promo label)		
LP	**MORE SONGS BY RICKY** (60) Black vinyl	Imperial 9122	$75
	(Mono)		
LP	**MORE SONGS BY RICKY** (60) Black vinyl	Imperial 12059	$100
	(Stereo)		
LP(P)	**MORE SONGS BY RICKY** (60) Black vinyl	Imperial 9122	$150
	(White promo label)		
LP	**MORE SONGS BY RICKY** (60) Red vinyl	Imperial 12059	$1,000
LP(P)	**MORE SONGS BY RICKY** (60) Blue vinyl	Imperial 12059	$1,250
	(White promo label, blue vinyl, also a poster was issued with some of these 12059 LPs and it is rare, worth $150 in mint condition)		
LP	**RICK IS 21** (61) Mono	Imperial 9152	$40
LP	**RICK IS 21** (61) Stereo	Imperial 12071	$75
LP(P)	**RICK IS 21** (61)	Imperial 9152	$100
	(White promo label)		
LP	**ALBUM SEVEN BY RICK** (62) Mono	Imperial 9167	$40
LP	**ALBUM SEVEN BY RICK** (62) Stereo	Imperial 12082	$75
LP(P)	**ALBUM SEVEN BY RICK** (62)	Imperial 9167	$100
	(White promo label)		
LP	**BEST SELLERS** (63) Stars on the label	Imperial 9218	$25

LP	**BEST SELLERS** (63) Black green label, mono	Imperial 9218	$15
LP	**BEST SELLERS** (63) Black green label, "stereo"	Imperial 12218	$10
LP(P)	**BEST SELLERS** (63)	Imperial 9218	$75
	(White promo label)		
LP	**IT'S UP TO YOU** (63) Stars on the label	Imperial 9223	$25
LP(P)	**IT'S UP TO YOU** (63)	Imperial 9223	$75
	(White promo label)		
LP	**MILLION SELLERS** (63) Stars on the label	Imperial 9232	$25
LP	**MILLION SELLERS** (63) Black green label	Imperial 9232	$15
LP	**MILLION SELLERS** (63) Black green label, "stereo"	Imperial 12232	$10
LP(P)	**MILLION SELLERS** (63)	Imperial 9232	$75
	(White promo label)		
LP	**A LONG VACATION** (63) Stars on the label, mono	Imperial 9244	$25
LP	**A LONG VACATION** (63) "Stereo"	Imperial 12244	$18
LP(P)	**A LONG VACATION** (63)	Imperial 9244	$75
	(White promo label)		
LP	**RICK NELSON SINGS FOR YOU** (64) Stars, mono	Imperial 9251	$25
LP	**RICK NELSON SINGS FOR YOU** (64) "Stereo"	Imperial 12251	$18
LP(P)	**RICK NELSON SINGS FOR YOU** (64)	Imperial 9251	$75
	(White promo label)		
LP	**FOR YOUR SWEET LOVE** (63)	Decca 4419	$25
	(All Decca listings are stereo or mono, the mono number is listed, stereos are in the 74000 series)		
LP	**RICK NELSON SINGS FOR YOU** (63)	Decca 4479	$25
LP(P)	**RICK NELSON SINGS FOR YOU** (63)	Decca 4479	$50
	(White promo label)		
LP	**THE VERY THOUGHT OF YOU** (64)	Decca 4559	$20
LP(P)	**THE VERY THOUGHT OF YOU** (64)	Decca 4559	$40
	(White promo label)		
LP	**SPOTLIGHT ON RICK** (64)	Decca 4608	$20
LP(P)	**SPOTLIGHT ON RICK** (64)	Decca 4608	$40
	(White promo label)		
LP	**BEST ALWAYS** (65)	Decca 4660	$20
LP(P)	**BEST ALWAYS** (65)	Decca 4660	$40
	(White promo label)		
LP	**LOVE AND KISSES** (65)	Decca 4678	$20
LP(P)	**LOVE AND KISSES** (65)	Decca 4678	$35
	(White promo label)		
LP	**BRIGHT LIGHTS AND COUNTRY MUSIC** (66)	Decca 4779	$25
LP(P)	**BRIGHT LIGHTS AND COUNTRY MUSIC** (66)	Decca 4779	$35
	(White promo label)		
LP	**RICKY NELSON** (66)	Sunset 4118	$18
LP	**COUNTRY FEVER** (67)	Decca 4827	$25
LP(P)	**COUNTRY FEVER** (67)	Decca 4827	$35
	(White promo label)		
LP	**ON THE FLIP SIDE** (67)	Decca 4836	$25
	(Soundtrack)		
LP(P)	**ON THE FLIP SIDE** (67)	Decca 4836	$35
	(White promo label)		
LP	**ANOTHER SIDE OF RICK** (67)	Decca 4944	$20
LP(P)	**ANOTHER SIDE OF RICK** (67)	Decca 4944	$30
	(White promo label)		
LP	**PERSPECTIVE** (68)	Decca 75014	$25
LP(P)	**PERSPECTIVE** (68)	Decca 75014	$35
	(White promo label)		
LP	**I NEED YOU** (68)	Sunset 5205	$18
LP	**RICK NELSON IN CONCERT** (70)	Decca 75162	$20
	(Add $5 for the poster)		
LP(P)	**RICK NELSON IN CONCERT** (70)	Decca 75162	$30
	(White promo label)		
LP	**RICK SINGS NELSON** (70)	Decca 75236	$20
LP(P)	**RICK SINGS NELSON** (70)	Decca 75236	$30
	(White promo label)		
LP	**RUDY THE FIFTH** (71)	Decca 75297	$15
LP(P)	**RUDY THE FIFTH** (71)	Decca 75297	$25
	(White promo label)		
2LP	**LEGENDARY MASTERS** (71)	United Artists 960	$20
2LP(P)	**LEGENDARY MASTERS** (71)	United Artists 960	$30
	(White promo labels)		
LP	**GARDEN PARTY** (72)	Decca 75391	$15
LP(P)	**GARDEN PARTY** (72)	Decca 75391	$25
	(White promo label)		
2LP	**RICK NELSON COUNTRY** (73)	MCA 4004	$15
10"LP	**FOUR YOU** (81)	Epic 36868	$15
	(Four tracks on a ten-inch LP)		

4LP(RS)	**ROCK, ROLL & REMEMBER** (Feb 87) Various artists (With Dick Clark, features many Nelson interviews in this four-hour show highlighting Rick Nelson)	United Stations	$20-40

TOMMY NELSON (R)

-singles-

45rpm	**HOBO HOP** (58)	Dixie 814	$125

WILLIE NELSON (CW)

Member of the Highwaymen (the country group)
Other United Artists 45s $3-6 each
Atlantic 45s $3 each
Other RCA Victor 45s $3-6 each
RCA Victor picture sleeves $5 each
MCA 45s $3 each
Other Columbia 45s $2 each
Delta 45s with Johnny Bush $5 each
Felicity 45s with Steven Fromholz $4 each
Columbia picture sleeves $2 each
Columbia promo picture sleeves $3 each
Epic 45s with Merle Haggard $2 each
Other RCA Victor LPs $4-8 each
Atlantic LPs $4-8 each
Other Columbia LPs $2-6 each
Other Pickwick LPs $3-5 each
HSRD, Delta, Potomac, Songbird, Plantation, Aura, Accord, Allegiance, Lone Star, Casino, Shotgun, Exact, and Tacoma LPs $2-4 each
Romulus, Delta, Plantation, Quicksilver, and Columbia duets LPs $4-6 each

-singles-

45rpm	**NO DOUGH** (60)	Liberty 55155	$25
45(P)	**NO DOUGH** (60) (White promo label)	Liberty 55155	$20
45rpm	**MISERY MOUNTAIN** (61) Red vinyl	Betty 5702	$75
45rpm	**MAN WITH THE BLUES** (62)	Betty 5703	$25
45rpm	**NIGHT LIFE** (63) Red vinyl	Bellaire 107	$75
45rpm	**NIGHT LIFE** (63)	United Artists 641	$20
45(P)	**NIGHT LIFE** (63) (White promo label)	United Artists 641	$15
45(P)	**WHAT'S IT ALL ABOUT** (Apr 77) Public service show (Flip side features the Manhattans)	W. I. A. A. 366	$15
45(P)	**WHITE CHRISTMAS** (79) (White label, green vinyl)	Columbia AE7-1182	$15
45(P)	**RUDOLPH THE RED-NOSED REINDEER** (79) (White label, red vinyl)	Columbia AE7-1183	$15
45(P)	**MOUNTAIN DEW** (81) (Blue promo label, red vinyl)	RCA Victor 12328	$15
45(P)	**JUST TO SATISFY YOU** (82) With Waylon Jennings (Silver label, blue vinyl)	RCA Victor 13073	$15
45(P)	**THE DOCK OF THE BAY** (82) With Waylon Jennings (Green label, red vinyl)	RCA Victor 13319	$15

-EPs-

33(P)	**VOTE 84** (84) PSA ads for election (Seven-inch record with small center hole, Nelson does one spot with Kristofferson)	Ad Council 884	$18

-albums-

LP	**AND THEN I WROTE** (62) With Leon Russell	Liberty 7239	$50
LP(P)	**AND THEN I WROTE** (62) (White promo label)	Liberty 7239	$75
LP	**HERE'S WILLIE NELSON** (63)	Liberty 7308	$40
LP(P)	**HERE'S WILLIE NELSON** (63) (White promo label)	Liberty 7308	$50
LP	**COUNTRY WILLIE-HIS OWN SONGS** (65)	RCA Victor 3418	$25
LP	**COUNTRY FAVORITES, WILLIE NELSON STYLE** (66)	RCA Victor 3528	$25
LP	**LIVE COUNTRY MUSIC CONCERT** (66)	RCA Victor 3659	$25
LP	**HELLO WALLS** (66) (Reissued on Pickwick)	Sunset 5138	$25
LP	**MAKE WAY FOR WILLIE NELSON** (67)	RCA Victor 3748	$25
LP	**THE PARTY'S OVER** (67)	RCA Victor 3858	$25
LP	**TEXAS IN MY SOUL** (67)	RCA Victor 3937	$25
LP	**GOOD TIMES** (68)	RCA Victor 4057	$25
LP	**MY OWN PECULIAR WAY** (69)	RCA Victor 4111	$25
LP	**BOTH SIDES NOW** (70)	RCA Victor 4294	$20
LP	**COLUMBUS STOCKADE BLUES** (70)	Camden 2444	$15
LP	**LAYING MY BURDENS DOWN** (70)	RCA Victor 4404	$20
LP	**WILLIE NELSON & FAMILY** (71)	RCA Victor 4489	$18
LP	**YESTERDAY'S WINE** (71) (Reissued in 1975 and 1980 on RCA Victor)	RCA Victor 4568	$18

LP	THE PICTURE (72)	RCA Victor 4653	$18
LP	THE WILLIE WAY (72)	RCA Victor 4760	$18
LP	THE BEST OF WILLIE NELSON (73)	United Artists 086	$15
LP(P)	THE BEST OF WILLIE NELSON (73)	United Artists 086	$18
	(White promo label)		
LP	COUNTRY WINNERS (73)	Camden 0326	$15
LP	SPOTLIGHT ON WILLIE NELSON (74)	Camden 0705	$15
LP	COUNTRY WILLIE (75)	United Artists 410	$18
LP(P)	COUNTRY WILLIE (75)	United Artists 410	$20
	(White promo label)		
LP	WHAT CAN YOU DO TO ME NOW (75)	RCA Victor 1234	$12
LP	THE SOUND IN YOUR MIND (76)	Columbia 34092	$10
LP(P)	THE SOUND IN YOUR MIND (76)	Columbia 34092	$12
	(White promo label)		
LP	THE TROUBLEMAKER (76)	Columbia 34112	$10
LP	WILLIE NELSON LIVE (76)	RCA Victor 1487	$10
LP	TO LEFTY, FROM WILLIE (77)	Columbia 34695	$10
LP	WILLIE BEFORE HIS TIME (77)	RCA Victor 2210	$10
LP(P)	STARDUST (78)	Columbia 35305	$10
	(White promo label)		
PD(P)	STARDUST (78)	Columbia 35305	$40
	(Promo-only picture disc)		
2LP(RS)	WILLIE & FAMILY LIVE (78)	Columbia 35642	$10
	(With Emmylou Harris and Johnny Paycheck)		
LP	THERE'LL BE NO TEARDROPS TONIGHT (78)	United Artists 930	$15
LP(P)	THERE'LL BE NO TEARDROPS TONIGHT (78)	United Artists 930	$18
	(White promo label)		
2LP	ONE FOR THE ROAD (79)	Columbia 36064	$15
	(With Leon Russell)		
2LP(P)	ONE FOR THE ROAD (79)	Columbia 36064	$18
	(White promo labels)		
LP	SWEET MEMORIES (79)	RCA Victor 3243	$12
2LP	HONEYSUCKLE ROSE (80)	Columbia 36752	$15
	(Soundtrack)		
2LP(P)	HONEYSUCKLE ROSE (80)	Columbia 36752	$18
	(White promo labels)		
LP	SOMEWHERE OVER THE RAINBOW (81)	Columbia 36883	$12
LP(P)	SOMEWHERE OVER THE RAINBOW (81)	Columbia 36883	$15
	(White promo label)		
2LP	GREATEST HITS AND SOME THAT WILL BE (82)	Columbia 37542	$12
3LP	COUNTRY & WESTERN CLASSICS (83)	Time-Life 16946	$20
10LP	WILLIE NELSON (83)	Columbia 38250	$125
	(Ten record box set)		

-radio shows-

3LP(RS)	WILLIE NELSON & MERLE HAGGARD (Jun 82) Box set	Mutual Broadcasting	$25-40
	(Price includes scripts)		
4LP(RS)	WILLIE AND FRIENDS Four-hour show	Creative Radio	$15-30
	(Music and interviews)		
LP(RS)	LIVE AT GILLEY'S (Nov 88)	Westwood One	$50-100
	(Rare live concert)		
3LP(RS)	WILLIE NELSON SILVER ANNIVERSARY (Dec 86) Box set	United Stations	$25-40
	(Music and interviews)		
LP(RS)	WESTWOOD ONE PRESENTS (May 89) With Parton and Rogers	Westwood One	$25-40
	(Live concert)		

NERVOUS NORVUS (N)

Jimmy Drake
Apollo and MGM 45s by the Four Jokers $30 each
Embee and Big Ben 45s by Nervous Norvus $25 each

-singles-

45rpm	TRANSFUSION (56) The Four Jokers	Diamond 3004	$75
	(R & B original version)		
78rpm	TRANSFUSION (56)	Dot 15470	$40
45rpm	TRANSFUSION (56) Maroon label	Dot 15470	$30
45rpm	TRANSFUSION (56) Black label	Dot 15470	$25
78rpm	APE CALL (56)	Dot 15485	$30
45rpm	APE CALL (56) Maroon label	Dot 15485	$25
45rpm	APE CALL (56) Black label	Dot 15485	$20
78rpm	THE FANG (56)	Dot 15500	$40
45rpm	THE FANG (56) Maroon label	Dot 15500	$25
45rpm	THE FANG (56) Black label	Dot 15500	$20

EDDIE NESBITT (C)

-albums-

LP	THE SONGS OF BRADLEY KINCAID (70s)	Bluebonnet 103	$15
LP	LOST TREASURES (70s)	Bluebonnet 116	$15

JIM NESBITT (C)
Chart 45s $3-6 each
Capricorn 45s $4 each
Scorpion 45s $3 each

-albums-

LP	YOUR FAVORITE COMEDY & HEART SONGS (64)	Chart 6500	$18
LP	TRUCK DRIVIN' CAT WITH NINE WIVES (68)	Chart 1005	$15
LP	RUNNIN' BARE (70)	Chart 1031	$15
LP	THE BEST OF JIM NESBITT (71)	Chart 1044	$15
LP	PHONE CALL FROM THE DEVIL (76)	Scorpion 0001	$10

JOE NETTLES (RB)

-singles-

45rpm	OH BABY (58)	Circle 1174	$40

NEW LOST CITY RAMBLERS (CW)
Folkways EPs $8 each
Other Folkways LPs $4-8 each

-albums-

LP	RURAL DELIVERY (64)	Verve 9003	$15
2LP	20 YEARS OF CONCERT PERFORMANCES (80)	Flying Fish 102	$12

MICKEY NEWBURY (C)
RCA Victor 45s $3 each
Mercury 45s $3 each
Elektra 45s $2 each
MCA and ABC 45s $1 each
Other Elektra LPs $4-6 each
MCA and ABC LPs $3 each

-albums-

LP	HARLEQUIN MELODIES (68)	RCA Victor 4043	$15
2LP	LIVE AT MONTEZUMA HALL (73)	Elektra 2007	$12
2LP(P)	LIVE AT MONTEZUMA HALL (73)	Elektra 2007	$15
	(White promo labels)		

JIMMY NEWMAN (CW)
Jimmy C. Newman
Dot 45s, black label reissues of 1200 series $4-8 each
Decca 45s $3 each
Other MGM yellow label 45s $3-6 each
MGM black label 45s $3 each
Plantation 45s $1 each

-singles-

45rpm	CRY, CRY DARLING (54)	Dot 1195	$15
	(Reissued in 1957, Dot 15659)		
45rpm	DAYDREAMING (55)	Dot 1237	$15
45rpm	BLUE DARLIN' (55)	Dot 1260	$15
45rpm	GOD WAS SO GOOD (55)	Dot 1270	$15
45rpm	SEASONS OF MY HEART (56)	Dot 1278	$15
45rpm	COME BACK TO ME (56)	Dot 1283	$12
45rpm	LET THE WHOLE WORLD TALK (56) Maroon label	Dot 1286	$12
	(Reissued on a black label)		
45rpm	A FALLEN STAR (57)	Dot 1289	$18
45rpm	A FALLEN STAR (57)	Dot 15574	$15
45rpm	CRY, CRY DARLING (57)	Dot 15659	$12
45rpm	CARRY ON (58)	Dot 15766	$25
45rpm	YOU'RE MAKING A FOOL OUT OF ME (58)	MGM 12707	$15
45(P)	YOU'RE MAKING A FOOL OUT OF ME (58)	MGM 12707	$12
	(Yellow promo label)		
45rpm	WHAT'CHA GONNA DO (58)	MGM 12749	$10
45rpm	LONELY GIRL (59)	MGM 12790	$15
45(P)	LONELY GIRL (59)	MGM 12790	$12
	(Yellow promo label)		
45rpm	THE BALLAD OF BABY DOE (59)	MGM 12812	$15
45(P)	THE BALLAD OF BABY DOE (59)	MGM 12812	$12
	(Yellow promo label)		
45rpm	WHAT ABOUT ME (60)	MGM 12894	$12
45(P)	WHAT ABOUT ME (60)	MGM 12894	$10
	(Yellow promo label)		

-EPs-

EP	JIMMY NEWMAN (64)	Decca 2772	$12

-albums-

LP	THIS IS JIMMY NEWMAN (59) Mono	MGM 3777	$25
LP	THIS IS JIMMY NEWMAN (59) Stereo	MGM 3777	$30
LP(P)	THIS IS JIMMY NEWMAN (59)	MGM 3777	$30
	(Yellow promo label)		

LP	**SONGS BY JIMMY NEWMAN** (62)	MGM 4045	$25
LP(P)	**SONGS BY JIMMY NEWMAN** (62)	MGM 4045	$30
	(Yellow promo label)		
LP	**FOLK SONGS OF THE BAYOU COUNTRY** (63)	Decca 4398	$40
LP(P)	**FOLK SONGS OF THE BAYOU COUNTRY** (63)	Decca 4398	$50
	(Pink promo label)		
LP	**ARTIFICIAL ROSE** (66)	Decca 4748	$20
LP(P)	**ARTIFICIAL ROSE** (66)	Decca 4748	$25
	(Pink promo label)		
LP	**JIMMY NEWMAN SINGS COUNTRY SONGS** (66)	Decca 4781	$20
LP(P)	**JIMMY NEWMAN SINGS COUNTRY SONGS** (66)	Decca 4781	$25
	(Pink promo label)		
LP	**A FALLEN' STAR** (66)	Dot 3690	$30
LP	**COUNTRY CROSSROADS** (66)	Dot 25736	$25
LP	**THE WORLD OF COUNTRY MUSIC** (67)	Decca 4885	$18
LP(P)	**THE WORLD OF COUNTRY MUSIC** (67)	Decca 4885	$20
	(Pink promo label)		
LP	**THE JIMMY NEWMAN WAY** (67)	Decca 4960	$15
LP(P)	**THE JIMMY NEWMAN WAY** (67)	Decca 4960	$18
	(Pink promo label)		
LP	**BORN TO LOVE YOU** (68)	Decca 5065	$15
LP(P)	**BORN TO LOVE YOU** (68)	Decca 5065	$18
	(Pink promo label)		
LP	**JIMMY NEWMAN STYLE** (69)	Decca 5136	$15
LP(P)	**JIMMY NEWMAN STYLE** (69)	Decca 5136	$18
	(Pink promo label)		
LP	**COUNTRY TIME** (70)	Decca 5220	$15
LP(P)	**COUNTRY TIME** (70)	Decca 5220	$18
	(Pink promo label)		
LP	**GUEST STAR OF THE GRAND OLE OPRY** (70s)	Crown 329	$15
LP	**ALLIGATOR MAN** (72)	Hilltop 6171	$15
LP	**THE HAPPY CAJUN** (79)	Plantation 544	$12
	(Green vinyl)		

-radio shows-

16"(RS)	**COUNTRY MUSIC TIME** (60s)	U.S. Army 116	$20-40
	(Music and interviews)		
16"(RS)	**U.S. ARMY BAND** (60s)	U.S. Army	$15-25
	(Music and interviews)		
LP(RS)	**GRAND OL' OPRY** (63)	WSM Radio 59	$20-40
	(Music and interviews)		
LP(RS)	**GRAND OL' OPRY** (64)	WSM Radio 73	$20-40
	(Music and interviews)		
LP(RS)	**GRAND OL' OPRY** (64)	WSM Radio 87	$15-30
	(Music and interviews)		
LP(RS)	**GRAND OL' OPRY** (64)	WSM Radio 94	$15-30
	(Music and interviews)		
LP(RS)	**GRAND OL' OPRY** (64)	WSM Radio 111	$15-30
	(Music and interviews)		

JUICE NEWTON (C)
Capitol 45s $2 each
Capitol picture sleeves $2 each
Other RCA Victor 45s $1 each
RCA Victor picture sleeves $1 each
RCA Victor promo picture sleeves $2 each

-singles-

45(P)	**A LITTLE LOVE** (84)	RCA Victor 13823	$10
	(Orange promo label, red vinyl)		

-radio shows-

LP(RS)	**LIVE AT GILLEY'S** (July 88)	Westwood One	$10-20
	(Live concert)		
LP(RS)	**WESTWOOD ONE PRESENTS** (July 88)	Westwood One	$30-60
	(Live concert)		
LP(RS)	**WESTWOOD ONE PRESENTS** (Jan 89)	Westwood One	$25-50
	(Live concert)		

BETTY NICKELL (RB)

-singles-

45rpm	**HOT DOG** (58)	Abbey 102	$25

ROCKY NIGHT (RB)

-singles-

45rpm	**TEEN AGE HOP** (58)	Pearl 708	$60

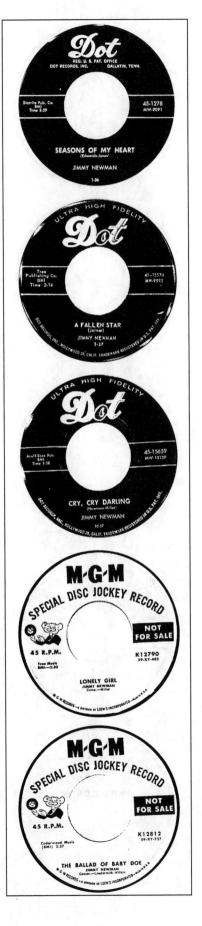

VARIOUS ARTISTS

-albums-

LP(P)	**NIGHT AT THE GRAND OLE OPRY** (64)	Harmony 7369	$25
	(White promo label)		

NITE ROCKETS (RB)

-singles-

45rpm	**LITTLE MAMA** (58)	Super 003	$40

NITTY GRITTY DIRT BAND (C)

The Dirt Band
Liberty 45s $5 each (55000 series)
United Artists 45s $3-6 each
United Artists picture sleeves $4 each
United Artists 45s duets with Doc Watson $5 each
Liberty (Capitol) 45s $2 each (1600 series)
MCA 45s $2 each
Warner 45s $2 each
Warner picture sleeves $2 each

-singles-

45(P)	**WHAT'S IT ALL ABOUT** (Oct 75) Public service show	W. I. A. A. 287	$12
	(Flip side is Waylon Jennings)		

-albums-

LP	**THE NITTY GRITTY DIRT BAND** (67)	Liberty 7501	$25
LP	**RICOCHET** (67)	Liberty 7516	$20
LP	**RARE JUNK** (68)	Liberty 7540	$18
LP	**ALIVE** (69)	Liberty 7611	$18
LP	**UNCLE CHARLIE & HIS DOG TEDDY** (70)	Liberty 7642	$18
	(Includes "Mr. Bojangles")		
LP	**ALL THE GOOD TIMES** (71)	United Artists 5553	$15
LP(P)	**ALL THE GOOD TIMES** (71)	United Artists 5553	$18
	(White promo label)		
3LP	**WILL THE CIRCLE BE UNBROKEN** (72)	United Artists 9801	$15
3LP	**WILL THE CIRCLE BE UNBROKEN** (72)	United Artists 9801	$20
	(White promo labels)		
2LP(P)	**STARS & STRIPES FOREVER** (74)	United Artists 184	$15
2LP(P)	**STARS & STRIPES FOREVER** (74)	United Artists 184	$20
	(White promo labels)		
LP(P)	**INTERVIEW** (75)	United Artists SP-117	$40
	(Promo-only release)		
LP	**DREAM** (75)	United Artists 469	$12
LP(P)	**DREAM** (75)	United Artists 469	$15
	(White promo label)		
3LP	**DIRT, SILVER & GOLD** (77)	United Artists 670	$20
3LP(P)	**DIRT, SILVER & GOLD** (77)	United Artists 670	$25
	(White promo labels)		
LP	**THE DIRT BAND** (78)	United Artists 830	$12
LP(P)	**THE DIRT BAND** (78)	United Artists 830	$15
	(White promo label)		
LP	**THE NITTY GRITTY DIRT BAND** (78)	United Artists 854	$12
LP(P)	**THE NITTY GRITTY DIRT BAND** (78)	United Artists 854	$15
	(White promo label)		

-radio shows-

LP(RS)	**COUNTRY MUSIC TIME** (80s)	U.S. Air Force	$10-20
	(Music and interviews)		
LP(RS)	**WESTWOOD ONE PRESENTS** (Apr 90)	Westwood One	$40-75
	(Rare live concert)		

FORD NIX (RB)

-singles-

45rpm	**NINE TIMES OUT OF TEN** (58)	Clix 621	$60

EDDIE NOACK (CW)

-singles-

45rpm	**TAKE IT AWAY LUCKY** (54)	Starday 159	$12
45rpm	**WALK EM OFF** (57)	D 1037	$20
45rpm	**A THINKING MAN'S WOMAN** (58)	D 1060	$10

TERRY NOLAND (RB)

-singles-

45rpm	**LONG GONE BABY** (57)	Apt 25065	$18
45(P)	**LONG GONE BABY** (57)	Apt 25065	$20
	(White promo label)		
45rpm	**HYPNOTIZED** (57)	Brunswick 55010	$15
45(P)	**HYPNOTIZED** (57)	Brunswick 55010	$12
	(Yellow promo label)		

45rpm	**PATTY BABY** (58)	Brunswick 55036	$12
45(P)	**PATTY BABY** (58)	Brunswick 55036	$10
	(Yellow promo label)		
45rpm	**LOOK AT ME** (58)	Brunswick 55054	$15
45(P)	**LOOK AT ME** (58)	Brunswick 55054	$12
	(Yellow promo label)		
45rpm	**EVERYONE BUT ONE** (58)	Brunswick 55069	$12
45(P)	**EVERYONE BUT ONE** (58)	Brunswick 55069	$10
	(Yellow promo label)		
45rpm	**THERE WAS A FUNGUS AMONG US** (59)	Brunswick 55092	$15
45(P)	**THERE WAS A FUNGUS AMONG US** (59)	Brunswick 55092	$12
	(Yellow promo label)		
45rpm	**GUESS I'M GONNA FALL** (59)	Brunswick 55122	$18
45(P)	**GUESS I'M GONNA FALL** (59)	Brunswick 55122	$15
	(Yellow promo label)		
45rpm	**THERE WAS A FUNGUS AMONG US** (59)	Coral 62274	$12
45(P)	**THERE WAS A FUNGUS AMONG US** (59)	Coral 62274	$10
	(Blue promo label)		
LP	**TERRY NOLAND** (58)	Brunswick 54041	$100
LP(P)	**TERRY NOLAND** (58)	Brunswick 54041	$85
	(Yellow promo label)		

NORMA JEAN (C)
Norma Jean Taylor
RCA Victor 45s $2-4 each
Other RCA Victor LPs $4-8 each
RCA Victor LP with Bobby Bare and Liz Anderson $5 each

-albums-

LP	**LET'S GO ALL THE WAY** (64)	RCA Victor 2961	$25
LP	**PRETTY MISS NORMA JEAN** (65)	RCA Victor 3449	$20
LP	**COUNTRY'S FAVORITE** (66)	Harmony 11163	$15
LP(P)	**COUNTRY'S FAVORITE** (66)	Harmony 11163	$18
	(White promo label)		
LP	**PLEASE DON'T HURT ME** (66)	RCA Victor 3541	$15
LP	**NORMA JEAN SINGS A TRIBUTE TO KITTY WELLS** (66)	RCA Victor 3664	$18
LP	**NORMA JEAN SINGS PORTER WAGONER** (67)	RCA Victor 3700	$15
LP	**JACKSON AIN'T A VERY BIG TOWN** (67)	RCA Victor 3836	$15
LP	**HEAVEN'S JUST A PRAYER AWAY** (68)	RCA Victor 3910	$15
LP	**NORMA JEAN THE BODY AND MIND** (68)	RCA Victor 3977	$15
LP	**LOVE'S A WOMAN'S JOB** (68)	RCA Victor 4060	$15
LP	**COUNTRY GIANTS** (69)	RCA Victor 4146	$15
LP	**HEAVEN HELP THE WORKING GIRL** (68)	Camden 2218	$15
LP	**THE BEST OF NORMA JEAN** (69)	RCA Victor 4227	$12

GENE NORMAN (RB)

-singles-

45rpm	**SNAGGLE TOOTH ANN** (58)	Snag 101	$100

NORMAN PETTY TRIO See Petty

JOE NORRIS (RB)

-singles-

45rpm	**ROCK OUT OF THIS WORLD** (58)	Soma 1001	$60

NORVAL & IVY (N)
Imperial 45s $3 each

-albums-

LP	**WINGIN' IT WITH NORVAL & IVY** (67)	Imperial 12349	$15

CECIL NULL (G)
Decca 45s $3 each

-albums-

LP	**INSTRUMENTAL COUNTRY HYMNS** (67)	Decca 4934	$15
LP(P)	**INSTRUMENTAL COUNTRY HYMNS** (67)	Decca 4934	$12
	(Pink promo label)		

O

OAK RIDGE BOYS (G)
Oak Ridge Quartet
Other Impact 45s $5-8 each
Columbia 45s $2-4 each

ABC/Dot 45s $2-3 each
ABC/Dot 45s with insert (17710) $5 each
Other MCA 45s $2 each
MCA picture sleeves $2 each
MCA poster picture sleeves (52419) $4 each
ABC/Dot LPs $4-8 each
Phonorama, Intermedia, Power Pak, and 51 West LPs $3 each
MCA LPs $2-4 each

-singles-

45rpm	**JESUS IS A SOUL MAN** (72)	Impact 5093	$10
45(P)	**THE BOY SCOUT WAY** (81)	MCA 1741	$12
	(Public service ad for the Boy Scouts)		
45(P)	**SANTA'S SONG/HAPPY CHRISTMAS EVE** (82)	MCA 1154	$12
	(Promo-only release)		
45(P)	**THANK GOD FOR KIDS/JESUS IS BORN TODAY** (82)	MCA 1250	$12
	(Promo-only release)		
45(P)	**COME ON IN** (85)	MCA 52722	$10
	(White promo label, blue vinyl)		
45(P)	**WHEN YOU GIVE IT AWAY** (86)	MCA 17233	$15
	(White promo-only release, green vinyl)		
45(P)	**THERE'S A NEW KID IN TOWN** (86)	MCA 17450	$10
	(Promo-only release, Nancy Griffith song on flip)		
45(P)	**JULIET** (86)	MCA 52801	$12
	(White promo label, green vinyl)		
45(P)	**THIS CRAZY LOVE** (87)	MCA 53023	$10
	(White promo label, blue vinyl)		

-EPs-

33(P)	**NEW MINIMUM WAGE PSA'S** (82) Orange label	U.S. Dept Labor 80021	$15
	(Oak Ridge Boys sing on two of the eleven PSA ads, issued with paper cover)		
33(P)	**PREVENTION OF CHILD ABUSE** (86) Blue label	Ad Council 1285	$15
	(Oak Ridge Boys do all four PSA ads, with song "Thank God for Kids")		

-albums-

LP	**THE OAK RIDGE QUARTET** (59)	Cadence 3019	$30
LP	**WITH SOUNDS OF NASHVILLE** (63)	Warner 1497	$15
LP(P)	**WITH SOUNDS OF NASHVILLE** (63)	Warner 1497	$20
	(White promo label)		
LP	**FOLK MINDED SPIRITUALS** (63)	Warner 1521	$15
LP(P)	**FOLK MINDED SPIRITUALS** (63)	Warner 1521	$20
	(White promo label)		
LP	**THE OAK RIDGE BOYS SING FOR YOU** (64)	Skylite 6020	$15
LP	**I WOULDN'T TAKE NOTHING FOR MY JOURNEY NOW** (65)	Skylite 6030	$15
LP	**THE SENSATIONAL OAK RIDGE BOYS** (65)	Starday 356	$15
LP	**THE OAK RIDGE BOYS AT THEIR BEST** (66)	United Artists 6554	$15
LP(P)	**THE OAK RIDGE BOYS AT THEIR BEST** (66)	United Artists 6554	$18
	(White promo label)		
LP	**SOLID GOSPEL SOUND OF THE OAK RIDGE QUARTET** (66)	Skylite 6040	$15
LP	**TOGETHER** (66) With the Harvesters	Canaan 9625	$15
LP	**THE OAK RIDGE QUARTET SINGS RIVER OF LOVE** (67)	Skylite 6045	$15
LP	**HIGHER POWER** (70)	Nashville 2086	$12
LP	**INTERNATIONAL** (71)	Heartwarming 3091	$12
LP	**THE LIGHT** (72)	Heartwarming 3159	$12
LP	**THE OAK RIDGE BOYS** (74)	Columbia 32742	$10
LP(P)	**THE OAK RIDGE BOYS** (74)	Columbia 32742	$12
	(White promo label)		
LP	**SKY HIGH** (75)	Columbia 33057	$12
LP(P)	**SKY HIGH** (75)	Columbia 33057	$15
	(White promo label)		
LP	**OLD FASHIONED, DOWN HOME, QUARTET MUSIC** (76)	Columbia 33935	$15
LP(P)	**OLD FASHIONED, DOWN HOME, QUARTET MUSIC** (76)	Columbia 33935	$18
	(White promo label)		
2LP(P)	**STEP ON OUT WORLD PREMIERE** (85)	MCA 1276	$25
	(White promo-only labels, no script or cover)		

-radio shows-

LP(RS)	**COUNTRY MUSIC TIME** (80s)	U.S. Air Force	$10-15
	(Music and interviews)		
LP(P)	**COUNTRY GREATS IN CONCERT** (81)	ABC Radio 107	$20-30
	(Live concert)		
LP(P)	**COUNTRY SESSIONS** (81)	NBC Radio	$12-25
	(Live concert)		
3LP(RS)	**COUNTRY MUSIC COUNTDOWN** (81) Various Artists	Mutual Radio	$20-30
	(Hosted by the Oak Ridge Boys, price includes box set and script)		
3LP(RS)	**SILVER EAGLE** (81) "The Oaks for the Arts"	DIR (No #)	$25-50
	(Live concert)		
3LP(RS)	**SILVER EAGLE** (82)	DIR	$30-60
	(Live concert, released several times)		

LP(RS)	**SILVER EAGLE II** (82) For Canadian broadcast	TBS Syndications	$25-40
	(Live concert)		
3LP(RS)	**SILVER EAGLE** (82) With Sylvia	DIR	$20-40
	(Live concert)		
LP(RS)	**LIVE AT GILLEY'S** (May 87)	Westwood One	$25-50
	(Live concert)		
LP(RS)	**WESTWOOD ONE PRESENTS** (July 87)	Westwood One	$30-60
	(Live concert)		
3LP(RS)	**CHRISTMAS WITH THE OAK RIDGE BOYS** (Dec 91)		$20-30
	(Music and interviews)		

VARIOUS ARTISTS
-EPs-

33(P)	**OCTOBER IS COUNTRY MUSIC MONTH** (73) PSA radio	CMA Nashville	$15
	(Twenty cuts featuring top country artists)		
33(P)	**OCTOBER IS COUNTRY MUSIC MONTH** (74) PSA radio	CMA Nashville	$12
	(Twenty-two cuts featuring top country artists and a CMA jingle)		
33(P)	**OCTOBER IS COUNTRY MUSIC MONTH** (75) PSA radio	CMA Nashville	$15
	(Twenty-two cuts)		

MOLLY O'DAY (CW)
LaVerne Williamson
Columbia 45s $8 each

-EPs-

EP	**MOLLY O'DAY** (59)	Columbia 2826	$18

-albums-

LP	**HYMNS FOR THE COUNTRY FOLKS** (60)	Audio Lab 1544	$25
LP	**THE UNFORGETTABLE MOLLY O'DAY** (63)	Harmony 7299	$18
LP(P)	**THE UNFORGETTABLE MOLLY O'DAY** (63)	Harmony 7299	$25
	(White promo label)		
LP	**THE LIVING LEGEND OF COUNTRY MUSIC** (66)	Starday 367	$25
	(Reissued on Pine Mountain label)		

KENNY O'DELL (C)
Mar-Kay 45s $8 each
Capricorn and Vegas 45s $4-6 each

-albums-

LP	**BEAUTIFUL PEOPLE** (68)	Vegas 401	$20
LP	**KENNY O'DELL** (73)	Capricorn 0140	$12
LP(P)	**KENNY O'DELL** (73)	Capricorn 0140	$15
	(Light yellow promo label)		
LP	**LET'S SHAKE HANDS & COME OUT LOVIN'** (78)	Capricorn 0211	$10

MAC O'DELL (G)
-albums-

LP	**HYMNS FOR THE COUNTRY FOLKS** (61)	Audio Lab 1544	$20

JIM OERTLING (RB)
-singles-

45rpm	**OLD MOSS BACK** (60)	Hammond 267	$100

JAMES O'GWYNN (CW)
Mercury 45s $5-10 each
Plantation 45s $2 each
Plantation 45s green vinyl $4 each

-albums-

LP	**THE BEST OF JAMES O'GWYNN** (62)	Mercury 60727	$40
LP(P)	**THE BEST OF JAMES O'GWYNN** (62)	Mercury 20727	$50
	(White promo label)		
LP	**HEARTACHES & MEMORIES** (64)	Mercury Wing 16290	$25
LP(P)	**HEARTACHES & MEMORIES** (64)	Mercury Wing 16290	$30
	(White promo label)		
LP	**JAMES O'GWYNN'S GREATEST HITS** (76)	Plantation 21	$10
LP	**COUNTRY DANCE TIME** (78)	Plantation 525	$12
	(Green vinyl)		

BEV OILAR (RB)
-singles-

45rpm	**SIXTEEN** (58)	G & G 120	$40

JOHNNY O'KEEFE (RB)
-singles-

45rpm	**REAL WILD CHILD** (57)	Brunswick 55067	$30
45(P)	**REAL WILD CHILD** (57)	Brunswick 55067	$25
	(Yellow promo label)		
45rpm	**IT'S TOO LATE** (58)	Liberty 55228	$12

45(P)	**IT'S TOO LATE** (58)	Liberty 55228	$10
	(White promo label)		

OKLAHOMA WRANGLERS (CW)
-albums-

LP	**SONGS OF THE OLD WEST** (63)	Cumberland 69504	$20

JOHNNY OLENN (R)
-singles-

45rpm	**TEENIE** (57)	Personality 1002	$12

-albums-

LP	**JUST ROLLIN' WITH JOHNNY OLENN** (58)	Liberty 3029	$300
LP(P)	**JUST ROLLIN' WITH JOHNNY OLENN** (58)	Liberty 3029	$400
	(White promo label)		

SHADIE OLLER (RB)
-singles-

45rpm	**COME TO ME BABY** (58)	Summit 114	$60

GRADY O'NEIL (RB)
-singles-

45rpm	**BABY OH BABY** (58)	Bella 2205	$60

WOLF OPPER (RB)
-singles-

45rpm	**STOMPIN' TO THE BEAT** (58)	Academy 1437	$40

THE ORANGE BLOSSOM SOUND (BG)
-albums-

LP	**BLUEGRASS & ORANGE BLOSSOMS** (69)	Epic 26494	$15
LP(P)	**BLUEGRASS & ORANGE BLOSSOMS** (69)	Epic 26494	$18
	(White promo label)		

ROY ORBISON (R)
Of the Teen Kings
One of the Traveling Wilburys (See Traveling Wilburys)
Other Monument 45s (500 series) $4-8 each
Monument 45s (8000 and 200 series) $3 each
Other Monument promo 45s $2-6 each
Other MGM 45s $4-8 each
Mercury 45s $5 each
Warner duet 45s $3 each
Asylum 45s $3 each
Virgin 45s $3 each
Virgin picture sleeves $4 each
Virgin 12-inch singles $5-8 each
Spectrum LPs $10 each

-singles-

45rpm	**OOBY DOOBY** (56)	Je-Wel 101	$6,000
	(Teen Kings with Roy Orbison)		
45rpm	**TELL ME IF YOU KNOW** (56)	Bee 1115	$2,000
	(Teen Kings)		
78rpm	**OOBY DOOBY** (57)	Sun 242	$100
45rpm	**OOBY DOOBY** (57)	Sun 242	$100
45rpm	**OOBY DOOBIE** (70s)	Sun 8	$10
	(Notice the different spelling)		
78rpm	**ROCKHOUSE** (57)	Sun 251	$100
45rpm	**ROCKHOUSE** (57)	Sun 251	$40
45rpm	**ROCKHOUSE** (70s)	Sun 12	$10
45rpm	**DEVIL DOLL** (58)	Sun 265	$50
45rpm	**CHICKEN HEARTED** (58)	Sun 284	$40
45rpm	**DEVIL DOLL** (60)	Sun 353	$300
45(P)	**DEVIL DOLL** (60)	Sun 353	$150
	(White promo label)		
45rpm	**DEVIL DOLL** (70s)	Sun 16	$10
45rpm	**SWEET & INNOCENT** (58)	RCA Victor 7381	$40
45rpm	**ALMOST EIGHTEEN** (59)	RCA Victor 7447	$40
45rpm	**PAPER BOY** (59)	Monument 409	$30
45(P)	**PAPER BOY** (59)	Monument 409	$50
	(Brown/white promo label)		
45rpm	**UPTOWN** (59)	Monument 412	$15
45(P)	**UPTOWN** (59)	Monument 412	$40
	(Brown/white promo label)		
45rpm	**ONLY THE LONELY** (60)	Monument 421	$15
45(P)	**ONLY THE LONELY** (60)	Monument 421	$30
	(Brown/white promo label)		

45rpm	**BLUE ANGEL** (60)	Monument 425	$15
45(P)	**BLUE ANGEL** (60)	Monument 425	$25
	(Brown/white promo label)		
45rpm	**I'M HURTIN'** (60)	Monument 433	$15
45rpm	**I'M HURTIN'** (60)	Monument 433	$50
	(Price includes picture sleeve)		
45(P)	**I'M HURTIN'** (60)	Monument 433	$20
	(Brown/white promo label)		
45rpm	**RUNNING SCARED** (61)	Monument 438	$15
45rpm	**RUNNING SCARED** (61)	Monument 438	$50
	(Price includes picture sleeve)		
45(P)	**RUNNING SCARED** (61)	Monument 438	$18
	(Brown/white promo label)		
45rpm	**CRYING** (61)	Monument 447	$15
45rpm	**CRYING** (61)	Monument 447	$50
	(Price includes picture sleeve)		
45(P)	**CRYING** (61)	Monument 447	$18
	(Brown/white promo label)		
45rpm	**DREAM BABY** (62)	Monument 456	$15
45rpm	**DREAM BABY** (62)	Monument 456	$50
	(Price includes picture sleeve)		
45(P)	**DREAM BABY** (62)	Monument 456	$18
	(Brown/white promo label)		
45rpm	**THE CROWD** (62)	Monument 461	$15
45rpm	**THE CROWD** (62)	Monument 461	$50
	(Price includes picture sleeve)		
45(P)	**THE CROWD** (62)	Monument 461	$15
	(Brown/white promo label)		
45rpm	**WORKIN' FOR THE MAN** (62)	Monument 467	$15
45rpm	**WORKIN' FOR THE MAN** (62)	Monument 467	$50
	(Price includes picture sleeve)		
45(P)	**WORKIN' FOR THE MAN** (62)	Monument 467	$15
	(Brown/white promo label)		
45rpm	**IN DREAMS** (63)	Monument 806	$10
45(P)	**IN DREAMS** (63)	Monument 806	$12
	(Brown/white promo)		
45rpm	**FALLING** (63)	Monument 815	$12
45rpm	**FALLING** (63)	Monument 815	$40
	(Price includes picture sleeve)		
45(P)	**FALLING** (63)	Monument 815	$15
	(Brown/white promo label)		
45rpm	**MEAN WOMAN BLUES** (63)	Monument 824	$12
45rpm	**PRETTY PAPER** (63)	Monument 830	$12
45rpm	**IT'S OVER** (63)	Monument 837	$12
45rpm	**IT'S OVER** (63)	Monument 837	$40
	(Price includes picture sleeve)		
45rpm	**OH, PRETTY WOMAN** (64)	Monument 851	$12
45rpm	**GOODNIGHT** (65)	Monument 873	$12
45rpm	**YOU'RE MY GIRL** (65)	Monument 891	$12
45rpm	**LET THE GOOD TIMES ROLL** (65)	Monument 906	$10
45rpm	**LANA** (66)	Monument 939	$10
45rpm	**PAPER BOY** (66)	Monument 503	$18
45rpm	**UP TOWN** (66)	Monument 505	$15
45rpm	**RIDE AWAY** (66)	MGM 13386	$12
45rpm	**RIDE AWAY** (66)	MGM 13386	$25
	(Price includes picture sleeve)		
45(P)	**RIDE AWAY** (66)	MGM 13386	$15
	(Yellow promo label)		
45rpm	**CRAWLING BACK** (66)	MGM 13410	$10
45rpm	**CRAWLING BACK** (66)	MGM 13410	$25
	(Price includes picture sleeve)		
45(P)	**CRAWLING BACK** (66)	MGM 13410	$12
	(Yellow promo label)		
45rpm	**BREAKIN' UP IS BREAKIN' MY HEART** (66)	MGM 13446	$10
45rpm	**BREAKIN' UP IS BREAKIN' MY HEART** (66)	MGM 13446	$25
	(Price includes picture sleeve)		
45(P)	**BREAKIN' UP IS BREAKIN' MY HEART** (66)	MGM 13446	$12
	(Yellow promo label)		
45rpm	**TWINKLE TOES** (66)	MGM 13498	$10
45rpm	**TWINKLE TOES** (66)	MGM 13498	$20
	(Price includes picture sleeve)		
45(P)	**TWINKLE TOES** (66)	MGM 13498	$12
	(Yellow promo label)		
45rpm	**TOO SOON TO KNOW** (66)	MGM 13549	$10
45rpm	**TOO SOON TO KNOW** (66)	MGM 13549	$20
	(Price includes picture sleeve)		
45(P)	**TOO SOON TO KNOW** (66)	MGM 13549	$12
	(Yellow promo label)		

45s(P)	**MGM CELEBRITY SERIES** (66) Box set	MGM CS9-5	$100
	(Five-record promo set, yellow promo labels)		
45rpm	**CRY SOFTLY, LONELY ONE** (67)	MGM 13764	$20
	(Price includes picture sleeve)		
12"(P)	**YOU GOT IT** (89)	Virgin 99245	$10
	(Promo twelve-inch single)		

-EPs-

EP(P)	**ROY ORBISON & THE TEEN KINGS** (59)	Stars 101	$150
	(Promo-only EP shipped to fan club members)		
EP(P)	**IN DREAMS** Vol 1 (62)	Monument 003	$100
	(Special promo paper sleeve)		
EP(P)	**IN DREAMS** Vol 2 (62)	Monument 004	$100
	(Special promo paper sleeve)		
EP(JB)	**ROY ORBISON'S GREATEST HITS** (67) Jukebox LLP	Monument	$40
	(Price includes cover and title strips)		
EP(JB)	**MORE OF ROY ORBISON'S GREATEST HITS** (67) Jukebox	Monument 506	$40
	(Price includes cover and title strips)		
EP(P)	**SWING THE JINGLE** (60s) Various artists	Coca-Cola	$400
	(Radio ads, price includes picture sleeve)		
EP(P)	**COKE** (60s) Various artists	Coca-Cola	$400
	(Radio ads, artists include Roy Orbison)		
EP(JB)	**ORBISONGS** (67) Jukebox LLP	Monument 512	$40
	(Price includes soft cover and title strips)		
EP(JB)	**THE CLASSIC ROY ORBISON** (67) Jukebox LLP	MGM 4379	$40
	(Price includes hard cover and title strips)		

-albums-

LP	**ROY ORBISON AT THE ROCKHOUSE** (61)	Sun 1260	$500
LP	**LONELY & BLUE** (61) Mono	Monument 4002	$100
LP	**LONELY & BLUE** (61) Stereo	Monument 14002	$300
LP	**CRYING** (62) Mono	Monument 4007	$75
LP	**CRYING** (62) Stereo	Monument 14007	$200
LP	**ROY ORBISON'S GREATEST HITS** (62) Mono	Monument 4009	$25
LP	**ROY ORBISON'S GREATEST HITS** (62) Stereo	Monument 14009	$35
LP	**ROY ORBISON'S GREATEST HITS** (63) Mono	Monument 8000	$25
LP	**ROY ORBISON'S GREATEST HITS** (64) Stereo	Monument 18000	$35
LP	**IN DREAMS** (63) Mono	Monument 8003	$75
LP	**IN DREAMS** (63) Stereo	Monument 18003	$150
LP	**EARLY ORBISON** (64) Mono	Monument 8023	$25
LP	**EARLY ORBISON** (64) Stereo	Monument 18023	$40
LP	**MORE OF ROY ORBISON'S GREATEST HITS** (64) Mono	Monument 8024	$25
LP	**MORE OF ROY ORBISON'S GREATEST HITS** (64) Stereo	Monument 18024	$30
LP	**SPECIAL DELIVERY** (64) with Bobby Bare and Joey Powers	RCA Camden 820	$25
	(RCA Victor material)		
LP	**ORBISONGS** (65) Mono	Monument 8035	$20
LP	**ORBISONGS** (65) Stereo	Monument 18035	$25
LP	**THE VERY BEST OF ROY ORBISON** (65) Mono	Monument 8045	$18
LP	**THE VERY BEST OF ROY ORBISON** (65) Stereo	Monument 18045	$20
LP	**THERE IS ONLY ONE ROY ORBISON** (65)	MGM 4308	$12
LP(P)	**THERE IS ONLY ONE ROY ORBISON** (65)	MGM 4308	$25
	(Yellow promo label)		
LP	**THE ORBISON WAY** (66)	MGM 4322	$12
LP(P)	**THE ORBISON WAY** (66)	MGM 4322	$25
	(Yellow promo label)		
LP	**THE CLASSIC ROY ORBISON** (66)	MGM 4379	$12
LP(P)	**THE CLASSIC ROY ORBISON** (66)	MGM 4379	$25
	(Yellow promo label)		
LP	**ROY ORBISON SINGS DON GIBSON** (66)	MGM 4424	$12
LP(P)	**ROY ORBISON SINGS DON GIBSON** (66)	MGM 4424	$25
	(Yellow promo label)		
LP	**THE FASTEST GUITAR ALIVE** (67) Mono	MGM 4475	$20
	(Soundtrack)		
LP	**THE FASTEST GUITAR ALIVE** (67) Stereo	MGM 4475	$25
	(Soundtrack)		
LP(P)	**THE FASTEST GUITAR ALIVE** (67)	MGM 4475	$30
	(Yellow promo label)		
LP	**CRY SOFTLY, LONELY ONE** (67)	MGM 4514	$15
LP(P)	**CRY SOFTLY, LONELY ONE** (67)	MGM 4514	$25
	(Yellow promo label)		
LP	**THE ORIGINAL SUN SOUND OF ROY ORBISON** (69)	Sun 113	$20
LP	**THE MANY MOODS OF ROY ORBISON** (69)	MGM 4636	$12
LP(P)	**THE MANY MOODS OF ROY ORBISON** (69)	MGM 4636	$25
	(Yellow promo label)		
LP	**HANK WILLIAMS THE ROY ORBISON WAY** (70)	MGM 4683	$12
LP(P)	**HANK WILLIAMS THE ROY ORBISON WAY** (70)	MGM 4683	$25
	(Yellow promo label)		
LP	**ROY ORBISON SINGS** (72)	MGM 4835	$12

LP(P)	**ROY ORBISON SINGS** (72)	MGM 4835	$25
	(White promo label)		
LP	**MEMPHIS** (72)	MGM 4867	$10
LP(P)	**MEMPHIS** (72)	MGM 4867	$20
	(White promo label)		
LP	**MILESTONES** (73)	MGM 4934	$10
LP(P)	**MILESTONES** (73)	MGM 4934	$20
	(White promo label)		
2LP(P)	**A HISTORY: MONUMENT RECORD CORP.** (73)	Columbia AS-25	$40
	(Promo-only release features Roy Orbison)		
2LP	**ALL TIME GREATEST HITS** (73)	Monument 31484	$20
LP	**I'M STILL IN LOVE WITH YOU** (75)	Mercury 1045	$15
LP(P)	**I'M STILL IN LOVE WITH YOU** (75)	Mercury 1045	$20
	(White promo label)		
LP	**REGENERATION** (76)	Monument 7600	$10
2LP	**ALL TIME GREATEST HITS** (77)	Monument 8600	$10
LP	**ROY ORBISON'S GREATEST HITS** (77)	Monument 6619	$10
LP	**IN DREAMS** (77)	Monument 6620	$10
LP	**MORE OF ROY ORBISON'S GREATEST HITS** (77)	Monument 6621	$10
LP	**THE VERY BEST OF ROY ORBISON** (77)	Monument 6622	$10
2LP	**THE LIVING LEGEND OF ROY ORBISON** (77)	Candlelite 12946	$15
2LP(P)	**ALL TIME GREATEST HITS** (82)	Monument 38384	$40
	(Gatefold double LP with promo labels)		

-radio shows-

3LP(RS)	**INTERNATIONAL FESTIVAL OF COUNTRY MUSIC** (Oct 82)	Mutual Radio	$50-125
	(Live concert)		
LP(RS)	**LIVE AT GILLEY'S** (80s)	Westwood One	$50-100
	(Very rare live concerts)		
4LP(RS)	**ROCK, ROLL & REMEMBER** (Aug 87) With Dick Clark	United Stations	$20-40
	(Includes interviews with Orbison)		
4LP(RS)	**ROCK, ROLL & REMEMBER** (Mar 89) With Dick Clark	United Stations	$20-40
	(Includes interviews with Orbison)		
2LP(RS)	**OFF THE RECORD** (89) With the Traveling Wilburys	Westwood One	$50-75
	(Includes Orbison's final interviews)		
2LP(RS)	**OFF THE RECORD** (Apr 89) With Roy Orbison	Westwood One	$50-80
	(Includes Orbison's final interview and new LP material)		

ORIGINAL WASHBOARD BAND (BG)
-albums-

LP	**SCRUBBIN' & PICKIN'** (59)	RCA Victor 1958	$18

ORION (R)
Orion Eckley Darnell
Jimmy Ellis
The "King" of Elvis sound-alikes
Other 45s $5-8 each

-singles-

45(P)	**THAT'S ALL RIGHT** (71) No artist	Sun 1129	$40
	(First pressing, no artist listed, no mention on label of Ellis or Orion, flip side is "Blue Moon of Kentucky"; a lot of people thought this was Sun #209)		
45rpm	**THAT'S ALL RIGHT** (71) Jimmy Ellis	Sun 1129	$15
	("Blue Moon of Kentucky" on flip)		
45(P)	**THAT'S ALL RIGHT** (71) Jimmy Ellis	Sun 1129	$15
	(Yellow promo label)		
45rpm	**I USE HER TO REMIND ME OF YOU** (73) Jimmy Ellis	Sun 1131	$12
45(P)	**I USE HER TO REMIND ME OF YOU** (73)	Sun 1131	$10
	(Yellow promo label)		
45rpm	**THERE YA GO** (73) Jimmy Ellis	MCA 40060	$25
45(P)	**THERE YA GO** (73)	MCA 40060	$15
	(White promo label)		

45rpm	**THAT'S ALL RIGHT/BLUE MOON OF KENTUCKY** (77) No artist	Sun 1136	$15
	("D.O.A." by Misty on flip)		
45rpm	**HERE COMES THAT WONDERFUL FEELING AGAIN** (77)	Boblo 531	$12
	(By Jimmy Ellis)		
45(P)	**HERE COMES THAT WONDERFUL FEELING AGAIN** (77)	Boblo 531	$10
	(Blue/white promo label)		
45(P)	**I'M NOT TRYING TO BE LIKE ELVIS** (78) Jimmy Ellis	Boblo 636	$50
	(Price includes promo-only picture sleeve with a letter to the DJ on the back side)		
45rpm	**HONEY** (79) Orion	Sun 1142	$12
45(P)	**HONEY** (79)	Sun 1142	$10
	(White promo label)		
45rpm	**BEFORE THE NEXT TEARDROP FALLS** (79)	Sun 1147	$12
45(P)	**BEFORE THE NEXT TEARDROP FALLS** (79)	Sun 1147	$10
	(White promo label)		
45rpm	**REMEMBER BETHLEHEM** (79) Orion	Sun 1148	$15

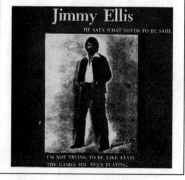

45(P)	**REMEMBER BETHLEHEM** (79)	Sun 1148	$12
	(White promo label)		
45rpm	**IT AIN'T NO MYSTERY** (80) Orion	Sun 1152	$12
45(P)	**IT AIN'T NO MYSTERY** (80)	Sun 1152	$10
	(White promo label)		
45rpm	**TEXAS TEA** (80) Orion	Sun 1153	$12
45(P)	**TEXAS TEA** (80)	Sun 1153	$10
	(White promo label)		
45rpm	**AM I THAT EASY TO FORGET** (80) Orion	Sun 1156	$12
45(P)	**AM I THAT EASY TO FORGET** (80)	Sun 1156	$10
	(White promo label, yellow vinyl)		
45rpm	**ROCKABILLY REBEL** (80) Orion	Sun 1159	$15
45(P)	**ROCKABILLY REBEL** (80)	Sun 1159	$12
	(White promo label, yellow vinyl)		
45rpm	**MATCHBOX** (81) Orion	Sun 1162	$12
45(P)	**MATCHBOX** (81)	Sun 1162	$10
	(White promo label)		
45rpm	**BORN** (81) Orion	Sun 1165	$12
45(P)	**BORN** (81)	Sun 1165	$10
	(White promo label, yellow vinyl)		
45rpm	**SOME YOU WIN, SOME YOU LOSE** (81) Orion	Sun 1170	$12
45(P)	**SOME YOU WIN, SOME YOU LOSE** (81)	Sun 1170	$10
	(White promo label, yellow vinyl)		
45rpm	**FEELINGS** (82) Orion	Sun 1172	$12
45(P)	**FEELINGS** (82)	Sun 1172	$10
	(White promo label)		
45rpm	**HONKY TONK HEAVEN** (82) Orion	Sun 1175	$12
45(P)	**HONKY TONK HEAVEN** (82)	Sun 1175	$10
	(White promo label, yellow vinyl)		
45rpm	**LISTEN TO DADDY** (82) Orion with Shana Stacy Singleton	Sun 1177	$12
45(P)	**LISTEN TO DADDY** (82)	Sun 1177	$10
	(White promo label)		
45rpm	**100 POUNDS OF CLAY** (85) Orion	Kristal 2338	$10

-EPs-

EP(P)	**A STRANGER IN MY PLACE** (80) Orion	Sun 1152	$50
	(Promo only, six cuts of radio ads to use with play of latest single, "Stranger in My Place," price includes insert, EP issued without a cover)		

-albums-

LP	**BY REQUEST, ELLIS SINGS ELVIS** (78) Jimmy Ellis	Boblo 829	$125
LP	**ORION REBORN** (78) Orion	Sun 1012	$40
	(Coffin cover is white, gold vinyl)		
LP	**ORION REBORN** (78) Orion	Sun 1012	$12
	(The more common blue cover, gold vinyl)		
LP	**SUNRISE** (79) Orion	Sun 1017	$12
	(Gold vinyl)		
LP	**ORION COUNTRY** (80) Orion	Sun 1019	$12
	(Gold vinyl)		
LP	**ROCKABILLY** (80) Orion	Sun 1021	$18
	(Gold vinyl)		
LP(P)	**ROCKABILLY** (80) No name on label	Sun 1021	$75
	(White label, black vinyl, no cover, not a test pressing, promo sampler with inserts and poster of Orion)		
LP	**GLORY** (80) Orion	Sun 1025	$12
	(Gold vinyl)		
LP	**FRESH** (81) Orion	Sun 1028	$12
	(Gold vinyl)		
LP	**FEELINGS** (81) Orion	Sun 144	$10
LP	**20 ALL-TIME FAVORITES** (81) Orion	Suffolk 27	$20
	(TV mail-in album)		

J. D. ORR (R)
And the Lonesome Valley Boys

-singles-

45rpm	**HULA HOOP BOOGIE** (58)	Summit 105	$125

SONNY OSBORN (BG)
And His Sunny Mountain Boys
Gateway LPs $8 each
Hollywood, Ultra Sonic, and Mount Vernon LPs $6 each

ARTHUR OSBORNE (RB)
-singles-

45rpm	**HEY RUBY** (57)	Brunswick 55068	$25
45(P)	**HEY RUBY** (57)	Brunswick 55068	$20
	(Yellow promo label)		

JIMMY OSBORNE (CW)

Jimmie Osborne
Other King 78s $5-10 each
Other King 45s $4-8 each

-singles-

78rpm	**THE DEATH OF LITTLE KATHY FISCUS** (49)	King 788	$18
78rpm	**GOD, PLEASE PROTECT AMERICA** (50)	King 893	$15
45rpm	**MAMA DON'T AGREE** (53)	King 1117	$15
45rpm	**HILLS OF ROAN COUNTY** (54)	King 1231	$12

-EPs-

EP	**JIMMY OSBORNE** (59)	Audio Lab 3	$15

-LPs-

LP	**JIMMY OSBORNE, SINGING SONGS HE WROTE** (59)	Audio Lab 1527	$30
LP	**THE LEGENDARY JIMMY OSBORNE** (61)	King 730	$25
LP	**GOLDEN HARVEST** (63)	King 782	$25
LP	**THE VERY BEST OF JIMMY OSBORNE** (64)	King 892	$20
LP	**JIMMY OSBORNE'S GOLDEN HARVEST** (65)	King 941	$20

OSBORNE BROTHERS (BG)

With Red Allen
Other MGM 78s and 45s $4-8 each

-singles-

45rpm	**RUBY, ARE YOU MAD?** (56) With Red Allen	MGM 12308	$15
45rpm	**SHE'S NO ANGEL** (57) With Red Allen	MGM 12583	$12
45(P)	**SHE'S NO ANGEL** (57)	MGM 12583	$10
	(Yellow promo label)		

-EPs-

EP	**COUNTRY PICKIN' & HILLSIDE SINGIN'** Vol 1 (59)	MGM 1645	$18
EP	**COUNTRY PICKIN' & HILLSIDE SINGIN'** Vol 2 (59)	MGM 1646	$18
EP	**COUNTRY PICKIN' & HILLSIDE SINGIN'** Vol 3 (59)	MGM 1647	$18

-albums-

LP	**COUNTRY PICKIN' AND HILLSIDE SINGIN'** (59)	MGM 3734	$40
LP(P)	**COUNTRY PICKIN' AND HILLSIDE SINGIN'** (59)	MGM 3734	$50
	(Yellow promo label)		
LP	**THE OSBORNE BROTHERS & RED ALLEN** (80)	Rounder 03	$10
	See Osborne Brothers		

OSBORNE BROTHERS (BG)

Bobby and Sonny
Decca 45s $3-5 each

-albums-

LP	**BLUEGRASS MUSIC** (62)	MGM 4018	$25
LP(P)	**BLUEGRASS MUSIC** (62)	MGM 4018	$30
	(Yellow promo label)		
LP	**BLUEGRASS INSTRUMENTALS** (62)	MGM 4090	$20
LP(P)	**BLUEGRASS INSTRUMENTALS** (62)	MGM 4090	$25
	(Yellow promo label)		
LP	**CUTTIN' GRASS** (63)	MGM 4149	$20
LP(P)	**CUTTIN' GRASS** (63)	MGM 4149	$25
	(Yellow promo label)		
LP	**VOICES IN BLUEGRASS** (65)	Decca 4602	$18
LP(P)	**VOICES IN BLUEGRASS** (65)	Decca 4602	$20
	(Pink promo label)		
LP	**MODERN SOUNDS OF BLUEGRASS MUSIC** (67)	Decca 4903	$12
LP(P)	**MODERN SOUNDS OF BLUEGRASS MUSIC** (67)	Decca 4903	$15
	(White promo label)		
LP	**YESTERDAY, TODAY & THE OSBORNE BROTHERS** (68)	Decca 4993	$12
LP(P)	**YESTERDAY, TODAY & THE OSBORNE BROTHERS** (68)	Decca 4993	$15
	(White promo label)		
LP	**FAVORITE HYMNS BY THE OSBORNE BROTHERS** (69)	Decca 5079	$12
LP(P)	**FAVORITE HYMNS BY THE OSBORNE BROTHERS** (69)	Decca 5079	$15
	(White promo label)		
LP	**UP TO DATE & DOWN TO EARTH** (69)	Decca 5128	$12
LP(P)	**UP TO DATE & DOWN TO EARTH** (69)	Decca 5128	$15
	(White promo label)		
LP	**RU-BE-EEEE** (70)	Decca 5204	$12
LP(P)	**RU-BE-EEEE** (70)	Decca 5204	$15
	(White promo label)		
LP	**THE OSBORNE BROTHERS** (71)	Decca 5271	$12
LP(P)	**THE OSBORNE BROTHERS** (71)	Decca 5271	$15
	(White promo label)		
LP	**COUNTRY ROADS** (71)	Decca 5321	$12
LP(P)	**COUNTRY ROADS** (71)	Decca 5321	$15
	(White promo label)		
LP	**BOBBY & SONNY** (72)	Decca 5356	$10
LP(P)	**BOBBY & SONNY** (72)	Decca 5356	$15
	(White promo label)		

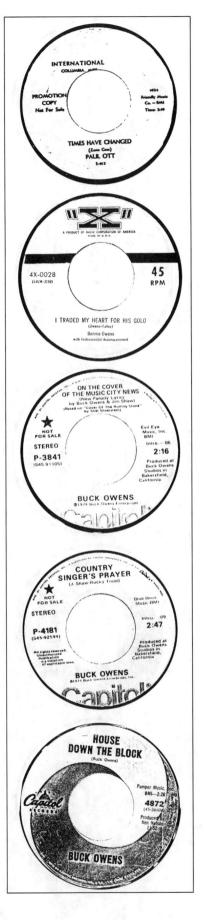

YOU'RE FOR ME (Buck Owens-Tommy Collins) Central Songs, Inc. BMI-2:11 Capitol 4872 (45-36511) Produced by Ken Nelson BUCK OWENS

Capitol PROMOTIONAL DEBUT RECORD — First Record 1957 — Central Songs, Inc. BMI-2:15 F3824 Vocal with Instrumental Accompaniment (45-17415) COME BACK (Al Edgar) BUCK OWENS

Capitol PROMOTIONAL DEBUT RECORD M.M. Central Songs, Inc. BMI-2:06 F3824 Vocal with Instrumental Accompaniment (45-17414) I KNOW WHAT IT MEANS (Al Edgar) BUCK OWENS

SANTA LOOKED A LOT LIKE DADDY (Buck Owens-Don Rich) Capitol Bluebook Music Publishing BMI-2:13 5537 (45-53783) Produced by Ken Nelson BUCK OWENS

Capitol © 1989 Capitol Records, Inc. NOT FOR SALE P-B-44409 Tree Pub. Co., Inc.-BMI intro:06 2:59 Produced by JERRY CRUTCHFIELD and JIM SHAW Recorded at Abbey Road Studios BUCK OWENS AND RINGO STARR ACT NATURALLY (V. Morrison-J. Russell)

2LP	THE BEST OF THE OSBORNE BROTHERS (75)	MCA 4086	$10
2LP	OSBORNE BROTHERS BLUEGRASS COLLECTION (78)	CMH 9011	$10
LP	THE ESSENTIAL BLUEGRASS ALBUM (79)	CMH 9016	$15
	(With Mac Wiseman)		
	See Osborne Brothers and Red Allen		

K. T. OSLIN (C)
Elektra 45s $2 each
RCA Victor 45s $1 each
RCA Victor promo picture sleeves $4 each
Elektra and RCA Victor LPs $4 each

-radio shows-

LP(RS)	WESTWOOD ONE PRESENTS (Oct 89) With Don Williams	Westwood One	$15-25
	(Live concert)		
LP(RS)	WESTWOOD ONE PRESENTS (Dec 89)	Westwood One	$15-25
	(Live concert)		
LP(RS)	LIVE AT GILLEY'S (Nov 89)	Westwood One	$10-20
	(Live concert)		

BROTHER OSWALD (CW)
Pete Kirby
Bashful Brother Oswald

-albums-

LP	BASHFUL BROTHER OSWALD (62)	Starday 192	$20

PAUL OTT (RB)

-singles-

45rpm	KITTY KAT (57)	Thunder 1022	$30
45rpm	TIMES HAVE CHANGED (58)	Thunder 1024	$10

BONNIE OWENS (C)
Once married to Buck Owens
Later married to Merle Haggard
Capitol 45s $2 each
Capitol LPs $8-10 each

-singles-

45rpm	I TRADED MY HEART FOR HIS GOLD (53)	"X" 0028	$25

BUCK OWENS (CW)
With the Buckaroos
Corky Jones
Other Capitol 45s $3-6 each
Capitol picture sleeves $3-6 each
Warner 45s $1 each
Other Capitol jukebox LLPs $8 each
Hilltop LPs $6 each
Hall of Music LPs $5 each
Warner LPs $4 each
Capitol duet LPs $5-8 each
  (Buddy Alan or Susan Raye)
Hilltop LPs with Young and Husky $10 each

-singles-

45rpm	GOOSE ROCK (53) Bud Hobbs	MGM 11579	$75
	(Features That Man About Town, Buck Owens)		
45(P)	GOOSE ROCK (53)	MGM 11579	$60
	(Yellow promo label)		
45rpm	DOWN ON THE CORNER OF LOVE (56)	Pep 105	$25
45rpm	DOWN ON THE CORNER OF LOVE (56)	Starday 588	$10
45rpm	RIGHT AFTER THE DANCE (56)	Pep 106	$20
45rpm	THERE GOES MY LOVE (56)	Pep 109	$15
45rpm	HOT DOG (56) Corky Jones	Pep 107	$100
45rpm	HOT DOG (57) Corky Jones	New Star 6418	$100
45rpm	HOT DOG (57)	Hilltop 6027	$15
	(Re-recorded for Capitol in 1990)		
45rpm	LEAVIN' DIRTY TRACKS (57)	Chesterfield	$12
45rpm	COME BACK (57)	Capitol 3824	$15
45(P)	COME BACK (57)	Capitol 3824	$18
	(Promotional debut record label)		
45rpm	SWEET THING (58)	Capitol 3957	$20
	(Flip side "I Only Know That I Love You")		
45(P)	SWEET THING (58)	Capitol 3957	$15
	(White promo label)		
45rpm	PUPPY LOVE (59) With Dolly Parton	Goldband 1086	$50
45rpm	SANTA LOOKED A LOT LIKE DADDY (65)	Capitol 5537	$10
	(Price includes picture sleeve)		
45rpm	ACT NATURALLY (89) With Ringo Starr	Capitol 44409	$15
	(Purple label)		

45(P)	**ACT NATURALLY** (89) (White promo label)	Capitol 44409	$25

-EPs-

EP	**FOOLIN' AROUND** (61) (Issued with a hard cover)	Capitol 1550	$25
EP	**FOUR BY BUCK OWENS** (65) (Issued with a hard cover)	Capitol 5446	$18
EP(JB)	**ROLL OUT THE RED CARPET** (66) Jukebox LLP (Issued with hard cover)	Capitol 2443	$15
EP(JB)	**CARNEGIE HALL CONCERT** (67) Jukebox LLP (Issued with hard cover)	Capitol 2556	$15
EP(JB)	**OPEN UP YOUR HEART** (68) Jukebox LLP (Issued with hard cover)	Capitol 2640	$15

-albums-

LP	**BUCK OWENS** (61) (Yellow label)	La Brea 8017	$100
LP	**BUCK OWENS** (61) (Blue and White label)	La Brea 8017	$50
LP	**BUCK OWENS SINGS HARLAN HOWARD** (61)	Capitol 1482	$50
LP	**UNDER YOUR SPELL AGAIN** (61)	Capitol 1489	$40
LP	**FAMOUS COUNTRY MUSIC SOUND OF BUCK OWENS** (62)	Starday 172	$50
LP	**YOU'RE FOR ME** (62)	Capitol 1777	$40
LP	**BUCK OWENS ON THE BANDSTAND** (63)	Capitol 1879	$40
LP	**BUCK OWENS SINGS TOMMY COLLINS** (63) (Owens played in Tommy Collins band in the '50s)	Capitol 1989	$50
LP	**THE BEST OF BUCK OWENS** (64)	Capitol 2105	$25
LP	**COUNTRY HIT MAKER #1** (64)	Starday 327	$25
LP	**TOGETHER AGAIN** (64)	Capitol 2135	$20
LP	**I DON'T CARE** (64)	Capitol 2186	$20
LP	**I'VE GOT A TIGER BY THE TAIL** (65)	Capitol 2283	$20
LP	**BEFORE YOU GO** (65)	Capitol 2353	$18
LP	**INSTRUMENTAL HITS** (65)	Capitol 2367	$15
LP	**CHRISTMAS WITH BUCK OWENS** (65)	Capitol 2396	$20
LP	**ROLL OUT THE RED CARPET** (66)	Capitol 2443	$15
LP	**DUST ON MOTHER'S BIBLE** (66)	Capitol 2497	$15
LP(P)	**BUCK OWENS MINUTE MASTERS** (66) (White promo label edited versions)	Capitol 2980	$50
LP	**CARNEGIE HALL CONCERT** (66)	Capitol 2556	$15
LP	**OPEN UP YOUR HEART** (67)	Capitol 2640	$15
LP	**BUCK OWENS & HIS BUCKAROOS IN JAPAN** (67)	Capitol 2715	$15
LP	**YOUR TENDER LOVING CARE** (67)	Capitol 2760	$15
LP	**IT TAKES PEOPLE LIKE YOU** (68)	Capitol 2841	$12
LP	**THE BEST OF BUCK OWENS** Vol 2 (68)	Capitol 2897	$12
LP	**A NIGHT ON THE TOWN** (68)	Capitol 2902	$12
LP	**SWEET ROSIE JONES** (68)	Capitol 2962	$12
LP	**CHRISTMAS SHOPPING** (68)	Capitol 2977	$15
LP	**THE GUITAR PLAYER** (69)	Capitol 2994	$12
2LP	**CLOSE UP** (69)	Capitol 257	$12
3LP	**BUCK OWENS** (70)	Capitol 574	$18
2LP	**A MERRY HEE HAW CHRISTMAS** (70)	Capitol 486	$15

-radio shows-

LP(RS)	**HERE'S TO VETERANS** (60s) (Rare music and interviews)	Veterans Administration	$50-100

GLEN OWENS (RB)

-singles-

45rpm	**GOT A RIGHT TO CRY** (58)	Rocket 500	$50

JIM OWENS (C)
And the (original) Drifting Cowboys

-albums-

2LP	**SONG FOR US ALL** (77)	Epic 34852	$20
2LP(P)	**SONG FOR US ALL** (77) (White promo labels)	Epic 34852	$30

KENNY OWENS (RB)

-singles-

45rpm	**I GOT THE BUG** (57)	Poplar 106	$60
45rpm	**FROG MAN HOP** (58)	Ruth 442	$25

VERNON OXFORD (CW)
RCA Victor 45s $2 each
Rounder LPs $5 each

-albums-

LP	**WOMAN, LET ME SING YOU A SONG** (67)	RCA Victor 3704	$35

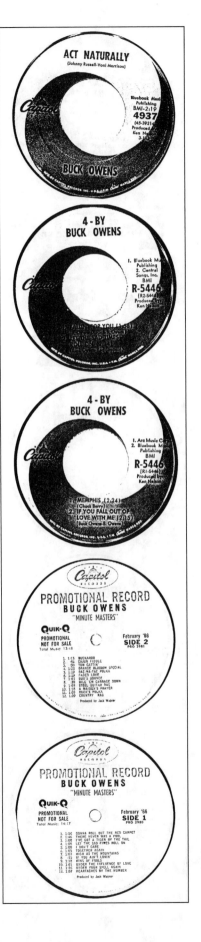

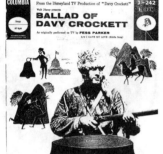

OZARK OPRY GROUP (CW)

-albums-

LP	**AN EVENING ON BUFORD MOUNTAIN** (65)	Fontana 67535	$15
LP(P)	**AN EVENING ON BUFORD MOUNTAIN** (65)	Fontana 67535	$18
	(White promo label)		

P

ALAN PAGE (RB)

-singles-

45rpm	**DATELESS NIGHT** (58)	Moon 302	$10
45rpm	**SHE'S THE ONE THAT'S GOT IT** (58)	Moon 303	$25

PATTI PAGE (Pop)

Mercury 78s $3 each
Mercury red label 45s $4-8 each
Mercury black label 45s $3-6 each
Mercury picture sleeves $8 each
Columbia 45s $2 each
Columbia colored vinyl 45s $6 each
Columbia picture sleeves $5 each
Plantation 45s $1 each
Plantation color vinyl 45s $3 each
Other Mercury 10-inch pop LPs $25-40 each
Other Mercury 12-inch pop LPs $8-25 each
Columbia LPs $3-6 each
Plantation LPs $3 each

-singles-

45(P)	**HOLIDAY GREETINGS VOICE TRACKS** (60s) Green vinyl	Columbia 111921	$15
	(Thirteen cuts, all less than ten seconds each, two Page)		

-EPs-

EP	**ROMANCE ON THE RANGE** (55)	Mercury 3034	$12
EP	**THE RAGE AND THE RUSTY** (57) With Rusty Draper	Mercury 3129	$15

-country albums-

10"LP	**FOLKSONG FAVORITES** (51)	Mercury 25101	$40
10"LP	**TENNESSEE WALTZ** (52)	Mercury 25154	$40
LP	**ROMANCE ON THE RANGE** (55)	Mercury 20075	$25
LP	**THE WALTZ QUEEN** (57)	Mercury 20318	$18
LP(P)	**THE WALTZ QUEEN** (57)	Mercury 20318	$20
	(White promo label)		
LP	**COUNTRY & WESTERN GOLDEN HITS** (61)	Mercury 20615	$12
LP(P)	**COUNTRY & WESTERN HITS** (61)	Mercury 20615	$15
	(White promo label)		

TOM PALEY (BG)

-albums-

LP	**FOLK SONGS FROM THE SOUTH APPALACHIAN MOUNTAINS** (59)	Elektra 12	$25

FESS PARKER (CW)

Played part of Davy Crockett for Disney Productions

-singles-

78rpm	**BALLAD OF DAVY CROCKETT** (54) Children's series	Columbia J-242	$10
	(Original soundtrack version)		
78rpm	**BALLAD OF DAVY CROCKETT** (54) Picture sleeve	Columbia J-242	$35
	(Same price for the 45rpm version of Columbia J-242, price includes picture sleeve)		
78rpm	**BALLAD OF DAVY CROCKETT** (54)	Columbia 40449	$20
78(P)	**BALLAD OF DAVY CROCKETT** (54)	Columbia 40449	$25
	(White promo label)		
45rpm	**BALLAD OF DAVY CROCKETT** (54)	Columbia 40449	$15
45(P)	**BALLAD OF DAVY CROCKETT** (54)	Columbia 40449	$20
	(White promo label)		

-EPs-

EP	**THE ORIGINAL DAVY CROCKETT** (56)	Columbia 2031	$40
	(At the Alamo)		
EP	**THE ORIGINAL DAVY CROCKETT** (56)	Columbia 2032	$40
	(Goes to Congress)		
EP	**THE ORIGINAL DAVY CROCKETT** (56)	Columbia 2033	$40
	(Indian Fighter)		

-albums-

LP	**TV SWEETHEARTS** (55)	Columbia 576	$75
	(With Marion Marlowe)		

Type	Title	Label	Price
LP	**DAVY CROCKETT** (55)	Columbia 666	
LP	**THREE ADVENTURES OF DAVY CROCKETT** (55)	Disneyland 3007	$40
LP	**YARNS AND SONGS** (56)	Disneyland 3602	$40
LP	**COWBOY AND INDIAN SONGS** (57)	Disneyland 1336	$30
LP	**FESS PARKER SINGS** (64)	RCA Victor 2973	$20
	See Davy Crockett		

PARKER FAMILY (CW)
Audio Lab LPs $8 each

-albums-

| LP | **JUST A REAL NICE FAMILY** (65) | King 923 | $15 |

GENE PARSON (RB)

-singles-

| 45rpm | **NIGHTCLUB ROCK & ROLL** (59) | Southfield 4501 | $125 |

BILL PARSONS See Bobby Bare

GRAM PARSONS (R)
Member of the International Submarine Band
Recorded with the Byrds and the Flying Burrito Brothers
Other Reprise 45s $2-6 each
A&M 45s $3 each
Warner 45s $5 each
Sierra 45s $5 each
Sierra LPs $8-10 each

-singles-

| 45(P) | **CRY ONE MORE TIME** (73) | Reprise PRO-557 | $10 |

-EPs-

| EP | **THE BIG FINISH** (82) | Sierra 104 | $12 |

-albums-

LP	**SAFE AT HOME** (68) International Submarine Band	L. H. I. 12001	$100
	(Multicolored label)		
LP	**GRAM PARSONS** (73)	Shiloh 4088	$20
	(Reissue of L. H. I. 12001, artist listed as Gram Parsons)		
LP	**GRAM PARSONS** (73)	Reprise 2123	$15
LP(P)	**GRAM PARSONS** (73)	Reprise 2123	$18
	(White promo label)		
LP	**GRIEVOUS ANGEL** (74) With Emmylou Harris	Reprise 2171	$12
LP(P)	**GRIEVOUS ANGEL** (74)	Reprise 2171	$15
	(White promo label)		

DOLLY PARTON (CW)
Other Monument 45s $5 each
Other Monument promo 45s $7 each
Other RCA Victor 45s $2-5 each
RCA Victor picture sleeves $3-8 each
Other Columbia 45s $2 each
Columbia picture sleeves $2 each
Other RCA Victor LPs $6-10 each
Alshire and Camden LPs $10 each
Time-Life LPs $8 each

-singles-

45rpm	**PUPPY LOVE** (59)	Goldband 1086	$50
	(Her first single, with Buck Owens on guitar)		
45rpm	**DUMB BLONDE** (67)	Monument 982	$10
	(First hit single)		
45(P)	**DUMB BLONDE** (67)	Monument 982	$12
	(White promo label)		
45(P)	**WHAT'S IT ALL ABOUT** (Sept 77) Public service show	W. I. A. A. 389	$15
	(Flip side features B. J. Thomas)		
45(P)	**STARTING OVER AGAIN** (80)	RCA Victor 11926	$12
	(Green label, green vinyl)		
45(P)	**9 TO 5** (80)	RCA Victor 12133	$18
	(Pink label, blue vinyl)		
45(P)	**SINGLE WOMAN** (82)	RCA Victor 13057	$15
	(Red label, red vinyl)		
45(P)	**HARD CANDY CHRISTMAS** (82)	RCA Victor 13361	$10
	(Pink label, red vinyl)		
45(P)	**POTENTIAL NEW BOYFRIEND** (83)	RCA Victor 13514	$15
	(Mustard label, yellow vinyl)		
45(P)	**POTENTIAL NEW BOYFRIEND** (83)	RCA Victor 13514	$15
	(Purple label, blue vinyl)		
45(P)	**SAVE THE LAST DANCE FOR ME** (83) With Jordanaires	RCA Victor 13703	$12
	(Pink label, green vinyl)		
PS(JB)	**(GENERIC HARD COVER CARDBOARD PICTURE SLEEVE)**	Bally Pinball Division	$25
	(Photo of Dolly standing by Bally pinball machine, for generic use		
	by jukebox vendors, a souvenir and quite rare)		

45(P)	**HE'S ALIVE** (89)	No label (CBS)	$10
	(Not a test press, looks like one)		
45(P)	**HE'S ALIVE** (89)	Columbia 01929	$10
	(Columbia red/orange promo label, small center hole)		

-EPs-

EP(P)	**PORTER WAYNE AND DOLLY REBECCA** (70) Jukebox LLP	RCA Victor 4305	$50
	(Price includes unusual hard cover that opens from the left side, title strips)		

-albums-

LP	**HITS MADE FAMOUS BY COUNTRY QUEENS** (63)	Somerset 19700	$30
	(With Faye Tucker, Dolly sings hits of Kitty Wells)		
LP	**COUNTRY & WESTERN SOUL** (63) With Faye Tucker	Time 2108	$40
	(One side for each artist)		
LP	**HELLO, I'M DOLLY** (67)	Monument 18085	$30
LP	**DOLLY PARTON & GEORGE JONES** (68)	Starday 429	$75
LP	**DOLLY PARTON SINGS COUNTRY OLDIES** (68)	Somerset 29400	$15
	(With Faye Tucker)		
LP	**JUST BECAUSE I'M A WOMAN** (69) Mono	RCA Victor 3949	$100
	(Very rare in mono)		
LP	**JUST BECAUSE I'M A WOMAN** (69) Stereo	RCA Victor 3949	$20
	(Black label)		
LP	**JUST BECAUSE I'M A WOMAN** (69) Stereo	RCA Victor 3949	$20
	(Orange label)		
LP	**IN THE GOOD OLD DAYS** (69)	RCA Victor 4099	$20
LP	**MY BLUE RIDGE MOUNTAIN BOY** (69)	RCA Victor 4188	$20
LP	**THE FAIREST OF THEM ALL** (70)	RCA Victor 4288	$20
LP	**A REAL LIVE DOLLY** (70)	RCA Victor 4387	$20
LP	**AS LONG AS I LOVE** (70)	Monument 18136	$20
LP	**GOLDEN STREETS OF GLORY** (70)	RCA Victor 4398	$20
LP	**THE BEST OF DOLLY PARTON** (70)	RCA Victor 4449	$15
LP	**JOSHUA** (71)	RCA Victor 4507	$15
LP	**COAT OF MANY COLORS** (71)	RCA Victor 4603	$15
LP	**TOUCH YOUR WOMAN** (71)	RCA Victor 4686	$15
LP	**MY FAVORITE SONG WRITER: PORTER WAGONER** (72)	RCA Victor 4752	$15
LP	**THE WORLD OF DOLLY** (72)	Monument 31913	$15
LP	**DOLLY PARTON SINGS** (72)	RCA Victor 4762	$12
LP	**MY TENNESSEE MOUNTAIN HOME** (73) Quad	RCA Victor 0033	$15
2LP	**HELLO I'M DOLLY** (75)	Monument 33876	$18
	(Reissues, also LP "As Long As I Love")		
LP	**GREAT BALLS OF FIRE** (79)	RCA Victor 3413	$18
	(Picture disc)		
LP(P)	**HBO PRESENTS DOLLY PARTON** (83)	RCA Victor 812	$25
	(Picture disc from HBO)		

-radio shows-

3LP(RS)	**DOLLY & DON** (Aug 83) Box set radio show	Mutual Broadcasting	$20-30
	(Dolly Parton and Don Williams)		
3LP(RS)	**AMERICAN EAGLE** (Sept 86) With Loretta Lynn	DIR	$75-125
	(Live concert)		
LP(RS)	**RADIO SPECIAL** (87) With Emmylou Harris		$50-75
	(Music and interviews)		
LP(RS)	**A PERSONAL MUSIC DIALOG**		$15-25
	(Music and interviews)		
LP(RS)	**LIVE AT GILLEY'S** (Feb 90) Live concert	Westwood One	$15-25
	(With Willie Nelson and Kenny Rogers)		

RANDY PARTON (C)
Dolly's brother
Other RCA Victor 45s $2 each

-singles-

45(P)	**SHOT FULL OF LOVE** (81)	RCA Victor 12271	$10
	(Yellow promo label, red vinyl)		
45(P)	**OH, NO** (82)	RCA Victor 13087	$10
	(Gold promo label, yellow vinyl)		
45(P)	**OH, NO** (82)	RCA Victor 13087	$15
	(Gold promo label, yellow vinyl, price includes rare hard promo cover)		
45(P)	**ROLL ON EIGHTEEN WHEELER** (82)	RCA Victor 13309	$10
	(Green promo label, yellow vinyl)		

STELLA PARTON (C)
Dolly's sister
Elektra 45s $2 each
Elektra, Townhouse LPs $4-8 each

-albums-

LP	**I WANT TO HOLD YOU IN MY DREAMS TONIGHT** (75)	Soul Country & Blues 6006	$20

		-radio shows-		
LP(RS)	**COUNTRY MUSIC TIME** (80s)		U.S. Air Force	$10-15
	(Music and interviews)			

PAT & DEE (R)

		-singles-		
45rpm	**GEE WIZ** (57)		Dixie 2006	$50

RAY PATE (RB)

		-singles-		
45rpm	**MY SHADOW** (58)		Gulfstream 6654	$100

JIMMY PATTON (RB)

		-singles-		
45rpm	**YAH! I'M MOVIN' ON** (58)		Sage 261	$100
45rpm	**GUILTY** (59)		Sims 103	$15
45rpm	**OKIE'S IN THE POKIE** (60)		Hilligan 001	$150
45rpm	**OKIE'S IN THE POKIE** (61)		Sims 117	$75
		-EPs-		
EP	**JIMMY PATTON** (80s)		Rollin' Rock 001	$10
		-albums-		
LP	**BLUE DARLIN'** (64)		Sourdough 127	$50
LP	**BLUE DARLIN'** (65)		Sims 127	$25
LP	**MAKE ROOM FOR THE BLUES** (66)		Moon 101	$45

GLEN PAUL (RB)

		-singles-		
45rpm	**WATERMELON THUMP** (57)		Sarg 120	$15
45rpm	**RUNNING LATE** (58)		Mercury 71296	$15
45(P)	**RUNNING LATE** (58)		Mercury 71296	$10
	(White promo label)			

EVERETT PAULEY (RB)

		-singles-		
45rpm	**LITTLE GIRL** (58)		(No name) 11429	$60

BUTCH PAULSON (RB)

		-singles-		
45rpm	**MAN FROM MARS** (58)		Virgelle 708	$50

LEX PAXTON (RB)

		-singles-		
45rpm	**TALL TEXAS WOMAN** (58)		Springdale 102	$18

JOHNNY PAYCHECK (C)

Donald Lytle
Also recorded as Jimmy Dallas
Little Darlin' 45s $3 each
Hilltop 45s $3 each
Epic 45s $1 each
Epic LPs $4-8 each

		-singles-		
45rpm	**HURTIN' IN MY HEART** (61) Jimmy Dallas		Decca 31133	$18
45(P)	**HURTIN' IN MY HEART** (61)		Decca 31133	$15
	(White promo label)			
		-albums-		
LP	**JOHNNY PAYCHECK AT CARNEGIE HALL** (66)		Little Darlin' 8001	$20
LP	**THE LOVIN' MACHINE** (66)		Little Darlin' 8003	$18
LP	**GOSPELTIME IN MY FASHION** (66)		Little Darlin' 8004	$18
LP	**JOHNNY PAYCHECK SINGS JUKEBOX CHARLIE** (67)		Little Darlin' 8006	$18
LP	**COUNTRY SOUL** (68)		Little Darlin' 8010	$15
LP	**WHEREVER YOU ARE** (69)		Little Darlin' 8023	$15
LP	**JOHNNY PAYCHECK AGAIN** (70)		Centron 7002	$15
		-radio shows-		
LP(RS)	**COUNTRY SESSIONS** (80s)		NBC Radio	$10-15
	(Music and interviews)			
LP(RS)	**LIVE AT GILLEY'S** (Nov 85)		Westwood One	$10-15
	(Live concert)			

DON PAYNE (CW)

		-singles-		
45rpm	**POGO THE HOBO** (53)		Starday 150	$10

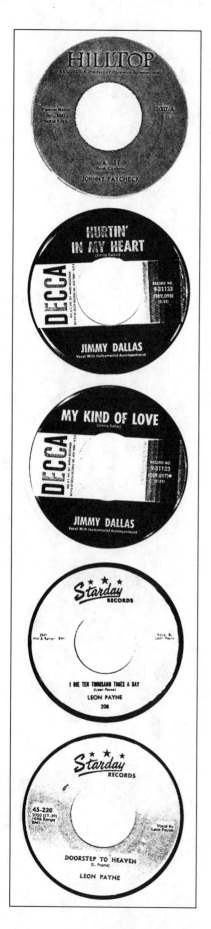

DUSTY PAYNE (RB)

-singles-

45rpm	LONG TIME GONE (58)	Bakersfield 119	$25

LEON PAYNE (CW)

-singles-

78rpm	I LOVE YOU BECAUSE (49)	Capitol 40238	$10
	(His only major country hit)		
45rpm	I WANT YOU TO LOVE ME (50)	Capitol 1910	$10
45rpm	I DIE TEN THOUSAND TIMES A DAY (53)	Starday 208	$12
45rpm	DOORSTEP TO HEAVEN (54)	Starday 220	$12
45rpm	TWO BY FOUR (54)	Starday 232	$10
	(Impersonation of "You Know Who")		
45rpm	LUMBERJACK (57)	Mercury 71063	$12
45(P)	LUMBERJACK (57)	Mercury 71063	$10
	(White promo label)		

-albums-

LP	LEON PAYNE: A LIVING LEGEND OF COUNTRY MUSIC (63)	Starday 231	$75
LP	AMERICANA (63)	Starday 236	$50

BUFORD PEAK (RB)

-singles-

45rpm	KNOCK DOWN, DRAG OUT (58)	Fernwood 102	$60

MIKE PEDICIN QUINTET (R)

Other RCA Victor 45s $10 each
20th Century Fox 45s $10 each

-singles-

45rpm	MAMBO ROCK (55)	RCA Victor 6051	$15
45(P)	MAMBO ROCK (55)	RCA Victor 6051	$12
	(White promo label)		
45rpm	HEY POP GIVE ME THE KEYS (57)	Apollo 534	$18
45(P)	HEY POP GIVE ME THE KEYS (57)	Apollo 534	$20
	(White promo label)		
45rpm	HOTTER THAN A PISTOL (57)	RCA Victor 6369	$18
45rpm	THE BEAT (57)	RCA Victor 6546	$18
45rpm	CLOSE ALL THE DOORS (57)	RCA Victor 6676	$18
45rpm	SHAKE A HAND (57)	Cameo 125	$15

PAUL PEEK AND THE CAPS (RB)

-singles-

45rpm	DADDY DEAN (59) the Caps	White Star 102	$15
45rpm	SWEET SKINNY JENNY (59) Paul Peek	NRC 001	$20
45(P)	SWEET SKINNY JENNY (59)	NRC 001	$15
	(White promo label)		
45rpm	HURTIN' INSIDE (60) Paul Peek	NRC 048	$15
	(Written and orchestrated by Ray Stevens)		
45(P)	HURTIN' INSIDE (60)	NRC 048	$12
	(White promo label)		
45rpm	BROTHER-IN-LAW (61) Paul Peek	Fairlane 702	$15
45(P)	BROTHER-IN-LAW (61)	Fairlane 702	$10
	(White promo label)		
45rpm	WATERMELON (61) Paul Peek	Fairlane 21005	$10
	(White promo label)		
	See Gene Vincent		

PEGGY SUE (C)

Peggy Sue Wells
Sister of Loretta Lynn and Crystal Gayle
Decca 45s $3 each
Door Knob LPs $4-8 each
Country International duet LPs $5 each

-albums-

LP	DYNAMITE (69)	Decca 75153	$15
LP(P)	DYNAMITE (69)	Decca 75153	$18
	(White promo label)		
LP	ALL AMERICAN HUSBAND (70)	Decca 75215	$15
LP(P)	ALL AMERICAN HUSBAND (70)	Decca 75215	$18
	(White promo label)		

DENNIS PENNA (RB)

-singles-

45rpm	BATTLE OF THE DUALS (58)	Musitron 105	$40

RAY PENNINGTON (C)
Monument 45s $2 each

-albums-

LP	**RAY PENNINGTON SINGS FOR THE OTHER WOMAN** (70)	Monument 18145	$15

JOE PENNY (RB)

-singles-

45rpm	**BIP A LITTLE, BOP A LITTLE** (58)	Federal 12322	$50

CARL PERKINS (RB)
Dollie 45s $8-10 each
Other Columbia 45s (44723-45694) $5-8 each
  (Including NRBQ singles)
Mercury 45s $5 each
Suede 45s $4 each
Music Hill and MMI 45s $ 3 each
Jet (CBS) 45s $4 each
America (Smash) 45s $3 each
America picture sleeves $3 each
Universal (MCA) 45s $2 each
Trip, Accord, Album Globe, Koala, Allegiance LPs $3 each

-singles-

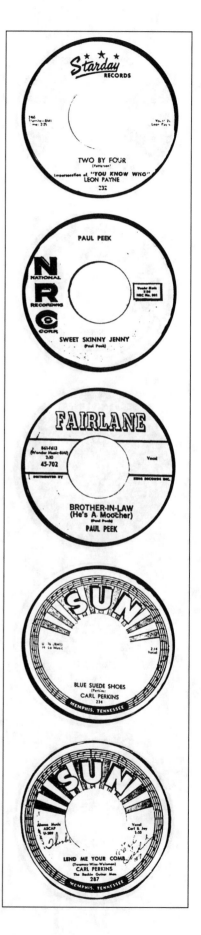

78rpm	**MOVIE MAGG** (55)	Flip 501	$400
45rpm	**MOVIE MAGG** (55)	Flip 501	$600
78rpm	**GONE GONE GONE** (56)	Sun 224	$75
45rpm	**GONE GONE GONE** (56)	Sun 224	$100
78rpm	**BLUE SUEDE SHOES** (57)	Sun 234	$75
45rpm	**BLUE SUEDE SHOES** (57)	Sun 234	$30
78rpm	**BOPPIN' THE BLUES** (57)	Sun 243	$60
45rpm	**BOPPIN' THE BLUES** (57)	Sun 243	$30
78rpm	**DIXIE FRIED** (57)	Sun 249	$30
45rpm	**DIXIE FRIED** (57)	Sun 249	$25
78rpm	**MATCHBOX** (58)	Sun 261	$30
45rpm	**MATCHBOX** (58)	Sun 261	$25
78rpm	**THAT'S RIGHT** (58)	Sun 274	$30
45rpm	**THAT'S RIGHT** (58)	Sun 274	$25
45rpm	**LEND ME YOUR COMB** (58)	Sun 287	$20
45rpm	**PINK PEDAL PUSHERS** (59)	Columbia 41131	$25
45rpm	**PINK PEDAL PUSHERS** (59)	Columbia 41131	$100
	(Price includes picture sleeve)		
45(P)	**PINK PEDAL PUSHERS** (59)	Columbia 41131	$20
	(White promo label)		
45rpm	**LEVI JACKET** (59)	Columbia 41207	$18
45(P)	**LEVI JACKET** (59)	Columbia 41207	$15
	(Blue promo label)		
45rpm	**THIS LIFE I LIVE** (60)	Columbia 41296	$18
45(P)	**THIS LIFE I LIVE** (60)	Columbia 41296	$12
	(Blue promo label)		
45rpm	**POINTED TOE SHOES** (60)	Columbia 41379	$18
45(P)	**POINTED TOE SHOES** (60)	Columbia 41379	$12
	(White promo label)		
45rpm	**ONE TICKET TO LONELINESS** (59)	Columbia 41449	$15
45(P)	**ONE TICKET TO LONELINESS** (59)	Columbia 41449	$12
	(White promo label)		
45rpm	**L-O-V-E-V-I-L-L-E** (60)	Columbia 41651	$15
45(P)	**L-O-V-E-V-I-L-L-E** (60)	Columbia 41651	$12
	(White promo label)		
45rpm	**HONEY 'CAUSE I LOVE YOU** (61)	Columbia 41825	$15
45(P)	**HONEY 'CAUSE I LOVE YOU** (61)	Columbia 41825	$12
	(White promo label)		
45rpm	**ANYWAY THE WIND BLOWS** (61)	Columbia 42061	$15
45(P)	**ANYWAY THE WIND BLOWS** (61)	Columbia 42061	$12
	(White promo label)		
45rpm	**HOLLYWOOD CITY** (62)	Columbia 42405	$15
45rpm	**HOLLYWOOD CITY** (62)	Columbia 42405	$75
	(Price includes picture sleeve)		
45(P)	**HOLLYWOOD CITY** (62)	Columbia 42405	$12
	(White promo label)		
45rpm	**SISTER TWISTER** (62)	Columbia 42514	$15
45rpm	**SISTER TWISTER** (62)	Columbia 42514	$200
	(Price includes picture sleeve)		
45rpm	**FORGET ME NEXT TIME AROUND** (63)	Columbia 42753	$15
45(P)	**FORGET ME NEXT TIME AROUND** (63)	Columbia 42753	$12
	(White promo label)		
45rpm	**HELP ME FIND MY BABY** (63)	Decca 31548	$15
45(P)	**HELP ME FIND MY BABY** (63)	Decca 31548	$12
	(Pink promo label)		

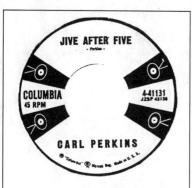

45rpm	AFTER SUNDOWN (64)	Decca 31591	$15
45(P)	AFTER SUNDOWN (64)	Decca 31591	$12
	(Pink promo label)		
45rpm	LET MY BABY BE (64)	Decca 31709	$15
45(P)	LET MY BABY BE (64)	Decca 31709	$12
	(Pink promo label)		
45rpm	ONE OF THESE DAYS (65)	Decca 31786	$12
45(P)	ONE OF THESE DAYS (65)	Decca 31786	$10
	(Pink promo label)		
45rpm	TENNESSEE (75)	Sun #5	$10
	(Golden Treasure Series)		

-EPs-

EP	DANCE ALBUM (56)	Sun 115	$500
EP	WHOLE LOTTA SHAKIN' (58)	Columbia 12341	$600
EP(P)	DIG THIS (72) Various artists	Columbia AS 3	$25
	(One Perkins/NRBQ cut, "Boppin' the Blues")		

-albums-

LP	DANCE ALBUM (57)	Sun 1225	$600
LP	TEEN BEAT (61)	Sun 1225	$500
	(Repackage)		
LP	WHOLE LOTTA SHAKIN' (58)	Columbia 1234	$300
LP(P)	WHOLE LOTTA SHAKIN' (58)	Columbia 1234	$400
	(White promo label)		
LP	TENNESSEE (63) Various artists	Design 611	$20
	(Budget label)		
LP	BLUE SUEDE SHOES (69)	Sun 112	$15
LP(P)	BLUE SUEDE SHOES (69)	Sun 112	$18
	(White promo label)		
LP	CARL PERKINS GREATEST HITS (69)	Columbia 9833	$18
LP(P)	CARL PERKINS GREATEST HITS (69)	Columbia 9833	$25
	(White promo label)		
LP	ON TOP (69)	Columbia 9931	$18
LP(P)	ON TOP (69)	Columbia 9931	$25
	(White promo label)		
LP	BOPPIN' THE BLUES (70) With NRBQ	Columbia 9981	$18
LP(P)	BOPPIN' THE BLUES (70)	Columbia 9981	$25
	(White promo label)		
LP	BROWN EYED HANDSOME MAN (72)	Harmony 31179	$15
LP(P)	BROWN EYED HANDSOME MAN (72)	Harmony 31179	$18
	(White promo label)		
LP	CARL PERKINS (72)	Harmony 31185	$12
LP(P)	CARL PERKINS (72)	Harmony 31185	$15
	(White promo label)		
LP	THE GREATEST HITS OF CARL PERKINS (72)	Harmony 31192	$12
LP(P)	THE GREATEST HITS OF CARL PERKINS (72)	Harmony 31192	$15
	(White promo label)		
LP	MY KIND OF COUNTRY (73)	Mercury 691	$12
LP	THE SUN STORY, VOL 3: CARL PERKINS (77)	Sunnyvale 330-903	$10
LP	OL' BLUE SUEDE'S BACK (78)	Jet (CBS) 856	$12
LP(P)	OL' BLUE SUEDE'S BACK (78)	Jet 856	$15
	(White promo label)		
LP	LIVE AT AUSTIN CITY LIMITS (81)	Suede 002	$10

-radio shows-

LP(RS)	COUNTRY MUSIC TIME (80s)	U.S. Air Force 940	$20-30
	(Music and interviews)		
LP(RS)	COUNTRY CROSSROADS (Nov 81)	Southern Baptist	$20-30
	(Music and interviews)		
3LP(RS)	AMERICAN EAGLE (Jun 83) With Tanya Tucker	DIR	$50-100
	(Live concert)		

ROY PERKINS (RB)

-singles-

45rpm	I'VE GOT A GIRL NAMED DEE (61)	Nusound	$65

PETE & JIMMY (RB)

-singles-

45rpm	SO WILD (58)	Castle 504	$40

EARL PETERSON (R)

-singles-

45rpm	BOOGIE BLUES (55)	Sun 197	$40

NORMAN PETTY TRIO (AC)
-singles-

Only the Buddy Holly related records
45rpm	**MOONDREAMS** (58)	Columbia 41039	$20
45(P)	**MOONDREAMS** (58)	Columbia 41039	$15
	(White promo label)		
45rpm	**TRUE LOVE WAYS** (59)	Nor Va Jak 1325	$25

-EPs-

EP	**MOONDREAMS** (59)	Columbia 1092	$30

-albums-

LP	**MOONDREAMS** (59)	Columbia 1092	$25
LP(P)	**MOONDREAMS** (59)	Columbia 1092	$30
	(White promo label)		

THE PHANTOM (RB)
-singles-

45rpm	**LOVE ME** (61)	Dot 16056	$60

JACKIE PHELPS (C)
-albums-

LP	**TEN TALENTED FINGERS OF JACKIE PHELPS** (63)	Starday 265	$20

TERRY PHILIPS (R)
-singles-

45rpm	**HANDS OF A FOOL** (58)	V.A. 351	$40

BILL PHILLIPS (CW)
Decca 45s $3 each
-albums-

LP	**BILL PHILLIPS' BEST** (64)	Harmony 7309	$20
LP(P)	**BILL PHILLIPS' BEST** (64)	Harmony 7309	$25
	(White promo label)		
LP	**PUT IT OFF UNTIL TOMORROW** (66)	Decca 4792	$50
LP(P)	**PUT IT OFF UNTIL TOMORROW** (66)	Decca 4792	$40
	(White promo label)		
LP	**BILL PHILLIPS' STYLE** (67)	Decca 4897	$25
LP(P)	**BILL PHILLIPS' STYLE** (67)	Decca 4897	$25
	(Decca promo label)		
LP	**COUNTRY ACTION** (68)	Decca 5022	$18
LP(P)	**COUNTRY ACTION** (68)	Decca 5022	$25
	(Decca promo label)		
LP	**LITTLE BOY SAD** (70)	Decca 5182	$15
LP(P)	**LITTLE BOY SAD** (70)	Decca 5182	$20
	(Decca promo label)		

CARL PHILLIPS (RB)
-singles-

45rpm	**WIGWAM WILLIE** (58)	Bobbin 110	$75

PHIL PHILLIPS (R)
-singles-

45rpm	**SEA OF LOVE** (59)	Khourys 711	$150
45rpm	**SEA OF LOVE** (59)	Mercury 71465	$12
45(P)	**SEA OF LOVE** (59)	Mercury 71465	$15
	(White promo label)		
45rpm	**TAKE THIS HEART** (59)	Mercury 71531	$10
45rpm	**WHAT WILL I TELL MY HEART** (60)	Mercury 71611	$10
45rpm	**NOBODY KNOWS AND NOBODY CARES** (60)	Mercury 71657	$10

STU PHILLIPS (C)
Capitol 45s $3 each
RCA Victor 45s $2 each
-albums-

LP	**FEELS LIKE LOVIN'** (65)	Capitol 2356	$20
LP	**SINGING STU PHILLIPS** (66)	RCA Victor 3619	$18
LP	**GRASS ROOTS COUNTRY** (66)	RCA Victor 3717	$18
LP	**OUR LAST RENDEZVOUS** (68)	RCA Victor 4012	$15

PHIPPS FAMILY (G)
Pine Mountain LPs $5-10 each
-albums-

LP	**THE MOST REQUESTED SACRED SONGS OF THE CARTER FAMILY** (61)	Starday 139	$40
LP	**OLD TIME PICKIN' & SINGIN'** (62)	Starday 195	$25
LP	**ECHOS OF THE CARTER FAMILY** (63)	Starday 248	$20

LEE PICKETT (RB)

-singles-

45rpm	**FATTY PATTY** (58)	Jolt 331	$75

PETE PICO (RB)

-singles-

45rpm	**HOT DOG** (58)	Jet 100	$40

WEBB PIERCE (CW)

4-Star 78s $8 each
Other Decca 78s $4-8 each
Other Decca 45s $3-6 each
Plantation, Coral, MCA, Era, and Skylite LPs $3-6 each

-singles-

45rpm	**JILTED LOVE** (52)	4-Star 1629	$25
45rpm	**WONDERING** (52)	Decca 46364	$20
45rpm	**YOU KNOW I'M STILL IN LOVE WITH YOU** (52)	Decca 46385	$20
45rpm	**THAT HEART BELONGS TO ME** (52)	Decca 28091	$15
45rpm	**BACK STREET AFFAIR** (52)	Decca 28369	$15
45rpm	**I'LL GO ON ALONE** (53)	Decca 28534	$15
45rpm	**THE LAST WALTZ** (53)	Decca 28594	$15
45rpm	**IT'S BEEN SO LONG** (53)	Decca 28725	$12
45rpm	**THERE STANDS THE GLASS** (53)	Decca 28834	$12
45rpm	**SLOWLY** (54)	Decca 28991	$12
45rpm	**EVEN THO** (54)	Decca 29107	$12
45(P)	**EVEN THO** (54)	Decca 29107	$10
	(Pink promo label)		
45rpm	**IT'S ALL BETWEEN THE LINES** (54)	King 5366	$12
45(P)	**IT'S ALL BETWEEN THE LINES** (54)	King 5366	$10
	(White promo label)		
45rpm	**JILTED LOVE** (55)	King 5429	$12
45(P)	**JILTED LOVE** (55)	King 5429	$10
	(White promo label)		
45rpm	**MORE AND MORE** (55)	Decca 29252	$12
45(P)	**MORE AND MORE** (55)	Decca 29252	$10
	(Pink promo label)		
45rpm	**IN THE JAILHOUSE NOW** (55)	Decca 29391	$15
45(P)	**IN THE JAILHOUSE NOW** (55)	Decca 29391	$12
	(Pink promo label)		
45rpm	**I DON'T CARE** (55)	Decca 29480	$10
45rpm	**SATISFIED MIND** (55) With Betty Foley	Decca 29526	$10
45rpm	**IF YOU WERE ME** (55)	Decca 29662	$10
45rpm	**WHY BABY WHY** (55) With Red Sovine	Decca 29755	$15
45(P)	**WHY BABY WHY** (55)	Decca 29755	$12
	(Pink promo label)		
45rpm	**'CAUSE I LOVE YOU** (56)	Decca 29805	$10
45rpm	**LITTLE ROSA** (56) With Red Sovine	Decca 29876	$10
45rpm	**ANY OLD TIME** (56)	Decca 29974	$10
78rpm	**TEENAGE BOOGIE** (56)	Decca 30045	$25
78(P)	**TEENAGE BOOGIE** (56)	Decca 30045	$30
	(Pink promo label)		
45rpm	**TEENAGE BOOGIE** (56)	Decca 30045	$25
45(P)	**TEENAGE BOOGIE** (56)	Decca 30045	$18
	(Pink promo label)		
45rpm	**I'M TIRED** (57)	Decca 30155	$10
45rpm	**DON'T DO IT DARLIN'** (57)	Decca 30419	$10
45rpm	**YOU'LL COME BACK** (57)	Decca 30623	$10
45rpm	**TUPELO COUNTY JAIL** (58)	Decca 30711	$10
45rpm	**I AIN'T NEVER** (59)	Decca 30923	$15
45(P)	**I AIN'T NEVER** (59)	Decca 30923	$10
	(Pink promo label)		
5-33s	**HIDEAWAY HEART** (62) Five stereo singles	Decca 34014-34018	$8 each
	(Set of five for jukeboxes, $40 for the set)		
5-33s	**I'VE GOT A NEW HEARTACHE** (63) Five stereo singles	Decca 34135-34139	$8 each
	(Set of five for jukeboxes, $40 for the set)		

-EPs-

EP(P)	**WEBB PIERCE SINGS** (55)	Sesac AD 33	$40
	(Promo-only EP issued with hard cover)		
EP	**THE WONDERING BOY** Vol 1 (55)	Decca 2144	$30
EP	**THE WONDERING BOY** Vol 2 (55)	Decca 2145	$30
EP	**WEBB PIERCE** Vol 1 (55)	Decca 2241	$25
EP	**WEBB PIERCE** Vol 2 (55)	Decca 2242	$25
EP	**WEBB PIERCE** Vol 3 (55)	Decca 2243	$25
EP	**THE COUNTRY CHURCH** (56)	Decca 2355	$20
EP	**THE WONDERING BOY** (56)	Decca 2364	$18
EP	**JUST IMAGINATION** (58)	Decca 2581	$18

EP	**WEBB** (59) Mono	Decca 2653	$15
EP	**WEBB** (59) Stereo	Decca 2653	$18
EP	**WEBB PIERCE & KITTY WELLS** (59)	Decca 2666	$15
EP	**I AIN'T NEVER** (59) Mono	Decca 2668	$15
EP	**I AIN'T NEVER** (59) Stereo	Decca 2668	$20
EP	**WALKING THE STREETS** (60)	Decca 2685	$15
EP	**IS IT WRONG** (61)	Decca 2694	$15
EP	**HIDEAWAY HEART** (62)	Decca 2709	$15
EP	**WEBB PIERCE** (62)	Decca 2719	$15
EP	**CRAZY WILD DESIRE** (62)	Decca 2734	$15
EP	**FALLEN' ANGEL** (63)	Decca 2748	$15
EP	**COW TOWN** (64)	Decca 2761	$15
EP	**NOBODY'S DARLIN' BUT MINE** (65)	Decca 2785	$12
EP	**SOFTLY & TENDERLY** (65)	Decca 2786	$12
EP	**LOVING YOU THEN LOSING YOU** (65)	Decca 2799	$12

-albums-

10"LP	**THAT WONDERING BOY** (53)	Decca 5536	$125
LP	**WEBB PIERCE** (55)	Decca 8129	$50
LP(P)	**WEBB PIERCE** (55)	Decca 8129	$75
	(Pink promo label)		
LP	**THAT WONDERING BOY** (56)	Decca 8295	$50
LP(P)	**THAT WONDERING BOY** (56)	Decca 8295	$40
	(Pink promo label)		
LP	**JUST IMAGINATION** (57)	Decca 8728	$40
LP(P)	**JUST IMAGINATION** (57)	Decca 8728	$30
	(Pink promo label)		
LP	**SING FOR YOU** (58)	Audio Lab 1563	$75
	(With Marvin Rainwater and Stuart Hamblen)		
LP	**BOUND FOR THE KINGDOM** (59) Mono	Decca 8889	$25
LP	**BOUND FOR THE KINGDOM** (59) Stereo	Decca 78889	$40
LP(P)	**BOUND FOR THE KINGDOM** (59)	Decca 8889	$30
	(Pink promo label)		
LP	**WEBB!** (59) Mono	Decca 8899	$25
LP	**WEBB!** (59) Stereo	Decca 8899	$40
LP(P)	**WEBB!** (59)	Decca 8899	$30
	(Pink promo label)		
LP	**THE ONE AND ONLY WEBB PIERCE** (59)	King 648	$75
LP	**WEBB WITH A BEAT** (60)	Decca 4015	$20
LP(P)	**WEBB WITH A BEAT** (60)	Decca 4015	$25
	(Pink promo label)		
LP	**WALKING THE STREETS** (60)	Decca 4079	$20
LP(P)	**WALKING THE STREETS** (60)	Decca 4079	$25
	(Pink promo label)		
LP	**GOLDEN FAVORITES** (61)	Decca 4110	$18
LP(P)	**GOLDEN FAVORITES** (61)	Decca 4110	$20
	(Pink promo label)		
LP	**FALLEN ANGEL** (61)	Decca 4144	$18
LP(P)	**FALLEN ANGEL** (61)	Decca 4144	$20
	(Pink promo label)		
LP	**HIDEAWAY HEART** (62)	Decca 4218	$15
LP(P)	**HIDEAWAY HEART** (62)	Decca 4218	$18
	(Pink promo label)		
LP	**CROSS COUNTRY** (62)	Decca 4294	$15
LP(P)	**CROSS COUNTRY** (62)	Decca 4294	$18
	(Pink promo label)		
LP	**WEBB PIERCE & WYNN STEWART** (62)	Design 604	$20
	(Rare budget label)		
LP	**I'VE GOT A NEW HEARTACHE** (63)	Decca 4358	$15
LP(P)	**I'VE GOT A NEW HEARTACHE** (63)	Decca 4358	$18
	(Pink promo label)		
LP	**BOW THY HEAD** (63)	Decca 4384	$15
LP(P)	**BOW THY HEAD** (63)	Decca 4384	$18
	(Pink promo label)		
2LP	**THE WEBB PIERCE STORY** (64)	Decca 181	$25
	(Price includes booklet)		
2LP(P)	**THE WEBB PIERCE STORY** (64)	Decca 181	$40
	(White promo labels)		
LP	**SANDS OF GOLD** (64)	Decca 4486	$15
LP(P)	**SANDS OF GOLD** (64)	Decca 4486	$18
	(Decca promo label)		
LP	**MEMORY NO. 1** (65)	Decca 4604	$12
LP(P)	**MEMORY NO. 1** (65)	Decca 4604	$15
	(Decca promo label)		
LP	**COUNTRY MUSIC TIME** (65)	Decca 4659	$12
LP(P)	**COUNTRY MUSIC TIME** (65)	Decca 4659	$15
	(Decca promo label)		
LP	**JUST WEBB PIERCE** (65)	Hilltop 6002	$15

LP	**SWEET MEMORIES** (66)	Decca 4739	$12
LP(P)	**SWEET MEMORIES** (66)	Decca 4739	$15
	(Decca promo label)		
LP	**WEBB'S CHOICE** (66)	Decca 4782	$12
LP(P)	**WEBB'S CHOICE** (66)	Decca 4782	$15
	(White promo label)		
LP	**WEBB PIERCE** (66)	Vocalion 3766	$15
	(Material recorded for 4-Star)		
LP(P)	**WEBB PIERCE** (66)	Vocalion 3766	$18
	(White promo label)		
LP	**WHERE'D YA STAY LAST NIGHT?** (67)	Decca 74844	$12
LP(P)	**WHERE'D YA STAY LAST NIGHT?** (67)	Decca 74844	$15
	(White promo label)		
LP	**FOOL, FOOL, FOOL** (68)	Decca 74964	$12
LP(P)	**FOOL, FOOL, FOOL** (68)	Decca 74964	$15
	(White promo label)		
LP	**WEBB PIERCE'S GREATEST HITS** (68)	Decca 74999	$10
LP(P)	**WEBB PIERCE'S GREATEST HITS** (68)	Decca 74999	$15
	(White promo label)		
LP	**COUNTRY SONGS** (68)	Vocalion 3830	$12
LP(P)	**COUNTRY SONGS** (68)	Vocalion 3830	$15
	(White promo label)		
LP	**SATURDAY NIGHT** (69)	Decca 75071	$12
LP(P)	**SATURDAY NIGHT** (69)	Decca 75071	$15
	(White promo label)		
LP	**WEBB PIERCE SINGS THIS THING** (69)	Decca 75132	$10
LP(P)	**WEBB PIERCE SINGS THIS THING** (69)	Decca 75132	$12
	(White promo label)		
LP	**LOVE AIN'T NEVER GONNA BE NO BETTER** (70)	Decca 75168	$10
LP(P)	**LOVE AIN'T NEVER GONNA BE NO BETTER** (70)	Decca 75168	$12
	(White promo label)		
LP	**COUNTRY FAVORITES** (70)	Vocalion 3911	$12
LP(P)	**COUNTRY FAVORITES** (70)	Vocalion 3911	$15
	(White promo label)		
LP	**MERRY-GO-ROUND WORLD** (70)	Decca 75210	$10
LP	**WEBB PIERCE ROAD SHOW** (71)	Decca 75280	$10
LP(P)	**DOUBLE STAR SERIES** (70s) With Loretta Lynn	MCA 734585	$20
	(MCA Special Market offer from Philco)		
LP	**I'M GONNA BE A SWINGER** (72)	Decca 75393	$10

-radio shows-

16"(RS)	**COUNTRY STYLE USA** (55)	Country Style USA 117	$40-75
	(Music and interviews)		
16"(RS)	**COUNTRY STYLE USA** (56)	Country Style USA 186	$40-75
	(Music and interviews)		
16"(RS)	**COUNTRY MUSIC TIME** (50s)	U.S. Army 81	$20-30
	(Music and interviews)		
16"(RS)	**COUNTRY MUSIC TIME** (60S)	U.S. Army 94	$20-30
	(Music and interviews)		
16"(RS)	**U.S. AIR FORCE SHOW** (60s)	U.S. Air Force	$20-30
	(Music and interviews)		

PETE PIKE (C)

-albums-

LP	**PETE PIKE** (60)	Audio Lab 1559	$25

RAY PILLOW (C)
Capitol and ABC 45s $2 each
Plantation 45s $1 each
ABC, Mega, Plantation, Hilltop LPs $2-4 each

-albums-

LP	**PRESENTING RAY PILLOW** (65)	Capitol 2417	$18
LP	**EVEN WHEN IT'S BAD, IT'S GOOD** (67)	Capitol 2738	$15

PINKARD & BOWDEN (N)
Warner 45s $3 each
Warner LPs $5-8 each

-radio shows-

LP(RS)	**COUNTRY MUSIC TIME** (80s-90s)	U.S. Air Force	$15-25
	(Music and interviews)		

PLAINSMEN (G)
Hickory and Mercury 45s $2-3 each

-albums-

LP	**SOMEONE'S WATCHING OVER YOU** (61)	Mercury 60625	$15
LP(P)	**SOMEONE'S WATCHING OVER YOU** (61)	Mercury 20625	$18
	(White promo label)		

LP	THE WORLD'S GREATEST GOSPEL SONGS (62)	Mercury 60699	$12
LP(P)	THE WORLD'S GREATEST GOSPEL SONGS (62)	Mercury 20699	$15
	(White promo label)		
LP	BOTH SIDES OF THE PLAINSMEN (74)	Hickory 4513	$10

PO' BOYS (C)
Back-up group for Bill Anderson
Decca 45s $2 each

-albums-

LP	BILL ANDERSON PRESENTS THE PO' BOYS (66)	Decca 4725	$15
LP(P)	BILL ANDERSON PRESENTS THE PO' BOYS (66)	Decca 4725	$18
	(Pink promo label)		
LP	THE PO' BOYS PICK AGAIN (67)	Decca 4884	$12
LP(P)	THE PO' BOYS PICK AGAIN (67)	Decca 4884	$15
	(Pink promo label)		
LP	THAT CASUAL COUNTRY FEELING (71)	Decca 5278	$10
LP(P)	THAT CASUAL COUNTRY FEELING (71)	Decca 5278	$12
	(White promo label)		
	See Bill Anderson		

POCO (R)
Epic 45s $2 each
ABC, MCA 45s $1 each
RCA Victor 45s $1 each
Any label LPs $2-4 each

-singles-

45(P)	WHAT'S IT ALL ABOUT (Jan 76) Public service show	W. I. A. A. 299	$10
	(Flip side features Roger Whitaker)		
45(P)	WHAT'S IT ALL ABOUT (June 79) Public service show	W. I. A. A. 476	$10
	(Flip side features Judy Collins)		

-radio shows-

LP(RS)	ROBERT W. MORGAN (June 80)	Watermark	$15-25
	(Music and interviews)		
CD(RS)	KING BISCUIT FLOWER HOUR (Oct 88) With Foghat	DIR	$30-40
	(Live concert)		

BOBBY POE (RB)

-singles-

45rpm	ROCK & ROLL RECORD GIRL (58)	White Rock 1112	$50

JOHNNY POOLE (RB)

-singles-

45rpm	BAREFOOTED BABY (58)	Wide 430	$40

JOE POOVEY (RB)

-singles-

45rpm	TEN LONG FINGERS (58)	Dixie 2018	$100
45rpm	MOVE AROUND (58)	Dixie 733	$75

ROYCE PORTER (RB)

-singles-

45rpm	LOOKIN' (57)	D 1026	$20
45rpm	A WOMAN CAN MAKE YOU BLUE (58)	Spade 1931	$65
45rpm	YES I DO (58)	Look 1001	$50
45rpm	GOOD TIME (58)	Mercury 71314	$30
45(P)	GOOD TIME (58)	Mercury 71314	$25
	(White promo label)		

SANDY POSEY (C)
Backed Elvis Presley
Currently backing Elvis Wade
MGM 45s $5 each
MGM picture sleeves $5 each
Columbia 45s $2 each
Other MGM LPs $8 each
51 West LPs $4 each
Gusto duet LPs $3 each

-albums-

LP	BORN A WOMAN (66)	MGM 4418	$15
LP(P)	BORN A WOMAN (66)	MGM 4418	$18
	(Yellow promo label)		
LP	SINGLE GIRL (67)	MGM 4455	$15
LP(P)	SINGLE GIRL (67)	MGM 4455	$18
	(Yellow promo label)		
LP	SANDY POSEY (67)	MGM 4480	$15
LP(P)	SANDY POSEY (67)	MGM 4480	$18
	(Yellow promo label)		

LP	**THE BEST OF SANDY POSEY** (67)	MGM 4509	$12
LP(P)	**THE BEST OF SANDY POSEY** (67)	MGM 4509	$15
	(Yellow promo label)		
LP	**LOOKING AT YOU** (68)	MGM 4525	$12
LP(P)	**LOOKING AT YOU** (68)	MGM 4525	$15
	(Yellow promo label)		
LP	**WHY DON'T WE GO SOMEWHERE AND LOVE** (72)	Columbia 31594	$10

POSSUM HUNTERS (BG)
-albums-

LP	**DEATH ON LEE HIGHWAY** (70)	Takoma 1010	$18
LP	**IN THE PINES** (71)	Takoma 1025	$15

CURTIS POTTER (R)
-singles-

45rpm	**I'M A REAL GLAD DADDY** (58)	Fox 409	$75

JOHNNY POWERS (RB)
-singles-

45rpm	**ROCK ROCK** (57)	Fox 916	$125
45rpm	**BE MINE ALL MINE** (58)	Sun 327	$12
45rpm	**ROCK THE UNIVERSE** (58)	Fortune 199	$30
45rpm	**ROCK THE UNIVERSE** (58)	Hi-Q 5044	$25

POZO SECO SINGERS See Don Williams

LYNN PRATT (RB)
-singles-

45rpm	**TOM CAT BOOGIE** (58)	Hornet 1000	$65
45rpm	**TROUBLES** (58)	Hornet 1001	$55
45rpm	**COME HERE MAMA** (59)	Hornet 1002	$50
45rpm	**RED HEADED WOMAN** (59)	Hornet 1003	$55

ELVIS PRESLEY (RB)
The King of Rock 'N' Roll was first a country-western artist
Other RCA Victor 45s after 9791 $4-8 each
RCA Victor 11099-11113 45s and picture sleeves $4 for each record/sleeve combination
Other RCA Victor dog-on-side reissues $4-8 each
Other RCA Victor orange label reissues $50-100 each
    (Rare, do not confuse with regular releases after 1972)
Other RCA Victor red label reissues 3-6 each
-78s-

78rpm	**THAT'S ALL RIGHT** (54)	Sun 209	$750
	(Worth around $100 in good, $250 in VG)		
78rpm	**THAT'S ALL RIGHT** (55)	RCA Victor 6380	$100
78rpm	**GOOD ROCKIN' TONIGHT** (55)	Sun 210	$750
	(Worth around $100 in good, $250 in VG)		
78rpm	**GOOD ROCKIN' TONIGHT** (55)	RCA Victor 6381	$100
78rpm	**MILKCOW BLUES BOOGIE** (55)	Sun 215	$1,000
	(Worth around $200 in good, $500 in VG)		
78rpm	**MILKCOW BLUES BOOGIE** (55)	RCA Victor 6382	$100
78rpm	**BABY, LET'S PLAY HOUSE** (55)	Sun 217	$600
	(Worth around $100 in good, $150 in VG)		
78rpm	**BABY, LET'S PLAY HOUSE** (55)	RCA Victor 6383	$75
78rpm	**MYSTERY TRAIN** (55)	Sun 223	$250
	(The most common Sun single)		
78rpm	**MYSTERY TRAIN** (55)	RCA Victor 6357	$75
	(This is the first RCA Victor Presley single)		
78(P)	**MYSTERY TRAIN** (55)	RCA Victor 6357	$800
	(White promo label)		
78rpm	**HEARTBREAK HOTEL** (56)	RCA Victor 6420	$75
78(P)	**HEARTBREAK HOTEL** (56)	RCA Victor 6420	$750
	(White promo label)		
78rpm	**I WANT YOU, I NEED YOU, I LOVE YOU** (56)	RCA Victor 6540	$75
78(P)	**I WANT YOU, I NEED YOU, I LOVE YOU** (56)	RCA Victor 6540	$750
	(White promo label)		
78rpm	**DON'T BE CRUEL** (56)	RCA Victor 6604	$75
78(P)	**DON'T BE CRUEL** (56)	RCA Victor 6604	$750
	(White promo label)		
78rpm	**BLUE SUEDE SHOES** (56)	RCA Victor 6636	$75
78rpm	**I GOT A WOMAN** (56)	RCA Victor 6637	$75
78rpm	**I'LL NEVER LET YOU GO** (56)	RCA Victor 6638	$75
78rpm	**TRYING TO GET OVER YOU** (56)	RCA Victor 6639	$80
78rpm	**BLUE MOON** (56)	RCA Victor 6640	$75
78rpm	**MONEY HONEY** (56)	RCA Victor 6641	$75
78rpm	**SHAKE RATTLE AND ROLL** (56)	RCA Victor 6642	$75
78rpm	**LOVE ME TENDER** (56)	RCA Victor 6643	$60

78(P)	**LOVE ME TENDER** (56)	RCA Victor 6643	$750
	(White promo label)		
78rpm	**TOO MUCH** (57)	RCA Victor 6800	$60
78(P)	**TOO MUCH** (57)	RCA Victor 6800	$750
	(White promo label)		
78rpm	**ALL SHOOK UP** (57)	RCA Victor 6870	$60
78(P)	**ALL SHOOK UP** (57)	RCA Victor 6870	$750
	(White promo label)		
78rpm	**TEDDY BEAR** (57)	RCA Victor 7000	$75
78(P)	**TEDDY BEAR** (57)	RCA Victor 7000	$750
	(White promo label)		
78rpm	**JAILHOUSE ROCK** (57)	RCA Victor 7035	$75
78(P)	**JAILHOUSE ROCK** (57)	RCA Victor 7035	$750
	(White promo label)		
78rpm	**DON'T** (58)	RCA Victor 7150	$75
78rpm	**WEAR MY RING AROUND YOUR NECK** (58)	RCA Victor 7240	$75
78rpm	**HARD HEADED WOMAN** (58)	RCA Victor 7280	$100
78rpm	**ONE NIGHT** (58)	RCA Victor 7410	$250

-singles-

45rpm	**THAT'S ALL RIGHT** (54)	Sun 209	$1,500
45rpm	**THAT'S ALL RIGHT** (54)	RCA Victor 6380	$50
45rpm	**THAT'S ALL RIGHT** (54)	RCA Victor 6380	$150
	(Horizontal lines on the label)		
45rpm	**THAT'S ALL RIGHT** (65)	RCA Victor 0601	$400
	(Price is for the picture sleeve and record)		
45(P)	**THAT'S ALL RIGHT** (65)	RCA Victor 0601	$100
	(White promo label)		
45rpm	**THAT'S ALL RIGHT** (68) Orange label	RCA Victor 0601	$50
45rpm	**GOOD ROCKIN' TONIGHT** (55)	Sun 210	$1,500
45rpm	**GOOD ROCKIN' TONIGHT** (55)	RCA Victor 6381	$50
45rpm	**GOOD ROCKIN' TONIGHT** (55)	RCA Victor 6381	$150
	(Horizontal lines on the label)		
45rpm	**GOOD ROCKIN' TONIGHT** (65)	RCA Victor 0602	$400
	(Price includes picture sleeve)		
45(P)	**GOOD ROCKIN' TONIGHT** (65)	RCA Victor 0602	$100
	(White promo label)		
45rpm	**GOOD ROCKIN' TONIGHT** (68) Orange label	RCA Victor 0602	$35
45rpm	**MILKCOW BLUES BOOGIE** (55)	Sun 215	$2,000
	(Rarest Presley Sun single)		
45rpm	**MILKCOW BLUES BOOGIE** (55)	RCA Victor 6382	$50
45rpm	**MILKCOW BLUES BOOGIE** (55)	RCA Victor 6382	$150
	(Horizontal lines on label)		
45rpm	**BABY, LET'S PLAY HOUSE** (55)	Sun 217	$1,200
45rpm	**BABY, LET'S PLAY HOUSE** (55)	RCA Victor 6386	$50
45rpm	**BABY, LET'S PLAY HOUSE** (55)	RCA Victor 6386	$150
	(Horizontal lines on label)		
45rpm	**MYSTERY TRAIN** (55)	Sun 223	$500
	(Most common Presley Sun single)		
45rpm	**MYSTERY TRAIN** (55)	RCA Victor 6357	$40
45rpm	**MYSTERY TRAIN** (55)	RCA Victor 6357	$150
	(Horizontal lines on the label)		
45(P)	**MYSTERY TRAIN** (55)	RCA Victor 6357	$500
	(First Presley white promo label single)		
45(P)	**MYSTERY TRAIN** (65)	RCA Victor 0600	$100
	(White promo label)		
45rpm	**MYSTERY TRAIN** (68) Orange label	RCA Victor 0600	$40
45rpm	**HEARTBREAK HOTEL** (65)	RCA Victor 6420	$25
45rpm	**HEARTBREAK HOTEL** (65)	RCA Victor 0605	$400
	(Price includes picture sleeve)		
45(P)	**HEARTBREAK HOTEL** (65)	RCA Victor 0605	$100
	(White promo label)		
45rpm	**I WANT YOU, I NEED YOU, I LOVE YOU** (56)	RCA Victor 6540	$25
45rpm	**I WANT YOU, I NEED YOU, I LOVE YOU** (56)	RCA Victor 6540	$50
	(Horizontal lines on label)		
PS(P)	**I WANT YOU, I NEED YOU, I LOVE YOU** (56)	RCA Victor 6540	$2,000
	(Promo-only sleeve issued to radio stations with a stock copy of the record)		
45(P)	**OLD SHEP** (56) Promo label	RCA Victor CR 15	$1,500
	(Promo-only release from the EP for radio only)		
45rpm	**DON'T BE CRUEL** (56)	RCA Victor 6604	$20
45rpm	**DON'T BE CRUEL** (56)	RCA Victor 6604	$50
	(Horizontal lines on label)		
45rpm	**DON'T BE CRUEL** (56)	RCA Victor 6604	$125
	(Price includes picture sleeve, on coated paper)		
45rpm	**DON'T BE CRUEL** (56)	RCA Victor 6604	$200
	(Price includes picture sleeve, on uncoated paper)		
45rpm	**DON'T BE CRUEL** (65)	RCA Victor 0607	$400
	(Price includes picture sleeve)		

45(P)	**DON'T BE CRUEL** (65)	RCA Victor 0607	$100
	(White promo label)		
45rpm	**BLUE SUEDE SHOES** (56)	RCA Victor 6636	$50
45rpm	**BLUE SUEDE SHOWS** (56)	RCA Victor 6636	$75
	(Horizontal lines on label)		
45rpm	**I GOT A WOMAN** (56)	RCA Victor 6637	$50
45rpm	**I GOT A WOMAN** (56)	RCA Victor 6637	$75
	(Horizontal lines on label)		
45rpm	**I'LL NEVER LET YOU GO** (56)	RCA Victor 6638	$50
45rpm	**I'LL NEVER LET YOU GO** (56)	RCA Victor 6638	$75
	(Horizontal lines on label)		
45rpm	**TRYING TO GET TO YOU** (56)	RCA Victor 6639	$50
45rpm	**TRYING TO GET TO YOU** (56)	RCA Victor 6639	$75
	(Horizontal lines on label)		
45rpm	**BLUE MOON** (56)	RCA Victor 6640	$40
45rpm	**BLUE MOON** (56)	RCA Victor 6640	$50
	(Horizontal lines on label)		
45rpm	**MONEY HONEY** (56)	RCA Victor 6641	$40
45rpm	**MONEY HONEY** (56)	RCA Victor 6641	$50
	(Horizontal lines on label)		
45rpm	**SHAKE RATTLE AND ROLL** (56)	RCA Victor 6642	$40
45rpm	**SHAKE RATTLE AND ROLL** (56)	RCA Victor 6642	$50
	(Horizontal lines on label)		
45rpm	**SHAKE RATTLE AND ROLL** (56)	RCA Victor 6642	$150
	(No dog on the label)		
45rpm	**LOVE ME TENDER** (56)	RCA Victor 6643	$20
45rpm	**LOVE ME TENDER** (56)	RCA Victor 6643	$50
	(Horizontal lines on label)		
45rpm	**LOVE ME TENDER** (56)	RCA Victor 6643	$60
	(Price includes black and light pink picture sleeve)		
45rpm	**LOVE ME TENDER** (56)	RCA Victor 6643	$75
	(Price includes black and dark pink picture sleeve)		
45rpm	**LOVE ME TENDER** (56)	RCA Victor 6643	$100
	(Price includes black and green picture sleeve)		
45rpm	**LOVE ME TENDER** (56)	RCA Victor 6643	$175
	(Price includes black and white picture sleeve, the rarest version)		
Flexi	**ELVIS PRESLEY SPEAKS-IN-PERSON** (56)	Rainbow	$150
	(Price is for the flexi-disc only)		
Flexi	**ELVIS PRESLEY SPEAKS-IN-PERSON** (56)	Rainbow	$250
	(Price is for the flexi-disc AND magazine)		
Flexi	**THE TRUTH ABOUT ME** (56)	Rainbow	$150
	(Price is for the flexi-disc only)		
Flexi	**THE TRUTH ABOUT ME** (56)	Rainbow	$250
	(Price is for flexi-disc and magazine)		
Flexi	**THE TRUTH ABOUT ME** (56)	Rainbow 1404	$100
	(Flexi-disc only, from the *Teen Parade* magazine)		
Flexi	**THE TRUTH ABOUT ME** (56)	Rainbow 1404	$175
	(Price is for flexi-disc and *Teen Parade* magazine)		
45rpm	**TOO MUCH** (57)	RCA Victor 6800	$20
45rpm	**TOO MUCH** (57)	RCA Victor 6800	$40
	(Horizontal lines on label)		
45rpm	**TOO MUCH** (57)	RCA Victor 6800	$60
	(Price includes picture sleeve)		
45rpm	**TOO MUCH** (57)	RCA Victor 6800	$125
	(No dog on the label)		
45rpm	**ALL SHOOK UP** (57)	RCA Victor 6870	$20
45rpm	**ALL SHOOK UP** (57)	RCA Victor 6870	$40
	(Horizontal lines on label)		
45rpm	**ALL SHOOK UP** (57)	RCA Victor 6870	$75
	(Price includes picture sleeve)		
45rpm	**ALL SHOOK UP** (65)	RCA Victor 0618	$55
	(Price includes picture sleeve)		
45(P)	**ALL SHOOK UP** (65)	RCA Victor 0618	$100
	(White promo label)		
45rpm	**TEDDY BEAR** (57)	RCA Victor 7000	$15
45rpm	**TEDDY BEAR** (57)	RCA Victor 7000	$40
	(Horizontal lines on label)		
45rpm	**TEDDY BEAR** (57)	RCA Victor 7000	$75
	(Price includes picture sleeve)		
45rpm	**JAILHOUSE ROCK** (57)	RCA Victor 7035	$15
45rpm	**JAILHOUSE ROCK** (57)	RCA Victor 7035	$40
	(Horizontal lines on label)		
45rpm	**JAILHOUSE ROCK** (57)	RCA Victor 7035	$75
	(Price includes picture sleeve)		
45(P)	**JAILHOUSE ROCK** (57)	RCA Victor 7035	$750
	(Very limited promo-only picture sleeve)		
45(P)	**AMAZING WORLD OF SHORTWAVE LISTENING** (57)	Hall'ctrs 4434	$75
	(Contains excerpts from several Presley songs)		

45(P)	**BLUE CHRISTMAS** (57) Promo label	RCA Victor 0808	$1,500
	(Promo-only release for radio stations only, must have 7W-0808 label number)		
45(P)	**BLUE CHRISTMAS** (64) White promo label	RCA Victor 0720	$75
	(Price is for promo record and stock picture sleeve)		
45rpm	**BLUE CHRISTMAS** (64)	RCA Victor 0720	$50
	(Price is for stock record and stock picture sleeve)		
45(P)	**BLUE CHRISTMAS** (65) White promo label	RCA Victor 0647	$50
	(Price is for promo record and stock picture sleeve)		
45rpm	**DON'T** (58)	RCA Victor 7150	$15
45rpm	**DON'T** (58)	RCA Victor 7150	$60
	(Price includes picture sleeve)		
45(P)	**DON'T** (58)	RCA Victor SP45-76	$750
	(White promo label, very limited)		
PS(P)	**DON'T** (58)	RCA Victor SP45-76	$2,000
	(Promo picture sleeve for the record listed above)		
45rpm	**WEAR MY RING AROUND YOUR NECK** (58)	RCA Victor 7240	$15
45rpm	**WEAR MY RING AROUND YOUR NECK** (58)	RCA Victor 7240	$60
	(Price includes picture sleeve)		
45rpm	**HARD HEADED WOMAN** (58)	RCA Victor 7280	$15
45rpm	**HARD HEADED WOMAN** (58)	RCA Victor 7280	$60
	(Price includes picture sleeve)		
45rpm	**ONE NIGHT** (58)	RCA Victor 7410	$15
45rpm	**ONE NIGHT** (58)	RCA Victor 7410	$60
	(Price includes picture sleeve)		
45rpm	**A FOOL SUCH AS I** (59)	RCA Victor 7506	$15
45rpm	**A FOOL SUCH AS I** (59)	RCA Victor 7506	$1,750
	(Price includes picture sleeve, which advertises "Elvis Sails" EP on back)		
45rpm	**A FOOL SUCH AS I** (59)	RCA Victor 7506	$50
	(Price includes picture sleeve, no ad for "Elvis Sails" EP)		
45rpm	**A BIG HUNK O' LOVE** (59)	RCA Victor 7600	$15
45rpm	**A BIG HUNK O' LOVE** (59)	RCA Victor 7600	$50
	(Price includes picture sleeve)		
45rpm	**STUCK ON YOU** (60)	RCA Victor 7740	$12
PS	**STUCK ON YOU** (60)	RCA Victor 7740	$40
	(Picture sleeve)		
45(S)	**STUCK ON YOU** (60) Stereo single	RCA Victor 7740	$400
	(Stereo singles must include the "61"-prefix with the label number)		
45rpm	**IT'S NOW OR NEVER** (60)	RCA Victor 7777	$15
PS	**IT'S NOW OR NEVER** (60)	RCA Victor 7777	$50
	(Picture sleeve)		
45(S)	**IT'S NOW OR NEVER** (60) Stereo single	RCA Victor 7777	$400
45(P)	**IT'S NOW OR NEVER** (61)	U.S. Air Force 125	$250
	(Green promo label)		
45rpm	**ARE YOU LONESOME TONIGHT** (60)	RCA Victor 7810	$12
PS	**ARE YOU LONESOME TONIGHT** (60)	RCA Victor 7810	$40
	(Picture sleeve)		
45(S)	**ARE YOU LONESOME TONIGHT** (60) Stereo single	RCA Victor 7810	$400
45rpm	**SURRENDER** (61)	RCA Victor 7850	$12
PS	**SURRENDER** (61)	RCA Victor 7850	$40
	(Picture sleeve)		
45(S)	**SURRENDER** (61) Stereo single	RCA Victor 7850	$400
	(Price is for the STEREO, 45rpm version)		
33rpm	**SURRENDER** (61) Stereo compact single	RCA Victor 7850	$800
33rpm	**SURRENDER** (61) Stereo compact single	RCA Victor 7850	$3,000
	(This record has a "68" prefix)		
33rpm	**SURRENDER** (61) Compact single	RCA Victor 7850	$500
	(This record has a "37" prefix)		
PS	**SURRENDER** (61) Picture sleeve	RCA Victor 7850	$1,250
	(This picture sleeve has the "37" prefix)		
45(P)	**SURRENDER** (61) Green label	U.S. Air Force 159	$250
	(Public service five-minute program)		
45rpm	**I FEEL SO BAD** (61)	RCA Victor 7880	$12
45rpm	**I FEEL SO BAD** (61)	RCA Victor 7880	$40
	(Price includes picture sleeve)		
33rpm	**I FEEL SO BAD** (61) Compact single	RCA Victor 7880	$500
	(This record has a "37" prefix number)		
PS	**I FEEL SO BAD** (61) Picture sleeve	RCA Victor 7880	$1,500
	(This compact single sleeve has a "37" prefix)		
45rpm	**LITTLE SISTER** (61)	RCA Victor 7908	$12
45rpm	**LITTLE SISTER** (61)	RCA Victor 7908	$40
	(Price includes picture sleeve)		
33rpm	**LITTLE SISTER** (61) Compact single	RCA Victor 7908	$500
	(This record has a "37" prefix number)		
PS	**LITTLE SISTER** (61) Picture sleeve	RCA Victor 7908	$1,500
	(This compact single sleeve has a "37" prefix)		

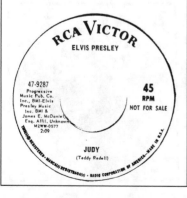

45rpm	**CAN'T HELP FALLING IN LOVE** (61)	RCA Victor 7968	$12
45rpm	**CAN'T HELP FALLING IN LOVE** (61)	RCA Victor 7968	$40
	(Price includes picture sleeve)		
33rpm	**CAN'T HELP FALLING IN LOVE** (61) Compact single	RCA Victor 7968	$1,500
	(This record has a "37" prefix number)		
PS	**CAN'T HELP FALLING IN LOVE** (61) Picture sleeve	RCA Victor 7968	$2,500
	(This compact single sleeve has a "37" prefix)		
45rpm	**GOOD LUCK CHARM** (62)	RCA Victor 7992	$12
45rpm	**GOOD LUCK CHARM** (62)	RCA Victor 7992	$40
	(Price includes picture sleeve)		
33rpm	**GOOD LUCK CHARM** (62) Compact single	RCA Victor 7992	$1,500
	(This record has a "37" prefix number)		
PS	**GOOD LUCK CHARM** (62)	RCA Victor 7992	$3,000
	(Picture sleeve)		
45(P)	**KING OF THE WHOLE WIDE WORLD** (62) Record only	RCA Victor SP 118	$200
	(Promo-only version for radio stations)		
PS(P)	**KING OF THE WHOLE WIDE WORLD** (62) Picture sleeve	RCA Victor SP 118	$300
	(Promo-only sleeve for the record above)		
45rpm	**SHE'S NOT YOU** (62)	RCA Victor 8041	$12
45rpm	**SHE'S NOT YOU** (62)	RCA Victor 8041	$40
	(Price includes picture sleeve)		
45rpm	**RETURN TO SENDER** (63)	RCA Victor 8100	$12
45rpm	**RETURN TO SENDER** (63)	RCA Victor 8100	$40
	(Price includes picture sleeve)		
45rpm	**ONE BROKEN HEART FOR SALE** (63)	RCA Victor 8134	$12
45rpm	**ONE BROKEN HEART FOR SALE** (63)	RCA Victor 8134	$35
	(Price includes picture sleeve)		
45rpm	**DEVIL IN DISGUISE** (63)	RCA Victor 8188	$10
45rpm	**DEVIL IN DISGUISE** (63)	RCA Victor 8188	$30
	(Price includes picture sleeve)		
45rpm	**DEVIL IN DISGUISE** (63) Label error	RCA Victor 8188	$75
	(Flip side, ALONG is in title instead of corrected AROUND)		
45rpm	**BOSSA NOVA BABY** (63)	RCA Victor 8243	$10
45rpm	**BOSSA NOVA BABY** (63)	RCA Victor 8243	$25
	(Price includes picture sleeve)		
45rpm	**KISSIN' COUSINS** (63)	RCA Victor 8307	$10
45rpm	**KISSIN' COUSINS** (63)	RCA Victor 8307	$25
	(Price includes picture sleeve)		
45rpm	**VIVA LAS VEGAS** (64)	RCA Victor 8360	$10
45rpm	**VIVA LAS VEGAS** (64)	RCA Victor 8360	$25
	(Price includes picture sleeve)		
45rpm	**SUCH A NIGHT** (64)	RCA Victor 8400	$10
45rpm	**SUCH A NIGHT** (64)	RCA Victor 8400	$25
	(Price includes picture sleeve)		
45(P)	**SUCH A NIGHT** (64) White promo label	RCA Victor 8400	$3,000
	(Rarest Presley promo of a commercial release, also the first promo since Mystery Train on RCA)		
45rpm	**ASK ME** (64)	RCA Victor 8440	$10
45rpm	**ASK ME** (64)	RCA Victor 8440	$25
	(Price includes picture sleeve)		
45(P)	**ASK ME** (64)	RCA Victor 8440	$50
	(White promo label)		
45rpm	**DO THE CLAM** (64)	RCA Victor 8500	$10
45rpm	**DO THE CLAM** (64)	RCA Victor 8500	$25
	(Price includes picture sleeve)		
45(P)	**DO THE CLAM** (64)	RCA Victor 8500	$50
	(White promo label)		
45(P)	**ROUSTABOUT** (64) White promo label	RCA Victor SP 139	$300
	(Promo-only release for radio stations)		
45(P)	**ROUSTABOUT** (64) Radio ads	Paramount 2414	$1,000
	(Promo-only release for selected theaters)		
45rpm	**EASY QUESTION** (64)	RCA Victor 8585	$10
45rpm	**EASY QUESTION** (64)	RCA Victor 8585	$25
	(Price includes picture sleeve)		
45(P)	**EASY QUESTION** (64)	RCA Victor 8585	$50
	(White promo label)		
45rpm	**I'M YOURS** (65)	RCA Victor 8657	$10
45rpm	**I'M YOURS** (65)	RCA Victor 8657	$25
	(Price includes picture sleeve)		
45(P)	**I'M YOURS** (65)	RCA Victor 8657	$50
	(White promo label)		
45rpm	**TELL ME WHY** (66)	RCA Victor 8740	$10
45rpm	**TELL ME WHY** (66)	RCA Victor 8740	$25
	(Price includes picture sleeve)		
45(P)	**TELL ME WHY** (66)	RCA Victor 8740	$50
	(White promo label)		
45rpm	**FRANKIE AND JOHNNY** (66)	RCA Victor 8780	$10

45rpm	**FRANKIE AND JOHNNY** (66)	RCA Victor 8780	$25
	(Price includes picture sleeve)		
45(P)	**FRANKIE AND JOHNNY** (66)	RCA Victor 8780	$50
	(White promo label)		
45rpm	**LOVE LETTERS** (66)	RCA Victor 8870	$10
45rpm	**LOVE LETTERS** (66)	RCA Victor 8870	$25
	(Price includes picture sleeve)		
45(P)	**LOVE LETTERS** (66)	RCA Victor 8870	$50
	(White promo label)		
45rpm	**SPINOUT** (66)	RCA Victor 8941	$10
45rpm	**SPINOUT** (66)	RCA Victor 8941	$40
	(Price includes picture sleeve)		
45(P)	**SPINOUT** (66)	RCA Victor 8941	$50
	(White promo label)		
45rpm	**IF EVERY DAY WAS LIKE CHRISTMAS** (66)	RCA Victor 8950	$18
45rpm	**IF EVERY DAY WAS LIKE CHRISTMAS** (66)	RCA Victor 8950	$100
	(Price includes picture sleeve)		
45(P)	**IF EVERY DAY WAS LIKE CHRISTMAS** (66)	RCA Victor 8950	$50
	(White promo label)		
45rpm	**JOSHUA FIT THE BATTLE** (66)	RCA Victor 0651	$18
45rpm	**JOSHUA FIT THE BATTLE** (66)	RCA Victor 0651	$150
	(Price includes picture sleeve)		
45rpm	**JOSHUA FIT THE BATTLE** (70)	RCA Victor 0651	$25
	(Red label reissue)		
45(P)	**JOSHUA FIT THE BATTLE** (66)	RCA Victor 0651	$50
	(White promo label)		
45rpm	**MILKY WHITE WAY** (66)	RCA Victor 0652	$18
45rpm	**MILKY WHITE WAY** (66)	RCA Victor 0652	$100
	(Price includes picture sleeve)		
45rpm	**MILKY WHITE WAY** (70)	RCA Victor 0652	$25
	(Red label reissue)		
45(P)	**MILKY WHITE WAY** (66)	RCA Victor 0652	$50
	(White promo label)		
45(P)	**I'LL BE BACK** (67) One-sided 45rpm	RCA Victor 4-834-115	$1,500
	(Alternate take promo only, very rare)		
45rpm	**INDESCRIBABLY BLUE** (67)	RCA Victor 9056	$10
45rpm	**INDESCRIBABLY BLUE** (67)	RCA Victor 9056	$20
	(Price includes picture sleeve)		
45rpm	**INDESCRIBABLY BLUE** (70)	RCA Victor 0659	$15
	(Red label reissue)		
45(P)	**INDESCRIBABLY BLUE** (67)	RCA Victor 9056	$50
	(White promo label)		
45rpm	**LONG LEGGED GIRL** (67)	RCA Victor 9115	$10
45rpm	**LONG LEGGED GIRL** (67)	RCA Victor 9115	$20
	(Price includes picture sleeve)		
45rpm	**LONG LEGGED GIRL** (70)	RCA Victor 0660	$30
	(Rarest of the red label reissues)		
45(P)	**LONG LEGGED GIRL** (67)	RCA Victor 9115	$50
	(White promo label)		
45rpm	**THERE'S ALWAYS ME** (67)	RCA Victor 9287	$10
45rpm	**THERE'S ALWAYS ME** (67)	RCA Victor 9287	$20
	(Price includes picture sleeve)		
45rpm	**THERE'S ALWAYS ME** (70)	RCA Victor 0661	$20
	(Red label reissue)		
45(P)	**THERE'S ALWAYS ME** (67)	RCA Victor 9287	$50
	(White promo label)		
45rpm	**BIG BOSS MAN** (67)	RCA Victor 9341	$10
45rpm	**BIG BOSS MAN** (67)	RCA Victor 9341	$20
	(Price includes picture sleeve)		
45(P)	**BIG BOSS MAN** (67)	RCA Victor 9341	$50
	(White promo label)		
45rpm	**GUITAR MAN** (68)	RCA Victor 9425	$10
45rpm	**GUITAR MAN** (68)	RCA Victor 9425	$20
	(Price includes picture sleeve)		
45(P)	**GUITAR MAN** (68)	RCA Victor 9425	$40
	(Yellow promo label)		
45rpm	**U. S. MALE** (68)	RCA Victor 9465	$10
45rpm	**U. S. MALE** (68)	RCA Victor 9465	$20
	(Price includes picture sleeve)		
45(P)	**U. S. MALE** (68)	RCA Victor 9465	$40
	(Yellow promo label)		
45rpm	**LET YOURSELF GO** (68)	RCA Victor 9547	$10
45rpm	**LET YOURSELF GO** (68)	RCA Victor 9547	$20
	(Price includes picture sleeve)		
45rpm	**LET YOURSELF GO** (70)	RCA Victor 0666	$15
	(Red label reissue)		
45(P)	**LET YOURSELF GO** (68)	RCA Victor 9547	$40
	(Yellow promo label)		

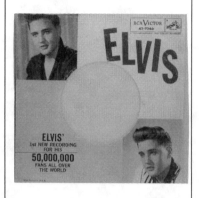

45rpm	**YOU'LL NEVER WALK ALONE** (68)	RCA Victor 9600	$18
45rpm	**YOU'LL NEVER WALK ALONE** (68)	RCA Victor 9600	$150
	(Price includes picture sleeve)		
45rpm	**YOU'LL NEVER WALK ALONE** (70)	RCA Victor 0665	$25
	(Red label reissue)		
45(P)	**YOU'LL NEVER WALK ALONE** (68)	RCA Victor 9600	$40
	(White promo label)		
45rpm	**ALMOST IN LOVE** (68)	RCA Victor 9610	$10
45rpm	**ALMOST IN LOVE** (68)	RCA Victor 9610	$20
	(Price includes picture sleeve)		
45(P)	**ALMOST IN LOVE** (68)	RCA Victor 9610	$40
	(Yellow promo label)		
45rpm	**IF I CAN DREAM** (69)	RCA Victor 9670	$10
45rpm	**IF I CAN DREAM** (69)	RCA Victor 9670	$20
	(Price includes picture sleeve)		
45(P)	**IF I CAN DREAM** (69)	RCA Victor 9670	$30
	(Yellow promo label)		
PS(P)	**IF I CAN DREAM** (69) Picture sleeve	RCA Victor 9670	$300
	(Experimental cardboard picture sleeve)		
45(P)	**HOW GREAT THOU ART** (67)	RCA Victor SP-162	$200
	(Promo record only)		
PS(P)	**HOW GREAT THOU ART** (67)	RCA Victor SP-162	$200
	(Promo sleeve only)		
45rpm	**HOW GREAT THOU ART** (69)	RCA Victor 0130	$20
45rpm	**HOW GREAT THOU ART** (69)	RCA Victor 0130	$150
	(Price includes picture sleeve)		
45rpm	**HOW GREAT THOU ART** (70)	RCA Victor 0670	$25
	(Red label reissue)		
45(P)	**HOW GREAT THOU ART** (69)	RCA Victor 0130	$50
	(Yellow promo label)		
45rpm	**MEMORIES** (69)	RCA Victor 9731	$10
45rpm	**MEMORIES** (69)	RCA Victor 9731	$20
	(Price includes picture sleeve)		
45(P)	**MEMORIES** (69)	RCA Victor 9731	$30
	(Yellow promo label)		
45rpm	**IN THE GHETTO** (69)	RCA Victor 9741	$10
45rpm	**IN THE GHETTO** (69)	RCA Victor 9741	$20
	(Price includes picture sleeve)		
45(P)	**IN THE GHETTO** (60)	RCA Victor 9741	$30
	(Yellow promo label)		
45rpm	**CLEAN UP YOUR OWN BACK YARD** (69)	RCA Victor 9747	$10
45rpm	**CLEAN UP YOUR OWN BACK YARD** (69)	RCA Victor 9747	$20
	(Price includes picture sleeve)		
45(P)	**CLEAN UP YOUR OWN BACK YARD** (69)	RCA Victor 9747	$30
	(Yellow promo label)		
45rpm	**SUSPICIOUS MINDS** (69)	RCA Victor 9764	$10
45rpm	**SUSPICIOUS MINDS** (69)	RCA Victor 9764	$18
	(Price includes picture sleeve)		
45(P)	**SUSPICIOUS MINDS** (69)	RCA Victor 9764	$30
	(Yellow promo label)		
45rpm	**DON'T CRY DADDY** (69)	RCA Victor 9768	$10
45rpm	**DON'T CRY DADDY** (69)	RCA Victor 9768	$18
	(Price includes picture sleeve)		
45(P)	**DON'T CRY DADDY** (69)	RCA Victor 9768	$30
	(Yellow promo label)		
45rpm	**KENTUCKY RAIN** (70)	RCA Victor 9791	$10
45rpm	**KENTUCKY RAIN** (70)	RCA Victor 9791	$18
	(Price includes picture sleeve)		
45(P)	**KENTUCKY RAIN** (70)	RCA Victor 9791	$25
	(Yellow promo label)		
45rpm	**THE WONDER OF YOU** (70)	RCA Victor 9835	$15
	(Price includes picture sleeve)		
45(P)	**THE WONDER OF YOU** (70)	RCA Victor 9835	$25
	(Yellow promo label)		
45rpm	**I'VE LOST YOU** (70)	RCA Victor 9873	$15
	(Price includes picture sleeve)		
45(P)	**I'VE LOST YOU** (70)	RCA Victor 9873	$20
	(Yellow promo label)		
45rpm	**YOU DON'T HAVE TO SAY YOU LOVE ME** (70)	RCA Victor 9916	$15
	(Price includes picture sleeve)		
45(P)	**YOU DON'T HAVE TO SAY YOU LOVE ME** (70)	RCA Victor 9916	$20
	(Yellow promo label)		
45rpm	**RAGS TO RICHES** (71)	RCA Victor 9980	$20
	(Price includes picture sleeve)		
45(P)	**RAGS TO RICHES** (71)	RCA Victor 9980	$25
	(Yellow promo label)		
45rpm	**LIFE** (71)	RCA Victor 9985	$18
	(Price includes picture sleeve)		

45(P)	**LIFE** (71)	RCA Victor 9985	$25
	(Yellow promo label)		
45rpm	**I'M LEAVIN'** (71)	RCA Victor 9998	$15
	(Price includes picture sleeve)		
45(P)	**I'M LEAVIN'** (71)	RCA Victor 9998	$20
	(Yellow promo label)		
45rpm	**IT'S ONLY LOVE** (71)	RCA Victor 1017	$15
	(Price includes picture sleeve)		
45(P)	**IT'S ONLY LOVE** (71)	RCA Victor 1017	$20
	(Yellow promo label)		
45rpm	**MERRY CHRISTMAS BABY** (71)	RCA Victor 0572	$15
45rpm	**MERRY CHRISTMAS BABY** (71)	RCA Victor 0572	$40
	(Price includes picture sleeve)		
45(P)	**MERRY CHRISTMAS BABY** (71)	RCA Victor 0572	$50
	(Yellow promo label)		
45rpm	**UNTIL IT'S TIME FOR YOU TO GO** (71)	RCA Victor 0619	$20
	(Price includes picture sleeve)		
45(P)	**UNTIL IT'S TIME FOR YOU TO GO** (71)	RCA Victor 0619	$30
	(Promo label)		
45(P)	**THAT'S THE WAY IT IS** (71)	MGM WLC-448	$500
	(White label one-sided movie spots)		
45rpm	**HE TOUCHED ME** (72)	RCA Victor 0651	$18
45rpm	**HE TOUCHED ME** (72)	RCA Victor 0651	$100
	(Price includes picture sleeve)		
45(P)	**HE TOUCHED ME** (72)	RCA Victor 0651	$50
	(Yellow promo label)		
45rpm	**HE TOUCHED ME** (72) Pressing error	RCA Victor 0651	$75
	(Plays at about 35rpm, to identify you'll have to play the record)		
45rpm	**AN AMERICAN TRILOGY** (72)	RCA Victor 0672	$12
45rpm	**AN AMERICAN TRILOGY** (72)	RCA Victor 0672	$50
	(Price includes picture sleeve)		
45(P)	**AN AMERICAN TRILOGY** (72)	RCA Victor 0672	$30
	(Yellow promo label)		
45rpm	**BURNING LOVE** (72) Gray label	RCA Victor 0769	$150
45rpm	**BURNING LOVE** (72) Orange label	RCA Victor 0769	$15
	(Price includes picture sleeve)		
45(P)	**BURNING LOVE** (72)	RCA Victor 0769	$15
	(Cream-colored promo label)		
45rpm	**SEPARATE WAYS** (72)	RCA Victor 0815	$15
	(Price includes picture sleeve)		
45(P)	**SEPARATE WAYS** (72)	RCA Victor 0815	$15
	(Cream-colored promo label)		
45rpm	**STEAMROLLER BLUES** (73)	RCA Victor 0910	$15
	(Price includes picture sleeve)		
45(P)	**STEAMROLLER BLUES** (73)	RCA Victor 0910	$15
	(Cream-colored promo label)		
45rpm	**RAISED ON ROCK** (73)	RCA Victor 0088	$15
	(Price includes picture sleeve)		
45(P)	**RAISED ON ROCK** (73)	RCA Victor 0088	$15
	(Cream-colored promo label)		
45rpm	**I'VE GOT A THING ABOUT YOU BABY** (74)	RCA Victor 0196	$15
	(Price includes picture sleeve)		
45(P)	**I'VE GOT A THING ABOUT YOU BABY** (74)	RCA Victor 0196	$15
	(Cream-colored promo label)		
45rpm	**IF YOU TALK IN YOUR SLEEP** (74)	RCA Victor 0280	$15
	(Price includes picture sleeve)		
45(P)	**IF YOU TALK IN YOUR SLEEP** (74)	RCA Victor 0280	$15
	(Cream-colored promo label)		
45rpm	**PROMISED LAND** (74) Brown label	RCA Victor 10074	$30
	(Record only)		
45rpm	**PROMISED LAND** (74) Gray label	RCA Victor 10074	$12
	(Record only)		
45rpm	**PROMISED LAND** (74) Orange label	RCA Victor 10074	$15
	(Price includes picture sleeve)		
45(P)	**PROMISED LAND** (74)	RCA Victor 10074	$15
	(Cream-colored promo label)		
45rpm	**MY BOY** (75) Brown or orange label	RCA Victor 10191	$15
	(Price includes picture sleeve)		
45(P)	**MY BOY** (75)	RCA Victor 10191	$15
	(Cream-colored promo label)		
45rpm	**T-R-O-U-B-L-E** (75) Brown label	RCA Victor 10278	$10
	(Record only)		
45rpm	**T-R-O-U-B-L-E** (75) Orange label	RCA Victor 10278	$15
	(Price includes picture sleeve)		
45(P)	**T-R-O-U-B-L-E** (75)	RCA Victor 10278	$15
	(Cream-colored promo label)		
45rpm	**BRINGIN' IT BACK** (75) Orange label	RCA Victor 10401	$75
	(Record only)		

45rpm	**BRINGIN' IT BACK** (75) Brown label (Price includes picture sleeve)	RCA Victor 10401	$12
45(P)	**BRINGIN' IT BACK** (75) (Cream-colored promo label)	RCA Victor 10401	$15
45rpm	**HURT** (76) Black label (Record only)	RCA Victor 10601	$100
45rpm	**HURT** (76) Brown label (Price includes picture sleeve)	RCA Victor 10601	$12
45(P)	**HURT** (76) Cream-colored promo label	RCA Victor 10601	$15
45rpm	**MOODY BLUE** (77) Black vinyl (Price includes picture sleeve)	RCA Victor 10857	$12
45(P)	**MOODY BLUE** (77) (Cream-colored promo label)	RCA Victor 10857	$15
45(P)	**MOODY BLUE** (77) (Red vinyl)	RCA Victor 10857	$1,250
45(P)	**MOODY BLUE** (77) (White vinyl)	RCA Victor 10857	$1,250
45(P)	**MOODY BLUE** (77) (Blue vinyl)	RCA Victor 10857	$1,250
45(P)	**MOODY BLUE** (77) (Green vinyl)	RCA Victor 10857	$1,250
45(P)	**MOODY BLUE** (77) (Gold vinyl)	RCA Victor 10857	$1,250
45(P)	**MOODY BLUE** (77) (Swirl color vinyl)	RCA Victor 10857	$1,500
45(P)	**MOODY BLUE** (77) (Multicolored vinyl)	RCA Victor 10857	$2,000
45(P)	**LET ME BE THERE** (77) Promo label (Promo-only release for radio stations)	RCA Victor 10951	$300
45rpm	**WAY DOWN** (77) (Price includes picture sleeve)	RCA Victor 10998	$12
45(P)	**WAY DOWN** (77) (White promo label)	RCA Victor 10998	$150
45(P)	**WAY DOWN** (77) (Cream-colored promo label)	RCA Victor 10998	$15
15-45s	**FIFTEEN GOLDEN RECORDS** (77) Box set (Fifteen singles with picture sleeves, price is for all fifteen records and sleeves)	RCA Victor 11301/+	$50
10-45s	**TWENTY GOLDEN HITS** (77) Box set (Ten singles with picture sleeves, price is for all ten records and sleeves)	RCA Victor 11340/+	$60
45rpm	**MY WAY/AMERICA** (77) (Price includes picture sleeve)	RCA Victor 11165	$12
45rpm	**MY WAY/AMERICA** (77) (Cream-colored promo label)	RCA Victor 11165	$10
45rpm	**MY WAY/AMERICA THE BEAUTIFUL** (77) Record only (Error appears on record label)	RCA Victor 11165	$15
45rpm	**MY WAY/AMERICA THE BEAUTIFUL** (77) Sleeve only	RCA Victor 11165	$75
45rpm	**UNCHAINED MELODY** (78) (Price includes picture sleeve)	RCA Victor 11212	$12
45(P)	**UNCHAINED MELODY** (78) (Cream-colored promo label)	RCA Victor 11212	$10
45rpm	**TEDDY BEAR** (78) (Price includes picture sleeve)	RCA Victor 11320	$12
45(P)	**TEDDY BEAR** (78) (Cream-colored promo label)	RCA Victor 11320	$10
45rpm	**ARE YOU SINCERE** (78) (Price includes picture sleeve)	RCA Victor 11533	$12
45(P)	**ARE YOU SINCERE** (78) (Cream-colored promo label)	RCA Victor 11533	$10
45rpm	**THERE'S A HONKY TONK ANGEL** (79) (Price includes picture sleeve)	RCA Victor 11679	$10
45(P)	**THERE'S A HONKY TONK ANGEL** (79) (Cream-colored promo label)	RCA Victor 11679	$10
45(P)	**WHAT'S IT ALL ABOUT** (77) Presbyterian Church (Music profile plus interview, featured song is "Life")	W. I. A. A. 78	$50
45(P)	**WHAT'S IT ALL ABOUT** (80) Presbyterian Church (Part 1 and part 2, shows 555 and 556, profile and interview)	W. I. A. A. 1840	$75
45(P)	**WHAT'S IT ALL ABOUT** (80) Presbyterian Church (Part 1 and part 2, shows 633 and 634, profile and interview)	W. I. A. A. 3025	$75
Flexi	**THE KING IS DEAD** (78) (Flexi plastic soundsheet)	Evatone 52578	$125
45rpm	**GUITAR MAN** (81) (Price includes picture sleeve)	RCA Victor 12158	$10
45(P)	**GUITAR MAN** (81) (Cream-colored promo label)	RCA Victor 12158	$10
45(P)	**GUITAR MAN** (81) (Red vinyl)	RCA Victor 12158	$200

45rpm	**LOVIN' ARMS** (81)	RCA Victor 12205	$10
	(Price includes picture sleeve)		
45(P)	**LOVIN' ARMS** (81)	RCA Victor 12205	$10
	(Cream-colored promo label)		
45(P)	**LOVIN' ARMS** (81)	RCA Victor 12205	$225
	(Yellow promo label, green vinyl)		
45rpm	**THERE GOES MY EVERYTHING** (82)	RCA Victor 13058	$10
	(Price includes picture sleeve)		
45(P)	**THERE GOES MY EVERYTHING** (82)	RCA Victor 13058	$10
	(Cream-colored promo label)		
45rpm	**THE IMPOSSIBLE DREAM** (82)	RCA Victor 13302	$10
	(Price includes picture sleeve)		
45(P)	**THE IMPOSSIBLE DREAM** (82)	RCA Victor 13302	$10
	(Cream-colored promo label)		
45(P)	**THE IMPOSSIBLE DREAM** (82)	RCA Victor 13302	$100
	(Gold vinyl, giveaway item)		
PS(P)	**THE IMPOSSIBLE DREAM** (82) Picture sleeve	RCA Victor 13302	$100
	(Picture sleeve for the giveaway record above)		
45rpm	**THE ELVIS MEDLEY** (82)	RCA Victor 13351	$15
	(Price includes picture sleeve)		
45(P)	**THE ELVIS MEDLEY** (82)	RCA Victor 13351	$200
	(Gold promo label, gold vinyl)		
45(P)	**THE ELVIS MEDLEY** (82)	RCA Victor 13351	$10
	(Cream-colored promo label)		
45rpm	**I WAS THE ONE** (83)	RCA Victor 13500	$10
	(Price includes picture sleeve)		
45(P)	**I WAS THE ONE** (83)	RCA Victor 13500	$200
	(Yellow promo label, gold vinyl)		
45(P)	**I WAS THE ONE** (83)	RCA Victor 13500	$10
	(Cream-colored, promo label)		
45rpm	**LITTLE SISTER** (83)	RCA Victor 13547	$30
	(Price includes picture sleeve)		
45(P)	**LITTLE SISTER** (83)	RCA Victor 13547	$150
	(Blue promo label, blue vinyl)		
45(P)	**LITTLE SISTER** (83)	RCA Victor 13547	$10
	(Cream-colored promo label)		
12"(P)	**LITTLE SISTER** (83)	RCA Victor 0517	$150
	(Promo-only twelve-inch single)		
45(P)	**BABY, LET'S PLAY HOUSE** (84)	RCA Victor 13875	$200
	(Special release, yellow vinyl)		
PS(P)	**BABY, LETS PLAY HOUSE** (84) Picture sleeve	RCA Victor 13875	$40
	(Picture sleeve for the record above)		
45rpm	**BLUE SUEDE SHOES** (85) Blue vinyl	RCA Victor 13929	$15
	(Price includes picture sleeve)		
45(P)	**BLUE SUEDE SHOES** (85)	RCA Victor 13929	$20
	(Gold promo label, blue vinyl)		
45rpm	**ALWAYS ON MY MIND** (85) Purple vinyl	RCA Victor 14090	$15
	(Price includes picture sleeve)		
45(P)	**ALWAYS ON MY MIND** (85)	RCA Victor 14090	$20
	(Gold promo label, purple vinyl)		
45rpm	**MERRY CHRISTMAS BABY** (85) Green vinyl	RCA Victor 14237	$15
	(Price includes picture sleeve)		
45(P)	**MERRY CHRISTMAS BABY** (85)	RCA Victor 14237	$25
	(Gold promo label, green vinyl)		
45rpm	**HEARTBREAK HOTEL** (88)	RCA Victor 8760	$10
	(Price includes picture sleeve)		
45(P)	**HEARTBREAK HOTEL** (88) Presley/David Keith	RCA Victor 8760	$15
	(Elvis version on "A" side, Keith version on flip)		
45(P)	**HEARTBREAK HOTEL** (88) David Keith	RCA Victor 8760	$10
	(Both sides by David Keith)		
PS(P)	**HEARTBREAK HOTEL** (88) Promo picture sleeve	RCA Victor 8760	$50
	(Sleeve used for either promo version)		
CD(P)	**MY HAPPINESS** (94)	RCA Victor	$40
	(Promo-only release on CD)		

-EPs-

EP	**ELVIS PRESLEY** (56) Black label, dog on top	RCA Victor 747	$60
	(RCA Victor EPs all have the EPA prefix)		
PS	**ELVIS PRESLEY** (56)	RCA Victor 747	$450
	(Limited paper sleeve)		
EP	**ELVIS PRESLEY** (56) Black label	RCA Victor 747	$175
	(No dog on label)		
EP	**ELVIS PRESLEY** (65) Black label, dog on label	RCA Victor 747	$40
EP	**ELVIS PRESLEY** (68) Orange label	RCA Victor 747	$45
2EP	**ELVIS PRESLEY** (56) No horizontal lines on label	RCA Victor 1254	$250
	(Dog on label, several varieties of back covers, all about the same value)		
2EP	**ELVIS PRESLEY** (56) With horizontal lines on labels	RCA Victor 1254	$275
	(Dog on label)		

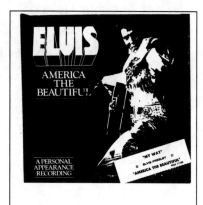

2EP	**ELVIS PRESLEY** (56) NO DOG on label	RCA Victor 1254	$350
	(These 1254 double-EP sets carry the EPB prefix)		
PS(P)	**MOST TALKED ABOUT NEW PERSONALITY** (56)	RCA Victor 1254	$3,000
	(Promo-only paper picture sleeve, single pocket for both records)		
2EP(P)	**ELVIS PRESLEY/JAYE P. MORGAN** (56)	RCA Victor 992/689	$4,000
	(Promotional item for in-store play)		
EP(P)	**DEALER'S PREVUE** (56) Two cuts by Presley	RCA Victor 7-2	$600
	(White promo label)		
PS(P)	**DEALER'S PREVUE** (56) Envelope	RCA Victor 7-2	$300
	(Also known as RCA Victor SDS-39)		
EP(P)	**SAVE-ON-RECORDS** (June 56) Sampler	RCA Victor 7-27	$150
	(RCA promo label)		
PS(P)	**SAVE-ON-RECORDS** (56) Paper sleeve	RCA Victor 7-27	$400
	(Promo-only sleeve)		
EP(P)	**OLD SHEP** (56) Single disc	RCA Victor 15	$1,500
	(Not to be confused with EP set 15, promo label)		
EP(P)	**PERFECT FOR PARTIES** (56) With horizontal lines	RCA Victor 37	$150
	(Black promo label)		
EP(P)	**PERFECT FOR PARTIES** (56) No horizontal lines	RCA Victor 37	$150
	(Black promo label)		
PS(P)	**PERFECT FOR PARTIES** (56) Paper sleeve	RCA Victor 37	$100
	(Promo picture sleeve)		
10EP(P)	**(EP BOX SET)** (56) Ten EPs	RCA Victor 15	$1,750
	(One of the EPs is Presley, price is for the entire set plus box, black labels)		
10EP(P)	**(EP BOX SET)** (56) Ten EPs	RCA Victor 15	$1,500
	(Gray labels)		
EP(P)	**(EP BOX SET)** (56) Elvis disc only	RCA Victor 9089 (15)	$900
	(Black label, dog on top)		
EP(P)	**(EP BOX SET)** (56) Elvis disc only	RCA Victor 9089 (15)	$750
	(Gray label, dog on top)		
8EP(P)	**SOUND OF LEADERSHIP** (56) Eight EPs	RCA Victor 19	$1,600
	(One of the EPs by Presley)		
EP(P)	**SOUND OF LEADERSHIP** (56) Elvis disc only	RCA Victor 9113 (19)	$750
	(Black label, dog on top)		
2EP(P)	**(SPD 22)** Giveaway with phonograph purchase	RCA Victor SPD 22	$1,500
	(Black label, phonograph was a $33 RCA Victrola, light pink cover)		
2EP(P)	**(SPD 22)** Giveaway	RCA Victor SPD 22	$1,500
	(Dark pink cover)		
3EP(P)	**(SPD 23)** Giveaway with phonograph purchase	RCA Victor SPD 23	$4,000
	(Black label, phonograph was a $48 RCA Victrola)		
10EP	**GREAT COUNTRY WESTERN HITS** (56) Ten-EP set	RCA Victor 26	$850
	(One Presley disc, price is for 10EP set)		
EP(P)	**GREAT COUNTRY WESTERN HITS** (56) Elvis disc only	RCA Victor 9141 (260)	$200
	(Black label)		
EP(P)	**LOVE ME TENDER/ANY WAY YOU WANT ME** (56)	RCA Victor DJ-7	$300
	(Two songs by another artist on flip side, white promo label)		
EP(P)	**TOO MUCH/PLAYING FOR KEEPS** (56)	RCA Victor DJ-56	$300
	(Two songs by another artist on flip side, white promo label)		
EP(P)	**TV GUIDE PRESENTS ELVIS PRESLEY** (56) Blue label	RCA Victor 8705	$1,500
	(Issued without a picture sleeve)		
EP(P)	**TV GUIDE PRESENTS ELVIS PRESLEY** (56) White label	RCA Victor 8705	$1,200
	(Issued without a picture sleeve)		
EP(P)	**TV GUIDE PRESENTS ELVIS PRESLEY** (56) With insert	RCA Victor 8705	$1,750
	(Either white or blue label record)		
EP(P)	**SAMPLER** (56) Includes Elvis track	RCA Victor 61	$1,000
	(Black promo label)		
EP	**HEARTBREAK HOTEL** (56) Black label, dog on top	RCA Victor 821	$60
EP	**HEARTBREAK HOTEL** (56) Black label, NO DOG on label	RCA Victor 821	$175
EP	**HEARTBREAK HOTEL** (65) Black label, dog on side	RCA Victor 821	$40
EP	**HEARTBREAK HOTEL** (68) Orange label	RCA Victor 821	$45
EP	**ELVIS PRESLEY** (56) Black label, dog on top	RCA Victor 830	$60
EP	**ELVIS PRESLEY** (56) Black label, NO DOG	RCA Victor 830	$150
EP	**ELVIS PRESLEY** (65) Black dog, dog on side	RCA Victor 830	$40
EP	**ELVIS PRESLEY** (68) Orange label	RCA Victor 830	$45
EP	**THE REAL ELVIS** (56) Black label, dog on top	RCA Victor 940	$60
EP	**THE REAL ELVIS** (56) Black label, NO DOG	RCA Victor 940	$175
EP	**THE REAL ELVIS** (59) Gold Standard, dog on top	RCA Victor 5120	$60
EP	**THE REAL ELVIS** (59) Gold Standard, MAROON label	RCA Victor 5120	$250
EP	**THE REAL ELVIS** (65) Gold Standard, dog on side	RCA Victor 5120	$40
EP	**THE REAL ELVIS** (68) Gold Standard, orange label	RCA Victor 5120	$45
EP	**ANY WAY YOU WANT ME** (56) Black label, dog on top	RCA Victor 965	$60
EP	**ANY WAY YOU WANT ME** (56) Black label, NO DOG	RCA Victor 965	$175
EP	**ANY WAY YOU WANT ME** (65) Black label, dog on side	RCA Victor 965	$40
EP	**ANY WAY YOU WANT ME** (68) Orange label	RCA Victor 965	$45
EP	**ELVIS VOL. 1** (56) Black label, dog on top	RCA Victor 992	$60
EP	**ELVIS VOL. 1** (56) Black label, NO DOG	RCA Victor 992	$175

EP	**ELVIS VOL. 1** (65) Black label, dog on side	RCA Victor 992	$40
EP	**ELVIS VOL. 1** (68) Orange label	RCA Victor 992	$45
EP	**ELVIS VOL. 2** (56) Black label, dog on top	RCA Victor 993	$60
EP	**ELVIS VOL. 2** (56) Black label, NO DOG	RCA Victor 993	$175
EP	**ELVIS VOL. 2** (65) Black label, dog on side	RCA Victor 993	$40
EP	**ELVIS VOL. 2** (68) Orange label	RCA Victor 993	$45
EP	**STRICTLY ELVIS** (56) Black label, dog on top	RCA Victor 994	$60
EP	**STRICTLY ELVIS** (56) Black label, NO DOG	RCA Victor 994	$175
EP	**STRICTLY ELVIS** (65) Black label, dog on side	RCA Victor 994	$40
EP	**STRICTLY ELVIS** (68) Orange label	RCA Victor 994	$45
	(Some of the 992, 993, and 994 EP covers were printed without the black strip across the top, these were for the later releases)		
EP	**LOVE ME TENDER** (56) Black label, dog on top	RCA Victor 4006	$60
EP	**LOVE ME TENDER** (56) Black label, NO DOG	RCA Victor 4006	$150
EP	**LOVE ME TENDER** (65) Black label, dog on side	RCA Victor 4006	$40
EP	**LOVE ME TENDER** (68) Orange label	RCA Victor 4006	$45
EP	**LOVING YOU VOL. 1** (57) Black label, dog on top	RCA Victor 1-1515	$50
EP	**LOVING YOU VOL. 1** (65) Black label, dog on side	RCA Victor 1-1515	$40
EP	**LOVING YOU VOL. 1** (68) Orange label	RCA Victor 1-1515	$45
EP	**LOVING YOU VOL. 2** (57) Black label, dog on top	RCA Victor 2-1515	$50
EP	**LOVING YOU VOL. 2** (65) Black label, dog on side	RCA Victor 2-1515	$40
EP	**LOVING YOU VOL. 2** (68) Orange label	RCA Victor 2-1515	$45
EP	**JUST FOR YOU** (57) Black label, dog on top	RCA Victor 4041	$60
EP	**JUST FOR YOU** (57) Black label, NO DOG on label	RCA Victor 4041	$150
EP	**JUST FOR YOU** (65) Black label, dog on side	RCA Victor 4041	$40
EP	**JUST FOR YOU** (68) Orange label	RCA Victor 4041	$45
EP	**PEACE IN THE VALLEY** (57) Black label, dog on top	RCA Victor 4054	$60
EP	**PEACE IN THE VALLEY** (59) Gold Standard, black, dog on top	RCA Victor 5121	$50
EP	**PEACE IN THE VALLEY** (59) Gold Standard, MAROON label	RCA Victor 5121	$275
EP	**PEACE IN THE VALLEY** (65) Gold Standard, black, dog on side	RCA Victor 5121	$40
EP	**PEACE IN THE VALLEY** (68) Gold Standard, orange label	RCA Victor 5121	$45
EP	**JAILHOUSE ROCK** (57) Black label, dog on top	RCA Victor 4114	$60
EP	**JAILHOUSE ROCK** (65) Black label, dog on side	RCA Victor 4114	$40
EP	**JAILHOUSE ROCK** (68) Orange label	RCA Victor 4114	$45
EP	**KING CREOLE** (58) Black label, dog on top	RCA Victor 4319	$50
EP	**KING CREOLE** (59) Gold Standard, black, dog on top	RCA Victor 5122	$50
EP	**KING CREOLE** (59) Gold Standard, MAROON label	RCA Victor 5122	$275
EP	**KING CREOLE** (65) Gold Standard, black, dog on side	RCA Victor 5122	$40
EP	**KING CREOLE** (68) Gold Standard, orange label	RCA Victor 5122	$45
EP	**KING CREOLE VOL. 2** (58) Black label, dog on top	RCA Victor 4321	$50
EP	**KING CREOLE VOL. 2** (65) Black label, dog on side	RCA Victor 4321	$40
EP	**KING CREOLE VOL. 2** (68) Orange label	RCA Victor 4321	$45
EP	**ELVIS SAILS** (58) Black label, dog on top	RCA Victor 4325	$75
EP	**ELVIS SAILS** (59) Gold Standard, black, dog on top	RCA Victor 5157	$125
EP	**ELVIS SAILS** (65) Gold Standard, black, dog on side	RCA Victor 5157	$50
EP	**ELVIS SAILS** (68) Orange label	RCA Victor 5157	$50
EP	**CHRISTMAS WITH ELVIS** (58) Black label, dog on top	RCA Victor 4340	$100
EP	**CHRISTMAS WITH ELVIS** (65) Black label, dog on side	RCA Victor 4340	$40
EP	**CHRISTMAS WITH ELVIS** (68) Orange label	RCA Victor 4340	$75
EP	**A TOUCH OF GOLD** (59) Black label, dog on top	RCA Victor 5088	$75
EP	**A TOUCH OF GOLD** (59) MAROON label	RCA Victor 5088	$300
EP	**A TOUCH OF GOLD** (66) Black label, dog on side	RCA Victor 5088	$50
EP	**A TOUCH OF GOLD** (69) Orange label	RCA Victor 5088	$75
EP	**A TOUCH OF GOLD VOL. II** (59) Black label, dog on top	RCA Victor 5101	$75
EP	**A TOUCH OF GOLD VOL. II** (59) MAROON label	RCA Victor 5101	$300
EP	**A TOUCH OF GOLD VOL. II** (66) Black label, dog on side	RCA Victor 5101	$50
EP	**A TOUCH OF GOLD VOL. II** (68) Orange label	RCA Victor 5101	$75
EP	**A TOUCH OF GOLD VOL. III** (60) Black label, dog on top	RCA Victor 5141	$75
EP	**A TOUCH OF GOLD VOL. III** (60) MAROON label	RCA Victor 5141	$300
EP	**A TOUCH OF GOLD VOL. III** (66) Black label, dog on side	RCA Victor 5141	$50
EP	**A TOUCH OF GOLD VOL. III** (69) Orange label	RCA Victor 5141	$75
EP	**ELVIS BY REQUEST** (61) Compact-33	RCA Victor 128	$75
	(Because of small hole, this EP was commonly used by jukebox vendors, has LPC prefix)		
EP	**FOLLOW THAT DREAM** (62) Black label, dog on top	RCA Victor 4368	$50
PS(P)	**FOLLOW THAT DREAM** (62) Paper sleeve	RCA Victor 4368	$200
	(Paper picture sleeve used on some stock EPs and for the promo listed below)		
EP(P)	**FOLLOW THAT DREAM** (62) Promo label	RCA Victor 4368	$200
	(Promo version for radio, label must read "Not for Sale")		
EP	**FOLLOW THAT DREAM** (66) Black label, dog on side)	RCA Victor 4368	$40
EP	**FOLLOW THAT DREAM** (68) Orange label	RCA Victor 4368	$65
EP	**KID GALAHAD** (62) Black label, dog on top	RCA Victor 4371	$50
EP	**KID GALAHAD** (65) Black label, dog on side	RCA Victor 4371	$40
EP	**KID GALAHAD** (68) Orange label	RCA Victor 4371	$65
EP(P)	**RCA FAMILY RECORD CENTER** (62)	RCA Victor 121	$1,000
	(Excerpts from several songs including Presley, promo-only sampler)		

EP	**VIVA LAS VEGAS** (64) Black label, dog on top	RCA Victor 4382	$50
EP	**VIVA LAS VEGAS** (65) Black label, dog on side	RCA Victor 4382	$40
EP	**VIVA LAS VEGAS** (68) Orange label	RCA Victor 4382	$65
EP	**ELVIS SINGS CHRISTMAS SONGS** (65) Black label, dog on top	RCA Victor 4108	$50
EP	**ELVIS SINGS CHRISTMAS SONGS** (68) Black label, dog on side	RCA Victor 4108	$40
EP	**ELVIS SINGS CHRISTMAS SONGS** (68) Orange label	RCA Victor 4108	$65
EP	**TICKLE ME** (65) Black label, dog on side	RCA Victor 4383	$40
EP	**TICKLE ME** (68) Orange label	RCA Victor 4383	$60
EP	**EASY COME, EASY GO** (67) Black label, dog on side	RCA Victor 4387	$50
EP(P)	**EASY COME, EASY GO** (67) White promo label (The only white promo label EP of a stock release, issued without a cover)	RCA Victor 4387	$100
EP	**EASY COME, EASY GO** (68) Orange label	RCA Victor 4387	$60
EP(JB)	**ALOHA FROM HAWAII VIA SATELLITE** (73) Jukebox LLP (With hard cover, price includes title strips)	RCA Victor 2006	$100
EP(P)	**TUPPERWARE'S HIT PARADE** (73) Sampler (Tupperware sales tool, includes Presley song)	Tupperware 11973	$50
EP(P)	**THE ELVIS HOUR** (86) Demo disc EP (Seven-inch sample of promo radio show, there are two versions, same value)	Creative Radio	$40

-ads-

16"(P)	**MARCH OF DIMES** (56) Public service spots (Sixteen-inch 33rpm disc, spots by twenty artists including one by Presley)	March of Dimes 0653	$2,500
16"(P)	**MARCH OF DIMES** (56) Public service interviews (Sixteen-inch 33rpm disc, interviews and songs by six artists including Presley)	March of Dimes 0657	$2,500
16"(P)	**ARMED FORCES RADIO & TELEVISION SERVICE** (57) (Seven songs from the Christmas LP)	AFRTS Service	$500
16"(P)	**ARMED FORCES RADIO & TELEVISION SERVICE** (59) (Two Elvis songs on the "A" side)	AFRTS Service 6743	$500

-early promo samplers-

10"LP	**E-Z COUNTRY PROGRAMMING #2** (55) Various artists (Promo-only sampler including Presley)	RCA Victor 0108	$300
10"LP	**E-Z POP PROGRAMMING #5** (55) Various artists (Promo-only sampler including Presley)	RCA Victor 9681	$300
10"LP	**E-Z PROGRAMMING #3** (56) Various artists (Promo-only sampler including Presley)	RCA Victor 0199	$250
10"LP	**E-Z PROGRAMMING #6** (56) Various artists (Promo-only sampler including Presley)	RCA Victor 0197	$250
LP(P)	**(SP-33-4)** (Jul 56) Various artists (Promo-only sampler of twenty-one artists including Elvis Presley)	RCA Victor SP-33-4	$800
LP(P)	**RCA VICTROLA SPOTS** (56) Radio ads (One-sided disc advertising SPD 22, SPD 23)	RCA Victor 401	$500
LP(P)	**JAILHOUSE ROCK INTERVIEW** (57) (Issued in plain cardboard jacket)	MGM (No number)	$1,000
LP(P)	**(SP-33-10)** (Aug 58) Various artists (Promo-only sampler including Presley)	RCA Victor SP-33-10	$750
LP(P)	**(SP-33-27)** (Aug 59) Various artists (Promo-only sampler of thirteen artists including Elvis Presley)	RCA Victor SP-33-27	$650
LP(P)	**(SP-33-54)** (Oct 59) Various artists (Promo-only sampler including Presley)	RCA Victor SP-33-54	$500
LP(P)	**(SP-33-59)** (59) Various artists including Presley (Promo-only sampler)	RCA Victor SP-33-59	$450
LP(P)	**(SP-33-66)** (Dec 59) Various artists (Promo-only Christmas sampler including one Presley cut)	RCA Victor SP-33-66	$500
PS(P)	**(SP-33-66)** (Dec 59) Paper sleeve (Promo-only paper sleeve for record above, Santa is pictured at a console)	RCA Victor SP-33-66	$500
LP(P)	**(SPS-33-96)** (Oct 60) Various artists (Promo-only sampler including Presley)	RCA Victor SPS-33-96	$400
LP(P)	**(SPS-33-141)** (62) Various artists (Promo-only sampler including Presley)	RCA Victor SPS-33-141	$400
LP(P)	**(SPS-33-191)** (62) Various artists (Promo-only sampler including Presley)	RCA Victor SPS-33-191	$400
LP(P)	**(SPS-33-219)** (Oct 63) Various artists (Promo-only sampler including Presley)	RCA Victor 33-219	$400
LP(P)	**(SPS-33-247)** (Dec 63) Various artists (Promo-only sampler including Presley)	RCA Victor 33-247	$400
LP(P)	**(SPS-33-272)** (Oct 64) Various artists (Promo-only sampler including Presley)	RCA Victor 33-272	$400
LP(P)	**(SPS-33-331)** (Apr 65) Various artists (Promo-only sampler including Presley)	RCA Victor 33-331	$400
LP(P)	**(SPS-33-347)** (Aug 65) Various artists (Promo-only sampler including Presley)	RCA Victor 33-347	$400
LP(P)	**(SPS-33-403)** (Apr 66) Various artists (Promo-only sampler including Presley)	RCA Victor 33-403	$400

-albums-

LP	**ELVIS PRESLEY** (56) Mono (First pressing, reads "Long Play" on bottom of the label, "Elvis" in pale pink on cover)	RCA Victor 1254	$250
LP	**ELVIS PRESLEY** (56) Mono ("Long Play" on bottom of label, "Elvis" in dark pink letters on cover)	RCA Victor 1254	$150
LP	**ELVIS PRESLEY** (63) Mono (Later pressing, reads "Mono" at the bottom of the label)	RCA Victor 1254	$60
LP	**ELVIS PRESLEY** (65) Mono ("Monaural" on the bottom of label)	RCA Victor 1254	$50
LP	**ELVIS PRESLEY** (62) Stereo ("Stereo Electronically Reprocessed" on bottom of label)	RCA Victor 1254	$60
LP	**ELVIS PRESLEY** (68) Orange label	RCA Victor 1254	$25
LP	**ELVIS** (56) Mono ("Long Play" on bottom, ads on back cover)	RCA Victor 1382	$200
LP	**ELVIS** (56) Mono (First pressing, reads "Long Play" on bottom of label, catalog number under logo, no ads)	RCA Victor 1382	$150
LP	**ELVIS** (56) Mono ("Long Play" at the bottom of label, NO catalog number under the logo, cuts are identified as Bands)	RCA Victor 1382	$500
LP	**ELVIS** (56) Mono ("Long Play" at the bottom of the label, 17S in trailoff area of record)	RCA Victor 1382	$1,250
LP	**ELVIS** (63) Mono ("Mono" at bottom of the label)	RCA Victor 1382	$60
LP	**ELVIS** (62) Mono ("Monaural" on bottom of label)	RCA Victor 1382	$50
LP	**ELVIS** (63) Stereo ("Stereo Electronically Reprocessed" on bottom of label, RCA in silver)	RCA Victor 1382	$50
LP	**ELVIS** (65) Stereo ("Stereo Electronically Reprocessed" on bottom, RCA in white)	RCA Victor 1382	$40
LP	**ELVIS** (68) Orange label	RCA Victor 1382	$25
LP	**ELVIS' CHRISTMAS ALBUM** (57) Mono w/photos and sticker (Fold-open cover with ten pages of photos and gift certificate sticker on cover)	RCA Victor 1035	$1,000
LP	**ELVIS' CHRISTMAS ALBUM** (57) Mono, no sticker (Fold-open cover with ten pages of photos)	RCA Victor 1035	$500
LP	**ELVIS' CHRISTMAS ALBUM** (58) Mono (First pressing of RCA 1951, "Long Play" at bottom of the label)	RCA Victor 1951	$75
LP	**ELVIS' CHRISTMAS ALBUM** (63) Mono (Later pressing, "Mono" at bottom of the label)	RCA Victor 1951	$50
LP	**ELVIS' CHRISTMAS ALBUM** (63) Stereo (Later pressing, "Stereo" at the bottom of the label)	RCA Victor 1951	$25
LP	**ELVIS' CHRISTMAS ALBUM** (68) Orange label	RCA Victor 1951	$30
LP	**LOVING YOU** (57) Mono (First pressing, "Long Play" at bottom of the label)	RCA Victor 1515	$150
LP	**LOVING YOU** (63) Mono ("Mono" on the bottom of label)	RCA Victor 1515	$60
LP	**LOVING YOU** (63) Mono ("Monaural" on bottom of label)	RCA Victor 1515	$50
LP	**LOVING YOU** (62) Stereo ("Stereo Electronically Reprocessed" on bottom of label, RCA in silver)	RCA Victor 1515	$60
LP	**LOVING YOU** (65) Stereo ("Stereo Electronically Reprocessed" on bottom of label, RCA in white)	RCA Victor 1515	$40
LP(P)	**JAILHOUSE ROCK** (57) Interview (Radio interview with Leiber and Stoller, red vinyl)	MGM 12-232	$500
LP	**ELVIS' GOLDEN RECORDS** (58) Mono ("Long Play" on bottom of label)	RCA Victor 1707	$150
LP	**ELVIS' GOLDEN RECORDS** (59) Mono ("Long Play" on the bottom of label, "RE" printed on the back)	RCA Victor 1707	$100
LP	**ELVIS' GOLDEN RECORDS** (63) Mono ("Mono" on the bottom)	RCA Victor 1707	$60
LP	**ELVIS' GOLDEN RECORDS** (65) Mono ("Monaural" on bottom of label)	RCA Victor 1707	$50
LP	**ELVIS' GOLDEN RECORDS** (62) Stereo ("Stereo Electronically Reprocessed" on bottom of label, RCA in silver)	RCA Victor 1707	$60
LP	**ELVIS' GOLDEN RECORDS** (65) Stereo ("Stereo Electronically Reprocessed" on bottom of label, RCA in white)	RCA Victor 1707	$40
LP	**KING CREOLE** (58) Mono (First pressing, "Long Play" at the bottom of the label)	RCA Victor 1884	$150

LP	**KING CREOLE** (58) Mono (First pressing, "Long Play" at bottom of label and bonus photo included)	RCA Victor 1884	$300
LP	**KING CREOLE** (63) Mono ("Mono" at bottom of the label)	RCA Victor 1884	$60
LP	**KING CREOLE** (65) Mono ("Monaural" on the bottom of label)	RCA Victor 1884	$50
LP	**KING CREOLE** (63) Stereo ("Stereo Electronically Reprocessed" on bottom of label, RCA in silver)	RCA Victor 1884	$60
LP	**KING CREOLE** (65) Stereo ("Stereo Electronically Reprocessed" on bottom of label, RCA in white)	RCA Victor 1884	$40
LP	**ELVIS' CHRISTMAS ALBUM** (58) Mono ("Long Play" on the bottom of label)	RCA Victor 1951	$100
LP	**ELVIS' CHRISTMAS ALBUM** (58) Mono ("Mono" on the bottom on label)	RCA Victor 1951	$60
LP	**ELVIS' CHRISTMAS ALBUM** (65) Mono ("Monaural" on the bottom of label)	RCA Victor 1951	$60
LP	**ELVIS' CHRISTMAS ALBUM** (65) Stereo ("Stereo Electronically Reprocessed" on the bottom of the label)	RCA Victor 1951	$40
LP	**FOR LP FANS ONLY** (59) Mono (First pressing, "Long Play" at bottom, front and back cover the same)	RCA Victor 1990	$250
LP	**FOR LP FANS ONLY** (59) Mono (First pressing, "Long Play" at bottom, front and back covers different like other RCA LPs)	RCA Victor 1990	$150
LP	**FOR LP FANS ONLY** (63) Mono ("Mono" at bottom of the label)	RCA Victor 1990	$60
LP	**FOR LP FANS ONLY** (65) Mono ("Monaural" on the bottom of label)	RCA Victor 1990	$50
LP	**FOR LP FANS ONLY** (65) Stereo ("Stereo Electronically Reprocessed" on bottom of label)	RCA Victor 1990	$40
LP	**FOR LP FANS ONLY** (68) Orange label	RCA Victor 1990	$25
LP	**A DATE WITH ELVIS** (59) Mono	RCA Victor 2011	$200
	(First pressing, "Long Play" at bottom of label, gatefold cover)		
LP	**A DATE WITH ELVIS** (59) Mono (Same as above, with a red sticker)	RCA Victor 2011	$300
LP	**A DATE WITH ELVIS** (63) Mono ("Mono" at bottom of the label)	RCA Victor 2011	$60
LP	**A DATE WITH ELVIS** (65) Mono ("Monaural" on the bottom of label)	RCA Victor 2011	$50
LP	**A DATE WITH ELVIS** (63) Stereo ("Stereo Electronically Reprocessed" at bottom of label)	RCA Victor 2011	$40
LP	**ELVIS' GOLDEN RECORDS VOL 2** (59) Mono (First pressing "Long Play" on bottom of the label)	RCA Victor 2075	$150
LP	**ELVIS' GOLDEN RECORDS VOL 2** (63) Mono ("Mono" on bottom of label)	RCA Victor 2075	$60
LP	**ELVIS' GOLDEN RECORDS VOL 2** (65) Mono ("Monaural" on bottom of label)	RCA Victor 2075	$50
LP	**ELVIS' GOLDEN RECORDS VOL 2** (62) Stereo ("Stereo Electronically Reprocessed" on bottom of the label, RCA in silver)	RCA Victor 2075	$60
LP	**ELVIS' GOLDEN RECORDS VOL 2** (65) Stereo ("Stereo Electronically Reprocessed" on bottom of the label, RCA in white)	RCA Victor 2075	$40
LP	**ELVIS IS BACK** (60) Mono (Gatefold cover, "Long Play" on bottom of label)	RCA Victor 2231	$125
LP	**ELVIS IS BACK** (60) Mono (Gatefold cover, "Long Play," song titles on cover)	RCA Victor 2231	$100
LP	**ELVIS IS BACK** (60) Mono (Gatefold cover, "Mono" on bottom of label)	RCA Victor 2231	$60
LP	**ELVIS IS BACK** (65) Mono (Gatefold cover, "Monaural" on bottom)	RCA Victor 2231	$50
LP	**ELVIS IS BACK** (60) Stereo ("Living Stereo" on bottom of label, no song titles on cover)	RCA Victor 2231	$150
LP	**ELVIS IS BACK** (60) Stereo ("Living Stereo" on bottom, song titles on cover)	RCA Victor 2231	$125
LP	**ELVIS IS BACK** (65) Stereo ("Stereo" on the bottom of label)	RCA Victor 2231	$50
LP	**ELVIS IS BACK** (77) Stereo (Brown label, green vinyl)	RCA Victor 2231	$500
LP	**G.I. BLUES** (60) Mono ("Long Play" on bottom of label)	RCA Victor 2256	$50
LP	**G.I. BLUES** (60) Mono (Same as above, with heart-shaped sticker on cover)	RCA Victor 2256	$100
LP	**G.I. BLUES** (63) Mono ("Mono" on the bottom of label)	RCA Victor 2256	$60

LP	**G.I. BLUES** (65) Mono ("Monaural" on bottom of label)	RCA Victor 2256	$50
LP	**G.I. BLUES** (60) Stereo ("Living Stereo" on bottom of label)	RCA Victor 2256	$75
LP	**G.I. BLUES** (60) Stereo (Same as above, with heart-shaped sticker)	RCA Victor 2256	$125
LP	**G.I. BLUES** (63) Stereo ("Stereo" on the bottom of label)	RCA Victor 2256	$50
LP	**HIS HAND IN MINE** (60) Mono ("Long Play" on bottom of label)	RCA Victor 2328	$60
LP	**HIS HAND IN MINE** (60) Mono ("Mono" on bottom of label)	RCA Victor 2328	$50
LP	**HIS HAND IN MINE** (65) Mono ("Monaural" on bottom of label)	RCA Victor 2328	$40
LP	**HIS HAND IN MINE** (60) Stereo ("Living Stereo" on bottom of label)	RCA Victor 2328	$100
LP	**HIS HAND IN MINE** (63) Stereo ("Stereo" on bottom of label)	RCA Victor 2328	$50
LP	**SOMETHING FOR EVERYBODY** (61) Mono ("Long Play" on bottom of label)	RCA Victor 2370	$60
LP	**SOMETHING FOR EVERYBODY** (61) Mono ("Mono" on bottom of label)	RCA Victor 2370	$50
LP	**SOMETHING FOR EVERYBODY** (65) Mono ("Monaural" on bottom of label)	RCA Victor 2370	$40
LP	**SOMETHING FOR EVERYBODY** (61) Stereo ("Living Stereo" on bottom of label)	RCA Victor 2370	$100
LP	**SOMETHING FOR EVERYBODY** (63) Stereo ("Stereo" on bottom of label)	RCA Victor 2370	$50
LP	**BLUE HAWAII** (61) Mono ("Long Play" on bottom of label)	RCA Victor 2426	$60
LP	**BLUE HAWAII** (61) Mono (Same as above, with red sticker on cover)	RCA Victor 2426	$100
LP	**BLUE HAWAII** (63) Mono ("Mono" on bottom of label)	RCA Victor 2426	$50
LP	**BLUE HAWAII** (65) Mono ("Monaural" on bottom of label)	RCA Victor 2426	$40
LP	**BLUE HAWAII** (61) Stereo ("Living Stereo" on bottom of label)	RCA Victor 2426	$60
LP	**BLUE HAWAII** (61) Stereo (Same as above, with red sticker on cover)	RCA Victor 2426	$125
LP	**BLUE HAWAII** (63) Stereo ("Stereo" on the bottom of label)	RCA Victor 2426	$50
LP(P)	**BLUE HAWAII** (61) Movie Ads (Four ads on one-sided record)	Paramount 1796	$750
LP	**POT LUCK** (62) Mono ("Long Play" on bottom of label)	RCA Victor 2523	$60
LP	**POT LUCK** (63) Mono ("Mono" on bottom of label)	RCA Victor 2523	$50
LP	**POT LUCK** (65) Mono ("Monaural" on bottom of label)	RCA Victor 2523	$40
LP	**POT LUCK** (62) Stereo ("Living Stereo" on bottom of label)	RCA Victor 2523	$100
LP	**POT LUCK** (63) Stereo ("Stereo" on bottom of label)	RCA Victor 2523	$50
LP(P)	**KID GALAHAD** (62) Movie ads (Four ads on one-sided promo record)	Paramount 1964	$750
LP	**GIRLS! GIRLS! GIRLS!** (62) Mono ("Long Play" on bottom of label)	RCA Victor 2621	$60
LP	**GIRLS! GIRLS! GIRLS!** (62) Mono (Same as above with calendar with LP ads on back)	RCA Victor 2621	$100
LP	**GIRLS! GIRLS! GIRLS!** (62) Mono (Same as above with calendar with 45s ads on back)	RCA Victor 2621	$125
LP	**GIRLS! GIRLS! GIRLS!** (62) Mono (Same as above with calendar with Santa Claus on back)	RCA Victor 2621	$300
LP	**GIRLS! GIRLS! GIRLS!** (65) Mono ("Monaural" on bottom of label)	RCA Victor 2621	$40
LP	**GIRLS! GIRLS! GIRLS!** (62) Stereo ("Living Stereo" on bottom of label)	RCA Victor 2621	$75
LP	**GIRLS! GIRLS! GIRLS!** (65) Stereo (Same as above with calendar with LP ads)	RCA Victor 2621	$100
LP	**GIRLS! GIRLS! GIRLS!** (65) Stereo (Same as above with calendar with 45s ads)	RCA Victor 2621	$125
LP	**GIRLS! GIRLS! GIRLS!** (65) Stereo (Same as above with calendar with Santa Claus on the back)	RCA Victor 2621	$300
LP	**GIRLS! GIRLS! GIRLS!** (63) Stereo ("Stereo" on bottom of label)	RCA Victor 2621	$50

LP(P)	**GIRLS! GIRLS! GIRLS!** (62) Movie ads	Paramount 2014	$750
	(Four ads on one-sided promo record)		
LP	**IT HAPPENED AT THE WORLD'S FAIR** (63) Mono	RCA Victor 2697	$60
	("Long Play" on bottom of label)		
LP	**IT HAPPENED AT THE WORLD'S FAIR** (63) Mono	RCA Victor 2697	$200
	(Same as above, with bonus photo)		
LP	**IT HAPPENED AT THE WORLD'S FAIR** (65) Mono	RCA Victor 2697	$40
	("Monaural" on bottom of label)		
LP	**IT HAPPENED AT THE WORLD'S FAIR** (63) Stereo	RCA Victor 2697	$75
	("Living Stereo" on bottom of label)		
LP	**IT HAPPENED AT THE WORLD'S FAIR** (63) Stereo	RCA Victor 2697	$225
	(Same as above, with bonus photo)		
LP	**FUN IN ACAPULCO** (63) Mono	RCA Victor 2756	$50
	("Mono" on bottom of label)		
LP	**FUN IN ACAPULCO** (65) Mono	RCA Victor 2756	$40
	("Monaural" on bottom of label)		
LP	**FUN IN ACAPULCO** (63) Stereo	RCA Victor 2756	$50
	("Stereo" on bottom of label)		
LP	**ELVIS' GOLDEN RECORDS VOL 3** (63) Mono	RCA Victor 2765	$50
	("Mono" on bottom of label)		
LP	**ELVIS' GOLDEN RECORDS VOL 3** (63) Mono	RCA Victor 2765	$90
	(Same as above, with attached photo)		
LP	**ELVIS' GOLDEN RECORDS VOL 3** (65) Mono	RCA Victor 2765	$40
	("Monaural" on bottom of label)		
LP	**ELVIS' GOLDEN RECORDS VOL 3** (63) Stereo	RCA Victor 2765	$50
	("Stereo" on bottom of label)		
LP	**ELVIS' GOLDEN RECORDS VOL 3** (63) Stereo	RCA Victor 2765	$90
	(Same as above with attached photo)		
LP	**KISSIN' COUSINS** (64) Mono	RCA Victor 2894	$100
	("Mono" on bottom of the label, NO photo of cast on the cover)		
LP	**KISSIN' COUSINS** (64) Mono	RCA Victor 2894	$50
	("Mono" on bottom of the label, WITH photo of cast on the cover)		
LP	**KISSIN' COUSINS** (65) Mono	RCA Victor 2894	$40
	("Monaural" on bottom of label)		
LP	**KISSIN' COUSINS** (64) Stereo	RCA Victor 2894	$100
	("Stereo" on bottom of the label, NO photo of cast on the cover)		
LP	**KISSIN' COUSINS** (64) Stereo	RCA Victor 2894	$50
	("Stereo" on bottom of the label, WITH photo of cast on the cover)		
LP	**ROUSTABOUT** (64) Mono	RCA Victor 2999	$60
	("Mono" on bottom of label)		
LP	**ROUSTABOUT** (65) Mono	RCA Victor 2999	$40
	("Monaural" on bottom of label)		
LP	**ROUSTABOUT** (64) Stereo	RCA Victor 2999	$50
	(RCA logo is in white, like most RCA Victor LPs)		
LP	**ROUSTABOUT** (64) Stereo	RCA Victor 2999	$400
	(RCA logo is in SILVER, very rare label version)		
7"(P)	**ROUSTABOUT** (64) Radio ads	Paramount 2414	$1,000
	(Theater spots for radio, 45rpm)		
LP	**GIRL HAPPY** (65) Mono	RCA Victor 3338	$50
	("Monaural" on bottom of label)		
LP	**GIRL HAPPY** (65) Stereo	RCA Victor 3338	$50
	("Stereo" on bottom of label)		
LP	**GIRL HAPPY** (68) Stereo	RCA Victor 3338	$25
	(Orange label)		
LP	**ELVIS FOR EVERYONE** (65) Mono	RCA Victor 3450	$50
	("Monaural" on bottom of label)		
LP	**ELVIS FOR EVERYONE** (65) Stereo	RCA Victor 3450	$40
	("Stereo" on bottom of label)		
LP	**ELVIS FOR EVERYONE** (68) Stereo	RCA Victor 3450	$25
	(Orange label)		
LP	**HARUM SCARUM** (65) Mono	RCA Victor 3468	$40
	("Monaural" on bottom of the label, with NO bonus photo)		
LP	**HARUM SCARUM** (65) Mono	RCA Victor 3468	$60
	("Monaural" on bottom of the label, WITH bonus photo)		
LP	**HARUM SCARUM** (65) Stereo	RCA Victor 3468	$40
	("Stereo" on bottom of the label, with NO bonus photo)		
LP	**HARUM SCARUM** (65) Stereo	RCA Victor 3468	$60
	("Stereo" on bottom of the label, WITH bonus photo)		
LP	**FRANKIE AND JOHNNY** (66) Mono	RCA Victor 3553	$40
	("Monaural" on bottom of label)		
LP	**FRANKIE AND JOHNNY** (66) Mono	RCA Victor 3553	$60
	(With bonus photo)		
LP	**FRANKIE AND JOHNNY** (66) Stereo	RCA Victor 3553	$40
	("Stereo" on bottom of label)		
LP	**FRANKIE AND JOHNNY** (66) Stereo	RCA Victor 3553	$60
	(With bonus photo)		

LP	**PARADISE HAWAIIAN STYLE** (66) Mono ("Monaural" on bottom of label)	RCA Victor 3643	$40
LP	**PARADISE HAWAIIAN STYLE** (66) Stereo ("Stereo" on bottom of label)	RCA Victor 3643	$40
LP	**SPINOUT** (66) Mono ("Monaural" on bottom of label)	RCA Victor 3702	$40
LP	**SPINOUT** (66) Mono (With bonus photo)	RCA Victor 3702	$60
LP	**SPINOUT** (66) Stereo ("Stereo" on bottom of label)	RCA Victor 3702	$40
LP	**SPINOUT** (66) Stereo (With bonus photo)	RCA Victor 3702	$60
LP	**HOW GREAT THOU ART** (67) Mono ("Mono Dynagroove" on bottom of the label)	RCA Victor 3758	$50
LP	**HOW GREAT THOU ART** (67) Stereo ("Stereo Dynagroove" on bottom of label)	RCA Victor 3758	$40
LP	**HOW GREAT THOU ART** (67) Stereo (Same as above, with RIAA gold record stamp on cover)	RCA Victor 3758	$30
LP	**DOUBLE TROUBLE** (67) Mono ("Monaural" on the bottom of the label, NO bonus photo)	RCA Victor 3787	$40
LP	**DOUBLE TROUBLE** (67) Mono ("Monaural" on bottom of the label, WITH bonus photo)	RCA Victor 3787	$60
LP	**DOUBLE TROUBLE** (67) Stereo ("Stereo" on bottom of label, NO bonus photo)	RCA Victor 3787	$40
LP	**DOUBLE TROUBLE** (67) Stereo ("Stereo" on bottom of label, WITH bonus photo)	RCA Victor 3787	$60
LP	**CLAMBAKE** (67) Mono ("Monaural" on bottom of label, NO bonus photo, very rare in mono)	RCA Victor 3893	$200
LP	**CLAMBAKE** (67) Mono ("Monaural" on bottom of label, WITH bonus photo)	RCA Victor 3893	$225
LP	**CLAMBAKE** (67) Stereo ("Stereo" on bottom of label, NO bonus photo)	RCA Victor 3893	$40
LP	**CLAMBAKE** (67) Stereo ("Stereo" on bottom of label, WITH bonus photo)	RCA Victor 3893	$60
LP(P)	**SPECIAL CHRISTMAS PROGRAMMING** (67) (Promo-only for radio stations, price includes inserts, white promo label)	RCA Victor 5697	$1,500
LP(P)	**SPECIAL PALM SUNDAY PROGRAMMING** (67) (For radio stations, price is for record only)	RCA Victor 461	$1,400
LP(P)	**SPECIAL PALM SUNDAY PROGRAMMING** (67) (For radio stations, price is for record AND programming booklet)	RCA Victor 461	$1,500
LP	**SINGER PRESENTS FLAMING STAR & OTHERS** (68) (Price is for record only)	RCA Victor 279	$40
LP	**SINGER PRESENTS FLAMING STAR & OTHERS** (68) (Price includes booklet)	RCA Victor 279	$100
LP	**SINGER PRESENTS FLAMING STAR & OTHERS** (68) (Price includes bonus photo)	RCA Victor 279	$50
LP	**SINGER PRESENTS FLAMING STAR & OTHERS** (68) (Price includes four-by-six-inch ticket)	RCA Victor 279	$60
LP	**ELVIS SINGS FLAMING STAR** (69) (Orange label, non-flexi vinyl)	Camden 2304	$20
LP	**ELVIS SINGS FLAMING STAR** (69) (Orange label, flexi vinyl)	Camden 2304	$10
LP	**ELVIS' GOLDEN RECORDS VOL 4** (68) Mono (Very rare in mono)	RCA Victor 3921	$1,000
LP	**ELVIS' GOLDEN RECORDS VOL 4** (68) Mono (With bonus photo)	RCA Victor 3921	$1,100
LP	**ELVIS' GOLDEN RECORDS VOL 4** (68) Stereo ("Stereo" on bottom of label)	RCA Victor 3921	$40
LP	**ELVIS' GOLDEN RECORDS VOL 4** (68) Stereo (Includes bonus photo)	RCA Victor 3921	$60
LP	**SPEEDWAY** (68) Mono ("Monaural" on bottom of the label, NO bonus photo)	RCA Victor 3989	$1,000
LP	**SPEEDWAY** (68) Mono ("Monaural" on bottom of the label, WITH bonus photo, very rare in mono)	RCA Victor 3989	$1,040
LP	**SPEEDWAY** (68) Stereo ("Stereo" on bottom of the label, NO bonus photo)	RCA Victor 3989	$40
LP	**SPEEDWAY** (68) Stereo ("Stereo" on bottom of the label, with bonus photo)	RCA Victor 3989	$80
LP	**SPEEDWAY** (68) Stereo (Orange label)	RCA Victor 3989	$30
LP(P)	**AGE OF ROCK** (69) Various artists (Various artists LP features three songs by Presley)	EMR 8	$75
LP	**INTERNATIONAL HOTEL PRESENTS ELVIS** (69) (Orange label, non-flex vinyl)	RCA Victor 4088	$25

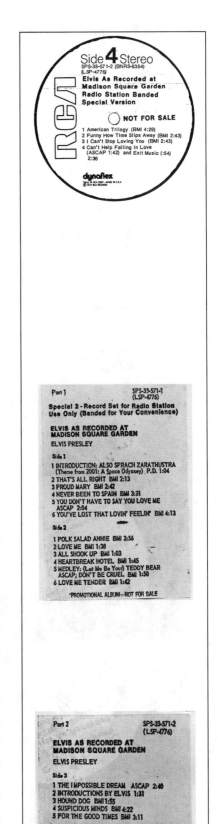

BOX(P)	**INTERNATIONAL HOTEL PRESENTS ELVIS** (69) (Two LPs plus misc items specially boxed, price is mostly for box)	RCA Victor 4088/4155	$2,500
BOX(P)	**INTERNATIONAL HOTEL PRESENTS ELVIS** (70) (LP and 45rpm plus misc items specially boxed, price is mostly for box and the 45 [9791])	RCA Victor 6020	$2,500
2LP	**FROM MEMPHIS TO VEGAS** (69) Orange label (Flexi vinyl)	RCA Victor 6020	$20
2LP	**FROM MEMPHIS TO VEGAS** (69) Orange label (NON-flex vinyl)	RCA Victor 6020	$25
2LP(P)	**SHELBY SINGLETON PRESENTS SONGS FOR THE 70S** (69) (White promo label record plus sixty-six-page booklet)	Shelby Singleton 1	$150
LP	**FROM ELVIS IN MEMPHIS** (69) (Orange)	RCA Victor 4155	$15
LP	**FROM ELVIS IN MEMPHIS** (69) (Includes bonus photo)	RCA Victor 4155	$30
4LP	**WORLDWIDE 50 GOLD AWARDS HITS** (70) Box set (Orange labels)	RCA Victor 6401	$60
4LP	**WORLDWIDE 50 GOLD AWARDS HITS** (70) Book (Records and bonus book)	RCA Victor 6401	$85
4LP	**WORLDWIDE 50 GOLD AWARDS HITS** (70) Box set (Tan labels)	RCA Victor 6401	$25
4LP	**WORLDWIDE 50 GOLD AWARDS HITS** (71) Box set (Orange labels)	RCA Victor 6402	$25
LP	**ON STAGE-FEBRUARY 1970** (70) (Orange label, non-flexi vinyl)	RCA Victor 4362	$20
LP	**ON STAGE-FEBRUARY 1970** (70) (Orange label, flexi vinyl)	RCA Victor 4362	$10
LP	**ELVIS IN PERSON AT THE INTERNATIONAL HOTEL** (70) (Orange label, non-flexi vinyl)	RCA Victor 4428	$20
LP	**ELVIS IN PERSON AT THE INTERNATIONAL HOTEL** (70) (Orange label, flexi vinyl)	RCA Victor 4428	$10
LP	**BACK IN MEMPHIS** (70) (Orange label, non-flexi vinyl)	RCA Victor 4429	$20
LP	**BACK IN MEMPHIS** (70) (Orange label, flexi vinyl)	RCA Victor 4429	$10
LP	**THAT'S THE WAY IT IS** (70) (Orange label, non-flexi vinyl)	RCA Victor 4445	$25
LP	**THAT'S THE WAY IT IS** (70) (Orange label, flexi vinyl)	RCA Victor 4445	$10
LP	**LET'S BE FRIENDS** (70) (Blue label, non-flexi vinyl)	Camden 2408	$20
LP	**LET'S BE FRIENDS** (70) (Blue label, flexi vinyl)	Camden 2408	$10
LP	**ELVIS' CHRISTMAS ALBUM** (70) (Blue label, non-flexi vinyl)	Camden 2428	$20
LP	**ELVIS' CHRISTMAS ALBUM** (70) (Blue label, flexi vinyl)	Camden 2428	$10
LP	**ALMOST IN LOVE** (70) (Blue label, non-flexi vinyl)	Camden 2440	$20
LP	**ALMOST IN LOVE** (70) (Blue label, flexi vinyl)	Camden 2440	$10
LP	**ELVIS COUNTRY** (71) (Orange label, non-flexi vinyl)	RCA Victor 4460	$20
LP	**ELVIS COUNTRY** (71) (Same as above, with bonus photo)	RCA Victor 4460	$30
LP	**ELVIS COUNTRY** (71) (Orange label, flexi vinyl)	RCA Victor 4460	$10
LP	**ELVIS COUNTRY** (71) (Brown label, blue vinyl)	RCA Victor 4460	$500
LP	**YOU'LL NEVER WALK ALONE** (71) (Blue label)	Camden 2472	$12
LP	**C'MON EVERYBODY** (71) (Blue label)	Camden 2518	$10
LP	**I GOT LUCKY** (71) (Blue label)	Camden 2533	$10
LP	**LOVE LETTERS FROM ELVIS** (71) Orange label (Cover title is split with "Love Letters from" on top)	RCA Victor 4530	$40
LP	**LOVE LETTERS FROM ELVIS** (71) Orange label (Cover title is split with "Love Letters" on top)	RCA Victor 4530	$30
4LP	**THE OTHER SIDES** (71) Box set (a.k.a. "Worldwide Gold Award Hits Vol 2")	RCA Victor 6402	$40
4LP	**THE OTHER SIDES** (71) Poster (Same as above, includes poster or envelope)	RCA Victor 6402	$50
LP	**THE WONDERFUL WORLD OF CHRISTMAS** (71) (Orange label)	RCA Victor 4579	$25
LP	**THE WONDERFUL WORLD OF CHRISTMAS** (71) (Includes Christmas photo)	RCA Victor 4579	$40

LP	**ELVIS NOW** (72) (Orange label)	RCA Victor 4671	$20
LP	**ELVIS NOW** (72) (Cover has TIMING STRIP, record is stock copy)	RCA Victor 4671	$150
LP	**ELVIS NOW** (72) (Brown label, green vinyl)	RCA Victor 4671	$500
LP	**HE TOUCHED ME** (72) (Orange label)	RCA Victor 4690	$20
LP	**HE TOUCHED ME** (72) (Cover has TIMING STRIP, record is stock copy)	RCA Victor 4690	$150
LP	**ELVIS SINGS HITS FROM HIS MOVIES VOL 1** (72) (Blue label)	Camden 2567	$10
LP	**ELVIS SINGS BURNING LOVE** (72) (Price includes bonus photo and star on cover advertising the photo)	Camden 2595	$75
LP	**ELVIS SINGS BURNING LOVE** (72) (No bonus photo, or mention of)	Camden 2595	$10
LP	**RECORDED AT MADISON SQUARE GARDEN** (72) (Orange label)	RCA Victor 4776	$15
2LP	**RECORDED AT MADISON SQUARE GARDEN** (72) (White promo label, plain cover)	RCA Victor SPS-571	$250
LP	**ROCK ROCK ROCK** (72) Various artists (Includes one Presley cut)	Original Sound 11	$40
2LP	**ALOHA FROM HAWAII** (73) Quad (Chicken of the Sea sticker of the cover)	RCA Victor 6089	$2,500
2LP	**ALOHA FROM HAWAII** (73) Quad (Cover has TIMING STRIP, record is stock copy)	RCA Victor 6089	$200
2LP	**ALOHA FROM HAWAII** (73) Quad (Either orange or red-orange label)	RCA Victor 6089	$25
2LP	**ALOHA FROM HAWAII** (73) Quad (RCA Record Club issue)	RCA Victor 213736	$40
2LP	**ALOHA FROM HAWAII** (73) Quad (Solid orange color label)	RCA Victor 6089	$25
LP	**ELVIS** (73) (Orange label)	RCA Victor 0283	$40
2LP	**ELVIS** (73) (Blue labels, TV mail-in offer, do not confuse with the gold vinyl set that is also RCA 0056)	RCA Victor 0056	$50
LP	**SEPARATE WAYS** (73) (Without the bonus photo)	Camden 2611	$10
LP	**SEPARATE WAYS** (73) (Price includes bonus photo)	Camden 2611	$20
LP	**RAISED ON ROCK** (73) (Orange label)	RCA Victor 0388	$20
LP	**RAISED ON ROCK** (73) (Brown label)	RCA Victor 0388	$10
LP(P)	**ROBERT W. SARNOFF: 25 YEARS OF LEADERSHIP** (73) (Various RCA artists, four Presley songs)	RCA Victor 0001	$250
LP	**A LEGENDARY PERFORMER VOL 1** (74) (Black label)	RCA Victor 0341	$20
LP(PD)	**A LEGENDARY PERFORMER VOL 1** (74) (Very rare picture disc with one of twenty-four pictures)	RCA Victor 0341	$500
LP	**GOOD TIMES** (74) (Orange label)	RCA Victor 0475	$20
LP	**RECORDED LIVE ON STAGE IN MEMPHIS** (74) (Orange label)	RCA Victor 0606	$15
LP(P)	**RECORDED LIVE ON STAGE IN MEMPHIS** (74) (No mention of promo, but is BANDED and includes DJL-prefix on label number)	RCA Victor DJL 0606	$250
LP	**RECORDED LIVE ON STAGE IN MEMPHIS** (74) Quad (Orange label, NOT banded, rare quad issue)	RCA Victor 0606	$200
LP	**HAVING FUN WITH ELVIS ON STAGE** (74) (Sold at Presley concerts, later released on RCA Victor)	Boxcar	$200
LP	**HAVING FUN WITH ELVIS ON STAGE** (74) (Orange label)	RCA Victor 0818	$20
LP	**HAVING FUN WITH ELVIS ON STAGE** (74) (Brown label)	RCA Victor 0818	$15
2LP	**WORLDWIDE GOLD AWARD HITS PARTS 1 & 2** (74) (RCA Record Club release)	RCA Victor 213690	$40
2LP	**WORLDWIDE GOLD AWARD HITS PARTS 3 & 4** (78) (RCA Record Club release)	RCA Victor 214657	$20
LP	**PROMISED LAND** (75) (Orange label)	RCA Victor 0873	$50
LP	**PROMISED LAND** (75) (Brown label, black vinyl)	RCA Victor 0873	$15
LP	**PROMISED LAND** (75) (Brown label, blue vinyl)	RCA Victor 0873	$500

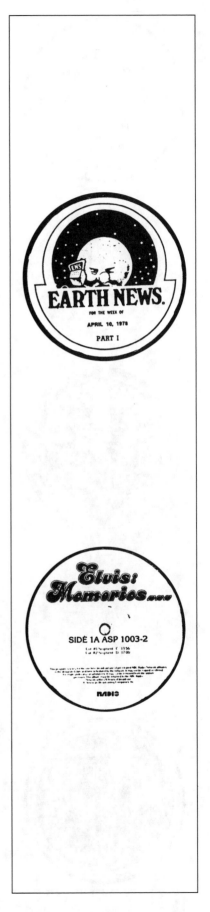

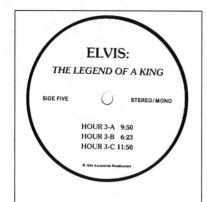

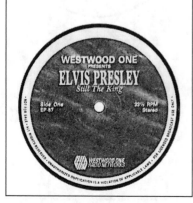

LP	**PROMISED LAND** (75) Quad (Orange label)	RCA Victor 0873	$200
LP	**PROMISED LAND** (75) Quad (Black label)	RCA Victor 0873	$75
LP	**ELVIS TODAY** (75) (Orange label)	RCA Victor 1039	$50
LP	**ELVIS TODAY** (75) (Brown label)	RCA Victor 1039	$15
LP	**ELVIS TODAY** (75) Quad (Orange label)	RCA Victor 1039	$200
LP	**ELVIS TODAY** (75) Quad (Black label)	RCA Victor 1039	$75
LP	**A LEGENDARY PERFORMER VOL 2** (76) (Black label)	RCA Victor 1349	$20
2LP	**ELVIS IN HOLLYWOOD** (76) (TV mail-in offer)	RCA Victor 0168	$25
LP(P)	**LET'S BE FRIENDS** (76) Gold vinyl (Special release gold vinyl for record VIPs in promotion)	Pickwick 2408	$350
LP	**THE SUN SESSIONS** (76) (Brown label)	RCA Victor 1675	$15
LP	**THE SUN SESSIONS** (76) (Brown label, blue vinyl)	RCA Victor 1675	$500
LP	**FROM ELVIS PRESLEY BOULEVARD** (76) (Brown label)	RCA Victor 1506	$15
LP	**COUNTRY MUSIC IN THE MODERN ERA** (76) Various (Includes songs by Presley)	New World 207	$50
6LP	**EPIC OF THE 70S** (76) Various artists (This set includes at least one Presley song)	Century 21	$75
5LP	**ELVIS: A COLLECTORS EDITION** (77) (Box set)	RCA Victor TB-1	$30
LP	**THE SUN YEARS** (77) First pressing ("Memphis, Tennessee" on the bottom of label)	Sun 1001	$50
LP	**THE SUN YEARS** (77) Later pressings (May have yellow or white label)	Sun 1001	$10
LP	**MOODY BLUE** (77) Blue vinyl (The common version)	RCA Victor 2428	$10
LP	**MOODY BLUE** (77) Purple/white vinyl (Experimental issues, only a few copies made)	RCA Victor 2428	$2,000
LP	**MOODY BLUE** (77) Red/white vinyl (Experimental issues, only a few copies made)	RCA Victor 2428	$2,000
LP	**MOODY BLUE** (77) Yellow/white vinyl (Experimental issues, only a few copies made)	RCA Victor 2428	$2,000
LP	**MOODY BLUE** (77) White vinyl (Experimental issues, only a few copies made)	RCA Victor 2428	$1,500
LP	**MOODY BLUE** (77) Green vinyl (Experimental issues, only a few copies made)	RCA Victor 2428	$1,500
LP	**MOODY BLUE** (77) Red vinyl (Experimental issues, only a few copies made)	RCA Victor 2428	$1,500
LP	**MOODY BLUE** (77) Gold vinyl (Experimental issues, only a few copies made)	RCA Victor 2428	$1,500
LP	**MOODY BLUE** (77) Black vinyl (Very limited on black vinyl)	RCA Victor 2428	$300
LP	**INTERVIEWS WITH ELVIS** (77)	Starday 995	$30
2LP	**EXCLUSIVE LIVE PRESS CONFERENCE** (77)	Green Valley 2001	$25
2LP	**ELVIS SPEAKS TO YOU** (77) (Gatefold cover with bonus photo)	Green Valley 2002	$25
2LP	**ELVIS SPEAKS TO YOU** (77) (Single pocket cover with bonus photo)	Green Valley 2002	$15
5LP	**ALL TIME CHRISTMAS FAVORITES** (78) Various artists (One of the records is exclusive Presley, price is for the five-record set)	Collectors 505	$150
LP	**ALL TIME CHRISTMAS FAVORITES** (78) (Presley record only)	Collectors 505	$100
5LP	**THE ELVIS PRESLEY STORY** (78) (Box set)	Candlelight 0263	$25
5LP	**MEMORIES OF ELVIS** (78) (Box set)	Candlelight 0347	$25
2LP	**COUNTRY CLASSICS** (78) (RCA Record Club release)	RCA Victor 233299	$15
2LP	**FROM ELVIS WITH LOVE** (78) (RCA Record Club release)	RCA Victor 234340	$15
2LP	**LEGENDARY CONCERT PERFORMANCES** (78) (RCA Record Club release)	RCA Victor 244047	$15
2LP	**ELVIS COMMEMORATIVE ALBUM** (78) Gold vinyl (TV marketing)	RCA Victor 0056	$30
7LP	**THE PICKWICK PACK** (78) Reissue of RCA LPs (Includes "Frankie & Johnny" LP)	Pickwick (RCA)	$40

7LP	**THE PICKWICK PACK** (79) Reissue of RCA LPs	Pickwick (RCA)	$50
	(Includes Christmas Album)		
LP(P)	**MICHELOB PRESENTS HIGHLIGHTS** (78)	ABC Radio	$200
	(Highlights from the ABC radio show, released for Michelob executives)		
LP	**THE GREATEST SHOW ON EARTH** (78)	RCA Victor 0348	$15
LP(P)	**PURE ELVIS** (78)	RCA Victor 3455	$250
	(White promo label)		
6LP	**THE LEGENDARY RECORDINGS OF ELVIS PRESLEY** (79)	Candlelight 0412	$30
	(Box set)		
2LP	**PERSONALLY ELVIS** (79)	Silhouette 1001/1002	$25
LP	**THE FIRST YEARS** (79)	HALW 00001	$15
	(Pink label)		
LP	**A LEGENDARY PERFORMER VOL 3** (79)	RCA Victor 3078	$20
	(Black label)		
LP(PD)	**A LEGENDARY PERFORMER VOL 3** (79)	RCA Victor 3078	$25
	(Picture disc)		
8LP	**ELVIS ARON PRESLEY** (80) Silver box set	RCA Victor 3699	$60
	(The common commercial version, includes book)		
LP(P)	**ELVIS ARON PRESLEY** (80) Promo edit	RCA Victor (No number)	$200
	(Early edited version sent to radio, no record number)		
LP(P)	**ELVIS ARON PRESLEY** (80) Promo edit	RCA Victor 3729	$100
	(Has record number)		
LP(P)	**ELVIS ARON PRESLEY** (80) Promo edit	RCA Victor 3781	$150
	(Has record number)		
LP	**FROM ELVIS IN MEMPHIS** (80)	Mobile Fidelity 059	$35
2LP	**COUNTRY MEMORIES** (80)	RCA Victor 244069	$15
	(RCA Record Club release)		
6LP	**THE LEGENDARY RECORDINGS OF ELVIS PRESLEY** (80)	RCA Victor 0412	$40
	(Issued with book and print)		
LP	**GREATEST MOMENTS IN MUSIC** (80)	RCA Victor 0413	$15
LP	**THE LEGENDARY MAGIC OF ELVIS PRESLEY** (80)	RCA Victor 0461	$15
LP	**LIGHTNING STRIKES TWICE** (81) With the Beatles	United Distributors 2382	$50
	(Side one is live Presley tracks, side two features early Beatles recordings)		
LP(P)	**FELTON JARVIS TALKS ABOUT ELVIS** (81)	RCA Victor 1981	$75
	(Open end interview)		
LP(P)	**FELTON JARVIS TALKS ABOUT ELVIS** (81)	RCA Victor 1981	$100
	(Price includes belt buckle)		
LP	**ELVIS SINGS INSPIRATIONAL FAVORITES** (82)	RCA Victor 181	$15
8LP	**ELVIS! HIS GREATEST HITS** (83) Box set	RCA Victor 010	$400
	(White box set)		
7LP	**ELVIS! HIS GREATEST HITS** (83) Box set	RCA Victor 010	$40
	(Yellow box set)		
7LP	**THE LEGEND LIVES ON** (84) Box set	RCA Victor 191	$40
	(Box set)		
6LP	**A GOLDEN CELEBRATION** (84) Box set	RCA Victor 5172	$30
	(Price includes bonus photo)		
3LP	**FIFTY YEARS/FIFTY HITS** (85)	RCA Victor 0710	$15
	(Box set)		
LP	**ELVIS SINGS COUNTRY FAVORITES** (85)	RCA Victor 242	$50
	(Bonus album with *Readers Digest* box set)		
LP	**ONE NIGHT WITH YOU** (85)	RCA Victor 0704	$30
	(No poster)		
LP	**ONE NIGHT WITH YOU** (85)	RCA Victor 0704	$40
	(With bonus poster)		
2LP	**HIS SONGS OF FAITH AND INSPIRATION** (85)	RCA Victor 0728	$15
2LP	**GOOD ROCKIN' TONIGHT** (85)	RCA Victor 0824	$10
LP(P)	**AUDIO SELF PORTRAIT** (85)	RCA Victor 0835	$75
	(White promo label)		
LP	**ELVIS TALKS** (88)	RCA Victor 0835	$25
	(Reissue of RCA 0835)		
LP	**ELVIS, SCOTTY & BILL** (88)	Mavenco (No number)	$15
	(No copy of contract)		
LP	**ELVIS, SCOTTY & BILL** (88)	Mavenco (No number)	$50
	(Includes a copy of contract with Scotty)		
	-radio shows-		
LP(RS)	**FRANTIC FIFTIES** Radio show	Mutual Radio	$50-100
	(Includes Presley music)		
8LP(RS)	**COUNTRY EXPRESS** (With Gene Price) (75)	U.S. Air Force	$25-50
	(Price is for the four 2LP sets that feature Presley songs … of the twenty-eight 2LP sets)		
13LP(RS)	**ELVIS PRESLEY STORY** (75)	Watermark	$400-750
	(Price includes manual, labels have pink letters)		
13LP(RS)	**ELVIS PRESLEY STORY** (75)	Watermark	$350-700
	(Price includes manual, labels have blue letters)		
LP(RS)	**LOUISIANA HAYRIDE** (76)	La Hayride 8454	$250-500
	(Yellow label, for radio stations, various artists)		

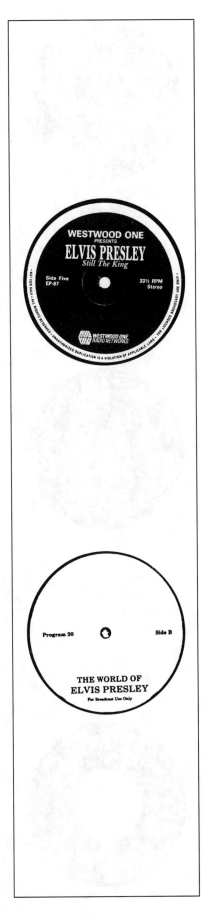

LP(RS)	**LOUISIANA HAYRIDE** (81)	La Hayride 8454	$125-250
	(Gold label repeat of the show above)		
LP(RS)	**LOUISIANA HAYRIDE** (84)	(RCA Victor) 3061	$125-250
	(White promo label advance from RCA, non white label version worth around $12)		
5LP(RS)	**BILLBOARD SOUND OF '77** (Dec 77) Box set	Billboard Magazine	$75-125
	(Country version of the countdown of top records of the year)		
5LP(RS)	**BILLBOARD SOUND OF '77** (Dec 77) Box set	Billboard Magazine	$75-150
	(Rock version of countdown, both shows feature Presley tribute)		
3LP(RS)	**REFLECTIONS OF ELVIS** (77)	Diamond P	$200-350
	(Tribute to Elvis Presley)		
3LP(RS)	**ELVIS, A THREE HOUR SPECIAL** (77)	Drake-Chenault	$125-250
	(Tribute to Elvis Presley)		
LP(RS)	**EARTH NEWS** (Aug 77) Daily news shows	Earth News	$125-250
	(The whole week dedicated to Presley)		
LP(P)	**ON THE RECORD** (77) Top news of '77	Caedmon 1572	$25-40
	(Available to radio stations from United Press International)		
LP(P)	**WORLD OF SOUND** (77) Top news of '77	AP 1977	$25-50
	(Available to radio stations from Associated Press)		
6LP(RS)	**ROCK ROLL & REMEMBER** (77) Dick Clark	United Stations	$50-75
	(Special "Presley Remembered" show of the weekly series)		
3LP(RS)	**ELVIS REMEMBERED** (78)	Creative Radio	$150-225
	(Music and interviews, price includes scripts)		
3LP(RS)	**50TH ANNIVERSARY SPECIAL** (Jan 85)	Creative Radio	$75-125
	(Creative shows are designed to air anytime during the year)		
6LP(RS)	**50TH ANNIVERSARY SPECIAL** (Jan 85)	Creative Radio	$175-250
	(Price includes scripts)		
3LP(RS)	**MEMORIES OF ELVIS** (Jan 87)	Creative Radio	$75-125
	(Music and interviews)		
6LP(RS)	**ELVIS' 10TH ANNIVERSARY RADIO TRIBUTE** (Jan 87)	Creative Radio	$150-250
	(Price includes scripts)		
LP(RS)	**CHRISTMAS WITH ELVIS** (Dec 87)	Creative Radio	$20-40
	(Music and interviews)		
LP(RS)	**THE ELVIS HOUR** (June 86-Dec 87)	Creative Radio	$15-20
	(Price is for each show)		
78LP(RS)	**THE ELVIS HOUR** (June 86-Dec 87) Complete set	Creative Radio	$1,000-1,250
	(One weekly LP, price good through Dec 1987, any shows after that date add $15 each)		
LP(P)	**MICHELOB PRESENTS HIGHLIGHTS** (78)	ABC Radio	$125-200
	(Advance material from "Elvis Memories" radio show)		
3LP(RS)	**ELVIS MEMORIES** (Jan 79) Box set	ABC Radio 1003	$250-400
	(Price includes scripts, programming booklet and box)		
LP(RS)	**LEGEND OF A KING** (80)	Associated Broadcasters	$40-75
	(White promo label sent to radio stations)		
3LP(RS)	**LEGEND OF A KING** (85)	Associated Broadcasters	$100-175
	(Radio show, NOT a box set)		
3LP(RS)	**LEGEND OF A KING** (85) Box set	Associated Broadcasters	$150-225
	(Radio show version that is a BOX SET)		
3LP(RS)	**LEGEND OF A KING** (86) Box set	Associated Broadcasters	$150-225
	(Radio show version, box set)		
CD(RS)	**LEGEND OF A KING** (89) w/scripts	Associated Broadcasters	$75-150
	(CD version of the same show)		
CD(RS)	**LEGEND OF A KING** (90) w/scripts	Associated Broadcasters	$75-150
	(Same show as above, different date)		
LP(RS)	**COUNTRY SESSIONS** (83) Show 126	Country Sessions	$100-200
	(Elvis Tribute)		
LP(RS)	**COUNTRY SESSIONS** (83) Show 122	Country Sessions	$40-75
	(Various artists, includes two Presley songs)		
LP(RS)	**COUNTRY CROSSROADS** (May 82) Show 21-82	Southern Baptist	$100-150
	(Includes Presley song and interview from Louisiana Hayride)		
LP(RS)	**COUNTRY CROSSROADS** (Aug 83) Show 32-83	Southern Baptist	$30-60
	(Includes Presley song)		
3LP(RS)	**A GOLDEN CELEBRATION** (84) Box set	Westwood One	$100-175
	(Price includes cue sheets and box)		
4LP(RS)	**STILL THE KING** (Aug 87)	Westwood One	$75-125
	(Red label, Presley tribute radio show)		
4LP(RS)	**STILL THE KING** (Aug 88) Repeat show	Westwood One	$75-125
	(Presley tribute radio show)		
LP(RS)	**THE WORLD OF ELVIS PRESLEY** (Jan 85-Dec 85)	NBC Radio	$20-40
	(Price is for each show)		
30LP(RS)	**THE WORLD OF ELVIS PRESLEY** (Jan 85-Dec 85)	NBC Radio	$1,250-2,000
	(Price is for a complete set, only a few collectors claim a complete set of these weekly shows)		
CD(RS)	**TICKET TO RIDE** (Aug 88) Beatles show	DIR	$25-50
	(This one show of the series is The Beatles Meet the King)		
7LP(RS)	**SOUNDS OF SOLID COUNTRY** (Through 85) Box set	U.S. Marines	$25-40
	(Price is for any 7LP box set that contains at least one Presley cut)		

7LP(RS)	**SOUNDS OF SOLID GOLD** (Through 85) Box set (Price is for any 7LP box set that contains at least one Presley cut)	U.S. Marine	$25-40
7LP(RS)	**SOUNDS OF SOLID GOLD** (Through 85) Box set (Price is for VOL. 51, which includes three sides of Presley exclusive)	U.S. Marines	$50-100
3LP(RS)	**BILLBOARD'S OFFICIAL TOP 40 PRESLEY HITS** (May 87) (All the Presley hits ranked by *Billboard* magazine)	United Stations	$50-100
LP(RS)	**BBC TRANSCRIPTION DISC** (93) (The other artist profiled is Sid Vicious)	BBC Transcription	$500-750
3CD(RS)	**THE BIOGRAPHY** (94) (Music and interviews)	Entertainment Radio	$50-100

JOHNNY PRESTON (R)

Other Mercury 45s $5-10 each
Mercury Celebrity series 45s $3 each
TCF/Fox 45s $4 each
Hall 45s $5 each
Hallway/ABC 45s $3 each

-singles-

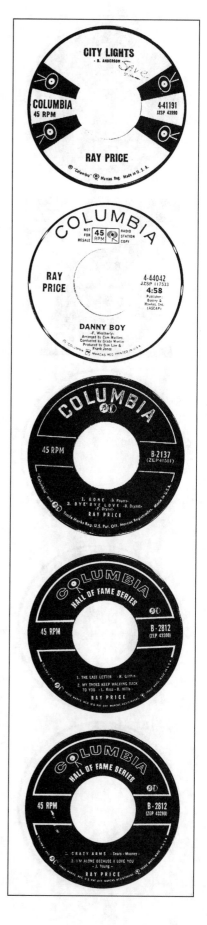

45rpm	**RUNNING BEAR** (59)	Mercury 71474	$15
45(P)	**RUNNING BEAR** (59) (White promo label)	Mercury 71474	$20
45rpm	**CRADLE OF LOVE** (60)	Mercury 71598	$15
45rpm	**CRADLE OF LOVE** (60) (Price includes picture sleeve)	Mercury 71598	$40
45(S)	**CRADLE OF LOVE** (60) (Stereo single)	Mercury 10027	$50
45(P)	**CRADLE OF LOVE** (60) (White promo label)	Mercury 71598	$15
45rpm	**FEEL SO FINE** (60)	Mercury 71651	$12
45(P)	**FEEL SO FINE** (60) (White promo label)	Mercury 71651	$18
45rpm	**CHARMING BILLY** (60)	Mercury 71691	$12
45(P)	**CHARMING BILLY** (60) (White promo label)	Mercury 71691	$15
45rpm	**ROCK AND ROLL GUITAR** (60)	Mercury 71728	$18
45(P)	**ROCK AND ROLL GUITAR** (60) (White promo label)	Mercury 71728	$15
45rpm	**LEAVE MY KITTEN ALONE** (61)	Mercury 71761	$18
45rpm	**LEAVE MY KITTEN ALONE** (61) (Price includes picture sleeve)	Mercury 71761	$40
45(P)	**LEAVE MY KITTEN ALONE** (61) (White promo label)	Mercury 71761	$15
45rpm	**I FEEL GOOD** (61)	Mercury 71803	$10
45(P)	**I FEEL GOOD** (61) (Price includes picture sleeve)	Mercury 71803	$40
45(P)	**I FEEL GOOD** (61) (White promo label)	Mercury 71803	$12
45rpm	**KISSIN' TREE** (61) (Price includes picture sleeve)	Mercury 71908	$30
45rpm	**BROKEN HEARTS ANONYMOUS** (62) (Price includes picture sleeve)	Mercury 71951	$30
45rpm	**THIS LITTLE BITTY TEAR** (63)	Imperial 5924	$10

-EPs-

EP	**JOHNNY PRESTON** (60)	Mercury 3397	$300

-albums-

LP	**RUNNING BEAR** (60) Black label, mono	Mercury 20592	$75
LP	**RUNNING BEAR** (60) Black label, stereo	Mercury 60250	$100
LP(P)	**RUNNING BEAR** (60) (White promo label)	Mercury 20592	$125
LP	**COME ROCK WITH ME** (61) Black label, mono	Mercury 20609	$50
LP	**COME ROCK WITH ME** (61) Black label, stereo	Mercury 60609	$75
LP(P)	**COME ROCK WITH ME** (61) (White promo label)	Mercury 20609	$100

FRANK PRICE (CW)

Country Artist LPs $8-10 each

MEL PRICE (RB)

-singles-

45rpm	**LITTLE BOY BLUES** (58)	Dixie 2016	$75

RAY PRICE (CW)

Columbia 78s $3-6 each
Other Columbia 45s $5-10 each
Columbia green label HOF 45s $3 each

ABC 45s $2 each
Dimension 45s $1 each
Dimension red vinyl 45s $4 each
Myrrh 45s $1 each
Other Columbia LPs $5-8 each
Other Harmony LPs $4-8 each
Dimension and Myrrh LPs $3-5 each
Other ABC LPs $5 each
Monument, MCA, Radiant, Word, Warner, and 51 West LPs $3 each

-singles-

45rpm	**IF YOU'RE ONLY LONELY** (54)	Columbia 20810	$15
45rpm	**I SAW MY CASTLES FALL** (54)	Columbia 20833	$15
45rpm	**TALK TO YOUR HEART** (55)	Columbia 20913	$12
45rpm	**I CAN'T ESCAPE** (55)	Columbia 21015	$12
45rpm	**DON'T LET THE STARS GET IN YOUR EYES** (55)	Columbia 21025	$15
45rpm	**THAT'S WHAT I GET FOR LOVING YOU** (56)	Columbia 21089	$12
45rpm	**COLD SHOULDER** (56)	Columbia 21117	$12
45rpm	**RELEASE ME** (56)	Columbia 21214	$12
45rpm	**I COULD LOVE YOU MORE** (56)	Columbia 21299	$12
45rpm	**IF YOU DON'T SOMEONE ELSE WILL** (56)	Columbia 21315	$12
45rpm	**ONE BROKEN HEART** (56)	Columbia 21354	$12
45rpm	**SWEET LITTLE MISS BLUE EYES** (56)	Columbia 21402	$12
45rpm	**CRAZY ARMS** (56)	Columbia 21510	$10
	(One of country's all-time greatest hits)		
45(P)	**CRAZY ARMS** (56)	Columbia 21510	$12
	(White promo label)		
33rpm	**CRAZY ARMS** (64) Hall of Fame singles series	Columbia 33017	$15
	(Seven-inch, small center hole, black label, orange paper sleeve)		
45rpm	**I'LL BE THERE** (58)	Columbia 40889	$10
45rpm	**MY SHOES KEEP WALKING BACK TO YOU** (58)	Columbia 40951	$10
45rpm	**CITY LIGHTS** (58)	Columbia 41191	$10
	(Another country mega-hit)		
45(P)	**MAKE THE WORLD GO AWAY** (63)	Columbia 42827	$15
	(White promo label, red vinyl)		
PS(P)	**MAKE THE WORLD GO AWAY** (63) Promo-only sleeve	Columbia 42827	$15
	(Special typewritten sleeve from Bob Thompson)		
45rpm	**DANNY BOY** (67)	Columbia 44042	$10
	(Price includes picture sleeve)		
45(P)	**DANNY BOY** (67)	Columbia 44042	$18
	(White promo label, green vinyl)		

-EPs-

EP	**RAY PRICE** (53)	Columbia 1786	$25
EP	**FOUR HITS BY RAY PRICE** (56)	Columbia 2118	$20
EP	**RAY PRICE SINGS FOUR HITS** (57)	Columbia 2137	$18
EP	**RAY PRICE** (57)	Columbia 2809	$15
EP	**RAY PRICE** (57)	Columbia 2812	$15
EP	**RAY PRICE SINGS HEART SONGS** Vol 1 (57)	Columbia 10051	$15
EP	**RAY PRICE SINGS HEART SONGS** Vol 2 (57)	Columbia 10052	$15
EP	**RAY PRICE SINGS HEART SONGS** Vol 3 (57)	Columbia 10053	$15
EP	**TALK TO YOUR HEART** (58)	Columbia 11481	$15
EP	**FAITH** Vol 1 (60)	Columbia 14941	$12
EP	**FAITH** Vol 2 (60)	Columbia 14942	$12
EP	**FAITH** Vol 3 (60)	Columbia 14943	$12
EP(JB)	**FOR THE GOOD TIMES** (70) Jukebox LLP	Columbia 30106	$18
	(Price includes hard cover and title strips)		
EP(JB)	**I WON'T MENTION IT AGAIN** (71) Jukebox LLP	Columbia 30510	$15
	(Price includes hard cover and title strips)		

-albums-

LP	**RAY PRICE SINGS HEART SONGS** (57)	Columbia 1015	$50
LP	**TALK TO YOUR HEART** (58)	Columbia 1148	$40
LP	**FAITH** (60) Mono	Columbia 1494	$30
LP	**FAITH** (60) Stereo	Columbia 8285	$40
LP(P)	**FAITH** (60)	Columbia 1494	$40
	(White promo label)		
LP	**RAY PRICE'S GREATEST HITS** (61)	Columbia 1566	$25
LP(P)	**RAY PRICE'S GREATEST HITS** (61)	Columbia 1566	$30
	(White promo label)		
LP	**SAN ANTONIO ROSE** (62) Mono	Columbia 1758	$20
LP	**SAN ANTONIO ROSE** (62) Stereo	Columbia 8556	$25
LP(P)	**SAN ANTONIO ROSE** (62)	Columbia 1758	$25
	(White promo label)		
LP	**NIGHT LIFE** (63)	Columbia 1971	$15
LP(P)	**NIGHT LIFE** (63)	Columbia 1971	$20
	(White promo label)		
LP	**GREATEST WESTERN HITS VOL 1** (63)	Columbia 1976	$15
	(With Lefty Frizzell and Carl Smith)		
LP(P)	**GREATEST WESTERN HITS VOL 1** (63)	Columbia 1976	$20

	(White promo label)		
LP	**LOVE LIFE** (64)	Columbia 2189	$15
LP(P)	**LOVE LIFE** (64)	Columbia 2189	$18
	(White promo label)		
LP	**BURNING MEMORIES** (65)	Columbia 2289	$15
LP(P)	**BURNING MEMORIES** (65)	Columbia 2289	$18
	(White promo label)		
LP	**WESTERN STRINGS** (65)	Columbia 2339	$15
LP(P)	**WESTERN STRINGS** (65)	Columbia 2339	$18
	(White promo label)		
LP	**THE OTHER WOMAN** (65)	Columbia 2382	$12
LP	**ANOTHER BRIDGE TO BURN** (66)	Columbia 2528	$12
LP	**COLLECTOR'S CHOICE** (66)	Harmony 7372	$18
	(Package of early singles from Columbia)		
LP(P)	**COLLECTOR'S CHOICE** (66)	Harmony 7372	$20
	(White promo label)		
LP	**TOUCH MY HEART** (67)	Columbia 2606	$12
LP	**BORN TO LOSE** (67)	Harmony 11240	$12
LP(P)	**BORN TO LOSE** (67)	Harmony 11240	$15
	(White promo label)		
LP	**RAY PRICE'S GREATEST HITS VOL 2** (67)	Columbia 2670	$12
LP	**DANNY BOY** (67)	Columbia 2677	$12
LP	**TAKE ME AS I AM** (68)	Columbia 2806	$12
LP	**SHE WEARS MY RING** (68)	Columbia 9733	$10
LP	**SWEETHEART OF THE YEAR** (69)	Columbia 9822	$10
LP	**RAY PRICE'S CHRISTMAS ALBUM** (69)	Columbia 9861	$10
LP	**I FALL TO PIECES** (69)	Harmony 11373	$12
	(Best known for the LP's stereo tracks)		
LP(P)	**I FALL TO PIECES** (69)	Harmony 11373	$10
	(White promo label)		
LP	**YOU WOULDN'T KNOW LOVE** (70)	Columbia 9918	$10
LP	**FOR THE GOOD TIMES** (70) Quad version	Columbia 30106	$10
LP	**MAKE THE WORLD GO AWAY** (70)	Harmony 30272	$10
LP	**HANK 'N' ME** (76)	ABC 2062	$10

-radio shows-

16"(RS)	**COUNTRY MUSIC TIME** (60s)	U.S. Army 86	$20-30
	(Music and interviews)		
16"(RS)	**COUNTRY MUSIC TIME** (60s)	U.S. Army 90	$20-30
	(Music and interviews)		
16"(RS)	**COUNTRY MUSIC TIME** (60s)	U.S. Army 97	$20-30
	(Music and interviews)		
16"(RS)	**COUNTRY MUSIC TIME** (60s)	U.S. Army 108	$20-30
	(Music and interviews)		
16"(RS)	**U.S. ARMY BAND SHOW** (60s)	U.S. Army	$20-30
	(Music and interviews)		

CHARLEY PRIDE (CW)

Country Charley Pride
And the Pridesmen
RCA Victor 45s by Country Charley Pride $4 each
RCA Victor 45s $2-3 each
RCA Victor picture sleeves $3 each
16th Avenue 45s $1 each
Other RCA Victor jukebox LLPs $5-8 each
Other RCA Victor LPs $4-8 each
Time-Life and Camden LPs $5-10 each

-singles-

45(P)	**WHAT'S IT ALL ABOUT** (Jul 77) Public service show	W. I. A. A. 1080	$15
	(Flip side artist is the Kinks)		
45(P)	**I DON'T THINK SHE'S IN LOVE ANYMORE** (82)	RCA Victor 13096	$10
	(Yellow promo label, red vinyl)		
45(P)	**YOU'RE SO GOOD WHEN YOU'RE BAD** (82)	RCA Victor 13293	$10
	(Orange promo label, red vinyl)		
45(P)	**MORE AND MORE** (83)	RCA Victor 13451	$10
	(Orange promo label, green vinyl)		
45(P)	**NIGHT GAMES** (83)	RCA Victor 13542	$10
	(Orange promo label, red vinyl)		
45(P)	**DOWN ON THE FARM** (85)	RCA Victor 14045	$12
	(Green promo label, blue vinyl)		
45(P)	**MOODY WOMAN** (No year listed)	(No label)	$10
	(Special copy, blue label, red vinyl)		

-EPs-

EP(JB)	**IN PERSON** (69) Jukebox LLP	RCA Victor 4094	$12
	(Issued with a hard cover)		
EP(JB)	**SINGS HEART SONGS** (71) Jukebox LLP	RCA Victor 4617	$12
	(Issued with a hard cover)		
EP(JB)	**THE BEST OF CHARLEY PRIDE** (72) Jukebox LLP	RCA Victor 4223	$10

	(Issued with a soft cover)			
33(P)	**IN CONCERT WITH CHARLEY PRIDE** (No year)		RCA Victor 10287	$10
	(Singles number, with Milsap, Parton, Stewart, Atkins, and Reed,			
	Pride is host, no cover)			

-albums-

LP	**COUNTRY CHARLEY PRIDE** (66) Mono		RCA Victor 3645	$15
LP	**COUNTRY CHARLEY PRIDE** (66) Stereo		RCA Victor 3645	$20
LP	**THE PRIDE OF COUNTRY MUSIC** (67) Mono		RCA Victor 3775	$20
	(Very hard to find in mono)			
LP	**THE PRIDE OF COUNTRY MUSIC** (67) Stereo		RCA Victor 3775	$15
LP	**THE COUNTRY WAY** (67) Mono		RCA Victor 3895	$20
	(Mono is rare)			
LP	**THE COUNTRY WAY** (67) Stereo		RCA Victor 3895	$12
LP	**MAKE MINE COUNTRY** (68) Mono		RCA Victor 3952	$50
	(The rarest mono)			
LP	**MAKE MINE COUNTRY** (68) Stereo		RCA Victor 3952	$12
LP	**SONGS OF PRIDE, CHARLEY THAT IS** (68)		RCA Victor 4041	$10
LP	**SWEET COUNTRY** (73) Quad version		RCA Victor 0217	$12
LP	**AMAZING LOVE** (73) Quad version		RCA Victor 0397	$12
LP	**PRIDE OF AMERICA** (74) Quad version		RCA Victor 0757	$12
LP	**CHARLEY** (75) Quad version		RCA Victor 1038	$12
LP	**THE HAPPINESS OF HAVING YOU** (75) Quad version		RCA Victor 1241	$12
LP	**SUNDAY MORNING WITH CHARLEY PRIDE** (76) Quad version		RCA Victor 1359	$12

-radio shows-

3LP(RS)	**SILVER EAGLE** (81) With Sylvia and John Conley		DIR	$18-35
	(Live concert)			
	See the Pridesmen			

THE PRIDESMEN (C)
Back-up group for Charley Pride
RCA Victor 45s $2 each
Other RCA Victor LPs $8 each

-albums-

LP	**THE PRIDESMEN** (73)		RCA Victor 0315	$12
	See Charley Pride			

JIMMY PRITCHETT (RB)

-singles-

45rpm	**THAT'S THE WAY I FEEL** (58)		Crystal 503	$55

ORVAL PROPHET (CW)
Other Decca 45s $4-8 each

-singles-

45rpm	**THE JUDGEMENT DAY EXPRESS** (52)		Decca 28206	$12

RONNIE PROPHET (C)
RCA Victor 45s $1 each
RCA Victor LPs $3 each

JEANNE PRUETT (C)
Decca 45s $2-3 each
Other label LPs $3 each

-albums-

LP	**LOVE ME** (72)		Decca 75360	$10

LEWIS PRUITT (RB)

-singles-

45rpm	**PRETTY BABY** (58)		Peach 703	$40
45rpm	**THIS LITTLE GIRL** (59)		Peach 710	$40

RALPH PRUITT (RB)

-singles-

45rpm	**HEY MR. PORTER** (58)		Lark 1506	$150
45rpm	**HEY MR. PORTER** (58)		Meridan 1507	$125
45rpm	**LOUISE** (58)		B.B. 226	$60

CACTUS PRYOR (N)

-singles-

45rpm	**WHAT'S THE SCORE, PODNER** (53)		4-Star 1676	$25
	(Dizzy Dean type play-by-play parody)			

DENNIS PUCKET (RB)

-singles-

45rpm	**ROCKIN' TEENS** (58)		Emerald 2018	$100

DWIGHT PULLEN (RB)

-singles-

45rpm	**SUNGLASSES AFTER DARK** (58)	Carlton 455	$250
45(P)	**SUNGLASSES AFTER DARK** (58)	Carlton 455	$175
	(Green promo label)		

WHITEY PULLEN (RB)

-singles-

45rpm	**WALK MY WAY BACK HOME** (57)	Sage 274	$40
45rpm	**LET'S ALL GO WILD TONIGHT** (58)	Sage 294	$40

-albums-

LP	**WHITEY PULLEN, COUNTRY MUSIC STAR** (63) Mono	Crown 5332	$40
LP	**WHITEY PULLEN, COUNTRY MUSIC STAR** (63) Stereo	Crown 32	$15

VERN PULLENS (RB)

-singles-

45rpm	**MAMA DON'T ALLOW NO BOPPIN'** (58)	Spade	$85
45rpm	**BOP CRAZY BABY** (58)	Spade 1927	$85

LEROY PULLINS (C)
Kapp 45s $2 each

-albums-

LP	**I'M A NUT** (66)	Kapp 3488	$12
LP	**FUNNY BONES & HEARTS** (68)	Kapp 3557	$10

PURE PRAIRIE LEAGUE (C)
Casablanca 45s $3-5 each
   (Vince Gill is lead singer)
RCA Victor 45s $1-2 each
Casablanca LPs $5-10 each
   (Gill is lead singer)
RCA Victor LPs $3-6 each
   (Gill sings lead on the first RCA LP)
See Vince Gill

CURLEY PUTNAM (C)
ABC 45s $2 each
ABC LPs $3 each

Q

RAY QUAL (RB)

-singles-

45rpm	**GOING ROCKIN' TONIGHT** (58)	Apache 1836	$150

DOUG QUATTLEBAUM (RB)

-singles-

45rpm	**DON'T BE FUNNY BABY** (53)	Gotham 7519	$60

R

EDDIE RABBITT (C)
Other Elektra 45s $2 each
Warner 45s $2 each
RCA Victor 45s $2 each including duets
RCA Victor promo-only picture sleeves $3 each
Elektra and Warner LPs $3-5 each
RCA Victor LPs $3 each

-singles-

45rpm	**THE BED** (68)	Date 1599	$10
45(P)	**THE BED** (68)	Date 1599	$15
	(White promo label)		
45(P)	**SONG OF IRELAND** (78)	Elektra 1A-378	$12
	(Shamrock promo-only label with small center hole, green vinyl)		

		-albums-		
LP(P)	**EDDIE RABBITT AN AUDIOBIOGRAPHY** (79)		Elektra 279	$25
	(White promo label, issued with special hard cover)			
		-radio shows-		
LP(RS)	**COUNTRY GREATS IN CONCERT** (81) Eddie Rabbitt		ABC Radio 108	$25-40
	(Live concert, also broadcast in Canada, price includes script)			
Reel(P)	**BARTENDER SONG** (81) Radio spots		Trackworks 703	$15-20
	(Five-inch reel 7.5 ips, spot for Miller High Life)			
LP(RS)	**ROBERT W. MORGAN** (Feb 81)		Watermark	$10-15
	(Music and interviews)			
Reel(P)	**BARTENDER SONG/GOIN' OUT FOR A BEER** (82) Radio spots		Trackworks 1036	$15-20
	(Five-inch reel 7.5 ips, spots for Miller High Life)			
3LP(RS)	**THE EDDIE RABBITT STORY** (May 83) Box set		United Stations	$20-40
	(Price includes scripts)			
2LP(RS)	**STARTRACK PROFILE** (Aug 84)		Westwood One	$10-15
	(Music and interviews)			
LP(RS)	**WESTWOOD ONE PRESENTS** (Jun 89)		Westwood One	$10-15
	(Music and interviews)			

BUZZ RABIN (C)
Elektra 45s $2 each

-albums-

LP	**CROSS COUNTRY COWBOY** (73)		Elektra 75076	$10

JIMMY RAGSDALE (CW)

-singles-

45rpm	**ENGINEER'S SONG** (53)		Columbia 21123	$12

MARVIN RAINWATER (CW)
Other MGM black label 45s (after 12865) $4-8 each
Wesco 45s $4 each
Brave 45s $5 each
  (Including 45s by Taller O'Shea)
Kajak, United Artists 45s $4 each
Nu Trayl 45s $3 each
Okie 45s $2 each
Little Ralph Himself 33s $3 each

-singles-

45(P)	**ESPECIALLY FOR FRIENDS** (55) White promo label		(No Label) MR 1-A	$75
	(An MGM promo-only tribute to Hank Williams including			
	dialogue and three songs with "Hearts Hall of Fame")			
45rpm	**STICKS AND STONES** (55)		MGM 12071	$15
45(P)	**STICKS AND STONES** (55)		MGM 12071	$10
	(Yellow promo label)			
45rpm	**TENNESSEE HOUN' DOG YODEL** (55)		MGM 12090	$15
45(P)	**TENNESSEE HOUN' DOG YODEL** (55)		MGM 12090	$10
	(Yellow promo label)			
45rpm	**DEM LOW DOWN BLUES** (55)		MGM 12152	$15
45(P)	**DEM LOW DOWN BLUES** (55)		MGM 12152	$10
	(Yellow promo label)			
45rpm	**HOT AND COLD** (56)		MGM 12240	$25
45(P)	**HOT AND COLD** (56)		MGM 12240	$20
	(Yellow promo label)			
45rpm	**WHY DID YOU HAVE TO GO AND LOVE ME** (56)		MGM 12313	$15
45(P)	**WHY DID YOU HAVE TO GO AND LOVE ME** (56)		MGM 12313	$10
	(Yellow promo label)			
45rpm	**GET OFF THE STOOL** (56)		MGM 12370	$15
45(P)	**GET OFF THE STOOL** (56)		MGM 12370	$10
	(Yellow promo label)			
78rpm	**GONNA FIND ME A BLUEBIRD** (56)		MGM 12412	$15
78(P)	**GONNA FIND ME A BLUEBIRD** (56)		MGM 12412	$18
	(Yellow promo label)			
45rpm	**GONNA FIND ME A BLUEBIRD** (56)		MGM 12412	$15
45(P)	**GONNA FIND ME A BLUEBIRD** (56)		MGM 12412	$10
	(Yellow promo label)			
45rpm	**I GOTTA GO GET MY BABY**		Coral 61342	$12
45(P)	**I GOTTA GO GET MY BABY**		Coral 61342	$10
	(Blue promo label)			
45rpm	**MY BRAND OF BLUES** (57)		MGM 12511	$15
45(P)	**MY BRAND OF BLUES** (57)		MGM 12511	$10
	(Yellow promo label)			
45rpm	**THE MAJESTY OF LOVE** (57)		MGM 12555	$15
	(Marvin Rainwater and Connie Francis)			
45(P)	**THE MAJESTY OF LOVE** (57)		MGM 12555	$10
	(Yellow promo label)			

45rpm	**LUCKY STAR** (57)	MGM 12586	$15
45(P)	**LUCKY STAR** (57)	MGM 12586	$10
	(Yellow promo label)		
45rpm	**BABY, DON'T GO** (57)	MGM 12609	$15
45(P)	**BABY, DON'T GO** (57)	MGM 12609	$10
	(Yellow promo label)		
45rpm	**TWO FOOLS IN LOVE** (58)	MGM 12625	$15
	(Marv and Patty)		
45(P)	**TWO FOOLS IN LOVE** (58)	MGM 12625	$10
	(Yellow promo label)		
45rpm	**I DIG YOU BABY** (58)	MGM 12665	$15
45(P)	**I DIG YOU BABY** (58)	MGM 12665	$10
	(Yellow promo label)		
45rpm	**A NEED FOR LOVE** (58)	MGM 12701	$15
45(P)	**A NEED FOR LOVE** (58)	MGM 12701	$10
	(Yellow promo label)		
45rpm	**CAN I COUNT ON YOU** (58)	MGM 12728	$15
	(Marv and Patty)		
45(P)	**CAN I COUNT ON YOU** (58)	MGM 12728	$10
	(Yellow promo label)		
45rpm	**BORN TO BE LONESOME** (58)	MGM 12739	$15
45(P)	**BORN TO BE LONESOME** (58)	MGM 12739	$10
	(Yellow promo label)		
45rpm	**LOVE ME BABY** (59)	MGM 12773	$15
45(P)	**LOVE ME BABY** (59)	MGM 12773	$10
	(Yellow promo label)		
45rpm	**HALF BREED** (59)	MGM 12803	$15
45(P)	**HALF BREED** (59)	MGM 12803	$10
	(Yellow promo label)		
45rpm	**THE PALE FACED INDIAN** (59) Black label	MGM 12865	$15
45(P)	**THE PALE FACED INDIAN** (59)	MGM 12865	$10
	(Yellow promo label)		
45rpm	**BOO HOO** (62)	Warwick 666	$12
45(P)	**BOO HOO** (62)	Warwick 666	$10
	(White promo label)		
45rpm	**TOUGH TOP CAT** (63)	Warwick 674	$15
45(P)	**TOUGH TOP CAT** (63)	Warwick 674	$10
	(White promo label)		
45rpm	**I GOTTA GO GET MY BABY** (63)	Coral 61342	$15
45(P)	**I GOTTA GO GET MY BABY** (63)	Coral 61342	$10
	(Blue promo label)		
	(Later version on Hilltop worth $5)		

-EPs-

EP	**SONGS BY MARVIN RAINWATER VOL 1** (57)	MGM 1464	$30
EP	**SONGS BY MARVIN RAINWATER VOL 2** (57)	MGM 1465	$30
EP	**SONGS BY MARVIN RAINWATER VOL 3** (57)	MGM 1466	$30

-albums-

LP	**SONGS BY MARVIN RAINWATER** (57)	MGM 3534	$100
LP(P)	**SONGS BY MARVIN RAINWATER** (57)	MGM 3534	$125
	(Yellow promo label)		
LP	**MARVIN RAINWATER SINGS WITH A BEAT** (58)	MGM 3721	$100
LP(P)	**MARVIN RAINWATER SINGS WITH A BEAT** (58)	MGM 3721	$125
	(Yellow promo label)		
LP	**SING FOR YOU** (60) With Webb Pierce	Audio Lab 1653	$75
LP	**GONNA FIND ME A BLUEBIRD** (62)	MGM 4046	$75
LP(P)	**GONNA FIND ME A BLUEBIRD** (62)	MGM 4046	$100
	(Yellow promo label)		
LP	**COUNTRY'S FAVORITE SINGER** (70)	Mount Vernon 146	$15
LP	**GOLDEN COUNTRY HITS SUNG BY MARVIN RAINWATER** (72)	Spinorama 109	$12
	(Other side of the LP has songs sung by Wade Holmes)		
LP	**MARVIN RAINWATER** (74)	Crown 307	$20
LP	**MARVIN RAINWATER & MIKE COWDERY** (81)	Hoky 107	$15

BONNIE RAITT (C)
Any 45s $2 each
Any LPs $4 each

-radio shows-

| Cass(RS) | **AUSTIN ENCORE** (92) With Ricky Skaggs | Main Street | $30-60 |
| | (Live concert) | | |

OBRAY RAMSEY (BG)
ABC 45s $2 each

-albums-

LP	**OBRAY RAMSEY SINGS JIMMIE RODGERS FAVORITES** (60)	Prestige 13009	$30
LP	**FOLK SONGS FROM THE THREE LAURELS** (61)	Prestige 13020	$25
LP	**BANJO SONGS FOR THE BLUE RIDGE & SMOKY** (60s)	Riverside 649	$20

LP	WHITE LIGHTNING (69)	ABC 690	$12
LP(P)	WHITE LIGHTNING (60)	ABC 690	$15
	(White promo label)		
LP	WHITE LIGHTNING FRESH AIR (70s)	Polydor 4047	$10
LP(P)	WHITE LIGHTNING FRESH AIR (70s)	Polydor 4047	$12
	(White promo label)		
LP	BLUE RIDGE BANJO (70s)	Washington 707	$15

BOOTS RANDOLPH (C)
Monument 45s $2 each
Monument jukebox LLPs $5 each
Other Monument LPs $3-6 each
Other Camden LPs $5-10 each

-albums-

LP	YAKETY SAX (60)	RCA Victor 2165	$18
	(Includes the original "Yakety Sax")		
LP	THE YAKIN' SAX MAN (64)	Camden 825	$15
	(Also includes original "Yakety Sax," the hit version of the song was released after the RCA sessions on Monument)		
LP	SWEET TALK (65)	Camden 865	$15

WAYNE RANEY (CW)
Other King 78s and 45s $4-8 each
Starday 45s $3-5 each
Old Homestead LPs $3-5 each

-singles-

78rpm	LOST JOHN BOOGIE (48)	King 719	$15
78rpm	JACK AND JILL BOOGIE (48)	King 732	$12
78rpm	WHY DON'T YOU HAUL OFF AND LOVE ME (49)	King 791	$10
45rpm	THE CHILD'S SIDE OF LIFE (52)	King 1149	$18
45rpm	POWERFUL LOVE (52)	King 1160	$10

-EPs-

EP	WAYNE RANEY & THE RANEY FAMILY (60)	Starday 124	$15
EP	WAYNE RANEY & HIS TALKING HARMONICA (60)	Starday 126	$15

-albums-

LP	SONGS FROM THE HILLS (58)	King 588	$40
LP	WAYNE RANEY & THE RANEY FAMILY (60)	Starday 124	$30
LP	WAYNE RANEY & THE RANEY FAMILY (70s)	Nashville 2002	$18
LP	DON'T TRY TO BE WHAT YOU AIN'T (64)	Starday 279	$20
LP	GATHERING IN THE SKY (70)	Rimrock 492	$12
LP	WE NEED A LOT MORE OF JESUS (70s)	Rimrock	$15

RANGERS QUARTET (G)

-singles-

45rpm	HEAVENLY CANNON BALL (55)	Capitol 3035	$25
45(P)	HEAVENLY CANNON BALL (55)	Capitol 3035	$15
	(White promo label)		
45rpm	GLORYLAND BOOGIE (55)	Capitol 3142	$25
45(P)	GLORYLAND BOOGIE (55)	Capitol 3142	$15
	(White promo label)		

OLE RASMUSSEN (CW)
And His Nebraska Cornhuskers
Capitol 78s and 45s $5 each

BOZO RATLIFF (RB)

-singles-

45rpm	LET ME IN (58)	Space 100	$50

RAUNCH HANDS (C)
Epic 45s $3 each

-albums-

LP	PICKIN' & SINGIN' (60)	Epic 3698	$18
LP(P)	PICKIN' & SINGIN' (60)	Epic 3698	$25
	(White promo label)		
LP	THE RAUNCH HANDS AGAINST THE WORLD (61)	Epic 586	$18
LP(P)	THE RAUNCH HANDS AGAINST THE WORLD (61)	Epic 586	$25
	(White promo label)		

EDDY RAVEN (C)
Other RCA Victor and ABC 45s $1 each
Any LPs $3-5 each

-singles-

45(P)	I GOT MEXICO (84)	RCA Victor 13746	$10
	(Orange promo label, red vinyl)		

-radio shows-

3LP(RS)	**AMERICAN EAGLE** (Oct 86)	DIR	$10-15
	(Live concert)		
LP(RS)	**WESTWOOD ONE PRESENTS** (Jan 87)	Westwood One	$10-15
	(Live concert)		
LP(RS)	**LIVE AT GILLEY'S** (Jan 87)	Westwood One	$10-15
	(Live concert)		

DAVID RAY (RB)

-singles-

45rpm	**LONESOME BABY BLUES** (58)	Kliff 101	$60
45rpm	**JITTER BUGGIN' BABY** (58)	Kliff 102	$60

DON RAY (RB)

-singles-

45rpm	**THOSE ROCK AND ROLL BLUES** (58)	Rodeo 129	$50
45rpm	**DONCHA' BABY MY BABY** (59)	Rodeo 130	$50

RONNIE RAY (RB)

-singles-

45rpm	**MEAN MAMA BLUES** (58)	Circle Dot 1002	$60

WADE RAY (CW)
Other Capitol 45s $5-10 each
Other RCA Victor 45s $4-8 each
ABC Paramount 45s $3 each

-singles-

45rpm	**FLOP-EARED MULE** (49)	Capitol 40204	$12
45rpm	**HEART OF A CLOWN** (52)	RCA Victor 4429	$10
45rpm	**THAT LOVE MAKIN' MELODY** (53)	RCA Victor 5377	$10

-EPs-

EP(P)	**WHEN I LOST YOU/ALL OR NOTHIN' MAN** (57)	RCA Victor DJ-66	$18
	(Two songs on each side, flip side is by Del Wood)		

-albums-

LP	**A RAY OF COUNTRY SUN** (66)	ABC Paramount 539	$15
LP(P)	**A RAY OF COUNTRY SUN** (66)	ABC Paramount 539	$25
	(White promo label)		
LP	**WALK SOFTLY** (66)	Camden 2107	$25
	(Early RCA Victor material)		

SUSAN RAYE (C)
Capitol 45s $1-2 each
United Artists 45s $1 each
Capitol LPs $4-6 each
United Artists LPs $3-6 each

REBEL ROUSERS (RB)

-singles-

45rpm	**RED HEADED WOMAN** (58)	Jan 11959	$100

RED RIVER DAVE (CW)
Dave McEnery

-singles-

45rpm	**RED RIVER VALLEY** (51)	Royale 4516	$25
45rpm	**NEW YEAR BELLS** (52)	MGM 11070	$20
45rpm	**COTTON EYED JOE** (54)	Remington 1031	$18
45rpm	**THE RED DECK OF CARDS** (54)	Decca 29002	$15
45(P)	**THE RED DECK OF CARDS** (54)	Decca 29002	$12
	(Pink promo label)		

-EPs-

EP	**SADDLE SONGS OF THE WEST** (60s)	Varsity 7	$18
	(With Jesse Rogers)		

-albums-

10"LP	**RED RIVER DAVE** (51)	Varsity 6962	$75
LP	**RED RIVER DAVE SINGS** (62)	Continental 1507	$25
LP	**RED RIVER DAVE VOL 1** (70s)	Bluebonnet 119	$18
LP	**RED RIVER DAVE VOL 2** (70s)	Bluebonnet 122	$18
LP	**SONGS OF THE RODEO** (70s) With the Texas Tophands	Place 714	$12

TEDDY REDELL (RB)

-singles-

45rpm	**KNOCKING ON THE BACKSIDE** (58)	Vaden 110	$40

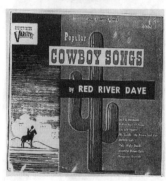

JERRY REED (CW)
Jerry Hubbard
RCA Victor white promo label 45s $4 each
Other RCA Victor 45s $2-4 each
RCA Victor picture sleeves $5-8 each
Other RCA Victor LPs, including duets, $5-10 each

-singles-

45rpm	SOLDIER'S JOY (57)	NRG 5008	$25
45(P)	SOLDIER'S JOY (57)	NRG 5008	$30
	(White promo label)		
45rpm	IF THE LORD'S WILLING AND THE CREEKS DON'T RISE (57)	Capitol 3294	$12
45(P)	IF THE LORD'S WILLING AND THE CREEKS DON'T RISE (57)	Capitol 3294	$10
	(White promo label)		
45rpm	I'M A LOVER, NOT A FIGHTER (57)	Capitol 3381	$15
45(P)	I'M A LOVER, NOT A FIGHTER (57)	Capitol 3381	$10
	(White promo label)		
45rpm	MISTER WHIZ (57)	Capitol 3429	$12
45(P)	MISTER WHIZ (57)	Capitol 3429	$10
	(White promo label)		
45rpm	JUST A ROMEO (57)	Capitol 3504	$12
45(P)	JUST A ROMEO (57)	Capitol 3504	$10
	(White promo label)		
45rpm	YOU'RE BRAGGIN' BOY (58)	Capitol 3592	$15
45(P)	YOU'RE BRAGGIN' BOY (58)	Capitol 3592	$10
	(White promo label)		
45rpm	IT'S HIGH TIME (58)	Capitol 3657	$15
45(P)	IT'S HIGH TIME (58)	Capitol 3657	$10
	(White promo label)		
45rpm	ROCKIN' IN BAGDAD (58)	Capitol 3731	$18
45(P)	ROCKIN' IN BAGDAD (58)	Capitol 3731	$15
	(Yellow promo label)		
45rpm	IN MY OWN BACK YARD (58)	Capitol 3823	$12
45(P)	IN MY OWN BACK YARD (58)	Capitol 3823	$10
	(Yellow promo label)		
45rpm	BESSIE BABY (58)	Capitol 3882	$15
45(P)	BESSIE BABY (58)	Capitol 3882	$12
	(White promo label)		
45rpm	YOUR MONEY MAKES YOU PURTY (59)	Capitol 3992	$12
45(P)	YOUR MONEY MAKES YOU PURTY (59)	Capitol 3992	$10
	(White promo label)		
45rpm	GOODNIGHT IRENE (62)	Columbia 42417	$12
45(P)	GOODNIGHT IRENE (62)	Columbia 42417	$15
	(White promo label)		
45rpm	HULLY GULLY GUITAR (62)	Columbia 42533	$12
45rpm	HULLY GULLY GUITAR (62)	Columbia 42533	$25
	(Price includes picture sleeve)		
33rpm	HULLY GULLY GUITAR (62)	Columbia 42533	$20
	(Single 33)		
45(P)	HULLY GULLY GUITAR (62)	Columbia 42533	$15
	(White promo label)		
45rpm	JUNE NIGHT (64)	Columbia 43052	$12
	(With the Hully Girlies)		
45(P)	JUNE NIGHT (64)	Columbia 43052	$10
	(White promo label)		
45(P)	HIGH BALLIN' (77) Two movie promo spots	American International 7808	$25
	(Radio spots, one sided)		
45(P)	THE LINE IN GASOLINE (79)	RCA Victor 11638	$15
	(Red promo label, red vinyl)		
45(P)	THE MAN WITH THE GOLDEN THUMB (82)	RCA Victor 13081	$12
	(Gold promo label, green vinyl)		
45(P)	THE BIRD (82)	RCA Victor 13355	$12
	(Cream-colored promo label, blue vinyl)		
45(P)	DOWN ON THE CORNER (82)	RCA Victor 13422	$15
	(Gold promo label, green vinyl)		
45(P)	SHE'S READY FOR SOMEONE TO LOVE HER (83)	RCA Victor 13527	$12
	(Gold promo label, blue vinyl)		
45(P)	GOOD OLE BOYS (83)	RCA Victor 13527	$15
	(Gold promo label, green vinyl)		

-EPs-

33(P)	SMOKEY AND THE BANDIT (77)	MCA S33-1961	$18
	(Four songs from the soundtrack, by Reed, issued with a hard printed cover)		
33(P)	FOREST FIRE PREVENTION (82)	Advertising Council	$20
	(Includes "Jerry Reed's Friends" as one of eight PSA radio spots)		

-albums-

LP	THE UNBELIEVABLE GUITAR & VOICE OF JERRY REED (67)	RCA Victor 3756	$15

LP	I'M MOVIN' ON (71)	Harmony 30547	$10
LP(P)	I'M MOVIN' ON (71)	Harmony 30547	$12
	(White promo label)		
LP	OH WHAT A WOMAN (72)	Camden 2585	$12
LP	TUPELO, MISSISSIPPI FLASH (74)	Camden 0331	$12

BILL REEDER (RB)
-singles-

45rpm	TILL I WALTZ AGAIN WITH YOU (58)	Voll Para 100	$50

DEL REEVES (C)
And the Good Time Charlies
United Artists 45s $2-4 each
United Artists picture sleeves $4 each
Reprise 45s $3 each
Other United Artists LPs, including duets, $4-8 each
Liberty duet LPs $8 each
Koala and Exact duet LPs $5 each
-albums-

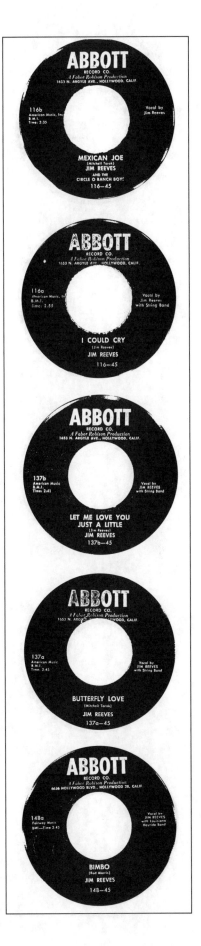

LP	GIRL ON THE BILLBOARD (65)	United Artists 6441	$18
LP(P)	GIRL ON THE BILLBOARD (65)	United Artists 6441	$20
	(White promo label)		
LP	DOODLE-OO-DOO-DOO (65)	United Artists 6458	$18
LP(P)	DOODLE-OO-DOO-DOO (65)	United Artists 6458	$20
	(White promo label)		
LP	DEL REEVES SINGS JIM REEVES (66)	United Artists 6468	$15
LP(P)	DEL REEVES SINGS JIM REEVES (66)	United Artists 6468	$18
	(White promo label)		
LP	SPECIAL DELIVERY (66)	United Artists 6488	$12
LP(P)	SPECIAL DELIVERY (66)	United Artists 6488	$15
	(White promo label)		
LP	SANTA'S BOY (66)	United Artists 6528	$15
LP(P)	SANTA'S BOY (66)	United Artists 6528	$18
	(White promo label)		
LP	GETTIN' ANY FEED FOR YOUR CHICKENS? (66)	United Artists 6530	$15
LP(P)	GETTIN' ANY FEED FOR YOUR CHICKENS? (66)	United Artists 6530	$18
	(White promo label)		
LP	STRUTTIN' MY STUFF (67)	United Artists 6571	$12
LP(P)	STRUTTIN' MY STUFF (67)	United Artists 6571	$15
	(White promo label)		
LP	SIX OF ONE, HALF-A-DOZEN OF THE OTHER (67)	United Artists 6595	$12
LP(P)	SIX OF ONE, HALF-A-DOZEN OF THE OTHER (67)	United Artists 6595	$15
	(White promo label)		
LP	THE BEST OF DEL REEVES (67)	United Artists 6635	$15
LP(P)	THE BEST OF DEL REEVES (67)	United Artists 6635	$18
	(White promo label)		
LP	RUNNING WILD (67)	United Artists 6673	$12
LP(P)	RUNNING WILD (67)	United Artists 6673	$15
	(White promo label)		
LP	LOOKING AT THE WORLD THROUGH A WINDSHIELD (67)	United Artists 6674	$12
LP(P)	LOOKING AT THE WORLD THROUGH A WINDSHIELD (67)	United Artists 6674	$15
	(White promo label)		
LP	THE LITTLE CHURCH IN THE DELL (67)	United Artists 6612	$15
LP(P)	THE LITTLE CHURCH IN THE DELL (67)	United Artists 6612	$18
	(White promo label)		
LP	OUR WAY OF LIFE (67) With Bobby Goldsboro	United Artists 6615	$12
LP(P)	OUR WAY OF LIFE (67)	United Artists 6615	$15
	(White promo label)		
LP	DOWN AT GOOD TIME CHARLIE'S (69)	United Artists 6705	$12
LP(P)	DOWN AT GOOD TIME CHARLIE'S (69)	United Artists 6705	$15
	(White promo label)		
LP	THE WONDERFUL WORLD OF COUNTRY MUSIC (69)	Sunset 5230	$15

GLENN REEVES (RB)
-singles-

45rpm	ROCKIN' COUNTRY STYLE (57)	Atco 6080	$18
45rpm	ROCK-A-BILLY LOU (58) Stock or promo copy	Decca 30589	$12
45rpm	I'M JOHNNY ON THE SPOT	TNT 120	$30
45rpm	I AIN'T GOT ROOM TO ROCK	TNT 129	$25

JIM REEVES (CW)
Other RCA Victor 78s $8-10 each
Other RCA Victor 45s $2-8 each
RCA 447 series, dog on top 45s $3 each
Other RCA Victor promo 45s $3-8 each
MCA duet 45s $2 each
Pair 2LP sets $10
Pickwick LPs $4-8 each
MCA and RCA Victor duet LPs with Patsy Cline $5 each

-singles-

78rpm	**WAGON LOAD OF LOVE** (53)	Abbott 115	$30
45rpm	**WAGON LOAD OF LOVE** (53)	Abbott 115	$40
78rpm	**MEXICAN JOE** (53)	Abbott 116	$25
45rpm	**MEXICAN JOE** (53) Black vinyl	Abbott 116	$40
	(Answer song is Carolyn Bradshaw's "Marriage of Mexican Joe," Abbott 141)		
45rpm	**MEXICAN JOE** (53) Red vinyl	Abbott 116	$100
	(With the "Circle O Ranch Boys")		
78rpm	**BUTTERFLY LOVE** (53)	Abbott 137	$25
45rpm	**BUTTERFLY LOVE** (53) Red label	Abbott 137	$25
45rpm	**BUTTERFLY LOVE** (53) Brown label	Abbott 137	$30
78rpm	**EL RANCHO DEL RIO** (53)	Abbott 143	$25
45rpm	**EL RANCHO DEL RIO** (53)	Abbott 143	$25
78rpm	**BIMBO** (54)	Abbott 148	$20
45rpm	**BIMBO** (54)	Abbott 148	$25
78rpm	**I LOVE YOU** (54) Ginny Wright and Jim Reeves	Fabor 101	$25
45rpm	**I LOVE YOU** (54)	Fabor 101	$30
	(Jim Reeves does recitation)		
45(P)	**I LOVE YOU** (54)	Fabor 101	$40
	(Black promo label)		
78rpm	**THEN I'LL STOP LOVING YOU** (54)	Abbott 160	$20
45rpm	**THEN I'LL STOP LOVING YOU** (54)	Abbott 160	$25
78rpm	**BEATIN' ON THE DING DONG** (54)	Abbott 164	$20
45rpm	**BEATIN' ON THE DING DONG** (54)	Abbott 164	$25
78rpm	**PADRE OF OLD SAN ANTONE** (54)	Abbott 168	$20
45rpm	**PADRE OF OLD SAN ANTONE** (54)	Abbott 168	$25
78rpm	**PENNY CANDY** (54)	Abbott 170	$20
45rpm	**PENNY CANDY** (54)	Abbott 170	$25
78rpm	**WHERE DOES A BROKEN HEART GO** (55)	Abbott 174	$20
45rpm	**WHERE DOES A BROKEN HEART GO** (55)	Abbott 174	$25
78rpm	**DRINKING TEQUILA** (55)	Abbott 178	$20
45rpm	**DRINKING TEQUILA** (55)	Abbott 178	$25
78rpm	**TAHITI** (55)	Abbott 180	$25
45rpm	**TAHITI** (55)	Abbott 180	$25
78rpm	**ARE YOU THE ONE** (55)	Abbott 184	$25
45rpm	**ARE YOU THE ONE** (55)	Abbott 184	$25
78rpm	**HILLBILLY WALTZ** (55)	Abbott 186	$25
45rpm	**HILLBILLY WALTZ** (55)	Abbott 186	$18
78rpm	**YONDER COMES A SUCKER** (55)	RCA Victor 6200	$15
45rpm	**YONDER COMES A SUCKER** (55)	RCA Victor 6200	$10
45(P)	**YONDER COMES A SUCKER** (55)	RCA Victor 6200	$20
	(White promo label, includes promo-only intro)		
78rpm	**JIMBO JENKINS** (55)	RCA Victor 6274	$15
45rpm	**JIMBO JENKINS** (55)	RCA Victor 6274	$12
45(P)	**JIMBO JENKINS** (55)	RCA Victor 6274	$15
	(White promo label)		
78rpm	**IF YOU WERE MINE** (55)	RCA Victor 6401	$12
45rpm	**IF YOU WERE MINE** (55)	RCA Victor 6401	$10
45(S)	**HE'LL HAVE TO GO** (59) Stereo single	RCA Victor 7643	$20
	(Black label stereo single)		
45rpm	**I'M GETTIN' BETTER** (60)	RCA Victor 7756	$15
	(Price includes picture sleeve)		
45rpm	**I MISSED ME** (60)	RCA Victor 7800	$15
	(Price includes picture sleeve)		
33rpm	**THE BLIZZARD** (60) Compact single	RCA Victor 7855	$40
	(Small center hole, must have a "37" prefix)		
45rpm	**PRIDE GOES BEFORE A FALL** (62)	RCA Victor 8080	$18
	(Price includes picture sleeve)		
5-45s	**A TOUCH OF VELVET** (62) Five jukebox singles	RCA Victor (1-5) 2487	$12 each
	($60 for the set of stereo singles, including paper envelope cover)		
45rpm	**IS THIS ME?** (62)	RCA Victor 8127	$15
	(Price includes picture sleeve)		
45rpm	**GUILTY** (63)	RCA Victor 8193	$15
	(Price includes picture sleeve)		
5-45s	**DIAMONDS BY THE DOZEN** (63) Five jukebox singles	RCA Victor (1-5) 2668	$12 each
	($60 for the set of stereo singles, including paper envelope cover)		
45(P)	**A STRANGER'S JUST A FRIEND** (64)	RCA Victor SP-143	$25
	(White promo label, release as a promo only)		
45rpm	**IS IT REALLY OVER?** (65)	RCA Victor 8625	$10
	(Price includes picture sleeve)		

-EPs-

EP	**SINGING DOWN THE LANE** (56)	RCA Victor 757	$50
2EP	**SINGING DOWN THE LANE** (56)	RCA Victor 1256	$100
EP	**BIMBO** (57)	RCA Victor 1410	$40
EP	**JIM REEVES** (57)	RCA Victor 1576	$40

EP	**FOUR WALLS** (57)	RCA Victor 4062	$30
EP(P)	**AM I LOSING YOU/WAITIN' FOR A TRAIN** (57)	RCA Victor 6749 DJ-42	$30
	(Promo-only EP, Dave Rich is on the flip side)		
EP	**HE'LL HAVE TO GO** (59)	RCA Victor 4357	$25
EP	**JIM REEVES' HITS** (59)	RCA Victor 5124	$25
EP	**AM I LOSING YOU** (60)	RCA Victor 5145	$25
33rpm	**TALL TALES & SHORT TEMPERS** (61)	RCA Victor 133	$50
	(Compact-33)		
EP(P)	**MOONLIGHT AND ROSES** (64) Jukebox LLP	RCA Victor 2854	$40
	(First pressing with dog in logo on cover)		
EP(P)	**MOONLIGHT AND ROSES** (76) Jukebox LLP	RCA Victor 2854	$25
	(Second pressing, NO dog in logo on cover)		
EP(P)	**THE BEST OF JIM REEVES** (66) Jukebox LLP	RCA Victor 289	$25
	(Issued with a hard cover)		
EP(P)	**THE JIM REEVES WAY** (65) Jukebox LLP	RCA Victor 2968	$25
	(Issued with a hard cover)		
EP(P)	**THE BEST OF JIM REEVES VOL. II** (66) Jukebox LLP	RCA Victor 3482	$25
	(Issued with a hard cover)		
EP(P)	**BLUE SIDE OF LONESOME** (67) Jukebox LLP	RCA Victor 3793	$25
	(This LLP opens from the left)		
EP(P)	**JIM REEVES** (74)	RCA Victor 10133	$25
	(Promo only, cream-colored label)		

-albums-

LP	**JIM REEVES SINGS** (56)	Abbott 5001	$1,500
	(Mono only)		
LP	**SINGING DOWN THE LANE** (56) Mono	RCA Victor 1256	$150
	(Price is for first pressing with LPM prefix)		
LP	**BIMBO** (57) Mono	RCA Victor 1410	$75
	(LPM prefix, repackage of Abbott-label LP)		
LP	**JIM REEVES** (57) Mono	RCA Victor 1576	$50
	(Must have LPM prefix)		
LP	**GIRLS I HAVE KNOWN** (58) Mono	RCA Victor 1685	$40
LP	**GOD BE WITH YOU** (58) Mono	RCA Victor 1950	$30
	(Must have prefix LSP)		
LP	**GOD BE WITH YOU** (58) Stereo	RCA Victor 1950	$50
LP	**SONGS TO WARM THE HEART** (59) Mono	RCA Victor 2001	$30
LP	**SONGS TO WARM THE HEART** (59) Stereo	RCA Victor 2001	$40
LP	**THE INTIMATE JIM REEVES** (60) Mono	RCA Victor 2216	$25
LP	**THE INTIMATE JIM REEVES** (60) Stereo	RCA Victor 2216	$30
LP	**HE'LL HAVE TO GO** (60) Mono	RCA Victor 2223	$30
LP	**HE'LL HAVE TO GO** (60) Stereo	RCA Victor 2223	$18
	(Rechanneled stereo)		
LP	**ACCORDING TO MY HEART** (60)	Camden 583	$20
LP	**TALL TALES & SHORT TEMPERS** (61) Mono	RCA Victor 2284	$20
LP	**TALL TALES & SHORT TEMPERS** (61) Stereo	RCA Victor 2284	$30
LP	**TALKIN' TO YOUR HEART** (61) Mono	RCA Victor 2339	$20
LP	**TALKIN' TO YOUR HEART** (61) Stereo	RCA Victor 2339	$30
LP	**A TOUCH OF VELVET** (62) Mono	RCA Victor 2487	$20
LP	**A TOUCH OF VELVET** (62) Stereo	RCA Victor 2487	$30
LP	**WE THANK THEE** (62) Mono	RCA Victor 2552	$20
LP	**WE THANK THEE** (62) Stereo	RCA Victor 2552	$30
LP	**THE COUNTRY SIDE OF JIM REEVES** (62)	RCA Victor 686	$20
LP	**GENTLEMAN JIM** (63) Mono	RCA Victor 2605	$20
LP	**GENTLEMAN JIM** (63) Stereo	RCA Victor 2605	$30
LP	**THE INTERNATIONAL JIM REEVES** (63) Mono	RCA Victor 2704	$20
LP	**THE INTERNATIONAL JIM REEVES** (63) Stereo	RCA Victor 2704	$30
LP	**TWELVE SONGS OF CHRISTMAS** (63) Mono	RCA Victor 2758	$20
LP	**TWELVE SONGS OF CHRISTMAS** (63) Stereo	RCA Victor 2758	$30
LP	**GOOD 'N COUNTRY** (63)	Camden 784	$18
LP	**DIAMONDS IN THE SAND** (63)	Camden 0123	$12
LP	**KIMBERLY JIM** (64) Mono	RCA Victor 2780	$15
	(Soundtrack)		
LP	**KIMBERLY JIM** (64) Stereo	RCA Victor 2780	$20
LP	**MOONLIGHT AND ROSES** (64) Mono	RCA Victor 2854	$15
LP	**MOONLIGHT AND ROSES** (64) Stereo	RCA Victor 2854	$20
LP	**THE BEST OF JIM REEVES** (64) Mono	RCA Victor 2890	$15
LP	**THE BEST OF JIM REEVES** (64) Stereo	RCA Victor 2890	$20
LP	**HAVE I TOLD YOU LATELY THAT I LOVE YOU** (64)	Camden 842	$18
LP	**I LOVE YOU** (64)	Guest Star 1471	$15
	(Budget label, includes the Ginny Wright track)		
LP	**THE JIM REEVES WAY** (65) Mono	RCA Victor 2968	$15
LP	**THE JIM REEVES WAY** (65) Stereo	RCA Victor 2968	$20
LP	**UP THROUGH THE YEARS** (65) Mono	RCA Victor 3427	$15
LP	**UP THROUGH THE YEARS** (65) Stereo	RCA Victor 3427	$20
LP(P)	**SOMETHING SPECIAL FOR DISC JOCKEYS** (66)	RCA Victor SP-33-479	$150
	(White promo label, promo-only release)		
LP	**THE BEST OF JIM REEVES VOL 2** (66) Mono	RCA Victor 3482	$15

LP	**THE BEST OF JIM REEVES VOL 2** (66) Stereo	RCA Victor 3482	$20
LP	**DISTANT DRUMS** (66) Mono	RCA Victor 3542	$15
LP	**DISTANT DRUMS** (66) Stereo	RCA Victor 3542	$20
LP	**YOURS SINCERELY, JIM REEVES** (66) Mono	RCA Victor 3709	$15
LP	**YOURS SINCERELY, JIM REEVES** (66) Stereo	RCA Victor 3709	$20
LP	**THE BLUE SIDE OF LONESOME** (67) Mono	RCA Victor 3793	$25
	(Scarce in mono)		
LP	**THE BLUE SIDE OF LONESOME** (67) Stereo	RCA Victor 3793	$20
LP	**MY CATHEDRAL** (67) Mono	RCA Victor 3903	$25
LP	**MY CATHEDRAL** (67) Stereo	RCA Victor 3903	$20
LP	**A TOUCH OF SADNESS** (68) Mono	RCA Victor 3987	$75
	(Very rare in mono)		
LP	**A TOUCH OF SADNESS** (68) Stereo	RCA Victor 3987	$20
LP	**JIM REEVES ON STAGE** (68)	RCA Victor 4062	$20
LP	**JIM REEVES AND SOME FRIENDS** (69)	RCA Victor 4112	$18
LP	**THE BEST OF JIM REEVES VOL 3** (69)	RCA Victor 4187	$18
4LP	**THE UNFORGETTABLE JIM REEVES** (69)	RCA Victor 0644	$25
	(Box set)		
LP	**JIM REEVES WRITES YOU A RECORD** (71)	RCA Victor 4475	$15
LP	**YOUNG & COUNTRY** (71)	Camden 2532	$15
	(Some of the Abbott material included)		
LP	**SOMETHING SPECIAL** (72)	RCA Victor 4528	$15
LP	**MY FRIEND** (72)	RCA Victor 4646	$12
2LP	**JIM REEVES** (72)	Camden 9001	$15
LP	**AM I THAT EASY TO FORGET** (73)	RCA Victor 0039	$12
	(Price includes bonus photo)		
5LP	**JIM REEVES GOLDEN RECORD COLLECTION** (74)	RCA Victor 0587	$40
	(RCA Special Products release)		
LP	**I LOVE YOU BECAUSE** (76)	RCA Victor 1224	$12
	(Price includes bonus photo)		
6LP	**THE UNFORGETTABLE JIM REEVES** (76) Box set	RCA Victor 210	$40
	(Released for *Readers Digest*)		

-radio shows-

16"(RS)	**LEATHERNECK JAMBOREE** Fifteen-minute show	Leatherneck	$100-150
	(Music and interviews)	Jamboree 14	
16"(RS)	**COUNTRY MUSIC TIME** Fifteen-minute show	U.S. Army 105	$50-100
	(Music and interviews)		
16"(RS)	**COUNTRY MUSIC TIME** Fifteen-minute show	U.S. Army 112	$50-100
	(Music and interviews)		
LP(RS)	**COUNTRY CROSSROADS** (Jul 82) Tribute show	Southern Baptist	$25-50
	(Music and interviews)		
LP(RS)	**COUNTRY MUSIC TIME** (60s-70S)	U.S. Air Force	$25-50
	Also see the Blue Boys		

HERB REMMINGTON (C)
United Artists 45s $2 each

-albums-

LP	**STEEL GUITAR HOLIDAY** (61)	United Artists 6167	$20
LP(P)	**STEEL GUITAR HOLIDAY** (61)	United Artists 6167	$25
	(White promo label)		
LP	**HERB REMMINGTON PLAYS THE STEEL** (65)	D 1115	$25
LP	**REMMINGTON RIDES AGAIN** (65)	Hilltop 6020	$18

JACK RENO (C)
Atco 45s $3-4 each
Dot 45s $3 each
Target 45s $2 each

-albums-

LP	**MEET JACK RENO** (68)	Atco 251	$15
LP(P)	**MEET JACK RENO** (68)	Atco 251	$18
	(White promo label)		
LP	**I WANT ONE** (68)	Dot 25921	$15
LP	**I'M A GOOD MAN IN A BAD FRAME OF MIND** (69)	Dot 25946	$15
LP	**HITCHIN' A RIDE** (72)	Target 1313	$12
LP	**INTERSTATE 7** (78)	Derbytown 106	$10

RENO & SMILEY (CW)
Don Reno
Don Reno and Red Smiley
Other King 45s $4-8 each
King-Bluegrass LPs with Bill Harrell $8-10 each
Rural Rhythm LPs with Bill Harrell $5-8 each
Rural Rhythm LPs with Buck Ryan $8 each
Rural Rhythm LPs by Red Smiley $8-10 each
Other CMH LPs with Bill Harrell $4-8 each
Cabin Creek LPs with Benny Martin $5 each
Rebel LPs with Eddie Adcock $5 each

RESTLESS HEART (C)

RCA Victor 45s $1 each
RCA Victor picture sleeves $3 each
RCA Victor LPs $3 each

EDDIE REYNOLDS (RB)

-singles-

45rpm	**WHAT WAS IT** (57)	Dixie 838	$40

WESTLEY REYNOLDS (RB)

-singles-

45rpm	**TRIP TO THE MOON** (58)	Rose 108	$45
45rpm	**RAG MOP** (58)	Rose 117	$30

RED RHODES (CW)
Crown, Exact, Happy Tiger, and Alshire LPs $4-8 each

SLIM RHODES (RB)

-singles-

45rpm	**UNCERTAIN LOVE** (55)	Sun 216	$12
45rpm	**HOUSE OF SIN** (56)	Sun 225	$18
45rpm	**GONNA ROMP & STOMP** (56)	Sun 238	$25
45rpm	**DO WHAT I DO** (57)	Sun 256	$15

RHYTHM ROUSERS (RB)

-singles-

45rpm	**JUST BECAUSE** (58)	Rouser 7423	$40

BOBBY G. RICE (C)
Royal American, GRT, and Metromedia 45s $2 each
Any label LPs $4-8 each

ELDON RICE (RB)

-singles-

45rpm	**DON'T LET LOVE BREAK YOUR HEART** (58)	El Rio 413	$150

CHARLIE RICH (CW)
Also recorded as Bobby Sheridan
Other Smash 45s $4-8 each
Sun reissue series 45s $3 each
  (Recorded as Bobby Sheridan, released as Charlie Rich)
RCA Victor 45s $2-4 each
Epic 45s $1 each
Elektra and United Artists 45s $1 each
Epic promo EPs $3 each
Sun LPs $5 each
Other RCA Victor LPs $3 each
Other Epic LPs $1-2 each
Epic quad LPs $5-10 each
Buckboard, Pickwick, United Artists, Harmony, Elektra, Camden, and Power Pak LPs $1-3 each

-singles-

45rpm	**PHILADELPHIA BABY** (59)	Philips 3532	$25
45rpm	**REBOUND** (59)	Philips 3542	$20
45rpm	**RED MAN** (60) Bobby Sheridan	Sun 354	$30
45rpm	**LONELY WEEKENDS** (60)	Philips 3552	$20
45rpm	**GONNA BE WAITING** (60)	Philips 3560	$20
45rpm	**STAY** (60)	Philips 3562	$20
45rpm	**WHO WILL THE NEXT FOOL BE** (60)	Philips 3566	$20
45rpm	**JUST A LITTLE SWEET** (61)	Philips 3572	$20
45rpm	**MIDNIGHT BLUES** (62)	Philips 3576	$20
45rpm	**WHO WILL THE NEXT FOOL BE** (59)	Philips 3577	$15
45rpm	**SITTIN' AND THINKIN'** (63)	Philips 3582	$15
45rpm	**I NEED YOUR LOVE NOW** (63)	Philips 3584	$15
45rpm	**SHE LOVED EVERYBODY BUT ME** (63)	Groove 0020	$12
45rpm	**SHE LOVED EVERYBODY BUT ME** (63)	Groove 0020	$35
	(Price includes picture sleeve)		
45(P)	**SHE LOVED EVERYBODY BUT ME** (63)	Groove 0020	$18
	(White promo label)		
45rpm	**BIG BOSS MAN** (63)	Groove 0025	$12
45(P)	**BIG BOSS MAN** (63)	Groove 0025	$15
	(White promo label)		
45rpm	**THE WAYS OF A WOMAN IN LOVE** (64)	Groove 0035	$12
45(P)	**THE WAYS OF A WOMAN IN LOVE** (64)	Groove 0035	$15
	(White promo label)		
45rpm	**MOHAIR SAM** (65)	Smash 1993	$10
45(P)	**MOHAIR SAM** (65)	Smash 1993	$12
	(White promo label)		
45(P)	**THE DANCE OF LOVE** (65)	Smash 2012	$10
	(White promo label)		
45(P)	**SOMETHING JUST CAME OVER ME** (66)	Smash 2022	$10
	(White promo label)		
45(P)	**TEARS AGO** (66)	Smash 2038	$10
	(White promo label)		

-albums-

LP	**LONELY WEEKENDS** (60)	Philips 1970	$400
LP	**CHARLIE RICH** (64) Mono	Groove 1000	$100
LP	**CHARLIE RICH** (64) Stereo	Groove 1000	$250
LP	**THAT'S RICH** (65) Mono	RCA Victor 3352	$25
LP	**THAT'S RICH** (65) Stereo	RCA Victor 3352	$40
LP	**THE MANY SIDES OF CHARLIE RICH** (65) Mono	Smash 27070	$20
LP	**THE MANY SIDES OF CHARLIE RICH** (65) Stereo	Smash 67070	$30
LP(P)	**THE MANY SIDES OF CHARLIE RICH** (65)	Smash 27070	$25
	(White promo label)		
LP	**BIG BOSS MAN** (66) Mono	RCA Victor 3537	$25
LP	**BIG BOSS MAN** (66) Stereo	RCA Victor 3537	$40
LP	**THE BEST YEARS** (66) Mono	Smash 27078	$15
LP	**THE BEST YEARS** (66) Stereo	Smash 67078	$20
LP(P)	**THE BEST YEARS** (66)	Smash 27078	$25
	(White promo label)		
LP	**CHARLIE RICH SINGS COUNTRY & WESTERN** (67)	Hi 32037	$18
LP(P)	**CHARLIE RICH SINGS COUNTRY & WESTERN** (67)	Hi 32037	$20
	(White promo label)		
LP	**A LONELY WEEKEND** (69)	Mercury 16375	$15
LP(P)	**A LONELY WEEKEND** (69)	Mercury 16375	$18
	(White promo label)		
LP(P)	**CHARLIE RICH** (72)	Epic AS-50	$18
	(White promo label)		
LP	**CHARLIE RICH** (74)	Hi 32084	$12
2LP	**FULLY REALIZED** (74)	Mercury 7505	$10
LP(P)	**EVERYTHING YOU WANTED TO HEAR** (76)	Epic AS-139	$15
	(White promo label)		

DAVE RICH (RB)

-singles-

45rpm	**AIN'T IT FINE** (57)	RCA Victor 6595	$18
45rpm	**LONELY STREET** (57)	RCA Victor 6753	$15
45rpm	**CHICKEN HOUSE** (58)	RCA Victor 7045	$15
45rpm	**SCHOOL BLUES** (58)	RCA Victor 7141	$12

-EPs-

EP(P)	**LONELY STREET/DIDN'T WORK OUT, DID IT?** (57)	RCA Victor 6753 DJ-42	$30
	(Flip side features two songs by Jim Reeves)		

-radio shows-

16"(RS)	**U.S. ARMY BAND** (60s)	U.S. Army	$50-75
	(Music and interviews)		

RICHARD & JIM (C)
Richard Lockmiller and Jim Connor

-albums-

LP	**FOLK SONGS & COUNTRY SOUNDS** (64)	Capitol 2058	$25
LP	**TWO BOYS FROM ALABAMA** (65)	Capitol 2287	$25

JIMMY RICHARDSON (C)

-albums-

LP	**SWEET WITH A BEAT** (60)	Starday 126	$18

MERLE RICHARDSON (RB)

-singles-

45rpm	**MEAN AND CRUEL** (58)	Caron 6103	$40

PAT RICHMOND (RB)

-singles-

45rpm	**DON'T STOP THE ROCKIN'** (58)	Vulco 1500	$50

ALMEDA RIDDLE (C)

-albums-

LP	**SONGS & BALLADS OF THE OZARKS** (64)	Vanguard 9158	$15

RIDERS OF THE PURPLE SAGE (CW)
Featuring Foy Willing
Other 78s $5-10 each
Other 45s $10 each

-singles-

78rpm	**TEXAS BLUES** (44) Foy Willing	Capitol 162	$15
78rpm	**DETOUR** (46) Foy Willing	Decca 9000	$12
78rpm	**HAVE I TOLD YOU LATELY THAT I LOVE YOU** (46)	Majestic 6000	$12
	(Foy Willing)		
45rpm	**DIVORCE ME C. O. D.** (50)	Varsity 45241	$25
45rpm	**SONG OF THE SIERRAS** (52)	Royale 4520	$15

45rpm	COOL WATER (54)	Varsity 45212	$15

-albums-

10"LP	RIDERS OF THE PURPLE SAGE (50)	Varsity 6032	$100
10"LP	RIDERS OF THE PURPLE SAGE (52)	Royale 6032	$100
LP	COWBOY (58) Foy Williing	Roulette 25035	$40
LP	THE NEW SOUND OF AMERICAN FOLK (62)	Jubilee 5021	$25

-radio shows-

16"(RS)	ARMED FORCES RADIO (60s)	Armed Forces 400	$25-50
	(Music and interview)		

TOMMY RIDGLEY (R & B)

-singles-

45rpm	I LIVE MY LIFE (52)	Imperial 5198	$45
45rpm	LOOPED (52)	Imperial 5203	$40
45rpm	MONKEY MAN (53)	Imperial 5214	$40
45rpm	GOOD TIMES (53)	Imperial 5223	$40

BILLY RILEY (RB)

-singles-

45rpm	FLIP FLOP & FLY (57)	Home of the Blues 233	$12
45rpm	ROCKIN' ON THE MOON (57)	Brunswick 55085	$50
45(P)	ROCKIN' ON THE MOON (57)	Brunswick 55085	$45
	(Yellow promo label)		
45rpm	ROCK WITH ME BABY (57)	Sun 245	$25
45rpm	FLYING SAUCERS ROCK AND ROLL (58)	Sun 260	$30
45rpm	RED HOT (58)	Sun 277	$15
45rpm	BABY PLEASE DON'T GO (58)	Sun 289	$10
45rpm	NO NAME GIRL (58)	Sun 313	$10
45rpm	GOT THE WATER BOILING (59)	Sun 322	$20

BOB RILEY (RB)

-singles-

45rpm	WANDA JEAN (57)	MGM 12612	$25
45(P)	WANDA JEAN (57)	MGM 12612	$18
	(Yellow promo label)		
45rpm	WITHOUT YOUR LOVE (57)	Dot 15625	$10

JEANNIE C. RILEY (C)
Other Plantation 45s $2-4 each

-singles-

45(P)	MY MAN (70) Promo copy	Plantation 65	$12
	(Green promo label, green vinyl)		
45(P)	MY MAN (70) Does not mention promo	Plantation 65	$10
	(Green promo label, green vinyl)		
45(P)	OH, SINGER (70)	Plantation 72	$10
	(Green promo label, green vinyl)		
45(P)	THE LION'S CLUB (71)	Plantation 85	$10
	(Green promo label, green vinyl)		
45(P)	HARPER VALLEY P. T. A. (78) Reissue	Plantation 173	$10
	(Green promo label, green vinyl, price includes picture sleeve)		
45(P)	HARPER VALLEY P. T. A. (78) Reissue	Plantation 173	$10
	(White promo label, green vinyl)		

-EPs-

EP	HARPER VALLEY P. T. A. (68)	Plantation 1	$15

-albums-

LP	HARPER VALLEY P. T. A. (68)	Plantation 1	$10
LP(P)	HARPER VALLEY P. T. A. (68)	Plantation 1	$15
	(White promo label)		

TEX RITTER (CW)
Other Capitol 78s $4-8 each
Other Capitol 45s $3-8 each
Capitol Starline 45s $3 each
Spin-O-Rama, Coronet, Hilltop LPs $5-10 each
Album Globe, Camay, and Shasta LPs $4-8 each

-singles-

78rpm	I'M WASTIN' MY TEARS ON YOU (44)	Capitol 174	$10
78rpm	YOU TWO TIMED ME ONE TIME TOO OFTEN (45)	Capitol 206	$10
78rpm	DECK OF CARDS (48)	Capitol 40114	$10
	(First issue of this Ritter classic)		
2-45s	CHILDREN'S SONGS AND STORIES (50)	Capitol 3010	$25
	(Two 45s issued in double sleeve color jacket)		
3-45s	SONGS FOR CHILDREN (50) Box set	Capitol 3027	$30
	(Three 45s issued in a box set)		
2-45s	CHILDREN'S SONGS AND STORIES (50)	Capitol 3045	$25
	(Two 45s issued in double sleeve color jacket)		

78rpm	**DADDY'S LAST LETTER** (50)	Capitol 1267	$10
45rpm	**DADDY'S LAST LETTER** (50)	Capitol 1267	$18
	(One of Capitol's first 45rpm releases)		
78rpm	**DECK OF CARDS** (51)	Capitol 1665	$15
78(P)	**DECK OF CARDS** (51)	Capitol 1665	$12
	(Capitol promo label)		
45rpm	**DECK OF CARDS** (51)	Capitol 1665	$20
	(Reissue of Capitol 40114)		
78rpm	**HIGH NOON** (52)	Capitol 2120	$12
78(P)	**HIGH NOON** (52)	Capitol 2120	$10
	(Capitol promo label)		
45rpm	**HIGH NOON** (52)	Capitol 2120	$15
45rpm	**THE MARSHAL'S DAUGHTER** (53)	Capitol 2120	$12
78(P)	**THE RED DECK OF CARDS** (54)	Capitol 2686	$10
	(Capitol promo label)		
78rpm	**THE RED DECK OF CARDS** (54)	Capitol 2686	$15
78(P)	**THE RED DECK OF CARDS** (54)	Capitol 2686	$10
	(Yellow promo label)		
45rpm	**THE RED DECK OF CARDS** (54)	Capitol 2686	$18
45(P)	**THE RED DECK OF CARDS** (54)	Capitol 2686	$12
	(White promo label)		
45rpm	**LOVELY VEIL OF WHITE** (54)	Capitol 2836	$12
45(P)	**LOVELY VEIL OF WHITE** (54)	Capitol 2836	$10
	(White promo label)		
45rpm	**THE BANDIT** (54)	Capitol 2916	$15
45(P)	**THE BANDIT** (54)	Capitol 2916	$12
	(White promo label)		
45rpm	**IS THERE A SANTA CLAUS?** (55)	Capitol 2957	$12
45(P)	**IS THERE A SANTA CLAUS?** (55)	Capitol 2957	$10
	(White promo label)		
45rpm	**WICHITA** (55)	Capitol 3179	$12
45(P)	**WICHITA** (55)	Capitol 3179	$10
	(White promo label)		
45rpm	**GUNSMOKE** (55)	Capitol 3230	$15
45(P)	**GUNSMOKE** (55)	Capitol 3230	$10
	(White promo label)		
45rpm	**THE SEARCHERS** (56)	Capitol 3430	$10
45rpm	**DECK OF CARDS** (60)	Capitol 4285	$12
45(P)	**DECK OF CARDS** (60)	Capitol 4285	$10
	(Red promo label)		
45rpm	**I DREAMED OF A HILL-BILLY HEAVEN** (61) Purple label	Capitol 4567	$15
45rpm	**I DREAMED OF A HILL-BILLY HEAVEN** (61) Swirl label	Capitol 4567	$12
45(P)	**I DREAMED OF A HILL-BILLY HEAVEN** (61)	Capitol 4567	$10
	(Capitol promo label)		
33(S)	**I DREAMED OF A HILL-BILLY HEAVEN** (61) Compact-33	Capitol 1623	$20
	(Stereo single issued for jukebox use)		

-EPs-

EP	**TEX RITTER SINGS** (53)	Capitol 431	$30
EP	**PSALMS** (59)	Capitol 1100	$25
EP	**BLOOD IN THE SADDLE VOL 1** (60)	Capitol 1-1292	$20
EP	**BLOOD IN THE SADDLE VOL 2** (60)	Capitol 2-1292	$20
EP	**BLOOD IN THE SADDLE VOL 3** (60)	Capitol 3-1292	$20
EP	**DECK OF CARDS** (60)	Capitol 1323	$25

-albums-

10"LP	**COWBOY FAVORITES** (54)	Capitol 4004	$125
LP	**SONGS FROM THE WESTERN SCREEN** (58)	Capitol 971	$75
LP(P)	**SONGS FROM THE WESTERN SCREEN** (58)	Capitol 971	$60
	(Yellow promo label)		
LP	**PSALMS** (59)	Capitol 1100	$50
LP(P)	**PSALMS** (59)	Capitol 1100	$40
	(Yellow promo label)		
LP	**BLOOD ON THE SADDLE** (60) Mono	Capitol 1292	$30
LP	**BLOOD ON THE SADDLE** (60) Stereo	Capitol 1292	$40
LP(P)	**BLOOD ON THE SADDLE** (60)	Capitol 1292	$40
	(Yellow promo label)		
LP	**THE LINCOLN HYMNS** (61) Mono	Capitol 1562	$30
LP	**THE LINCOLN HYMNS** (61) Stereo	Capitol 1562	$40
LP(P)	**THE LINCOLN HYMNS** (61)	Capitol 1562	$40
	(Yellow promo label)		
LP	**HILLBILLY HEAVEN** (61) Mono	Capitol 1623	$30
LP	**HILLBILLY HEAVEN** (61) Stereo	Capitol 1623	$40
LP(P)	**HILLBILLY HEAVEN** (61)	Capitol 1623	$30
	(Capitol promo label)		
LP	**STAN KENTON-TEX RITTER** (62)	Capitol 1757	$25
LP(P)	**STAN KENTON-TEX RITTER** (62)	Capitol 1757	$25
	(Capitol promo label)		

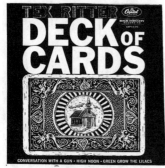

LP	BORDER AFFAIR (63)	Capitol 1910	$20
LP(P)	BORDER AFFAIR (63)	Capitol 1910	$25
	(Capitol promo label)		
LP	THE FRIENDLY VOICE OF TEX RITTER (65)	Capitol 2402	$18
LP	THE BEST OF TEX RITTER (65)	Capitol 2402	$15
LP	SWEET LAND OF LIBERTY (67)	Capitol 2743	$15
LP	JUST BEYOND THE MOON (67)	Capitol 2786	$15
LP	BUMP TIDDLI DEE BUM BUM! (68) Mono	Capitol 2890	$30
	(Very hard to find in mono)		
LP	BUMP TIDDLI DEE BUM BUM! (68) Stereo	Capitol 2890	$15
LP	TEX RITTER'S WILD WEST (68)	Capitol 2974	$15
LP	JAMBOREE, NASHVILLE STYLE (60s)	La Brea 8036	$12
2LP	MY KINDA SONGS (70s)	Hilltop 2020	$12
LP	CHUCK WAGON DAYS (69)	Capitol 213	$12
LP	GREEN GREEN VALLEY (71)	Capitol 467	$12
LP	SUPER COUNTRY LEGENDARY TEX RITTER (72)	Capitol 11037	$12
3LP	AN AMERICAN LEGEND (73) Box set	Capitol 11241	$25

-radio shows-

16"(RS)	NAVY HOEDOWN (60s)	U.S. Navy	$25-50
	(Music and interviews)		
LP(RS)	HOOTENAVY (60s)	U.S. Navy 17/18	$25-50
	(With Johnny Bond Band, two shows, one on each side)		
LP(RS)	COUNTRY CROSSROADS (80s)	Southern Baptist	$10-15
	(Music and interviews)		

JERRY RIVERS (C)
Of the Drifting Cowboys

-albums-

LP	FANTASTIC FIDDLIN' & TALL TALES (64)	Starday 281	$20

DENNIS ROBBINS (C)
MCA color vinyl 45s $5 each
MCA LPs $3 each

HARGUS ROBBINS (C)
Hargus "Pig" Robbins
Time, Chart, and Elektra 45s $1-2 each
Elektra LPs $3-5 each

-albums-

LP	A BIT OF COUNTRY PIANO (63)	Time 2107	$18
LP	ONE MORE TIME (69)	Chart 1011	$15

MARTY ROBBINS (CW)
Martin Robinson
Other Columbia 78s $4-8 each
Other Columbia 45s $3-8 each
Columbia red label Hall of Fame 45s $2-4 each
Warner 45s $3 each
MCA 45s $2 each
Other Columbia LPs $4-8 each
K-Tel LPs $5 each
Pickwick LPs $6 each
Other MCA LPs $6 each
Time-Life and Gusto LPs $4 each
Sunrise Media and Orbit LPs $4 each

-singles-

78rpm	I'LL GO ON ALONE (52)	Columbia 21022	$15
	(Huge country-western hit)		
78(P)	I'LL GO ON ALONE (52)	Columbia 21022	$18
	(Columbia promo label)		
45rpm	I'LL GO ON ALONE (52)	Columbia 21022	$30
78rpm	I COULDN'T KEEP FROM CRYING (53)	Columbia 21075	$15
78(P)	I COULDN'T KEEP FROM CRYING (53)	Columbia 21075	$18
	(Columbia promo label)		
45rpm	I COULDN'T KEEP FROM CRYING (53)	Columbia 21075	$25
78rpm	A CASTLE IN THE SKY (53)	Columbia 21111	$15
78(P)	A CASTLE IN THE SKY (53)	Columbia 21111	$18
	(Columbia promo label)		
45rpm	A CASTLE IN THE SKY (53)	Columbia 21111	$25
78rpm	SING ME SOMETHING SENTIMENTAL (53)	Columbia 21145	$12
78(P)	SING ME SOMETHING SENTIMENTAL (53)	Columbia 21145	$15
	(Columbia promo label)		
45rpm	SING ME SOMETHING SENTIMENTAL (53)	Columbia 21145	$25
78rpm	DON'T MAKE ME ASHAMED (54)	Columbia 21176	$12
78(P)	DON'T MAKE ME ASHAMED (54)	Columbia 21176	$15
	(White promo label)		
45rpm	DON'T MAKE ME ASHAMED (54)	Columbia 21176	$20

78rpm	**MY ISLE OF GOLDEN DREAMS** (54)	Columbia 21213	$10
78(P)	**MY ISLE OF GOLDEN DREAMS** (54)	Columbia 21213	$12
	(White promo label)		
45rpm	**MY ISLE OF GOLDEN DREAMS** (54)	Columbia 21213	$10
78rpm	**PRETTY WORDS** (54)	Columbia 21246	$10
78(P)	**PRETTY WORDS** (54)	Columbia 21246	$12
	(White promo label)		
78rpm	**I'M TOO BIG TO CRY** (54)	Columbia 21291	$10
78(P)	**I'M TOO BIG TO CRY** (54)	Columbia 21291	$12
	(White promo label)		
45rpm	**I'M TOO BIG TO CRY** (54)	Columbia 21291	$15
78rpm	**IT'S A PITY WHAT MONEY CAN DO** (54)	Columbia 21324	$10
78(P)	**IT'S A PITY WHAT MONEY CAN DO** (54)	Columbia 21324	$12
	(White promo label)		
45rpm	**IT'S A PITY WHAT MONEY CAN DO** (54)	Columbia 21324	$12
45(P)	**IT'S A PITY WHAT MONEY CAN DO** (54)	Columbia 21324	$15
	(White promo label)		
78rpm	**THAT'S ALL RIGHT** (55)	Columbia 21351	$75
78(P)	**THAT'S ALL RIGHT** (55)	Columbia 21351	$50
	(White promo label)		
45rpm	**THAT'S ALL RIGHT** (55)	Columbia 21351	$50
45(P)	**THAT'S ALL RIGHT** (55)	Columbia 21351	$40
	(White promo label)		
78rpm	**PRAY FOR ME MOTHER OF MINE** (55)	Columbia 21388	$10
78(P)	**PRAY FOR ME MOTHER OF MINE** (55)	Columbia 21388	$12
	(White promo label)		
45rpm	**PRAY FOR ME MOTHER OF MINE** (55)	Columbia 21388	$10
45(P)	**PRAY FOR ME MOTHER OF MINE** (55)	Columbia 21388	$12
	(White promo label)		
78rpm	**IT LOOKS LIKE I'M JUST IN YOUR WAY** (55)	Columbia 21414	$10
78(P)	**IT LOOKS LIKE I'M JUST IN YOUR WAY** (55)	Columbia 21414	$12
	(White promo label)		
45rpm	**IT LOOKS LIKE I'M JUST IN YOUR WAY** (55)	Columbia 21414	$10
45(P)	**IT LOOKS LIKE I'M JUST IN YOUR WAY** (55)	Columbia 21414	$12
	(White promo label)		
78rpm	**MAYBELLENE** (55)	Columbia 21446	$50
78(P)	**MAYBELLENE** (55)	Columbia 21446	$40
	(White promo label)		
45rpm	**MAYBELLENE** (55)	Columbia 21446	$50
45(P)	**MAYBELLENE** (55)	Columbia 21446	$40
	(White promo label)		
78rpm	**PRETTY MAMA** (56)	Columbia 21461	$50
78(P)	**PRETTY MAMA** (56)	Columbia 21461	$40
	(White promo label)		
45rpm	**PRETTY MAMA** (56)	Columbia 21461	$50
45(P)	**PRETTY MAMA** (56)	Columbia 21461	$40
	(White promo label)		
78rpm	**TENNESSEE TODDY** (56)	Columbia 21477	$50
78(P)	**TENNESSEE TODDY** (56)	Columbia 21477	$40
	(White promo label)		
45rpm	**TENNESSEE TODDY** (56)	Columbia 21477	$50
45(P)	**TENNESSEE TODDY** (56)	Columbia 21477	$40
	(White promo label)		
78rpm	**SINGING THE BLUES** (56)	Columbia 21545	$20
78(P)	**SINGING THE BLUES** (56)	Columbia 21545	$25
	(White promo label)		
45rpm	**SINGING THE BLUES** (56)	Columbia 21545	$30
45(P)	**SINGING THE BLUES** (56)	Columbia 21545	$25
	(White promo label)		
78rpm	**LONG TALL SALLY** (57)	Columbia 40679	$50
78(P)	**LONG TALL SALLY** (57)	Columbia 40679	$40
	(White promo label)		
45rpm	**LONG TALL SALLY** (57)	Columbia 40679	$50
45(P)	**LONG TALL SALLY** (57)	Columbia 40679	$40
	(White promo label)		
78rpm	**RESPECTFULLY MISS BROOKS** (57)	Columbia 40706	$25
78(P)	**RESPECTFULLY MISS BROOKS** (57)	Columbia 40706	$20
	(White promo label)		
45rpm	**RESPECTFULLY MISS BROOKS** (57)	Columbia 40706	$30
45rpm	**RESPECTFULLY MISS BROOKS** (57)	Columbia 40706	$25
	(White promo label)		
78rpm	**KNEE DEEP IN THE BLUES** (57)	Columbia 40815	$30
78(P)	**KNEE DEEP IN THE BLUES** (57)	Columbia 40815	$25
	(White promo label)		
45rpm	**KNEE DEEP IN THE BLUES** (57)	Columbia 40815	$25
45(P)	**KNEE DEEP IN THE BLUES** (57)	Columbia 40815	$20
	(White promo label)		

78rpm	**A WHITE SPORT COAT** (57)	Columbia 40864	$40
78(P)	**A WHITE SPORT COAT** (57)	Columbia 40864	$25
	(White promo label)		
45rpm	**A WHITE SPORT COAT** (57)	Columbia 40864	$20
45rpm	**A WHITE SPORT COAT** (57)	Columbia 40864	$50
	(Price includes picture sleeve)		
45(P)	**A WHITE SPORT COAT** (57)	Columbia 40864	$18
	(White promo label)		
45rpm	**TEEN AGE DREAM** (57)	Columbia 40969	$20
45(P)	**TEEN AGE DREAM** (57)	Columbia 40969	$15
	(White promo label)		
45rpm	**THE STORY OF MY LIFE** (57)	Columbia 41013	$20
45rpm	**THE STORY OF MY LIFE** (57)	Columbia 41013	$45
	(Price includes picture sleeve)		
45rpm	**JUST MARRIED** (58)	Columbia 41143	$18
45(P)	**JUST MARRIED** (58)	Columbia 41143	$15
	(White promo label)		
45rpm	**SHE WAS ONLY SEVENTEEN** (58)	Columbia 41208	$18
45rpm	**SHE WAS ONLY SEVENTEEN** (58)	Columbia 41208	$40
	(Price includes picture sleeve)		
45(P)	**SHE WAS ONLY SEVENTEEN** (58)	Columbia 41208	$15
	(White promo label)		
45rpm	**AIN'T I THE LUCKY ONE** (58)	Columbia 41325	$20
45(P)	**AIN'T I THE LUCKY ONE** (58)	Columbia 41325	$18
	(White promo label)		
45rpm	**THE HANGING TREE** (59)	Columbia 41325	$20
45rpm	**THE HANGING TREE** (59)	Columbia 41325	$40
	(Price includes picture sleeve)		
45(P)	**THE HANGING TREE** (58)	Columbia 41325	$18
	(White promo label)		
45rpm	**CAP AND GOWN** (59)	Columbia 41408	$18
45(P)	**CAP AND GOWN** (59)	Columbia 41408	$15
	(White promo label)		
45rpm	**EL PASO** (60)	Columbia 41511	$15
45rpm	**EL PASO** (60)	Columbia 41511	$40
	(Price includes picture sleeve)		
45(P)	**EL PASO** (60)	Columbia 41511	$12
	(White promo label)		
45rpm	**BIG IRON** (60)	Columbia 41589	$12
45rpm	**BIG IRON** (60)	Columbia 41589	$35
	(Price includes picture sleeve)		
45(P)	**BIG IRON** (60)	Columbia 41589	$10
	(White promo label)		
45rpm	**IS THERE ANY CHANCE?** (60)	Columbia 41686	$12
45(P)	**IS THERE ANY CHANCE?** (60)	Columbia 41686	$10
	(White promo label)		
45rpm	**FIVE BROTHERS** (60)	Columbia 41771	$12
45(P)	**FIVE BROTHERS** (60)	Columbia 41771	$10
	(White promo label)		
45rpm	**BALLAD OF THE ALAMO** (61)	Columbia 41809	$12
45rpm	**BALLAD OF THE ALAMO** (61)	Columbia 41809	$30
	(Price includes picture sleeve)		
45(P)	**BALLAD OF THE ALAMO** (61)	Columbia 41809	$10
	(White promo label)		
33rpm	**BALLAD OF THE ALAMO** (61) 33rpm single	Columbia 41809	$25
45rpm	**DON'T WORRY** (61)	Columbia 41922	$12
45rpm	**DON'T WORRY** (61)	Columbia 41922	$30
	(Price includes picture sleeve)		
45(P)	**DON'T WORRY** (61)	Columbia 41922	$10
	(White promo label)		
33rpm	**DON'T WORRY** (61) 33rpm single	Columbia 41922	$25
45rpm	**JIMMY MARTINEZ** (61)	Columbia 42008	$12
45rpm	**JIMMY MARTINEZ** (61)	Columbia 42008	$25
	(Price includes picture sleeve)		
45(P)	**JIMMY MARTINEZ** (61)	Columbia 42008	$10
	(White promo label)		
33rpm	**JIMMY MARTINEZ** (61) 33rpm single	Columbia 42008	$25
45rpm	**IT'S YOUR WORLD** (61)	Columbia 42065	$12
45rpm	**IT'S YOUR WORLD** (61)	Columbia 42065	$25
	(Price includes picture sleeve, which has two versions of the ads on the back)		
45(P)	**IT'S YOUR WORLD** (61)	Columbia 42065	$10
	(White promo label)		
33rpm	**IT'S YOUR WORLD** (61) 33rpm single	Columbia 42065	$25
45rpm	**I TOLD THE BROOK** (62)	Columbia 42246	$12
45rpm	**I TOLD THE BROOK** (62)	Columbia 42246	$25
	(Price includes picture sleeve)		

45(P)	**I TOLD THE BROOK** (62)	Columbia 42246	$10
	(White promo label)		
33rpm	**I TOLD THE BROOK** (62) 33rpm single	Columbia 42246	$25
45rpm	**DEVIL WOMAN** (62)	Columbia 42486	$12
45rpm	**DEVIL WOMAN** (62)	Columbia 42486	$30
	(Price includes picture sleeve, green photo)		
45rpm	**DEVIL WOMAN** (62)	Columbia 42486	$25
	(Price includes picture sleeve, brown photo)		
45(P)	**DEVIL WOMAN** (62)	Columbia 42486	$10
	(White promo label)		
33rpm	**DEVIL WOMAN** (62) 33rpm single	Columbia 42486	$25
45rpm	**RUBY ANN** (62)	Columbia 42614	$12
45rpm	**RUBY ANN** (62)	Columbia 42614	$25
	(Price includes picture sleeve)		
45(P)	**RUBY ANN** (62)	Columbia 42614	$10
	(White promo label)		
33rpm	**RUBY ANN** (62) 33rpm single	Columbia 42614	$25
45rpm	**HAWAII'S CALLING ME** (62)	Columbia 42672	$18
45(P)	**HAWAII'S CALLING ME** (62)	Columbia 42672	$15
	(White promo label)		
45rpm	**TEENAGER'S DAD** (63)	Columbia 42701	$12
45rpm	**TEENAGER'S DAD** (63)	Columbia 42701	$25
	(Price includes picture sleeve)		
45(P)	**TEENAGER'S DAD** (63)	Columbia 42701	$10
	(White promo label)		
33rpm	**TEENAGER'S DAD** (63) 33rpm single	Columbia 42701	$25
45rpm	**NO SIGNS OF LONELINESS** (63)	Columbia 42781	$20
	(Price includes picture sleeve)		
33rpm	**NO SIGNS OF LONELINESS** (63) 33rpm single	Columbia 42781	$25

-EPs-

EP	**MARTY ROBBINS** (53)	Columbia 1785	$125
	(Includes "I'll Go on Alone," his first hit)		
EP	**MARTY ROBBINS & GEORGE MORGAN** (55)	Columbia 2069	$75
	(Two songs by each artist)		
EP	**SINGING THE BLUES** (56)	Columbia 2116	$100
EP	**A WHITE SPORT COAT** (56)	Columbia 2134	$75
EP	**MARTY ROBBINS** (57)	Columbia 2153	$50
EP	**THE SONG OF ROBBINS VOL 1** (57)	Columbia 9761	$25
EP	**THE SONG OF ROBBINS VOL 2** (57)	Columbia 9762	$25
EP	**THE SONG OF ROBBINS VOL 3** (57)	Columbia 9763	$25
EP	**SONG OF THE ISLANDS** (57)	Columbia 10871	$25
EP	**MARTY ROBBINS** (57)	Columbia 2808	$200
	(Includes "Tennessee Toddy")		
EP	**MARTY ROBBINS** (58)	Columbia 2814	$20
	(Hall of Fame series)		
EP	**MARTY ROBBINS** (58)	Columbia 11891	$25
EP	**GUNFIGHTER BALLADS & TRAIL SONGS VOL 1** (59)	Columbia 13491	$30
EP	**GUNFIGHTER BALLADS & TRAIL SONGS VOL 2** (59)	Columbia 13492	$30
EP	**GUNFIGHTER BALLADS & TRAIL SONGS VOL 3** (59)	Columbia 13493	$30
EP	**MORE GUNFIGHTER BALLADS & TRAIL SONGS VOL 1** (60)	Columbia 14811	$25
EP	**MORE GUNFIGHTER BALLADS & TRAIL SONGS VOL 2** (60)	Columbia 14812	$25
EP	**MORE GUNFIGHTER BALLADS & TRAIL SONGS VOL 3** (60)	Columbia 14813	$25

-albums-

10"LP	**CARL, LEFTY & MARTY** (56)	Columbia 2544	$250
	(Smith, Frizzell, and Robbins)		
10"LP	**ROCK'N ROLL'N ROBBINS** (57)	Columbia 2601	$800
	(Marty's early rockabilly recordings)		
LP	**THE SONG OF ROBBINS** (57) Mono	Columbia 976	$100
LP	**THE SONG OF ROBBINS** (67) Mono	Columbia 2621	$30
LP	**THE SONG OF ROBBINS** (67) Stereo	Columbia 9421	$25
LP(P)	**THE SONG OF ROBBINS** (57)	Columbia 976	$125
	(White promo label)		
LP	**SONG OF THE ISLANDS** (57) Mono	Columbia 1087	$125
LP	**SONG OF THE ISLANDS** (67) Mono	Columbia 2625	$30
LP	**SONG OF THE ISLANDS** (57) Stereo	Columbia 9425	$25
LP(P)	**SONG OF THE ISLANDS** (57)	Columbia 1087	$125
	(White promo label)		
LP	**SONG OF THE ISLANDS** (72)	Harmony 31258	$25
LP(P)	**SONG OF THE ISLANDS** (72) White promo label	Harmony 31258	$30
	(White promo label)		
LP	**MARTY ROBBINS** (58) Mono	Columbia 1189	$75
LP(P)	**MARTY ROBBINS** (58) White promo label	Columbia 1189	$100
	(White promo label)		
LP	**MARTY'S GREATEST HITS** (59) Mono	Columbia 1325	$75
LP(P)	**MARTY'S GREATEST HITS** (59)	Columbia 1325	$100
	(White promo label)		

LP	**GUNFIGHTER BALLADS & TRAIL SONGS** (59) Mono	Columbia 1599	$30
LP	**GUNFIGHTER BALLADS & TRAIL SONGS** (59) Stereo	Columbia 8158	$40
LP(P)	**GUNFIGHTER BALLADS & TRAIL SONGS** (59) (White promo label)	Columbia 1599	$50
LP	**MORE GUNFIGHTER BALLADS & TRAIL SONGS** (60) Mono	Columbia 1713	$20
LP	**MORE GUNFIGHTER BALLADS & TRAIL SONGS** (60) Stereo	Columbia 8272	$30
LP(P)	**MORE GUNFIGHTER BALLADS & TRAIL SONGS** (60) (White promo label)	Columbia 1713	$35
LP	**THE ALAMO** (61) Mono (Soundtrack)	Columbia 1799	$25
LP	**THE ALAMO** (61) Stereo	Columbia 8358	$35
LP(P)	**THE ALAMO** (61) (White promo label)	Columbia 1799	$50
LP	**MORE GREATEST HITS** (61) Mono	Columbia 1635	$20
LP	**MORE GREATEST HITS** (61) Stereo	Columbia 8435	$30
LP(P)	**MORE GREATEST HITS** (61) (White promo label)	Columbia 1635	$40
LP	**JUST A LITTLE SENTIMENTAL** (61) Mono	Columbia 1666	$20
LP	**JUST A LITTLE SENTIMENTAL** (61) Stereo	Columbia 8466	$30
LP(P)	**JUST A LITTLE SENTIMENTAL** (61) (White promo label)	Columbia 1666	$40
LP	**MARTY AFTER MIDNIGHT** (62) Mono	Columbia 1801	$50
LP	**MARTY AFTER MIDNIGHT** (62) Stereo	Columbia 8601	$75
LP(P)	**MARTY AFTER MIDNIGHT** (62) (White promo label)	Columbia 1801	$50
LP	**PORTRAIT OF MARTY** (62) Mono	Columbia 1855	$35
LP	**PORTRAIT OF MARTY** (62) Mono (Price includes bonus photo)	Columbia 1855	$60
LP	**PORTRAIT OF MARTY** (62) Stereo	Columbia 8655	$50
LP	**PORTRAIT OF MARTY** (62) Stereo (Price includes bonus photo)	Columbia 8655	$75
LP(P)	**PORTRAIT OF MARTY** (62) (White promo label)	Columbia 1855	$50
LP	**DEVIL WOMAN** (62) Mono	Columbia 1918	$20
LP	**DEVIL WOMAN** (62) Stereo	Columbia 8718	$30
LP(P)	**DEVIL WOMAN** (62) (White promo label)	Columbia 1918	$40
LP	**HAWAII'S CALLING ME** (63) Mono	Columbia 2040	$30
LP	**HAWAII'S CALLING ME** (63) Stereo	Columbia 8840	$40
LP(P)	**HAWAII'S CALLING ME** (63) (White promo label)	Columbia 8840	$40
LP	**THE RETURN OF THE GUNFIGHTER** (63) Mono	Columbia 2072	$20
LP	**THE RETURN OF THE GUNFIGHTER** (63) Stereo	Columbia 8872	$30
LP(P)	**THE RETURN OF THE GUNFIGHTER** (63) (White promo label)	Columbia 2072	$40
LP	**ISLAND WOMAN** (64) Mono	Columbia 2167	$30
LP	**ISLAND WOMAN** (64) Stereo	Columbia 8976	$40
LP(P)	**ISLAND WOMAN** (64) (White promo label)	Columbia 2167	$40
LP	**R.F.D.** (64) Mono	Columbia 2220	$30
LP	**R.F.D.** (64) Stereo	Columbia 9020	$40
LP	**TURN THE LIGHTS DOWN LOW** (65) Mono	Columbia 2304	$20
LP	**TURN THE LIGHTS DOWN LOW** (65) Stereo	Columbia 9104	$30
LP	**SADDLE TRAMP** (65) Mono (Columbia Record Club issue)	Columbia 237	$15
LP	**SADDLE TRAMP** (65) Stereo	Columbia 237	$20
LP	**WHAT GOD HAS DONE** (65) Mono	Columbia 2448	$15
LP	**WHAT GOD HAS DONE** (65) Stereo	Columbia 9248	$20
LP	**THE DRIFTER** (66) Mono	Columbia 2527	$15
LP	**THE DRIFTER** (66) Stereo	Columbia 9327	$20
LP	**BEND IN THE RIVER** (66) Mono (Columbia Special Products)	Columbia 445	$30
LP	**BEND IN THE RIVER** (66) Stereo	Columbia 445	$40
LP(P)	**BEND IN THE RIVER** (66) (Unusual promo version)	Columbia 445	$40
LP	**MY KIND OF COUNTRY** (67) Mono	Columbia 2645	$30
LP	**MY KIND OF COUNTRY** (67) Stereo	Columbia 9445	$20
LP	**TONIGHT CARMEN** (67) Mono	Columbia 2725	$30
LP	**TONIGHT CARMEN** (67) Stereo	Columbia 9525	$20
LP	**CHRISTMAS WITH MARTY ROBBINS** (67) Mono	Columbia 2735	$50
LP	**CHRISTMAS WITH MARTY ROBBINS** (67) Stereo	Columbia 9535	$30
LP	**BY THE TIME I GET TO PHOENIX** (68) Mono	Columbia 2817	$50
LP	**BY THE TIME I GET TO PHOENIX** (68) Stereo	Columbia 9617	$20
LP	**BY THE TIME I GET TO PHOENIX** (71)	Columbia 11513	$15
LP	**I WALK ALONE** (68)	Columbia 9725	$15
2LP	**THE HEART OF MARTY ROBBINS** (69)	Columbia 2016	$75
LP	**IT'S A SIN** (69)	Columbia 9811	$25
LP	**MARTY'S COUNTRY** (69)	Columbia 15	$15

LP	SINGING THE BLUES (69)	Harmony 11338	$15
LP(P)	SINGING THE BLUES (69)	Harmony 11338	$18
	(White promo label)		
LP	MY WOMAN, MY WOMAN, MY WIFE (70)	Columbia 9978	$15
LP	EL PASO (70)	Columbia 30316	$15
LP	EL PASO (70)	Harmony 30316	$12
LP(P)	EL PASO (70)	Harmony 30316	$15
	(White promo label)		
LP	COUNTRY HYMNS (70)	Columbia 30324	$15
	(With Johnny Cash and Ray Price)		
LP	THE STORY OF MY LIFE (70)	Harmony 11409	$12
LP(P)	THE STORY OF MY LIFE (70)	Harmony 11409	$15
	(White promo label)		
2LP	THE WORLD OF MARTY ROBBINS (71)	Columbia 30811	$18
LP	MARTY'S GREATEST HITS VOL 3 (71)	Columbia 30571	$15
LP	MARTY ROBBINS TODAY (71)	Columbia 30816	$15
LP	BOUND FOR OLD MEXICO (71)	Columbia 31341	$15
2LP	ALL TIME GREATEST HITS (72)	Columbia 31361	$15
LP	I'VE GOT A WOMAN'S LOVE (72)	Columbia 31628	$15
5LP	MARTY (72) Box set	Columbia 5812	$40
LP	CHRISTMAS WITH MARTY ROBBINS (72)	Columbia 10980	$15
LP	MARTY ROBBINS' FAVORITES (72)	Harmony 31257	$12
LP(P)	MARTY ROBBINS' FAVORITES (72)	Harmony 31257	$15
	(White promo label)		
LP	THE JOY OF CHRISTMAS (72)	Columbia 11087	$15
LP	THIS MUCH A MAN (72)	Decca 75389	$12
LP(P)	THIS MUCH A MAN (72)	Decca 75389	$15
	(White promo label)		
LP	THE BEST OF MARTY ROBBINS (73)	Artco 110	$18
LP	THE STREETS OF LAREDO (73)	Harmony 32286	$18
LP(P)	THE STREETS OF LAREDO (73)	Harmony 32286	$25
	(White promo label)		
LP	MARTY ROBBINS' OWN FAVORITES (74)	Columbia 12416	$12
LP	HAVE I TOLD YOU LATELY THAT I LOVE YOU (74)	Columbia 32586	$12
LP	GOOD 'N COUNTRY (74)	MCA 421	$15
3LP	COUNTRY & WESTERN CLASSICS (83)	Readers Digest	$25
	(Box set includes a book)		
5LP	HIS GREATEST HITS (83)	Readers Digest 054	$30
	(Box set and booklet)		

-radio shows-

16"(RS)	LEATHERNECK JAMBOREE (60s)	Jamboree 20	$150-250
	(Music and interviews)		
LP(RS)	HOOTENAVY (60s)	U.S. Navy show 43	$100-150
	(Both sides feature Marty Robbins and Marion Worth)		
LP(RS)	COUNTRY SESSIONS (82)	NBC Radio	$25-50
	(Marty Robbins tribute, music and interviews)		
LP(RS)	GRAND OL' OPRY (61) Fifteen-minute show	WSM Radio 11	$100-150
	(Live concert)		
LP(RS)	GRAND OL' OPRY (62)	WSM Radio 75	$100-150
	(Live concert)		
LP(RS)	GRAND OL' OPRY (63)	WSM Radio 81	$100-150
	(Live concert)		
LP(RS)	GRAND OL' OPRY (63)	WSM Radio 92	$100-150
	(Live concert)		
LP(RS)	HERE'S TO VETERANS (60s)	V.A. 1352	$100-125
	(Music and interviews)		
3LP(RS)	AMERICAN EAGLE (80s) With others	DIR	$200-300
	(Live concert)		
2LP(RS)	COUNTRY COOKIN' (Nov 86)	Army Reserve 287	$40-75
	(Four shows with Robbins, Freddie Hart, Doug Sahm, and Byron Berline, music and interviews)		
3LP(RS)	INTERNATIONAL FESTIVAL OF COUNTRY MUSIC (Oct 82)	Mutual Radio	$100-200
	(Robbins live on nine songs, also Terri Gibbs, Porter Wagoner, Mel Tillis, Billy Swan, and Kris Kristofferson)		

MEL ROBBINS (RB)
-singles-

| 45rpm | SAVE IT (58) | Argo 5340 | $40 |

RONNY ROBBINS (C)
Marty Robbins Jr.
Columbia 45s $4 each
-albums-

LP	COLUMBIA RECORDS PRESENTS MARTY ROBBINS JR. (70)	Columbia 9944	$25
LP(P)	COLUMBIA RECORDS PRESENTS MARTY ROBBINS JR. (70)	Columbia 9944	$30
	(White promo label)		
LP	REACH FOR ALL YOU CAN GET (81)	Thunder 7774	$10

WARREN ROBBINS (RB)

-singles-

45rpm	**MY CHICKEN PEN** (58)	Mystic 730	$25
45rpm	**SINGLE MAN**	Mystic 811	$25

DICK ROBINSON (RB)

-singles-

45rpm	**THE BOPPIN' MARTIAN** (58)	MCI 1006	$30

BOBBY ROBERTS (RB)

-singles-

45rpm	**BIG SANDY** (58)	Sky 101	$125
45rpm	**HOP, SKIP AND JUMP** (58)	Hut 4707	$75

KENNY ROBERTS (C)
Starday 45s $2 each
Longhorn, MCA, and Point LPs $3-5 each

-albums-

LP	**INDIAN LOVE CALL** (65)	Starday 336	$30
LP	**YODELIN' KENNY ROBERTS SINGS COUNTRY SONGS** (66)	Vocalion 3770	$15
LP(P)	**YODELIN' KENNY ROBERTS SINGS COUNTRY SONGS** (66)	Vocalion 3770	$18
	(White promo label)		
LP	**THE INCREDIBLE KENNY ROBERTS** (67)	Starday 406	$25
LP	**COUNTRY MUSIC SINGING SENSATION** (69)	Starday 434	$18
LP	**JEALOUS HEART** (70)	Starday 470	$15
LP	**I NEVER SEE MAGGIE ALONE** (71)	Nashville 2095	$12

DON ROBERTSON (C)
Capitol 45s $3-5 each
RCA Victor 45s $2-4 each

-albums-

LP	**HEART ON MY SLEEVE** (65)	RCA Victor 3348	$15

TEXAS JIM ROBERTSON (CW)
Coral 78s and 45s $8-10 each

-EPs-

EP	**ROUND THE CAMPFIRE** (59)	Camden 114	$15

-albums-

10"LP	**EIGHT TOP WESTERN HITS** (58)	Masterseal	$50
	(Budget label)		
LP	**TEXAS JIM ROBERTSON** (61)	Strand 1016	$40
LP	**GOLDEN HITS OF COUNTRY WESTERN MUSIC** (60s)	Design 115	$15
	(Design is also a budget label)		
LP	**SACRED COUNTRY & WESTERN SONGS** (60s)	Design 132	$15
LP	**GREAT HITS OF COUNTRY & WESTERN MUSIC** (60s)	Grand Prix 185	$15
	(Budget label)		
LP	**GREAT HITS OF COUNTRY & WESTERN MUSIC** (60s)	International Award 185	$12
	(Budget reissue)		

BETTY JEAN ROBINSON (CW)

-albums-

LP	**ON THE WAY HOME** (76)	4-Star 004	$10

CARSON ROBISON (RB)
Square dances
Other RCA Victor and MGM 45s $5-10 each
Glendale and Old Homestead LPs $5-10 each

-singles-

45rpm	**ROCKIN' AND ROLLIN' WITH GRANDMA** (57)	MGM 12266	$50
45(P)	**ROCKIN' AND ROLLIN' WITH GRANDMA** (57)	MGM 12266	$40
	(Yellow promo label)		
3-45s	**SQUARE DANCE** (54) 45rpm box set	RCA Victor 155	$18

-EPs-

EP	**LIFE GETS TEE-JUS, DON'T IT VOL 1** (58)	MGM 1533	$20
EP	**LIFE GETS TEE-JUS, DON'T IT VOL 2** (58)	MGM 1534	$20
EP	**LIFE GETS TEE-JUS, DON'T IT VOL 3** (58)	MGM 1535	$20

-albums-

10"LP	**SQUARE DANCE** (55)	Columbia 2551	$75
LP	**LIFE GETS TEE-JUS, DON'T IT** (58)	MGM 3594	$50
LP(P)	**LIFE GETS TEE-JUS, DON'T IT** (58)	MGM 3594	$40
	(Yellow promo label)		

ROCK 'N ROLLERS (RB)

-singles-

45rpm	**FOR YOU** (58)	Van 100	$60

BILLY ROCKA (RB)

-singles-

45rpm	**LISTEN PRETTY BABY** (57)	Brunswick 55049	$15
45(P)	**LISTEN PRETTY BABY** (57)	Brunswick 55049	$12
	(Yellow promo label)		

ROCKIN' CHAIRS (RB)

-singles-

45rpm	**ROCKIN' CHAIR BOOGIE** (58)	Recorte 5402	$50

ROCKY FELLOWS (RB)

-singles-

45rpm	**PAINT THE TOWN RED** (58)	Goldwater 424	$50

JIMMIE RODGERS (CW)

The Father of Country Music
Other 78s $25-40 each
78s on Bluebird and Montgomery Ward worth $25-$50 each, Victor to 22554 $25 each,
    Victor 23503 to 23796 $60-$75 each, and Victor 40000 series $10-15 each
The original 1928 version of "Blue Yodel" is Victor 21142
The original 1928 version of In the "Jail House Now" is Victor 21245

-singles-

78rpm	**THE SOUTHERN CANNON BALL** (33)	Victor 23811	$100
78rpm	**MISSISSIPPI DELTA BLUES** (33)	Victor 23816	$100
78rpm	**THE YODELING RANGER** (34)	Victor 23830	$125
78rpm	**OLD LOVE LETTERS** (34)	Victor 23840	$125
78rpm	**BLUE YODEL NO. 12** (35)	Victor 24456	$100
78(PD)	**BLUE YODEL NO. 12**	Victor 6000	$1,000
	(This picture disc is one of the most collectible records		
	of any format)		
45rpm	**BLUE YODEL** (49)	RCA Victor 0017	$18
45rpm	**PISTOL PACKIN' PAPA** (50)	RCA Victor 0027	$10
45rpm	**YOU AND MY OLD GUITAR** (50)	RCA Victor 0028	$10
45rpm	**OLD PAL OF MY HEART** (50)	RCA Victor 0029	$10
45rpm	**HOW DO YOU THINK I FEEL** (54)	RCA Victor 5900	$10
45rpm	**IN THE JAILHOUSE NOW NO. 2** (55)	RCA Victor 6092	$18
	(Only country charted hit)		
45(P)	**IN THE JAILHOUSE NOW NO. 2** (55)	RCA Victor 6092	$18
	(White promo label, re-recorded version features Chet Atkins and		
	Hank Snow overdub)		
45rpm	**SOMEBODY ELSE'S HEARTACHE** (56)	RCA Victor 6130	$10
45rpm	**MULESKINNER BLUES** (56)	RCA Victor 6205	$10
45rpm	**NEVER NO MO' BLUES** (56)	RCA Victor 6408	$18
45(P)	**NEVER NO MO' BLUES** (56)	RCA Victor 6408	$15
	(White promo label)		

-EPs-

EP	**IMMORTAL PERFORMANCES** (51)	RCA Victor 6	$125
EP	**JIMMIE RODGERS VOL 1** (51)	RCA Victor 10	$100
EP	**JIMMIE RODGERS VOL 2** (51)	RCA Victor 11	$100
EP	**JIMMIE RODGERS MEMORIAL ALBUM VOL 1** (50)	RCA Victor EPAT 21	$100
EP	**JIMMIE RODGERS MEMORIAL ALBUM VOL 1** (52)	RCA Victor WPT 21	$75
	(Second pressing)		
EP	**JIMMIE RODGERS MEMORIAL ALBUM VOL 2** (50)	RCA Victor EPAT 22	$100
EP	**JIMMIE RODGERS MEMORIAL ALBUM VOL 2** (52)	RCA Victor WPT 22	$75
	(Second pressing)		
EP	**JIMMIE RODGERS MEMORIAL ALBUM VOL 3** (50)	RCA Victor EPAT 23	$100
EP	**JIMMIE RODGERS MEMORIAL ALBUM VOL 3** (52)	RCA Victor WPT 23	$75
	(Second pressing)		
EP	**JIMMIE RODGERS MEMORIAL ALBUM VOL 4** (52)	RCA Victor 409	$100
EP	**JIMMIE RODGERS MEMORIAL ALBUM VOL 5** (52)	RCA Victor 410	$100
EP	**JIMMIE RODGERS MEMORIAL ALBUM VOL 6** (52)	RCA Victor 411	$100
2EP	**TRAVELIN' BLUES** (52) Double EP	RCA Victor 3073	$150
2EP	**NEVER NO MO' BLUES** (55) Double EP	RCA Victor 1232	$100
EP	**NEVER NO MO' BLUES** (56)	RCA Victor 793	$75

-albums-

10"LP	**JIMMIE RODGERS MEMORIAL ALBUM VOL 1** (52)	RCA Victor 3037	$250
10"LP	**JIMMIE RODGERS MEMORIAL ALBUM VOL 2** (52)	RCA Victor 3038	$250
10"LP	**JIMMIE RODGERS MEMORIAL ALBUM VOL 3** (52)	RCA Victor 3039	$250
10"LP	**TRAVELIN' BLUES** (52)	RCA Victor 3073	$250
LP	**NEVER NO MO' BLUES** (55)	RCA Victor LPM 1232	$150
LP	**NEVER NO MO' BLUES** (75)	RCA Victor AHM 1232	$25
	(Second pressing)		
LP	**TRAIN WHISTLE BLUES** (57)	RCA Victor LPM 1640	$125

LP	**TRAIN WHISTLE BLUES** (75)	RCA Victor AHM 1640	$25
	(Second pressing)		
LP	**MY ROUGH AND ROWDY WAYS** (60)	RCA Victor LPM 2112	$75
LP	**MY ROUGH AND ROWDY WAYS** (75)	RCA Victor ANL 1209	$30
	(Second pressing)		
LP	**JIMMIE THE KID** (61)	RCA Victor LPM 2213	$75
LP	**COUNTRY MUSIC HALL OF FAME** (62)	RCA Victor LPM 2531	$75
LP	**COUNTRY MUSIC HALL OF FAME** (77)	RCA Victor AHM 2531	$20
	(Second pressing)		
LP	**SHORT BUT BRILLIANT LIFE OF JIMMIE RODGERS** (63)	RCA Victor LPM 2634	$75
LP	**SHORT BUT BRILLIANT LIFE OF JIMMIE RODGERS** (76)	RCA Victor AHM 2634	$20
	(Second pressing)		
LP	**MY TIME AIN'T LONG** (64)	RCA Victor LPM 2865	$50
LP	**MY TIME AIN'T LONG** (78)	RCA Victor AHM 2865	$20
	(Second pressing)		
LP	**BEST OF THE LEGENDARY JIMMIE RODGERS** (65)	RCA Victor LPM 3315	$40
LP	**BEST OF THE LEGENDARY JIMMIE RODGERS** (80)	RCA Victor AHL 3315	$15
	(Second pressing)		
LP	**JIMMIE RODGERS SINGS & PLAYS 12 IMMORTAL HITS** (65)	Hamilton 148	$30
LP	**A LEGENDARY PERFORMER** (70s)	RCA Victor 2504	$15
2LP	**THE LEGENDARY JIMMIE RODGERS VOL 1** (74)	RCA Victor 0075	$40
	(Mail-order Special Products release)		
2LP	**THIS IS- JIMMIE RODGERS** (83)	RCA Victor 6091	$15
LP	**UNISSUED JIMMIE RODGERS** (83)	Anthology 11	$25

MRS. JIMMIE RODGERS (CW)
Wife of Jimmie Rodgers

-singles-

78rpm	**WE MISS HIM WHEN THE EVENING SHADOWS FALL** (33)	Bluebird 6698	$50
78rpm	**MY RAINBOW TRAIL**	Bluebird 7339	$40

JOHNNY RODRIGUEZ (C)
Mercury and Epic 45s $2 each
Mercury and Epic LPs $2-4 each
K-Tel LPs $3 each

-radio shows-

3LP(RS)	**SILVER EAGLE** (Feb 84)	DIR	$15-30
	(Live concert)		
LP(RS)	**LIVE AT GILLEY'S** (Jan 87)	Westwood One	$10-15
	(Live concert)		
LP(RS)	**COUNTRY SESSIONS** (80s)	NBC Radio	$10-15
	(Live concert)		
Cass(RS)	**AUSTIN ENCORE** (92)	Main Street	$20-40
	(Live concert with Alabama)		

DAVID ROGERS (C)
Atlantic and Columbia 45s $2 each
Other Columbia and Atlantic LPs $3-6 each

-albums-

LP	**THE WORLD CALLED YOU** (70)	Columbia 1023	$12
LP(P)	**THE WORLD CALLED YOU** (70)	Columbia 1023	$15
	(White promo label)		

KENNY ROGERS (C)
Kenny Rogers and the First Edition
Other Jolly Rogers 45s $4-8 each
  (Kenny Rogers and the First Edition)
Reprise 45s $3 each
  (Kenny Rogers and the First Edition)
Reprise promo 45s $4 each
United Artists 45s $1-2 each
United Artists picture sleeves $2 each
Allied Record Company 45s $10 each
  (Test pressings)
Liberty 45s $1 each
Liberty picture sleeves $2 each
RCA Victor 45s $1 each
RCA Victor poster fold-out picture sleeves $4 each
RCA Victor picture sleeves $2 each
United Artists LPs $3-6 each
Liberty LPs $2-4 each
RCA Victor LPs $2-3 each
Other Reprise LPs $4-8 each
  (Kenny Rogers and the First Edition)

-singles-

45(P)	**JOLE BLON** (58)	Ken-Lee 102	$25
	(Promo-only release)		
45rpm	**WE'LL ALWAYS HAVE EACH OTHER** (59)	Carlton 454	$50

45(P)	WE'LL ALWAYS HAVE EACH OTHER (59)	Carlton 454	$40
	(Green promo label)		
45rpm	I'VE GOT A LOT TO LEARN (59)	Carlton 468	$50
45(P)	I'VE GOT A LOT TO LEARN (59)	Carlton 468	$40
	(Green promo label)		
45rpm	HERE'S THAT RAINY DAY (66)	Mercury 72545	$20
45(P)	HERE'S THAT RAINY DAY (66)	Mercury 72545	$15
	(White promo label)		
45rpm	THERE'S AN OLD MAN IN OUR TOWN (72) Wolfman Jack	Wooden Nickel 0110	$15
	(Background vocals by Kenny Rogers)		
45(P)	THERE'S AN OLD MAN IN OUR TOWN (72)	Wooden Nickel 0110	$12
	(Brown promo label)		
45rpm	THERE'S AN OLD MAN IN OUR TOWN (72)	Jolly Rogers 1001	$15
	(Kenny Rogers and the First Edition)		
45rpm	SHE THINKS I STILL CARE (72)	Jolly Rogers 1004	$10
	(Kenny Rogers and the First Edition)		
45(P)	WHAT'S IT ALL ABOUT (July 79) Public service show	W. I. A. A. 1641	$20
	(Flip side features Ray Charles)		

-EPs-

| EP(P) | THE GAMBLER (80) | Creative 422 | $10 |
| | (Demo disc for the radio show) | | |

-albums-

LP	THE FIRST EDITION (67) The First Edition	Reprise 6276	$15
LP(P)	THE FIRST EDITION (67)	Reprise 6276	$18
	(White promo label)		
LP	THE FIRST EDITION'S 2ND (68) The First Edition	Reprise 6302	$10
LP(P)	THE FIRST EDITION'S 2ND (68)	Reprise 6302	$12
	(White promo label)		
LP	RUBY DON'T TAKE YOUR LOVE TO TOWN (69)	Reprise 6352	$10
	(Kenny Rogers and the First Edition)		
LP(P)	RUBY DON'T TAKE YOUR LOVE TO TOWN (69)	Reprise 6352	$12
	(White promo label)		
LP(P)	BACKROADS (72) Kenny Rogers and the First Edition	Jolly Rogers 5001	$150
	(Test pressing picture disc)		
LP	ROLLIN' (72) Kenny Rogers and the First Edition	Jolly Rogers 5003	$15
LP	MONUMENTAL (72) Kenny Rogers and the First Edition	Jolly Rogers 5004	$15
2LP	THE BALLAD OF CALICO (72)	Reprise 6476	$12
2LP(P)	THE BALLAD OF CALICO (72)	Reprise 6476	$15
	(White promo labels)		
LP(P)	THE GAMBLER (78)	United Artists 934	$25
	(Promo-only picture disc)		
LP(P)	HBO SPECIAL (82)	HBO Cable Television	$30
	(Promo-only picture disc)		

-radio shows-

| 3LP(RS) | CHRISTMAS IN AMERICA (Dec 89) Box set | | $15-25 |
| | (Music and interviews) | | |

ROCK ROGERS (RB)

-singles-

| 45rpm | THAT AIN'T IT (58) | Starday 245 | $30 |

ROY ROGERS (CW)
Member of the Sons of the Pioneers
Roy Rogers and Dale Evans
Vocalion 78s $10-15 each
RCA Victor 78s $5-10 each
Other 78s $10-15 each
Other Aqua black vinyl box set reissues and singles reissues $5-10 each
Other RCA Victor 45s $5-10 each
Other RCA Victor colored vinyl 45s $15 each
Other Capitol 45s $2-4 each
Warner duets with Rex Allen Jr. $3 each
20th Century 45s $3-5 each
MCA 45s $2 each

-singles-

78rpm	HI-YO, SILVER (38)	Vocalion 4190	$12
78rpm	THINK OF ME (43)	Decca 6092	$10
45rpm	DON'T FENCE ME IN (50)	RCA Victor 0008	$25
	(Green vinyl)		
45rpm	THE YELLOW ROSE OF TEXAS (50)	RCA Victor 0009	$25
	(Green vinyl)		
45rpm	SAN FERNANDO VALLEY (50)	RCA Victor 0010	$25
	(Green vinyl)		
3-45s	SOUVENIR ALBUM (50) Box set	RCA Victor 215	$100
	(Records are green vinyl)		
45rpm	BLUE SHADOWS ON THE TRAIL (50)	RCA Victor 0035	$25
	(Green vinyl, with the Sons of the Pioneers)		

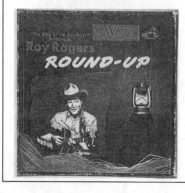

45rpm	THAT PALOMINO PAL OF MINE (51)	RCA Victor 0074	$20
45rpm	MY CHICKASHAY GAL (51)	RCA Victor 0115	$25
	(Green vinyl)		
45rpm	I WISH I HAD NEVER MET SUNSHINE (51)	RCA Victor 0116	$25
	(Green vinyl)		
45rpm	MY HEART WENT THAT-A-WAY (51)	RCA Victor 0117	$25
	(Green vinyl)		
2-45s	LORE OF THE WEST (51) Box set	RCA Victor 388	$40
	(Records are yellow vinyl, numbers 0158 and 0159)		
2-45s	PECOS BILL (51) Box set	RCA Victor 389	$40
	(Records are yellow vinyl)		
3-45s	ROUND-UP (51) Box set	RCA Victor 253	$75
	(Records are green vinyl)		
45rpm	CHRISTMAS ON THE PLAINS (51) Roy Rogers and Dale Evans	RCA Victor 0128	$25
	(Green vinyl, with Foy Willing and the Riders of the Purple Sage)		
45rpm	WHAT A FRIEND WE HAVE IN JESUS (52) Roy & Dale	RCA Victor	$20
45rpm	SINCE JESUS CAME INTO MY HEART (52) Roy & Dale	RCA Victor	$20
45rpm	WHERE HE LEADS ME (52) Roy Rogers and Dale Evans	RCA Victor	$20
3-45s	HYMNS OF FAITH (52) Roy Rogers and Dale Evans	RCA Victor 286	$60
	(Price is for the box set complete)		
2-45s	ROY ROGERS' RODEO (52) Box set	RCA Victor 413	$40
	(Records are yellow vinyl, numbers are 0228 and 0229)		
45rpm	FROSTY THE SNOW MAN (52)	RCA Victor 0255	$20
	(Yellow vinyl)		
45rpm	PETER COTTONTAIL (52)	RCA Victor 0262	$12
	(Yellow vinyl)		
45rpm	THIRTY-TWO FEET, EIGHT LITTLE TAILS (52) Dale Evans	RCA Victor 0293	$20
	(Yellow vinyl)		
45rpm	YELLOW BONNETS AND POLKA DOT SHOES (52)	RCA Victor 0399	$15
	(Green vinyl, Roy Rogers and Dale Evans)		
45rpm	RIDE, SON, RIDE (53)	RCA Victor 0414	$15
45rpm	HAPPY TRAILS (53) Roy Rogers and Dale Evans	RCA Victor 65	$15
	(Bluebird Children's Records series)		

-EPs-

2EP	ROY ROGERS SOUVENIR ALBUM (50)	RCA Victor 3041	$40
EP	ROY ROGERS ROUNDUP (50)	RCA Victor 253	$30
2EP	HYMNS OF FAITH (51)	RCA Victor 3168	$40
EP	PECOS BILL (51)	Bluebird 5	$20
EP	SWEET HOUR OF PRAYER (57)	RCA Victor 1439	$25

-albums-

10"LP	ROY ROGERS SOUVENIR ALBUM (52)	RCA Victor 3041	$75
10"LP	HYMNS OF FAITH (54)	RCA Victor 3168	$50
LP	SWEET HOUR OF PRAYER (57)	RCA Victor 1439	$40
LP	JESUS LOVES ME (59)	RCA Victor 1022	$30
	(Children's Bluebird series)		
LP	JESUS LOVES ME (60)	Camden 1022	$20
LP	JESUS LOVES ME (70s)	Pickwick 7021	$10
LP	THE BIBLE TELLS ME SO (62) Roy Rogers and Dale Evans	Capitol 1745	$25
LP	PETER COTTONTAIL (62) And Mitch Miller Orchestra	Golden 81	$25
LP	16 GREAT SONGS OF THE OLD WEST (63)	Golden 198	$20
LP	16 GREAT SONGS OF THE OLD WEST (64)	Golden 6	$20
	(With Mitch Miller & His Orchestra)		
LP	PECOS BILL (64) And Sons of the Pioneers	Camden 1054	$20
LP	LORE OF THE WEST (66)	Camden 1074	$15
LP	CHRISTMAS IS ALWAYS (67)	Capitol 2818	$15
LP	PETER COTTONTAIL & HIS FRIENDS (68)	Camden 1097	$15
	(With Emile Renan and the All Toy Orchestra)		
LP	THE COUNTRY SIDE OF ROY ROGERS (70)	Capitol 594	$15
LP	A MAN FROM DUCK RUN (71)	Capitol 785	$12
LP	TAKE A LITTLE LOVE (72)	Capitol 11020	$12
LP	IN THE SWEET BY AND BY (73)	Word 8589	$12
LP	THE BEST OF ROY ROGERS (70s)	Camden 0953	$15
LP	HAPPY TRAILS TO YOU (75)	20th Century 467	$15
LP	GOOD LIFE (77)	Word 8761	$10
LP	ROY ROGERS (84)	Columbia 38907	$10

-radio shows-

LP(RS)	COUNTRY CROSSROADS (80s)	Southern Baptist	$10-15
	(Music and interviews)		

Many early Sons of the Pioneers records feature Roy Rogers as
lead singer; those records are not included above
See Sons of the Pioneers

WELDON ROGERS (RB)

A country singer

-singles-

45rpm	EVERYBODY WANTS YOU (56)	Jewel 103	$1,000
	(Weldon Rogers and Wanda Wolfe; Jewel Records was, at this time, releasing Roy Orbison and the Teen Kings, Jewel 101)		

45rpm	**SO LONG, GOOD LUCK AND GOODBYE** (57)	Imperial 5451	$250
	(Flip side is actually "Trying to Get to You" by Roy Orbison, which was the result of a mix-up of master tapes)		
45(P)	**SO LONG, GOOD LUCK AND GOODBYE** (57)	Imperial 5451	$100
	(Cream-colored promo label)		

DANNY ROSS (RB)
-singles-

45rpm	**LOOK AT YOU GO** (58)	Minor 107	$60

JACK ROUBIK (RB)
-singles-

45rpm	**LIVE IT UP** (58)	Lindy 741	$40

DAVE ROWLAND (C)
Dave & Sugar
Used to back Elvis as a member of the Imperials
Elektra 45s $1
Elektra LPs $3 each
See Dave & Sugar

ROXSTER (RB)
-singles-

45rpm	**GOODBYE BABY** (58)	Art 175	$60

BILL ROYAL (RB)
-singles-

45rpm	**CAFFEINE, NICOTINE, GASOLINE** (58)	Odessa 504	$60

BILLY JOE ROYAL (C)
Only his country listed

-radio shows-

LP(RS)	**WESTWOOD ONE PRESENTS** (July 89)	Westwood One	$15-20
	(Live concert)		

JOE RUMORE (CW)
-albums-

45rpm	**TRIBUTE TO HANK WILLIAMS** (58) Special release	Republic 100	$30
	(Not in the regular Republic numbering order)		

IRVIN RUSS (RB)
-singles-

45rpm	**CRAZY ALLIGATOR** (58)	Felco 201	$150

JOHNNY RUSSELL (C)
RCA Victor 45s $2 each
RCA Victor LPs $3-5 each

-radio shows-

LP(RS)	**COUNTRY MUSIC TIME** (80s)	U.S. Air Force	$10-12
	(Music and interviews)		

LEON RUSSELL (R)
Hank Wilson
Shelter and Paradise 45s $3 each
Shelter and Paradise LPs $4-8 each

RUSTY & DOUG (CW)
Rusty and Doug Kershaw
Doug Kershaw
Other Hickory 45s $4-8 each
RCA Victor 45s $5-10 each
Reprise 45s by Doug Kershaw $3-6 each
Warner 45s by Doug Kershaw $2-4 each

-singles-

45rpm	**SO LOVELY BABY** (55)	Hickory 1027	$20
45(P)	**SO LOVELY BABY** (55)	Hickory 1027	$15
	(Yellow promo label)		
45rpm	**MONEY** (56) With Al Terry	Hickory 1061	$20
45(P)	**MONEY** (56)	Hickory 1061	$15
	(Yellow promo label)		
45rpm	**LOVE ME TO PIECES** (57)	Hickory 1068	$15
45(P)	**LOVE ME TO PIECES** (57)	Hickory 1068	$15
	(Yellow or white promo label)		
45rpm	**HEY, SHERIFF** (58)	Hickory 1083	$12
45(P)	**HEY, SHERIFF** (58)	Hickory 1083	$10
	(White promo label)		
45rpm	**KAW-LIGA** (59)	Hickory 1095	$12

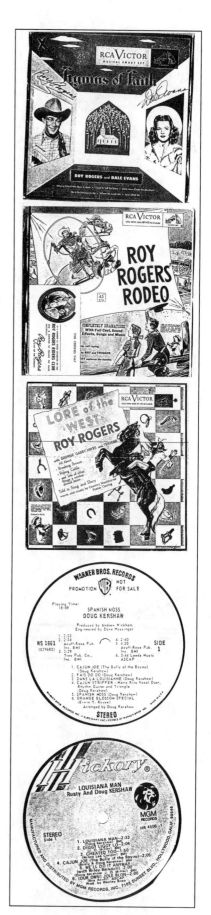

45(P)	**KAW-LIGA** (59)	Hickory 1095	$10
	(White promo label)		
45rpm	**LOUISIANA MAN** (61)	Hickory 1137	$15
	(Reissued as Hickory 1575)		
45(P)	**LOUISIANA MAN** (61)	Hickory 1137	$12
	(White promo label)		
45rpm	**HEY MAE** (61)	Hickory 1151	$12
45(P)	**HEY MAE** (61)	Hickory 1151	$10
	(White promo label)		
45rpm	**CAJUN JOE** (63)	Hickory 1177	$12
45(P)	**CAJUN JOE** (63)	Hickory 1177	$10
	(White promo label)		

-albums-

LP	**RUSTY & DOUG SING LOUISIANA MAN** (60)	Hickory 103	$100
LP	**THE CAJUN WAY** (69) Doug Kershaw	Warner 1820	$15
LP(P)	**THE CAJUN WAY** (69)	Warner 1820	$18
	(White promo label)		
LP	**SPANISH MOSS** (70) Doug Kershaw	Warner 1861	$10
LP	**CAJUN IN THE BLUES COUNTRY** (70) Rusty Kershaw	Cotillion 9030	$12
LP(P)	**CAJUN IN THE BLUES COUNTRY** (70)	Cotillion 9030	$15
	(White promo label)		
LP	**GREAT STARS OF THE GRAND OL' OPRY** (70s)	Crown 5331	$15
	(Rusty and Doug and Jerry and Glen)		
LP	**SWAMP GRASS** (71) Doug Kershaw	Warner 2581	$10
LP	**DEVIL'S ELBOW** (72) Doug Kershaw	Warner 2649	$10
LP	**KERSHAW** (72) Doug Kershaw	Hickory 163	$12
LP(P)	**KERSHAW** (72)	Hickory 163	$15
	(White promo label)		
LP	**DOUGLAS JAMES KERSHAW** (73) Doug Kershaw	Warner 2725	$10
LP	**LOUISIANA MAN** (74)	Hickory 4506	$15
LP(P)	**LOUISIANA MAN** (74)	Hickory 4506	$18
	(White promo label)		
LP	**MAMA KERSHAW'S BOY** (74) Doug Kershaw	Warner 2793	$10
LP	**ALIVE & PICKIN'** (75) Doug Kershaw	Warner 2851	$10
LP	**RAJIN' CAJUN** (76) Doug Kershaw	Warner 2910	$10
LP	**FLIP, FLOP & FLY** (77) Doug Kershaw	Warner 3025	$10
LP	**LOUISIANA MAN** (78) Doug Kershaw	Warner 3166	$10

-radio shows-

2LP(RS)	**COUNTRY COOKIN'** (75)	U.S. Air Force	$15-25
	(Music and interviews)		

BUCK RYAN (BG)

-albums-

LP	**BALLADS & BLUEGRASS** (65)	Monument 18031	$15
	(With Smitty Irvin)		

CHARLIE RYAN (R)
Other 45s $5-10 each

-singles-

45rpm	**HOT ROD LINCOLN** (55)	Souvenir 101	$50
45rpm	**HOT ROD LINCOLN** (59)	4-Star 1733	$15
45(P)	**HOT ROD LINCOLN** (59)	4-Star 1733	$25
	(White promo label)		
45rpm	**SIDE CAR CYCLE** (60)	4-Star 1745	$12
45(P)	**SIDE CAR CYCLE** (60)	4-Star 1745	$15
	(White promo label)		
45rpm	**HOT ROD HADES** (61)	4-Star 1749	$15
45(P)	**HOT ROD HADES** (61)	4-Star 1749	$12
	(White promo label)		

-albums-

LP	**HOT ROD LINCOLN** (61)	King 751	$150
LP	**HOT ROD LINCOLN DRAGS AGAIN** (64) Mono	Hilltop 6006	$50
LP	**HOT ROD LINCOLN DRAGS AGAIN** (64) Stereo	Hilltop 6006	$40
LP	**HOT ROD LINCOLN** (67) Mono	Pickwick 417	$25
LP	**HOT ROD LINCOLN** (67) Stereo	Pickwick 417	$28

JOHN WESLEY RYLES (C)
Columbia 45s $3 each
Other Columbia LPs $4 each
MCA, Plantation, and Dot LPs $3 each

-albums-

LP	**KAY** (69)	Columbia 9788	$12

S

DOUG SAHM (R)

Sir Doug of the Sir Douglas Quintet
Atlantic 45s $5-10 each
Warner 45s $8 each
Dot 45s $6 each

-singles-

45rpm	**CRAZY DAISY** (57)	Satin 100	$50
45rpm	**CRAZY DAISY** (58)	Warrior 507	$75
45rpm	**HENRIETTA** (58)	Texas Record 108	$12
45rpm	**WHY WHY WHY** (60) With the Markays	Harlem 107	$150
45rpm	**WHY WHY WHY** (60) With the Markays	Swingin' 625	$25
45rpm	**BABY, TELL ME** (60)	Harlem 108	$50
45(P)	**BABY, TELL ME** (60)	Harlem 108	$150
45rpm	**SLOWDOWN** (60)	Harlem 113	$40
45rpm	**JUST A MOMENT** (61)	Cobra 116	$40
45rpm	**MAKES NO DIFFERENCE** (61)	Renner 212	$30
45(P)	**MAKES NO DIFFERENCE** (61)	Renner 212	$100
	(Red vinyl)		
45rpm	**BABY, WHAT'S ON YOUR MIND** (61)	Renner 215	$30
45(P)	**BABY, WHAT'S ON YOUR MIND** (61)	Renner 215	$100
	(Red vinyl)		
45rpm	**BABY, WHAT'S ON YOUR MIND** (62) w/The Spirits	Personality 260	$25
45rpm	**BABY, WHAT'S ON YOUR MIND** (62) w/The Spirits	Personality 3504	$30
45rpm	**JUST BECAUSE** (62)	Renner 226	$40
45rpm	**CRY** (63)	Renner 232	$40
45rpm	**CRY** (64)	Soft 1031	$20
45rpm	**LUCKY ME** (63)	Renner 240	$40
45rpm	**MR. KOOL** (64)	Renner 247	$40

-albums-

LP	**DOUG SAHM & BAND** (73)	Atlantic 7254	$15
	(Bob Dylan is featured on some of the tracks)		
LP(P)	**DOUG SAHM & BAND** (73)	Atlantic 7254	$20
	(White promo label)		
LP	**GROOVER'S PARADISE** (74)	Warner 2810	$50
	(Includes members of Creedence Clearwater Revival)		
LP(P)	**GROOVER'S PARADISE** (74)	Warner 2810	$60
	(White promo label)		
LP	**HELL OF A SPELL** (80)	Takoma 7075	$12

MAC SALES (RB)

-singles-

45rpm	**YAKETY YAK** (58)	Meteor 5022	$40

JOE SAMPLE (C)

ABC 45s $1 each
ABC promo EP $3 each
ABC LPs $3 each

JUNIOR SAMPLES (C)

-albums-

LP	**THE WORLD OF JUNIOR SAMPLES** (67)	Chart 1002	$18
LP	**THE BEST OF JUNIOR SAMPLES** (71)	Chart 1045	$15

ED SANDERS (C)

-albums-

LP	**SANDERS' TRUCKSTOP** (69)	Reprise 6374	$15
LP(P)	**SANDERS' TRUCKSTOP** (69)	Reprise 6374	$12
	(White promo label)		

HANK SANDERS (RB)

-singles-

45rpm	**BEEN GONE A LONG TIME** (57)	Crest 1039	$25
45(P)	**BEEN GONE A LONG TIME** (57)	Crest 1039	$20
	(White promo label)		

RAY SANDERS (C)

a.k.a. Curly Sanders
Imperial and United Artists 45s $1-2 each

-albums-

LP	**FEELING GOOD IS EASY** (69)	Imperial 12447	$15
LP	**RAY SANDERS** (72)	United Artists 6822	$12

FRANKIE SANDS (RB)

-singles-

45rpm	BLUEBIRDS OVER THE MOUNTAIN (58)	Imperial 5495	$15
45(P)	BLUEBIRDS OVER THE MOUNTAIN (58)	Imperial 5495	$10
	(Cream-colored promo label)		

FRANK SANDY (RB)

Tops 45s $5 each
(Budget label)

-singles-

45rpm	TARRENTELLA ROCK (58)	MGM 12626	$15
45(P)	TARRENTELLA ROCK (58)	MGM 12626	$12
	(Yellow promo label)		
45rpm	LET'S GO ROCK N' ROLL (58)	MGM 12678	$25
45(P)	LET'S GO ROCK N' ROLL (58)	MGM 12678	$20
	(Yellow promo label)		

JOHNNY SARDO (RB)

-singles-

45rpm	HIP HOP TAKE A RIDE WITH ME	Chock Full of Hits 104	$20
45rpm	I WANNA ROCK (57)	Warner Bros 5014	$15
45(P)	I WANNA ROCK (57)	Warner Bros 5014	$12
	(White promo label)		

MIKE SARGE (RB)

-singles-

45rpm	BOBBY SOX BABY (57)	Mercury 70945	$15
45(P)	BOBBY SOX BABY (57)	Mercury 70945	$10
	(White promo label)		

HENDER SAUL (RB)

-singles-

45rpm	I AIN'T GONNA ROCK TONIGHT (58)	Liberty Tone 104	$150

SAWYER BROWN (C)

Capitol 45s $2 each
Capitol picture sleeves $2 each
Curb 45s $1 each
LPs $3 each

-radio shows-

3LP(RS)	AMERICAN EAGLE (Aug 86)	DIR	$20-30
	(Live concert)		
LP(RS)	WESTWOOD ONE PRESENTS (Feb 90)	Westwood One	$20-30
	(Live concert)		
Cass(RS)	AUSTIN ENCORE (92) With Tanya Tucker	Main Street	$30-45
	(Live concert)		

TYRONE SCHMIDLING (RB)

-singles-

45rpm	YOU'RE GONE, I'M LEFT (58)	Andex 4022	$60

JOHN SCHNEIDER (C)

Scotti Bros 45s $3 each
MCA 45s $1-2 each
MCA color vinyl 45s $6 each
MCA picture sleeves $2 each

SCHOOLBOY CLEVE (R)

-singles-

45rpm	SHE'S GONE (58)	Feature 3013	$75

JACK SCOTT (R)

With the Chantones
Dot 45s $4-8 each
Ponie 45s $3 each

-singles-

45rpm	BABY, SHE'S GONE (57)	ABC Paramount 9818	$100
45(P)	BABY, SHE'S GONE (57)	ABC Paramount 9818	$80
	(White promo label)		
45rpm	TWO TIMIN' WOMAN (57)	ABC Paramount 9860	$100
45(P)	TWO TIMIN' WOMAN (57)	ABC Paramount 9860	$75
	(White promo label)		
45rpm	MY TRUE LOVE (58)	Carlton 462	$18
45(P)	MY TRUE LOVE (58)	Carlton 462	$50
	(Red promo label)		
45rpm	WITH YOUR LOVE (58)	Carlton 483	$15

45rpm	**WITH YOUR LOVE** (58)	Carlton 483	$50
	(Price includes picture sleeve)		
45(P)	**WITH YOUR LOVE** (58)	Carlton 483	$40
	(Red promo label)		
45rpm	**GOODBYE, BABY** (58)	Carlton 493	$15
45rpm	**GOODBYE, BABY** (58)	Carlton 493	$50
	(Price includes picture sleeve)		
45(P)	**GOODBYE, BABY** (58)	Carlton 493	$40
	(Red promo label)		
45rpm	**I NEVER FELT LIKE THIS** (59)	Carlton 504	$12
45rpm	**THE WAY I WALK** (59)	Carlton 514	$12
45rpm	**THERE COMES A TIME** (59)	Carlton 519	$12
45rpm	**WHAT AM I LIVING FOR** (60)	Guaranteed 209	$12
45(P)	**WHAT AM I LIVING FOR** (60)	Guaranteed 209	$25
	(White promo label)		
45rpm	**GO WILD, LITTLE SADIE** (60)	Guaranteed 211	$12
45(P)	**GO WILD, LITTLE SADIE** (60)	Guaranteed 211	$25
	(White promo label)		
45rpm	**WHAT IN THE WORLD'S COME OVER YOU** (60)	Top Rank 2028	$12
45(P)	**WHAT IN THE WORLD'S COME OVER YOU** (60)	Top Rank 2028	$25
	(White promo label)		
45rpm	**BURNING BRIDGES** (60)	Top Rank 2041	$12
45rpm	**BURNING BRIDGES** (60)	Top Rank 2041	$50
	(Price includes picture sleeve)		
45(P)	**BURNING BRIDGES** (60)	Top Rank 2041	$25
	(White promo label)		
45rpm	**IT ONLY HAPPENED YESTERDAY** (60)	Top Rank 2055	$12
45(P)	**IT ONLY HAPPENED YESTERDAY** (60)	Top Rank 2055	$25
	(White promo label)		
45rpm	**PATSY** (60)	Top Rank 2075	$12
45(P)	**PATSY** (60)	Top Rank 2075	$25
	(White promo label)		
45rpm	**IS THERE SOMETHING ON YOUR MIND** (60)	Top Rank 2093	$10
45rpm	**IS THERE SOMETHING ON YOUR MIND** (60)	Top Rank 2093	$50
	(Price includes picture sleeve)		
45(P)	**IS THERE SOMETHING ON YOUR MIND** (60)	Top Rank 2093	$20
	(White promo label)		
45rpm	**A LITTLE FEELING** (61)	Capitol 4554	$15
45rpm	**A LITTLE FEELING** (61)	Capitol 4554	$50
	(Price includes picture sleeve)		
45rpm	**MY DREAMS COME TRUE** (61)	Capitol 4597	$15
45rpm	**MY DREAMS COME TRUE** (61)	Capitol 4597	$50
	(Price includes picture sleeve)		
45rpm	**STEPS 1 AND 2** (61)	Capitol 4637	$15
45rpm	**STEPS 1 AND 2** (61)	Capitol 4637	$50
	(Price includes picture sleeve)		
45rpm	**CRY, CRY, CRY** (62)	Capitol 4689	$15
45rpm	**CRY, CRY, CRY** (62)	Capitol 4689	$50
	(Price includes picture sleeve)		
45rpm	**THE PART WHERE I CRY** (62)	Capitol 4738	$15
45rpm	**THE PART WHERE I CRY** (62)	Capitol 4738	$50
	(Price includes picture sleeve)		
45rpm	**SAD STORY** (62)	Capitol 4796	$15
45rpm	**IF ONLY** (63)	Capitol 4855	$15
45rpm	**STRANGERS** (63)	Capitol 4903	$15
45rpm	**ALL I SEE IS YOU** (63)	Capitol 4955	$15
45rpm	**JINGLE BELL SLIDE** (63)	Groove 0027	$10
45(P)	**JINGLE BELL SLIDE** (63)	Groove 0027	$20
	(White promo label)		
45rpm	**I KNEW YOU FIRST** (64)	Groove 0031	$10
45(P)	**I KNEW YOU FIRST** (64)	Groove 0031	$20
	(White promo label)		
45rpm	**WHAT A WONDERFUL NIGHT OUT** (64)	Groove 0037	$10
45(P)	**WHAT A WONDERFUL NIGHT OUT** (64)	Groove 0037	$20
	(White promo label)		
45rpm	**THOU SHALT NOT STEAL** (64)	Groove 0042	$10
45(P)	**THOU SHALT NOT STEAL** (64)	Groove 0042	$20
	(White promo label)		
45rpm	**TALL TALES** (64)	Groove 0049	$10
45(P)	**TALL TALES** (64)	Groove 0049	$18
	(White promo label)		
45rpm	**I DON'T BELIEVE IN TEA LEAVES** (65)	RCA Victor 8505	$10
45(P)	**I DON'T BELIEVE IN TEA LEAVES** (65)	RCA Victor 8505	$15
	(White promo label)		
45rpm	**LOOKING FOR LINDA** (65)	RCA Victor 8685	$10
45(P)	**LOOKING FOR LINDA** (65)	RCA Victor 8685	$15
	(White promo label)		

45rpm	**DON'T HUSH THE LAUGHTER** (65)	RCA Victor 8724	$10
45(P)	**DON'T HUSH THE LAUGHTER** (65) (White promo label)	RCA Victor 8724	$15
45rpm	**BEFORE THE BIRD FLIES** (66)	ABC Paramount 10843	$15
45(P)	**BEFORE THE BIRD FLIES** (66) (White promo label)	ABC Paramount 10843	$25
45rpm	**MY SPECIAL ANGEL** (67)	Jubilee 5606	$15
45(P)	**MY SPECIAL ANGEL** (67) (White promo label)	Jubilee 5606	$25

-EPs-

EP	**PRESENTING JACK SCOTT** (59)	Carlton 1070	$300
EP	**PRESENTING JACK SCOTT** (59)	Carlton 1071	$300
EP	**JACK SCOTT SINGS** (59)	Carlton 1072	$250
EP	**STARRING JACK SCOTT** (59)	Carlton 1073	$250
EP	**JACK SCOTT** (60)	Top Rank 1001	$250

-albums-

LP	**JACK SCOTT** (59) Mono	Carlton 107	$100
LP	**JACK SCOTT** (59) Stereo (STEREO in letters on cover down left side)	Carlton 107	$300
LP	**JACK SCOTT** (59) Stereo (STEREO in felt letters across top of cover)	Carlton 107	$250
LP	**JACK SCOTT** (59) Stereo	Carlton 107	$200
LP	**WHAT AM I LIVING FOR** (59) Mono	Carlton 122	$100
LP	**WHAT AM I LIVING FOR** (59) Stereo	Carlton 122	$200
LP	**I REMEMBER HANK WILLIAMS** (60) Mono	Top Rank 319	$100
LP	**I REMEMBER HANK WILLIAMS** (60) Stereo	Top Rank 619	$200
LP	**WHAT IN THE WORLD'S COME OVER YOU** (60) Mono	Top Rank 326	$100
LP	**WHAT IN THE WORLD'S COME OVER YOU** (60) Stereo	Top Rank 626	$200
LP	**THE SPIRIT MOVES ME** (60) Mono	Top Rank 348	$100
LP	**THE SPIRIT MOVES ME** (60) Stereo	Top Rank 648	$200
LP	**GREAT SCOTT** (60s)	Jade 202	$100
LP	**BURNING BRIDGES** (64) Mono	Capitol 2035	$75
LP	**BURNING BRIDGES** (64) Stereo (Black label)	Capitol 2035	$150
LP	**BURNING BRIDGES** (64) Stereo (Green label)	Capitol 2035	$75
LP(P)	**SOUL STIRRING** (60s) Black and yellow label (Promo only released to radio stations)	Sesac 4201	$175

RAY SCOTT (R)

-singles-

45rpm	**YOU DRIVE ME CRAZY** (57)	Satellite 104	$125
45rpm	**BOY MEETS GIRL** (58)	Stompertime 1161	$75
45rpm	**BOPPIN' WIGWAM WILLIE** (58)	Erwin 700	$60

RICKY SCOTT (RB)

-singles-

45rpm	**I DIDN'T MEAN IT** (58)	X-Clusive 1001	$40

RODNEY SCOTT (RB)

-singles-

45rpm	**GRANNY WENT ROCKIN'** (58)	Cannon 225	$75
45rpm	**YOU'RE SO SQUARE** (58)	Cannon 231	$50

SANDY SCOTT (RB)

-singles-

45rpm	**MISTER BIG** (57) (White promo label)	Choice 5605	$30
45rpm	**SHAKE IT UP** (58) (White promo label)	Choice 5606	$35

SHERREE SCOTT (RB)

-singles-

45rpm	**FASCINATING BABY** (57)	Rocket 1036	$60
45rpm	**WHOLE LOTTA SHAKIN'** (58)	Rocket 101	$50
45rpm	**WHOLE LOTTA SHAKIN'** (58) (Price includes picture sleeve)	Rocket 101	$100

TOM SCOTT (RB)

-singles-

45rpm	**RECORD HOP** (59)	Hep 2140	$60

RAMBLIN' TOMMY SCOTT (CW)

-singles-

45rpm	**WHAT DO YOU KNOW-I LOVE HER** (53)	King 1129	$10

EARL SCRUGGS See Flatt & Scruggs

JOHNNY SEA (C)
Philips and Warner 45s $3 each
Guest Star and Pickwick LPs $3-5 each

-albums-

LP	JOHNNY SEA (64)	Philips 200139	$15
LP(P)	JOHNNY SEA (64)	Philips 200139	$18
	(White promo label)		
LP	LIVE AT THE BITTER END (65)	Philips 200194	$15
LP(P)	LIVE AT THE BITTER END (65)	Philips 200194	$18
	(White promo label)		
LP	DAY FOR DECISION (66)	Warner 1659	$15
LP(P)	DAY FOR DECISION (66)	Warner 1659	$18
	(White promo label)		

DAN SEALS (C)
EMI 45s $2 each
EMI picture sleeves $2 each
EMI LPs $3 each

-radio shows-

LP(RS)	COUNTRY MUSIC TIME (80s)	U.S. Air Force	$10-12
	(Music and interviews)		

JEANNIE SEELY (C)
Monument and Decca 45s $2-4 each
Other Monument LPs $4-8 each
Decca LPs $4-8 each
Harmony and MCA LPs $2-4 each

-albums-

LP	SEELY STYLE (66)	Monument 18057	$15
LP	THANKS HANK (67)	Monument 18073	$12
	(Hank Cochran songs)		

RONNIE SELF (RB)

-singles-

45rpm	PRETTY BAD BLUES (56)	ABC Paramount 9714	$100
45(P)	PRETTY BAD BLUES (56)	ABC Paramount 9714	$50
	(White promo label)		
45(P)	SWEET LOVE (56)	ABC Paramount 9768	$50
	(White promo-only label)		
45rpm	AIN'T I'M A DOG (58)	Columbia 40989	$30
45(P)	AIN'T I'M A DOG (58)	Columbia 40989	$25
	(White promo label)		
45rpm	BOP-A-LENA (59)	Columbia 41101	$30
45(P)	BOP-A-LENA (59)	Columbia 41101	$25
	(White promo label)		
45rpm	BIG BLON' BABY (58)	Columbia 41166	$30
45(P)	BIG BLON' BABY (58)	Columbia 41166	$25
	(White promo label)		
45rpm	YOU'RE SO RIGHT FOR ME (58)	Columbia 41241	$30
45(P)	YOU'RE SO RIGHT FOR ME (58)	Columbia 41241	$25
	(White promo label)		
45rpm	THIS MUST BE THE PLACE (59)	Decca 30958	$20
45(P)	THIS MUST BE THE PLACE (59)	Decca 30958	$15
	(Pink promo label)		
45rpm	I'VE BEEN THERE (60)	Decca 31131	$18
45(P)	I'VE BEEN THERE (60)	Decca 31131	$15
	(Pink promo label)		
45rpm	SOME THINGS YOU CAN'T CHANGE (60)	Decca 31351	$15
45(P)	SOME THINGS YOU CAN'T CHANGE (60)	Decca 31351	$12
	(Pink promo label)		
45rpm	OH ME, OH MY (62)	Decca 31431	$10
45rpm	BLESS MY BROKEN HEART (63)	Kapp 546	$10

-EPs-

EP	AIN'T I'M A DOG (58)	Columbia 2149	$500

CHARLES SENNS (RB)

-singles-

45rpm	GEE WHIZ LIZ (58)	DJ 1014	$60

ORDEN SEXTON (RB)

-singles-

45rpm	ROCK-A-WAY (58)	Camellia 100	$125

HENRY SHARPE (RB)

-singles-

45rpm	**SHORTNIN' ROCK AND ROLL** (58)	Global 717	$60

MIKE SHAW (RB)

-singles-

45rpm	**LONG GONE BABY** (58)	Perfect 111	$100

MERLE SHELTON (CW)

-singles-

45rpm	**I LOVE YOU BECAUSE** (57)	Lin 1006	$18

SHENANDOAH (C)
Columbia 45s $1 each
Columbia LPs $3 each

-radio shows-

LP(RS)	**WESTWOOD ONE PRESENTS** (Dec 89) (Live concert)	Westwood One	$15-25

JEAN SHEPARD (CW)
Capitol 78s $3-6 each
Other Capitol 45s $4-8 each
Other Capitol LPs $5-10 each
United Artists LPs $4-8 each
Mercury LPs $8 each
Power Pak and Pickwick LPs $3-5 each

-singles-

45rpm	**TWICE THE LOVIN'** (53) With Speedy West	Capitol 2358	$15
45rpm	**FORGIVE ME, JOHN** (55) With Ferlin Husky (Country mega-hit)	Capitol 2586	$10
5-33s	**HEARTACHES AND TEARS** (62) (Set of five stereo jukebox singles)	Capitol 1663	$8 each

-EPs-

EP	**COUNTRY BALLADS** (56)	Capitol 687	$40
EP	**SONGS OF A LOVE AFFAIR VOL 1** (58)	Capitol 1-728	$20
EP	**SONGS OF A LOVE AFFAIR VOL 2** (58)	Capitol 2-728	$20
EP	**SONGS OF A LOVE AFFAIR VOL 3** (58)	Capitol 3-728	$20
EP	**LONESOME LOVE VOL 1** (59)	Capitol 1-1126	$18
EP	**LONESOME LOVE VOL 2** (59)	Capitol 2-1127	$18
EP	**LONESOME LOVE VOL 3** (59)	Capitol 3-1128	$18
EP	**THIS IS JEAN SHEPARD VOL 1** (59)	Capitol 1-1253	$15
EP	**THIS IS JEAN SHEPARD VOL 2** (59)	Capitol 2-1253	$15
EP	**THIS IS JEAN SHEPARD VOL 3** (59)	Capitol 3-1253	$15
EP	**GOT YOU ON MY MIND VOL 1** (61)	Capitol 1-1525	$15
EP	**GOT YOU ON MY MIND VOL 2** (61)	Capitol 2-1525	$15
EP	**GOT YOU ON MY MIND VOL 3** (61)	Capitol 3-1525	$15

-albums-

LP	**SONGS OF A LOVE AFFAIR** (58)	Capitol 728	$60
LP	**LONESOME LOVE** (59)	Capitol 1126	$40
LP(P)	**LONESOME LOVE** (59) (Yellow promo label)	Capitol 1126	$50
LP	**THIS IS JEAN SHEPARD** (59)	Capitol 1253	$40
LP(P)	**THIS IS JEAN SHEPARD** (59) (Yellow promo label)	Capitol 1253	$50
LP	**GOT YOU ON MY MIND** (61) Mono	Capitol 1525	$25
LP	**GOT YOU ON MY MIND** (61) Stereo	Capitol 1525	$30
LP(P)	**GOT YOU ON MY MIND** (61) (Blue promo label)	Capitol 1525	$30
LP	**HEARTACHES AND TEARS** (62) Mono	Capitol 1663	$25
LP	**HEARTACHES AND TEARS** (62) Stereo	Capitol 1663	$30
LP(P)	**HEARTACHES AND TEARS** (62) (Blue promo label)	Capitol 1663	$30
LP	**THE BEST OF JEAN SHEPARD** (63) Mono	Capitol 1922	$15
LP	**THE BEST OF JEAN SHEPARD** (63) Stereo	Capitol 1922	$20
LP	**LIGHTHEARTED AND BLUE** (64)	Capitol 2187	$15
LP	**IT'S A MAN EVERYTIME** (65)	Capitol 2416	$12
LP	**I'LL TAKE THE DOG** (66) (With Ray Pillow)	Capitol 2537	$12
LP	**MANY HAPPY HANGOVERS** (66)	Capitol 2547	$12
LP	**HEART, WE DID ALL THAT WE COULD** (67)	Capitol 2690	$12
LP	**YOUR FOREVERS DON'T LAST VERY LONG** (67)	Capitol 2765	$10
LP	**HEART TO HEART** (68)	Capitol 2871	$10
LP	**A REAL GOOD WOMAN** (68)	Capitol 2966	$10

-radio shows-

16"(RS)	**COUNTRY STYLE USA** (56) Fifteen-minute show (Show number 175)	Country Style USA	$25-40

LP(RS)	**HOOTENAVY** (60s) Fifteen-minute show (Music and interviews, with the Wilburn Brothers)	U.S. Navy 19/20	$25-40
16"(RS)	**U.S. ARMY BAND** (60s) (Music and interviews)	U.S. Army	$25-40
16"(RS)	**NAVY HOEDOWN** (60s) (Music and interviews)	U.S. Navy	$25-40

T. G. SHEPPARD (C)
Hitsville 45s $3 each
Warner and Columbia 45s $1-2 each
Warner, Curb, and Columbia LPs $3-5 each

-albums-

LP	**T. G. SHEPPARD** (75)	Melodyland 401	$15
LP	**MOTELS & MEMORIES** (76)	Melodyland 403	$12
LP	**SOLITARY MAN** (76)	Hitsville 404	$10

-radio shows-

2LP(RS)	**COUNTRY COOKIN'** (Mar 77) (One show of four, music and interviews)	U.S. Air Force	$20-30
3LP(RS)	**SILVER EAGLE** (Apr 83) (Live concert)	DIR	$15-25
LP(RS)	**LIVE AT GILLEY'S** (Oct 85) (Live concert)	Westwood One	$15-25

BILLY SHERRILL (RB)
One of Nashville's best known producers

-singles-

45rpm	**DON'T YOU ROCK ME DADDY-O** (58)	Tyme 101	$50
45rpm	**CADILLAC BABY** (58)	Tyme 102	$60
45rpm	**ROCK ON BABY** (58)	Tyme 103	$40
45rpm	**KOOL KAT** (58)	Tyme 104	$100
45rpm	**DRAG RACE** (63)	ABC Paramount 10465	$20
45(P)	**DRAG RACE** (63) (White promo label)	ABC Paramount 10465	$15
45rpm	**WHIRLAWAY** (64)	ABC Paramount 10535	$20
45(P)	**WHIRLAWAY** (64) (White promo label)	ABC Paramount 10535	$15

-albums-

LP	**CLASSICAL COUNTRY** (67)	Epic 24232	$15
LP(P)	**CLASSICAL COUNTRY** (67) (White promo label)	Epic 24232	$18

ARKIE SHIBLEY (RB)

-singles-

45rpm	**PICK PICK PICKIN' MY GUITAR** (57)	Four Star 1737	$25
45rpm	**HOT ROD RACE** (58)	Giltedge 5021	$25
45rpm	**ARKIE MEETS THE JUDGE** (58)	Giltedge 5036	$18

HAROLD SHUTTERS (R)

-singles-

45rpm	**ROCK 'N ROLL MR. MOON** (56)	Golden Rod 204	$175
45rpm	**BUNNY HONEY** (56)	Golden Rod 300	$150

SID SILVER (RB)

-singles-

45rpm	**BUMBLE RUMBLE** (58)	Bakersfield 510	$18

GENE SIMMONS (RB)

-singles-

45rpm	**DRINKIN' WINE** (58)	Sun 299	$60

FRANK SIMON (C)
4-Star 45s $5-10 each

-EPs-

EP	**FRANK SIMON** (57)	4-Star P-36-A	$12

-albums-

LP	**FOUR STAR HITS** (60)	Audio Lab 1552	$20

DONALD SIMPSON (RB)

-singles-

45rpm	**SAVE ME YOUR LOVE** (58)	Major 1002	$65

RED SIMPSON (C)
Capitol 45s $2-4 each
Other Capitol LPs $6-10 each

-albums-

LP	ROLL TRUCK, ROLL (66)	Capitol 2468	$18
LP	THE MAN BEHIND THE BADGE (66)	Capitol 2569	$15
LP	TRUCK DRIVIN' FOOL (67)	Capitol 2691	$12
LP	RED SIMPSON SINGS A BAKERSFIELD DOZEN (67)	Capitol 2829	$12

JIMMY SINGLETON (R)

-singles-

45rpm	SALLY (58)	Devere	$65

MARGIE SINGLETON (C)
United Artists 45s $2 each

-albums-

LP	CRYING TIME (65)	United Artists 6459	$15
LP(P)	CRYING TIME (65)	United Artists 6459	$18
	(White promo label)		
LP	MARGIE SINGLETON SINGS COUNTRY MUSIC WITH SOUL (67)	Ashley 3003	$15

BOBBY SISCO (RB)

-singles-

45rpm	HONKY TONKIN' RHYTHM (58)	Mar-Vel 111	$50
45rpm	GO GO GO (58)	Chess 1650	$50

SIX FAT DUTCHMEN (OT)
RCA Victor 78s and 45s $1-10 each
RCA Victor colored vinyl 45s $5-10 each
Dot 45s $1 each
RCA Victor and Dot LPs $2-5 each

ARTHUR SIZEMORE (CW)
Other 78s $10-20 each
Decca 45s and 78s $4-8 each

-singles-

78rpm	LITTLE JIMMIE'S GOODBYE TO JIMMIE RODGERS	Bluebird 5445	$40

-albums-

LP	MOUNTAIN BALLADS & OLD HYMNS (66)	Decca 4785	$40
LP(P)	MOUNTAIN BALLADS & OLD HYMNS (66)	Decca 4785	$30
	(Pink promo label)		

RICKY SKAGGS (BG)
Epic 45s $2-4 each
Epic AE7 series promo 45s $3-6 each
Epic one-sided small center hole 45s $4 each
Other Sugar Hill duet LPs $5 each
Epic LPs $3-6 each

-albums-

LP	SWEET TEMPTATION (79)	Sugar Hill 3706	$10

-radio shows-

3LP(RS)	AMERICAN EAGLE (Jan 82)	DIR	$25-40
	(Live concert)		
3LP(RS)	SILVER EAGLE (Jun 83) With the Whites	DIR	$25-40
	(Live concert)		
3LP(RS)	TRIPLE (May 83) Box set, w/Alabama and J. Fricke	Mutual Broadcasting	$25-30
	(Music and interviews)		
3LP(RS)	THE GREAT ENTERTAINER (July 86) Box set	United Stations	$20-30
	(Music and interviews)		
LP(RS)	WESTWOOD ONE PRESENTS (Jun 90)	Westwood One	$15-25
	(Live concert)		
LP(RS)	LIVE AT GILLEY'S (Jul 90)	Westwood One	$15-25
	(Live concert)		
Cass(RS)	AUSTIN CITY LIMITS (92)	Main Street	$30-60
	(Live concert with Bonnie Raitt)		

THE SKEE BROTHERS (RB)

-singles-

45rpm	THAT'S ALL SHE WROTE (57)	Okeh 7108	$12
45rpm	BIG DEAL (57)	Epic 9275	$30
45(P)	BIG DEAL (57)	Epic 9275	$25
	(White promo label)		

EDDIE SKELTON (RB)
-singles-
45rpm	GOTTA KEEP IT SWINGING (58)	Dixie 2011	$125
45rpm	MY HEART GETS LONELY (58)	Starday 294	$50

JIMMY SKILES (RB)
-singles-
45rpm	IS MY BABY COMIN' BACK (58)	Rural Rhythm 518	$65

JIMMIE SKINNER (CW)
Mercury 45s $3-6 each
Decca and Starday 45s $2-4 each
Vetco and Jewel LPs $5-10 each
Jewel duet LPs $6 each
QCA LPs $6 each

-EPs-
EP	SONGS THAT MAKE THE JUKEBOX PLAY (57)	Mercury 4037	$20

-albums-
LP	SONGS THAT MADE THE JUKEBOX PLAY (57)	Mercury 20352	$75
LP(P)	SONGS THAT MADE THE JUKEBOX PLAY (57) (White promo label)	Mercury 20352	$60
LP	COUNTRY SINGER (64)	Decca 4132	$50
LP(P)	COUNTRY SINGER (64) (Pink promo label)	Decca 4132	$40
LP	JIMMIE SKINNER SINGS JIMMIE RODGERS (62)	Mercury 60700	$25
LP(P)	JIMMIE SKINNER SINGS JIMMIE RODGERS (62) (White promo label)	Mercury 20700	$30
LP	JIMMIE SKINNER (63)	Starday 240	$40
LP	COUNTRY BLUES (64)	Mercury 16277	$25
LP(P)	COUNTRY BLUES (64) (White promo label)	Mercury 16277	$30

MACY SKIPPER (RB)
-singles-
45rpm	WHO PUT THE SQUEEZE ON ELOISE (58)	Light 2020	$40

NORM SKYLAR (RB)
-singles-
45rpm	ROCK AND ROLL BLUES (58)	Crest 1044	$60

SLIM JIM (CW)
-albums-
LP	SLIM JIM SINGS (58) Black label (Other label versions are worth $10-$15 each)	Soma 1225	$35

JACK SMEDLEY (RB)
-singles-
45rpm	SWEET SUE ANN (58)	Key 1186	$225

AUSTIN SMILEY (RB)
-singles-
45rpm	PRETTY BABY-OH (57)	Brunswick 55061	$15
45(P)	PRETTY BABY-OH (57) (Yellow promo label)	Brunswick 55061	$12

ARTHUR SMITH (CW)
Arthur Guitar Boogie Smith
And His Crakerjacks
The Crossroads Quartet
Bluebird 78s $8-$12 each
MGM 78s $6-10 each
Other MGM 45s $5-10 each
MGM Golden Circle 45s $3 each
Starday 45s $2-4 each
Monument 45s $2 each
Dot 45s $4 each
Monument LPs $5-10 each
County LPs $4-6 each

-singles-
78rpm	BANJO BOOGIE (48)	MGM 10229	$25
78rpm	GUITAR BOOGIE (49)	MGM 10293	$25
45rpm	LISTEN TO THE MOCKING BIRD (51)	MGM 11096	$30
45rpm	INDIAN BOOGIE (53)	MGM 11413	$25
45rpm	BECAUSE YOU LOVE ME (53) (Vocal by Tommy Faile)	MGM 11503	$25
45rpm	THE HONEYMOON IS OVER (53)	MGM 11657	$20

45rpm	**HALF-MOON** (54)	MGM 11817	$25
45rpm	**TRUCK STOP GRILL** (54)	MGM 11879	$20
	(Flip side is "Hi-Lo Boogie")		
45rpm	**MIDNIGHT RAG** (55)	MGM 11945	$20
	(Reissue of 1951 release)		
45rpm	**'BYE 'BYE BLACK SMOKE CHOO CHOO** (55)	MGM 12006	$15
45rpm	**YOUR WAY** (55)	MGM 12064	$15
45rpm	**JACOB'S LADDER** (56) Crossroads Quartet	MGM 12208	$15
45(P)	**JACOB'S LADDER** (56)	MGM 12208	$10
	(Yellow promo label)		
45rpm	**YOU ARE THE FINGER OF GOD** (56) Crossroads Quartet	MGM 12346	$15
45(P)	**YOU ARE THE FINGER OF GOD** (56)	MGM 12346	$10
	(Yellow promo label)		
45rpm	**COAT OF MANY COLORS** (56) Crossroads Quartet	MGM 12411	$12
	(Later recorded by Dolly Parton)		
45(P)	**COAT OF MANY COLORS** (56)	MGM 12411	$10
	(Yellow promo label)		
45rpm	**FREEZE IT BOOGIE** (56)	MGM 12436	$15
45(P)	**FREEZE IT BOOGIE** (56)	MGM 12436	$12
	(Yellow promo label)		
45rpm	**STAMPS** (57)	MGM 12458	$15
45(P)	**STAMPS** (57)	MGM 12458	$12
	(White promo label)		
45rpm	**NOT MY WILL** (57) Crossroads Quartet	MGM 12528	$12
45(P)	**NOT MY WILL** (57)	MGM 12528	$10
	(Yellow promo label)		
45rpm	**TEEN-AGE REBEL** (57)	MGM 12544	$20
45(P)	**TEEN-AGE REBEL** (57)	MGM 12544	$18
	(Yellow promo label)		
45rpm	**ROCKIN' THE NEWS** (58)	MGM 12618	$20
45(P)	**ROCKIN' THE NEWS** (58)	MGM 12618	$18
	(Yellow promo label)		
45rpm	**THE SHADOW OF THE CROSS** (58)	MGM 12675	$15
45(P)	**THE SHADOW OF THE CROSS** (58)	MGM 12675	$10
	(Yellow promo label)		
45rpm	**HARD BROILED BOOGIE** (59)	MGM 12791	$15
45(P)	**HARD BROILED BOOGIE** (59)	MGM 12791	$10
	(Yellow promo label)		
45rpm	**OUR PILOT KNOWS THE SEA** (59) Crossroads Quartet	Choice 5609	$15
45(P)	**OUR PILOT KNOWS THE SEA** (59)	Choice 5609	$10
	(White promo label)		
45rpm	**DO YOUR BEST** (59) Crossroads Quartet	Choice 5802	$15
45(P)	**DO YOUR BEST** (59)	Choice 5802	$10
	(White promo label)		
45rpm	**THE SUNSHINE OF HIS LOVE** (59) Crossroads Quartet	Choice 5803	$12
45(P)	**THE SUNSHINE OF HIS LOVE** (59)	Choice 5803	$10
	(White promo label)		
45rpm	**SHHH** (60) With dialog/without dialog	Choice 6101	$15
45(P)	**SHHH** (60)	Choice 6101	$10
	(White promo label)		
45rpm	**HOSPITALITY BLUES** (62)	Starday 615	$12

-EPs-

EP	**GUITAR JAMBOREE** (55)	MGM 1009	$50
EP	**FINGERS ON FIRE** (55)	MGM 1043	$50
EP	**ARTHUR GUITAR BOOGIE SMITH** (62)	Starday 207	$18
	(Six-song EP)		

-albums-

10"LP	**FOOLISH QUESTIONS** (54)	MGM 236	$125
10"LP	**FINGERS ON FIRE** (55)	MGM 533	$100
LP	**SPECIALS** (55)	MGM 3301	$75
LP(P)	**SPECIALS** (55)	MGM 3301	$100
	(Yellow promo label)		
LP	**FINGERS ON FIRE** (57)	MGM 3525	$75
LP(P)	**FINGERS ON FIRE** (57)	MGM 3525	$100
	(Yellow promo label)		
LP	**MISTER GUITAR** (62)	Starday 173	$30
LP	**ARTHUR SMITH & THE CROSSROADS QUARTET** (62)	Starday 186	$40
LP	**RARE OLD TIME FIDDLE TUNES** (62)	Starday 202	$25
	(With the Dixieliners)		
LP	**ARTHUR GUITAR BOOGIE SMITH GOES TO TOWN** (63)	Starday 216	$25
LP	**IN PERSON** (63)	Starday 241	$25
LP	**DOWN HOME** (64)	Starday 266	$25
LP	**THE GUITARS OF ARTHUR SMITH** (68)	Starday 415	$15
LP	**ARTHUR GUITAR SMITH AND VOICES** (68)	ABC Paramount 441	$15
LP(P)	**ARTHUR GUITAR SMITH AND VOICES** (68)	ABC Paramount 441	$18
	(White promo label)		

LP	**OLD TIMERS OF THE GRAND OL' OPRY** (64)	Folkways 2379	$15
	(With Sam and Kirk McGee)		
LP	**THE ARTHUR SMITH SHOW** (64)	Hamilton 12134	$12
LP	**ORIGINAL GUITAR BOOGIE** (64)	Dot 3600	$25
LP	**GREAT COUNTRY & WESTERN HITS** (65)	Dot 3636	$15
LP	**SINGING ON THE MOUNTAIN** (65)	Dot 3642	$12
	(With the Crossroads Quartet)		
LP	**A TRIBUTE TO JIM REEVES** (66)	Dot 3769	$15
LP	**GUITAR BOOGIE** (68)	Nashville 2060	$12

BETTY SMITH (RB)

-singles-

45rpm	**OH YEAH** (58)	Echo 584	$15

CAL SMITH (C)
Kapp and MCA 45s $2-4 each
Kapp LPs $5-10 each
MCA LPs $2-4 each

CARL SMITH (CW)
Columbia 78s $4-8 each
Other Columbia LPs $4-8 each
Other Harmony LPs $3-6 each
Gusto, Lake Shore, and ABC LPs $3-5 each
ABC LPs $4 each

-singles-

45rpm	**LET MOTHER NATURE HAVE HER WAY** (51)	Columbia 20862	$20
45(P)	**LET MOTHER NATURE HAVE HER WAY** (51)	Columbia 20862	$15
	(White promo label)		
45rpm	**DON'T JUST STAND THERE** (52)	Columbia 20893	$18
45(P)	**DON'T JUST STAND THERE** (52)	Columbia 20893	$12
	(White promo label)		
45rpm	**ARE YOU TEASING ME** (52)	Columbia 20922	$15
45(P)	**ARE YOU TEASING ME** (52)	Columbia 20922	$12
	(White promo label)		
45rpm	**OUR HONEYMOON** (53)	Columbia 21008	$15
45(P)	**OUR HONEYMOON** (53)	Columbia 21008	$12
	(White promo label)		
45rpm	**THAT'S THE KIND OF LOVE I'M LOOKING FOR** (53)	Columbia 21051	$15
45(P)	**THAT'S THE KIND OF LOVE I'M LOOKING FOR** (53)	Columbia 21051	$12
	(White promo label)		
45rpm	**ORCHIDS MEAN GOODBYE** (53)	Columbia 21087	$15
45(P)	**ORCHIDS MEAN GOODBYE** (53)	Columbia 21087	$10
	(White promo label)		
45rpm	**TRADEMARK** (53)	Columbia 21119	$15
45(P)	**TRADEMARK** (53)	Columbia 21119	$10
	(White promo label)		
45rpm	**HEY JOE!** (53)	Columbia 21129	$15
45(P)	**HEY JOE!** (53)	Columbia 21129	$10
	(White promo label)		
45rpm	**SATISFACTION GUARANTEED** (53)	Columbia 21166	$12
45(P)	**SATISFACTION GUARANTEED** (53)	Columbia 21166	$10
	(White promo label)		
78rpm	**DOG-GONE IT, BABY, I'M IN LOVE** (53)	Columbia 21197	$25
78(P)	**DOG-GONE IT, BABY, I'M IN LOVE** (53)	Columbia 21197	$20
	(Columbia promo label)		
45rpm	**DOG-GONE IT, BABY, I'M IN LOVE** (53)	Columbia 21197	$25
45(P)	**DOG-GONE IT, BABY, I'M IN LOVE** (53)	Columbia 21197	$20
	(White promo label)		
45rpm	**BACK UP BUDDY** (54)	Columbia 21226	$12
45(P)	**BACK UP BUDDY** (54)	Columbia 21226	$10
	(White promo label)		
78rpm	**GO, BOY GO** (54)	Columbia 21266	$25
78(P)	**GO, BOY GO** (54)	Columbia 21266	$20
	(Columbia promo label)		
45rpm	**GO, BOY GO** (54)	Columbia 21266	$25
45(P)	**GO, BOY GO** (54)	Columbia 21266	$20
	(White promo label)		
45rpm	**LOOSE TALK** (54)	Columbia 21317	$10
45rpm	**OLD LONESOME TIMES** (54)	Columbia 21382	$10
45rpm	**DON'T TEASE ME** (55)	Columbia 21429	$10
45rpm	**I FEEL LIKE CRYIN'** (55)	Columbia 21462	$10
45rpm	**WICKED LIES** (55)	Columbia 21552	$10
45rpm	**YOU CAN'T HURT ME ANYMORE** (56)	Columbia 40823	$10
45rpm	**TRY TO TAKE IT LIKE A MAN** (56)	Columbia 40918	$10
45rpm	**EMOTIONS** (57)	Columbia 40984	$10
45rpm	**YOU'RE SO EASY TO LOVE** (58)	Columbia 41092	$10

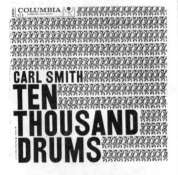

45rpm	GUESS I'VE BEEN AROUND TOO LONG (58)	Columbia 41170	$10
45rpm	TEN THOUSAND DRUMS (59)	Columbia 41417	$20
	(Price includes picture sleeve)		

-EPs-

EP	CARL SMITH (57)	Columbia 2801	$25
EP	CARL SMITH (57)	Columbia 2810	$20
EP	CARL SMITH (57)	Columbia 2821	$20
EP	FOUR HITS BY CARL SMITH (57)	Columbia 2131	$25
EP	SUNDAY DOWN SOUTH (57)	Columbia 9591	$20
EP	SMITH'S THE NAME VOL 1 (57)	Columbia 10221	$18
EP	SMITH'S THE NAME VOL 2 (57)	Columbia 10222	$18
EP	SMITH'S THE NAME VOL 3 (57)	Columbia 10223	$18
EP	LET'S LIVE A LITTLE (58)	Columbia 11721	$18

-albums-

10"LP	CARL SMITH (56)	Columbia 2579	$100
10"LP	SENTIMENTAL SONGS (56)	Columbia 9023	$100
10"LP	SOFTLY & TENDERLY (56)	Columbia 9026	$75
10"LP	CARL, LEFTY AND MARTY (56)	Columbia 2544	$250
	(With Lefty Frizzel and Marty Robbins)		
LP	SUNDAY DOWN SOUTH (57)	Columbia 959	$50
LP	SMITH'S THE NAME (57)	Columbia 1022	$50
LP	LET'S LIVE A LITTLE (58)	Columbia 1172	$40
LP	THE CARL SMITH TOUCH (60) Mono	Columbia 1532	$20
LP	THE CARL SMITH TOUCH (60) Stereo	Columbia 8332	$25
LP(P)	THE CARL SMITH TOUCH (60)	Columbia 1532	$30
	(White promo label)		
LP	EASY TO PLEASE (62) Mono	Columbia 1740	$20
LP	EASY TO PLEASE (62) Stereo	Columbia 8540	$25
LP(P)	EASY TO PLEASE (62)	Columbia 1740	$30
	(White promo label)		
LP	CARL SMITH'S GREATEST HITS (62)	Columbia 1937	$18
LP(P)	CARL SMITH'S GREATEST HITS (62)	Columbia 1937	$25
	(White promo label)		
LP	TALL, TALL GENTLEMAN (63)	Columbia 2091	$20
LP(P)	TALL, TALL GENTLEMAN (63)	Columbia 2091	$25
	(White promo label)		
LP	THERE STANDS THE GLASS (64)	Columbia 2173	$18
LP(P)	THERE STANDS THE GLASS (64)	Columbia 2173	$20
	(White promo label)		
LP	CARL SMITH'S BEST (64)	Harmony 7310	$15
LP(P)	CARL SMITH'S BEST (64)	Harmony 7310	$18
	(White promo label)		
LP	I WANT TO LIVE AND LOVE (65)	Columbia 2293	$18
LP(P)	I WANT TO LIVE AND LOVE (65)	Columbia 2293	$20
	(White promo label)		
LP	KISSES DON'T LIE (65)	Columbia 2358	$18
LP(P)	KISSES DON'T LIE (65)	Columbia 2358	$20
	(White promo label)		
LP	MAN WITH A PLAN (66)	Columbia 2501	$15
LP(P)	MAN WITH A PLAN (66)	Columbia 2501	$18
	(White promo label)		
LP	THE COUNTRY GENTLEMAN (67)	Columbia 2610	$15
LP(P)	THE COUNTRY GENTLEMAN (67)	Columbia 2610	$18
	(White promo label)		
LP	THE COUNTRY GENTLEMAN SINGS (67)	Columbia 2687	$15
LP(P)	THE COUNTRY GENTLEMAN SINGS (67)	Columbia 2687	$18
	(White promo label)		
LP	SATISFACTION GUARANTEED (67)	Harmony 11218	$10
LP	DEEP WATER (68)	Columbia 2822	$12
LP(P)	DEEP WATER (68)	Columbia 2822	$15
	(White promo label)		
LP	COUNTRY ON MY MIND (68)	Columbia 9688	$10
LP	GENTLEMAN IN LOVE (68)	Harmony 11251	$10
LP	FADED LOVE AND WINTER ROSES (69)	Columbia 9786	$10
LP	CARL SMITH'S GREATEST HITS VOL 2 (69)	Columbia 9807	$10
LP	A TRIBUTE TO ROY ACUFF (69)	Columbia 9870	$10
LP	TAKE IT LIKE A MAN (69)	Harmony 11317	$10
LP	I LOVE YOU BECAUSE (70)	Columbia 9898	$10
2LP	ANNIVERSARY ALBUM (70)	Columbia 31	$12
LP	THE WAY I LOSE MY MIND (75)	Hickory 4518	$12

CHESTER SMITH (CW)
Other Capitol 45s $5-10 each

-singles-

45rpm	WISHING MY LIFE AWAY (54)	Capitol 2572	$10
45rpm	HOLIDAY FOR TEARS (55)	Capitol 2858	$10

CONNIE SMITH (C)

RCA Victor 45s $3-6 each
RCA Victor picture sleeves $5 each
Monument and Columbia 45s $2-3 each
Other RCA Victor LPs $5-10 each
Other Camden LPs $5-8 each
Columbia LPs $5 each

-albums-

LP	THE OTHER SIDE OF CONNIE SMITH (65)	RCA Victor 3341	$20
LP	CUTE 'N COUNTRY (65)	RCA Victor 3444	$18
LP	MISS SMITH GOES TO NASHVILLE (66)	RCA Victor 3520	$18
LP	CONNIE SMITH SINGS GREAT SACRED SONGS (66)	RCA Victor 3589	$18
LP	BORN TO SING (66)	RCA Victor 3628	$18
LP	DOWNTOWN COUNTRY (67)	RCA Victor 3725	$15
LP	CONNIE SMITH SINGS BILL ANDERSON (67)	RCA Victor 3768	$15
LP	THE BEST OF CONNIE SMITH (67)	RCA Victor 3848	$15
LP	CONNIE IN THE COUNTRY (67)	Camden 2120	$12
LP	SOUL OF COUNTRY MUSIC (68)	RCA Victor 3889	$12
LP	I LOVE CHARLIE BROWN (68)	RCA Victor 4002	$12
LP	SUNSHINE & RAIN (68)	RCA Victor 4077	$12
LP	CONNIE'S COUNTRY (69)	RCA Victor 4132	$12
LP	YOUNG LOVE (69)	RCA Victor 4190	$12
LP	BACK IN BABY'S ARMS (69)	RCA Victor 4229	$15

-radio shows-

16"(RS)	U.S. AIR FORCE (60s)	U.S. Air Force	$20-40
	(Music and interviews)		
16"(RS)	U.S. ARMY BAND (60s)	U.S. Army	$20-40
	(Music and interviews)		
LP(RS)	LIVE AT GILLEY'S (Mar 87)	Westwood One	$15-25
	(Live concert)		

EDDIE SMITH (CW)

Other King 45s $5-10 each

-singles-

45rpm	THE PREACHER AND THE BEAR (54)	King 1095	$10
	(With the Super Chiefs)		
45rpm	BACK IN YOUR OWN BACK YARD (54)	King 1171	$10
	(With the Seven Chiefs)		
45rpm	WHEN YOU AND I WERE YOUNG MAGGIE (54)	King 1204	$10

HANK SMITH See George Jones

JERRY SMITH (C)

Decca 45s $1 each
Decca, Ranwood, and ABC LPs $2-3 each

JIMMY SMITH (RB)

-singles-

45rpm	PINCH ME QUICK (58)	Wonder 110	$65

KENNY SMITH (R)

-singles-

45rpm	I'M SO LONESOME BABY (58)	Top-per 281	$75

LEON SMITH (RB)

-singles-

45rpm	LITTLE FORTY FORD (58)	Williamette 101	$50
45rpm	LITTLE FORTY FORD (59)	Williamette 105	$25

RAY SMITH (RB)

Smash 45s $5-10 each
Zircon, Infinity, Warner, Celebrity Circle, Diamond, and BC 45s $4-8 each

-singles-

45rpm	GONE BABY GONE (58)	Heart 250	$2,000
45rpm	RIGHT BEHIND YOU BABY (58)	Sun 298	$25
45rpm	YOU MADE A HIT (58)	Sun 308	$25
45rpm	ROCKIN' BANDIT (61)	Sun 319	$25
45rpm	CANDY DOLL (62)	Sun 375	$20
45(P)	CANDY DOLL (62)	Sun 375	$25
	(White promo label)		
45rpm	ROCKIN' LITTLE ANGEL (60)	Judd 1016	$25
45rpm	PUT YOUR ARMS AROUND ME, HONEY (60)	Judd 1017	$18
45rpm	ONE WONDERFUL LOVE (60)	Judd 1019	$15
45rpm	BLOND HAIR, BLUE EYES (61)	Judd 1021	$15
45rpm	DID WE HAVE A PARTY (63)	Tollie 9029	$15
45(P)	DID WE HAVE A PARTY (63)	Tollie 9029	$12
	(White promo label)		

45rpm	**ALMOST ALONE** (62)	Toppa 1071	$15
45rpm	**ROBBIN' THE CRADLE** (64)	Vee Jay 579	$15
45(P)	**ROBBIN' THE CRADLE** (64)	Vee Jay 579	$12
	(White promo label)		
45rpm	**DEEP IN MY HEART** (64)	Ne-Tone 1182	$12

-albums-

LP	**TRAVELIN' WITH RAY** (60)	Judd 701	$500
LP	**THE BEST OF RAY SMITH** (62)	T 56062	$100
	(Reissue of the Judd LP)		
LP	**RAY SMITH'S GREATEST HITS** (63) Mono	Columbia 1937	$25
LP	**RAY SMITH'S GREATEST HITS** (63) Stereo	Columbia 8737	$40
LP(P)	**RAY SMITH'S GREATEST HITS** (63)	Columbia 1937	$50
	(White promo label)		
LP	**RAY SMITH AND PAY CUPP** (63) Mono	Crown 5364	$30
LP	**RAY SMITH AND PAT CUPP** (63) Stereo	Crown 364	$25
LP	**I'M GONNA ROCK SOME MORE** (70s)	Wix 1000	$15

SAMMI SMITH (C)
Mega 45s $2 each
Mega LPs $5 each
United Artists, Harmony, and Elektra LPs $4 each

SAMMY SMITH (RB)

-singles-

45rpm	**SATELLITE ROCK** (58)	Wee Rebel 102	$60

WARREN SMITH (RB)
Liberty 45s $5-10 each

-singles-

45rpm	**ROCK 'N ROLL RUBY** (56)	Sun 239	$50
45rpm	**ROCK 'M ROLL RUBY** (56)	Sun 239	$75
	(Error in the title, "M" instead of "N")		
45rpm	**UBANGI STOMP** (57)	Sun 250	$40
45rpm	**MISS FROGGIE** (57)	Sun 268	$40
45rpm	**I'VE GOT LOVE IF YOU WANT IT** (58)	Sun 286	$30
45rpm	**SWEET SWEET GIRL** (59)	Sun 314	$30

-albums-

LP	**THE FIRST COUNTRY COLLECTION** (61) Mono	Liberty 3199	$50
LP	**THE FIRST COUNTRY COLLECTION** (61) Stereo	Liberty 7199	$75
LP(P)	**THE FIRST COUNTRY COLLECTION** (61)	Liberty 7199	$40
	(White promo label)		

LONNIE SMITHSON (RB)

-singles-

45rpm	**IT TAKES TIME** (58)	Starday 330	$15

EDDIE SNOW (RB)

-singles-

45rpm	**AIN'T THAT RIGHT** (55)	Sun 226	$75

HANK SNOW (CW)
And the Rainbow Ranch Boys
Bluebird 78s are worth $10-$15 each
RCA Victor 78s $5-10 each
RCA Victor white promo label 78s $15-20 each
Other black label, dog on top RCA Victor 45s $4-8 each
Other RCA Victor 45s $2-4 each
Other RCA Victor LPs $5-10 each
Pickwick and Other Camden LPs $4-8 each
RCA Victor duet LPs with Kelly Foxton $8 each

-singles-

45rpm	**MARRIAGE VOW** (49)	RCA Victor 0056	$25
	(One of the first RCA Victor 45s)		
45rpm	**I'M MOVING ON** (50)	RCA Victor 0328	$20
45rpm	**THE GOLDEN ROCKET** (50)	RCA Victor 0400	$18
45rpm	**THE RHUMBA BOOGIE** (51)	RCA Victor 0431	$18
45rpm	**BLUEBIRD ISLAND** (51)	RCA Victor 0441	$18
45rpm	**UNWANTED SIGN UPON YOUR HEART** (51)	RCA Victor 0498	$18
45rpm	**ONE MORE RIDE** (52)	RCA Victor 4097	$15
45rpm	**MUSIC MAKIN' MAMA FROM MEMPHIS** (52)	RCA Victor 4346	$15
	(All of the above are on aqua-color labels)		
45rpm	**THE GOLD RUSH IS OVER** (52)	RCA Victor 4522	$15
45(P)	**THE GOLD RUSH IS OVER** (52)	RCA Victor 4522	$20
	(White promo label)		
45rpm	**MARRIED BY THE BIBLE, DIVORCED BY THE LAW** (52)	RCA Victor 4733	$15
45(P)	**MARRIED BY THE BIBLE, DIVORCED BY THE LAW** (52)	RCA Victor 4733	$20
	(White promo label)		

45rpm	**I WENT TO YOUR WEDDING** (52)	RCA Victor 4909	$15
45(P)	**I WENT TO YOUR WEDDING** (52)	RCA Victor 4909	$20
	(White promo label)		
45rpm	**A FOOL SUCH AS I** (52)	RCA Victor 5034	$15
45(P)	**A FOOL SUCH AS I** (52)	RCA Victor 5034	$20
	(White promo label)		
45rpm	**HONEYMOON ON A ROCKET SHIP** (53)	RCA Victor 5155	$15
45(P)	**HONEYMOON ON A ROCKET SHIP** (53)	RCA Victor 5155	$18
	(White promo label)		
45rpm	**THE GLORY LAND MARCH** (53)	RCA Victor 5249	$15
	(Hank Snow and the Jordaniares)		
45(P)	**THE GLORY LAND MARCH** (53)	RCA Victor 5249	$18
	(White promo label)		
45rpm	**SPANISH FIRE BALL** (53)	RCA Victor 5296	$15
45(P)	**SPANISH FIRE BALL** (53)	RCA Victor 5296	$18
	(White promo label)		
45rpm	**CHRISTMAS ROSES** (53)	RCA Victor 5340	$15
45(P)	**CHRISTMAS ROSES** (53)	RCA Victor 5340	$18
	(White promo label)		
45rpm	**FOR NOW AND ALWAYS** (53)	RCA Victor 5380	$15
45(P)	**FOR NOW AND ALWAYS** (53)	RCA Victor 5380	$18
	(Whiter promo label)		
45rpm	**WHEN MEXICAN JOE MET JOLE BLON** (53)	RCA Victor 5490	$15
45(P)	**WHEN MEXICAN JOE MET JOLE BLON** (53)	RCA Victor 5490	$15
	(White promo label)		
45rpm	**INVISIBLE HANDS** (53)	RCA Victor 5548	$15
	(Hank Snow and the Blackwood Brothers)		
45(P)	**INVISIBLE HANDS** (53)	RCA Victor 5548	$15
	(White promo label)		
45rpm	**PANAMAMA** (53)	RCA Victor 5592	$15
45(P)	**PANAMAMA** (53)	RCA Victor 5592	$12
	(White promo label)		
3-45s	**RAILROADING SONGS** (54) Box set	RCA Victor 310 (3)	$50
	(Price is for box and three 45s)		
45rpm	**I DON'T HURT ANYMORE** (54)	RCA Victor 5698	$12
	(End of the dogless labels)		
45(P)	**I DON'T HURT ANYMORE** (54)	RCA Victor 5698	$10
	(White promo label)		
45rpm	**THAT CRAZY MAMBO THING** (54)	RCA Victor 5912	$12
	(First of the dog on top labels)		
45rpm	**KEEP YOUR PROMISE, WILLIE THOMAS** (56)	RCA Victor 6500	$10
	(Hank Snow and Anita Carter)		
45rpm	**HULA ROCK** (56)	RCA Victor 6578	$10
33rpm	**POOR LITTLE JIMMIE** (58)	RCA Victor 7869	$25
	(Compact-33 single)		
45rpm	**THE MAN WHO ROBBED THE BANK AT SANTA FE** (63)	RCA Victor 8151	$15
	(Price includes picture sleeve)		
45(P)	**1980 9TH ANNUAL FANFAIR** (80) Radio ads	CMA/CBS	$25
	(Seventeen cuts, Snow does one spot, a station tour)		

-EPs-

2EP	**COUNTRY CLASSICS** (52) Double EP, w/Anita Carter	RCA Victor 3026	$75
	(RCA Victor EP 1233 is also the same title but different songs)		
2EP	**HANK SNOW SINGS** (52)	RCA Victor 3070	$75
2EP	**HANK SNOW SALUTES JIMMIE RODGERS** (53)	RCA Victor 3131	$100
	(Hank named his son Jimmie Rodgers Snow, who also recorded for RCA Victor)		
EP	**RAILROADING SONGS** (54)	RCA Victor 310	$30
EP	**CANADIAN FAVORITES OF SNOW** (55)	RCA Victor 443	$30
EP	**COUNTRY CHRISTMAS** (55)	RCA Victor 472	$40
	(Bell shaped cover)		
2EP	**JUST KEEP A-MOVIN'** (55)	RCA Victor 1113	$50
2EP	**OLD DOC BROWN AND OTHER NARRATIONS** (55)	RCA Victor 1156	$75
	(Various LP ads appear on the back side of the EP cover, each with same value)		
2EP	**COUNTRY CLASSICS** (55)	RCA Victor 1233	$30
	(Not the same EP as RCA 3026)		
EP	**THESE THINGS SHALL PASS** (55)	RCA Victor 503	$25
EP	**COUNTRY PICKIN'** (55)	RCA Victor 546	$25
EP	**HANK SNOW'S COUNTRY GUITAR** (58)	RCA Victor 582	$25
EP	**GOD'S LITTLE CANDLES** (55)	RCA Victor 591	$25
EP	**COUNTRY CLASSICS** (56)	RCA Victor 794	$25
EP	**COUNTRY & WESTERN JAMBOREE VOL 1** (57)	RCA Victor 1-1419	$25
EP	**COUNTRY & WESTERN JAMBOREE VOL 2** (57)	RCA Victor 2-1419	$25
EP	**HANK SNOW'S COUNTRY GUITAR VOL 2** (57)	RCA Victor 1435	$25
EP	**HANK SNOW** (58)	RCA Victor 5062	$25
EP	**THE GOLDEN ROCKET** (58)	RCA Victor 5086	$25
EP	**HANK SNOW SINGS SACRED SONGS** (58)	RCA Victor 4158	$25

EP	MUSIC MAKIN' HANK SNOW (59)	RCA Victor 5151	$25
EP	MORE HANK SNOW SOUVENIRS (64) Jukebox LLP	RCA Victor 2812	$30
	(Price includes title strips and hard cover)		
EP(P)	CALYPSO SWEETHEART/MARRIAGE AND DIVORCE (59)	RCA Victor 6831 DJ-76	$75
	(Two songs on each side, flip is Janis Martin)		

-albums-

10"LP	COUNTRY CLASSICS (52)	RCA Victor 3026	$175
10"LP	HANK SNOW SINGS (52)	RCA Victor 3070	$150
10"LP	HANK SNOW SALUTES JIMMIE RODGERS (53)	RCA Victor 3131	$150
10"LP	HANK SNOW COUNTRY GUITAR (54)	RCA Victor 3267	$150
LP	JUST KEEP A-MOVIN' (55)	RCA Victor 1113	$100
2LP	OLD DOC BROWN AND OTHER NARRATIONS (55)	RCA Victor 1156	$100
LP	COUNTRY CLASSICS (55)	RCA Victor 1233	$75
	(Reissue of ten-inch LP with four additional cuts)		
LP	COUNTRY AND WESTERN JAMBOREE (57)	RCA Victor 1419	$75
LP	HANK SNOW'S COUNTRY GUITAR (57)	RCA Victor 1435	$75
LP	HANK SNOW SINGS SACRED SONGS (58)	RCA Victor 1638	$60
	(Later on the Pickwick label this LP is worth around $10)		
LP	THE GUITAR (58)	School Of Music 1149	$250
	(Includes booklet)		
LP	WHEN TRAGEDY STRUCK (58)	RCA Victor 1861	$75
LP(P)	SHOP AT THE STORE (58) One record from set	RCA Thesaurus 5119	$200
	(Radio jingle, one thirty-second cut by Snow, from a sound effects library)		
LP(P)	SHOP AT THE STORE (58) One record from set	RCA Thesaurus	$200
	(Radio jingles, two cuts by Snow, :06 and :09, from a sound effects library)		
LP	THE SINGING STRANGER (59)	Camden 514	$20
LP	HANK SNOW SINGS JIMMIE RODGERS' SONGS (59) Mono	RCA Victor 2043	$50
LP	HANK SNOW SINGS JIMMIE RODGERS' SONGS (60) Stereo	RCA Victor 2043	$75
6LP	I'M MOVIN' ON Box set	Reader's Digest 216	$125
	(Six-record box set ordered through the mail)		
LP	HANK SNOW'S SOUVENIRS (61) Mono	RCA Victor 2285	$25
LP	HANK SNOW'S SOUVENIRS (61) Stereo	RCA Victor 2285	$40
LP	BIG COUNTRY HITS (61) Mono	RCA Victor 2458	$25
LP	BIG COUNTRY HITS (61) Stereo	RCA Victor 2458	$40
LP	THE SOUTHERN CANNONBALL (61)	Camden 680	$20
LP	TOGETHER AGAIN (62) Mono	RCA Victor 2580	$25
	(Hank Snow and Anita Carter)		
LP	TOGETHER AGAIN (62) Stereo	RCA Victor 2580	$40
LP	THE ONE AND ONLY HANK SNOW (62)	Camden 722	$20
LP	I'VE BEEN EVERYWHERE (63) Mono	RCA Victor 2675	$20
LP	I'VE BEEN EVERYWHERE (63) Stereo	RCA Victor 2675	$30
LP	RAILROAD MAN (63) Mono	RCA Victor 2705	$20
LP	RAILROAD MAN (63) Stereo	RCA Victor 2705	$30
LP	THREE COUNTRY GENTLEMEN (63) Mono	RCA Victor 2723	$20
	(With Porter Wagoner and Hank Locklin)		
LP	THREE COUNTRY GENTLEMEN (63) Stereo	RCA Victor 2723	$30
LP	THE LAST RIDE (63)	Camden 782	$20
LP	MORE HANK SNOW SOUVENIRS (64) Mono	RCA Victor 2812	$20
LP	MORE HANK SNOW SOUVENIRS (64) Stereo	RCA Victor 2812	$30
LP	SONGS OF TRAGEDY (64) Mono	RCA Victor 2901	$30
LP	SONGS OF TRAGEDY (64) Stereo	RCA Victor 2901	$40
LP	REMINISCING (64) Mono	RCA Victor 2952	$20
	(Hank Snow and Chet Atkins)		
LP	REMINISCING (64) Stereo	RCA Victor 2952	$30
LP	OLD AND GREAT SONGS BY HANK SNOW (64) Mono	Camden 836	$15
LP	OLD AND GREAT SONGS BY HANK SNOW (64) Stereo	Camden 836	$18
LP	YOUR FAVORITE COUNTRY HITS (65) Mono	RCA Victor 3317	$20
LP	YOUR FAVORITE COUNTRY HITS (65) Stereo	RCA Victor 3317	$30
LP	GLORYLAND MARCH (65) Mono	RCA Victor 3378	$25
LP	GLORYLAND MARCH (65) Stereo	RCA Victor 3378	$30
LP	HEARTBREAK TRAIL (65) Mono	RCA Victor 3471	$18
	(With the Jordanaires)		
LP	HEARTBREAK TRAIL (65) Stereo	RCA Victor 3471	$25
LP	THE HIGHEST BIDDER AND OTHER FAVORITES (65) Mono	Camden 910	$15
LP	THE HIGHEST BIDDER AND OTHER FAVORITES (65) Stereo	Camden 910	$18
LP	THE BEST OF HANK SNOW (66) Mono	RCA Victor 3478	$18
LP	THE BEST OF HANK SNOW (66) Stereo	RCA Victor 3478	$25
LP	THE GUITAR STYLINGS OF HANK SNOW (66) Mono	RCA Victor 3548	$20
LP	THE GUITAR STYLINGS OF HANK SNOW (66) Stereo	RCA Victor 3548	$25
LP	GOSPEL TRAIN (66) Mono	RCA Victor 3595	$20
LP	GOSPEL TRAIN (66) Stereo	RCA Victor 3595	$25
2LP	THIS IS MY STORY (66) Mono	RCA Victor 6014	$40
LP	THIS IS MY STORY (66) Stereo	RCA Victor 6014	$50
	(Part of the LP is dialog)		
LP	TRAVELIN' BLUES (66) Mono	Camden 964	$15

LP	**TRAVELIN' BLUES** (66) Stereo	Camden 964	$18
LP	**SNOW IN HAWAII** (67) Mono	RCA Victor 3737	$30
LP	**SNOW IN HAWAII** (67) Stereo	RCA Victor 3737	$25
LP	**CHRISTMAS WITH HANK SNOW** (67) Mono	RCA Victor 3826	$40
LP	**CHRISTMAS WITH HANK SNOW** (67) Stereo	RCA Victor 3826	$30
LP	**SPANISH FIREBALL** (67) Mono	RCA Victor 3857	$30
LP	**SPANISH FIREBALL** (67) Stereo	RCA Victor 3857	$25
LP	**MY EARLY COUNTRY FAVORITES** (67) Mono	Camden 2160	$15
LP	**MY EARLY COUNTRY FAVORITES** (67) Stereo	Camden 2160	$18
LP	**HITS, HITS AND MORE HITS** (68) Mono	RCA Victor 3965	$100
	(From this point on, mono LPs are very scarce)		
LP	**HITS, HITS AND MORE HITS** (68) Stereo	RCA Victor 3965	$20
LP	**TALES OF THE YUKON** (68)	RCA Victor 4032	$20
LP	**SNOW IN ALL SEASONS** (69)	RCA Victor 4122	$25
LP	**BY SPECIAL REQUEST** (70) C. B. Atkins and C. E. Snow	RCA Victor 4254	$20
	(Hank Snow and Chet Atkins)		
LP	**HANK SNOW SINGS** (70)	RCA Victor 4306	$20
	(Jimmie Rodgers tribute LP)		
LP	**CURE FOR THE BLUES** (70)	RCA Victor 4379	$20
LP	**TRACKS AND TRAINS** (71)	RCA Victor 4501	$15
LP	**AWARD WINNERS** (71)	RCA Victor 4601	$15
LP	**THE JIMMIE RODGERS STORY** (72)	RCA Victor 4708	$18
LP	**THE BEST OF HANK SNOW VOL. 2** (72)	RCA Victor 4798	$15
2LP	**THE WRECK OF THE OLD 97** (72)	Camden 9009	$25
LP	**ALL ABOUT TRAINS** (75)	RCA Victor 1052	$15
	(With Jimmie Rodgers)		
2LP	**THE LIVING LEGEND** (78)	RCA Victor 0134	$100
	(RCA Victor Special Products release)		
LP	**BY REQUEST** (81)	RCA Victor 0482	$25
	(RCA Special Products)		

-radio shows-

16"(RS)	**HANK SNOW** (55) RCA Thesaurus Library Series	RCA Victor	$40-75 each
	(Show numbers include 1649, 1657, 1660, 1676, 1680, 1870, 1921, 1933, 1986)		
9LP(RS)	**HANK SNOW** (55) RCA Thesaurus Library Series	RCA Victor	$300-500
	(The complete set)		
16"(RS)	**COUNTRY STYLE USA** (55) Fifteen-minute show	Country Style #181	$40-75
	(Music and interviews)		
16"(RS)	**COUNTRY STYLE USA** (55)	Country Style #198	$40-75
	(Music and interviews)		
16"(RS)	**COUNTRY STYLE USA** (55)	Country Style #208	$40-75
	(Music and interviews)		
16"(RS)	**NAVY HOEDOWN** (60s)	U.S. Navy	$40-75
	(Music and interviews)		
16"(RS)	**U.S. ARMY** (60s)	U.S. Army	$40-75
	(Music and interviews)		
LP(RS)	**GRAND OL' OPRY** (63) Fifteen-minute show	WSM Radio 76	$50-100
	(Music and interviews)		
LP(RS)	**GRAND OL' OPRY** (63)	WSM Radio 83	$50-100
	(Music and interviews)		
LP(RS)	**GRAND OL' OPRY** (63)	WSM Radio 109	$50-100
	(Music and interviews)		

JIMMIE RODGERS SNOW (CW)

And His Tennessee Playboys
Son of Hank Snow
Other RCA Victor 78s $10-15 each
Other RCA Victor 45s $5-10 each

-singles-

78rpm	**WHY DON'T YOU LET ME GO** (54)	RCA Victor 5900	$25
78(P)	**WHY DON'T YOU LET ME GO** (54)	RCA Victor 5900	$15
	(White promo label)		
45rpm	**WHY DON'T YOU LET ME GO** (54)	RCA Victor 5900	$15
45(P)	**WHY DON'T YOU LET ME GO** (54)	RCA Victor 5900	$10
	(White promo label)		
78rpm	**LOVE ME** (55)	RCA Victor 5986	$20
78(P)	**LOVE ME** (55)	RCA Victor 5986	$15
	(White promo label)		
45rpm	**LOVE ME** (55)	RCA Victor 5986	$15
45(P)	**LOVE ME** (55)	RCA Victor 5986	$10
	(White promo label)		
78rpm	**GO BACK YOU FOOL** (55)	RCA Victor 6189	$20
78(P)	**GO BACK YOU FOOL** (55)	RCA Victor 6189	$15
	(White promo label)		
45rpm	**GO BACK YOU FOOL** (55)	RCA Victor 6189	$15
45(P)	**GO BACK YOU FOOL** (55)	RCA Victor 6189	$10
	(White promo label)		

78rpm	**THE MEANEST THING IN THE WORLD IS THE BLUES** (56)	RCA Victor 6303	$20
78(P)	**THE MEANEST THING IN THE WORLD IS THE BLUES** (56)	RCA Victor 6303	$15
	(White promo label)		
45rpm	**THE MEANEST THING IN THE WORLD IS THE BLUES** (56)	RCA Victor 6303	$15
45(P)	**THE MEANEST THING IN THE WORLD IS THE BLUES** (560	RCA Victor 6303	$10
	(White promo label)		
45rpm	**MILKCOW BLUES** (57)	RCA Victor 6430	$12

SONS OF THE PIONEERS (CW)

Originally the Pioneers, with Roy Rogers and Tim Spencer
Records by Roy Rogers listed separately under Rogers
Decca 78s are worth $5-$8 each, Vocalion $5-$8 each
RCA Victor 78rpm box set same as 45s
Other RCA Victor aqua green vinyl 45s $20 each
Other RCA Victor aqua black vinyl 45s $10 each
Other RCA Victor black label, no dog 45s $5-10 each
RCA Gold Standard 45s $3-5 each
Granite 45s $2 each
Other RCA Victor and Camden LPs $5-10 each
American Folk Music LPs $8 each
   (Recordings of old radio programs)
Pickwick and MCA LPs $2-4 each
Granite LPs $3 each

-singles-

78rpm	**TUMBLING TUMBLEWEEDS** (34) Original version	Decca 5047	$15
	(Re-recorded many times on several labels)		
78rpm	**COOL WATER** (41) Original version	Decca 5939	$15
	(Like "Tumbleweeds," re-recorded often on several labels)		
78rpm	**STARS AND STRIPES ON IWO JIMA** (45)	Victor 1724	$15
45rpm	**COOL WATER** (49) Green label	RCA Victor 0004	$25
	(Green vinyl)		
45rpm	**COOL WATER** (51) Green label	RCA Victor 0004	$18
	(Black vinyl)		
45rpm	**COOL WATER** (53) Black label	RCA Victor 0004	$15
	(Black vinyl, no dog on label)		
45rpm	**TUMBLING TUMBLEWEEDS** (49) Green label	RCA Victor 0005	$25
	(Green vinyl)		
45rpm	**TUMBLING TUMBLEWEEDS** (51) Green label	RCA Victor 0005	$18
	(Black vinyl)		
45rpm	**TUMBLING TUMBLEWEEDS** (53) Black label	RCA Victor 0005	$15
	(Black vinyl, no dog on label)		
45rpm	**THE TIMBER TRAIL** (49) Green label	RCA Victor 0006	$25
	(Green vinyl)		
45rpm	**THE TIMBER TRAIL** (51) Green label	RCA Victor 0006	$18
	(Black vinyl)		
45rpm	**THE TIMBER TRAIL** (53) Black label	RCA Victor 0006	$15
	(Black vinyl, no dog on label)		
3-45s	**COWBOY CLASSICS** (49) Box set	RCA Victor 168	$75
	(Green vinyl, price is for three 45s and box)		
3-45s	**COWBOY CLASSICS** (49) Box set	RCA Victor 168	$60
	(Black vinyl, price is for three 45s and box)		
45rpm	**TOO HIGH, TOO WIDE, TOO LOW** (50)	RCA Victor 0094	$25
	(Green vinyl)		
45rpm	**LEAD ME GENTLY HOME, FATHER** (50)	RCA Victor 0095	$25
	(Green vinyl)		
45rpm	**THE OLD RUGGED CROSS** (50)	RCA Victor 0096	$25
	(Green vinyl)		
3-45s	**COWBOY HYMNS AND SPIRITUALS** (50) Box set	RCA Victor 168	$75
	(Price is for three 45s and box)		
45rpm	**ROOM FULL OF ROSES** (52)	RCA Victor 0060	$18
45rpm	**WEDDING DOLLS** (53)	RCA Victor 0171	$25
	(Green vinyl)		
45rpm	**LET'S GO WEST AGAIN** (53)	RCA Victor 0184	$25
	(Green vinyl)		
45rpm	**WHAT THIS COUNTRY NEEDS** (53)	RCA Victor 0388	$25
	(Green vinyl)		
45rpm	**LITTLE WHITE CROSS** (54)	RCA Victor 3983	$15
45rpm	**SAN ANTONIO ROSE** (54)	RCA Victor 4073	$15
3-45s	**GARDEN OF ROSES** (54) Box set	RCA Victor 309	$45
	(Price is for three 45s and box)		
45rpm	**LAND BEYOND THE SUN** (54)	RCA Victor 4571	$12
45rpm	**HOME ON THE RANGE** (54)	Bluebird 46	$15
45rpm	**COWBOY COUNTRY** (54)	Bluebird 104	$10
45rpm	**MONTANA** (55)	Coral 61316	$12
45(P)	**MONTANA** (55)	Coral 61316	$10
	(Blue promo label)		
45rpm	**THE TENNESSEE ROCK AND ROLL** (55)	RCA Victor 6123	$15

45(P)	THE TENNESSEE ROCK AND ROLL (55)	RCA Victor 6123	$12
	(White promo label)		
45rpm	COOL WATER/TUMBLING TUMBLEWEEDS (56)	Decca 29814	$12
45(P)	COOL WATER/TUMBLING TUMBLEWEEDS (56)	Decca 29814	$10
	(Pink promo label)		

-EPs-

2EP	COWBOY CLASSICS (52) Double EP	RCA Victor 3032	$50
2EP	COWBOY HYMNS & SPIRITUALS (52)	RCA Victor 3095	$50
2EP	WESTERN CLASSICS (53)	RCA Victor 3162	$50
EP	GARDEN OF ROSES (54)	RCA Victor 309	$30
EP	WESTERN FAVORITES (55)	RCA Victor 422	$25
EP	SONGS OF REVERENCE (55)	RCA Victor 493	$25
EP	FAVORITE COWBOY SONGS VOL 1 (55)	RCA Victor 650	$25
EP	FAVORITE COWBOY SONGS VOL 2 (55)	RCA Victor 651	$25
EP	FAVORITE COWBOY SONGS VOL 3 (55)	RCA Victor 652	$25
EP	HOW GREAT THOU ART (57)	RCA Victor 1431	$20
EP	ONE MAN'S SONGS (57)	RCA Victor 1483	$20
EP	SONS OF THE PIONEERS SING FRED ROSE (58)	RCA Victor 4218	$20
EP	COOL WATER (59)	RCA Victor 5116	$25
EP	TUMBLING TUMBLEWEEDS (61)	RCA Victor 103	$20
	(Compact-33 double)		
EP(JB)	OUR MEN OUT WEST (63) Stereo Jukebox LLP	RCA Victor 2603	$25
	(Price includes hard cover and title strips)		

-albums-

10"LP	COWBOY CLASSICS (52)	RCA Victor 3032	$100
10"LP	COWBOY HYMNS & SPIRITUALS (52)	RCA Victor 3095	$100
10"LP	WESTERN CLASSICS (53)	RCA Victor 3162	$100
LP	FAVORITE COWBOY SONGS (55)	RCA Victor 1130	$50
LP	HOW GREAT THOU ART (57)	RCA Victor 1431	$50
LP	ONE MAN'S SONGS (57)	RCA Victor 1483	$50
LP	WAGONS WEST (58) Mono	Camden 413	$20
LP	WAGONS WEST (63) Stereo	Camden 413	$15
LP	COOL WATER (59) Mono	RCA Victor 2118	$25
LP	COOL WATER (59) Stereo	RCA Victor 2118	$30
LP	ROOM FULL OF ROSES (60)	Camden 587	$18
LP	LURE OF THE WEST (61) Mono	RCA Victor 2356	$20
LP	LURE OF THE WEST (61) Stereo	RCA Victor 2356	$25
LP	WESTWOOD HO! (61)	RCA Victor 108	$25
LP	TUMBLEWEED TRAILS (62) Mono	RCA Victor 2456	$20
LP	TUMBLEWEED TRAILS (62) Stereo	RCA Victor 2456	$25
LP	OUR MEN OUT WEST (63) Mono	RCA Victor 2603	$20
LP	OUR MEN OUT WEST (63) Stereo	RCA Victor 2603	$25
LP	HYMNS OF THE COWBOY (63) Mono	RCA Victor 2652	$20
LP	HYMNS OF THE COWBOY (63) Stereo	RCA Victor 2652	$25
LP	TRAIL DUST (63) Mono	RCA Victor 2737	$20
LP	TRAIL DUST (63) Stereo	RCA Victor 2737	$25
LP	GOOD OLD COUNTRY MUSIC (63)	Camden 723	$15
LP	COUNTRY FARE (64) Mono	RCA Victor 2855	$20
LP	COUNTRY FARE (64) Stereo	RCA Victor 2855	$25
LP	DOWN MEMORY TRAIL (64) Mono	RCA Victor 2957	$15
LP	DOWN MEMORY TRAIL (64) Stereo	RCA Victor 2957	$20
LP	SONS OF THE PIONEERS BEST (64)	Harmony 7317	$15
LP(P)	SONS OF THE PIONEERS BEST (64)	Harmony 7317	$18
	(White promo label)		
LP	TUMBLEWEED TRAILS (64)	Vocalion 3715	$15
LP(P)	TUMBLEWEED TRAILS (64)	Vocalion 3715	$18
	(White promo label)		
LP	LEGENDS OF THE WEST (65) Mono	RCA Victor 3351	$15
LP	LEGENDS OF THE WEST (65) Stereo	RCA Victor 3351	$20
LP	BEST OF THE SONS OF THE PIONEERS (66) Mono	RCA Victor 3476	$15
LP	BEST OF THE SONS OF THE PIONEERS (66) Stereo	RCA Victor 3476	$20
LP	THE SONGS OF BOB NOLAN (66) Mono	RCA Victor 3554	$15
LP	THE SONGS OF BOB NOLAN (66) Stereo	RCA Victor 3554	$20
LP	CAMPFIRE FAVORITES (67) Mono	RCA Victor 3714	$20
LP	CAMPFIRE FAVORITES (67) Stereo	RCA Victor 3714	$20
LP	SOUTH OF THE BORDER (68) Mono	RCA Victor 3967	$75
	(Rare in mono)		
LP	SOUTH OF THE BORDER (68) Stereo	RCA Victor 3967	$20
LP	SAN ANTONIO ROSE (68)	Camden 2205	$15
LP	TUMBLING TUMBLEWEEDS (69)	RCA Victor 4119	$15
LP	VISIT THE SOUTH SEAS (69)	RCA Victor 4194	$10
2LP	RIDERS IN THE SKY (73)	Camden 587	$15

-radio shows-

16"(RS)	SONS OF THE PIONEERS (55) RCA Thesaurus Library	RCA Victor 8	$40-75
	(Special audition show, not for regular broadcast)		

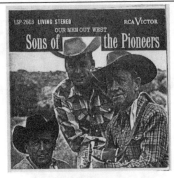

16"(RS)	**SONS OF THE PIONEERS** (55) RCA Thesaurus Library	RCA Victor	$25-50 each
	(Shows include 1653, 1675, 1728, 1731, 1740, 1751, 1776, 1790, 1981, 2010)		
11LP(RS)	**SONS OF THE PIONEERS** (55) RCA Thesaurus Library	RCA Victor	$300-500
	(For the complete set)		
16"(RS)	**SMOKEY THE BEAR** (57) Fifteen-minute show for Smokey	U.S. Forest Dept 4	$75-150
	(Red vinyl)		
16"(RS)	**HERE'S TO VETS** (58) Fifteen-minute show	Vets Administration	$25-50
	(Music and interviews)		
LP(RS)	**HOOTENAVY** (65) Public service shows 49 and 50	U.S. Navy	$50-75 each
	(Both sides are shows by the Sons of the Pioneers and Marian Hall)		
LP(RS)	**NAVY HOEDOWN** (66) Public service shows 15 and 16	U.S. Navy	$50-75 each
	(Both sides have Ralph Emery as the emcee)		
LP(RS)	**HERE'S TO VETERANS** Public service show 1416	Vets Administration	$40-75
	(Members of the group are co-hosts for the program)		
LP(RS)	**HERE'S TO VETERANS** Public service show 1430	Vets Administration	$40-75
	(Members of the group are co-hosts for the program)		
LP(RS)	**COUNTRY CROSSROADS** (Jan 85) Two thirty-minute shows	Southern Baptist	$25-40 each
	(Tribute shows with members of the group)		
	See Roy Rogers		

SONS OF THE PURPLE SAGE (CW)
Not to be confused with Riders of the Purple Sage or Sons of the Pioneers

-albums-

10"LP	**SONGS OF THE GOLDEN WEST** (55)	Waldorf 143	$50
LP	**SONS OF THE PURPLE SAGE AT WESTERN CAMPFIRES** (60s)	Somerset 11900	$15
LP	**WESTERN FAVORITES** (60s) With Linna Shane	Tops 1588	$15
	(All of the above are budget labels)		

VARIOUS ARTISTS
-radio shows-

364LP(RS)	**SOUNDS OF SOLID GOLD COUNTRY** (81-Jun 85) 52 Box set	U.S. Marine Corps	$400-500
	(Complete set of all fifty-two box sets, all country music, and is a monthly 7LP box set series)		
7LP(RS)	**SOUNDS OF SOLID GOLD COUNTRY** (through Jun 85)	U.S. Marine Corps	$40-50
	(Any show including at least one Presley cut)		
7LP(RS)	**SOUNDS OF SOLID GOLD** (85) Presley shows Vol. 51	U.S. Marine Corps	$100-125
	(Three sides, shows, are exclusive Elvis Presley)		

HAL SOUTHERN (CW)
Hal wrote "Hillbilly Heaven"

-singles-

45rpm	**I'LL NEVER ROAM AGAIN** (62)	Sage 361	$10
	(With Joanie & the Frontiersmen)		

-albums-

LP	**YOU GOT A MAN ON YOUR HANDS** (67)	Sage & Sound 46	$25

SOUTHERN PACIFIC (C)
Warner 45s and picture sleeves $1 each
Warner LPs $3 each

-radio shows-

LP(RS)	**COUNTRY MUSIC TIME** (80s)	U.S. Air Force	$10-15
	(Live concert)		
3LP(RS)	**AMERICAN EAGLE** (Nov 86)	DIR	$25-40
	(Live concert)		
LP(RS)	**WESTWOOD ONE PRESENTS** (May 89)	Westwood One	$20-30
	(Live concert)		

RED SOVINE (CW)
Other Decca 45s $5-10 each
Gusto 45s $4 each
Starday 45s $3 each
Chart 45s $2-4 each
Other Starday LPs $5-10 each
Other Chart and Nashville LPs $4-8 each
Gusto and Power Pak LPs $3-6 each

-singles-

45rpm	**A QUARTER'S WORTH OF HEARTACHES** (53)	MGM 11402	$10
45rpm	**JUKE JOINT JOHNNY** (58)	Decca 30239	$25
45(P)	**JUKE JOINT JOHNNY** (58)	Decca 30239	$18
	(Pink promo label)		

-EPs-

EP	**RED SOVINE VOL 1** (55)	MGM 1367	$20
EP	**RED SOVINE VOL 2** (55)	MGM 1368	$20
EP	**RED SOVINE VOL 3** (55)	MGM 1369	$20

-albums-

LP	**RED SOVINE** (57)	MGM 3465	$75
LP(P)	**RED SOVINE** (57)	MGM 3465	$100
	(Yellow promo label)		
LP	**THE ONE AND ONLY** (61)	Starday 132	$40
LP	**COUNTRY HITS MADE FAMOUS BY ATKINS & FORD** (63)	Somerset 18400	$20
	(With Jerry Shook)		
LP	**RED SOVINE** (64)	Decca 4445	$25
	(Includes duet with Webb Pierce)		
LP(P)	**RED SOVINE** (64)	Decca 4445	$30
	(Decca promo label)		
LP	**COUNTRY MUSIC TIME** (66)	Decca 4736	$25
LP(P)	**COUNTRY MUSIC TIME** (66)	Decca 4736	$20
	(White promo label)		
LP	**LITTLE ROSA** (66)	Starday 341	$15
LP	**GIDDY-UP GO** (66)	Starday 363	$15
	(Reissues on Nashville and Gusto)		
LP	**TOWN & COUNTRY ACTION** (66)	Starday 383	$15
LP	**THE NASHVILLE SOUND OF RED SOVINE** (67)	Starday 396	$15
LP	**I DIDN'T JUMP THE FENCE** (67)	Starday 405	$12
LP	**PHANTOM 309** (67)	Starday 414	$12
LP	**FAREWELL, SO LONG, GOODBYE** (67)	Metro 618	$18
LP(P)	**FAREWELL, SO LONG, GOODBYE** (67)	Metro 618	$25
	(White promo label)		
LP	**TELL MAUDE I SLIPPED** (68)	Starday 420	$18
LP	**SUNDAY WITH SOVINE** (68)	Starday 427	$15
LP	**TEDDY BEAR** (68)	Starday 968	$12
	(Reissues on Starday 989 and Gusto)		
LP	**THE COUNTRY WAY** (69)	Vocalion 3829	$15
LP(P)	**THE COUNTRY WAY** (69)	Vocalion 3829	$18
	(White promo label)		
LP	**WHO AM I** (69)	Starday 445	$15
LP	**A DEAR JOHN LETTER** (70)	Nashville 2044	$15
LP	**ANYTIME** (70)	Nashville 2056	$12
2LP	**THE BEST OF RED SOVINE** (70s)	Lake Shore 11	$12
LP	**THE GREATEST GRAND OL' OPRY** (72)	Chart 1052	$12

-radio shows-

16"(RS)	**U.S. AIR FORCE** (60s)	U.S. Air Force	$20-40
	(Music and interviews)		

RANDY SPANGLER (RB)

-singles-

45rpm	**ROCK AND ROLL BABY** (58)	Mart 112	$60

BILLIE JO SPEARS (C)

Capitol and United Artists 45s $2 each
Other Capitol and United Artists LPs $6 each

-albums-

LP	**THE VOICE OF BILLIE JO SPEARS** (68)	Capitol 114	$15

SPECK & DOYLE (RB)

-singles-

45rpm	**BIG NOISE, BRIGHT LIGHTS** (57)	Syrup Bucket 1000	$50

THE SPROUTS (RB)

-singles-

45rpm	**TEEN BILLY BABY** (58)	RCA Victor 7080	$10

TOMMY SPURLIN (RB)

-singles-

45rpm	**HANG LOOSE** (56)	Perfect 109	$125
45rpm	**ONE EYED SAM** (57)	Art 109	$50

TOMMY ST. JOHN (C)

RCA Victor 45s $2 each
RCA Victor color vinyl 45s $5 each

CLYDE STACY (R)

-singles-

45rpm	**SURE DO LOVE YOU BABY** (57)	Bullseye 1008	$25
45rpm	**DREAM BOY** (58)	Candlelight 1018	$18

JOE STAMPLEY (C)
ABC, Dot, Columbia, and Epic 45s $1-2 each
ABC 2LP sets $8 each
ABC, Dot, and Epic LPs $3-5 each
Columbia duet LPs $3 each

HOWARD STANGE (RB)
-singles-

45rpm	**REAL GONE DADDY**	Jenn 101	$50

STANLEY BROTHERS (BG)
Ralph and Carter with the Clinch Mountain Boys
Includes listings of Ralph Stanley
78s $5-10 each
King 45s $4-8 each
Other King LPs by Ralph Stanley $6-10 each
Other Rebel LPs by Ralph Stanley $4-8 each
Rounder LPs by Ralph Stanley $4-8 each
Blue Jay, County, Plantation, and Stanley Sound LPs by Ralph Stanley $3-5 each
Other Copper Creek LPs $5-10 each
Other Nashville, Wango, Rounder, and Rimrock LPs $5-10 each
Gusto, Melodeon, Collector's Classics, County Power Pak LPs $3-5 each

-singles-

45rpm	**NO SCHOOL BUS IN HEAVEN** (58)	Mercury 71302	$10
45rpm	**ANGEL OF DEATH** (62)	King 5441	$10

-EPs-

EP	**THE STANLEY BROTHERS** (58)	Columbia 2833	$50
EP	**THE STANLEY BROTHERS** (59)	Starday 107	$30
EP	**THE STANLEY BROTHERS & CLINCH MOUNTAIN BOYS** (59)	Starday 707	$30
EP	**FOR THE GOOD PEOPLE VOL 1** (61)	King 461	$20
EP	**FOR THE GOOD PEOPLE VOL 2** (61)	King 462	$20
EP	**FOR THE GOOD PEOPLE VOL 3** (61)	King 463	$20
EP	**THE STANLEYS IN PERSON VOL 1** (62)	King 467	$20
EP	**THE STANLEYS IN PERSON VOL 2** (62)	King 468	$20
EP	**THE STANLEYS IN PERSON VOL 3** (62)	King 469	$20
EP	**OLD TIME CAMP MEETING VOL 1** (62)	King 479	$20
EP	**OLD TIME CAMP MEETING VOL 2** (61)	King 480	$20

(All EPs above are by the Stanley Brothers)

-albums-

LP	**COUNTRY PICKIN' AND SINGIN'** (58)	Mercury 20349	$75
LP(P)	**COUNTRY PICKIN' AND SINGIN'** (58)	Mercury 20349	$100
	(White promo label)		
LP	**THE STANLEY BROTHERS** (59)	King 615	$75
LP	**MOUNTAIN SONG FAVORITES** (59)	Starday 106	$50
LP	**MOUNTAIN SONG FAVORITES** (60s)	Nashville 2014	$15
	(Reissue)		
LP	**SACRED SONGS OF THE HILLS** (60)	Starday 122	$50
LP	**HYMNS & SACRED SONGS** (60)	King 645	$50
LP	**STANLEY BROTHERS LIVE AT ANTIOCH COLLEGE** (61)	Vintage 002	$75
LP	**SING EVERYBODY'S COUNTRY FAVORITES** (61)	King 690	$50
LP	**FOR THE GOOD PEOPLE** (61)	King 698	$50
LP	**THE STANLEYS IN PERSON** (61)	King 719	$50
LP	**THE STANLEY BROTHERS & THE CLINCH MOUNTAIN BOYS SING THE SONGS THEY LIKE BEST** (61)	King 772	$50
LP	**OLD TIME CAMP MEETING** (61)	King 750	$50
LP	**THE STANLEY BROTHERS** (61)	Harmony 7291	$25
LP(P)	**THE STANLEY BROTHERS** (61)	Harmony 7291	$30
	(White promo label)		
LP	**THE MOUNTAIN MUSIC SOUND** (62)	Starday 201	$50
LP	**AWARD WINNERS** (62)	King 791	$50
LP	**GOOD OLD CAMP MEETING SONGS** (62)	King 805	$50
LP	**JUST BECAUSE** (64)	King 834	$25
LP	**HARD TIMES** (63)	Mercury 60884	$25
LP(P)	**HARD TIMES** (63)	Mercury 20884	$30
	(White promo label)		
LP	**HARD TIMES** (66)	Wing 16327	$15
	(Reissue of Mercury 20884)		
LP(P)	**HARD TIMES** (66)	Wing 16327	$18
	(White promo label)		
LP	**COUNTRY-FOLK MUSIC SPOTLIGHT** (63)	King 864	$25
LP	**WORLD'S FINEST 5-STRING BANJO** (63)	King 872	$40
LP	**HYMNS OF THE CROSS** (64)	King 918	$25
LP	**SING AND PLAY BLUEGRASS SONGS FOR YOU** (65)	King 924	$20
LP	**BLUEGRASS GOSPEL FAVORITES** (66)	Cabin Creek 203	$75
LP	**THE ANGELS ARE SINGING** (66)	Harmony 11177	$20
LP(P)	**THE ANGELS ARE SINGING** (66)	Harmony 11177	$25
	(White promo label)		

LP	**THE GREATEST COUNTY & WESTERN SHOW ON EARTH** (66)	King 963	$20
LP	**JACOB'S VISION** (66)	Starday 384	$20
LP	**BEST LOVED SACRED SONGS OF THE CARTER FAMILY** (67)	King 1013	$18
LP	**BRAND NEW COUNTRY SONGS BY RALPH STANLEY** (68)	King 1028	$18
LP	**OVER THE SUNSET HILL** (68) Ralph Stanley	King 1032	$15
LP	**SWEETER THAN THE FLOWERS** (70)	Nashville 2078	$15
LP	**HILLS OF HOME** (69) Ralph Stanley	King 1069	$15
LP	**ON AND ON** (70s) Ralph Stanley	Jalyn 118	$25
2LP	**LIVE AT MCCLURE** (70s) Ralph Stanley	Rebel 1554	$15
LP	**THE BLUEGRASS SOUND** (70s) Ralph Stanley	Jalyn 120	$25
LP	**RALPH STANLEY & THE CLINCH MOUNTAIN BOYS** (70s)	Jalyn 129	$18
	(With Keith Whitely and Ricky Skaggs, black cover)		
LP	**RALPH STANLEY & THE CLINCH MOUNTAIN BOYS** (70s)	Jalyn 129	$15
	(Orange cover)		
6LP	**THE STANLEY BROTHERS** (83) Pack of six LPs	GTO 103-108	$100
	(Price is for all six LPs)		
4LP	**THE STANLEY SERIES VOL 1** (70s)	Copper Creek 1	$50
	(Set of four LPs)		
4LP	**THE STANLEY SERIES VOL 2** (80s)	Copper Creek 2	$40
	(Set of four LPs)		

BUDDY STARCHER (C)
Starday and Decca 45s $3 each
Heartwarming LPs $5 each

-EPs-

EP(P)	**THE BOY FROM DOWN HOME** (57)	Four Star 21	$15
	(Radio promo copy)		
EP	**BUDDY AND MAY ANN STARCHER** (61)	Starday 158	$20

-albums-

LP	**BUDDY STARCHER AND HIS MOUNTAIN GUITAR** (62)	Starday 211	$25
LP	**HISTORY REPEATS ITSELF** (66)	Decca 4796	$20
LP(P)	**HISTORY REPEATS ITSELF** (66)	Decca 4796	$25
	(Pink promo label)		
LP	**HISTORY REPEATS ITSELF** (66)	Starday 382	$25
	(With Minnie Pearl)		
LP	**BUDDY STARCHER VOL 1** (70s)	Bluebonnet 121	$15

ANDY STARR (RB)

-singles-

45rpm	**I LOVE MY BABY** (53)	Arcade 115	$250
45rpm	**ROCKIN' ROLLIN' STONE** (56)	MGM 12263	$100
45(P)	**ROCKIN' ROLLIN' STONE** (56)	MGM 12263	$75
	(Yellow promo label)		
45rpm	**SHE'S A-GOIN' JESSIE** (56)	MGM 12315	$100
45(P)	**SHE'S A-GOIN' JESSIE** (56)	MGM 12315	$75
	(Yellow promo label)		
45rpm	**ROUND AND ROUND** (57)	MGM 12364	$150
45(P)	**ROUND AND ROUND** (57)	MGM 12364	$125
	(Yellow promo label)		
45rpm	**NO ROOM FOR YOUR KIND** (57)	MGM 12421	$100
45(P)	**NO ROOM FOR YOUR KIND** (57)	MGM 12421	$75
	(Yellow promo label)		

CHARLIE STARR (C)
Mercury 45s $2 each

-albums-

LP	**JUST PLAIN CHARLIE** (69)	Mercury 61209	$15
LP(P)	**JUST PLAIN CHARLIE** (69)	Mercury 21209	$18
	(White promo label)		

FRANK STARR (RB)

-singles-

45rpm	**DIG THEM SQUEEKY SHOES** (55)	Lin 1009	$125
45rpm	**TELL ME WHY** (57)	Lin 1013	$25
45(P)	**TELL ME WHY** (57)	Lin 1013	$20
	(Bio promo label)		

FRANKIE STARR (RB)

-singles-

45rpm	**ELEVATOR ROCK** (64)	Starwin 7008	$50

VARIOUS ARTISTS (CW)

-albums-

2LP	**STARS OF THE GRAND OLE OPRY** (67) Box set version	RCA Victor 6015	$30
	(Top RCA artists from Opry with original hits)		
2LP	**STARS OF THE GRAND OLE OPRY** (68) Double LP	RCA Victor 6015	$20

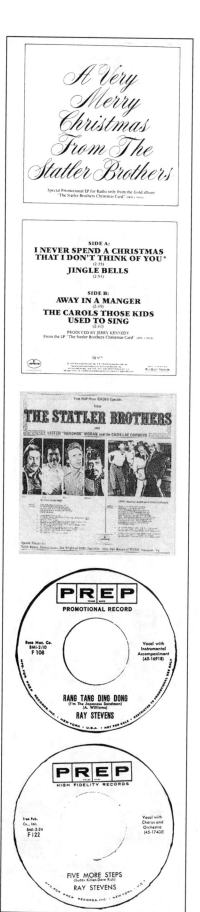

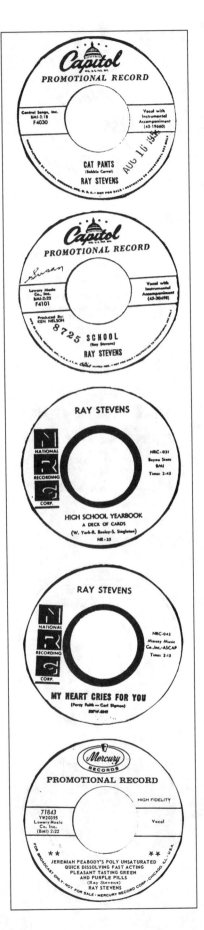

STATLER BROTHERS (C, G)
Other Columbia 45s $3-5 each
Other Mercury 45s $2-3 each
Mercury picture sleeves $2-3 each
Other Columbia LPs $5-10 each
Harmony LPs $8-10 each
Other Mercury LPs $2-5 each
Time-Life, 51 West, and Priority LPs $2-4 each

-singles-

45(P)	FLOWERS ON THE WALL (65)	Columbia 43315	$20
	(White promo label, red vinyl)		
45(P)	ATLANTA BLUE (84)	Mercury 818-700	$12
	(Black promo label, blue vinyl)		

-EPs-

EP(P)	A VERY MERRY CHRISTMAS (78)	Mercury DJ 577	$12
	(Promo only, seven-inch with small center hole and promo picture sleeve)		

-albums-

LP	FLOWERS ON THE WALL (66)	Columbia 9249	$25
	(With CS-prefix)		
LP(P)	FLOWERS ON THE WALL (66)	Columbia 9249	$30
	(White promo label)		
LP	THE STATLER BROTHERS SING THE BIG HITS (67)	Columbia 9519	$15
LP(P)	THE STATLER BROTHERS SING THE BIG HITS (67)	Columbia 9519	$20
	(White promo label)		
LP	OH HAPPY DAY (69)	Columbia 9878	$15
LP(P)	OH HAPPY DAY (69)	Columbia 9878	$20
	(White promo label)		
2LP	THE WORLD OF THE STATLER BROTHERS (72)	Columbia 31557	$12
LP(P)	INTERVIEW WITH THE STATLER BROTHERS (72)	Mercury 61358	$25
	(White promo label, promo-only release)		
2LP(P)	TWO HALF HOUR SPECIALS (74)	Mercury MK-5	$25
	(Each of the LPs above includes a promo-only hard cover)		

-radio shows-

LP(RS)	COUNTRY CROSSROADS (80s)	Southern Baptist	$10-15
	(Music and interviews)		

JIMMY STAYTON (RB)
-singles-

45rpm	HOT HOT MAMA (60)	Blue Hen 220	$200
45rpm	YOU'RE GONNA TREAT ME RIGHT (60)	Blue Hen 224	$150

JUNE STEARNS (C)
Columbia 45s $2 each

-albums-

LP	RIVER OF REGRET (69)	Columbia 9783	$15

SONDRA & JON STEELE (CW)
Cardinal 45s $4-8 each

WILBER STEINBERG (RB)
-singles-

45rpm	MOP BOP BOOGIE (58)	Hut 4401	$50

RAY STEVENS (N)
Other Mercury 45s $4-8 each
Monument 45s $4-8 each
Other Barnaby 45s $2-5 each
Warner 45s $3 each
Warner picture sleeves $4 each
Warner 45s by Henhouse Five Plus Too $4 each
Other RCA Victor 45s $2-4 each
Other MCA 45s $2 each
Curb 45s $1 each
Barnaby and Warner LPs $5-10 each
RCA Victor and Priority LPs $5 each

-singles-

45rpm	RANG TANG DING DONG (57)	Prep 108	$20
45(P)	RANG TANG DING DONG (57)	Prep 108	$25
	(White promo label)		
45rpm	FIVE MORE STEPS (57)	Prep 122	$15
45(P)	FIVE MORE STEPS (57)	Prep 122	$18
	(White promo label)		
45rpm	CAT PANTS (58)	Capitol 4030	$15
45(P)	CAT PANTS (58)	Capitol 4030	$12
	(White promo label)		
45rpm	SCHOOL (58)	Capitol 4101	$18

45(P)	**SCHOOL** (58) (White promo label)	Capitol 4101	$12
45rpm	**HIGH SCHOOL YEARBOOK** (59) (To the tune of "A Deck of Cards")	NRC 35	$15
45(P)	**HIGH SCHOOL YEARBOOK** (59) (White promo label)	NRC 35	$18
45rpm	**MY HEART CRIES FOR YOU** (60) (Written by Percy Faith)	NRC 42	$12
45(P)	**MY HEART CRIES FOR YOU** (60) (White promo label)	NRC 42	$15
45rpm	**SERGENT PRESTON OF THE YUKON** (60)	NRC 57	$15
45(P)	**SERGENT PRESTON OF THE YUKON** (60) (White promo label)	NRC 57	$18
45rpm	**HAPPY BLUE YEAR** (60)	NRC 63	$18
45(P)	**HAPPY BLUE YEAR** (60) (White promo label)	NRC 63	$25
45rpm	**JEREMIAH PEABODY'S POLY UNSATURATED QUICK DISSOLVING FAST ACTING PLEASANT TASTING GREEN AND PURPLE PILLS** (61)	Mercury 71843	$10
45rpm	**JEREMIAH PEABODY'S POLY UNSATURATED QUICK DISSOLVING FAST ACTING PLEASANT TASTING GREEN AND PURPLE PILLS** (61) (Price includes picture sleeve)	Mercury 71843	$40
45(P)	**JEREMIAH PEABODY'S POLY UNSATURATED QUICK DISSOLVING FAST ACTING PLEASANT TASTING GREEN AND PURPLE PILLS** (61) (White promo label)	Mercury 71843	$15
45rpm	**SCRATCH MY BACK** (61)	Mercury 71888	$10
45rpm	**SCRATCH MY BACK** (61) (Price includes picture sleeve)	Mercury 71808	$25
45(P)	**SCRATCH MY BACK** (61) (White promo label)	Mercury 71808	$12
45rpm	**AHAB, THE ARAB** (61)	Mercury 71966	$10
45rpm	**AHAB, THE ARAB** (61) (Price includes picture sleeve)	Mercury 71966	$25
45(P)	**AHAB, THE ARAB** (61) (White promo label)	Mercury 71966	$12
45rpm	**FURTHER MORE** (62)	Mercury 72039	$10
45rpm	**SANTA CLAUS IS WATCHING YOU** (62)	Mercury 72058	$10
45rpm	**SANTA CLAUS IS WATCHING YOU** (62) (Price includes picture sleeve)	Mercury 72058	$25
45(P)	**SANTA CLAUS IS WATCHING YOU** (62) (White promo label)	Mercury 72058	$15
45rpm	**HARRY THE HAIRY APE** (63)	Mercury 72125	$10
45rpm	**HARRY THE HAIRY APE** (63) (Price includes picture sleeve)	Mercury 72125	$25
45rpm	**BUTCH BARBARIAN** (63)	Mercury 72255	$10
45rpm	**BUTCH BARBARIAN** (63) (Price includes picture sleeve)	Mercury 72255	$25
45(P)	**BUTCH BARBARIAN** (63)	Mercury DJ-66	$15
45(P)	**BUTCH BARBARIAN** (63) (Promo record and promo picture sleeve, which is not the same as the stock copy above)	Mercury DJ-66	$40
45rpm	**BUBBLE GUM THE BUBBLE DANCER** (64)	Mercury 72307	$15
45rpm	**BUBBLE GUM THE BUBBLE DANCER** (64) (Price includes picture sleeve)	Mercury 72307	$25
45rpm	**ROCKIN' TEENAGE MUMMIES** (65)	Mercury 72382	$18
45(P)	**ROCKIN' TEENAGE MUMMIES** (65) (White promo label)	Mercury 72382	$15
45rpm	**MR. BAKER THE UNDERTAKER** (65)	Mercury 72430	$18
45(P)	**MR. BAKER THE UNDERTAKER** (65) (White promo label)	Mercury 72430	$15
45rpm	**FUNNY MAN** (65)	Mercury 72816	$10
45rpm	**BRIDGET THE MIDGET** (70) (Price includes picture sleeve)	Barnaby 2024	$12
33(P)	**FIND YOURSELF A STAR** (74) PSA ads on seven-inch (Ray Stevens featured on two spots, thirty-second and sixty-second, issued with a hard cover)	USAF #42	$18
45(P)	**WHAT'S IT ALL ABOUT** (Jan 75) Public service show (Flip side features Gladys Knight & the Pips)	W. I. A. A. 250	$25
45(P)	**WHAT'S IT ALL ABOUT** (Dec 75) Public service show (Flip side features the 5th Dimension)	W. I. A. A. 295	$18
45(P)	**SHRINER'S CONVENTION** (80) (Long 5:33 and short 4:10 versions, white promo label, red vinyl)	RCA Victor 11911	$12
45(P)	**NIGHT GAMES** (80) (Silver promo label, blue vinyl)	RCA Victor 12069	$18

45(P)	**ONE MORE LAST CHANCE** (81)	RCA Victor 12170	$18
	(Silver promo label, blue vinyl)		
45(P)	**WRITTEN DOWN IN MY HEART** (81)	RCA Victor 13038	$15
	(Yellow promo label, yellow vinyl)		
33(P)	**HOME BUYERS ALERT** (82) PSA ads on seven-inch	Housing Adm 82-1	$10
	(Ray featured on all spots, issued with a paper cover)		
45(P)	**SANTA CLAUS IS WATCHING YOU** (85)	MCA 52738	$15
	(Green promo and red vinyl, price includes picture sleeve)		
45(P)	**SANTA CLAUS IS WATCHING YOU** (85)	MCA 52738	$10
	(White promo label, black vinyl, price includes picture sleeve issued with the black vinyl)		
45(P)	**THE BALLAD OF THE BLUE CYCLONE** (85)	MCA 52771	$12
	(White promo label, blue vinyl)		
45(P)	**SOUTHERN AIR** (86)	MCA 52906	$10
	(White promo label, red vinyl)		
45(P)	**CAN HE LOVE YOU HALF AS MUCH AS I** (87)	MCA 53007	$10
	(White promo label, blue vinyl)		
45rpm	**WOULD JESUS WEAR A ROLEX** (87)	MCA 53101	$10
	(White promo label, black-dark gray see-thru vinyl)		

-EPs-

33(P)	**SAVE THE CHILDREN** (87) PSA ads on seven-inch	DWP 126	$20
	(Twenty spots including one thirty-second by Stevens)		

-albums-

LP	**1,837 SECONDS OF HUMOR** (62) Black label, mono	Mercury 20732	$40
	(Also known as "Ahab the Arab")		
LP	**1,837 SECONDS OF HUMOR** (62) Black label, stereo	Mercury 60732	$50
LP	**1,837 SECONDS OF HUMOR** (62) Red label	Mercury 60732	$18
LP(P)	**1,837 SECONDS OF HUMOR** (62)	Mercury 20732	$60
	(White promo label)		
LP	**THIS IS RAY STEVENS** (63) Mono	Mercury 20828	$25
LP	**THIS IS RAY STEVENS** (63) Stereo	Mercury 60828	$30
LP(P)	**THIS IS RAY STEVENS** (63)	Mercury 20828	$30
	(White promo label)		
LP	**THE BEST OF RAY STEVENS** (63) Mono	Wing 20828	$15
LP	**THE BEST OF RAY STEVENS** (63) Stereo	Wing 60828	$18
LP(P)	**THE BEST OF RAY STEVENS** (63)	Wing 20828	$20
	(White promo label)		
LP	**RAY STEVENS AND HAL WINTERS** (63) Mono	Crown 5333	$18
LP	**RAY STEVENS AND HAL WINTERS** (63) Stereo	Crown 333	$12
	(Budget label)		
LP	**EVEN STEVENS** (68)	Monument 18102	$15
LP	**GITARZAN** (69)	Monument 18115	$15
LP	**HAVE A LITTLE TALK WITH MYSELF** (69)	Monument 18134	$15

-radio shows-

LP(RS)	**HERE'S TO VETERANS** (60s)	Vets Administration	$40-75
	(Show 1414, music and interviews)		
LP(RS)	**COUNTRY MUSIC TIME** (80s)	U.S. Air Force	$10-20
	(Music and interviews)		

CLIFF STEWARD (CW)
And the San Francisco Boys
Other Coral 45s $5-10 each

-singles-

45rpm	**ALABAMA JUBILEE** (54)	Coral 60228	$15
45rpm	**I DON'T WANNA GO HOME** (56)	Coral 60924	$12
45rpm	**RED HEAD** (57) With the Boro Lounge Boys	Coral 61399	$10

FRANKLIN STEWART (RB)

-singles-

45rpm	**THAT LONG BLACK TRAIN** (58)	Lu 501	$50

GARY STEWART (C)
Other RCA Victor 45s $2 each
RCA Victor picture sleeves $2 each
Hightone 45s $2 each
RCA Victor LPs $2-4 each

-singles-

45(P)	**CACTUS AND A ROSE** (80)	RCA Victor 11960	$15
	(Yellow promo label, yellow vinyl)		
45(P)	**LET'S FORGET THAT WE'RE MARRIED** (81)	RCA Victor 12203	$15
	(Silver promo label, blue vinyl)		
45(P)	**SHE SINGS AMAZING GRACE** (82)	RCA Victor 13261	$12
	(Orange promo label, blue vinyl)		

JIMMY STEWART (RB)

-singles-

45rpm	**ROCK ON THE MOON** (58)	Crystal	$60
45rpm	**ROCK ON THE MOON** (58)	Eko	$50

REDD STEWART (CW)

Lead singer with Pee Wee King's band
Hickory LPs $5-10 each

-albums-

LP	**REDD STEWART SINGS FAVORITE OLD TIME SONGS** (59)	Audio Lab 1528	$40

Also see Pee Wee King

WYNN STEWART (CW)

And the Tourists
Other Capitol 45s and 78s $5-10 each
Playboy 45s $3 each
Other Capitol LPs $5-10 each
Forum LPs $5 each

-singles-

45rpm	**WALTZ OF THE ANGELS** (58)	Capitol 2408	$12
	(Original version, re-released several times)		
45rpm	**DONNA ON MY MIND** (58)	Jackpot 9164	$20
45(P)	**DONNA ON MY MIND** (58)	Jackpot 9164	$18
	(White promo label)		
45rpm	**COME ON** (58)	Jackpot 48005	$15
45(P)	**COME ON** (58)	Jackpot 48005	$12
	(White promo label)		
45rpm	**YANKEE, GO HOME** (60)	Jackpot 48014	$15
	(Wynn Stewart and Jan Howard)		
45(P)	**YANKEE, GO HOME** (60)	Jackpot 48014	$10
	(White promo label)		
45rpm	**ABOVE AND BEYOND** (60)	Jackpot 48019	$12
45(P)	**ABOVE AND BEYOND** (60)	Jackpot 48019	$10
	(White promo label)		
45rpm	**WISHFUL THINKING** (61)	Challenge 59061	$15
45(P)	**WISHFUL THINKING** (61)	Challenge 59061	$12
	(White promo label)		
45rpm	**HALF OF THIS, HALF OF THAT** (64)	Capitol 5271	$10
	(Price includes picture sleeve)		
45rpm	**'CAUSE I HAVE YOU** (67)	Capitol 5937	$10
	(Price includes picture sleeve)		
45rpm	**WALTZ OF THE ANGELS** (67)	Capitol 2012	$12
	(Price includes picture sleeve, flip side is "Love's Gonna Happen to Me")		
45rpm	**SOMETHING PRETTY** (68)	Capitol 2437	$10
	(Price includes picture sleeve)		

-EPs-

EP(JB)	**IT'S SUCH A PRETTY WORLD TODAY** (67) Jukebox LLP	Capitol 2737	$15
	(Issued with a hard cover)		

-albums-

LP	**SWEETHEARTS OF COUNTRY MUSIC** (61)	Challenge 611	$50
	(Wynn Stewart and Jan Howard)		
LP	**WYNN STEWART** (62)	Wrangler 1006	$40
LP	**THE SONGS OF WYNN STEWART** (65)	Capitol 2332	$20
LP	**IT'S SUCH A PRETTY WORLD TODAY** (67)	Capitol 2737	$18
LP	**LOVE'S GONNA HAPPEN TO ME** (68)	Capitol 2849	$15
LP	**SOMETHING PRETTY** (68)	Capitol 2921	$15
LP	**IN LOVE** (68)	Capitol 113	$15
LP	**WYNN STEWART & JAN HOWARD SING THEIR HITS** (68)	Starday 421	$20
LP	**LET THE WHOLE WORLD SING WITH ME** (69)	Capitol 214	$15
LP	**YOURS FOREVER** (69)	Capitol 324	$15
LP	**YOU DON'T CARE WHAT HAPPENS TO ME** (70)	Capitol 453	$15
LP	**IT'S A BEAUTIFUL DAY** (70)	Capitol 561	$15
LP	**BABY, IT'S YOURS** (71)	Capitol 687	$15

THE STEWART FAMILY (G)

King 45s $3 each

-albums-

LP	**THE STEWART FAMILY SINGS COUNTRY SACRED SONGS** (60)	King 687	$25
LP	**GOLDEN COUNTRY FAVORITES** (60)	King 695	$20

CLIFFIE STONE (CW)

Best known for square dance music
Other Capitol 78s $4-8 each
Other Capitol 45s $5-10 each

-singles-

45rpm	SOLDIERS JOY (51)	Capitol 40165	$10
45rpm	CRIPPLE CREEK (51)	Capitol 40166	$10
45rpm	THE GAL I LEFT BEHIND ME (51)	Capitol 40167	$10
45rpm	RAGTIME ANNIE (51)	Capitol 40168	$10
3-45s	SQUARE DANCES (51) Box set	Capitol 4002	$40
45rpm	THE LAST ROUND-UP (53)	Capitol 2407	$12
45rpm	IN A SHANTY IN OLD SHANTY TOWN (53)	Capitol 2497	$15
	(On the flip side, "The Bunny Hop")		
45rpm	ROCKY MOUNTAIN EXPRESS (54)	Capitol 2571	$10
78rpm	BLUE MOON OF KENTUCKY (54)	Capitol 2910	$40
78(P)	BLUE MOON OF KENTUCKY (54)	Capitol 2910	$30
	(Capitol promo label)		
45rpm	BLUE MOON OF KENTUCKY (54)	Capitol 2910	$25
45(P)	BLUE MOON OF KENTUCKY (54)	Capitol 2910	$20
	(White promo label)		

-albums-

10"LP	SQUARE DANCES (55)	Capitol 4009	$50
LP	THE PARTY'S ON ME (58)	Capitol 1080	$30
LP(P)	THE PARTY'S ON ME (58)	Capitol 1080	$35
	(Yellow promo label)		
LP	COOL COWBOY (59)	Capitol 1230	$25
LP(P)	COOL COWBOY (59)	Capitol 1230	$30
	(Yellow promo label)		
LP	SQUARE DANCE PROMENADE (60)	Capitol 1286	$25
LP(P)	SQUARE DANCE PROMENADE (60)	Capitol 1286	$30
	(Yellow promo label)		
LP	ORIGINAL COWBOY SING-A-LONG (61)	Capitol 1555	$25
LP(P)	ORIGINAL COWBOY SING-A-LONG (61)	Capitol 1555	$30
	(Capitol promo label)		
LP	TOGETHER AGAIN (67)	Capitol 5073	$10

JEFF STONE (RB)

-singles-

45rpm	EVERYBODY ROCK (57)	Sarg 151	$35

JIMMY STONE (RB)

-singles-

45rpm	FOUND (58)	Cross Country 523	$60

STONE COUNTRY (C)

-albums-

LP	STONE COUNTRY (68)	RCA Victor 3958	$15

ERNEST STONEMAN (CW)

Victor 78s are worth $15 each
Any 45s $2-4 each

-albums-

LP	COOL COWBOY (59)	Capitol 1230	$18
LP(P)	COOL COWBOY (59)	Capitol 1230	$25
	(Capitol promo label)		
LP	THE POP STONEMAN MEMORIAL ALBUM (69)	MGM 4588	$15
LP(P)	THE POP STONEMAN MEMORIAL ALBUM (69)	MGM 4588	$18
	(Yellow promo label)		
	See the Stonemans		

THE STONEMANS (C)

RCA Victor and MGM 45s $2-4 each
RCA Victor LPs $8-10 each
Folkways LPs $5-10 each
CMH LPs $5 each

-albums-

LP	BIG BALL IN MONTEREY (64)	World Pacific 1828	$25
LP	WHITE LIGHTNING (64)	Starday 393	$30
LP	THOSE SINGIN' SWINGIN' STOMPIN' SENSATIONAL STONEMANS (66)	MGM 4363	$15
LP	THOSE SINGIN' SWINGIN' STOMPIN' SENSATIONAL STONEMANS (66)	MGM 4363	$18
	(Yellow promo label)		
LP	STONEMANS' COUNTRY (67)	MGM 4453	$15
LP(P)	STONEMANS' COUNTRY (67)	MGM 4453	$18
	(Yellow promo label)		

LP	**ALL IN THE FAMILY** (68)	MGM 4511	$15
LP(P)	**ALL IN THE FAMILY** (68)	MGM 4511	$18
	(Yellow promo label)		
LP	**THE GREAT STONEMANS** (68)	MGM 4578	$12
LP(P)	**THE GREAT STONEMANS** (68)	MGM 4578	$15
	(White promo label)		
LP	**A STONEMAN CHRISTMAS** (68)	MGM 4613	$12
LP(P)	**A STONEMAN CHRISTMAS** (68)	MGM 4613	$15
	(White promo label)		
LP	**THE STONEMAN FAMILY LIVE** (68)	Sunset 5203	$15
LP	**THE STONEMANS** (68)	Nashville 2063	$12
LP	**THE STONEMANS** (70)	MGM 125	$10

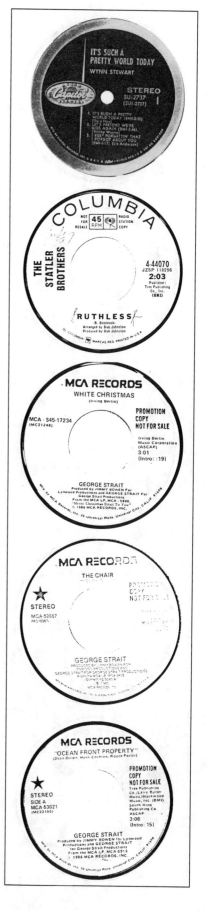

CARL STORY (G)
Other Columbia 45s $5-10 each
Mercury 45s $4-8 each
Starday 45s $3-6 each
Other Starday LPs $5-10 each
Diplomat, CMH, Old Homestead, Atteiram, Songs of Faith, Scripture, Puritan, Rimrock, Buckboard, and Spar LPs $3-5 each

-singles-

45rpm	**WHAT A LINE** (55)	Columbia 21444	$15
45(P)	**WHAT A LINE** (55)	Columbia 21444	$12
	(White promo label)		

-EPs-

EP	**CARL STORY** (59)	Starday 101	$20
EP	**CARL STORY** (59)	Starday 113	$15

-albums-

LP	**GOSPEL QUARTET FAVORITES** (58)	Mercury 20323	$25
LP(P)	**GOSPEL QUARTET FAVORITES** (58)	Mercury 20323	$30
	(White promo label)		
LP	**PEACHIN' PRAYIN' SHOUTIN' & SINGIN'** (59)	Starday 105	$30
LP	**AMERICA'S FAVORITE COUNTRY GOSPEL ARTIST** (59)	Starday 107	$30
LP	**ALL DAY SINGING WITH DINNER ON THE GROUND** (61)	Starday 137	$20
LP	**ALL DAY SINGING WITH DINNER ON THE GROUND** (69)	Nashville 2007	$12
LP	**GET RELIGION** (61)	Starday 152	$18
LP	**MIGHTY CLOSE TO HEAVEN** (63)	Starday 219	$18
LP	**GOOD OLE GOSPEL MOUNTAIN MUSIC** (64)	Wing 16291	$15
LP(P)	**GOOD OLE GOSPEL MOUNTAIN MUSIC** (64)	Wing 16291	$18
	(White promo label)		
LP	**ALL DAY SACRED SINGING** (64)	Starday 278	$18
LP	**SACRED SONGS OF LIFE AND THE HEREAFTER** (65)	Starday 315	$15
LP	**THERE'S NOTHING ON EARTH** (65)	Starday 348	$15
LP	**SONGS FOR OUR SAVIOR** (66)	Sims 136	$15
	See the Sunshine Boys		

VARIOUS ARTISTS

-radio shows-

48LP(RS)	**THE STORY OF COUNTRY MUSIC** (82)	TM Special Products	$250
	(Forty-eight hour show, one hour each disc, the history of country music; music and interviews)		

VERN STOVALL (CW)
Other Crest 45s $4-8 each

-singles-

45rpm	**LONG BLACK LIMOUSINE** (59)	Crest 1080	$10

GEORGE STRAIT (C)
Other MCA 45s $1 each
MCA picture sleeves $3 each
MCA LPs $2-4 each

-singles-

45(P)	**THE CHAIR** (85)	MCA 52667	$12
	(White promo label, blue vinyl)		
45(P)	**OCEAN FRONT PROPERTY** (86)	MCA 53021	$12
	(White promo label, yellow vinyl)		
45(P)	**MERRY CHRISTMAS STRAIT TO YOU** (86)	MCA 17234	$18
	(White promo label, red vinyl, promo only)		
45(P)	**ALL MY EX'S LIVE IN TEXAS** (87)	MCA 53087	$12
	(White promo label, yellow vinyl)		
45(P)	**AM I BLUE** (87)	MCA 53165	$12
	(White promo label, blue vinyl)		
45(P)	**FOR CHRIST'S SAKE, IT'S CHRISTMAS** (87)	MCA 17451	$15
	(White promo label, red vinyl, promo only)		

-radio shows-

LP(RS)	**LIVE AT GILLEY'S** (Feb 85)	Westwood One	$20-30
	(Live concert)		

MEL STREET (C)
Metromedia, GRT, Mercury, and Polydor 45s $2 each
Mercury LPs $5 each
Metromedia, GRT, and Polydor LPs $4 each
Sunbird LPs $3 each

TEXAS BILL STRENGTH (CW)

-albums-

LP	**GREATEST HITS** (67)	Re-Car (Soma) 2022	$25

JOHNNY STRICKLAND (RB)

-singles-

45rpm	**SHE'S MINE** (58)	Roulette 4119	$25
45(P)	**SHE'S MINE** (58)	Roulette 4119	$30
	(Includes a promo letter insert from Roulette)		
45rpm	**I'VE HEARD THAT LINE BEFORE** (58)	Roulette 4147	$15
45(P)	**I'VE HEARD THAT LINE BEFORE** (58)	Roulette 4147	$18
	(White promo label)		

STRIKES (RB)

-singles-

45rpm	**IF YOU CAN'T ROCK ME** (57)	Imperial 5433	$15
45(P)	**IF YOU CAN'T ROCK ME** (57)	Imperial 5433	$12
	(Cream-colored promo label)		
45rpm	**ROCKIN'** (57)	Imperial 5446	$15
45(P)	**ROCKIN'** (57)	Imperial 5446	$12
	(Cream-colored promo label)		

STRINGBEAN (CW)
David Akeman
Starday 45s $3-5 each

-EPs-

EP	**STRINGBEAN & HIS BANJO** (60)	Starday 131	$25

-albums-

LP	**OLD TIME PICKIN' AND SINGIN' WITH STRINGBEAN** (61)	Starday 142	$75
LP	**STRINGBEAN** (62)	Starday 179	$50
LP	**A SALUTE TO UNCLE DAVE MACON** (63)	Starday 215	$50
LP	**WAY BACK IN THE HILLS OF OLD KENTUCKY** (64)	Starday 260	$40
LP	**HEE HAW CORNSHUCKER** (71)	Nashville 2100	$12
LP	**ME AND MY OLD CROWE** (72)	Nugget 102	$15
LP	**STRINGBEAN GOIN' TO THE GRAND OLE OPRY** (77)	Ovation 1726	$12

JUD STRUNK (C)
MGM, Columbia, and MCA 45s $1-2 each
MGM and Columbia LPs $6-10 each
MCA LPs $4 each

MARTY STUART (C)
Other Columbia 45s $2-3 each
MCA 45s $2 each
MCA LPs $3 each

-singles-

45rpm	**ARLENE** (85)	Columbia 05724	$10
	(Price includes picture sleeve)		

-albums-

LP	**BUSY BEE CAFE** (80s)	Sugar Hill 3726	$15
	(With Johnny Cash, Earl Scruggs, Merle Watson, Doc Watson, and others)		

SCOTTIE STUART (RB)

-singles-

45rpm	**NIGHTMARE** (58)	MMC 006	$50

NAT STUCKEY (C)
Paula 45s $2-4 each
RCA Victor 45s $2 each
Other RCA Victor LPs $4-8 each

-albums-

LP	**ALL MY TOMORROWS** (67)	Paula 2196	$20
LP(P)	**ALL MY TOMORROWS** (67)	Paula 2196	$25
	(White promo label)		
LP	**COUNTRY FAVORITES** (67)	Paula 2203	$20
LP(P)	**COUNTRY FAVORITES** (67)	Paula 2203	$25
	(White promo label)		
LP	**NAT STUCKEY SINGS** (68)	RCA Victor 4090	$18
LP	**KEEP 'EM COUNTRY** (69)	RCA Victor 4123	$18

LP	NEW COUNTRY ROADS (69)	RCA Victor 4226	$18
LP	OLD MAN WILLIS (70)	RCA Victor 4330	$15
LP	SHE WAKES ME UP WITH A KISS EVERY MORNING (71)	RCA Victor 4477	$15
LP	COUNTRY FEVER (70)	RCA Victor 4389	$15
LP	ONLY A WOMAN LIKE YOU (71)	RCA Victor 4559	$15
LP	FORGIVE ME FOR CALLING YOU DARLING (72)	RCA Victor 4635	$15
LP	IS IT ANY WONDER THAT I LOVE YOU (72)	RCA Victor 4743	$15

BRAD SUGGS (RB)

-singles-

| 45rpm | CHARCOAL SUIT (56) | Meteor 5034 | $75 |

NIKI SULLIVAN (RB)
Member of the Crickets

-singles-

| 45rpm | IT'S ALL OVER (58) | Dot 15751 | $50 |
| 45rpm | IT REALLY DOESN'T MATTER | Joli 075 | $45 |

GENE SUMMERS (RB)
Not the lead singer of KISS

-singles-

45rpm	BLUE DIAMOND (57)	Capri 502	$10
45rpm	ALABAMA SHAKE (57)	Capri 507	$12
45rpm	SCHOOL OF ROCK N' ROLL (58)	Jan 100	$18
45rpm	NERVOUS (58)	Jan 102	$15
45rpm	TWIXTEEN (59)	Jan 106	$10
45rpm	DRINKIN' WINE (59)	Sun 299	$12
45rpm	ALMOST 12 O'CLOCK (59)	Lafayette 1001	$10

JOE SUN (C)
Elektra and Ovation 45s $2 each
Elektra and Ovation LPs $4 each

SUN VALLEY TRIO (CW)
Other King 45s $5-10 each

-singles-

| 45rpm | THE HOKEY POKEY (55) | King 1505 | $10 |

THE SUNSHINE BOYS (G)
With Carl Story
Starday 45s $3-6 each

-EPs-

| EP | GOSPEL SONGS (59) | Starday 112 | $20 |

-albums-

LP	PREACHIN' PRAYIN' SHOUTIN' & SINGIN' (59)	Starday 105	$30
LP	SING UNTO HIM (59)	Dot 3189	$40
LP	AMERICA'S NUMBER ONE GOSPEL GROUP (60)	Starday 113	$40
LP	MORE COUNTRY MUSIC SING ALONG (62)	Starday 166	$30
LP	HAPPY HOME UP THERE (65)	Starday 349	$25
	See Carl Story		

CECIL SURRATT (CW)
With Smitty Smith
King 45s $4-6 each

-albums-

LP	SONGS EVERYBODY KNOWS (61)	Audio Lab 1565	$30
LP	COUNTRY MUSIC FROM THE HEART OF COUNTRY (63)	King 860	$25
LP	GOOD COUNTRY SINGING AND PICKING (66)	King 966	$20

SWANEE RIVER BOYS (CW)

-albums-

| LP | OLD VIRGINNY (68) | Skylite 6066 | $18 |

BOBBY SWANSON (RB)

-singles-

| 45rpm | ROCKIN' LITTLE ESKIMO (58) | Igloo 1003 | $40 |

HANK SWATLEY (RB)

-singles-

| 45rpm | OAKIE BOOGIE (58) | Aaron 101 | $100 |

AL SWEATT (RB)

-singles-

| 45rpm | LET'S PAINT THE TOWN RED (58) | Keen 289 | $65 |

SWEETHEARTS OF THE RODEO (C)
Columbia 45s $2 each
Columbia LPs $3 each

-radio shows-

LP(RS)	**WESTWOOD ONE PRESENTS** (July 89) (Live concert)		Westwood One	$10-20

SYLVIA (C)
Other RCA Victor 45s $2-3 each
Other RCA Victor color vinyl 45s $8 each
RCA Victor LPs $3 each

-singles-

45(P)	**VICTIMS OF GOODBYE** (84) (Green promo label, blue vinyl)		RCA Victor 13755	$10
45(P)	**FALLIN' IN LOVE** (85) (Yellow promo label, green vinyl)		RCA Victor 13997	$10
45(P)	**FALLIN' IN LOVE** (85) (Yellow promo label, blue vinyl)		RCA Victor 13997	$10

-radio shows-

LP(RS)	**COUNTRY MUSIC TIME** (80s) (Music and interviews)		U.S. Air Force	$10-12
3LP(RS)	**SILVER EAGLE** (Apr 83) (Live concert)		DIR	$10-20
LP(RS)	**WESTWOOD ONE PRESENTS** (Sept 86) (Live concert)		Westwood One	$10-20
Cass(RS)	**AUSTIN ENCORE** (92) (Live concert on cassette)		Main Street	$25-50

T

T. TOMMY (CW)
Other Mercury 45s $4-8 each

-singles-

45rpm	**FREE, FREE** (58)	Mercury 70955	$12
45(P)	**FREE, FREE** (58) (White promo label)	Mercury 70955	$10

DICK TACKER (RB)

-singles-

45rpm	**ROCK ALL NIGHT WITH ME** (58)	Kingston 1364	$60

TOM TALL (RB)
Chart 45s $3 each
Scorpion 45s $2 each

-singles-

45rpm	**STACK-A-RECORDS** (58)	Crest 1038	$40

ROY TAN (RB)

-singles-

45rpm	**ISABELLA** (57)	Tan 3002	$18
45rpm	**ISABELLA** (57)	Dot 15551	$10

SID TANNER (CW)
Bluebird 78s $12 each
Columbia 78s $18 each

FRANKIE TARO (RB)

-singles-

45rpm	**SUZY ANN** (58)	G & G 111	$40

BILL TAYLOR (R & B)

-singles-

45rpm	**SPLIT PERSONALITY** (55)	Flip 502	$500
45rpm	**BORDER TOWN** (56)	Pen 117	$15
45(P)	**BORDER TOWN** (56) (Rare promo copy)	Pen 117	$18
45rpm	**NELDA JANE** (57)	Trophy 500	$12
45rpm	**BANDSTAND** (57)	Felsted 8564	$10

BOB TAYLOR (RB)

-singles-

45rpm	**DON'T BE UNFAIR** (58)	Yucca 110	$40

EARL TAYLOR (CW)
Vetco LPs $5 each

-EPs-

EP	**EARL TAYLOR** (63)	Capitol 2090	$15
	(Issued with a hard cover)		

-albums-

LP	**ALAN LOMAX PRESENTS FOLK SONGS FROM BLUEGRASS** (60)	United Artists 6049	$18
LP(P)	**ALAN LOMAX PRESENTS FOLK SONGS FROM BLUEGRASS** (60)	United Artists 6049	$25
	(White promo label)		
LP	**BLUEGRASS TAYLOR-MADE** (63)	Capitol 2090	$45
LP(P)	**BLUEGRASS TAYLOR-MADE** (63)	Capitol 2090	$50
	(Capitol promo label)		

TUT TAYLOR (C)
World Pacific 45s $2 each
Tune, Old Homestead, Tacoma, Rounder, and Flying Fish LPs $3-6 each

-albums-

LP	**12 STRING DOBRO** (64)	World Pacific 1816	$50
	(Very limited red vinyl)		
LP	**12 STRING DOBRO** (64)	World Pacific 1816	$25
	(Black vinyl)		
LP	**DOBRO COUNTRY** (64)	World Pacific 1829	$25

VERNON TAYLOR (RB)

-singles-

45rpm	**MYSTERY TRAIN** (58)	Sun 325	$10

TEDDY & JOHNNY (R)

-singles-

45rpm	**TEENAGE PARTY** (57)	Peach 0566	$40

TENNESSEE EXPRESS (C)
RCA Victor 45s $2 each
RCA Victor color vinyl 45s $5-8 each

TENNESSEE GUITARS See Gordon Terry

TENNESSEE TWISTERS (C)
Smash 45s $2 each

-albums-

LP	**TWIST COUNTRY HITS** (62)	Smash 67009	$15
LP(P)	**TWIST COUNTRY HITS** (62)	Smash 67009	$12
	(White promo label)		

AL TERRY (CW)
Other Hickory 45s $4-8 each
Crown LPs (With Johnny Tyler) $5 each
Index LPs $4 each

-singles-

45rpm	**GOOD DEAL, LUCILLE** (54)	Hickory 1003	$15
45(P)	**GOOD DEAL, LUCILLE** (54)	Hickory 1003	$10
	(Yellow promo label)		
45rpm	**HEY, WHATTA Y'SAY** (54)	Hickory 1017	$12
45(P)	**HEY, WHATTA Y'SAY** (54)	Hickory 1017	$10
45rpm	**HATE ME NOT** (55)	Hickory 1022	$10
45rpm	**MY BABY KNOWS** (55) Hickory 1088		
45rpm	**WATCH DOG** (55)	Hickory 1111	$10

DON TERRY (RB)
Other Columbia 45s $4-8 each
Other Columbia LPs $10 each

-singles-

45rpm	**KNEES SHAKIN**	Lin 5018	$50

-EPs-

EP	**TEEN-AGE DANCE SESSION** (55)	Columbia 1853	$15

-albums-

10"LP	**TEEN-AGE DANCE SESSION** (55)	Columbia 6288	$50

GENE TERRY (RB)

-singles-

45rpm	**CINDY LOU** (58)	Goldband 1066	$40

GORDON TERRY (C)
Also with the Tennessee Guitars
Cadence 45s $5 each
Liberty 45s $4 each
Capitol 45s $3 each
Plantation 45s $2 each
Plantation LPs $5 each
   (With the Tennessee Guitars)

-singles-

45rpm	A LOTTA LOTTA WOMAN (59)	RCA Victor 7632	$20
45rpm	TROUBLE ON THE TURNPIKE (60)	RCA Victor 7741	$12
45rpm	GONNA GO DOWN THE RIVER (60)	RCA Victor 7788	$10
45rpm	AND THEN I HEARD THE BAD NEWS (60)	RCA Victor 7875	$10
45rpm	HOW MY BABY CAN LOVE (60)	RCA Victor 7944	$10
45rpm	LONG BLACK LIMOUSINE (61)	RCA Victor 7989	$10

-albums-

LP	LIBERTY SQUARE DANCE CLUB (62) With Homer Garrett	Liberty 3218	$15
	(With square dance calls)		
LP(P)	LIBERTY SQUARE DANCE CLUB (62)	Liberty 3218	$18
	(White promo label)		
LP	LIBERTY SQUARE DANCE CLUB (62)	Liberty 3219	$12
	(No square dance calls)		
LP(P)	LIBERTY SQUARE DANCE CLUB (62)	Liberty 3219	$15
	(White promo label)		
LP	SQUARE DANCE PARTY WITH GORDON TERRY (62)	RCA Victor 2530	$15
LP	GUITAR STYLINGS OF THOSE NASHVILLE CATS (67)	Bell 6005	$15
	(The Tennessee Guitars)		
LP(P)	GUITAR STYLINGS OF THOSE NASHVILLE CATS (67)	Bell 6005	$18
	(White promo label)		

LARRY TERRY (RB)

-singles-

45rpm	HEP CAT (58)	Testa 006	$125

THE TEXAS RANGERS (CW)

-albums-

LP	THE BEST OF WESTERN SWING (63)	Cumberland 69505	$25

TEXAS RUBY (CW)
King 45s $5 each

-albums-

LP	FAVORITE SONGS OF TEXAS RUBY (63)	King 840	$25

THE TEXAS TROUBADORS (CW)

-albums-

LP	SONGS OF THE OPEN RANGE (58)	Promenade 2078	$25

TEXAS VOCAL COMPANY See David Wills

CHUCK THARP (RB)

-singles-

45rpm	I DON'T KNOW (57)	Kapp 248	$50
45(P)	I DON'T KNOW (57)	Kapp 248	$40
	(White promo label)		

JOE THERRIEN (RB)

-singles-

45rpm	I AIN'T GONNA BE AROUND	Jat 101	$50
45rpm	HEY BABE! LET'S GO DOWNTOWN (56)	Brunswick 55005	$18
45(P)	HEY BABE! LET'S GO DOWNTOWN (56)	Brunswick 55005	$12
	(Yellow promo label)		
45rpm	YOU'RE LONG GONE (57)	Brunswick 55017	$30
45(P)	YOU'RE LONG GONE (57)	Brunswick 55017	$25
	(Yellow promo label)		

ERNEST THOMPSON (CW)
Columbia 78s are worth $10-$12 each

HANK THOMPSON (CW)
And His Brazos Valley Boys
Other Capitol 78s $4-8 each
Other Capitol blue label 45s $4-8 each
Capitol yellow swirl label 45s $2-4 each
Dot 45s $2 each
Other Churchill 45s $2 each
Other Capitol LPs $4-8 each
Other Dot/ABC LPs $3-6 each
Pickwick, Churchill, Gusto, MCA, and Waco LPs $3 each

-singles-

78rpm	WHOA SAILOR (46)	Globe 124	$20
78rpm	MY STARRY-EYED TEXAS GIRL (47)	Blue Bonnet 107	$15
78rpm	CALIFORNIA WOMEN (47)	Blue Bonnet 123	$15
78rpm	HUMPTY DUMPTY HEART (48) (Original version)	Capitol 40065	$10
78rpm	WHAT ARE WE GOING TO DO ABOUT THE MOONLIGHT (48)	Capitol 15132	$10
45rpm	THE WILD SIDE OF LIFE (52)	Capitol 1942	$12
45rpm	WAITING IN THE LOBBY OF YOUR HEART (52)	Capitol 2063	$20
45rpm	NO HELP WANTED (53)	Capitol 2376	$12
45rpm	RUB-A-DUB-DUB (53)	Capitol 2445	$10
45rpm	YESTERDAY'S GIRL (54)	Capitol 2553	$15
45(P)	YESTERDAY'S GIRL (54) (White promo label)	Capitol 2553	$10
45rpm	WAKE UP, IRENE (54)	Capitol 2646	$10
45(P)	WAKE UP, IRENE (54) (White promo label)	Capitol 2646	$10
45rpm	A FOOLER, A FAKER (55)	Capitol 2758	$15
45(P)	A FOOLER, A FAKER (55)	Capitol 2758	$10
45rpm	JERSEY BOUNCE (55) (Instrumental)	Capitol 2792	$10
45rpm	WE'VE GONE TOO FAR (55)	Capitol 2823	$12
45(P)	WE'VE GONE TOO FAR (55) (White promo label)	Capitol 2823	$10
45rpm	THE NEW GREEN LIGHT (55)	Capitol 2920	$12
45(P)	THE NEW GREEN LIGHT (55) (White promo label)	Capitol 2920	$10
45rpm	JOHNSON RAG (55) (Instrumental)	Capitol 2998	$10
45rpm	IF LOVIN' YOU IS WRONG (56)	Capitol 3030	$12
45(P)	IF LOVIN' YOU IS WRONG (56) (White promo label)	Capitol 3030	$10
45rpm	BREAKIN' IN ANOTHER HEART (56)	Capitol 3106	$10
45rpm	SIMPLE SIMON (56)	Capitol 3188	$10
45rpm	RED SKIN GAL (56) (Instrumental)	Capitol 3235	$10
45rpm	HONEY, HONEY BEE BALL (56)	Capitol 3275	$10
45rpm	THE BLACKBOARD OF MY HEART (56)	Capitol 3347	$10
45rpm	WEEPING WILLOW (56) With Merle Travis (Instrumental)	Capitol 3440	$10
45rpm	IT MAKES NO DIFFERENCE NOW (57)	Capitol 3536	$10
78rpm	ROCKIN' IN THE CONGO (57)	Capitol 3623	$20
78(P)	ROCKIN' IN THE CONGO (57) (White promo label)	Capitol 3623	$25
45rpm	ROCKIN' IN THE CONGO (57)	Capitol 3623	$18
45(P)	ROCKIN' IN THE CONGO (57) (White promo label)	Capitol 3623	$15
45rpm	A GIRL IN THE NIGHT (57)	Capitol 3709	$10
45rpm	TEARS ARE ONLY PAIN (57)	Capitol 3781	$10
45rpm	IF I'M NOT TOO LATE (57)	Capitol 3850	$10
45rpm	LITTLE LIZA JANE (58)	Capitol 3950	$10
45rpm	SQUAWS ALONG THE YUKON (58)	Capitol 4017	$18
45(P)	SQUAWS ALONG THE YUKON (58) (White promo label)	Capitol 4017	$15
45rpm	YOU'RE GOING BACK TO YOUR OLD WAYS AGAIN (58)	Capitol 4085	$10
45rpm	LOST JOHN (61)	Capitol 4649	$18
45rpm	LOST JOHN (61) (Price includes picture sleeve)	Capitol 4649	$30
45rpm	ROCKIN' IN THE CONGO (81) (Price includes picture sleeve)	Churchill 7779	$10
45rpm	COCAINE BLUES (82) (Price includes picture sleeve)	Churchill 94003	$10
5-33s	HANK THOMPSON AT THE GOLDEN NUGGET (62) Jukebox 33s (Set of five singles for jukebox use)	Capitol 1632	$8 each

-EPs-

EP	SONGS OF THE BRAZOS VALLEY VOL 1 (53)	Capitol 1-418	$25
EP	SONGS OF THE BRAZOS VALLEY VOL 2 (53)	Capitol 2-418	$25
EP	SONGS OF THE BRAZOS VALLEY VOL 3 (53)	Capitol 3-418	$25
EP	HANK THOMPSON (55)	Capitol 601	$25
EP	NORTH OF THE RIO GRANDE VOL 1 (55)	Capitol 1-618	$20
EP	NORTH OF THE RIO GRANDE VOL 2 (55)	Capitol 2-618	$20
EP	NORTH OF THE RIO GRANDE VOL 3 (55)	Capitol 3-618	$20
EP	DANCING WESTERN STYLE (56)	Capitol 705	$20
EP	NEW RECORDINGS OF HANK'S ALL-TIME HITS (56)	Capitol 1-729	$20
EP	NEW RECORDINGS OF HANK'S ALL-TIME HITS (56)	Capitol 2-729	$20
EP	NEW RECORDINGS OF HANK'S ALL-TIME HITS (56)	Capitol 3-729	$20

EP	HANK! VOL 1 (57)	Capitol 1-826	$20
EP	HANK! VOL 2 (57)	Capitol 2-826	$20
EP	HANK! VOL 3 (57)	Capitol 3-826	$20
EP	DANCE RANCH VOL 1 (58)	Capitol 1-975	$20
EP	DANCE RANCH VOL 2 (58)	Capitol 2-975	$20
EP	DANCE RANCH VOL 3 (58)	Capitol 3-975	$20
EP	FAVORITE WALTZES BY HANK THOMPSON VOL 1 (59)	Capitol 1-1111	$20
EP	FAVORITE WALTZES BY HANK THOMPSON VOL 2 (59)	Capitol 2-1111	$20
EP	FAVORITE WALTZES BY HANK THOMPSON VOL 3 (59)	Capitol 3-1111	$20
EP	SONGS FOR ROUNDERS VOL 1 (59)	Capitol 1-1246	$20
EP	SONGS FOR ROUNDERS VOL 2 (59)	Capitol 2-1246	$20
EP	SONGS FOR ROUNDERS VOL 3 (59)	Capitol 3-1246	$20
EP	MOST OF ALL (60)	Capitol 1360	$18
33EP	HANK THOMPSON & THE BRAZOS VALLEY BOYS (61)	Capitol 1590	$20
	(Compact-33 double)		
EP(P)	GOLDEN COUNTRY HITS (64) Jukebox LLP	Capitol 2089	$15
	(Issued with a hard cover)		
EP(P)	BREAKIN' IN ANOTHER HEART (65) Jukebox LLP	Capitol 2274	$15
	(Issued with a hard cover)		

-albums-

10"LP	SONGS OF THE BRAZOS VALLEY (53)	Capitol 418	$100
LP	SONGS OF THE BRAZOS VALLEY (56)	Capitol 418	$75
LP(P)	SONGS OF THE BRAZOS VALLEY (56)	Capitol 418	$125
	(Yellow promo label)		
10"LP	NORTH OF THE RIO GRANDE (53)	Capitol 618	$100
LP	NORTH OF THE RIO GRANDE (56)	Capitol 618	$75
LP(P)	NORTH OF THE RIO GRANDE (56)	Capitol 618	$100
	(Yellow promo label)		
10"LP	NEW RECORDINGS OF HANK'S ALL-TIME HITS (53)	Capitol 729	$100
LP	NEW RECORDINGS OF HANK'S ALL-TIME HITS (56)	Capitol 729	$75
LP(P)	NEW RECORDINGS OF HANK'S ALL-TIME HITS (56)	Capitol 729	$100
	(Yellow promo label)		
LP	HANK! (57)	Capitol 826	$30
LP(P)	HANK! (57) Capitol 826		
LP(P)	HANK! (57)	Capitol 826	$100
	(Yellow promo label)		
10"LP	HANK THOMPSON FAVORITES (53)	Capitol 911	$100
LP	HANK THOMPSON FAVORITES (57)	Capitol 911	$75
LP(P)	HANK THOMPSON FAVORITES (57)	Capitol 911	$100
	(Yellow promo label)		
LP	HANK THOMPSON'S DANCE RANCH (58)	Capitol 975	$75
LP(P)	HANK THOMPSON'S DANCE RANCH (58)	Capitol 975	$80
	(Capitol promo label)		
LP	FAVORITE WALTZES BY HANK THOMPSON (59)	Capitol 1111	$60
LP(P)	FAVORITE WALTZES BY HANK THOMPSON (59)	Capitol 1111	$75
	(Capitol promo label)		
LP	SONGS FOR ROUNDERS (59) Mono	Capitol 1246	$30
LP	SONGS FOR ROUNDERS (59) Stereo	Capitol 1246	$40
LP(P)	SONGS FOR ROUNDERS (59)	Capitol 1246	$50
	(Capitol promo label)		
LP	MOST OF ALL (60) Mono	Capitol 1360	$25
LP	MOST OF ALL (60) Stereo	Capitol 1360	$30
LP(P)	MOST OF ALL (60)	Capitol 1360	$40
	(Capitol promo label)		
LP	THIS BROKEN HEART OF MINE (60) Mono	Capitol 1469	$25
LP	THIS BROKEN HEART OF MINE (60) Stereo	Capitol 1469	$30
LP(P)	THIS BROKEN HEART OF MINE (60)	Capitol 1469	$40
	(Capitol promo label)		
LP	AN OLD LOVE AFFAIR (61) Mono	Capitol 1544	$25
LP	AN OLD LOVE AFFAIR (61) Stereo	Capitol 1544	$30
LP(P)	AN OLD LOVE AFFAIR (61)	Capitol 1544	$35
	(Blue promo label)		
LP	AT THE GOLDEN NUGGET (61) Mono	Capitol 1632	$20
LP	AT THE GOLDEN NUGGET (61) Stereo	Capitol 1632	$25
LP(P)	AT THE GOLDEN NUGGET (61)	Capitol 1632	$30
	(Blue promo label)		
LP	THE #1 COUNTRY & WESTERN BAND (62) Mono	Capitol 1741	$20
LP	THE #1 COUNTRY & WESTERN BAND (62) Stereo	Capitol 1741	$25
LP(P)	THE #1 COUNTRY & WESTERN BAND (62)	Capitol 1741	$30
	(Blue promo label)		
LP	CHEYENNE FRONTIER DAYS (62) Mono	Capitol 1775	$18
LP	CHEYENNE FRONTIER DAYS (62) Stereo	Capitol 1775	$20
LP(P)	CHEYENNE FRONTIER DAYS (62)	Capitol 1775	$25
	(Blue promo label)		
LP	THE BEST OF HANK THOMPSON (63) Mono	Capitol 1878	$15
LP	THE BEST OF HANK THOMPSON (63) Stereo	Capitol 1878	$18
LP(P)	THE BEST OF HANK THOMPSON (63)	Capitol 1878	$20
	(Blue promo label)		

LP	**AT THE STATE FAIR OF TEXAS** (63) Mono	Capitol 1955	$18
LP	**AT THE STATE FAIR OF TEXAS** (63) Stereo	Capitol 1955	$20
LP(P)	**AT THE STATE FAIR OF TEXAS** (63)	Capitol 1955	$25
	(Blue promo label)		
LP	**GOLDEN COUNTRY HITS** (64) Mono	Capitol 2089	$15
LP	**GOLDEN COUNTRY HITS** (64) Stereo	Capitol 2089	$18
LP(P)	**GOLDEN COUNTRY HITS** (64)	Capitol 2089	$20
	(Blue promo label)		
LP	**IT'S CHRISTMAS TIME** (64) Mono	Capitol 2154	$18
LP	**IT'S CHRISTMAS TIME** (64) Stereo	Capitol 2154	$20
LP(P)	**IT'S CHRISTMAS TIME** (64)	Capitol 2154	$25
	(Blue promo label)		
LP	**BREAKIN' IN ANOTHER HEART** (65) Mono	Capitol 2274	$15
LP	**BREAKIN' IN ANOTHER HEART** (65) Stereo	Capitol 2274	$18
LP	**THE LUCKIEST HEARTACHE IN TOWN** (65) Mono	Capitol 2342	$12
LP	**THE LUCKIEST HEARTACHE IN TOWN** (65) Stereo	Capitol 2342	$15
LP	**A SIX PACK TO GO** (66) Mono	Capitol 2460	$12
LP	**A SIX PACK TO GO** (66) Stereo	Capitol 2460	$15
LP	**BREAKIN' THE RULES** (66) Mono	Capitol 2575	$12
LP	**BREAKIN' THE RULES** (66) Stereo	Capitol 2575	$15
LP	**WHERE IS THE CIRCUS** (66)	Warner 1664	$15
LP(P)	**WHERE IS THE CIRCUS** (66)	Warner 1664	$18
	(White promo label)		
LP	**THE BEST OF HANK THOMPSON VOL 2** (67) Mono	Capitol 2661	$10
LP	**THE BEST OF HANK THOMPSON VOL 2** (67) Stereo	Capitol 2661	$12
LP	**JUST AN OLD FLAME** (67) Mono	Capitol 2826	$10
LP	**JUST AN OLD FLAME** (67) Stereo	Capitol 2826	$12
LP	**COUNTRYPOLITAN SOUND OF HANK'S BRAZOS BOYS** (67)	Warner 1679	$12
LP(P)	**COUNTRYPOLITAN SOUND OF HANK'S BRAZOS BOYS** (67)	Warner 1679	$15
	(White promo label)		
LP	**GOLD STANDARD COLLECTION OF HANK THOMPSON** (67)	Warner 1686	$12
LP(P)	**GOLD STANDARD COLLECTION OF HANK THOMPSON** (67)	Warner 1686	$15
	(White promo label)		
LP	**COUNTRY BLUES** (68) Mono	Tower 5120	$15
LP	**COUNTRY BLUES** (68) Stereo	Tower 5120	$18
LP	**THE GOLD STANDARDS** (68)	Dot 25864	$10
LP	**ON TAP, IN THE CAN OR IN THE BOTTLE** (68)	Dot 25894	$10
LP	**SMOKEY THE BAR** (69)	Dot 25932	$10
LP	**HANK THOMPSON SALUTES OKLAHOMA** (69)	Dot 25971	$10
LP	**NEXT TIME I FALL IN LOVE, I WON'T** (71)	Dot 25991	$10
LP	**CAB DRIVER, A SALUTE TO THE MILLS BROTHERS** (72)	Dot 25996	$10
2LP	**25TH ANNIVERSARY ALBUM** (72)	Dot 2000	$12
LP	**HANK THOMPSON'S GREATEST HITS** (72)	Dot 26004	$10
LP	**KINDLY KEEP IT COUNTRY** (73)	Dot 26015	$10

HAYDEN THOMPSON (RB)

-singles-

45rpm	**WHAT CHA' GONNA DO** (58)	Profile 4015	$40
45rpm	**LOVE MY BABY** (58)	Philips 3517	$25

-albums-

LP	**HERE'S HAYDEN THOMPSON** (66)	Kapp 3507	$15
LP(P)	**HERE'S HAYDEN THOMPSON** (66)	Kapp 3507	$18
	(White promo label)		

JUNIOR THOMPSON (R)

-singles-

45rpm	**HOW COME YOU DO ME** (58)	Tune (no #)	$50
45rpm	**MAMA'S LITTLE BABY** (58)	Meteor 5029	$100

SUE THOMPSON (CW)
Other Decca 45s $4-8 each
Other Hickory 45s $3-6 each

-singles-

45rpm	**RED HOT HENRY BROWN** (58)	Decca 30435	$15
45(P)	**RED HOT HENRY BROWN** (58)	Decca 30435	$12
	(Pink promo label)		
45rpm	**SAD MOVIES** (61)	Hickory 1153	$15
45(P)	**SAD MOVIES** (61)	Hickory 1153	$10
	(White promo label)		
45rpm	**NORMAN** (61)	Hickory 1159	$12
45(P)	**NORMAN** (61)	Hickory 1159	$10
	(White promo label)		
45rpm	**WHAT'S WRONG, BILL?** (63)	Hickory 1204	$25
	(Price includes record and picture sleeve)		
45rpm	**TRUE CONFESSIONS** (63)	Hickory 1217	$25
	(Price includes record and picture sleeve)		

	-EPs-		
EP(P)	TWO OF A KIND (62) Six-song promo-only EP	Hickory 107	$15
	-albums-		
LP	MEET SUE THOMPSON (62) Mono	Hickory 104	$30
LP	MEET SUE THOMPSON (62) Stereo	Hickory 104	$40
LP(P)	MEET SUE THOMPSON (62)	Hickory 104	$35
	(White promo label)		
LP	TWO OF A KIND (62) Mono	Hickory 107	$20
LP	TWO OF A KIND (62) Stereo	Hickory 107	$25
LP(P)	TWO OF A KIND (62)	Hickory 107	$30
	(White promo label)		
LP	SUE THOMPSON'S GOLDEN HITS (63) Mono	Hickory 111	$20
LP	SUE THOMPSON'S GOLDEN HITS (63) Stereo	Hickory 111	$25
LP(P)	SUE THOMPSON'S GOLDEN HITS (63)	Hickory 111	$30
	(White promo label)		
LP	THE COUNTRY SIDE OF SUE THOMPSON (64) Mono	Wing 12317	$20
LP	THE COUNTRY SIDE OF SUE THOMPSON (64) Stereo	Wing 16317	$25
LP(P)	THE COUNTRY SIDE OF SUE THOMPSON (64)	Wing 12317	$30
	(White promo label)		
LP	PAPER TIGER (65) Mono	Hickory 121	$18
LP	PAPER TIGER (65) Stereo	Hickory 121	$20
LP(P)	PAPER TIGER (65)	Hickory 121	$25
	(White promo label)		
LP	SUE THOMPSON WITH STRINGS ATTACHED (66) Mono	Hickory 130	$15
LP	SUE THOMPSON WITH STRINGS ATTACHED (66) Stereo	Hickory 130	$12
LP(P)	SUE THOMPSON WITH STRINGS ATTACHED (66)	Hickory 130	$18
	(White promo label)		
LP	THIS IS SUE THOMPSON (69)	Hickory 148	$12
LP	SWEET MEMORIES (74)	Hickory 4511	$12
LP	... AND LOVE ME (74)	Hickory 4515	$12

CHUCK THORP (RB)
-singles-

45rpm	LONG LONG PONYTAIL (58)	Jaro 79029	$20

THREE ACES & JOKER (RB)
-singles-

45rpm	BOOZE PARTY (58)	GRC 104	$50

TIFFANYS (R)
-singles-

45rpm	I'VE GOT A GIRL (57)	Rockin' Robin 1	$45

MEL TILLIS (CW)
With the Statesiders
Kapp 45s $2-4 each
MGM 45s $2-4 each
Elektra 45s $2-3 each
MCA 45s $2 each
Other Columbia LPs $8 each
Other Kapp LPs $4-8 each
MGM LPs $4-8 each
  (Including duet LPs with Sherry Bryce)
MGM 2LP sets $10 each
Elektra LPs $5 each
MCA LPs $3-4 each
MCA 2LP sets $5 each
TeeVee, Gusto, and Coral LPs $3 each
Power Pac LPs with Sovine and Felts $6 each
-singles-

45rpm	IT TAKES A WORRIED MAN TO SING A WORRIED SONG (57)	Columbia 40845	$15
45(P)	IT TAKES A WORRIED MAN TO SING A WORRIED SONG (57)	Columbia 40845	$10
	(White promo label)		
45rpm	JUKE BOX MAN (57)	Columbia 40944	$20
45(P)	JUKE BOX MAN (57)	Columbia 40944	$15
	(White promo label)		
45rpm	TEENAGE WEDDING (58)	Columbia 41115	$20
45(P)	TEENAGE WEDDING (58)	Columbia 41115	$15
	(White promo label)		
45rpm	NO SONG TO SING (59)	Columbia 41189	$12
45(P)	NO SONG TO SING (59)	Columbia 41189	$10
	(White promo label)		
45rpm	THE BROOKLYN BRIDGE (59)	Columbia 41277	$12
45(P)	THE BROOKLYN BRIDGE (59)	Columbia 41277	$10
	(White promo label)		
45rpm	GEORGIA TOWN BLUES (59)	Columbia 41530	$12
45(P)	GEORGIA TOWN BLUES (59)	Columbia 41530	$10
	(White promo label)		

45rpm	**IT'S SO EASY** (60)	Columbia 41632	$12
45(P)	**IT'S SO EASY** (60)	Columbia 41632	$10
	(White promo label)		
45rpm	**WALK ON BOY** (61)	Columbia 41863	$12
45(P)	**WALK ON BOY** (61)	Columbia 41863	$10
	(White promo label)		
45rpm	**HEARTS OF STONE** (61)	Columbia 41986	$12
45(P)	**HEARTS OF STONE** (61)	Columbia 41986	$10
	(White promo label)		
45(P)	**THERE'S NO TURNING BACK** (77)	KFC (MCA) 001	$10
	(Kentucky Fried Chicken songwriting contest)		

-EPs-

EP(P)	**WE'VE FLIPPED** (76) Various artists	MCA 1943	$10
	(Tillis does one song, price includes cover)		

-albums-

LP	**HEART OVER MIND** (62) Mono	Columbia 1724	$30
LP	**HEART OVER MIND** (62) Stereo	Columbia 8524	$40
LP(P)	**HEART OVER MIND** (62)	Columbia 1724	$50
	(White promo label)		
LP	**STATESIDE** (66) Mono	Kapp 1492	$15
LP	**STATESIDE** (66) Stereo	Kapp 3492	$20
LP(P)	**STATESIDE** (66)	Kapp 1492	$25
	(White promo label)		
LP	**LIFE TURNED HER THAT WAY** (67)	Kapp 1514	$12
LP(P)	**LIFE TURNED HER THAT WAY** (67)	Kapp 1514	$15
	(White promo label)		
LP	**LIFE'S THAT WAY** (67)	Kapp 1514	$10
	(Same record, different title)		
LP	**MR. MEL** (67)	Kapp 1535	$10
LP	**LET ME TALK TO YOU** (68)	Kapp 3543	$10
LP	**SOMETHING SPECIAL** (68)	Kapp 3570	$10
LP	**MEL TILLIS' GREATEST HITS** (69)	Kapp 3589	$10
LP	**WHO'S JULIE?** (69)	Kapp 3594	$10
LP	**OLD FAITHFUL** (69)	Kapp 3609	$10
LP	**SHE'LL BE HANGING 'ROUND SOMEWHERE** (70)	Kapp 3630	$10
LP	**BIG 'N COUNTRY** (70)	Vocalion 3914	$12
LP(P)	**BIG 'N COUNTRY** (70)	Vocalion 3914	$15
	(White promo label)		
LP	**WALKING ON NEW GRASS** (70)	Vocalion 3928	$12
LP(P)	**WALKING ON NEW GRASS** (70)	Vocalion 3928	$15
	(White promo label)		
LP	**MEL TILLIS' GREATEST HITS VOL 2** (71)	Kapp 3653	$10
LP	**STATESIDE** (72)	Starday 471	$12
LP	**MEL TILLIS** (72)	Harmony 31952	$10
LP(P)	**MEL TILLIS** (72)	Harmony 31952	$12
	(White promo label)		

-radio shows-

16"(RS)	**U.S. AIR FORCE BAND** (60s)	U.S. Air Force	$25-50
	(Music and interviews)		
LP(RS)	**HOOTENAVY** (60s)	U.S. Navy	$25-50
	(Music and interviews)		
LP(RS)	**COUNTRY MUSIC TIME** (70s)	U.S. Air Force	$10-15
	(Music and interviews)		
3LP(RS)	**THE SILVER EAGLE** (81) With Gail Davies	DIR	$40-75
	(Live concert)		
3LP(RS)	**INTERNATIONAL FESTIVAL** (Oct 82)	Mutual Radio	$100-200
	(Live concert, includes Billy Swan, Marty Robbins, and Kris Kristofferson)		
3LP(RS)	**AMERICAN EAGLE** (May 87)	DIR	$40-75
	(Live concert)		
LP(RS)	**WESTWOOD ONE PRESENTS** (Apr 90)	Westwood One	$15-25
	(Live concert)		
Cass(RS)	**AUSTIN ENCORE** (92)	Mainstreet	$30-60
	(Live concert on cassette)		

PAM TILLIS (C)
Warner and Arista 45s $1 each
Warner and Arista LPs $3 each

FLOYD TILLMAN (CW)
Columbia and RCA Victor 45s $3-5 each
Bagatelle and Crazy Cajun LPs $3-5 each
Columbia LPs $5 each

-albums-

LP	**FLOYD TILLMAN'S GREATEST** (58)	RCA Victor 1686	$50
LP	**LET'S MAKE MEMORIES** (62)	Cimarron 2003	$30

LP	FLOYD TILLMAN'S BEST (64)	Harmony 7316	$18
LP(P)	FLOYD TILLMAN'S BEST (64)	Harmony 7316	$25
	(White promo label)		
LP	FLOYD TILLMAN SINGS HIS GREAT HITS OF LOVIN' (65)	Hilltop 6017	$15
LP	LET'S MAKE MEMORIES (65)	Starday 310	$18
LP	FLOYD TILLMAN'S COUNTRY (67)	Musicor 313	$18
LP	DREAM ON (68)	Musicor 3157	$18
LP	I'LL STILL BE LOVIN' YOU (69)	Harmony 11297	$10
LP	FLOYD TILLMAN & FRIENDS (70s)	Gilley's 504	$15
	(Includes Tubb, Haggard, Nelson, and Lee)		

CARL TIPTON (C)
-albums-

LP	THE CARL TIPTON SHOW (70s)	Sims 143	$18

JOHNNY TODD (R)
-singles-

45rpm	PINK CADILLAC (56)	Modern 1003	$50

TOM & JERRY (C)
Charlie Tomlinson and Jerry Kennedy
Mercury 45s $5-10 each
-albums-

LP	GUITAR'S GREATEST HITS (61)	Mercury 60626	$20
LP(P)	GUITAR'S GREATEST HITS (61)	Mercury 60626	$25
	(White promo label)		
LP	GUITARS PLAY THE SOUND OF RAY CHARLES (62)	Mercury 60671	$18
LP(P)	GUITARS PLAY THE SOUND OF RAY CHARLES (62)	Mercury 60671	$20
	(White promo label)		
LP	GUITAR'S GREATEST HITS VOL 2 (62)	Mercury 60756	$18
LP(P)	GUITAR'S GREATEST HITS VOL 2 (62)	Mercury 60756	$20
	(White promo label)		
LP	SURFIN' HOOTENANNY (63)	Mercury 60842	$20
LP(P)	SURFIN' HOOTENANNY (63)	Mercury 60842	$25
	(White promo label)		
	Do not confuse this group with the Tom & Jerry that became		
	better known as Simon & Garfunkel		

MITCHELL TOROK (CW)
-singles-

45rpm	HOOTCHY KOOTCHY HENRY (53)	Abbott 150	$40
	(Red vinyl)		
45rpm	RED LIGHT, GREEN LIGHT (57)	Decca 29863	$12
45(P)	RED LIGHT, GREEN LIGHT (57)	Decca 29863	$10
	(Pink promo label)		
45rpm	PLEDGE OF LOVE (57)	Decca 30230	$12
45(P)	PLEDGE OF LOVE (57)	Decca 30230	$10
	(Pink promo label)		
45rpm	THE P. T. A. ROCK AND ROLL (59)	Decca 30901	$15
45(P)	THE P. T. A. ROCK AND ROLL (59)	Decca 30901	$12
	(Pink promo label)		
45rpm	CARIBBEAN (59)	Abbott 140	$25
45rpm	CARIBBEAN (59)	Guyden 2018	$15
45rpm	MEXICAN JOE (60)	Guyden 2028	$12
45rpm	PINK CHIFFON (60)	Guyden 2034	$10
	-albums-		
LP	CARIBBEAN (60)	Guyden 502	$75
LP	GUITAR COURSE (66)	Reprise 6223	$15
LP(P)	GUITAR COURSE (66)	Reprise 6223	$18
	(White promo label)		

BUCK TRAIL (RB)
-singles-

45rpm	HONKY TONK ON 2ND STREET (57)	Trail 100	$75
45rpm	KNOCKED OUT JOINT ON MARS (58)	Trail 103	$150
45rpm	CHATTANOOGA DRUMMER MAN (58)	Trail 105	$50

REX TRAILER (CW)
And the Playboys
-albums-

LP	COUNTRY & WESTERN (58)	Crown 5158	$15

TRAILBLAZERS (RB)
-singles-

45rpm	GRANDPA'S ROCK (58)	Watson 500	$75

BOBBY LEE TRAMMELL (RB)
Sun 45s $3 each

-singles-

45rpm	SHIMMY LOU (57)	Hot 101	$25
45rpm	BETTY JEAN (57)	Hot 102	$25
45rpm	ARKANSAS TWIST (57)	Alley 1001	$20
45rpm	COME ON BABY (57)	Alley 1004	$20
45rpm	SALLY TWIST (57)	Atlanta 1501	$20
45rpm	YOU MOSTEST GIRL (57)	Fabor 127	$20
45rpm	SHIRLEY LEE (57)	Fabor 4038	$100
45rpm	YOU MOSTEST GIRL (57)	Radio 102	$25
45rpm	MY SUSIE J.-MY SUSIE JANE (57)	Radio 114	$25
45rpm	SHIRLEY LEE (58)	ABC Paramount 9890	$50
45(P)	SHIRLEY LEE (58)	ABC Paramount 9890	$40
	(White promo label)		
45rpm	WOE IS ME (59)	Warrior 1554	$50
45rpm	HI-YO SILVER	Santo 9052	$20
45rpm	HI-YO SILVER	Vaden 304	$20

-albums-

LP	ARKANSAS TWIST (62)	Atlantic 1503	$400
LP	I DARE AMERICA TO BE GREAT (71)	Souncot 1102	$10
LP	LOVE ISN'T LOVE TILL YOU GIVE IT AWAY (71)	Souncot 1141	$10

MERLE TRAVIS (CW)
Other Capitol 78s $5-8 each
Other Capitol blue label 45s $5-10 each
Other Capitol swirl label 45s $2-4 each

-singles-

78rpm	CINCINNATI LOU (46)	Capitol 258	$15
78rpm	DIVORCE ME C. O. D. (46)	Capitol 290	$12
78rpm	SO ROUND, SO FIRM, SO FULLY PACKED (47)	Capitol 349	$15
78rpm	FAT GAL/MERLE'S BOOGIE WOOGIE (48)	Capitol 40026	$10
45rpm	SPOONIN' MOON (50)	Capitol 1146	$12
45rpm	EL RENO (51)	Capitol 1241	$10
45rpm	DRY BREAD (52)	Capitol 1337	$10
45rpm	DEEP SOUTH (52)	Capitol 1519	$10
45rpm	CANNON BALL RAG (53)	Capitol 2245	$15
45rpm	BAJOU BABY (53)	Capitol 2336	$18
78rpm	GAMBLER'S GUITAR (54)	Capitol 2544	$15
78(P)	GAMBLER'S GUITAR (54)	Capitol 2544	$18
	(White promo label)		
45rpm	GAMBLER'S GUITAR (54)	Capitol 2544	$15
45(P)	GAMBLER'S GUITAR (54)	Capitol 2544	$12
	(White promo label)		
78rpm	DANCE OF THE GOLDEN ROD (54)	Capitol 2563	$15
78(P)	DANCE OF THE GOLDEN ROD (54)	Capitol 2563	$18
	(White promo label)		
45rpm	DANCE OF THE GOLDEN ROD (54)	Capitol 2563	$15
45(P)	DANCE OF THE GOLDEN ROD (54)	Capitol 2563	$12
	(White promo label)		
45rpm	LOUISIANA BOOGIE (54)	Capitol 2902	$15
45(P)	LOUISIANA BOOGIE (54)	Capitol 2902	$10
	(White promo label)		
45rpm	BEER BARREL POLKA (56)	Capitol 3194	$10

-EPs-

EP	THE MERLE TRAVIS GUITAR VOL 1 (56)	Capitol 1-650	$30
EP	THE MERLE TRAVIS GUITAR VOL 2 (56)	Capitol 2-650	$30
EP	THE MERLE TRAVIS GUITAR VOL 3 (56)	Capitol 3-650	$30
EP	BACK HOME (57)	Capitol 891	$25

-albums-

LP	THE MERLE TRAVIS GUITAR (56)	Capitol 650	$125
LP(P)	THE MERLE TRAVIS GUITAR (56)	Capitol 650	$125
	(Yellow promo label)		
LP	BACK HOME (57)	Capitol 891	$100
LP(P)	BACK HOME (57)	Capitol 891	$100
	(Yellow promo label)		
LP	WALKIN' THE STRINGS (60)	Capitol 1391	$75
LP(P)	WALKIN' THE STRINGS (60)	Capitol 1391	$100
	(Yellow promo label)		
LP	TRAVIS (62) Mono	Capitol 1664	$40
LP	TRAVIS (62) Stereo	Capitol 1664	$50
LP(P)	TRAVIS (62)	Capitol 1664	$75
	(Capitol promo label)		
LP	SONGS OF THE COAL MINES (63)	Capitol 1956	$50
LP	I'M A NATURAL BORN GAMBLING MAN (64)	Spin-O-Rama 176	$15
	(Only one side of this budget label record is by Merle Travis)		

LP	**MERLE TRAVIS & JOE MAPHIS** (64)	Capitol 2102	$40
	(First pressing)		
LP	**GREAT SONGS OF THE DELMORE BROTHERS** (69)	Capitol 249	$15
	(With Johnny Bond)		
2LP	**COUNTRY GUITAR GIANTS** (70s) Travis and Maphis	CHM 9017	$15
2LP	**THE CLAYTON MCMICHEN STORY** (82)	CHM 9028	$15
	(With Mac Wiseman)		

-radio shows-

LP(RS)	**COUNTRY CROSSROADS** (Apr 83)	Southern Baptist	$10-20
	(Music and interviews)		

RANDY TRAVIS (C)
Randy Traywick
Other Warner 45s $1-2 each
Warner picture sleeves $2 each
Warner LPs $2-4 each

-singles-

45rpm	**SHE'S MY WOMAN** (78) Randy Traywick	Paula 431	$50
45(P)	**SHE'S MY WOMAN** (78)	Paula 431	$40
	(Red promo label)		
45(P)	**WHITE CHRISTMAS MAKES ME BLUE** (87)	Warner Bros PRO 2842	$12
	(Promo-only release)		

-radio shows-

3LP(RS)	**AMERICAN EAGLE** (Mar 87)	DIR	$25-50
	(Live concert)		
3LP(RS)	**THE STORY OF RANDY TRAVIS** (88)	United Stations	$20-30
	(Music and interviews)		

BUCK TRENT (C)
Smash 45s $3 each
RCA Victor, Dot, and Boone 45s $1-2 each
Boone and RCA Victor LPs $5 each
ABC/Dot LPs $4 each

-albums-

LP	**THE SOUND OF A BLUEGRASS BANJO** (62) Charles Trent	Smash 67002	$18
LP(P)	**THE SOUND OF A BLUEGRASS BANJO** (62)	Smash 27002	$25
	(White promo label)		
LP	**THE SOUND OF A FIVE STRING BANJO** (62) Charles Trent	Smash 67017	$18
LP(P)	**THE SOUND OF A FIVE STRING BANJO** (62)	Smash 67017	$25
	(White promo label)		

VAN TREVOR (C)
Other Royal American 45s $2 each

-singles-

45(P)	**CHRISTMAS IN THE COUNTRY** (60s)	Band Box 373	$15
	(Promo-only release with holiday greetings by other Band Box artists on the flip side)		

-albums-

LP	**FUNNY FAMILIAR FORGOTTEN FEELINGS** (69)	Royal American 2800	$15
LP	**COME ON OVER TO OUR SIDE** (70s)	Band Box	$12

TRAVIS TRITT (C)
Warner 45s $1 each
Warner LPs $3 each

-radio shows-

3LP(RS)	**CHRISTMAS WITH TRAVIS TRITT** (Dec 92)		$20-30
	(Music and interviews)		

JIMMY TROTTER (RB)

-singles-

45rpm	**EVERYBODY'S GOT A BABY BUT ME** (57)	Swade 103	$40

ERNEST TUBB (CW)
And the Texas Troubadors
Other Decca 78s $4-8 each
Other Decca 45s before 30000 $8 each
Decca 45s after 30000 $4-8 each
Decca 45s after 31000 $2-4 each
First Generation 45s $2 each
MCA and Coral LPs $4-6 each
Radiola LPs $5 each
  (By the Texas Troubadors)
Pickwick and other First Generation LPs $4 each

-singles-

78rpm	**THE PASSING OF JIMMIE RODGERS** (36)	Bluebird 6693	$175
78rpm	**SINCE THAT BLACK CAT CROSSED MY PATH** (38)	Bluebird 7000	$125

78rpm	**MEAN OLD BED BUG BLUES** (41)	Bluebird 8899	$100
78rpm	**MY MOTHER IS LONELY** (41)	Bluebird 8966	$100
78rpm	**TRY ME ONE MORE TIME** (44)	Decca 6093	$25
78rpm	**SOLDIER'S LAST LETTER** (44)	Decca 6098	$25
78rpm	**IT'S BEEN SO LONG, DARLIN'** (45)	Decca 6110	$25
78rpm	**RAINBOW AT MIDNIGHT** (46)	Decca 46018	$20
45rpm	**RAINBOW AT MIDNIGHT** (49)	Decca 46018	$25
45rpm	**FILIPINO BABY** (49)	Decca 46019	$20
3-45s	**ERNEST TUBB** (49) Three 45s in a set	Decca 146	$75
	(Price is for all three records and box)		
78rpm	**SOLDIER'S LAST LETTER** (49)	Decca 46047	$18
78(P)	**SOLDIER'S LAST LETTER** (49)	Decca 46047	$25
	(Decca promo label)		
45rpm	**SOLDIER'S LAST LETTER** (49)	Decca 46047	$20
45rpm	**HAVE YOU EVER BEEN LONELY?** (49)	Decca 46144	$20
45rpm	**I'M BITING MY FINGERNAILS AND THINKING OF YOU** (49)	Decca 24592	$20
	(With the Andrews Sisters and Ernest Tubb)		
45rpm	**SLIPPIN' AROUND** (49)	Decca 46173	$15
45rpm	**BLUE CHRISTMAS** (49)	Decca 46186	$15
45rpm	**LETTERS HAVE NO ARMS** (50)	Decca 46207	$12
45rpm	**I LOVE YOU BECAUSE** (50)	Decca 46213	$12
45rpm	**DON'T STAY TOO LONG** (50)	Decca 46296	$12
45rpm	**TOO OLD TO CUT THE MUSTARD** (50) With Red Foley	Decca 46387	$10
78rpm	**A HEARTSICK SOLDIER ON HEARTBREAK RIDGE** (52)	Decca 46389	$20
78(P)	**A HEARTSICK SOLDIER ON HEARTBREAK RIDGE** (52)	Decca 46389	$25
	(Pink promo label)		
45rpm	**A HEARTSICK SOLDIER ON HEARTBREAK RIDGE** (52)	Decca 46389	$25
45(P0	**A HEARTSICK SOLDIER ON HEARTBREAK RIDGE** (52)	Decca 46389	$20
	(Pink promo label)		
45rpm	**MY MOTHER MUST HAVE BEEN A GIRL LIKE YOU** (52)	Decca 28067	$15
45rpm	**DEAR JUDGE** (53)	Decca 28550	$15
78rpm	**HANK, IT WILL NEVER BE THE SAME WITHOUT YOU** (53)	Decca 28630	$20
78(P)	**HANK, IT WILL NEVER BE THE SAME WITHOUT YOU** (53)	Decca 28630	$25
	(Pink promo label)		
45rpm	**HANK, IT WILL NEVER BE THE SAME WITHOUT YOU** (53)	Decca 28630	$25
	(Written by Justin and Ernest, royalties from this record were contributed by Ernest Tubb to the Hank Williams Jr. Trust fund)		
45(P)	**HANK, IT WILL NEVER BE THE SAME WITHOUT YOU** (53)	Decca 28630	$20
	(Pink promo label)		
45rpm	**NO HELP WANTED #2** (53) With Red Foley	Decca 28634	$18
45(P)	**NO HELP WANTED #2** (53)	Decca 28634	$10
	(Pink promo label)		
78rpm	**WHEN JIMMIE RODGERS SAID GOOD-BYE** (53)	Decca 28696	$20
78(P)	**WHEN JIMMIE RODGERS SAID GOOD-BYE** (53)	Decca 28696	$25
	(Pink promo label)		
45rpm	**WHEN JIMMIE RODGERS SAID GOOD-BYE** (53)	Decca 28696	$25
45(P)	**WHEN JIMMIE RODGERS SAID GOOD-BYE** (53)	Decca 28696	$20
	(Pink promo label)		
45rpm	**JEALOUS LOVING HEART** (54)	Decca 29020	$12
45(P)	**JEALOUS LOVING HEART** (54)	Decca 29020	$10
	(Pink promo label)		
45rpm	**YOUR MOTHER, YOUR FRIEND, YOUR LOVER** (54)	Decca 29103	$10
45rpm	**DOUBLE-DATIN'** (54) With Red Foley	Decca 29195	$10
45rpm	**TWO GLASSES, JOE** (54)	Decca 29220	$10
45rpm	**I MET A FRIEND** (55)	Decca 29624	$10
45rpm	**THE YELLOW ROSE OF TEXAS** (55)	Decca 29633	$10
45rpm	**THIRTY DAYS** (55)	Decca 29731	$12
45(P)	**THIRTY DAYS** (55)	Decca 29731	$10
	(Pink promo label)		
45rpm	**SO DOGGONE LONESOME** (55)	Decca 29836	$10
5-33s	**ERNEST TUBB'S GOLDEN FAVORITES** (61)	Decca 74118	$8 each
	(Five stereo jukebox 33rpm singles)		

-EPs-

EP	**JIMMIE RODGERS SONGS SUNG BY ERNEST TUBB** (51)	Decca 588	$50
EP	**ERNEST TUBB SINGS** (53)	Decca 2026	$40
EP	**SING A SONG OF CHRISTMAS** (53)	Decca 2089	$40
EP	**ERNEST TUBB FAVORITES VOL 1** (56)	Decca 2356	$20
EP	**ERNEST TUBB FAVORITES VOL 2** (56)	Decca 2357	$20
EP	**SING JIMMIE RODGERS FAVORITES** (57)	Decca 2422	$20
	(Ernest and Justin Tubb)		
EP	**THE DADDY OF 'EM ALL** (57)	Decca 2521	$20
EP	**ERNEST TUBB ENCORES** (57)	Decca 2522	$20
EP	**MY HILLBILLY BABY** (57)	Decca 2523	$20
EP	**ERNEST TUBB SINGS THE HITS** (58)	Decca 2563	$20
EP	**ERNEST TUBB** (59)	Decca 2626	$20
EP	**ERNEST TUBB & THE WILBURN BROTHERS** (59)	Decca 2627	$20
EP	**THE IMPORTANCE OF BEING ERNEST** (59)	Decca 2643	$20

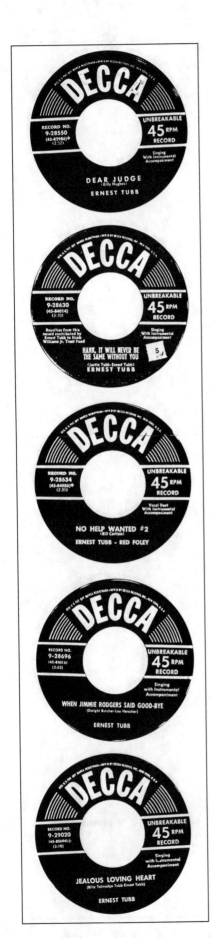

EP	THE ERNEST TUBB STORY (59) Mono	Decca 2655	$20
EP	THE ERNEST TUBB STORY (59) Stereo	Decca 2655	$20
EP	THE ERNEST TUBB RECORD SHOP (60)	Decca 2680	$18
EP	ERNEST TUBB (61)	Decca 2691	$18
EP	ERNEST TUBB (62)	Decca 2706	$18
EP	ERNEST TUBB (62)	Decca 2718	$18
EP	SHOW HER LOTS OF GOLD (62)	Decca 2728	$15
EP	ERNEST TUBB (63)	Decca 2739	$15
EP	ERNEST TUBB (64)	Decca 2769	$15
EP	THANKS A LOT (64)	Decca 2774	$15
EP(JB)	MY PICK OF THE HITS (65) Jukebox LLP	Decca 34329	$20
	(Jukebox LLP, price includes hard cover)		
EP	BE BETTER TO YOUR BABY (65)	Decca 2787	$15
EP	PASS THE BOOZE (65)	Decca 2797	$15
	-albums-		
10"LP	ERNEST TUBB FAVORITES (51)	Decca 5301	$125
10"LP	JIMMIE RODGERS SONGS SUNG BY ERNEST TUBB (51)	Decca 5336	$100
10"LP	OLD RUGGED CROSS (51)	Decca 5334	$100
10"LP	SING A SONG OF CHRISTMAS (52)	Decca 5497	$100
LP	ERNEST TUBB FAVORITES (56)	Decca 8291	$50
LP(P)	ERNEST TUBB FAVORITES (56)	Decca 8291	$75
	(Pink promo label)		
LP	THE DADDY OF 'EM ALL (56)	Decca 8553	$50
LP(P)	THE DADDY OF 'EM ALL (56)	Decca 2521	$75
	(Pink promo label)		
2LP	THE ERNEST TUBB STORY (58)	Decca 159	$75
	(Price includes booklet)		
2LP(P)	THE ERNEST TUBB STORY (58)	Decca 159	$100
	(Decca promo labels)		
LP	THE IMPORTANCE OF BEING ERNEST (59) Mono	Decca 8834	$40
LP	THE IMPORTANCE OF BEING ERNEST (59) Stereo	Decca 78834	$50
LP(P)	THE IMPORTANCE OF BEING ERNEST (59)	Decca 8834	$50
	(Decca promo label)		
LP	ERNEST TUBB RECORD SHOP (60) Mono	Decca 4042	$30
LP	ERNEST TUBB RECORD SHOP (60) Stereo	Decca 74042	$30
LP(P)	ERNEST TUBB RECORD SHOP (60)	Decca 4042	$50
	(Decca promo label)		
LP	MIDNIGHT JAMBOREE (60) Mono	Decca 4045	$40
	(Includes Kitty Wells, Patsy Cline, Wilburn Brothers, and others)		
LP	MIDNIGHT JAMBOREE (60) Stereo	Decca 74045	$40
LP(P)	MIDNIGHT JAMBOREE (60)	Decca 4045	$50
	(Pink promo label)		
LP	ERNEST TUBB & HIS TEXAS TROUBADORS (60)	Vocalion 3684	$20
LP(P)	ERNEST TUBB & HIS TEXAS TROUBADORS (60)	Vocalion 3684	$25
	(White promo label)		
LP	ALL TIME HITS (61) Mono	Decca 4046	$25
LP	ALL TIME HITS (61) Stereo	Decca 74046	$30
LP(P)	ALL TIME HITS (61)	Decca 4046	$40
	(Pink promo label)		
LP	ERNEST TUBB'S GOLDEN FAVORITES (61) Mono	Decca 4118	$25
LP	ERNEST TUBB'S GOLDEN FAVORITES (61) Stereo	Decca 74118	$30
LP(P)	ERNEST TUBB'S GOLDEN FAVORITES (61)	Decca 4118	$40
	(Pink promo label)		
LP	ON TOUR (62) Mono	Decca 4321	$20
LP	ON TOUR (62) Stereo	Decca 74321	$25
LP(P)	ON TOUR (62)	Decca 4321	$30
	(Pink promo label)		
LP	JUST CALL ME LONESOME (63) Mono	Decca 4385	$20
LP	JUST CALL ME LONESOME (63) Stereo	Decca 74385	$25
LP(P)	JUST CALL ME LONESOME (63)	Decca 4385	$30
	(Pink promo label)		
LP	THE FAMILY BIBLE (63) Mono	Decca 4397	$18
LP	THE FAMILY BIBLE (63) Stereo	Decca 74397	$20
LP(P)	THE FAMILY BIBLE (63)	Decca 4397	$25
	(Pink promo label)		
LP	THE TEXAS TROUBADORS (64) Mono	Decca 4459	$18
LP	THE TEXAS TROUBADORS (64) Stereo	Decca 74459	$20
LP(P)	THE TEXAS TROUBADORS (64)	Decca 4459	$25
	(Pink promo label)		
LP	THANKS A LOT (64) Mono	Decca 4514	$18
LP	THANKS A LOT (64) Stereo	Decca 74514	$20
LP(P)	THANKS A LOT (64)	Decca 4514	$25
	(Pink promo label)		
LP	BLUE CHRISTMAS (64) Mono	Decca 4518	$20
LP	BLUE CHRISTMAS (64) Stereo	Decca 74518	$25
LP(P)	BLUE CHRISTMAS (64)	Decca 4518	$30
	(White promo label)		

2LP	**THE ERNEST TUBB STORY** (64) Mono	Decca 159	$25
2LP	**THE ERNEST TUBB STORY** (64) Stereo	Decca 7159	$30
2LP(P)	**THE ERNEST TUBB STORY** (64)	Decca 159	$40
	(White promo labels)		
LP	**ERNEST TUBB & LORETTA LYNN** (65) Mono	Decca 4639	$25
LP	**ERNEST TUBB & LORETTA LYNN** (65) Stereo	Decca 74639	$30
LP(P)	**ERNEST TUBB & LORETTA LYNN** (65)	Decca 4639	$30
	(White promo label)		
LP	**MY PICK OF THE HITS** (65) Mono	Decca 4640	$15
LP	**MY PICK OF THE HITS** (65) Stereo	Decca 74640	$20
LP(P)	**MY PICK OF THE HITS** (65)	Decca 4640	$25
	(White promo label)		
LP	**COUNTRY DANCE TIME** (65) Mono	Decca 4644	$15
	(The Texas Troubadors)		
LP	**COUNTRY DANCE TIME** (65) Stereo	Decca 74644	$20
LP(P)	**COUNTRY DANCE TIME** (65)	Decca 4644	$25
	(White promo label)		
LP	**HITTIN' THE ROAD** (65) Mono	Decca 4681	$15
LP	**HITTIN' THE ROAD** (65) Stereo	Decca 74681	$20
LP(P)	**HITTIN' THE ROAD** (65)	Decca 4681	$25
	(White promo label)		
LP	**ERNEST TUBB'S FABULOUS TEXAS TROUBADORS** (66) Mono	Decca 4745	$15
LP	**ERNEST TUBB'S FABULOUS TEXAS TROUBADORS** (66) Stereo	Decca 74745	$20
LP(P)	**ERNEST TUBB'S FABULOUS TEXAS TROUBADORS** (66)	Decca 4745	$25
	(White promo label)		
LP	**BY REQUEST** (66) Mono	Decca 4746	$15
LP	**BY REQUEST** (66) Stereo	Decca 74746	$20
LP(P)	**BY REQUEST** (66)	Decca 4746	$25
	(White promo label)		
LP	**COUNTRY HITS, OLD & NEW** (67) Mono	Decca 4772	$15
LP	**COUNTRY HITS, OLD & NEW** (67) Stereo	Decca 74772	$20
LP(P)	**COUNTRY HITS, OLD & NEW** (67)	Decca 4772	$25
	(White promo label)		
LP	**ANOTHER STORY** (67) Mono	Decca 4867	$12
LP	**ANOTHER STORY** (67) Stereo	Decca 74867	$15
LP(P)	**ANOTHER STORY** (67)	Decca 4867	$18
	(White promo label)		
LP	**STAND BY ME** (67)	Vocalion 3765	$15
LP(P)	**STAND BY ME** (67)	Vocalion 3765	$18
	(White promo label)		
LP	**ERNEST TUBB & LORETTA LYNN SINGIN' AGAIN** (67)	Decca 4872	$15
LP(P)	**ERNEST TUBB & LORETTA LYNN SINGIN' AGAIN** (67)	Decca 4872	$18
	(White promo label)		
LP	**ERNEST TUBB SINGS HANK WILLIAMS** (68)	Decca 74957	$15
LP(P)	**ERNEST TUBB SINGS HANK WILLIAMS** (68)	Decca 74957	$20
	(White promo label)		
LP	**ERNEST TUBB'S GREATEST HITS** (68)	Decca 75006	$10
LP(P)	**ERNEST TUBB'S GREATEST HITS** (68)	Decca 75006	$15
	(White promo label)		
LP	**THE TERRIFIC TEXAS TROUBADORS** (68)	Decca 75017	$10
LP(P)	**THE TERRIFIC TEXAS TROUBADORS** (68)	Decca 75017	$12
	(White promo label)		
LP	**COUNTRY HIT TIME** (68)	Decca 75072	$12
LP(P)	**COUNTRY HIT TIME** (68)	Decca 75072	$15
	(White promo label)		
LP	**LET'S TURN BACK THE YEARS** (69)	Decca 75114	$12
LP(P)	**LET'S TURN BACK THE YEARS** (69)	Decca 75114	$15
	(White promo label)		
LP	**IF WE PUT OUR HEADS TOGETHER** (69)	Decca 75115	$15
	(With Loretta Lynn)		
LP(P)	**IF WE PUT OUR HEADS TOGETHER** (69)	Decca 75115	$18
	(White promo label)		
LP	**SATURDAY SATAN, SUNDAY SAINT** (69)	Decca 75122	$12
LP(P)	**SATURDAY SATAN, SUNDAY SAINT** (69)	Decca 75122	$15
	(White promo label)		
LP	**GREAT COUNTRY** (69)	Vocalion 3877	$12
LP(P)	**GREAT COUNTRY** (69)	Vocalion 3877	$15
	(White promo label)		
LP	**A GOOD YEAR FOR THE WINE** (70)	Decca 75222	$12
LP(P)	**A GOOD YEAR FOR THE WINE** (70)	Decca 75222	$15
	(White promo label)		
LP	**ERNEST TUBB'S GREATEST HITS VOL 2** (70)	Decca 75252	$10
LP(P)	**ERNEST TUBB'S GREATEST HITS VOL 2** (70)	Decca 75252	$12
	(White promo label)		
LP	**ONE SWEET HELLO** (71)	Decca 75301	$12
LP(P)	**ONE SWEET HELLO** (71)	Decca 75301	$15
	(White promo label)		

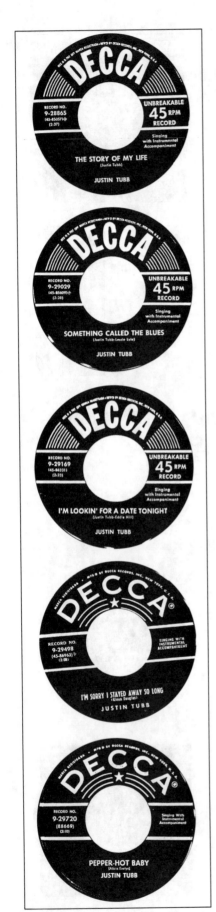

LP	SAY SOMETHING NICE TO SARAH (72)	Decca 75345	$12
LP(P)	SAY SOMETHING NICE TO SARAH (72)	Decca 75345	$15
	(White promo label)		
LP	BABY, IT'S SO HARD TO BE GOOD (72)	Decca 75388	$10
LP(P)	BABY, IT'S SO HARD TO BE GOOD (72)	Decca 75388	$12
	(White promo label)		
2LP	THE LEGEND AND THE LEGACY (79)	First Generation 0002	$50
	(First pressing)		
2LP	THE LEGEND AND THE LEGACY (79)	TV 1033	$25
	(TV mail-order item)		
LP	THE LEGEND AND THE LEGACY (79)	Cachet 3001	$10

-radio shows-

16"(RS)	LEATHERNECK JAMBOREE (60s)	Show 15	$40-75
	(Music and interviews)		
16"(RS)	NAVY HOEDOWN (60s)	U.S. Navy	$40-75
	(Music and interviews)		
16"(RS)	U.S. ARMY BAND (60s)	U.S. Army	$40-75
	(Music and interviews)		
LP(RS)	GRAND OL' OPRY (60s)	WSM Radio	$40-75
	(Music and interviews)		
LP(RS)	HOOTENAVY (60s)	U.S. Navy	$40-75
	(Music and interviews)		

JUSTIN TUBB (CW)
His dad is Ernest Tubb
Decca 78s $5-8 each
Other Decca 45s $4-8 each
Dot 45s $3 each
First Generation and Hilltop LPs $5 each

-singles-

45rpm	THE STORY OF MY LIFE (53)	Decca 28865	$15
45(P)	THE STORY OF MY LIFE (53)	Decca 28865	$10
	(Pink promo label)		
45rpm	SOMETHING CALLED THE BLUES (54)	Decca 29029	$15
45(P)	SOMETHING CALLED THE BLUES (54)	Decca 29029	$10
	(Pink promo label)		
45rpm	I'M LOOKING FOR A DATE TONIGHT (54)	Decca 29169	$12
45(P)	I'M LOOKING FOR A DATE TONIGHT (54)	Decca 29169	$10
	(Pink promo label)		
45rpm	SURE FIRE KISSES (54) With Goldie Hill	Decca 29349	$12
45(P)	SURE FIRE KISSES (54)	Decca 29349	$10
	(Pink promo label)		
45rpm	I'M SORRY I STAYED AWAY SO LONG (54)	Decca 29498	$12
45(P)	I'M SORRY I STAYED AWAY SO LONG (54)	Decca 29498	$10
	(Pink promo label)		
45rpm	WITHIN YOUR ARMS (55)	Decca 29590	$10
45rpm	PEPPER HOT BABY (55)	Decca 29720	$12
45(P)	PEPPER HOT BABY (55)	Decca 29720	$10
	(Pink promo label)		
45rpm	LUCKY LUCKY SOMEONE ELSE (56)	Decca 29895	$10
45rpm	I'M JUST FOOL ENOUGH (56)	Decca 30062	$10
45rpm	I'M A BIG BOY NOW (56)	Decca 30229	$10
45rpm	THE PARTY IS OVER (57)	Decca 30408	$10
45rpm	TAKE A LETTER, MISS GRAY (58)	Groove 0017	$10
45rpm	TAKE A LETTER, MISS GRAY (58)	Groove 0017	$30
	(Price includes picture sleeve)		
45(P)	TAKE A LETTER, MISS GRAY (58)	Groove 0017	$12
	(White promo label)		
45rpm	LITTLE MISS LONESOME (58)	Groove 0019	$10
45rpm	PREMATURELY BLUE (58)	Groove 0047	$10
45rpm	BIG FOOL OF THE YEAR (59)	Challenge 59081	$12
45(P)	BIG FOOL OF THE YEAR (59)	Challenge 59081	$10
	(White promo label)		

-EPs-

EP	ERNEST & JUSTIN TUBB (57)	Decca 2422	$20
	(Jimmie Rodgers songs)		
EP	COUNTRY BOY IN LOVE (57)	Decca 2559	$20

-albums-

LP	COUNTRY BOY IN LOVE (57)	Decca 8644	$50
LP(P)	COUNTRY BOY IN LOVE (57)	Decca 2559	$40
	(Pink promo label)		
LP	JUSTIN TUBB STAR OF THE GRAND OLE OPRY (62)	Starday 160	$30
LP	THE MODERN COUNTRY SOUND OF JUSTIN TUBB (62)	Starday 198	$30
LP	THE BEST OF JUSTIN TUBB (65)	Starday 334	$25
LP	WHERE YOU'RE CONCERNED (65) Mono	RCA Victor 3339	$15
LP	WHERE YOU'RE CONCERNED (65) Stereo	RCA Victor 3339	$20

LP	**JUSTIN TUBB** (65)	Vocalion 3741	$15
LP(P)	**JUSTIN TUBB** (65)	Vocalion 3741	$18
	(White promo label)		
LP	**TOGETHER AND ALONE** (66) Mono	RCA Victor 3591	$30
	(With Lorene Mann)		
LP	**TOGETHER AND ALONE** (66) Stereo	RCA Victor 3591	$40
LP	**THINGS I STILL REMEMBER VERY WELL** (69)	Dot 25922	$15

BILLY JOE TUCKER (RB)
-singles-

45rpm	**BOOGIE WOOGIE BILL** (58)	Maha 103	$50
45rpm	**BOOGIE WOOGIE BILL** (58)	Dot	$25

FAYE TUCKER (CW)
-albums-

LP	**BLUES FROM A BROKEN HEARTED GAL** (60s)	Somerset 28700	$12
	(Budget label)		
LP	**COUNTRY & WESTERN SOUL** (63) With Dolly Parton	Time 2108	$40

TANYA TUCKER (C)
Columbia 45s $3-4 each
MCA 45s $2-3 each including duets
MCA picture sleeves $4 each
Arista 45s $2 each
Capitol 45s $1-2 each including duets
Other Columbia LPs $6-8 each
Arista LPs $6 each
MCA and Capitol LPs $4 each

-singles-

45rpm	**D. O. A.** (77) Misty	Sun 1136	$10
	(Mystery Elvis tribute)		

-albums-

LP	**DELTA DAWN** (72)	Columbia 31742	$15
LP(P)	**DELTA DAWN** (72)	Columbia 31742	$18
	(White promo label)		

-radio shows-

LP(RS)	**LIVE AT GILLEY'S** (May 88)	Westwood One	$15-25
	(Live concert)		
CD(RS)	**THE TANYA TUCKER STORY** (94)	R. H. Entertainment	$15-25
	(Music and interviews)		
Cass(RS)	**AUSTIN ENCORE** (92)	Mainstreet	$30-45
	(Live concert, on cassette, with Sawyer Brown)		

RICHARD TURLEY (RB)
-singles-

45rpm	**MAKIN' LOVE WITH MY BABY** (57)	Fraternity 845	$20
45(P)	**MAKIN' LOVE WITH MY BABY** (57)	Fraternity 845	$15
	(White promo label)		
45rpm	**I WANNA DANCE** (60)	Dot 16231	$10

HANK TURNER (CW)
-albums-

LP	**GOLDEN COUNTRY & WESTERN HITS** (63)	Columbia 8758	$18
LP(P)	**GOLDEN COUNTRY & WESTERN HITS** (63)	Columbia 8758	$20
	(White promo label)		
LP	**COUNTRY & WESTERN HITS** (68)	Harmony 11250	$12
LP(P)	**COUNTRY & WESTERN HITS** (68)	Harmony 11250	$15
	(White promo label)		

HOUSTON TURNER (CW)
-singles-

45rpm	**UNCLE JOHN'S BONGOS** (59)	Do-Ra-Me 1416	$15

JACK TURNER (CW)
-singles-

78rpm	**HOUND DOG** (54)	RCA Victor 5267	$15
78(P)	**HOUND DOG** (54)	RCA Victor 5267	$18
	(White promo label)		
45rpm	**HOUND DOG** (54)	RCA Victor 5267	$25
78rpm	**MODEL T BABY** (54)	RCA Victor 5997	$15
78(P)	**MODEL T BABY** (54)	RCA Victor 5997	$18
	(White promo label)		
45rpm	**MODEL T BABY** (55)	RCA Victor 5997	$15
45(P)	**MODEL T BABY** (54)	RCA Victor 5997	$12
	(White promo label)		
45rpm	**EVERYBODY'S ROCKIN' BUT ME** (57)	Hickory 1050	$20

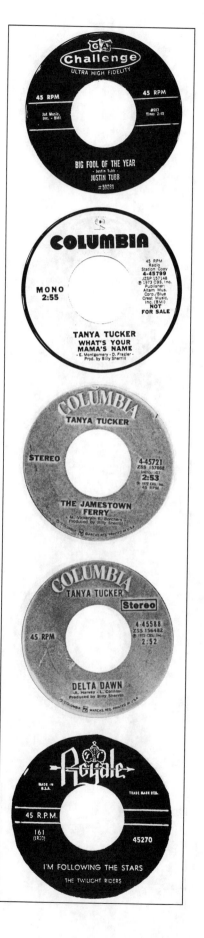

45(P)	**EVERYBODY'S ROCKIN' BUT ME** (57) (White promo label)	Hickory 1050		$12

ZEB TURNER (CW)
-albums-

LP	**COUNTRY MUSIC IN THE TURNER STYLE** (59)	Audio Lab 1537		$18

THE TWILIGHT RIDERS (CW)
-singles-

45rpm	**I'M FOLLOWING THE STARS** (54) Red vinyl	Royale 161		$15

THE TWINS (TWIN-TONES) (RB)
Jim and John

-singles-

45rpm	**THE FLIP SKIP** (58) Twin-Tones	RCA Victor 7148		$10
45rpm	**JO-ANN'S SISTER** (58) Twins	RCA Victor 7235		$12
45rpm	**JO-ANN'S SISTER** (58) (Price includes picture sleeve)	RCA Victor 7235		$30

CONWAY TWITTY (RB/CW)
Harold Jenkins
Later MGM 45s $2-3 each
Elektra 45s $1-2 each
Elektra picture sleeves $3 each
Other Warner 45s $1-2 each
Warner picture sleeves $4 each
Other MCA 45s $1 each
Other MCA color vinyl 45s $8 each
Other MCA LPs $3-6 each
   (Including Loretta Lynn duets)
Warner and Elektra LPs $2-5 each
Candlelite 2LP sets $10 each
Demand, Trolley Car, Accord, Coral, Pickwick, and Allegiance LPs $2-4 each

-singles-

45rpm	**I NEED YOUR LOVIN'** (57) Maroon label	Mercury 71086		$35
45rpm	**I NEED YOUR LOVIN'** (57) Black label	Mercury 71086		$30
45(P)	**I NEED YOUR LOVIN'** (57) (White promo label)	Mercury 71086		$50
45rpm	**SHAKE IT UP** (58)	Mercury 71148		$30
45(P)	**SHAKE IT UP** (58) (White promo label)	Mercury 71148		$40
45rpm	**DOUBLE TALK BABY** (58)	Mercury 71384		$40
45(P)	**DOUBLE TALK BABY** (58) (White promo label)	Mercury 71384		$50
45rpm	**IT'S ONLY MAKE BELIEVE** (58)	MGM 12677		$20
45(S)	**IT'S ONLY MAKE BELIEVE** (58) Stereo single	MGM 50107		$100
45(P)	**IT'S ONLY MAKE BELIEVE** (58) (Yellow promo label)	MGM 12677		$35
45rpm	**THE STORY OF MY LOVE** (59)	MGM 12748		$15
45(P)	**THE STORY OF MY LOVE** (59) (Yellow promo label)	MGM 12748		$25
45rpm	**HEY LITTLE LUCY** (59)	MGM 12748		$15
45(P)	**HEY LITTLE LUCY** (59) (Yellow promo label)	MGM 12785		$20
45rpm	**MONA LISA** (59)	MGM 12804		$15
45(P)	**MONA LISA** (59) (Yellow promo label)	MGM 12804		$18
45rpm	**DANNY BOY** (59) Yellow label	MGM 12826		$15
45(S)	**DANNY BOY** (59) Stereo single	MGM 50130		$100
45(P)	**DANNY BOY** (59) Yellow promo label	MGM 12826		$15
45rpm	**LONELY BLUE BOY** (60)	MGM 12857		$15
45(P)	**LONELY BLUE BOY** (60) (Yellow promo label)	MGM 12857		$12
45rpm	**WHAT AM I LIVING FOR** (60)	MGM 12886		$12
45rpm	**WHAT AM I LIVING FOR** (60) (Price includes picture sleeve)	MGM 12886		$50
45(P)	**WHAT AM I LIVING FOR** (60) (Yellow promo label)	MGM 12886		$10
45rpm	**IS A BLUEBIRD BLUE** (60)	MGM 12911		$12
45rpm	**IS A BLUEBIRD BLUE** (60) (Price includes picture sleeve)	MGM 12911		$50
45(P)	**IS A BLUEBIRD BLUE** (60)	MGM 12911		$10
45rpm	**TELL ME ONE MORE TIME** (60)	MGM 12918		$12
45(P)	**TELL ME ONE MORE TIME** (60) (Yellow promo label)	MGM 12918		$10
5-33s	**CONWAY TWITTY'S GREATEST HITS** (60) Five singles (Five stereo 33rpm jukebox singles, $200 for set)	MGM SB-2		$40 each

5-33s	CONWAY TWITTY'S GREATEST HITS (60) Five singles	MGM SB-5	$40 each
	(Five stereo 33rpm jukebox singles, $200 for set)		
45rpm	WHOLE LOT OF SHAKIN' GOING ON (60)	MGM 12962	$12
45(P)	WHOLE LOT OF SHAKIN' GOING ON (60)	MGM 12962	$10
	(Yellow promo label)		
45rpm	C'EST SI BON (61)	MGM 12969	$12
45rpm	C'EST SI BON (61)	MGM 12969	$50
	(Price includes picture sleeve)		
45(P)	C'EST SI BON (61)	MGM 12969	$10
	(Yellow promo label)		
45rpm	THE NEXT KISS (61)	MGM 12998	$10
45rpm	THE NEXT KISS (61)	MGM 12998	$50
	(Price includes picture sleeve)		
45(P)	THE NEXT KISS (61)	MGM 12998	$10
	(Yellow promo label)		
45rpm	A MILLION TEARDROPS (61)	MGM 13011	$12
45(P)	A MILLION TEARDROPS (61)	MGM 13011	$10
	(Yellow promo label)		
45rpm	IT'S DRIVING ME WILD (61)	MGM 13034	$12
45rpm	IT'S DRIVING ME WILD (61)	MGM 13034	$40
	(Price includes picture sleeve)		
45(P)	IT'S DRIVING ME WILD (61)	MGM 13034	$10
	(Yellow promo label)		
45rpm	PORTRAIT OF A FOOL (62)	MGM 13050	$10
45rpm	COMFY 'N COZY (62)	MGM 13072	$10
45rpm	THERE'S SOMETHING ON YOUR MIND (62)	MGM 13089	$10
45rpm	THE PICKUP (62)	MGM 13112	$10
45rpm	GOT MY MOJO WORKING (62)	MGM 13149	$10
45rpm	GO ON AND CRY (63)	ABC Paramount 10507	$20
45(P)	GO ON AND CRY (63)	ABC Paramount 10507	$15
	(White promo label)		
45rpm	SUCH A NIGHT (64)	ABC Paramount 10550	$25
45(P)	SUCH A NIGHT (64)	ABC Paramount 10550	$18
	(White promo label)		
45(PD)	SEASON'S GREETINGS (72) Promo-only picture disc	(Decca) 7211281	$75
	(With Loretta Lynn, promo seven-inch picture disc)		
45(P)	HELLO DARLIN' (75)	MCA 60180	$15
	(White promo label, Russian/English version)		
45(P)	JULIA (87)	MCA 53034	$10
	(White promo label, red vinyl)		
45(P)	I WANT TO KNOW YOU BEFORE WE MAKE LOVE (87)	MCA 53134	$10
	(White promo label, blue vinyl)		

-EPs-

EP	IT'S ONLY MAKE BELIEVE (58) Yellow label	MGM 1623	$300
EP	CONWAY TWITTY SINGS VOL 1 (59)	MGM 1640	$250
EP	CONWAY TWITTY SINGS VOL 2 (59) Black label	MGM 1641	$250
EP	CONWAY TWITTY SINGS VOL 3 (59)	MGM 1642	$250
EP	SATURDAY NIGHT WITH CONWAY TWITTY VOL 1 (59)	MGM 1678	$250
EP	SATURDAY NIGHT WITH CONWAY TWITTY VOL 2 (59)	MGM 1679	$250
EP	SATURDAY NIGHT WITH CONWAY TWITTY VOL 3 (59)	MGM 1680	$250
EP	LONELY BLUE BOY (60)	MGM 1701	$200
EP(JB)	CONWAY TWITTY (66) Jukebox LLP	MGM 5	$40
	(Issued with hard cover)		
EP(JB)	LOOK INTO MY TEARDROPS (66) Jukebox LLP	Decca 34437	$25
	(Issued with a hard cover)		
EP(JB)	TO SEE MY ANGEL CRY (70) Jukebox LLP	Decca 34732	$25
	(Issued with a hard cover)		
EP(JB)	FIFTEEN YEARS AGO (70) Jukebox LLP	Decca LLP #130	$20
	(Issued with a soft cover)		

-albums-

LP	CONWAY TWITTY SINGS (59) Yellow label, mono	MGM 3744	$75
LP	CONWAY TWITTY SINGS (59) Black label, mono	MGM 3744	$40
LP	CONWAY TWITTY SINGS (59) Yellow label, stereo	MGM 3744	$125
LP	CONWAY TWITTY SINGS (59) Black label, stereo	MGM 3744	$50
LP(P)	CONWAY TWITTY SINGS (59)	MGM 3744	$150
	(Yellow promo label)		
LP	SATURDAY NIGHT WITH CONWAY TWITTY (59) Mono	MGM 3786	$75
LP	SATURDAY NIGHT WITH CONWAY TWITTY (59) Stereo	MGM 3786	$100
LP(P)	SATURDAY NIGHT WITH CONWAY TWITTY (59)	MGM 3786	$125
	(Yellow promo label)		
LP	LONELY BLUE BOY (60) Mono	MGM 3818	$75
LP	LONELY BLUE BOY (60) Stereo	MGM 3818	$100
LP(P)	LONELY BLUE BOY (60)	MGM 3818	$125
	(Yellow promo label)		
LP	CONWAY TWITTY'S GREATEST HITS (60) Mono	MGM 3849	$40
LP	CONWAY TWITTY'S GREATEST HITS (60) Stereo	MGM 3849	$50
	(Prices are for first pressing black label)		

LP(P)	CONWAY TWITTY'S GREATEST HITS (61)	MGM 3849	$75
	(Yellow promo label)		
LP	THE ROCK & ROLL STORY (61) Mono	MGM 3907	$50
LP	THE ROCK & ROLL STORY (61) Stereo	MGM 3907	$75
LP(P)	THE ROCK & ROLL STORY (61)	MGM 3907	$75
	(Yellow promo label)		
LP	THE CONWAY TWITTY TOUCH (61) Mono	MGM 3943	$50
LP	THE CONWAY TWITTY TOUCH (61) Stereo	MGM 3943	$75
LP(P)	THE CONWAY TWITTY TOUCH (61)	MGM 3943	$75
	(Yellow promo label)		
LP	PORTRAIT OF A FOOL AND OTHERS (62) Mono	MGM 4019	$40
LP	PORTRAIT OF A FOOL AND OTHERS (62) Stereo	MGM 4019	$50
LP(P)	PORTRAIT OF A FOOL AND OTHERS (62)	MGM 4019	$75
	(Yellow promo label)		
LP	R & B '63 (63) Mono	MGM 4089	$40
LP	R & B '63 (63) Stereo	MGM 4089	$50
LP(P)	R & B '63 (63)	MGM 4089	$60
	(Yellow promo label)		
LP	HIT THE ROAD (64) Mono	MGM 4217	$18
LP	HIT THE ROAD (64) Stereo	MGM 4217	$20
LP(P)	HIT THE ROAD (64)	MGM 4217	$25
	(Yellow promo label)		
LP	IT'S ONLY MAKE BELIEVE (65) Mono	Metro 512	$15
LP	IT'S ONLY MAKE BELIEVE (65) Stereo	Metro 512	$20
LP(P)	IT'S ONLY MAKE BELIEVE (65)	Metro 512	$25
	(Yellow promo label)		
LP	CONWAY TWITTY SINGS (66) Mono	Decca 4724	$15
LP	CONWAY TWITTY SINGS (66) Stereo	Decca 74724	$20
LP(P)	CONWAY TWITTY SINGS (66)	Decca 4724	$25
	(White promo label)		
LP	LOOK INTO MY TEARDROPS (66) Mono	Decca 4828	$15
LP	LOOK INTO MY TEARDROPS (66) Stereo	Decca 74828	$18
LP(P)	LOOK INTO MY TEARDROPS (66)	Decca 4828	$20
	(White promo label)		
LP	CONWAY TWITTY COUNTRY (67) Mono	Decca 4913	$12
LP	CONWAY TWITTY COUNTRY (67) Stereo	Decca 74913	$15
LP(P)	CONWAY TWITTY COUNTRY (67)	Decca 4913	$18
	(White promo label)		
LP	HERE'S CONWAY TWITTY & HIS LONELY BLUE BOYS (68)	Decca 74990	$10
LP	NEXT IN LINE (68)	Decca 75062	$10
LP	DARLING, YOU KNOW I WOULDN'T LIE (69)	Decca 75105	$10
LP	I LOVE YOU MORE TODAY (69)	Decca 75131	$10
LP	TO SEE MY ANGEL CRY (70)	Decca 75172	$10
LP	HELLO DARLIN' (70)	Decca 75209	$10
LP	FIFTEEN YEARS AGO (71)	Decca 75248	$10
LP	CONWAY TWITTY (71)	MGM 110	$20
LP(P)	CONWAY TWITTY (71)	MGM 110	$25
	(White promo label)		
LP	WE ONLY MAKE BELIEVE (71) With Loretta Lynn	Decca 75251	$10
LP	CONWAY TWITTY'S GREATEST HITS VOL 1 (71)	Decca 75252	$10
LP	HOW MUCH MORE CAN SHE STAND (71)	Decca 75276	$10
LP	I WONDER WHAT SHE'LL THINK ABOUT ME LEAVING (71)	Decca 75292	$10
LP	CONWAY TWITTY HITS (71)	MGM 4799	$10
LP	LEAD ME ON (72)	Decca 75326	$10
LP	I CAN'T SEE ME WITHOUT YOU (72)	Decca 75335	$10
LP	CONWAY TWITTY'S GREATEST HITS (72)	Decca 75352	$10
LP	CONWAY TWITTY (72)	Decca 75361	$10
LP	CONWAY TWITTY SINGS THE BLUES (72)	MGM 4837	$10
2LP	TWENTY GREAT HITS (73)	MGM 4884	$12
2LP(P)	TWENTY GREAT HITS (73)	MGM 4884	$15
	(White promo labels)		
LP	STEAL AWAY (73)	MCA 376	$50
2LP	CONWAY & LORETTA SING THE GREAT COUNTRY HITS (76)	TVP 1010	$15

-radio shows-

2LP(RS)	COUNTRY COOKIN' (Sept 74) Various artists	Army Reserve	$25-40
	(Music and interviews)		
6LP(RS)	CONWAY TWITTY THEN & NOW (70s)	Opryland 12636	$100-150
	(Music and interviews)		

JOHNNY TYLER (RB)

-singles-

45rpm	DEVIL'S HOT ROD (55) Red vinyl	Ekko 1000	$150
45rpm	LIE TO ME, BABY (59) Red vinyl	Rural Rhythm 515	$100
45rpm	LIE TO ME, BABY (59) Black vinyl	Rural Rhythm 515	$25

T. TEXAS TYLER (CW)
David Myrick
Other King 78s $5-10 each
Decca and 4-Star 78s $4-8 each
Other King 45s $5-10 each
Other Decca and 4-Star 45s $3-6 each
Starday 45s $3 each
Gusto 45s $2 each

-singles-

78rpm	**FILIPINO BABY** (46)	4-Star 1008	$25
78rpm	**DECK OF CARDS** (48)	4-Star 1228	$25
78rpm	**DAD GAVE MY DOG AWAY** (48)	4-Star 1248	$10
78rpm	**MY BUCKET'S GOT A HOLE IN IT** (49)	4-Star 1383	$10
45rpm	**OKLAHOMA HILLS** (51)	4-Star 1008 (45)	$18
45rpm	**DECK OF CARDS** (51)	4-Star 1228	$25
45rpm	**TIRED OF IT ALL** (53)	4-Star 1649	$10
45rpm	**HE DONE HER WRONG** (54)	Decca 28544	$15
45rpm	**BUMMING AROUND** (54)	Decca 28579	$15
45rpm	**LET'S GET MARRIED** (54)	Decca 28760	$15
45rpm	**COURTIN' IN THE RAIN** (54)	4-Star 1660	$10
45rpm	**DECK OF CARDS** (55)	King 5249	$12
45(P)	**DECK OF CARDS** (55) (Black promo label)	King 5249	$25
45rpm	**THAT'S WHAT YOU MEAN TO ME** (56)	Decca 29598	$10

-albums-

LP	**DECK OF CARDS** (58)	Sound 607	$50
LP	**T. TEXAS TYLER** (59)	King 664	$75
LP	**THE GREAT TEXAN** (60)	King 689	$75
LP	**T. TEXAS TYLER** (61)	King 721	$50
LP	**SONGS ALONG THE WAY** (61)	King 734	$50
LP	**SALVATION** (62) Mono	Capitol 1662	$25
LP	**SALVATION** (62) Stereo	Capitol 1662	$35
LP(P)	**SALVATION** (62) (Blue promo label)	Capitol 1662	$40
LP	**T. TEXAS TYLER** (62)	Wrangler 1002	$35
LP	**TEN SONGS HE MADE FAMOUS** (62) (Budget label)	Design 602	$18
LP	**TEN SONGS HE MADE FAMOUS** (62) (Another budget label)	International Award 209	$15
LP	**HITS OF T. TEXAS TYLER** (65) Mono	Capitol 2344	$20
LP	**HITS OF T. TEXAS TYLER** (65) Stereo	Capitol 2344	$25
LP	**THE MAN WITH A MILLION FRIENDS** (66)	Starday 379	$25
LP	**GREAT HITS** (67)	Hilltop 6402	$15

-radio shows-

16"(RS)	**LEATHERNECK JAMBOREE** Fifteen-minute show (Music and interviews)	Leatherneck Jamboree 16	$40

U

UNCLE JOSH & COUSIN JAKE (CW)
-albums-

LP	**JUST JOSHING** (58)	Cotton Town 101	$100

UNIQUES (C)
Featuring Joe Stampley
Paula 45s $4-6 each

V

BLACKY VALE (RB)
-singles-

45rpm	**IF I HAD ME A WOMAN** (58)	Hurricane 100	$65

RITCHIE VALENS (R)
Also recorded as Arvee Allens
Del-Fi blue label 45s $10-15 each

-singles-

45rpm	**COME ON, LET'S GO** (58) Green label	Del-Fi 4106	$50
45(P)	**COME ON, LET'S GO** (58)	Del-Fi 4106	$75
	(White promo label)		
45rpm	**DONNA** (58) Green label first pressing	Del-Fi 4110	$30
45rpm	**DONNA** (58) Green/black label w/circles	Del-Fi 4110	$25
45(P)	**DONNA** (58)	Del-Fi 4110	$50
	(White promo label)		
45rpm	**FAST FREIGHT** (59) Ritchie Valens	Del-Fi 4111	$35
45rpm	**FAST FREIGHT** (59) Arvee Allens	Del-Fi 4111	$40
45(P)	**FAST FREIGHT** (59) Arvee Allens	Del-Fi 4111	$50
	(White promo label)		
45rpm	**THAT'S MY LITTLE SUSIE** (59)	Del-Fi 4114	$25
45rpm	**THAT'S MY LITTLE SUSIE** (59)	Del-Fi 4114	$100
	(Price includes picture sleeve)		
45(P)	**THAT'S MY LITTLE SUSIE** (59)	Del-Fi 4114	$50
	(White promo label)		
45rpm	**LITTLE GIRL** (59) Gold label	Del-Fi 4117	$25
45rpm	**LITTLE GIRL** (59)	Del-Fi 4117	$100
	(Price includes picture sleeve)		
45(P)	**LITTLE GIRL** (59)	Del-Fi 4117	$30
	(White promo label)		
45rpm	**BIG BABY BLUES** (60)	Del-Fi 4128	$20
45rpm	**BIG BABY BLUES** (60)	Del-Fi 4128	$75
	(Price includes picture sleeve)		
45(P)	**BIG BABY BLUES** (60)	Del-Fi 4128	$20
	(White promo label)		
45rpm	**CRY CRY CRY** (60)	Del-Fi 4133	$20
45(P)	**CRY CRY CRY** (60)	Del-Fi 4133	$25
	(White promo label)		
45rpm	**DONNA** (60s)	Kasey 7040	$10
45rpm	**DONNA** (60s)	Kasey 7040	$40
	(Price includes picture sleeve)		

-EPs-

EP	**RITCHIE VALENS** (59)	Del-Fi 1	$300
EP	**RITCHIE VALENS** (59)	Del-Fi 101	$300
	(Cardboard cover)		
EP	**RITCHIE VALENS** (59)	Del-Fi 101	$300
	(Paper cover)		
EP	**RITCHIE VALENS** (59)	Del-Fi 111	$250

-albums-

LP	**RITCHIE VALENS** (59)	Del-Fi 1201	$150
LP	**RITCHIE** (59)	Del-Fi 1206	$150
LP	**IN CONCERT AT PACOIMA** (60)	Del-Fi 1214	$200
LP	**HIS GREATEST HITS** (63)	Del-Fi 1225	$250
	(Black cover)		
LP	**HIS GREATEST HITS** (63)	Del-Fi 1225	$100
	(White cover)		
LP	**HIS GREATEST HITS VOL. 2** (65)	Del-Fi 1247	$100
LP	**THE ORIGINAL RITCHIE VALENS** (63) Mono	Guest Star 1469	$25
	(Budget label)		
LP	**THE ORIGINAL RITCHIE VALENS** (63) Stereo	Guest Star 1469	$15
LP	**THE ORIGINAL LA BAMBA** (63) Mono	Guest Star 1484	$25
LP	**THE ORIGINAL LA BAMBA** (63) Stereo	Guest Star 1484	$15
LP	**RITCHIE VALENS & JERRY KOLE** (63) Mono	Crown 5336	$25
	(Budget label)		
LP	**RITCHIE VALENS & JERRY KOLE** (63) Stereo	Crown 336	$15
LP	**RITCHIE VALENS** (70)	MGM 117	$30
LP(P)	**RITCHIE VALENS** (70) Yellow promo label	MGM 117	$40

BILLY VALENTINE (CW)
Other Capitol 78s and 45s $2-4 each

-singles-

78rpm	**YOUR LOVE HAS GOT ME REELIN' AND ROCKIN'** (55)	Capitol 3145	$10
45rpm	**YOUR LOVE HAS GOT ME REELIN' AND ROCKIN'** (55)	Capitol 3145	$25
45(P)	**YOUR LOVE HAS GOT ME REELIN' AND ROCKIN'** (55)	Capitol 3145	$18
	(Capitol promo label)		

LEROY VAN DYKE (CW)
Other Mercury 45s $5-10 each
Decca 45s $2-4 each
Kapp and MCA 45s $2 each
Plantation and Warner 45s $1-2 each
Warner, MGM, and Kapp LPs $10 each

-singles-

78rpm	**AUCTIONEER** (57)	Dot 15503	$25
45rpm	**AUCTIONEER** (57)	Dot 15503	$18
45rpm	**THE POCKET BOOK SONG** (57)	Dot 15561	$15
45rpm	**ONE HEART** (57)	Dot 15652	$15
45rpm	**LEATHER JACKET** (58)	Dot 15698	$50
45rpm	**WALK ON BY** (58)	Mercury 71834	$10
45(P)	**WALK ON BY** (61)	Mercury 71834	$12
	(White promo label)		

-albums-

LP	**WALK ON BY** (62)	Mercury 60682	$25
LP(P)	**WALK ON BY** (62)	Mercury 20682	$30
	(White promo label)		
LP	**MOVIN' VAN DYKE** (63)	Mercury 20716	$15
LP(P)	**MOVIN' VAN DYKE** (63)	Mercury 20716	$20
	(White promo label)		
LP	**LEROY VAN DYKE'S GREATEST HITS** (63)	Mercury 20802	$12
LP(P)	**LEROY VAN DYKE'S GREATEST HITS** (63)	Mercury 20802	$15
	(White promo label)		
LP	**SONGS FOR MOM & DAD** (64)	Mercury 20922	$12
LP(P)	**SONGS FOR MOM & DAD** (64)	Mercury 20922	$15
	(White promo label)		

-radio shows-

LP(RS)	**GRAND OL' OPRY** (60s)	WSM Radio 70	$20-40
	(Music and interviews)		
LP(RS)	**NAVY HOEDOWN** (60s)	U.S. Navy	$20-40
	(Music and interviews)		

DALE VAUGHAN (RB)

-singles-

45rpm	**HIGH STEPPIN** (58)	Von 480	$125

VEGA BROTHERS (C)
MCA 45s $1 each
MCA color vinyl 45s $5 each
MCA LPs $3 each

RAY VERNON (RB)

-singles-

45rpm	**I'M COUNTING ON YOU** (58)	Cameo 115	$15

RAY VICT (R & B)

-singles-

45rpm	**WE'RE GONNA BOP STOP ROCK** (58)	Zip 1042	$75
45rpm	**WE'RE GONNA BOP STOP ROCK** (58)	Goldband 1042	$50

GENE VINCENT (RB)

-singles-

78rpm	**BE-BOP-A-LULA** (56)	Capitol 3450	$100
78(P)	**BE-BOP-A-LULA** (56)	Capitol 3450	$125
	(White promo label)		
45rpm	**BE-BOP-A-LULA** (56)	Capitol 3450	$50
	(Large Capitol logo on label)		
45rpm	**BE-BOP-A-LULA** (56)	Capitol 3450	$25
	(Small Capitol logo on label)		
45(P)	**BE-BOP-A-LULA** (56)	Capitol 3450	$75
	(White promo label)		
78rpm	**RACE WITH THE DEVIL** (56)	Capitol 3530	$100
78(P)	**RACE WITH THE DEVIL** (56)	Capitol 3530	$125
	(Yellow promo label)		
45rpm	**RACE WITH THE DEVIL** (56)	Capitol 3530	$30
45(P)	**RACE WITH THE DEVIL** (56)	Capitol 3530	$40
	(Yellow promo label)		
78rpm	**BLUEJEAN BOP** (57)	Capitol 3558	$100
78(P)	**BLUEJEAN BOP** (57)	Capitol 3558	$125
	(White promo label)		
45rpm	**BLUEJEAN BOP** (57)	Capitol 3558	$25
45(P)	**BLUEJEAN BOP** (57)	Capitol 3558	$30
	(White promo label)		
78rpm	**CRAZY LEGS** (57)	Capitol 3617	$100

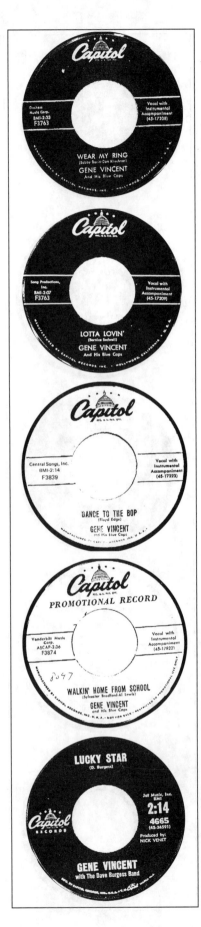

78(P)	**CRAZY LEGS** (57)	Capitol 3617	$125
	(White promo label)		
45rpm	**CRAZY LEGS** (57)	Capitol 3617	$30
45(P)	**CRAZY LEGS** (57)	Capitol 3617	$35
	(White promo label)		
78rpm	**B-I-BICKEY-BI-BO-BO-GO** (58)	Capitol 3678	$100
78(P)	**B-I-BICKEY-BI-BO-BO-GO** (58)	Capitol 3678	$125
	(White promo label)		
45rpm	**B-I-BICKEY-BI-BO-BO-GO** (58)	Capitol 3678	$30
45(P)	**B-I-BICKEY-BI-BO-BO-GO** (58)	Capitol 3678	$40
	(White promo label)		
78rpm	**LOTTA LOVIN'** (58)	Capitol 3763	$150
78(P)	**LOTTA LOVIN'** (58)	Capitol 3763	$175
	(White promo label)		
45rpm	**LOTTA LOVIN'** (58)	Capitol 3763	$25
45(P)	**LOTTA LOVIN'** (58)	Capitol 3763	$25
	(White promo label)		
45rpm	**DANCE TO THE BOP** (58)	Capitol 3839	$25
45(P)	**DANCE TO THE BOP** (57)	Capitol 3839	$25
	(White promo label)		
45rpm	**WALKIN' HOME FROM SCHOOL** (58)	Capitol 3874	$25
45(P)	**WALKIN' HOME FROM SCHOOL** (58)	Capitol 3874	$20
	(White promo label)		
45rpm	**BABY BLUE** (58)	Capitol 3959	$50
45(P)	**BABY BLUE** (58)	Capitol 3959	$40
	(White promo label)		
45rpm	**YES I LOVE YOU, BABY** (58)	Capitol 4010	$40
45(P)	**YES I LOVE YOU, BABY** (58)	Capitol 4010	$30
	(White promo label)		
45rpm	**LITTLE LOVER** (58)	Capitol 4051	$25
45(P)	**LITTLE LOVER** (59)	Capitol 4051	$20
	(White promo label)		
45rpm	**SAY MAMA** (59)	Capitol 4105	$50
45(P)	**SAY MAMA** (59)	Capitol 4105	$40
	(White promo label)		
45rpm	**WHO'S PUSHIN' YOUR SWING** (59)	Capitol 4153	$50
45(P)	**WHO'S PUSHIN' YOUR SWING** (59) Promo label	Capitol 4153	$40
	(White promo label)		
45rpm	**RIGHT NOW** (59)	Capitol 4237	$50
45rpm	**RIGHT NOW** (59)	Capitol 4237	$2,000
	(Price includes this picture sleeve, which is one of the most collectible known for any artist)		
45(P)	**RIGHT NOW** (59)	Capitol 4237	$40
	(White promo label)		
45rpm	**WILD CAT** (60)	Capitol 4313	$50
45(P)	**WILD CAT** (60)	Capitol 4313	$40
	(Red promo label)		
45rpm	**PISTOL PACKIN' MAMA** (60)	Capitol 4442	$40
45(P)	**PISTOL PACKIN' MAMA** (60)	Capitol 4442	$30
	(Red promo label)		
45rpm	**IF YOU WANT MY LOVIN'** (60)	Capitol 4525	$25
45(P)	**IF YOU WANT MY LOVIN'** (60)	Capitol 4525	$20
	(Red promo label)		
45rpm	**LUCKY STAR** (61)	Capitol 4665	$25
45(P)	**LUCKY STAR** (61)	Capitol 4665	$20
	(Red promo label)		
45rpm	**BE-BOP-A-LULA** (65) Black label	Capitol 6042	$20
45rpm	**BIRD DOGGIN'** (66)	Challenge 59337	$20
45(P)	**BIRD DOGGIN'** (66)	Challenge 59337	$15
	(White promo label)		
45rpm	**LONELY STREET** (66)	Challenge 59347	$20
45(P)	**LONELY STREET** (66)	Challenge 59347	$15
	(White promo label)		
45rpm	**BORN TO BE A ROLLING STONE** (67)	Challenge 59365	$20
45(P)	**BORN TO BE A ROLLING STONE** (67)	Challenge 59365	$15
	(White promo label)		
45rpm	**STORY OF THE ROCKERS** (68)	Playground 100	$75
	(Written by Jim Pewter)		
45rpm	**STORY OF THE ROCKERS** (69)	Forever 6001	$50
45rpm	**SUNSHINE** (71)	Kama Sutra 514	$10
45(P)	**SUNSHINE** (71)	Kama Sutra 514	$12
	(Promo label)		
45rpm	**HIGH ON LIFE** (71)	Kama Sutra 518	$10
45(P)	**HIGH ON LIFE** (71)	Kama Sutra 518	$12
	(Promo label)		
45rpm	**BE-BOP-A-LULA** (74) Orange label	Capitol 3871	$10

-EPs-

EP	BLUEJEAN BOP VOL 1 (57)	Capitol 764	$300
EP	BLUEJEAN BOP VOL 2 (57)	Capitol 764	$300
EP	BLUEJEAN BOP VOL 3 (57)	Capitol 764	$300
EP	GENE VINCENT & HIS BLUECAPS VOL 1 (57)	Capitol 811	$300
EP	GENE VINCENT & HIS BLUECAPS VOL 2 (57)	Capitol 811	$300
EP	GENE VINCENT & HIS BLUECAPS VOL 3 (57)	Capitol 811	$300
EP	GENE VINCENT ROCKS & THE BLUE CAPS ROLL VOL 1 (58)	Capitol 970	$300
EP	GENE VINCENT ROCKS & THE BLUE CAPS ROLL VOL 2 (58)	Capitol 970	$300
EP	GENE VINCENT ROCKS & THE BLUE CAPS ROLL VOL 3 (58)	Capitol 970	$300
EP(P)	DANCE TO THE BOP (58)	Capitol 438	$500
	(Promo-only release, no cover)		
EP(P)	HOT ROD GANG (58)	Capitol 985	$750
	(Soundtrack, promo-only release)		
EP	A GENE VINCENT RECORD DATE VOL 1 (58)	Capitol 1059	$250
EP	A GENE VINCENT RECORD DATE VOL 2 (58)	Capitol 1059	$250
EP	A GENE VINCENT RECORD DATE VOL 3 (58)	Capitol 1059	$250

-albums-

LP	BLUEJEAN BOP (57) Green label	Capitol 764	$300
LP(P)	BLUEJEAN BOP (57)	Capitol 764	$250
	(Yellow promo label)		
LP	GENE VINCENT & HIS BLUECAPS (57) Black label	Capitol 811	$300
LP(P)	GENE VINCENT & HIS BLUECAPS (57)	Capitol 811	$250
	(Yellow promo label)		
LP	GENE VINCENT ROCKS & THE BLUECAPS ROLL (58)	Capitol 970	$300
LP(P)	GENE VINCENT ROCKS & THE BLUECAPS ROLL (58) Promo	Capitol 970	$250
	(Yellow promo label)		
LP	A GENE VINCENT RECORD DATE (58)	Capitol 1059	$300
LP(P)	A GENE VINCENT RECORD DATE (58)	Capitol 1059	$250
	(Blue promo label)		
LP	SOUNDS LIKE GENE VINCENT (59)	Capitol 1207	$300
LP(P)	SOUNDS LIKE GENE VINCENT (59)	Capitol 1207	$250
	(Blue promo label)		
LP	CRAZY TIMES (60) Mono	Capitol 1342	$300
LP	CRAZY TIMES (60) Stereo	Capitol 1342	$500
LP(P)	CRAZY TIMES (60)	Capitol 1342	$250
	(Blue promo label)		
LP	GENE VINCENT'S GREATEST (69) Green label	Capitol 380	$25
LP	GENE VINCENT'S GREATEST (70s) Orange label	Capitol 380	$10
LP	I'M BACK AND I'M PROUD (70)	Dandelion 102	$20
LP	IF ONLY YOU COULD SEE ME TODAY (70)	Kama Sutra 2019	$20
LP	THE DAY THE WORLD TURNED BLUE (71)	Kama Sutra 2027	$20

VIRGIN SLEEP (R)

-singles-

45rpm	HALLIFORD HOUSE (67)	Dream 7514	$40

VIRGINIA MOUNTAIN BOYS (BG)
Folkway LPs $10-15 each

VIRGINIANS (BG)

-albums-

LP	THE WONDERFUL WORLD OF BLUEGRASS MUSIC (63)	United Artists 6293	$18
LP(P)	THE WONDERFUL WORLD OF BLUEGRASS MUSIC (63)	United Artists 6293	$20
	(White promo label)		
LP	BALLADS & BLUEGRASS (65)	Monument 18031	$15

VAL VOLK (RB)

-singles-

45rpm	A ROCKIN' PARTY TONIGHT (58)	Rocket 1050	$50

W

WGN'S BARN DANCE TROUPE (CW)

-albums-

LP	SATURDAY NIGHT AT THE OLD BARN DANCE (65)	Kapp 3442	$15

RONNIE WADE (RB)

-singles-

45rpm	GOTTA MAKE HER MINE	King 5061	$25

45rpm	I'LL NEVER FALL IN LOVE AGAIN	King 5078	$12
45rpm	ANNIE DON'T WORK	King 5099	$12
45rpm	ALL I WANT	King 5112	$10

MIKE WAGGONER (RB)
And the Bops

-singles-

45rpm	BABY BABY (58)	Vee 7002	$250

TV SOUNDTRACK

-albums-

LP	WAGON TRAIN (59) Mono	Mercury 20179	$40
LP	WAGON TRAIN (59) Stereo	Mercury 60179	$50
LP(P)	WAGON TRAIN (59)	Mercury 20179	$75
	(White promo label)		

PORTER WAGONER (CW)
And the Wagonmasters, Porter Wagoner Trio
RCA Victor 78s $4-8 each
Other RCA Victor 45s $2-8 each
Other RCA Victor LPs $5-10 each
   (Including duets)
Other Camden LPs $5-8 each
Warner LPs $5-8 each
Other Pickwick, Accord, HRSD, Tudor LPs $2-4 each

-singles-

45rpm	THAT'S IT (53)	RCA Victor 5215	$25
45(P)	THAT'S IT (53)	RCA Victor 5215	$12
	(White promo label)		
45rpm	COMPANY'S COMIN' (55)	RCA Victor 5848	$20
45(P)	COMPANY'S COMIN' (55)	RCA Victor 5848	$12
	(White promo label)		
45rpm	A SATISFIED MIND (55)	RCA Victor 6105	$15
45rpm	EAT, DRINK & BE MERRY (55)	RCA Victor 6289	$12
45rpm	WHAT WOULD YOU DO (56)	RCA Victor 6421	$12
45rpm	UNCLE PEN (56)	RCA Victor 6494	$10
45rpm	TRYIN' TO FORGET THE BLUES (56)	RCA Victor 6598	$10
45rpm	SEEING HER ONLY REMINDED ME OF YOU (56)	RCA Victor 6697	$10
45rpm	I SHOULD BE WITH YOU (56)	RCA Victor 6803	$10
45rpm	I THOUGHT I HEARD YOUR NAME (57)	RCA Victor 6964	$10
45rpm	DOLL FACE (57)	RCA Victor 7073	$12

-EPs-

EP(P)	I SHOULD BE WITH YOU/I'M DAY DREAMIN' TONIGHT (59)	RCA Victor 6803 DJ-60	$15
	(Two songs by Anita Carter on the flip side)		
EP	A SATISFIED MIND (56)	RCA Victor 937	$18
EP	COMPANY'S COMIN' (56)	RCA Victor 938	$18
EP(JB)	PORTER WAGONER AND DOLLY REBECCA (70) Jukebox LLP	RCA Victor 4305	$50
	(Issued with a hard cover)		
33(P)	HIGH BLOOD PRESSURE (83) Public service radio ads	NR 14463	$10
	(One ad features Porter Wagoner)		

-albums-

LP	A SATISFIED MIND (56)	RCA Victor 1358	$200
LP	A SLICE OF LIFE (63) Mono	RCA Victor 2447	$30
LP	A SLICE OF LIFE (63) Stereo	RCA Victor 2447	$40
LP	DUETS (62) Mono	RCA Victor 2529	$25
	(With Skeeter Davis)		
LP	DUETS (62) Stereo	RCA Victor 2529	$30
LP	THE PORTER WAGONER SHOW (63) Mono	RCA Victor 2650	$25
LP	THE PORTER WAGONER SHOW (63) Stereo	RCA Victor 2650	$30
LP	Y'ALL COME (63) Mono	RCA Victor 2706	$25
LP	Y'ALL COME (63) Stereo	RCA Victor 2706	$30
LP	A SATISFIED MIND (63) Mono	Camden 769	$15
LP	IN PERSON (64) Mono	RCA Victor 2840	$20
	(With Norma Jean)		
LP	IN PERSON (64) Stereo	RCA Victor 2840	$25
LP	THE BLUEGRASS STORY (65) Mono	RCA Victor 2960	$20
LP	THE BLUEGRASS STORY (65) Stereo	RCA Victor 2960	$25
LP	THE THIN MAN FROM WEST PLAINS (65)	RCA Victor 3389	$15
LP	OLD LOG CABIN FOR SALE (65)	Camden 861	$18
LP	GRAND OLD GOSPEL (66)	RCA Victor 3488	$15
LP	LIVE ON THE ROAD (66) With Norma Jean	RCA Victor 3509	$15
LP	THE BEST OF PORTER WAGONER (66)	RCA Victor 3560	$12
LP	CONFESSIONS OF A BROKEN MAN (66)	RCA Victor 3593	$15
LP	I'M DAY DREAMING TONIGHT (66)	RCA Victor 2116	$15
LP	A SATISFIED MIND (66) Stereo	Camden 769	$10
LP	YOUR OLD LOVE LETTERS (66)	Camden 942	$12

LP	SOUL OF A CONVICT (67)	RCA Victor 3683	$15
LP	THE COLD HARD FACTS OF LIFE (67)	RCA Victor 3797	$15
LP	MORE GRAND OLD GOSPEL (67)	RCA Victor 3855	$15
LP	PORTER WAGONER SINGS BALLADS OF HEART & SOUL (67)	Camden 2116	$15
LP	JUST BETWEEN YOU & ME (68) Mono	RCA Victor 3926	$100
	(Rare in mono, with Dolly Parton)		
LP	JUST BETWEEN YOU & ME (68) Stereo	RCA Victor 3926	$20
LP	THE BOTTOM OF THE BOTTLE (68) Mono	RCA Victor 3968	$100
	(Rare in mono)		
LP	THE BOTTOM OF THE BOTTLE (68) Stereo	RCA Victor 3968	$15
LP	GOSPEL COUNTRY (68)	RCA Victor 4034	$15
LP	JUST THE TWO OF US (68) With Dolly Parton	RCA Victor 4039	$18
LP	GREEN, GREEN GRASS OF HOME (68)	Camden 2191	$12
LP	THE CARROLL COUNTY ACCIDENT (69)	RCA Victor 4116	$12
LP	ME AND MY BOYS (69)	RCA Victor 4181	$12
LP	ALWAYS, ALWAYS (69) With Dolly Parton	RCA Victor 4186	$15
LP	COUNTRY FEELING (69)	Camden 2321	$15
LP	YOU GOT TA HAVE A LICENSE (70)	RCA Victor 4286	$10
LP	PORTER WAGONER & DOLLY PARTON (70) With Dolly Parton	RCA Victor 4305	$12
LP	THE BEST OF PORTER WAGONER VOL 2 (70)	RCA Victor 4321	$10
LP	SKIDROW JOE (70)	RCA Victor 4386	$10
LP	ONCE MORE (70) With Dolly Parton	RCA Victor 4388	$12
LP	HOWDY NEIGHBOR, HOWDY (70)	Camden 2409	$12
LP	TWO OF A KIND (71) With Dolly Parton	RCA Victor 4490	$12
LP	PORTER WAGONER COUNTRY (71)	Camden 2478	$10
2LP	BLUE MOON OF KENTUCKY (71)	Camden 9010	$18
LP	THE BEST OF PORTER WAGONER & DOLLY PARTON (71)	RCA Victor 4556	$10
LP	THE SILENT KIND (71)	Camden 2588	$10
LP	THE RIGHT COMBINATION (72) With Dolly Parton	RCA Victor 4628	$12
LP	TOGETHER ALWAYS (72) With Dolly Parton	RCA Victor 4761	$10
LP	WE FOUND IT (73) With Dolly Parton	RCA Victor 4841	$10
2LP	BLUE MOON OF KENTUCKY (76)	Pickwick 9010	$10

-radio shows-

16"(RS)	U.S. ARMY BAND (60s)	U.S. Army	$25-40
	(Music and interviews)		
16"(RS)	COUNTRY STYLE USA (60s)	Country Style	$25-40
	(Music and interviews)		
LP(RS)	GRAND OL' OPRY (62)	WSM Radio	$20-30
	(Music and interviews)		
LP(RS)	COUNTRY MUSIC TIME (80s)	U.S. Air Force	$10-15
	(Music and interviews)		

JIMMY WAKELY (CW)

Other Decca, Coral, and Capitol 78s $2-4 each
Shasta 78s $4 each
Other Shasta 45s $5 each
Other Capitol 45s $4-8 each
Other Coral 45s $5-8 each
Other Decca 45s $2-4 each
Other Shasta LPs $5-10 each
MCA, Coral, MCR, Danny, Album Globe LPs $3-6 each

-singles-

78rpm	I'M SENDING YOU RED ROSES (44)	Decca 6095	$15
78rpm	SIGNED, SEALED AND DELIVERED (48)	Capitol 40088	$12
78rpm	ONE HAS MY NAME (48)	Capitol 15162	$12
78rpm	I LOVE YOU SO MUCH IT HURTS (48)	Capitol 15243	$12
78rpm	MINE ALL MINE (48)	Capitol 15236	$10
78rpm	FOREVER MORE (49)	Capitol 15333	$10
78rpm	TILL THE END OF THE WORLD (49)	Capitol 15368	$10
78rpm	I WISH I HAD A NICKEL (49)	Capitol 40153	$10
78rpm	SLIPPING AROUND (49) With Margaret Whiting	Capitol 40224	$10
	(Later 45rpm versions worth $3-10 each)		
78rpm	I'LL NEVER SLIP AROUND AGAIN (49)	Capitol 40246	$10
	(With Margaret Whiting)		
45rpm	BROKEN DOWN MERRY-GO-ROUND (50) With Margaret Whiting	Capitol 800	$15
78rpm	PETER COTTONTAIL (50)	Capitol 929	$10
45rpm	PETER COTTONTAIL (50)	Capitol 929	$15
45rpm	BY THE WATERS OF THE MINNETONKA (50)	Shasta 104	$25
45rpm	LET'S GO TO CHURCH (50) With Margaret Whiting	Capitol 960	$12
45rpm	I DON'T HAVE TO DIE TO GO TO HEAVEN (50)	Capitol 1066	$15
45rpm	MONA LISA (50)	Capitol 1151	$15
45rpm	A BUSHEL AND A PECK (50) With Margaret Whiting	Capitol 1234	$10
45rpm	SILVER BELLS (50) With Margaret Whiting	Capitol 1255	$12
45rpm	MY HEART CRIED FOR YOU (51)	Capitol 1328	$12
45rpm	EASTER PARADE (51) With Margaret Whiting	Capitol 1382	$10
45rpm	BEAUTIFUL BROWN EYES (51)	Capitol 1393	$10
45rpm	WHEN YOU AND I WERE YOUNG MAGGIE BLUES (51)	Capitol 1500	$10
	(With Margaret Whiting)		

45rpm	I'LL NEVER DO A THING TO HURT YOU (51)	Capitol 1554	$12
45rpm	THE SOLID SOUTH (51)	Capitol 1762	$12
45rpm	I DON'T WANT TO BE FREE (51)	Capitol 1816	$10
45rpm	TOMORROW (51)	Shasta 105	$15
45rpm	THAT'S SANTA CLAUS (51)	Shasta 106	$18
45rpm	THERE'S THAT SAME OLD LOVELIGHT IN YOUR EYES (52)	Capitol 2172	$10
45rpm	I WENT TO YOUR WEDDING (52)	Capitol 2221	$10
45rpm	RAINBOW AT MIDNIGHT (53)	Capitol 2272	$12
45rpm	SLIPPING AROUND (54)	Shasta 107	$10
45rpm	SLIPPING AROUND (54)	Shasta 107	$25
	(Price includes picture sleeve)		
45rpm	IT'S LONELY ON THE TRAIL TONIGHT (55)	Coral 61220	$15
45(P)	IT'S LONELY ON THE TRAIL TONIGHT (55)	Coral 61220	$10
	(Blue promo label)		
45rpm	HIS NAME WAS DEAN/GIANT (57)	Coral 61706	$20
	(Tribute record to James Dean)		
45(P)	HIS NAME WAS DEAN/GIANT (57)	Coral 61706	$15
	(Blue promo label)		

-EPs-

EP	SLIPPIN' AROUND (53)	Capitol 403	$25
	(Jimmy Wakely and Margaret Whiting)		
EP	CHRISTMAS ON THE RANGE (54)	Capitol 9004	$15
EP	COUNTRY HITS (57)	Coral 81080	$15
EP	ENTER & REST & PRAY (58)	Decca 2614	$12

-albums-

10"LP	SONGS OF THE WEST (54)	Capitol 4008	$50
10"LP	CHRISTMAS ON THE RANGE (54)	Capitol 9004	$50
LP	SANTA FE TRAIL (56)	Decca 8409	$75
LP(P)	SANTA FE TRAIL (56)	Decca 8409	$60
	(Pink promo label)		
LP	ENTER & REST & PRAY (57) Mono	Decca 8680	$40
LP(P)	ENTER & REST & PRAY (57)	Decca 8680	$30
	(Pink promo label)		
LP	COUNTRY MILLION SELLERS (59)	Shasta 501	$20
LP	MERRY CHRISTMAS (59)	Shasta 502	$20
LP	A COWBOY SERENADE (59)	Tops 1601	$10
	(The classic budget label)		
LP	JIMMY WAKELY SINGS (60)	Shasta 505	$20
LP	SLIPPIN' AROUND (66)	Dot 25711	$12
LP	CHRISTMAS WITH JIMMY WAKELY (66)	Dot 25754	$15
LP	ENTER & REST & PRAY (67) Stereo	Decca 8680	$15
LP	ENTER & REST & PRAY (67)	Decca 8680	$18
	(White promo label)		
LP	I'LL NEVER SLIP AROUND AGAIN (67)	Hilltop 6053	$12
	(With Margaret Whiting)		
LP	HEARTACHES (69)	Decca 75077	$15
LP(P)	HEARTACHES (69)	Decca 5077	$18
	(White promo label)		
LP	HERE'S JIMMY WAKELY (69)	Vocalion 3857	$12
LP(P)	HERE'S JIMMY WAKELY (69)	Vocalion 3857	$15
	(White promo label)		
LP	BIG COUNTRY SONGS (70)	Vocalion 3904	$10
LP(P)	BIG COUNTRY SONGS (70)	Vocalion 3904	$12
	(White promo label)		
LP	NOW AND THEN (70)	Decca 75192	$10

-radio shows-

16"(RS)	JIMMY WAKELY RCA Thesaurus Library	RCA Victor 1469	$25
	(Recorded music)		

JOHN WAKELY (C)
Jimmy Wakely is his dad

-albums-

LP	PLEASE DON'T HURT ME ANYMORE (69)	Decca 75139	$15
LP(P)	PLEASE DON'T HURT ME ANYMORE (69)	Decca 75139	$12
	(White promo label)		

BILLY WALKER (CW)
Other Columbia 45s $3-6 each
Monument 45s $2 each
Other Columbia, Harmony, and Monument LPs $4-8 each
MGM LPs $6-8 each
HSRD, RCA Victor, Gusto LPs $3-5 each

-singles-

45rpm	THANK YOU FOR CALLING (54)	Columbia 21256	$15
45(P)	THANK YOU FOR CALLING (54)	Columbia 21256	$12
	(White promo label)		

45rpm	I'VE GOT LEAVIN' ON MY MIND (56)	Columbia 21531	$15
45(P)	I'VE GOT LEAVIN' ON MY MIND (56)	Columbia 21531	$10
	(White promo label)		
45(P)	CROSS THE BRAZOS AT WACO (65) Red vinyl promo	Columbia 43120	$15
	(Price includes promo-only picture sleeve)		

-albums-

LP	EVERYBODY'S HITS BUT MINE (61) Mono	Columbia 1624	$20
LP	EVERYBODY'S HITS BUT MINE (61) Stereo	Columbia 8424	$30
LP(P)	EVERYBODY'S HITS BUT MINE (61)	Columbia 1624	$40
	(White promo label)		
LP	BILLY WALKER'S GREATEST HITS (63) Mono	Columbia 1935	$15
LP	BILLY WALKER'S GREATEST HITS (63) Stereo	Columbia 8735	$20
LP	THANK YOU FOR CALLING (64) Mono	Columbia 2206	$15
LP	THANK YOU FOR CALLING (64) Stereo	Columbia 9006	$18
LP	ANYTHING YOUR HEART DESIRES (64)	Harmony 7306	$18
LP(P)	ANYTHING YOUR HEART DESIRES (64)	Harmony 7306	$25
	(White promo label)		
LP	A MILLION & ONE (66)	Monument 18047	$15
LP	BIG COUNTRY HITS (67)	Harmony 11210	$12
LP	THE WALKER WAY (670	Monument 18072	$15
LP	I TAUGHT HER EVERYTHING SHE KNOWS (68)	Monument 18090	$15
LP	PORTRAIT OF BILLY (69)	Monument 18116	$15
LP	HOW BIG IS GOD (69)	Monument 18132	$15
LP	DARLING DAYS (70)	Monument 18143	$12

BRYAN WALKER (RB)

-singles-

45rpm	I STUBBED MY TOE (58)	Piper 501	$12

CHARLIE WALKER (CW)
Other Columbia 45s and 78s $3-6 each
Epic and Plantation 45s $2-3 each
RCA Victor, Columbia, and Vocalion LPs $5-10 each
Other Epic and Plantation LPs $3-6 each

-singles-

45rpm	PICK ME UP ON YOUR WAY DOWN (58)	Columbia 41211	$15
45(P)	PICK ME UP ON YOUR WAY DOWN (58)	Columbia 41211	$10
	(White promo label)		
45rpm	I'LL NEVER LET IT SHOW (57)	Mercury 71111	$10

-albums-

LP	CHARLIE WALKER'S GREATEST HITS (61) Mono	Columbia 1691	$20
LP	CHARLIE WALKER'S GREATEST HITS (61) Stereo	Columbia 8491	$20
LP(P)	CHARLIE WALKER'S GREATEST HITS (61)	Columbia 1691	$25
	(White promo label)		
LP	CLOSE ALL THE HONKY TONKS (65)	Epic 26137	$15
LP(P)	CLOSE ALL THE HONKY TONKS (65)	Epic 26137	$18
	(White promo label)		
LP	BORN TO LOSE (65)	Epic 26153	$15
LP(P)	BORN TO LOSE (65)	Epic 26153	$18
	(White promo label)		
LP	WINE, WOMEN & WALKER (66)	Epic 26209	$12
LP(P)	WINE, WOMEN & WALKER (66)	Epic 26209	$15
	(White promo label)		
LP	DON'T SQUEEZE MY CHARMIN (67)	Epic 26328	$12
LP(P)	DON'T SQUEEZE MY CHARMIN (67)	Epic 26328	$15
	(White promo label)		
LP	CHARLIE WALKER RECORDED LIVE IN DALLAS, TEXAS (69)	Epic 26483	$12
LP(P)	CHARLIE WALKER RECORDED LIVE IN DALLAS, TEXAS (69)	Epic 26483	$15
	(White promo label)		

CINDY WALKER (C)

-albums-

LP	WORDS & MUSIC (64)	Monument 18020	$18

JACKIE WALKER (RB)

-singles-

45rpm	ONLY TEENAGERS ALLOWED (58)	Imperial 5490	$20
45rpm	GOOD GOOD FEELIN' (58)	Imperial 5521	$15

JERRY JEFF WALKER (CW)
Any 45s $2-4 each
Other Atco LPs $10-15 each
Vanguard and Decca LPs $4-8 each

-albums-

LP	MR. BOJANGLES (68)	Atco 259	$25
LP(P)	MR. BOJANGLES (68)	Atco 259	$30
	(White promo label)		

LP	FIVE YEARS GONE (69)	Atco 297	$30
LP(P)	FIVE YEARS GONE (69)	Atco 297	$40
	(White promo label)		

-radio shows-

LP(RS)	LIVE AT GILLEY'S (Mar 85)	Westwood One	$25-35
	(Live concert)		

LANIE WALKER (RB)

-singles-

45rpm	DROP IN (58)	Blue Hen 123	$30
45rpm	SIDE TRACK DADDY (58)	Blue Hen 209	$12

WAYNE WALKER (RB)
Other ABC and Brunswick 45s $6-10 each
Coral 45s $5-10 each

-singles-

45rpm	ALL I CAN DO IS CRY (57)	ABC Paramount 9735	$40
45(P)	ALL I CAN DO IS CRY (57)	ABC Paramount 9735	$30
	(White promo label)		
45rpm	YOU'VE GOT ME (58)	Brunswick 55133	$12
45(P)	YOU'VE GOT ME (58)	Brunswick 55133	$10
	(Yellow promo label)		

JERRY WALLACE (CW)
Other Challenge 45s $5-10 each
Other 45s $2 each
United Artists, Liberty, and Wing LPs $5-10 each
MGM, MCA, Four Star, BMA, and Decca LPs $4-8 each

-singles-

45rpm	LITTLE MISS ONE (51)	Allied 5015	$30
45rpm	BLUE JEAN BABY (58)	Challenge 1003	$20
45(P)	BLUE JEAN BABY (58)	Challenge 1003	$18
	(White promo label)		
45rpm	THE OTHER ME (58)	Challenge 59000	$18
45(P)	THE OTHER ME (58)	Challenge 59000	$15
	(White promo label)		
45rpm	HOW THE TIME FLIES (58)	Challenge 59013	$12
45(P)	HOW THE TIME FLIES (58)	Challenge 59013	$10
	(White promo label)		
45rpm	DIAMOND RING (58)	Challenge 59027	$12
45(P)	DIAMOND RING (58)	Challenge 59027	$10
	(White promo label)		
45rpm	A TOUCH OF PINK (59)	Challenge 59040	$12
45(P)	A TOUCH OF PINK (59)	Challenge 59040	$10
	(White promo label)		
45rpm	PRIMROSE LANE (59)	Challenge 59047	$15
45(P)	PRIMROSE LANE (59)	Challenge 59047	$18
	(White promo label)		
45rpm	LITTLE COCO PALM (60)	Challenge 59060	$10
45rpm	LITTLE COCO PALM (60)	Challenge 59060	$25
	(Price includes picture sleeve)		
45rpm	IN THE MISTY MOONLIGHT (64)	Challenge 59246	$15

-EPs-

EP	THERE SHE GOES (60)	Challenge 7104	$30

-albums-

LP	JUST JERRY (59)	Challenge 606	$75
LP	THERE SHE GOES (60) Mono	Challenge 612	$25
LP	THERE SHE GOES (60) Stereo	Challenge 612	$35
LP	SHUTTERS & BOARDS (62) Mono	Challenge 616	$20
LP	SHUTTERS & BOARDS (62) Stereo	Challenge 616	$25
LP	IN THE MISTY MOONLIGHT (64) Mono	Challenge 619	$15
LP	IN THE MISTY MOONLIGHT (64) Stereo	Challenge 619	$20
LP	THE BEST OF JERRY WALLACE (66)	Mercury 61072	$10
LP(P)	THE BEST OF JERRY WALLACE (66)	Mercury 61072	$12
	(White promo label)		

JOE WALLACE (RB)

-singles-

45rpm	LEOPARD MAN (58)	Moon 304	$60

TRAVIS WAMMACK (RB)

-singles-

45rpm	ROCK AND ROLL BLUES (58)	Fernwood 103	$50

WALTON & THE SILVER LAKE BOYS (RB)
-singles-

45rpm	**MAN WHAT A PARTY** (58)	Lael 1137	$60

STEVE WARINER (C)
RCA Victor and MCA black vinyl 45s $2 each
Other RCA Victor and MCA colored vinyl 45s $8 each
MCA picture sleeves $2 each
Liberty 45s $1-2 each
RCA Victor and MCA LPs $3 each

-singles-

45(P)	**THE PARTY'S OVER** (80) (Green promo label, green vinyl)	RCA Victor 12029	$12
45(P)	**DON'T IT BREAK YOUR HEART** (82) (Yellow promo label, green vinyl)	RCA Victor 13308	$10
45(P)	**KANSAS CITY LIGHTS** (82) (Yellow promo label, yellow vinyl)	RCA Victor 13072	$10
45(P)	**DON'T YOUR MEM'RY EVER SLEEP AT NIGHT** (83) (Green promo label, blue vinyl)	RCA Victor 13515	$10
45(P)	**YOU CAN DREAM OF ME** (85) (White promo label, yellow vinyl)	MCA 52721	$10
45(P)	**STARTING OVER AGAIN** (86) (White promo label, red vinyl)	MCA 52837	$10
45(P)	**SMALL TOWN GIRL** (86) (White promo label, blue vinyl)	MCA 53006	$10

-radio shows-

3LP(RS)	**SILVER EAGLE** (Jan 83) With Mel McDaniel (Live concert)	DIR	$30-60
3LP(RS)	**AMERICAN EAGLE** (Nov 86) (Live concert)	DIR	$40-75
LP(RS)	**LIVE AT GILLEY'S** (Nov 86) (Live concert)	Westwood One	$20-30
LP(RS)	**WESTWOOD ONE PRESENTS** (July 87) (Live concert)	Westwood One	$20-30

JUNIOR WARREN (RB)
-singles-

45rpm	**ROCK & ROLL FEVER** (58)	Sherba 1500	$100

BILL WATKINS (R)
-singles-

45rpm	**I GOT TROUBLES** (58)	Tip Tock 14321	$40

CLAYTON WATSON (RB)
-singles-

45rpm	**EVERYBODY BOPPIN** (58)	Lavender 2454	$75

DOC WATSON (C)
Arthel Watson
United Artists 45s $2 each
Other Folkways LPs $4-8 each
Other Vanguard LPs $5-10 each
 (Including duet LPs with Merle)
Other United Artists LPs $5-10 each
 (Including duet LPs with Merle)
Liberty and Flying Fish LPs $5 each
Poppy and Sugar Hill LPs, Doc and Merle, $3-6 each

-albums-

LP	**DOC WATSON & FAMILY** (63)	Folkways 2366	$15
LP	**DOC WATSON** (64)	Vanguard 9152	$20
LP	**DOC WATSON & SON** (65)	Vanguard 9170	$18
LP	**SOUTHBOUND** (66)	Vanguard 9213	$15
LP	**HOME AGAIN** (67)	Vanguard 9239	$15
LP	**GOOD DEAL** (68)	Vanguard 9276	$15
2LP	**THE BEST OF DOC WATSON** (73)	Vanguard 45	$15
2LP(P)	**THE BEST OF DOC WATSON** (73) (White promo labels)	Vanguard 45	$18
2LP	**MEMORIES** (75)	United Artists 423	$18
2LP(P)	**MEMORIES** (75) (White promo labels)	United Artists 423	$20
2LP	**OLD TIME CONCERT** (77)	Vanguard 107	$10

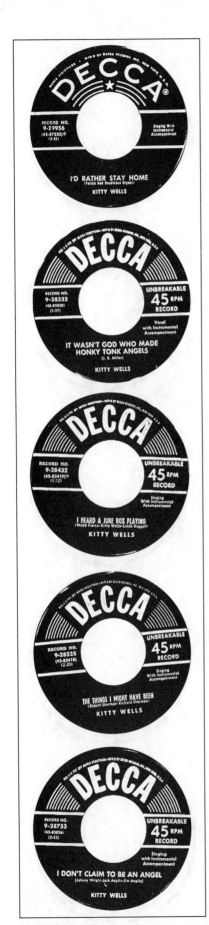

GENE WATSON (RB)
MCA, Curb, and Capitol 45s $1 each
Capitol and MCA LPs $3-6 each

-singles-

45rpm	**MY ROCKIN' BABY** (58)	Tri Dec 8357	$60

-radio shows-

LP(RS)	**COUNTRY MUSIC TIME** (77)	U.S. Air Force	$10-12
	(Music and interviews)		
3LP(RS)	**ON A COUNTRY ROAD** (Sept 83)	Mutual Radio	$10-15
	(Live segment features Gene Watson)		
LP(RS)	**LIVE AT GILLEY'S** (Oct 87)	Westwood One	$10-15
	(Live concert)		

AL WAYNE (RB)

-singles-

45rpm	**SWING BOP BOOGIE** (56)	Westport 132	$60
45rpm	**DON'T MEAN MAYBE BABY** (57)	Westport 138	$40
45rpm	**YOU ARE THE ONE** (58)	Westport 140	$50

BILLY WAYNE (RB)

-singles-

45rpm	**WALKING AND STROLLING** (58)	Hill Crest 778	$60

JIMMY WAYNE (RB)

-singles-

45rpm	**YOU SHAKE ME** (58)	Corwin 6618	$50

VARIOUS ARTISTS

-radio ads-

CD(P)	**WE ONLY HAVE 10 YEARS TO SAVE OUR PLANET** (90)	ECO-Nashville	$15
	(A series of sixty-three public service radio commercials with Roseanne Cash and many others)		

HOYT WEBB (RB)

-singles-

45rpm	**BABY WON'T YOU SLOW DOWN** (59)	Cotton Club 177	$60

JAY LEE WEBB (C)
Brother of Loretta Lynn, Crystal Gayle, and Peggy Sue
Decca 45s $2 each

-albums-

LP	**I COME HOME A-DRINKIN'** (67)	Decca 74933	$15
LP(P)	**I COME HOME A-DRINKIN'** (67)	Decca 4933	$12
	(Pink promo label)		
LP	**SHE'S LOOKING BETTER BY THE MINUTE** (69)	Decca 75121	$15
LP(P)	**SHE'S LOOKING BETTER BY THE MINUTE** (69)	Decca 5121	$12
	(Pink promo label)		

ERIC WEISSBERG (BG)

-albums-

LP	**NEW DIMENSIONS IN BANJO & BLUEGRASS** (63)	Elektra 238	$20

JIMMY WELFORD (RB)

-singles-

45rpm	**MY NAME IS JIMMY** (58)	Four Star 1714	$25

FREDDY WELLER (C)
Member of Paul Revere & the Raiders
Columbia 45s $2-4 each
Other Columbia LPs $4-8 each

-albums-

LP	**GAMES PEOPLE PLAY** (69)	Columbia 9904	$15
LP(P)	**GAMES PEOPLE PLAY** (69)	Columbia 9904	$18
	(White promo label)		

KITTY WELLS (CW)
Muriel Deason
Other Decca 78s $2-5 each
Other Decca 45s $2-5 each
 (Including duets)
Ruboca 45s $1 each
Other Decca jukebox LLPs $8-15 each
MCA 2LP sets $8 each
Other MCA, Imperial House, Pickwick, Suffolk, Kaola, Ruboca, Exact, and Mistletoe LPs $2-5 each

-singles-

45rpm	**IT WASN'T GOD WHO MADE HONKY TONK ANGELS** (52)	Decca 28232	$20

45rpm	**I HEARD A JUKEBOX PLAYING** (53)	Decca 28432	$15
45rpm	**THE THINGS I MIGHT HAVE BEEN** (53)	Decca 28525	$15
45rpm	**PAYING FOR THAT BACK STREET AFFAIR** (53)	Decca 28578	$12
45rpm	**I DON'T CLAIM TO BE AN ANGEL** (53)	Decca 28753	$12
45rpm	**HEY JOE** (53)	Decca 28797	$12
45rpm	**CHEATIN'S A SIN** (54)	Decca 28911	$12
45rpm	**RELEASE ME** (54)	Decca 29023	$12
45rpm	**ONE BY ONE** (54) With Red Foley	Decca 29065	$10
45rpm	**THOU SHALT NOT STEAL** (54)	Decca 29313	$10
45rpm	**MAKIN' BELIEVE** (55)	Decca 29419	$10
45rpm	**THERE'S POISON IN YOUR HEART** (55)	Decca 29577	$10
45rpm	**LONELY SIDE OF TOWN** (55)	Decca 29728	$10
45rpm	**HOW FAR IS HEAVEN** (56)	Decca 29823	$10
45rpm	**SEARCHING** (56)	Decca 29956	$10
78rpm	**FRAULEIN** (57)	Decca 30415	$15
78(P)	**FRAULEIN** (57)	Decca 30415	$10
	(Pink promo label)		
45rpm	**FRAULEIN** (57)	Decca 30415	$10
5-33s	**KITTY'S CHOICE** (60) Stereo singles	Decca 78987	$10 each
	(Five singles-set issued for jukeboxes, $50 for the set)		
5-33s	**SEASONS OF MY HEART** (60) Stereo singles	Decca 74075	$8 each
	(Five singles-set issued for jukeboxes, $40 for the set)		
5-33s	**CHRISTMAS DAY WITH KITTY WELLS** (62) Stereo singles	Decca 74349	$8 each
	(Five singles-set issued for jukeboxes, $40 for the set)		
45rpm	**GUILTY STREET** (69)	Decca 32455	$15
	(Price includes picture sleeve)		

-EPs-

EP	**KITTY WELLS SINGS** (55)	Decca 2163	$25
EP	**KITTY WELLS VOL 1** (56)	Decca 2361	$20
EP	**KITTY WELLS VOL 2** (56)	Decca 2362	$20
EP	**KITTY WELLS VOL 3** (56)	Decca 2363	$20
EP	**WINNER OF YOUR HEART** (56)	Decca 2518	$20
EP	**WINNER OF YOUR HEART** (56)	Decca 2519	$20
EP	**WINNER OF YOUR HEART** (56)	Decca 2520	$20
EP	**LONELY STREET** (58)	Decca 2584	$20
EP	**DUST ON THE BIBLE** (59) Mono	Decca 2646	$20
EP	**DUST ON THE BIBLE** (59) Stereo	Decca 2646	$30
EP	**KITTY WELLS & RED FOLEY** (59)	Decca 2667	$20
EP	**KITTY'S CHOICE** (60)	Decca 2677	$18
EP	**SEASONS OF MY HEART** (60)	Decca 2684	$18
EP	**HEARTBREAK USA** (61)	Decca 2699	$18
EP	**KITTY WELLS** (62)	Decca 2710	$18
EP	**KITTY WELLS** (62)	Decca 2717	$18
EP	**KITTY WELLS** (62)	Decca 2732	$18
EP	**WICKED WORLD** (63)	Decca 2737	$18
EP	**ALL THE TIME** (63)	Decca 2749	$18
EP	**KITTY WELLS** (64)	Decca 2763	$15
EP	**TALK BACK TREMBLING LIPS** (64)	Decca 2777	$15
EP	**COUNTRY MUSIC TIME** (65)	Decca 2780	$15
EP	**THIS WHITE CIRCLE** (65)	Decca 2781	$15
EP	**BURNING MEMORIES** (65)	Decca 2804	$15
EP(JB)	**THE KITTY WELLS STORY** (66) Jukebox LLP	Decca 4031	$15
	(Issued with a hard cover)		
EP(JB)	**COUNTRY MUSIC TIME** (66) Jukebox LLP	Decca 4554	$15
	(Issued with a hard cover)		
EP(JB)	**SONGS MADE FAMOUS BY JIM REEVES** (66) Jukebox LLP	Decca 4741	$15
	(Issued with a hard cover)		
EP(JB)	**SHOWCASE** (66) Jukebox LLP	Decca 74961	$15
	(Issued with a hard cover)		

-albums-

LP	**KITTY WELLS' COUNTRY HIT PARADE** (56)	Decca 8293	$50
LP(P)	**KITTY WELLS' COUNTRY HIT PARADE** (56)	Decca 8293	$40
	(Pink promo label)		
LP	**WINNER OF YOUR HEART** (56)	Decca 8552	$50
LP(P)	**WINNER OF YOUR HEART** (56)	Decca 8552	$40
	(Pink promo label)		
LP	**DUST ON THE BIBLE** (59)	Decca 8858	$50
LP(P)	**DUST ON THE BIBLE** (59)	Decca 8858	$40
	(Pink promo label)		
LP	**AFTER DARK** (59)	Decca 8888	$40
LP(P)	**AFTER DARK** (59)	Decca 8888	$30
	(Pink promo label)		
LP	**KITTY'S CHOICE** (60) Mono	Decca 8979	$30
LP	**KITTY'S CHOICE** (60) Stereo	Decca 78979	$40
LP(P)	**KITTY'S CHOICE** (60)	Decca 8979	$30
	(Pink promo label)		

LP	**COUNTRY HIT PARADE** (60) Mono	Decca 8293	$20
LP	**COUNTRY HIT PARADE** (60) Stereo	Decca 78293	$15
LP(P)	**COUNTRY HIT PARADE** (60)	Decca 8293	$25
	(Pink promo label)		
LP	**WINNER OF YOUR HEART** (60) Mono	Decca 8552	$20
LP	**WINNER OF YOUR HEART** (60) Stereo	Decca 78552	$15
LP(P)	**WINNER OF YOUR HEART** (60)	Decca 8552	$25
	(Pink promo label)		
LP	**DUST ON THE BIBLE** (60) Mono	Decca 8858	$20
LP	**DUST ON THE BIBLE** (60) Stereo	Decca 78858	$15
LP(P)	**DUST ON THE BIBLE** (60)	Decca 8858	$25
	(Pink promo label)		
LP	**AFTER DARK** (60) Mono	Decca 8888	$20
LP	**AFTER DARK** (60) Stereo	Decca 78888	$15
LP(P)	**AFTER DARK** (60)	Decca 8888	$25
	(Pink promo label)		
LP	**SEASONS OF MY HEART** (60) Mono	Decca 4075	$20
LP	**SEASONS OF MY HEART** (60) Stereo	Decca 74075	$15
LP(P)	**SEASONS OF MY HEART** (60)	Decca 4075	$25
	(Pink promo label)		
LP	**KITTY WELLS' GOLDEN FAVORITES** (61) Mono	Decca 4108	$20
LP	**KITTY WELLS' GOLDEN FAVORITES** (65) Stereo	Decca 4108	$15
LP(P)	**KITTY WELLS' GOLDEN FAVORITES** (61)	Decca 4108	$25
	(Pink promo label)		
LP	**KITTY WELLS & RED FOLEY'S GREATEST HITS** (61) Mono	Decca 4109	$20
LP	**KITTY WELLS & RED FOLEY'S GREATEST HITS** (65) Stereo	Decca 74109	$25
LP(P)	**KITTY WELLS & RED FOLEY'S GREATEST HITS** (65)	Decca 4109	$30
	(Pink promo label)		
LP	**HEARTBREAK U. S. A.** (61) Mono	Decca 4141	$20
LP	**HEARTBREAK U. S. A.** (61) Stereo	Decca 74141	$25
LP(P)	**HEARTBREAK U. S. A.** (61)	Decca 4141	$30
	(Pink promo label)		
LP	**KITTY WELLS, QUEEN OF COUNTRY MUSIC** (62) Mono	Decca 4197	$20
LP	**KITTY WELLS, QUEEN OF COUNTRY MUSIC** (62) Stereo	Decca 74197	$25
LP(P)	**KITTY WELLS, QUEEN OF COUNTRY MUSIC** (62)	Decca 4197	$30
	(Pink promo label)		
LP	**SINGING ON SUNDAY** (62) Mono	Decca 4270	$20
LP	**SINGING ON SUNDAY** (62) Stereo	Decca 74270	$25
LP(P)	**SINGING ON SUNDAY** (62)	Decca 4270	$30
	(Decca promo label)		
LP	**CHRISTMAS WITH KITTY WELLS** (62) Mono	Decca 4349	$20
LP	**CHRISTMAS WITH KITTY WELLS** (62) Stereo	Decca 74349	$25
LP(P)	**CHRISTMAS WITH KITTY WELLS** (62)	Decca 4349	$30
	(Decca promo label)		
2LP	**THE KITTY WELLS STORY** (63) Mono	Decca 174	$20
2LP	**THE KITTY WELLS STORY** (63) Stereo	Decca 7174	$25
2LP(P)	**THE KITTY WELLS STORY** (63)	Decca 174	$30
	(White promo labels)		
LP	**ESPECIALLY FOR YOU** (64) Mono	Decca 4493	$20
LP	**ESPECIALLY FOR YOU** (64) Stereo	Decca 74493	$25
LP(P)	**ESPECIALLY FOR YOU** (64)	Decca 4493	$30
	(White promo label)		
LP	**COUNTRY MUSIC TIME** (64) Mono	Decca 4554	$18
LP	**COUNTRY MUSIC TIME** (64) Stereo	Decca 74554	$20
LP(P)	**COUNTRY MUSIC TIME** (64)	Decca 4554	$25
	(White promo label)		
LP	**BURNING MEMORIES** (65) Mono	Decca 4612	$18
LP	**BURNING MEMORIES** (65) Stereo	Decca 74612	$20
LP(P)	**BURNING MEMORIES** (65)	Decca 4612	$25
	(White promo label)		
LP	**LONESOME, SAD & BLUE** (65) Mono	Decca 4658	$18
LP	**LONESOME, SAD & BLUE** (65)	Decca 74658	$20
LP(P)	**LONESOME, SAD & BLUE** (65)	Decca 4658	$25
	(White promo label)		
LP	**KITTY WELLS FAMILY GOSPEL SING** (65) Mono	Decca 4679	$18
LP	**KITTY WELLS FAMILY GOSPEL SING** (65) Stereo	Decca 74679	$20
LP(P)	**KITTY WELLS FAMILY GOSPEL SING** (65)	Decca 4679	$25
	(White promo label)		
LP	**LONELY STREET** (65) Mono	Decca 8732	$20
LP	**LONELY STREET** (65) Stereo	Decca 8732	$20
LP(P)	**LONELY STREET** (65)	Decca 8732	$25
	(White promo label)		
LP	**SONGS MADE FAMOUS BY JIM REEVES** (66) Mono	Decca 4741	$20
LP	**SONGS MADE FAMOUS BY JIM REEVES** (66) Stereo	Decca 74741	$25
LP	**SONGS MADE FAMOUS BY JIM REEVES** (66)	Decca 4741	$30
	(White promo label)		
LP	**COUNTRY ALL THE WAY** (66) Mono	Decca 4776	$18

LP	COUNTRY ALL THE WAY (66) Stereo	Decca 74776	$20
LP(P)	COUNTRY ALL THE WAY (66)	Decca 4776	$25
	(White promo label)		
LP	THE KITTY WELLS SHOW (66) Mono	Decca 4831	$18
LP	THE KITTY WELLS SHOW (66) Stereo	Decca 74831	$20
LP(P)	THE KITTY WELLS SHOW (66)	Decca 4831	$25
	(White promo label)		
LP	KITTY WELLS (66)	Vocalion 3786	$15
LP(P)	KITTY WELLS (66)	Vocalion 3786	$20
	(White promo label)		
LP	LOVE MAKES THE WORLD GO AROUND (67) Mono	Decca 4857	$15
LP	LOVE MAKES THE WORLD GO AROUND (67) Stereo	Decca 4857	$18
LP(P)	LOVE MAKES THE WORLD GO AROUND (67)	Decca 4857	$25
	(White promo label)		
LP	TOGETHER AGAIN (67) With Red Foley	Decca 4906	$15
LP(P)	TOGETHER AGAIN (67)	Decca 4906	$18
	(White promo label)		
LP	QUEEN OF HONKY TONK STREET (67)	Decca 4929	$15
LP(P)	QUEEN OF HONKY TONK STREET (67)	Decca 4929	$20
	(White promo label)		
LP	SHOWCASE (68)	Decca 74961	$15
LP(P)	SHOWCASE (68)	Decca 74961	$20
	(White promo label)		
LP	KITTY WELLS' GREATEST HITS (68)	Decca 75001	$12
LP(P)	KITTY WELLS' GREATEST HITS (68)	Decca 75001	$15
	(White promo label)		
LP	WE'LL STICK TOGETHER (68) With Johnny Wright	Decca 75026	$12
LP(P)	WE'LL STICK TOGETHER (68)	Decca 75026	$10
	(White promo label)		
LP	CREAM OF COUNTRY HITS (68)	Decca 75067	$12
LP(P)	CREAM OF COUNTRY HITS (68)	Decca 75067	$10
	(White promo label)		
LP	GUILTY STREET (68)	Decca 75098	$12
LP(P)	GUILTY STREET (68)	Decca 75098	$10
	(White promo label)		
LP	BOUQUET OF COUNTRY HITS (69)	Decca 75164	$10
LP	COUNTRY HEART (69)	Vocalion 3875	$12
LP(P)	COUNTRY HEART (69)	Vocalion 3875	$15
	(White promo label)		
LP	SINGIN' 'EM COUNTRY (70)	Decca 75221	$10
LP	YOUR LOVE IS THE WAY (70)	Decca 75245	$10
LP	THEY'RE STEPPING ALL OVER MY HEART (71)	Decca 75277	$10
LP	PLEDGING MY LOVE (71)	Decca 75313	$10
LP	HEARTWARMING GOSPEL SONGS (72)	Decca 75325	$10
LP	SINCERELY (72)	Decca 75350	$10
LP	I'VE GOT YESTERDAY (72)	Decca 75382	$10

-radio shows-

LP(RS)	HERE'S TO VETS (60s)	Vets Administration	$25-40
	(Music and interviews)		

WEST (C)

-albums-

LP	WEST (68)	Epic 26380	$10

CLINT WEST

-singles-

45rpm	TAKE A RIDE (58)	Jin 107	$75

DOTTIE WEST (C)
RCA Victor 45s $2-4 each
United Artists 45s $1 each
Other RCA Victor LPs $5-10 each
United Artists LPs $4-8 each
Camden and Liberty LPs $3-6 each

-EPs-

EP(JB)	HERE COMES MY BABY (65) Jukebox LLP	RCA Victor 3368	$18
	(Issued with a hard cover)		

-albums-

LP	COUNTRY GIRL SINGING SENSATION (64)	Starday 302	$25
LP	QUEENS OF COUNTRY MUSIC (65) With Melba Montgomery	Starday 352	$25
LP	HERE COMES MY BABY (65)	RCA Victor 3368	$18
LP	DOTTIE WEST SINGS (66)	RCA Victor 3490	$12
LP	WHAT I'M CUT OUT TO BE (68) Mono	RCA Victor 3932	$30
	(Rare mono recording)		

SHELLY WEST (C)
Daughter of Dottie West
Warner and Viva 45s $1 each
Warner and Viva LPs $3 each
   (Including duets with David Frizzell)

-radio shows-

3LP(RS)	**SILVER EAGLE** (Apr 85)	DIR	$15-25
	(Live concert)		

JIMMY WEST (RB)

-singles-

45rpm	**BINGO BLUES** (58)	Skyline 752	$60

SPEEDY WEST (CW)
Speedy West and Jimmy Bryant
Capitol 78s $3-6 each
Other Capitol 45s $5-10 each

-singles-

45rpm	**TWICE THE LOVIN'** (52) With Jean Shepard	Capitol 2358	$15
45rpm	**STEEL GUITAR RAG** (53) With Cliffe Stone	Capitol 2620	$12
45rpm	**STRATOSPHERE BOOGIE** (54) With Jimmy Bryant	Capitol 2964	$10
45rpm	**STEELIN' MOONLIGHT** (55) With Jimmy Bryant	Capitol 3208	$10
45rpm	**ROLLING SKY** (56) With Jimmy Bryant	Capitol 3635	$10

-EPs-

EP	**TWO GUITARS COUNTRY STYLE** (54) With Jimmy Bryant	Capitol 1-520	$50
EP	**TWO GUITARS COUNTRY STYLE** (54)	Capitol 2-520	$50

-albums-

10"LP	**TWO GUITARS COUNTRY STYLE** (54) With Jimmy Bryant	Capitol 520	$200
LP	**TWO GUITARS COUNTRY STYLE** (54)	Capitol 520	$100
LP	**WEST OF HAWAII** (58)	Capitol 956	$40
LP(P)	**WEST OF HAWAII** (58)	Capitol 956	$30
	(Yellow promo label)		
LP	**STEEL GUITAR** (60)	Capitol 1341	$30
LP(P)	**STEEL GUITAR** (60)	Capitol 1341	$25
	(Blue promo label)		
LP	**GUITAR SPECTACULAR** (62)	Capitol 1835	$25
LP(P)	**GUITAR SPECTACULAR** (62)	Capitol 1835	$25
	(Blue promo label)		

KENT WESTBURY (RB)

-singles-

45rpm	**MY BABY DON'T ROCK ME NOW** (59)	Art 172	$60

JOHNNY WESTERN (CW)
The Rainbow Rider
Other Columbia 45s $5-10 each
Hep 45s $5 each

-singles-

45rpm	**GIVE ME MORE, MORE, MORE** (54)	Joco 301	$50
	(Red vinyl)		
45rpm	**LITTLE BUFFALO BILL** (55)	Joco 302	$50
	(Red vinyl)		
45rpm	**THE BALLAD OF PALADIN** (58)	Columbia 41260	$25
45(P)	**THE BALLAD OF PALADIN** (58)	Columbia 41260	$18
	(White promo label; flip side, "The Guns of Rio Muerto," features Richard Boone; both tracks from "Have Gun, Will Travel")		
45rpm	**THE BALLAD OF PALADIN** (60)	Columbia 42161	$15
	(Issued with "The Echo of Your Voice" on flip)		
45(P)	**THE BALLAD OF PALADIN** (60)	Columbia 42161	$12
	(White promo label)		
45rpm	**THE GUNFIGHTER** (62)	Columbia 42525	$15
	(White promo label)		

-albums-

LP	**HAVE GUN, WILL TRAVEL** (58)	Columbia 8588	$50
LP(P)	**HAVE GUN, WILL TRAVEL** (58)	Columbia 8588	$40
	(White promo label)		

GEORGE WESTON (RB)

-singles-

45rpm	**HEY LITTLE CAR HOP** (58)	Jackpot 48013	$40
45(P)	**HEY LITTLE CAR HOP** (58)	Jackpot 48013	$25
	(White promo label)		
45rpm	**DEAD MAN** (59)	Challenge 59066	$10

CHUCK WHEELER (RB)

-singles-

45rpm	**CHEROKEE ROCK** (59)	Stevens 103	$75

BILLY EDD WHEELER (C)

Kapp 45s $3-5 each
United Artists and Flying Fish LPs $4-8 each
RCA Victor LPs $6 each
Avalanche LPs $4 each

-albums-

LP	**BILLY EDD** (61)	Monitor 354	$20
LP	**BLUEGRASS TOO** (62)	Monitor 367	$18
LP	**NEW BAG OF SONGS** (64)	Kapp 3351	$15
LP	**MEMORIES OF AMERICA** (65)	Kapp 3425	$20
LP	**WHEELER MAN** (65)	Kapp 3443	$15
LP	**GOIN' TOWN & COUNTRY** (66)	Kapp 3479	$15
LP	**PAPER BIRDS** (67)	Kapp 3533	$15
LP	**I AIN'T THE WORRYIN' KIND** (68)	Kapp 3567	$15

KAREN WHEELER (C)

RCA Victor 45s $3 each
RCA Victor picture sleeves $5 each

ONIE WHEELER (RB)

All other 45s $1-2 each

-singles-

45rpm	**LITTLE MAMA** (53)	Okeh Records	$15
45rpm	**LITTLE MAMA** (53)	Columbia 21371	$15
45(P)	**LITTLE MAMA** (53)	Columbia 21371	$10
	(White promo label)		
45rpm	**ONIE'S BOP** (54)	Columbia 21523	$15
45(P)	**ONIE'S BOP** (54)	Columbia 21523	$10
	(White promo label)		
45rpm	**GOING BACK TO THE CITY** (56)	Columbia 40911	$12
45(P)	**GOING BACK TO THE CITY** (56)	Columbia 40911	$10
	(White promo label)		

-albums-

LP	**JOHN'S BEEN SHUCKIN' MY CORN** (70s)	Onie 100	$15

WHITES (C)

Buck, Sharon, and Cheryl
Warner and MCA 45s $1 each
Warner and MCA LPs $3 each

-singles-

45(P)	**LOVE WON'T WAIT** (86)	MCA 52825	$10
	(White promo label, blue vinyl)		
45(P)	**IT SHOULD HAVE BEEN EASY** (86)	MCA 52953	$10
	(White promo label, yellow vinyl)		

-radio shows-

LP(RS)	**COUNTRY MUSIC TIME** (80s)	U.S. Air Force	$10-12
	(Music and interviews)		
LP(RS)	**LIVE AT GILLEY'S** (Mar 83)	Westwood One	$10-15
	(Live concert)		

KEITH WHITLEY (C)

RCA Victor 45s $1-2 each
Rebel LPs $6 each
RCA Victor LPs $3 each

-albums-

LP	**TRIBUTE TO THE STANLEY BROTHERS** (60s)	Jalyn 129	$25
	(Featuring Ricky Skaggs)		

-radio shows-

LP(RS)	**COUNTRY MUSIC TIME** (80s)	U.S. Air Force	$20-30
	(Live concert)		
LP(RS)	**LIVE AT GILLEY'S** (Mar 87)	Westwood One	$30-60
	(Live concert)		
LP(RS)	**WESTWOOD ONE PRESENTS** (June 89)	Westwood One	$30-60
	(Live concert)		
2CD(RS)	**THE KEITH WHITLEY STORY** (90s)	RH Entertainment	$40-75
	(Music and interviews)		

SLIM WHITMAN (CW)

Otis Whitman
With the Light Crust Doughboys in 1949-50
Okeh 78s by the Light Crust Doughboys $8-12 each, on Vocalion $6-$12 each
Other Imperial 45s $2-8 each
Cleveland International 45s $2 each
United Artists 45s $2 each
Epic and Liberty LPs $5-8 each
United Artists LPs $5-10 each
Other RCA Victor and Sunset LPs $5-8 each
Other Suffolk 2LP sets $8 each
Pickwick LPs $4 each

-singles-

45rpm	BIRMINGHAM JAIL (49) Green vinyl	RCA Victor 0145	$75
78rpm	THERE'S A RAINBOW IN EVERY TEARDROP (53)	RCA Victor 5431	$25
78(P)	THERE'S A RAINBOW IN EVERY TEARDROP (53)	RCA Victor 5431	$30
	(White promo label)		
45rpm	THERE'S A RAINBOW IN EVERY TEARDROP (53)	RCA Victor 5431	$50
45(P)	THERE'S A RAINBOW IN EVERY TEARDROP (53)	RCA Victor 5431	$40
	(White promo label)		
78rpm	BIRMINGHAM JAIL (54)	RCA Victor 5557	$25
78(P)	BIRMINGHAM JAIL (54)	RCA Victor 5557	$30
	(White promo label)		
45rpm	BIRMINGHAM JAIL (54)	RCA Victor 5557	$50
45(P)	BIRMINGHAM JAIL (54)	RCA Victor 5557	$40
	(White promo label)		
78rpm	PLEASE PAINT A ROSE ON THE GARDEN WALL (54)	RCA Victor 5724	$25
78(P)	PLEASE PAINT A ROSE ON THE GARDEN WALL (54)	RCA Victor 5724	$30
	(White promo label)		
45rpm	PLEASE PAINT A ROSE ON THE GARDEN WALL (54)	RCA Victor 5742	$50
45(P)	PLEASE PAINT A ROSE ON THE GARDEN WALL (54)	RCA Victor 5742	$40
	(White promo label)		
78rpm	LOVE SONG OF THE WATERFALL (54)	Imperial 8134	$18
45rpm	LOVE SONG OF THE WATERFALL (52)	Imperial 8134	$25
78rpm	BANDERA WALTZ (52)	Imperial 8144	$15
45rpm	BANDERA WALTZ (52)	Imperial 8144	$30
78rpm	INDIAN LOVE CALL (52)	Imperial 8156	$15
45rpm	INDIAN LOVE CALL (52)	Imperial 8156	$25
78rpm	BY THE WATERS OF THE MINNETONKA (52)	Imperial 8163	$15
45rpm	BY THE WATERS OF THE MINNETONKA (52)	Imperial 8163	$25
78rpm	KEEP IT A SECRET (52)	Imperial 8169	$15
45rpm	KEEP IT A SECRET (52)	Imperial 8169	$25
78rpm	HOW CAN I TELL (52)	Imperial 8180	$12
45rpm	HOW CAN I TELL (53)	Imperial 8180	$25
78rpm	SONG OF THE OLD WATER WHEEL (53)	Imperial 8189	$12
45rpm	SONG OF THE OLD WATER WHEEL (53)	Imperial 8189	$25
78rpm	THERE'S A RAINBOW IN EVERY TEARDROP (53)	Imperial 8201	$12
45rpm	THERE'S A RAINBOW IN EVERY TEARDROP (53)	Imperial 8201	$20
78rpm	NORTH WIND (53)	Imperial 8208	$12
45rpm	NORTH WIND (53)	Imperial 8208	$20
78rpm	STAIRWAY TO HEAVEN (53)	Imperial 8220	$12
45rpm	STAIRWAY TO HEAVEN (53)	Imperial 8220	$20
78rpm	SECRET LOVE (54)	Imperial 8223	$12
45rpm	SECRET LOVE (54)	Imperial 8223	$20
78rpm	ROSE-MARIE (54)	Imperial 8236	$12
45rpm	ROSE-MARIE (54)	Imperial 8236	$20
	(All of the Imperial 45s above have a blue script label)		
78rpm	RIDE AWAY (54)	Imperial 8257	$10
45rpm	RIDE AWAY (54)	Imperial 8257	$18
78rpm	SINGING HILLS (55)	Imperial 8267	$10
45rpm	SINGING HILLS (55)	Imperial 8267	$18
78rpm	CATTLE CALL (55)	Imperial 8281	$10
45rpm	CATTLE CALL (55)	Imperial 8281	$18
78rpm	ROLL ON SILVERY MOON (55)	Imperial 8290	$10
45rpm	ROLL ON SILVERY MOON (55)	Imperial 8290	$18
45(P)	ROLL ON SILVERY MOON (55)	Imperial 8290	$15
	(Cream-colored promo label)		
78rpm	I'LL NEVER TAKE YOU BACK AGAIN (55)	Imperial 8298	$10
45rpm	I'LL NEVER TAKE YOU BACK AGAIN (55)	Imperial 8298	$18
45(P)	I'LL NEVER TAKE YOU BACK AGAIN (55)	Imperial 8298	$15
	(Cream-colored promo label)		
78rpm	YOU HAVE MY HEART (56)	Imperial 8299	$10
45rpm	YOU HAVE MY HEART (56)	Imperial 8299	$18
45(P)	YOU HAVE MY HEART (56)	Imperial 8299	$15
	(Cream-colored promo label)		
78rpm	TUMBLING TUMBLEWEEDS (56)	Imperial 8304	$10

45rpm	**TUMBLING TUMBLEWEEDS** (56)	Imperial 8304	$15
	(Imperial 8257 through 8304 have red labels)		
45(P)	**TUMBLING TUMBLEWEEDS** (56)	Imperial 8304	$12
	(Cream-colored promo label)		
78rpm	**I'M A FOOL** (56)	Imperial 8305	$10
45rpm	**I'M A FOOL** (56)	Imperial 8305	$15
45(P)	**I'M A FOOL** (56)	Imperial 8305	$12
	(Cream-colored promo label)		
78rpm	**THE WHIFFENPOOF SONG** (56)	Imperial 8307	$10
45rpm	**THE WHIFFENPOOF SONG** (56)	Imperial 8307	$15
45(P)	**THE WHIFFENPOOF SONG** (56)	Imperial 8307	$12
	(Cream-colored promo label)		
78rpm	**CURTAIN OF TEARS** (56)	Imperial 8308	$10
45rpm	**CURTAIN OF TEARS** (56)	Imperial 8308	$15
45(P)	**CURTAIN OF TEARS** (56)	Imperial 8308	$12
	(Cream-colored promo label, black vinyl)		
45(P)	**CURTAIN OF TEARS** (56) Red vinyl	Imperial 8308	$200
	(Cream-colored promo label, red vinyl)		
78rpm	**I MUST HAVE BEEN BLIND** (57)	Imperial 8309	$15
45rpm	**I MUST HAVE BEEN BLIND** (57)	Imperial 8309	$15
45(P)	**I MUST HAVE BEEN BLIND** (57)	Imperial 8309	$12
	(Cream-colored promo label)		
78rpm	**I'LL TAKE YOU HOME AGAIN KATHLEEN** (57)	Imperial 8310	$25
45rpm	**I'LL TAKE YOU HOME AGAIN KATHLEEN** (57)	Imperial 8310	$12
45(P)	**I'LL TAKE YOU HOME AGAIN KATHLEEN** (57)	Imperial 8310	$10
	(Cream-colored promo label)		
45rpm	**UNCHAIN MY HEART** (57)	Imperial 8312	$12
45(P)	**UNCHAIN MY HEART** (57)	Imperial 8312	$10
	(Cream-colored promo label)		
45rpm	**CARELESS HANDS** (57)	Imperial 8316	$12
45(P)	**CARELESS HANDS** (57)	Imperial 8316	$10
	(Cream-colored promo label)		
45rpm	**TORMENTED** (58)	Imperial 8317	$10
45rpm	**PUT YOUR TRUST IN ME** (58)	Imperial 8318	$10
45rpm	**AT THE END OF NOWHERE** (58)	Imperial 8319	$10
45rpm	**THE LETTER EDGED IN BLACK** (59)	Imperial 8320	$10
45rpm	**WHAT KIND OF GOD** (59)	Imperial 8321	$10
45rpm	**A FOOL SUCH AS I** (59)	Imperial 8322	$10
45rpm	**INDIAN LOVE CALL** (59)	Imperial 8323	$10
45rpm	**TWILLA LEE** (59)	Imperial 8326	$10
45rpm	**I'LL WALK WITH GOD** (59)	Imperial 8327	$10
45rpm	**VAYA CON DIOS** (59)	Imperial 8329	$10
45rpm	**I'D CLIMB THE HIGHEST MOUNTAIN** (60)	Imperial 5746	$10
45rpm	**VALLEY OF TEARS** (61)	Imperial 5821	$10

-EPs-

EP	**AMERICA'S FAVORITE FOLK ARTIST** (54)	Imperial 106	$100
EP(P)	**AMERICA'S FAVORITE FOLK ARTIST** (54)	Imperial 106	$150
	(Cream-colored promo label)		
2EP	**SLIM WHITMAN SINGS & YODELS** (54)	RCA Victor 3217	$200
	(Double record EP)		
EP	**SLIM WHITMAN SINGING** (56)	Imperial 130	$75
EP(P)	**SLIM WHITMAN SINGING** (56)	Imperial 130	$100
	(Cream-colored promo label)		
EP	**SONGS BY SLIM WHITMAN** (56)	Imperial 131	$75
EP(P)	**SONGS BY SLIM WHITMAN** (56)	Imperial 131	$100
	(Cream-colored promo label)		
EP	**SONGS BY SLIM WHITMAN** (56)	Imperial 132	$50
EP(P)	**SONGS BY SLIM WHITMAN** (56)	Imperial 132	$75
	(Cream-colored promo label)		
EP	**SONGS BY SLIM WHITMAN** (56)	Imperial 133	$50
EP(P)	**SONGS BY SLIM WHITMAN** (56)	Imperial 133	$75
	(Cream-colored promo label)		
EP	**SONGS BY SLIM WHITMAN** (56)	Imperial 134	$50
EP(P)	**SONGS BY SLIM WHITMAN** (56)	Imperial 134	$75
	(Cream-colored promo label)		
EP	**SLIM WHITMAN** (56)	Imperial 135	$50
EP	**SLIM WHITMAN** (56)	Imperial 135	$75
	(Cream-colored promo label)		
EP	**SONGS BY SLIM WHITMAN** (56)	Imperial 136	$50
EP	**SONGS BY SLIM WHITMAN** (56)	Imperial 136	$75
	(Cream-colored promo label)		
EP	**SLIM WHITMAN** (56)	Imperial 137	$50
EP(P)	**SLIM WHITMAN** (56)	Imperial 137	$75
	(Cream-colored promo label)		
EP(JB)	**COUNTRY SONGS** (64) Jukebox LLP	Imperial 42268	$50
	(Issued with a hard cover)		

EP(JB)	**MORE THAN YESTERDAY** (65) Jukebox LLP	Imperial 42303	$50
	(Issued with a hard cover)		

-albums-

10"LP	**AMERICA'S FAVORITE FOLK ARTIST** (54)	Imperial 3004	$300
10"LP	**SLIM WHITMAN SINGS & YODELS** (54)	RCA Victor 3217	$200
LP	**SLIM WHITMAN FAVORITES** (56) Maroon label	Imperial 9003	$50
LP	**SLIM WHITMAN FAVORITES** (56) Black label	Imperial 9003	$30
LP	**SLIM WHITMAN SINGS** (57) Maroon label	Imperial 9026	$50
LP	**SLIM WHITMAN SINGS** (57) Black label	Imperial 9026	$30
LP	**SLIM WHITMAN SINGS** (58) Maroon label	Imperial 9056	$50
LP	**SLIM WHITMAN SINGS** (58) Black label	Imperial 9056	$30
LP	**SLIM WHITMAN SINGS** (59) Maroon label	Imperial 9064	$50
LP	**SLIM WHITMAN SINGS** (59) Black label	Imperial 9064	$30
LP	**ANNIE LAURIE** (59)	Imperial 9077	$30
LP	**I'LL WALK WITH GOD** (60) Mono	Imperial 9088	$30
LP	**I'LL WALK WITH GOD** (66) Stereo	Imperial 12032	$15
LP	**COUNTRY HITS VOL 1** (60)	Imperial 9100	$15
LP	**MILLION RECORD HITS** (60)	Imperial 9102	$30
LP	**SONG OF THE OLD WATERWHEEL** (66)	Imperial 9102	$15
LP	**COUNTRY HITS VOL 2** (66)	Imperial 9104	$15
LP	**MY BEST TO YOU** (66)	Imperial 9105	$15
LP	**COUNTRY FAVORITES** (66)	Imperial 9106	$15
LP	**FIRST VISIT TO BRITAIN** (60)	Imperial 9135	$15
LP	**JUST CALL ME LONESOME** (61)	Imperial 9137	$15
LP	**ONCE IN A LIFETIME** (61)	Imperial 9156	$15
LP	**FOREVER** (66)	Imperial 9171	$15
LP	**SLIM WHITMAN SINGS** (61) Mono	Imperial 9194	$25
LP	**SLIM WHITMAN SINGS** (61) Stereo	Imperial 12194	$30
LP(P)	**SLIM WHITMAN SINGS** (61)	Imperial 9171	$50
	(White promo label)		
LP	**HEART SONGS AND LOVE SONGS** (61)	Imperial 9209	$25
LP(P)	**HEART SONGS AND LOVE SONGS** (62)	Imperial 9209	$50
	(White promo label)		
LP	**I'M A LONELY WANDERER** (62)	Imperial 9226	$25
LP(P)	**I'M A LONELY WANDERER** (62)	Imperial 9226	$50
	(White promo label)		
LP	**YODELING** (63)	Imperial 9235	$25
LP(P)	**YODELING** (63)	Imperial 9235	$40
	(White promo label)		
LP	**IRISH SONGS, THE WHITMAN WAY** (63)	Imperial 9245	$25
LP(P)	**IRISH SONGS, THE WHITMAN WAY** (63)	Imperial 9245	$30
	(White promo label)		
LP	**ALL TIME FAVORITES** (64)	Imperial 9252	$25
LP(P)	**ALL TIME FAVORITES** (64)	Imperial 9252	$30
	(White promo label)		
LP	**COUNTRY SONGS CITY HITS** (64)	Imperial 9268	$15
LP(P)	**COUNTRY SONGS CITY HITS** (64)	Imperial 9268	$20
	(White promo label)		
LP	**LOVE SONG OF THE WATERFALL** (64)	Imperial 9277	$10
LP(P)	**LOVE SONG OF THE WATERFALL** (64)	Imperial 9277	$15
	(White promo label)		
LP	**REMINISCING** (65)	Imperial 9288	$10
LP(P)	**REMINISCING** (65)	Imperial 9288	$12
	(White promo label)		
LP	**MORE THAN YESTERDAY** (65)	Imperial 9303	$10
LP	**BIRMINGHAM JAIL** (66) Mono	Camden 954	$25
	(Early RCA Victor material)		
LP	**BIRMINGHAM JAIL** (66) Stereo	Camden 954	$18
LP	**GOD'S HAND IN MINE** (66)	Imperial 9308	$10
LP	**A TRAVELIN' MAN** (66)	Imperial 9313	$10
LP	**A TIME FOR LOVE** (66)	Imperial 9333	$10
LP	**15TH ANNIVERSARY** (67)	Imperial 9342	$10
LP	**COUNTRY MEMORIES** (67)	Imperial 9356	$10
LP	**A LONESOME HEART** (67)	Sunset 5167	$15
LP	**IN LOVE, THE WHITMAN WAY** (68)	Imperial 12356	$10
LP	**UNCHAIN YOUR HEART** (68)	Sunset 1112	$12
LP	**HAPPY STREET** (69)	Imperial 12375	$10
LP	**SLIM** (69)	Imperial 12436	$10
LP	**SLIM WHITMAN CHRISTMAS ALBUM** (69)	Imperial 12448	$10
2LP	**ALL MY BEST** (79)	Suffolk 8128	$15
	(Television offer)		

ROY WIGGINS (C)

Starday 45s $3-6 each
Power Pak and Diplomat LPs $3-5 each

-albums-

LP	**MISTER STEEL GUITAR** (62)	Starday 188	$25
LP	**EIGHTEEN ALL TIME HITS** (66)	Starday 392	$18

WALLY WIGGINS (RB)

-singles-

45rpm	**MAYBELLINE** (59)	Mercury 71713	$20
45(P)	**MAYBELLINE** (59)	Mercury 71713	$15
	(White promo label)		

WILBURN BROTHERS (CW)
Teddy and Doyle
Decca 78s $4-8 each
Other Decca 45s $5-8 each
Other Decca LPs $8-10 each
Other Vocalion LPs $8 each
MCA LPs $3 each

-singles-

45rpm	**I WANNA, WANNA, WANNA** (55)	Decca 29459	$18
45(P)	**I WANNA, WANNA, WANNA** (55)	Decca 29459	$15
	(Pink promo label)		
45rpm	**DEEP ELM BLUES** (56)	Decca 29887	$10
45rpm	**CRY BABY CRY** (58)	Decca 30686	$10

-EPs-

EP	**THE WILBURN BROTHERS** (57)	Decca 2537	$20
EP	**THE WILBURN BROTHERS** (57)	Decca 2551	$20
EP	**THE WILBURN BROTHERS** (58)	Decca 2588	$15
EP	**SIDE BY SIDE** (59)	Decca 2617	$15
EP	**BIG HEARTBREAK** (60)	Decca 2681	$15
EP	**WILBURN BROTHERS** (61)	Decca 2689	$15
EP	**TROUBLE'S BACK IN TOWN** (62)	Decca 2727	$15
EP	**WILBURN BROTHERS** (63)	Decca 2756	$15
EP	**ROLL MUDDY RIVER** (65)	Decca 2782	$15
EP	**TAKE UP THY CROSS** (65)	Decca 2783	$15
EP	**I'M GONNA TIE ONE ON TONIGHT** (65)	Decca 2803	$15
EP	**THE WILBURN BROTHERS** (66) Jukebox LLP	Decca 34371	$25
	(Price includes hard cover and title strips)		

-albums-

LP	**THE WILBURN BROTHERS** (57)	Decca 8576	$50
LP(P)	**THE WILBURN BROTHERS** (57)	Decca 8576	$40
	(Pink promo label)		
LP	**SIDE BY SIDE** (58) Mono	Decca 8774	$30
LP	**SIDE BY SIDE** (58) Stereo	Decca 78774	$50
LP(P)	**SIDE BY SIDE** (58)	Decca 8774	$40
	(Pink promo label)		
LP	**LIVIN' IN GOD'S COUNTRY** (59) Mono	Decca 8959	$30
LP	**LIVIN' IN GOD'S COUNTRY** (59) Stereo	Decca 8959	$50
LP(P)	**LIVIN' IN GOD'S COUNTRY** (59)	Decca 78959	$40
	(Pink promo label)		
LP	**THE BIG HEARTBREAK** (60)	Decca 4058	$25
LP(P)	**THE BIG HEARTBREAK** (60)	Decca 4058	$30
	(Pink promo label)		
LP	**CITY LIMITS** (61)	Decca 4122	$20
LP(P)	**CITY LIMITS** (61)	Decca 4122	$25
	(Pink promo label)		
LP	**THE WILBURN BROTHERS SING** (61)	Decca 4142	$20
LP(P)	**THE WILBURN BROTHERS SING** (61)	Decca 4142	$25
	(Pink promo label)		
LP	**THE WONDERFUL WILBURN BROTHERS** (61)	King 746	$75
LP	**FOLK SONGS** (62)	Decca 4225	$15
LP(P)	**FOLK SONGS** (62)	Decca 4225	$20
	(Pink promo label)		
LP	**CAREFREE MOMENTS** (62)	Vocalion 3691	$15
LP(P)	**CAREFREE MOMENTS** (62)	Vocalion 3691	$18
	(White promo label)		
LP	**TROUBLE'S BACK IN TOWN** (63)	Decca 4391	$15
LP(P)	**TROUBLE'S BACK IN TOWN** (63)	Decca 4391	$18
	(Pink promo label)		
LP	**TAKE UP THY CROSS** (64)	Decca 4464	$15
LP(P)	**TAKE UP THY CROSS** (64)	Decca 4464	$15
	(Decca promo label)		
LP	**NEVER ALONE** (64)	Decca 4544	$10
LP	**COUNTRY GOLD** (65)	Decca 4615	$10
LP	**I'M GONNA TIE ONE ON TONIGHT** (65)	Decca 4645	$10
LP	**THE WILBURN BROTHERS SHOW** (66) Mono	Decca 4721	$30
	(Includes Loretta Lynn and Ernest Tubb)		
LP	**THE WILBURN BROTHERS SHOW** (66) Stereo	Decca 74721	$75
LP(P)	**THE WILBURN BROTHERS SHOW** (66)	Decca 4721	$50
	(Decca promo label)		

LP	LET'S GO COUNTRY (66)		Decca 4764	$10
LP	TWO FOR THE SHOW (67)		Decca 4824	$10
LP	COOL COUNTRY (67)		Decca 4871	$10
LP	IT'S ANOTHER WORLD (68)		Decca 74954	$10
LP	THE WILBURN BROTHERS' GREATEST HITS (68)		Decca 75002	$10
LP	I WALK THE LINE (68)		Vocalion 3889	$10
LP	WE NEED A LOT MORE HAPPINESS (69)		Decca 75087	$10
LP	IT LOOKS LIKE THE SUN'S GONNA SHINE (69)		Decca 75123	$10

-radio shows-

16"(RS)	U.S. NAVY BAND (50s)		U.S. Navy	$25-40
	(Music and interviews)			
16"(RS)	COUNTRY STYLE USA (56) Fifteen-minute show		CStyle USA 184	$25-40
	(Music and interviews)			
LP(RS)	GRAND OL' OPRY (63) Fifteen-minute show		WSM Radio 62	$25-40
	(Music and interviews)			
LP(RS)	HOOTENAVY (60s) Fifteen-minute show		U.S. Navy 19/20	$25-40
	(Music and interviews)			

CHUCK WILEY (RB)

-singles-

45rpm	TEAR IT UP (58)		United Artists 113	$25

SLIM WILLET (CW)

-singles-

45rpm	DON'T LET THE STARS (52)		4-Star 1614	$10
45rpm	LET ME KNOW (53)		4-Star 1625	$10
45rpm	THE RED ROSE (53)		4-Star 1637	$10
45rpm	DON'T WASTE YOUR HEART (54)		4-Star 1645	$10

-EPs-

EP	SLIM WILLET (59)		Audio Lab 9	$30

-albums-

LP	SLIM WILLET (59)		Audio Lab 1542	$20

WALLY WILLETTE (RB)

-singles-

45rpm	EENIE MEENIE (58)		Flag 118	$125

DON WILLIAMS (CW)

A member of The Pozo Seco Singers
Other JMI 45s $3-$5 each
Columbia 45s by The Pozo Seco Singers $5 each
Certron 45s by The Pozo Seco Singers $3 each
Dot 45s $2-3 each
Warner duet 45s $2 each
Capitol 45s $1 each
Dot/ABC and MCA LPs $3-5 each
Power Pak LPs $3 each

-singles-

45rpm	AMANDA (73)		JMI 24	$10
45(P)	A SPECIAL MESSAGE FROM DON WILLIAMS (82)		MCA 1763	$12
	(Promo-only "For your radio station and audience")			

-albums-

LP	TIME (66) The Pozo Seco Singers		Columbia 9315	$20
LP(P)	TIME (66)		Columbia 9315	$25
	(White promo label)			
LP	I CAN MAKE IT WITH YOU (67) Pozo Seco Singers		Columbia 9315	$15
LP	SHADES OF TIME (68) The Pozo Seco Singers		Columbia 9656	$18
LP(P)	SHADES OF TIME (68)		Columbia 9656	$25
	(White promo label)			
LP	SPEND SOME TIME WITH ME (72) Pozo Seco Singers		Certron 7007	$15
LP	DON WILLIAMS (73)		JMI 4004	$25
LP	DON WILLIAMS VOL 2 (74)		JMI 4006	$20
LP(P)	DON WILLIAMS (77)		ABC 28	$15
	(Promo-only 3-track mini LP)			

-radio shows-

3LP(RS)	THE SILVER EAGLE (81) Live concert		DIR 006	$35
	(Don Williams and Roseanne Cash and Rodney Crowell)			
3LP(RS)	INTERNATIONAL FESTIVAL OF COUNTRY MUSIC (Oct 82)		Mutual Radio	$40
	(Williams, Boxcar Willie, Razzy Bailey, and others)			
3LP(RS)	DON & DOLLY (Aug 83) Box set		Mutual Radio	$20-30
	(Music and interviews with Dolly Parton)			
LP(RS)	WESTWOOD ONE PRESENTS (Dec 86)		Westwood One	$25-50
	(Live concert)			

HANK WILLIAMS (CW)
Also recorded as Luke the Drifter
Audrey was his first wife and mother of Hank Jr.
MGM Golden Circle 45s with black bar on label $5-10 each
MGM Golden Circle 45s $3-5 each
MGM Band of Gold 45s $2-3 each
Other MGM 45s $2-3 each
MGM blue and gold label LPs $5-10 each
Other MGM LPs $5-10 each
Polydor LPs $4-8 each
Blaine House, Sunrise Media, Other Time-Life, Golden Country, Country Music Foundation LPs $4-8 each

-singles-

78rpm	**CALLING YOU** (47)	Sterling 201	$750
78rpm	**WEALTH WON'T SAVE YOUR SOUL** (47)	Sterling 204	$500
	(Flip side "When God Comes and Gathers His Jewels")		
78rpm	**WEALTH WON'T SAVE YOUR SOUL** (47)	Sterling 204	$500
	(Flip side "When God Comes and Fathers His Jewels," which is a label misprint)		
78rpm	**I DON'T CARE IF TOMORROW NEVER COMES** (47)	Sterling 208	$500
78rpm	**HONKY TONKIN'** (47)	Sterling 210	$400
78rpm	**MOVE IT ON OVER** (47)	MGM 10033	$75
78(P)	**MOVE IT ON OVER** (47)	MGM 10033	$100
	(Yellow promo label)		
78rpm	**FLY TROUBLE** (47)	MGM 10073	$50
78(P)	**FLY TROUBLE** (47)	MGM 10073	$75
	(Yellow promo label)		
78rpm	**ROOTIE TOOTIE** (48)	MGM 10124	$50
78(P)	**ROOTIE TOOTIE** (48)	MGM 10124	$75
	(Yellow promo label)		
78rpm	**HONKY TONKIN'** (48)	MGM 10171	$50
78(P)	**HONKY TONKIN'** (48)	MGM 10171	$75
	(Yellow promo label)		
78rpm	**I'M A LONG GONE DADDY** (48)	MGM 10212	$40
78(P)	**I'M A LONG GONE DADDY** (48)	MGM 10212	$60
	(Yellow promo label)		
78rpm	**PAN AMERICAN** (48)	MGM 10226	$40
78(P)	**PAN AMERICAN** (48)	MGM 10226	$60
	(Yellow promo label)		
78rpm	**I SAW THE LIGHT** (48)	MGM 10271	$40
78(P)	**I SAW THE LIGHT** (48)	MGM 10271	$60
	(Yellow promo label)		
78rpm	**A MANSION ON THE HILL** (48)	MGM 10328	$40
78(P)	**A MANSION ON THE HILL** (48)	MGM 10328	$60
	(Yellow promo label)		
78rpm	**LOVESICK BLUES** (49)	MGM 10352	$30
78(P)	**LOVESICK BLUES** (49)	MGM 10352	$60
	(Yellow promo label)		
78rpm	**WEDDING BLESS** (49)	MGM 10401	$30
78(P)	**WEDDING BLESS** (49)	MGM 10401	$60
	(Yellow promo label)		
78rpm	**DEAR BROTHER** (49)	MGM 10434	$35
78(P)	**DEAR BROTHER** (49)	MGM 10434	$60
	(Yellow promo label)		
78rpm	**MIND YOUR OWN BUSINESS** (49)	MGM 10461	$30
78(P)	**MIND YOUR OWN BUSINESS** (49)	MGM 10461	$60
	(Yellow promo label)		
45rpm	**MIND YOUR OWN BUSINESS** (50)	MGM 10461	$25
45(P)	**MIND YOUR OWN BUSINESS** (50)	MGM 10461	$20
	(Yellow promo label)		
78rpm	**LOST HIGHWAY** (50)	MGM 10506	$30
78(P)	**LOST HIGHWAY** (50)	MGM 10506	$60
	(Yellow promo label)		
45rpm	**LOST HIGHWAY** (50)	MGM 10506	$25
45(P)	**LOST HIGHWAY** (50)	MGM 10506	$20
	(Yellow promo label)		
78rpm	**HONKY TONKIN'** (50) Audrey Williams	Decca 46233	$50
45rpm	**HONKY TONKIN'** (50) Audrey Williams	Decca 46233	$40
78rpm	**MY TIGHT WAD DADDY** (50) Audrey Williams	Decca 46264	$40
45rpm	**MY TIGHT WAD DADDY** (50) Audrey Williams	Decca 46264	$30
45rpm	**HELP ME UNDERSTAND** (50) Audrey Williams	Decca 46275	$25
78rpm	**I'M SO LONESOME I COULD CRY** (50)	MGM 10560	$30
78(P)	**I'M SO LONESOME I COULD CRY** (50)	MGM 10560	$60
	(Yellow promo label)		
45rpm	**I'M SO LONESOME I COULD CRY** (50)	MGM 10560	$25
45(P)	**I'M SO LONESOME I COULD CRY** (50)	MGM 10560	$20
	(Yellow promo label)		
78rpm	**MAY YOU NEVER BE ALONE** (50)	MGM 10609	$30

78(P)	**MAY YOU NEVER BE ALONE** (50)	MGM 10609	$60
	(Yellow promo label)		
45rpm	**MAY YOU NEVER BE ALONE** (50)	MGM 10609	$25
45(P)	**MAY YOU NEVER BE ALONE** (50)	MGM 10609	$20
	(Yellow promo label)		
78rpm	**BEYOND THE SUNSET** (50) Luke the Drifter	MGM 10630	$30
78(P)	**BEYOND THE SUNSET** (50)	MGM 10630	$60
	(Yellow promo label)		
45rpm	**BEYOND THE SUNSET** (50)	MGM 10630	$25
45(P)	**BEYOND THE SUNSET** (50)	MGM 10630	$20
	(Yellow promo label)		
78rpm	**LONG GONE LONESOME BLUES** (50)	MGM 10645	$30
78(P)	**LONG GONE LONESOME BLUES** (50)	MGM 10645	$60
	(Yellow promo label)		
45rpm	**LONG GONE LONESOME BLUES** (50)	MGM 10645	$25
45(P)	**LONG GONE LONESOME BLUES** (50)	MGM 10645	$20
	(Yellow promo label)		
78rpm	**WHY DON'T YOU LOVE ME** (50)	MGM 10696	$25
78(P)	**WHY DON'T YOU LOVE ME** (50)	MGM 10696	$60
	(Yellow promo label)		
45rpm	**WHY DON'T YOU LOVE ME** (50)	MGM 10696	$25
45(P)	**WHY DON'T YOU LOVE ME** (50)	MGM 10696	$20
	(Yellow promo label)		
78rpm	**EVERYTHING'S OK** (50) Luke the Drifter	MGM 10718	$25
78(P)	**EVERYTHING'S OK** (50)	MGM 10718	$60
	(Yellow promo label)		
45rpm	**EVERYTHING'S OK** (50)	MGM 10718	$25
45(P)	**EVERYTHING'S OK** (50)	MGM 10718	$20
	(Yellow promo label)		
78rpm	**WHY SHOULD WE TRY ANYMORE** (50)	MGM 10760	$30
78(P)	**WHY SHOULD WE TRY ANYMORE** (50)	MGM 10760	$60
	(Yellow promo label)		
45rpm	**WHY SHOULD WE TRY ANYMORE** (50)	MGM 10760	$25
45(P)	**WHY SHOULD WE TRY ANYMORE** (50)	MGM 10760	$20
	(Yellow promo label)		
78rpm	**NO NO, JOE** (50) Luke the Drifter	MGM 10806	$25
78(P)	**NO NO, JOE** (50)	MGM 10806	$60
	(Yellow promo label)		
45rpm	**NO NO, JOE** (50)	MGM 10806	$25
45(P)	**NO NO, JOE** (50)	MGM 10806	$20
	(Yellow promo label)		
78rpm	**I HEARD MY MOTHER PRAYING FOR ME** (50)	MGM 10813	$30
78(P)	**I HEARD MY MOTHER PRAYING FOR ME** (50)	MGM 10813	$60
	(Yellow promo label)		
45rpm	**I HEARD MY MOTHER PRAYING FOR ME** (50)	MGM 10813	$25
45(P)	**I HEARD MY MOTHER PRAYING FOR ME** (50)	MGM 10813	$20
	(Yellow promo label)		
78rpm	**MOANIN' THE BLUES** (50)	MGM 10832	$25
78(P)	**MOANIN' THE BLUES** (50)	MGM 10832	$50
	(Yellow promo label)		
45rpm	**MOANIN' THE BLUES** (50)	MGM 10832	$25
45(P)	**MOANIN' THE BLUES** (50)	MGM 10832	$20
	(Yellow promo label)		
78rpm	**COLD, COLD HEART** (51)	MGM 10904	$25
78(P)	**COLD, COLD HEART** (51)	MGM 10904	$50
	(Yellow promo label)		
45rpm	**COLD, COLD HEART** (51)	MGM 10904	$25
45(P)	**COLD, COLD HEART** (51)	MGM 10904	$20
	(Yellow promo label)		
78rpm	**JUST WAITIN'** (51) Luke the Drifter	MGM 10932	$25
78(P)	**JUST WAITIN'** (51)	MGM 10932	$50
	(Yellow promo label)		
45rpm	**JUST WAITIN'** (51)	MGM 10932	$25
45(P)	**JUST WAITIN'** (51)	MGM 10932	$20
	(yellow promo label)		
78rpm	**I CAN'T HELP IT** (51)	MGM 10961	$25
78(P)	**I CAN'T HELP IT** (51)	MGM 10961	$50
	(Yellow promo label)		
45rpm	**I CAN'T HELP IT** (51)	MGM 10961	$25
45(P)	**I CAN'T HELP IT** (51)	MGM 10961	$20
	(Yellow promo label)		
78rpm	**HEY, GOOD LOOKIN'** (51)	MGM 11000	$25
78(P)	**HEY, GOOD LOOKIN'** (51)	MGM 11000	$50
	(Yellow promo label)		
45rpm	**HEY, GOOD LOOKIN'** (51)	MGM 11000	$18
45(P)	**HEY, GOOD LOOKIN'** (51)	MGM 11000	$20
	(Yellow promo label)		

78rpm	**I DREAMED ABOUT MAMA LAST NIGHT** (51)	MGM 11017	$25
	(Luke the Drifter)		
78(P)	**I DREAMED ABOUT MAMA LAST NIGHT** (51)	MGM 11017	$50
	(Yellow promo label)		
45rpm	**I DREAMED ABOUT MAMA LAST NIGHT** (51)	MGM 11017	$20
45(P)	**I DREAMED ABOUT MAMA LAST NIGHT** (51)	MGM 11017	$20
	(Yellow promo label)		
78rpm	**LONESOME WHISTLE** (51)	MGM 11054	$30
78(P)	**LONESOME WHISTLE** (51)	MGM 11054	$50
	(Yellow promo label)		
45rpm	**LONESOME WHISTLE** (51)	MGM 11054	$20
45(P)	**LONESOME WHISTLE** (51)	MGM 11054	$20
	(Yellow promo label)		
78rpm	**LEAVE US WOMEN ALONE** (51)	MGM 11083	$30
78(P)	**LEAVE US WOMEN ALONE** (51)	MGM 11083	$50
	(Yellow promo label)		
45rpm	**LEAVE US WOMEN ALONE** (51)	MGM 11083	$20
45(P)	**LEAVE US WOMEN ALONE** (51)	MGM 11083	$20
	(Yellow promo label)		
78rpm	**BABY, WE'RE REALLY IN LOVE** (51)	MGM 11100	$30
78(P)	**BABY, WE'RE REALLY IN LOVE** (51)	MGM 11100	$50
	(Yellow promo label)		
45rpm	**BABY, WE'RE REALLY IN LOVE** (51)	MGM 11100	$20
45(P)	**BABY, WE'RE REALLY IN LOVE** (51)	MGM 11100	$20
	(Yellow promo label)		
78rpm	**RAMBLIN' MAN** (52) Luke the Drifter	MGM 11120	$30
78(P)	**RAMBLIN' MAN** (52)	MGM 11120	$50
	(Yellow promo label)		
45rpm	**RAMBLIN' MAN** (52)	MGM 11120	$15
45(P)	**RAMBLIN' MAN** (52)	MGM 11120	$20
	(Yellow promo label)		
78rpm	**HONKY TONK BLUES** (52)	MGM 11160	$30
78(P)	**HONKY TONK BLUES** (52)	MGM 11160	$50
	(Yellow promo label)		
45rpm	**HONKY TONK BLUES** (52)	MGM 11160	$15
45(P)	**HONKY TONK BLUES** (52)	MGM 11160	$20
	(Yellow promo label)		
78rpm	**HALF AS MUCH** (52)	MGM 11202	$25
78(P)	**HALF AS MUCH** (52)	MGM 11202	$50
	(Yellow promo label)		
45rpm	**HALF AS MUCH** (52)	MGM 11202	$15
45(P)	**HALF AS MUCH** (52)	MGM 11202	$20
	(Yellow promo label)		
78rpm	**JAMBALAYA** (52)	MGM 11283	$25
78(P)	**JAMBALAYA** (52)	MGM 11283	$50
	(Yellow promo label)		
45rpm	**JAMBALAYA** (52)	MGM 11283	$15
45(P)	**JAMBALAYA** (52)	MGM 11283	$20
	(Yellow promo label)		
78rpm	**BE CAREFUL OF STONES** (52) Luke the Drifter	MGM 11309	$25
78(P)	**BE CAREFUL OF STONES** (52)	MGM 11309	$50
	(Yellow promo label)		
45rpm	**BE CAREFUL OF STONES** (52)	MGM 11309	$25
45(P)	**BE CAREFUL OF STONES** (52)	MGM 11309	$20
	(Yellow promo label)		
78rpm	**SETTIN' THE WOODS ON FIRE** (52)	MGM 11318	$25
78(P)	**SETTIN' THE WOODS ON FIRE** (52)	MGM 11318	$50
	(Yellow promo label)		
45rpm	**SETTIN' THE WOODS ON FIRE** (52)	MGM 11318	$20
45(P)	**SETTIN' THE WOODS ON FIRE** (52)	MGM 11318	$20
	(Yellow promo label)		
78rpm	**I'LL NEVER GET OUT OF THIS WORLD ALIVE** (53)	MGM 11366	$30
78(P)	**I'LL NEVER GET OUT OF THIS WORLD ALIVE** (53)	MGM 11366	$50
	(Yellow promo label)		
45rpm	**I'LL NEVER GET OUT OF THIS WORLD ALIVE** (53)	MGM 11366	$18
45(P)	**I'LL NEVER GET OUT OF THIS WORLD ALIVE** (53)	MGM 11366	$20
	(Yellow promo label)		
78rpm	**KAW-LIGA** (53)	MGM 11416	$30
78(P)	**KAW-LIGA** (53)	MGM 11416	$50
	(Yellow promo label)		
45rpm	**KAW-LIGA** (53)	MGM 11416	$15
45(P)	**KAW-LIGA** (53)	MGM 11416	$20
	(Yellow promo label)		
78rpm	**TAKE THESE CHAINS FROM MY HEART** (53)	MGM 11479	$25
78(P)	**TAKE THESE CHAINS FROM MY HEART** (53)	MGM 11479	$50
	(Yellow promo label)		
45rpm	**TAKE THESE CHAINS FROM MY HEART** (53)	MGM 11479	$15

45(P)	**TAKE THESE CHAINS FROM MY HEART** (53)	MGM 11479	$18
	(Yellow promo label)		
78rpm	**I WON'T BE HOME NO MORE** (53)	MGM 11533	$25
78(P)	**I WON'T BE HOME NO MORE** (53)	MGM 11533	$50
	(Yellow promo label)		
45rpm	**I WON'T BE HOME NO MORE** (53)	MGM 11533	$15
45(P)	**I WON'T BE HOME NO MORE** (53)	MGM 11533	$18
	(Yellow promo label)		
78rpm	**WEARY BLUES FROM WAITIN'** (53)	MGM 11574	$25
78(P)	**WEARY BLUES FROM WAITIN'** (53)	MGM 11574	$50
	(Yellow promo label)		
45rpm	**WEARY BLUES FROM WAITIN'** (53)	MGM 11574	$15
45(P)	**WEARY BLUES FROM WAITIN'** (53)	MGM 11574	$18
	(Yellow promo label)		
78rpm	**WHEN GOD COMES AND GATHERS HIS JEWELS** (54)	MGM 11628	$25
78(P)	**WHEN GOD COMES AND GATHERS HIS JEWELS** (54)	MGM 11628	$50
	(Yellow promo label)		
45rpm	**WHEN GOD COMES AND GATHERS HIS JEWELS** (54)	MGM 11628	$15
45(P)	**WHEN GOD COMES AND GATHERS HIS JEWELS** (54)	MGM 11628	$18
	(Yellow promo label)		
78rpm	**LOW DOWN BLUES** (54)	MGM 11675	$25
78(P)	**LOW DOWN BLUES** (54)	MGM 11675	$50
	(Yellow promo label)		
45rpm	**LOW DOWN BLUES** (54)	MGM 11675	$15
45(P)	**LOW DOWN BLUES** (54)	MGM 11675	$18
	(Yellow promo label)		
78rpm	**HOW CAN YOU REFUSE HIM NOW** (54)	MGM 11707	$25
78(P)	**HOW CAN YOU REFUSE HIM NOW** (54)	MGM 11707	$50
	(Yellow promo label)		
45rpm	**HOW CAN YOU REFUSE HIM NOW** (54)	MGM 11707	$15
45(P)	**HOW CAN YOU REFUSE HIM NOW** (54)	MGM 11707	$18
	(Yellow promo label)		
78rpm	**I AIN'T GOT NOTHIN' BUT TIME** (54)	MGM 11768	$25
78(P)	**I AIN'T GOT NOTHIN' BUT TIME** (54)	MGM 11768	$50
	(Yellow promo label)		
45rpm	**I AIN'T GOT NOTHIN' BUT TIME** (54)	MGM 11768	$15
45(P)	**I AIN'T GOT NOTHIN' BUT TIME** (54)	MGM 11768	$18
	(Yellow promo label)		
78rpm	**ANGEL OF DEATH** (54)	MGM 11861	$25
78(P)	**ANGEL OF DEATH** (54)	MGM 11861	$50
	(Yellow promo label)		
45rpm	**ANGEL OF DEATH** (54)	MGM 11861	$15
45(P)	**ANGEL OF DEATH** (54)	MGM 11861	$18
	(Yellow promo label)		
78rpm	**FADED LOVE AND WINTER ROSES** (55)	MGM 11928	$25
78(P)	**FADED LOVE AND WINTER ROSES** (55)	MGM 11928	$50
	(Yellow promo label)		
45rpm	**FADED LOVE AND WINTER ROSES** (55)	MGM 11928	$25
45(P)	**FADED LOVE AND WINTER ROSES** (55)	MGM 11928	$20
	(Yellow promo label)		
78rpm	**MAKING BELIEVE** (55) Audrey Williams	MGM 11935	$25
78(P)	**MAKING BELIEVE** (55)	MGM 11935	$40
	(Yellow promo label)		
45rpm	**MAKING BELIEVE** (55)	MGM 11935	$25
45(P)	**MAKING BELIEVE** (55)	MGM 11935	$20
	(Yellow promo label)		
78rpm	**MESSAGE TO MY MOTHER** (54)	MGM 11975	$25
78(P)	**MESSAGE TO MY MOTHER** (54)	MGM 11975	$50
	(Yellow promo label)		
45rpm	**MESSAGE TO MY MOTHER** (54)	MGM 11975	$25
45(P)	**MESSAGE TO MY MOTHER** (54)	MGM 11975	$20
	(Yellow promo label)		
78rpm	**ALONE AND FORSAKEN** (55)	MGM 12029	$25
78(P)	**ALONE AND FORSAKEN** (55)	MGM 12029	$50
	(Yellow promo label)		
45rpm	**ALONE AND FORSAKEN** (55)	MGM 12029	$25
45(P)	**ALONE AND FORSAKEN** (55)	MGM 12029	$20
	(Yellow promo label)		
78rpm	**SOMEDAY YOU'LL CALL MY NAME** (55)	MGM 12077	$25
78(P)	**SOMEDAY YOU'LL CALL MY NAME** (55)	MGM 12077	$50
	(Yellow promo label)		
45rpm	**SOMEDAY YOU'LL CALL MY NAME** (55)	MGM 12077	$25
45(P)	**SOMEDAY YOU'LL CALL MY NAME** (55)	MGM 12077	$20
	(Yellow promo label)		
78rpm	**LITTLE BOSEPHUS** (55) Audrey Williams	MGM 12082	$25
	(A song about six-year old Hank Jr.)		

78(P)	**LITTLE BOSEPHUS** (55)	MGM 12082	$40
	(Yellow promo label)		
45rpm	**LITTLE BOSEPHUS** (55)	MGM 12082	$20
45(P)	**LITTLE BOSEPHUS** (55)	MGM 12082	$25
	(Yellow promo label)		
78rpm	**THE BATTLE OF ARMAGEDDON** (55)	MGM 12127	$25
78(P)	**THE BATTLE OF ARMAGEDDON** (55)	MGM 12127	$50
	(Yellow promo label)		
45rpm	**THE BATTLE OF ARMAGEDDON** (55)	MGM 12127	$20
45(P)	**THE BATTLE OF ARMAGEDDON** (55)	MGM 12127	$25
	(Yellow promo label)		
78rpm	**THY BURDENS ARE GREATER THAN MINE** (55)	MGM 12185	$25
78(P)	**THY BURDENS ARE GREATER THAN MINE** (55)	MGM 12185	$50
	(Yellow promo label)		
45rpm	**THY BURDENS ARE GREATER THAN MINE** (55)	MGM 12185	$25
45(P)	**THY BURDENS ARE GREATER THAN MINE** (55)	MGM 12185	$20
	(Yellow promo label)		
4-45s	**HANK WILLIAMS SINGS** (55) Box set	MGM K-107	$25 each
	(Box set of four singles from the ten-inch LP, price for the complete set $125)		
4-45s	**THE MEMORIAL ALBUM** (55) Box set	MGM K-202	$25 each
	(Box set of four singles from the ten-inch LP, price for the complete set $125)		
4-45s	**HANK WILLIAMS AS LUKE THE DRIFTER** (55) Box set	MGM K-203	$25 each
	(Box set of four singles from the ten-inch LP, price for the complete set $125)		
78rpm	**LIVIN' IT UP AND HAVIN' A BALL** (55) Audrey Williams	MGM 12210	$25
78(P)	**LIVIN' IT UP AND HAVIN' A BALL** (55)	MGM 12210	$40
	(Yellow promo label)		
45rpm	**LIVIN' IT UP AND HAVIN' A BALL** (55)	MGM 12210	$25
45(P)	**LIVIN' IT UP AND HAVIN' A BALL** (55)	MGM 12210	$20
	(Yellow promo label)		
78rpm	**I WISH I HAD A NICKEL** (56)	MGM 12244	$25
78(P)	**I WISH I HAD A NICKEL** (56)	MGM 12244	$50
	(Yellow promo label)		
45rpm	**I WISH I HAD A NICKEL** (56)	MGM 12244	$25
45(P)	**I WISH I HAD A NICKEL** (56)	MGM 12244	$20
	(Yellow promo label)		
78rpm	**LET ME SIT ALONE** (56) Hank and Audrey	MGM 12314	$25
78(P)	**LET ME SIT ALONE** (56)	MGM 12314	$50
	(Yellow promo label)		
45rpm	**LET ME SIT ALONE** (56)	MGM 12314	$25
45(P)	**LET ME SIT ALONE** (56)	MGM 12314	$20
	(Yellow promo label)		
78rpm	**SINGING WATERFALL** (56)	MGM 12332	$25
78(P)	**SINGING WATERFALL** (56)	MGM 12332	$50
	(Yellow promo label)		
45rpm	**SINGING WATERFALL** (56)	MGM 12332	$25
45(P)	**SINGING WATERFALL** (56)	MGM 12332	$20
	(Yellow promo label)		
78rpm	**A HOME IN HEAVEN** (57) Hank and Audrey	MGM 12394	$25
78(P)	**A HOME IN HEAVEN** (57)	MGM 12394	$50
	(Yellow promo label)		
45rpm	**A HOME IN HEAVEN** (57)	MGM 12394	$25
45(P)	**A HOME IN HEAVEN** (57)	MGM 12394	$20
	(Yellow promo label)		
78rpm	**ALIMONY BLUES** (57)	MGM 12431	$25
78(P)	**ALIMONY BLUES** (57)	MGM 12431	$50
	(Yellow promo label)		
45rpm	**ALIMONY BLUES** (57)	MGM 12431	$25
45(P)	**ALIMONY BLUES** (57)	MGM 12431	$20
	(Yellow promo label)		
78rpm	**LEAVE ME ALONE WITH THE BLUES** (57)	MGM 12484	$25
78(P)	**LEAVE ME ALONE WITH THE BLUES** (57)	MGM 12484	$50
	(Yellow promo label)		
45rpm	**LEAVE ME ALONE WITH THE BLUES** (57)	MGM 12484	$20
45(P)	**LEAVE ME ALONE WITH THE BLUES** (57)	MGM 12484	$25
	(Yellow promo label)		
78rpm	**NO ONE WILL EVER KNOW** (58)	MGM 12535	$25
78(P)	**NO ONE WILL EVER KNOW** (58)	MGM 12535	$50
	(Yellow promo label)		
45rpm	**NO ONE WILL EVER KNOW** (58)	MGM 12535	$25
45(P)	**NO ONE WILL EVER KNOW** (58)	MGM 12535	$20
	(Yellow promo label)		
78rpm	**WHY DON'T YOU LOVE ME** (58)	MGM 12611	$30
78(P)	**WHY DON'T YOU LOVE ME** (58)	MGM 12611	$60
	(Yellow promo label)		

45rpm	**WHY DON'T YOU LOVE ME** (58)	MGM 12611	$20
45(P)	**WHY DON'T YOU LOVE ME** (58)	MGM 12611	$18
	(Yellow promo label)		
78rpm	**WE LIVE IN TWO DIFFERENT WORLDS** (58)	MGM 12635	$40
78(P)	**WE LIVE IN TWO DIFFERENT WORLDS** (58)	MGM 12635	$75
	(Yellow promo label)		
45rpm	**WE LIVE IN TWO DIFFERENT WORLDS** (58)	MGM 12635	$18
45(P)	**WE LIVE IN TWO DIFFERENT WORLDS** (58)	MGM 12635	$15
	(Yellow promo label)		
78rpm	**JUST WAITIN'** (58)	MGM 12727	$50
78(P)	**JUST WAITIN'** (58)	MGM 12727	$75
	(Yellow promo label)		
45rpm	**JUST WAITIN'** (58)	MGM 12727	$15
	(All stock copy singles above are on yellow labels, other color labels are reissues and second pressings, worth less than $10 each)		
45(P)	**JUST WAITIN'** (58)	MGM 12727	$12
	(Yellow promo label)		
45rpm	**YOUR CHEATIN' HEART** (65)	MGM 13305	$15
	(Price includes picture sleeve)		
CD(P)	**THERE'S A TEAR IN MY BEER** (89) With Hank Jr.	Warner PRO-CD 3399	$10
	(Hank Williams Sr. on a promo CD single)		

-EPs-

2EP	**MOANIN' THE BLUES** (53) Double EP	MGM 168	$150
	(First pressing yellow labels)		
2EP	**MOANIN' THE BLUES** (60) Double EP	MGM 168	$75
	(Second pressing black labels)		
EP	**CRAZY HEART** (53) Yellow label	MGM 1014	$75
EP	**CRAZY HEART** (60) Black label	MGM 1014	$25
2EP	**MEMORIAL ALBUM** (54) Double EP	MGM 202	$150
	(First pressing yellow labels)		
2EP	**MEMORIAL ALBUM** (60) Double EP	MGM 202	$75
	(Second pressing black labels)		
2EP	**HANK WILLIAMS AS LUKE THE DRIFTER** (55) Double EP	MGM 203	$150
	(First pressing yellow labels)		
2EP	**HANK WILLIAMS AS LUKE THE DRIFTER** (60) Double EP	MGM 203	$75
	(Second pressing black labels)		
EP	**HANK WILLIAMS AS LUKE THE DRIFTER** (55)	MGM 1047	$75
	(First pressing yellow label)		
EP	**HANK WILLIAMS AS LUKE THE DRIFTER** (60)	MGM 1047	$25
	(Second pressing black label)		
2EP	**HONKY TONKIN'** (55) Double EP	MGM 242	$150
	(First pressing yellow label)		
2EP	**HONKY TONKIN'** (60) Double EP	MGM 242	$75
	(Second pressing black labels)		
2EP	**I SAW THE LIGHT** (55) Double EP	MGM 243	$150
	(First pressing yellow label)		
2EP	**I SAW THE LIGHT** (60) Double EP	MGM 243	$75
EP	**MOVE IT ON OVER** (55) Yellow label	MGM 1076	$50
EP	**MOVE IT ON OVER** (60) Black label	MGM 1076	$25
EP	**I SAW THE LIGHT** (55) Yellow label	MGM 4110	$50
EP	**I SAW THE LIGHT** (60) Black label	MGM 4110	$25
EP	**I SAW THE LIGHT** (55) Yellow label	MGM 4111	$50
EP	**I SAW THE LIGHT** (60) Black label	MGM 4111	$25
EP	**THERE'LL BE NO TEARDROPS TONIGHT** (55) Yellow label	MGM 1082	$50
EP	**THERE'LL BE NO TEARDROPS TONIGHT** (60) Black label	MGM 1082	$25
EP	**HANK WILLIAMS SINGS** (55) Yellow label	MGM 1101	$50
EP	**HANK WILLIAMS SINGS** (60) Black label	MGM 1101	$25
EP	**HANK WILLIAMS SINGS** (55) Yellow label	MGM 1102	$50
EP	**HANK WILLIAMS SINGS** (55) Black label	MGM 1102	$25
2EP	**RAMBLIN' MAN** (55) Double EP	MGM 291	$150
	(First pressing yellow labels)		
2EP	**RAMBLIN' MAN** (60) Double EP	MGM 291	$75
	(Second press black label)		
EP	**RAMBLIN' MAN** (55) Yellow label	MGM 1135	$50
EP	**RAMBLIN' MAN** (60) Black label	MGM 1135	$25
EP	**RAMBLIN' MAN** (55) Yellow label	MGM 1136	$50
EP	**RAMBLIN' MAN** (60) Black label	MGM 1136	$25
EP	**HANK WILLIAMS AS LUKE THE DRIFTER** (56) Yellow label	MGM 1165	$50
EP	**HANK WILLIAMS AS LUKE THE DRIFTER** (60) Black label	MGM 1165	$25
EP	**MOANIN' THE BLUES** (56) Yellow label	MGM 1215	$50
EP	**MOANIN' THE BLUES** (60) Black label	MGM 1215	$25
EP	**MOANIN' THE BLUES** (56) Yellow label	MGM 1216	$50
EP	**MOANIN' THE BLUES** (60) Black label	MGM 1216	$25
EP	**MOANIN' THE BLUES** (56) Yellow label	MGM 1217	$50
EP	**MOANIN' THE BLUES** (60) Black label	MGM 1217	$25
EP	**I SAW THE LIGHT** (56) Yellow label	MGM 1218	$50
EP	**I SAW THE LIGHT** (56) Black label	MGM 1218	$25

EP	**HONKY TONKIN'** (57) Yellow label	MGM 1317	$50
EP	**HONKY TONKIN'** (60) Black label	MGM 1317	$25
EP	**HONKY TONKIN'** (57) Yellow label	MGM 1318	$50
EP	**HONKY TONKIN'** (60) Black label	MGM 1318	$25
EP	**HONKY TONKIN'** (57) Yellow label	MGM 1319	$50
EP	**HONKY TONKIN'** (60) Black label	MGM 1319	$25
EP	**SING ME A BLUE SONG** (58) Yellow label	MGM 1491	$50
EP	**SING ME A BLUE SONG** (60) Black label	MGM 1491	$25
EP	**SING ME A BLUE SONG** (58) Yellow label	MGM 1492	$50
EP	**SING ME A BLUE SONG** (60) Black label	MGM 1492	$25
EP	**SING ME A BLUE SONG** (58) Yellow label	MGM 1493	$50
EP	**SING ME A BLUE SONG** (60) Black label	MGM 1493	$25
EP	**THE IMMORTAL HANK WILLIAMS** (58) Yellow label	MGM 1554	$50
EP	**THE IMMORTAL HANK WILLIAMS** (60) Black label	MGM 1554	$25
EP	**THE IMMORTAL HANK WILLIAMS** (58) Yellow label	MGM 1555	$50
EP	**THE IMMORTAL HANK WILLIAMS** (60) Black label	MGM 1555	$25
EP	**THE IMMORTAL HANK WILLIAMS** (58) Yellow label	MGM 1556	$50
EP	**THE IMMORTAL HANK WILLIAMS** (60) Black label	MGM 1556	$25
EP	**HANK WILLIAMS MEMORIAL ALBUM** (59) Yellow label	MGM 1612	$50
EP	**HANK WILLIAMS MEMORIAL ALBUM** (60) Black label	MGM 1612	$25
EP	**HANK WILLIAMS MEMORIAL ALBUM** (59) Yellow label	MGM 1613	$50
EP	**HANK WILLIAMS MEMORIAL ALBUM** (60) Black label	MGM 1613	$25
EP	**HANK WILLIAMS MEMORIAL ALBUM** (59) Yellow label	MGM 1614	$50
EP	**HANK WILLIAMS MEMORIAL ALBUM** (60) Black label	MGM 1614	$25
EP	**THE UNFORGETTABLE HANK WILLIAMS** (59) Yellow label	MGM 1637	$50
EP	**THE UNFORGETTABLE HANK WILLIAMS** (60) Black label	MGM 1637	$25
EP	**THE UNFORGETTABLE HANK WILLIAMS** (59) Yellow label	MGM 1638	$50
EP	**THE UNFORGETTABLE HANK WILLIAMS** (60) Black label	MGM 1638	$25
EP	**THE UNFORGETTABLE HANK WILLIAMS** (59) Yellow label	MGM 1639	$50
EP	**THE UNFORGETTABLE HANK WILLIAMS** (60) Black label	MGM 1639	$25
EP	**HANK WILLIAMS AS LUKE THE DRIFTER** (59) Yellow label	MGM 1643	$50
EP	**HANK WILLIAMS AS LUKE THE DRIFTER** (60) Black label	MGM 1644	$25
EP	**HANK WILLIAMS AS LUKE THE DRIFTER** (59) Yellow label	MGM 1644	$50
EP	**HANK WILLIAMS AS LUKE THE DRIFTER** (60) Black label	MGM 1644	$25
EP	**I SAW THE LIGHT** (59) Yellow label	MGM 1648	$50
EP	**I SAW THE LIGHT** (60) Black label	MGM 1649	$25
EP	**I SAW THE LIGHT** (59) Yellow label	MGM 1649	$50
EP	**I SAW THE LIGHT** (60) Black label	MGM 1649	$25
EP	**RAMBLIN' MAN** (59) Yellow label	MGM 1650	$50
EP	**RAMBLIN' MAN** (60) Black label	MGM 1650	$25
EP	**THE LONESOME SOUND OF HANK WILLIAMS** (60)	MGM 1698	$40
EP	**THE LONESOME SOUND OF HANK WILLIAMS** (60)	MGM 1699	$40
EP	**THE LONESOME SOUND OF HANK WILLIAMS** (60)	MGM 1700	$40
EP(JB)	**THE VERY BEST OF HANK WILLIAMS** (67) Jukebox LLP	MGM 4168	$40
	(Issued with a hard cover)		
EP(JB)	**THE LEGEND LIVES ON** (67) Jukebox LLP	MGM 4377	$40
	(Issued with a hard cover)		

-albums-

10"LP	**HANK WILLIAMS SINGS** (52)	MGM 107	$300
10"LP	**MOANIN' THE BLUES** (52)	MGM 168	$300
LP	**MOANIN' THE BLUES** (56) Yellow label	MGM 3330	$150
LP	**MOANIN' THE BLUES** (60) Black label	MGM 3330	$25
10"LP	**HANK WILLIAMS AS LUKE THE DRIFTER** (53)	MGM 203	$300
LP	**HANK WILLIAMS AS LUKE THE DRIFTER** (55)	MGM 3267	$150
	(Yellow label)		
LP	**HANK WILLIAMS AS LUKE THE DRIFTER** (60)	MGM 3267	$25
	(Black label)		
10"LP	**HANK WILLIAMS MEMORIAL ALBUM** (53)	MGM 202	$300
LP	**HANK WILLIAMS MEMORIAL ALBUM** (55) Yellow label	MGM 3272	$150
LP	**HANK WILLIAMS MEMORIAL ALBUM** (60) Black label	MGM 3272	$25
10"LP	**HONKY TONKIN'** (54)	MGM 242	$300
LP	**HONKY TONKIN'** (57) Yellow label	MGM 3412	$150
LP	**HONKY TONKIN'** (60) Black label	MGM 3412	$25
10"LP	**I SAW THE LIGHT** (54)	MGM 243	$300
LP	**I SAW THE LIGHT** (56)	MGM 3331	$200
	(Green cover, first pressing)		
LP	**I SAW THE LIGHT** (59) Yellow label	MGM 3331	$150
	(Church on the cover, second pressing)		
LP	**I SAW THE LIGHT** (60) Black label	MGM 3331	$25
10"LP	**RAMBLIN' MAN** (54)	MGM 291	$300
LP	**RAMBLIN' MAN** (55) Yellow label	MGM 3219	$150
LP	**RAMBLIN' MAN** (60) Black label	MGM 3219	$25
LP	**SING ME A BLUE SONG** (58) Yellow label	MGM 3560	$150
LP	**SING ME A BLUE SONG** (60) Black label	MGM 3560	$25
LP	**THE IMMORTAL HANK WILLIAMS** (58) Yellow label	MGM 3605	$150
LP	**THE IMMORTAL HANK WILLIAMS** (60) Black label	MGM 3560	$25

LP(P)	**SPECIAL DJ SAMPLER** (59) Various artists	MGM DJ-2	$50
	(Includes one Hank Williams song)		
3LP	**36 OF HANK WILLIAMS GREATEST HITS** (57)	MGM 3E-2	$250
	(Yellow label)		
3LP	**36 OF HANK WILLIAMS GREATEST HITS** (60)	MGM 3E-2	$125
	(Black label)		
3LP	**36 MORE GREATEST HITS** (58) Yellow label	MGM 3E-4	$200
3LP	**36 MORE GREATEST HITS** (60) Black label	MGM 3E-4	$100
LP	**THE UNFORGETTABLE HANK WILLIAMS** (59) Yellow label	MGM 3733	$150
LP	**THE UNFORGETTABLE HANK WILLIAMS** (60) Black label	MGM 3733	$25
LP	**THE LONESOME SOUND OF HANK WILLIAMS** (60)	MGM 3803	$25
LP(P)	**THE LONESOME SOUND OF HANK WILLIAMS** (60)	MGM 3803	$100
	(Yellow promo label)		
LP	**WAIT FOR THE LIGHT TO SHINE** (60)	MGM 3850	$40
LP(P)	**WAIT FOR THE LIGHT TO SHINE** (60)	MGM 3850	$75
	(Yellow promo label)		
LP	**HANK WILLIAMS' GREATEST HITS** (61)	MGM 3918	$25
LP(P)	**HANK WILLIAMS' GREATEST HITS** (61)	MGM 3918	$75
	(Yellow promo label)		
LP	**HANK WILLIAMS LIVES AGAIN** (61)	MGM 3923	$25
LP(P)	**HANK WILLIAMS LIVES AGAIN** (61)	MGM 3923	$75
	(Yellow promo label)		
LP	**SING ME A BLUE SONG** (61)	MGM 3924	$25
LP(P)	**SING ME A BLUE SONG** (61)	MGM 3924	$60
	(Yellow promo label)		
LP	**WANDERIN' AROUND** (61)	MGM 3925	$25
LP(P)	**WANDERIN' AROUND** (61)	MGM 3925	$60
	(Yellow promo label)		
LP	**I'M BLUE INSIDE** (61)	MGM 3926	$25
LP(P)	**I'M BLUE INSIDE** (61)	MGM 3926	$60
	(Yellow promo label)		
LP	**FIRST, LAST & ALWAYS** (61)	MGM 3928	$25
LP(P)	**FIRST, LAST & ALWAYS** (61)	MGM 3928	$50
	(Yellow promo label)		
LP	**THE SPIRIT OF HANK WILLIAMS** (61)	MGM 3955	$25
LP(P)	**THE SPIRIT OF HANK WILLIAMS** (61)	MGM 3955	$50
	(Yellow promo label)		
LP	**HANK WILLIAMS ON STAGE-RECORDED LIVE** (62) Mono	MGM 3999	$25
LP	**HANK WILLIAMS ON STAGE-RECORDED LIVE** (62) Stereo	MGM 3999	$15
LP(P)	**HANK WILLIAMS ON STAGE-RECORDED LIVE** (62)	MGM 3999	$50
	(Yellow promo label)		
LP	**14 MORE GREATEST HITS** (62)	MGM 4040	$25
LP(P)	**14 MORE GREATEST HITS** (62)	MGM 4040	$50
	(Yellow promo label)		
LP	**HANK WILLIAMS ON STAGE** (63) Mono	MGM 4109	$25
LP	**HANK WILLIAMS ON STAGE** (63) Stereo	MGM 4109	$15
LP(P)	**HANK WILLIAMS ON STAGE** (63)	MGM 4109	$50
	(Yellow promo label)		
LP	**BEYOND THE SUNSET** (63) Mono	MGM 4138	$25
LP	**BEYOND THE SUNSET** (63) Stereo	MGM 4138	$15
LP(P)	**BEYOND THE SUNSET** (63)	MGM 4138	$50
	(Yellow promo label)		
LP	**14 MORE GREATEST HITS** (63)	MGM 4140	$25
LP(P)	**14 MORE GREATEST HITS** (63)	MGM 4140	$50
	(Yellow promo label)		
LP	**THE VERY BEST OF HANK WILLIAMS** (63) Mono	MGM 4168	$25
LP	**THE VERY BEST OF HANK WILLIAMS** (63) Stereo	MGM 4168	$15
LP(P)	**THE VERY BEST OF HANK WILLIAMS** (63)	MGM 4168	$50
	(Yellow promo label)		
LP	**THE VERY BEST OF HANK WILLIAMS** (63) Mono	MGM 4227	$25
LP	**THE VERY BEST OF HANK WILLIAMS** (63) Stereo	MGM 4227	$15
LP(P)	**THE VERY BEST OF HANK WILLIAMS** (63)	MGM 4227	$50
	(Yellow promo label)		
LP	**LOST HIGHWAY** (64)	MGM 4254	$40
LP(P)	**LOST HIGHWAY** (64)	MGM 4254	$60
	(Yellow promo label)		
LP	**HANK WILLIAMS SR. & HANK WILLIAMS JR.** (65) Mono	MGM 4276	$15
LP	**HANK WILLIAMS SR. & HANK WILLIAMS JR.** (65) Stereo	MGM 4276	$20
LP(P)	**HANK WILLIAMS SR. & HANK WILLIAMS JR.** (65)	MGM 4276	$50
	(Yellow promo label)		
4LP	**THE HANK WILLIAMS STORY** (65) Box set	MGM 4267	$50
4LP(P)	**THE HANK WILLIAMS STORY** (65) Box set	MGM 4267	$100
	(Yellow promo labels)		
LP	**KAW-LIGA AND OTHER HUMOROUS SONGS** (65) Mono	MGM 4300	$25
LP	**KAW-LIGA AND OTHER HUMOROUS SONGS** (65) Stereo	MGM 4300	$15
LP(P)	**KAW-LIGA AND OTHER HUMOROUS SONGS** (65)	MGM 4300	$50
	(Yellow promo label)		

LP	**HANK WILLIAMS** (65) Mono	Metro 509	$25
LP	**HANK WILLIAMS** (65) Stereo	Metro 509	$15
LP(P)	**HANK WILLIAMS** (65)	Metro 509	$30
	(Yellow promo label)		
LP	**MR. & MRS. HANK WILLIAMS** (65) Mono	Metro 547	$25
LP	**MR. & MRS. HANK WILLIAMS** (65) Stereo	Metro 547	$15
LP(P)	**MR. & MRS. HANK WILLIAMS** (65)	Metro 547	$30
	(Yellow promo label)		
LP	**THE LEGEND LIVES ANEW** (66) Mono	MGM 4377	$20
	(With strings)		
LP	**THE LEGEND LIVES ANEW** (66) Stereo	MGM 4377	$25
	(The strings are in stereo)		
LP(P)	**THE LEGEND LIVES ANEW** (66)	MGM 4377	$50
	(Yellow promo label)		
LP	**AGAIN** (66) With Hank Jr.	MGM 4378	$25
	(Mono)		
LP	**AGAIN** (66) Stereo	MGM 4378	$15
LP(P)	**AGAIN** (66)	MGM 4378	$40
	(Yellow promo label)		
LP	**LUKE THE DRIFTER** (66) Mono	MGM 4380	$25
LP	**LUKE THE DRIFTER** (66) Stereo	MGM 4380	$15
LP(P)	**LUKE THE DRIFTER** (66)	MGM 4380	$40
	(Yellow promo label)		
LP	**MORE HANK WILLIAMS AND STRINGS** (66) Mono	MGM 4429	$20
LP	**MORE HANK WILLIAMS AND STRINGS** (66) Stereo	MGM 4429	$25
	(The strings are in stereo)		
LP(P)	**MORE HANK WILLIAMS AND STRINGS** (66)	MGM 4429	$40
	(Yellow promo label)		
LP	**THE IMMORTAL HANK WILLIAMS** (67) Mono	Metro 602	$25
LP	**THE IMMORTAL HANK WILLIAMS** (67) Stereo	Metro 602	$15
LP(P)	**THE IMMORTAL HANK WILLIAMS** (67)	Metro 602	$30
	(Yellow promo label)		
LP	**I WON'T BE HOME NO MORE** (67) Mono	MGM 4481	$25
LP	**I WON'T BE HOME NO MORE** (67) Stereo	MGM 4481	$15
LP(P)	**I WON'T BE HOME NO MORE** (67)	MGM 4481	$40
	(Yellow promo label)		
LP	**HANK WILLIAMS AND STRINGS** (68)	MGM 4529	$18
LP(P)	**HANK WILLIAMS AND STRINGS** (68)	MGM 4529	$40
	(MGM promo label)		
LP	**HANK WILLIAMS IN THE BEGINNING** (68) Mono	MGM 4576	$25
LP	**HANK WILLIAMS IN THE BEGINNING** (68) Stereo	MGM 4576	$15
LP(P)	**HANK WILLIAMS IN THE BEGINNING** (68)	MGM 4576	$40
	(MGM promo label)		
LP	**THE ESSENTIAL HANK WILLIAMS** (69)	MGM 4651	$12
LP(P)	**THE ESSENTIAL HANK WILLIAMS** (69)	MGM 4651	$40
	(MGM promo label)		
LP	**LIFE TO LEGEND** (70)	MGM 4680	$12
LP(P)	**LIFE TO LEGEND** (70)	MGM 4680	$40
	(MGM promo label)		
2LP	**24 OF HANK WILLIAMS' GREATEST HITS** (70)	MGM 4755	$15
2LP(P)	**24 OF HANK WILLIAMS' GREATEST HITS** (70)	MGM 4755	$50
	(MGM promo labels)		
2LP	**24 KARAT HITS** (70)	MGM 240	$18
2LP(P)	**24 KARAT HITS** (70)	MGM 240	$50
	(MGM promo labels)		
LP	**THE LAST PICTURE SHOW** (71)	MGM 1SE-33ST	$25
	(Soundtrack)		
LP(P)	**THE LAST PICTURE SHOW** (71)	MGM 1SE-33ST	$40
	(MGM promo label)		
LP(P)	**THE LEGEND OF HANK WILLIAMS** (73)	MGM 4865	$20
	(White promo label)		
LP(P)	**ARCHETYPES** (74)	MGM 4954	$18
	(White promo label)		
3LP	**HANK WILLIAMS/ROY ACUFF** (70s)	Lamb & Lion 707	$20
	(Three records, three artists)		
2LP(P)	**INSIGHTS INTO HANK WILLIAMS IN SONG & STORY** (74)	MGM 4976	$25
	(White promo labels)		
3LP(P)	**REFLECTIONS OF THOSE WHO LOVED HIM** (75) Box set	MGM 912	$250
	(Music and interviews, white promo labels)		
4LP	**THE HANK WILLIAMS TREASURY** (76) Box set	Columbia 5616	$40
	(Columbia Record Club release)		
LP(P)	**ON STAGE RECORDED LIVE** (76)	MGM 1042	$15
	(White promo label)		
LP(P)	**A HOME IN HEAVEN** (76)	MGM 4991	$15
	(White promo label)		
LP(P)	**HANK WILLIAMS SR. LIVE AT THE GRAND OLE OPRY** (76)	MGM 5019	$15
	(White promo label)		

3LP	**COUNTRY & WESTERN CLASSICS** (81)	Time-Life 3003	$25
	(Part of a series of box sets)		
3CD	**THE ORIGINAL SINGLES COLLECTION** (90)	Polydor 847-194-2	$25
	(Box set)		

-radio shows-

3LP(RS)	**AMERICAN EAGLE** (Sept 86)	DIR	$100-150
	(Special live tribute show)		
	See Hank Williams Jr.		

HANK WILLIAMS JR. (C)

Parents are Hank and Audrey Williams
Recorded as Luke the Drifter Jr.
MGM black label 45s $3-5 each
MGM promo 45s $3-5 each
MGM picture sleeves $5 each
MGM green/gold label 45s $2 each
MGM Golden Circle 45s $3-5 each
Elektra 45s $2 each
Warner 45s $1 each
Warner picture sleeves $1-2 each
Other MGM LPs $8-10 each
   (Including duets with Lois Johnson)
Elektra, Warner, and Curb LPs $3-6 each

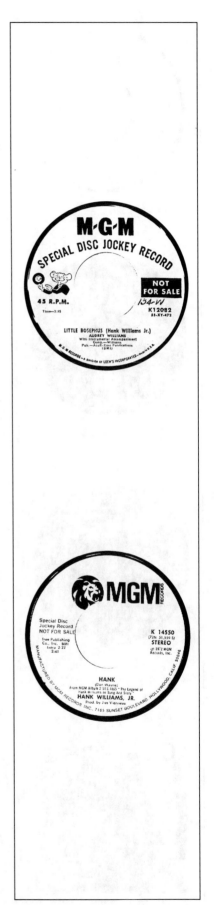

-singles-

45(P)	**THE LAST PICTURE SHOW** (71) Movie ads	Columbia Pictures	$75
	(Radio spots for the movie, five cuts)		
33(P)	**USO'S 40TH ANNIVERSARY** (82) Public service spots	USO	$25
	(Thirty-two cuts, one by Hank Jr.)		
CD(P)	**THERE'S A TEAR IN MY BEER** (89) With Hank Sr.	Warner PRO-CD 3399	$10
	(CD promo single features Hank Williams Sr.)		
CD(P)	**ALL MY ROWDY FRIENDS ARE COMING OVER FOR MONDAY NIGHT FOOTBALL** (90)	Warner PRO-CD 4484	$25
	(For ABC Football, promo-only release)		
45(P)	**DON'T GIVE US A REASON** (90)	Warner PRO-449	$10
	(Promo-only version)		

-EPs-

EP	**BALLADS OF THE HILLS & PLAINS** (65) Jukebox LLP	MGM 4316	$40
	(Issued with a hard cover)		

-albums-

LP	**SONGS OF HANK WILLIAMS** (63) Mono	MGM 4213	$18
LP	**SONGS OF HANK WILLIAMS** (63) Stereo	MGM 4213	$25
LP(P)	**SONGS OF HANK WILLIAMS** (63)	MGM 4213	$30
	(Yellow promo label)		
LP	**YOUR CHEATIN' HEART** (64) Mono	MGM 4260	$15
	(Soundtrack)		
LP	**YOUR CHEATIN' HEART** (64) Stereo	MGM 4260	$20
LP(P)	**YOUR CHEATIN' HEART** (64)	MGM 4260	$25
	(Yellow promo label)		
LP	**HANK WILLIAMS SR. & HANK WILLIAMS JR.** (65) Mono	MGM 4276	$15
LP	**HANK WILLIAMS SR. & HANK WILLIAMS JR.** (65) Stereo	MGM 4276	$20
LP(P)	**HANK WILLIAMS SR. & HANK WILLIAMS JR.** (65)	MGM 4276	$50
	(Yellow promo label)		
LP	**BALLADS OF HILLS & PLAINS** (65) Mono	MGM 4316	$15
LP	**BALLADS OF HILLS & PLAINS** (65) Stereo	MGM 4316	$20
LP(P)	**BALLADS OF HILLS & PLAINS** (65)	MGM 4316	$25
	(Yellow promo label)		
LP	**BLUE'S MY NAME** (66) Mono	MGM 4344	$12
LP	**BLUE'S MY NAME** (66) Stereo	MGM 4344	$18
LP(P)	**BLUE'S MY NAME** (66)	MGM 4344	$20
	(Yellow promo label)		
LP	**COUNTRY SHADOWS** (66) Mono	MGM 4391	$12
LP	**COUNTRY SHADOWS** (66) Stereo	MGM 4391	$18
LP(P)	**COUNTRY SHADOWS** (66)	MGM 4391	$20
	(Yellow promo label)		
LP	**IN MY OWN WAY** (67) Mono	MGM 4428	$12
LP	**IN MY OWN WAY** (67) Stereo	MGM 4428	$18
LP(P)	**IN MY OWN WAY** (67)	MGM 4428	$20
	(Yellow promo label)		
LP	**THE BEST OF HANK WILLIAMS JR.** (67) Mono	MGM 4513	$10
LP	**THE BEST OF HANK WILLIAMS JR.** (67) Stereo	MGM 4513	$12
LP(P)	**THE BEST OF HANK WILLIAMS JR.** (67)	MGM 4513	$15
	(Yellow promo label)		
LP	**MY SONGS** (68)	MGM 4527	$10
LP(P)	**MY SONGS** (68)	MGM 4527	$12
	(Yellow promo label)		
LP	**TIME TO SING** (68)	MGM 4540	$15
	(Soundtrack)		

LP(P)	**TIME TO SING** (68)	MGM 4540	$18
	(Yellow promo label)		
LP	**LUKE THE DRIFTER JR.** (69)	MGM 4559	$10
LP(P)	**LUKE THE DRIFTER JR.** (69)	MGM 4559	$12
	(Yellow promo label)		
LP	**SONGS MY FATHER LEFT ME** (69)	MGM 4621	$10
LP(P)	**SONGS MY FATHER LEFT ME** (69)	MGM 4621	$12
	(Yellow promo label)		
LP	**LUKE THE DRIFTER JR. VOL 2** (69)	MGM 4632	$10
LP(P)	**LUKE THE DRIFTER JR. VOL 2** (69)	MGM 4632	$12
	(Yellow promo label)		
LP	**LIVE AT COBO HALL** (69)	MGM 4644	$10
LP(P)	**LIVE AT COBO HALL** (69)	MGM 4644	$12
	(Yellow promo label)		
LP	**HANK WILLIAMS JR.'S GREATEST HITS** (70)	MGM 4656	$10
LP(P)	**HANK WILLIAMS JR.'S GREATEST HITS** (70)	MGM 4656	$12
	(Yellow promo label)		
LP	**SUNDAY MORNING** (70)	MGM 4657	$10
LP(P)	**SUNDAY MORNING** (70)	MGM 4657	$12
	(Yellow promo label)		
LP	**LUKE THE DRIFTER JR. VOL 3** (70)	MGM 4673	$10
LP(P)	**LUKE THE DRIFTER JR. VOL 3** (70)	MGM 4673	$12
	(Yellow promo label)		
LP	**SINGING MY SONGS** (70)	MGM 4675	$10
LP(P)	**SINGING MY SONGS** (70)	MGM 4675	$12
	(MGM promo label)		
LP	**REMOVING THE SHADOW** (70)	MGM 4721	$10
LP(P)	**REMOVING THE SHADOW** (70)	MGM 4721	$12
	(MGM promo label)		
LP	**ALL FOR THE LOVE OF SUNSHINE** (70)	MGM 4750	$10
LP(P)	**ALL FOR THE LOVE OF SUNSHINE** (70)	MGM 4750	$12
	(MGM promo label)		
LP	**HANK WILLIAMS JR.** (70)	MGM 119	$10
LP(P)	**HANK WILLIAMS JR.** (70)	MGM 119	$12
	(MGM promo label)		
LP(P)	**I'VE GOT A RIGHT TO CRY** (71)	MGM 4774	$12
	(MGM promo label)		
LP(P)	**GREATEST HITS-VOLUME 2** (72)	MGM 4822	$12
	(White swirl promo label)		
LP(P)	**AFTER YOU/PRIDE'S NOT HARD TO SWALLOW** (73)	MGM 4862	$12
	(White swirl promo label)		

-radio shows-

LP(RS)	**LIVE FROM THE LONE STAR** (Jan 79)		$50-100
	(Rare live concert)		
LP(RS)	**LIVE FROM THE LONE STAR** (Aug 80)		$40-75
	(Live concert)		
3LP(RS)	**THE SILVER EAGLE** (81)	ABC Radio	$50-100
	(Live concert)		
2LP(RS)	**COUNTRY CLOSE-UP** (Apr 84)	Supertracks	$20-40
	(Music and interviews)		
3LP(RS)	**THE SILVER EAGLE** (June 85) Cross Country Show	DIR/ABC	$40-75
	(Various artists including Hank Jr., live concert)		
LP(RS)	**COUNTRY SESSIONS** (80s)	NBC Radio	$25-50
	(Live concert)		
LP(RS)	**COUNTRY MUSIC TIME** (80s)	U.S. Air Force	$25-50
	(Live show version)		
LP(RS)	**COUNTRY MUSIC TIME** (80s)	U.S. Air Force	$10-20
	(Music and interviews version)		
3LP(RS)	**AMERICAN EAGLE** (Mar 86)	DIR	$40-75
	(Live concert)		
3LP(RS)	**MEMORIAL DAY SPECIAL** (May 88)		$50-100
	(Music and interviews, some live)		
LP(RS)	**LIVE AT GILLEY'S** (Oct 88)	Westwood One	$20-40
	(Live concert)		
LP(RS)	**WESTWOOD ONE PRESENTS** (Oct 88)	Westwood One	$20-40
	(Live concert)		
Cass(RS)	**AUSTIN ENCORE** (92)	Mainstreet	$25-50
	(Live concert on cassette)		

JIM WILLIAMS (BG)
Recorded with Red Ellis
Starday 45s $5-10 each
Jessup LPs $8-10 each

-singles-

45rpm	**YOU'RE ALWAYS LATE**	Dub 2842	$25

-EPs-

EP	JIMMY WILLIAMS & RED ELLIS (59)	Starday 105	$18
EP	JIMMY WILLIAMS & RED ELLIS (59)	Starday 110	$18
EP	JIMMY WILLIAMS & RED ELLIS (59)	Starday 120	$15
EP	JIMMY WILLIAMS & RED ELLIS (60)	Starday 124	$15
EP	JIMMY WILLIAMS & RED ELLIS (60)	Starday 132	$12
EP	JIMMY WILLIAMS & RED ELLIS (60)	Starday 138	$12
EP	JIMMY WILLIAMS & RED ELLIS (60)	Starday 156	$12

-albums-

LP	HOLY CRY FROM THE HILLS (62)	Starday 165	$20

JOHNNY WILLIAMS (CW)

-albums-

LP	A SALUTE TO HANK WILLIAMS (63)	Crown 5186	$25
LP	THE ERA OF HANK WILLIAMS (64)	Crown 5327	$18

LEONA WILLIAMS (C)
Hickory LPs $5-10 each
Mercury LPs $3-6 each
MCA LPs $2-3 each

LEW WILLIAMS (RB)

-singles-

45rpm	I'LL PLAY YOUR GAME (57)	Imperial 8306	$15
45rpm	GONE APE MAN (57)	Imperial 5394	$20
45(P)	GONE APE MAN (57)	Imperial 5394	$15
	(Cream-colored promo label)		
45rpm	BOP BOP BA DOO BOP (57)	Imperial 5411	$25
45(P)	BOP BOP BA DOO BOP (57)	Imperial 5411	$20
	(Cream-colored promo label)		
45rpm	CENTIPEDE (57)	Imperial 5429	$25
45(P)	CENTIPEDE (57)	Imperial 5429	$20
	(Cream-colored promo label)		

LOIS WILLIAMS (CW)
Starday 45s $3 each

-albums-

LP	A GIRL NAMED SAM (70)	Starday 448	$15

OTIS WILLIAMS (C)
(Of the Charms R & B group)
And the Midnight Cowboys

-albums-

LP	OTIS WILLIAMS & THE MIDNIGHT COWBOYS (71)	Stop 1022	$15
	(His only country effort)		

RON WILLIAMS (RB)

-singles-

45rpm	SUE SUE BABY (59)	Ty-Tex 100	$50

TEX WILLIAMS (CW)
Other Capitol 78s and 45s $5-10 each
Shasta, Monument, and Liberty 45s $4 each
Other Decca 78s and 45s $4-8 each
Boone 45s $3 each
Shasta, Monument, Granite, and Garu LPs $4-8 each

-singles-

78rpm	SMOKE! SMOKE! SMOKE! (47)	Capitol 40001	$15
45rpm	OLD BETSY (55) From Davy Crockett movie	Decca 29578	$10
45rpm	YOU ROCKED WHEN YOU SHOULD'A ROLLED (59)	Decca 30774	$18
45(P)	YOU ROCKED WHEN YOU SHOULD'A ROLLED (59)	Decca 30774	$15
	(Pink promo label)		

-EPs-

EP	ALL TIME GREATS (55)	Decca 2174	$18
EP	DANCE-O-RAMA: TEX WILLIAMS (55)	Decca 2229	$15
EP	POLKA! (56)	Capitol 4005	$12
EP	ROUND DANCE FAVORITES (57)	Capitol 4016	$12
EP	TEX WILLIAMS' BEST (58)	Camden 414	$12

-albums-

10"LP	DANCE-O-RAMA: TEX WILLIAMS (55)	Decca 5565	$250
LP	TEX WILLIAMS' BEST (58)	Camden 363	$25
LP	SMOKE! SMOKE! SMOKE! (60) Mono	Capitol 1463	$25
LP	SMOKE! SMOKE! SMOKE! (60) Stereo	Capitol 1463	$40
LP(P)	SMOKE! SMOKE! SMOKE! (60)	Capitol 1463	$50
	(Blue promo label)		
LP	COUNTRY MUSIC TIME (62) Mono	Decca 4295	$20

LP	**COUNTRY MUSIC TIME** (62) Stereo	Decca 4295	$25
LP(P)	**COUNTRY MUSIC TIME** (62)	Decca 4295	$30
	(Pink promo label)		
LP	**TEX WILLIAMS IN LAS VEGAS** (63) Mono	Liberty 3304	$18
LP	**TEX WILLIAMS IN LAS VEGAS** (63) Stereo	Liberty 7304	$20
LP(P)	**TEX WILLIAMS IN LAS VEGAS** (63)	Liberty 3304	$25
	(White promo label)		
LP	**THE VOICE OF AUTHORITY** (66) Mono	Imperial 9309	$18
LP	**THE VOICE OF AUTHORITY** (66) Stereo	Imperial 12309	$20
LP(P)	**THE VOICE OF AUTHORITY** (66)	Imperial 9309	$25
	(White promo label)		
LP	**TEX WILLIAMS** (66)	Sunset 5144	$15
LP	**TWO SIDES OF TEX WILLIAMS** (66)	Boone 1210	$15

-radio shows-

LP(RS)	**HOOTENAVY** (60s) Fifteen-minute show	U.S. Navy 27/28	$25
	(Two shows, one on each side, each with Joannie Hall and Frontiersmen)		

WAYNE WILLIAMS (RB)

-singles-

45rpm	**RED HOT MAMA** (58)	Sure 1001	$150

BILL WILLIS (RB)

-singles-

45rpm	**BOOGIE WOOGIE ALL NIGHT** (58)	Dixie 825	$150

DON WILLIS (RB)

-singles-

45rpm	**BOPPIN' HIGH SCHOOL BABY** (58)	Satellite 101	$200

HAL WILLIS (RB)

-singles-

45rpm	**WALKIN' DOWN** (57)	Athens 704	$75
45rpm	**BOP-A-DEE, BOP-A-DOO** (57)	Atlantic 1114	$150

RALPH WILLIS (BG)

-albums-

LP	**FADED PICTURE BLUES** (70)	King 1098	$15
	(Recorded with Paul Howard)		

RAY WILLIS (RB)

-singles-

45rpm	**WHATTA YOU DO** (58)	Jane 103	$18

-albums-

LP	**COUNTRY HITS** (69)	Alshire 5146	$15

ROD WILLIS (RB)

-singles-

45rpm	**SOMEBODY'S BEEN ROCKING MY BABY** (57)	Chic 1010	$25

WILLIS BROTHERS (C)
Starday 45s $3-6 each

-albums-

LP	**THE WILLIS BROTHERS IN ACTION** (62)	Starday 163	$50
LP	**CODE OF THE WEST** (63)	Starday 229	$40
LP	**LET'S HIT THE ROAD** (65)	Starday 306	$30
LP	**GIVE ME 40 ACRES** (65)	Starday 323	$30
LP	**ROAD STOP JUKE BOX HITS** (65)	Starday 353	$25
LP	**THE WILD SIDE OF LIFE** (66)	Starday 369	$20
LP	**THE SENSATIONAL WILLIS BROTHERS** (65)	Hilltop 6035	$15
LP	**THE WILLIS BROTHERS GOIN' TO TOWN** (66)	Starday 387	$20
LP	**BOB** (67)	Starday 403	$20
LP	**HEY, MISTER TRUCK DRIVER** (68)	Starday 428	$20
LP	**BUMMIN' AROUND** (69)	Starday 442	$25
LP	**TRUCK DRIVER HITS** (69)	Nashville 2040	$12
LP	**Y'ALL** (69)	Nashville 2053	$12
LP	**COUNTRY HITS** (69)	Alshire 5146	$15
LP	**THE BEST OF THE WILLIS BROTHERS** (70)	Starday 466	$18
LP	**FOR THE GOOD TIMES** (71)	Starday 472	$15

BILLY JACK WILLS (RB)

-singles-

45rpm	**THERE'S GOOD ROCKING TONIGHT** (54)	MGM 11966	$25
45(P)	**THERE'S GOOD ROCKING TONIGHT** (54)	MGM 11966	$20
	(Yellow promo label)		

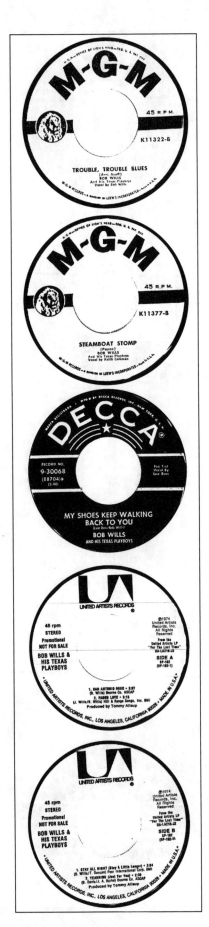

45rpm	**ALL SHE WANTS TO DO IS ROCK** (55)	MGM 12172	$25
45(P)	**ALL SHE WANTS TO DO IS ROCK** (55)	MGM 12172	$20
	(Yellow promo label)		

BOB WILLS (CW)

Vocalion 78s $15-20 each
Other 78s $5-10 each
Other MGM 45s $5-10 each
Other Decca and Coral 45s $5-8 each
Other United Artists, ABC, Capitol, and Liberty 45s $2-4 each
Western Heritage, Time-Life, and Delta LPs $6-10 each
MCA, Texas Rose, Kaleidoscope, Pickwick, and Coral LPs $4-8 each
Other Longhorn LPs $4-6 each

-singles-

78rpm	**NANCY JANE**	Bluebird 5257	$100
	(By the Fort Worth Doughboys)		
78rpm	**NEW SAN ANTONIO ROSE** (41)	Okeh 5694	$10
	(The original version)		
78rpm	**STARS AND STRIPES ON IWO JIMA** (45)	Okeh 6742	$15
78rpm	**NEW SPANISH TWO-STEP** (46)	Columbia 36966	$10
78rpm	**HAVE I STAYED AWAY TOO LONG?** Fan club release	Antone's 501	$25
45rpm	**IDA RED LIKES THE BOOGIE** (50)	MGM 10570	$25
45rpm	**FADED LOVE** (50)	MGM 10786	$15
45rpm	**TROUBLE, TROUBLE BLUES** (52)	MGM 11322	$10
45rpm	**STEAMBOAT STOMP** (52)	MGM 11377	$12
45rpm	**MY SHOES KEEP WALKING BACK TO YOU** (57)	Decca 30068	$10
45rpm	**SAN ANTONIO ROSE** (55) Tommy Duncan	Coral 61391	$10
45rpm	**BUFFALO TWIST** (64)	Longhorn 544	$15
	(Bob Wills photo on label)		

-EPs-

EP	**DANCE-O-RAMA** (55)	Decca 2223	$25
EP	**DANCE-O-RAMA** (55)	Decca 2224	$25
EP	**RANCH HOUSE FAVORITES VOL 1** (56)	MGM 1237	$20
EP	**RANCH HOUSE FAVORITES VOL 2** (56)	Decca 1238	$20
EP	**RANCH HOUSE FAVORITES VOL 3** (56)	Decca 1239	$20
EP	**BOB WILLS** (57)	Columbia 2805	$20
EP(P)	**FOR THE LAST TIME** (74)	United Artists 102	$20
	(Promo release with promo picture cover)		

-albums-

10"LP	**BOB WILLS ROUNDUP** (49)	Columbia 9003	$250
10"LP	**RANCH HOUSE FAVORITES** (51)	MGM 91	$250
10"LP	**DANCE-O-RAMA** (55)	Decca 5562	$250
10"LP	**OLD TIME FAVORITES**	Antone's 6000	$400
	(Fan club release)		
10LP	**OLD TIME FAVORITES**	Antone's 6010	$400
	(Fan club release)		
LP	**RANCH HOUSE FAVORITES** (56)	MGM 3352	$125
LP	**BOB WILLS & HIS TEXAS PLAYBOYS** (57)	Decca 8727	$75
LP(P)	**BOB WILLS & HIS TEXAS PLAYBOYS** (57)	Decca 8727	$100
	(Pink promo label)		
LP	**BOB WILLS SPECIAL** (57)	Harmony 7036	$40
	(First press maroon label)		
LP	**BOB WILLS SPECIAL** (57)	Harmony 7036	$50
	(White promo label)		
LP	**BOB WILLS & TOMMY DUNCAN** (61)	Liberty 1912	$25
LP(P)	**BOB WILLS & TOMMY DUNCAN** (61)	Liberty 1912	$30
	(White promo label)		
LP	**TOGETHER AGAIN** (60) Mono	Liberty 3173	$25
	(With Tommy Duncan)		
LP	**TOGETHER AGAIN** (60) Stereo	Liberty 7173	$30
LP(P)	**TOGETHER AGAIN** (60)	Liberty 3173	$40
	(White promo label)		
LP	**A LIVING LEGEND** (61) Mono	Liberty 3182	$30
LP	**A LIVING LEGEND** (61) Stereo	Liberty 7182	$40
LP(P)	**A LIVING LEGEND** (61)	Liberty 3182	$50
	(White promo label)		
LP	**MR. WORDS & MR. MUSIC** (61) Mono	Liberty 3194	$30
LP	**MR. WORDS & MR. MUSIC** (61) Stereo	Liberty 7194	$40
LP(P)	**MR. WORDS & MR. MUSIC** (61)	Liberty 7194	$50
	(White promo label)		
LP	**BOB WILLS SINGS & PLAYS** (63) Mono	Liberty 3303	$25
LP	**BOB WILLS SINGS & PLAYS** (63) Stereo	Liberty 7303	$30
LP(P)	**BOB WILLS SINGS & PLAYS** (63)	Liberty 3303	$40
	(White promo label)		
LP	**THE BEST OF BOB WILLS** (63)	Harmony 7304	$25
LP(P)	**THE BEST OF BOB WILLS** (63)	Harmony 7304	$30
	(White promo label)		

LP	THE GREAT BOB WILLS (65)	Harmony 7345	$20
LP(P)	THE GREAT BOB WILLS (65)	Harmony 7345	$25
	(White promo label)		
LP	SAN ANTONIO ROSE (65)	Starday 375	$25
LP	MY KEEPSAKE ALBUM (65)	Longhorn 001	$75
	(First pressing)		
LP	MY KEEPSAKE ALBUM (65)	Longhorn 001	$50
	(Second pressing has orange cover)		
LP	WESTERN SWING BAND (65)	Vocalion 3735	$20
LP(P)	WESTERN SWING BAND (65)	Vocalion 3735	$25
	(White promo label)		
LP	TOGETHER AGAIN (66) With Tommy Duncan	Sunset 1108	$15
LP	BOB WILLS (67) Mono	Metro 594	$15
LP	BOB WILLS (67) Stereo	Metro 594	$10
LP(P)	BOB WILLS (67)	Metro 594	$18
	(Yellow promo label)		
LP	FROM THE HEART OF TEXAS (67) Mono	Kapp 1506	$18
LP	FROM THE HEART OF TEXAS (67) Stereo	Kapp 3506	$25
LP	KING OF WESTERN SWING (67) Mono	Kapp 1523	$18
	(With Mel Tillis)		
LP	KING OF WESTERN SWING (67) Stereo	Kapp 3523	$25
LP	HERE'S THAT MAN AGAIN (68)	Kapp 3542	$20
LP	TIME CHANGES EVERYTHING (69)	Kapp 3569	$20
LP	THE LIVING LEGEND (69)	Kapp 3587	$20
LP	THE GREATEST STRING BAND HITS (69)	Kapp 3601	$20
LP	A COUNTRY WALK (69)	Sunset 5248	$18
LP	BOB WILLS SPECIAL (69)	Harmony 11358	$15
LP	BOB WILLS IN PERSON (70)	Kapp 3639	$20
LP	THE BOB WILLS STORY (70)	Starday 469	$15
LP	THE BEST OF BOB WILLS (71)	Kapp 3641	$20
2LP	LEGENDARY MASTERS (71)	United Artists 9962	$25
LP(P)	LEGENDARY MASTERS (71)	United Artists 9962	$40
	(White promo labels)		
LP	A TRIBUTE TO BOB WILLS (71)	MGM 141	$25
LP(P)	A TRIBUTE TO BOB WILLS (71)	MGM 141	$30
	(Yellow promo label)		
LP	HISTORY OF BOB WILLS & HIS TEXAS PLAYBOYS (73)	MGM 4866	$12
LP(P)	HISTORY OF BOB WILLS & HIS TEXAS PLAYBOYS (73)	MGM 4866	$15
	(Yellow promo label)		
2LP	BOB WILLS ANTHOLOGY (73)	Columbia 32416	$12
2LP	FOR THE LAST TIME (74)	United Artists 216	$12
	(Price includes book)		
2LP(P)	FOR THE LAST TIME (74)	United Artists 216	$18
	(White promo labels)		
2LP	THE LEGENDARY BOB WILLS (75)	Columbia 12924	$12
2LP	BOB WILLS & HIS TEXAS PLAYBOYS IN CONCERT (76)	Capitol 11550	$15
LP	THE TIFFANY TRANSCRIPTIONS (77)	Lariat 1	$75
	(Shows from 1945-48)		
LP	THE TIFFANY TRANSCRIPTIONS (78)	Tishomingo 01	$50
2LP	ORIGINAL TEXAS PLAYBOYS LIVE FROM AUSTIN CITY LIMITS (70s)		
	(The Texas Playboys)	Delta 1164	$15
2LP	BOB WILLS DAY (70s) Original Texas Playboys	Delta 1177	$15
LP	SAN ANTONIO ROSE (71)	Vocalion 3922	$15
LP(P)	SAN ANTONIO ROSE (71)	Vocalion 3922	$18
	(White promo label)		
LP	THE LATE BOB WILLS ORIGINAL TEXAS PLAYBOYS (77)	Capitol 11612	$12
	(The Original Texas Playboys)		
LP	LIVE & KICKIN' (78) Original Texas Playboys	Capitol 11725	$12
LP	ORIGINAL TEXAS PLAYBOYS LIVE & KICKIN' (79)	Capitol 11917	$12
	(The Original Texas Playboys)		

-radio shows-

Cass(RS)	AUSTIN ENCORE (92)	Mainstreet Radio	$40-75
	(Concert material on cassette)		

CHILL WILLS (CW)
TV and movie actor
Metromedia and Atlantic 45s $2-5 each
Metromedia and Atlantic LPs $5-10 each

DAVID WILLS (C)
Texas Vocal Company
Epic 45s $1-2 each
Other RCA Victor 45s $2 each
Epic and RCA Victor LPs $3 each

-singles-

45(P)	THOSE NIGHTS, THOSE DAYS (83)	RCA Victor 13460	$10
	(Green promo label, red vinyl)		

45(P)	**TWO HEARTS** (83) Texas Vocal Company	RCA Victor 13504	$10
	(Green promo label, green vinyl)		
45(P)	**THE EYES OF A STRANGER** (83)	RCA Victor 13541	$10
	(Green promo label, yellow vinyl)		
45(P)	**IT HAD TO BE YOU** (83) Texas Vocal Company	RCA Victor 13566	$10
	(Yellow promo label, yellow vinyl)		
45(P)	**THANK GOD FOR FRIDAY** (84)	RCA Victor 13833	$10
	(Blue promo label, blue vinyl)		

JOHNNY LEE WILLS (CW)
Brother of Bob Wills

-albums-

LP	**WHERE THERE'S A WILLS THERE'S A WAY** (62)	Sims 101	$40
LP	**JOHNNY LEE WILLS AT THE TULSA STAMPEDE** (63)	Sims 108	$30
LP	**THE BEST OF JOHNNY LEE WILLS** (70s)	Crown 565	$15

TOMMY WILLS (RB)

-singles-

45rpm	**LET 'EM ROLL** (58)	Club Miami 501	$100

ANDY WILSON (RB)

-singles-

45rpm	**MY LOVE MY LOVE** (56)	Bullseye 1012	$18
45rpm	**HILLBILLY BOOGIE** (56)	Dot 1127	$12

LONNIE WILSON (CW)

-albums-

LP	**THE PLAYBOY FARMER** (59)	Starday 217	$20

PEANUTS WILSON (RB)

-singles-

45rpm	**CAST IRON MAN** (58)	Brunswick 55039	$200
45(P)	**CAST IRON MAN** (58) Yellow promo label	Brunswick 55039	$125
	(Buddy Holly on guitar)		

MAGGIE SUE WIMBERLY (RB)

-singles-

45rpm	**DAYDREAMS COME TRUE** (59)	Sun 229	$25

JACK WINSTON (RB)

-singles-

45rpm	**IT'S ROCK & ROLL** (58)	Jay Wing 5806	$50

GAIL WINTERS (C)

-albums-

LP	**GIRL FOR ALL SEASONS** (67)	Hickory 138	$15
LP(P)	**GIRL FOR ALL SEASONS** (67)	Hickory 138	$18
	(White promo label)		

CHUBBY WISE (BG)
Stoneway and Guest Star LPs $5 each

-albums-

LP	**THE TENNESSEE FIDDLER CHUBBY WISE** (61)	Starday 154	$50
2LP	**GIVE ME MY SMOKIES & THE TENNESSEE WALTZ** (70s)	Gilley's 500	$20
	(Recorded with Mac Wiseman)		

MAC WISEMAN (CW)
Other Dot 45s $4-8 each
Capitol 45s $3-6 each
ABC and RCA Victor 45s $2-3 each
ABC and RCA Victor LPs $5-10 each
Vetco and Rural Rhythm LPs $4-8 each
Gusto, CMH, Pickwick, Ridge Runner, and MCA LPs $5 each

-singles-

45rpm	**SIX MORE MILES** (51)	Dot 1146	$10
45rpm	**CRAZY BLUES** (54)	Dot 1168	$12
45rpm	**THE LITTLE OLD CHURCH IN THE VALLEY** (55)	Dot 1236	$10
78rpm	**BALLAD OF DAVY CROCKETT** (55)	Dot 1240	$12
45rpm	**BALLAD OF DAVY CROCKETT** (55)	Dot 1240	$12
45rpm	**I HEAR YOU KNOCKING** (55)	Dot 1273	$10
45rpm	**THESE HANDS** (56)	Dot 1276	$10
45rpm	**THE MEANEST BLUES IN THE COUNTRY** (56)	Dot 1282	$10
45rpm	**SMILIN' THROUGH** (56)	Dot 1285	$10
45rpm	**ONE MINUTE JULIP** (56)	Dot 15497	$15
	(Maroon labels on all singles listed above)		
45rpm	**STEP IT UP AND GO** (57) Black label	Dot 15544	$25

45rpm	LOVE LETTERS IN THE SAND (57)	Dot 15578	$10
45rpm	I'LL STILL WRITE YOUR NAME IN THE SAND (57)	Dot 15638	$10
45rpm	WHEN THE WORK'S ALL DONE THIS FALL (58)	Dot 15731	$10
45rpm	JIMMY BROWN THE NEWSBOY (59)	Dot 15946	$20

-EPs-

| EP | SONGS FROM THE HILLS (55) | Dot 1027 | $25 |

-albums-

LP	TIS SWEET TO BE REMEMBERED (58) Mono	Dot 3084	$50
LP	TIS SWEET TO BE REMEMBERED (58) Stereo	Dot 25084	$20
LP	BESIDE THE STILL WATERS (59) Mono	Dot 25135	$30
LP	BESIDE THE STILL WATERS (59) Stereo	Dot 25135	$40
LP	GREAT FOLK BALLADS (59) Mono	Dot 25213	$30
LP	GREAT FOLK BALLADS (59) Stereo	Dot 25213	$40
LP	MAC WISEMAN SINGS 12 GREAT HITS (60) Mono	Dot 25313	$30
LP	MAC WISEMAN SINGS 12 GREAT HITS (60) Stereo	Dot 25313	$40
LP	KEEP ON THE SUNNY SIDE (60) Mono	Dot 3336	$40
LP	KEEP ON THE SUNNY SIDE (60) Stereo	Dot 25336	$20
LP	FIREBALL MAIL (61) Mono	Dot 3408	$30
LP	FIREBALL MAIL (61) Stereo	Dot 25408	$20
LP	BLUEGRASS FAVORITES (62) Mono	Capitol 1800	$30
LP	BLUEGRASS FAVORITES (62) Stereo	Capitol 1800	$40
LP(P)	BLUEGRASS FAVORITES (62)	Capitol 1800	$40
	(Blue promo label)		
LP	SINCERELY (64)	Hamilton 12130	$20
LP	SONGS OF THE DEAR OLD DAYS (66)	Hamilton 12167	$18
LP	THIS IS MAC WISEMAN (66)	Dot 25697	$18
LP	A MASTER AT WORK (66)	Dot 25730	$18
LP	BLUEGRASS (68)	Dot 25731	$18
LP	GOLDEN HITS OF MAC WISEMAN (68)	Dot 25896	$15
2LP	GIVE ME MY SMOKIES & THE TENNESSEE WALTZ (70s)	Gilley's 500	$20
	(Recorded with Chubby Wise)		
LP	LESTER 'N' MAC (71) With Lester Flatt	RCA Victor 4547	$20
LP	ON THE SOUTHBOUND (72) With Lester Flatt	RCA Victor 4688	$20
LP	OVER THE HILLS TO THE POORHOUSE (73)	RCA Victor 0309	$20
	(With Lester Flatt)		

-radio shows-

16"(RS)	COUNTRY STYLE USA (55) Fifteen-minute show	Country Style 195	$40-60
	(Music and interviews)		
16"(RS)	COUNTRY STYLE USA (56) Fifteen-minute show	Country Style 213	$40-60
	(Music and interviews)		
16"(RS)	U.S. ARMY BAND (60s)	U.S. Army	$40-60
	(Music and interviews)		

NORMAN WITCHER (RB)

-singles-

| 45rpm | SOMEBODY'S BEEN ROCKIN' MY BOAT (58) | Poor Boy 102 | $60 |

JIMMY WITTER (RB)

-singles-

| 45rpm | IF YOU LOVE MY WOMAN (58) | Elvis 900 | $125 |

JIMMY WOLFORD (RB)

-singles-

| 45rpm | MY NAME IS JIMMY (58) | Four Star 1714 | $100 |

AUSTIN WOOD (CW)
And His Missouri Swingsters

-singles-

45rpm	GRAY EAGLE (54)	Sure 0398	$18
45rpm	TRUCK DRIVERS NIGHT RUN BLUES (54)	Sure 0405	$15

BOBBY WOOD (C)

-albums-

| LP | BOBBY WOOD (64) | Joy 1001 | $18 |

DEL WOOD (CW)
Adelaide Hazelwood
Any 78s and 45s $2-4 each
Republic EPs $5-10 each
Other RCA Victor EPs $4-8 each
RCA Victor promo EPs $8 each
Other RCA Victor, Camden, Republic, Mercury LPs $4-8 each
Vocalion and Columbia LPs $2-5 each

-EPs-

| 2EP | DOWN YONDER (55) | RCA Victor 1129 | $15 |

-albums-

LP	**DOWN YONDER** (55)	RCA Victor 1129	$10

JERRY WOODARD (RB)

-singles-

45rpm	**SIX LONG WHEELS** (58)	Fad 901	$40
45rpm	**WHO'S GONNA ROCK MY BABY** (58)	Reed 1017	$40

WOODHULL'S OLD TYME MASTERS (CW)

Floyd C. Woodhull
Other RCA Victor 45s $2-4 each
RCA Victor title sleeves $2 each

-singles-

4-45s	**SQUARE DANCES** (50) Box set of five 45s	RCA Victor WDC 36	$15
	(With and without square dance calls)		

-albums-

LP	**SQUARE DANCES** (62)	Camden 220	$15

BILL WOODS (RB)

-singles-

45rpm	**BOP** (58)	Fire 100	$50

DON WOODY (RB)

-singles-

45rpm	**YOU'RE BARKING UP THE WRONG TREE** (58)	Decca 30277	$40

SHEB WOOLEY (CW)

Also recorded as Ben Colder
Other MGM 45s $5-10 each
MGM 45s by Ben Colder $4-8 each

-singles-

78rpm	**TEXAS TANGO** (53) With His Calumet Indians	MGM 11580	$10
78(P)	**TEXAS TANGO** (53)	MGM 11580	$12
	(Yellow promo label)		
45rpm	**TEXAS TANGO** (53)	MGM 11580	$25
45rpm	**THE BIRTH OF ROCK 'N' ROLL** (56)	MGM 12202	$15
45(P)	**THE BIRTH OF ROCK 'N' ROLL** (56)	MGM 12202	$10
	(Yellow promo label)		
45rpm	**FIRST DAY OF SCHOOL** (56)	MGM 12328	$15
45(P)	**FIRST DAY OF SCHOOL** (56)	MGM 12328	$10
45rpm	**THE PURPLE PEOPLE EATER** (58)	MGM 12651	$18
45(P)	**THE PURPLE PEOPLE EATER** (58)	MGM 12651	$25
	(Yellow promo label)		
45rpm	**SANTA AND THE PURPLE PEOPLE EATER** (58)	MGM 12733	$15
45(P)	**SANTA AND THE PURPLE PEOPLE EATER** (58)	MGM 12733	$12
	(Yellow promo label)		
45(P)	**THE PURPLE PEOPLE EATER** (73)	MGM 14647	$10
	(White promo label)		

-EPs-

EP	**SHEB WOOLEY VOL 1** (56)	MGM 1188	$75
EP	**SHEB WOOLEY VOL 2** (56)	MGM 1189	$75
EP	**SHEB WOOLEY VOL 3** (56)	MGM 1190	$75
EP	**THE PURPLE PEOPLE EATER PLAYS EARTH MUSIC** (58)	MGM 1607	$75
EP	**THE PURPLE PEOPLE EATER** (58)	MGM 1608	$75

-albums-

LP	**SHEB WOOLEY** (56)	MGM 3299	$100
LP(P)	**SHEB WOOLEY** (56)	MGM 3299	$125
	(Yellow promo label)		
LP	**THAT'S MY MA AND THAT'S MY PA** (62) Mono	MGM 4026	$25
LP	**THAT'S MY MA AND THAT'S MY PA** (62) Stereo	MGM 4026	$30
LP(P)	**THAT'S MY MA AND THAT'S MY PA** (62)	MGM 4026	$25
	(Yellow promo label)		
LP	**SPOOFING THE BIG ONES** (62) Mono	MGM 4117	$18
	(As Ben Colder)		
LP	**SPOOFING THE BIG ONES** (62) Stereo	MGM 4117	$25
LP(P)	**SPOOFING THE BIG ONES** (62)	MGM 4117	$25
	(Yellow promo label)		
LP	**TALES OF HOW THE WEST WAS WON** (63) Mono	MGM 4136	$18
LP	**TALES OF HOW THE WEST WAS WON** (63) Stereo	MGM 4136	$25
LP(P)	**TALES OF HOW THE WEST WAS WON** (63)	MGM 4136	$20
	(Yellow promo label)		
LP	**BEN COLDER** (63) Mono	MGM 4173	$18
LP	**BEN COLDER** (63) Stereo	MGM 4173	$25
LP(P)	**BEN COLDER** (63)	MGM 4173	$20
	(Yellow promo label)		

LP	THE VERY BEST OF SHEB WOOLEY (65)	MGM 4275	$18
LP(P)	THE VERY BEST OF SHEB WOOLEY (65)	MGM 4275	$20
	(Yellow promo label)		
LP	IT'S A BIG LAND (65)	MGM 4325	$18
LP(P)	IT'S A BIG LAND (65)	MGM 4325	$20
	(Yellow promo label)		
LP	BIG BEN STRIKES AGAIN (66)	MGM 4421	$15
LP(P)	BIG BEN STRIKES AGAIN (66)	MGM 4421	$18
	(Yellow promo label)		
LP	WINE, WOMEN & SONG (67) As Ben Colder	MGM 4482	$15
LP(P)	WINE, WOMEN & SONG (67)	MGM 4482	$18
	(Yellow promo label)		
LP	WARM AND WOOLEY (69)	MGM 4615	$10
LP(P)	WARM AND WOOLEY (69)	MGM 4615	$12
	(White promo label)		

-albums-

LP(RS)	HOOTENAVY (60s)	U.S. Navy	$25-50
	(Music and interviews)		

WAYNE WORLEY (RB)

-singles-

45rpm	RED HEADED WOMAN (58)	Elbridge 11016	$40

MARION WORTH (C)
Mary Ann Ward
Columbia 45s $2-3 each
Columbia picture sleeves $8 each

-albums-

LP	MARION WORTH'S GREATEST HITS (63)	Columbia 8811	$15
LP(P)	MARION WORTH'S GREATEST HITS (63)	Columbia 8811	$20
	(White promo label)		
LP	MARION WORTH SINGS MARTY ROBBINS (64)	Columbia 9087	$15
LP(P)	MARION WORTH SINGS MARTY ROBBINS (64)	Columbia 9087	$20
	(White promo label)		
LP	A WOMAN NEEDS LOVE (67)	Decca 4936	$15
LP(P)	A WOMAN NEEDS LOVE (67)	Decca 4936	$18
	(Pink promo label)		

JOHN WORTHAM (RB)

-singles-

45rpm	THE CATS WERE JUMPIN' (58)	Peach 722	$60

LINK WRAY (R)
Lucky Wray
Cadence 45s $20 each
Other Epic 45s $15-20 each
Rumble 45s $20 each
Trans Atlas 45s $15 each
Other Okeh 45s $10-15 each
Swan 45s $10-20 each
Heavy and Mr. G 45s $8-15 each
Polydor 45s $2-4 each
Polydor LPs $10-15 each

-singles-

45rpm	I SEZ BABY (56)	Kay 3690	$250
45rpm	SICK & TIRED (56) Lucky Wray	Starday 552	$250
45rpm	GOT ANOTHER BABY (57) Lucky Wray	Starday 575	$250
45rpm	TEENAGE CUTIE (57) Lucky Wray	Starday 608	$250
45rpm	SLINKY (59)	Epic 9343	$60
	(Price includes picture sleeve)		
45rpm	RUMBLE MAMBO (63)	Okeh 7166	$50
	(Price includes picture sleeve)		

-albums-

LP	LINK WRAY & THE WRAYMEN (60)	Epic 3361	$150
LP(P)	LINK WRAY & THE WRAYMEN (60)	Epic 3661	$125
	(White promo label)		
LP	JACK THE RIPPER (63)	Swan 510	$150
LP	GREAT GUITAR HITS (63)	Vermillion 1924	$150
LP	LINK WRAY SINGS AND PLAYS GUITAR (64)	Vermillion 1925	$150
LP	YESTERDAY & TODAY (70s)	Record Factory 1929	$50

BOBBY WRIGHT (C)
Son of Kitty Wells and Johnny Wright
Cast member of *McHale's Navy*

-albums-

LP	HERE I GO AGAIN (71)	Decca 75319	$15

LP(P)	**HERE I GO AGAIN** (71) (Pink promo label)	Decca 75319	$12

DALE WRIGHT (RB)
-singles-

45rpm	**I'M THE LOVIN' TYPE** (58)	Fraternity 761	$15
45(P)	**I'M THE LOVIN' TYPE** (58) (White promo label)	Fraternity 761	$20
45rpm	**THAT'S MY GAL** (59)	Fraternity 837	$12
45(P)	**THAT'S MY GAL** (59) (White promo label)	Fraternity 837	$18

JOHNNY WRIGHT (CW)
Married to Kitty Wells
 Decca 45s $2-3 each
-albums-

LP	**HELLO VIET NAM** (65)	Decca 4698	$18
LP(P)	**HELLO VIET NAM** (65) (Pink promo label)	Decca 4698	$15
LP	**COUNTRY MUSIC SPECIAL** (66)	Decca 4770	$15
LP(P)	**COUNTRY MUSIC SPECIAL** (66) (Pink promo label)	Decca 4770	$12
LP	**COUNTRY THE WRIGHT WAY** (67)	Decca 4846	$15
LP(P)	**COUNTRY THE WRIGHT WAY** (67) (Pink promo label)	Decca 4846	$12
LP	**JOHNNY WRIGHT SINGS COUNTRY FAVORITES** (68)	Decca 5019	$15
LP(P)	**JOHNNY WRIGHT SINGS COUNTRY FAVORITES** (68) (Pink promo label)	Decca 5019	$12

-radio shows-

LP(RS)	**GRAND OL' OPRY** (62) (Music and interviews)	WSM Radio	$20-40

RUBY WRIGHT (CW)
Other King 78s and 45s $5-10 each
-singles-

45rpm	**THREE STARS** (58) (Narrative by Dick Pike)	King 5192	$25
45(S)	**THREE STARS** (58) (Stereo single)	King S-5192	$30

-albums-

LP	**DERN YA** (66)	Kapp 3508	$15

SONNY WRIGHT (C)
-albums-

LP	**I LOVE YOU, LORETTA LYNN** (69)	Kapp 3614	$15

GENE WYATT (R)
-singles-

45rpm	**LOVER BOY** (57)	Ebb 123	$40

TAMMY WYNETTE (CW)
Other Epic 45s $1-2 each
 Other Epic LPs $4-6 each
 Other Epic promo LPs $5-8 each
 Epic 2LP sets $8-10 each
 Time-Life LPs $8 each
-singles-

45(P)	**THE WONDERS YOU PERFORM** (70) (Promo-only white label, red vinyl)	Epic TW 1	$18
45(P)	**WHITE CHRISTMAS** (73) (Promo-only orange label, price includes promo-only picture sleeve)	Epic AS 60	$12

-EPs-

EP(P)	**THE FIRST LADY** (70) Jukebox LLP (Issued with a hard cover, yellow cover)	Epic 30213	$15
EP(P)	**WE SURE CAN LOVE EACH OTHER** (71) Jukebox LLP (Issued with a hard cover, orange label)	Epic 30658	$15

-albums-

LP	**YOUR GOOD GIRL'S GONNA GO BAD** (67)	Epic 26305	$15
LP(P)	**YOUR GOOD GIRL'S GONNA GO BAD** (67) (White promo label)	Epic 26305	$20
LP	**TAKE ME TO YOUR WORLD** (68)	Epic 26353	$15
LP(P)	**TAKE ME TO YOUR WORLD** (68) (White promo label)	Epic 26353	$18
LP	**D-I-V-O-R-C-E** (68)	Epic 26392	$15
LP(P)	**D-I-V-O-R-C-E** (68)	Epic 26392	$18

	(White promo label)		
LP	**TAMMY WYNETTE** (70)	Harmony 30096	$12
LP	**IT'S JUST A MATTER OF TIME** (71)	Harmony 30914	$12
LP(P)	**IT'S JUST A MATTER OF TIME** (71)	Harmony 30914	$15
	(White promo label)		
5LP	**THE VERY BEST OF TAMMY WYNETTE** (73) Box set	Columbia 5856	$50
	(Five record box set)		

-radio shows-

3LP(RS)	**THE SILVER EAGLE** (81)	DIR	$20-40
	(Live concert)		
LP(RS)	**COUNTRY SESSIONS** (82)	NBC Radio	$15-25
	(Live concert)		
LP(RS)	**LIVE AT GILLEY'S** (Nov 84)	Westwood One	$10-20
	(Live concert)		
LP(RS)	**WESTWOOD ONE PRESENTS** (Nov 89)	Westwood One	$10-20
	(Live concert)		
Cass(RS)	**AUSTIN ENCORE** (92)	Mainstreet Radio	$20-40
	(Live concert on cassette)		

Y

FRANKIE YANKOVIC & HIS YANKS (Polka)

Other Continental and Remington 78s and 45s $5-10 each
Columbia 45s before 40000 $5-10 each
Columbia 45s after 40000 $2-5 each
V Records 45s $2 each
Polka City 45s $1 each
Columbia LPs $5-10 each

-singles-

45rpm	**GOLDEN STARS POLKA** (50)	Continental 009	$10
45rpm	**HERKULOVIC** (50)	Continental 036	$10
45rpm	**TO THE LEFT TO THE RIGHT** (52)	Remington 1017	$10
	(Maroon label)		
45rpm	**JOLLY POLKA** (53)	Remington 1062	$10
45rpm	**MY GIRL FRIEND JULAYDA** (53)	Columbia 39116	$10
45rpm	**CHARLIE WAS A BOXER/BLUE SKIRT WALTZ** (52)	Columbia 10016	$10
45rpm	**WHO STOLE THE KEESHKA** (72)	Columbia 45555	$10

-EPs-

EP	**TV POLKAS** (55)	Columbia 10382	$12
EP	**FRANKIE YANKOVIC** (55)	Columbia 1570	$12
EP	**FRANKIE YANKOVIC'S WALTZ FAVORITES** (55)	Columbia 1652	$12
EP	**DANCE THE POLKA** (57)	Columbia 1753	$10
EP	**FRANKIE YANKOVIC** (57)	Columbia 2548	$12
	(Columbia Hall of Fame series)		
EP(JB)	**JUST FOR FUN** (65) Jukebox LLP	Columbia 9223	$10
	(Issued with a paper cover)		

LAFAYETTE YARBROUGH (RB)

-singles-

45rpm	**COOL COOL BABY** (57)	Bart 7625	$60

MALCOLM YELVINGTON (RB)

-singles-

45rpm	**DRINKIN' WINE SPODEE-O-DEE** (54)	Sun 211	$50
45rpm	**ROCKIN' WITH MY BABY** (55)	Sun 246	$15

DWIGHT YOAKAM (C)

Reprise 45s $1 each
Reprise picture sleeves $1 each
Reprise LPs $3 each

-radio shows-

3LP(RS)	**AMERICAN EAGLE** (80s)	DIR	$40-75
	(Live concert)		
Cass(RS)	**AUSTIN ENCORE** (92)	Mainstreet Radio	$40-75
	(Live concert on cassette)		

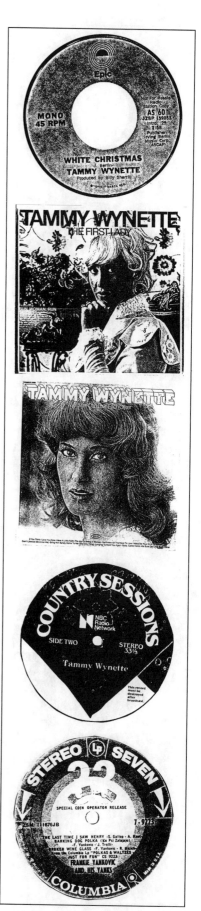

RUSTY YORK (CW)
Capitol 45s $5-10 each
Blue Grass Special and Queen City LPs $5-10 each
Rural Rhythm LPs with J. D. Jarvis $8 each

YORK BROTHERS (CW)
King 78s and 45s $5-10 each

-EPs-

EP	THE YORK BROTHERS SING THEIR HITS (58)	King 216	$18

-albums-

LP	THE YORK BROTHERS (58)	King 586	$40
LP	THE YORK BROTHERS VOL 2 (58)	King 591	$30
LP	16 GREAT COUNTRY WESTERN SONGS (63)	King 820	$20

FARON YOUNG (CW)
The Sheriff & His Deputies
Capitol 78s $3-6 each
Other Capitol 45s $3-8 each
Capitol picture sleeves $4-8 each
Mercury 45s $2-4 each
Mercury picture sleeves $2-4 each
Union 45s $2 each
Union picture sleeves $1 each
Exact, Album Globe, MCA, Allegiance, and Castle LPs $4-8 each
Faron Young (label) LPs $10 each

-singles-

45rpm	FOOLISH PRIDE (52)	Capitol 2133	$18
45rpm	GOIN' STEADY (53)	Capitol 2299	$15
45rpm	I CAN'T WAIT (53)	Capitol 2461	$12
45rpm	THAT'S WHAT I'D DO FOR YOU (54)	Capitol 2570	$12
45rpm	I HARDLY KNEW IT WAS YOU (54)	Capitol 2690	$12
45rpm	YOU'RE RIGHT (54)	Capitol 2780	$10
45rpm	IN THE CHAPEL IN THE MOONLIGHT (55)	Capitol 2859	$10
45rpm	KING OF A LONELY CASTLE (55)	Capitol 2914	$10
45rpm	IF YOU AIN'T LOVIN' (55)	Capitol 2953	$10
45rpm	LIVE FAST, LOVE HARD, DIE YOUNG (55)	Capitol 3056	$10
45rpm	HONEY STOP! (57)	Capitol 3805	$15
45(P)	HONEY STOP! (57) White promo label	Capitol 3805	$12
45rpm	HELLO WALLS (58)	Capitol 4533	$10
45(P)	HELLO WALLS (58)	Capitol 4533	$12
	(Red promo label)		
5-33s	FARON YOUNG AIMS AT THE WEST (63) Jukebox singles	Mercury 11001	$8 each
	(Five blue label stereo singles, $40 for the set)		

-EPs-

EP	GOIN' STEADY (54)	Capitol 450	$25
EP(P)	AND NOW (55)	Sesac AD 1	$50
	(Released to radio stations only)		
EP	FARON YOUNG (56)	Capitol 611	$25
EP(P)	NO GREATER LOVE (57) With Chet Atkins	Sesac AD 48	$25
	(Released to radio stations only)		
EP	SWEETHEARTS OR STRANGERS VOL 1 (57)	Capitol 1-778	$25
EP	SWEETHEARTS OR STRANGERS VOL 2 (57)	Capitol 2-778	$25
EP	SWEETHEARTS OR STRANGERS VOL 3 (57)	Capitol 3-778	$25
EP	THE SHRINE OF ST. CECILIA (57)	Capitol 869	$25
EP	COUNTRY MUSIC HOLIDAY VOL 1 (58)	Capitol 1-921	$20
EP	COUNTRY MUSIC HOLIDAY VOL 2 (58)	Capitol 2-921	$20
EP	COUNTRY MUSIC HOLIDAY VOL 3 (58)	Capitol 3-921	$20
EP	THIS IS FARON YOUNG VOL 1 (59)	Capitol 1-1096	$18
EP	THIS IS FARON YOUNG VOL 2 (59)	Capitol 2-1096	$18
EP	THIS IS FARON YOUNG VOL 3 (59)	Capitol 3-1096	$18
EP	MY GARDEN OF PRAYER VOL 1 (59)	Capitol 1-1185	$15
EP	MY GARDEN OF PRAYER VOL 2 (59)	Capitol 2-1185	$15
EP	MY GARDEN OF PRAYER VOL 3 (59)	Capitol 3-1185	$15
EP	TALK ABOUT HITS VOL 1 (59)	Capitol 1-1245	$15
EP	TALK ABOUT HITS VOL 2 (59)	Capitol 2-1245	$15
EP	TALK ABOUT HITS VOL 3 (59)	Capitol 3-1245	$15
EP	FAN CLUB FAVORITES (61)	Capitol 1528	$18
EP	HELLO WALLS (61)	Capitol 1549	$18
EP(JB)	COUNTRY DANCE FAVORITES (64) Jukebox LLP	Mercury 60931	$10
	(Issued with a hard cover)		

-albums-

LP	SWEETHEARTS OR STRANGERS (57)	Capitol 778	$60
LP(P)	SWEETHEARTS OR STRANGERS (57)	Capitol 778	$75
	(Yellow promo label)		
LP	THE OBJECT OF MY AFFECTION (58)	Capitol 1004	$50
LP(P)	THE OBJECT OF MY AFFECTION (58)	Capitol 1004	$50
	(Yellow promo label)		

LP	**THIS IS FARON YOUNG** (59)	Capitol 1096	$50
LP(P)	**THIS IS FARON YOUNG** (59)	Capitol 1096	$40
	(Yellow promo label)		
LP	**MY GARDEN OF PRAYER** (59)	Capitol 1185	$30
LP(P)	**MY GARDEN OF PRAYER** (59)	Capitol 1185	$30
	(Blue promo label)		
LP(P)	**FARON YOUNG CHURCH SONGS** (59)	Sesac LP	$75
	(Yellow and black label, released to radio only)		
LP(P)	**FARON YOUNG SINGS ON STAGE FOR MARY CARTER PAINTS**	Mary Carter 1000	$50
	(Released by Mary Carter Paints for radio only)		
LP	**TALK ABOUT HITS** (59) Mono	Capitol 1245	$25
LP	**TALK ABOUT HITS** (59) Stereo	Capitol 1245	$40
LP(P)	**TALK ABOUT HITS** (59)	Capitol 1245	$30
	(Blue promo label)		
LP	**THE BEST OF FARON YOUNG** (60) Mono	Capitol 1450	$15
LP	**THE BEST OF FARON YOUNG** (60) Stereo	Capitol 1450	$20
LP(P)	**THE BEST OF FARON YOUNG** (60)	Capitol 1450	$30
	(Blue promo label)		
LP	**HELLO WALLS** (61) Mono	Capitol 1528	$18
LP	**HELLO WALLS** (61) Stereo	Capitol 1528	$20
LP(P)	**HELLO WALLS** (61)	Capitol 1528	$25
	(Blue promo label)		
LP	**THE YOUNG APPROACH** (61) Mono	Capitol 1634	$18
LP	**THE YOUNG APPROACH** (61) Stereo	Capitol 1634	$20
LP(P)	**THE YOUNG APPROACH** (61)	Capitol 1634	$25
	(Blue promo label)		
LP	**THE ALL TIME GREAT HITS** (63)	Capitol 1876	$18
LP(P)	**THE ALL TIME GREAT HITS** (63)	Capitol 1876	$25
	(Blue promo label)		
LP	**MEMORY LANE** (65) Mono	Capitol 2037	$18
LP	**MEMORY LANE** (65) Stereo	Capitol 2037	$20
LP(P)	**MEMORY LANE** (65)	Capitol 2037	$25
	(Blue promo label)		
LP	**FALLING IN LOVE** (65) Mono	Capitol 2307	$15
LP	**FALLING IN LOVE** (65) Stereo	Capitol 2307	$18
LP(P)	**FALLING IN LOVE** (65)	Capitol 2307	$20
	(Blue promo label)		
LP	**FARON, CARL & CLAUDE** (65)	Hilltop 6011	$15
	(With Claude King and Carl Perkins)		
LP	**IF YOU AIN'T LOVIN' YOU AIN'T LIVIN'** (66) Mono	Capitol 2536	$12
LP	**IF YOU AIN'T LOVIN' YOU AIN'T LIVIN'** (66) Stereo	Capitol 2536	$15
LP(P)	**IF YOU AIN'T LOVIN' YOU AIN'T LIVIN'** (66)	Capitol 2536	$18
	(Blue promo label)		
LP	**THIS IS FARON** (63) Mono	Mercury 20785	$12
LP	**THIS IS FARON** (63) Stereo	Mercury 60785	$15
LP(P)	**THIS IS FARON** (63)	Mercury 20785	$15
	(White promo label)		
LP	**FARON YOUNG AIMS AT THE WEST** (63)	Mercury 60840	$12
LP(P)	**FARON YOUNG AIMS AT THE WEST** (63)	Mercury 20840	$15
	(White promo label)		
LP	**STORY SONGS FOR COUNTRY FANS** (64)	Mercury 60896	$12
LP(P)	**STORY SONGS FOR COUNTRY FANS** (64)	Mercury 20896	$15
	(White promo label)		
LP	**COUNTRY DANCE FAVORITES** (64)	Mercury 60931	$12
LP(P)	**COUNTRY DANCE FAVORITES** (64)	Mercury 20931	$15
	(White promo label)		
LP	**STORY SONGS OF MOUNTAINS & VALLEYS** (64)	Mercury 60971	$10
LP(P)	**STORY SONGS OF MOUNTAINS & VALLEYS** (64)	Mercury 20971	$12
	(White promo label)		
LP	**PEN AND PAPER** (65)	Mercury 61007	$10
LP(P)	**PEN AND PAPER** (65)	Mercury 21007	$12
	(White promo label)		
LP	**FARON YOUNG'S GREATEST HITS** (65)	Mercury 61047	$10
LP(P)	**FARON YOUNG'S GREATEST HITS** (65)	Mercury 21047	$12
	(White promo label)		
LP	**FARON YOUNG SINGS THE BEST OF JIM REEVES** (66)	Mercury 61058	$10
LP(P)	**FARON YOUNG SINGS THE BEST OF JIM REEVES** (66)	Mercury 21058	$12
	(White promo label)		
LP	**IT'S A GREAT LIFE** (66)	Tower 5022	$18
LP	**FARON YOUNG** (66)	Hilltop 6037	$12
LP	**UNMITIGATED GALL** (67)	Mercury 61110	$10
LP(P)	**UNMITIGATED GALL** (67)	Mercury 21110	$12
	(White promo label)		
LP	**THE WORLD OF FARON YOUNG** (68)	Tower 5121	$15
LP	**I'LL BE YOURS** (68)	Hilltop 6073	$12
LP	**CANDY KISSES** (70s)	Sears 124	$15

-radio shows-

16"(RS)	**U.S. NAVY BAND** (60s)		U.S. Navy	$25-50
	(Music and interviews)			
16"(RS)	**NAVY HOEDOWN** (60s)		U.S. Navy	$25-50
	(Music and interviews)			
16"(RS)	**LEATHERNECK JAMBOREE**		Leatherneck 17	$20-40
	(Music and interviews)			
16"(RS)	**COUNTRY STYLE USA** (56)		Country Style 173	$20-40
	(Music and interviews)			
16"(RS)	**COUNTRY STYLE USA** (57)		Country Style 183	$20-40
	(Music and interviews)			
16"(RS)	**COUNTRY STYLE USA** (57)		Country Style 192	$20-40
	(Music and interviews)			
16"(RS)	**COUNTRY STYLE USA** (57)		Country Style 278	$20-40
	(Music and interviews)			
16"(RS)	**COUNTRY MUSIC TIME** (57)		U.S. Army 80	$20-40
	(Music and interviews)			
16"(RS)	**COUNTRY MUSIC TIME** (57)		U.S. Army 102	$20-40
	(Music and interviews)			
16"(RS)	**COUNTRY MUSIC TIME** (57)		U.S. Army 117	$20-40
	(Music and interviews)			
LP(RS)	**GRAND OL' OPRY** (63)		WSM Radio 82	$20-40
	(Music and interviews)			
LP(RS)	**GRAND OL' OPRY** (64)		WSM radio 106	$20-40
	(Music and interviews)			
LP(RS)	**HOOTENAVY** (60s)		U.S. Navy 31/32	$20-40
	(Music and interviews)			
	Also see the Deputies			

GEORGE YOUNG (R)

-singles-

45rpm	**CAN'T STOP ME** (58)		Mercury 71259	$50
45(P)	**CAN'T STOP ME** (58)		Mercury 71259	$40
	(White promo label)			

NELSON YOUNG (RB)

-singles-

45rpm	**ROCK OLD SPUTNIK** (58)		Lucky 0002	$65

VICKI YOUNG (R)

Other Capitol 78s and 45s $4-8 each

-singles-

45rpm	**RIOT IN CELL BLOCK NUMBER NINE** (54)		Capitol 2865	$25
45(P)	**RIOT IN CELL BLOCK NUMBER NINE** (54)		Capitol 2865	$20
	(White promo label)			

Z

EDDIE ZACK (R)

-singles-

45rpm	**ROCKY ROAD BLUES** (55)		Columbia 21387	$75
45(P)	**ROCKY ROAD BLUES** (55)		Columbia 21387	$50
	(White promo label)			

TEX ZARIO (RB)

-singles-

45rpm	**GO MAN** (58)		Skyrocket 1001	$40